STATE AND FEDERAL ADMINISTRATIVE LAW

Fourth Edition

■ ■ ■

by

Michael Asimow

Visiting Professor of Law, Stanford Law School

Professor of Law Emeritus
University of California, Los Angeles

Ronald M. Levin

William R. Orthwein Distinguished Professor of Law
Washington University in St. Louis

AMERICAN CASEBOOK SERIES®

Mat #41314756

To
Merrie
and
Anne Carol

PREFACE TO THE FOURTH EDITION

The present edition of this book, like its predecessors, has several features that we believe distinguish it from the many other administrative law coursebooks on the market.

Most saliently, we give serious attention to state administrative law along with federal law where it is possible to do so. Our coverage of federal law is, we believe, sufficiently thorough that it can stand up well on its own terms. But we think that exposing students to the additional dimension of state administrative law has several benefits. First, state and federal law often differ. These differences add an important perspective to the study of administrative law by suggesting solutions to problems that are not otherwise apparent. Second, most law students will deal with state and local administrative agencies in their practice much more frequently than with federal agencies. They're quite likely to appear before state medical licensing boards or local zoning boards but are unlikely ever to see the inside of the FCC. As a result, for most students there is a clear professional advantage to a study of state law.

A recent development that has special significance for our casebook is the approval of a new Model State Administrative Procedure Act in July 2010. This action by the Uniform Law Commission was the culmination of more than six years' work to update the Act, which was last revised in 1981. During this lengthy gestation period, each of your authors served as American Bar Association advisor to the drafting committee that was charged with preparing the new Act. Numerous revisions in this edition reflect the advent of a new Model Act.

In another respect this book is relatively traditional. It is a book about administrative procedure and does not attempt to combine that subject matter with a study of one or more regulated industries. The basic goal of the book is to teach the administrative process: adjudication, rulemaking, political controls of agency action, freedom of information, and judicial review. The substantive law that agencies apply is left for other courses, such as environmental law, securities law, or the like. This approach keeps the book relatively short and also makes it possible to organize the course clearly. As we see it, there really isn't time in the typical administrative law course to cover the basics as well as the substantive law that agencies apply.

A potential disadvantage of the straight-procedure approach is that students might feel that the course is too abstract, that it jumps around among cases that describe wildly dissimilar agencies and functions, and that it does not adequately take account of the important relationship between procedure and substantive law. To counteract this potential reaction, our book makes extensive use of teaching problems. Most of the problems are practical and professionally-oriented. They take the students into the law office or into an agency, where they must deal with a client who has a specific problem involving a government agency. Problems can help to bring the subject down to earth, root it in real experience, teach client counseling skills, and demonstrate the important relationship between substantive law and procedure. Some users, including one of the authors, teach the course almost entirely through the problems, starting each discussion with the relevant problem and using the cases and text as resources to discuss that problem.

The basic conception of this book was that of Arthur Earl Bonfield, who participated only in the first edition. We gratefully acknowledge Arthur's contributions and hope the book continues to live up to his original aspiration.

We have tried to keep our book relatively short and the length of assignments manageable for students. As a result, we have edited the cases quite heavily. We have freely deleted citations and footnotes without ellipses. We also have tried to make it easy for instructors to use the book in a variety of ways. Some instructors have used past editions of the book to teach a basically federal law course. We have selected and arranged the materials in a manner that we believe will enable them to continue to use that approach without difficulty. But we invite teachers to draw liberally on the state law material, to the extent their individual tastes may dictate. We believe it offers perspectives that are frequently interesting and frequently illuminating.

MICHAEL ASIMOW
RONALD M. LEVIN

April 2014

ACKNOWLEDGMENTS

Fourth editions are easier to produce than first editions, but we have benefitted from the help of a number of people in preparing this revision. In particular, we appreciate the feedback we have received over the years from law students who have studied from the past editions; their ideas have improved this edition in ways too numerous to track. In addition, we are grateful for a host of thoughtful suggestions made by professional colleagues, including Craig Oren, Jeffrey Lubbers, and Arthur Wolf.

Finally, we thank the following publishers and journals for their generous permission to reprint excerpts from their copyrighted publications indicated below:

(1) American Bar Association: THE COST-BENEFIT STATE: THE FUTURE OF REGULATORY PROTECTION, by Cass R. Sunstein (2002); A GUIDE TO FEDERAL AGENCY RULEMAKING, by Jeffrey S. Lubbers (5th ed. 2012); A BLACKLETTER STATEMENT OF FEDERAL ADMINISTRATIVE LAW, by the Section of Administrative Law and Regulatory Practice (2d ed. 2013); and the following articles from the Administrative Law Review, published by the Section of Administrative Law and Regulatory Practice (formerly the Section of Administrative Law), American Bar Association: Newton Minow, *Letter to President Kennedy*, 15 Administrative Law Review 146 (1963); Richard J. Pierce, Jr., *Seven Ways to Deossify Agency Rulemaking*, 47 Administrative Law Review 59 (1995). Copyright 1963, 1995, 2002, 2012, 2013, American Bar Association. Reprinted with permission.

(2) Cato Institute: Antonin Scalia, *A Note on the Benzene Case*, Regulation 27 (July–Aug. 1980). Copyright 1980 by Cato Institute.

(3) Columbia Law Review: Nicholas Bagley & Richard L. Revesz, *Centralized Oversight of the Regulatory State*, 106 Columbia Law Review 1260 (2006). Copyright 2006 by Columbia Law Review Association, Inc.

(4) Cornell Law Review and Fred B. Rothman & Co.: Ralph F. Fuchs, *The Hearing Officer Problem-Symptom and Symbol*, 40 Cornell Law Quarterly 281 (1955). Copyright 1955 by Cornell University. All rights reserved.

(5) Duke Law Journal: Thomas O. McGarity, *Some Thoughts on Deossifying the Rulemaking Process*, 41 Duke Law Journal 1385 (1992).

(6) Environmental Law: William F. Funk, *When Smoke Gets In Your Eyes: Regulatory Negotiation and the Public Interest—EPA's Woodstove Standards*, 18 Environmental Law 55 (1987).

(7) Georgetown Environmental Law and Policy Institute: Lisa Heinzerling & Frank Ackerman, PRICING THE PRICELESS: COST-BENEFIT ANALYSIS OF ENVIRONMENTAL PROTECTION (2002).

(8) Northwestern University Law Review: George B. Shepard, *Fierce Compromise: The Administrative Procedure Act Emerges from New Deal Politics*, 90 Northwestern University Law Review 1557 (1996). Reprinted by special permission of Northwestern University School of Law, Northwestern University Law Review, vol. 90, 1996.

(9) Temple Law Review: John Devlin, *Toward a State Constitutional Analysis of Allocation of Powers: Legislators and Legislative Appointees Performing Administrative Functions*, 66 Temple Law Review 1205 (1993).

(10) Uniform Law Commission: REVISED MODEL STATE ADMINISTRATIVE PROCEDURE ACT, Copyright © 1961, 1981, 2010 by the Uniform Law Commission.

(11) University of Michigan Press: Glen O. Robinson, AMERICAN BUREAUCRACY: PUBLIC CHOICE AND PUBLIC LAW (1991). Copyright © by the University of Michigan 1991.

SUMMARY OF CONTENTS

TABLE OF CONTENTS

TABLE OF CASES

The principal cases are in bold type.

STATE AND FEDERAL ADMINISTRATIVE LAW

Fourth Edition

CHAPTER 1

INTRODUCTION

■ ■ ■

§ 1.1 ADMINISTRATIVE AGENCIES AND ADMINISTRATIVE LAW

Administrative agencies are units of government other than the legislature or the courts. Agencies usually have legal power to affect the rights or duties of persons outside the government. Agencies administer or execute law under powers delegated to them by statute. There are thousands of agencies at all levels of government—federal, state, and local.

Administrative agencies may be headed by a single official or by several officials, and may be called a department, commission, board or some other name. Most agencies are part of the executive branch of government but others are independent of the executive. While the heads of most agencies are appointed by the chief executive (meaning the U. S. President or a state governor or local mayor or other official), in some states agency heads are directly elected or are appointed by the legislature.

Agencies vary in size from units with no full time officials or employees and minuscule budgets to units with many thousands of employees and budgets in the billions of dollars. Some agencies make millions of decisions each year that affect the public (such as Social Security), while others make only a handful of such decisions. Agencies are specialists. Some specialize in a particular problem wherever it occurs, like labor-management relations or consumer protection, while others specialize in problems arising in particular industries, like energy or securities.

Most agencies are *regulatory*, meaning that they enforce a mandatory scheme of prohibitions or obligations, such as environmental protection or local planning and zoning. Other agencies distribute *benefits* such as food stamps or Social Security. To carry out these missions, agencies are authorized by statute to exercise a variety of powers such as investigation, prosecution, adoption of legally binding regulations, adjudication, or licensing.

Administrative law deals with the legal principles common to all administrative agencies, including the procedures that agencies use to carry out their functions and the principles of judicial review of agency actions. Administrative law also defines the role of the courts, the legislature, and the chief executive, vis-à-vis agencies. It does not deal with the *substantive law* enforced by agencies. Substantive issues relating to labor relations, land-use planning, or environmental law, for instance, are covered in courses on those particular subjects.

A course in administrative law, therefore, has much in common with a course on civil procedure. It cuts across many substantive law areas and assumes that administrative agencies have enough in common to be worth studying. In short, administrative law is a course in procedural law rather than a course in substantive law.

§ 1.2   REASONS FOR STUDYING ADMINISTRATIVE LAW

You're probably asking yourself, right about now, why should I take a course in administrative law? One answer is emblazoned on t-shirts distributed by the American Bar Association's Section on Administrative Law and Regulatory Practice "administrative law—everybody does it." That's because the laws administered by agencies affect our lives in so many profound ways. Think about it—agencies administer laws relating to our taxes, government benefits, education, environment, professional or driver's licenses, banking, transportation by air or land, communications by phone, internet, or television, or immigration status. Virtually every lawyer routinely encounters federal, state and local administrative agencies and thus must grapple with administrative law problems.

If you do real estate work, you'll deal with agencies administering the local zoning and land use planning laws as well as environmental law. If you practice tax, immigration, or labor law, you will be in intimate contact with administrative bureaucracies at every stage of your practice. A general business lawyer deals with many different agencies—agencies that license occupations and professions, regulate the issuance of securities or the protection of intellectual property, enforce anti-discrimination laws, administer consumer protection laws, oversee environmental protection laws, and apply safety in the workplace laws. If you represent hospitals or banks, you'll grapple with a maze of regulatory agencies. If you represent clients receiving Social Security or veterans' benefits or clients involved in government contracting or seeking government grants, you'll be up against the agencies administering those programs.

Every time this happens, proper representation of your clients requires you to understand the applicable substantive law as well as administrative procedure and judicial review of agency action. For all these reasons, lawyers need to know administrative law as much as civil procedure.

§ 1.3   STATE AND FEDERAL ADMINISTRATIVE LAW

This course book differs from other books that use predominantly federal materials to introduce students to the subject. In contrast, this book constantly compares federal, state and local materials. One reason for doing so is that there are many differences between them. As a result, a comparison of state and federal law can stimulate insights into problems and solutions in the administrative process that cannot be obtained from federal materials alone. Of course, the administrative law of other countries provides still more interesting comparisons to domestic law, but space limitations preclude us from discussing foreign materials.

A second reason to study state administrative materials is to better prepare yourself to deal with the realities of law practice. Most lawyers confront state and local agencies much more often than federal agencies. Most lawyers will never get anywhere near the Federal Communications Commission, but they are likely to encounter state licensing and regulatory agencies all the time. As a result, knowing something about state and local administrative practice is essential to prepare for the kind of law you will probably practice.

§ 1.4   ADMINISTRATIVE PROCEDURE ACTS

The principal sources of administrative law are federal and state constitutions, statutes, and judge-made common law. Of special importance are administrative procedure acts (APAs). The federal government and all of the states have general and comprehensive APAs. We will be considering APA provisions in most classes. APAs are general, meaning that they apply to most agencies rather than to just one or a few. And they are comprehensive, meaning that they deal with the main problems in administrative law—that is, rulemaking, adjudication, and judicial review.

Some people opposed the enactment of APAs, because there are enormous differences between agencies. The opponents of the APA concept believed that each agency should have its own procedural statute. However, others believed that a code that dealt only with fundamental principles rather than with details was both desirable and feasible. Once the federal APA was adopted, the states followed suit.

Here is some background on the federal Act:

> The landmark [federal APA] was the bill of rights for the new regulatory state. Enacted in 1946, the APA established the

fundamental relationship between regulatory agencies and those whom they regulate—between government, on the one hand, and private citizens, business, and the economy, on the other hand. The balance that the APA struck between promoting individuals' rights and maintaining agencies' policymaking flexibility has continued in force, with only minor modifications, until the present. The APA's impact has been large. It has provided agencies with broad freedom, limited only by relatively weak procedural requirements and judicial review, to create and implement policies in the many areas that agencies touch: from aviation to the environment, from labor relations to the securities markets. The APA permitted the growth of the modern regulatory state.

The APA and its history are central to the United States' economic and political development. In the 1930s and 1940s when the APA was debated, much in the United States was uncertain. Many believed that communism was a real possibility, as were fascism and dictatorship. Many supporters of the New Deal favored a form of government in which expert bureaucrats would influence even the details of the economy, with little recourse for the people and businesses that felt the impacts of the bureaucrats' commands. To New Dealers, this was efficiency. To the New Deal's opponents, this was dictatorial central planning. The battle over the APA helped to resolve the conflict between bureaucratic efficiency and the rule of law, and permitted the continued growth of government regulation. The APA expressed the nation's decision to permit extensive government, but to avoid dictatorship and central planning. . . .

Since the time of the APA's adoption, and even before, some commentators have suggested that the APA was universally beloved legislation. . . . This widely held perception of the APA's history is inaccurate. The APA's development was not primarily a search for administrative truth and efficiency. Nor was it a theoretically centered debate on appropriate roles for government and governed. Instead, the fight over the APA was a pitched political battle for the life of the New Deal. The more than a decade of political combat that preceded the adoption of the APA was one of the major political struggles in the war between supporters and opponents of the New Deal. Republicans and Southern Democrats sought to crush New Deal programs by means of administrative controls on agencies. . . .

The APA that finally emerged in 1946 did not represent a unanimous social consensus about the proper balance between individual rights and agency powers. The APA was a hard-fought compromise that left many legislators and interest groups far from completely satisfied. Congressional support for the bill was unanimous only because many legislators recognized that, although the bill was imperfect, it was better than no bill. The APA passed only with much grumbling.

George B. Shepherd, *Fierce Compromise: The Administrative Procedure Act Emerges from New Deal Politics,* 90 Nw. U. L. REV. 1557, 1558–60 (1996).

State APAs apply to most or all agencies of the state but do not cover local agencies. The APAs of more than half of the states are based in whole or in part on the 1961 Model State APA (MSAPA). In 1981 the Commissioners on Uniform State Laws adopted a much more ambitious and detailed MSAPA, but few states adopted any of its provisions and no state adopted all of them. The Commissioners have now adopted a 2010 MSAPA, which has been submitted to the states. It comes closer to the approach of the 1961 Act, in that it is less ambitious and detailed than the 1981 Act. Relevant portions of all three Model Acts are set forth in Appendices to this book.

The Administrative Conference of the United States (referred to throughout this book as ACUS) generates proposals for improvement of the federal administrative process. ACUS is a small federal agency that has effectively used its staff plus academic consultants and volunteer members to produce a large volume of reports and recommendations. Congress defunded ACUS in 1995, but it rose from the dead in 2009 and is again studying the federal administrative process and proposing improvements.

§ 1.5   A SNAPSHOT OF THE ADMINISTRATIVE PROCESS

Suppose that the state legislature has been deluged with complaints about unfair practices in the automobile insurance industry. The legislature isn't sure exactly what the problem is (much less how to solve it), so it enacts a vaguely worded statute ("the Act") prohibiting unfair and discriminatory automobile insurance practices. The Act, of course, will not enforce itself. So the Act creates an agency called the Automobile Insurance Commission (AIC) to enforce it. According to the Act, the AIC will have a director (or perhaps several agency heads), a staff, and a budget.

How will AIC go about enforcing the statute?

i.   *Research and publicity.* AIC will research the auto insurance industry and identify both problems and solutions. It may commission research by its staff or by outside consultants. AIC might publicize its findings. For example, it could publish a directory of insurance premiums or a study of consumer complaints against insurance companies. Publicity of this kind can help consumers make their own decisions and thus can help the market work more efficiently.

ii. *Rulemaking.* Often, the only way to enact a regulatory statute is to strike a compromise between proponents and opponents. Such statutes resolve very few of the hard issues and provide no specifics about problems or solutions. For example, the Act bans unfair and discriminatory auto insurance practices, but doesn't say what those practices might be. Instead, such statutes delegate authority to an agency to identify and solve the problems. The political process, which was not completed in the legislature, resumes in the agency when it takes up these issues.

The Act will authorize AIC to adopt rules to identify and prohibit unfair and discriminatory practices. For instance, suppose AIC believes that it is unfair for insurers to charge different premiums to consumers with different ZIP codes. It will first study the problem. Then it will propose, and later adopt, rules prohibiting such conduct.

In practical effect, agency rules are like statutes because they determine legal rights and duties. (Incidentally, the words "rule" and "regulation" mean the same thing and will be used interchangeably in this book.) Broadly speaking, rules are agency statements of general applicability and future effect that implement law or policy. APAs require agencies to give public notice of proposed rules, invite public comment, and to consider and respond to the public's input. The agency must publish the rules after they are adopted. Although rules are legally binding like statutes (assuming the rule is consistent with the statute that it is interpreting or enforcing), the differences between legislative and administrative lawmaking are profound. Legislatures are not required to seek input from the general public before passing a law and are not required to explain the laws, but the APA requires agencies to notify the public and seek its comments and to explain their regulations. The administrative process is much more structured and transparent than the legislative process.

Administrative rules are a very important part of the legal landscape today. There are rules relating to taxation, safety in the workplace, air and water pollution, Medicare benefits, automobile safety, civil rights, and much, much more. Next time you're in the law library, look at the many bookshelves containing the Code of Federal Regulations (CFR). While the official United States Code is contained in perhaps two dozen volumes, CFR comprises hundreds of volumes. And those volumes contain only federal regulations; the rules of your state and city agencies fill many more volumes. In addition to these published rules, agencies issue many guidance documents (sometimes called interpretive rules, bulletins, rulings, policy statements, or other names) to guide the public and their own staff. These documents are also considered rules but are not legally binding and, at least under federal law, can be adopted with no formalities at all. In contrast, some states subject guidance documents to the same procedural requirements as legally binding rules.

iii. *Licensing.* A license authorizes an individual or entity to engage in a specified activity. The statute creating AIC might authorize it to license auto insurance companies or insurance brokers. The AIC will issue rules establishing the qualifications for obtaining a license (such as financial qualifications, education, experience, or an exam). The rules will also specify what licensees may and may not do and will set forth the sanctions for violating the rules, such as revocation of the licenses.

Licensing schemes can be beneficial. They help to assure that consumers are served only by properly qualified persons. But such schemes also have costs. They are a barrier to entry, often requiring licensees to have more education, experience or financial resources than they really need. In that case, licensing tends to decrease competition and increase prices without compensating public benefit. A regulated industry may have "captured" an agency so that the agency power is turned against the interests of the public rather than the regulated industry. For these reasons, we suggest close scrutiny when analyzing the desirability of licensing schemes.

Permits are a form of license. An agency may be authorized to require a permit before specified action may occur. If AIC adopted a permit system, for example, an automobile insurance company might be required to secure permission from that agency before changing its rates or the terms of its policies. Permit systems are sometimes necessary, as in the case of a dangerous activity like selling a new drug. Permit systems are also used in connection with environmental regulation (for example, a permit is required before pollutants can be discharged into rivers). Permit schemes are costly to administer, often entail long delays, may be harmful to the competitive system (which requires competitors to respond promptly to market conditions), and may in practice allow administrators to substitute their wisdom for that of the market. And note that a staff member who must make a decision to grant a permit is likely to be conservative and cautious; that might mean that some beneficial products or projects are never approved.

A less intrusive approach is sometimes referred to as a clearance system. Under that approach, an agency requires a regulated party to take certain steps before proceeding with a planned course of action. If the agency does nothing, the party may proceed. Thus the agency must take affirmative steps to stop the project. For example, a corporation may be required to file disclosure documents and issue a prospectus before selling securities. Under the clearance approach, AIC might require automobile insurance companies to notify AIC before changing the rates or the terms of their policies, but if AIC does nothing, the change goes into effect.

iv. *Investigation and law enforcement.* An agency needs to ensure that its rules are followed. It will require regulated parties to file routine reports and it must be prepared to receive complaints from the public. It needs formal investigatory powers to subpoena documents and inspect premises. If a violation is detected, the agency must be empowered to initiate enforcement action, because statutes and rules will not enforce themselves, and members of the public may lack the resources, the will, or the information to do so. For practical purposes, therefore, an agency functions much like a police department and a prosecutor.

v. *Adjudication.* An adjudication is an agency determination of *particular applicability* that affects the legal rights or duties of a specified person or persons (as distinguished from rules which have *general applicability*). For example, AIC might adjudicate whether the license of a particular insurance broker should be suspended or revoked because of a violation of AIC rules. When it conducts adjudication, AIC operates much like a court.

The AIC might also be empowered to resolve disputes between consumers and insurance companies over questions of coverage, rates, or unjust cancellation. In other words, agencies are sometimes authorized to decide private-party disputes that would ordinarily be decided in court. For example, agencies administering workers' compensation schemes resolve disputes between employers and employees over compensation for job-related injuries.

State and federal APAs prescribe the procedures that agencies must follow when engaging in adjudication. In addition, the due process clauses of state and federal constitutions require agencies to provide fair procedures and impartial adjudicators; due process is particularly important as a constraint on local government adjudication, because local governments usually have no APAs. The APA or due process typically requires agencies to afford private parties a trial-type hearing. That hearing will normally be conducted by a person called an administrative judge or similar title. The administrative judge's decision usually may be appealed to the agency head. This part of administrative law may seem familiar, because it is not unlike civil procedure, but there are deep differences between courts and adjudicating agencies.

An agency is usually (though not always) a party to the dispute it is adjudicating (as when it considers whether to revoke a license). A court, on the other hand, is an uninvolved arbiter. In civil litigation, the lawyers control many aspects of the proceedings and the judge is relatively passive. Administrative judges take a greater role in controlling their proceedings, especially because there are no juries. In addition, because an agency specializes in its particular regulatory process, it acquires experience and technical expertise. Judges, on the other hand, are usually generalists, not specialists. Finally, an agency makes the rules, investigates violations, prosecutes cases, and adjudicates cases; a court only adjudicates cases and therefore is not subject to conflicts between potentially inconsistent functions. These differences raise serious problems in assuring fair and impartial agency adjudication.

vi. *Ratemaking.* Suppose the legislature wants to regulate auto insurance rates. It cannot set the rates itself, because the process is extremely time-consuming and the rates require constant adjustment as market conditions change. Therefore, it will have to delegate the ratemaking power to AIC.

Administrative price fixing is a common technique, particularly in situations of natural monopoly (such as local phones, gas, or electricity) or when market failures of one sort or another prevent the market from functioning properly. Some cities engage in rent control, which is a form of ratemaking. In the recent past we have partially or completely abandoned government price fixing of transportation (trucking, airlines, busses, railroads, pipelines) and financial services (banking, stock brokerage). Increasingly, utility services are being deregulated.

In order to fix prices on either an industry-wide or a company-specific basis, AIC must observe appropriate procedures. Depending on whether the rates are industry-wide or company-specific, the appropriate process may look more like rulemaking or adjudication. Either way, the process will be a lengthy one since the rates can be set only after detailed economic information is collected and analyzed and a fair rate of return is determined. In any case, it seems doubtful whether rate fixing is needed or even useful in a competitive market like automobile insurance.

vii. *Judicial review.* Judicial review of administrative action occurs very frequently. Generally speaking, judicial review occurs in regular courts (whereas, in some countries such as France, judicial review occurs in specialized courts). Broadly speaking, courts review final agency action (both rules and adjudication) for errors of law and for reasonableness in finding facts or exercising discretion. A typical challenge to agency action may include allegations that it was procedurally improper, that it was unconstitutional or inconsistent with applicable substantive law, that it was unsupported factually, or that it was arbitrary. How to divide power between agencies and reviewing courts is a major subject of this course.

viii. *Freedom of information.* Both the federal and state governments have adopted Freedom of Information Acts (often referred as FOIA statutes). FOIA requires government agencies to publish their rules and adjudicatory decisions (most such publication is now on-line). In addition, FOIA allows any member of the public to request any document in the possession of government agencies (with limited exceptions) and go to court to enforce the demands if the agency refuses to comply. FOIA statutes greatly increase the transparency of government but are quite costly to administer.

ix. *Legislative and executive review.* Both the legislative and executive branches of government scrutinize agency actions. The legislature investigates agency action and often amends or repeals agency enabling statutes. In some states, the legislature has other powers to control agencies by delaying or vetoing agency rules. The legislature can also influence agency action by increasing or decreasing the agency's budget or defunding it altogether.

The chief executive (the governor in our example) will appoint the head or heads of AIC. The governor's staff will keep track of AIC's activities. The governor may have the authority to remove the AIC agency head or heads for any reason. However, if AIC is an "independent" agency, the governor can remove the heads only for good cause. Governors also can exercise control over AIC by requesting the legislature to increase or to cut the agency's budget.

The above snapshot of the administrative process is meant only to convey a general idea of what agencies do and how they are controlled. In fact, the administrative process is very diverse. Each agency has its own way of doing business. As a result, when a client has a problem with a particular agency, you have to consult not only general principles of administrative law but also that agency's enabling act, its substantive and procedural rules, and the administrative and judicial precedents relating to the regulatory scheme in question. And it's also a good idea to make some phone calls to find out how things actually work in practice.

§ 1.6 AGENCY LEGITIMACY AND ADMINISTRATIVE LAW

The administrative process should be lawful and fair and produce accurate results at acceptable cost. In addition, the process must strive for *legitimacy,* meaning that the exercise of power by administrative agencies is recognized by regulated parties and the community at large as politically acceptable.

Federal and state constitutions do not usually mention administrative agencies and agency heads are not elected (with a few exceptions at the state level). As a result, many people question whether the exercise of rulemaking and adjudicatory power by agencies is legitimate. Theorists have long struggled with the legitimacy problem.

See generally Richard B. Stewart, *The Reformation of American Administrative Law,* 88 HARV. L. REV. 1667 (1975), for an excellent treatment of legitimacy theories.

An early theory to legitimate agency power was the claim that they serve as a *transmission belt* for implementing specific statutes. In this view, the politically responsible legislature has already answered the major policy questions; unelected agencies just fill in the details. According to the transmission belt model, the role of administrative law is to protect private liberty and property interests by making agencies stay within statutory bounds and follow fair procedures. However, as indicated in § 7.2, that model is unsatisfactory, because many statutes creating administrative agencies do not answer the major policy questions with which the agency must grapple. Instead (as in the example of auto insurance regulation discussed in § 1.5), statutes often delegate broad discretionary powers to agencies without providing any significant guidance as to how the power should be exercised. Generally people who believe in the transmission belt approach are in favor of narrowing delegations of discretionary power to government agencies and requiring the legislature to supply clear and meaningful standards for agencies to apply.

In the 1930's the New Deal arose out of the economic chaos of the Great Depression. While many important federal agencies already existed before the 1930's, the New Deal spawned numerous new ones. These agencies regulated areas of the economy that had previously been governed by the market. The epochal events surrounding the Depression and the New Deal gave rise to a new theory of administrative law that prevailed until the 1970's. Agencies were expected to solve the nation's economic and social problems on the basis of their *expertise*. This approach suggests that agencies should be allowed to function as teams of experts, and the purpose of administrative law should be to protect agency action from unwarranted legislative, judicial or executive intrusion. Today, our faith in expertise has declined, since many of the problems that agencies attempt to solve are obviously political rather than technical.

The *pluralist* or interest representation model views the activities of agencies as legitimate if they engage in a fair political process. This model suggests that a desirable outcome reconciles the claims of all affected interests in a way that reflects their political influence. Judicial review assures that everyone who should have been at the table was invited. In this model, therefore, the role of administrative law is to insure that agencies use a process that approximates the political process. However, there are a number of serious problems with this approach, which seems to neglect the public interest in favor of striking political deals. In addition, many political interests, such as environmental or consumer groups, may not be represented because they lack the resources to engage in full participation. Moreover, agencies may be captured by the special interests they are supposed to be regulating.

Under the *civic republican* model, the role of government is to encourage a deliberative process in which the views of all citizens are respected in pursuit of the common good. Civic republicans believe that broad delegations to administrative agencies are a good thing. The role of administrative law should be to facilitate the deliberative process, minimize political influences over the administrative process, and assure that agency decisions are well explained and rational. Civic republicans reject the pluralist notion that the role of government is to broker deals according to the political influence of interest groups. Civic republicans like notice and comment rulemaking, because everyone is invited to participate and the agency must explain why it rejected public suggestions. Others have criticized the civil republican model, arguing that piling up deliberative procedures simply delays agency action, thus harming the members of the public who would benefit from regulation. For discussion of both sides of the debate, see Mark Seidenfeld, *A Civic Republican Justification for the Bureaucratic State*, 105 HARV. L. REV. 1511 (1992); Thomas O. McGarity, *The Courts and the Ossification of Rulemaking: A Response to Professor Seidenfeld*, 75 TEX. L. REV. 525 (1997).

A number of theorists reject all these models and argue that most programs of federal regulation should be repealed as an infringement on separation of powers and an unwarranted interference with individual liberty, market forces and the common law. These arguments are made by libertarians and classical liberals and are voiced politically by many Republicans, particularly those of the Tea Party persuasion. These groups disagree on many points but share a deep suspicion of regulatory programs. They tend to favor administrative law reforms that make it more difficult for agencies to adopt regulations or that increase judicial scrutiny of the regulations. *See, e.g.*, Richard A. Epstein, *Why the Modern Administrative State is Inconsistent with the Rule of Law*, 3 N.Y.U. J.L. & LIBERTY 491 (2008).

Lacking a comprehensive theory that provides legitimacy for agency exercise of political power, scholars often turn to *procedural regularity* and to *checks and balances*. The procedural regularity idea holds that agency rulemaking is legitimate because agencies must employ APA notice and comment procedure which guarantees a measure of direct democratic participation. As discussed in Chapter 5, courts have vastly elaborated the simple APA rulemaking provisions, so that private interests have many opportunities to influence the result.

The checks and balances idea emphasizes that agency power is subject to a variety of important controls that help to ensure both legality and political responsiveness. Judicial review (especially so-called "hard look" review discussed in § 9.3.2) functions as a meaningful check on agency discretion. The legislature can and often does control agency action through oversight, new legislation, or cutting the budget. At both federal and state levels, the executive branch has numerous tools to scrutinize and control agency rulemaking, up to and including removal of the agency heads. Legislative and executive controls on agency action are discussed in Chapter 7.

However, legislative and executive branch controls and imposition of sanctions on agencies involve extensive and costly monitoring of agency activity. As a result they are not very effective in preventing abuse of power by agencies. There is a link between the procedural regularity theory and the checks and balances theory. One way to view administrative procedure is that it serves to facilitate the exercise of judicial, legislative and executive political controls. The notice, comment, and explanation requirements of the APA build a record suitable for searching judicial review. Moreover, special interest groups that were instrumental in securing the passage of legislation remain interested in agency rulemaking under that legislation. The APA notice and comment procedure alerts these groups to the possibility that an agency might deviate from the compromises that led to the legislation in question. As a result, these interested groups can use the APA comment procedure to change the agency's course before it is too late. Moreover, once alerted to the problem, these groups are likely to seek legislative or executive assistance to bring the agency back to the correct path. This "fire alarm" theory is most closely associated with public choice theorists. *See* Matthew McCubbins, et. al. *Administrative Procedures as Instruments of Political Control*," 3 J. L. ECON. & ORG. 243 (1987).

§ 1.7 PROBLEM

Your state has recently adopted a voter initiative that legalizes the use and possession of medical marijuana. The statute contains no provisions relating to what government agencies should administer the law and gives no specific details about how the marijuana should be grown and distributed and who can purchase it. The initiative provides that the state legislature and local governments should adopt statutes governing these matters.

One unresolved problem with the new law is that the federal criminal law prohibits all aspects of producing, selling and using marijuana. However, the federal authorities tend not to enforce federal law in states that legalize medical marijuana if the production or distribution complies with state law and the state adequately administers the law and controls abuses.

You are a member of the staff of a state legislator who is the chair of the committee that will be responsible for adopting legislation to implement the medical marijuana law. Some legislators believe that the state legislature should keep its hands off medical marijuana. They believe that any necessary regulation should occur at the local level or through state criminal law. Other legislators believe that the state legislature should regulate medical marijuana and impose taxes on growers and distributors. They believe the legislature should create a new agency to engage in research, rulemaking, licensing, law enforcement, and adjudication.

Please prepare a memo to your boss that discusses whether the state legislature should establish an agency to regulate medical marijuana. Assuming that the state legislature decides to create such an entity, what provisions should the state law contain?

CHAPTER 2

THE CONSTITUTIONAL RIGHT TO
A HEARING

■ ■ ■

The Fifth Amendment (which applies to the federal government) provides that no person shall "be deprived of life, liberty, or property, without due process of law." Section 1 of the Fourteenth Amendment (which applies to state and local government) contains similar language. State constitutions also provide for due process and may provide more (but not less) protection than the federal Constitution. Both provisions require "state action," meaning that they do not apply to private action.

You are familiar with the *judicial* procedures required before the state imposes a criminal sanction or a civil remedy. However, a vast number of governmental decisions that negatively impact persons outside the government are not administered through courts (although courts can usually *review* these decisions). Chapter 2 concerns the constitutional requirements imposed on government agencies that take such decisions. Chapter 3 concerns statutory rights to a hearing. Here are some examples of the sorts of decisions that involve millions of people every year:

• *Benefit decisions.* An agency refuses to grant or terminates government benefits such as social security disability payments, welfare, or food stamps.

• *Access to services.* A state educational institution expels a student, asserting poor academic performance or violation of rules.

• *Licenses.* An agency revokes a driver's license or the license to practice of a lawyer or doctor.

• *Jobs or contracts.* Government fires an employee or terminates a contract.

Almost all of such disputes are resolved informally. But if they are not resolved informally, an adversely affected person is often entitled by due process or by a statute to a fair hearing at which an impartial decisionmaker adjudicates the conflict.

This chapter introduces several themes that recur throughout the book:

• *Administrative law matters.* An administrative hearing is vital to persons who believe they are the victims of wrong decisions taken by a clumsy and insensitive bureaucracy.

• *Administrative procedure is costly.* Take welfare hearings—the subject considered next. It costs a lot of money and staff time to provide hearings before terminating the benefits of unqualified recipients. The hearing right encourages people to appeal just to delay the termination of their payments.

• *Issues of administrative law involve fundamental value conflicts.* Your position on administrative law issues will often be determined by your own political viewpoint, but a study of administrative law can inform these positions. Some of the value conflicts illuminated by this chapter are: Should nontraditional forms of property and liberty (like welfare benefits, reputation, or a government job) receive the same procedural protection that we give to traditional kinds of property or liberty? Where should we draw the line between full procedural protection and conflicting interests such as efficiency or cost? Is adversarial procedure the best way to protect people's interests against detrimental administrative action?

The chapter opens with an important and dramatic administrative law decision. The majority and dissenting opinions in *Goldberg v. Kelly* illuminate these value conflicts with stirring rhetoric in a setting of great practical importance: the conflict between an individual and a state welfare bureaucracy. Much of the material that follows in this chapter is a retreat from Justice Brennan's opinion in *Goldberg.* Did Justice Brennan promise more than government can deliver?

§ 2.1   HEARINGS AND WELFARE TERMINATION: DUE PROCESS AND MASS JUSTICE

Before turning to the *Goldberg* decision, we supply some background about welfare, meaning government benefits distributed according to need. There are numerous federal, state and local welfare programs, including Medicaid, food stamps, general relief, and rent supplements. Aid for Families with Dependent Children (AFDC), the welfare program involved in *Goldberg,* was fundamentally altered and renamed Temporary Assistance for Needy Families (TANF) in 1996. Under TANF, welfare is no longer an "entitlement," and the states are permitted to design their own programs. TANF is heavily oriented toward getting welfare recipients into the work force. These changes to the welfare system may cast doubt on the underlying theories and arguments set forth in *Goldberg.*

Established in 1935, AFDC furnished federal money to the states; the states provided additional funds, set their own level of benefits, and administered the program (within the constraints of federal law). In 1994, there were over 14 million recipients of AFDC, but by 2010, only about 4 million adults and children received TANF benefits. The great majority of AFDC and TANF recipients live in single-parent households, usually headed by females with one or more children.

Qualification for welfare programs is based on need, and the welfare bureaucracy must constantly assess and reassess the need of vast numbers of people. Although benefits under AFDC or TANF vary from state to state, even in the most generous states a family must be nearly destitute to qualify. The benefits may be denied, reduced, or terminated for various reasons, such as a change in resources or refusal to cooperate in obtaining support from an absent parent. Under TANF, recipients risk a loss of benefits if they fail to meet work or community service requirements or required participation in drug rehab programs. The issue in *Goldberg* is what sort of appeal procedure a state must provide when it terminates benefits and the recipient disagrees.

GOLDBERG V. KELLY

397 U.S. 254 (1970)

BRENNAN, J.:

The question for decision is whether a State that terminates public assistance payments to a particular recipient without affording him the opportunity for an evidentiary hearing prior to termination denies the recipient procedural due process in violation of the Due Process Clause of the Fourteenth Amendment.

[Recipients of AFDC and of New York's general relief program allege that New York state and city officials terminated their aid without prior notice and hearing, thereby denying them due process of law. They complained that they had been dropped from the rolls for illegal or incorrect reasons. Under recently adopted procedural rules] a caseworker who has doubts about the recipient's continued eligibility must first discuss them with the recipient. If the caseworker concludes that the recipient is no longer eligible, he recommends termination of aid to a unit supervisor. If the latter concurs, he sends the recipient a letter stating the reasons for proposing to terminate aid and notifying him that within seven days he may request that a higher official review the record, and may support the request with a written statement prepared personally or with the aid of an attorney or other person. If the reviewing official affirms the determination of ineligibility, aid is stopped immediately and the recipient is informed by letter of the reasons for the action.

Appellees' challenge to this procedure emphasizes the absence of any provisions for the personal appearance of the recipient before the reviewing official, for oral presentation of evidence, and for confrontation and cross-examination of adverse witnesses. However, the letter does inform the recipient that he may request a post-termination "fair hearing." This is a proceeding before an independent state hearing officer at which the recipient may appear personally, offer oral evidence, confront and cross-examine the witnesses against him, and have a record made of the hearing. If the recipient prevails at the "fair hearing" he is paid all funds erroneously withheld. A recipient whose aid is not restored by a "fair hearing" decision may have judicial review. . . .

I

The constitutional issue to be decided, therefore, is the narrow one whether the Due Process Clause requires that the recipient be afforded an evidentiary hearing *before* the termination of benefits. The District Court held that only a pre-termination evidentiary hearing would satisfy the constitutional command, and rejected the argument of the state and city officials that the combination of the post-termination "fair hearing" with the informal pre-termination review disposed of all due process claims. The court said: "While post-termination review is relevant, there is one overpowering fact which controls here. By hypothesis, a welfare recipient is destitute, without funds or assets. . . . Suffice it to say that to cut off a welfare recipient in the face of . . . brutal need without a prior hearing of some sort is unconscionable, unless overwhelming considerations justify it." The court rejected the argument that the need to protect the public's tax revenues supplied the requisite "overwhelming consideration." "Against the justified desire to protect public funds must be weighed the individual's overpowering need in this unique situation not to be wrongfully deprived of assistance. . . . While the problem of additional expense must be kept in mind, it does not justify denying a hearing meeting the ordinary standards of due process. Under all the circumstances, we hold that due process requires an adequate hearing before termination of welfare benefits, and the fact that there is a later constitutionally fair proceeding does not alter the result." . . .

Appellant does not contend that procedural due process is not applicable to the termination of welfare benefits. Such benefits are a matter of statutory entitlement for persons qualified to receive them.[8]

---

[8] It may be realistic today to regard welfare entitlements as more like "property" than a "gratuity." Much of the existing wealth in this country takes the form of rights that do not fall within traditional common-law concepts of property. It has been aptly noted that "[s]ociety today is built around entitlement. The automobile dealer has his franchise, the doctor and lawyer their professional licenses, the worker his union membership, contract, and pension rights, the executive his contract and stock options; all are devices to aid security and independence. Many of the most important of these entitlements now flow from government: subsidies to farmers and businessmen, routes for airlines and channels for television stations; long term contracts for defense, space, and education; social security pensions for individuals. Such sources of security,

Their termination involves state action that adjudicates important rights. The constitutional challenge cannot be answered by an argument that public assistance benefits are a "privilege" and not a "right." Relevant constitutional restraints apply as much to the withdrawal of public assistance benefits as to disqualification for unemployment compensation . . . or to discharge from public employment. . . . The extent to which procedural due process must be afforded the recipient is influenced by the extent to which he may be "condemned to suffer grievous loss," *Joint Anti-Fascist Refugee Committee v. McGrath*, 341 U.S. 123 (1951). (Frankfurter, J., concurring), and depends upon whether the recipient's interest in avoiding that loss outweighs the governmental interest in summary adjudication. Accordingly, as we said in *Cafeteria & Restaurant Workers Union v. McElroy*, 367 U.S. 886 (1961), "consideration of what procedures due process may require under any given set of circumstances must begin with a determination of the precise nature of the government function involved as well as of the private interest that has been affected by governmental action."

It is true, of course, that some governmental benefits may be administratively terminated without affording the recipient a pre-termination evidentiary hearing.[10] But we agree with the District Court that when welfare is discontinued, only a pre-termination evidentiary hearing provides the recipient with procedural due process.

For qualified recipients, welfare provides the means to obtain essential food, clothing, housing, and medical care. Thus the crucial factor in this context—a factor not present in the case of the black-listed government contractor, the discharged government employee, the taxpayer denied a tax exemption, or virtually anyone else whose governmental entitlements are ended—is that termination of aid pending resolution of a controversy over eligibility may deprive an *eligible* recipient of the very means by which to live while he waits. Since he lacks independent resources, his situation becomes immediately desperate. His need to concentrate upon finding the means for daily subsistence, in turn, adversely affects his ability to seek redress from the welfare bureaucracy.

Moreover, important governmental interests are promoted by affording recipients a pre-termination evidentiary hearing. From its founding the Nation's basic commitment has been to foster the dignity

---

whether private or public, are no longer regarded as luxuries or gratuities; to the recipients they are essentials, fully deserved, and in no sense a form of charity. It is only the poor whose entitlements, although recognized by public policy, have not been effectively enforced." Reich, Individual Rights and Social Welfare: The Emerging Legal Issues, 74 YALE L.J. 1245, 1255 (1965). See also Reich, The New Property, 73 YALE L.J. 733 (1964).

[10] [The Court referred to decisions upholding administrative action taken before providing a hearing in emergency situations such as securities fraud, mislabeled vitamins, or seizure of spoiled food.]

and well-being of all persons within its borders. . . . Welfare, by meeting the basic demands of subsistence, can help bring within the reach of the poor the same opportunities that are available to others to participate meaningfully in the life of the community. At the same time, welfare guards against the societal malaise that may flow from a widespread sense of unjustified frustration and insecurity. Public assistance, then, is not mere charity, but a means to "promote the general Welfare, and secure the Blessings of Liberty to ourselves and our Posterity." The same governmental interests that counsel the provision of welfare, counsel as well its uninterrupted provision to those eligible to receive it; pre-termination evidentiary hearings are indispensable to that end.

Appellant does not challenge the force of these considerations but argues that they are outweighed by countervailing governmental interests in conserving fiscal and administrative resources. These interests, the argument goes, justify the delay of any evidentiary hearing until after discontinuance of the grants. Summary adjudication protects the public fisc by stopping payments promptly upon discovery of reason to believe that a recipient is no longer eligible. Since most terminations are accepted without challenge, summary adjudication also conserves both the fisc and administrative time and energy by reducing the number of evidentiary hearings actually held.

We agree with the District Court, however, that these governmental interests are not overriding in the welfare context. The requirement of a prior hearing doubtless involves some greater expense, and the benefits paid to ineligible recipients pending decision at the hearing probably cannot be recouped, since these recipients are likely to be judgment-proof. But the State is not without weapons to minimize these increased costs. Much of the drain on fiscal and administrative resources can be reduced by developing procedures for prompt pre-termination hearings and by skillful use of personnel and facilities. Indeed, the very provision for a post-termination evidentiary hearing in New York's Home Relief program is itself cogent evidence that the State recognizes the primacy of the public interest in correct eligibility determinations and therefore in the provision of procedural safeguards. Thus, the interest of the eligible recipient in uninterrupted receipt of public assistance, coupled with the State's interest that his payments not be erroneously terminated, clearly outweighs the State's competing concern to prevent any increase in its fiscal and administrative burdens. . . .

II

We also agree with the District Court, however, that the pre-termination hearing need not take the form of a judicial or quasi-judicial trial. We bear in mind that the statutory "fair hearing" will provide the recipient with a full administrative review.[14] Accordingly, the pre-termination hearing has one function only: to produce an initial determination of the validity of the welfare department's grounds for discontinuance of payments in order to protect a recipient against an erroneous termination of his benefits. Thus, a complete record and a comprehensive opinion, which would serve primarily to facilitate judicial review and to guide future decisions, need not be provided at the pre-termination stage. We recognize, too, that both welfare authorities and recipients have an interest in relatively speedy resolution of questions of eligibility, that they are used to dealing with one another informally, and that some welfare departments have very burdensome caseloads. These considerations justify the limitation of the pre-termination hearing to minimum procedural safeguards, adapted to the particular characteristics of welfare recipients, and to the limited nature of the controversies to be resolved. We wish to add that we, no less than the dissenters, recognize the importance of not imposing upon the States or the Federal Government in this developing field of law any procedural requirements beyond those demanded by rudimentary due process. . . .

The hearing must be "at a meaningful time and in a meaningful manner." In the present context these principles require that a recipient have timely and adequate notice detailing the reasons for a proposed termination, and an effective opportunity to defend by confronting any adverse witnesses and by presenting his own arguments and evidence orally. These rights are important in cases such as those before us, where recipients have challenged proposed terminations as resting on incorrect or misleading factual premises or on misapplication of rules or policies to the facts of particular cases.[15]

We are not prepared to say that the seven-day notice currently provided by New York City is constitutionally insufficient per se, although there may be cases where fairness would require that a longer time be given. Nor do we see any constitutional deficiency in the content or form of the notice. New York employs both a letter and a personal conference with a caseworker to inform a recipient of the precise questions raised about his continued eligibility. Evidently the recipient is told the legal and factual bases for the Department's doubts. This combination is probably the most effective method of communicating with recipients.

---

[14] Due process does not, of course, require two hearings. If, for example, a State simply wishes to continue benefits until after a "fair" hearing there will be no need for a preliminary hearing.

[15] This case presents no question requiring our determination whether due process requires only an opportunity for written submission, or an opportunity both for written submission and oral argument, where there are no factual issues in dispute or where the application of the rule of law is not intertwined with factual issues.

The city's procedures presently do not permit recipients to appear personally with or without counsel before the official who finally determines continued eligibility. Thus a recipient is not permitted to present evidence to that official orally, or to confront or cross-examine adverse witnesses. These omissions are fatal to the constitutional adequacy of the procedures.

The opportunity to be heard must be tailored to the capacities and circumstances of those who are to be heard. It is not enough that a welfare recipient may present his position to the decisionmaker in writing or secondhand through his caseworker. Written submissions are an unrealistic option for most recipients, who lack the educational attainment necessary to write effectively and who cannot obtain professional assistance. Moreover, written submissions do not afford the flexibility of oral presentations; they do not permit the recipient to mold his argument to the issues the decisionmaker appears to regard as important. Particularly where credibility and veracity are at issue, as they must be in many termination proceedings, written submissions are a wholly unsatisfactory basis for decision. The secondhand presentation to the decisionmaker by the caseworker has its own deficiencies; since the caseworker usually gathers the facts upon which the charge of ineligibility rests, the presentation of the recipient's side of the controversy cannot safely be left to him. Therefore a recipient must be allowed to state his position orally. Informal procedures will suffice; in this context due process does not require a particular order of proof or mode of offering evidence.

In almost every setting where important decisions turn on questions of fact, due process requires an opportunity to confront and cross-examine adverse witnesses. . . . Welfare recipients must therefore be given an opportunity to confront and cross-examine the witnesses relied on by the department.

"The right to be heard would be, in many cases, of little avail if it did not comprehend the right to be heard by counsel." We do not say that counsel must be provided at the pre-termination hearing, but only that the recipient must be allowed to retain an attorney if he so desires. Counsel can help delineate the issues, present the factual contentions in an orderly manner, conduct cross-examination, and generally safeguard the interests of the recipient. We do not anticipate that this assistance will unduly prolong or otherwise encumber the hearing. . . . Finally, the decisionmaker's conclusion as to a recipient's eligibility must rest solely on the legal rules and evidence adduced at the hearing. To demonstrate compliance with this elementary requirement, the decisionmaker should state the reasons for his determination and indicate the evidence he relied on, though his statement need not amount to a full opinion or even formal findings of fact and conclusions of law. And, of course, an impartial decisionmaker is essential. We agree with the District Court that prior involvement in some aspects of a case will not necessarily bar a welfare official from acting as a decisionmaker. He should not, however, have participated in making the determination under review.

Affirmed.

BLACK, J., dissenting. . . .

The Court [today] relies upon the Fourteenth Amendment and in effect says that failure of the government to pay a promised charitable installment to an individual deprives that individual of *his own property,* in violation of the Due Process Clause of the Fourteenth Amendment. It somewhat strains credulity to say that the government's promise of charity to an individual is property belonging to that individual when the government denies that the individual is honestly entitled to receive such a payment.

I would have little, if any, objection to the majority's decision in this case if it were written as the report of the House Committee on Education and Labor, but as an opinion ostensibly resting on the language of the Constitution I find it woefully deficient. Once the verbiage is pared away it is obvious that this Court today adopts the views of the District Court "that to cut off a welfare recipient in the face of . . . 'brutal need' without a prior hearing of some sort is unconscionable," and therefore, says the Court, unconstitutional. The majority reaches this result by a process of weighing "the recipient's interest in avoiding" the termination of welfare benefits against "the governmental interest in summary adjudication." Today's balancing act requires a "pre-termination evidentiary hearing," yet there is nothing that indicates what tomorrow's balance will be. Although the majority attempts to bolster its decision with limited quotations from prior cases, it is obvious that today's result does not depend on the language of the Constitution itself or the principles of other decisions, but solely on the collective judgment of the majority as to what would be a fair and humane procedure in this case. . . .

The Court apparently feels that this decision will benefit the poor and needy. In my judgment the eventual result will be just the opposite. While today's decision requires only an administrative, evidentiary hearing, the inevitable logic of the approach taken will lead to constitutionally imposed, time-consuming delays of a full adversary process of administrative and judicial review. In the next case the welfare recipients are bound to argue that cutting off benefits before judicial review of the agency's decision is also a denial of due process. Since, by hypothesis, termination of aid at that point may still "deprive an *eligible* recipient of the very means by which to live while he waits," I would be surprised if the weighing process did not compel the conclusion that termination without full judicial review would be unconscionable. After all, at each step, as the majority seems to feel, the issue is only one of weighing the government's pocketbook against the actual survival of the recipient, and surely that balance must always tip in favor of the individual.

Similarly today's decision requires only the opportunity to have the benefit of counsel at the administrative hearing, but it is difficult to believe that the same reasoning process would not require the appointment of counsel, for otherwise the right to counsel is a meaningless one since these people are too poor to hire their own advocates. Thus the end result of today's decision may well be that the government, once it decides to give welfare benefits, cannot reverse that decision until the recipient has had the benefits of full administrative and judicial review, including, of course, the opportunity to present his case to this Court. Since this process will usually entail a delay of several years, the inevitable result of such a constitutionally imposed burden will be that the government will not put a claimant on the rolls initially until it has made an exhaustive investigation to determine his eligibility. While this Court will perhaps have insured that no needy person will be taken off the rolls without a full "due process" proceeding, it will also have insured that many will never get on the rolls, or at least that they will remain destitute during the lengthy proceedings followed to determine initial eligibility.

For the foregoing reasons I dissent from the Court's holding. The operation of a welfare state is a new experiment for our Nation. For this reason, among others, I feel that new experiments in carrying out a welfare program should not be frozen into our constitutional structure. They should be left, as are other legislative determinations, to the Congress and the legislatures that the people elect to make our laws.

[BURGER, C.J., and STEWART, J., also dissented.]

NOTES AND QUESTIONS

1. *The Goldberg decision.* Because nearly everything that follows in this chapter is a reaction to *Goldberg*, be clear on the issues determined:

    i.   The right to a continued flow of welfare benefits is an interest protected by procedural due process.

    ii. Due process requires a hearing *before* welfare benefits are terminated.

    iii. A pre-termination hearing must include the ingredients specified in the last paragraphs of the opinion.

2. *The purposes of due process.* A due process right to a trial-type hearing might serve various interests. Evaluate each of the following propositions in the context of welfare pre-termination hearings:

i. A hearing serves a *dignitary* function. It treats the individual as important, not just a cog in a giant machine. It affirms the value of fair procedure *for its own sake.*

ii. A right to a hearing serves an *empowerment* function. By demanding a hearing, people can seize the attention of a bureaucratic institution and prevent their problems from slipping through the cracks. On a practical level, a person who has a right to demand a hearing has leverage in settlement negotiations since the bureaucracy wants to avoid a time-consuming hearing.

iii. A hearing helps the individual *to understand and accept* a negative government decision. Therefore it tends to enhance people's satisfaction with government and to diminish their desire to resist it.

iv. A hearing is a good way to reach an *accurate* decision—to find out what happened and to apply law and policy correctly. Therefore, it protects individuals against governmental errors.

v. The decisions of administrative judges create a system of agency precedents. This helps to assure that agency decisions are *consistent.*

vi. Front-line officials are more likely to act seriously and carefully if they know that the people affected by their decisions can demand a hearing.

vii. A hearing is a good way to help government exercise *discretion* wisely.

viii. The use of hearings may *serve the purposes* of the substantive programs in which they occur. For instance, in the welfare context, hearings may help assure that the right people get benefits and the wrong ones don't.

ix. Hearings may help *identify recurring problems* and thus improve the system. For example, they may suggest that a problem might better be solved by adopting a rule or a guideline, rather than resolving disputes on a case-by-case basis.

x. A hearing facilitates *judicial review* because it produces a decision based exclusively on a record made at the hearing and results in a written decision.

Which of these rationales are persuasive in the context of welfare? What *disadvantages* should be set off against these advantages?

3. *In the wake of Goldberg. Goldberg* triggered a massive increase in the number of AFDC hearings. The decision occurred in March, 1970. In 1969, the New York Department of Social Services employed 11 hearing officers and a support staff of 20. In 1989, the Department employed 105 hearing officers and a support staff of 141. In 1969, 1300 appellants sought

hearings and 1000 decisions resulted. In 1989, recipients requested more than 150,000 hearings and 77,000 decisions were issued. In 1969, hearing officers held an average of 5 hearings a week and drafted decisions in longhand. In 1989, hearing officers faced calendars of 28 to 35 scheduled hearings daily and drafted decisions on a statewide computer system that could print and issue a decision in Albany the same day. *See* Cesar A. Perales, *The Fair Hearings Process: Guardian of the Social Service System*, 56 BROOK. L. REV. 889, 891 (1990).

Of the requests that go to a hearing, the recipient prevailed in about half of the cases (either through winning on the merits or because the agency withdrew its proposed action). However, nearly half of clients who request a hearing never follow through on their request, which suggests that the request for hearing was being used to keep the checks coming as long as possible. *See* Vicki Lens, *Bureaucratic Disentitlement After Welfare Reform*, 12 GEO. J. ON POVERTY L. & POL'Y 13, 42–49 (2005).

Consider the arguments made by Justice Black in his dissent. Did welfare recipients as a group gain or lose as a result of *Goldberg?*

4.   *Adversariness and mass justice.* One fundamental question raised by *Goldberg* is whether adversarial hearings are a good way to protect the rights of benefit recipients. The first year of law school tends to teach students that adversary civil and criminal trials are the best way to achieve justice. But we should recall that 90% or more of civil and criminal cases are settled, not tried. *Walters v. Radiation Survivors*, § 2.4 N.4, expresses skepticism about the utility of the adversary system in mass justice situations.

For a hearing system to work, welfare recipients have to have the resources and determination to fight back by demanding a hearing. They must determine that the costs of pursuing a remedy (considering the bother and lost time as well as the risk of antagonizing the bureaucracy) are worth the benefits. Do you think most welfare recipients would prefer a system of trial-type hearings as spelled out in *Goldberg* or a system of informal conferences with social workers, like the one used by New York prior to *Goldberg?* Consider that very few welfare recipients will have lawyers to represent them in the hearings. *See* Jason Parkin, *Adaptable Due Process,* 160 U. PA. L. REV. 1309, 1352–56 (2012).

§ 2.2   INTERESTS PROTECTED BY DUE PROCESS: LIBERTY AND PROPERTY

The balance of this chapter discusses three approaches to limiting the scope of procedural due process as articulated by *Goldberg*. The first approach (§ 2.2) excludes certain interests from the categories of "liberty" and "property." The second approach provides contextual rather than absolute rules for the timing and the elements of due process hearings

(§§ 2.3 and 2.4). The third approach identifies the action in question as generalized rather than individualized (§ 2.5).

§ 2.2.1 LIBERTY AND PROPERTY AS DEFINED IN *ROTH*

BOARD OF REGENTS V. ROTH
408 U.S. 564 (1972)

STEWART, J.

In 1968 the respondent, David Roth, was hired for his first teaching job as assistant professor of political science at Wisconsin State University–Oshkosh. He was hired for a fixed term of one academic year. The notice of his faculty appointment specified that his employment would begin on September 1, 1968, and would end on June 30, 1969. The respondent completed that term. But he was informed that he would not be rehired for the next academic year.

The respondent had no tenure rights to continued employment. Under Wisconsin statutory law a state university teacher can acquire tenure as a "permanent" employee only after four years of year-to-year employment. Having acquired tenure, a teacher is entitled to continued employment "during efficiency and good behavior." A relatively new teacher without tenure, however, is under Wisconsin law entitled to nothing beyond his one-year appointment. There are no statutory or administrative standards defining eligibility for re-employment. State law thus clearly leaves the decision whether to rehire a nontenured teacher for another year to the unfettered discretion of university officials.

The procedural protection afforded a Wisconsin State University teacher before he is separated from the University corresponds to his job security. As a matter of statutory law, a tenured teacher cannot be "discharged except for cause upon written charges" and pursuant to certain procedures. A nontenured teacher, similarly, is protected to some extent *during* his one-year term. Rules promulgated by the Board of Regents provide that a nontenured teacher "dismissed" before the end of the year may have some opportunity for review of the "dismissal." But the Rules provide no real protection for a nontenured teacher who simply is not re-employed for the next year. He must be informed by February 1 "concerning retention or non-retention for the ensuing year." But "no reason for non-retention need be given. No review or appeal is provided in such case."

In conformance with these Rules, the President of Wisconsin State University–Oshkosh informed the respondent before February 1, 1969, that he would not be rehired for the 1969–1970 academic year. He gave the respondent no reason for the decision and no opportunity to challenge it at any sort of hearing.

The respondent then brought this action in Federal District Court alleging that the decision not to rehire him for the next year infringed his Fourteenth Amendment rights. He attacked the decision both in substance and procedure. First, he alleged that the true reason for the decision was to punish him for certain statements critical of the University administration, and that it therefore violated his right to freedom of speech. Second, he alleged that the failure of University officials to give him notice of any reason for nonretention and an opportunity for a hearing violated his right to procedural due process of law.

The District Court granted summary judgment for the respondent on the procedural issue, ordering the University officials to provide him with reasons and a hearing. The Court of Appeals, with one judge dissenting, affirmed this partial summary judgment. The only question presented to us at this stage in the case is whether the respondent had a constitutional right to a statement of reasons and a hearing on the University's decision not to rehire him for another year. We hold that he did not.

I

The requirements of procedural due process apply only to the deprivation of interests encompassed by the Fourteenth Amendment's protection of liberty and property. When protected interests are implicated, the right to some kind of prior hearing is paramount.[7] But the range of interests protected by procedural due process is not infinite.

The District Court decided that procedural due process guarantees apply in this case by assessing and balancing the weights of the particular interests involved. It concluded that the respondent's interest in re-employment at Wisconsin State University–Oshkosh outweighed the University's interest in denying him re-employment summarily. Undeniably, the respondent's re-employment prospects were of major concern to him—concern that we surely cannot say was insignificant. And a weighing process has long been a part of any determination of the *form* of hearing required in particular situations by procedural due process. But, to determine whether due process requirements apply in the first place, we must look not to the "weight" but to the *nature* of the interest at stake. We must look to see if the interest is within the Fourteenth Amendment's protection of liberty and property.

"Liberty" and "property" are broad and majestic terms. They are among the "[g]reat [constitutional] concepts . . . purposely left to gather meaning from experience. . . ." For that reason, the Court has fully and finally rejected the wooden distinction between "rights" and "privileges"

---

[7]   Before a person is deprived of a protected interest, he must be afforded opportunity for some kind of a hearing, "except for extraordinary situations where some valid governmental interest is at stake that justifies postponing the hearing until after the event."

that once seemed to govern the applicability of procedural due process rights. The Court has also made clear that the property interests protected by procedural due process extend well beyond actual ownership of real estate, chattels, or money. By the same token, the Court has required due process protection for deprivations of liberty beyond the sort of formal constraints imposed by the criminal process.

Yet, while the Court has eschewed rigid or formalistic limitations on the protection of procedural due process, it has at the same time observed certain boundaries. For the words "liberty" and "property" in the Due Process Clause of the Fourteenth Amendment must be given some meaning. . . .

II

"While this court has not attempted to define with exactness the liberty . . . guaranteed [by the Fourteenth Amendment], the term has received much consideration and some of the included things have been definitely stated. Without doubt, it denotes not merely freedom from bodily restraint but also the right of the individual to contract, to engage in any of the common occupations of life, to acquire useful knowledge, to marry, establish a home and bring up children, to worship God according to the dictates of his own conscience, and generally to enjoy those privileges long recognized . . . as essential to the orderly pursuit of happiness by free men." *Meyer v. Nebraska*, 262 U.S. 390, 399. In a Constitution for a free people, there can be no doubt that the meaning of "liberty" must be broad indeed.

There might be cases in which a State refused to re-employ a person under such circumstances that interests in liberty would be implicated. But this is not such a case.

The State, in declining to rehire the respondent, did not make any charge against him that might seriously damage his standing and associations in his community. It did not base the nonrenewal of his contract on a charge, for example, that he had been guilty of dishonesty, or immorality. Had it done so, this would be a different case. For "[w]here a person's good name, reputation, honor, or integrity is at stake because of what the government is doing to him, notice and an opportunity to be heard are essential." *Wisconsin v. Constantineau*, 400 U.S. 433, 437. In such a case, due process would accord an opportunity to refute the charge before University officials.[12] In the present case, however, there is no suggestion whatever that the respondent's "good name, reputation, honor, or integrity" is at stake.

---

[12] The purpose of such notice and hearing is to provide the person an opportunity to clear his name. Once a person has cleared his name at a hearing, his employer, of course, may remain free to deny him future employment for other reasons.

Similarly, there is no suggestion that the State, in declining to re-employ the respondent, imposed on him a stigma or other disability that foreclosed his freedom to take advantage of other employment opportunities. The State, for example, did not invoke any regulations to bar the respondent from all other public employment in state universities. Had it done so, this, again, would be a different case. For "[t]o be deprived not only of present government employment but of future opportunity for it certainly is no small injury. . . ." The Court has held, for example, that a State, in regulating eligibility for a type of professional employment, cannot foreclose a range of opportunities "in a manner . . . that contravene[s] . . . Due Process," and, specifically, in a manner that denies the right to a full prior hearing. *Willner v. Committee on Character,* 373 U.S. 96 [bar admission]. In the present case, however, this principle does not come into play.[13]

To be sure, the respondent has alleged that the nonrenewal of his contract was based on his exercise of his right to freedom of speech. But this allegation is not now before us. The District Court stayed proceedings on this issue, and the respondent has yet to prove that the decision not to rehire him was, in fact, based on his free speech activities.

Hence, on the record before us, all that clearly appears is that the respondent was not rehired for one year at one university. It stretches the concept too far to suggest that a person is deprived of "liberty" when he simply is not rehired in one job but remains as free as before to seek another.

III

The Fourteenth Amendment's procedural protection of property is a safeguard of the security of interests that a person has already acquired in specific benefits. These interests—property interests—may take many forms.

Thus, the Court has held that a person receiving welfare benefits under statutory and administrative standards defining eligibility for them has an interest in continued receipt of those benefits that is safeguarded by procedural due process. *Goldberg v. Kelly.* Similarly, in the area of public employment, the Court has held that a public college

---

[13] The District Court made an *assumption* "that non-retention by one university or college creates concrete and practical difficulties for a professor in his subsequent academic career." And the Court of Appeals based its affirmance of the summary judgment largely on the premise that "the substantial adverse effect non-retention is likely to have upon the career interests of an individual professor" amounts to a limitation on future employment opportunities sufficient to invoke procedural due process guarantees. But even assuming, *arguendo,* that such a "substantial adverse effect" under these circumstances would constitute a state-imposed restriction on liberty, the record contains no support for these assumptions. There is no suggestion of how nonretention might affect the respondent's future employment prospects. Mere proof, for example, that his record of nonretention in one job, taken alone, might make him somewhat less attractive to some other employers would hardly establish the kind of foreclosure of opportunities amounting to a deprivation of "liberty."

professor dismissed from an office held under tenure provisions, and college professors and staff members dismissed during the terms of their contracts have interests in continued employment that are safeguarded by due process. . . .

Certain attributes of "property" interests protected by procedural due process emerge from these decisions. To have a property interest in a benefit, a person clearly must have more than an abstract need or desire for it. He must have more than a unilateral expectation of it. He must, instead, have a legitimate claim of entitlement to it. It is a purpose of the ancient institution of property to protect those claims upon which people rely in their daily lives, reliance that must not be arbitrarily undermined. It is a purpose of the constitutional right to a hearing to provide an opportunity for a person to vindicate those claims.

Property interests, of course, are not created by the Constitution. Rather, they are created and their dimensions are defined by existing rules or understandings that stem from an independent source such as state law—rules or understandings that secure certain benefits and that support claims of entitlement to those benefits. Thus, the welfare recipients in *Goldberg v. Kelly* had a claim of entitlement to welfare payments that was grounded in the statute defining eligibility for them. The recipients had not yet shown that they were, in fact, within the statutory terms of eligibility. But we held that they had a right to a hearing at which they might attempt to do so.

Just as the welfare recipients' "property" interest in welfare payments was created and defined by statutory terms, so the respondent's "property" interest in employment at Wisconsin State University–Oshkosh was created and defined by the terms of his appointment. Those terms secured his interest in employment up to June 30, 1969. But the important fact in this case is that they specifically provided that the respondent's employment was to terminate on June 30. They did not provide for contract renewal absent "sufficient cause." Indeed, they made no provision for renewal whatsoever.

Thus, the terms of the respondent's appointment secured absolutely no interest in re-employment for the next year. They supported absolutely no possible claim of entitlement to re-employment. Nor, significantly, was there any state statute or University rule or policy that secured his interest in re-employment or that created any legitimate claim to it. In these circumstances, the respondent surely had an abstract concern in being rehired, but he did not have a *property* interest sufficient to require the University authorities to give him a hearing when they declined to renew his contract of employment.

IV

Our analysis of the respondent's constitutional rights in this case in no way indicates a view that an opportunity for a hearing or a statement of reasons for nonretention would, or would not, be appropriate or wise in public colleges and universities. For it is a written Constitution that we apply. Our role is confined to interpretation of that Constitution.

We must conclude that the summary judgment for the respondent should not have been granted, since the respondent has not shown that he was deprived of liberty or property protected by the Fourteenth Amendment. The judgment of the Court of Appeals, accordingly, is reversed and the case is remanded for further proceedings consistent with this opinion.

[DOUGLAS, J., dissented, arguing that Roth was entitled to a hearing because he alleged that the dismissal was based upon expression protected by the First Amendment. Also dissenting, MARSHALL, J. contended that due process requires a statement of reasons and, if need be, a hearing whenever the government denies an individual a job. He argued that the job is "property" and that "liberty" protects the right to work.]

NOTES AND QUESTIONS

1.   *The right-privilege doctrine.* A government job was once considered a "privilege" and not a "right," meaning that a deprivation of the job did not trigger procedural due process. *Bailey v. Richardson,* 182 F.2d 46 (D.C. Cir. 1950), *aff'd by equally divided Court,* 341 U.S. 918 (1951). *Bailey* clearly reflected the cold war attitudes of the time.

Ms. Bailey was dismissed from her "non-sensitive" job in the U.S. Employment Service on the basis that reasonable grounds existed for the belief that she was disloyal. She received a hearing but was not allowed to confront the unnamed FBI informants who stated that there was reason to believe she was a member of the Communist Party. She denied this under oath, affirmed her loyalty to the United States, and placed a great deal of evidence of her loyalty on record. The Court of Appeals held that a government job is not property and that a dismissal for disloyalty is not an infringement of liberty, despite its stigmatic effect. Consequently, the government need not provide any procedure at all, much less confrontation of informants.

In addition to government jobs, many other relationships between private parties and government were treated as "privileges." Among them were licenses to do the sort of business that the state could prohibit entirely (like selling liquor), subsidies, welfare benefits, and the ability to contract with the government. The theory of the right-privilege distinction was that since government did not have to give a person a job, a license, welfare benefits, or a contract, due process did not apply to the withdrawal of these benefits.

Goldberg v. Kelly discarded the right-privilege distinction. In a footnote in *Roth* (not reproduced in the text), the Court said: "The basis of the [*Bailey*] holding has been thoroughly undermined in the ensuing years ... [T]his Court now has rejected the concept that constitutional rights turn upon whether a governmental benefit is characterized as a 'right' or a 'privilege.'" 408 U.S. at 571 n.9. Is the distinction between tenured and untenured government jobs in *Roth* a modern counterpart to the right-privilege distinction?

2. *New property.* Procedural due process has always protected a person's interest in traditional forms of property (such as land, money, or the right to own and use goods). Justice Stewart's definition of property broke new ground. Under *Roth,* the right to receive welfare benefits is a statutory "entitlement" and thus "property." Similarly, *Perry,* discussed in N.7, held that a professor's right under implied contract to keep his job is "property." However, these sorts of "new property" interests are very different from "old property" like money, land, or chattels. For example, they cannot be divided, inherited, or sold like old property. They can be legislatively abolished without the need for government to pay compensation.

New property depends upon an *entitlement* created and defined by an *independent source* of law such as a state or federal statute. We call this a "positivist" approach to identifying property. because no rights to new property exist in the absence of a specific statute or other source of positive law. This means that the state can modify or eliminate the property right by modifying or repealing its positive law source.

In a footnote (not quoted in text), the *Roth* decision cited with approval an old case in which a procedural *regulation* created an entitlement that triggered due process rights. In *Goldsmith v. Board of Tax Appeals,* 270 U.S. 117 (1926), the Board's regulation made attorneys licensed to practice under state law eligible to practice before the Board. The Board denied admission to an attorney without a hearing or statement of reasons. The Supreme Court held that a hearing was required.

In the 1996 statute that abandoned AFDC and adopted TANF (see the text preceding *Goldberg*), Congress declared that welfare is no longer an entitlement: "NO INDIVIDUAL ENTITLEMENT. This part shall not be interpreted to entitle any individual or family to assistance under any State program funded under this part." 42 U.S.C. § 601(b). Of course, welfare might still be an entitlement under state law even if it is not an entitlement under federal law. TANF requires states to "provide opportunities for recipients who have been adversely affected to be heard in a State administrative or appeal process." 42 U.S.C. § 602(a)(1)(B)(iii). Does all this mean that a state can now design a welfare system that involves discretion rather than entitlement and thus dispense with pre-termination welfare hearings? This question remains unanswered at present (though some decisions hold that state law provides an entitlement to welfare even if federal law does not). *See Weston v. Cassata*, 37 P.2d 469 (Colo. App. 2002).

3.   *What is liberty? Roth* defined "liberty" as a form of "natural" rather than "positive" law, in sharp contrast to its definition of "property." Justice Stewart relied upon the open-ended natural law analysis of *Meyer v. Nebraska* in sketching the contours of liberty. *Meyer* was a 1923 decision that declared invalid a Nebraska law prohibiting the teaching of foreign languages to young children. Note that *Meyer* involved *substantive* rather than *procedural* due process. The state law was invalid, not because of the procedure that Nebraska used, but because it "materially" interfered "with the calling of modern language teachers, with the opportunities of pupils to acquire knowledge, and with the power of parents to control the education of their own." *Roth* establishes that this definition of "liberty" applies to *both* procedural and substantive due process. In addition, it adds the imposition of a stigma by government as an element of liberty.

This course concerns *procedural* rather than *substantive* due process. Elements of substantive due process (studied in constitutional law classes) survive in cases that require a compelling state interest in order to interfere with people's "fundamental" interests such as control over their bodies or family relations. *See, e.g., Roe v. Wade*, 410 U.S. 113 (1973) (right to have an abortion). In the economic area, there is little left of substantive due process (or of its close counterpart, substantive equal protection). The courts accept any rational justification for statutes that limit economic rights. *See, e.g., Williamson v. Lee Optical Inc.*, 348 U.S. 483 (1955) (imagining reasons why state law regulating optometry might be rational).

4.   *Free speech rights.* Roth argued that he lost his job because the University disapproved of constitutionally protected speeches he gave. The majority believed that issue was not before the Court and thus did not reach it. Because "liberty" includes First Amendment rights, government invades liberty if it refuses to rehire employees (tenured or untenured) because of disagreement with their political speeches. The decision remands the case to the trial court to decide whether Roth was discharged in violation of his first amendment rights. Why is this claim to be resolved in the federal district court rather than in an administrative hearing?

Roth's claim was plausible. Of 442 non-tenured teachers, the University failed to renew the teaching contracts of only four. Roth had been involved in demonstrations against the Vietnam War and had caustically criticized the university administration. He ultimately prevailed on his First Amendment claim in the district court and was awarded $6746 in damages. By that time he had another teaching job at Purdue. *Chronicle of Higher Education*, Nov. 26, 1973.

5.   *Discretion and due process.* The Court held that Wisconsin infringed no liberty or property rights, so Roth was entitled to no process. Nevertheless, the effect of a decision not to renew a young professor's contract is quite drastic. Do you think that there should be a right to a hearing whenever

government exercises discretionary power in a way that drastically and negatively affects a person's life? Is a hearing *more important* when the government exercises discretionary power than when it applies a non-discretionary standard? If so, should federal courts adopt the California approach discussed in the next note?

6.   *State constitutional law.* Although the language of the California constitutional due process clause is the same as the federal, the California Supreme Court rejected the *Roth* approach. It held that denial of a statutory benefit under a discretionary standard triggered due process protection. *Saleeby v. State Bar*, 702 P.2d 525 (Cal. 1985), involved a claim by a defrauded client for reimbursement from the California Bar's Client Security Fund. By statute, "any payments from the fund shall be discretionary and shall be subject to such regulation and conditions as the [State Bar] shall prescribe." The Bar denied Saleeby's claim for payment from the Fund and declined to provide a hearing or any statement of reasons. After summarizing *Roth*, the court said:

> California has expanded upon the federal analytical base by focusing on the administrative process itself. . . . [D]ue process safeguards required for protection of an individual's statutory interests must be analyzed in the context of the principle that *freedom from arbitrary adjudicative procedures* is a substantive element of one's liberty.

> No firm rule can be established to ascertain what protections are necessary in a particular situation. Rather the relief to be afforded depends upon balancing the various interests involved. Generally, the dictates of due process necessitate considering (1) the private interest that will be affected by the official action, (2) the risk of an erroneous deprivation of such interest through the procedures used, and the probable value, if any, of additional or substitute procedural safeguards, (3) *the dignitary interest in informing individuals of the nature, grounds, and consequences of the action and in enabling them to present their side of the story before a responsible governmental official*, and (4) the governmental interest, including the function involved and the fiscal and administrative burdens that the additional or substitute procedural requirement would entail. . . . [emphasis added]

The court held that Saleeby had a right to be heard and to respond (orally or in writing) to the Bar's determination and the Bar must issue sufficient findings to afford judicial review. What is the "dignitary interest" to which the court refers and how does a hearing vindicate that interest?

7.   *De facto tenure. Perry v. Sindermann*, 408 U.S. 593 (1972) was decided the same day as *Roth*. Both cases involved untenured professors whose contracts were not renewed, but Sindermann alleged a right to re-employment based on *implied contract*. The contract arose from guidelines on which he had relied during his ten-year teaching career and on the practice of

the institution not to discharge professors without good cause. The Court held that an entitlement could be based on implied as well as express contract, since implied contract rights are protected in state courts. The Court said: "[T]here may be an unwritten 'common law' in a particular university that certain employees shall have the equivalent of tenure. This is particularly likely in a college or university, like Odessa Junior College, that has no explicit tenure system even for senior members of its faculty, but that nonetheless may have created such a system in practice." *Id.* at 602.

8. *Deprivation.* The Constitution requires the state to provide due process only if a person is "deprived" of life, liberty, or property. There may be a constitutional distinction between being "deprived" of what you already have and being "denied" something that you want but do not yet have. Thus, for example, the Court might deny that due process applies to a person whose *application* for welfare is rejected even though due process applies to a *termination* of an existing right to welfare payments.

American Manufacturers Mutual Ins. Co. v. Sullivan, 526 U.S. 40 (1999), concerned the Pennsylvania workers' compensation law. The law entitled an employee to payment of reasonable and necessary medical expenses arising out of an on-the-job injury. However, if the employer or insurance company believed that a particular medical procedure was not reasonable and necessary, it could refuse to pay until the issue was determined through a hearing procedure. Employees argued that this procedure violated due process, since they should be entitled to a hearing *before* being deprived of payment of the benefits (in other words, that the benefits should be paid before a hearing was provided, not after).

The Supreme Court decided that due process was inapplicable because the action was taken by a private company rather than by the state. In dictum, the Court discussed the due process issues that would have arisen if the state action requirement had been met. It might have disposed of those issues by finding that due process applied, but that a post-deprivation hearing was adequate in the circumstances, as in *Mathews v. Eldridge*, § 2.3.

However, the Court took a different approach. Part III of the opinion by Chief Justice Rehnquist stated that due process was inapplicable. The opinion distinguished *Goldberg v. Kelly* and *Mathews v. Eldridge*.

> In both cases, an individual's entitlement to benefits had been established, and the question presented was whether pre-deprivation notice and a hearing were required before the individual's interest in *continued* payment of benefits could be terminated. Respondent's property interest in this case, however, is fundamentally different. . . . [Pennsylvania] law expressly limits an employee's entitlement to 'reasonable' and 'necessary' medical treatment, and requires that disputes over the reasonableness and necessity of particular treatment must be resolved *before* an employer's obligation to pay—and an employee's entitlement to benefits—arise. . . . Thus for an employee's property interest in the

payment of medical benefits to attach under state law . . . he must establish that the particular medical treatment is reasonable and necessary. Only then does the employee's interest parallel that of the beneficiary of welfare assistance in *Goldberg* and the recipient of disability benefits in *Mathews* . . ."

Justice Ginsburg's concurring opinion provided the fifth vote: "I join Part III of the Court's opinion on the understanding that the Court rejects specifically, and only, respondents' demands for constant payment of each medical bill, within 30 days of receipt, pending determination of the necessity or reasonableness of the medical treatment. I do not doubt, however, that due process requires fair procedures for the adjudication of respondents' claims for workers' compensation benefits, including medical care." Lower court cases have consistently applied due process to an agency's ultimate rejection of an application for an entitlement. *See, e.g., Cushman v. Shinseki,* 576 F.3d 1290 (Fed. Cir. 2009) (due process applies to the rejection by the VA of a claim for veterans' benefits). However, the question remains unresolved at the Supreme Court level.

§ 2.2.2 REFINING THE *ROTH* APPROACH TO PROPERTY AND LIBERTY

The *Roth* case held that a tenured professor's job or the continued flow of welfare benefits is "property" while an untenured professor's job is not. According to *Roth,* property interests are created and limited by positive law such as state statutes. Does it follow that a statute that creates "property" can also prescribe the procedure for taking it away?

CLEVELAND BOARD OF EDUCATION V. LOUDERMILL
470 U.S. 532 (1985)

[Respondents worked for cities in Ohio. One was a security guard, the other a bus mechanic. By law, they could be discharged only for cause. They were discharged without any opportunity to respond to the charges against them prior to the discharge. One was discharged for lying on his employment application, one failed an eye examination. Ohio law provided no pre-termination hearing, only a post-termination hearing and judicial review. The post-termination hearing occurred about nine months after the discharge.]

WHITE, J.:

. . . . Respondents' federal constitutional claim depends on their having had a property right in continued employment. *Board of Regents v. Roth.* If they did, the State could not deprive them of this property without due process.

Property interests are not created by the Constitution, "they are created and their dimensions are defined by existing rules or understandings that stem from an independent source such as state law. . . ." *Roth.* The Ohio statute plainly creates such an interest. Respondents were "classified civil service employees," entitled to retain their positions "during good behavior and efficient service," who could not be dismissed "except . . . for . . . misfeasance, malfeasance, or nonfeasance in office." The statute plainly supports the conclusion, reached by both lower courts, that respondents possessed property rights in continued employment. . . .

The Parma Board argues, however, that the property right is defined by, and conditioned on, the legislature's choice of procedures for its deprivation. The Board stresses that in addition to specifying the grounds for termination, the statute sets out procedures by which termination may take place. The procedures were adhered to in these cases. According to petitioner, "[t]o require additional procedures would in effect expand the scope of the property interest itself."

This argument, which was accepted by the District Court, has its genesis in the plurality opinion in *Arnett v. Kennedy*, 416 U.S. 134 (1974). *Arnett* involved a challenge by a former federal employee to the procedures by which he was dismissed. The plurality reasoned that where the legislation conferring the substantive right also sets out the procedural mechanism for enforcing that right, the two cannot be separated:

> The employee's statutorily defined right is not a guarantee against removal without cause in the abstract, but such a guarantee as enforced by the procedures which Congress has designated for the determination of cause . . . [W]here the grant of a substantive right is inextricably intertwined with the limitations on the procedures which are to be employed in determining that right, a litigant in the position of appellee must take the bitter with the sweet.

This view garnered three votes in *Arnett,* but was specifically rejected by the other six Justices. Since then, this theory has at times seemed to gather some additional support. More recently, however, the Court has clearly rejected it. . . . In light of these holdings, it is settled that the "bitter with the sweet" approach misconceives the constitutional guarantee. If a clearer holding is needed, we provide it today. The point is straightforward: the Due Process Clause provides that certain substantive rights—life, liberty, and property—cannot be deprived except pursuant to constitutionally adequate procedures. The categories of substance and procedure are distinct. Were the rule otherwise, the Clause would be reduced to a mere tautology. "Property" cannot be defined by the procedures provided for its deprivation any more than can life or liberty. The right to due process "is conferred, not by legislative grace, but by constitutional guarantee. While the legislature may elect not to confer a property interest in [public] employment, it may not constitutionally authorize the deprivation of such an interest, once conferred, without appropriate procedural safeguards."

In short, once it is determined that the Due Process Clause applies, "the question remains what process is due." The answer to that question is not to be found in the Ohio statute. . . . [The Court found that Ohio's pre-termination procedures did not provide due process. See § 2.3 N.3.]

REHNQUIST, C.J., dissenting.

. . . . We ought to recognize the totality of the State's definition of the property right in question, and not merely seize upon one of several paragraphs in a unitary statute to proclaim that in that paragraph the State has inexorably conferred upon a civil service employee something which it is powerless under the United States Constitution to qualify in the next paragraph of the statute. This practice ignores our duty under *Roth* to rely on state law as the source of property interests for purposes of applying the Due Process Clause of the Fourteenth Amendment. While it does not impose a federal definition of property, the Court departs from the full breadth of the holding in *Roth* by its selective choice from among the sentences the Ohio legislature chooses to use in establishing and qualifying a right. . . .

NOTES AND QUESTIONS

1. *The bitter with the sweet.* Since "property" does not exist in the abstract but arises only from statute, contract, or other interest protected by law, what's wrong with Rehnquist's contention that the state should be allowed to create the procedural as well as the substantive contours of property interests? In other words, why shouldn't the property-holder take "the bitter with the sweet?"

In the portion of the opinion discussed in § 2.3 N.3, the Court held that a *written* pre-termination proceeding is sufficient protection for a discharged employee, if a full hearing with *oral* testimony is provided after the discharge. Was this determination a factor in persuading the majority justices to reject the "bitter with the sweet" approach?

2. *Consequences of Loudermill.* Do decisions like *Perry v. Sindermann* (§ 2.2.1 N.7) and *Loudermill* go too far in rigidifying public employment? It might be argued that the Court's due process rulings relating to public employment force government to choose between a spoils system (under which government employees have no job protection) and a tenure system that is highly protective of employee job security. As a practical matter, government managers are often unable or unwilling to take the trouble and expense of attempting to fire incompetent employees whose jobs are protected by due process. Moreover, these cases encourage government to contract out

to the private sector such traditional governmental tasks as trash collection, playground maintenance, public transportation and the like. Since job security is a matter of employer-employee bargaining in the private sector, private employers may be able to furnish such services more efficiently than government.

3.   *Jobs and licenses as property.* Among the most important forms of "new property" are government jobs that protect the employee from discharge without cause. Many government jobholders have less protection than a tenured college professor but more protection than Mr. Roth. For example, in *Bishop v. Wood,* 426 U.S. 341 (1976), a policeman was classified as a "permanent employee." The ordinance provided that "if a permanent employee fails to perform work up to the standard of the classification held, or continues to be negligent, inefficient, or unfit to perform his duties, he may be dismissed by the City manager. Any discharged employee shall be given written notice of his discharge setting forth the effective date and reasons for his discharge if he shall request such a notice." No North Carolina cases had interpreted this ordinance.

The federal trial judge, "who of course sits in North Carolina and practiced law there for many years," concluded that the policeman "held his position at the will and pleasure of the city." The Supreme Court deferred to this construction and held that the job was not "property." This decision requires trial courts to conduct a detailed analysis of the parameters of the job in question and there have been many such reported cases.

Besides certain jobs and welfare benefits, what other relationships between persons and government are *entitlements*? Among the most important are *licenses* to do what cannot be done without governmental permission (for example, to drive a car or practice medicine). *See, e.g. Barry v. Barchi,* 443 U.S. 55 (1979) (suspension of horse trainer's license). Equally important is the right to public *services* such as education. *See, e.g. Memphis Light, Gas and Water Div. v. Craft,* 436 U.S. 1 (1978) (right to continued service from municipal utility).

4.   *Standards plus discretion. Bishop v. Wood* illustrates a larger problem with the *Roth* entitlement analysis: a statute creating a benefit often contains a legal standard for granting or terminating the benefit but also gives the decisionmaker some discretion in applying the standard. Is such a benefit "property" like the job in *Loudermill* or non-property like the job in *Roth*?

Town of Castle Rock v. Gonzales, 545 U.S. 748 (2005), raised this issue in an unusual context—a domestic violence restraining order (DVRO) under Colorado law. By statute, a police officer "shall arrest" a restrained person if the officer has probable cause to believe that the person has violated or attempted to violate a DVRO. Jessica Gonzales got a DVRO against her estranged husband, Simon, ordering him to remain 100 yards from the family home. Simon violated the DVRO and kidnapped their three children. Jessica frantically asked the police to find and arrest Simon, but they did nothing.

Later that night, Simon murdered the children. Jessica sued the town, alleging that it had a practice of non-enforcement of DVROs and that this practice deprived her of procedural due process. However, the Supreme Court found that Jessica had not been deprived of "property," so there was no violation of due process. Despite the "shall" language in the statute, the majority opinion held that it did not create an "entitlement" to police enforcement. Instead, the police's decision to arrest or not arrest Simon was discretionary. The Court was influenced by the "deep-rooted nature of law enforcement discretion."

The opinion continued: "Even if we were to think otherwise concerning the creation of an entitlement by Colorado, it is by no means clear that an individual entitlement to enforcement of a [DVRO] could constitute a 'property' interest for purposes of the Due Process Clause. Such a right would not, of course, resemble any traditional conception of property. Although that alone does not disqualify it from due process protection, as *Roth* and its progeny show, the right to have a restraining order enforced does not 'have some ascertainable monetary value,' as even our '*Roth*-type property-as-entitlement' cases have implicitly required. . . . Perhaps most radically, the alleged property interest here arises incidentally, not out of some new species of government benefit or service, but out of a function that government actors have always performed—to wit, arresting people who they have probable cause to believe have committed a criminal offense."

Justice Stevens (joined by Justice Ginsburg) dissented. They argued that the statute created an entitlement to police protection that should be considered a species of property (like any other form of municipal services to which a person is entitled, such as education or utility service). The police deprived Jessica of this property right by ignoring her pleas to arrest Simon without providing any sort of hearing or other process. If the Court had ruled the other way in *Castle Rock,* what sort of procedure would have been appropriate to protect Jessica's entitlement?

5. *Does required procedure create liberty or property? Loudermill* establishes that if state law creates a property interest, the process that is due is determined by federal rather than state law. What about the reverse situation: suppose state law prescribes procedures to protect an interest that qualifies as neither liberty nor property? If the state then fails to provide those procedures, it violates state law but *not* due process. For example, in *Bishop,* the statute required the employer to provide a statement of reasons for dismissal of the employee, but this provision by itself did not elevate the job into "property" for due process purposes and the failure to provide reasons was not a due process violation. *See Cain v. Larson,* 879 F.2d 1424, 1426 (7th Cir. 1989) (making this point explicit, on facts similar to those of *Bishop*).

6. *De minimis deprivations. Goss v. Lopez,* 419 U.S. 565, 576 (1975), involved a ten-day suspension of a high school student. The Court held that this interest was not de minimis and the suspended student had a right to

due process. We discuss the process that must be provided in §§ 2.3 and 2.4 and discuss *Goss* further in § 2.4 N.1.

What sort of deprivation of property might be *de minimis* (that is, too trivial to bother with)? *See Swick v. City of Chicago,* 11 F.3d 85 (7th Cir. 1993). The court held that placing a police officer on paid sick leave, so that he could not wear a badge or carry a gun or arrest people, is a *de minimis* deprivation. "Otherwise we shall be hearing appeals next in cases in which the public employer reneged on a promise to give the employee an office with a view, or a second secretary, or leave to coach a Little League team."

7.   *Stigma plus.* In *Roth,* the Court stated that the imposition of a stigma by government could be a deprivation of liberty. It relied on an earlier case holding that a person was entitled to a prior hearing before the state posted his name as a "public drunkard." *Wisconsin v. Constantineau,* 400 U.S. 433 (1971).

However, in *Paul v. Davis,* 424 U.S. 693 (1976), the police circulated a flyer bearing Davis' photo and labeling him as an "active shoplifter." This action might have defamed Davis but did not deprive him of liberty. A stigma qualifies as a deprivation of liberty only if the state makes it in connection with *some other change of right or status recognized by state law*—such as discharge from a job. This something-more requirement is often called "stigma plus." The *Paul* decision distinguished *Constantineau* because state law prevented a "public drunkard" from purchasing alcoholic beverages (thus meeting the "stigma-plus" test).

Numerous cases have dealt with the stigma-plus requirement as well as the nature of the "name-clearing hearing" required by *Roth.* A public employee who has been discharged for reasons that are stigmatic in nature has no right to a hearing unless the employer publicizes the reasons for the discharge on its own initiative. *Bishop v. Wood, supra.* Even where the employer has publicized the stigmatic information, the Court has applied the stigma-plus test narrowly. In *Siegert v. Gilley,* 500 U.S. 226 (1991), Siegert quit his government job (as a psychologist at St. Elizabeth's Hospital in Washington, D.C.) to avoid being fired. Siegert requested that St. Elizabeth's furnish information about him to another hospital. Several weeks later, in response to this request, Siegert's former supervisor furnished adverse comments about him. These facts did not meet the "stigma-plus" requirement. The stigmatizing statements were not uttered "incident to" the termination of Siegert's employment, because he had quit his job (rather than being fired) and had himself requested his former employer to furnish the information.

8.   *Prisoners' rights as liberty.* After *Roth,* the Court experienced difficulty deciding whether prisoners are deprived of liberty when prison officials make decisions adversely affecting them. For example, does the prison need to provide a hearing before disciplining a prisoner by placing him in solitary confinement? Early cases suggested that a hearing is required before imposing discipline. *Wolff v. McDonnell,* 418 U.S. 539 (1974). More

recently, however, the Court decided that prisoners have no liberty interest (and thus no right to a hearing) in most situations involving prison discipline. *Sandin v. Conner,* 515 U.S. 472 (1995). However, *Sandin* provided for a couple of exceptions. The prison deprives a prisoner of a liberty interest if the decision inevitably lengthens the term of imprisonment or imposes "atypical and significant hardship on the inmate in relation to the ordinary incidents of prison life." Examples of such hardships include transfer to a mental hospital, *Vitek v. Jones*, 445 U.S. 480 (1980); involuntary administration of psychotropic drugs, *Washington v. Harper,* 494 U.S. 210 (1990); and transfer to an extremely harsh "supermax" prison. *Wilkinson v. Austin*, 545 U.S. 209 (2005).

9. *Problem—property.* Seaside High School hires part-time athletic coaches to work less than 20 hours per week. The contracts provide that if a coach's work is satisfactory and the coach's services are needed for the next academic year, the contract will be renewed. If a contract is not renewed because of unsatisfactory service, the principal must furnish a written explanation of the decision.

Rex, the principal of Seaside High, hired Doris to coach girls' tennis for the spring semester. The contract called for compensation of $400 per month for four months. Rex's daughter, Ann, was on the team. Doris did not allow Ann to play in several important matches because of poor attitude. However, Seaside's team was undefeated, and most of the girls were pleased with Doris. Rex declined to renew Doris' contract for the following academic year, even though a coach was needed. He stated no reasons and refused to discuss the matter with Doris. What are Doris' rights? *See Vail v. Board of Educ.,* 706 F.2d 1435 (7th Cir. 1983), *aff'd by equally divided Court,* 466 U.S. 377 (1984).

10. *Problem—liberty.* The Madison Social Welfare Department (MSWD) maintains a hotline to receive information about child abuse. A Madison statute requires that the names of all persons suspected of child abuse must be placed on a registry maintained by MSWD. Any employer engaged in education of children or child care must consult the registry before hiring a new employee. Any such employer who hires a person whose name appears on the list must notify MSWD in writing. The statute provides that MSWD must notify any person whose name is placed on the list. Such person can write to MSWD and show cause why his or her name should be removed from the list.

Anna slapped her child in the face because she suspected him of stealing from her wallet. A neighbor who observed the incident phoned the hotline. Based on this information, Anna's name was added to the child abuse list. Anna sent a letter to MSWD asking that her name be removed, but MSWD declined to do so. Anna has recently completed a course in school counseling and hopes to get a job with her local school district.

Anna sues MSWD in federal court, arguing that she has been deprived of due process. How should the court rule? *See Valmonte v. Bane,* 18 F.3d 992 (2d Cir. 1994).

§ 2.3   TIMING OF TRIAL-TYPE HEARINGS

If a court determines that government action has deprived a person of liberty or property, thus triggering due process protection, it must decide what process is due. *Goldberg* determined that a trial-type hearing must be held *before* termination of benefits. The timing question is often critical, because a hearing after the event may do little to repair the damage caused by an administrative error. Yet a requirement that an agency hold a hearing before it can terminate benefits, employment, or some other entitlement may be quite costly.

Mathews v. Eldridge asks whether trial-type hearings must be provided *before* termination of benefits to *disabled* persons under Title II of the Social Security Act. The complex state-federal system that adjudicates disability claims is described in the *Mathews* opinion. Some additional background on the disability program is helpful in evaluating the decision.

The Social Security Administration (SSA) operates the largest system of administrative adjudication in the Western world. It processed about 2.8 million applications for disability benefits in fiscal 2011. Many thousands of state agency personnel make the initial decisions whether to grant or deny disability claims. Close to 1500 federal administrative law judges hear administrative appeals from state agency denials or benefit terminations. These ALJs dispose of nearly 800,000 cases each year. The backlog of undecided cases was nearly 800,000 at the end of 2011. The claims that these officials adjudicate are not small. The average disability recipient receives $1110 per month. More than 8.8 million disabled workers and their dependents drew annual benefits in 2011. The benefits total over $114 billion annually. When the Medicaid and Medicare payments for which these beneficiaries are automatically eligible are included, the total figure is much larger.

MATHEWS V. ELDRIDGE
424 U.S. 319 (1976)

POWELL, J.:

The issue in this case is whether the Due Process Clause of the Fifth Amendment requires that prior to the termination of Social Security disability benefit payments the recipient be afforded an opportunity for an evidentiary hearing. . . . Respondent Eldridge was first awarded benefits in June 1968. In March 1972, he received a questionnaire from the state agency charged with monitoring his medical condition. Eldridge completed the questionnaire, indicating that his condition had not improved and identifying the medical sources, including physicians, from whom he had received treatment recently. The state agency then obtained reports from his physician and a psychiatric consultant. After considering these reports and other information in his file the agency informed Eldridge by letter that it had made a tentative determination that his disability had ceased in May 1972. The letter included a statement of reasons for the proposed termination of benefits, and advised Eldridge that he might request reasonable time in which to obtain and submit additional information pertaining to his condition.

In his written response, Eldridge disputed one characterization of his medical condition and indicated that the agency already had enough evidence to establish his disability. The state agency then made its final determination that he had ceased to be disabled in May 1972. This determination was accepted by the Social Security Administration (SSA), which notified Eldridge in July that his benefits would terminate after that month. The notification also advised him of his right to seek reconsideration by the state agency of this initial determination within six months.

Instead of requesting reconsideration Eldridge commenced this action challenging the constitutional validity of the administrative procedures established by the Secretary of Health, Education, and Welfare for assessing whether there exists a continuing disability. He sought an immediate reinstatement of benefits pending a hearing on the issue of his disability. . . . In support of his contention that due process requires a pretermination hearing, Eldridge relied exclusively upon this Court's decision in *Goldberg v. Kelly*. . . .

A

Procedural due process imposes constraints on governmental decisions which deprive individuals of "liberty" or "property" interests within the meaning of the Due Process Clause of the Fifth or Fourteenth Amendment. The Secretary does not contend that procedural due process is inapplicable to terminations of Social Security disability benefits. He recognizes . . . that the interest of an individual in continued receipt of these benefits is a statutorily created "property" interest protected by the Fifth Amendment. Rather, the Secretary contends that the existing administrative procedures, detailed below, provide all the process that is constitutionally due before a recipient can be deprived of that interest. . . . In only one case, *Goldberg v. Kelly,* has the Court held that a hearing closely approximating a judicial trial is necessary. In other cases requiring some type of pretermination hearing as a matter of constitutional right the Court has spoken sparingly about the requisite procedures. . . .

[O]ur prior decisions indicate that identification of the specific dictates of due process generally requires consideration of three distinct factors: First, the private interest that will be affected by the official action; second, the risk of an erroneous deprivation of such interest through the procedures used, and the probable value, if any, of additional or substitute procedural safeguards; and finally, the Government's interest, including the function involved and the fiscal and administrative burdens that the additional or substitute procedural requirement would entail. . . .

B

The disability insurance program is administered jointly by state and federal agencies. State agencies make the initial determination whether a disability exists, when it began, and when it ceased. . . . In order to establish initial and continued entitlement to disability benefits a worker must demonstrate that he is unable "to engage in any substantial gainful activity by reason of any medically determinable physical or mental impairment which can be expected to result in death or which has lasted or can be expected to last for a continuous period of not less than 12 months. . . ."

To satisfy this test the worker bears a continuing burden of showing, by means of "medically acceptable clinical and laboratory diagnostic techniques," that he has a physical or mental impairment of such severity that "he is not only unable to do his previous work but cannot, considering his age, education, and work experience, engage in any other kind of substantial gainful work which exists in the national economy, regardless of whether such work exists in the immediate area in which he lives, or whether a specific job vacancy exists for him, or whether he would be hired if he applied for work."

. . . . If there is a conflict between the information provided by the beneficiary and that obtained from medical sources such as his physician, or between two sources of treatment, the agency may arrange for an examination by an independent consulting physician. Whenever the agency's tentative assessment of the beneficiary's condition differs from his own assessment, the beneficiary is informed that benefits may be terminated, provided a summary of the evidence upon which the proposed determination to terminate is based, and afforded an opportunity to review the medical reports and other evidence in his case file. He also may respond in writing and submit additional evidence. The state agency then makes its final determination, which is reviewed by an examiner in the SSA Bureau of Disability Insurance. If, as is usually the case, the SSA accepts the agency determination it notifies the recipient in writing, informing him of the reasons for the decision, and of his right to seek *de novo* reconsideration by the state agency. Upon acceptance by the SSA, benefits are terminated effective two months after the month in which medical recovery is found to have occurred. . . . He then has a right to an evidentiary hearing before an SSA administrative law judge.

The hearing is nonadversary, and the SSA is not represented by counsel. As at all prior and subsequent stages of the administrative process, however, the claimant may be represented by counsel or other spokesmen. If this hearing results in an adverse decision, the claimant is entitled to request discretionary review by the SSA Appeals Council and finally may obtain judicial review.

Should it be determined at any point after termination of benefits, that the claimant's disability extended beyond the date of cessation initially established, the worker is entitled to retroactive payments. . . . If, on the other hand, a beneficiary receives any payments to which he is later determined not to be entitled, the statute authorizes the Secretary to attempt to recoup these funds in specified circumstances.

C

Despite the elaborate character of the administrative procedures provided by the Secretary, the courts below held them to be constitutionally inadequate, concluding that due process requires an evidentiary hearing prior to termination. In light of the private and governmental interests at stake here and the nature of the existing procedures, we think this was error.

Since a recipient whose benefits are terminated is awarded full retroactive relief if he ultimately prevails, his sole interest is in the uninterrupted receipt of this source of income pending final administrative decision on his claim. His potential injury is thus similar in nature to that of the welfare recipient in *Goldberg.* . . .

Only in *Goldberg* has the Court held that due process requires an evidentiary hearing prior to a temporary deprivation. It was emphasized there that welfare assistance is given to persons on the very margin of subsistence . . . Eligibility for disability benefits, in contrast, is not based upon financial need. Indeed, it is wholly unrelated to the worker's income or support from many other sources, such as earnings of other family members, workmen's compensation awards, tort claims awards, savings, private insurance, public or private pensions, veterans' benefits, food stamps, public assistance, or the "many other important programs, both public and private, which contain provisions for disability payments affecting a substantial portion of the work force. . . ."

As *Goldberg* illustrates, the degree of potential deprivation that may be created by a particular decision is a factor to be considered in assessing the validity of any administrative decisionmaking process. The potential deprivation here is generally likely to be less than in *Goldberg,* although the degree of difference can be overstated. As the District Court emphasized, to remain eligible for benefits a recipient must be "unable to engage in substantial gainful activity." Thus, in contrast to the discharged federal employee in *Arnett,* there is little possibility that the terminated recipient will be able to find even temporary employment to ameliorate the interim loss.

. . . . [T]he possible length of wrongful deprivation of . . . benefits [also] is an important factor in assessing the impact of official action on the private interests. The Secretary concedes that the delay between a request for a hearing before an administrative law judge and a decision on the claim is currently between 10 and 11 months. Since a terminated recipient must first obtain a reconsideration decision as a prerequisite to invoking his right to an evidentiary hearing, the delay between the actual cutoff of benefits and final decision after a hearing exceeds one year.

In view of the torpidity of this administrative review process and the typically modest resources of the family unit of the physically disabled worker,[26] the hardship imposed upon the erroneously terminated disability recipient may be significant. Still, the disabled worker's need is likely to be less than that of a welfare recipient. In addition to the possibility of access to private resources, other forms of government assistance will become available where the termination of disability benefits places a worker or his family below the subsistence level.

In view of these potential sources of temporary income, there is less reason here than in *Goldberg* to depart from the ordinary principle, established by our decisions, that something less than an evidentiary hearing is sufficient prior to adverse administrative action.

D

An additional factor to be considered here is the fairness and reliability of the existing pretermination procedures, and the probable value, if any, of additional procedural safeguards. Central to the evaluation of any administrative process is the nature of the relevant inquiry. In order to remain eligible for benefits the disabled worker must demonstrate by means of "medically acceptable clinical and laboratory diagnostic techniques" that he is unable "to engage in any substantial gainful activity by reason of any *medically determinable* physical or mental impairment. . . ." In short, a medical assessment of the worker's physical or mental condition is required. This is a more sharply focused and easily documented decision than the typical determination of welfare entitlement. In the latter case, a wide variety of information may be deemed relevant, and issues of witness credibility and veracity often are critical to the decisionmaking process. *Goldberg* noted that in such circumstances "written submissions are a wholly unsatisfactory basis for decision."

---

[26] Amici cite statistics compiled by the Secretary which indicate that in 1965 the mean income of the family unit of a disabled worker was $3,803, while the median income for the unit was $2,836. The mean liquid assets—*i.e.* cash, stocks, bonds—of those family units was $4,862; the median was $940. These statistics do not take into account the family unit's nonliquid assets—*i.e.* automobile, real estate, and the like.

By contrast, the decision whether to discontinue disability benefits will turn, in most cases, upon "routine, standard, and unbiased medical reports by physician specialists" concerning a subject whom they have personally examined. In *Richardson v. Perales,* 402 U.S. 389, 404 (1971), the Court recognized the "reliability and probative worth of written medical reports," emphasizing that while there may be "professional disagreement with the medical conclusions" the "specter of questionable credibility and veracity is not present." To be sure, credibility and veracity may be a factor in the ultimate disability assessment in some cases. But procedural due process rules are shaped by the risk of error inherent in the truthfinding process as applied to the generality of cases, not the rare exceptions. The potential value of an evidentiary hearing, or even oral presentation to the decisionmaker, is substantially less in this context than in *Goldberg.*

The decision in *Goldberg* also was based on the Court's conclusion that written submissions were an inadequate substitute for oral presentation because they did not provide an effective means for the recipient to communicate his case to the decisionmaker. Written submissions were viewed as an unrealistic option, for most recipients lacked the "educational attainment necessary to write effectively" and could not afford professional assistance. In addition, such submissions would not provide the "flexibility of oral presentations" or "permit the recipient to mold his argument to the issues the decision maker appears to regard as important." In the context of the disability-benefits-entitlement assessment the administrative procedures under review here fully answer these objections.

The detailed questionnaire which the state agency periodically sends the recipient identifies with particularity the information relevant to the entitlement decision, and the recipient is invited to obtain assistance from the local SSA office in completing the questionnaire. More important, the information critical to the entitlement decision usually is derived from medical sources, such as the treating physician. Such sources are likely to be able to communicate more effectively through written documents than are welfare recipients or the lay witnesses supporting their cause. The conclusions of physicians often are supported by X-rays and the results of clinical or laboratory tests, information typically more amenable to written than to oral presentation.

A further safeguard against mistake is the policy of allowing the disability recipient's representative full access to all information relied upon by the state agency. In addition, prior to the cutoff of benefits the agency informs the recipient of its tentative assessment, the reasons therefor, and provides a summary of the evidence that it considers most relevant. Opportunity is then afforded the recipient to submit additional evidence or arguments, enabling him to challenge directly the accuracy of information in his file as well as the correctness of the agency's tentative conclusions. These procedures, again as contrasted with those before the Court in *Goldberg,* enable the recipient to "mold" his argument to respond to the precise issues which the decisionmaker regards as crucial.

Despite these carefully structured procedures, *amici* point to the significant reversal rate for appealed cases as clear evidence that the current process is inadequate. Depending upon the base selected and the line of analysis followed, the relevant reversal rates urged by the contending parties vary from a high of 58.6% for appealed reconsideration decisions to an overall reversal rate of only 3.3%. Bare statistics rarely provide a satisfactory measure of the fairness of a decisionmaking process. Their adequacy is especially suspect here since the administrative review system is operated on an open-file basis. A recipient may always submit new evidence, and such submissions may result in additional medical examinations. Such fresh examinations were held in approximately 30% to 40% of the appealed cases, in fiscal 1973, either at the reconsideration or evidentiary hearing stage of the administrative process. In this context, the value of reversal rate statistics as one means of evaluating the adequacy of the pretermination process is diminished. Thus, although we view such information as relevant, it is certainly not controlling in this case.

E

In striking the appropriate due process balance the final factor to be assessed is the public interest. This includes the administrative burden and other societal costs that would be associated with requiring, as a matter of constitutional right, an evidentiary hearing upon demand in all cases prior to the termination of disability benefits. The most visible burden would be the incremental cost resulting from the increased number of hearings and the expense of providing benefits to ineligible recipients pending decision. No one can predict the extent of the increase, but the fact that full benefits would continue until after such hearings would assure the exhaustion in most cases of this attractive option. Nor would the theoretical right of the Secretary to recover undeserved benefits result, as a practical matter, in any substantial offset to the added outlay of public funds. The parties submit widely varying estimates of the probable additional financial cost. We only need say that experience with the constitutionalizing of government procedures suggests that the ultimate additional cost in terms of money and administrative burden would not be insubstantial.

Financial cost alone is not a controlling weight in determining whether due process requires a particular procedural safeguard prior to some administrative decision. But the Government's interest, and hence that of the public, in conserving scarce fiscal and administrative resources is a factor that must be weighed. At some point the benefit of an additional safeguard to the individual affected by the administrative action and to society in terms of increased assurance that the action is just may be outweighed by the cost. Significantly, the cost of protecting those whom the preliminary administrative process has identified as likely to be found undeserving may in the end come out of the pockets of the deserving since resources available for any particular program of social welfare are not unlimited.

But more is implicated in cases of this type than ad hoc weighing of fiscal and administrative burdens against the interests of a particular category of claimants. The ultimate balance involves a determination as to when, under our constitutional system, judicial-type procedures must be imposed upon administrative action to assure fairness. We reiterate the wise admonishment of Mr. Justice Frankfurter that differences in the origin and function of administrative agencies "preclude wholesale transplantation of the rules of procedure, trial and review which have evolved from the history and experience of courts." The judicial model of an evidentiary hearing is neither a required, nor even the most effective, method of decisionmaking in all circumstances. The essence of due process is the requirement that "a person in jeopardy of serious loss [be given] notice of the case against him and opportunity to meet it." All that is necessary is that the procedures be tailored, in light of the decision to be made, to "the capacities and circumstances of those who are to be heard," *Goldberg v. Kelly,* to insure that they are given a meaningful opportunity to present their case. In assessing what process is due in this case, substantial weight must be given to the good-faith judgments of the individuals charged by Congress with the administration of social welfare programs that the procedures they have provided assure fair consideration of the entitlement claims of individuals. This is especially so where, as here, the prescribed procedures not only provide the claimant with an effective process for asserting his claim prior to any administrative action, but also assure a right to an evidentiary hearing, as well as to subsequent judicial review, before the denial of his claim becomes final.

We conclude that an evidentiary hearing is not required prior to the termination of disability benefits and that the present administrative procedures fully comport with due process.

The judgment of the Court of Appeals is *Reversed.*

[BRENNAN and MARSHALL, JJ. dissented. They observed:] ... The Court's consideration that a discontinuance of disability benefits may cause the recipient to suffer only a limited deprivation is no argument. It is speculative. ... Indeed in the present case, it is indicated that because disability benefits were terminated, there was a foreclosure on the

Eldridge home and the family's furniture was repossessed, forcing Eldridge, his wife and children to sleep in one bed. . . .

NOTES AND QUESTIONS

1. *Dispensing with prior hearings in emergencies.* In case of emergency, a state can deprive an individual of liberty or property without a prior hearing, even if a later remedy is inadequate. *See* note 10 in *Goldberg.* The classic case is *North American Cold Storage Co. v. Chicago,* 211 U.S. 306 (1908), in which the Court upheld a state law providing for the destruction without prior hearing of food held in cold storage which the authorities, after inspection, believed to be rotting and creating a menace to public health. The Court stated that an adequate remedy is provided by a tort action in which the authorities who destroyed the food would have to prove that the food was unfit. However, under present law the officials are likely to be immune from liability. *See* § 10.2.

A number of Supreme Court decisions allow an agency to act first and provide a hearing later. "An important government interest, accompanied by a substantial assurance that the deprivation is not baseless or unwarranted, may in limited cases demanding prompt action justify postponing the opportunity to be heard until after the initial deprivation." *FDIC v. Mallen,* 486 U.S. 230 (1988) (suspension of banking executive under indictment for felony involving dishonesty).

For example, an agency closed a mine because an inspection determined that it was unsafe or risked imminent environmental harm. A hearing on the propriety of the closure was available promptly thereafter. *Hodel v. Virginia Surface Mining Ass'n,* 452 U.S. 264 (1981). Similarly, a state racing board acted properly when it summarily suspended the license of a horse trainer after a test showed one of his horses to have been drugged. Here, too, a prompt post-suspension hearing was available. *Barry v. Barchi,* 443 U.S. 55 (1979). It can be argued that in these cases the inspection or audit that triggered the summary action is an adequate substitute for a pre-deprivation hearing.

Mathews permitted an agency to terminate disability payments prior to an evidentiary hearing in order to save the government money, not because of an emergency. This was a new departure. Are Justice Powell's arguments distinguishing *Goldberg* from *Mathews* persuasive?

2. *Pre-termination hearings after Mathews.* Surprisingly, Social Security regulations allow recipients to file an election that keeps their checks coming until the ALJ hearing if the dispute concerns whether the recipient remains physically or mentally impaired. *See* 20 C.F.R. § 404.1597a. If the termination of benefits is upheld at the hearing, Social Security is entitled to recoup the benefits it has paid after the notice of termination, but even then it will waive the recovery if the recipient's request for continuation of benefits was in good faith. 20 C.F.R. § 416.996. Thus Social Security

decided not to cut off disability payments before a hearing, *despite its victory in Mathews.*

3. *Timing and employment decisions. Roth* indicated that a *prior* hearing must be provided before an employee is discharged from a tenured government job. Later cases have been more cautious and recognize government's interest in immediate removal of an objectionable employee. In these cases, the Court has accepted abbreviated pre-termination procedures designed to insure only that the government has probable cause for its decision—not that the decision was right. However, a full-fledged trial-type hearing must be provided promptly after removal.

In *Cleveland Board of Education v. Loudermill,* § 2.2.2, the Court held that pre-termination procedure serves as an "initial check against mistaken decisions—essentially, a determination of whether there are reasonable grounds to believe that the charges against the employee are true and support the proposed action." This means that an employee must receive oral or written notice of the charges against him, an explanation of the employer's evidence (although it is not clear how detailed this must be), and an opportunity to present his side of the story—orally or in writing. But this procedure falls far short of the pre-termination hearing required by *Goldberg v. Kelly.*

4. *How long is too long?* How long can the employer delay in providing a post-termination hearing? The government has an incentive to stall. The longer a hearing is delayed, the fewer hearings must be held since many petitioners will get discouraged, move away, or get other jobs. Yet it is difficult for a court to say exactly how long is too long. In *Mathews,* the Court tolerated a delay of well over one year before the post-termination hearing occurred. In *Loudermill,* the Court noted that a delay in the post-termination hearing could itself be a constitutional violation, but held that a wait of about nine months was not unreasonable.

5. *Suspension without pay.* In employment cases, a government employer often suspends employees with pay rather than firing them outright. It provides no procedural protection prior to the suspension but furnishes a trial-type hearing after the suspension. In *Gilbert v. Homar,* 520 U.S. 924 (1997), the Court held that due process allows the suspension of a tenured campus policeman who was charged with drug offenses without providing *any* process prior to the suspension and *without pay.* Applying *Mathews* balancing, the Court gave little weight to the policeman's private interest in receiving an uninterrupted flow of paychecks for the relatively brief period until a post-suspension hearing was provided. On the other hand, the state has a substantial interest in immediately suspending employees in positions of public trust who are charged with felonies. "Government does not have to give an employee charged with a felony a paid leave at taxpayer expense." The risk of erroneous deprivation was low because the criminal charges against the policeman were independently verifiable and provided a reasonable basis for the action. Similarly, states often suspend a professional

license because of exigent circumstances. For example, in cases involving danger to patients, a medical licensing board ordinarily has power to suspend a physician's license rather than allow the physician to continue practicing until a hearing is provided.

6. *Problem.* Elm City constructed and operated Elm Grove, a large apartment project for low income residents. The relevant statute recites that the problem of low income housing is critical and that poor people have a right to decent housing. Muriel and her four teenage children are tenants in Elm Grove. Her sole source of income is TANF and food stamps. When she moved in on January 1, she signed a one-year lease which stated that the lease could be renewed only by agreement between Elm Grove and the tenant. It also stated that tenants could be evicted at any time if they fail to follow the rules of Elm Grove. The rules require that tenants refrain from disturbing other tenants. The lease provided that tenants must vacate their apartment within 10 days of receiving an eviction notice. It also stated that Elm Grove would furnish a hearing within two weeks after the apartment is vacated due to eviction.

Muriel received a notice of eviction on April 19 which stated that occupants of her apartment had violated the rules by constantly playing loud music late at night. The notice furnished no specific details. It ordered her to move out by April 29 and informed her that a hearing would be held on May 6 if she requested one. Muriel seeks an injunction in federal district court against her eviction, denying that she or her family had violated the rules and arguing that she has been denied procedural due process. Should the injunction be granted? *See HUD v. Rucker*, 535 U.S. 125 (2002); *Richmond Tenants Org. v. Kemp*, 956 F.2d 1300 (4th Cir. 1992); *Lopez v. Henry Phipps Plaza South, Inc.*, 498 F.2d 937 (2d Cir. 1974); *United States v. One Tract of Real Property*, 803 F. Supp. 1080 (E.D.N.C. 1992).

§ 2.4   ELEMENTS OF A HEARING

Courts employ the balancing formula of *Mathews v. Eldridge* to determine *what process* is due as well as *when* it is due. Recall the list in *Goldberg* of the precise elements of a due process hearing. Does a *Goldberg* pre-termination hearing differ in any substantial way from a normal civil trial before a judge? From a *post*-termination welfare hearing? The cases following *Mathews* are much less demanding than *Goldberg* and in many situations call for less elaborate process or none at all.

INGRAHAM V. WRIGHT

430 U.S. 651 (1977)

POWELL, J.

This case presents questions concerning the use of corporal punishment in public schools: First, whether the paddling of students as a means of maintaining school discipline constitutes cruel and unusual punishment in violation of the Eighth Amendment; and, second, to the extent that paddling is constitutionally permissible, whether the Due Process Clause of the Fourteenth Amendment requires prior notice and an opportunity to be heard. [The plaintiffs were eighth and ninth grade students who were subject to disciplinary paddling at their Florida junior high school. The punishment consisted of paddling the student on the buttocks with a flat wooden paddle measuring less than two feet long, three to four inches wide, and about one-half inch thick.

One plaintiff testified that because he was slow to respond to his teacher's instructions, he was subjected to more than 20 licks with a paddle while being held over a table in the principal's office. The paddling was so severe that he suffered a hematoma requiring medical attention and keeping him out of school for several days. The second plaintiff was paddled several times for minor infractions. On two occasions he was struck on his arms, once depriving him of the full use of his arm for a week.

The lower court rejected both the cruel and unusual punishment and due process claims. The Supreme Court held that corporal punishment was not cruel and unusual in light of the long history of its use and the common law rule that teachers could impose reasonable but not excessive force to discipline a child. The Court then turned to the due process claim.]

Application of [due process] requires the familiar two-stage analysis: We must first ask whether the asserted individual interests are encompassed within the Fourteenth Amendment's protection of "life, liberty or property"; if protected interests are implicated, we then must decide what procedures constitute "due process of law." Following that analysis here, we find that corporal punishment in public schools implicates a constitutionally protected liberty interest, but we hold that the traditional common-law remedies are fully adequate to afford due process.

A

.... The Due Process Clause of the Fifth Amendment, later incorporated into the Fourteenth, was intended to give Americans at least the protection against governmental power that they had enjoyed as Englishmen against the power of the Crown. The liberty preserved from deprivation without due process included the right "generally to enjoy those privileges long recognized at common law as essential to the orderly pursuit of happiness by free men." *Meyer v. Nebraska.* . . . Among the historic liberties so protected was a right to be free from, and to obtain judicial relief for, unjustified intrusions on personal security. . . . It is fundamental that the state cannot hold and physically punish an individual except in accordance with due process of law.

This constitutionally protected liberty interest is at stake in this case. There is, of course, a de minimis level of imposition with which the Constitution is not concerned. But at least where school authorities, acting under color of state law, deliberately decide to punish a child for misconduct by restraining the child and inflicting appreciable physical pain, we hold that Fourteenth Amendment liberty interests are implicated.

B

"[The] question remains what process is due." Were it not for the common-law privilege permitting teachers to inflict reasonable corporal punishment on children in their care, and the availability of the traditional remedies for abuse, the case for requiring advance procedural safeguards would be strong indeed. But here we deal with a punishment—paddling—within that tradition, and the question is whether the common-law remedies are adequate to afford due process. . . . Whether in this case the common-law remedies for excessive corporal punishment constitute due process of law must turn on an analysis of the competing interests at stake, viewed against the background of "history, reason, [and] the past course of decisions." The analysis requires consideration of three distinct factors. . . . *Mathews v. Eldridge.*

1

Because it is rooted in history, the child's liberty interest in avoiding corporal punishment while in the care of public school authorities is subject to historical limitations. Under the common law, an invasion of personal security gave rise to a right to recover damages in a subsequent judicial proceeding. But the right of recovery was qualified by the concept of justification. Thus, there could be no recovery against a teacher who gave only "moderate correction" to a child. . . . Under that longstanding accommodation of interests, there can be no deprivation of substantive rights as long as disciplinary corporal punishment is within the limits of the common-law privilege.

This is not to say that the child's interest in procedural safeguards is insubstantial. . . . In any deliberate infliction of corporal punishment on a child who is restrained for that purpose, there is some risk that the intrusion on the child's liberty will be unjustified and therefore unlawful. In these circumstances the child has a strong interest in procedural safeguards that minimize the risk of wrongful punishment and provide for the resolution of disputed questions of justification. We turn now to a consideration of the safeguards that are available under applicable Florida law.

2

. . . . Florida has preserved the traditional judicial proceedings for determining whether the punishment was justified. If the punishment inflicted is later found to have been excessive—not reasonably believed at the time to be necessary for the child's discipline or training—the school authorities inflicting it may be held liable in damages to the child and, if malice is shown, they may be subject to criminal penalties. . . .

Although students have testified in this case to specific instances of abuse, there is every reason to believe that such mistreatment is an aberration. The uncontradicted evidence suggests that corporal punishment in the Dade County schools was, "[w]ith the exception of a few cases . . . unremarkable in physical severity." Moreover, because paddlings are usually inflicted in response to conduct directly observed by teachers in their presence, the risk that a child will be paddled without cause is typically insignificant. . . . In those cases where severe punishment is contemplated, the available civil and criminal sanctions for abuse—considered in light of the openness of the school environment—afford significant protection against unjustified corporal punishment. Teachers and school authorities are unlikely to inflict corporal punishment unnecessarily or excessively when a possible consequence of doing so is the institution of civil or criminal proceedings against them.[46]

It still may be argued, of course, that the child's liberty interest would be better protected if the common-law remedies were supplemented by the administrative safeguards of prior notice and a hearing. We have found frequently that some kind of prior hearing is necessary to guard against arbitrary impositions on interests protected by the Fourteenth Amendment. But where the State has preserved what "has always been the law of the land," the case for administrative safeguards is significantly less compelling. . . .

---

[46] The low incidence of abuse, and the availability of established judicial remedies in the event of abuse, distinguish this case from *Goss v. Lopez,* 419 U.S. 565 (1975). The Ohio law struck down in *Goss* provided for suspensions from public school of up to 10 days without "any written procedure applicable to suspensions." Although Ohio law provided generally for administrative review, the Court assumed that the short suspensions would not be stayed pending review, with the result that the review proceeding could serve neither a deterrent nor a remedial function. In these circumstances, the Court held the law authorizing suspensions unconstitutional for failure to require "that there be at least an informal give-and-take between student and disciplinarian, preferably prior to the suspension. . . ." The subsequent civil and criminal proceedings available in this case may be viewed as affording substantially greater protection to the child than the informal conference mandated by *Goss.*

3

But even if the need for advance procedural safeguards were clear, the question would remain whether the incremental benefit could justify the cost. Acceptance of petitioners' claims would work a transformation in the law governing corporal punishment in Florida and most other States. Given the impracticability of formulating a rule of procedural due process that varies with the severity of the particular imposition, the prior hearing petitioners seek would have to precede any paddling, however moderate or trivial.

Such a universal constitutional requirement would significantly burden the use of corporal punishment as a disciplinary measure. Hearings—even informal hearings—require time, personnel, and a diversion of attention from normal school pursuits. School authorities may well choose to abandon corporal punishment rather than incur the burdens of complying with the procedural requirements. Teachers, properly concerned with maintaining authority in the classroom, may well prefer to rely on other disciplinary measures—which they may view as less effective—rather than confront the possible disruption that prior notice and a hearing may entail. Paradoxically, such an alteration of disciplinary policy is most likely to occur in the ordinary case where the contemplated punishment is well within the common-law privilege.

Elimination or curtailment of corporal punishment would be welcomed by many as a societal advance. But when such a policy choice may result from this Court's determination of an asserted right to due process, rather than from the normal processes of community debate and legislative action, the societal costs cannot be dismissed as insubstantial. We are reviewing here a legislative judgment, rooted in history and reaffirmed in the laws of many States, that corporal punishment serves important educational interests. This judgment must be viewed in light of the disciplinary problems commonplace in the schools. . . .

"At some point the benefit of an additional safeguard to the individual affected . . . and to society in terms of increased assurance that the action is just, may be outweighed by the cost." *Mathews v. Eldridge.* We think that point has been reached in this case. In view of the low incidence of abuse, the openness of our schools, and the common-law safeguards that already exist, the risk of error that may result in violation of a schoolchild's substantive rights can only be regarded as minimal. Imposing additional administrative safeguards as a constitutional requirement might reduce that risk marginally, but would also entail a significant intrusion into an area of primary educational responsibility. We conclude that the Due Process Clause does not require notice and a hearing prior to the imposition of corporal punishment in the public schools, as that practice is authorized and limited by the common law.

AFFIRMED

[WHITE, J., joined by BRENNAN, MARSHALL, and STEVENS, JJ., dissented. He argued that traditional tort remedies do nothing to prevent punishment based on mistaken facts, so long as the punishment was reasonable from the disciplinarian's point of view. More important, the lawsuit occurs after the punishment has been finally imposed; the infliction of physical pain cannot be undone. "There is every reason to require, as the court did in *Goss,* a few minutes of 'informal give-and-take between student and disciplinarian' as a 'meaningful hedge' against the erroneous infliction of irreparable injury."]

NOTES AND QUESTIONS

1. *Due process at school. Ingraham* established that state common law tort remedies provide the *only* process due to high school students deprived of liberty by the infliction of corporal punishment. Can *Ingraham* be distinguished from *Goss v. Lopez,* as the Court asserts in footnote 46? *Goss* preceded *Mathews* by one year and is also discussed in § 2.2.2 N.6. It held that a disciplinary suspension of high school students for ten days or less deprived them of property (because state law created an entitlement to public education) and of liberty (because the suspensions "could seriously damage the students' standing with fellow pupils and teachers as well as interfere with later opportunities for higher education and employment").

In *Goss,* the Court called for a proceeding quite different from the adversary hearing mandated by *Goldberg.* The school must provide "fundamentally fair procedures," but that means only "*some* kind of notice and . . . *some* kind of hearing." The student must receive "oral or written notice of the charges against him and, if he denies them, an explanation of the evidence the authorities have and an opportunity to present his side of the story." The discussion with the student could take place minutes after the alleged misconduct occurs and, except in the case of exigent circumstances, it should occur before the student is removed from school. A student does not have the right "to secure counsel, to confront and cross-examine witnesses supporting the charge, or to call his own witnesses to verify his version of the incident." The Court said:

> Brief disciplinary suspensions are almost countless. To impose in each such case even truncated trial-type procedures might well overwhelm administrative facilities in many places and, by diverting resources, cost more than it would save in educational effectiveness. Moreover, further formalizing the suspension process and escalating its formality and adversary nature may not only make it too costly as a regular disciplinary tool but also destroy its effectiveness as part of the teaching process.

Essentially, the "hearing" required in *Goss* is a conversation between the student and the disciplinarian. The *Ingraham* dissenters argued that the *Goss* model should be followed in paddling cases, instead of dispensing entirely with an administrative hearing as the majority allowed. Which opinion has the better of the argument?

2. *Judicial remedies as a form of due process.* In *Ingraham,* the Supreme Court held that due process can sometimes be provided by a post-deprivation *judicial remedy* as opposed to a pre-deprivation administrative hearing.

Judicial remedies provide due process when a prior administrative proceeding is infeasible. In *Parratt v. Taylor,* 451 U.S. 527 (1981), prison officials negligently lost a prisoner's hobby kit worth $23. The Court did not hold that a $23 loss was a *de minimis* deprivation of property. Instead, it decided that a state tort action after such a "random and unauthorized" deprivation of property satisfied due process. After all, how could the state provide a hearing prior to the deprivation when the deprivation was negligent? The same reasoning applies to an *intentional* destruction of a prisoner's property by a prison guard on a vendetta against the prisoner. *Hudson v. Palmer,* 468 U.S. 517 (1984). Later, overruling *Parratt* on a different issue, the Court held that a merely *negligent* deprivation of property is not a due process violation at all. *Daniels v. Williams,* 474 U.S. 327 (1986).

Judicial remedies may also provide due process in a contract dispute between government and a private contractor. Suppose the government withholds contractual payments because it believes the contractor is in breach. Such withholding might be treated as a deprivation of property (that is, money). However, no prior administrative hearing is required; a state court breach of contract remedy is sufficient (even though it might take several years to come to trial). *Lujan v. G & G Fire Sprinklers,* 532 U.S. 189 (2001). The Court reasoned that a private party should not have greater contract remedies against the government than it would have against another private contracting party.

3. *De novo judicial trial as due process.* In lieu of an administrative hearing, a statute might provide for a de novo judicial trial that occurs before the deprivation of a property interest. The judicial remedy would satisfy due process requirements. This principle arose in a controversial setting involving orders by the Environmental Protection Agency (EPA) to clean up hazardous waste conditions. By statute, the EPA can issue "unilateral administrative orders" (UAOs) to "potentially responsible parties" (PRPs) to remediate hazardous waste conditions that pose an imminent danger to health. To issue a UAO to a PRP, EPA had to assemble an administrative record through a notice-and-comment type procedure, including a public meeting, but *not* an administrative trial-type hearing.

The statute provided two choices to a PRP that receives a UAO. First, the PRP could comply with the UAO and then seek reimbursement from EPA by suing in federal district court to recover the costs because it was not liable for the cleanup or because the UAO was arbitrary and capricious. Second it could refuse to comply, in which case EPA could bring an action in federal district court to enforce the UAO or clean the site itself and sue the PRP to recover costs. In either proceeding, the court has power to impose fines or punitive damages but it is not required to do so. In *General Electric Co. v. Jackson*, 610 F.3d 110 (D.C. Cir. 2010), the court upheld this scheme against a due process attack.

GE contended that it was entitled to a trial-type administrative hearing on whether it is liable for remediation costs before performing the cleanup. EPA responded that the district court de novo hearing satisfies due process. The problem is that if GE loses before the district court, it could be liable for fines or punitive damages. GE argued that this scheme created a Hobson's choice—it was just too risky to refuse to comply. However, the court rejected this argument because the court cannot impose fines or penalties unless the PRP "willfully" failed to comply with the UAO without "sufficient cause." Moreover, whether to impose fines and penalties is discretionary with the district court. Consequently, the statute does not impose a Hobson's choice and the risk of fines and penalties for non-compliance does not prevent the district court hearing from satisfying due process. *But see* Recent Case, 124 HARV. L. REV. 1572 (2011) (criticizing *GE v. Jackson*).

4. *The right to counsel in administrative hearings.* There is no right to have counsel appointed at public expense in an administrative proceeding, since the proceeding is civil rather than criminal. See, e.g., *Turner v. Rogers*, 131 S. Ct. 2507 (2011) (no right to appointed counsel in case of civil contempt for non-payment of child support, even though party can be imprisoned).

Does a party have a due process right to be represented by a lawyer that the party pays for itself (or a lawyer working pro bono or that is provided by a legal service agency)? The answer is usually but not necessarily.

Walters v. National Ass'n of Radiation Survivors, 473 U.S. 305 (1985), involved a statute (first enacted in 1862 and now repealed) that limited an attorney's fee to $10 in a veteran's benefit case. This statute prevented veterans from retaining counsel to represent them during the process of consideration of a benefit claim by the Veterans Administration (VA) and at benefit hearings before the Board of Veterans Appeals (BVA). Veterans' organizations such as the American Legion provide non-lawyer claims agents free of charge to assist claimants. Veterans represented by these lay advocates had about the same success rate as those represented by attorneys. (Present law prohibits attorneys from charging a fee for representing a veteran during the informal process of VA review of a benefit claim, but it does allow payment of fees after proceedings are initiated before the BVA— *see* 38 U.S.C. § 5904(c)(2).)

The Supreme Court assumed without deciding that an *applicant* for government benefits is entitled to due process. (This issue is still not resolved—*see* § 2.2.1 N.8.) Using *Mathews* balancing, the Court upheld the statute limiting fees to $10. It refused to follow the *Goldberg* dictum that a welfare claimant must be allowed to retain an attorney. Instead, the Court honored Congress' desire that veterans keep their entire award rather than dividing it with attorneys. It also deferred to the government's interest in keeping VA hearings as informal and non-adversarial as possible. The introduction of lawyers would not further this goal. However, two of the Justices who concurred in Justice Rehnquist's opinion suggested that there might be a "special circumstances" rule allowing individuals to retain attorneys in complex cases. Three Justices dissented.

5. *Academic decisionmaking.* A student at a state educational institution (K–12 or college) who is subject to expulsion or a lengthy suspension for disciplinary reasons is entitled to a trial-type due process hearing. However, a student dismissed for *academic* rather than *disciplinary* reasons is entitled to much less process—perhaps none at all. In *Board of Curators, Univ. of Mo. v. Horowitz,* 435 U.S. 78 (1978), the Court stated:

> The decision to dismiss respondent . . . rested on the academic judgment of school officials that she did not have the necessary clinical ability to perform adequately as a medical doctor. . . . Such [an academic] judgment is by its nature more subjective and evaluative than the typical factual questions presented in the average disciplinary decision. Like the decision of an individual professor as to the proper grade for a student in his course, the determination whether to dismiss a student for academic reasons requires an expert evaluation of cumulative information and is not readily adapted to the procedural tools of judicial or administrative decision-making.

The Court was reluctant to "formalize" the educational process and to "further enlarge the judicial presence in the academic community and thereby risk deterioration of many beneficial aspects of the faculty-student relationship." Do you think there should be any required administrative process when a student questions a University's academic judgment?

6. *Confrontation.* When a person is entitled by due process to a trial-type hearing, is there a right to confront and cross-examine one's accuser? Usually, but not necessarily. In *Van Harken v. City of Chicago,* 103 F.3d 1346 (7th Cir. 1997), the City decriminalized its system of adjudicating parking ticket disputes. Parking cases, carrying a maximum fine of $100, are heard by private lawyers serving as part-time hearing officers. The police officer who wrote the ticket is not expected to participate in the hearing other than through the ticket itself, which is treated as an affidavit. The hearing officer can choose to subpoena the officer in unusual cases and is expected to conduct a "searching" cross-examination of the alleged violator.

Reducing the *Mathews* balancing to a straightforward cost-benefit analysis, the court upheld this procedure. Requiring officers to appear at the hearings, the court calculated, would cost the city 134,000 police hours per year—the equivalent of 67 full-time officers. Moreover, if a case must be dismissed because the officer fails to show up, the dismissal would undermine the deterrent effect of parking laws and deprive the city of revenue to which it was entitled.

On the benefit side of requiring confrontation, the court figured the average fine was about $55. Suppose the probability of an erroneous determination is 5% and an officer's presence at the hearing would cut that probability to 2.5%. "Then the average saving to the innocent respondent from this additional procedural safeguard would be only $1.38 ($55 x .025)—a trivial amount."

Should *Mathews* balancing be reduced to an equation of this kind? Or should confrontation and cross-examination of one's accuser be provided regardless of its costs and benefits?

7. *When due process requires only a paper hearing—or no hearing at all.* The Court has occasionally held that due process permits an agency to conduct a "hearing" on paper. For example, *Hewitt v. Helms,* 459 U.S. 460 (1983) (later overruled on different issues by *Sandin v. Conner,* discussed in § 2.2.2 N.8), concerned the process owed to a prisoner placed in administrative segregation. Applying a *Mathews* balancing analysis, the Court required only an informal, non-adversary review of the information supporting the decision, including a prisoner's written statement, within a reasonable time after the prisoner was placed in segregation. The Court refused to require an oral conference, of the sort prescribed by *Goss,* finding that the issues to be resolved were based on "purely subjective evaluations and predictions of future behavior" and on "intuitive judgments" rather than on specific facts. As a result, an auditory trial-type hearing would not be particularly helpful.

Indeed, due process requires no hearing at all unless there is a factual issue in dispute. In *Conn. Dep't of Public Safety v. Doe,* 538 U.S. 1 (2003), Doe was a convicted sex offender. Connecticut's version of "Megan's Law" requires that all convicted sex offenders must register and be listed on a publicly available website (with address and photo). Doe alleged that publicizing this information was a deprivation of his liberty. He claimed that he was not dangerous to anyone and demanded a hearing to establish this fact.

The Supreme Court assumed that listing information about sex offenders on the website invaded a liberty interest. (This assumption was defensible. The requirement that offenders register with the state might provide the "plus" needed to satisfy the stigma-plus test of *Paul v. Davis,* § 2.2.2 N.7.) Even so, there was no right to a hearing, because dangerousness was not relevant to the statutory scheme. All convicted sex offenders had to register and be placed on the website, regardless of any fact other than their conviction. Therefore, a hearing on the subject of dangerousness would be a "bootless exercise." Due process does not require a hearing unless there is a relevant issue of disputed fact.

Must there be a hearing if the only issue to be resolved is how the decisionmaker should exercise discretion? In *Loudermill,* Justice White wrote: "Even where the facts are clear, the appropriateness or necessity of the discharge may not be; in such cases, the only meaningful opportunity to invoke the discretion of the decisionmaker is likely to be before the termination takes effect." 470 U.S. at 543. It is unclear whether the Supreme Court would follow this dictum under current law.

8.   *Adversary systems.* One fundamental issue posed by *Walters* (N.4 above) is whether due process means an adversarial trial-type hearing. *Goldberg v. Kelly* was the high-water mark for that view. *Goss* opened the way for allowing informal meetings to substitute for trial-type hearings. And *Walters* establishes that Congress can choose a sharply different model for disbursing government benefits: an informal, investigatory meeting without lawyers, formal testimony, or cross-examination. Could a state provide for a non-adversary hearing when the issue is the revocation of a physician's license to practice?

9.   *New and old property.* The cases discussed in §§ 2.3 and **Error! Reference source not found.** involve "new property" (meaning statutory entitlements) as opposed to "old property" (meaning money or real or personal property). *See* § 2.2.1 N.2. Do cases like *Mathews v. Eldridge* balancing apply to deprivations of old property as well as new property? Cases involving seizures of money or property seem to apply *Mathews* without drawing a distinction between old and new property. *See, e.g., Al Haramain Islamic Found. v. U. S. Dep't of Treasury,* 686 F.3d 965 (9th Cir. 2012), involving the seizure of the assets (including cash in bank accounts) of a non-profit corporation suspected of supporting international terrorism. The court applied *Mathews.* It upheld the seizure of the assets without a prior hearing, because of the emergency nature of the situation and the risk the assets would disappear. On the other hand, the court held that *Mathews* was violated by the failure to give notice of the reasons for the seizure and a meaningful opportunity to respond during the four-year period after the seizure but before a hearing was finally provided.

10.   *Problem.* Madison wants to cut the cost of pre-termination hearings in cases involving the various types of welfare benefit programs administered by the state. It also wants to make the process more convenient and pleasant for all concerned, including recipients and social workers who often have to sit around all day waiting for their hearing to be called. It therefore proposes new procedural regulations providing that hearings may be conducted on the Internet in cases where the benefits agency wishes to reduce or terminate benefits. Each case would be the subject of a password-protected Internet file. The agency must state clearly the reason for the proposed reduction or termination of benefits and post all testimony and relevant reports. The parties can post questions for social workers or other witnesses on the net, which must be answered within ten days. The agency could also post questions that welfare recipient would have to answer within ten days. The decisionmaker would make a decision based on the posted materials but would have the option of calling for a telephone or a live hearing if necessary to resolve a credibility dispute. Computer terminals will be provided in

libraries for the use of welfare recipients who don't own a computer. You work for a legal service office that provides assistance to welfare claimants. You have been asked to submit comments about these proposed regulations. What arguments should your comments make?

§ 2.5 THE DISTINCTION BETWEEN RULEMAKING AND ADJUDICATION

This subchapter introduces a fundamental distinction between government action that has *particular applicability* (meaning that it affects only specific persons) and government action that has *general applicability* (meaning that it affects a class of persons). The first kind of action is called "adjudication." An example of adjudication is a welfare agency's decision to terminate A's benefits because A's income is too high. Procedural due process applies to adjudications in which a person is deprived of liberty or property. (§ 2.2). The second kind of action is called "rulemaking." An example is the establishment by the welfare agency of a standard for determining how to compute the income of welfare recipients. Procedural due process does not apply to rulemaking.

§ 2.5.1 PARTICULAR AND GENERAL APPLICABILITY

Our exploration of the distinction between rulemaking and adjudication begins with two old Supreme Court cases that concerned Denver property tax disputes. Much of the structure of procedural due process has been erected upon the foundation of these two cases.

LONDONER V. DENVER
210 U.S. 373 (1908)

[A Denver ordinance allowed the City Council, on recommendation of the Board of Public Works, to establish a special assessment district for the purpose of paving streets. After the paving was completed, the total cost of the job was apportioned among the property owners in the district. The ordinance provided that the Council's determination was binding on the Colorado courts. The Board recommended an apportionment to the Council. Objecting owners were permitted to file written complaints with the Council. The Council considered the complaints and enacted an ordinance assessing each owner an amount the council believed to be appropriate. The complainants were not granted an opportunity for an oral hearing. Londoner filed a lengthy complaint with the council. One of his objections was that individual parcels in the district, including his property, were assessed arbitrarily because those with equal assessments had not benefitted equally from the paving.]

MOODY, J.:

. . . . The first step in the assessment proceedings was by the certificate of the board of public works of the cost of the improvement and a preliminary apportionment of it. The last step was the enactment of the assessment ordinance. From beginning to end of the proceedings the landowners, although allowed to formulate and file complaints and objections, were not afforded an opportunity to be heard upon them. Upon these facts was there a denial by the State of the due process of law guaranteed by the Fourteenth Amendment to the Constitution of the United States?

In the assessment, apportionment and collection of taxes upon property within their jurisdiction the Constitution of the United States imposes few restrictions upon the States. In the enforcement of such restrictions as the Constitution does impose this court has regarded substance and not form. But where the legislature of a State, instead of fixing the tax itself, commits to some subordinate body the duty of determining whether, in what amount, and upon whom it shall be levied, and of making the assessment and apportionment, due process of law requires that at some stage of the proceedings before the tax becomes irrevocably fixed, the taxpayer shall have an opportunity to be heard, of which he must have notice, either personal, by publication, or by a law fixing the time and place of the hearing. It must be remembered that the law of Colorado denies the landowner the right to object in the courts to the assessment, upon the ground that the objections are cognizable only by the [Council].

If it is enough that, under such circumstances, an opportunity is given to submit in writing all objections to and complaints of the tax to the [Council], then there was a hearing afforded in the case at bar. But we think that something more than that, even in proceedings for taxation, is required by due process of law. Many requirements essential in strictly judicial proceedings may be dispensed with in proceedings of this nature. But even here a hearing, in its very essence, demands that he who is entitled to it shall have the right to support his allegations by argument however brief, and, if need be, by proof, however informal. It is apparent that such a hearing was denied to [Londoner]. . . . The assessment was therefore void, and [Londoner was] entitled to a decree discharging [his land] from a lien on account of it.

THE CHIEF JUSTICE and JUSTICE HOLMES dissent.

BI-METALLIC INVESTMENT CO. V. STATE BD. OF EQUALIZATION

239 U.S. 441 (1915)

HOLMES, J.:

This is a suit to enjoin the State Board of Equalization and the Colorado Tax Commission from putting in force and the defendant Pitcher, as assessor of Denver, from obeying, an order of the boards, increasing the valuation of all taxable property in Denver 40 per cent. . . . The plaintiff is the owner of real estate in Denver, and brings the case here on the ground that it was given no opportunity to be heard, and that therefore its property will be taken without due process of law. . . .

For the purposes of decision we assume that the constitutional question is presented in the baldest way—that neither the plaintiff nor the assessor of Denver, who presents a brief on the plaintiff's side, nor any representative of the city and county, was given an opportunity to be heard. . . . On this assumption it is obvious that injustice may be suffered if some property in the county already has been valued at its full worth. But if certain property has been valued at a rate different from that generally prevailing in the county, the owner has had his opportunity to protest and appeal as usual in our system of taxation so that it must be assumed that the property owners in the county all stand alike. The question, then, is whether all individuals have a constitutional right to be heard before a matter can be decided in which all are equally concerned— here, for instance, before a superior board decides that the local taxing officers have adopted a system of undervaluation throughout a county, as notoriously often has been the case. . . .

Where a rule of conduct applies to more than a few people, it is impracticable that everyone should have a direct voice in its adoption. The Constitution does not require all public acts to be done in town meeting or an assembly of the whole. General statutes within the state power are passed that affect the person or property of individuals, sometimes to the point of ruin, without giving them a chance to be heard. Their rights are protected in the only way that they can be in a complex society, by their power, immediate or remote, over those who make the rule. If the result in this case had been reached, as it might have been, by the state's doubling the rate of taxation, no one would suggest that the 14th Amendment was violated unless every person affected had been allowed an opportunity to raise his voice against it before the body entrusted by the state Constitution with the power. In considering this case in this court we must assume that the proper state machinery has been used, and the question is whether, if the state Constitution had declared that Denver had been undervalued as compared with the rest of the state, and had decreed that for the current year the valuation should be 40 per cent higher, the objection now urged could prevail. It appears to us that to put the question is to answer it. There must be a limit to individual argument in such matters if government is to go on. In *Londoner v. Denver* a local board had to determine "whether, in what amount, and upon whom" a tax for paving a street should be levied for special benefits. A relatively small number of persons was concerned, who were exceptionally affected, in each case upon individual grounds, and it was held that they had a right to a hearing. But that decision is far from reaching a general determination dealing only with the principle upon which all the assessments in a county had been laid.

Judgment affirmed.

NOTES AND QUESTIONS

1.   *An oral hearing?* Londoner was entitled to a trial-type hearing with respect to the amount he would be assessed for street paving ("the right to support his allegations by argument however brief, and, if need be, by proof, however informal"). He had been allowed to file a written complaint, but that was not enough. If the case came up today, do you think that a trial-type oral hearing would be required?

2.   *General v. particular applicability.* Londoner gets a hearing; Bi-Metallic Investment Co. does not. Both are protesting higher property taxes. What's the difference?

One way to distinguish the two cases is that *Bi-Metallic* involved a proceeding in which the rights of all the taxpayers in Denver were at stake and all were equally affected. We call this a proceeding of "general applicability." *Londoner* involved a proceeding in which Londoner's individual assessment was at issue. We call this a proceeding of "particular applicability."

A modern restatement of the *Bi-Metallic* doctrine, based on the distinction between general and particular, occurs in *United States v. Florida East Coast Ry. Co.,* 410 U.S. 224, 244–46 (1973), a case considered in detail in § 5.4.2. *Florida East Coast* involved regulations that raised the rates that railroads must pay for the use of freight cars owned by other railroads. The issue was whether a trial-type hearing was required for adoption of these regulations. The Court observed:

> The basic distinction between rulemaking and adjudication is illustrated by this Court's treatment of two related cases under the Due Process Clause of the Fourteenth Amendment. In *Londoner v. Denver* . . . the Court held that due process had not been accorded a landowner who objected to the amount assessed against his land as its share of the benefit resulting from the paving of a street . . . But in the later case of *Bi-Metallic Investment Co.* . . . the Court held that no hearing at all was constitutionally required prior to a decision by state tax officers in Colorado to increase the valuation of

all taxable property by a substantial percentage. The Court distinguished *Londoner* by stating that there a small number of persons "were exceptionally affected, in each case upon individual grounds. . . ."

Later decisions have continued to observe the distinction adverted to in *Bi-Metallic Investment Co., supra.* In *Ohio Bell Telephone Co. v. Public Utilities Commission,* 301 U.S. 292, 304–05 (1937), the Court noted the fact that the administrative proceeding there involved was designed to require the utility to refund previously collected rate charges. The Court held that in such a proceeding the agency could not, consistently with due process, act on the basis of undisclosed evidence which was never made a part of the record before the agency. The case is thus more akin to *Interstate Commerce Commission v. Louisville & Nashville R. Co.,* 227 U.S. 88 (1913), holding that due process applied to a decision by the ICC that a specific railroad rate was unreasonable than it is to this case. . . . While the line dividing them may not always be a bright one, these decisions represent a recognized distinction in administrative law between proceedings for the purpose of promulgating policy-type rules or standards, on the one hand, and proceedings designed to adjudicate disputed facts in particular cases on the other.

Here the incentive payments proposed by the Commission . . . were applicable across the board to all . . . railroads . . . No effort was made to single out any particular railroad for special consideration based on its own peculiar circumstances. . . . Though the Commission obviously relied on factual inferences as a basis for its order . . . [these] factual inferences were used in the formulation of a basically legislative-type judgment, for prospective application only, rather than in adjudicating a particular set of disputed facts.

3. *Legislative and adjudicative facts.* "Adjudicative facts" concern a particular party and frequently concern questions of who did what and why they did it. When an adjudicative fact is disputed, trial-type procedure typically calls for the individual to testify and be subjected to cross-examination. In contrast, "legislative facts" do not describe an individual but are the general facts that help government decide questions of law, policy, and discretion. Disputes concerning legislative facts are best resolved through published literature and through expert testimony. Some authorities distinguish *Londoner* and *Bi-Metallic* by focusing on the nature of the facts in issue. *Bi-Metallic* involved an issue of legislative fact—whether all taxpayers in Denver were being systematically under-assessed. *Londoner* involved an issue of adjudicative fact—how much did a particular property owner benefit from paving of a street? In general, due process does not apply to a proceeding (such as rulemaking) the purpose of which is to determine legislative facts. Due process does apply to a proceeding (such as adjudication) the purpose of which is to determine adjudicative facts. *See* 2

RICHARD J. PIERCE, JR., ADMINISTRATIVE LAW TREATISE 741 (5th ed. 2010). Professor Pierce restates a theory first advanced by Professor Kenneth Davis, formerly the co-author of the Pierce treatise, who is often identified with the legislative/adjudicative fact distinction.

Note that the third paragraph of the *Florida East Coast* decision, quoted in N. 2, specifically refers to the type of facts at issue in that case. In deciding whether due process applies to a particular proceeding, is it helpful to ask whether the facts at issue are legislative or adjudicative?

4. *Rulemaking hearings.* Justice Holmes argued in *Bi-Metallic* that no hearing would be required if the state constitution or the state legislature had doubled Denver's tax rate. Therefore, it followed that there was no right to a hearing when the same action was taken by the State Board of Equalization. Holmes's premise about legislatures is right as a matter of constitutional law. Under modern administrative procedure acts, however, a notice-and-comment procedure is generally required before an agency adopts rules, whereas a legislature can use whatever procedure it wants in adopting legislation.

5. *Problem.* A major political issue in Elm City is whether rapid development of residential neighborhoods with high rise apartments and shopping centers should be slowed down.

a) A newly elected city council conducts a hearing on a proposed zoning ordinance. The ordinance would provide that no new development (other than single-family dwellings) could occur in large areas of the city, including the Brentwood neighborhood. Ben, who owns an empty lot in Brentwood, seeks to cross-examine the city planner at a hearing in order to show that the ordinance is too restrictive and that the ambiance of Brentwood can be preserved if small shopping centers are permitted. Is Ben entitled to cross-examine the planner?

b) Assume the council adopts the ordinance. Later, Ben requests issuance of a variance to allow the construction of a small shopping center on his lot. The ordinance provides that a variance can be issued in cases of "unusual hardship." Ben argues that he could make five times as much on his investment if he could build a shopping center. Moreover, it would be a great convenience for the neighborhood because there is no nearby shopping. Finally, he makes the same arguments that he made earlier in opposing the citywide ordinance. The council proposes to deny the request. Is Ben entitled to a trial-type hearing?

c) Assume instead that the council proposes to grant Ben's request for a variance. Mary, Ben's neighbor, is outraged at the extra noise and traffic that a shopping center would bring to her street and to Brentwood generally. Is Mary entitled to a trial-type hearing? *See Horn v. County of Ventura,* 596 P.2d 1134 (Cal. 1979);

High Horizons Dev. Co. v. New Jersey Dep't of Transp., 575 A.2d
1360, 1367–68 (N.J. 1990); *River Park, Inc. v. City of Highland
Park*, 23 F.3d 164 (7th Cir. 1994).

§ 2.5.2 REGULATIONS APPLICABLE TO A SINGLE ENTITY

ANACONDA CO. V. RUCKELSHAUS

482 F.2d 1301 (10th Cir. 1973)

DOYLE, J.:

. . . . The crucial aspect of the case is the validity of the proposed EPA
regulation for the control of sulfur oxide emissions in Deer Lodge County,
Montana where Anaconda operates its smelter. The company is the only
significant source of sulfur oxide pollution in the county and so
concededly the proposed regulation, although general in form, would
apply to Anaconda alone. . . . Anaconda immediately demanded an
adjudicatory hearing on EPA's proposed regulation, but EPA's reply was
that the public hearings were to be legislative or informational and not
adjudicatory. Subsequently, it was further explained that the hearing
would not be conducted in the nature of a trial. Instead, any interested
persons or corporations could make a statement and all relevant
testimony would be received. Also, the hearing record would remain open
until October 7, 1972, for written statements or other submissions. After
that there would be a further hearing to allow further public statements.

Anaconda's position expressed at the hearing was that it was
spending large sums of money on its own initiative in an effort to control
sulfur oxide emissions; that it was preparing to restrict them from the
current rate of 64,000 pounds per hour to 50,000 pounds per hour. Its
position was further expressed that the 7,040 pounds per hour would be
technologically and economically unfeasible and would create a
significant water pollution problem. . . .

Our final question is whether there was sufficient substance to
Anaconda's contention so that it would appear that it has been deprived
of procedural due process by EPA's refusal to grant a trial type
adjudicatory hearing. . . . The fact that Anaconda alone is involved is not
conclusive on the question as to whether the hearing should be
adjudicatory, for there are many other interested parties and groups who
are affected and are entitled to be heard. So the guidelines enunciated by
Mr. Justice Holmes in *Bi-Metallic* are not applicable. We have also
examined the early decision in *Londoner* and nothing therein imposes the
adjudicatory requirement. . . .

From our examination of the Act and the related case law and
statutes, it would appear that the congressional requirement of a public

hearing [in § 110(c) of the Clean Air Act] has been satisfied. Notice has been given and the proposed regulation has been issued. Anaconda appeared at that hearing and submitted material and was given an opportunity to submit more material and information for a period of 75 days following the public hearing. We perceive no violation of Anaconda's right to procedural due process.

Unending procedure could be produced by an adjudicatory hearing. This could bring about unending delay which would not only impede but completely stifle congressional policy. We do not, of course, condemn the trial court's concern for the rights of Anaconda. Those rights are important and the court should be sensitive to them, but those rights are not of such magnitude as to overcome congressional policy and the rights of the remainder of the community.

The judgment of the district court is reversed. . . .

NOTES AND QUESTIONS

1. *Adjudicative v. legislative facts.* The facts at issue in *Anaconda* concerned the harm done by sulfur dioxide pollution and the costs that Anaconda would have to pay to meet the EPA standards. Are these legislative or adjudicative facts? Should the distinction matter for deciding the *Anaconda* case?

2. *Rules applicable to a single party.* Should due process apply to agency rulemaking when a rule is applicable only to a single party? Professor Schwartz criticized *Anaconda* and maintained that if a facially general pronouncement is individual in impact, the affected person should be given a trial-type hearing. BERNARD SCHWARTZ, ADMINISTRATIVE LAW § 5.8 at 241 (3d ed. 1991). Do you agree?

CHAPTER 3

ADMINISTRATIVE ADJUDICATION: FUNDAMENTAL PROBLEMS

■ ■ ■

Chapter 2 examined the constitutional right to a trial-type hearing. This chapter also explores the right to a hearing, but the source of the right is statutory rather than constitutional. In many situations, constitutional and statutory rights overlap because both due process and the applicable APA may require hearings. However, statutory hearings are likely to be more formalized than due process hearings. Often there is no overlap, because a statute may require a hearing even though due process does not or (particularly at the local level) due process may require a hearing even though no statute does so.

This chapter addresses fundamental problems concerning agency hearings required by statute: When does a statute require an agency to hold a hearing? What is the relationship between statutory and constitutionally required hearings? Can an agency adjudicate a case impartially when it investigated and prosecuted the very case it is about to decide? When is an agency decisionmaker disabled by bias or by having received off-the-record communications?

Chapter 4 takes up many practical problems of agency adjudication. It begins with investigation and discovery arising in the pre-hearing phase, continues with the hearing itself, and concludes with the principles relating to an agency's final decision.

§ 3.1 STATUTORY RIGHTS TO AN ADJUDICATORY HEARING

Every APA, whether federal or state, contains a predefined set of ground rules for evidentiary or trial-type hearings. In federal practice, a hearing conducted according to these ground rules is called "formal adjudication;" state APAs generally use the term "contested case." A key issue for many litigants, therefore, is whether they will be eligible for one of these APA hearings. We call this issue the "gateway" problem.

Administrative procedure statutes have taken two different approaches to this problem. Under the federal APA (discussed in § 3.1.1) and most state statutes (discussed in § 3.1.2), agencies are required to use these procedures *only if* an *external source* (such as *another* statute or the state or federal constitution) requires an evidentiary hearing. If no external source requires an agency to conduct an evidentiary hearing, the agency is free to choose its own dispute resolution procedure (unless due process or some other statute or the agency's own regulations require it to use a particular procedure). Such adjudication is often called "informal adjudication" (although, as we will see, this is a misnomer, because the procedures for non-APA adjudication are often quite formal—*see* § 3.4).

In contrast, the APAs of several states take a different approach to the gateway problem. Rather than looking to an external source to decide whether an evidentiary hearing is required, these APAs themselves prescribe when evidentiary hearings must occur.

§ 3.1.1 FEDERAL LAW—RIGHT TO A HEARING UNDER THE APA

Read APA § 554(a). This is the APA's "gateway" provision. It applies only to "adjudication required by statute to be determined on the record after opportunity for an agency hearing ..." When a federal statute outside the APA calls for an agency hearing that is "on the record," these are code words signaling that Congress intends that the formal adjudication sections of the APA come into play. Thus the gateway provision in the federal APA depends on an external source to trigger the APA's adjudicatory provisions. That external source must either provide explicitly that the APA applies or must use the code words "on the record" or their equivalent.

The fact that a "record" is maintained at a hearing (meaning that everything said is transcribed and turned into a written transcript) does not mean the hearing is "on the record" for purposes of deciding whether the APA formal adjudication provisions apply. The phrase "on the record" really means "on the exclusive record," which in turn means that the trier of fact is allowed to consider only evidence that has been admitted at the hearing. *See* APA § 556(e). However, many hearings that are not required to be conducted as APA formal adjudicatory hearings also respect the "exclusive record" requirement. So in the end, the words "on the record" in § 554(a) really don't mean anything except to signal the intent of Congress that the APA should apply.

The most important APA formal adjudication provisions require that:

•   The hearing must be conducted by an administrative law judge (ALJ). An ALJ is a special kind of presiding officer who works for the agency that is a party to the case. An ALJ is hired by the Office of Personnel Management according to strict merit selection standards. An ALJ's independence from agency pressures is protected by a variety of statutory provisions. See APA §§ 3105, 7521, discussed in § 3.4.

• An agency must separate its prosecuting and adjudicating functions (§ 554(d)) and no party can engage in ex parte contact with decisionmakers (§ 557(d)).

• An agency must allow such cross-examination at the hearing as "may be required for a full and true disclosure of the facts" (§ 556(d)).

• If the private party wins and the agency's position was not substantially justified, the private party is often entitled to recover attorney fees under the Equal Access to Justice Act (discussed in § 10.3).

But what happens if Congress merely calls for a "hearing" or a "public hearing" without using the code words "on the record?" Might such a statute be interpreted as *implicitly* contemplating formal adjudication? Or does a case governed by such a statute necessarily fall into the residual category of "informal adjudication?" If the latter is true, an agency is limited in its choice of procedures only by due process (if it is applicable), by the statutory requirement that it provide a "hearing," and by its own procedural rules.

DOMINION ENERGY BRAYTON POINT, LLC v. JOHNSON
443 F.3d 12 (1st Cir. 2006)

SELYA, J.:

[Dominion owns an electric generating facility that draws water from several rivers for use in the plant's cooling system and discharges the heated water back into the rivers. Under the federal Clean Water Act (CWA), heating the water is considered a form of water pollution. As a result, Dominion must secure a National Pollution Discharge Elimination System (NPDES) permit from the Environmental Protection Agency (EPA) that authorizes it to heat the water.

EPA issued permits to Dominion that contained a "thermal variance." The CWA provides that, in deciding whether to issue a thermal variance, the EPA must offer an "opportunity for public hearing." The agency can issue the variance if, "taking into account the interaction of such thermal component with other pollutants," the variance "will assure the protection and propagation of a balanced, indigenous population of shellfish, fish, and wildlife in and on that body of water." Dominion's permit was up for renewal, but there was a dispute concerning the terms of the renewed permit. In accordance with procedural regulations it had adopted in 2000, EPA refused to conduct a formal APA adjudicatory hearing.]

On appeal, the central question presented concerns the effect of this court's decision in *Seacoast Anti-Pollution League v. Costle*, 572 F.2d 872

(1st Cir. 1978), in light of the Supreme Court's subsequent decision in *Chevron, U.S.A. Inc. v. Natural Resources Defense Council, Inc.*, 467 U.S. 837 (1984). Concluding, as we do, that *Seacoast* does not control, we affirm the judgment below. . . .

II. THE LEGAL LANDSCAPE

We set the stage for our substantive discussion by undertaking a brief review of the legal rules that frame the controversy at hand. Before the EPA either issues an NPDES permit or authorizes a thermal variance, it must offer an "opportunity for public hearing." 33 U.S.C. §§ 1326(a), 1342(a). No definition of "public hearing" is contained within the four corners of the CWA.

The [APA] is also part of the relevant legal landscape. Most pertinent here are those sections that combine to describe the procedures for formal administrative adjudications. *See* §§ 554, 556, 557. These procedures apply "in every case of adjudication required by statute to be determined on the record after opportunity for an agency hearing." § 554(a). The APA does not directly address whether these procedures apply when a statute simply calls for an "opportunity for public hearing" without any specific indication that the hearing should be "on the record."

In *Seacoast,* this court interpreted "public hearing" . . . to mean "evidentiary hearing"—in other words, a hearing that comports with the APA's requirements for a formal adjudication. Examining the legislative history of the APA, we adopted a presumption that "unless a statute otherwise specifies, an adjudicatory hearing subject to judicial review must be [an evidentiary hearing] on the record." Applying that presumption to the CWA, we concluded that "the statute certainly does not indicate that the determination need *not* be on the record."

So viewed, *Seacoast* established a rebuttable presumption that, in the context of an adjudication, an organic statute that calls for a "public hearing" should be read to require an evidentiary hearing in compliance with the formal adjudication provisions of the APA. . . . Acquiescing in this construction, the EPA promulgated regulations that memorialized the use of formal evidentiary hearings in the NPDES permit process.

In 1984, a sea change occurred in administrative law and, specifically, in the interpretation of organic statutes such as the CWA. The Supreme Court held that "[w]hen a court reviews an agency's construction of the statute which it administers," the reviewing court first must ask "whether Congress has directly spoken to the precise question at issue." If Congress's intent is clear, that intent governs—both the court and the agency must give it full effect. If, however, Congress has not directly addressed the question and the agency has stepped into the vacuum by promulgating a . . . regulation, a reviewing court may "not simply impose its own construction on the statute," but, rather, ought to ask "whether the agency's answer is based on a permissible construction of the statute."

This paradigm, sometimes called the *Chevron* two-step, increases the sphere of influence of agency action. If congressional intent is unclear and an agency's interpretation of a statute that it administers is reasonable, an inquiring court must defer to that interpretation. That is so even if the agency's interpretation is not the one that the court considers to be the best available interpretation.

Armed with the *Chevron* decision and a presidential directive to streamline regulatory programs, the EPA [adopted a rule] to eliminate formal evidentiary hearings from the NPDES permitting process. This revision depended heavily on a *Chevron* analysis. The agency began by "finding no evidence that Congress intended to require formal evidentiary hearings or that the text [of the relevant statute] precludes informal adjudication of permit review petitions." Then, it weighed the risks and benefits of employing informal hearing procedures for NPDES permit review, "determining that these procedures would not violate the Due Process Clause." Finally, it "concluded that informal hearing procedures satisfy the hearing requirement of [the relevant section]. . . ." Thus, it was under this scheme that the EPA denied Dominion's request for an evidentiary hearing.

III. ANALYSIS

. . . The only piece left to this puzzle is to confirm that the EPA's new regulations are, in fact, entitled to *Chevron* deference. This inquiry is a straightforward one. As our earlier discussion suggests (and as the *Seacoast* court correctly deduced), Congress has not spoken directly to the precise question at issue here. *See, e.g.,* . . . *Chemical Waste Mgmt., Inc. v. EPA,* 873 F.2d 1477, 1480–82 (D.C. Cir.1989) (concluding that Congress's intent behind the words "public hearing" in [a different environmental statute] was ambiguous for *Chevron* purposes). Accordingly, we must defer to the EPA's interpretation of the CWA as long as that interpretation is reasonable.

In this instance, the administrative interpretation took into account the relevant universe of factors [referring by analogy to the *Mathews* due process test]. . . . The agency's conclusion that evidentiary hearings are unnecessary and that Congress, in using the phrase "opportunity for public hearing," did not mean to mandate evidentiary hearings seems reasonable—and Dominion, to its credit, has conceded the point. . . .

Dominion exhorts us to find that *Seacoast's* holding is actually an interpretation of the APA, not the CWA (and, therefore, the EPA's regulation is also an interpretation of the APA, not entitled to *Chevron* deference). Such a reading of *Seacoast* is plainly incorrect. While the *Seacoast* court relied on a presumption borrowed from the APA, the court's holding is an interpretation of the CWA and, specifically, of the term "public hearing" contained in [the relevant CWA provisions]. . . . Because those changes implicate the statute that the EPA administers (i.e., the CWA), *Chevron* deference is appropriate. . . . [Affirmed].

NOTES AND QUESTIONS

1.   *EPA's reasons for adopting informal procedure in NPDES cases.* In 2000, the EPA adopted procedural regulations that dispensed with trial-type hearings in NPDES cases and substituted a less formal procedure. Staff members seek written comments and provide a "public hearing" in which the applicant for the permit or anybody else can present written or oral statements. If any interested persons disagree with the permitting decision, they can appeal to the Environmental Appeals Board (EAB). EAB does not conduct a trial but reviews the permitting decision based on the written record. All this falls far short of APA requirements. In particular, the EPA regulations do not provide for a formal trial-type hearing presided over by an ALJ.

Many agencies besides EPA have sought to avoid APA adjudication procedures. Agencies consider these procedures too formal and inflexible. In addition, agencies wish to avoid having to use ALJs as presiding officers, because the agencies have far more flexibility if they can use their own staff members as administrative judges. Just to mention one frequent objection, the APA gives agencies very little choice in hiring ALJs, and thus the agencies can't select judges with the needed technical competence. See further discussion of this issue in § 3.4.1.

2.   *Hearings required by statute.* When a statute calls for a "hearing" or a "public hearing" but does not use the magic words "on the record," does the statute trigger § 554(a) of the APA? In cases of *rulemaking*, the Supreme Court has held that formal procedures are not triggered by a requirement that the ICC act "after hearing." Congress must use the words "on the record" or their equivalent. *United States v. Florida East Coast Ry.*, 410 U.S. 224 (1973), discussed in § 5.4.2.

However, in cases of *adjudication*, several decisions prior to *Dominion* required formal adjudicatory procedures under statutes that call only for a "hearing" or a "public hearing." The leading case in that line was *Seacoast Anti-Pollution League* which was overruled in *Dominion*. *Seacoast* involved the same statutory scheme at issue in *Dominion* and similar factual issues.

Also prior to *Dominion*, several court of appeals decisions had disagreed with *Seacoast*. These cases held that the APA does not apply to adjudication unless Congress requires a hearing "on the record" or otherwise explicitly indicates an intention that the APA should apply. *See, e.g., City of West Chicago v. NRC*, 701 F.2d 632 (7th Cir. 1983) (no APA hearing is required for Nuclear Regulatory Commission's decision relating to storage of radioactive material by a manufacturing company).

Seacoast relied in part on the *Attorney General's Manual on the Administrative Procedure Act* (1947), a respected interpretive guide that the Justice Department published shortly after the APA was enacted. The Manual states:

> [A] statutory provision that rules be issued after a hearing, without more, should not be construed as requiring agency action "on the record," but rather as merely requiring an opportunity for the expression of views. That conclusion [is] based on the legislative nature of rulemaking. . . . No such rationale applies to administrative adjudication. In fact, it is assumed that where a statute specifically provides for administrative adjudication (such as the suspension or revocation of a license) after opportunity for an agency hearing, such specific requirement for a hearing ordinarily implies the further requirement of decision in accordance with evidence adduced at the hearing. *Id.* at 42–43.

Should the *Attorney General's Manual* be followed as a reflection of the likely original intent behind the APA? Or is the Manual outdated because it did not anticipate the great increase in cases like *Dominion, Seacoast,* or *West Chicago*? The following note considers the latter possibility.

3.   *Technical and complex cases.* There is a policy issue of whether the APA formal hearing requirements *should* apply to cases like *Dominion, Seacoast,* or *West Chicago*. The disputed issues in such cases are technical, scientific, or economic. Decisionmakers must make difficult judgments that involve great uncertainty and have significant political repercussions. Such cases do not depend on judgments of witness credibility or any charges of wrongdoing.

Should cases of this type be resolved through informal procedure (like the process prescribed in the EPA regulations at issue in *Dominion*)? That procedure would involve an opportunity for public comment and the exchange of written reports by experts, followed by oral arguments. Or should such cases be resolved through trial-type procedures? In the adjudicatory model, there is a trial in which expert witnesses testify and are cross-examined. The trial is conducted by an ALJ and the decisionmakers cannot consult with staff members who played adversary roles in the case. (See § 3.3.4 for discussion of separation of functions).

4.   *Deferring to the agency's choice.* The First Circuit in *Dominion* and the D. C. Circuit in *Chemical Waste* (which was cited in Dominion) took a different tack from either *West Chicago* or *Seacoast*. *Dominion* and *Chemical Waste* indicate that the words "hearing" or "public hearing" are ambiguous with respect to whether the APA should apply.

However, *Chevron* does not apply to an agency's interpretation of the APA. Was the First Circuit correct in asserting that *Dominion* involved only an interpretation of the CWA as opposed to an interpretation of the APA? *Cf.* Cooley R. Howarth, Jr., *Restoring the Applicability of the APA's Adjudicatory*

Procedures, 56 ADMIN. L. REV. 1043, 1052 (2004) (arguing that, in a case of this kind, "a reviewing court will, of necessity, be required to interpret not only the agency's empowering statute, but the APA as well. A court cannot determine whether particular language in an agency's statute triggers compliance with the APA unless it first understands what kind of statutory language the APA requires as the triggering mechanism for compliance." We discuss *Chevron* in detail at § 9.2.2.

With *Seacoast* overruled, the law now seems fairly clear: courts must defer to reasonable agency interpretations of ambiguous words like "hearing" or "public hearing" in the agency's statute. Cases like *City of West Chicago* come out at the same place by ruling that the APA does not apply at all unless the statute calls for an on-the-record hearing or otherwise explicitly declares that the APA should apply. Only a fairly dubious Ninth Circuit precedent is to the contrary. *Marathon Oil Co. v. EPA,* 564 F.2d 1253 (9th Cir. 1977). As a result, agencies will be strongly influenced to adopt regulations defining the words "hearing" or "public hearing" in their statutes to avoid application of the APA, as the EPA did in *Dominion* and *Chemical Waste.*

5. *Informal adjudication and judicial creativity.* As we point out in the introductory paragraphs of § 3.1.1 and in greater detail in § 3.4.1, the term "informal adjudication" is somewhat of a misnomer. The common usage of the term informal adjudication is that it includes all adjudication not covered by the APA. However, federal statutes often require agencies to provide evidentiary hearings that are not covered by the APA. Such non-APA adjudication is often relatively "formal" in structure but it is presided over by administrative judges (AJs) rather than by ALJs. It is estimated that over half a million federal adjudications consist of evidentiary hearings that are not covered by the APA. Examples are hearings by the Board of Veterans Appeals, immigration and deportation cases, cases involving government contract disputes, security clearance revocation cases, and many others.

A large amount of other non-APA adjudication is not conducted through evidentiary hearings and is truly informal. There are countless examples in the areas of federal grants, contracts and land management, and in decisions by consular officials to deny a visa to visit the U. S. APA §§ 558 and 555 provide a few meager protections applicable to true informal adjudication, and due process sometimes applies. Other than these constraints, the APA leaves agencies free to design their own informal adjudication procedures.

Assume that a statute requires an agency to provide a "hearing" before deciding a certain type of case (but that neither the APA nor due process applies). A reviewing court believes that the agency's procedures are not fair to the private party—for example, because the agency decisionmakers received ex parte communications. The court cannot fall back on any statute or regulation to provide the necessary protection. Can the court interpret the statutory word "hearing" to require the agency to provide at least some procedural protections? *See United States Lines, Inc. v. FMC,* 584 F.2d 519

(D.C. Cir. 1978) ("hearing" includes limits on ex parte contacts with the decisionmaker). In order to facilitate judicial review, some case law has required a system of notice, comment, and explanation, like that required in informal rulemaking, before an agency completes informal adjudication. *Indep. U.S. Tanker Owners Comm. v. Lewis*, 690 F.2d 908, 922–26 (D.C. Cir. 1982).

In an important case involving rulemaking, the Supreme Court held that courts cannot mandate procedures beyond those set forth in the APA. *See Vermont Yankee,* § 5.4.3. Later, it extended *Vermont Yankee* to adjudication. *Pension Benefit Guaranty Corp. v. LTV Corp.*, 496 U.S. 633 (1990), discussed in § 5.4.3 N.5. As a result, the agency, and not the courts, decides what procedure to employ if due process or a statute specific to the agency does not otherwise dictate the procedure. In the wake of *Vermont Yankee* and *PBGC,* the D. C. Circuit has expressed serious doubt about the reasoning of the cases cited in the preceding paragraph. *District No. 1, Pacific Coast Dist. Marine Eng'rs' Beneficial Ass'n v. Maritime Admin.*, 215 F.3d 37, 42–43 (D.C. Cir. 2000).

Do you agree with the *Pension Benefit Guaranty* case? Note the major difference between rulemaking and adjudication. In the case of informal rulemaking, the APA provides a series of adequate procedural protections, so judicial tinkering may be unnecessary. (Rulemaking procedures are discussed in Chapter 5.) But in the case of informal adjudication, the APA provides virtually no protection at all.

6. *ABA recommendations.* The ABA House of Delegates has adopted several recommendations relevant to the gateway problem. First, the ABA recommended in 2000 that Congress enact a statute providing that the APA adjudication provisions will apply to *future* statutes that call for a "hearing." Thus if Congress does not want the APA to apply, it would have to say so. This would reverse the status quo; under *Dominion* if the agency interprets the ambiguous word "hearing" to permit informal adjudication, the courts must defer to that choice. The supporting report, submitted by the ABA's Judicial Division (which includes ALJs), explained:

> Congressional failure to state whether adjudications are to be conducted under APA mandates has caused needless confusion, controversy and judicial review over the years. This has detracted from the acceptance of Federal agency adjudication as a model. For example, in legislation creating a number of adjudications in which substantial civil money penalties may be imposed, it was not clear whether Congress intended that ALJs should preside over the hearings or whether other APA requirements should apply. The result was a vacuum in which the implementing agencies themselves made the legislative decision; they decided not to conduct such proceedings subject to the independence and formality of APA adjudications, much to the consternation of some who

perceived that decision as an attempt to maximize agency advantages and deny due process.

125–2 A.B.A. REP. 251 (2000). For an opposing view, see Gary J. Edles, *An APA-Default Presumption for Administrative Hearings: Some Thoughts on "Ossifying" the Adjudication Process*, 55 ADMIN. L. REV. 787, 815–16 (2003). Edles wrote:

> Evolutionary developments in the administrative hearing process are not a coincidence. They reflect decades of common sense experimentation, experience, and, eventually, judicial and congressional acceptance and encouragement. The shift away from formal adjudication, and the emergence of informal hearings as a new category, has occurred, in large measure, because the governmental tasks have changed since the 1940s and formal hearings are seen as ill suited to the myriad adjudicatory needs of modern government. Public attentiveness to the cost implications of government programs has also heightened. In an era of limited and diminishing resources, agencies should not be deprived automatically of the opportunity to craft the most cost effective methods for administering their programs—consistent, of course, with fundamental fairness.

> Formal hearings are still used—and should be used—in cases for which they are suited. . . . However, informal hearings have emerged because informal procedures can be conducted fairly and efficiently as agencies, under judicial and congressional supervision, tailor procedural elements to the requirements of their substantive missions. . . . Is a wholesale return to a regime predicated on the environment of the 1940s really the most sensible solution to perceived inadequacies?

Second, the ABA recommended in 2004 that Congress provide limited procedural protections when Congress calls for an evidentiary hearing but the APA does not apply. For example, the APA's ban on ex parte contacts and its requirement of separation of prosecution from adjudicatory functions would apply in these cases. However, the recommendation would not require that ALJs preside at the hearing. *See* Michael Asimow, *The Spreading Umbrella: Extending the APA's Adjudication Provisions to All Evidentiary Hearings Required by Statute*, 56 ADMIN. L. REV. 1003 (2004).

7. *Constitutionally required hearings.* What happens if *due process* requires a trial-type hearing but the APA formal adjudication provisions do not apply? This was the situation in *Wong Yang Sung v. McGrath*, 339 U.S. 33 (1950). *Wong* was a deportation case. The statute did not require the agency (then called the Immigration & Naturalization Service or INS) to provide any kind of hearing. However, due process requires a hearing before a person can be deported.

The Court held that the APA formal adjudication provisions applied to deportation cases, because the words "required by statute" in § 554(a) were intended to include *hearings required by the Constitution as well as hearings required by statute.* The Court refused to "attribute to Congress a purpose to be less scrupulous about the fairness of a hearing necessitated by the Constitution than one granted as a matter of expediency." Congress swiftly overturned the narrow holding of *Wong* and made clear that the APA did not apply to deportation cases. *See Marcello v. Bonds*, 349 U.S. 302 (1955) (upholding this statute). However, this legislation did not foreclose the Court from applying the *Wong* principle in other regulatory contexts.

In recent decades the courts have often ignored or evaded *Wong. See* Robert E. Zahler, Note, *The Requirement of Formal Adjudication under Section 5 of the Administrative Procedure Act*, 12 HARV. J. LEGIS. 194, 218–41 (1975). A good example is *Clardy v. Levi*, 545 F.2d 1241 (9th Cir. 1976), which declined to apply APA formal adjudication to federal prison disciplinary cases, even though due process then required a hearing in such cases (see § 2.2.2 N.8).

Does the eclipse of *Wong* make sense? Recall that, under *Mathews* balancing (*see* §§ 2.3 and § 2.4), many of the procedures called for by the APA need not be employed in hearings required by due process. Arguably, applying *Wong* in such situations would unnecessarily formalize due process hearings. On the other hand, *Mathews* balancing is difficult and unpredictable. Applying the APA might avoid that unpredictability, so that courts and agencies would know exactly what procedures were required. *See* William Funk, *The Rise and Demise of* Wong Yang Sung, 58 ADMIN. L. REV. 881 (2006) (arguing that *Wong* was rightly decided and should not be overruled).

8.   *Problem.* Mel wished to dredge and fill a swampy area on his farm that is useless for farming and is a breeding ground for mosquitoes. Once this wetland is filled, the area would be suitable for farming or for building homes. The wetland drains into a navigable river. Under § 404 of the federal Clean Water Act, Mel must obtain a dredging permit from the Army Corps of Engineers. The statute provides that the Corps may issue permits for the discharge of dredged or fill material into navigable waters, after "notice and opportunity for public hearings."

Ed (the Corps' District Engineer) did not conduct a hearing on Mel's application but did provide public notice. Ed received letters from a local environmental group charging that the project would increase the risk of downstream flooding and would destroy wildlife breeding habitats. Mel argued that the project would decrease the risk of flooding, would not destroy any breeding habitats, and would assist in mosquito control. He submitted letters from community leaders and from an environmental engineer in support of his position.

Ed visited Mel's farm. He also conducted informal meetings with Mel and with several opponents of the application. He did not take any notes of what was said at these meetings. Mel was not present at the meeting with the opponents. Based on the file, the informal conferences, and the site visit, Ed denied the application, writing a one-paragraph explanation of this decision. Mel requested a formal hearing under the APA or at least an oral argument, but Ed declined to provide them. The procedural regulations of the Corps of Engineers require only public notice and the opportunity to submit written comments in § 404 cases.

To what additional procedure, if any, is Mel entitled? *See Buttrey v. United States,* 690 F.2d 1170, 1174–83 (5th Cir. 1982).

§ 3.1.2 RIGHTS TO A HEARING UNDER STATE LAW

All states have their own APAs, the majority of which are based on the 1961 Model State APA. See § 1.4 for discussion of the 1961, 1981, and 2010 MSAPAs. The gateway provision of the 1961 Act is similar to the external source requirement in § 554(a) of the federal APA (discussed in § 3.1.1). The 1961 MSAPA defines a "contested case," to which its formal adjudication provisions apply, as a "proceeding, including but not restricted to ratemaking and licensing, in which the legal rights, duties or privileges of a party are required *by law* to be determined by an agency after an opportunity for hearing." 1961 MSAPA § 1(2) (emphasis added). The word "law" is not defined. The 1961 Act provides only for a single adjudication format: a formal, trial-type hearing. The 2010 MSAPA continues this approach by defining a contested case as "an adjudication in which an opportunity for an evidentiary hearing is required by the federal constitution, a federal statute, or the constitution or a statute of this state." § 102(7).

A number of recent state statutes and the 1981 MSAPA take a different approach to the gateway issue. These statutes provide an *inclusive* definition of adjudication. With only narrow exceptions, *all* adjudicatory decisions are covered by these APAs, regardless of whether an external source requires a hearing. *See* 1981 MSAPA § 4–201. The Florida statute, applied in *Metsch,* uses an inclusive definition of adjudication.

Some state statutes strike a compromise between the 1961 and 1981 MSAPA approaches. For example, Oregon defines a "contested case" to include cases in which a statute or constitutional provision requires an evidentiary hearing but adds some additional categories—a contested case includes any agency discretionary decision to suspend or revoke a right or privilege or to refuse to renew or issue a license, regardless of whether any other law requires a hearing. In addition, a contested case arises if a rule or order of the agency provides for procedures like those called for by the APA. The *Oregon Environmental Council* case which follows illustrates the operation of the Oregon statute.

OREGON ENVIRONMENTAL COUNCIL V. OREGON STATE BOARD OF EDUCATION

761 P.2d 1322 (Ore. 1988)

GILLETTE, J.:

The Oregon Environmental Council and the Portland Audubon Society seek to overturn a decision of the State Board of Education (Board) approving a textbook, *Get Oregonized*, for use in Oregon's public elementary schools. The issue is whether the Board's decision is a rule or an order and, if an order, whether in a contested case or otherwise. The answer implicates, among other things, the scope of judicial review, the procedures by which the decision was made, the criteria by which the decision must be measured and whether petitioners can seek review in the appellate courts at this time. The Court of Appeals decided that the Board's decision was a rule and upheld its validity. We hold that the decision was an order in other than a contested case, *i.e.*, a matter not reviewable in the Court of Appeals, and therefore reverse the decision of that court and remand the case to it with instructions to dismiss the petition for judicial review.

BACKGROUND

We begin with some background on the textbook approval process. The Board, whose decision is here challenged, has three responsibilities with regard to textbook selection. First, it appoints the seven members of the State Textbook Commission (Commission). Second, it establishes "guidelines and criteria for review and selection of textbooks." It has done so by rule. Finally, the Board ratifies or rejects the Commission's selection of textbooks for use in Oregon public schools. District school boards are required to select the books for use from the books on the approved list.

The textbook selection process begins when a publisher submits to the Commission its proposed text documenting how the text conforms to the guidelines and criteria adopted by the Board. The Commission must prepare a "multiple choice list" of approved texts periodically. The Commission meets in public meeting on a designated day every other year "for the purpose of reviewing and selecting textbooks." It may reject a text if the terms and conditions for furnishing the text are "unreasonable" or if the text is "unsuitable" pursuant to the Board's guidelines and criteria. . . .

The textbook selection statutes contain no directives about procedures to be used in the selection process . . . The Board has provided by rule that any person wishing to challenge approval (but not rejection) of a text selected by the Commission shall have an opportunity to be heard in advance of the Board's decision. . . .

The Commission selected *Get Oregonized* as a fourth grade social studies text ... A Board hearings officer held a public hearing on February 5 and 6, 1986, at which proponents and opponents of the textbook testified. Those speaking in favor asserted that the book provided needed information about Oregon's timber and agricultural industries. They contended that it compared well with other approved texts and that the minor errors of fact and grammar could be corrected in later editions. Those opposed criticized it as advocating exploitation of natural resources, as being of poor quality and grammatically incorrect. The Board was apprised of the competing positions by the written report of the hearings officer. In a six to one vote on March 6, the Board by resolution amended its rule to include *Get Oregonized* as an approved textbook and authorized contracts with the publisher. . . .

Petitioners argue that if the decision were a rule, the Board is obliged but has failed to explain how the book complied with its guidelines and criteria. They assert that, if it is an order in a contested case, the Board failed to provide contested case procedures and to support its decision with substantial evidence in the record. We consider each of these contentions in turn.

THE AGENCY DECISION WAS NOT A RULE

The Administrative Procedures Act (APA), defines rules and orders in part by the breadth of their respective applications. A rule is an "agency directive, standard, regulation or statement of general applicability." An order is an "agency action * * * directed to a named person or named persons."

The Court of Appeals held that the Board's decision to approve *Get Oregonized* was a rule, adopting the Board's characterization that it is "a 'directive of general applicability that implements [the] policy' embodied in [statutes and regulations]," the rationale being that the decision was generally applicable to all school districts. This analysis focuses on the wrong issue. Although the decision applies to all school districts, it concerns but one book. Viewed in that light, the Board's decision is functionally similar to individual licensing decisions made by professional licensing agencies. Such licensing decisions are orders, not rules, although they affect others beyond the individual seeking a license ... Thus, the decision is an order. The question becomes whether the order must be made in a contested case or by some other procedure.

THE ORDER WAS NOT AN ORDER IN A CONTESTED CASE

Orders may be issued either in contested cases or in less formalized circumstances, *i.e.*, in circumstances "other than" contested cases. Under *ORS 183.310(2)(a)*, a "contested case" means:

(a) A proceeding before an agency:

(A) In which the individual legal rights, duties or privileges of specific parties are required by statute or Constitution to be determined only after an agency hearing at which such specific parties are entitled to appear and be heard;

(B) Where the agency has discretion to suspend or revoke a right or privilege of a person;

(C) For the suspension, revocation or refusal to renew or issue a license where the licensee or applicant for a license demands such hearing; or

(D) Where the agency by rule or order provides for hearings substantially of the character required by [the adjudication provisions of the Oregon APA].

If a proceeding before an agency fits one of these four definitions, the APA binds the agency to certain procedures by which it must reach its decision, *viz.*, the agency must base its decision on a record of evidence that the contesting parties have an opportunity to develop, it must confine its decision to the evidence so developed, and it must explain how its decision complies with the law and is supported by the facts. Orders in contested cases are reviewed in the Court of Appeals for errors of legal interpretation, abuse of agency discretion and lack of substantial evidence to support the decision. Review is confined to the record. Court of Appeals review of contested cases presupposes a record developed by the agency.

The APA says little about that category of agency decisions called "orders in other than contested cases." All that is clear is that these decisions represent that large body of agency actions that are "orders" . . . but not orders resulting from one of the four kinds of proceedings defined as "contested cases. . . ." The legislature directed the Court of Appeals to review "contested cases" and send "orders other than contested cases" to the circuit courts [that is, trial courts]. The circuit court was to conduct its review "without a jury as a suit in equity."

Petitioner's theories. Deciding whether a proceeding is a contested case does not depend on the kind of hearing the agency actually conducted; the appropriate analysis is whether the proceeding qualified as a contested case under the APA . . . Respondents asserted that this case is not included in any of the four categories of contested cases listed therein. Petitioners counter that this case falls into the categories described in *ORS 183.310(2)(a)(A)* and *(D)*. Specifically, they contend that the textbook statute gives students a right to a certain standard of quality in textbooks and that the federal constitution bestows on them the right to be free from government interference with access to expressive materials. These are, according to petitioners, "individual legal rights, duties or privileges" which can be determined only after a contested case hearing. Alternatively, petitioners argue that the Board has provided by rule a hearing "substantially of the character required" in a contested case.

We agree with respondents that petitioners themselves do not come within the terms of any part of *ORS 183.310(2)(a)*. The legislature charged the Board with setting standards and evaluating texts for compliance before approval; it did not, however, grant to any individual the right or power to compel the Board to act. If petitioners were seeking access to expressive material, their claim of constitutional right might have force. However, petitioners do not seek access to expressive material; they seek to prevent its dissemination.

Even in the absence of constitutional or statutory individual rights, a refusal to issue a license is an independent basis for a contested case hearing, upon the applicant's demand. *ORS 183.310(2)(a)(C)*. The publisher, as the applicant seeking agency approval . . . could demand a contested case hearing, if the Commission had recommended and the Board was contemplating rejecting a text. But subsection (C) does not entitle petitioners, who are not "applicants" or "licensees," to a contested case hearing. Ordinarily, government's approval of a party's request to be permitted to pursue an activity need not be preceded by contested case proceedings.

Further, we disagree with petitioners that the Board's rule, OAR 581–11–070, provides a hearing "substantially of the character required" in a contested case, thus entitling them to such proceedings under *ORS 183.310(2)(a)(D)*. . . . The rule says only that challengers to adoption of a text may have an "opportunity to be heard" before the Board makes its decision . . . This could mean an opportunity as limited as submission of written views on a proposed decision. Or, in order to ensure its accountability to the public, an agency may proceed, as the Board did here, with a public hearing format so that persons may "be heard" and hear others in person with oral testimony. But this format does not require that all testimony and evidence be tested for relevance and truthfulness and challenged by cross-examination as would occur at a contested case hearing . . .

The decision of the Court of Appeals is reversed.

METSCH V. UNIVERSITY OF FLORIDA

550 So.2d 1149 (Fla. App. 1989)

PER CURIAM:

Benjamin Metsch appeals from an order of the University of Florida denying his request for an administrative hearing following his unsuccessful application for admission to the University of Florida College of Law. We affirm.

Metsch, while a student at Columbia University, applied for admission to the fall 1989 entering class of the University of Florida College of Law. Metsch was denied automatic admission based upon a computer projection of his law school grades derived from his undergraduate grade point average and his Law School Admissions Test score. Metsch was then placed in the "hold" category, and his application was reviewed by the Faculty Admissions Committee. In April, 1989, Metsch received a letter from the University informing him that he had not been admitted. The following month, Metsch wrote to the law school and requested a statement of the reasons for the denial of his application, reconsideration of his application, and a hearing pursuant to § 120.57(1), Florida Statutes (1987). In his request for a hearing, Metsch alleged that his "substantial interests" had been determined by the University, a state agency. The University reconsidered his application and, by letter, affirmed and explained the denial of admission, described the admissions process and suggested that he reapply for admission to the spring 1990 semester. On May 10, 1989, the University's Interim President denied Metsch's request for an administrative hearing. Metsch appeals that denial.

The formal hearing provisions of the Florida Administrative Procedure Act, § 120.57(1) "apply in all proceedings in which the substantial interests of a party are determined by an agency, unless such proceedings are exempt pursuant to subsection (5) . . ."

. . . [W]e believe that before one can be considered to have a substantial interest in the outcome of the proceeding he must show 1) that he will suffer injury in fact which is of immediate sufficiency to entitle him to a § 120.57 hearing, and 2) that his substantial injury is of a type or nature which the proceeding is designed to protect . . .

In his request for an administrative hearing, Metsch alleged no injury and specified no interest other than his "sincere desire to study law at the University of Florida College of Law and to become a practicing member of The Florida Bar." Obviously Metsch has an interest, as that term is ordinarily used, in admission to the University's College of Law; however, his "sincere desire to study law" at that institution does not rise to the level of a "substantial interest" within the meaning of section 120.57(1). In our view, Metsch's interest can best be described as a hope or a "unilateral expectation of admittance." *Ramos v. Texas Tech Univ.*, 441 F. Supp. 1050, 1054 (N.D. Tex. 1977) (applicant for admission to graduate program had no liberty or property interest in being admitted), *aff'd*, 566 F.2d 573 (5th Cir. 1978). . . . If such hopes and aspirations were deemed substantial interests, all unsuccessful applicants for admission to a state university would be entitled to a formal hearing upon the denial of their applications. While this scenario is not the basis for our denial of Metsch's claim, we cannot ignore the repercussions that would flow from granting the relief which he seeks . . .

AFFIRMED

NOTES AND QUESTIONS

1.   *Oregon Environmental.* Note the various holdings of the *Oregon Environmental* case: i) the Board's decision to approve the textbook was an order (meaning the product of adjudication) and not a rule, but ii) the order was not the result of a "contested case." As a result, the Board was not required to follow the adjudication provisions of the Oregon APA. The APA provides detailed procedural requirements for rulemaking and for contested cases, but none for "orders in other than contested cases." Thus "orders in other than contested cases" are a kind of administrative law black hole. In addition, the Oregon Court of Appeals could not hear the case but had to remand it to a trial court.

2.   *Oregon's definition of "contested case."* Like the federal APA and the 1961 and 2010 MSAPAs, Oregon defines a contested case as one in which an external source (statute or constitution) requires "an agency hearing at which such specific parties are entitled to appear and be heard." The petitioners argued that this was a contested case because students have a constitutional right to a certain standard of quality in textbooks and the right to be "free from governmental interference with access to expressive materials." Why did the court reject this argument?

Unlike the federal APA or the 1961 or 2010 MSAPAs, Oregon added a number of important types of disputes to the "contested case" category.

•   A contested case is one in which the agency has discretion to suspend or revoke a right or privilege. See *Morrison v. University of Oregon Health Sciences Ctr.*, 685 P.2d 439 (Or. App. 1984). In *Morrison*, the dismissal of a dental student for "lack of adequate clinical performance" triggered rights to a formal hearing, because the dismissal was a discretionary revocation of a privilege. (Compare *Board of Curators, Univ. of Missouri v. Horowitz*, § 2.4 N.5, which deals with the same issue under due process.)

•   A contested case includes an agency proceeding for the suspension, revocation, or refusal to renew or issue a license. If the board had *rejected* the textbook, instead of *approving* it, this action would have been the refusal to issue a license and would have turned the dispute into a "contested case." *Oregon Environmental Council* was a 4–3 decision; the dissenters argued that the petitioners who disagreed with approval of the textbook were "parties" to a case for the issuance of a license.

• The Oregon statute treated a dispute as a contested case if the agency adopts a rule or an order calling for "hearings substantially of the character required" by the APA. The Board's rule provided that challengers of a textbook approval have an "opportunity to be heard." Why did this rule not turn the dispute into a contested case?

3. *Due process and the APA.* Recall that the relationship between the federal APA and hearings required by due process is unclear. *See* § 3.1.1 N.7. Under *Wong Yang Sung,* when due process calls for a trial-type hearing, the federal APA's adjudicatory provisions are triggered. Perhaps because it might cause excessive proceduralization, *Wong* has been ignored by lower courts and might well be overruled by the Supreme Court if the issue came up today.

However, the issue cannot be ignored under state law. The Oregon APA's gateway provision explicitly provides that the APA applies if due process requires "an agency hearing at which such specific parties are entitled to appear and be heard." The 2010 MSAPA applies if a constitutional provision requires an "evidentiary hearing." Many states operating under the 1961 MSAPA have reached the same conclusion by determining that the word "law" in § 1(2) includes constitutional as well as statutory law. The advantage of sweeping hearings required by due process into the APA is that the APA provides clear guidelines for the hearings. This avoids the need to do a *Mathews v. Eldridge* balancing to decide exactly what a due process hearing actually entails.

The problem with gateway provisions that sweep due process hearings under the APA is that many due process hearings are, and should be, less formal than full-fledged APA proceedings. For example, *Goss v. Lopez* (§ 2.4 N.1) held that due process applies to a brief suspension of a student from school. However, the decision does not call for a trial, merely a conference between the student and the disciplinarian. To avoid holding that a brief student suspension triggers the APA, states following the 1961 or 2010 MSAPA model would need to interpret their gateway provisions so that the APA does not come into play unless due process itself requires a reasonably formal hearing.

4. *Florida's inclusive approach.* Note that, unlike the Oregon statute or the 1961 or 2010 MSAPA, the Florida APA provides for a hearing whenever the "substantial interests" of a person are determined by an agency, regardless of whether a hearing is required by any other statute or the constitution. This is an example of the "inclusive" approach to defining adjudication that was employed in the 1981 MSAPA. If the Florida statute applied to NPDES determinations instead of the federal APA, would a hearing have been required in *Dominion,* § 3.1.1? Given the choice, would you recommend your state follow the gateway provisions of the 1961 or 2010 Acts or the Florida alternative? How about the Oregon compromise?

5.   *The result in Metsch.* Do you agree that the Law School's decision rejecting Metsch did not determine "substantial interests?" Didn't Metsch think they were substantial? The court relied on *Ramos*, which held that a rejected applicant for a university program was not deprived of due process and so had no right to a hearing. Is that decision in point in applying the Florida statute?

6.   *Formal hearings for disappointed law school applicants?* The judges who decided *Metsch* were concerned that "all unsuccessful applicants for admission to a state university would be entitled to a formal hearing upon the denial of their applications. . . . [W]e cannot ignore the repercussions that would flow from granting the relief which he seeks."

This is a serious concern. One can imagine the Law School getting swamped by the need to hold thousands of trial-type hearings each year. But was this concern valid? Very few rejected applicants will ask for any sort of review of the decision. They'll just move on and attend a different school. Moreover, Florida law provides for "informal proceedings" where a case does not present a "disputed issue of material fact." In an informal proceeding, an agency is required only

•   to give a person notice of its decision together with a summary of the grounds for the decision;

•   to give the person an opportunity at a convenient time and place to present to the agency written or oral evidence in opposition to its action, or a written statement challenging the grounds which it chose to justify its action; and

•   if the person's objections are overruled, a written explanation within seven days.

Did Metsch's case present a "disputed issue of material fact"? If not, would providing an informal proceeding for anybody who wanted one really be a major problem for the law school?

7.   *Problem.* Our client Ralph is a permanent employee of Library engaged in classifying new books. By statute, a permanent employee cannot be discharged except for good cause. Library's rules for employees prohibit smoking anywhere in the building. The rules also provide for disciplinary sanctions in case of rule violations. For a first offense, a supervisor can place a warning letter in an employee's file and can also suspend the employee for a period not to exceed five days. A supervisor has discretion as to which sanctions should be applied, if any.

Martha, Ralph's supervisor, believes that Ralph was smoking at his desk. Ralph denies this (he says the cigarette butts in his trash can were left by a friend who stopped by to visit him). He claims that another employee who hates him told Martha that he had been smoking. Even if he did it, he wants to persuade Martha not to put a letter in his file or suspend him.

Assume that Library is operated by

    i)   a county which is not subject to any APA,

    ii) a state that has adopted the 2010 MSAPA,

    iii) a state that has adopted the Florida statute,

    iv) the federal government.

Is Ralph entitled to a hearing and, if so, of what sort? What do you advise him to do now?

§ 3.2 LIMITING THE ISSUES TO WHICH HEARING RIGHTS APPLY

A recurring theme in this book is the interplay between adjudication and rulemaking. Section 2.5 explored the applicability of due process to agency pronouncements of general applicability. Recall *Bi-Metallic*. This section considers the related issue of whether an agency must provide an adjudicatory hearing prescribed by statute if the agency has already addressed the disputed issue in a rule. A few other devices by which an agency can narrow the issues that are subject to hearing rights are also discussed. Sections 5.1 and 6.2 will return to the relationship between rulemaking and adjudication, taking up the circumstances in which rulemaking should, or must, displace adjudication as a tool of regulation.

HECKLER V. CAMPBELL
461 U.S. 458 (1983)

POWELL, J.

The issue is whether the Secretary of Health and Human Services may rely on published medical-vocational guidelines to determine a claimant's right to Social Security disability benefits.

The Social Security Act defines "disability" in terms of the effect a physical or mental impairment has on a person's ability to function in the workplace. It provides disability benefits only to persons who are unable "to engage in any substantial gainful activity by reason of any medically determinable physical or mental impairment." 42 U.S.C. § 423(d)(1)(A). And it specifies that a person must "not only [be] unable to do his previous work but [must be unable], considering his age, education, and work experience, [to] engage in any other kind of substantial gainful work which exists in the national economy, regardless of whether such work exists in the immediate area in which he lives, or whether a specific job vacancy exists for him, or whether he would be hired if he applied for work." 42 U.S.C. § 423(d)(2)(A).

In 1978, the Secretary of Health and Human Services promulgated regulations implementing this definition. The regulations recognize that certain impairments are so severe that they prevent a person from pursuing any gainful work. A claimant who establishes that he suffers from one of these impairments will be considered disabled without further inquiry. If a claimant suffers from a less severe impairment, the Secretary must determine whether the claimant retains the ability to perform either his former work or some less demanding employment. If a claimant can pursue his former occupation, he is not entitled to disability benefits. If he cannot, the Secretary must determine whether the claimant retains the capacity to pursue less demanding work.

The regulations divide this last inquiry into two stages. First, the Secretary must assess each claimant's present job qualifications. The regulations direct the Secretary to consider the factors Congress has identified as relevant: physical ability, age, education, and work experience. Second, she must consider whether jobs exist in the national economy that a person having the claimant's qualifications could perform.

Prior to 1978, the Secretary relied on vocational experts to establish the existence of suitable jobs in the national economy. After a claimant's limitations and abilities had been determined at a hearing, a vocational expert ordinarily would testify whether work existed that the claimant could perform. Although this testimony often was based on standardized guides, vocational experts frequently were criticized for their inconsistent treatment of similarly situated claimants. To improve both the uniformity and efficiency[2] of this determination, the Secretary promulgated medical-vocational guidelines as part of the 1978 regulations. These guidelines relieve the Secretary of the need to rely on vocational experts by establishing through rulemaking the types and numbers of jobs that exist in the national economy. They consist of a matrix of the four factors identified by Congress—physical ability, age, education, and work experience—and set forth rules that identify whether jobs requiring specific combinations of these factors exist in significant numbers in the national economy.[4] Where a claimant's qualifications correspond to the job requirements identified by a rule,[5] the guidelines direct a conclusion as to whether work exists that the claimant could perform. If such work exists, the claimant is not considered disabled.

---

[2] The Social Security hearing system is "probably the largest adjudicative agency in the Western world." J. Mashaw et al., Social Security Hearings and Appeals, p. xi (1978). Approximately 2.3 million claims for disability benefits were filed in fiscal year 1981. More than a quarter of a million of these claims require a hearing before an Administrative Law Judge. The need for efficiency is self-evident.

[4] For example, Rule 202.10 provides that a significant number of jobs exist for a person who can perform light work, is closely approaching advanced age, has a limited education but who is literate and can communicate in English, and whose previous work has been unskilled.

[5] The regulations recognize that the rules only describe "major functional and vocational patterns." If an individual's capabilities are not described accurately by a rule, the regulations make clear that the individual's particular limitations must be considered. Additionally, the regulations declare that the administrative law judge will not apply the age categories "mechanically in a borderline situation," and recognize that some claimants may possess limitations that are not factored into the guidelines. . . .

In 1979, Carmen Campbell applied for disability benefits because a back condition and hypertension prevented her from continuing her work as a hotel maid. After her application was denied, she requested a hearing *de novo* before an Administrative Law Judge. He determined that her back problem was not severe enough to find her disabled without further inquiry, and accordingly considered whether she retained the ability to perform either her past work or some less strenuous job. He concluded that even though Campbell's back condition prevented her from returning to her work as a maid, she retained the physical capacity to do light work. In accordance with the regulations, he found that Campbell was 52 years old, that her previous employment consisted of unskilled jobs, and that she had a limited education. He noted that Campbell, who had been born in Panama, experienced difficulty in speaking and writing English. She was able, however, to understand and read English fairly well. Relying on [line 202.10 of] the medical-vocational guidelines [described in n.4], the Administrative Law Judge found that a significant number of jobs existed that a person of Campbell's qualifications could perform. Accordingly, he concluded that she was not disabled.

This determination was upheld by both the Social Security Appeals Council, and the District Court for the Eastern District of New York. The Court of Appeals for the Second Circuit reversed. . . . The court noted that it has consistently required that the Secretary identify specific alternative occupations available in the national economy that would be suitable for the claimant and that these jobs be supported by a job description clarifying the nature of the job, [and] demonstrating that the job does not require exertion or skills not possessed by the claimant.

The court found that the medical-vocational guidelines did not provide the specific evidence that it previously had required. It explained that in the absence of such a showing, "the claimant is deprived of any real chance to present evidence showing that she cannot in fact perform the types of jobs that are administratively noticed by the guidelines." The court concluded that because the Secretary had failed to introduce evidence that specific alternative jobs existed, the determination that Campbell was not disabled was not supported by substantial evidence. . . .

The court's requirement that additional evidence be introduced on this issue prevents the Secretary from putting the guidelines to their intended use and implicitly calls their validity into question. Accordingly, we think the decision below requires us to consider whether the Secretary may rely on medical-vocational guidelines in appropriate cases.

The Social Security Act directs the Secretary to "adopt reasonable and proper rules and regulations to regulate and provide for the nature and extent of the proofs and evidence and the method of taking and furnishing the same" in disability cases. 42 U.S.C. § 405(a). Where, as here, the statute expressly entrusts the Secretary with the responsibility for implementing a provision by regulation, our review is limited to determining whether the regulations promulgated exceeded the Secretary's statutory authority and whether they are arbitrary and capricious.

We do not think that the Secretary's reliance on medical-vocational guidelines is inconsistent with the Social Security Act. It is true that the statutory scheme contemplates that disability hearings will be individualized determinations based on evidence adduced at a hearing. See 42 U.S.C. §§ 423(d)(2)(A) (specifying consideration of each individual's condition) and 405(b) (disability determination to be based on evidence adduced at hearing). But this does not bar the Secretary from relying on rulemaking to resolve certain classes of issues. The Court has recognized that even where an agency's enabling statute expressly requires it to hold a hearing, the agency may rely on its rulemaking authority to determine issues that do not require case-by-case consideration. See *FPC v. Texaco Inc.,* 377 U.S. 33, 41–44 (1964); *United States v. Storer Broadcasting Co.,* 351 U.S. 192, 205 (1956). A contrary holding would require the agency continually to relitigate issues that may be established fairly and efficiently in a single rulemaking proceeding.

The Secretary's decision to rely on medical-vocational guidelines is consistent with *Texaco* and *Storer.* As noted above, in determining whether a claimant can perform less strenuous work, the Secretary must make two determinations. She must assess each claimant's individual abilities and then determine whether jobs exist that a person having the claimant's qualifications could perform. The first inquiry involves a determination of historic facts, and the regulations properly require the Secretary to make these findings on the basis of evidence adduced at a hearing. We note that the regulations afford claimants ample opportunity both to present evidence relating to their own abilities and to offer evidence that the guidelines do not apply to them.[11] The second inquiry requires the Secretary to determine an issue that is not unique to each claimant—the types and numbers of jobs that exist in the national economy. This type of general factual issue may be resolved as fairly through rulemaking as by introducing the testimony of vocational experts at each disability hearing.

As the Secretary has argued, the use of published guidelines brings with it a uniformity that previously had been perceived as lacking. To require the Secretary to relitigate the existence of jobs in the national

---

[11] Both *Texaco* and *Storer Broadcasting Co.,* were careful to note that the statutory scheme at issue allowed an individual applicant to show that the rule promulgated should not be applied to him. The regulations here provide a claimant with equal or greater protection since they state that an Administrative Law Judge will not apply the rules contained in the guidelines when they fail to describe a claimant's particular limitations. See n. 5, *supra.*

economy at each hearing would hinder needlessly an already overburdened agency. We conclude that the Secretary's use of medical-vocational guidelines does not conflict with the statute, nor can we say on the record before us that they are arbitrary and capricious.

We now consider Campbell's argument that the Court of Appeals properly required the Secretary to specify alternative available jobs. [That holding] appears to be based on a principle of administrative law— that when an agency takes official or administrative notice of facts, a litigant must be given an adequate opportunity to respond. See 5 U.S.C. § 556(e).

This principle is inapplicable, however, when the agency has promulgated valid regulations. Its purpose is to provide a procedural safeguard: to ensure the accuracy of the facts of which an agency takes notice. But when the accuracy of those facts already has been tested fairly during rulemaking, the rulemaking proceeding itself provides sufficient procedural protection. . . .

REVERSED.

NOTES AND QUESTIONS

1. *Foreclosure of hearing rights through rulemaking. Campbell* holds that an agency can resolve an issue by adopting a rule and thereby displace an individual's statutory right to an evidentiary hearing on that issue. By statute, a disability determination must be based on evidence adduced at the hearing, but *Campbell* establishes that the determination can be based on evidence that was previously adduced in a rulemaking proceeding. The Social Security rule involved in *Campbell* is often referred to as "the grid," because it determines whether there are jobs available in the national economy for a person like the applicant, based on an analysis of a series of objectively determinable factors (physical impairments, age, education, and work experience).

The effect of a rule differs from the effect of official notice, which is also mentioned in *Campbell.* An agency can use official notice to meet its burden of proof in an adjudicatory proceeding, but the opposing party has the right to offer a rebuttal. *See* § 4.2.2. A valid rule, on the other hand, is conclusive and there is no right to rebut it (see, however, the discussion of "safety valves" in N.3). The Court says that the rulemaking proceeding itself offered sufficient procedural protection. Does that make sense?

2. *Issues suitable for rulemaking.* The Court in *Campbell* says that the Secretary may use rulemaking to resolve "certain classes of issues," meaning issues "that do not require case-by-case determination." *Campbell* suggests that the question of what jobs were available in the national economy for various categories of workers was "not unique to each claimant" but turned on a "general factual issue." Claimants like Ms. Campbell were not deprived of any right to present evidence "relating to their own abilities."

Does that mean that there are some situations in which the Court will not allow factual determinations made in a prior rulemaking to trump subsequent case-by-case determinations? A later case endorses a presumption that such rules are valid even in cases that present issues that would normally require case-by-case factual determinations. In *American Hospital Ass'n v. NLRB*, 499 U.S. 606 (1991), the Court heard a challenge to the first substantive rule issued by the NLRB since 1935. The rule defined an employee unit appropriate for collective bargaining in acute care hospitals. It was challenged on the ground that "the National Labor Relations Act required the board to make a separate bargaining unit determination 'in each case' and therefore prohibits the Board from using general rules to define bargaining units." In rejecting this challenge, the Court cited *Campbell,* as well as the *Storer* and *Texaco* cases mentioned therein. It said that those cases "confirm that, even if a statutory scheme requires individualized determinations, the decisionmaker has the authority to rely on rulemaking to resolve certain issues of general applicability *unless Congress clearly expresses an intent to withhold that authority." Id.* at 612 (emphasis added).

3.   *Safety valves.* In *Storer* and *Texaco,* the Court noted that the regulations at issue permitted affected persons to seek a waiver of the rules. This language suggested that a waiver or "safety valve" provision is important, or perhaps critical, to the validity of rules that foreclose hearing rights. *Campbell's* footnotes 5 and 11 observe that, although the grid regulations do not allow an applicant for disability benefits to request a waiver, they provide "equal or greater protection" because an ALJ is not supposed to apply them "when they fail to describe a claimant's particular limitations."

This loophole has caused the grid regulations to have less impact than one might at first suppose. The regulations do not take into account non-physical factors such as mental disabilities or the presence of constant pain. Such factors are present in a large number of cases, meaning that applicants for disability benefits can argue that there are no jobs available in the national economy for people like themselves and they can introduce evidence to that effect. With respect to a significant slice of the caseload, therefore, the efficiency benefits touted by the *Campbell* majority have not materialized in practice. For discussion of the confusion in the case law about how to take account of non-physical disabilities in applying the grid, see Jon C. Dubin, *Overcoming Gridlock:* Campbell *after a Quarter-Century and Bureaucratically Rational Gap-Filling in Mass Justice Adjudication in the Social Security Administration's Disability Programs,* 62 ADMIN. L. REV. 937 (2010).

Campbell indicates that adjudication-trumping rules are valid even without an explicit provision allowing people to apply for a waiver of the rules. Thus in *FCC v. WNCN Listeners Guild,* 450 U.S. 582 (1981), the Court upheld the Commission's rule that changes in programming format by radio stations would *never* be considered during license renewal proceedings because format decisions should be regulated exclusively by the market. The dissenting Justices argued that the rule was invalid, in part because it did not allow for waivers in unusual cases (such as where a specialized listening audience would otherwise lose access to a distinctive format such as classical music). The majority disagreed, noting that its prior cases "did not hold that the Commission may never adopt a rule that lacks a waiver provision." Similarly, the Federal Aviation Administration rebuffed all requests for waivers of its former rule that commercial airline pilots must retire at age 60, fearing that if it entertained such petitions it would have to make case-by-case judgments of the physical and mental health of every aging pilot. *See Yetman v. Garvey*, 261 F.3d 664 (7th Cir. 2001).

Of course, even if an agency has not said in advance that it will consider waiver requests, it might entertain them anyway. However, an explicit waiver provision is better calculated to ensure a reasoned decision and equal treatment to potential waiver applicants. Yet such provisions can trigger a flood of requests for special treatment; the benefits of using rules instead of case-by-case adjudication can be dissipated. We return to the FAA example and other issues surrounding waiver requests in § 6.4.

4. *No material issue of fact.* An agency can deny a hearing otherwise required by statute when there are no disputed issues of material fact. Thus agency rules may explicitly provide for a form of summary judgment. *See Weinberger v. Hynson, Westcott & Dunning, Inc.*, 412 U.S. 609 (1973). That case arose out of a massive examination by the FDA to determine whether thousands of existing drugs were effective for their claimed uses. A 1962 statute required FDA to withdraw the licenses for such drugs unless their effectiveness was established by "adequate and well-controlled investigations" and it provided for a hearing in case of withdrawal. Under FDA regulations, a request for a hearing would be dismissed when it clearly appeared from the application that there was no "genuine and substantial issue of fact," including evidence of effectiveness from well-controlled scientific studies.

The Supreme Court upheld these regulations. *Hynson* was of great practical importance to the FDA. Had the agency been forced to provide a full-fledged adjudicatory hearing before withdrawing any drug license, removal of all the ineffective drugs from the market might have taken many decades. For example, in the *Hynson* case itself, the Court decided that summary judgment was inappropriate. Lutrexin, the drug at issue in that case, was not ultimately withdrawn from the market until 1976—fourteen years after enactment of the 1962 amendments. In the wake of *Hynson* and other precedents, administrative summary judgment has become routine.

Even in the absence of a summary judgment procedure, agencies can dispense with useless hearings. For example, the Federal Energy Regulatory Commission (FERC) must rule on many applications and complaints relating to interstate natural gas shipments. In *Board of Water, Light & Sinking Fund Commissioners v. FERC*, 294 F.3d 1317, 1328 (11th Cir. 2002), a local gas company (Dalton) complained that Southern Natural Gas wanted to build a pipeline directly to a factory that was Dalton's biggest customer. FERC denied an evidentiary hearing since Dalton's arguments were directed at FERC policy, not at any disputed factual issues. As a result, live testimony would not have been helpful. In dictum, the court stated that the agency could dispense with an oral hearing even if there were disputed issues of fact if the issues could be adequately resolved on the written record. *See also Kourouma v. FERC*, 723 F.3d 274, 277–78 (D.C. Cir. 2013).

5.   *Class actions? Campbell* stresses the efficiency advantages for resolving recurring factual issues through adoption of a rule rather than through numerous adjudicatory proceedings. Is there another way to achieve that result? Agencies might adopt procedural rules authorizing private parties to bring administrative class actions to resolve recurring issues (such as whether a specific employer has a practice of sex discrimination or whether a specific mine is unsafe). Or would the complexities of the class action process overwhelm the system of administrative adjudication? *See* Michael D. Sant'Ambroglio & Adam S. Zimmerman, *The Agency Class Action*, 112 COLUM. L. REV. 1992 (2012).

6.   *Problem.* Madison has adopted the 2010 MSAPA. By statute, licensing decisions of the Madison Medical Board are contested cases that call for evidentiary hearings under the APA. Three months ago, Madison's Medical Board adopted a rule providing that no graduate of a foreign medical school (except one located in the United Kingdom or Canada) can be licensed to practice medicine in Madison. Prior to adopting this rule, the Board decided license applications by foreign medical school graduates on a case-by-case basis.

Our client Kate attended three years of medical school at Madison University. The fourth year of medical school is all clinical; she spent the year at a hospital in Madison. However, as the result of an unfortunate personal encounter with an administrator, she transferred to Caribbean University Medical School in the Dominican Republic for the fourth and last year of medical school. She took no courses at Caribbean; it merely awarded her a diploma based on her three years of course work at Madison University and her clinical work at the Madison hospital.

The Board refuses to grant Kate a license or even hold a hearing, stating that there are no exceptions to its rule. What do you suggest we do now?

§ 3.3   THE CONFLICT BETWEEN INSTITUTIONAL AND JUDICIALIZED DECISION-MAKING

Students of the administrative process have identified two conflicting models of adjudicative decision-making. Oversimplified statements of the two models follow:

The *judicial* model suggests that an agency's adjudicative decision resembles a judge's decision. Therefore, the administrative process should resemble judicial process as closely as possible. Litigants should be entitled to a full-fledged trial with cross-examination of witnesses. The decisionmakers should personally hear the evidence and argument, have no preconceptions about the case, receive no information about it except through on-the-record submissions, and be completely independent of investigators and prosecutors. Adherents of the judicial model argue that *fairness* and *acceptability* to private litigants should be the primary goals of the agency adjudication process.

The *institutional* model views an agency as if it were a single unit with the mission of implementing a regulatory scheme. Decisionmaking methodology should be whatever seems efficient and effective, not necessarily a trial. The entire staff are members of the decisionmaking team and all should be available for off-the-record consultation. Adjudication is a policymaking tool, along with rulemaking, advice-giving, and publicity. Each adjudicated case should promote the regulatory scheme and further agency policy. Adherents of the institutional model stress *accuracy* and *efficiency* as the dominant values to be pursued. As one commentator noted:

> . . . The "institutional method" . . . involves the cooperative effort of a number of officers with the agency head, bringing to bear the cumulative efforts of specialized officers . . . The safeguards to persons who have interests at stake . . . lie in the professional training and responsibility of the officers involved, in cross-checking among them, and in the responsibility of the agency heads who coordinate the entire operation, decide finally upon the result, and must answer for all that transpires.

> Outside of government, the preponderance of human affairs calling for more than individual action is conducted by a consultative method, with or without professional participation. Business decisions are reached, human ailments are diagnosed, and club and church problems are settled in this manner. . . . In government too, foreign policy, military affairs, and the management of public enterprises and property go forward in the same way. Often vital interests of people are at stake in what transpires . . . yet it is rarely suggested that the "hearing" of interested persons be attempted in connection with such matters, or, if it is, that more than an interview be accorded. Arguably, the same considerations as account for the acceptance of "institutional" methods in these contexts should point to their possible use in licensing, rate fixing, and kindred operations—for which, indeed, they were thought to suffice until relatively recently.

Ralph F. Fuchs, *The Hearing Officer Problem—Symptom and Symbol*, 40 CORNELL L.Q. 281, 289–90 (1955). © 1955 by Cornell University. All rights reserved.

The administrative process strikes many compromises between these two polar models, sacrificing the virtues of one of them to secure the virtues of the other. Sections 3.3 and 3.4 address a number of problems on the borderline between judicial and institutional decisionmaking: personal responsibility of decisionmakers, ex parte contacts, legislature pressures, separation of functions, bias, and independence of the administrative judges. As you read this material, try to analyze it as a set of tradeoffs between the judicial and institutional methods of adjudication.

§ 3.3.1 PERSONAL RESPONSIBILITY OF DECISIONMAKERS

In a judicial model, the judge hears all of the evidence and argument and makes a decision based on that input. In an institutional model, one or more persons might hear the evidence and argument but someone else might make the decision. Needless to say, the institutional approach makes lawyers uneasy.

During the 1930s and 1940s, in the first of four *Morgan* cases (*Morgan I*), the Supreme Court indicated a strong preference for the judicial model. The *Morgan* cases arose out of a proceeding begun by the Secretary of Agriculture in 1930 to fix the maximum rates of commission that all of the livestock agents working in a stockyard in Kansas City could charge. The applicable statute required that the Secretary provide a "full hearing." The ratemaking case could be considered rulemaking, rather than adjudication, since the agency action was generalized rather than individualized. However, the "full hearing" statute meant that the ratemaking process had to contain trial-type elements. Probably, due process did not apply, because the action was generalized. (Recall *Bi-Metallic*, § 2.5.) Yet in the *Morgan* cases, the Court seems to speak in constitutional terms.

MORGAN V. UNITED STATES (MORGAN I)
298 U.S. 468 (1936)

[*Morgan I* arose on a motion to dismiss. Plaintiff alleged that a hearing examiner took evidence but did not file a report. The Acting Secretary of Agriculture heard oral argument. The parties filed briefs. The Secretary of Agriculture made the final decision. The plaintiffs asserted that the Secretary had not heard or read any of the evidence or argument or read the briefs. Instead, he rubber-stamped a decision made by someone else. Thus, the Court assumed that the Agriculture

Department had used a purely institutional approach to making the rates. The Court noted that responsibility for making the final decision might have been delegated to the Acting Secretary who heard the argument, but no such delegation occurred. The Secretary, who had not heard the case, took responsibility for the final decision.]

HUGHES, C. J.:

. . . . There must be a full hearing. There must be evidence adequate to support pertinent and necessary findings of fact. Nothing can be treated as evidence which is not introduced as such. . . .

Facts and circumstances which ought to be considered must not be excluded. Facts and circumstances must not be considered which should not legally influence the conclusion. Findings based on the evidence must embrace the basic facts which are needed to sustain the order. . . .

A proceeding of this sort, requiring the taking and weighing of evidence, determinations of fact based upon the consideration of the evidence, and the making of an order supported by such findings, has a quality resembling that of a judicial proceeding. Hence it is frequently described as a proceeding of a quasi-judicial character. The requirement of a "full hearing" has obvious reference to the tradition of judicial proceedings in which evidence is received and weighed by the trier of the facts. The "hearing" is designed to afford the safeguard that the one who decides shall be bound in good conscience to consider the evidence, to be guided by that alone, and to reach his conclusion uninfluenced by extraneous considerations which in other fields might have play in determining purely executive action. The "hearing" is the hearing of evidence and argument. If the one who determines the facts which underlie the order has not considered evidence or argument, it is manifest that the hearing has not been given.

There is thus no basis for the contention that the authority conferred by Section 310 of the Packers and Stockyards Act is given to the Department of Agriculture, as a department in the administrative sense, so that one official may examine evidence, and another official who has not considered the evidence may make the findings and order. In such a view, it would be possible, for example, for one official to hear the evidence and argument and arrive at certain conclusions of fact, and another official who had not heard or considered either evidence or argument to overrule those conclusions and for reasons of policy to announce entirely different ones. It is no answer to say that the question for the court is whether the evidence supports the findings and the findings support the order. For the weight ascribed by the law to the findings—their conclusiveness when made within the sphere of the authority conferred—rests upon the assumption that the officer who makes the findings has addressed himself to the evidence and upon that evidence has conscientiously reached the conclusions which he deems it to justify. That duty cannot be performed by one who has not considered evidence or argument. It is not an impersonal obligation. It is a duty akin to that of a judge. The one who decides must hear.

This necessary rule does not preclude practicable administrative procedure in obtaining the aid of assistants in the department. Assistants may prosecute inquiries. Evidence may be taken by an examiner. Evidence thus taken may be sifted and analyzed by competent subordinates. Argument may be oral or written. The requirements are not technical. But there must be a hearing in a substantial sense. And to give the substance of a hearing, which is for the purpose of making determinations upon evidence, the officer who makes the determinations must consider and appraise the evidence which justifies them. That duty undoubtedly may be an onerous one, but the performance of it in a substantial manner is inseparable from the exercise of the important authority conferred. . . .

NOTES AND QUESTIONS

1. *"The one who decides must hear."* The first *Morgan* case strikes a powerful blow for the *judicial*, rather than the *institutional* method. Like a judge, an administrator who takes the responsibility for making the decision must personally hear the case. However, this language cannot be taken literally. The Secretary was not required to actually "hear" the case or even read all of the evidence. The last paragraph makes clear that an examiner may take the evidence and the evidence "can be sifted and analyzed by competent subordinates." However, the person making the decision "must consider and appraise the evidence" that justifies it. Why does the Court require the official taking final responsibility for an adjudicative decision to "consider and appraise the evidence?"

2. *Getting around Morgan I.* Although the *Morgan I* principle seems reasonable, it is completely unrealistic if taken literally. The Secretary of Agriculture is not like a trial or appellate judge whose only duty is to decide cases. The Secretary has a vast number of administrative and regulatory responsibilities, concerning every aspect of American agriculture, many of them extremely important to the public (and much more important than the commissions charged by livestock brokers in Kansas City). Officials at the level of the Secretary of Agriculture sit as members of the President's cabinet and must constantly deal with Congress and the media. If such officials were required to familiarize themselves with the voluminous and technical records in all of the ratemaking or other adjudicatory matters decided by their departments, they would have time for little else.

In light of that reality, how can an agency comply with *Morgan I?* Consider these options:

i.   An agency head can delegate the power to make final decisions. In fact, the Department of Agriculture has done exactly that; a "judicial officer" makes the final decision in all adjudicatory cases. However, such delegation is not always permissible. It depends on the terms of the agency's statute (although courts presume that delegation is permissible unless a statute specifically forbids it). More important, adjudication is sometimes a vehicle for making new law and policy. Realistically, the policymaking function cannot be carried out by staff below the level of the politically responsible agency head or heads.

ii.   The person who conducts the hearing and hears the evidence could decide the case. That decision would become final unless the agency head decides to consider an appeal. The agency head could decline to hear an appeal without examining the record. Under this approach, the agency head would personally consider appeals (and become familiar with the record) in only a few significant, precedent-making situations.

iii.   Decisions of hearing officers could be appealed to an intermediate review board within the agency. The agency head would have discretion to consider appeals from the intermediate review board.

iv.   The agency head might consider only a highly condensed summary of the evidence and arguments prepared by law clerks or other employees. The head would then decide the case solely on the basis of information contained in that summary.

Each of these approaches departs from the judicial model and approaches the institutional model. For a survey and comparison of the different approaches to the problem of appeals within the agency, see Russell L. Weaver, *Appellate Review in Executive Departments and Agencies*, 48 ADMIN. L. REV. 251 (1996).

In *Morgan II*, the Court determined that the Secretary had in fact complied with the dictates of *Morgan I*. (The Court had not reached that issue in *Morgan I* itself, because that appeal had been decided on the pleadings.) "The Secretary read the summary presented by appellants' briefs and he conferred with his subordinates who had sifted and analyzed the evidence." That was sufficient. *Morgan v. United States (Morgan II)*, 304 U.S. 1, 18 (1938).

3.   *Intermediate reports.* Suppose that a case is heard by an administrative judge but the agency head or heads make the final decision. Two issues arise: i) must the administrative judge prepare a proposed decision? ii) if there is a proposed decision, must it be disclosed to the litigants so they can object to it before the final decision?

Statutes generally require the administrative judge to prepare a proposed decision that is disclosed to the parties before the final decision. *See* APA §§ 557(b), (c). Under § 413(c) of MSAPA 2010, the presiding officer must serve an initial decision on each party within 90 days after the hearing ends, the record closes, or memoranda, briefs, or proposed findings are submitted, whichever is latest.

What happens, however, if no statutes are applicable? *Morgan II* concerned claims that the market agencies did not know the government's claims and therefore could not rebut them. "The right to submit argument implies that opportunity; otherwise the right may be but a barren one. Those who are brought into contest with the Government in a quasi-judicial proceeding aimed at the control of their activities are entitled to be fairly advised of what the Government proposes and to be heard upon its proposals before it issues its final command." 304 U.S. at 18–19.

One problem in *Morgan II* was the failure of the hearing examiner to prepare a proposed decision. The examiner simply submitted the lengthy record to the Secretary of Agriculture. In the absence of any pleadings or recommendations by the examiner, the issues remained unfocussed and the industry was unable to brief or argue them effectively. This problem was magnified because staff advocates prepared recommended findings and discussed them with the Secretary. Such advocacy raises an issue of separation of functions, which is discussed in § 3.3.4. The Court implied that due process (or at least a statutory "full hearing") requires the preparation of a proposed decision. A later case made clear that due process does not require a proposed decision without a showing of prejudice. *See NLRB v. Mackay Radio & Telegraph Co.,* 304 U.S. 333, 350–51 (1938).

4.   *The right to object to a proposed decision.* If a hearing examiner prepares a proposed decision, do the parties have a right to see and object to it in the absence of a statutory requirement? According to *Ballard v. Comm'r,* 544 U.S. 40 (2005), the answer is probably yes. U.S. Tax Court rules allow Tax Court judges to assign the hearing function to a "special trial judge" (STJ) who prepares an opinion after hearing the case. (For discussion of the appointment of STJs by the Chief Judge of the Tax Court, see *Freytag* at § 7.5.1a N.4.) The final decision is made by a Tax Court judge, who must give "due regard" to the STJ's opportunity to evaluate the credibility of the witnesses.

The STJ's opinion was not served on the parties and was not part of the record on judicial review. Instead, the Tax Court judge treated the STJ's opinion as a first draft and came to the opposite conclusion (including findings about the credibility of witnesses that differed from those of the STJ). As a result, neither the taxpayer nor an appellate judge could determine how the STJ's opinion was changed or whether the Tax Court judge paid any regard to the STJ's credibility assessments. The taxpayer, of course, wanted access to the STJ decision, so he could use it to show that the Tax Court judge had violated the "due regard" requirement.

In *Ballard,* the Supreme Court held that the Tax Court's rules did not permit the Tax Court to keep an STJ's opinion confidential, and it suggested that the opinion should be part of the record, even apart from those rules. The Court noted that ". . . it is routine in federal judicial and administrative decisionmaking both to disclose the initial report of a hearing officer, and to make that report part of the record available to an appellate forum. A departure of the bold character practiced by the Tax Court ... demands, at the very least, full and fair statement in the Tax Court's own rules." The decision refers to a wide variety of federal statutes relating to magistrate judges, special masters, and bankruptcy judges as well as APA provisions requiring disclosure of an ALJ's proposed decision and requiring reviewing courts to consider the "whole record." APA §§ 557(c), 706.

Ballard cited with approval the well-known New Jersey case of *Mazza v. Cavicchia*, 105 A.2d 545 (N.J. 1954). *Mazza* concerned revocation of a liquor license. A hearing officer submitted confidential proposed findings and recommendations to the agency head. The Court held this procedure denied the licensee due process, because "it is a fundamental principle of all adjudication, judicial and administrative alike, that the mind of the decider should not be swayed by materials which are not communicated to both parties and which they are not given an opportunity to controvert. In the instant case the [hearing officer] can be characterized as a 'witness' giving his evidence to the judge behind the back of the appellant, who has no way of knowing what has been reported to the judge.... Such conduct not only constitutes a violation of the principle of the exclusiveness of the record in deciding controversies, but it shocks one's sense of fair play on which our fundamental concepts of procedure are based...." Is keeping the hearing officer's report confidential really the same as allowing a witness to give testimony behind the licensee's back?

5. *Proving a violation of Morgan I.* Courts generally presume that deciding officials have complied with legal requirements, such as familiarizing themselves with the record. How can this presumption be rebutted? It is usually not permissible to subject decision-makers (or their staff or law clerks) to discovery or trial about how they made a decision. Such a trial occurred at one point in the *Morgan* saga, but in *Morgan IV,* the Court stated:

> [T]he district court authorized the market agencies to take the deposition of the Secretary. The Secretary ... was questioned at length regarding the process by which he reached the conclusions of his order, including the manner and extent of his study of the record and his consultation with subordinates ... [T]he short of the business is that the Secretary should never have been subjected to this examination. The proceeding before the Secretary "has a quality resembling that of a judicial proceeding" [citing *Morgan I*]. Such an examination of a judge would be destructive of judicial responsibility. Just as a judge cannot be subjected to such a scrutiny ... so the integrity of the administrative process must be equally respected.... It will bear repeating that although the administrative process has had a different development and pursues somewhat different ways from those of courts, they are to

be deemed collaborative instrumentalities of justice and the appropriate independence of each should be respected by the other.

United States v. Morgan (Morgan IV), 313 U.S. 409 (1941).

According to the Supreme Court, inquiry into the mental processes of decisionmakers must be avoided absent "a strong showing of bad faith or improper behavior." *Citizens to Preserve Overton Park v. Volpe,* 401 U.S. 402, 420 (1971). Obviously, the challenger must come up with some strong initial evidence of bad faith or impropriety *before* a court will inquire any further, such as by examining the transcript of the agency deliberative proceedings. *San Luis Obispo Mothers for Peace v. NRC,* 789 F.3d 26, 44–45 (D.C. Cir. 1986).

6.   *The exclusive record for decision.* In *Morgan I*, Hughes stated: "[A hearing] is designed to afford the safeguard that the one who decides shall be bound in good conscience to consider the evidence, to be guided by that alone . . ." A due process and APA fundamental is that the record made at a hearing is the exclusive basis for decision. The decisionmaker cannot rely on factual information that is not in the record. *See* APA § 556(e). One important exception to the exclusive record rule is that a decisionmaker can take official notice of information that is not in the record, but only after affording an opportunity for rebuttal to the opposing party. *See* § 4.2.2.

7.   *Problem.* The Mountain School District wished to discharge Rex, a tenured junior high school teacher, for drunkenness. No APA is applicable. Under the district's usual procedures, a review committee (consisting of educators) conducted a three-hour hearing from noon to 3 PM. At the hearing, Rex denied that his drinking problem affected his teaching and claimed he was always sober at school. The hearing was tape recorded. At 6 PM the same day, the review committee issued a brief written decision, recommending that the School Board not discharge Rex. The decision stated that Rex had a drinking problem but that it had not affected his teaching. The decision was not furnished to Rex.

Two hours later, at 8 PM, the Mountain School Board decided to fire Rex, finding that he was drunk or hung over at school on many occasions. It provided no opportunity for oral argument or the filing of briefs. The meeting of the Board was over by 9 PM. Should this decision be reversed? *See Bates v. Sponberg,* 547 F.2d 325 (6th Cir. 1976).

§ 3.3.2 EX PARTE COMMUNICATIONS

This section addresses another conflict between the judicial and institutional models. Judges have only one responsibility—to decide cases. In contrast, an agency is a law enforcement and regulatory body, with substantial responsibilities for rulemaking, research, investigation, and prosecution. An agency must also be acutely sensitive to prevailing political winds, because it is accountable to the legislative and executive branches. These responsibilities require a constant flow of communication between agency personnel and regulated parties, members of the public, the media, legislators, and high-level executive officials. Inevitably, some of this communication touches on matters that the agency is adjudicating. A word of clarification: this section concerns communications between agency decisionmakers and persons who are *outside the agency*. The section on separation of functions, § 3.3.4, concerns communications between decisionmakers and advisers *inside the agency*.

PROFESSIONAL AIR TRAFFIC CONTROLLERS ORG. (PATCO) v. FEDERAL LABOR RELATIONS AUTHORITY
685 F.2d 547 (D.C. Cir. 1982)

[The members of PATCO engaged in an illegal strike against the government. Under § 7120(f) of the Civil Service Reform Act, the FLRA "shall revoke the exclusive recognition status" of a union that calls such a strike (in effect, putting the union out of business). After a hearing, the FLRA's ALJ revoked PATCO's exclusive recognition status. This decision was affirmed by the three members of the FLRA agency head (Applewhaite, Frazier, and Haughton).

This case concerns communications between the agency heads and persons outside FLRA while the PATCO case was before FLRA. Concerned by possible impropriety, the Court of Appeals ordered the FLRA to conduct a hearing with the aid of a specially appointed ALJ from another agency (John Vittone) to determine the extent and effect of the following communications.

- Secretary of Transportation Andrew Lewis phoned member Frazier. Lewis said he was not calling about the substance of the case but wanted to tell Frazier that there were no meaningful efforts to settle the strike. He stated that he would appreciate expeditious handling of the appeal from the ALJ decision to the FLRA agency heads. Lewis called Applewhaite with the same message and Applewhaite told him that a written motion to expedite the appeal had to be filed. Later, such a motion was filed and FLRA shortened the filing period.

- Albert Shanker, head of the American Federation of Teachers met FLRA member Applewhaite (a long-time friend) for dinner. Shanker urged Applewhaite not to revoke PATCO's exclusive recognition status.

EDWARDS, J. wrote the panel opinion. ROBINSON, J. concurred, expressing stronger condemnation of the incidents.]

C. Applicable Legal Standards

1. The Statutory Prohibition of Ex Parte Contacts and the FLRA Rules

. . . Since FLRA unfair labor practice hearings are formal adjudications within the meaning of the APA, § 557(d) governs ex parte communications. Section 557(d) was enacted by Congress as part of the Government in the Sunshine Act (1976). The section prohibits ex parte communications "relevant to the merits of the proceeding" between an "interested person" and an agency decisionmaker. . . .

Three features of the prohibition on ex parte communications in agency adjudications are particularly relevant to the contacts here at issue. First, by its terms, section 557(d) applies only to ex parte communications to or from an "interested person." Congress did not intend, however, that the prohibition on ex parte communications would therefore have only a limited application. . . .

Second, the Government in the Sunshine Act defines an "ex parte communication" as "an oral or written communication not on the public record to which reasonable prior notice to all parties is not given, but . . . not includ[ing] requests for status reports on any matter or proceeding. . . ." APA § 551(14). Requests for status reports are thus allowed under the statute, even when directed to an agency decisionmaker rather than to another agency employee. Nevertheless, the legislative history of the Act cautions:

> A request for a status report or a background discussion may in effect amount to an indirect or subtle effort to influence the substantive outcome of the proceedings. The judgment will have to be made whether a particular communication could affect the agency's decision on the merits. In doubtful cases the agency official should treat the communication as ex parte so as to protect the integrity of the decision making process.

Third, and in direct contrast to status reports, section 557(d) explicitly prohibits communications "relevant to the merits of the proceeding." The congressional reports state that the phrase should "be construed broadly and . . . include more than the phrase 'fact in issue' currently used in [section 554(d)(1) of] the APA." While the phrase must be interpreted to effectuate the dual purposes of the Government in the Sunshine Act, *i.e.*, of giving notice of improper contacts and of providing all interested parties an opportunity to respond to illegal communications, the scope of this provision is not unlimited. Congress explicitly noted that the statute does not prohibit procedural inquiries, or other communications "not relevant to the merits."

In sum, Congress sought to establish common-sense guidelines to govern ex parte contacts in administrative hearings, rather than rigidly defined and woodenly applied rules. The disclosure of ex parte communications serves two distinct interests. Disclosure is important in its own right to prevent the appearance of impropriety from secret communications in a proceeding that is required to be decided on the record. Disclosure is also important as an instrument of fair decisionmaking; only if a party knows the arguments presented to a decisionmaker can the party respond effectively and ensure that its position is fairly considered. When these interests of openness and opportunity for response are threatened by an ex parte communication, the communication must be disclosed. It matters not whether the communication comes from someone other than a formal party or if the communication is clothed in the guise of a procedural inquiry. If, however, the communication is truly not relevant to the merits of an adjudication and, therefore, does not threaten the interests of openness and effective response, disclosure is unnecessary. . . .

2.   Remedies for Ex Parte Communications

Section 557(d) contains two possible administrative remedies for improper ex parte communications. The first is disclosure of the communication and its content. The second requires the violating party to "show cause why his claim or interest in the proceeding should not be dismissed, denied, disregarded, or otherwise adversely affected on account of [the] violation." Congress did not intend, however, that an agency would require a party to "show cause" after every violation or that an agency would dismiss a party's interest more than rarely. Indeed, the statutory language clearly states that a party's interest in the proceeding may be adversely affected only "to the extent consistent with the interests of justice and the policy of the underlying statutes."[30]

The Government in the Sunshine Act contains no specific provisions for judicial remedy of improper ex parte communications. However, we may infer from approving citations in the House and Senate Reports that Congress did not intend to alter the existing case law regarding ex parte communications and the legal effect of such contacts on agency decisions. Under the case law in this Circuit improper ex parte communications, even when undisclosed during agency proceedings, do not necessarily void an agency decision. Rather, agency proceedings that have been blemished by ex parte communications have been held to be *voidable*.

In enforcing this standard, a court must consider whether, as a result of improper ex parte communications, the agency's decisionmaking

---

[30] By way of example, the Senate Report suggested that:

   [T]he interests of justice might dictate that a claimant for an old age benefit not lose his claim even if he violates the ex parte rules. On the other hand, where two parties have applied for a license and the applications are of relatively equal merit, an agency may rule against a party who approached an agency head in an ex parte manner in an effort to win approval of his license. . . .

process was irrevocably tainted so as to make the ultimate judgment of the agency unfair, either to an innocent party or to the public interest that the agency was obliged to protect. In making this determination, a number of considerations may be relevant: the gravity of the ex parte communications; whether the contacts may have influenced the agency's ultimate decision; whether the party making the improper contacts benefitted from the agency's ultimate decision; whether the contents of the communications were unknown to opposing parties, who therefore had no opportunity to respond; and whether vacation of the agency's decision and remand for new proceedings would serve a useful purpose. Since the principal concerns of the court are the integrity of the process and the fairness of the result, mechanical rules have little place in a judicial decision whether to vacate a voidable agency proceeding. Instead, any such decision must of necessity be an exercise of equitable discretion.

D.   Analysis of the Alleged Ex Parte Communications with FLRA Members

. . . After extensive review of the . . . troubling incidents we believe that they provide insufficient reason to vacate the FLRA decision or to remand this case for further proceedings before the Authority. . . .

Secretary Lewis' Telephone Calls to Members Frazier and Applewhaite

Transportation Secretary Lewis was undoubtedly an "interested person" within the meaning of section 557(d) and the FLRA Rules when he called Members Frazier and Applewhaite on August 13. Secretary Lewis' call clearly would have been an improper ex parte communication if he had sought to discuss the merits of the PATCO case. The Secretary explicitly avoided the merits, however, and mentioned only his view on the possibility of settlement and his desire for a speedy decision. On this basis, Solicitor Freehling and Member Frazier concluded the call was not improper.

We are less certain that Secretary Lewis' call was permissible. Although Secretary Lewis did not in fact discuss the merits of the case, even a procedural inquiry may be a subtle effort to influence an agency decision. We do not doubt that Member Frazier and Solicitor Freehling concluded in good faith that the communications were not improper, but it would have been preferable for them to heed Congress' warning, to assume that close cases like these are improper, and to report them on the public record.

We need not decide, however, whether Secretary Lewis' contacts were in fact improper. Even if they were, the contacts did not taint the proceedings or prejudice PATCO. . . . [because, at Member Applewhaite's direction, Lewis filed his request to modify the time limits as a formal motion and PATCO had ample opportunity to oppose that motion].

Member Applewhaite's Dinner with Albert Shanker

Of course, the most troublesome ex parte communication in this case occurred during the September 21 dinner meeting between Member Applewhaite and American Federation of Teachers President Albert Shanker—the "well-known labor leader" mentioned in Assistant Attorney General McGrath's affidavit. . . .

At the outset, we are faced with the question whether Mr. Shanker was an "interested person" to the proceeding under section 557(d). Mr. Shanker argues that he was not. He suggests that his only connection with the unfair labor practice case was his membership on the Executive Council of the AFL–CIO which, unbeknownst to him, had participated as amicus curiae in the oral argument of the PATCO case before the FLRA. This relationship to the proceeding, Mr. Shanker contends, is too tenuous to qualify him as an "interested person" forbidden to make ex parte communications to the Authority Members.

As noted above, Congress did not intend such a narrow construction of the term "interested person." . . . The House and Senate Reports agreed that the term covers "any individual or other person with an interest in the agency proceeding that is greater than the general interest the public as a whole may have. The interest need not be monetary, nor need a person be a party to, or intervenor in, the agency proceeding. . . ."

We believe that Mr. Shanker falls within the intended scope of the term "interested person." Mr. Shanker was (and is) the President of a major public-sector labor union. As such, he has a special and well-known interest in the union movement and the developing law of labor relations in the public sector. The PATCO strike, of course, was the subject of extensive media coverage and public comment. Some union leaders undoubtedly felt that the hard line taken against PATCO by the Administration might have an adverse effect on other unions, both in the federal and in state and local government sectors. Mr. Shanker apparently shared this concern. . . .

Even if we were to adopt Mr. Shanker's position that he was not an interested person, we are astonished at his claim that he did nothing wrong. Mr. Shanker frankly concedes that he "desired to have dinner with Member Applewhaite because he felt strongly about the PATCO case and he wished to communicate directly to Member Applewhaite sentiments he had previously expressed in public." While we appreciate Mr. Shanker's forthright admission, we must wonder whether it is a product of candor or a failure to comprehend that his conduct was improper. In case any doubt still lingers, we take the opportunity to make one thing clear: *It is simply unacceptable behavior for any person directly to attempt to influence the decision of a judicial officer in a pending case outside of the formal, public proceedings.* This is true for the general public, for "interested persons," and for the formal parties to the case. This rule applies to administrative adjudications as well as to cases in Article III courts.

We think it a mockery of justice to even suggest that judges or other decisionmakers may be properly approached on the merits of a case during the pendency of an adjudication. Administrative and judicial adjudications are viable only so long as the integrity of the decisionmaking processes remains inviolate. There would be no way to protect the sanctity of adjudicatory processes if we were to condone direct attempts to influence decisionmakers through ex parte contacts.

We do not hold, however, that Member Applewhaite committed an impropriety when he accepted Mr. Shanker's dinner invitation. Member Applewhaite and Mr. Shanker were professional and social friends. We recognize, of course, that a judge "must have neighbors, friends and acquaintances, business and social relations, and be a part of his day and generation." Similarly, Member Applewhaite was not required to renounce his friendships, either personal or professional, when he was appointed to the FLRA. When Mr. Shanker called Member Applewhaite on September 21, Member Applewhaite was unaware of Mr. Shanker's purpose in arranging the dinner. He therefore had no reason to reject the invitation.

The majority of the dinner conversation was unrelated to the PATCO case. Only in the last fifteen minutes of the dinner did the discussion become relevant to the PATCO dispute, apparently when Mr. Shanker raised the topic of local approaches to public employee strikes in New York and Pennsylvania. At this point, and as the conversation turned to the discipline appropriate for a striking union like PATCO, Member Applewhaite should have promptly terminated the discussion. Had Mr. Shanker persisted in discussing his views of the PATCO case, Member Applewhaite should have informed him in no uncertain terms that such behavior was inappropriate. Unfortunately, he did not do so. . . .

We do not believe that it is necessary to vacate the FLRA Decision and remand the case. First, while Mr. Shanker's purpose and conduct were improper, and while Member Applewhaite should not have entertained Mr. Shanker's views on the desirability of decertifying a striking union, no threats or promises were made. Though plainly inappropriate, the ex parte communication was limited to a ten or fifteen minute discussion, often couched in general terms, of the appropriate discipline for a striking public employee union. This behavior falls short of the "corrupt tampering with the adjudicatory process" found by this court in *WKAT, Inc. v. FCC*, 296 F.2d 375 (D.C. Cir. 1961).

Second, ALJ Vittone found that the Applewhaite/Shanker dinner had no effect on the ultimate decision of Member Applewhaite or of the FLRA as a whole in the PATCO case. None of the parties have disputed this finding. Indeed, even Member Frazier, who initiated the FBI investigation of the dinner, testified that "in his opinion the Shanker-Applewhaite dinner did not have an effect on Member Applewhaite's ultimate decision in the PATCO case."

Third, no party benefitted from the improper contact. The ultimate decision was adverse to PATCO, the party whose interests were most closely aligned with Mr. Shanker's position. The final decision also rejected the position taken by the AFL–CIO as amicus curiae and by Mr. Shanker in his dinner conversation with Member Applewhaite. . . .

NOTES AND QUESTIONS

1. *Ex parte communications—source of law.* PATCO interprets the APA's ex parte communications provision. § 557(d). Section 408(b) of the 2010 Model State APA provides: "[W]hile a contested case is pending, the presiding officer and the final decision maker may not make to or receive from any person any communication concerning the case without notice and opportunity for all parties to participate in the communication. For the purpose of this section, a contested case is pending from the issuance of the agency's pleading or from an application for an agency decision, whichever is earlier." Note how § 408(b) prohibits more communications than does § 557(d).

Even where no APA is applicable, ex parte communications to a decisionmaker might violate due process. *See Idaho Historic Pres. Council, Inc. v. City of Boise,* 8 P.3d 646 (Idaho 2000), overturning the decision of the Boise City Council to allow demolition of a historic structure. The Council was considering an appeal from a decision of the Planning Commission that had rejected the application. The members of the Council received a number of phone calls from the community. The members disclosed that they had received the phone calls but not the names of the callers or the substance of the conversations. The court held that the decision denied due process (although it did not explain who suffered a deprivation of liberty or property). The dissenting judges remarked: "In any decision such as this, city council members will unavoidably receive unsolicited communications from their constituents—not only by telephone but even as they walk down the street. Requiring council members to record the name of each opinionated constituent and the substance of each conversation not only is unduly burdensome . . . but also does little to reduce the risk of erroneously depriving a party of its interest."

A number of federal cases decided before enactment of APA § 557(d) invalidated decisions of federal agencies tainted by ex parte communications. These were cases in which a number of applicants were competing for a valuable license (usually for a television station), and they wined and dined FCC commissioners. The cases spoke in terms of the responsibility of appellate courts for the "basic fairness" of the hearing, so it is unclear whether such holdings are based on due process or the supervisory authority of the federal courts. *See, e.g., Sangamon Valley TV Corp. v. United States*, 269 F.2d 221 (D.C. Cir. 1959).

2.   *Lewis' call to Frazier.* Did this call violate APA § 557(d)? Consider the definition of "ex parte communication" in § 551(14). The FLRA's rules permit ex parte contacts concerning settlement. 5 C.F.R. § 2414.6(b), (d). Why is a conversation concerning settlement not a violation of § 557(d)? Could an inquiry about the status of a case or a comment about settlement be a prohibited ex parte communication? *See* Judge Edwards' comments in part C.1. of the *PATCO* opinion.

3.   *Dinner with Shanker.* Judge Edwards indicates that Shanker's conduct was deplorable and that Applewhaite erred badly by failing to terminate the discussion when it turned to the *PATCO* matter. In his concurring opinion, Judge Robinson indicated that it was inappropriate for Applewhaite even to have dinner with Shanker. Do you agree? Is it likely that Shanker's views came as a surprise to Applewhaite? Should Applewhaite be removed from office? Why was Shanker an "interested person"? If you had run into Applewhaite (an old friend of your father's) at the airport and made the same statements that Shanker did, would you have violated § 557(d)?

4.   *The President as an interested person.* In *Portland Audubon Soc,y v. Endangered Species Comm.*, 984 F.2d 1534 (9th Cir. 1993), the court considered ex parte communications by the White House staff to the Endangered Species Committee, popularly known as the "God Squad." The God Squad was a seven-person group (consisting of cabinet secretaries and other high political officials) charged with deciding whether to make exceptions to the Endangered Species Act. The God Squad decided to allow timber cutting that would jeopardize the habitat of the northern spotted owl. The court decided that the APA adjudication provisions applied to God Squad proceedings. It then turned to whether the President and his staff were "interested persons" who are "outside the agency" as those terms are used in § 557(d)(1)(A):

> We believe the President's position at the center of the Executive Branch renders him, ex officio, an "interested person" for the purposes of APA § 557(d)(1). As the head of government and chief executive officer, the President necessarily has an interest in every agency proceeding. No ex parte communication is more likely to influence an agency than one from the President or a member of his staff. No communication from any other person is more likely to deprive the parties and the public of their right to effective participation in a key governmental decision at a most crucial time. The essential purposes of the statutory provision compel the conclusion that the President and his staff are "interested persons" within the meaning of § 557(d)(1). . . .

> [T]he Endangered Species Act explicitly vests discretion to make exemption decisions in the Committee and does not

contemplate that the President or the White House will become involved in Committee deliberations. The President and his aides are not a part of the Committee decision-making process. They are "outside the agency" for the purposes of the ex parte communications ban.

This case should be compared to *Sierra Club v. Costle*, which upholds the right of the President and the White House staff to engage in ex parte communication *in rulemaking. Sierra Club* is discussed in § 5.5.2.

5. *Remedies for ex parte communications.* What should FLRA have done about the violations of § 557(d) and its own ex parte rules? *See* § 557(d)(1)(C). What additional action could FLRA have taken? *See* § 557(d)(1)(D) and the fourth sentence of § 556(d).

The court of appeals was obviously troubled by what it should do aside from laying harsh criticism on all concerned. Certainly, the hearing before ALJ Vittone must have been a humbling experience. Ordinarily, it is improper to "probe the mind" of agency decisionmakers about how they made their decision. *Morgan IV,* discussed in § 3.3.1 N.5. However, in cases of alleged ex parte contacts, the agency staff and decisionmakers must submit to a grueling inquiry into exactly who said what to whom.

Should the Court have remanded the *PATCO* case for a new FLRA decision, even though it concluded that the ex parte contacts were not prejudicial to any party? In the *Idaho Historic Pres. Council* case, discussed in N.1, rather than remand for a hearing on the nature of the ex parte contacts or any consideration of whether they made any difference to the decision, the court overturned the Council's approval of the development application. The dissenting judges complained: "Because the telephone calls were of little gravity, did not seem to influence the council's decision, did not come from parties, and were disclosed at the public hearings [the receipt of the calls was disclosed but not the identity of the callers or the substance of the conversations], vacating the decision would serve no useful purpose."

6. *Communications to agency staff members.* Notice that § 557(d) prohibits ex parte communications between outsiders and *advisers to decisionmakers.* Thus Shanker's communication would have been equally inappropriate if directed to Applewhaite's attorney-adviser. And observe also that § 557(d) goes into effect no later than the time a proceeding is noticed for hearing (or, if an outsider knows that it will be noticed, at the time of acquiring such knowledge). § 557(d)(1)(E).

There is a conflict between the APA provisions that prohibit ex parte contacts and the goals of i) encouraging free communication between outsiders and regulatory agencies and ii) making available the largest possible pool of staff advisers from within the agency for decisionmakers to call on in difficult cases.

For example, suppose Secretary of Transportation Lewis wants to discuss the *PATCO* case with Max after it has been noticed for hearing. Max is an FLRA staff attorney who is experienced in dealing with the problem of public employee strikes. Both Max and Lewis think that Max will prosecute the union in the *PATCO* case. Such a conversation (between an agency prosecutor and an executive official who favors the prosecution) seems entirely appropriate. *See Galveston v. Texas Dep't of Health,* 724 S.W.2d 115 (Tex. App. 1987) (ex parte communications with non-decisionmaker staff are legal under Texas ex parte statute). After the discussion between Lewis and Max occurs, someone other than Max is selected to prosecute the case. When the time for decision arrives, Member Applewhaite wants to call upon Max for ex parte advice, which normally would be appropriate and permissible. (The use of staff advisers to agency decisionmakers is discussed in § 3.3.4.) Max might be disqualified from giving advice because of his earlier and innocent ex parte contact with Lewis. Alternatively, if Max serves as an adviser, Lewis' ex parte communication might violate § 557(d) and therefore would have to be placed on the record under § 557(d)(1)(C).

7.   *Problem.* The Madison Public Utilities Commission (PUC) sets the rate that telephone companies can charge for intrastate calls. Madison has adopted the 2010 MSAPA, and a statute calls for a hearing on the record in connection with ratemaking. The PUC conducts adjudicatory hearings before an ALJ to set the rates; then the five agency heads make the final decision. These proceedings determine such issues as whether a phone company's costs are reasonable and necessary (so that the rates will reimburse the company for those costs). Consumer groups participate extensively in these hearings. The hearings may go on for months or even years.

Madison Telephone Co. (MTC) has applied to the PUC to raise its base telephone rate from $15 to $19 per month. One issue is whether the rates should cover MTC's costs to clean up toxic wastes that it buried in the ground. Consumer groups claims that these costs should be borne by the company's shareholders rather than the ratepayers.

The five commissioners of the PUC are willing to listen to ex parte presentations by any party to a rate case. Several consumers who had not previously participated in the case paid a visit to Commissioner Smith and gave her a one-hour presentation on why the cleanup costs should not be part of the rate base. Ultimately, the Commission voted 3–2 in favor of the consumer group's position; Smith was in the majority.

Should a reviewing court set aside this decision—and, if so, what should it order on remand? Would the analysis be different if MTC had made the ex parte contact, the Commission voted in its favor, and consumer groups sought judicial review? Would the analysis be different if the members of the PUC were elected officials, as they are in some states? What if the PUC were a federal agency covered by the federal APA?

See Southwestern Bell Tel. Co. v. Okla. Corp. Comm'n, 873 P.2d 1001 (Okla. 1994); *In re Public Serv. Co.,* 454 A.2d 435 (N.H. 1982); *In re Minn. PUC,* 417 N.W.2d 274 (Minn. Ct. App. 1987); *Business & Professional People for the Public Interest v. Barnich,* 614 N.E.2d 341 (Ill. App. 1993).

§ 3.3.3 AGENCY ADJUDICATION AND LEGISLATIVE PRESSURE

PILLSBURY CO. V. FTC
354 F.2d 952 (5th Cir. 1966)

TUTTLE, C. J.:

[Pillsbury seeks review of an order of the Federal Trade Commission (FTC) requiring it to divest two baking companies that the FTC found it had acquired in 1951 and 1952 in violation of § 7 of the Clayton Act. Pillsbury claims it was deprived of due process by reason of improper interference by Congressional committees with the decisional process of the FTC. In 1953, an FTC hearing examiner dismissed the case against Pillsbury, but the FTC agency heads reversed this decision and ordered the examiner to proceed. The agency heads ruled that the examiner must consider economic evidence about whether the acquisitions would cause a "substantial lessening of competition" (the "rule of reason" approach). It rejected the argument that where a company having a substantial share of the market acquires a competitor, the acquisition automatically violates § 7 (the "per se" rule). The hearing examiner received economic evidence for several years and decided in 1959 that the acquisitions violated § 7. The FTC agency heads upheld that decision in 1960.

During 1955, the antitrust subcommittees of the House and Senate Judiciary Committees held hearings about antitrust policy. FTC Chairman Howrey and several of the members of his staff appeared including Earl Kintner, who was then General Counsel and later became FTC Chairman. Kintner wrote the 1960 opinion. Also present was Robert Secrest who was a Commissioner in both 1955 and 1960 and Joseph Sheehy who was Director of Litigation. Sheehy's assistant, William Kern, was a Commissioner in 1960. Thus, of the four commissioners who participated in the 1960 decision, Secrest and Kintner were exposed to whatever interference was embodied in the hearings, and Kern was indirectly affected.]

When Chairman Howrey appeared before the Senate subcommittee on June 1, 1955, he met a barrage of questioning by the members of the committee challenging his view of the requirements of § 7. [The court quotes the Senate hearing extensively. This is a sample of two of the exchanges:]

Senator Kefauver: "This [the Pillsbury case] illustrates what I have been talking about, Mr. Howrey. I think Congress expected that where there was manifestly a lessening of competition, under the amended Clayton Act a merger should not take place. Now, here in the Southeast, a section of the country, there is a lessening of competition because one firm had 20 and something percent and the other had 20 and something percent. It would seem to me by applying the rule of reason and running the record up to 9,000 pages with more to come, and bringing in every possible economic factor, this, that, and the other, that the Federal Trade Commission is rather taking over the prerogative of congressional intent."

Mr. Howrey: "I would not think so, Senator. I think a careful study of the legislative history of amended section 7 requires the law-enforcement agency, and the quasi-judicial agency, to examine the market facts. . . ."

[Mr. Howrey]: "Well, I think the question you are asking about the Pillsbury decision is a much greater challenge to judicial processes, because I am sitting as a quasi-judicial officer in that case. That is a much greater challenge to judicial processes than anything I did by participating in this committee of the Attorney General." [Howrey had participated in an Attorney General's committee that studied the antitrust laws.]

[Senator Kefauver]: "Maybe you should not have answered my questions."

[Mr. Howrey]: "I think I will disqualify myself in the Pillsbury case for the rest of the case because of the inquiry which you have made about my mental processes in it. But let me answer your other question, and I think I should because I do not think I can sit in a quasi-judicial capacity and—I think you have delved too deeply into the quasi-judicial mind in the Pillsbury matter. . . ."]

We conclude that the proceedings just outlined constituted an improper intrusion into the adjudicatory processes of the Commission and were of such a damaging character as to have required at least some of the members in addition to the chairman to disqualify themselves. . . .

[W]hen such a [Congressional] investigation focuses directly and substantially upon the mental decisional processes of a Commissioner *in a case which is pending before it*, Congress is no longer intervening in the agency's *legislative* function, but rather, in its *judicial* function. At this latter point, we become concerned with the right of private litigants to a fair trial and, equally important, with their right to the appearance of impartiality, which cannot be maintained unless those who exercise the judicial function are free from powerful external influences. . . .

To subject an administrator to a searching examination as to how and why he reached his decision in a case still pending before him, and to criticize him for reaching the "wrong" decision, as the Senate subcommittee did in this case, sacrifices the appearance of impartiality— the *sine qua non* of American judicial justice—in favor of some short-run notions regarding the Congressional intent underlying an amendment to a statute, unfettered administration of which was committed by Congress to the Federal Trade Commission.

It may be argued that such officials as members of the Federal Trade Commission are sufficiently aware of the realities of governmental, not to say "political," life as to be able to withstand such questioning as we have outlined here. However, this court is not so "sophisticated" that it can shrug off such a procedural due process claim merely because the officials involved should be able to discount what is said and to disregard the force of the intrusion into the adjudicatory process. We conclude that we can preserve the rights of the litigants in a case such as this without having any adverse effect upon the legitimate exercise of the investigative power of Congress. What we do is to preserve the integrity of the judicial aspect of the administrative process. . . .

[The rule of necessity does not apply because] the Commission is not permanently disqualified to decide this case. We are convinced that the passage of time, coupled with the changes in personnel on the Commission, sufficiently insulate the present members from any outward [sic] effect from what occurred in 1955.

It is extremely unfortunate that this complaint, seeking divestiture by Pillsbury of two other companies acquired by it, has taken this long to reach the present stage of the litigation. It commenced as a pioneer case under the new amendment to the law. However, in the meantime much law has been written as to the quantity and quality of proof needed under a Section 7 complaint while it has been pending. . . .

VACATED AND REMANDED.

NOTES AND QUESTIONS

1. *The Pillsbury reasoning.* Whether the 1955 hearings actually influenced the FTC's 1960 decision seems doubtful:

> In particular, (1) five years elapsed between the oversight hearing and the challenged decision; (2) the chairman had already disqualified himself, and the commissioners who joined in the final agency order (and whose "appearance of impartiality" was in question) had not spoken or been questioned at the oversight hearing; (3) the FTC had already spoken on the antitrust issue that the senators raised, and this issue was not even in controversy in the FTC decision after remand; and, most important, (4) the FTC did not adopt the senators' view at all, but instead adhered to the same position on the "per se" issue that it had taken originally.

Ronald M. Levin, *Congressional Ethics and Constituent Advocacy in an Age of Mistrust*, 95 MICH. L. REV. 1, 40 n.153 (1996). In this light, was the court justified in vacating the decision? On remand in *Pillsbury,* the Commission quickly dismissed the case, declaring that the record (now fourteen years old) was too stale, and the effects of the merger were too entrenched, to make divestiture a realistic possibility.

2. *Pillsbury and the APA.* In 1976, ten years after *Pillsbury*, Congress added § 557(d) to the APA. See § 3.3.2. The legislative history of that section indicates that the term "interested persons" includes members of Congress. Had it been applicable in 1966, how would § 557(d) apply to *Pillsbury*? Does *PATCO* suggest a different remedy from the one the *Pillsbury* court ordered?

3. *Congressional oversight.* *Pillsbury* involves a conflict between the norms of judicialized adjudication and the need for Congressional oversight. Since agencies like the FTC often set policy through the adjudicatory process, Congress needs to be able to conduct oversight of such policymaking. Does the *Pillsbury* rule prevent it from doing so? We consider the oversight function further in § 7.4.3.

4. *Legislative interference with non-adjudicatory decisions.* In *D.C. Federation of Civic Ass'ns v. Volpe*, 459 F.2d 1231 (D.C. Cir. 1971), Representative Natcher, the chairman of a House appropriations subcommittee, put pressure on the Secretary of Transportation to approve construction of a new bridge over the Potomac River. Natcher publicly threatened that the Committee would deny funding to build the D.C. subway until the bridge project was under way. Soon thereafter, the Secretary approved the bridge.

The court found the *Pillsbury* doctrine inapposite because that decision applied only to proceedings that were "judicial or quasi-judicial." The Secretary's decision did not fit that description, because he "was not required to base it solely on a formal record established at a public hearing." In other words, the *D.C. Federation* case held that the *Pillsbury* rule is limited, more or less, to decisions reached in evidentiary hearings (perhaps only to cases in which due process applies).

Nevertheless, the court continued, even outside the realm of adjudication, there are some limits on legislative intervention. The Secretary's decision whether or not to build the bridge should have been based on considerations of engineering and traffic, not the wishes of congressmen. Thus, if the Secretary had relied on congressional pressure in approving the bridge, his decision was arbitrary and capricious. (See § 9.3.1.) A majority of the court held that on remand "the Secretary must make new determinations based strictly on the merits and completely without regard to any considerations not made relevant by Congress in the applicable statutes."

According to Professor Pierce: "*D.C. Federation* is hard to explain in a democracy in which two politically accountable branches of government share the power to make policy. . . . Our nation would be ungovernable in the absence of constant policy compromises between the executive and legislative branches. . . . [A]ny agency policymaker who took seriously the D.C. Circuit's admonition to ignore the policy views of legislators would be rendered ineffective in a matter of months." Pierce argues that the court should have held that the Secretary could lawfully take account of Natcher's pressure, because the transportation legislation did not *expressly* prohibit such consideration. Richard J. Pierce, Jr., *Political Control Versus Impermissible Bias in Agency Decisionmaking: Lessons from Chevron and Mistretta*, 57 U. CHI. L. REV. 481, 496–98 (1990).

5.   *Preliminary investigations.* In light of the conflict between *Pillsbury* and legitimate congressional oversight, other cases have been more cautious about challenging legislative intervention in the administrative process. A good example is *DCP Farms v. Yeutter*, 957 F.2d 1183 (5th Cir. 1992). That case involved federal crop subsidies, which are limited to $50,000 per person. DCP Farms split itself up into 51 trusts to avoid this limitation. After a county committee approved subsidy payments to each trust, the Agriculture Department (USDA) began reviewing the case.

Congressman Huckaby, chairman of the relevant subcommittee, wrote USDA Secretary Yeutter that the DCP Farms arrangement violated the letter and spirit of the law and urged a careful review of this and similar cases. He threatened to introduce legislation to amend the law to outlaw any payments to trusts unless DCP were disqualified. USDA responded that it would take a very aggressive enforcement position toward the farms.

The court denied relief. It held *Pillsbury* was not applicable, because, when Huckaby wrote his letter, the DCP Farms matter had not yet reached the point of quasi-judicial proceedings. It would not reach that stage until the hearing, the court said. Moreover, erecting a barrier to such communications would infringe too far on Congressional oversight of administrative agencies. Huckaby's communication was part of a larger policy debate, not just a dispute about DCP Farms. The key point was that Huckaby's letter concerned a relevant issue (whether trusts can be used to avoid the $50,000 per person limit), rather than an extraneous issue as in *D.C. Federation*.

Do you agree that Huckaby was free to engage in ex parte contacts until the actual hearing? Consider APA § 557(d)(1)(E). Was the threat to seek changes in the law if USDA did not submit really a "relevant issue" in the case? More generally, is the *DCP Farms* case too permissive in allowing Congressional interference with pending cases? Or was this a legitimate exercise of the oversight function? For one view, see Levin, *supra*, at 51, 57–59.

6.   *Legislative casework.* Legislators often receive requests for assistance from their constituents who are embroiled in controversies with agencies. Congressional offices handle millions of such cases every year. Typically, the member's staff will call or write to the agency and ask about the "status" of the matter. These requests are often given priority treatment by agency staff. Members sometimes seek to influence the outcome of the matter. In extreme cases, interference with pending agency adjudication can raise serious ethical issues for legislators.

Could such requests be treated as ex parte contacts that would violate state or federal APAs? In drafting APA § 557(d), Congress was anxious to protect its right to make status inquiries, which explains the specific reference to them in APA § 551(14). Senator Everett Dirksen once said: "I have been calling agencies for 25 years . . . Are we to be put on the carpet because we represent our constituents, make inquiries, and find out what the status of matters is, and so serve our constituents? . . . I know these people, they are good, reliable operators; they are good solid citizens. I just want to know what the status of the matter is." 105 CONG. REC. 14,057 (1959).

Is legislative casework, such as status inquiries, a form of undesirable tampering with the adjudicative process? Or is it a desirable form of democracy in action? The policy issues are reviewed in Levin, *supra*, at 16–32.

7.   *Problem.* In order to open a new hospital in Madison, it is necessary to receive a "certificate of need" from the Madison Health Agency (MHA). The statute directs MHA to consider the current and future demand for additional facilities in the area before granting or denying a certificate of need.

Midway Corp. sought to open a new hospital in Oak City called Midway Hospital, but its application was opposed by City General, an existing hospital. Midway believed that an additional hospital was needed, since City General is often full and the area has been increasing in population owing to some new factories. After Midway filed its application with MHA, MHA conducted an economic study that lasted ten months and concluded that the application should be granted. Madison state law requires an evidentiary hearing before a certificate of need is issued or rejected. MHA conducted a hearing, following which the MHA Director reversed the staff decision and rejected the application.

Two days after Midway filed its application, ten Madison legislators wrote to the Director, urging her to reject Midway's application. The letter stated Oak City could not support two hospitals and that if Midway were built, both Midway and City General would fail. The letter concluded: "If MHA grants the Midway application, we would have to review the question of whether MHA should continue to exist. As you know, we will have to make budget cuts next year and MHA would be a prime candidate for defunding." The legislators did not send a copy of this letter to Midway, but the Director forwarded a copy to Midway immediately after she received it.

Midway seeks judicial review of the MHA decision. How should the court rule? Assume that i) no APA is applicable, ii) 2010 MSAPA is applicable (*see* § 3.3.2 N.1), or iii) the federal APA is applicable.

§ 3.3.4 SEPARATION OF FUNCTIONS AND INTERNAL AGENCY COMMUNICATIONS

People often criticize the administrative process because a single agency makes the rules, investigates violations, prosecutes cases, and then decides those very cases. It seems that the agency acts as a legislator, investigator, prosecutor, judge and jury all rolled into one. Nevertheless, the combination within a single body of all these functions is a hallmark of the administrative process and constitutional challenges to that combination have been unsuccessful. The functions are combined primarily for reasons of efficiency and effectiveness. Of course, these functions could be split up between different bodies (we call this "external separation"). Then a different set of problems arises. *See* § 3.4.3.

When a single agency has combined functions, the issue shifts to whether an *individual* within the agency can play an *adversary* role in a particular case (as investigator, prosecutor, or advocate), then serve an *adjudicatory role* (as administrative judge, agency head, or adviser to either of them) in the same case. For example, suppose that A both investigates a case and then serves as the administrative judge in the same case. Even though A tries to judge the case fairly, A may consciously or unconsciously rely on evidence that has not been introduced at the hearing or may be predisposed to decide the case in a way consistent with the conclusions A reached when investigating the case.

To meet objections of this kind, most agencies are structured to achieve an *internal separation of functions.* As illustrated by *Quintanar,* staff members who engaged in *adversary* conduct on the agency's behalf cannot serve as an administrative decisionmaker or furnish off-the-record advice to the decisionmakers in that same case. However, as illustrated by *Consumer Advocate Division,* staff members who did *not* play adversary roles in a particular case are permitted to furnish off-the-record advice to agency heads in that same case.

As background to this material, try to imagine purely judicial and institutional models of separation of functions. The criminal law completely separates its functions: it is unthinkable that a prosecutor could be a judge in the same case or advise a judge off-the-record about how to decide the case. Judge and prosecutor are not part of the same team. At the opposite extreme, the president of a corporation, deciding whether to produce a new product, is perfectly free to gather evidence, make the case for one side, and to seek confidential advice from anybody inside or outside the firm—no holds barred. That is a pure institutional model. The rules of administrative adjudication strike a compromise between these extremes.

DEPARTMENT OF ALCOHOLIC BEVERAGE CONTROL V. ALCOHOLIC BEVERAGE CONTROL APPEALS BOARD (QUINTANAR)

145 P.3d 462 (Cal. 2006)

WERDEGAR, J.

The Department of Alcoholic Beverage Control (Department) has exclusive licensing authority over entities that sell alcoholic beverages. Its procedures for adjudicating whether licensees have violated the terms of their licenses include an evidentiary hearing at which a Department prosecutor makes the Department's case to an administrative law judge (ALJ), and a second level of decisionmaking in which the Department's director or a delegee decides whether to adopt the ALJ's proposed decision. [The Department's prosecutors sought to suspend Quintanar's license for serving obviously intoxicated patrons. The ALJ found in favor of the licensee, but the Director reversed the ALJ decision and suspended the license. A separate body, the Alcoholic Beverage Control Appeals Board (Board), reversed the Director's decision. The court of appeal affirmed the Board's decision. Consistent with standard Department procedure, the prosecutor prepared a "reports of hearing," consisting of a summary of the evidentiary hearing and recommended resolution, which he then provided ex parte to Director.]

While the state's administrative agencies have considerable leeway in how they structure their adjudicatory functions, they may not disregard certain basic precepts. One fairness principle directs that in adjudicative matters, one adversary should not be permitted to bend the ear of the ultimate decision maker or the decision maker's advisors in private. Another directs that the functions of prosecution and adjudication be kept separate, carried out by distinct individuals. California's Administrative Procedure Act (APA), as overhauled in 1995, adopts these precepts by regulating and strictly limiting contacts between an agency's prosecutor and the officers the agency selects to preside over hearings and ultimately decide adjudicative matters. We conclude the Department's procedure violates the APA's bar against ex parte communications. . . .

The Department is a unitary agency with the exclusive authority to license the sale of alcoholic beverages in California and to suspend or revoke licenses. As a unitary agency, it carries out multiple functions: "It is in the nature of administrative regulatory agencies that they function both as accuser and adjudicator on matters within their particular jurisdiction. Administrative agencies are created to interpret and enforce the legislative enactments applicable to the field in which they operate. That role necessarily involves the administrative agency in both determining whether a licensee is in violation of the law, and taking action to correct such violations."

Like many state administrative agencies, the Department exercises its adjudicatory power through a two-stage process. In the first (trial) stage, a Department staff attorney, acting as prosecutor, and the licensee present their respective cases to an ALJ at an evidentiary hearing. The ALJ then makes factual findings, prepares a proposed decision, and submits it to the Department. In the second (decision) stage, the Department's director or a delegee considers the proposed decision and elects to adopt it, modify it, reject it and remand for a new hearing, or reject it and decide the case on the record. . . .

I.   *The California Administrative Procedure Act* . . .

A.   *The APA: Historical Background.* California's original APA [of 1945] was pioneering but limited. It applied principally to licensing cases and covered only certain aspects of administrative practice. In particular, it said nothing about either ex parte communications or agency separation of functions. In the absence of regulation, agency heads were free to discuss adjudicatory matters with whomever they pleased, both inside and outside the agency, subject only to whatever indefinite limits due process might impose. [The 1995 revision to the adjudicatory portions of the APA contained an Administrative Adjudication Bill of Rights including a provision on separation of functions.]

B.   *The APA's Ex Parte and Separation of Function Provisions.* Article 7, modeled on provisions of the federal Administrative Procedure Act and the 1981 Model State APA, broadly prohibits ex parte contacts between parties, including agency parties, and decision makers during administrative adjudicative proceedings. "While the proceeding is pending there shall be *no communication, direct or indirect, regarding any issue in the proceeding,* to the presiding officer from an employee or representative of an agency that is a party . . . without notice and opportunity for all parties to participate in the communication." A "presiding officer" is defined as an officer who presides over an evidentiary hearing, but other provisions of article 7 expressly extend this prohibition to all decision makers, including agency heads and their delegees, whether or not they preside over an evidentiary hearing. . . .

Other provisions slightly narrow this blanket prohibition. Two are pertinent here. First, communications are permitted regarding uncontroversial procedural matters. Second, an agency decision maker may receive advice from *nonadversarial* agency personnel: an otherwise prohibited ex parte communication will be allowed if it "is for the purpose of assistance and advice to the presiding officer from a person who has not served as investigator, prosecutor, or advocate in the proceeding or its preadjudicative stage. An assistant or advisor may evaluate the evidence in the record but shall not furnish, augment, diminish, or modify the evidence in the record. . . ." Thus, the APA sets out a clear rule: an agency prosecutor cannot secretly communicate with the agency decision maker or the decision maker's advisor about the substance of the case prior to issuance of a final decision.

This rule enforces two important procedural precepts. First, it promotes neutral decisionmaking by requiring a limited internal separation of functions. Procedural fairness does not mandate the dissolution of unitary agencies, but it does require some internal separation between advocates and decision makers to preserve neutrality. Second, the rule preserves record exclusivity. "The decision of the agency head should be based on the record and not on off-the-record discussions from which the parties are excluded." [The Court rejected the Department's argument that the limits on ex parte communications by agency prosecutors extend only to the trial stage, not the decision stage] . . .

C. Application of the APA to Reports of Hearing. . . . Did the Department's prosecutor and the Department's final decision maker or advisor have an impermissible ex parte contact? The Board and the Court of Appeal inferred as much. The Department's refusal to comply with the Board's order and produce its reports of hearing from these three cases leaves us somewhat in the dark. . . . [The Court concluded that the Department should have complied with the Appeal Board's demand that it produce the reports of hearing. While the Appeals Board, like a court, normally reviews the Department's decisions solely on the record, it is appropriate to supplement the record when a party makes a claim of procedural irregularity, as in this case]. . . .

The Department argues the record contains no proof the reports of hearing were actually *considered* by the ultimate decision maker or his advisors, but neither does it deny this occurred. Whether the decision maker considered the reports of hearing is in any event beside the point. On the one hand, proof as to how a particular ex parte contact weighed in an agency decision maker's calculus would be impossible to come by without inquiry into matters beyond the ken of any court. . . . The party faced with such a communication need not prove that it was considered; conversely, the agency engaging in ex parte discussions cannot raise as a shield that the advice was *not* considered. Under the APA, the mere submission of ex parte substantive comments, without more, is illegal. . . .

The Department and Attorney General express concern that a rule precluding prosecutor-decision maker contact will have dramatic consequences for this and other agencies, requiring agencies to split and depriving agency heads of the advice of their subordinates. Nothing about our interpretation of the APA requires splitting this agency or any other.

The Department may still function as a unitary agency. In doing so, however, it must afford licensees fundamentally fair hearings by observing a limited internal separation of functions. The agency head is free to speak with anyone in the agency and to solicit and receive advice from whomever he or she pleases—anyone except the personnel who served as adversaries in a specific case. Indeed, the agency head can even contact the prosecutor to discuss settlement or direct dismissal. Virtually the only contact that is forbidden is communication in the other direction: a prosecutor cannot communicate off the record with the agency decision maker or the decision maker's advisors about the substance of the case. But the one contact that is forbidden is the one contact that occurred here.[13]

II. *Remedy*

[The court reversed the Department's order, refusing to apply the harmless error rule.] We note, however, that the further remedy ordered by the Court of Appeal—mandatory screening procedures barring prosecutor-decision maker contacts and precluding use of reports of hearing in future cases—is overbroad. The APA bars only advocate-decision maker ex parte contacts, not all contacts. Thus, for example, nothing in the APA precludes the ultimate decision maker from considering posthearing briefs submitted by, and served on, each side. The Department if it so chooses may continue to use the report of hearing procedure, so long as it provides licensees a copy of the report and the opportunity to respond. [The decision of the Court of Appeal is affirmed.]

CONSUMER ADVOCATE DIVISION V. TENNESSEE REGULATORY AUTHORITY

1998 Tenn. App. LEXIS 428, 1998 WL 684536 (Tenn. Ct. App. 1998)

[The Tennessee Regulatory Authority (TRA) approved rate increases for Nashville Gas Co. TRA staff members who had not been previously involved in the case furnished off-the-record advice to the agency heads. The TRA's Consumer Advocate Division (CAD) moved for discovery of these communications.]

The TRA chairman moved to deny the motion with the following explanation: "I believe that as a director I have a right to have privileged communication with a member of my staff for the purpose of understanding issues and analyzing the evidence in the many complicated proceedings that this Agency has to hear. I reject your allegation that I have abdicated my responsibility as a decision maker. I rely on my staff expertise as the law permits me to do so. Therefore, I

---

[13] Because limited internal separation of functions is required as a statutory matter, we need not consider whether it is also required by due process. As a prudential matter, we routinely decline to address constitutional questions when it is unnecessary to reach them . . .

move that your motion be denied." The Agency members unanimously denied the CAD's motion.

On this part of the controversy we are persuaded that the TRA was correct. The TRA deals with highly complicated data involving principles of finance, accounting, and corporate efficiency; it also deals with the convoluted principles of legislative utility regulation. To expect the Authority members to fulfill their duties without the help of a competent and efficient staff defies all logic. And, we are convinced, the staff may make recommendations or suggestions as to the merits of the questions before the TRA. *See* Tenn. Code Ann. § 4–5–304(b). Otherwise, all support staff—law clerks, court clerks, and other specialists—would be of little service to the person(s) that hire them. We are satisfied that any report made by the agency staff based on the record before the TRA was not subject to the CAD's motion to discover it . . .

NOTES AND QUESTIONS

1. *Due process and separation of adjudicatory and adversarial functions.* In *Quintanar*, the Court did not decide whether the prosecutor's ex parte contact with the Director violated due process (see footnote 13). The leading case on the relationship between due process and separation of functions is *Withrow v. Larkin,* 421 U.S. 35 (1975). The Court stated:

> That is not to say that there is nothing to the argument that those who have investigated should not then adjudicate. The issue is substantial, it is not new, and legislators and others concerned with the operations of administrative agencies have given much attention to whether and to what extent distinctive administrative functions should be performed by the same persons. No single answer has been reached. Indeed, the growth, variety, and complexity of the administrative processes have made any one solution highly unlikely. Within the Federal Government itself, Congress has addressed the issue in several different ways, providing for varying degrees of separation from complete separation of functions to virtually none at all. For the generality of agencies, Congress has been content with § 554(d) of the APA which provides that no employee engaged in investigating or prosecuting may also participate or advise in the adjudicating function, but which also expressly exempts from this prohibition "the agency or a member or members of the body comprising the agency." It is not surprising, therefore, to find that "[t]he case law, both federal and state, generally rejects the idea that the combination [of] judging [and] investigating functions is a denial of due process. . . ."

According to *Withrow*, Dr. Larkin was not deprived of due process because the heads of a state agency first investigated him and then decided to revoke his license. (In fact, it appears that the investigation was carried out by agency staff, not by the agency heads, but the Court assumed that the heads had both investigated and adjudicated.) A contrary holding would have disabled countless state and local agencies in which agency heads both investigate and adjudicate.

Nevertheless, other authority suggests that a combination of functions *below the agency head level* could violate due process, because there is no need for prosecutors or investigators to serve as lower-level decisionmakers or to advise the agency heads. Probably, a court dealing with a due process challenge to a combination of functions would engage in a *Mathews v. Eldridge*-type balancing to decide the issue. (*See* §§ 2.3 and § 2.4). Recall the very end of *Goldberg v. Kelly*: "And, of course, an impartial decision maker is essential. We agree with the District Court that prior involvement in some aspects of a case will not necessarily bar a welfare official from acting as a decision maker. He should not, however, have participated in making the determination under review."

2.   *Pennsylvania view.* With *Withrow*, compare *Lyness v. State Bd. of Medicine*, 605 A.2d 1204 (Pa. 1992). In *Lyness*, 8 of the 11 members of the Medical Board met by emergency conference call, heard a presentation by the Board's prosecutor, and voted to allow the prosecutor to cite Lyness for sexually molesting patients. Later a hearing examiner heard the case and recommended suspension of Lyness' license. Three years later, the full Board affirmed the examiner's fact findings but changed the penalty to license revocation. The Board's vote was 6 in favor, 1 abstention (3 members were absent). Of the 7 members present, 3 (including the abstainer who presided at the hearing) had participated in the conference call.

The court held that the due process clause of the *state* constitution allowed it to grant greater procedural protection than *Withrow* granted under the *federal* constitution. Thus it prohibited agency heads from exercising the functions of both prosecution and decisionmaker. In the future, a wall of division must be erected within the agency so that the persons who make the ultimate adjudicatory decisions have not been involved in the decision to prosecute.

A dissenter argued that it makes sense to allow agency heads to make the decision to prosecute a case rather than leaving that decision to the agency prosecutors. "The majority obviously finds the Board short of professional ability and personal integrity, a shortage they think best supplied by prosecutors."

Federal cases are contrary to *Lyness*. *See Vanelli v. Reynolds School Dist. No. 7*, 667 F.2d 773 (9th Cir. 1982) (school board's participation in initial termination decision did not disable the board from deciding the subsequent termination case). Under § 402(b) of the 2010 MSAPA, "An agency head that has participated in a determination of probable cause or other preliminary determination in an adjudication may serve as the presiding officer or final decision maker in the adjudication unless a party demonstrates grounds for disqualification under subsection (c)."

3.   *External separation of functions.* California split its alcoholic beverage enforcement between two levels. The Department investigates cases and conducts an ALJ hearing followed by a decision by the Director. Then the licensee can appeal to the Board. The Board is a separate administrative appellate agency that hears only cases coming from the Department. Either the licensee or (as in *Quintanar*) the Department can appeal to the courts from a decision of the Board. This is an example of *external separation of functions*, meaning that the Board is untainted by adversarial functions. However, the number of separate decisions necessary to actually impose discipline on an alcoholic beverage licensee in California seems excessive. Usually external separation of functions means that prosecution is lodged in one agency and adjudication in a second agency. See § 3.4.3.

4.   *Advice from nonadversarial staff members. Consumer Advocate Division* upholds a common practice in administrative law—ex parte advice to agency heads by staff members who played no adversarial role in the case. Staff members who furnish the advice are not permitted to introduce new evidence (because that would violate the exclusive record rule discussed in § 3.3.1 N.6). The decision in *Consumer Advocate Division* was a straightforward application of two Tennessee APA provisions (and, by implication, it also upholds the advice-giving practice under due process):

4–5–303. Separation of functions

(a) A person who has served as an investigator, prosecutor or advocate in a contested case may not serve as an administrative judge or hearing officer or assist or advise an administrative judge or hearing officer in the same proceeding.

4–5–304. Ex parte communications . . .

(b) . . . an administrative judge, hearing officer or agency member may communicate with agency members regarding a matter pending before the agency or may receive aid from staff assistants, members of the staff of the attorney general and reporter, or a licensed attorney, if such persons do not receive ex parte communications of a type that the administrative judge, hearing officer or agency members would be prohibited from receiving, and do not furnish, augment, diminish or modify the evidence in the record.

These statutory provisions were based directly on provisions in 1981 MSAPA §§ 4–213(b), 4–214(a).

As the *Consumer Advocate Division* case makes clear, advice to decisionmakers by non-adversarial staff members is particularly valuable in cases involving lengthy records and complex legal, economic, scientific, and technical issues. The agency heads need the advice because they lack the necessary training and experience to deal with these issues. They are often part-time administrators and don't have time to master the entire record, including the conflicting reports of expert witnesses. (See discussion of

Morgan I in 3.4.1 N.2) Yet the issues involved are important, not only to the private party (in this case, a utility seeking a rate increase) but to the general public (that will have to pay the higher rates). In N.8, we return to the issue of whether off-the-record non-adversarial staff advice to decisionmakers should be prohibited.

5.   *Separation of functions under the federal APA.* Like the California and Tennessee statutes, the federal APA requires internal separation of functions. Look at the language which begins *after* § 554(d)(2): "An employee or agent engaged in the performance of investigative or prosecuting functions . . ." and runs to the end of (C). *See generally* Michael Asimow, *When the Curtain Falls: Separation of Functions in the Federal Administrative Agencies*, 81 COLUM. L. REV. 759, 761–79 (1981).

The California, Tennessee, and federal APA provisions essentially divide agency employees into three groups:

  • adversaries (that is, advocates, investigators and prosecutors)

  • adjudicators (meaning both the ALJ who hears the case and the agency heads who make the final decision)

  • everyone else.

APA § 554(d) prohibits staff members in the first group (adversaries) from serving as adjudicators *or* from advising the adjudicators off the record. As *Quintanar* and *Consumer Advocate Division* confirmed, staff members in the third group ("everyone else") can furnish off-record advice to the adjudicators. Thus a staff member could be an adversary in one case and serve as an adjudicator or furnish advice to an adjudicator in a different (but similar) case.

6.   *Additional separation of functions provisions in the APA.* The drafters of the federal APA were quite concerned by issues of separation of functions and with safeguarding the decisional independence of federal ALJs. APA § 554(d)(1) provides that an ALJ may not "consult a person or party on a fact in issue, unless on notice and opportunity for all parties to participate . . ." This provision disables an ALJ (but not other agency decisionmakers, such as intermediate review boards or agency heads) from receiving ex parte advice *on factual issues* from *any* agency staff member (whether or not they have been adversaries in the case). *See Butz v. Economou*, 438 U.S. 478, 514 (1978) (noting that APA prohibits ex parte communications to ALJs from agency staff members). But this provision does not prohibit the ALJ from receiving advice on *law or policy* from agency staff members. As a practical matter, however, federal ALJs seldom receive ex parte advice of any kind from any agency staff members. They regard themselves as judges and act accordingly.

APA § 554(d)(2) provides that an ALJ may not be *supervised* by a person engaged in performing adversary functions for the agency. Thus ALJs must be part of a separate unit within an agency, supervised only by someone who does not engage in investigation, prosecution, or advocacy. This provision is designed to prevent "command influence," since an ALJ should not have to worry that a decision against the agency would jeopardize the ALJ's career.

7. *Exceptions to separation of functions.* Congress exempted both initial licensing and proceedings involving the validity of rates charged by utilities or carriers from the three separation of functions provisions discussed in NN. 5–6. Congress also excepted "the agency" and "members of the body comprising the agency" from separation of functions. § 554(d)(A), (B), (C). In the (C) exception, the word "agency" refers to the agency *heads.* Recall that the (C) exception is referred to in the *Withrow* excerpt in N.1. Most separation of function provisions in state APAs and MSAPAs contain none of these exceptions.

The precise meaning of the (C) exception has never been clarified by case law. The Attorney General's Memorandum on the APA (a respected interpretive guide to the APA that was written just after its enactment) explained the exception as follows: "Thus, if a member of the Interstate Commerce Commission actively participates in or directs the investigation of an adjudicatory case, he will not be precluded from participating with his colleagues in the decision of that case." *Id.* at 58. This excerpt indicates that the (C) exception allows agency heads to *personally* engage in conflicting functions. The Attorney General's Memorandum also explains: "[O]n 'agency review' the agency heads, as well as the hearing examiner, will be precluded from consulting or obtaining advice from any officer or employee [who] has participated in the investigation or prosecution." *Id.* at 57. This excerpt indicates that the agency head exception does *not* allow adversary staff members to advise agency heads off the record about a pending case.

8. *Separation of functions under the 2010 MSAPA.* Section 408(e)(1) of the 2010 MSAPA prohibits ex parte communications from staff adversaries to decisionmakers. Section 408(e)(2) also limits the type of ex parte advice that a *non-adversarial* staff member can furnish to the agency heads. Such advice is permitted only if it is:

> (A) an explanation of the technical or scientific basis of, or technical or scientific terms in, the evidence in the agency hearing record;

> (B) an explanation of the precedent, policies, or procedures of the agency; or

> (C) any other communication *that does not address the quality or sufficiency of, or the weight that should be given to, evidence in the agency hearing record or the credibility of witnesses.*

The italicized language in (C) is an innovation and would require substantial changes in agency practice. It allows non-adversary staff members to explain technical evidence in the record but would not allow them to express any opinion about the quality or weight of the evidence or the credibility of witnesses.

The members of the drafting committee for the 2010 Model Act inserted this provision because they were concerned about the "black box" problem. They heard from lawyers who are troubled by off-the-record communications between agency heads and the staff about the issues in the case. They cannot find out what happened inside the "black box," and they suspect that their carefully prepared case is often be undercut by staff communications. The lawyers were particularly concerned by staff advice that criticizes the quality of expert testimony in the record.

The rather complex provisions in § 408(e)(2) are intended as a compromise between those who favor a total ban on ex parte non-adversarial staff advice to the agency heads (which earlier drafts of the provision sought to do) and those who think it is necessary to allow such advice to assist the agency heads in making difficult technical and policy decisions. Those who favor allowing such communications fear that if the communications must be placed on the record, the advisers will not provide uninhibited advice.

What do you think of the compromise language in § 408(e)? Will agency heads and staff be able to differentiate between explaining the scientific basis of the evidence (clause A) and expressing a view about how to deal with the conflicting expert opinions (clause C)? If agencies can't draw this distinction with any confidence, it might lead agencies to ban all consultation with non-adversarial staff or require all such advice to be placed on the record. *See* Michael Asimow, *Contested Issues in Contested Cases: Adjudication Under the 2010 Model State Administrative Procedure Act,* 20 WIDENER L. J. 707, 721–39 (2011) (opposing § 408(e)(2)). *But see* Ann Marshall Young, *Ex Parte Communications and the Exclusive Record Provision of the 2010 MSAPA,* ADMIN. & REG. L. NEWS, Wint. 2011, at 8 (supporting § 408(e)(2)).

9. *The principle of necessity.* Under the "principle of necessity," a biased or otherwise disqualified judge can decide a case if there is no legally possible substitute decisionmaker. Otherwise, nobody could make the decision and a wrongdoer might not be punished or the public might not be protected. Does the principle of necessity help to distinguish *Goldberg v. Kelly* from *Withrow v. Larkin?* Did *Lyness* overlook the principle of necessity?

Section 402(f) of the 2010 MSAPA contains a provision authorizing the authority that appointed agency heads to designate a substitute in case one or more of the heads must be disqualified. It provides: "If a substitute presiding officer is required, the substitute must be appointed . . . by: (1) the Governor, if the original presiding officer is an elected official; or (2) the appointing authority, if the original presiding officer is an appointed official."

10. *Problem.* The Madison Environmental Protection Agency (MEPA) regulates water pollution in Madison and issues licenses to factories that discharge any effluent into navigable waterways in the state. The objective of the water pollution statute is to achieve the best possible water quality that is economically feasible. A statute requires MEPA to conduct a hearing on the record before issuing, renewing, or revoking any water pollution license. MEPA hearings are presided over by Arthur, an administrative judge who

works part-time for MEPA (and is a practicing lawyer the rest of the time). The head of MEPA is Helen, who maintains a full-time architecture practice.

Baxter Co. wishes to build a new factory located on the Madison River that will require a water pollution license. The factory will hire about 200 employees. It will produce an entirely new type of computer chip to be used in smart phones. The production process requires the use of large amounts of water from the river. When the water is discharged back into the river, it will contain about 10 parts per billion (ppb) of a chemical called QZT, and there is at present no substitute for QZT in the chip making process. Under existing technology, there is no feasible way of removing QZT from the water. If MEPA denies a license, Baxter has made it clear that it will build the factory in some other state or foreign country where the discharge will be permitted. There are no state or federal rules regulating the discharge of QZT into the environment.

There have been only two animal studies of the health effects of QZT. One showed significant damage to embryonic mice at a level of 50 ppb. A second study showed no damage to embryonic mice at a level of 5 ppb.

At the hearing before Arthur on Baxter's application for a license, there is a sharp clash of expert testimony. Sam is a MEPA staff member who investigated the Baxter application and recommended that it be denied. Sam has a Ph.D. in public health and has published numerous articles about water pollution. He testifies at the hearing that MEPA should always err on the side of public health when the science is in doubt. Baxter presents the testimony of several well-qualified chemists and public health specialists to the effect that QZT is benign and will not harm any living creature. All of the experts submit lengthy written reports. Economists testify that the Baxter factory would provide a much-needed shot in the arm for the Madison economy. Experts on high tech manufacturing testify that the new chip could revolutionize the field of smart-phone manufacturing, making the phones much cheaper and better. The record of the hearing is 10,000 pages long. After the hearing concluded, Arthur proposed a decision that a license be granted to Baxter that would allow discharge of QZT at the level of 10 ppb.

Helen must make the final decision on the Baxter application. She receives off-the-record advice from staff members Sam and Nancy. Sam urged her to deny the application because of serious methodological flaws in the studies about embryonic mice. Nancy is a MEPA staff member who had not previously worked on the Baxter application. Nancy helped Helen understand some of the scientific expert testimony. Nancy said that the Baxter experts were not serious scientists and would testify to anything if they got paid enough to do so. Helen's final decision rejected the Baxter application because she believed that MEPA had failed to establish that any QZT discharge was safe, regardless of the economic impact of the decision.

Our firm represents Baxter, which plans to seek judicial review of the MEPA decision. What is the likelihood of a favorable court decision if the applicable law is i) due process, ii) the 2010 Model State APA, iii) the federal APA?

§ 3.3.5 BIAS: PERSONAL INTEREST, PREJUDGMENT, AND ANIMUS

The previous section considered one kind of bias: a person engaged as a prosecutor, investigator, or advocate may find it difficult to take off the adversary hat and put on an adjudicating hat. This section considers additional problems of decisionmaker impartiality: an adjudicator is disqualified if tainted by a personal stake in the decision, or by prejudgment of the issues, or by animus (meaning prejudice or hostility toward a party). As in the previous section, the fundamental question is whether an administrative adjudicator (either administrative judge or agency head) must be as impartial as a judge.

CINDERELLA CAREER AND FINISHING SCHOOLS, INC. V. FEDERAL TRADE COMMISSION
425 F.2d 583 (D.C. Cir. 1970)

TAMM, J.

This is a petition to review orders of the Federal Trade Commission which required petitioners Cinderella Career College and Finishing Schools, Inc. (hereinafter Cinderella) . . . to cease and desist from engaging in certain practices which were allegedly unfair and deceptive [such as falsely advertising that it was a college, that its graduates could get jobs as airline stewardesses, and that the school found jobs for most of its graduates. The FTC's ALJ—called a hearing examiner in the opinion—dismissed the complaint, but the FTC commissioners reversed that decision.]

An additional ground which requires remand of these proceedings— and which would have required reversal even in the absence of the above-described procedural irregularities [the court found that the Commission had ignored the ALJ's findings when it substituted its own judgment as to the deceptiveness of the ads]—is participation in the proceedings by the then Chairman of the FTC, Paul Rand Dixon.

Notice that the hearing examiner's dismissal of all charges would be appealed was filed by the Commission staff on February 1, 1968. On March 12, 1968, this court's decision was handed down in a prior appeal arising from this same complaint, in which we upheld the Commission's issuance of press releases which called attention to the pending proceedings. Then, on March 15, 1968, while the appeal from the examiner's decision was pending before him, Chairman Dixon made a speech before the Government Relations Workshop of the National Newspaper Association in which he stated:

. . . How about ethics on the business side of running a paper? What standards are maintained on advertising acceptance? What would be the attitude toward accepting good money for advertising by a merchant who conducts a "going out of business" sale every five months? What about carrying ads that offer college educations in five weeks, fortunes by raising mushrooms in the basement, getting rid of pimples with a magic lotion, or becoming an airline's hostess by attending a charm school? . . . Without belaboring the point, I'm sure you're aware that advertising acceptance standards could stand more tightening by many newspapers. Granted that newspapers are not in the advertising policing business, their advertising managers are savvy enough to smell deception when the odor is strong enough. And it is in the public interest, as well as their own, that their sensory organs become more discriminating. . . .

We indicated in our earlier opinion in this case that "there is in fact and law authority in the Commission, acting in the public interest, to alert the public to suspected violations of the law by factual press releases whenever the Commission shall have reason to believe that a respondent is engaged in activities made unlawful by the Act . . ." *FTC v. Cinderella Career & Finishing Schools, Inc.* 404 F.2d 1308 (1968). This does not give individual Commissioners license to prejudge cases or to make speeches which give the appearance that the case has been prejudged. Conduct such as this may have the effect of entrenching a Commissioner in a position which he has publicly stated, making it difficult, if not impossible, for him to reach a different conclusion in the event he deems it necessary to do so after consideration of the record. There is a marked difference between the issuance of a press release which states that the Commission has filed a complaint because it has "reason to believe" that there have been violations, and statements by a Commissioner after an appeal has been filed which give the appearance that he has already prejudged the case and that the ultimate determination of the merits will move in predestined grooves. While these two situations—Commission press releases and a Commissioner's pre-decision public statements—are similar in appearance, they are obviously of a different order of merit. . . .

We find it hard to believe that former Chairman Dixon is so indifferent to the dictates of the Courts of Appeals that he has chosen once again to put his personal determination of what the law requires ahead of what the courts have time and again told him the law requires. If this is a question of "discretion and judgment," Commissioner Dixon has exercised questionable discretion and very poor judgment indeed, in directing his shafts and squibs at a case awaiting his official action. We can use his own words in telling Commissioner Dixon that he has acted "irrespective of the law's requirements;" we will spell out for him once again, avoiding tired cliché and weary generalization, in no uncertain terms, exactly what those requirements are, in the fervent hope that this will be the last time we have to travel this wearisome road.

The test for disqualification has been succinctly stated as being whether "a disinterested observer may conclude that (the agency) has in some measure adjudged the facts as well as the law of a particular case in advance of hearing it." That test was cited with approval by this court in *Texaco, Inc. v. FTC*, 336 F.2d 754 (1964). In that case Chairman Dixon made a speech before the National Congress of Petroleum Retailers, Inc. while a case against Texaco was pending before the examiner on remand. After restating the test for disqualification, this court said: "A disinterested reader of Chairman Dixon's speech could hardly fail to conclude that he had in some measure decided in advance that Texaco had violated the Act." We further stated that such an administrative hearing "must be attended, not only with every element of fairness but with the very appearance of complete fairness." We therefore concluded that Chairman Dixon's participation in the *Texaco* case amounted to a denial of due process.

After our decision in *Texaco* the United States Court of Appeals for the Sixth Circuit was required to reverse a decision of the FTC because Chairman Dixon refused to recuse himself from the case even though he had served as Chief Counsel and Staff Director to the Senate Subcommittee which made the initial investigation into the production and sale of the "wonder drug" tetracycline. *American Cyanamid Co. v. FTC*, 363 F.2d 757 (1966). . . . It is appalling to witness such insensitivity to the requirements of due process; it is even more remarkable to find ourselves once again confronted with a situation in which Mr. Dixon, pouncing on the most convenient victim, has determined either to distort the holdings in the cited cases beyond all reasonable interpretation or to ignore them altogether. We are constrained to this harshness of language because of Mr. Dixon's flagrant disregard of prior decisions.

The rationale for remanding the case despite the fact that former Chairman Dixon's vote was not necessary for a majority is well established: Litigants are entitled to an impartial tribunal whether it consists of one man or twenty and there is no way which we know of whereby the influence of one upon the others can be quantitatively measured. . . .

We vacate the order of the Commission and remand with instructions that the Commissioners consider the record and evidence in reviewing the initial decision, without the participation of Commissioner Dixon.

NOTES AND QUESTIONS

1. *Disqualification for bias.* Under § 402(e) of the 2010 MSAPA, "A presiding officer or agency head acting as a final decision maker is subject to disqualification for bias, prejudice, financial interest, ex parte communications as provided in Section 408, *or any other factor that would cause a reasonable person to question the impartiality of the presiding officer or agency head.*" What is the meaning of the italicized language? Is it the same standard that is applicable to the disqualification of judges? A federal judge is disqualified "in any proceeding in which his impartiality might reasonably be questioned." 28 U.S.C. § 455(a). Should the standard for disqualifying administrative decisionmakers be the same as for disqualifying a judge?

2. *Personal interest.* An adjudicator is disqualified because of a "personal interest" in the case, meaning that the decisionmaker or her family has some kind of stake in the decision. In most cases, the personal interest is financial in nature. *See Tumey v. Ohio,* 273 U.S. 510 (1927). In *Tumey,* a judge was disqualified because he took his compensation from the fines he levied on defendants. *Tumey* was extended in *Ward v. Village of Monroeville,* 409 U.S. 57 (1972), which disqualified a small town mayor from serving as a traffic court judge. The fines went into the city treasury, not the mayor's pocket. However, the fines were a significant part of the town's budget; the more fines the mayor collected as traffic judge, the less taxes he would have to levy on his constituents. In *Ward,* unlike *Tumey,* the "personal interest" was political in nature rather than financial.

3. *Professional bias.* What if the decisionmakers *by profession* have a pecuniary interest? The Supreme Court disqualified an entire licensing agency for this reason. By law, a state optometry agency was composed solely of *independent* optometrists. The agency determined that optometrists would lose their licenses if they work for corporate employers (like Wal-Mart). The Court upheld a lower court's finding that the board members had a personal pecuniary interest in limiting entry into the field to independent optometrists like themselves and keeping corporate chain stores out. *Gibson v. Berryhill,* 411 U.S. 564 (1973). *Gibson* seems to ignore the rule of necessity, because it disqualified the agency from taking action against corporate optometry, even if that prohibition was otherwise desirable.

Later, the Court backed away from the broader implications of *Gibson.* It ruled that an optometry board consisting of a *majority* of independent optometrists was not invalid for all purposes. A bias for interest claim must be based on an analysis of the facts presented in a particular disciplinary proceeding. *Friedman v. Rogers,* 440 U.S. 1, 18–19 (1979). Perhaps the difference between the two cases is that *Gibson* was an as-applied challenge to a particular order of the board, while *Friedman* was a facial challenge that would have ousted the board from performing any of its regulatory functions. Or perhaps the Court was backing away from *Gibson.*

Would an independent optometrist sitting on a state board that disciplined corporate optometrists be disqualified if §402(e)(1) of the 2010 MSAPA were applicable? (See N.1).

4. *Campaign contributions.* The Supreme Court recognized an additional type of personal-interest bias in *Caperton v. A. T. Massey Coal Co., Inc.,* 556 U.S. 868 (2009). In *Caperton,* a West Virginia state trial court found that defendant Massey had committed fraud and awarded plaintiff Caperton $50 million in damages. The case was pending before the West Virginia Supreme Court. Blankenship, Massey's CEO, contributed $3 million to the campaign of Brent Benjamin, who was running against an incumbent for a spot on the Supreme Court. This amount dwarfed all of the contributions by other Benjamin supporters as well as by supporters of the incumbent. Benjamin won the election and cast the deciding vote in reversing the lower court judgment against Massey.

The Supreme Court decided that due process required Benjamin to recuse himself from deciding the Massey appeal, even though there was no evidence that Benjamin was biased against Caperton. Under the circumstances, where campaign contributions by a litigant to a judge have a significant and disproportionate influence in a judge's election, there is a serious and objective risk that the judge could be biased.

The *Caperton* case might have an impact on administrative law at the local level, because elected local officials often act as adjudicators, especially in land use disputes. Consequently, large campaign contributions to such officials by proponents of land development schemes might require the officials to disqualify themselves.

5. *Prejudgment.* Agency heads should believe strongly in the regulatory scheme they are charged with implementing. For that reason, they are legally entitled to have strong views about that scheme, including views on the interpretation of the law or policy. However, agency decisionmakers are disqualified if they have prejudged *adjudicative* facts (that is, facts specific to the parties that are critical to decision in the pending case). Whether the decisionmakers can be disqualified because of prejudgment of legislative facts (that is, facts that are not specific to the parties) is uncertain. Did Dixon's remarks quoted in *Cinderella* reflect prejudgment of adjudicative facts, as distinguished from legislative facts, law or policy?

Frequently a decisionmaker will be exposed to the facts of a case in the course of carrying out a regular agency function. A court is unlikely to find that statements about the case made when the decisionmaker is "in role" are evidence of prejudgment. Thus, for example, an ALJ who believes that a witness is dishonest is entitled to say so without being disqualified from the case and an ALJ who decides a case against a party is not disqualified from deciding it again after remand by the agency. *NLRB v. Donnelly Garment Co.,* 330 U.S. 219 (1947).

Similarly, a school board that conducts negotiations with a striking teachers' union is not disqualified from discharging teachers who participated in the illegal strike. *Hortonville Joint School District v. Hortonville Education Ass'n,* 426 U.S. 482 (1976). In *Hortonville*, the Court said: "Mere familiarity with the facts of a case gained by an agency in the performance of its statutory role does not, however, disqualify a decisionmaker . . ." It added: "Nor is a decisionmaker disqualified simply because he has taken a position, even in public, on a policy issue related to the dispute."

Can you distinguish *Cinderella, Texaco,* and *American Cyanamid* (the latter two cases are described in *Cinderella* and all three involved FTC Chairman Dixon) from *Donnelly Garment* and *Hortonville*?

6. *Personal animus.* Hostile comments by a judge or an agency decisionmaker normally do not establish personal animus, because the comments reflect adverse credibility or character judgments arising out of evidence introduced at the hearing. In order to disqualify the decisionmaker, the information giving rise to the animus must come from an "extrajudicial source" (that is, from events other than the trial or a previous trial) to trigger disqualification. *Liteky v. United States,* 510 U.S. 540 (1994). However, in an exceptional case, the decisionmaker might be disqualified by reason of personal animus arising from events occurring at a trial "if it is so extreme as to display clear inability to render fair judgment." *Id.* at 551.

Recently, appellate courts have reversed numerous immigration decisions because Immigration Judges (IJs) engaged in shoddy reasoning, because of abuses of official notice (see § 4.2.2), or because their comments were so extreme as to indicate animus against a litigant even though the information came from the hearing itself. For example, in *Wang v. Attorney General,* 423 F.3d 260 (3d Cir. 2005), Wang sought asylum because of forced sterilization of his wife under China's one-child policy. At the hearing and in her opinion, the IJ's comments reflected extreme hostility toward Wang. The IJ seemed fixated by the fact that Wang wanted to have a son and that he failed to care enough about his daughter who was disabled. For example, in her opinion, the IJ said that she was "comfortable denying asylum to the respondent as a matter of discretion because he's a horrible father as far as the Court's concerned because he pays no attention to his daughter." This demonstration of personal animus established that the IJ was biased against Wang (even though the information that led the IJ to her conclusions arose from evidence at Wang's hearing). In addition, this negative predisposition toward Wang severely undermined the IJ's finding concerning Wang's lack of credibility. The court remarked:

> Time and time again, we have cautioned immigration judges against making intemperate or humiliating remarks during immigration proceedings. . . . A disturbing pattern of IJ misconduct has emerged notwithstanding the fact that some of our sister circuits have repeatedly echoed our concerns. . . . That assurance [that a judge is not predisposed to find against a litigant] is

absent—and judicial conduct improper—whenever a judge appears biased, even if she actually is not biased. . . .

Nor were the IJ's editorial comments excused on the theory that her apparent bias arose in the course of the immigration hearing itself, rather than from an extrajudicial predisposition against Wang or all similarly situated asylum applicants. First, the IJ's comments seem related to her broader views about family obligations. Second, even if the IJ was reacting spontaneously to Wang's testimony, her attitude still may be characterized as "bias" or "prejudice" if her comments are so antagonistic or "so extreme as to display clear inability to render fair judgment. . . ."

[W]e are sorely disappointed that the IJ here chose to attack Wang's moral character rather than conduct a fair and impartial inquiry into his asylum claims. The tone, the tenor, the disparagement, and the sarcasm of the IJ seem more appropriate to a court television show than a federal court proceeding. But we hasten to emphasize that our concerns about the IJ's opinion are not limited to her choice of words. Substantively, many of the issues addressed by the IJ at length, and to which she gave substantial weight, were irrelevant to Wang's asylum . . . claims. . . . The IJ was not called upon to determine whether Wang was a good father and son.

7. *Agency publicity.* Agencies frequently issue press releases to inform the public about a pending investigation or the issuance of a complaint. The publicity warns consumers about a deceptive practice that the agency thinks may be injurious to them and may violate the law. In *Cinderella,* the court observed that the FTC had issued a press release at an earlier point in the case. In the first *Cinderella* case, the court held that a press release announcing that the FTC had "reason to believe" that Cinderella had violated the law did not evidence bias or prejudgment. Are the two *Cinderella* case consistent with each other?

Such pretrial publicity can be highly injurious to the entity being investigated. Even if the entity ultimately wins the case, the damage from the pre-trial publicity cannot be undone. *See generally* Ernest Gellhorn, *Adverse Publicity by Administrative Agencies,* 86 HARV. L. REV. 1380 (1973). In response to Gellhorn's study, ACUS recommended that agencies adopt published rules of policy and procedure concerning publicity of agency action. ACUS Recommendation 73–1, *Adverse Agency Publicity,* 38 Fed. Reg. 19,782 (1973). The rules should balance the need to serve the public interest while protecting persons affected by adverse publicity. In particular, publicity should be issued only if there is a significant risk that the public might suffer harm to its economic interests or its health or safety unless it is immediately notified of the pending case.

In a recent study, Cortez shows that Recommendation 73–1 has never been implemented and that adverse agency publicity remains a major problem. All efforts to challenge such publicity in court have failed. Today, adverse publicity is often distributed through agency websites as well as new media like podcasts, Facebook or Twitter. The announcements are instantly publicized world-wide, often with devastating effect on the stock price of the target companies. Nathan Cortez, *Adverse Publicity by Administrative Agencies in the Internet Era,* 2011 BYU L. REV. 1371. Adverse agency publicity is further discussed in connection with the Problem in § 4.1.2 N.8.

8. *Problem.* The Madison Agricultural Labor Board (MALB) adjudicates agricultural labor disputes. MALB's regulations require employers to allow unions to contact farm workers after hours to encourage them to join a union. MALB issues a complaint against farmer Smith for violating this regulation. Smith denies that he obstructed union organizers from contacting the workers. Smith's workers, like most Madison farm workers, are of Hispanic origin. MALB is swamped by its caseload and appoints temporary judges to hear some of its cases. It appoints a local lawyer, Jerry Perez, to hear the Smith case. Perez is of Hispanic origin and has represented farm worker unions in several cases. He has written three articles supportive of unionization of farm workers. Smith moves that Perez be disqualified as a judge but the MALB agency heads refuse to do so. Later, Perez finds that Smith violated the MALB regulation and imposed sanctions against Smith. The MALB agency heads affirm. Should a court reverse this decision on the ground that Perez was biased against Smith? *See Andrews v. Agric. Labor Relations Bd.*, 623 P.2d 151 (Cal. 1981).

§ 3.4   ADMINISTRATIVE JUDGES AND DECISIONAL INDEPENDENCE

In both federal and state agency adjudication, a single administrative judge normally makes a proposed decision. The head or heads of the agency make the final agency decision. There has been a longstanding controversy about whether to view administrative judges as real judges with independent status or as just one member of the agency's team. Answering this question brings us back to the fundamental conflict between the judicial and institutional models of adjudication. This subchapter explores that issue.

At the federal level, there is a distinction between administrative law judges (ALJs) and administrative judges (AJs). ALJs hear cases of *formal adjudication* governed by the APA (unless the statute specifically provides for some other arrangement). Although ALJs work for the agencies for which they decide cases, their independence is safeguarded by an elaborate web of statutory protections. These statutes relate to hiring of ALJs, their duties and assignment to cases, separation of functions within the agency, and the manner in which ALJs are evaluated, compensated, and discharged. Because of all these statutory protections of ALJ independence, the agencies that employ ALJs have little practical control over them.

However, this is far from the whole picture, because the APA does not cover a wide variety of hearings conducted by many federal agencies and required by statute. In common usage, all non-APA adjudication is referred to as "informal adjudication." As pointed out in § 3.1.1 N.5, this term is often a misnomer. Often, non-APA evidentiary hearings are conducted in just as *formal* a manner as the "formal adjudications" described by the APA. The difference is that the cases are heard by AJs whose independence is not protected by statute. Because agency officials dislike the statutory constraints relating to the hiring and evaluation of ALJs, many agencies induced Congress to take them out of the APA adjudication provisions altogether. The term "informal adjudication" should be reserved for the vast array of adjudicatory proceedings where no evidentiary hearing is required by statute. For discussion of an ABA recommendation to extend the APA's various procedural protections to hearings conducted by AJs (but without changing the AJs to ALJs), see § 3.1.1 N.6.

Traditionally, the states followed the federal model: administrative judges work for the agencies for which they decide cases. However, about half the states and several large cities have adopted a *central panel* model. Under a central panel, judges are not employed by agencies that are parties to pending cases. Instead the judges work for a separate agency consisting entirely of administrative judges. These judges are assigned as needed to agencies that wish to conduct hearings. Central panel judges normally write proposed decisions; the agency heads still make the final decisions. Even in central panel states, a number of agencies retain their own judges and their cases are not decided by the central panel. Legislation to adopt a federal central panel (often called an ALJ Corps) has frequently been introduced in Congress, but has never come close to passage. The following materials relate to the issue of decisional independence for administrative judges. Please consider these materials in light of the following questions:

•   Should there be any changes in the system by which federal ALJs are appointed and evaluated?

•   In Madison, each state agency employs its own administrative judges. You work for a legislator who is chair of the judiciary committee. That committee is responsible for changes in administrative procedure. Advise your boss about whether Madison should adopt a central panel system.

•   Another item on your boss' agenda concerns casino gambling. At present, the Gaming Board regulates gambling in Madison. It has three agency heads. The Board adopts regulations and issues casino licenses. It has power to revoke or suspend licenses or exclude casino managers with criminal records or ties to organized crime. The Board can also hear and decide cases brought by casino customers against the casinos. The agency heads review the decisions of Gaming Board AJs and often reverse them.

"Card counting" is a technique that expert blackjack players use to improve their odds at the gambling table. By keeping track of what cards have been played and increasing their bets when the odds are in their favor, these players can overcome the house advantage and often win large sums. Casinos in Madison have reacted by banning card counting. Several excluded players have filed complaints with the Gaming Board, but the Board's AJs have repeatedly held that casinos have the right to exclude players who engage in card counting. Their theory is that the casinos have a common law right to exclude anybody from their property.

The chair of the Board adopted an interpretive bulletin that prohibits the casinos from excluding card counters on the theory that the detailed Madison legislation relating to casinos preempts the common law right of exclusion. As a result, the Gaming Board AJs have changed their position and started following the interpretive bulletin.

The casino industry is urging the Legislature to crack down on the Gaming Board by adopting one or more of the following alternatives. Should the Legislature adopt any of them?

i)   The Gaming Board is prohibited from adopting guidance documents without following notice and comment rulemaking procedure under the Madison APA.

ii)   Assuming Madison adopts a central panel, ALJs from that panel will decide Gaming Board cases instead of the AJs that presently decide them.

iii)   An independent Gaming Court will review the decisions of the agency heads instead of such cases being decided by the general court system.

iv)   Gaming Board judges will make final agency decisions. The Agency heads will not have power to review their decisions. Cases decided by the judges will be directly reviewable in court.

§ 3.4.1 SELECTION AND INDEPENDENCE OF ALJS

ADMINISTRATIVE CONFERENCE OF THE UNITED STATES, THE FEDERAL ADMINISTRATIVE JUDICIARY
Recommendation 92–7, 57 Fed. Reg. 61,759 (1992)

[The federal APA originally provided for "hearing examiners." The examiners were later redesignated as "ALJs." Examiners were to be] impartial factfinders, with substantive expertise in the subjects relevant to the adjudications over which they preside, who would be insulated from the investigatory and prosecutorial efforts of employing agencies through protections concerning hiring, salary, and tenure, as well as separation-of-functions requirements. The decisions of such impartial factfinders were made subject to broad review by agency heads to ensure that the accountable appointee at the top of each agency has control over the policymaking for which the agency has responsibility.

The need for impartial factfinders in administrative adjudications is evident. To ensure the acceptability of the process, some degree of adjudicator independence is necessary in those adjudications involving some kind of hearing. The legitimacy of an adjudicatory process also depends on the consistency of its results and its efficiency. . . .

The number of ALJs in the Federal government has leveled off in the last decade, and has actually decreased outside of the Social Security Administration, but [the use of administrative judges (AJs) has increased. AJs are hearing officers who preside at adjudicatory hearings that are either not governed by the APA at all or are governed by the APA but are permitted by statute to use AJs rather than ALJs]. The amount of functional independence accorded to AJs varies with the particular agency and type of adjudication; however, AJs generally lack the statutory protections guaranteed to ALJs. . . . The movement away from the uniformity of qualifications, procedures, and protections of independence that derives from using ALJs in appropriate adjudications is unfortunate. . . . This movement away from ALJs toward AJs has been fueled by perceptions among agency management of difficulties in selecting and managing ALJs. . . .

Use of ALJs and AJs

There is no apparent rationale undergirding current congressional or agency decisions on the use of ALJs or non-ALJs in particular types of cases. . . . The uniform structure established by the APA for on-the-record hearings and for qualifications of presiding officers serves to provide a consistency that helps furnish legitimacy and acceptance of agency adjudication. . . . The Conference, therefore, recommends that Congress consider the conversion of AJ positions to ALJ positions in certain contexts. . . .

One critical factor is the nature of the interest being adjudicated. The separation of functions mandated by the APA, as well as the selection criteria designed to ensure the highest quality adjudicators, are of particular value in situations where the most important interests are at stake. [Hearings that might involve substantial impact on personal liberties or freedom, or those that might result in sanctions with a substantial economic effect or those involving discrimination under civil rights laws] represent categories of proceedings that may call for ALJ use. . . .

ALJ Selection

. . . The Office of Personnel Management (OPM) develops the criteria for selection, accepts applications for the register of eligibles, and rates the applicants. . . . The scores from this process determine an applicant's rank on the register of eligibles. . . . OPM rates and ranks eligibles on a scale from 70 to 100, and when an agency seeks to fill a vacancy, OPM certifies the top three names on the register to that agency [the so-called "rule of three"].

The Veterans' Preference Act . . . is applicable to selection of ALJs . . . Veterans are awarded an extra 5 points, and disabled veterans are awarded an extra 10 points in their scores. These extra points have had an extremely large impact, given the small range in unadjusted scores. In addition, under current law, agencies may not pass over a veteran to hire a nonveteran with the same or lower score on the certificate. As a consequence, application of the veterans' preference has almost always been determinative in the ALJ selection system. . . .

[T]he application of veterans' preference to the ALJ selection process has had a materially negative effect on the potential quality of the federal administrative judiciary primarily because it has effectively prevented agencies from being able to hire representative numbers of qualified women candidates as ALJs. There is also some evidence that application of the veterans' preference may have adversely affected the hiring of racial minorities. . . . [T]he Conference recommends that Congress abolish veterans' preference in the particular and limited context of ALJ selection. . . .

[In addition, ACUS recommends replacing the rule-of-three by allowing agencies to choose any applicant whose rankings placed them in the top 50% of all applicants.] [T]he Conference is attempting to balance two factors. The Conference recognizes the agencies' strong interest in having a substantially larger pool of qualified candidates from which to select ALJs who meet their varying criteria and needs. It also recognizes the importance of ensuring that such a pool is highly qualified, as measured by a uniform objective rating system. . . .

ALJ Evaluation and Discipline

At present, ALJs, virtually alone among Federal employees, are statutorily exempt from any performance appraisal. Although agencies may seek removal or discipline of ALJs "for good cause" by initiating a formal proceeding at the Merit Systems Protection Board (MSPB), the Board has applied standards that have strictly limited the contexts in which such actions may successfully be taken against an ALJ. For example, agency actions premised on low productivity have never been successful before the Board. . . .

The Conference . . . recommends that a system of review of ALJ performance be developed. Chief ALJs would be given the responsibility to coordinate development of case processing guidelines . . . These guidelines, which would address issues such as ALJ productivity . . . would be one of the bases upon which Chief ALJs would conduct regular . . . performance reviews. Judicial comportment and demeanor would be another basis for review. Another factor on the list of bases for performance review, which list is not intended to be exclusive, would be the existence of a clear disregard of, or pattern of nonadherence to, properly articulated and disseminated rules, procedures, precedents and other agency policy . . .

Recently, attention has been focused on allegations of prejudice against certain classes of litigants by some ALJs. While there is no known evidence that such a problem is widespread, the Conference's view is that it is important to have a mechanism for handling complaints or allegations relating to ALJ misconduct, including allegations of bias or prejudice . . .

NOTES AND QUESTIONS

1. *ACUS Recommendation 92–7.* The proposals in ACUS Recommendation 92–7 were never implemented. Indeed, federal ALJs (who are quite well organized) mounted a strenuous attack against them. In 1995, ACUS was defunded (in part because of the controversy over Recommendation 92–7) and disappeared from the scene until it was revived in 2009.

2. *Discharge of ALJs for low productivity.* As Recommendation 92–7 states, ALJs cannot be removed from office unless "good cause is established and determined by the Merit Systems Protection Board." 5 U.S.C. § 7521(a). The MSPB is an independent adjudicating agency that handles cases involving removal or other disciplinary action against all federal government employees protected by the civil service system. In cases of ALJ removal, the MSPB must employ an ALJ to hear the case (but AJs hear cases involving all other federal employees). MSPB decisions are judicially reviewed by the Court of Appeals for the Federal Circuit.

Although Recommendation 92–7 states that removals of ALJs based on low productivity have never been successful before the MSPB, this seems to have changed. MSPB recently upheld the removal of Richard Abrams, a Social Security ALJ in the Houston office who had a backlog of numerous undecided cases over three years old. The chief ALJ of the Houston office sent numerous memos to Abrams ordering him to clean up his backlog of old cases or explain why he had not done so. Abrams either ignored the memos or falsely stated that the cases were about to be decided. The Board determined that Social Security had established "good cause" for removing Abrams because his failure to decide the cases or respond to the memos "evidenced a neglect of his duties as an ALJ to provide prompt and orderly dispatch of public business."

The court of appeals upheld Abrams' dismissal. *Abrams v. Social Security Adm'n,* 703 F.3d 538 (Fed. Cir. 2012). The decision held that the agency could discharge an ALJ for failure to follow instructions, even without having first adopted performance standards for ALJs. The court stated that the dismissal did not interfere with Abrams' decisional independence or constitute a prohibited performance evaluation. The decisions by MSPB and the Court of Appeals in the *Abrams* case should greatly strengthen Social Security's hand in dealing with the problem of unproductive ALJs.

3.   *Discharge of ALJs for non-job related misconduct.* Can off-the-job misconduct justify removal of an ALJ under the "good cause" standard? Social Security ALJ Danvers Long was involved in a nasty case of domestic partner abuse. The MSPB found that he shoved and hit his domestic partner and pursued her through the neighborhood. He accidentally struck her child as well. The neighbors were involved and the police responded. Criminal charges against Long were dismissed.

The MSPB ALJ suspended Long for 45 days but MSPB ordered his removal. It held that good cause was established if an ALJ "undermines public confidence in the administrative adjudicatory process." It drew this standard from the ABA Model Code of Judicial Conduct. Because of the nature of the behavior and involvement of the police and the neighbors, Long's conduct undermined public confidence in the administrative adjudicatory process, even though it was completely unrelated to his job performance and received no press coverage. The Federal Circuit deferred to the MSPB's definition of the ambiguous term "good cause" and affirmed its decision. *Long v. Social Security Adm'n,* 635 F.3d 526 (Fed. Cir. 2011).

Does this standard permit an agency to sanction an ALJ for private behavior or personal lifestyle choices? Could it serve as cover to remove an ALJ whose decisions an agency head doesn't like? Judge Dyk's concurring opinion in *Long* expressed concern on this score. He called on the Board to articulate a standard for when off-duty actions may lead to workplace discipline and signaled that in future cases a failure to define the standard could trigger reversal of an MSPB decision removing an ALJ.

4.   *Presiding officers and agency policy.* The presiding officers (POs) in state and federal administrative adjudications (we are using the term POs to cover both ALJs and AJs) have decisional independence but they are less independent than judges. As noted above, in most cases (but not in all cases—*see* § 3.4.3), a PO conducts a hearing and writes a proposed decision. The agency head makes the final call on issues of law and policy and can override the PO's fact findings as well. See APA § 557(b), which provides that on agency head review, the head "has all the powers which it would have in making the initial decision." (There are some limits on the ability of the agency heads to second-guess PO determinations of witness credibility. See § 9.1.1 NN.3–4.)

Agencies often use the adjudication process to make or change determinations of policy. (We discuss adjudicatory policymaking further in §§ 5.1 and 6.2.) Although they are subordinate to the agency heads, POs can play an important role in the agency policy-making process by discussing legal and policy issues in their proposed decisions and criticizing existing agency policies. They can also build the record and make findings of legislative fact necessary to support agency policy determinations. *See* Charles H. Koch, Jr., *Policymaking by the Administrative Judiciary,* 56 ALA. L. REV. 693 (2005).

Nevertheless, POs must follow the precedents and rules set out by the agency heads even if they disagree with them (and even if they choose to criticize them). At least that is the view that ACUS expressed in Recommendation 92–7: "Where the agency has made its policies known in an appropriate fashion, ALJs and AJs are bound to apply them in individual cases. Policymaking is the realm of the agency, and the ALJ's (or AJ's) role is to apply such policies to the facts that the judge finds in an individual case."

The difficult issue is whether POs must follow what are called "guidance documents." As discussed in detail in § 6.1.4, guidance documents (such as rulings, policy statements, bulletins and similar materials) are "rules" as that term is defined in the APA. Such documents are adopted to furnish guidance to private parties and to the agency staff about legal interpretations or agency policies. Yet guidance documents lack the force of law. Under the federal system (but not the law of many states), guidance documents can be adopted without the notice and comment procedure required to adopt rules that have the force of law. POs often argue that they are not bound to follow guidance documents.

Asmussen v. Comm'r, N.H. Dep't of Safety, 766 A.2d 678 (N.H. 2000), maintains that POs must comply with agency policies expressed in guidance documents. The assistant commissioner of the state department of safety held a meeting with the "hearings examiners" who preside over drivers' license suspension hearings. The commissioner instructed the examiners that they had to admit hearsay evidence and ask questions of police officers to assist the state in meeting its burden of proof. He told the examiners to keep their hearings brief and not conduct them like courtroom trials. He cautioned them not to "act like judges." He followed up these instructions with a written memorandum. The assistant commissioner made it clear that these instructions were binding and that if the examiners disagreed with them, they could resign. He actually removed one recalcitrant examiner from conducting hearings until he could be "retrained."

In *Asmussen,* the New Hampshire Supreme Court held that the examiners must follow these instructions, even though they had not been formally adopted as agency rules, because the examiners were subordinate employees of the department of safety. "On issues of policy and legal interpretation, hearings examiners are subject to the direction of the agency by which they are employed, and their independence is accordingly qualified.

Influence ordinarily is not deemed improper *unless it is aimed at affecting the outcome of a particular proceeding." Id.* at 692–93 (emphasis added). For discussion, see Ronald M. Levin, *Administrative Judges and Agency Policy Development: The Koch Way*, 22 WM. & MARY BILL RTS. J. 407 (2013).

The 2010 MSAPA takes a different position on this issue. Section 311(e) provides: "A guidance document may be considered by a presiding officer or final decision maker in an agency adjudication, but it does not bind the presiding officer and the final decision maker in the exercise of discretion."

§ 3.4.2 CENTRAL PANELS

As stated in the introductory note to § 3.4, about half of the states and several major cities have adopted ALJ central panels. The 2010 MSAPA provides for a central panel in Article 6, but leaves the decision whether to adopt Article 6 to each state that adopts the Act.

Under a central panel system, agencies do not employ their own judges. Instead, an agency that wants to hold a hearing must arrange for a central panel ALJ to conduct the hearing and write a proposed decision. The agency heads have the power to review the central panel ALJ's decision and to substitute their own judgment on issues of law, fact and discretion for that of the ALJs. In the great majority of the cases, however, agency heads summarily affirm the ALJ decisions. (*But see* § 3.4.3 N.1, discussing the law in several states that strips the agency heads of decisionmaking power and allows central panel ALJs to make the final agency decision.) Even in states that have adopted a central panel, some agencies retain their own judges and are not required to use central panelists to decide their cases. This is particularly true for agencies whose cases are complex and time consuming and involve technical issues such as public utility ratemaking or environmental decisionmaking.

The primary advantage of the central panel approach is to enhance the perceived fairness of the adjudicatory system. Private parties are understandably concerned when the judge works for the agency against which they are litigating (and which often is prosecuting them for some sort of wrongdoing). They simply don't believe that such judges can act in an independent manner. In addition, central panels may be quite efficient. Suppose the state dental board conducts only a few hearings every year. If it has full-time AJs, the AJs would be idle most of the time. If it employs staff members with other responsibilities to serve as AJs when needed, these staff members may be inexperienced as judges and may carry over a prosecutor bias into the judging function. A central panel makes an experienced and independent judge available for the few hearings the dental board conducts.

In general, the state and local central panel systems are well accepted and function smoothly. No state that has adopted a central panel has gone back to the older model, and the legislature or executive branch of states typically expand rather than contract the number of agencies whose proposed decisions are made by the central panel ALJs. *See generally* James F. Flanagan, *An Update on Developments in Central Panels and ALJ Final Order Authority,* 38 IND. L. REV. 401 (2005), which cites the voluminous literature on the subject.

Nevertheless, there are substantial arguments against adoption of a central panel. These arguments have persuaded Congress as well as legislators in about half the states (including New York) not to adopt the central panel model. Of course, the failure of central panel proposals can also be attributed to the understandable reluctance of agency heads (or the state attorney general) to surrender control over any part of the adjudicatory process. But there are practical issues at stake in addition to turf protection. Agencies prefer the convenience of using their own staff members as presiding officers rather than having to schedule hearings by central panelists in competition against other agencies. If the panel is busy, it might be months before an ALJ is available at the time and place where the agency wants to conduct the hearing. In addition, the agency must pay for the services of the central panel judge which can create budgetary difficulties and deter the agency from bringing additional cases.

In the consultants' report that led to the adoption of ACUS Recommendation 92–7, Paul Verkuil and his co-authors made a forceful argument against a federal central panel. Do you find their arguments equally applicable to proposals for the adoption of a state central panel system?

PAUL VERKUIL ET AL., THE FEDERAL ADMINISTRATIVE JUDICIARY

Administrative Conference of the United States 773 (1992)

. . . Congress originally assigned adjudication of some types of disputes to Article I agencies rather than to Article III courts to further several goals: (1) to take advantage of specialized expertise; (2) to provide a less formal and less expensive means of resolving some types of disputes; (3) to attain a higher degree of interdecisional consistency in adjudicating disputes that arise in administering national regulatory and benefit programs; and (4) to allow agencies to control the policy components of administrative adjudications. Adoption of the Corps proposal would represent an abandonment of each of those goals in favor of an administrative adjudication system designed to replicate the Article III courts. . . .

We do not view that as a virtue, however. It would entail abandonment of the traditional goal of providing a less formal and less expensive means of resolving specialized classes of disputes with the government. Over time, the cost of administrative adjudication would move ever closer to the cost of judicial adjudication. The potential for increased costs attributable to adoption of the formal, judicial model of adjudication is enormous. Use of the judicial model of adjudication to resolve tort disputes creates a situation in which the dispute resolution process costs approximately fifty per cent of the total amount of money awarded as compensation. By contrast, the Social Security Administration spends only 3.7 per cent of its budget on administrative adjudication. Some of this enormous difference in cost is attributable to the somewhat different issues to be resolved in tort cases versus disability cases, but a substantial proportion of the difference is attributable to the greater procedural and evidentiary formality of judicial adjudication.

Proponents of the ALJ Corps are also candid in their rejection of the value of specialized expertise that is among the principal justifications for assigning adjudicatory functions to agencies rather than to Article III judges. . . . Rejection of specialized expertise as a justification for administrative adjudication would have major implications. Converting all ALJs (and potentially [AJs]) into generalist judges would impose major costs on the agency adjudicatory system in the form of lost expertise. ALJs preside in more than one hundred different types of adjudicatory disputes at scores of different agencies. AJs preside in another nearly one hundred different types of adjudicatory disputes at scores of other agencies. Each of the hundreds of regulatory and benefit programs in which ALJs participate are different and each is extremely complicated. A typical regulatory or benefit system can be understood only by mastering hundreds of pages of statutes and regulations, thousands of pages of judicial opinions, tens of thousands of pages of agency guidelines and decisions, and the principles of one or more disciplines other than law. . . .

§ 3.4.3 EXTERNAL SEPARATION OF FUNCTIONS

Another way to achieve adjudicatory impartiality is to strip prosecuting and investigating agencies of the adjudicating function and transfer that function to a separate agency engaged only in adjudication. In many countries, such as the UK and Australia, agencies virtually never do their own adjudication. That function is carried out by a separate tribunal. The tribunal might hear cases involving only a single agency (as in Canada) or all agencies (as in the UK or Australia).

This model exists in many states. For example, workers' compensation or unemployment compensation cases are typically heard by a body exclusively engaged in adjudication. At the federal level, the

U.S. Tax Court adjudicates tax cases and is completely separate from the Internal Revenue Service. Should this model be expanded to additional agencies—or to all of them?

NEWTON MINOW, LETTER TO PRESIDENT KENNEDY
15 ADMIN. L. REV. 146 (1963)

[On resigning as chair of the FCC, Newton Minow suggested that the adjudicatory functions of the FCC (and presumably of other federal regulatory agencies) be transferred to an independent administrative court. He also suggested that the multi-member FCC be replaced by a single administrator.] There are several advantages to assigning the hearing functions now exercised by the Commission to a new administrative court patterned, for example, after the Tax Court.

First, it is clearly desirable to separate the prosecutory function from the function of judging. An agency should not be called upon to investigate fully whether a violation has occurred, to become steeped in all kinds of investigative reports upon which it determines that a hearing is necessary, and then to judge the merits of the case. . . .

Second, the establishment of the administrative court would greatly improve the decisional process itself. . . . FCC Commissioners cannot spend several weeks analyzing the record of a case and drafting their own opinions . . . [Instead] the Commissioners determine the case largely upon the basis of the staff analysis and oral argument and adopt an institutional decision prepared by the staff. This may be a necessary process but it is clearly not an optimum one. [Under an administrative court structure] the decision-maker is wholly familiar with the record and pleadings and actually drafts his own opinion.

Finally, the administrative court will lead to better formulation of standards. Not only will the administrator be required to lay down definitive and clear policies, if the administrative court is to follow them, but the court could be expected to apply these policies in a meaningful manner which would build up a body of meaningful precedents. . . .

There is, however, one argument which does have some validity. It may be difficult, in practice, to confine the policy-making function to the administrator. The administrative court, in deciding particular cases, may find itself called upon to make policy or may take action which in the administrator's view is inconsistent with the policies he has established. In a division of responsibility such as this, there is always the possibility of some degree of friction between the administrator and the court. . . .

My purpose here has not been to present a detailed blueprint but rather to advance the principle of separation of regulatory and hearing functions, in the hope that as more voices declare for the principle, a serious study of it will be undertaken. I do not believe it is possible to be a good judge on Monday and Tuesday, a good legislator on Wednesday and Thursday, and a good administrator on Friday.

PAUL VERKUIL ET AL., THE FEDERAL ADMINISTRATIVE JUDICIARY

ADMINISTRATIVE CONFERENCE OF THE UNITED STATES 773 (1992)

The adjudicatory function can be placed in an institution that is independent of the agency that makes and enforces rules and policies. This institutional structure can increase the extent to which adjudicatory decisionmaking is insulated from potential sources of agency bias. Congress has chosen this institutional structure in three significant contexts—mine safety and health, occupational safety and health, and transportation safety. In each case, one agency makes all rules and enforcement decisions, while a second independent agency makes all adjudicatory decisions. . . . Various groups have urged general adoption of this institutional structure for all agency adjudication for decades.

The Administrative Conference conducted a study of this alternative in 1986. The study was unable to detect any improvement in adjudicatory decisionmaking attributable to the use of the independent adjudicating agency. It was able to document clear and significant costs and inefficiencies, however, attributable to lack of policy coordination, a high level of institutional conflict, frequent litigation between the two agencies, turf battles, and ambiguity with respect to the authority and responsibilities of the two agencies. . . .

NOTES AND QUESTIONS

1. *Making ALJ decisions final.* A noticeable trend in state administrative law is to make central panel ALJ decisions final, either eliminating or greatly curtailing the ability of the agency heads to alter an ALJ decision. The effect is to constitute ALJs as a separate administrative court. This structure prevents the agency heads from making policy through adjudication; they must set policy through rulemaking or not at all.

South Carolina led the way with its 1996 legislation, and variations of this approach have appeared in Louisiana, Texas, Florida, Oregon, and North Carolina. *See* James F. Flanagan, *An Update on Developments in Central Panels and ALJ Final Order Authority,* 38 IND. L. REV. 401 (2005); Jim Rossi, *Final but Often Fallible: Recognizing Problems with ALJ Finality,* 56 ADMIN. L. REV. 53 (2004).

Louisiana has gone further than other states by giving its central panel ALJs power to enter final orders in numerous areas of regulation. Moreover, in Louisiana, the agency has no power to seek judicial review of an ALJ decision against it. By stripping the agency heads *and the courts* of any power to review an ALJ decision, Louisiana has transferred enormous power to its central panel ALJs. The ALJs have the power to make unreviewable decisions of law, fact, policy, or discretion. An ALJ decision that construes the law in favor of a private party will be binding on the agency and will create a precedent for all other similar cases. The effect of a single ALJ decision could be to destroy or drastically impede an entire system of regulation. Yet an ALJ may well lack expertise in the area in which he or she is making a decision. The agency's only recourse in such a case is to seek an amendment of the statute from the legislature; it has no way to get to court.

The Louisiana Supreme Court upheld the constitutionality of the statute depriving the elected Insurance Commissioner of the right to seek judicial review of an ALJ decision against him. *Wooley v. State Farm Fire & Cas. Insurance Co.,* 893 So.2d 746, 768–70 (La. 2005). The Court held that the legislature could validly preclude the Commissioner from seeking judicial review. The *Wooley* decision hints (but without deciding) that the result might differ in the case of executive branch agencies not headed by an elected official. Precluding such agencies from seeking review of an ALJ decision might so impede the operation of the executive branch that the arrangement could be held invalid under separation of powers (*see* § 7.1).

The Court also suggested that the Insurance Commissioner could go to court in a separate declaratory judgment action, seeking a judicial interpretation of the statute that differed from the ALJ's interpretation. The decision in the separate declaratory judgment case could not change the result in the prior case decided by the ALJ, but it could change the way the statute is interpreted in all future cases, including those heard by ALJs.

In South Carolina, ALJs have power to make the final agency decision in many areas of regulation. In other cases, agency heads have review powers but cannot change an ALJ's fact finding if it was supported by substantial evidence. In Florida also, the agency heads cannot overturn an ALJ's fact findings if they are based on substantial evidence. In Texas, the agency heads lack power to overturn an ALJ's factual decision. In North Carolina, the agency heads cannot change an ALJ's fact finding unless the finding is "clearly contrary to the preponderance of the evidence." If the agency heads do overturn an ALJ fact finding under this standard, a reviewing court is not permitted to give any deference to the agency heads' decision and must find the facts for itself after a de novo review of the record. In Oregon, a similar pattern applies, but only with respect to "historic" facts (meaning fact findings concerning events that occurred before the hearing, as opposed to "predictive" facts, which are findings about what will happen in the future).

CHAPTER 4

THE PROCESS OF ADMINISTRATIVE ADJUDICATION

■ ■ ■

The previous chapter explored some fundamental and enduring problems of administrative adjudication. This chapter examines the elements of adjudication in chronological order, starting with the pre-hearing phase and exploring issues such as notice, parties, discovery and intervention. It continues with the hearing itself and the decisional process. It considers the effects of adjudicatory decisions (such as res judicata or stare decisis). It concludes with consideration of the degree to which the adjudicatory system must protect reliance interests. Thus this chapter might be likened to a civil procedure course—except that we consider adjudicatory procedure before an agency rather than in court.

§ 4.1 THE PRE-HEARING PHASE: NOTICE, INVESTIGATION AND DISCOVERY

§ 4.1.1 NOTICE AND PARTIES TO ADJUDICATION

BLOCK V. AMBACH
537 N.E.2d 181 (N.Y. 1989)

ALEXANDER, J.:

[Petitioner Ackerman was a licensed psychiatrist who co-founded and directed the Association for Counseling and Therapy (ACT). His license was revoked because of his alleged fraud, gross negligence, and incompetence in the practice of medicine. The charges were based on Ackerman's having induced] two of his patients (A and B) to engage in sexual intercourse with him, to engage in lewd conduct, and to use inappropriate drugs during time periods covering 26 months, 78 months, 46 months and 53 months. The charges against Block, a registered psychiatric nurse, were similar.

In the Ackerman case, thirty-five witnesses, including A, B and a third complainant, D, testified before a Hearing Panel of the State Board for Professional Medical Conduct. At this hearing, which continued over a period of some six years, petitioner denied that A, B and D were his patients or that he had engaged in sexual activity with any of them.

159

Instead, he claimed that the group sessions he led were merely gatherings of people engaged in the discussion of a variety of topics and did not involve any form of psychotherapy treatment.

The Panel found, inter alia, that A and B were petitioner's patients; that petitioner had conducted private sessions with A "on or about the year 1973," and "on numerous occasions" instigated and participated in sexual activities involving that patient; that he had sexual relations with her on a particular day when petitioner's wife was engaged in a radio broadcast; and that A had sexual intercourse and oral sex with petitioner "on approximately 25 occasions." With only minor exceptions, the Panel sustained the charges against petitioner and recommended permanent revocation of his license and a $25,000 fine . . . [The Regents Review Committee upheld the Panel's determination in both the Ackerman and Block cases.]

Ackerman similarly argues that the charges against him cannot be sustained because he was deprived of due process in that the charges spanned a period of more than six years without indicating any specific dates of the alleged misconduct, and, moreover, no witness was able to testify as to any specific dates on which any of the alleged acts took place. He contends that he was thus deprived of the ability to assert an alibi defense or to produce contrary evidence. . . .

It is axiomatic that due process precludes the deprivation of a person's substantial rights in an administrative proceeding because of uncharged misconduct and it necessarily follows, therefore, that a respondent in such a proceeding is entitled to fair notice of the charges against him or her so that he or she may prepare and present an adequate defense and thereby have an opportunity to be heard . . . The [Education Code] requires that a statement of administrative charges contain "a short and plain statement of the matters asserted."

It does not follow, however, that the due process requirements for the specificity of an indictment in a criminal proceeding are to be imported and fully applied in administrative proceedings. Unlike the provisions of the . . . APA, the Criminal Procedure Law requires that "[an] indictment must contain . . . [a] statement in each count that the offense charged therein was committed on, or on or about, a designated date, or during a designated period of time." . . .

[T]he consequences of a criminal proceeding are palpably more grave and justify a requirement of greater specificity. Moreover, criminal indictments must also be sufficiently specific to allow the accused, if convicted, to assert the defense of double jeopardy in subsequent prosecutions for the same conduct. Because administrative proceedings entail neither the dire consequences of criminal prosecutions nor the considerations of double jeopardy, there is generally no need to import the strict requirements of the criminal law and criminal trials into administrative proceedings. We hold, therefore, that in the administrative forum, the charges need only be reasonably specific, in light of all the relevant circumstances, to apprise the party whose rights are being determined of the charges against him for the preparation of an adequate defense.

In the circumstances of these administrative proceedings therefore, we reject petitioners' contentions that the general time periods alleged in the administrative charges against them violate due process . . . Much of the misconduct charged in both *Block* and *Ackerman* was capable of being committed through either a single act or multiple acts and therefore may properly be characterized as continuing offenses . . .

Furthermore, the other relevant circumstances in each case indicate that the general time periods alleged afforded both petitioners reasonable notice of the charges against them and enabled them to prepare and present adequate defenses. . . . Petitioner admitted conducting the group sessions during which much of the misconduct was alleged to have occurred and never sought to interpose an alibi defense for any particular incident. Instead, he denied the allegations of improper conduct and also contended that he could not be subject to discipline because the complainants were not his patients. Petitioner advanced these defenses at a comprehensive hearing which lasted over six years and entailed the testimony of 35 witnesses. In these circumstances, we cannot say that he was denied due process. [AFFIRMED.]

NOTES AND QUESTIONS

1. *Six years?* The *Block* opinion is unclear as to whether Ackerman was allowed to continue practicing during the incredibly long six-year period occupied by the Panel's hearing process, not to mention the additional years consumed by an administrative appeal and litigation through three levels of the New York courts.

As discussed in § 2.3 N.3, a licensing agency normally has power to suspend a licensee from practice during the pendency of the hearing process if the licensee poses a threat to the public. *See* 2010 MSAPA § 407; 1961 MSAPA § 14(c). However, this authority is often not utilized. As discussed in § 11.2.3 N.5, courts have authority to stay administrative action pending judicial review. Courts often grant such stays, since judicial review would not be very meaningful to the licensee if he is already out of business. Hence, it is possible that Ackerman went on practicing right up until the 1989 decision of the New York Court of Appeals, even though some of the acts charged occurred twenty years before that decision.

2. *Statute of limitations.* Ackerman's misconduct occurred between 1969 and 1975. Suppose the Board didn't start proceedings against him until 1985. Should there be any statute of limitations in this type of case?

Undoubtedly criminal charges or tort actions against Ackerman would be long since barred by limitations, but licensing statutes often do not include statutes of limitation. Typically, courts do not transplant limitation provisions applicable to judicial action into the administrative sphere. *See BP America Production Co. v. Burton*, 549 U.S. 84 (2006) (refusing to apply the six-year statute of limitations applicable when government sues to recover mineral royalties to administrative recovery of mineral royalties). Federal law does, however, include some default limitations periods that apply in administrative cases, including a five-year statute of limitations for enforcement suits *by* the government, 28 U.S.C. § 2462, and a six-year statute of limitations for suits *against* the government. 28 U.S.C. § 2401. Specific statutes can, of course, override these default provisions.

Sexual misconduct like that in *Block* often is not discovered by authorities until many years after the events in question. Thus there is good reason not to have a statute of limitations on license revocations. Yet the cases often involve credibility conflicts. The time lapse can pose substantial problems for the licensee's defense, because by then memories are fuzzy, witnesses have vanished or died, and it is difficult to disprove the charges.

Absent a statute of limitations, a court might overturn administrative action on the basis of laches, if a licensee can show that the delay was *both* unreasonable and caused prejudice. Unreasonable delay could be shown if the agency failed to take action within a reasonable time after obtaining the necessary information. Prejudice could be shown if the delay caused witnesses to be unavailable or otherwise made the defense more difficult. *See Lam v. Bureau of Security and Investigative Services*, 40 Cal.Rptr.2d 137 (Cal. App. 1995) (inadequate showing of prejudice). In Texas, only prejudice is required, not unreasonable delay. *See Granek v. Texas State Bd. of Med. Exam.*, 172 S.W.3d 761, 771–76 (Tex. App. 2005). In *Granek,* a charge that physician touched the breasts of one patient 13 years before charges were filed was barred by laches. However, a charge that he touched the breasts of a second patient six years before charges were filed was not barred, since she had raised the issue with him immediately, thus making it easier for both Granek and the second patient to remember the events in question.

3.   *Notice.* Due process requires the government to make a reasonable effort to give notice to a person who is to be deprived of liberty or property. In *Dusenbery v. United States,* 534 U.S. 161 (2002), the Court held that the adequacy of notice of an administrative forfeiture of the assets of a person convicted of drug dealing would not be determined under *Mathews v. Eldridge* balancing. Instead, the test is whether the notice is "reasonably calculated under all of the circumstances to apprise" the individual of the action. The Court held that sending a certified letter to a prisoner met that test, even though the prison apparently lost the letter and the prisoner did not actually receive it. On the other hand, if the certified letter is returned to sender and marked "unclaimed," the state must take "additional reasonable steps to attempt to provide notice . . . if it is practicable to do so." *Jones v. Flowers,* 547 U.S. 220 (2006).

Due process actually requires two different forms of notice. In this § 4.1.1, we discuss the agency's obligation to furnish notice about the charges in the case that is sufficiently detailed to enable a private party to prepare for the hearing. In addition, due process also requires that the legal standard under which a person is charged must furnish notice of what conduct is prohibited. The standard must be clear enough so that ordinary people can conform their behavior to it. The void for vagueness requirement is discussed in § 4.5.1.

All APAs require notice of pending adjudicatory action that informs the private party of the matters of fact and law asserted (as well as the time, place and nature of the hearing and the legal authority for the hearing). See APA § 554(b). However, neither the APAs nor due process require the agency to give notice of specific details such as the dates on which misconduct occurred. Instead, for example, 2010 MSAPA requires only a "short and plain statement of the matters asserted, including the issues involved." § 405(c)(2). Why did Ackerman claim that the notice should have included the dates? Why did the Medical Board not give notice of the dates?

Block indicates that the strict requirements of notice in criminal cases do not apply to licensing cases. Do you agree that "administrative proceedings entail neither the dire consequences of criminal prosecutions nor the considerations of double jeopardy?" Few criminal cases involve a sanction more dire than revocation of a physician's license and a $25,000 fine. And even though double jeopardy protection does not apply to civil cases, res judicata and collateral estoppel do apply. See § 4.4.1. If, for example, patient A sued Ackerman in tort for sexual misconduct, the Medical Board decision could preclude Ackerman from denying that the misconduct occurred.

Bd. of Regents of the Univ. of Wisconsin v. State Personnel Comm'n, 646 N.W.2d 759 (Wisc.2002), provides an example of insufficient notice. In this case, the University fired B, a campus police officer, for telling racist jokes at work. The State Personnel Commission reversed the University's decision because B stopped telling the jokes after being warned to do so.

Then the Commission had to decide the amount of back pay owed to B during the period between his discharge and reinstatement. On this issue, the University tried to introduce new evidence it had discovered of a separate offense for which B could have been fired (taking confidential files home). As a result, the University claimed, it did not owe B backpay after the date it could have fired him for the separate offense. The Commission refused to allow introduction of this evidence, and the Wisconsin Supreme Court affirmed.

The Court held that the Commission correctly excluded this evidence because B had received no notice that he might be penalized for the offense of taking confidential files home. Failure to give such notice violated both due process and the state civil service law. The dissenting judge argued that B had not been "ambushed" by the introduction of this evidence, since the parties had been arguing over return of the documents well before the back pay hearing. B assumed he would be sued in a separate action to return the documents and was surprised that the issue came up in his back pay hearing. The dissent argued that B's interests could have been protected if a brief continuance had been granted, so he could have prepared his rebuttal to the after-acquired evidence if he had one. Who has the better of this argument, the majority or dissent?

4. *Forcing a hearing.* Suppose that after investigating the charges against Ackerman, the Medical Board decided *not* to take any action. Can A, the victim of Ackerman's misconduct, force the Board to hold a hearing? This might be referred to as a right of private prosecution or a right of initiation. Aside from seeking personal vindication or wanting to protect other innocent victims, why would A seek a private prosecution? Why would Ackerman and the Medical Board resist a private prosecution?

The same issue arises frequently in cases involving applications for licenses or land use permission. An agency might grant an application for a license or a zoning variance without a hearing. Can persons who want the application to be denied force the agency to hold a hearing? For example, Bob might seek a zoning variance to build a guest house to rent out. Carmen, who is Bob's neighbor, opposes the application because she wants the neighborhood to remain entirely occupied by one family per lot. The zoning board grants Bob's application without a hearing and denies Carmen's request for a hearing.

Generally third parties like A (the victim in *Block*) or Carmen (the disgruntled neighbor) do not have power to compel an agency to initiate a law enforcement proceeding against a third party absent some statute providing such a power. In general, whether to undertake enforcement is within the agency's discretion. *See Heckler v. Chaney*, § 10.5, which held that a prisoner on death row who faced execution by lethal injection could not compel the Food & Drug Administration to take action against use of the drugs for this unapproved purpose. However, statutes that provide a right of initiation are not uncommon. For example, a number of state and local statutes entitle community members who object to a liquor license application or a land use application to require the granting agency to hold a hearing before granting the application. And the Communications Act provision discussed in *United Church of Christ* in N.5 confers initiation rights on consumers.

A related issue is whether third parties can bring an independent action in court against a wrongdoer to enforce legal rights created by a statute when that statute appears to give enforcement rights only to an agency. Such rights are called "private rights of action." The issue boils down to whether the Legislature wanted private enforcement in addition to administrative enforcement. We discuss private rights of action in § 11.2.5 N.4.

5. *Intervention.* Most cases—judicial and administrative—are initially contests between two parties. Sometimes, a third party wants to join the case and take part in the litigation, because the third party believes that the decision will affect its legal interests and the parties to the case will not

protect that interest. We refer to the process of becoming a party to ongoing litigation as "intervention." Fed. R. Civ. Proc. 24 governs intervention in civil cases and distinguishes between intervention as of right (when an intervenor claims that the decision in the case may impede its ability to protect its interests) and permissive intervention (when an intervenor has a claim or defense that is also involved in the pending litigation).

Suppose that the medical board decides to charge Ackerman with violations of the Medical Practice Act. A, who claims to be one of Ackerman's victims, feels that the board's attorneys are doing a poor job and wishes to intervene. Why would A want to intervene? Is there some way short of intervention by which A could make her position known? *See* APA § 555(b) (third sentence).

Why would Ackerman and the Board resist intervention? *See* Richard A. Manso, Comment, *Licensing of Nuclear Power Plants: Abuse of the Intervention Right,* 21 U.S.F. L. REV. 121 (1986). According to the Comment, in one nuclear licensing case, intervenors filed 1600 allegations—all of which were ultimately rejected. Intervention greatly prolonged the licensing process, and the delays caused serious increases in the cost of the power plant. Among the 25 most recently licensed nuclear plants, the length of time from filing the application through issuance of the license ranged from 11.5 to 24.7 years, in part because of delays caused by intervenors. *See* David A. Repka & Tyson R. Smith, *Proximity, Presumptions, and Public Participation: Reforming Standing at the Nuclear Regulatory Commission,* 62 ADMIN. L. REV. 583 (2010).

Federal cases involving administrative intervention sometimes link that issue to a different one: standing to seek judicial review of an adverse adjudicative decision, an issue discussed in § 11.1. In *United Church of Christ (UCC) v. FCC,* 359 F.2d 994 (D.C. Cir. 1966), the issue was whether TV watchers have a right to initiate and to participate in FCC licensing proceedings. Thus the case involves issues of a right of initiation and a right of intervention. African-American TV watchers in Jackson, Miss., protested the renewal of WLBT's license because the station engaged in racist programming. The FCC proposed to renew the license without a hearing and it denied the listeners' petition to hold a hearing and to intervene. The statute allowed intervention by a "party in interest," but the FCC thought that only economic competitors of the station qualified as parties in interest.

In *UCC,* the court assumed that the same legal standard applied to the issues of whether viewers had standing to initiate and intervene in a license renewal proceeding and standing to seek judicial review. However, the court's fundamental reason for compelling the FCC to allow viewers standing to initiate and intervene was based on concern about the FCC's weak enforcement of the interests of viewers. "The theory that the Commission can always effectively represent the listener interests in a renewal proceeding without the aid and participation of legitimate listener representatives fulfilling the role of private attorneys general is one of those assumptions we collectively try to work with so long as they are reasonably adequate. When it becomes clear, as it does to us now, that it is no longer a valid assumption which stands up under the realities of actual experience, neither we nor the Commission can continue to rely on it. The gradual expansion and evolution of concepts of standing in administrative law attests that experience rather than logic or fixed rules has been accepted as the guide." Incidentally, the decision was written by Warren Burger, who later became Chief Justice of the U.S. Supreme Court.

A subsequent case undermines *UCC* by breaking the link between standing to intervene and to seek judicial review. *See Envirocare of Utah, Inc. v. NRC*, 194 F.3d 72 (D.C. Cir. 1999). Envirocare had a Nuclear Regulatory Commission license to process radioactive waste. It feared that the NRC would give its competitor Quivira a new license to process radioactive waste but would impose fewer safeguards on Quivira than the Commission had imposed on Envirocare. As a result, Envirocare sought to intervene in Quivira's licensing proceeding.

The statute provides that the NRC "shall grant a hearing upon the request of any person whose *interest may be affected* by the proceeding, and shall admit any such person as a party to such proceeding." The NRC refused to allow Envirocare to intervene in the Quivira proceeding, regardless of whether Envirocare would have standing to seek judicial review of the NRC's decision (whether Envirocare would have had judicial review standing was disputed). The NRC interpreted the term "interest" to cover only those persons who are concerned with the health and safety effects of granting the license, not economic competitors. It feared that intervention by competitors "could readily burden our adjudicatory process with open-ended allegations designed not to advance public health and safety but as a dilatory tactic to interfere with and impose costs upon a competitor. Such an abuse of our hearing process would significantly divert limited agency resources, which ought to be squarely—genuinely—focused upon health and safety concerns."

The court upheld the NRC's decision. It stated that the term "interest" is ambiguous. The word could include any person who had any kind of interest in the proceeding (even a purely academic one), or it could mean any person who would have standing to seek judicial review of the NRC's decision, or it could mean any person concerned with economic or environmental harm that might be caused by an NRC decision involving some other person.

Under *Chevron*, discussed in §§ 3.1.1 and § 9.2.2, a court must accept reasonable agency interpretations of ambiguous statutory language. Since the court thought that NRC's interpretation of the ambiguous word "interest" was reasonable, the court felt compelled to accept it. It suggested that *UCC* and several similar cases were decided prior to *Chevron* and thus were not controlling. The reasoning of the *Envirocare* decision is similar to that in *Dominion* (§ 3.1.1), which gave *Chevron* deference to an agency's interpretation of the word "hearing" for purposes of determining whether the APA adjudication provisions applied.

As *Envirocare* shows, the issues of standing to seek judicial review and intervention in an administrative proceeding need not be linked. For example, a party who *lacks* standing to seek judicial review might still be allowed to intervene. *Koniag, Inc. v. Andrus,* 580 F.2d 601 (D.C. Cir. 1978) (party can be both "interested" and "aggrieved" for intervention purposes, even though lacking standing to sue because its claim was too speculative); *Legal Envtl. Assistance Found., Inc. v. Clark,* 668 So.2d 982 (Fla. 1996) (conservation group properly intervened to oppose utility construction but lacked standing to appeal the result). Indeed, contrary to *Envirocare,* it would seem that it should be *easier* to intervene in an ongoing administrative case than to trigger judicial review of an administrative decision that otherwise might not get to court at all.

6.   *Problem.* You are general counsel of a state agency (the Coastal Commission) that grants permits for the development of beachfront property. Without such a permit, owners of beachfront property cannot build on their property or even make changes to existing buildings.

The agency heads are concerned that a large number of persons sometimes ask to be parties to permitting hearings. These are persons who do not live near the beach but are interested in securing access to the beach for the general public or in preventing building projects at the beach. Until now, the Commission allowed anyone who applied to be a party. The result is that a few hearings became quite complicated. Each party wanted to put on its own witnesses, introduce its own economic and environmental analyses, and cross-examine the witnesses of other parties.

Do you advise the agency heads to prohibit intervention? To encourage it? To allow it but impose conditions? What conditions?

§ 4.1.2 INVESTIGATION AND DISCOVERY: AGENCY POWER TO OBTAIN INFORMATION

In order to enforce the law, an agency must secure massive amounts of information about the industry it regulates. The information is needed for a variety of tasks, such as preparation of proposed rules or legislative proposals or investigating possible violations of the law that might lead to enforcement action.

Most of the needed information is supplied voluntarily in periodic reports or in response to requests for information. The burdens of preparing required paperwork (such as tax returns or reports on various kinds of business transactions) are quite substantial and in the aggregate consume billions of hours and hundreds of billions of dollars each year. Nevertheless, various kinds of government programs cannot function without paperwork (imagine the IRS trying to collect income taxes without requiring people to file tax returns). The Paperwork Reduction Act of 1980 (PRA), 44 U.S.C. §§ 3501–3520, imposes some controls on agency decisions to require paperwork. The Office of Information and

Regulatory Affairs (OIRA) in the Office of Management and Budget (OMB) is authorized to disapprove agency demands for paperwork as unnecessary or to require that agencies collaborate in seeking information to avoid duplicative demands. (Other functions exercised by OIRA and OMB are discussed in greater detail in §§ 5.8 and § 7.6.)

Occasionally, an agency must compel disclosure of information. It does so through a *subpoena duces tecum*. Such subpoenas are sometimes called "civil investigative demands" or CIDs. An agency may also engage in *physical inspections* of homes or businesses. With respect to agency investigations, read APA §§ 555(c) and (d) and 556(c)(2). The key point is that agencies need a statutory basis other than the APA in order to compel the production of information. It is not an inherent power.

CRAIB V. BULMASH
777 P.2d 1120 (Cal. 1989)

EAGLESON, J.:

[Craib, the Labor Commissioner, is investigating Bulmash's alleged failure to pay minimum wages to caretakers of his sister Serena. Craib served a subpoena on Bulmash directing him to appear at the Santa Barbara office and produce records showing the names, addresses, and wages of all of Serena's caretakers for the last three years. The statute requires employers to maintain these records. Bulmash failed to appear so Craib filed a petition in court seeking to enforce the subpoena. The lower court quashed the subpoena on both Fourth and Fifth Amendment grounds.]

A.   FOURTH AMENDMENT

The Commissioner essentially concedes that the instant subpoena fails to comply with literal Fourth Amendment requirements for a criminal warrant . . . He insists, however, that judicial enforcement of the subpoena is constitutionally permissible under a standard which is less exacting than that required for a search in a criminal prosecution. Based on a recent line of cases by the United States Supreme Court, we agree.

As Bulmash suggests, it was once assumed that the compulsory production of records was a "search and seizure" in the literal Fourth Amendment sense and that subpoenas, like warrants, were enforceable only if issued pursuant to a formal "complaint" or at least upon probable cause to suspect "a specific breach of the law." However, it is now clear that such a restrictive view of the administrative process is not constitutionally compelled. As regulatory schemes have become increasingly important in enforcing laws designed to protect the public's health and welfare, reliance on "probable cause" as a means of restraining agency subpoena power has all but disappeared.

The Commissioner correctly argues that the leading case is *Oklahoma Press Pub. Co. v. Walling*, 327 U.S. 186 (1946). There, the Supreme Court rejected a Fourth Amendment challenge to judicial orders enforcing administrative subpoenas for payroll and sales records. The subpoenas were issued by the federal wage and hour administrator to determine whether certain publishing corporations were covered under, and had violated, the Fair Labor Standards Act of 1938 (FLSA). At the outset, the court observed that "no question of actual search and seizure" is raised where the agency has not sought "to enter [the subpoenaed parties'] premises against their will, to search them, or to seize or examine their books, records or papers without their assent, otherwise than pursuant to orders of court authorized by law and made after adequate opportunity to present objections . . ." The court further questioned whether the Fourth Amendment applied at all to the subpoenas at bar, noting that corporate records historically had been subject to the government's "broad visitorial power."

Accordingly, *Oklahoma Press* articulated a test which applied Fourth Amendment requirements only by analogy. The notion that a subpoena could be enforced only where a specific charge or complaint is pending was explicitly rejected. Instead, said the court, the investigation need only be for "a lawfully authorized purpose, within the power of [the legislative body] to command." In addition, the requirement of " 'probable cause, supported by oath or affirmation,' literally applicable in the case of a warrant," is satisfied as long as the subpoenaed documents are "relevant" to the inquiry. "Beyond this the requirement of reasonableness, including particularity in 'describing the place to be searched, and the persons or things to be seized,' also literally applicable to warrants, comes down to specification of the documents to be produced adequate, but not excessive, for the purposes of the relevant inquiry." In a later case, the court emphasized that, while the subpoena may be issued and served by the agency, the subpoenaed party must have the opportunity for judicial review before suffering any penalties for refusing to comply. . . .

[W]e apply the same test of "reasonableness" here. The instant record reveals no official action beyond issuance and service of the subpoena. The subpoena itself does not authorize actual entry or immediate inspection, but merely requests future production of specific records at the Commissioner's office in another city. Thus, Bulmash cannot insist upon a showing of probable cause.

To the extent Bulmash properly challenges the breadth and relevance of the subpoena, these claims are not well taken. There is no dispute, of course, that the Commissioner is entitled to investigate the type of alleged wage-order violations at issue here and that such investigations are within the power of the Legislature to command. The instant subpoena described the targeted records with particularity, and sought only those records which the Commissioner could minimally expect would be available in light of pertinent record keeping requirements. Bulmash does not suggest, nor do we find, that these requirements facially impose an unreasonable burden on employers subject to their terms. . . .

Bulmash nonetheless relies on cases upholding a form of "warrant" requirement for administrative inspections of residential and commercial property. See, e.g., *Marshall v. Barlow's, Inc.*. 436 U.S. 307 (1978). Even in these cases, however, the "probable cause" necessary for an administrative warrant is less stringent than that required in criminal cases. And [the *Barlow's* test] turned upon the effort of the government inspectors to make "nonconsensual entries into areas not open to the public. [Where] no such entry is made . . . the enforceability of [an] administrative subpoena duces tecum . . . is governed, not by our decision in *Barlow's* but rather by our decision in *Oklahoma Press*." Hence, Bulmash's reliance on inspection cases is misplaced.

Finally, Bulmash seeks to distinguish the cases cited by the Commissioner on grounds that they all involve corporate records. He suggests that the rules developed for administrative subpoenas were based in part on the state's traditional "visitorial power" over corporations. Hence, he reasons, these cases do not alter the criminal probable cause standard where, as here, "private household records" of an "individual" are involved. . . .

We decline to limit *Oklahoma Press* in the manner urged by Bulmash. The documents contain information presumably accumulated in the ordinary course of business, and uniformly requested of employers. . . . It would be anomalous to prevent the Division from enforcing lawful wage and hour provisions through use of its authorized subpoena power solely because the employer possessing such records is an "individual," rather than a corporation or large business. . . . In any event, we agree with the Commissioner that no Fourth Amendment "privacy" claim can be asserted against an administrative subpoena limited to the production of records which the subpoenaed party is required to maintain, for the express purpose of agency inspection, under lawful statutes or regulations. . . .

B. FIFTH AMENDMENT

Bulmash argues that, since the instant records could facially disclose noncompliance with wage and hour laws, the Fifth Amendment is a complete defense to court-ordered compliance with the subpoena. He insists that all prerequisites for asserting the privilege are present, i.e., he is an individual who has been statutorily compelled to make incriminating statements[14] which the Division could conceivably use as a basis for imposing civil and/or criminal penalties. . . .

The Commissioner counters that the privilege simply does not apply where, as here, the subpoenaed records are required to be kept pursuant to this kind of lawful regulatory scheme. He relies on a line of cases beginning with *Shapiro v. United States*, 335 U.S. 1 (1948).

[*Shapiro* involved a prosecution for violation of price control laws. The government subpoenaed business records that the law required Shapiro to maintain. The Court rejected a Fifth Amendment claim for records that are required to be kept in order to enforce regulatory schemes. *Shapiro* was limited by *Marchetti v. United States*, 390 U.S. 39 (1968). In *Marchetti*, a statute required gamblers to maintain business records; the court held that the Fifth Amendment applied to these records because they were directed to a selective group inherently suspect of criminal activities. *Shapiro*, which involved an essentially non-criminal and regulatory area of inquiry, was distinguishable.]

The [*Shapiro*] approach leads us to reject Bulmash's Fifth Amendment challenge to judicial enforcement of the Commissioner's subpoena. As contemplated by *Shapiro*, the information [demanded here] is the "appropriate" subject of a lawful regulatory scheme. The reporting law is obviously intended to encourage voluntary compliance with minimum labor standards designed for the mutual benefit of employees and employers. Such standards are enforced, not with an aim to punish, but to "ensure employees are not required or permitted to work under substandard unlawful conditions, and to protect employers who comply with the law from those who attempt to gain competitive advantage at the expense of their workers. . . ."

[REVERSED]

MOSK, J., dissenting: . . . I cannot join the [majority] in importing the questionable federal required-records exception into our state constitutional privilege against self-incrimination. Once again, the majority have construed the state constitutional privilege against self-incrimination narrowly and begrudgingly, treating it as a historic relic to be, at most, merely tolerated. I dissent because the fundamental protections afforded by the California Declaration of Rights are more than

---

[14] It is well settled that a person can assert the privilege only to prevent "being incriminated by his own compelled testimonial communications." The contents of subpoenaed business records which have been *voluntarily* prepared are not privileged, because they were not made under compulsion. *United States v. Doe*, 465 U.S. 605 (1984). . . . Bulmash also insists that producing the records under compulsion of the subpoena constitutes an incriminating, testimonial, and privileged act . . . because it "tacitly concedes" that the papers exist; that the subpoenaed party possesses them; and that they are authentic. However [Doe] made clear that the court was not referring to statutorily "required records . . ." And no high court case specifically addressing required records has distinguished between their *contents* and the *act* of production for purposes of determining whether the privilege applies.

mere antiquities which can be readily discarded in favor of the more limited protections provided by federal authority.... [I]t is incontrovertible that the California Constitution is, and always has been, a document of independent force which is the first line of protection for the individual against the excesses of state officials. . . .

In an effort to safeguard this fundamental privilege, we have traditionally resolved the conflict between the state's desire to obtain information and the individual's right to be free from self-incrimination by providing the individual with use immunity for any self-incriminating statements made in a civil or administrative proceeding. Such an accommodation is eminently reasonable in this case, and Bulmash should be ordered to comply with the subpoena only if he is assured that the People will not use the material he is requested to produce as evidence against him in any subsequent criminal prosecution. Use immunity would protect Bulmash's privilege against self-incrimination without impairing the Labor Commissioner's effective enforcement of the Labor Code. . . .

The defendant in a criminal trial "has an absolute, unqualified right to compel the State to investigate its own case, find its own witnesses . . . and convince a jury through its own resources." Rather than creating exceptions to that basic right, I believe that if Bulmash is to be prosecuted for violations of the Labor Code the Labor Commissioner should obtain evidence of his crime through the time-honored method of independent investigation.

NOTES AND QUESTIONS

1. *Judicial enforcement.* Note that Craib was required to go to court to enforce the subpoena. In *ICC v. Brimson,* 154 U.S. 447 (1894), the Court indicated that an agency could not be given power to enforce its own subpoenas. It is unclear whether *Brimson* would be followed today. Congress has abided by *Brimson* and assumed that judicial enforcement is needed. However, it might be a significant time-saver if agencies could enforce their own subpoenas without having to seek judicial enforcement. Even if *Brimson* prevents an agency from enforcing its own subpoena through the contempt power, could an adjudicating agency preclude a party who ignored a subpoena from introducing any evidence?

2. *Defenses to subpoena enforcement.* In subpoena enforcement proceedings, a demandee can raise all appropriate defenses. However, constitutional defenses are limited. Like virtually all recent federal cases, *Craib* defers to agency demands for information. Many such demands are burdensome and intrusive. Cases from the late 1940's like *Oklahoma Press* have long since removed the roadblocks. These cases make clear that agency demands for information are almost always "reasonable" under the Fourth Amendment if they are relevant to the investigation. The analogy is to a

grand jury subpoena, not to a search warrant. Older decisions that condemned agency "fishing expeditions" are no longer followed.

Nevertheless, demandees can assert a few defenses to a subpoena. For example, the face of the subpoena might disclose that the agency plainly has no jurisdiction over the matter to which the information relates. *See Major League Baseball v. Crist,* 331 F.3d 1177 (11th Cir. 2003), which refused to enforce a CID issued by the Florida Attorney General to investigate Major League Baseball's decision to dispense with two teams. Because baseball's federal antitrust exemption extends to state law, the CID revealed on its face that the Attorney General had no power to regulate and thus could not subpoena documents. Similarly, a court might find a request too vague, or not reasonably relevant to the investigation, or unreasonably broad or burdensome. However, these kinds of claims are difficult to sustain. *See, e.g., CAB v. Hermann,* 353 U.S. 322 (1957), which upheld a subpoena for all the books, records and documents of an airline and its stockholders for a period of 38 months. The only solace to the company was that inspection could take place at its place of business so that it did not have to copy or move the records. The demandee could also argue that the information is subject to an evidentiary privilege (see N.4).

In addition, a court may refuse to enforce a subpoena because the demandee sustains the burden of showing that the agency violated procedural requirements in the statute or its own regulations or that the agency is acting in bad faith for an improper purpose and thus abusing the court's process. For example, a court might find that an agency is trying to harass the demandee or put pressure on it to settle some collateral dispute. Similarly, a subpoena might be quashed to protect First Amendment associational interests. *Dole v. Service Employees Union,* 950 F.2d 1456 (9th Cir. 1991) (protecting confidential material in union's minutes not needed for administrative case).

An agency is not required to give notice to the person investigated when it subpoenas materials from a third party—even though the person investigated would lose the right to assert possible defenses once the third party turns over the material. *SEC v. Jerry T. O'Brien, Inc.,* 467 U.S. 735 (1984). California refuses to follow this case. In *Sehlmeyer v. Dep't of General Services,* 21 Cal. Rptr. 2d 840 (App. 1993), A complained to the Board of Psychology about T, who was a licensed therapist. T then served subpoenas on 17 of A's former psychotherapists and physicians. The court held that A had a right to be notified of the subpoenas and to claim that the information was privileged or otherwise protected from disclosure. This right was based on California's constitutional right of privacy.

3. *State law and investigative subpoenas.* With the authorities discussed in the previous note, compare *Levin v. Murawski,* 449 N.E.2d 730 (N.Y. 1983), involving an investigative subpoena to a physician for specific patient records issued by the New York Medical Board. The Board stated simply that it had received complaints from patients about the doctor. The

court of appeals held that the Board must meet a minimum threshold foundation before a court can enforce the subpoena. The foundation would resemble the requirement of probable cause in obtaining a search warrant and furnish at least some assurance of the complainants' reliability. Said the court:

> It is ancient law that no agency of government may conduct an unlimited and general inquisition into the affairs of persons within its jurisdiction solely on the prospect of possible violations of law being discovered, especially with respect to subpoenas duces tecum . . . There must be authority, relevancy, and some basis for inquisitorial action.

The three dissenters in the *Levin* case argued that this requirement would frustrate disciplinary investigations of physicians (which the legislature had been trying to streamline and strengthen). Who is correct? Which authority is more in line with current attitudes about bureaucracy and privacy—decisions like *Craib* and *Oklahoma Press* that give carte blanche to investigators, or decisions like *Levin* that require a higher threshold before investigators can compel production of documents or other records?

4.   *Privileges.* The attorney-client and work product privileges (as well as other evidentiary privileges) apply to agency investigations. *Upjohn Co. v. United States,* 449 U.S. 383 (1981). Courts will enforce these privileges at the time the agency brings a subpoena enforcement action. In addition, a demandee may assert the Fifth Amendment privilege against self-incrimination in order to withhold documents or refuse to testify. However, for a number of reasons, the Fifth Amendment privilege is usually not applicable to administrative investigations.

i.   In a criminal case, a defendant can refuse to take the stand. In contrast, in an administrative case, a witness cannot refuse to take the stand and be sworn. However, the witness may assert the privilege to refuse to answer specific questions on the ground of self-incrimination. In a criminal case, the fact-finder cannot draw adverse inferences against the defendant because of a claim of privilege, but an agency is permitted to draw an adverse inference. *See Baxter v. Palmigiano,* 425 U.S. 308, 316–20 (1976) (prisoner exercises his right to remain silent in prison disciplinary proceeding but silence can be held against him).

ii.   Suppose an administrative proceeding and a criminal case are pending at the same time. For example, the same act might lead to disbarment of an attorney and to conviction of a felony. The attorney wishes to defer disbarment proceedings until the criminal case is completed, because she might wish to testify in the administrative case but to rely on her privilege in the criminal case. A court has discretion to delay the administrative matter, but the attorney has no absolute right to a delay. *See Keating v. Office of Thrift Supervision,* 45 F.3d 322 (9th Cir. 1995), which balances the interests of the agency, the public, and the courts, and refuses to grant a stay.

iii.   An agency can compel a person to testify in an administrative
proceeding by granting use immunity. Immunized testimony cannot be used
against the person in any subsequent criminal proceeding, but the agency can
use the testimony to impose administrative sanctions (such as loss of
employment or license revocation). *See Lefkowitz v. Turley*, 414 U.S. 70
(1973) (state cannot coerce government contractors into surrendering their
privilege against self-incrimination in a grand jury proceeding without
furnishing immunity); 18 U.S.C. § 6002(2) (federal agency can compel
testimony by granting use immunity to person who refuses to testify or
provide other information). Under a related rule, if an agency compels a
person to testify and fails to provide immunity, the testimony cannot be used
against the person in a subsequent criminal proceeding. *Garrity v. New
Jersey,* 385 U.S. 493 (1967).

iv.   The privilege applies only to testimony that is produced by state
compulsion. As a result, the contents of private papers are not privileged,
because they were prepared voluntarily rather than in response to
compulsion. *See United States v. Doe,* 465 U.S. 605 (1984). However, the
privilege can be asserted if the *act* of producing the papers would be
incriminatory (because it would admit that the papers existed or were
authentic or that the demandee possessed them). See *Doe* and footnote 14 in
Craib.

v.   The privilege does not apply to corporations, partnerships or
unincorporated entities like unions. Thus the custodian of an entity's records
must disclose them and cannot claim any personal privilege relating to the
entity's records—even if the contents of the material (or the act of producing
it) might incriminate the custodian. *Braswell v. United States,* 487 U.S. 99
(1988) (collective entity doctrine applies even though custodian's act of
producing corporate documents could incriminate custodian); *Bellis v. United
States,* 417 U.S. 85 (1974) (applying collective-entity doctrine to records of a
three-person law partnership).

vi.   The privilege can be asserted only if the person fearing
incrimination (or his attorney, assuming the attorney-client privilege applies)
is in possession of the documents subpoenaed. *Couch v. United States,* 409
U.S. 322 (1973) (taxpayer cannot assert privilege with respect to papers in
possession of accountant).

vii.   The privilege does not apply to materials seized under a valid
search warrant, because the person from whom the documents are seized is
not compelled to admit anything about them. *Andresen v. Maryland,* 427 U.S.
463 (1976).

viii. The privilege is inapplicable to the production of records if a statute
requires those records to be prepared and maintained. *See Shapiro v. United
States,* 335 U.S. 1 (1948), which is discussed and applied in *Craib.* If *Shapiro*
applies, the documents must be produced even if the act of producing them
might be incriminating and the state is not required to provide immunity.
Again, see footnote 14 in *Craib.*

This note is intended only to alert you to the existence of common-law and constitutional privileges in administrative investigation; this major subject in constitutional and evidence law cannot be treated in detail here.

5. *Physical searches.* When an agency physically inspects or searches a home or business, it must ordinarily secure a search warrant. *Marshall v. Barlow's, Inc.,* which is discussed in *Craib,* holds that a warrant is required before OSHA can inspect business premises to check for violation of employee safety rules. To obtain an administrative search warrant, the inspector need not establish probable cause to believe that a violation has occurred. It is sufficient if the choice of the particular employer to be inspected was based on reasonable and neutral standards, such as a statistical sampling technique approved by the agency. The warrant can be obtained ex parte (i.e. without notice to the employer). Although the warrant requirement is easy to satisfy, at least it tends to prevent inspections motivated by harassment or other improper purposes.

The *Barlow's* rule does not apply to pervasively regulated businesses like liquor or gun dealers, since they have a reduced expectation of privacy. This exception was broadened in *New York v. Burger,* 482 U.S. 691 (1987). New York law required junk yards and vehicle dismantlers to be licensed, to keep records of purchases and sales, and to submit to periodic unannounced inspections. Of course, the reason for searching junkyards is to find stolen auto parts so that the licensees can be prosecuted for theft.

According to *Burger*, four criteria must be met to justify warrantless administrative inspections of pervasively regulated businesses: (i) There must be a substantial government interest in regulating the business, (ii) unannounced inspections must be necessary to further the regulatory scheme, (iii) the statute must advise the owner of the periodic inspection program, and (iv) searches must be limited in time, place and scope. The New York law met all of these criteria.

However, the New York Court of Appeals refused to follow *Burger* under the state constitution. *People v. Scott*, 593 N.E.2d 1328, 1339–46 (N.Y. 1992). Taking the tack advocated by Justice Mosk's dissent in *Craib* (and the dissenters in *Burger*), the *Scott* majority held that a warrant was required to inspect the premises of automobile dismantlers because "the search is undertaken solely to uncover evidence of criminality and the underlying regulatory scheme is in reality designed simply to give the police an expedient means of enforcing penal sanctions."

6. *The exclusionary rule in administrative law.* Evidence that was illegally seized in violation of the Fourth Amendment cannot be admitted in a criminal proceeding because of the exclusionary rule. However, the exclusionary rule does not apply to administrative proceedings. *See INS v. Lopez-Mendoza,* 468 U.S. 1032 (1984) (evidence unlawfully seized by federal agents admissible in deportation proceeding); *United States v. Janis,* 428 U.S. 433 (1976) (evidence obtained by unlawful state search admissible in federal civil tax case). However, the evidence should be excluded in administrative

proceedings if the manner in which it was obtained constituted egregious violations of the Fourth Amendment or other liberties. *See Almeida-Amaral v. Gonzales,* 461 F.3d 231 (2d Cir. 2006), which applies dictum from *Lopez-Mendoza* (stopping and searching a person without probable cause and based solely on that person's race would be an egregious violation).

7. *Discovery.* Once an adjudicatory proceeding has formally commenced, the agency and the private party may seek information through the discovery process The APA confers no right to discovery. *See Citizens Awareness Network v. United States,* 391 F.3d 338, 350 (1st Cir. 2004) (holding that NRC can dispense with its prior discovery practice). Nevertheless, agency rules frequently provide for some forms of discovery such as disclosure to a private party of an agency's files or witness lists. Depositions and interrogatories are rarely employed in administrative proceedings.

The right to issuance of post-complaint subpoenas is narrower than an agency's right to investigate before issuing a complaint (as discussed above). An administrative judge may refuse to issue a post-complaint subpoena (either to the agency staff or to a private party) if the information sought would not be relevant to the charges in the complaint or would be unduly burdensome.

8. *Problem.* In Madison, it is a crime for an insurance company to engage in "deceptive insurance practices." The Madison Insurance Commission (MIC) is headed by Gloria, an elected official, who is a strong advocate of consumer rights. MIC has power to order an insurance company doing business in Madison to desist from the practice of refusing to pay justified claims. It can also order the refund of premiums to persons who were denied payment of proper claims.

MIC has power to investigate any matter relating to insurance and can issue a civil investigative demand (CID) calling for the production of documents. It can also require any person to answer written questions or give oral testimony under oath if it has reason to believe that any law relating to insurance is being violated. If a CID is not obeyed, the Attorney General can seek a court order requiring compliance. Disregard of such an order is punishable as civil contempt. If a court orders compliance with a CID, the demandee must pay the attorneys' fees incurred by the Attorney General in enforcing the CID.

Your client, Security Insurance Co., employs 2700 persons. Its home office is in Madison but it sells insurance in other states through branch offices. It specializes in selling health insurance to elderly people to cover costs not paid by Medicare. The MIC staff believes that Security has a policy of refusing to pay clearly proper claims. Security denies that it has any such policy.

Bill is a vice president of Security. He received a CID ordering him to appear in three weeks and bring with him all of Security's files and other documents relating to health insurance on persons over the age of 55 for the last three years. In addition, he was ordered to appear three weeks later to give sworn testimony. Bill says there is a record of hostility between him and Gloria. Bill particularly fears adverse publicity; MIC often issues press releases when it begins an investigation but it has not yet done so.

Bill is distressed by the breadth of the CID which covers literally millions of pieces of paper. Much of the material has not been scanned and thus is not part of a computer database. There is no staff available to gather the documents (they are stored in several places and mixed with material on insured persons under 55 and with other kinds of insurance). Some of the older documents are on microfiche and thus difficult to read and easily lost. Many of the records involve currently insured persons and are needed for business. Moreover, management does not trust MIC to take proper care of the documents while they are inspected and copied. Many of the policies cover residents of other states. MIC believes that it has jurisdiction over non-resident insured persons because Security's home office is in Madison, but Security disagrees. What is your strategy?

§ 4.1.3 ALTERNATIVE DISPUTE RESOLUTION IN ADMINISTRATIVE ADJUDICATION

It is widely perceived that litigation has become too slow, too adversarial, too costly, and too formal. As a result, there has been an explosion of interest in alternative dispute resolution (or ADR). Unlike litigation, ADR can be quick, non-adversarial, cheap, and informal. Frequently, ADR can settle a dispute creatively in a way that benefits both parties; litigation, on the other hand, is usually a zero sum game in which one party is a big winner and the other a big loser. As a result, it is now common for litigants to resort to voluntary ADR to avoid or settle disputes before they enter the litigation system or before they go to trial. Only a tiny percentage of civil and criminal cases are actually tried rather than settled or plea bargained. Numerous state and federal statutes require litigants to resort to ADR before going forward with a case.

Essentially, ADR consists of three broad classifications:

• *Negotiation.* In negotiation, the litigants and their lawyers get together to work out the problem without the assistance of third parties.

• *Mediation.* In mediation, a third party mediator helps the litigants work out the problem but cannot impose a solution.

• *Arbitration.* In arbitration, a third party arbitrator has authority to impose a solution.

A powerful movement is now underway to expand the use of ADR in administrative adjudication. This is ironic since administrative adjudication was invented as a form of ADR—to get disputes out of the courts and into agencies which were seen as specialized, inexpensive, and informal dispute resolvers. Today, it is clear that administrative adjudication all too often is slow, costly, adversarial, and formalized.

In 1990 Congress amended the APA to require agencies to explore and utilize ADR in all agency functions, including adjudication and rulemaking. As to adjudication, the Administrative Dispute Resolution Act (ADR Act) of 1990 was a giant step in the direction of changing the culture of administrative law in the direction of using ADR. We explore negotiated rulemaking in § 5.9.

The ADR Act added APA §§ 556(c)(6), (7), and (8) plus §§ 571–83. These provisions authorize and encourage agencies to use the whole range of ADR techniques up to and including arbitration. These procedures are voluntary, so that neither agencies nor regulated parties can be compelled to utilize them. The statute also suggests that there are situations in which ADR is not appropriate. For example, ADR should not be used when a matter must be authoritatively resolved in order to create a precedent. § 572(b). ADR provisions are finding their way into state APAs as well.

Problem. Review the Problem about the dispute between the Madison Insurance Commission and Security Insurance Co. in § 4.1.2 N.8. The dispute over production of documents can be resolved in court. The underlying dispute about Security's failure to pay claims can be resolved through a hearing before an administrative judge followed by a decision of the agency head; no doubt, the agency head's decision will be subjected to judicial review. Thus final resolution of the underlying dispute is years away. Until then, assuming MIC is right, consumers will remain subject to abusive claims practices. Security will find it difficult to engage in business planning and capital raising because of the uncertainty created by the ongoing dispute. Security will be subjected to massive unfavorable publicity. Insured persons whose claims were denied will be encouraged to sue the company for bad faith. Large sums (perhaps running into the millions of dollars) will be spent by both sides on attorneys' and experts' fees. Is ADR appropriate to resolve the dispute about production of documents or for the underlying dispute? If so, what techniques of ADR should be employed?

§ 4.2   THE HEARING PHASE

This subsection addresses issues that arise during the formal adjudication process. That process closely resembles a judicial trial. The parties introduce documentary evidence, call and examine witnesses, cross-examine the witnesses called by their adversaries, make oral arguments, and submit briefs. See APA § 556(d).

§ 4.2.1 EVIDENCE AT THE HEARING

REGUERO V. TEACHER STANDARDS AND PRACTICES COMMISSION

822 P.2d 1171 (Ore. 1991)

UNIS, J.:

[Petitioner Reguero applied to reinstate his teaching license, but Oregon's Teacher Standards and Practices Commission (TSPC) denied the application because of his sexual misconduct toward sixth-grade pupils Michelle and Leasa. Neither Michelle nor Leasa testified. To support its allegations, TSPC introduced hearsay testimony by Minette (a school counselor), Castner (a deputy district attorney), and Costelow (a police officer), each of whom had interviewed Michelle and Leasa.] According to this testimony, petitioner touched Michelle's breast on one occasion and her buttocks on another occasion. TSPC also introduced hearsay and multiple hearsay testimony that petitioner had kept Leasa after school in September, locked her in the classroom, touched her "on the breast and in the vaginal area," and lowered his trousers. . . .

Petitioner presented countervailing evidence. He admitted touching Michelle's breast, but said that the contact was inadvertent. With respect to Leasa's complaint of a sexual assault, he contended that she had fabricated the story to punish him for telling the school counselor that Michelle, who was her friend, was involved with prostitution and drugs. A school employee testified that she had overheard Michelle say, "I'm gonna get [petitioner]." Two teachers testified that the doors of the classrooms could not be locked from the inside. A teacher's aide testified that she was usually present in petitioner's classroom after school and had never seen him alone with Leasa. . . .

We now consider whether TSPC's findings about sexual contact with Michelle and Leasa are supported by substantial evidence. Petitioner's primary claim is that TSPC may not rely entirely on hearsay that would not be admissible in a civil or criminal trial to support findings that petitioner had sexual contact with the students, when TSPC did not show that they were unavailable to testify. Petitioner asserts that such hearsay, in such circumstances, does not constitute substantial evidence. He urges us to adopt the "residuum rule," at least in cases where direct evidence is available.

A. Residuum rule

The New York Court of Appeals created the residuum rule in *Carroll v. Knickerbocker Ice Co.*, 113 N.E. 507 (1916). In that case, the court set aside a workers' compensation award that was based solely on a deceased worker's statements that he had been injured on the job. The relevant statute provided that "common law or statutory rules of evidence" were not binding on the agency that administered workers' compensation. The court interpreted that statute to mean that, although the agency could "accept any evidence that is offered, still in the end there must be a residuum of legal evidence to support the claim before an award can be made." The residuum rule requires that an administrative agency's findings be supported by some evidence that would be admissible in a civil or criminal trial. . . .

Some jurisdictions retain the residuum rule. Courts that adopt the rule do so in an effort to ensure reliability of evidence and cross-examination of witnesses. But legal scholars have severely criticized the rule and those rationales for it. [For example,] McCormick reasons that courts concerned about cross-examination fail to consider that much "legal" evidence within the hearsay exceptions is equally untested. Yet the latter is accepted even in jury trials because of its probable reliability. Consequently the residuum rule's mechanical prohibition against uncorroborated hearsay is unsound. Its sound objectives can be secured through the sensitivity of the hearings officers and the wise application of the substantial evidence test which measures the quantity and quality of the supporting evidence regardless of its category or label

Because of its flaws, many courts that once applied the residuum rule have now abandoned it. . . . The Oregon statutes governing evidence in administrative hearings reject the assumption that hearsay evidence is categorically so unreliable that it cannot be substantial. Hearsay evidence is as admissible . . . as any other evidence as long as it meets the statutory test of reliability.[20]

ORS § 183.482(8)(c) provides that "substantial evidence exists to support a finding of fact when the record, viewed as a whole, would permit a reasonable person to make that finding." That statute makes no provision for weighing some classes of evidence in the record more heavily as classes than other classes of evidence in the record—for example, weighing exhibits more heavily than testimony, or non-hearsay testimony more heavily than hearsay—as a matter of law. . . . [T]he legislature could not have intended that a certain type of evidence, although reliable enough to be admissible under ORS 183.450(1), is categorically incapable of being substantial enough to permit a reasonable person to find in accordance with it under ORS 183.482(8)(c). Accordingly, we reject the residuum rule and [hold] that hearsay evidence alone, even if

---

[20] Oregon Rev. Stat. § 183.450(1) provides: "Irrelevant, immaterial or unduly repetitious evidence shall be excluded, but erroneous rulings on evidence shall not preclude agency action on the record unless shown to have substantially prejudiced the rights of a party. All other evidence of a type commonly relied upon by reasonably prudent persons in conduct of their serious affairs shall be admissible. Agencies shall give effect to the rules of privilege recognized by law. Objections to evidentiary offers may be made and shall be noted in the record. Any part of the evidence may be received in written form."

inadmissible in a civil or criminal trial, is not incapable of being "substantial evidence."

B. *Substantiality*

Our inquiry does not end there, however. In rejecting the residuum rule, we reject any categorical method of determining substantiality. While our task is not to substitute our judgment for that of the agency, we must decide whether the finding of substantiality is reasonable in the light of countervailing as well as supporting evidence.

[As proponent of the sexual misconduct charge] TSPC had the burden of presenting substantial evidence to support its allegations that petitioner was guilty of sexual misconduct.

The "substantial evidence" inquiry necessarily is case specific. Davis suggests, and we agree, that in assessing the substantiality of the evidence or lack of it, variable circumstances may be considered, such as: the alternative to relying on the hearsay evidence; the importance of the facts sought to be proved by the hearsay statements to the outcome of the proceeding and considerations of economy; the state of the supporting or opposing evidence, if any; the degree of lack of efficacy of cross-examination with respect to the particular hearsay statements; and the consequences of the decision either way. "When the alternative to relying on hearsay is to get the better evidence that is readily available, refusing to rely on the hearsay is appropriate." In this case, there was a convenient and apparently inexpensive alternative to relying on the challenged hearsay. Michelle [and] Leasa were readily available to be called as witnesses. No reason was given why they did not testify.[22] ... TSPC had the authority to issue subpoenas to require the students to testify at the hearing. It is beyond question that the students' direct testimony is better evidence than their hearsay statements.

The importance of the facts asserted in the hearsay statements to the outcome of this proceeding is likewise indisputable. TSPC's findings of fact, conclusions of law, opinion, and order were based entirely on hearsay, particularly the hearsay testimony of Castner, Minette, and Costelow. Moreover, Castner, Minette, and Costelow were permitted to express their opinion, based on that hearsay, multiple hearsay, gossip, and rumors, that Michelle and Leasa were telling the truth ... We hold that TSPC's decision in this case was not based on substantial evidence ... We reverse the decision of the Court of Appeals and the modified order of TSPC and remand this case to TSPC for further consideration.

---

[22] While the dissent suggests that the petitioner had the opportunity to subpoena the students to testify, it was not the petitioner's burden to do so. Petitioner, therefore, should not be faulted for forcing TSPC to carry its burden.

PETERSON, J. concurring: . . . I would state this rule: Where the claim and the finding involve conduct that would constitute a crime, hearsay evidence alone is insufficient to establish the conduct . . .

GRABER, J. dissenting: . . . [T]he majority's disposition of the case . . . analyzes the substantiality of the evidence incorrectly. The majority has—contrary to its proper role and its protestations—conducted its own fact-finding. A proper evaluation of the agency's fact-finding would lead to an affirmance . . .

NOTES AND QUESTIONS

1. *Admission of evidence.* The *Reguero* case involves the agency's decision to admit hearsay evidence. In the law of evidence, hearsay is an out-of-court statement (written or oral) admitted to prove the truth of that statement. This type of testimony deprives a party to the case of the opportunity to cross-examine the person who made the out-of-court statement. Thus, the testimony by Minette, Castner, and Costelow repeated out-of-court statements by Michelle and Leasa and were admitted to prove the truth of those statements. Yet Reguero was unable to cross-examine Michelle and Leasa to challenge the truthfulness of their statements. The hearsay rules contain a large number of exceptions that permit the introduction of certain types of hearsay evidence that are likely to be truthful.

In thinking about *Reguero,* separate two issues: (i) what evidence should be admitted at administrative hearings and (ii) to what extent should an agency be able to rely *exclusively* on evidence that would not be admissible in court? The first of these questions is discussed in this note; the second is discussed in N.2.

As to the first issue, read APA § 556(d) (second and third sentences and last sentence); and Oregon Rev. Stat. § 183.450(1), quoted in note 20 of *Reguero.* These statutes make hearsay evidence admissible in administrative hearings. What's the difference between administrative cases and civil or criminal cases that justifies this distinction? Does the federal APA impose *any* limit on the admission of evidence?

In contrast to the federal and the Oregon APAs, § 404 of the 2010 MSAPA provides:

The following rules apply in a contested case:

(1) Except as otherwise provided in paragraph (2), all relevant evidence is admissible, including hearsay evidence, if it is of a type commonly relied on by a reasonably prudent individual in the conduct of the affairs of the individual.

(2) The presiding officer may exclude evidence in the absence of an objection if the evidence is irrelevant, immaterial, unduly repetitious, or excludable on constitutional or statutory grounds or

on the basis of an evidentiary privilege recognized in the courts of this state. The presiding officer shall exclude the evidence if objection is made at the time the evidence is offered.

Thus the 2010 Model Act allows the introduction of hearsay evidence in administrative cases *unless* the state has adopted a *statute* prohibiting hearsay in civil cases (but not if the state has adopted its hearsay rule through case law). About 45 states have adopted evidence codes (mostly based on the Federal Rules of Evidence). In those states, § 404(2) appears to require such states to rigidly apply the rules of evidence applicable in civil cases, including the hearsay rule. This result appears to be unintended and attributable to a drafting error in the 2010 MSAPA.

2.   *The residuum rule.* Since hearsay (and other evidence barred from judicial proceedings) is generally admitted in administrative proceedings, the second question becomes important: can an agency rely *exclusively* on evidence that would be inadmissible in court? Under the "residuum rule," findings cannot be based exclusively on hearsay evidence. Instead, the findings must be supported by some evidence admissible in civil cases although that evidence by itself need not be substantial enough to support the findings. Many states still adhere to the residuum rule, but Oregon rejects it in *Reguero.* Note the disagreement between Justice Unis and Justice Peterson on this issue. Peterson would preserve the residuum rule, but only in cases where the finding involves conduct that would constitute a crime.

Section 413(f) of the 2012 MSAPA presents two alternative versions— one accepts the residuum rule and the other rejects it. States will have to choose which version to adopt.

The residuum rule is not followed in the federal courts. *Richardson v. Perales,* 402 U.S. 389 (1971), reviewed a decision by Social Security rejecting a claim for disability benefits. The ALJ held that Perales (who complained of disabling back pain) was not disabled. The only evidence in support of this determination was written evaluations by Social Security doctors. The lower court held that substantial evidence did not support the decision because the written medical evaluations were hearsay. The Supreme Court reversed, holding that the reports alone could furnish substantial evidence to support the decision against Perales. Although he had not cross-examined the doctors, that was his own fault—his counsel had failed to subpoena them. Even if the witnesses could not have been subpoenaed to testify at the hearing, it appears that federal courts do not follow the residuum rule—but that point has not been definitively established.

3.   *Hearsay and substantial evidence.* A reviewing court must decide whether the evidence in the record supports the agency's findings of fact. The normal standard for judicial review of fact findings in contested cases (or formal adjudication at the federal level) is the "substantial evidence" test. This test, which was applied in *Reguero,* is discussed in detail in § 9.1.1. As the court noted, "substantial evidence exists to support a finding of fact when

the record, viewed as a whole, would permit a reasonable person to make that finding." Often, there is good evidence in a case on both sides, meaning that a reasonable person could decide in favor of either side. In such cases, the court should affirm the decision, even though the judges might have gone the other way if they had heard the case themselves.

In practice, however, a court applying the substantial evidence test is likely to overturn agency findings if it feels an injustice has been done—which seems to be exactly what happened in the *Reguero* case. Justice Unis thought that the hearsay evidence presented by Minette, Castner, and Costelow was insufficient to satisfy a "reasonable person" that Reguero had engaged in misconduct with Michelle and Leasa. Justice Graber thought it was sufficient. Evidently, the majority was suspicious of a case based entirely on hearsay, especially considering the high stakes involved, and it must have suspected that a serious injustice might have occurred.

An important factor here is that Michelle and Leasa *could* have been subpoenaed to testify directly to whether Reguero had sexually harassed them. The use of hearsay evidence was unnecessary. Do you agree with the majority that TSPC, rather than Reguero, should have been required to subpoena Michelle and Leasa?

Another way the court might have decided the *Reguero* case is to hold that the hearsay evidence should not have been admitted in the first place because it is not the type of evidence "commonly relied upon by reasonably prudent persons in conduct of their serious affairs?" (That is the test in the Oregon statute quoted in note 20). Would *you* rely on this evidence if you had to decide whether to hire Reguero when he applies for a teaching job in your private school?

4. *Hearsay and confrontation.* Reguero could have argued that the use of hearsay evidence violated his due process right to confront his accusers. A number of cases have so held, but the circumstances must be compelling. For example, in *Pouhova v. Holder,* 726 F.3d 1007 (7th Cir. 2013), the government sought to deport Pouhova because she had given her Bulgarian passport to another alien (Dimova) who tried to use it in 2000 to enter the U.S. Pouhova claimed that she had lost her Bulgarian passport and didn't know how Dimova got it. There were only two items of evidence against Pouhova: i) a written account of Dimova's interview with a U.S. immigration official (Weiler) in which Dimova said that she owed Pouhova $1500 for arranging her travel; and ii) a written statement by Weiler on Form I–213 about this interview that was prepared in 2007. Both items are hearsay and Pouhova was unable to cross examine either Dimova (who had returned to Bulgaria and was unavailable) or Weiler (whom the government refused to make available at the hearing for unexplained reasons).

The court held that the use of these documents denied Pouhova due process, because both were unreliable. The Dimova interview was unreliable because Dimova was apparently not fluent in English and no interpreter was available. Therefore, it was not clear whether Dimova understood the questions put to her or whether Weiler understood her answers. As to Weiler's statement on Form I–213, it was suspicious because it was based on the suspect interview and, in addition, was prepared seven years after the interview and was inconsistent in several important respects with the written account of the interview

5.   *Burden of proof.* Evidence law distinguishes between the burden of producing evidence and the burden of persuasion. The burden of producing evidence allocates to one party the obligation to come forward with evidence on a particular point. The burden of persuasion indicates how strong a party's evidence on an issue must be to avoid losing on that issue. *See* APA § 556(d) (first sentence), which allocates the burden of proof to the "proponent of an order." The words "burden of proof" in § 556(d) refer to the burden of persuasion, not the burden of producing evidence. *See Director, Office of Workers' Comp. v. Greenwich Collieries*, 512 U.S. 267 (1994),which held that an agency rule that allows applicant to receive benefits if the evidence of the applicant and the employer are of equal strength violates § 556(d). In *Schaffer v. Weast*, 546 U.S. 49 (2005), the Court held that parents have the burden of persuasion to establish unsuitability of a school district's plan for their handicapped child at the "impartial due process hearing" required by statute, even though the district has better access to the facts.

In general, the proponent must discharge its burden of persuasion by a "preponderance of the evidence" (meaning a more than 50% probability). *See Steadman v. SEC,* 450 U.S. 91 (1981). *Steadman* was a case in which the SEC had imposed disciplinary sanctions on a broker for securities fraud. Construing the third sentence of APA § 556(d), the Court held that the preponderance test applies to APA formal adjudications, except where Congress dictates otherwise. Thus the SEC did not have to satisfy the common law "clear and convincing" test that is commonly used in contract cases in which the defense of fraud is raised. Similarly, the SEC did not have to prove its case "beyond a reasonable doubt," which is the standard used in criminal cases, even though securities fraud can be a criminal offense.

In some administrative cases, the courts have manipulated the burden in order to provide a high degree of protection against error. For example, *Woodby v. INS,* 385 U.S. 276 (1966), involved an order of deportation. The APA does not apply to deportation cases. The Court required the government to prove its case by "clear, unequivocal and convincing evidence." Similarly, in *Ettinger v. Board of Medical Quality Assurance,* 185 Cal. Rptr. 601 (App.1982), the court held that a state agency seeking to revoke a physician's license had to prove its case by "clear and convincing proof to a reasonable certainty." Texas rejected an elevated burden in this situation. *Granek v. Texas State Bd. of Med. Exam'rs,* 172 S.W.3d 761, 777 (Tex. App. 2005).

Because Reguero applied for renewal of his certificate, he had the burden to establish all the elements required by the statute for renewal. However, since TSPC raised the sexual misconduct argument as an affirmative defense, it had the burden to establish that claim. Considering the personal and professional harm done to someone like Reguero by an administrative finding that he engaged in sexual misconduct toward sixth-grade girls, should a court require proof of TSPC's allegations by more than a preponderance of the evidence?

6. *Responsibility of judge to bring out evidence.* In judicial trials, the responsibility for producing evidence falls on the parties. Judges aren't required or expected to ask witnesses questions that the lawyers (or even an unrepresented party) should have but failed to ask. In administrative law, however, the rule is different. Administrative judges are expected to take an active role in developing the record. This is especially important when one of the parties is not represented by counsel. In a vast number of cases, such as government benefits, government personnel, or small business licensing, a majority of the private parties represent themselves. In such situations, the administrative judge may commit reversible error by failing to help the unrepresented party establish his or her case.

For example, in an unemployment compensation case, the court said: "Especially in the case of an uncounseled claimant, the Commission's responsibility involves asking the right questions. We do not think it is appropriate for the Commission to disqualify a *pro se* claimant from receiving benefits because she failed to produce evidence of facts that case law from other states says she must establish when the appeals referee never even asked her the relevant questions." *Hoke v. Brinlaw Mfg. Co.*, 327 S.E.2d 254, 258 (N.C. App. 1985). In Social Security cases, the ALJ is responsible for assisting the applicants to establish their claim, even if they are represented by counsel. *Smolen v. Chater*, 80 F.3d 1273, 1288 (9th Cir. 1996).

7. *Closed or open hearing.* Probably Reguero, as well as Michelle, Leasa and their parents, would have preferred that the hearing be closed to the public and the media. Should an administrative judge have discretion to close a hearing relating to sexual misconduct toward young girls? *See generally* Christopher McNeil, *The Public's Right of Access to "Some Kind of Hearing": Creating Policies that Protect the Right to Observe Agency Hearings*, 68 LA. L. REV. 1121 (2008).

In *Detroit Free Press v. Ashcroft*, 303 F.3d 681 (6th Cir. 2002), the court invalidated the Immigration Service's Creppy Directive. The Directive arose out of the 9/11 disaster and required the closure of deportation hearings involving persons suspected of possible terrorist involvement. The court held that deportation hearings are formal and adversarial in nature and have traditionally been open to the public. As a result, the First Amendment right of access to judicial proceedings applies, unless the agency can establish a compelling interest for closing the hearing. Although open hearings might result in disclosure of investigative information that could jeopardize the struggle against terrorism, the government could not make a blanket showing that complete closure was necessary in every case. Instead, such decisions must be made on a case-by-case basis and supported by findings sufficiently specific that a reviewing court can determine whether the closure order was properly entered.

In support of its holding, the court argued that public access to judicial proceedings is vitally important. First, it acts as a check on the actions of the executive branch by assuring that proceedings are conducted fairly and properly. Second, it helps to avoid mistaken decisions (particularly given the fact that many deportees are not represented by counsel). Third, after 9/11, open hearings have a cathartic, therapeutic effect. Fourth, openness enhances the perception of integrity and fairness. Fifth, public access insures that the individual citizen can participate in and contribute to our republican system of self-government. The court concluded that "democracy dies behind closed doors."

North Jersey Media Group, Inc. v. Ashcroft, 308 F.3d 198 (3rd Cir. 2002), declined to follow *Detroit Free Press*. It found that there was no unbroken tradition of open deportation hearings—they have sometimes been closed or held at places inaccessible to the public. It also held that, on balance, openness of deportation hearings involving persons with suspected terrorist involvement would have negative rather than positive policy implications. Terrorist organizations could piece together information learned at the hearings in order to decide what the government knows and doesn't know. The Third Circuit took strong exception to the Sixth Circuit's conclusion that "democracy dies behind closed doors." Instead, it said, the real threat to democracy comes "should the government fail in its mission to prevent another September 11. If that happens, the public will demand, and will get, immense restrictions on liberties." Certiorari was denied in *North Jersey*, so the circuit split remains unresolved.

8.   *Cross-examination under the APA.* The APA provides that a party is entitled "to conduct such cross-examination as may be required for a full and true disclosure of the facts." APA § 556(d) (fifth sentence). However, "[i]n [formal] rule making or determining claims for money or benefits or applications for initial licenses an agency may, when a party will not be prejudiced thereby, adopt procedures for the submission of all or part of the evidence in written form." APA § 556(d) (sixth sentence).

The Nuclear Regulatory Commission revised its rules for nuclear reactor licensing cases to dispense with full rights of cross-examination. Many, but not all, such cases involve initial licensing and thus fall within the sixth sentence of § 556(d). Under the new rules, a party seeking to cross-examine a witness must first seek permission from the hearing officer and must establish that cross is "necessary to ensure the development of an adequate record for decision." In *Citizens Awareness Network v. United States,* 391 F.3d 338, 353–54 (1st Cir. 2004), the court upheld the new rule. In deciding that the NRC had sufficiently explained the change, so as to meet the arbitrary-capricious test (*see* § 9.3.1), the court said:

> The new rules' outlook on cross-examination presents a closer
> question [than the changes relating to discovery, discussed in § 4.1

N.7]. The Commission reasons that restricting cross-examination will reduce the amount of testimony taken and make hearings more efficient. The Commission further observes that, in its experience, cross-examination is not always helpful to the resolution of scientific or technical issues.

The petitioners retort that cross-examination is a vital component of a citizen-intervenor's case. They note that citizen-intervenors often lack the resources to present their own expert testimony and must rely on cross-questioning of the adverse party's experts to make their case. They also stress the value of cross-examination as a means for bolstering public confidence in licensing hearings. Tellingly, the Commission's own administrative judges agree that cross-examination is helpful for the resolution of issues raised in many licensing hearings. In addition to the reasons advanced by the petitioners, the administrative judges note that the prospect of cross-examination discourages exaggeration in direct testimony because witnesses are aware that they will have to defend their statements later.

Experience in the courts has left no doubt that cross-examination can be a useful tool. Had the new rules abolished cross-examination entirely, we might well find the Commission's action insupportable. Importantly, however, the new rules do not completely do away with cross-examination. Rather, they leave its availability to the discretion of the hearing officer. Just as we will not ignore the fact that discovery is resource-consuming, we will not presume that all—or, perhaps, even most—cross-examination is essential to the just resolution of issues. With this in mind, we find no fault with the Commission's decision to attempt to curtail unnecessary cross-examination. . . . Accordingly, we cannot say that it is arbitrary and capricious for the Commission to leave the determination of whether cross-examination will further the truth-seeking process in a particular proceeding to the discretion of the individual hearing officer.

We do, however, add a caveat. The APA does require that cross-examination be available when "required for a full and true disclosure of the facts." If the new procedures are to comply in practice with the APA, cross-examination must be allowed in appropriate instances. Should the agency's administration of the new rules contradict its present representations or otherwise flout this principle, nothing in this opinion will inoculate the rules against future challenges.

§ 4.2.2 OFFICIAL NOTICE

A court is permitted to take *judicial notice*—*i.e.* treat as proven— various facts and propositions that are virtually indisputable (such as the moon was full on Aug. 1 because the almanac says so). Agency adjudicators are permitted to take *official notice* not only of indisputable facts but of some disputable facts as well, as in the *Circu* case that follows. By taking official notice of a fact, the agency avoids the delay and expense of establishing it through witness testimony.

However, an agency normally must furnish the opposing party with an opportunity to rebut the noticed fact. *See* APA § 556(e), second sentence—"When an agency decision rests on official notice of a material fact not appearing in the evidence in the record, a party is entitled, on timely request, to an opportunity to show the contrary." The 2010 MSAPA goes further by requiring the agency to furnish prior notice that it intends to take official notice and by requiring the agency to explain the source of its information. "A party must be notified at the earliest practicable time of the facts proposed to be noticed and their source, including any staff memoranda or data. The party must be afforded an opportunity to contest any officially noticed fact before the decision becomes final." § 404(7).

APA § 556(e) refers only to a "material fact," without indicating which facts are appropriate for official notice. 2010 MSAPA is more explicit on this point: "The presiding officer may take official notice of all facts of which judicial notice may be taken and of scientific, technical, or other facts within the specialized knowledge of the agency." § 404(7).

CIRCU V. GONZALES
450 F.3d 990 (9th Cir. 2006)

CALLAHAN, J.

[Violeta Circu applied for asylum in the United States. She and her family are Pentecostal Christians, while most Romanians are Orthodox Christians. They were subjected to numerous acts of persecution because of their religion.] The immigration judge ("IJ") held a hearing on the matter, where the U.S. State Department's 1997 Romania Country Report on Human Rights Practices ("1997 Report") and 1997 Profile of Asylum Claims and Country Conditions for Romania were admitted into evidence. Two years after the hearing, however, the IJ, relying on a 1999 Country Report on Human Rights Practices ("1999 Report") published by the State Department nineteen months after the matter was argued and submitted, denied Circu's petition. [The 1999 Report indicates that open worship is now possible and is marred only occasionally by unsanctioned harassment by local officials.] Circu did not receive notice that the IJ intended to take administrative notice of the 1999 Report and was not afforded an opportunity to respond to its contents before the IJ issued her decision. The Board of Immigration Appeals ("BIA") summarily denied Circu's appeal, in which she requested an opportunity to counter the 1999 Report. . . .

[N]otice of intent to take administrative notice of events occurring after the hearing is all that is required if extra-record facts and questions are legislative, indisputable, and general. On the other hand, more controversial or individualized facts require *both* notice to the [alien] that administrative notice will be taken *and* an opportunity to rebut the extra-record facts or to show cause why administrative notice should not be taken of those facts. It is not necessary to warn that administrative notice will be taken of the fact that water runs downhill. Some propositions, however, may require that notice not be taken, or that warning be given, or that rebuttal evidence be allowed. The agency's discretion must be exercised in such a way as to be fair in the circumstances. An IJ may take administrative notice of a change of government, but where it is plausible that the change does not eliminate the danger to the individual petitioner, the IJ must give the petitioner an opportunity to be heard on the question of the individual impact.

The 1999 Report contains extra-record facts that are controversial. Accordingly, Circu was entitled both to notice of the IJ's intent to take administrative notice of the 1999 Report and an opportunity to respond to that report. This point is made clear in [*Getachew v. INS*, 25 F.3d 841 (9th Cir. 1994), which] distinguished between "indisputable" facts and "controversial" facts. The sole example given of an "indisputable" fact is a political party's victory in an election. An example of a "controversial" fact is "whether the election has vitiated any previously well-founded fear of persecution." The 1999 Report plainly falls into the latter category because the IJ's assertion that "open worship is now possible [in Romania] and is only marred occasionally by unsanctioned harassment by local officials" is based on her determination that the 1999 Report vitiates Circu's previously well-founded fear of persecution. . . .

The government's argument that Circu was afforded notice of the IJ's intent to rely on the 1999 Report ignores the fact that Circu was not given notice prior to the IJ's taking administrative notice of the report. The only notice Circu received that the IJ would consider the 1999 Report was the IJ's opinion. This after-the-fact reference clearly fails to afford Circu warning that the IJ planned on taking administrative notice of the 1999 Report. The 1999 Report did not even exist at the time of Circu's hearing before the IJ, and the IJ explicitly relied on that report, noting the possibility for open worship, which differed from the information provided in the 1997 Report.

Furthermore, Circu was never given the opportunity to counter the 1999 Report before the IJ relied on the statements made therein to find that conditions in Romania had changed to allow Circu's return without an objective fear of persecution. While establishing a due process violation always requires a showing of prejudice, Circu satisfied her burden here by showing that the IJ perceived significant differences between the evidence in the record and the improperly noticed 1999 Report, and that the IJ relied on those differences in rendering a decision.

The BIA compounded the error by failing to remand the matter to the IJ to afford Circu an opportunity to rebut the 1999 Report. The government misses the point by arguing that Circu had an adequate opportunity to respond to the 1999 Report in her appeal to the BIA. As noted, due process requires notice and an opportunity to respond before the IJ renders her decision. The appeal to the BIA did not afford the procedural means by which Circu could submit evidence to refute the points asserted in the 1999 Report. Accordingly, Circu asked the BIA to remand her case to the IJ so that she could present rebuttal evidence. Because the BIA summarily affirmed the IJ's decision—and consequently we review the IJ's decision as the agency's final decision—the denial of procedural due process requires that we remand the case to the BIA with directions that it remand the case for further proceedings before the IJ.

NOTES AND QUESTIONS

1.   *Rebuttal opportunity.* As *Circu* points out, an agency ordinarily must notify a party that it intends to take official notice of a fact and must also allow the opposing party an opportunity to rebut facts that have been officially noticed. The court relied on due process, rather than on APA § 556(e), because the APA does not apply to immigration cases. (See § 3.1.1 N.7.) Note that federal APA § 556(e) does not explicitly require the agency to give notice that it intends to take official notice, but 2010 MSAPA § 404(7) does require the agency to give notice before it takes official notice.

Circu refers to the distinction between legislative and adjudicative facts as well as the distinction between indisputable and controversial facts. What is the relevance of these distinctions in deciding issues relating to official notice?

Generally, state and federal APAs and due process require an agency to furnish private parties with an opportunity to rebut officially noticed facts. For example, in *Ohio Bell Tel. Co. v. PUC of Ohio*, 301 U.S. 292 (1937), the Supreme Court held that a state agency's failure to offer an opportunity to rebut officially noticed legislative facts violated due process. In a ratemaking case, the agency had taken official notice of generalized land values during the Depression without furnishing specifics or offering an opportunity for rebuttal. However, *Market St. Ry. Co. v. Railroad Comm'n,* 324 U.S. 548 (1945), involved an agency's prediction that lowering fares would increase the number of passengers. The agency was not required to give the railroad an opportunity to rebut this prediction. What's the difference between these cases?

In *Circu,* the officially noticed fact was contained in the IJ's opinion, so Circu had no opportunity to challenge the noticed facts at the hearing. In her appeal to the BIA, Circu challenged the use by the IJ of the 1999 report to establish that Romania provided religious freedom. However, the BIA summarily affirmed the IJ's decision. Why did this procedure not provide Circu with an adequate response opportunity?

2. *Official notice or evaluation of the evidence?* Suppose that in *Circu* the asylum petitioner presented expert testimony to the effect that Romanian Pentecostals continue to be subject to severe persecution. Assume further that the government put on no evidence to the contrary and there was no Country Report available. In his (hypothetical) decision, the IJ declared that, based on his long experience in evaluating asylum cases, including dozens of cases involving Romanians, the expert testimony was not convincing. The IJ stated that the expert had appeared before him on several previous occasions and would testify to anything he was paid to say. Because the expert was not convincing, the IJ found that Circu had not sustained her burden of proof to show that Romanian Pentecostals were subject to persecution. The BIA summarily affirmed. Should this decision be upheld on appeal?

When an agency relies on background knowledge and experience to evaluate evidence or resolve conflicts between witnesses, it is not taking official notice of anything and need not notify the parties or afford an opportunity to contest the evaluation. As the 2010 MSAPA provides, "The experience, technical competence, and specialized knowledge of the presiding officer or members of an agency head that is a multi-member body that is hearing the case may be used in evaluating the evidence in the hearing record." § 404(8). As a result, an agency can reject uncontradicted expert testimony that it finds unpersuasive. One frequently cited authority for this proposition is *McCarthy v. Industrial Comm'n*, 215 N.W. 824 (Wis. 1927), which upheld the Commission's rejection of expert testimony concerning whether a hernia was caused by an industrial accident.

With *McCarthy*, compare *Davis & Randall, Inc. v. United States*, 219 F. Supp. 673 (W.D.N.Y. 1963), an opinion of a three-judge court written by Judge Friendly of the Second Circuit. In *Davis & Randall*, the ICC had rejected the testimony of an expert who predicted that a trucker would make a profit if it charged a certain rate. The ICC substituted its own view that the rate would not be profitable. Friendly wrote:

> [W]e suggest that a rejection of unopposed testimony by a qualified and disinterested expert on a matter susceptible of reasonably precise measurement, without the agency's developing its objections at a hearing, ought to be upheld only when the agency's uncommunicated criticisms appear to the reviewing court to be both so compelling and so deeply held that the court can be fairly sure the agency would not have been affected by anything the witness could have said had he known of them, *and* the court would have been bound to affirm, despite the expert's hypothetical rebuttal, out of deference to the agency's judgment on so technical a matter.

The distinction between taking official notice and evaluating evidence is often difficult to draw, as in the hypothetical that begins N.2. As *Davis &*

Randall suggests, in a borderline case, the agency should follow the official notice procedure and provide the private party with a rebuttal opportunity before utilizing its supposed expertise to reject expert testimony or otherwise make critical findings. *See, e.g., Cohen v. Ambach*, 490 N.Y.S.2d 908 (App. Div. 1985). *Cohen* involved a regulation that chiropractors could not solicit business through advertising that "is not in the public interest." Cohen sent out a newsletter entitled "Health Facts." On finding that this material was not in the public interest, the agency suspended her license. However, no witnesses testified that the newsletter was false or misleading or how it might have been contrary to the public interest. The court said:

> When the panel concluded, on the bare record, that petitioner violated the Department's regulation after employing their individual expertise to analyze the publication, they denied petitioner her right to an adjudicatory hearing . . . While the hearing panel could properly use its expertise to analyze and interpret evidence before it, it could not use such expertise to substitute for evidence. . . . Finally, in relying on their expertise to analyze petitioner's publication without the benefit of any expert testimony, the members of the panel were essentially relying on material outside the record. [The court quoted the official notice provision in the state APA.] Here, no such notice [that the agency intended to take official notice] was given.

3. *Problem.* An Elm City ordinance establishes rent control and provides that rents must "provide a fair return on the owner's investment." An elected three-person Rent Control Board can order rent increases or decreases. Assume the Board follows (a) the federal APA or (b) the 2010 MSAPA.

Your client Red owns an apartment house and sought a rent increase. At a hearing conducted before the full Board, Red testified that the cost of the building with all improvements was $2,000,000. His books and records were introduced into evidence to prove this figure. Max, a tenant in the building, testified that he knew Gloria, Red's mother, and Gloria had recently told Max that Red had told her that he actually had only $1,400,000 invested in the building and had falsified his records. Red denied that he had ever had any such conversation with Gloria and affirmed the accuracy of his records.

Red presented the testimony of Beth, an expert appraiser, that 12% per year would be a reasonable rate of return on investment. This figure was based on an analysis of the risks of the business and of sale prices of similar buildings. Beth was not cross examined and there was no other testimony on rate of return.

The Board found that Red's investment was $1,400,000 (based on Max's testimony). It also determined that a reasonable rate of return was 9% per year. The Board noted that it did not agree with Beth's analysis and it was basing its conclusion on its experience in rent control. It noted that the building was probably appreciating in value and that 9% was more than Red could get from investing in a long-term bank account. It was also the figure the Board had been using in all of its rent control cases. As a result of these findings, the Board ordered a 15% cut in rents rather than an increase.

On judicial review, should this decision be upheld? *See Whispering Pines Mobile Home Park, Ltd. v. City of Scotts Valley,* 225 Cal. Rptr. 364 (App. 1986).

§ 4.3   THE DECISION PHASE: FINDING FACTS AND STATING REASONS

Fundamental to any system of adjudicatory procedure is a requirement that the decisionmaker state findings of fact and reasons for the decision. Recall the elements of a constitutionally required adjudicative hearing in *Goldberg v. Kelly* ("the decision maker should state the reasons for his determination and indicate the evidence he relied on, though his statement need not amount to a full opinion or even formal findings of fact and conclusions of law"). All APAs include such requirements. *See* § 557(c) of the federal act and § 413(d) of the 2010 MSAPA, which provides: "A recommended, initial, or final order must separately state findings of fact and conclusions of law on all material issues of fact, law, or discretion, the remedy prescribed, and, if applicable, the action taken on a petition for a stay . . ." Indeed, § 555(e) requires a statement of reasons in certain cases of informal adjudication—one of the very few federal APA provisions applicable to informal adjudication.

Can a reviewing court require an agency to make findings and provide reasons if no statute calls for them? And what should a reviewing court do when it is dissatisfied with an agency's statement of findings and reasons (or the absence thereof)?

SHIP CREEK HYDRAULIC SYNDICATE V. STATE
685 P.2d 715 (Alaska 1984)

RABINOWITZ, J.:

In 1953, the Territorial Legislature authorized what has become known as the "quick-take" procedure, in which title to [property that is being condemned for a highway project] passes upon the filing of a "declaration of taking" and such matters as the necessity for a taking and the fair market value of the property taken are left for later determination. Twenty-two years later . . . the Legislature amended the "quick-take" statute, requiring a condemning authority to state as part of its declaration of taking that "the property is taken by necessity for a project located in a manner which is most compatible with the greatest public good and the least private injury." If this statement proves to be untrue, the superior court is expressly empowered to divest the condemnor of title or possession.

In [cases decided in 1980 and 1982] we held that statutory amendments required individualized consideration of the private injury a public project would cause each private landholder, and that in some cases this individualized consideration would have to include approximate cost estimates of alternatives to the proposed taking. By amending the statute, we concluded, the Legislature had altered the summary nature of the "quick-take."

How cumbersome this procedure may now be became apparent when Ship Creek Hydraulic Syndicate, petitioner here, sought review of the superior court's refusal to set aside the taking of its Anchorage property. Ship Creek's objections had precipitated a four-day hearing, during which engineers debated the merits of the State's decision about where to locate the A–C Couplet, an Anchorage highway project. We granted Ship Creek's petition in order to decide whether by summarizing their decisions in a "decisional document" condemning authorities might be able to simplify and rationalize the inquiries Alaska statutes and this Court's decisions have imposed upon them.

A "decisional document," to quote *SEACC v. State*, 665 P.2d 544, 549 (Alaska 1983), "reflects . . . the facts and premises on which [a] decision . . . [is] based." Thus [the] one-sentence "statement" which [the statute] requires a declaration of taking to include does not qualify as a decisional document. A decisional document should indicate "the determinative reason for the final action taken;" "although detailed findings of fact are not required, the statement of reasons should inform the court and the [private party] of both the grounds of decision and the essential facts upon which the [agency's] inferences are based." If serious objections are raised in relation to action the agency proposes, the decisional document should respond to them.

As we said in *SEACC*,

> A decisional document, done carefully and in good faith, serves several salutary purposes. It facilitates judicial review by demonstrating those factors which were considered. It tends to ensure careful and reasoned administrative deliberation. It assists interested parties in determining whether to seek judicial review. And it tends to restrain agencies from acting beyond the bounds of their jurisdiction.

Moreover, explanations of administrative action have "intrinsic" as well as "instrumental" value. As one commentator has put it:

> The very essence of arbitrariness is to have one's status redefined by the state without an adequate explanation of its

reason for doing so. [Footnote, citing Kafka's *The Trial*, omitted.] It is crucial that this value be seen as distinct from the concern about administrative accuracy—the interest in correcting wrong decisions. Obviously, the two are related since a reasoned explanation is a means of assuring the individual that the facts in his case are correctly perceived. But I would insist that the respect for individual autonomy that is at the foundation of procedural due process imposes a distinct obligation upon the government to explain fully its adverse status decision.

Rabin, *Job Security and Due Process: Monitoring Administrative Discretion Through a Reasons Requirement*, 44 U. CHI. L. REV. 60, 77–78 (1976).

Some decisions are relatively unimportant, and the trouble of explaining them in writing could possibly outweigh any value a written explanation would have. In other cases, the legislature may have specified the procedures an administrative agency must follow, and in order to avoid trespassing on the legislative domain courts should refrain from imposing their own notions of proper procedure on the agency. *Vermont Yankee Nuclear Power Corp. v. NRDC*, 435 U.S. 519 (1978). Furthermore, due process does not require an agency to explain and defend every decision it makes. *Cf. Citizens to Preserve Overton Park, Inc. v. Volpe*, 401 U.S. 402, 417 (1971).

Nevertheless, if a statute requires reasoned decisions, and the legislature has not expressly or by implication limited judicial authority to decide how to review administrative action, courts may and should require agencies to explain their decisions. We think that "quick-take" decisions deserve explanation, and that the necessary explanations be made in a decisional document filed contemporaneously with the declaration of taking.

As the facts of this case demonstrate, the questions our statutes require the taker to answer are complex. . . . In our view the decisions the Legislature has required condemnors to make will be better decisions if they are explained in a contemporaneous decisional document.

The document will also aid property owners in understanding why their property, and not someone else's, is being taken. In some cases this fact alone justifies the use of a decisional document. In others, in which property owners must decide whether or not to contest the authority and necessity for a taking, a reasoned explanation will help them determine whether or not to seek judicial review. . . .

Opposing a requirement that it prepare "quick-take" decisional documents, the Department of Transportation and Public Facilities (DOT/PF) notes that, although the Legislature has set out the procedures a condemnor must follow to use a "quick-take," the statutes do not mention any decisional document requirement. It follows, DOT/PF claims, that courts should not burden it with additional requirements. For this proposition DOT/PF relies on *Vermont Yankee*. But *Vermont Yankee* did not hold that courts could not aid their own review of agency actions by requiring agencies to prepare a comprehensible record. A decisional document organizes the record in ways that make it more easily reviewable. Moreover, the statutory scheme at issue here is far less detailed and comprehensive than was the federal Administrative Procedure Act at issue in *Vermont Yankee*. We thus conclude that *Vermont Yankee* is not controlling and that this court possesses the authority to require condemnors to file decisional documents in conjunction with their use of declarations of taking.

DOT/PF further contends that as a practical matter a decisional document requirement would impose unwarranted burdens on it as well as on other condemnors [because] most takings do not generate objections to their authority and necessity. Taking a narrow view of a decisional document's purpose, DOT/PF argues that most of the documents it might have to prepare would be useless. Whatever the cost of preparing them, it concludes, that expense would be wasted. We reject the argument for three reasons. First, it ignores the fact that decisional documents improve decision-making. Second, [e]ach taking must receive individualized consideration, and we reject any implication that DOT/PF may ignore the statutes' requirements when it thinks that its failure to observe them will not be examined in court. Finally, the fact that few property owners object to takings may be due in large part to the fact that if they object they face elaborate hearings like the one which took place below. If process is simpler, legitimate objections will be easier to make.

We will not impose detailed requirements as to how decisional documents must be structured or as to what they must contain. So long as a decisional document adequately reflects the facts and premises on which a decision is based . . . we will, at least in the first instance, allow takers to decide how this purpose should be implemented in the decisional document.

We must now decide how these general observations affect the case before us. . . . Although a decisional document would have simplified this litigation, requiring one now would only complicate it. We therefore decline to apply the rule we adopt today to the case before us. Our holding is one of first impression. DOT/PF has relied on its belief that state law did not require decisional documents, and forcing it to file such documents with respect to condemnations it has already made would impose a substantial burden on it. . . . [AFFIRMED]

NOTES AND QUESTIONS

1. *Legal authority.* In *Ship Creek,* the court relied on a previous decision, *SEACC v. State.* That case involved a discretionary decision by the Commissioner of Natural Resources to enter into a contract allowing timber cutting on state lands. The contract involved complex and technical decisions relating to the amount and location within the forest of trees that could be cut over a long period of years consistent with the requirement of sustained yield. The case indicated that the Commissioner should prepare a decisional document to facilitate judicial review of his decision (as well as for the other purposes mentioned in the material quoted from *SEACC*). In fact, the Commissioner had prepared such a document, so the language in that case about decisional documents was dictum.

What is the legal basis for the requirement that state agencies prepare a decisional document when making important discretionary decisions like contracting for timber cutting or using the quick-take procedure to condemn land for a highway project? Due process? The Alaska APA? Statutory construction? The needs of the reviewing court? Administrative common law? *See* Sidney A. Shapiro & Richard E. Levy, *Heightened Scrutiny of the Fourth Branch: Separation of Powers and the Requirement of Adequate Reasons for Agency Decisions,* 1987 DUKE L.J. 387 (requirement of findings and reasons is common law technique to promote rational administrative decisionmaking and facilitate judicial review).

Federal courts are precluded from imposing procedural rules on agencies as a matter of administrative common law. *Vermont Yankee Nuclear Power Corp. v. NRDC,* § 5.4.3; *Pension Benefit Guaranty Corp. v. LTV Corp.,* §§ 3.1.1 N.5 and 5.4.3 N.5. The *Vermont Yankee* decision (distinguished in *Ship Creek*) held that a court could not impose requirements for rulemaking procedures beyond those specified in the federal APA in order to improve decisionmaking or facilitate judicial review; *LTV* said the same for adjudication procedures (even though the decision involved informal adjudication as to which the APA requires next to nothing by way of procedure).

In *Vermont Yankee* itself, however, the Supreme Court remanded the case to the lower court, noting that if the lower court found the decision inadequately explained for purposes of judicial review, that court should remand the case to the agency to supply that explanation. Thus courts can require that an agency explain its decision so that it can be properly reviewed. For further discussion of these mixed signals, see § 5.4.3 N.5.

2. *Construing statutes to require findings.* To the *Ship Creek* case, compare *AT&T Wireless PCS, Inc. v. City Council of Virginia Beach,* 155 F.3d 423 (4th Cir. 1998). AT & T applied to a city council for a permit to build two cell phone towers in a residential area. The council held a hearing at which numerous residents opposed the permit, as did a councilman who represented the area in question. The council then voted to deny the application. The decision was recorded by stamping the word "DENIED" on a letter in which

the city planning commission had described the application to the council. The decision was also recorded in a two-page summary of the minutes of the meeting, which described the application, identified the names and views of persons who had testified, and recorded the votes of each councilman. The district court held that the council had violated the federal Telecommunications Act of 1996, which requires that a local government's denial of a permit "shall be in writing and supported by substantial evidence contained in a written record."

The court of appeals reversed, concluding that the above materials satisfied the statutory requirement of a decision in writing. "The simple requirement of a decision 'in writing' cannot reasonably be inflated into a requirement of a "statement of . . . findings and conclusions, and the reasons or basis therefor" [the language of APA § 557(c)]. Nor, according to the court, were findings and reasons required for judicial review; the separate statutory requirement of substantial evidence ensures that there will be sufficient information to serve that purpose.

In a later case, the same court reaffirmed *Virginia Beach* and added: "To require as a matter of federal law . . . that each of [North Carolina's] six hundred odd county and municipal authorities write formal opinions with respect to every zoning decision in every case in which like towers are involved, and file the same contemporaneously with the decision, would create an administrative morass which might not be subject to solution and might well even invite Tenth Amendment scrutiny." *AT&T Wireless PCS, Inc. v. Winston–Salem Zoning Board of Adjustment,* 172 F.3d 307, 313 (4th Cir. 1999).

3.   *Overton Park.* The famous case of *Citizens to Preserve Overton Park, Inc. v. Volpe,* 401 U.S. 402 (1971), raises the question of what a reviewing court should do when an agency decision fails to supply sufficient explanation to permit the decision to be judicially reviewed. (*Overton Park* is further discussed in §§ 9.3.1 and § 10.5.) The Secretary of Transportation granted funds to build an interstate highway through a park. The statute provided that a road should not be built through a park unless there is no feasible and prudent alternative route. The Secretary did not explain why there was no such alternative. As in *Virginia Beach,* and in contrast to *Ship Creek,* the U. S. Supreme Court held that the statute required no explanation.

But without any explanation or administrative record, how could courts review the Secretary's decision? The Supreme Court remanded the case to the district court to conduct a "plenary review" of the decision based on the full record that was before the agency when it made the decision. During that plenary review, the court could require the Secretary to provide an explanation by testimony if that were necessary. Two Justices dissented on the remedy issue. They believed that the case should be remanded to the Secretary to provide the necessary explanation—*not* to the district court to conduct a trial on that issue. Later cases generally follow the dissent on this point. When an agency's decision lacks an explanation and thus cannot be judicially reviewed for rationality, the court should remand the case to the agency to supply the necessary explanation. *See Camp v. Pitts,* 411 U.S. 138 (1973).

4.   *Link between facts and law.* In *Adams v. Board of Review,* 821 P.2d 1 (Utah Ct. App. 1991), the issue was whether a telemarketer's neck and back injuries resulted from repetitive use of the phone at work or from non-occupational causes. There was a large body of conflicting medical evidence. The Workers' Compensation Commission summarized the evidence and found that "the preponderance of medical evidence in this case establishes that the applicant's various listed symptoms are not related to her work as a telemarketer at Unicorp." Reversing the decision because of lack of "subsidiary findings," the court said:

> [T]he Commission's conclusion that Adams failed to prove causation, without supporting findings, is arbitrary. Administrative bodies may not rely upon findings that contain only ultimate conclusions. Given the numerous legal and factual questions regarding causation in this case, the Commission's solitary finding that Adams failed to prove causation does not give the parties any real indication as to the bases for its decision and the steps taken to reach it, nor does it give a reviewing court anything to review.
>
> While the purported "findings of fact" written by the ALJ contain an informative summary of the evidence presented, such a rehearsal of contradictory evidence does not constitute findings of fact. [A finding of fact] must indicate what the ALJ determines in fact occurred, not merely what the contradictory evidence indicates might have occurred . . . Since we cannot even determine why the Commission found there was no causation shown, we clearly cannot assume that the Commission actually made any of the possible subsidiary findings.

5.   *Post hoc rationalizations. Overton Park* and many other cases hold that if an agency has failed to make findings or to state reasons, the deficiency cannot be repaired by after-the-fact rationalizations. For example, courts routinely refuse to consider an explanation of the agency's decision that is provided by agency lawyers in a brief, because the agency heads must take responsibility for the decision, not the agency's lawyers. This rule follows from the fundamental principle that a reviewing court must judge the propriety of agency action solely on the grounds invoked by the agency heads. If those grounds are inadequate or improper, the court should not affirm the administrative action by substituting a different rationale. *SEC v. Chenery Corp.,* 318 U.S. 80 (1943). (This decision is referred to as *Chenery I; Chenery II* is discussed in § 6.2.) For a thorough review of the issues regarding the application of *Chenery I,* see Kevin M. Stack, *The Constitutional Foundations of* Chenery, 116 YALE L.J. 952, 960–81 (2007).

Does the resistance to post hoc rationalizations make sense? In many situations, it does. A poorly explained decision may be evidence of a poorly reasoned decision and the *Chenery I* doctrine compels the agency head to take a fresh look at the problem which might well lead to a different outcome.

However, in some cases, *Chenery I* requires a costly and useless Ping-Pong game. When there is little reason to think the agency would come out differently and either the agency lawyers or responsible agency officials supply a legally adequate post-hoc explanation, why remand the case to the agency for new findings? *See* Richard Murphy, *Chenery Unmasked: Reasonable Limits on the Duty to Give Reasons,* 80 U. CIN. L. REV. 817 (2012). After all, agency lawyers represent the agency. At the time of judicial review, why shouldn't they be allowed to consult with the agency heads and supply any findings or reasons missing in the agency decision, so long as the findings or reasons are supported by the administrative record?

Thus courts have occasionally ignored *Chenery* or made exceptions to it. *See, e.g., Bagdonas v. Dep't of Treasury,* 93 F.3d 422 (7th Cir. 1996). In this case, Bagdonas had been convicted of a gun-related crime. One of the penalties was a lifetime ban on possession of firearms. The Bureau of Alcohol, Tobacco & Firearms had power to relieve him of this restriction. BATF studied Bagdonas' application to lift the restriction carefully and rejected it without explanation. In the district court, the official who made the BATF decision supplied a detailed and persuasive explanation for the rejection decision. The court of appeals reluctantly upheld BATF's action, stating that a remand to the agency for reconsideration and a new explanation would be a waste of time. It was inconceivable that BATF would change its mind if the case were remanded to it. "Despite our disapproval of the agency's initial handling of this matter—and with the expectation that we shall not see a similar performance again—we must conclude that, as the case comes to us, the Director's determination was not arbitrary, capricious, or unreasonable." Ordinarily, however, a reviewing court cannot be certain about what would happen if the case were returned to the agency, and in those circumstances, the *Bagdonas* exception does not apply. *See Florida Power & Light Co. v. Lorion,* 470 U.S. 729, 744 (1985) ("if the reviewing court simply cannot evaluate the challenged agency action on the basis of the record before it, the proper course, except in rare circumstances, is to remand to the agency").

6.   *Findings at every level?* In a typical administrative adjudication, an administrative judge conducts the hearing and renders a proposed decision that contains findings of fact and conclusions of law. The matter is then considered by the agency heads. More often than not, the agency heads summarily affirm the proposed decision. The agency heads are not required to explain their decision to accept the proposed decision. One set of findings and conclusions is all that either due process or the APAs require. *See Guentchev v. INS,* 77 F.3d 1036 (7th Cir. 1996), which states:

> To adopt someone else's reasoned explanation *is* to give reasons. . . . Writing imposes mental discipline, but we lack any principled ground to declare that members of the Board must use words different from those the immigration judge selected. . . . The

point is that an appellate tribunal is entitled to adopt the opinion of its predecessor; the form of words it chooses to do so is irrelevant.

On the other hand, in *Armstrong v. Commodity Futures Trading Commission,* 12 F.3d 401 (3d Cir. 1993), the agency heads affirmed an ALJ opinion, finding that the ALJ "reached a substantially correct result on all the allegations." The court held that this decision failed to satisfy § 557(c) of the APA, since it left uncertain which specific findings by the ALJ were incorrect. In addition, the ALJ's decision violated § 557(c) for another reason: it relied on a specific statute to hold a commodities broker personally liable for offenses committed by his controlled corporation, but failed to include any findings on the elements required by that statute to hold a controlling person liable.

7. *Problem.* A statute permits the Nevada Gaming Board, in its discretion, to exclude from the premises of all casinos a person who has an "unsavory reputation that would adversely affect public confidence in the gaming industry." The Gaming Board has never adopted any rules that would clarify this statute but has entered about a dozen exclusion orders.

Sally, who lives in Pennsylvania, enjoys gambling and often visits Nevada casinos. After conducting a hearing, the Board entered an order excluding Sally from all Nevada casinos. Evidence presented at the hearing indicated that Sally had a long-term romantic relationship with Max. Max is generally considered to be an important figure in organized crime in Pennsylvania. Neither Max nor Sally has ever been convicted of a crime. At the hearing both Max and Sally denied any connection with organized crime. However, there was evidence that Sally often carried messages and did other chores for the members of Max's crime "family."

The Board's only finding was that Sally had an unsavory reputation that would adversely affect public confidence in the gaming industry. On judicial review, should the Board's order be reversed if a) no APA applies? b) Federal APA § 557(c) applies? c) 2010 MSAPA § 413(d) applies? *See Spilotro v. State ex rel. Nevada Gaming Comm'n,* 661 P.2d 467 (Nev. 1983); *Kraft v. Jacka,* 872 F.2d 862 (9th Cir. 1989).

§ 4.4   EFFECTS OF ADJUDICATORY DECISIONS: RES JUDICATA AND STARE DECISIS

This subchapter considers the subsequent effect of an agency adjudicatory decision. It first addresses the preclusive effect of a decision upon later adjudication—the doctrines of res judicata and collateral estoppel. Second, it takes up stare decisis and considers the extent to which an agency can depart from its own prior precedents.

§ 4.4.1 RES JUDICATA AND COLLATERAL ESTOPPEL

Under the rule of res judicata (sometimes called "claim preclusion"), a valid and final personal judgment is conclusive of a claim. If the judgment is for the plaintiff, the claim is extinguished and merged in the judgment; if the judgment is for the defendant, plaintiff is barred from reasserting the claim. *See* RESTATEMENT OF JUDGMENTS 2d § 17.

Under the related doctrine of collateral estoppel (or "issue preclusion"), when an issue of fact or law is actually litigated and determined by a valid and final judgment, and the determination is essential to the judgment, the determination is conclusive in a subsequent action between the parties, *even on a different claim. Id.* § 27. In administrative law, collateral estoppel arises more frequently than res judicata, because the second case generally concerns a different "claim" but depends upon a matter determined in the first case. The key question is whether an administrative adjudicatory hearing provided the private party with a full and fair opportunity to litigate the claim or issue in question.

J.S. v. BETHLEHEM AREA SCHOOL DISTRICT
794 A.2d 936 (Pa. Commw. Ct. 2002)

JIULIANTE, J.

[While an eighth grade student at Nitschmann Middle School, J.S. ("Student") created a web site entitled "Teacher Sux" on his home computer. It contained derogatory, profane, and threatening comments about his algebra teacher, Mrs. Fulmer, and the principal, Mr. Kartsotis. After two days of disciplinary hearings, the School Board concluded that Student violated the Student Code of Conduct by 1) making threats to a teacher, 2) harassing a teacher and 3) showing disrespect to a teacher. Consequently, the School Board voted to permanently expel Student. The decision was upheld by the trial court, the Commonwealth Court, and the Pennsylvania Supreme Court. *See J. S. v. Bethlehem Area School Dist.,* 807 A.2d 847 (Pa. 2002). Student filed a separate state court action for money damages under 42 U.S.C. § 1983, alleging that School District violated his First Amendment rights. The trial court dismissed this action on the grounds of res judicata and collateral estoppel. Discussion of "res judicata" is omitted.]

Collateral estoppel bars a subsequent lawsuit where (1) an issue decided in a prior action is identical to one presented in a later action, (2) the prior action resulted in a final judgment on the merits, (3) the party against whom collateral estoppel is asserted was a party to the prior action, or is in privity with a party to the prior action, and (4) the party against whom collateral estoppel is asserted had a full and fair opportunity to litigate the issue in the prior action.

Appellants contend only that they were denied an opportunity to fully and fairly litigate the issues before the School Board in that there was no discovery in the expulsion proceedings, the School Board was not an independent fact finder, Student was unable to testify on his own behalf and the School Board was not a court of competent jurisdiction. . . .

Student was represented by counsel during the hearings, which took place on August 19 and 26, 1998. Both Mr. Kartsotis and Mrs. Fulmer testified at the hearings and Appellants were given an opportunity to cross-examine them. Thus, Student was afforded the discovery due to him under the Code's regulations. [Student missed the second hearing because his parents had enrolled him at an out-of-state school but his counsel and parents were present.] . . .

Appellants further complain that the School Board was not a court of competent jurisdiction and that it was not an independent fact finder. The law, however, provides that where an agency is acting in a judicial capacity and resolves disputed issues of fact that the parties had an opportunity to fully litigate, the courts will not hesitate to apply preclusion principles. . . . Thus, the School Board was acting in a quasi-judicial capacity when it undertook expulsion proceedings against Student. We therefore agree that Appellants were granted a full and fair opportunity to litigate the alleged violations of Student's constitutional rights in the prior proceeding.

Notwithstanding, Appellants argue that an administrative agency's determination should only preclude subsequent litigation before another administrative agency. [Pennsylvania authority establishes] that collateral estoppel principles apply between an action before an administrative agency and a subsequent action before [a] court. . . . Because Appellants' underlying causes of action are precluded, their § 1983 claims are no longer viable. A § 1983 claim is not a cause of action separate from the underlying federal right, but rather, a vehicle for asserting one's rights. Accordingly, we affirm.

FRIEDMAN, J. dissenting.

[Judge Friedman argued that Student did not have a full and fair opportunity to litigate the expulsion case before the School Board. Consequently, the decision by the Board that expulsion did not violate Student's First Amendment rights should not be preclusive of that issue in the § 1983 action]. . . . First . . . this is a case of the highest magnitude involving Student's First Amendment right to free speech. Moreover, it is a complex matter because the case involves the effect on an entire school community of an alleged threat made against one teacher on a student's web site. [The dissenter found no precedents involving a threat made against a teacher on a student's web site.]

Second, with respect to urgency, the regulation governing a local school board's formal expulsion proceeding specifically states that the "proceeding must be held with all reasonable speed." Third, because pre-hearing discovery is not permitted, the parties have little, if any, opportunity to obtain evidence prior to the hearing. [The FBI and local police both declined to recommend prosecution but refused to release their files to Student.] Moreover, absent pre-hearing discovery, a party does not have a fair opportunity to rebut the evidence and argument of the opposing party. Considering these factors, I conclude that the final determination by the School Board in this case is not conclusive under the rules of res judicata. . . .

Indeed, the majority never addresses the fact that an administrative agency does not have authority to decide the constitutionality of its own action. Therefore, the local school board in this case could *not* fully litigate Student's constitutional challenge to the school board's action. . . .

NOTES AND QUESTIONS

1. *Full and fair opportunity to litigate.* In order for an administrative decision to have collateral estoppel effect, the private party must have had a full and fair opportunity to litigate. As the U. S. Supreme Court said, "Redetermination of issues is warranted if there is reason to doubt the quality, extensiveness, or fairness of procedures followed in prior litigation." *Montana v. United States,* 440 U.S. 147, 164 (1979). Nevertheless, as the *J.S.* case shows, the administrative decision need not include all of the procedural rights of a prior judicial decision. For example, in *J.S.* the student did not have the opportunity to engage in discovery by taking the depositions of the witnesses who would testify against him. There was no right to a jury. The student had no opportunity to testify, because he had left town to enroll in a different school by the time of the second hearing. The school board proceeding came much more quickly than a judicial trial would have. The Bethlehem Area School Board that made the decision was also the employer of the alleged victims, Fulmer and Kartsotis. In comparison, a trial judge has no connection with the dispute. Do you think it is fair for an administrative hearing of this kind to preclude subsequent litigation of a First Amendment issue in court?

2. *Constitutional issues and collateral estoppel.* The *J.S.* case involves important and difficult issues relating to the First Amendment rights of students. Presumably students have a constitutional right to criticize or mock their teachers in off-campus websites (as they have done for generations over the phone), but not to threaten them. If collateral estoppel applies, the student is precluded from relitigating constitutional issues in a separate damages action under § 1983 for violation of constitutional rights. The

dissent is correct that agencies in most states lack the power to hold statutes unconstitutional, but they normally have the power to decide the application of constitutional principles to the issues before them, such as whether the First Amendment protects J.S.'s website. (*See* § 11.2.3 N.5.) Should collateral estoppel apply to a school board's determination of whether student speech was protected by the First Amendment?

Could J.S. have avoided the collateral estoppel problem by skipping the school expulsion hearing (thus conceding that he would be expelled from Nitschmann) and going straight to the damage action? Normally a litigant is required to exhaust administrative remedies before seeking judicial relief, but there is an exception for § 1983 cases. See *Patsy v. Florida Bd. of Regents*, 457 U.S. 496, discussed in § 11.2.3 N.7.

3. *Collateral estoppel in unemployment hearings.* In the *J.S.* case, the majority distinguished an earlier Pennsylvania Supreme Court decision that refused collateral estoppel effect to a decision of the state unemployment compensation agency. *Rue v. K-Mart Corp.*, 713 A.2d 82 (Pa. 1998). In that case, employee Rue was fired for allegedly eating a bag of potato chips without paying for them. Rue won the employment hearing, because a referee decided that he did not misappropriate company property or eat a bag of potato chips. Rue collected unemployment benefits and then sued K-Mart for defamation. K-Mart was allowed to argue that Rue had stolen the chips, because collateral estoppel did not apply. Why would unemployment compensation cases be treated differently from student expulsion cases?

In contrast, under New York law, collateral estoppel applies to unemployment cases. In *Ryan v. New York Telephone Co.,* 467 N.E.2d 487 (N.Y. 1984), Ryan was fired for theft of company property. The unemployment agency denied benefits because it upheld the theft charge. Later criminal proceedings were dismissed "in the interests of justice." Ryan sued the company for false arrest, wrongful discharge, and slander. The court held that collateral estoppel applied. The issues resolved in the administrative proceeding were dispositive of his tort claims, and he had a full and fair opportunity to litigate them before the agency. It was his choice to appear without counsel.

4. *Criminal cases.* Suppose a welfare recipient is criminally prosecuted and convicted of welfare fraud. In a later case before the welfare agency, the state attempts to recoup the illegal payments. Can the welfare recipient relitigate the issue of whether she was entitled to the payments? Suppose she was acquitted in the criminal case. Can the state relitigate the issue of whether she was entitled to the payments?

Suppose the state's action before the agency to recoup the overpayments precedes the criminal case. The recipient wins before the agency. Can the prosecution relitigate the issue in the criminal case? *See United States v. Payne,* 2 F.3d 706, 707–10 (6th Cir.1993) (yes); *People v. Garcia,* 141 P.3d 197 (Cal. 2006) (no). Suppose the recipient loses the administrative case. Can she relitigate the issue in the subsequent criminal case?

Suppose an employer is criminally convicted for violating workplace safety laws. An agency then seeks to collect civil money penalties for the same offense. Should the agency be barred by the constitutional prohibition against double jeopardy? Probably not, because double jeopardy applies only to successive *criminal* prosecutions. Administrative monetary penalties, although punitive in some respects, are not a criminal sanction. *Hudson v. United States*, 522 U.S. 93 (1997).

5.   *Preclusion against the government on issues of law.* In *United States v. Stauffer Chemical Co.*, 464 U.S. 165 (1984), the Court held that the federal government could be barred from relitigating a *legal* issue it had lost in an action involving the same party. Stauffer had won a Tenth Circuit decision that it could exclude certain inspectors from its plant. The identical issue arose in the Sixth Circuit, where Stauffer had another plant. The government was precluded from relitigating the issue in the Sixth Circuit (which had not previously decided the issue).

Non-mutual collateral estoppel is generally allowable, in the trial court's discretion, against a private party that loses a case brought by A and is then sued by B in a case involving the same issue. *See Parklane Hosiery Co. v. Shore*, 439 U.S. 322 (1979), holding that a decision against Parklane in a civil case brought by the SEC based on a false proxy statement is preclusive in a later class action for damages brought by Parklane's shareholders.

However, non-mutual collateral estoppel does not lie against the federal government. *United States v. Mendoza,* 464 U.S. 154 (1984). In *Mendoza,* an earlier *trial court* decision (in the Ninth Circuit) held that certain Philippine nationals were entitled to U.S. citizenship. The government did not appeal. The present case (which also arose in the Ninth Circuit) involved the same issue but with different Philippine claimants. They argued that the government was precluded from relitigating the issue.

Mendoza held that the government should be allowed (or even encouraged) to relitigate the issue, in hope of creating a conflict between the circuits, so that the issue might "percolate" to the Supreme Court. Also, the Court was concerned with the realities of government litigation—the U.S. should not be forced to appeal every case it loses in a trial court, no matter how unimportant, in order to guard against preclusion in later (and perhaps far more important) litigation. Moreover, a new administration should be able to change the policy of a prior one (which had decided to accept a defeat and not appeal). *See* Note, *Collateral Estoppel and Non-Acquiescence: Precluding Government Relitigation*, 99 HARV. L. REV. 847 (1986).

6.   *Non-acquiescence.* The federal government argues that it can freely relitigate an issue, despite having lost an *appellate* decision on the identical point in the *same circuit* against a different party. This is referred to as intra-circuit non-acquiescence. Despite *Mendoza* (discussed in N.5, holding that the government is not subject to non-mutual collateral estoppel), the courts have rejected the practice of intracircuit non-acquiescence. *See, e.g., Lopez v. Heckler,* 713 F.2d 1432 (9th Cir. 1983) (preliminary injunction granted); 464

U.S. 879 (1983) (5–4 vote to stay the injunction); 725 F.2d 1489 (9th Cir. 1984) (narrower injunction issued).

The background of the *Lopez* case was a policy of the Department of Health and Human Services (HHS). HHS terminated large numbers of persons receiving federal disability payments without any new evidence that their conditions had improved. Earlier Ninth Circuit cases had held that this was improper. But HHS went right on terminating recipients, even though they lived in the Ninth Circuit. As a result the recipients (mostly poor and quite sick) had to go to the expense of litigating the issue; because of the prior cases, they were certain to win—if they could survive long enough. In *Lopez* (a class action brought by persons whose benefits had been terminated), the court affirmed a preliminary injunction against HHS' non-acquiescence policy.

A concurring opinion said:

> The Secretary's ill-advised policy of refusing to obey the decisional law of this circuit is akin to the repudiated pre-Civil War doctrine of nullification whereby rebellious states refused to recognize certain federal laws within their boundaries. The Secretary's non-acquiescence not only scoffs at the law of this circuit, but flouts some very important principles basic to our American system of government—the rule of law, the doctrine of separation of powers embedded in the constitution, and the tenet of judicial supremacy laid down in *Marbury v. Madison* ... The government expects its citizens to abide by the law—no less is expected of those charged with the duty to faithfully administer the law. 713 F.2d at 1441.

The first *Lopez* decision preceded *Mendoza;* the second *Lopez* opinion said that *Mendoza* was not applicable. 725 F.2d at 1497 n.5. Can you distinguish *Lopez* from *Mendoza?*

7. *Res judicata.* Although it is less common than collateral estoppel, courts do occasionally invoke res judicata (otherwise known as claim preclusion) in administrative law cases. In *Worthington v. United States*, 50 Fed. Cl. 712 (2001), *aff'd on other grounds*, 53 Fed. Appx. 77 (Fed. Cir. 2002), a former Agriculture Department employee filed suit in the Court of Federal Claims, seeking overtime pay pursuant to the Back Pay Act. He lost, in part because he had already unsuccessfully sought the same relief on an illegal discrimination theory from the department's Equal Employment Opportunity office but without raising the Back Pay Act issue. As a result, he was precluded from raising that issue in the second case, given that he could have raised it in the first case. In contrast, in *People v. Damon*, 59 Cal. Rptr. 504 (Cal. App. 1996), an ALJ in the state's Bureau of Consumer Affairs suspended the registration of Damon's auto repair shop because of his overcharging, performing unnecessary work, failing to keep required records, etc. Then the county district attorney filed a civil suit against Damon, seeking injunctive relief and restitution for consumers. The court held that

the earlier proceeding did not preclude this action, because the Bureau did not have authority to grant the relief sought by the district attorney.

8.   *Problem.* The Monroe Corporations Commission (MCC) licenses stockbrokers. It can impose penalties (such as license revocation) against brokers who engage in misconduct (such as insider trading).

Your client, Jed, is a stock broker in Monroe. MCC suspects that Jed used inside information about Z Corp. mergers to make large profits for himself and for clients. Jed denies that he engaged in insider trading (he says he received no tips and instead developed the information by his own shrewd analysis). Jed has very large potential liability in civil litigation that might be brought in federal court under SEC rules by persons who sold Z Corp. stock while Jed and his clients were buying it.

MCC staff told you that the agency is willing to negotiate a one-year suspension of Jed's license. Jed wants to fight the case before MCC. Do you advise him to take the deal? *See* Edmund H. Kerr & Robert J. Stillman, *Collateral Estoppel Implications of SEC Adjudications*, 42 BUS. LAW. 441 (1987).

§ 4.4.2 CONSISTENCY OF DECISIONS AND STARE DECISIS

Under the principle of stare decisis, courts generally follow their own precedents and lower courts must adhere to precedents established by higher courts. Stare decisis assures consistency and predictability in the law. By minimizing litigation it also serves the purpose of judicial economy. Yet courts occasionally reconsider and depart from prior precedents—and they do not always admit they are doing so. Do the reasons for stare decisis apply with equal force to agency adjudicatory decisions? Greater or less force? What must an agency do if it wishes to abandon its precedents and set a new course?

UNITED AUTOMOBILE WORKERS V. NLRB
802 F.2d 969 (7th Cir. 1986)

[A collective bargaining agreement provided that National Lock Co. would "discuss" any relocation of its plant with the Union. Applicable labor law provides that a company must negotiate a plant relocation with the union if it is motivated by concern over labor costs. However, this statutory protection can be waived. The Board held that the agreement to "discuss" relocation was a waiver of the Union's right to "negotiate" over the issue. Prior Board decisions hold that there is a presumption against waiver and that to overcome the presumption, an alleged waiver must be clear and unmistakable. The Board did not discuss or cite any of those prior decisions in this case.]

POSNER, J.:

. . . We grant that despite the strong judicial endorsement of the rule [creating a presumption against waiver] the Board—which knows more about the dynamics of collective bargaining than the courts—might be able to dilute or abandon it, since the rule is a nonobvious gloss on the statute. And there [is] evidence that a desire to abandon or dilute, rather than mere oversight, does indeed lie behind the Board's failure to mention the rule. . . . [T]he administrative law judge had relied heavily on the presumption against inferring the waiver of a statutory right and the union had argued the presumption vigorously throughout the case. So the Board could not just have forgotten about the rule; and if it didn't mention the rule just because it did not want to weaken the force of its opinion, this would be the equivalent of wanting to dilute or abandon the rule. . . .

All this is rather bootless conjecture, though. For it makes no difference what the Board may have had in mind but failed to express; an administrative agency is not allowed to change direction without some explanation of what it is doing and why. This general principle of administrative law . . . is applicable to adjudication as well as to explicit "notice and comment" rulemaking. The fact that the Board has such broad discretion in deciding which route to follow, *NLRB v. Bell Aerospace Co.* [§ 6.2, holding the Board can choose between rulemaking and adjudication when it wishes to make or change policy], shows that the Board cannot be allowed to escape the obligation of justifying changes in its policies merely by following the common law route; the fact that common law rulemaking is retroactive buttresses this conclusion. So while not bound by *stare decisis,* the Board can jettison its precedents only if it has "adequately explicated the basis of its [new] interpretation."

. . . Forcing an administrative agency to 'fess up to its changes of position may seem productive merely of paper shuffling, and also inconsistent with the genius of the common law, which allows new doctrines to be created implicitly and even surreptitiously by judges who deny all the while that they are changing the law. Yet agencies often are forced to explicate decisions that judges and juries, not to mention legislative and executive branch officials, are allowed to make without explanation. The reason may be that agencies unlike courts are not constrained to make policy by the common law route, but can use explicit rulemaking procedures. Indeed, agencies are often criticized (none more so than the Labor Board) for not making greater use of their rulemaking powers. . . .

Another consideration may be that independent agencies, such as the Labor Board, in combining legislative, executive, and judicial functions, seem somehow to elude the constitutional system of checks and balances.

But these agencies are checked by other organs of government (as a legislature with executive and judicial functions, or an executive with legislative and judicial functions, would not be), even if they lack internal checks and balances—and the Administrative Procedure Act creates some. Moreover, the rule that the agency must explain its about-faces is not limited to the independent agencies; it extends to administrative agencies within the executive branch . . .

The decision reversing the administrative law judge does not contain a reasoned analysis of the law and the evidence, and we therefore set aside the decision and return the case to the Board.

NOTES AND QUESTIONS

1.   *Agency failure to follow its precedents.* Why do you think the NLRB failed to 'fess up to its changes in position? And if courts can and often do avoid unwelcome prior precedents by ignoring them or confining them "to their facts," why can't an agency do so?

Is it a waste of time for a court to reverse an agency decision that makes an unexplained shift in position even though the decision is otherwise legally correct (i.e. both the old and the new positions are consistent with the underlying statute) and supported by substantial evidence? Isn't the agency likely to reach the same result over again, this time with the necessary explanation?

The *UAW* case observes that agencies can change course through rulemaking as well as through case-by-case adjudication, although traditionally the NLRB has refused to adopt rules (see § 6.2). Is the requirement that an agency identify and justify a change in position more important in adjudication than in rulemaking? Or less important?

2.   *Refusal to depart from precedent.* Suppose a party attacks an existing precedent as irrational. Is the agency required to reconsider the precedent and explain why it has decided to stay the course? Or can it just cite existing precedents without explanation? *See Flagstaff Broadcasting Found. v. FCC,* 979 F.2d 1566 (D.C. Cir. 1992). In that case, the FCC brushed aside Flagstaff's argument that the agency should abandon its criterion favoring "integration of ownership and management" in deciding which applicant for a broadcasting frequency is best qualified. That criterion disqualified Flagstaff, because its owners and directors (five women of color devoted to community activism) did not plan to manage the station on a day-to-day basis.

> The FCC denies that its decision was improper, and argues that it was merely applying established policy—an action that does not require an elaborate explanation or justification. . . . An agency's action will be set aside by a reviewing court whenever the agency fails to provide a reasoned basis for its decision . . . This principle applies to all agency action, regardless of whether it involves

established policy or the application of brand-new rules of interpretation . . . Conclusory statements of binding precedent and policy will not suffice.

Does the *Flagstaff* rule place an unduly heavy burden on agencies?

§ 4.5   PROTECTION OF RELIANCE INTERESTS

This subchapter considers whether an agency must respect reliance interests created by its prior adjudicatory decisions or by other acts, such as advice giving, on which people have relied.

§ 4.5.1 NOTICE OF THE APPLICABLE LEGAL STANDARD

In order to sanction a private party, an agency must give the party adequate notice of the charges against that party so that it can prepare a defense. *See* § 3.3.1 N.3. In addition, the agency must furnish the party with proper notice of the legal standard the agency is enforcing against the party, so it has an opportunity to conform its behavior to that standard. The most unequivocal way for the agency to establish a legal standard is through the adoption of a prospective rule that sets forth that standard. See §§ 5.1, § 6.2. However, a legal standard can also be established through an adjudicatory precedent. As we saw in § 4.4.2, when an agency decides not to follow its precedents, it must explicitly acknowledge that it has changed course. But where does that leave people who relied on the prior precedent?

FCC v. FOX TELEVISION STATIONS, INC. (FOX II)
132 S. Ct. 2307 (2012)

KENNEDY, J.

Title 18 U. S. C. § 1464 provides that "[w]hoever utters any obscene, indecent, or profane language by means of radio communication shall be fined . . . or imprisoned not more than two years, or both." The Federal Communications Commission [enforces] § 1464 . . . [In] *FCC v. Pacifica Foundation*, 438 U. S. 726 (1978), the Commission determined that [a radio broadcast of] George Carlin's "Filthy Words" monologue was indecent. It contained "language that describes, in terms patently offensive as measured by contemporary community standards for the broadcast medium, sexual or excretory activities and organs, at times of the day when there is a reasonable risk that children may be in the audience." This Court upheld the Commission's ruling [under the statute and the First Amendment]. . . .

From 1978 to 1987, the Commission did not go beyond the narrow circumstances of *Pacifica* and brought no indecency enforcement actions. . . . [T]he Commission distinguished between the "repetitive occurrence of the 'indecent' words" (such as in the Carlin monologue) and an "isolated" or "occasional" expletive, that would not necessarily be actionable. In 1987, the Commission . . . stated that in later cases [it would] assess the full context of allegedly indecent broadcasts [but] continued to note the important difference between isolated and repeated broadcasts of indecent material. [A 2001 policy statement by the Commission reaffirmed the relevance of that distinction.]

. . . It was against this regulatory background that the three incidents of alleged indecency at issue here took place. First, in the 2002 Billboard Music Awards, broadcast by respondent Fox Television Stations, Inc., the singer Cher exclaimed during an unscripted acceptance speech: "I've also had my critics for the last 40 years saying that I was on my way out every year. Right. So f* * * 'em." Second, Fox broadcast the Billboard Music Awards again in 2003. There, a person named Nicole Richie made the following unscripted remark while presenting an award: "Have you ever tried to get cow s* * * out of a Prada purse? It's not so f* * *ing simple." The third incident involved an episode of NYPD Blue, a regular television show broadcast by respondent ABC Television Network. The episode broadcast on February 25, 2003, showed the nude buttocks of an adult female character for approximately seven seconds and for a moment the side of her breast . . .

After these incidents, but before the Commission issued Notices of Apparent Liability to Fox and ABC, the Commission issued a decision sanctioning NBC for a comment made by the singer Bono during the 2003 Golden Globe Awards. Upon winning the award for Best Original Song, Bono exclaimed: "This is really, really, f* * *ing brilliant. Really, really great." [Acknowledging] the isolated nature of the expletive, the Commission reversed prior rulings that had found fleeting expletives not indecent.

Even though the incidents at issue in these cases took place before the *Golden Globes* Order, the Commission applied its new policy regarding fleeting expletives and fleeting nudity. It found the broadcasts by respondents Fox and ABC to be in violation of this standard. . . . [In the *Fox* proceeding, the Commission found the Cher and Richie comments "actionably indecent" under the *Golden Globes* ruling, but it declined to impose any monetary penalty.] The Commission acknowledged that "it was not apparent that Fox could be penalized for Cher's comment at the time it was broadcast."

[Fox appealed to the Second Circuit, which held under the APA that the FCC decision was] arbitrary and capricious, because "the FCC has made a 180-degree turn regarding its treatment of 'fleeting expletives' without providing a reasoned explanation justifying the about-face."

[However, in *FCC v. Fox Television Stations, Inc.*, 556 U.S. 502 (2009) (*Fox I*), by a 5–4 vote, the Supreme Court reversed that APA ruling. The Court's decision held an agency, in the ordinary course, should acknowledge that it is in fact changing its position and "show that there are good reasons for the new policy." See § 4.4.2. There is no need, however, for an agency to provide detailed justifications for every change or to show that the reasons for the new policy are better than the reasons for the old one. The *Fox I* opinion is discussed more fully in § 9.3.2 N.4.]

On remand from *Fox I*, the Court of Appeals held the Commission's indecency policy unconstitutionally vague and invalidated it in its entirety. [Meanwhile, the Commission had found ABC to have violated § 1464.] Unlike in the *Fox* case, the Commission imposed a forfeiture of $27,500 on each of the 45 ABC-affiliated stations that aired the indecent episode. [The] Second Circuit vacated the forfeiture order, determining that it was bound by its *Fox* decision. . . .

II

A fundamental principle in our legal system is that laws which regulate persons or entities must give fair notice of conduct that is forbidden or required. . . . A conviction or punishment fails to comply with due process if the statute or regulation under which it is obtained "fails to provide a person of ordinary intelligence fair notice of what is prohibited, or is so standardless that it authorizes or encourages seriously discriminatory enforcement."

Even when speech is not at issue, the void for vagueness doctrine addresses at least two connected but discrete due process concerns: first, that regulated parties should know what is required of them so they may act accordingly; second, precision and guidance are necessary so that those enforcing the law do not act in an arbitrary or discriminatory way. When speech is involved, rigorous adherence to those requirements is necessary to ensure that ambiguity does not chill protected speech. . . .

[The above] regulatory history, however, makes it apparent that the Commission policy in place at the time of the broadcasts gave no notice to Fox or ABC that a fleeting expletive or a brief shot of nudity could be actionably indecent; yet Fox and ABC were found to be in violation. The Commission's lack of notice to Fox and ABC that its interpretation had changed so the fleeting moments of indecency contained in their broadcasts were a violation of § 1464 as interpreted and enforced by the agency "fail[ed] to provide a person of ordinary intelligence fair notice of what is prohibited." This would be true with respect to a regulatory change this abrupt on any subject, but it is surely the case when applied to the regulations in question, regulations that touch upon "sensitive areas of basic First Amendment freedoms." . . .

The Government raises two arguments in response, but neither is persuasive. . . . [It argued that the FCC had not imposed any sanction against Fox for its violation of § 1464.] [I]t is true that the Commission declined to impose any forfeiture on Fox, and in its order the Commission claimed that it would not consider the indecent broadcasts either when considering whether to renew stations' licenses or "in any other context." [However, the Commission] has the statutory power to take into account "any history of prior offenses" when setting the level of a forfeiture penalty. Just as in the First Amendment context, the due process protection against vague regulations "does not leave [regulated parties] . . . at the mercy of *noblesse oblige*." Given that the Commission found it was "not inequitable to hold Fox responsible for [the 2003 broadcast]," and that it has the statutory authority to use its finding to increase any future penalties, the Government's assurance it will elect not to do so is insufficient to remedy the constitutional violation.

In addition, when combined with the legal consequence described above, reputational injury provides further reason for granting relief to Fox. Cf. *Paul v. Davis,* [§ 2.2.2 N.7] (explaining that an "alteration of legal status . . . combined with the injury resulting from the defamation" justifies the invocation of procedural safeguards). As respondent CBS points out, findings of wrongdoing can result in harm to a broadcaster's "reputation with viewers and advertisers . . ." The challenged orders could have an adverse impact on Fox's reputation that audiences and advertisers alike are entitled to take into account.

With respect to ABC, the Government with good reason does not argue no sanction was imposed. The fine against ABC and its network affiliates for the seven seconds of nudity was nearly $1.24 million. The Government argues instead that ABC had notice that the scene in NYPD Blue would be considered indecent in light of a 1960 decision where the Commission declared that the "televising of nudes might well raise a serious question of programming contrary to 18 U.S.C. § 1464." This argument does not prevail. An isolated and ambiguous statement from a 1960 Commission decision does not suffice for the fair notice required when the Government intends to impose over a $1 million fine for allegedly impermissible speech. . . .

Therefore, the Commission's standards as applied to these broadcasts were vague, and the Commission's orders must be set aside.

III

It is necessary to make three observations about the scope of this decision. First, because the Court resolves these cases on fair notice grounds under the Due Process Clause, it need not address the First Amendment implications of the Commission's indecency policy. It is argued that this Court's ruling in *Pacifica* . . . should be overruled because the rationale of that case has been overtaken by technological change and the wide availability of multiple other choices for listeners and viewers. . . . In light of the Court's holding that the Commission's policy failed to provide fair notice it is unnecessary to reconsider *Pacifica* at this time.

This leads to a second observation. Here, the Court rules that Fox and ABC lacked notice at the time of their broadcasts that the material they were broadcasting could be found actionably indecent under then-existing policies. Given this disposition, it is unnecessary for the Court to address the constitutionality of the current indecency policy as expressed in the *Golden Globes* Order and subsequent adjudications. . . .

Third, this opinion leaves the Commission free to modify its current indecency policy in light of its determination of the public interest and applicable legal requirements. And it leaves the courts free to review the current policy or any modified policy in light of its content and application.

[Court of Appeals judgment vacated. SOTOMAYOR, J., did not participate.]

GINSBURG, J., concurring in the judgment.

In my view, the Court's decision in *Pacifica* was wrong when it issued. Time, technological advances, and the Commission's untenable rulings in the cases now before the Court show why *Pacifica* bears reconsideration. [Justice Ginsburg cited to Justice Thomas's concurring opinion in *Fox I*, which had likewise called for reconsideration of *Pacifica*.]

NOTES AND COMMENTS

1. *Void for vagueness.* The void-for-vagueness doctrine had its origins in criminal law cases. Prior to *Fox II*, the Supreme Court had not clearly held that the doctrine applies in the administrative law context. Lower courts had already taken that step. An early application of vagueness doctrine occurred in *General Electric Co. v. EPA*, 53 F.3d 1324 (D.C. Cir. 1995). *GE* held that an agency denies due process if it imposes sanctions on a regulated party without having provided fair notice of what conduct it prohibits or requires. "Fair notice" could mean publishing an interpretation of an ambiguous rule or otherwise informing the party of the agency's view before a party takes the action that led the agency to impose sanction against it. In *GE*, a complex and ambiguous EPA regulation concerned permissible methods of disposing of PCBs. GE disposed of PCBs in a manner that represented a reasonable interpretation of the regulation. The EPA read the regulation differently and sought a $25,000 penalty from GE. The court held EPA's reading was reasonable and the court would defer to it on the merits. Nevertheless, EPA

had failed to give GE fair warning of its approach and could not penalize GE for violating the regulation.

A number of cases extended *GE* to cover non-monetary sanctions. For example, in *Trinity Broadcasting of Florida, Inc. v. FCC,* 211 F.3d 618 (D.C. Cir. 2000), the FCC refused to renew a broadcasting license because the licensee (in an application for a different license) had violated FCC regulations. However, this action was set aside because the regulations failed to give fair notice of the FCC's interpretation and its other pronouncements only added to the confusion.

2.   *Possible limitations.* Shortly before the Court's decision in *Fox II,* a lower court had warned: "Agencies cannot be expected to regulate with perfect clarity; this is especially the case with regard to complex regulatory regimes like Medicaid. If an agency were prevented on notice grounds from enforcing its interpretation of a regulation against any party who proffered a reasonable alternative interpretation and suffered any monetary loss, the practice of deferring to an agency's reasonable interpretation of its regulations would be rendered essentially meaningless. Courts would be flooded with challenges to administrative actions, and agencies would be unable to administer their regulations efficiently. The 'fair notice' doctrine has not been—and ought not be—extended this far." *Arkansas Dep't of Human Servs. v. Sebelius,* 818 F. Supp. 2d 107, 122 (D.D.C. 2011). Is this a fair criticism of the *Fox II* analysis?

Prompted by these concerns, the court in *Arkansas Dep't* observed that most cases applying the doctrine had involved explicit penalties. It concluded that a "disallowance of federal matching funds that had been provided to a state [under Medicaid] is categorically different from the kinds of sanctions courts have found 'sufficiently grave' to merit the application of the 'fair notice' doctrine." *Id.* at 121. After *Fox II,* is this a viable distinction? Is the *Fox II* holding persuasive in relation to the two fact situations involved in that case itself?

Consider the assertion in the *Fox II* opinion that the objection based on fair notice "would be true with respect to a regulatory change this abrupt on any subject, but it is surely the case when applied to the regulations in question, regulations that touch upon 'sensitive areas of basic First Amendment freedoms.'" Should the void for vagueness doctrine articulated in *Fox II* be applied with equal strictness in a case that does not raise First Amendment concerns?

3.   *First Amendment.* Why do you think the Supreme Court in *Fox II* refused to decide whether there is a First Amendment right to broadcast fleeting expletives?

4.   *Retroactive adjudication as an abuse of discretion.* "Retroactivity is the norm in agency adjudications no less than in judicial adjudications." *AT&T v. FCC,* 454 F.3d 329, 332 (D.C. Cir. 2006). Therefore, when an agency changes its legal interpretation or its policy through the adjudicatory process,

that change normally applies retroactively to the private party to that adjudication, even though that party might have relied on the prior law or policy. Similarly, the precedent created by that adjudicatory decision will be applied to other parties who might also have relied on the prior authority.

There are, however, some exceptions to the rule of retroactivity. Under some circumstances, a reviewing court may determine that retroactive application of a legal interpretation or policy is a "manifest injustice" and should be set aside as an abuse of discretion. (Abuse of discretion, otherwise known as arbitrary and capricious review, is discussed in § 9.3.) This approach represents a non-constitutional technique for protection of reliance interests (as opposed to the constitutional approach taken in *Fox II*). Are there good reasons why an agency should have less freedom to apply a new case law principle retroactively than a court would have?

According to a leading case, the question of whether retroactive application of a changed legal interpretation or policy is a manifest injustice entails balancing at least five factors: "(1) whether the particular case is one of first impression; (2) whether the new rule represents an abrupt departure from well-established practice or merely attempts to fill a void in an unsettled area of the law; (3) the extent to which the party against whom the new law is applied relied on the prior law; (4) the degree of the burden which a retroactive order imposes on a party; and (5) the statutory interest in applying the new rule to the case at hand despite the reliance of a party on the old standard." *Retail, Wholesale & Dep't Store Union v. NLRB,* 466 F.2d 380, 390 (D.C. Cir. 1972).

In *Retail Union,* Coca-Cola refused to rehire workers who had been on strike against it. The NLRB found that the employer had committed an unfair labor practice by failing to rehire the workers. As a result, it ordered Coca-Cola to rehire them and to compensate them with back pay. The company appealed, arguing that its refusal to rehire had been permissible under the Board's case law at the time it occurred. After Coca-Cola's refusal to reinstate the workers, the Board had overruled that case law. Its finding against Coca-Cola was based on the newly announced precedent. Applying the above factors to these circumstances, the court decided that the NLRB's reinstatement and back pay order added up to a "manifest injustice" and should be set aside as an abuse of discretion.

In subsequent years the D.C. Circuit has deemphasized the five-factor formula, but it has adhered to the same basic approach of weighing concerns about reliance and unfair surprise against countervailing factors. See *Verizon Tel. Co. v. FCC,* 269 F.3d 1098 (D.C. Cir. 2001). For example, in *Cassell v. FCC,* 154 F.3d 478 (D.C. Cir. 1998), the FCC adopted a "finder's preference" program applicable to licensing of private land mobile radio stations. Under this program, if an applicant for a license presented the FCC with evidence that an existing licensee was not complying with certain Commission regulations, the license would be canceled, and the applicant would have first priority for a license to broadcast on the freed-up frequency. In the 1994 *Lott* case, the Commission granted a finder's preference based on a showing that a current licensee was broadcasting five miles from the latitude and longitude coordinates specified in its license. The opinion in that case indicated that a deviation of sixty feet from the licensed location would be deemed unauthorized. Cassell and other entrepreneurs then filed applications for finder's preferences regarding other stations that were not in compliance with the *Lott* criterion. In these cases, however, the FCC decided to adopt a new benchmark: geographical deviations of less than a mile would be deemed insubstantial. Accordingly, the FCC denied these applications. The applicants appealed, arguing that the Commission had acted unfairly by applying its new benchmark to their cases. They said they had relied on the *Lott* rule by hiring surveyors to identify target licensees and lawyers to file their finder's preference applications.

The court upheld the Commission's decision. It saw "no need to plow laboriously through the [*Retail Union*] factors," because those factors "boil down to a question of concerns grounded in equity and fairness." In this case, the petitioners' reliance had not been reasonable, because the *Lott* benchmark had not been a "well established practice." On the contrary, the FCC had shown an intention in *Lott* to proceed on a case-by-case basis. Moreover, "[i]f there were any parties in these cases who did have a reasonable reliance interest, they were the existing licensees, [who] had been operating their stations for years at what they thought, apparently in good faith, were the correct geographic coordinates," with far more of an investment than the petitioners had made.

If the Court had applied the manifest injustice principle in *Fox II* instead of the void for vagueness-due process analysis, would the result have changed?

5.   *Problem.* The National Highway Traffic Safety Administration (NHTSA) adopted regulations setting forth safety standards for new cars. One such standard required that seatbelts be able to withstand forces of 3000 pounds over 30 seconds. The test procedure required use of a pelvic body block, meaning a metal block that represents a human pelvis. The regulation did not specify how the pelvic body block should be placed during the test. Argo Motors tested its new model, the Meridian, by placing the pelvic body block against the seat back and the Meridian passed. As Argo was aware, NHTSA had specifically approved of that test design in cases involving two other manufacturers.

Several months after the new model year had begun, NHTSA decided, on the basis of new research, that the pelvic body block should be moved away from the seat back. In crash simulations performed according to this new condition, the Meridian failed the test.

NHTSA has authority to seek recall of a motor vehicle when a vehicle either has a "defect related to motor vehicle safety" or "does not comply with an applicable motor vehicle safety standard." Alleging that Argo had failed to comply with the safety standard governing seat belts, NHTSA ordered a recall of all 100,000 Meridians on the road to strengthen the seat belt anchorage. Argo challenges this order on judicial review. Should a reviewing court set aside the recall order? On what grounds? Would your answer change if NHTSA alleged and proved that the Meridian had a safety defect? *See United States v. Chrysler Corp.,* 158 F.3d 1350 (D.C. Cir. 1998).

§ 4.5.2 EQUITABLE ESTOPPEL

The principle of equitable estoppel has been applied countless times in nearly every area of law. Under that principle, if A's statement or conduct reasonably induces B's detrimental reliance, A will not be permitted to act inconsistently with its statement or conduct. Under another commonly applied private law rule, a principal is bound by the actions of its agent under either actual or apparent authority. Apparent authority arises if the principal has caused third parties reasonably to believe that the agent has authority to act—even if the agent has no such authority. Should the government be bound by equitable estoppel and apparent authority when the action of its agent misleads a person to his detriment?

FOOTE'S DIXIE DANDY, INC. V. MCHENRY
607 S.W.2d 323 (Ark. 1980)

[Employers pay a tax to support the system of unemployment compensation for employees. Foote's operated two grocery stores (Hamburg and Crossett) within a single corporation. In 1971, it separately incorporated the Crossett store. Foote's had a good unemployment record, which resulted in a low tax. If Foote's had filed a request for a transfer of that record, the new corporation would also have a low tax rate.

In 1971, Foote's CPA asked Yates, a field auditor for the Employment Security Division, about the new corporation's employment tax status. Foote's had always dealt exclusively with Yates about such questions. Yates said to do nothing special. In 1976, Yates retired. A new auditor discovered that the required request for transfer had not been filed in 1971. As a result, the state assessed $20,000 in additional taxes for the 1971–76 period. Foote's filed suit to prevent the state from collecting the $20,000.]

The State's claim is simply that it cannot be estopped regardless of the facts. Its position is based on a series of cases which announce the principle that the State cannot be estopped by the actions of its agent ... We abandon the principle stated in those cases that the state can *never* be estopped by the actions of its agents. Estoppel is not a defense that should be readily available against the state, but neither is it a defense that should never be available. Estoppel of the state is a principle of law recognized in more and more jurisdictions [including Alabama, California, New York, and Pennsylvania] . . .

Estoppel is governed by fairness, as the court said in *United States v. Lazy FC Ranch*, 481 F.2d 985 (9th Cir. 1973): "We think the estoppel doctrine is applicable to the United States where justice and fair play require it . . ." In *Gestuvo v. Immigration and Naturalization Service*, 337 F. Supp. 1093 (C.D. Cal. 1971), the court recognized estoppel when certain essential elements were present. As the court stated:

> Four elements are necessary: (1) the party to be estopped must know the facts; (2) he must intend that his conduct shall be acted on or must so act that the party asserting the estoppel had a right to believe it is so intended; (3) the latter must be ignorant of the true facts; and (4) he must rely on the former's conduct to his injury.

In explaining the application of estoppel, the court in *Gestuvo* continued: "[T]he requirements of morals and justice demand that our administrative agencies be accountable for their mistakes. Detrimental reliance on their misrepresentations or mere unconscientiousness should create an estoppel, at least in cases where no serious damage to national policy would result . . ."

The decisions of the federal and state courts favoring estoppel of the government are closely aligned with the abandonment of the doctrine of sovereign immunity . . . Arkansas has not abandoned the doctrine of sovereign immunity which is in our constitution . . .

Estoppel will protect the citizen only to the extent that he relied upon actions or statements by an agent. In the present case there was good faith reliance by Foote's C.P.A. on the advice of the Employment Security Division's field agent. There was no reason for the C.P.A. to question the agent's credibility since he had dealt with him frequently on Employment Security Division matters and no problems had arisen. Fairness has to be a two edged sword. People who deal with the state must be fair and the same principle should apply to the state. Justice Holmes made the remark many years ago that "Men must turn square corners when they deal with the government." Years later, two commentators added the logical corollary to Holmes' remark: "It is hard to see why the government should not be held to a like standard of rectangular rectitude when dealing with its citizens." We agree with both ideas.

We are satisfied that all the circumstances of this case warrant applying the doctrine of equitable estoppel. The facts are that *only* a form was not filed which would have been routinely approved if it had been filed; that there was not a scintilla of evidence of bad faith; and that an important agent of the State of Arkansas, clothed with considerable authority, had told Foote's that it did not have to file any further documentation. . . .

Because the State was entitled to rely upon a principle of law that we now abandon, it should be allowed to offer proof as to whether its auditor Yates did in fact make the statements attributed to him. Therefore, the cause is remanded for the sole purpose of permitting the State the opportunity of calling Yates as a witness on this fact issue. If Yates agrees that he did so advise the C.P.A., then the chancellor will enter a decree for the appellant; if Yates disagrees, or if it appears the facts are in dispute, the chancellor will make a finding and enter a decree consistent with this opinion. [REVERSED AND REMANDED.]

NOTES AND QUESTIONS

1. *Federal law of estoppel.* The *Foote's* opinion gives the impression that federal cases support its holding that the government can be estopped. While there are numerous lower court cases like *Lazy FC Ranch* or *Gestuvo,* the U.S. Supreme Court has *never* accepted an estoppel claim and has rejected them on numerous occasions. The *Foote's* case ignores these Supreme Court decisions, including several that decline to estop the government in tax cases.

For example, in *Office of Personnel Management v. Richmond*, 496 U.S. 414 (1990), a Navy personnel officer advised Richmond (orally and in writing) that he could safely take an extra job without jeopardizing his Navy retirement benefits. The advice was erroneous; Congress had changed the law. Accordingly, Richmond's benefits were cut off for six months. He sued to recover them on the basis of estoppel, but the Court rejected his claim. The opinion suggests that the Court is unlikely to uphold a claim for estoppel against the government but did not totally slam the door.

> From our earliest cases [dating to 1813] we have recognized that equitable estoppel will not lie against the Government as against private litigants. . . . Despite the clarity of these earlier decisions, dicta in our more recent cases have suggested the possibility that there might be some situation in which estoppel against the Government could be appropriate. . . . Our own opinions have continued to mention the possibility, in the course of rejecting estoppel arguments, that some type of "affirmative misconduct" might give rise to estoppel against the Government. . . . The language in our decisions has spawned numerous claims for equitable estoppel in the lower courts. . . .

> The Solicitor General proposes to remedy the present confusion in this area of the law with. . . . "a flat rule that estoppel may not in any circumstances run against the Government." The Government bases its broad rule first upon the doctrine of sovereign immunity, [asserting] that the courts are without jurisdiction to entertain a

suit to compel the Government to act contrary to a statute, no matter what the context or circumstances. The Government advances as a second basis for this rule the doctrine of separation of powers: . . . to recognize estoppel based on the misrepresentations of Executive Branch officials would give those misrepresentations the force of law, and thereby invade the legislative province reserved to Congress. . . .

We have recognized before that the "arguments the Government advances for the rule are substantial." And we agree that this case should be decided under a clearer form of analysis than "we will know an estoppel when we see one." But it remains true that we need not embrace a rule that no estoppel will lie against the Government in any case in order to decide this case. We leave for another day whether an estoppel claim could ever succeed against the Government. A narrower ground of decision is sufficient to address the type of suit presented here [namely that in no circumstances can estoppel require the payment of money from the Treasury contrary to statutory appropriation. The Court derived this proposition from the Appropriations Clause of the Constitution, Art. I, § 9, cl.7: "No Money shall be drawn from the Treasury, but in Consequence of Appropriations made by Law."] . . .

Respondent would have us ignore these obstacles on the ground that estoppel against the Government would have beneficial effects . . . [His] attempts to justify estoppel on grounds of public policy are suspect on their own terms. Even short of collusion by individual officers or improper Executive attempts to frustrate legislative policy, acceptance of estoppel claims for Government funds could have pernicious effects. It ignores reality to expect that the Government will be able to "secure perfect performance from its hundreds of thousands of employees scattered throughout the continent." To open the door to estoppel claims would only invite endless litigation over both real and imagined claims of misinformation by disgruntled citizens, imposing an unpredictable drain on the public fisc. Even if most claims were rejected in the end, the burden of defending such estoppel claims would itself be substantial.

Also questionable is the suggestion that if the Government is not bound by its agents' statements, then citizens will not trust them, and will instead seek private advice from lawyers, accountants, and others, creating wasteful expenses. Although mistakes occur, we may assume with confidence that Government agents attempt conscientious performance of their duties, and in most cases provide free and valuable information to those who seek advice about Government programs. A rule of estoppel might create not more reliable advice, but less advice. The natural consequence of a rule that made the Government liable for the statements of its agents would be a decision to cut back and impose strict controls upon Government provision of information in order to limit liability. Not only would valuable informational programs be lost to the public, but the greatest impact of this loss would fall on those of limited means, who can least afford the alternative of private advice. The inevitable fact of occasional individual hardship cannot undermine the interest of the citizenry as a whole in the ready availability of Government information.

2.   A *contrary view.* With *Richmond*, compare these views:

It is no longer realistic or just, if it ever was, to hold every person dealing with the government to knowledge of everything in the statute books and the Federal Register. As a matter of practice, most agencies consider themselves bound by erroneous advice. . . . Thus it may well be that the legal doctrines to the contrary serve no useful purpose. It no longer seems credible that the government will be ruined by a judicious application of estoppel. . . . The application of estoppel hardly means the repeal of a statute; it would simply preclude the retroactive correction as to particular individuals of a particular mistake, spreading the loss over all the taxpayers rather than the unfortunate individuals who relied to their detriment upon a governmental error or misrepresentation.

MICHAEL ASIMOW, ADVICE TO THE PUBLIC FROM FEDERAL ADMINISTRATIVE AGENCIES 60–61 (1973). Why is the Supreme Court so reluctant to accept claims of estoppel against the government? Why are the courts of many states (such as Arkansas) willing to go the other way?

3.   *Prerequisites for estoppel.* What must be shown to justify estoppel, if it is to be available at all? *Heckler v. Community Health Services*, 467 U.S. 51 (1984), states a stricter set of criteria than *Foote's*. The *CHS* case involved a charitable clinic that used federal job training money to fund its home visits to Medicare patients. Travelers Insurance (a private company that handled Medicare claims for the Department of Health and Human Services) orally advised CHS that it could use these funds without reducing its Medicare reimbursement. In reliance on that advice, CHS increased its spending for home visits. Later HHS explained that Travelers' advice had been mistaken and sought to recover a portion of the payments made to CHS.

The Court assumed for the sake of argument that the government could be bound by estoppel, but it held that the basic elements of estoppel were absent. Estoppel requires reasonable reliance. CHS did not reasonably rely on the advice it received because the advice was oral rather than written, and because it came from a private intermediary rather than from HHS. Moreover, CHS' showing of detrimental reliance was insufficient. It was only being asked to repay government reimbursement funds that it should never have received in the first place. Thus, CHS had not suffered the loss of a legal right or any adverse change in status.

4.   *Advice-giving.* Every government agency furnishes advice to the public on how to comply with the agency's law. Every day agencies advise taxpayers about whether a transaction is taxable, whether an issuance of stock must be registered, whether an alien might jeopardize her immigration status by leaving the country, or whether action taken by a professional licensee might jeopardize the license.

Advice-giving is an extraordinarily valuable service to the public (and, since it diminishes inadvertent violations of law, to the agency as well). The advice is usually correct and, when it is incorrect, the government often protects reliance interests created by the mistake even though in many cases it is not legally required to do so.

The *Richmond* decision (quoted in N.1) says that if the government could be estopped by mistaken advice, agencies would be deterred from advising the public. If that happened, the public as a whole would be worse off even though some individuals who had detrimentally relied on the advice would be better off. Do you agree with the prediction in *Richmond?*

5.   *Declaratory orders.* Declaratory orders are the administrative equivalent of judicial declaratory judgments. Declaratory orders normally apply the law to stipulated facts; therefore no trial-type hearing is necessary and the matter can usually be disposed of swiftly. Unlike an agency advice letter, a declaratory order is an administrative adjudication that binds all parties, including the agency. A party can rely on a declaratory order without concern about the nebulous doctrine of equitable estoppel against the government. Also, a party who disagrees with an agency's declaratory decision can seek judicial review. Can you think of situations in which you would suggest that a client seek a declaratory order?

Section 554(e) of the federal APA authorizes agencies to issue declaratory orders. *See* Jeffrey S. Lubbers & Blake D. Morant, *A Reexamination of Federal Agency Use of Declaratory Orders,* 56 ADMIN. L. REV. 1097 (2004). Does § 554(e) suggest that an agency is not authorized to issue a declaratory order in cases that fail to satisfy the gateway requirement in § 554(a)? (See § 3.1.1 for discussion of the gateway.) In contrast, the 2010 Model State APA, § 204, provides that an agency can issue a declaratory order in any case, whether or not it is a "contested case" to which the MSAPA's adjudication provisions apply.

6.   *Problem.* Under a Madison welfare program, Ann and her two children received benefit checks for two years. Welfare Department regulations provide that female applicants for benefits must name a child's father and furnish assistance to the Department in tracking him down. When Ann applied for welfare, she told Courtney, her social worker, that she was afraid of the father, who had battered her and the children, and she did not wish to name him. Courtney said that was no problem and approved the application. This was incorrect; Courtney had no discretion to waive the requirement of naming the father. Ann has now withdrawn from the welfare program and is supporting her children without government assistance. An

official audit has revealed the error. By statute, the Department is empowered to recover any welfare overpayments. The Department has demanded that Ann repay $14,000. It intends to garnish her paychecks until the full amount is recovered. Does Ann have any defense? *Cf. Lentz v. McMahon*, 777 P.2d 83 (Cal. 1989).

CHAPTER 5

RULEMAKING PROCEDURES

■ ■ ■

Statutes and case law divide the administrative process into two principal processes, each governed by separate procedures. The first resembles the judicial process and is called "adjudication." Its product is an "order." Adjudication was the subject of the prior three chapters. The second process resembles the legislative process and is called "rulemaking." Its product is a "rule." (Recall § 2.5, which traced the constitutional roots of the rulemaking-adjudication distinction.) Rulemaking is the subject of this and the next chapter.

§ 5.1 INTRODUCTION: THE RISE OF RULEMAKING

In 1978, while he was still a professor of administrative law, the future Justice Scalia wrote that "perhaps the most notable development in federal government administration during the past two decades" had been "the constant and accelerating flight away from individualized, adjudicatory proceedings to generalized disposition through rulemaking." Antonin Scalia, *Vermont Yankee: The APA, the D.C. Circuit, and the Supreme Court*, 1978 SUP. CT. REV. 345, 376. "The increased use of rulemaking," he continued, "has changed the whole structure of administrative law...." *Id.* A similar trend has occurred in the states. There, too, courts and agencies have had to confront questions about the extent to which they should adhere, during rulemaking proceedings, to traditional norms of administrative law that developed in an adjudication context. Much of the material in this chapter explores the federal and state governments' responses to that problem.

Part of the explanation for the spread of rulemaking during the past generation was that agencies, courts, and legislatures have come to understand that, in many situations at least, rulemaking has definite advantages over adjudication as a tool for agency lawmaking and policymaking. To generalize broadly, those advantages include the following;

a. Participation by all affected parties: In adjudication, only those persons who are parties to a particular dispute normally have a right to participate in the proceeding to resolve it. Yet the decision in such a proceeding can serve as precedent for similar cases involving other parties, and those parties may find it difficult to persuade the agency to distinguish or overrule the prior case. In contrast, anyone who wishes to do so can participate in rulemaking. Notice is given to all concerned, and anyone can submit comments.

b.   Apt procedure: When an agency makes new law or policy, the procedures of rulemaking (which resemble legislation) have advantages over those of adjudication (which resemble trials). Trials and trial records are good for establishing individualized facts, but not particularly suitable for determining broad questions of legislative fact and for ventilating important issues of policy. Moreover, at least in formal adjudication, the law relating to official notice, separation of functions, and internal and external communications with decisionmakers, may insulate the decisionmakers from important factual and policy data needed to make new agency law or policy. In contrast, the procedures of rulemaking have been designed for the precise purpose of exploring issues of law, policy, and legislative fact.

c.   Retroactivity: When an agency adopts a new principle in an adjudication, the agency usually has broad (but not unlimited) authority to apply it retroactively to the parties to the proceeding. As a result, the agency may upset important reliance interests. Rules, in contrast, normally apply prospectively only, thus providing fair warning to those whose conduct is affected.

d.   Uniformity: Agency law made by rule addresses classes of persons, and all persons falling within any such class will become subject to its terms at the same time and in the same way. The same is not true of agency law made in the course of adjudication, because an agency precedent technically binds only the specific parties to that adjudication. In addition, lawmaking by adjudication—often driven by the unique facts of individual cases—can tempt agencies to draw distinctions between otherwise similarly situated individuals on the basis of differences that may not be significant enough to justify those distinctions.

e.   Political input: Lawmaking is a highly political process. Rulemaking provides a regularized opportunity for politically active persons and groups to participate in the process and to mobilize political pressures for or against a proposed agency policy. The procedures utilized in adjudication are less well suited for the making of essentially political decisions.

f.   Agency agenda setting: When agencies make law through adjudications, their agenda is controlled by the happenstance of whatever cases come before them. As a result, they may be forced to spend time on relatively trivial problems and fail to address more important ones. Even if the agency has discretion to choose which cases to consider, the facts of a given case may not shape up as the agency had anticipated. When an agency decides to make law through rulemaking, it has more control over its own agenda, so that it can attack higher priority problems first. In rulemaking, the agency also avoids becoming distracted by the particular facts of each case or the particular problems of litigants; it can focus directly on the central policy issue.

g.   Definitiveness: Although rulemaking can be time consuming, it at least gives the agency the opportunity to settle an issue in a single proceeding, instead of litigating the same issue in numerous proceedings in order to accomplish that result.

h.   Accessibility: Rules are published and, therefore, are widely available, while agency case law is often unpublished and hard to track down. Indeed, even when case precedents can be found, it is often difficult to distill agency law from them. Agency cases are often inconsistent, and they may contain dicta of uncertain authority. Cases that make new law often do not clearly say they are doing so. But when law is set forth in rules, it is easier to ascertain and understand.

i.   Oversight: For the reasons just stated, it is far easier for the executive and legislative branches to exercise oversight over the merits and legality of agency-made law when the law is made through rulemaking rather than adjudication. In addition, federal law, as well as that of most states, provides formal schemes for the legislative and executive review of rules; these schemes may be bypassed if agencies make law through adjudication, because there are no comparable formal schemes for the legislative and executive review of agency law embodied in individual cases.

Nevertheless, lawmaking through adjudication can also have advantages. For example:

a.   Flexibility: Adjudication leads an agency to make law on a step-by-step basis, so that it can observe the actual operation of that law in concrete situations. As a result, law made in adjudication tends to be sensitive to differences in the circumstances of persons to whom the law will apply. Rulemaking leads the agency to prescribe principles divorced from the specific facts of particular cases. These principles are sometimes too broad, too narrow, or too rigid, because the agency fails to make allowances for some of the situations to which the rule will ultimately apply.

b.   The new and unexpected: A case-by-case approach may be better where the agency is not yet in a position to make generally applicable law, due to lack of sufficient expertise or because the distinctions in the area are likely to be so numerous or complex that they resist generalized treatment in a rule.

Moreover, especially in the case of newer statutes, an agency may discover a pattern of harmful behavior that has already occurred and that should be addressed through enforcement action. If the problem was unanticipated, the agency could not have adopted a prospective rule to deal with it. Only retroactively effective adjudication can solve the problem.

c.   Resource savings: The investigation and analysis required to examine a policy area comprehensively through rulemaking may put strains on the agency's resources. Adjudication is often less expensive and time-consuming, because the agency can resolve the individual case and leave further decisions to a later time.

d.   Resolution of disagreements: Policy differences among decisionmakers within an agency (or other officials with whom the agency interacts) are often sharp and fundamental. Case by case adjudication allows the agency to dispose of cases as they arise, without the need to resolve internal disagreements on a broader basis.

e.   Residual adjudication: Regardless of how many rules an agency makes, it can never dispense entirely with adjudication. There will always be ambiguities in rules that need to be answered in individual cases, thereby inevitably creating new precedents.

For a more extensive catalog of the advantages and disadvantages of rulemaking and adjudication, *see* Arthur Earl Bonfield, *State Administrative Policy Formulation and the Choice of Lawmaking Methodology*, 42 ADMIN. L. REV. 121, 122–33 (1990).

NOTES AND QUESTIONS

1.   *Rulemaking "ossification."* There are increasing concerns about resource constraints as an impediment to rulemaking. As Professor McGarity explains:

> As the "rulemaking era" dawned in the early 1970s, agencies agreed that informal rulemaking under section 553 of the Administrative Procedure Act (APA) offered an ideal vehicle for making regulatory policy. Professor Kenneth Culp Davis captured the prevailing sentiment only somewhat hyperbolically when he called informal rulemaking "one of the greatest inventions of modern government." Twenty years later, the bloom is off the rose. Although informal rulemaking is still an exceedingly effective tool for eliciting public participation in administrative policymaking, it has not evolved into the flexible and efficient process that its early supporters originally envisioned. During the last fifteen years the rulemaking process has become increasingly rigid and burdensome. An assortment of analytical requirements have been imposed on the simple rulemaking model, and evolving judicial doctrines have

obliged agencies to take greater pains to ensure that the technical bases for rules are capable of withstanding judicial scrutiny. Professor E. Donald Elliott, former General Counsel of the Environmental Protection Agency, refers to this troublesome phenomenon as the "ossification" of the rulemaking process, and many observers from across the political spectrum agree with him that it is one of the most serious problems currently facing regulatory agencies.

. . . The informal rulemaking process of the 1990s is so heavily laden with additional procedures, analytical requirements, and external review mechanisms that its superiority to case-by-case adjudication is not as apparent now as it was before it came into heavy use. Perhaps of even more concern to regulatees and the general public is recent evidence that agencies are beginning to seek out alternative, less participatory regulatory vehicles to circumvent the increasingly stiff and formalized structures of the informal rulemaking process.

Thomas O. McGarity, *Some Thoughts on 'Deossifying' the Rulemaking Process*, 41 DUKE L.J. 1385, 1385–86 (1992). For a similar diagnosis, see Richard J. Pierce, Jr., *Seven Ways to Deossify Agency Rulemaking*, 47 ADMIN. L. REV. 59 (1995); for a more skeptical perspective, see Jason Webb Yackee & Susan Webb Yackee, *Testing the Ossification Thesis: An Empirical Examination of Federal Regulatory Volume and Speed, 1950–1990,* 80 GEO. WASH. L. REV. 1414 (2012).

The precise dimensions of the ossification phenomenon are not entirely clear. As Pierce notes, "[o]ssification has been identified as a problem only with respect to major rules predicated on assumptions concerning complicated factual and scientific relationships. Agencies continue to issue hundreds of rules annually in other contexts expeditiously and at a relatively low cost." *Id.* at 62. Nevertheless, ossification has become a prominent and widely discussed theme in current administrative law scholarship. Many of the doctrines that will be examined in this chapter can be evaluated in light of this critique.

Not everyone, of course, regards developments that discourage rulemaking in a negative light. After all, a prominent theme in modern political debate is that agencies promulgate *too many* regulations. Consequently, proposals to restrain the growth of regulation are a familiar feature of current political discourse and will be examined frequently in the following pages.

2. *Rulemaking authority.* Because of the recognized advantages of rulemaking in the administrative process, the enabling statutes of most agencies allow them to exercise rulemaking power in appropriate cases. Many such statutes include a "general rulemaking clause" authorizing the agency to "make rules and regulations for the purpose of carrying out the provisions of this Act" (or words to similar effect). Some statutes also, or

alternatively, contain provisions that specifically empower the agency to make rules to accomplish a particular task.

Courts generally presume that a general rulemaking clause gives an agency the option of issuing rules that have the force of law. An important milestone in the development of this presumption was *National Petroleum Refiners Ass'n v. FTC*, 482 F.2d 672 (D.C. Cir. 1973), which upheld the FTC's rule requiring gas stations to post octane ratings. The language of section 6(g) of the FTC Act was similar to the verbal formula quoted in the preceding paragraph. For five decades the Commission had used rulemaking under § 6(g) for housekeeping and procedural matters only. In developing substantive trade regulation policies, it had always relied exclusively on case-by-case adjudication. Nevertheless, the court of appeals held that § 6(g) empowered the FTC to adopt substantive rules that would have the force of law. In reaching this conclusion, the court emphasized the enormous advantages of rulemaking over case-by-case adjudication in implementing a program of consumer protection. The presumption embodied in *National Petroleum Refiners* and like cases has long been entrenched, although not everyone endorses it. *See* Thomas W. Merrill & Kathryn Tongue Watts, *Agency Rules With the Force of Law: The Original Convention*, 116 HARV. L. REV. 467 (2002) (contending that, as applied to early administrative statutes, the presumption is historically inaccurate).

3. *Scope of rulemaking power.* The conclusion that an agency has some substantive rulemaking authority does not automatically resolve the question of how broad that power is. However, the dominant view in the federal system is that rulemaking clauses should be construed generously: "Where the empowering provision of a statute states simply that the agency may 'make . . . such rules and regulations as may be necessary to carry out the provisions of this Act,' we have held that the validity of a regulation promulgated thereunder will be sustained so long as it is 'reasonably related to the purposes of the enabling legislation.'" *Mourning v. Family Pubs. Serv., Inc.*, 411 U.S. 356 (1973). The dominant tendency in federal courts is to regard a rulemaking provision as, in Judge Posner's words, "a necessary and proper clause [that] empowers the Commission to deal with the unforeseen—even if that means straying a little way beyond the apparent boundaries of the Act—to the extent necessary to regulate effectively those matters already within the boundaries." *North Am. Telecomms. Ass'n v. FCC*, 772 F.2d 1282 (7th Cir. 1985).

Of course, courts and agencies have to make judgment calls about how to interpret rulemaking statutes in particular cases, and judges periodically decide that an agency has gone too far. For example, in *Chamber of Commerce v. NLRB*, 721 F.3d 152 (4th Cir. 2013), the National Labor Relations Board adopted a rule requiring employers to post notices in workplaces to inform employees of their rights under the National Labor Relations Act. The Board relied on § 6 of the Act, which empowers the Board to promulgate "such rules and regulations as may be necessary to carry out the provisions of [this Act]." The court held, however, that the posting rule exceeded the Board's powers under § 6. It stated that "*Mourning* applies only after a court has determined that Congress has indeed delegated interpretative powers to that agency. . . . [T]here is no general grant of power to the NLRB outside the roles of addressing ULP [unfair labor practice] charges and conducting representation elections." In the court's view, § 6 was intended to authorize rules that are "necessary" to implement the Board's specific functions under the Act, not rules that would promote the Act's purposes in a broader sense. *Accord, National Ass'n of Mfrs. v. NLRB*, 717 F.3d 947, 965–67 (D.C. Cir. 2013) (Henderson, J., joined by Brown, J., concurring). Is this reasoning a logical qualification of *Mourning*, or a misconceived narrowing of it?

Many states follow the *Mourning* approach, but Florida has taken a different path. In legislation enacted in 1996, and then strengthened afterwards, the legislature amended the state's APA to provide as follows:

> A grant of rulemaking authority is necessary but not sufficient to allow an agency to adopt a rule; a specific law to be implemented is also required. An agency may adopt only rules that implement or interpret the specific powers and duties granted by the enabling statute. No agency shall have authority to adopt a rule only because it is reasonably related to the purpose of the enabling legislation and is not arbitrary and capricious or is within the agency's class of powers and duties, nor shall an agency have the authority to implement statutory provisions setting forth general legislative intent or policy. Statutory language granting rulemaking authority or generally describing the powers and functions of an agency shall be construed to extend no further than implementing or interpreting the specific powers and duties conferred by the enabling statute.

Fla. Stat. Ann. § 120.536(1). The court relied on this provision in *St. Petersburg Kennel Club v. Dep't of Bus. and Prof. Reg.*, 719 So.2d 1210 (Fla. Dist. Ct. App.1998), appeal after remand, 757 So.2d 1240 (Fla. Dist. Ct. App.2000). Florida's Cardroom Act allowed dog racing tracks to operate cardrooms featuring certain listed "penny-ante games," including poker, pinochle, and rummy. One of these tracks applied for permission to offer a game called Big Poker 21. In this game, a player would draw a series of cards, trying to bring the sum of their face value as close as possible to 21. In fact, Big Poker 21 looked a lot like blackjack, which the Act did not allow cardrooms to offer. The department denied the application, relying on a rule in which it had defined poker to mean a game that adhered to the standard poker-hand rankings and afforded players an opportunity to bluff after seeing their hands. The court reversed, noting that, although the Cardroom Act authorized the department to regulate the cardrooms' operations, and to make rules to carry out and enforce the Act, it did not specifically confer authority to make rules that would set forth a definition of poker. (Later, however, the department denied the track's application without relying on its former rule, and the court affirmed.)

The Florida legislation is discussed in Jim Rossi, *"Statutory Nondelegation": Learning from Florida's Recent Experience in Administrative Procedure Reform,* 8 WIDENER J. PUB. L. 301 (1999). Whose approach to rulemaking clauses do you prefer—that of federal decisions like *Mourning,* or that of Florida?

4. *Problem.* Auto insurance companies in the state of Madison typically rate customers by the ZIP Code in which they reside. Insurance in some neighborhoods is much more expensive, and much less available, than in other neighborhoods. The Madison Insurance Commission has authority to deal with "unfair insurance practices." Its authorizing statute also provides that "the Commission may prescribe such rules and regulations as may be necessary in the public interest to carry out the provisions of this Act," but the Commission has never made policy by invoking that provision. The Commission also has power to enter cease-and desist orders on a case by case basis, a power it has often used. If it finds that an "unfair insurance practice" has occurred, it can order refunds of premiums or provide other appropriate relief to consumers.

You are the law clerk for one of the commissioners. At this morning's meeting between the commissioners and the enforcement staff, the staff presented data it has gathered on the practices of Ranchers Insurance Co. Ranchers is one of the larger auto insurance companies in Madison, and it utilizes ZIP Code pricing. The staff seeks authorization to issue an administrative complaint against Ranchers in the hope that this will produce a good test case on ZIP Code pricing. Your co-clerk, however, recommends a rulemaking proceeding.

What is your advice to your boss? What considerations would support his voting to authorize issuance of the complaint in this case? What considerations suggest that he should insist that the Commission commence a rulemaking proceeding to deal with the ZIP Code pricing problem? What other facts might be relevant to his decision?

Your co-clerk also suggests that, if rulemaking is pursued, the Commission should adopt a rule that would grant victims of ZIP Code pricing the right to sue auto insurers for damages in court. Do you think the Commission would have authority to adopt such a rule?

§ 5.2   DEFINITION OF "RULE"

§ 5.2.1 GENERALITY AND PARTICULARITY

All APAs define the term "rule" to which their rulemaking procedures apply. *See, e.g.,* 5 U.S.C. § 551(4); 2010 MSAPA § 102(30); 1961 MSAPA § 1(7). For example, the federal APA definition reads as follows:

(4) "rule" means the whole or a part of an agency statement of general or particular applicability and future effect designed

to implement, interpret, or prescribe law or policy or describing the organization, procedure, or practice requirements of an agency and includes the approval or prescription for the future of rates, wages, corporate or financial structures or reorganizations thereof, prices, facilities, appliances, services or allowances therefor or of valuations, costs, or accounting, or practices bearing on any of the foregoing;

Consider the following analysis of that provision.

JEFFREY S. LUBBERS, A GUIDE TO FEDERAL AGENCY RULEMAKING
43–45, 48 (5th ed. 2012)

Standing alone, the APA's definition of rule may not be too helpful. For example, an agency order directing Company X to cease and desist from engaging in a certain unlawful practice would fall within the literal terms of this definition. Yet, it is reasonably clear under the APA that a proceeding leading to the issuance of a cease-and-desist order ordinarily is adjudication and not rulemaking.

The definition of *adjudication* sheds little additional light, for it is defined as the agency process for formulating an *order*, which in turn is defined as "a final disposition, whether affirmative, negative, injunctive, or declaratory in form, of an agency in a matter other than rule making but including licensing." Thus, the APA's definitional structure is largely circular, because the definition of adjudication is residual.

To understand the thrust of the APA's distinction between rulemaking and adjudication, one must turn to the discussion in the *Attorney General's Manual on the APA*:

[T]he entire Act is based upon a dichotomy between rule making and adjudication. Examination of the legislative history of the definitions and of the differences in the required procedures for rule making and for adjudication discloses highly practical concepts of rule making and adjudication. Rule making is agency action which regulates the future conduct of either groups of persons or a single person; it is essentially legislative in nature, not only because it operates in the future but also because it is primarily concerned with policy considerations. The object of the rule making proceeding is the implementation or prescription of law or policy for the future, rather than the evaluation of a respondent's past conduct. Typically, the issues relate not to the evidentiary facts, as to which the veracity and demeanor of witnesses would often be important, but rather to the policy-making conclusions to be drawn from the facts. . . .

Given the breadth of the definitions of *rulemaking* and *adjudication* in the APA, it is not surprising that some confusion exists with respect to the proper classification of certain agency proceedings. . . .

[T]he inclusion of agency statements of "particular applicability" in the APA's definition of rule probably creates the most difficulty because most people think of rules as addressing general situations and adjudication as addressing particular situations. Although it is true that the great majority of rules have some general application and adjudication is nearly always particularized in its immediate application, the drafters of the APA wished certain actions of a particular nature, such as the setting of future rates or the approval of corporate reorganizations, to be carried out under the relatively flexible procedures governing rulemaking. Consequently, the words "or particular" were included in the definition.

. . . [P]robably no great change would occur if the words "or particular" were deleted from the definition of rule in section 551 of the APA.[32] . . .

NOTES AND QUESTIONS

1.   *The "or particular" language.* The curious draftsmanship of § 551(4) once led then-Professor Scalia to remark that "it is generally acknowledged that the only responsible judicial attitude toward this central APA definition is one of benign disregard." Antonin Scalia, Vermont Yankee: *The APA, the D.C. Circuit, and the Supreme Court*, 1978 SUP. CT. REV. 345, 383. The words "or particular" were added to the definition of "rule" at a late stage in the drafting of the APA. As Lubbers suggests, the change occurred because many administrative lawyers of that era thought of individualized ratemaking (that is, agency proceedings to set rates to be charged by a named public utility) as rulemaking. One reason to call these matters "rulemaking" was that they would thereby be exempted from the APA's separation of functions provisions, which apply only to adjudications. Look at the full text of § 551(4). Did the drafters need to include the words "or particular" in order to achieve that objective?

Although § 551(4) defines ratemaking as rulemaking for all purposes, a number of federal enabling acts require a hearing on the record before ratemaking of particular applicability. This triggers the process of "formal rulemaking," discussed in § 5.4.2, in which the agency must observe most, though not all, of the same requirements as in APA formal adjudication. *See* APA §§ 551(4), 553(c). Would due process permit individualized ratemaking

---

[32]   . . . The American Bar Association has long recommended revising the definition to delete the words "or particular." The Administrative Conference endorsed the ABA proposal with the understanding that "[a] matter may be considered of 'general applicability' even though it is directly applicable to a class which consists of only one or a few persons if the class is open in the sense that in the future the number of members of the class may be increased."

for a telephone company or a cable television franchise without a hearing? Without a trial-type hearing?

2. *State law definitions.* Section 102(30) of the 2010 MSAPA defines a "rule" as "the whole or a part of an agency statement of *general applicability* that implements, interprets, or prescribes (i) law or policy, or (ii) the organization, procedure, or practice requirements of an agency and has the force of law" (emphasis added). In contrast, that Act defines "order" as "an agency decision that determines or declares the rights, duties, privileges, immunities or other interests of *a specific person*." § 102(23) (emphasis added). Thus, the 2010 MSAPA (like its predecessors) draws a more clear-cut distinction than the federal APA does. Ratemaking proceedings are treated according to the same principles as other proceedings. A ratemaking proceeding of general applicability, i.e., addressed to all members of a described class of providers, is a "rule." But a ratemaking proceeding of particular applicability, i.e., addressed to a named party or parties, is adjudication.

A few state APAs define the term "rule" more narrowly than the APA provisions just described. For example, the Washington APA definition enumerates several categories of statements that constitute rules, and the state courts have held the list to be exclusive. Therefore, certain pronouncements of general applicability that implement law or policy have been held not to be rules, even if they would have been rules under the federal definition. *See* Wash. Rev. Code § 34.05.010(16) (2013); *State v. Straka*, 810 P.2d 888, 893 (Wash. 1991) (holding that definition of "rule" did not include a set of procedures approved by the state toxicologist for evaluating and maintaining breath testing machines for use in prosecutions for driving while intoxicated).

3. *Other criteria.* Review the *Bi-Metallic* and *Anaconda* cases in § 2.5. In the due process context, as in the APA context, courts often cite a variety of factors, in addition to the general-particular dichotomy, as they try to distinguish rulemaking from adjudication. Some examples: A rule is usually, if not always, prospective, but an order will often be retroactive (this test is the subject of § 5.2.2). A rule usually requires a further proceeding (an adjudication) to make it concretely effective against a particular individual, while an order typically needs no further proceeding to make it effective. A rule is usually directed at and binds a described class that may open to admit new members, while an order is directed at and binds only those who were parties to the adjudicative proceeding. A rule ordinarily is based on findings of fact that are legislative or general in nature and is often based on predictions about the future; an adjudication may well be based, at least in part, on facts specific to the parties and on findings of past events. Finally, in close cases a court might determine whether a particular proceeding is rulemaking or adjudication by asking whether rulemaking or adjudication procedures are most appropriate for its efficient, effective, and fair operation.

4. *Consequences of rulemaking label.* In the due process context, the private litigant normally would prefer to characterize the challenged action as an order rather than a rule, because the *Bi-Metallic* doctrine militates against due process rights in rulemaking. In the context of an APA, however, the private party may well prefer for a court to label the challenged action a rule. As you will recall from § 3.1, the federal APA and many state APAs specify few procedures for informal adjudication. Thus, when the private party has no hope of qualifying for *formal* (trial-type) adjudication, he or she may gain more procedural rights if the proceeding is deemed to be rulemaking than if it is deemed to be an adjudication.

For example, in *Yesler Terrace Community Council v. Cisneros*, 37 F.3d 442, 448–49 (9th Cir. 1994), the Department of Housing and Urban Development (HUD) determined that the State of Washington's eviction procedure provided tenants with various procedural protections. This determination allowed local public housing authorities to dispense with an informal grievance procedure that would otherwise have been available to tenants in the projects who were facing eviction because of suspected drug dealing. The issue was whether HUD's determination was rulemaking (which would make APA notice and comment procedure applicable) or informal adjudication (subject to no procedural requirements).

The court held that the determination was rulemaking. After quoting the APA definitions of "rule" and "order," the court said:

> Two principal characteristics distinguish rulemaking from adjudication. First, adjudications resolve disputes among specific individuals in specific cases, whereas rulemaking affects the rights of broad classes of unspecified individuals [citing the passage in *Florida East Coast Ry.* reprinted in § 2.5]. Second, because adjudications involve concrete disputes, they have an immediate effect on specific individuals (those involved in the dispute). Rulemaking, in contrast, is prospective, and has a definitive effect on individuals only after the rule subsequently is applied . . .
>
> Here, HUD's determination that Washington's state-court eviction procedures met HUD's due process requirements has all the hallmarks of a rule. HUD's determination had no immediate, concrete effect on anyone, but merely permitted [local public housing authorities] to evict tenants in the future without providing them with informal grievance hearings. At the same time, the determination affected the rights of a broad category of individuals not yet identified. Before the decision was made, all public housing tenants in Washington had a statutory right to a pre-eviction grievance hearing. After the decision, no public housing tenant accused of certain criminal activity had such a right. We conclude that HUD's determination was a rule.

Do you agree with the court's argument that the HUD determination had "no immediate, concrete effect on anyone" and was therefore rulemaking?

Indeed, couldn't it be argued that HUD's decision applied general standards to a single entity—the Washington state court system—and was therefore an adjudication? Is *Yesler* any different from a situation in which a federal agency grants a state permission to build a highway in a certain location? The highway will indirectly affect millions of citizens, but the Supreme Court has declared that this sort of decision is not rulemaking. *Citizens to Preserve Overton Park, Inc. v. Volpe,* 401 U.S. 402, 414 (1971). Recall also the *Oregon Environmental* case, § 3.1.2, in which the court concluded that the decision by a state board of education to approve a textbook for use in all of the state's elementary schools was an order, not a rule. Was the court right?

5.   *Critiques of the rulemaking-adjudication dichotomy.* The distinction between rules and orders has its limitations. As Dean Ronald Cass, among others, has pointed out, the metaphors that compare rulemaking with what legislatures do and adjudication with what courts do are far from perfect. Society expects the National Labor Relations Board to carry out its adjudicative functions in a much more political manner than would be legitimate for a court. Conversely, rulemaking by technically specialized agencies like the Occupational Safety and Health Administration is supposed to rest on far more rigorous scientific investigation than anyone could expect from a legislature. Ronald A. Cass, *Models of Administrative Action,* 72 VA. L. REV. 363, 396–97 (1986); *see also* Glen O. Robinson, *The Making of Administrative Policy: Another Look at Rulemaking and Adjudication and Administrative Procedure Reform,* 118 U. PA. L. REV. 485, 536–38 (1970). Notwithstanding these critiques, however, all of the states do have APAs that adhere to the traditional rulemaking-adjudication dichotomy, and most administrative lawyers seem to feel that these categories work acceptably most of the time.

6.   *Legislative rules and guidance documents.* Most of the rules discussed so far in this chapter are "legislative rules." Legislative rules are rules issued by an agency pursuant to an express or implied grant of authority to issue rules with the binding force of law. Guidance documents, often called nonlegislative rules or interpretive rules or statements of policy, are agency rules that do not have the force of law because they are not based upon delegated authority to issue such rules. *See* 1 RICHARD J. PIERCE, JR., ADMINISTRATIVE LAW TREATISE §§ 6.3, 6.4 (4th ed. 2002). The distinction between legislative rules and guidance documents is explored in § 6.1.4. But both types fall within the federal APA's definition of "rule," because even a guidance document is "designed to implement, interpret or prescribe law or policy," as provided in that Act. The same is generally true under state APAs. See, e.g., 1961 MSAPA § 1(7). The 2010 MSAPA, however, defines "rule" to mean only statements that have the force of law; pronouncements that would otherwise meet the definition of "rule" but lack the force of law are designated "guidance documents." *See* 2010 MSAPA §§ 102(14), (30). Even though, under federal law and the law of many states, an agency need not promulgate a guidance document using APA rulemaking procedure, other

APA provisions may apply to such a rule. The agency may be required to publish it, and private persons may be entitled to judicial review of it.

7. *Lesser pronouncements.* Sometimes a court will conclude that an agency's pronouncement does not rise to the level of being either a rule or an order (or any other kind of "agency action"). The issue can be important, because the APA provides that "agency actions" are subject to judicial review. *See* 5 U.S.C. §§ 701(2), 702. For example, in *Independent Equipment Dealers Ass'n v. EPA*, 372 F.3d 420 (D.C. Cir. 2004). EPA sent a letter to a trade association reaffirming its longstanding enforcement policy regarding emission standards for imported engines. The court, in an opinion by Judge (now Chief Justice) John Roberts, concluded that the letter was not a reviewable agency action, in part because it did not fit the APA's definition of a rule. "By *restating* EPA's established interpretation of the certificate of conformity regulation, the EPA Letter tread [sic] no new ground. It left the world just as it found it, and thus cannot be fairly described as implementing, interpreting, or prescribing law or policy." Is that persuasive?

Another example is *Industrial Safety Equipment Ass'n v. EPA*, 837 F.2d 1115 (D.C. Cir. 1988). The court held that a "Guide to Respiratory Protection for the Asbestos Abatement Industry," published by the Environmental Protection Agency and the National Institute for Occupational Safety and Health, was not a rule and therefore was not subject to judicial review. The guide explained that one important method of minimizing workers' exposure to asbestos is the use of respirators. "Air purifying" respirators filter asbestos particles out of the air; "supplied-air" respirators contain their own air supply. The guide listed the thirteen respirators that NIOSH had certified under its regulations, but declared that, as a matter of public health policy, NIOSH and EPA recommended only two of them—the "supplied-air" kind. Manufacturers of the other eleven respirators filed suit. They contended that the guide was a rule because it had in effect decertified their devices, yet had not been promulgated according to rulemaking procedures. The court disagreed. The guide was simply an educational publication that did not "implement, interpret, or prescribe law or policy" within the meaning of the APA. The guide had, after all, made clear that all thirteen devices were perfectly lawful.

In a state in which guidance documents are *not* exempt from rulemaking obligations, a court that wants to excuse an agency from those obligations has an incentive to say that a document that might be most easily characterized as a policy statement was not a rule at all. *See, e.g., Pacific Gas & Elec. Co. v. State Dep't of Water Resources*, 5 Cal. Rptr. 3d 283 (Ct. App. 2003); *Missouri Soybean Ass'n v. Mo. Clean Water Comm'n*, 102 S.W.3d 10 (Mo. 2003).

8. *Unwritten rules.* Can a policy that has never been committed to writing be a "rule" for APA purposes? Some cases have so held. *School Bd. of Broward County v. Bennett*, 771 So.2d 1270 (Fla. Dist. Ct. App. 2000); *C.P. v. Utah Office of Crime Victims' Reparations*, 966 P.2d 1226 (Utah 1998); *Dep't of Highway Safety & Motor Vehicles v. Schluter*, 705 So.2d 81 (Fla. Dist. Ct.

App. 1997). In *Schluter* the court found that the motor vehicle department had an unwritten policy of not allowing a law enforcement officer to consult with his counsel during an interview that could lead to disciplinary action. The court pointed out that, according to the reporter for the state's APA, the goals of that Act had included "prescribing due process minima for the operation of Florida administrative agencies [and] broadening public access to the precedents and activities of agencies." The court continued: "Obviously, an interpretation of the ... Act which fails to require an agency to comply with rulemaking simply because its policy statements were unwritten could not be said to have complied [with either purpose]." Is that so obvious?

9. *Problem.* The Madison Department of Public Works approved the sale of bonds to finance construction of a new highway bridge spanning the Publius River. The department also passed a resolution stating that, in view of the anticipated structural limitations of the new facility, the bridge would be declared off limits to trucks weighing ten tons or more. Was either of these decisions a rule? *Cf. Faulkner v. California Toll Bridge Auth.*, 253 P.2d 659 (Cal. 1953); ARTHUR EARL BONFIELD, STATE ADMINISTRATIVE RULE MAKING 79–80 (1986).

§ 5.2.2 PROSPECTIVITY AND RETROACTIVITY

Rules normally establish law or policy for the future, while orders generally concern past events and have retroactive effect. The federal APA and those of many states explicitly define rules as having "future effect." APA § 551(4). On the other hand, all of the MSAPAs omit the "future effect" language from the definition of "rule." Can a rule have retroactive effect? What do we mean by retroactive effect? And when is retroactivity good policy?

BOWEN V. GEORGETOWN UNIVERSITY HOSPITAL
488 U.S. 204 (1988)

[In 1981 the Department of Health and Human Services (HHS) adopted a rule that revised the formula for calculating its reimbursement to hospitals for services rendered to Medicare beneficiaries. Seven hospitals, including Georgetown, challenged the rule in a district court, which invalidated the rule because it had been adopted without notice and comment procedure. HHS then readopted the rule in 1984, using proper procedures. The 1984 rule was retroactive, in that it purported to allow HHS to recoup from hospitals the amounts that the agency would have saved if the 1981 rule had never been set aside. For the seven plaintiff hospitals, the recoupments would have added up to two million dollars.

In holding the retroactive effect of the 1984 rule to be invalid, KENNEDY, J., stated for the Court:]

Retroactivity is not favored in the law. Thus, congressional enactments and administrative rules will not be construed to have retroactive effect unless their language requires this result. By the same principle, a statutory grant of legislative rulemaking authority will not, as a general matter, be understood to encompass the power to promulgate retroactive rules unless that power is conveyed by Congress in express terms. Even where some substantial justification for retroactive rulemaking is presented, courts should be reluctant to find such authority absent an express statutory grant.

The Secretary contends that the Medicare Act provides the necessary authority to promulgate retroactive cost-limit rules in the unusual circumstances of this case. [The Court rejected this argument, finding that the Medicare Act did not provide authority for retroactive regulations, only for retroactivity in case-by-case adjudication.]

The Secretary nonetheless suggests that, whatever the limits on his power to promulgate retroactive regulations in the normal course of events, judicial invalidation of a prospective rule [like the 1981 HHS rule] is a unique occurrence that creates a heightened need, and thus a justification, for retroactive curative rulemaking. The Secretary warns that congressional intent and important administrative goals may be frustrated unless an invalidated rule can be cured of its defect and made applicable to past time periods. The argument is further advanced that the countervailing reliance interests are less compelling than in the usual case of retroactive rulemaking, because the original, invalidated rule provided at least some notice to the individuals and entities subject to its provisions.

Whatever weight the Secretary's contentions might have in other contexts, they need not be addressed here. The case before us is resolved by the particular statutory scheme in question. Our interpretation of the Medicare Act compels the conclusion that the Secretary has no authority to promulgate retroactive cost-limit rules. . . .

SCALIA, J., concurring.

I agree with the Court [but write separately in order to add] that the APA independently confirms the judgment we have reached.

The first part of the APA's definition of "rule" states that a rule "means the whole or a part of an agency statement of general or particular applicability *and future effect* designed to implement, interpret, or prescribe law or policy or describing the organization, procedure, or practice requirements of an agency. . . ." 5 U.S.C. § 551(4) (emphasis added).

The only plausible reading of the italicized phrase is that rules have legal consequences only for the future. It could not possibly mean that merely *some* of their legal consequences must be for the future, though they may also have legal consequences for the past, since that description would not enable rules to be distinguished from "orders," *see* 5 U.S.C. § 551(6), and would thus destroy the entire dichotomy upon which the most significant portions of the APA are based. (Adjudication—the process for formulating orders, *see* § 551(7)—has future as well as past legal consequences, since the principles announced in an adjudication cannot be departed from in future adjudications without reason.)

Nor could "future effect" in this definition mean merely *"taking effect in the future,"* that is, having a future effective date even though, once effective, altering the law applied in the past. That reading, urged by the [Government], produces a definition of "rule" that is meaningless, since obviously *all* agency statements have "future effect" in the sense that they do not take effect until after they are made. . . . Thus this reading, like the other one, causes § 551(4) to fail in its central objective, which is to distinguish rules from orders. All orders have "future effect" in the sense that they are not effective until promulgated. In short, there is really no alternative except the obvious meaning, that a rule is a statement that has legal consequences only for the future. . . .

[Although a rule cannot be retroactive, in the sense of making illegal past conduct which was formerly legal, a rule can legitimately affect past transactions.] That is not retroactivity in the sense at issue here, i.e., in the sense of altering the *past* legal consequences of past actions. Rather, it is what has been characterized as "secondary" retroactivity. A rule with exclusively future effect (taxation of future trust income) can unquestionably *affect* past transactions (rendering the previously established trusts less desirable in the future), but it does not for that reason cease to be a rule under the APA. . . .

A rule that has unreasonable secondary retroactivity—for example, altering future regulation in a manner that makes worthless substantial past investment incurred in reliance upon the prior rule—may for that reason be "arbitrary" or "capricious," and thus invalid. . . . It is erroneous, however, to extend this "reasonableness" inquiry to purported rules that not merely affect past transactions but change what was the law in the past. . . .

This case cannot be disposed of, as the [Government] suggests, by simply noting that retroactive rulemaking is similar to retroactive legislation, and that the latter has long been upheld against constitutional attack where reasonable. The issue here is not constitutionality, but rather whether there is any good reason to doubt that the APA means what it says. For purposes of resolving that question, it does not at all follow that, since Congress itself possesses the power retroactively to change its laws, it must have meant agencies to possess the power retroactively to change their regulations. Retroactive legislation has always been looked upon with disfavor, and even its constitutionality has been conditioned upon a rationality requirement beyond that applied to other legislation. It is entirely unsurprising, therefore, that even though Congress wields such a power itself, it has been unwilling to confer it upon the agencies. Given the traditional attitude towards retroactive legislation, the regime established by the APA is an entirely reasonable one: Where quasi-legislative action is required, an agency cannot act with retroactive effect without some special congressional authorization. That is what the APA says, and there is no reason to think Congress did not mean it.

The dire consequences that the [Government] predicts will ensue from reading the APA as it is written . . . are not credible. . . . It is important to note that the retroactivity limitation applies *only* to rulemaking. Thus, where legal consequences hinge upon the interpretation of statutory requirements, and where no pre-existing interpretive rule construing those requirements is in effect, nothing prevents the agency from acting retroactively through adjudication. Moreover, if and when an agency believes that the extraordinary step of retroactive rulemaking is crucial, all it need do is persuade Congress of that fact to obtain the necessary *ad hoc* authorization. It may even be that implicit authorization of particular retroactive rulemaking can be found in existing legislation. If, for example, a statute prescribes a deadline by which particular rules must be in effect, and if the agency misses that deadline, the statute may be interpreted to authorize a reasonable retroactive rule despite the limitation of the APA.

. . . I might add that even if I felt free to construct my own model of desirable administrative procedure, I would assuredly not sanction "curative" retroactivity. I fully agree with the District of Columbia Circuit that acceptance of the Secretary's position would "make a mockery . . . of the APA," since "agencies would be free to violate the rulemaking requirements of the APA with impunity if, upon invalidation of a rule, they were free to 'reissue' that rule on a retroactive basis." . . .

NOTES AND QUESTIONS

1. *Literalism.* Justice Scalia was not always so insistent on reading § 551(4) literally. *See* § 5.2.1 N.1. In this instance, however, he argues that "future effect" has to be given its literal meaning because, otherwise, nothing in § 551(4) would distinguish rules from orders. Is his argument persuasive? For a critique, see Ronald M. Levin, *The Case for (Finally) Fixing the APA's Definition of "Rule,"* 56 ADMIN. L. REV. 1077, 1085–88 (2004).

As mentioned earlier, the MSAPA definitions do not contain the "future effect" language found in § 551(4) of the federal APA. Under Scalia's approach, should the *Georgetown* case be decided differently under state law?

2. *Consequences of the Scalia view.* If, as Justice Scalia maintained, the Secretary's action was not a "rule" within the meaning of the federal APA, what was it? *See* § 551(6). Since no statute required the Secretary to make his decision using formal proceedings, what procedures does the APA prescribe in such circumstances?

In the past, courts have freely given retroactive effect to *interpretive* rules, in which an agency states what it thinks existing law means but does not purport to change the law. *See, e.g., Meritor Savings Bank, FSB v. Vinson,* 477 U.S. 57 (1986) (relying on 1980 EEOC sexual harassment guidelines in assessing legality of events occurring between 1974 and 1977). Is this allowable under Scalia's view?

3. *The majority's canons.* The majority articulates two canons or presumptions of statutory interpretation. First, there is a presumption that statutes and rules do not apply retroactively. The Court reaffirmed this teaching of *Georgetown* in *Landgraf v. USI Film Products,* 511 U.S. 244 (1994). The Court explained:

> Elementary considerations of fairness dictate that individuals should have an opportunity to know what the law is and to conform their conduct accordingly; settled expectations should not be lightly disrupted. For that reason, the "principle that the legal effect of conduct should ordinarily be assessed under the law that existed when the conduct took place has timeless and universal appeal." . . . The presumption against statutory retroactivity has consistently been explained by reference to the unfairness of imposing new burdens on persons after the fact.

Second (and of more immediate relevance to the actual controversy in *Georgetown*), an agency may not, "as a general matter," issue retroactive legislative rules unless Congress expressly authorizes retroactivity.

However, as the Court noted in *Landgraf,* "deciding when a statute operates 'retroactively' is not always a simple or mechanical task." The Court continued:

> A statute does not operate "retrospectively" merely because it is applied in a case arising from conduct antedating the statute's enactment or upsets expectations based in prior law. Rather, the court must ask whether the new provision attaches new legal consequences to events completed before its enactment. The conclusion that a particular rule operates "retroactively" comes at the end of a process of judgment. . . . However, retroactivity is a matter on which judges tend to have "sound . . . instinct[s]," and familiar considerations of fair notice, reasonable reliance, and settled expectations offer sound guidance.

The Court in *Landgraf* also mentioned several situations in which it had frequently held that a court should "apply the law in effect at the time it renders its decision... even though that law was enacted after the events that gave rise to the suit." Among these situations were statutes that make changes in procedural rules, statutes that authorize or affect the propriety of prospective relief and statutes conferring or ousting jurisdiction.

Courts often draw upon the analysis of *Landgraf* when they implement the two *Georgetown* canons. How would you resolve the following cases? (Assume that none of the rules involved in these cases spoke directly to the issue of retroactivity, and none of the agencies had express authority to issue retroactive rules.)

a. Combs applied for Social Security disability benefits in 1996. At that time, her obesity and related medical impairments would have entitled her to a presumption of disability, according to listing 9.09 of the medical-vocational guidelines (the same rules as were involved in *Heckler v. Campbell*, § 3.2). However, the Social Security Administration deleted listing 9.09 from the guidelines in 1999. When SSA finally adjudicated Combs' case in 2003, it found that she was not disabled and, therefore, denied her claim for benefits running from the date she applied, i.e., 1996. Should Combs have been permitted to invoke the presumption that was on the books when she became disabled and applied for benefits? *See Combs v. Comm'r of Social Security*, 459 F.3d 640 (6th Cir. 2006) (en banc).

b. Bernklau applied for an increase in his veterans benefits. The Department of Veterans Affairs rejected his application, and he filed for judicial review. While his appeal was pending, Congress passed the Veterans Claims Assistance Act of 2000, which provides in § 3(a) that the department must make reasonable efforts to assist claimants in obtaining evidence to support their claims. Should the case be reopened so that Bernklau can get the benefit of § 3(a)? *See Bernklau v. Principi*, 291 F.3d 795 (Fed. Cir. 2002). (This case concerns a statute rather than a regulation; at most, therefore, it involves only the first *Georgetown* canon, not the second.)

c. Figueroa applied for unemployment benefits, which are available to unemployed persons in an approved training program. A departmental regulation said that, to remain eligible, she needed to be enrolled in twelve credit hours' worth of courses at her community college. She had only nine classroom hours, but she sought to count computer lab time as class time. While her case was pending, the department amended its regulation to require twelve credit hours "or the equivalent." The department ultimately rejected her claim, applying the old regulation. Should it have applied the new regulation instead? *Compare Figueroa v. Director, Dep't of Labor & Workforce Devel.*, 763 N.E.2d 537 (Mass. App. 2002), *with id.* at 543–44 (Rapoza, J., dissenting).

4. *Reasonableness limitations.* Apart from the principle of the *Georgetown* case, the law has other doctrines that protect citizens against retroactive agency action in various circumstances. For example, as Justice Scalia remarked in his concurring opinion, a test of reasonableness is used to determine whether rules that involve "secondary retroactivity" are arbitrary and capricious. Essentially, this is a balancing test that weighs the possible

unfairness of retroactive application against the statutory interest in applying a new rule to the situation at hand.

For example, in *Nat'l Cable & Telecomms. Ass'n v. FCC*, 567 F.3d 659 (D.C. Cir. 2009), the FCC at one time allowed apartment building owners to enter into contracts whereby a cable company would agree to install wiring in their buildings in exchange for exclusive rights to provide service to the tenants. In a later rulemaking, the Commission changed its mind and required building owners to permit competition among multiple providers, even where this policy would mean overriding existing contracts. The court held, first, that this rule involved mere "secondary retroactivity." "Here the Commission has impaired the future value of past bargains but has not rendered past actions illegal or otherwise sanctionable. 'It is often the case that a business will undertake a certain course of conduct based on the current law, and will then find its expectations frustrated when the law changes.' Such expectations, however legitimate, cannot furnish a sufficient basis for identifying impermissibly retroactive rules." Then, applying the balancing test, the court found that the cable companies and building owners had some equities on their side, because the rule altered the bargained-for benefits of now-unenforceable contracts. But the rule was not arbitrary, because these harms were outweighed by the facts that cable companies could have seen this change coming, that they could continue to profit from providing service to at least some customers, and that increased competition would benefit tenants as a group.

Note that this analysis is largely the same as the arbitrariness test applied to retroactive adjudication under *Retail, Wholesale & Dept. Store Union v. NLRB*, § 4.5.1 N.4. Presumably, the same test would also apply to any rule that involves "true" retroactivity but is issued under express statutory authority as *Georgetown* requires. In *Georgetown*, would the Court have been better advised to rely exclusively on the reasonableness test to handle possibly unfair retroactivity in rulemaking, instead of adopting its strict presumption? *See* William V. Luneburg, *Retroactivity and Administrative Rulemaking*," 1991 DUKE L.J. 106, 140–41 (answering yes).

5.   *Problem*. According to the Madison Mining Control Act of 1980, companies that wish to engage in surface mining in the state of Madison must first obtain a permit from the Department of Natural Resources (DNR). Section 22 of the Act states that an applicant must be "law-abiding with respect to the environmental protection requirements of this Act" in order to receive a permit. Section 3 of the Act provides that DNR "may issue such rules as are necessary or appropriate to implement this Act."

In January of last year, DNR cited Colossal Coal Co. for violating the Act by failing to restore an abandoned mining property to its pre-mining condition. Colossal took no immediate action to cure this violation, because the expenses needed to rectify it would be very high. Moreover, it felt that the violation was merely technical, and DNR's practice had been to overlook technical violations for purposes of § 22. Thus, although Colossal had already filed with DNR an application to commence mining in Eden County, it was not worried.

In September, a departmental press release announced the adoption of DNR Directive 14–1. The directive stated that any uncorrected environmental violation of the Act committed by an applicant for a mining permit—including any violation committed prior to the issuance of the directive—would result in a denial of the permit. The explanatory statement accompanying the directive declared: "All three of Madison's coal mining companies, especially Colossal Coal, are continuing to thumb their noses at the Mining Control Act. Today we take a stand against such indifference to the environment." Madison law requires that all new rules be published in the Madison Register, but DNR did not publish the new directive in the Register.

One month later, DNR rejected Colossal's pending mining application for Eden County on the basis of § 22 and Directive 14–1.

a) Is DNR Directive 14–1 a "rule," and thus subject to the publication obligation?

b) Assume now that DNR adopted and published the directive using all necessary procedures. Can it lawfully invoke the directive to justify denying the Eden County permit? *Cf. National Mining Ass'n v. United States Dep't of Interior*, 177 F.3d 1 (D.C. Cir. 1999).

§ 5.3   INITIATING RULEMAKING PROCEEDINGS

§ 5.3.1 GIVING NOTICE OF THE PROPOSED RULE

CHOCOLATE MANUFACTURERS ASS'N V. BLOCK
755 F.2d 1098 (4th Cir.1985)

SPROUSE, J.:

Chocolate Manufacturers Association (CMA) appeals from the decision of the district court denying it relief from a rule promulgated by the Food and Nutrition Service (FNS) of the United States Department of Agriculture (USDA or Department). CMA protests that part of the rule that prohibits the use of chocolate flavored milk in the federally funded Special Supplemental Food Program for Women, Infants and Children (WIC Program). Holding that the Department's proposed rulemaking did not provide adequate notice that the elimination of flavored milk would be considered in the rulemaking procedure, we reverse.

. . . The WIC Program was established by Congress in 1972 to assist pregnant, postpartum, and breastfeeding women, infants and young children from families with inadequate income whose physical and mental health is in danger because of inadequate nutrition or health care.

Under the program, the Department designs food packages reflecting the different nutritional needs of women, infants, and children and provides cash grants to state or local agencies, which distribute cash or vouchers to qualifying individuals in accordance with Departmental regulations as to the type and quantity of food.

In 1978 Congress, in extending the WIC Program through fiscal year 1982, [stated]:

> The Secretary shall prescribe by regulation supplemental foods to be made available in the program under this section. To the degree possible, the Secretary shall assure that the fat, sugar, and salt content of the prescribed foods is appropriate.

To comply with this statutory redefinition ... the Department in November 1979 published for comment the proposed rule at issue in this case. Along with the proposed rule, the Department published a preamble discussing the general purpose of the rule and acknowledging the congressional directive that the Department design food packages containing the requisite nutritional value and appropriate levels of fat, sugar, and salt. Discussing the issue of sugar at length, it noted, for example, that continued inclusion of high sugar cereals may be "contrary to nutrition education principles and may lead to unsound eating practices." It also noted that high sugar foods are more expensive than foods with lower sugar content, and that allowing them would be "inconsistent with the goal of teaching participants economical food buying patterns."

The rule proposed a maximum sugar content specifically for authorized cereals. The preamble also contained a discussion of the sugar content in juice, but the Department did not propose to reduce the allowable amount of sugar in juice because of technical problems involved in any reduction. Neither the rule nor the preamble discussed sugar in relation to flavoring in milk. Under the proposed rule, the food packages for women and children without special dietary needs included milk that could be "flavored or unflavored."

The notice allowed sixty days for comment and specifically invited comment on the entire scope of the proposed rules: "The public is invited to submit written comments in favor of or in objection to the proposed regulations or to make recommendations for alternatives not considered in the proposed regulations." Over 1,000 comments were received from state and local agencies, congressional offices, interest groups, and WIC Program participants and others. Seventy-eight commenters, mostly local WIC administrators, recommended that the agency delete flavored milk from the list of approved supplemental foods.

In promulgating the final rule, the Department, responding to these public comments, deleted flavored milk from the list, explaining:

In the previous regulations, women and children were allowed to receive flavored or unflavored milk. No change in this provision was proposed by the Department. However, 78 commenters requested the deletion of flavored milk from the food packages since flavored milk has a higher sugar content than unflavored milk. They indicated that providing flavored milk contradicts nutrition education and the Department's proposal to limit sugar in the food packages. Furthermore, flavored milk is more expensive than unflavored milk. The Department agrees with these concerns. . . . Therefore, to reinforce nutrition education, for consistency with the Department's philosophy about sugar in the food packages, and to maintain food package costs at economic levels, the Department is deleting flavored milk from the food packages for women and children. Although the deletion of flavored milk was not proposed, the comments and the Department's policy on sugar validate this change. . . .

On this appeal, CMA contends . . . that the Department did not provide notice that the disallowance of flavored milk would be considered. . . . The Department responds . . . by arguing that its notice advised the public of its general concern about high sugar content in the proposed food packages and that this should have alerted potentially interested commenters that it would consider eliminating any food with high sugar content. It also argues in effect that the inclusion of flavored milk in the proposed rule carried with it the implication that both inclusion and exclusion would be considered in the rulemaking process. . . .

[The APA, § 553(b)] requires that the notice in the Federal Register of a proposed rulemaking contain "either the terms or substance of the proposed rule or a description of the subjects and issues involved." The purpose of the notice-and-comment procedure is both "to allow the agency to benefit from the experience and input of the parties who file comments . . . and to see to it that the agency maintains a flexible and open-minded attitude towards its own rules." The notice-and-comment procedure encourages public participation in the administrative process and educates the agency, thereby helping to ensure informed agency decisionmaking. . . .

There is no question that an agency may promulgate a final rule that differs in some particulars from its proposal. Otherwise the agency "can learn from the comments on its proposals only at the peril of starting a new procedural round of commentary." An agency, however, does not have carte blanche to establish a rule contrary to its original proposal simply because it receives suggestions to alter it during the comment period. An interested party must have been alerted by the notice to the possibility of the changes eventually adopted from the comments.

Although an agency, in its notice of proposed rulemaking, need not identify precisely every potential regulatory change, the notice must be sufficiently descriptive to provide interested parties with a fair opportunity to comment and to participate in the rulemaking. . . .

The test devised by the First Circuit for determining adequacy of notice of a change in a proposed rule occurring after comments appears to us to be sound: notice is adequate if the changes in the original plan "are in character with the original scheme," and the final rule is a "logical outgrowth" of the notice and comments already given. Other circuits also have adopted some form of the "logical outgrowth" test. Stated differently, if the final rule materially alters the issues involved in the rulemaking or . . . "substantially departs from the terms or substance of the proposed rule," the notice is inadequate.

There can be no doubt that the final rule in the instant case was the "outgrowth" of the original rule proposed by the agency, but the question of whether the change in it was in character with the original scheme and whether it was a "logical outgrowth" is not easy to answer. In resolving this difficult issue, we recognize that, although helpful, verbal formulations are not omnipotent talismans, and we agree that in the final analysis each case "must turn on how well the notice that the agency gave serves the policies underlying the notice requirement." Under either view, we do not feel that CMA was fairly treated or that the administrative rulemaking process was well served by the drastic alteration of the rule without an opportunity for CMA to be heard. . . .

Chocolate flavored milk has been a permissible part of the WIC Program diet since its inception and there have been no proposals for its removal until the present controversy.

The Department sponsored commendable information-gathering proceedings prior to publishing its proposed rule. . . . The National Advisory Council on Maternal, Infant, and Fetal Nutrition provided information and advice. Regional council meetings were open to the public and held in diverse areas of the country. Department of Agriculture personnel attended a number of regional, state, and local meetings and gathered opinions concerning possible changes in the food packages. The agency also gathered a food package advisory panel of experts seeking their recommendations. Food packages were designed based on the information and advice gleaned from these sources. In all of these activities setting out and discussing food packages, including the proposed rule and its preamble, the Department never suggested that flavored milk be removed from the WIC Program.

At the time the proposed rulemaking was published, neither CMA nor the public in general could have had any indication from the history of either the WIC Program or any other food distribution programs that flavored milk was not part of the acceptable diet for women and children without special dietary needs. The discussion in the preamble to the proposed rule was very detailed and identified specific foods which the agency was examining for excess sugar. This specificity, together with total silence concerning any suggestion of eliminating flavored milk, strongly indicated that flavored milk was not at issue. The proposed rule positively and unqualifiedly approved the continued use of flavored milk. Under the specific circumstances of this case, it cannot be said that the ultimate changes in the proposed rule were in character with the original scheme or a logical outgrowth of the notice. We can well accept that, in general, an approval of a practice in a proposed rule may properly alert interested parties that the practice may be disapproved in the final rule in the event of adverse comments. The total effect of the history of the use of flavored milk, the preamble discussion, and the proposed rule, however, could have led interested persons only to conclude that a change in flavored milk would not be considered. Although ultimately their comments may well have been futile, CMA and other interested persons at least should have had the opportunity to make them. We believe that there was insufficient notice that the deletion of flavored milk from the WIC Program would be considered if adverse comments were received, and, therefore, that affected parties did not receive a fair opportunity to contribute to the administrative rulemaking process. . . .

The judgment of the district court is therefore reversed, and the case is remanded to the administrative agency with instructions to reopen the comment period and thereby afford interested parties a fair opportunity to comment on the proposed changes in the rule.

NOTES AND QUESTIONS

1. *Formulation of proposed rules.* Note the steps that USDA took to obtain input from the public even before it published its proposed rule. These steps were not unusual. Although proposed rules are sometimes formulated entirely on the basis of intra-agency consultations, administrative judgment, and expertise, practice varies widely. Often agencies will publish informational notices (commonly called "advance notices of proposed rulemaking" or ANPRMs) identifying a subject with respect to which they contemplate future rulemaking and soliciting public comment thereon. At other times, in formulating the text of proposed rules, agencies incorporate prior efforts of the private sector by relying upon standards originally created and adopted by trade associations or other private standard-setting organizations. Some agencies also consult standing advisory committees or potentially affected individuals or organizations prior to the formulation of particular proposed rules. The Federal Advisory Committee Act is discussed in § 8.2.2.

The 2010 MSAPA expressly authorizes ANPRMs, § 303(a), following the lead of some of the states. *See* 5 ILL. COMP. STAT. 100/5–30; R.I. GEN. LAWS § 42–35–2.5. Under these provisions, as under federal law, the decision about whether to solicit comment prior to the rulemaking proposal is usually entirely within the agency's discretion. However, a presidential executive order requires federal agencies to publish a semiannual list, called the Unified Agenda of Regulatory and Deregulatory Actions, identifying all regulations under development and providing detailed information about upcoming "significant" regulatory actions (usually rules that will have an annual effect on the economy of at least $100 million). Exec. Order 12,866, § 4(b)–(c), 58 Fed.Reg. 51,735 (1993). The agenda is available online at *www.reginfo.gov.*

2. *Detail required.* How informative must a notice of proposed rulemaking (or NPRM) be? Section 553(b)(3) says that "either the terms or substance of the proposed rule or a description of the subjects and issues involved" must be disclosed, and many state APAs contain parallel language. Suppose a welfare department announces that it is revising its eligibility regulations. The published notice does not specify the anticipated changes but says that anyone may obtain a free copy of the new provisions on request. Is the notice valid? *Compare Richard v. Commissioner of Income Maintenance,* 573 A.2d 712 (Conn.1990) (upholding such a notice), *with* Melanie B. Abbott, *Notice of Rulemaking in Connecticut Administrative Law: What Remains After* Richard?, 13 BRIDGEPORT L. REV. 1 (1992) (criticizing this result). Should states follow the lead of 2010 MSAPA § 304(a)(3) and require that the text of the proposed rule be published?

3. *The logical outgrowth test.* The issue addressed in *Chocolate Mfrs.* is one of the most frequently litigated issues in court challenges to agency rules. *See* Phillip M. Kannen, *The Logical Outgrowth Doctrine in Rulemaking,* 48 ADMIN. L. REV. 213 (1996); Annotation, 96 A.L.R. FED. 411. Is the case correctly decided? Consider this critique of the Fourth Circuit's decision:

> Anyone whose product appeared on the proposal was invited by the notice itself to submit comments in favor of retaining their product on the list. Everyone knew or should have known that there was the possibility that negative comments could convince the agency to take any product off of the list. There was nothing whatsoever misleading about the notice, and it was unfair of the Court of Appeals to characterize the notice as such. . . .

> It has become very time consuming to engage in rulemaking, and agencies should not worry that every difference between the proposal and the final rule is likely to lead to reversal on judicial review for lack of proper notice. The process can be highly unpredictable, forcing agencies to grapple with just how much change is allowed before a court will declare that the final rule is a material alteration and no longer a logical outgrowth of the proposal. This gives agencies a strong incentive to overproceduralize

rulemaking by issuing, as we see today, highly detailed proposed rules with voluminous supporting material, and by conducting additional comment periods whenever a significant change is warranted by the comments.

Jack M. Beermann & Gary Lawson, *Reprocessing* Vermont Yankee, 75 GEO. WASH. L. REV. 856, 898–99 (2007).

4. *U-turns.* The Supreme Court seemed to endorse the logical outgrowth test as the key inquiry under § 553(b) in *Long Island Care at Home, Ltd. v. Coke*, 551 U.S. 158 (2007). In a unanimous opinion by Justice Breyer, the Court noted with apparent approval that the courts of appeals had applied that test, and it added: "The object, in short, is fair notice."

However, the manner in which the Court applied the test in *Long Island Care* was not very demanding. Plaintiff Coke was a companionship worker who attended to the needs of elderly or ailing persons in their homes. She sued her employer, Long Island Care (LIC), for overtime and minimum wage payments alleged to be due under the Fair Labor Standards Act. A 1974 amendment to the Act had extended its coverage to certain domestic service workers but exempted "any employee employed in domestic service employment to provide companionship services" like Coke's. The crucial question was whether the exemption applied to someone who, like Coke, worked for a third-party employer rather than directly for the family at whose home the services were performed. LIC relied on a Department of Labor regulation that said that such workers were exempt from FLSA coverage. Coke replied that, even if the regulation was intended to be legally binding (which was a controverted issue in the case), the Department had adopted it without giving adequate prior notice in the Federal Register.

As initially proposed, the rule would have provided that employers of companionship workers were required to comply with FLSA if they had been "covered enterprises" prior to the 1974 legislation, because "it was not the purpose of [the 1974] Amendments to deny the Act's protection to previously covered domestic service employees." Had the Department adopted that rule, LIC would have been deemed to be subject to the Act. The final rule took the opposite position (i.e., favoring employers), but the Court upheld it, finding the logical outgrowth test satisfied:

> Since the proposed rule was simply a proposal, its presence meant that the Department was *considering* the matter; after that consideration the Department might choose to adopt the proposal or to withdraw it. As it turned out, the Department did withdraw the proposal for special treatment of "covered enterprises." The result was a determination that exempted *all* third-party-employed companionship workers from the Act. We do not see why such a possibility was not reasonably foreseeable.

Does this mean that the NPRM in *Chocolate Mfrs.*—which listed flavored milk in some of the food packages that USDA contemplated authorizing under the revised WIC program—necessarily gave the industry fair notice that the Department might eliminate its eligibility? Would that be a sound result? *Cf. Envtl. Integrity Project v. EPA*, 425 F.3d 992, 998 (D.C. Cir. 2005) ("Whatever a 'logical outgrowth' of this proposal may include, it certainly does not include the Agency's decision to repudiate its proposed interpretation and adopt its inverse.").

5.   *Logical outgrowth of what?* Observe that at one point the court in *Chocolate Mfrs.* phrased its test as "whether the final rule is a 'logical outgrowth' of the notice and comments already given." Yet one can also find statements in the case law that "notice necessarily must come—if at all—from the agency." *Horsehead Resource Devel. Co. v. Browner*, 16 F.3d 1246 (D.C. Cir. 1994); *see Ass'n of Private Sector Colls. & Univs. v. Duncan*, 681 F.3d 427 (D.C. Cir. 2012). Can comments from interested persons put the public on constructive notice of a possible change in a proposed rule? For an affirmative answer, see Beermann & Lawson, *supra*, at 898: "Applying the logical outgrowth test without reference to the comments responding to the original notice dramatically restricts the ability of agencies to make changes between notice and rule without providing a second notice and conducting an additional period of comment. This transforms the logical outgrowth test from a requirement that agencies stay within the bounds of the notice and the comments received to a requirement that agencies predict, in the initial notice, all of the possible directions in which the comments may lead." Do you agree?

6.   *State provisions.* The 2010 MSAPA borrows the "logical outgrowth" test from federal law. § 308. Some states, however, have codified the language of § 3–107 of the 1981 MSAPA, which created a "substantially different" test. Is that criterion more helpful or desirable than the "logical outgrowth test"? *Cf.* Marcia J. Oddi, *Environmental Rulemaking in Indiana: The Impact of the Substantial Difference Requirement on Public Input*, 24 IND. L. REV. 845, 860 (1991) (discussing Indiana's experience with each test).

The states' responses to the issue of variance between proposed and final rules span a wide spectrum. Some states require an agency to offer a new round of comment whenever it wishes to adopt a rule that differs "substantively" from the rule originally proposed. *See* Md. Code Ann., State Gov't § 10–113(a) (1993); *cf.* 5 Ill. Comp. Stat. Ann. 100/5–40(c) (1993). Would you expect this approach to work well? Under what circumstances might it prove to be most advantageous? California requires notice and an additional 15-day comment period if the agency makes any change to a proposed rule (other than trivial changes such as grammatical corrections). Cal. Gov't Code § 11346.8. On the other hand, some jurisdictions apply a "logical outgrowth" test or similar formula leniently, rejecting allegations of unfair notice. *See, e.g., Texas Workers' Compensation Comm'n v. Patient Advocates of Texas*, 136 S.W.3d 643 (Tex. 2004); *In re Dep't of Public Service*, 632 A.2d 1373 (Vt.1993); *Iowa Citizen/Labor Energy Coalition v. Iowa State Commerce Comm'n*, 335 N.W.2d 178, 181 (Iowa 1983). In *Brocal Corp. v. Pa. Dep't of Transp.*, 528 A.2d 114, 119–20 (Pa. 1987), the agency adopted a schedule for reimbursement of transit companies participating in a "shared ride" program for senior citizens. Among the differences between the proposed rules and the final rules were these: uniform, industry-wide limits on reimbursement replaced a system in which limits would be set individually for each carrier; special rates were set for trips to or from Philadelphia or Pittsburgh; and limits involving non-ambulatory passengers were increased by 33%.

The court held, 4–3, that the agency was not required to solicit additional comments before making these changes. The Pennsylvania Documents Law provides that a final rule "may contain such modifications to the proposed text . . . as do not enlarge its original purpose." The court said: "Appellants argue that the term 'enlarge the purpose' . . . should be construed to include fundamental changes in methodologies. When, as here, a statute's words are clear and unambiguous, the plain language should not be disregarded under the pretext of pursuing its spirit. Purpose refers to the reason for enacting legislation, not the particular course or scheme chosen to achieve that end." Here, "[t]he method for calculating reimbursement limits was changed, not the reason for creating limits."

The court said that the Pennsylvania provision was based on the federal APA and that its holding was consistent with interpretations of the federal APA that require "additional notice [only] when the changes are significant and do not grow out of the rulemaking process." In a footnote the court observed that if the legislature had wished to provide more expansive notice, it could have chosen language such as that in the 1981 MSAPA. Is the court's reasoning persuasive?

7. *Problem.* The Madison Medical Board became concerned about private hospitals' practice of subjecting psychiatric patients to restraints (such as straitjackets, ankle cuffs, or drugs) for the purpose of managing or controlling their behavior. Overuse of these techniques, the Board believed, led to physical injuries, prolongation of hospital stays, psychological harms, and even some deaths. Accordingly, the Board proposed a rule that would forbid hospitals from using these techniques except where necessary to prevent immediate injury to the patient or others. The Board also requested comments on whether additional restrictions were needed. It listed several possibilities, including a requirement that a physician or other licensed practitioner must conduct a face-to-face evaluation of a patient before renewing an order to impose such restraints. The Board cited two professional articles that outlined the health risks of behavior-controlling restraints.

The Board has now issued its final rule, prescribing a number of safeguards. Among other measures, the rule requires a face-to-face evaluation by a physician or other licensed practitioner, not only when an order authorizing restraints is *renewed*, but also within one hour of when the restraint is *initially imposed*. This latter condition had not been specifically mentioned in the initial notice; and, unlike the provision relating to renewals, it goes beyond the standards prescribed by the hospitals' national accreditation organization.

The Mental Health Coalition, an association of psychiatric hospitals, plans to challenge the new rule in court. Many staff doctors at these hospitals are disturbed by the one-hour requirement. They believe that the requirement is not necessary in all cases, because approval of the restraint by a physician after a telephone briefing from a trained nurse would sometimes provide sufficient protection. Moreover, they think, the requirement could prove harmful to some patients (such as those who might be asleep or highly agitated during the one-hour period). Can the Coalition successfully challenge the rule on the basis of variance between the proposed and final rules? *Cf. National Ass'n of Psychiatric Health Systems v. Shalala*, 120 F. Supp. 2d 33 (D.D.C. 2000).

§ 5.3.2 DISCLOSING SUPPORTING DATA

UNITED STATES V. NOVA SCOTIA FOOD PRODUCTS CORP.
568 F.2d 240 (2d Cir. 1977)

GURFEIN, J.:

This appeal involving a regulation of the Food and Drug Administration is . . . from a judgment of the District Court for the Eastern District of New York . . . enjoining the appellants, after a hearing, from processing hot smoked whitefish except in accordance with time-temperature-salinity (T–T–S) regulations contained in 21 C.F.R. Part 122 (1977). [These regulations required warming of the fish to kill botulism spores.] . . .

Government inspection of appellants' plant established without question that the minimum T–T–S requirements were not being met. . . . Appellants, on their part, do not defend on the ground that they were in compliance, but rather that the requirements could not be met if a marketable whitefish was to be produced. . . .

The key issues were (1) whether, in the light of the rather scant history of botulism in whitefish, that species should have been considered separately rather than included in a general regulation which failed to distinguish species from species; (2) whether the application of the proposed T–T–S requirements to smoked whitefish made the whitefish commercially unsaleable; and (3) whether the agency recognized that prospect, but nevertheless decided that the public health needs should prevail even if that meant commercial death for the whitefish industry. The procedural issues were whether, in the light of these key questions, the agency procedure was inadequate because (i) it failed to disclose to interested parties the scientific data and the methodology upon which it relied; and (ii) because it failed utterly to address itself to the pertinent question of commercial feasibility.

The history of botulism occurrence in whitefish, as established in the trial record, which we must assume was available to the FDA in 1970, is as follows. Between 1899 and 1964 there were only eight cases of botulism reported as attributable to hot-smoked whitefish. In all eight instances, vacuum-packed whitefish was involved. All of the eight cases occurred in 1960 and 1963. The industry has abandoned vacuum-packing, and there has not been a single case of botulism associated with commercially prepared whitefish since 1963, though 2,750,000 pounds of whitefish are processed annually. Thus, in the seven-year period from 1964 through 1970, 17.25 million pounds of whitefish have been commercially processed in the United States without a single reported case of botulism. The evidence also disclosed that defendant Nova Scotia has been in business some 56 years, and that there has never been a case of botulism illness from the whitefish processed by it.

Interested parties were not informed of the scientific data, or at least of a selection of such data deemed important by the agency, so that comments could be addressed to the data. Appellants argue that unless the scientific data relied upon by the agency are spread upon the public records, criticism of the methodology used or the meaning to be inferred from the data is rendered impossible.

We agree with appellants in this case, for although we recognize that an agency may resort to its own expertise outside the record in an informal rulemaking procedure, we do not believe that when the pertinent research material is readily available and the agency has no special expertise on the precise parameters involved, there is any reason to conceal the scientific data relied upon from the interested parties. As Judge Leventhal said in *Portland Cement Ass'n v. Ruckelshaus*, 486 F.2d 375, 393 (D.C. Cir. 1973): "It is not consonant with the purpose of a rulemaking proceeding to promulgate rules on the basis of inadequate data, or on data that [in] critical degree, *is known only to the agency*." (Emphasis added.) This is not a case where the agency methodology was based on material supplied by the interested parties themselves. Here all the scientific research was collected by the agency, and none of it was disclosed to interested parties as the material upon which the proposed rule would be fashioned. . . .

Though a reviewing court will not match submission against counter-submission to decide whether the agency was correct in its conclusion on scientific matters (unless that conclusion is arbitrary), it will consider whether the agency has taken account of all "relevant factors and whether there has been a clear error of judgment." [*Citizens to Preserve Overton Park, Inc., v. Volpe*, 401 U.S. 402, 415–16 (1971), excerpted in

§ 9.3.] In this circuit we have said that "it is 'arbitrary or capricious' for an agency not to take into account all relevant factors in making its determination." *Hanly v. Mitchell*, 460 F.2d 640, 648 (2d Cir. 1972) (an enforcement action under NEPA).

If the failure to notify interested persons of the scientific research upon which the agency was relying actually prevented the presentation of relevant comment, the agency may be held not to have considered all "the relevant factors." We can think of no sound reasons for secrecy or reluctance to expose to public view (with an exception for trade secrets or national security) the ingredients of the deliberative process. Indeed, the FDA's own regulations now specifically require that every notice of proposed rulemaking contain "references to all data and information on which the Commissioner relies for the proposal (copies or a full list of which shall be a part of the administrative file on the matter . . .)." And this is, undoubtedly, the trend.

We think that the scientific data should have been disclosed to focus on the proper interpretation of "insanitary conditions." When the basis for a proposed rule is a scientific decision, the scientific material which is believed to support the rule should be exposed to the view of interested parties for their comment. One cannot ask for comment on a scientific paper without allowing the participants to read the paper. Scientific research is sometimes rejected for diverse inadequacies of methodology; and statistical results are sometimes rebutted because of a lack of adequate gathering technique or of supportable extrapolation. Such is the stuff of scientific debate. To suppress meaningful comment by failure to disclose the basic data relied upon is akin to rejecting comment altogether. For unless there is common ground, the comments are unlikely to be of a quality that might impress a careful agency. The inadequacy of comment in turn leads in the direction of arbitrary decision-making. We do not speak of findings of fact, for such are not technically required in the informal rulemaking procedures. We speak rather of what the agency should make known so as to elicit comments that probe the fundamentals. Informal rulemaking does not lend itself to a rigid pattern. Especially, in the circumstance of our broad reading of statutory authority in support of the agency, we conclude that the failure to disclose to interested persons the scientific data upon which the FDA relied was procedurally erroneous. . . .

[The court also found the agency's explanatory statement deficient. On the basis of both procedural errors, it ordered that the injunction be vacated and the complaint dismissed.]

NOTES AND QUESTIONS

1. *Enforcement review.* Apart from its teachings about rulemaking procedure, *Nova Scotia* is a revealing case because it illustrates a regulated person's ability to obtain judicial review of a rule in an enforcement proceeding. That is, a private person who is sued for violating a rule can defend on the ground that the rule is (and always has been) unlawful. The upshot may be that a court will invalidate the rule years after it was promulgated. Today this is a relatively uncommon route to judicial review. More often, a regulated person seeks review of a rule immediately after it was issued, on a "pre-enforcement" basis. Actually, however, enforcement review was the norm in administrative law until the 1960s, when the barriers to pre-enforcement review were lowered significantly. *See* § 11.2.4.

2. *Information that forms basis of rule.* Many cases have endorsed the Second Circuit's position that an agency's notice of rulemaking must include scientific data or methodology upon which the agency relied in formulating its proposal. This expectation was first articulated in the leading case of *Portland Cement Ass'n v. Ruckelshaus,* 486 F.2d 375, 392–94 (D.C. Cir. 1973), cited in *Nova Scotia,* and it is therefore known as the *Portland Cement* doctrine. The principle of *Portland Cement* remains alive and well in the D.C. Circuit. *American Radio Relay League, Inc. v. FCC,* 524 F.3d 227, 236–40 (D.C. Cir. 2008). The scope of this requirement is, however, somewhat indeterminate. An opinion by then-Judge Scalia once described it by saying that "at least the most critical factual material that is used to support the agency's position on review must have been made public in the proceeding." *Ass'n of Data Processing Serv. Orgs. v. Bd. of Govs.,* 745 F.2d 677, 684 (D.C. Cir. 1984). Another court has suggested some limits:

> The APA requires notice of the "substance of the proposed rule" or a "description of the subjects or issues involved." 5 U.S.C. § 553. Title 5 does not, however, expressly require that interested parties receive notice of, and an opportunity to comment on, antecedent factual underpinnings for agency rule making. Our sister circuits have invalidated rule-making procedures for agency failure to disclose critical factual underpinnings for rule making, but . . . the information withheld [in those instances] was so central to the decisional process that its nondisclosure was tantamount to refusing to describe the subject or issues in the rule-making proceeding. In such rare instances, nondisclosure . . . can violate the APA. . . . [In this case, however,] the record does not show that DVA relied on any specific data, and particularly not the withheld data, in promulgating its rule. . . . [I]t is hard to conclude that a single intra-agency memo is evidence of agency-wide reliance on its content.

Mortgage Investors Corp. v. Gober, 220 F.3d 1375 (Fed. Cir. 2000); *see also Time Warner Entm't Co. v. FCC,* 240 F.3d 1126, 1140 (D.C. Cir. 2001).

3. *Legality.* Although the *Portland Cement* principle has broad appeal on a policy level, its legal bona fides are controversial, to say the least. In

Nova Scotia the Second Circuit seemed to find support for it in the "relevant factors" test that courts apply on judicial review in deciding whether an agency action is arbitrary and capricious. That theory has attracted little if any favor in subsequent cases, perhaps because courts feel that the doctrine ought to rest on a basis that applies directly to agencies, regardless of whether judicial review is sought in a particular case. A more natural place to look for a basis would be the APA's rulemaking provision, § 553.

As the above quotation from *Mortgage Investors* suggests, however, the sufficiency of § 553 to undergird the *Portland Cement* doctrine is not very clear, either. At least, the Third Circuit does not think so:

> Finally, AARP challenges the regulation based on the notice and comment requirements of the APA, asserting that the proposed regulation was based on comments and information that were not publicly available during the notice and comment period. The plain language of section 553 of the APA fails to support this claim. For notice and comment rulemaking, as here, the APA requires only "[g]eneral notice of proposed rule making ... in the Federal Register," including "either the terms or substance of the proposed rule," and "an opportunity to participate in the rule making through submission of written data, views, or arguments." 5 U.S.C. § 553(b)–(c). Here, the EEOC provided general notice of the proposed rulemaking, including the terms of the rule and a lengthy explanation of its rationale, and provided an opportunity for interested parties to participate in the rulemaking through the submission of comments. Therefore, the EEOC fulfilled the requirements of section 553.

AARP v. EEOC, 489 F.3d 558, 567 (3d Cir. 2007). Is the court correct? *See American Radio, supra*, at 245–47 (Kavanaugh, J., concurring in part and dissenting in part) (also questioning legality of *Portland Cement*); Richard J. Pierce, Jr., *Waiting for* Vermont Yankee *III, IV, and V? A Response to Beermann and Lawson*, 75 GEO. WASH. L. REV. 902, 916–17 (2007) (supporting the doctrine).

4. *Information disclosure and the administrative record.* The drafters of the 2010 MSAPA were persuaded by the arguments for the *Portland Cement* principle. They specifically incorporated into that Act a requirement that a rulemaking notice must contain "a citation to and summary of each scientific or statistical study, report, or analysis that served as a basis for the proposed rule, together with an indication of how the full text of the study, report, or analysis may be obtained." § 304(a)(6). A parallel provision establishes and prescribes the contents of the rulemaking record, including "all factual material, studies, and reports agency personnel relied on or consulted in formulating the proposed or final rule." § 302(b)(6). The federal APA has no corresponding provision prescribing the contents of the rulemaking record, but uncodified federal practice has developed along similar lines. The Administrative Conference has issued a recommendation

identifying "best practices" in the compilation and use of rulemaking records. ACUS Recommendation 2013–4, *The Administrative Record in Informal Rulemaking*, 78 Fed. Reg. 41352 (2013). Today, agencies typically post rulemaking materials online, as will be discussed in detail in § 5.4.1b. The role of the rulemaking record in judicial review is discussed in § 9.4.

5. *Subsequent additions to the record.* What if relevant information comes to the agency's attention after the close of the comment period, and members of the public are given no additional opportunity to comment on the new material? In *Rybachek v. EPA*, 904 F.2d 1276, 1286 (9th Cir. 1990), the EPA added 6000 pages to the rulemaking record in response to comments made during that period. The court held that the addition of these materials after the close of the comment period did not entitle the public to an opportunity to comment upon them. The court stated:

> Nothing prohibits the Agency from adding supporting documentation for a final rule in response to public comments. In fact, adhering to the [plaintiff's] view might result in the EPA's never being able to issue a final rule capable of standing up to review: every time the Agency responded to public comments, such as those in this rulemaking, it would trigger a new comment period. Thus, either the comment period would continue in a never-ending circle, or, if the EPA chose not to respond to the last set of public comments, any final rule could be struck down for lack of support in the record.

See also Kern County Farm Bureau v. Allen, 450 F.3d 1072 (9th Cir. 2006) ("supplementary" data may be added to record after the comment period if no prejudice is shown); *Building Industry Ass'n v. Norton*, 247 F.3d 1241 (D.C. Cir. 2001) (same).

However, in *Chamber of Commerce v. SEC*, 443 F.3d 890 (D.C. Cir. 2006), the court distinguished this line of cases and overturned SEC rules that would have required mutual funds to have boards of directors composed mainly of independent directors. In an earlier appeal, the court had directed the agency to consider the costs that mutual funds would have to bear in order to comply with the new rules. On remand, the Commission declared that these costs would be insignificant, relying primarily on salary and compensation surveys that were not part of the rulemaking record. The court held that the agency had erred by relying on these surveys without reopening the record for new comments.

6. *Prejudicial impact.* In alleging a violation of *Portland Cement*, a challenger is required to explain why the lack of disclosure was prejudicial. *See West Virginia v. EPA*, 362 F.3d 861, 868–69 (D.C. Cir. 2004) (prejudice not shown): *Personal Watercraft Ass'n v. Dept. of Commerce*, 48 F.3d 540, 544 (D.C. Cir. 2005). For example, in *Chamber of Commerce*, the court noted that the Chamber had identified specific objections that it would have lodged, as well as additional information it would have brought forward, if it had known that the Commission might rely on the salary surveys. However, in *Shell Oil*

Co. v. EPA, 950 F.2d 741 (D.C. Cir. 1991), the court held that a challenger's obligation to show prejudice does not apply to a violation of the "logical outgrowth" principle; it is up to the agency to show that comments on the changes it made between the proposed and final rules would have been useless. *See also Sprint Corp. v. FCC*, 315 F.3d 369, 376–77 (D.C. Cir. 2003). Is this distinction persuasive? *Shell Oil* is a dramatic example of the potency of the "logical outgrowth" doctrine, because the court used that test as the basis for invalidating eleven-year-old rules that had served as a cornerstone of EPA's regulation of hazardous waste facilities.

7.   *Problem.* Reconsider the Problem in § 5.3.1 N.7 arising out of the Madison Medical Board's rule on subjecting psychiatric patients to physical or chemical restraints. Assume that, in the preamble to the final rule, the Board referred to five additional articles in medical journals documenting the risks of restraints. Board staff had consulted these five articles in formulating the proposed rule but had not previously cited them or incorporated them into the rulemaking record. Can the Mental Health Coalition successfully challenge the rule in court on the ground that the Board did not disclose five of the medical studies on which it relied in preparing its notice of proposed rulemaking?

§ 5.4   PUBLIC PARTICIPATION

The federal APA provides for two kinds of rulemaking—"formal" and "informal." *Formal rulemaking* involves an opportunity for a trial-type hearing, including the right to present evidence, conduct cross-examination, and submit rebuttal evidence, conducted according to most of the adjudication provisions of the federal act. Formal rulemaking procedures are spelled out in §§ 556 and 557, but these provisions come into play only "[w]hen rules are required by statute to be made on the record after opportunity for an agency hearing." APA § 553(c). *Informal rulemaking,* often called notice and comment rulemaking, is governed by far less rigorous procedural requirements. As seen in § 5.3, the process usually revolves around an exchange of documents—a so-called "paper hearing" (although in recent years the dialogue has increasingly been digital rather than on paper). In contrast to the federal APA, state APAs explicitly recognize only one type of rulemaking—informal rulemaking of the notice and comment variety.

During the 1970s, Congress occasionally departed from the two APA models in the enabling acts of certain federal agencies. It created statutory schemes that resembled the basic notice and comment process, but included additional or alternate procedural requirements that were designed to broaden opportunities for public participation. This intermediate approach has often been called *hybrid rulemaking.*

The informal, formal, and hybrid varieties of rulemaking are the subject of this section. Over time, as will be seen, the prevalence of formal and hybrid rulemaking has sharply declined. In practice, therefore, informal rulemaking has become the standard model in the federal system, just as had been true all along in the states.

§ 5.4.1 INFORMAL RULEMAKING

§ 5.4.1a Traditional Procedures

NOTES AND QUESTIONS

1. *Extending notice and comment.* The APA requires at least a single round of notice and comment in informal rulemaking. Often, however, agencies extend a comment period beyond its originally announced expiration date in order to solicit further input on issues of interest or to allow stakeholders to reply to comments that have already been filed. *See* ACUS Recommendation 2011–2, *Rulemaking Comments*, ¶ 6, 76 Fed. Reg. 48,789 (2011) (encouraging allowance of reply comments where appropriate). In fact, agencies often will accept submissions from interested persons regarding a pending rulemaking even after the announced period for submitting comments has elapsed. In this latter situation, agencies are often thought to need discretion to reject some such submissions. *See id.* ¶ 5 ("The agency may make clear that late comments are disfavored and will only be considered to the extent practicable.") The 2010 MSAPA tacitly takes a similar position: An agency "*shall* consider all information and comment on a proposed rule which is submitted . . . within the comment period" and "*may* consider any other information it receives concerning a proposed rule during the rulemaking." § 306(a)–(b) (emphasis added). Do these authorities concede too much to agency preferences?

2. *Written or oral comment.* In informal rulemaking under the federal APA, the agency is free to limit public participation to written submissions unless the agency determines otherwise or some other species of law requires more. Nevertheless, federal agencies frequently exercise their discretion to conduct oral hearings on proposed rules.

The typical state APA follows 1961 MSAPA § 3(a)(2) and requires an opportunity to make written submissions to the agency concerning a proposed rule and also, if properly demanded, an opportunity for an "oral hearing." An oral hearing is construed to be an argument or legislative style hearing rather than a trial-type hearing. It must be demanded by 25 persons, a government subdivision, another agency, or an association with 25 or more members. A few states *require* a public hearing as part of their standard rulemaking processes (with limited exemptions). Hawaii Rev. Stat. § 91–3; Neb. Rev. Stat. 84–907; Mich. Comp. Laws § 24.24(1).

Consider the following justifications for oral proceedings in rulemaking:

It must be admitted that in some situations oral presentations will be more effective than written submissions to communicate to an agency relevant information or arguments, and also to enable the agency to resolve any questions it may have through the oral questioning process. In some situations, oral presentations in rule making may be more effective simply because they are delivered in person, they allow a direct and instantaneous interplay of information and argument between members of the public and the agency, and they are better than written presentations to express depth of feeling or emotion. In addition, oral proceedings may be more effective than proceedings limited entirely to written submissions for provoking broad-based public opposition to a proposed rule. Oral presentations are also likely to be more effective than written submissions for persons who lack the ability to engage in effective written communication.

ARTHUR EARL BONFIELD, STATE ADMINISTRATIVE RULE MAKING 194 (1986). In addition, an opportunity for members of the public to make oral submissions can engender greater public satisfaction with the process. Given these potential benefits from oral proceedings in rulemaking, what considerations might make an agency reluctant to allow them?

3. *Impact of comments.* The notice and comment process of § 553 can have an impact on the contents of agency rules, but inertia is often not easily overcome. One researcher studied all final rules issued by federal agencies during a two-month period and reported that "proposed rules that received comments were more likely to be changed than proposed rules that didn't receive them. . . . However, 72% of the proposed rules that received comments underwent only minor or clarifying changes." The rest of these rules did undergo significant changes, but only rarely did the agency alter the entire direction of its proposed rule. Stuart Shapiro, *Two Months in the Life of the Regulatory State*, ADMIN. & REG. L. NEWS, Spring 2005, at 12, 14. The same scholar later found a similar pattern in a study of rulemaking in New Jersey. In that state, when an agency wishes to make a substantive change in a proposed rule, it must propose it again. In practice, "[f]ewer than two percent of all rules are reproposed, the most significant category of changes. Of the remaining rules, very few have anything but the most minor changes." Stuart Shapiro & Deborah Borie-Holtz, *Lessons from New Jersey*, REGULATION, Spring 2011, at 14, 19. Does it follow that APA procedure should be scaled back, or at least not expanded?

§ 5.4.1b Electronic Rulemaking

NOTES AND QUESTIONS

1. *E-rulemaking structures.* The growth of Internet technology has ushered in dramatic changes in the rulemaking process and opened up possibilities for more. At many agencies, electronic submission of rulemaking comments is now the norm, and paper comments are the rare exception. Many federal agencies have established "electronic dockets"—websites at which members of the general public can learn about pending rulemaking proceedings and submit online comments in these proceedings. The sites link

to the proposed rules and, sometimes, other documents supporting them. Some of the sites also allow members of the public to view all previous comments about a proposed rule and to write responses, resulting in a sort of "threaded discussion." In addition, the federal government maintains a central website, *www.regulations.gov*, on which users can search for pending rules in a given subject area at multiple agencies. Frequently they are able to use this site to obtain documentation on these rules and participate directly in the proceedings.

The Obama administration has been forthright in promoting the use of Internet technology in rulemaking. In 2011 President Obama called upon agencies, "[t]o the extent feasible and permitted by law, [to] afford the public a meaningful opportunity to comment through the Internet on any proposed regulation, [and] to provide, for both proposed and final rules, timely online access to the rulemaking docket on regulations.gov . . ." Exec. Order 13,563, § 2(b), 76 Fed. Reg. 3821 (2011). Moreover, the administration has been encouraging agencies to increase participation by designing

> website content that is dynamic and broadly interactive, rather than static and hierarchically controlled by the site owner. Examples include blogs and discussion fora in which content is created through initial and reactive postings; wikis and collaboration tools such as Google Docs that make it possible for multiple users to author a single text, simultaneously if they wish; and social networking services such as Facebook and Twitter that permit users to share information in the form of text and images and react to the information provided by others.

Cynthia Farina et al., *Rulemaking vs. Democracy: Judging and Nudging Public Participation That Counts*, 2 MICH. J. ENVTL. & ADMIN. L. 123, 128 (2012). *See also* ACUS Recommendation 2013–5, *Social Media in Rulemaking*, 78 Fed. Reg. 76,269 (2013).

There are also parallel developments at the state level, such as in Virginia, *townhall.virginia.gov*, and Florida, *www.flrules.org*. The 2010 MSAPA was drafted to be fully compatible with e-rulemaking. *See, e.g.,* §§ 102(29), 202, 303(a).

2. *E-rulemaking in practice.* Studies indicate that, to date, most rulemaking proceedings have been barely affected by the new opportunities for electronic participation. Most attract little attention, and the comments come primarily from the organized interest groups that have traditionally participated in the process. *See, e.g.,* Cary Coglianese, *Citizen Participation in Rulemaking: Past, Present, and Future*, 55 DUKE L.J. 943 (2006). Would you expect that, as electronic dockets become more sophisticated and user-friendly, the number of rulemaking proceedings that will attract comment from the citizenry at large will increase substantially?

Occasionally, however, a pending rule provokes widespread public controversy. In such high-profile proceedings, the opportunity to comment online does frequently result in a flood of rulemaking comments. In 2012 a coalition of environmentalist groups claimed a new record by generating more than two million comments in support of a proposed EPA air quality rule. Rachel Arenstein, *Two Million Comments to Cut Carbon Pollution*, WILDLIFE PROMISE, June 28, 2012, *blog.nwf.org/2012/06/2–1–million-comments-to-cut-carbon-pollution/*. In order to manage mass comments on this scale, some agencies are now resorting to software that can group identical comments together and identify small differences among similar submissions. *See* 73 Fed.Reg. 28,212, 28,235 (Fish and Wildlife Service 2008) (noting use of such software to cope with 670,000 comments submitted regarding listing of polar bear as an endangered species). Is computerized screening consistent with APA § 553(c), which requires "consideration of the relevant matter presented" by *all* rulemaking comments? For one answer, see ACUS Recommendation 2011–1, *Legal Considerations in Rulemaking*, 76 Fed. Reg. 48,789, ¶ 1(a)(1) (2011) (asserting that the APA "does not require agencies to ensure that a person reads each one of multiple identical or nearly identical comments.")

3.   *Vox populi.* Is the broad public participation that policymakers have been striving to elicit in rulemaking proceedings worth its costs? Professor Funk is dubious:

> [T]elling the public they can have a voice in the rulemaking process verges on misleading. The notice-and-comment procedure of rulemaking isn't supposed to be a political exercise. Of course, politics may be involved in a controversial rulemaking, but it's not exercised in the comments filed with the agency during the period for public comment. Connected players in the Washington scene, whether from public or special interest groups, may bring political pressure to bear . . . by instigating congressional pressure, and by direct contacts with agency officials. But that's not an argument for encouraging more citizen input in public comments on rulemakings. That's an argument for citizens to support the organized groups they believe further their (or the public's) interests, because public comments on agency rulemakings are not political pressure to which agencies will respond.

> If rulemaking were to be decided by direct democracy, then getting out the vote might be relevant, but there is virtually no statutory requirement or authorization for rulemaking that states the agency is to consider the number of people who support or oppose the rule, or even the depth of intensity identified by those on either side.

> . . . Public participation via comments in rulemaking may make people *feel* better, knowing that they can participate in this agency activity, but it may only be giving the public false hope. How will people feel about their experience participating in government when they discover that their comments in fact have no impact whatsoever on the rulemaking?

Bill Funk, *The Public Needs a Voice in Policy. But is Involving the Public in Rulemaking a Workable Idea?*, CPR BLOG, April 13, 2010, *progressivereform.org/CPRBlog.cfm?idBlog=F74D5F86–B44E–2CBB–ED1507624B63809E.*

Professor Shulman goes further, suggesting that mass comments may actually impair the rulemaking process. He cites EPA's experience in a 2004 proceeding to set limits on emissions of airborne mercury. The agency's proposal for a "cap and trade" system was widely viewed as too weak, and EPA received about a half million comments. Shulman sampled these comments and reported: "[F]or every brief but substantive comment tacked onto a form letter e-mail, a reviewer will also have to read at least 90–95 pithy, pleading, condescending, name calling, or otherwise useless comments. It may therefore do more harm than good when hastily typed[, u]nreflective tirades are the bulk of the comments and they drown out the people whose carefully drawn comments might actually make a difference." Stuart W. Shulman, *Whither Deliberation?: Mass E-Mail Campaigns and U.S. Regulatory Rulemaking*, 3 J. E-GOVERNMENT 41, 58 (2006). *See also* Farina et al., *supra*, at 137–41, 150–51.

Sometimes, however, members of the general public submit sophisticated or informative comments, and those comments are the most likely to have influence on the rulemaking agency, according to Mariano-Florentino Cuéllar, *Rethinking Regulatory Democracy*, 52 ADMIN. L. REV. 411 (2005). More broadly speaking, Professor Mendelson believes that agencies *should* give significant weight to mass comments. She argues that the notice and comment process "can help us view the agency decision as democratic and thus essentially self-legitimating." Yet, she says,

> [a]n agency's dismissal or pro forma treatment of significant numbers of public comments would be very hard to square with a vision of rulemaking as a democratic process. . . .

> This is not to say that an agency should tally up the total number of comments for or against a particular issue and have that serve as a referendum or a dispositive vote of some sort on the policy issue at hand. . . . But in view of the focused, crystallized and thus likely useful nature of many of these comments, there is a case to be made that a democratically responsive agency process should attend to, incorporate, and engage value-laden points, especially when they are made in a significant number of comments. . . .

> For example, especially where the comments point in a direction different from the agency's proposed path, such comments have to be understood as an important signal—perhaps even akin to a straw poll—that further investigation of some sort into public values and policy direction is needed. . . .

> [E]ven if not perfectly representative of the public at large, the level of participation in mass commenting is surely an improvement

over a nation without citizen engagement. This is especially true given the general underrepresentation of diffuse beneficiary groups. Public comment campaigns may serve to roughly counterbalance the long-time advantage enjoyed by regulated entities.

Nina A. Mendelson, *Rulemaking, Democracy, and Torrents of E-Mail*, 79 GEO. WASH. L. REV. 1343, 1343, 1359, 1374, 1375, 1376 (2011). In light of these commentaries, is mass public participation in rulemaking proceedings a boon or a bane?

4. *Management difficulties.* Implementation of e-rulemaking poses multiple challenges to administrators, over and above the burdens of coping with large quantities of comments. If a comment from a member of the public contains indecent material, must the agency allow it to be posted? What if a comment includes an entire copyrighted book? *See* ACUS Recommendation 2013–4, *The Administrative Record in Informal Rulemaking*, 78 Fed. Reg. 41,358, 41,359 (2013); 2010 MSAPA § 302(a). Another question that has arisen is whether an agency should allow people to comment anonymously. Some agencies require a signature, and others do not. Professor Noveck sees merit on both sides of the question:

> Does designing for participation mean that the general public should know my views on a particular topic or those of General Motors or the Audubon Society? When my name is "googled," should my response to an open rulemaking be the first item returned for the world to see? Should commercial data miners have access to my postings? Should a political party or a public interest group be allowed to mine for comments? Accountability is desirable in order to foster responsible participation, yet the overwhelmingly public nature of open comment on the Internet may undermine informational self-determination. On the other hand, rulemaking is designed to be a public process, and the public enjoys the right of access to all documents, including comments. Making comments readily and publicly available promotes accountability.

Beth Simone Noveck, *The Electronic Revolution in Rulemaking*, 53 EMORY L.J. 433, 488 (2004).

5. *Problem.* The Office of Administration in the state of Madison has developed software that individual agencies can use to conduct rulemaking proceedings online. The agency can allow members of the public to submit comments online; to read other submitters' comments and reply to them; and to signify, with a mouse click, that they "approve" or "disapprove" of an existing comment. Moreover, the Office has available a series of central portals that agencies can use to encourage public participation by publicizing their ongoing rulemaking proceedings. These portals have search engines that enhance citizens' ability to find out about proceedings that may be of interest to them. However, each of these features is entirely optional with the particular rulemaking agency.

Deborah is the head of a Madison park agency that is about to launch a rulemaking proceeding to govern the use of snowmobiles in state parks. Experience in neighboring states suggests that if the proceeding is opened up to electronic commenting, the agency will receive a blizzard of comments, mainly from opponents of snowmobile use. The agency's staff, however, is inclined to allow and perhaps even expand permission for use of snowmobiles in the parks. The staff believes that modern machines are cleaner and quieter than earlier models, although, to judge from other states' experience, many citizens do not seem to believe this.

You are Deborah's staff assistant. She asks your advice as to whether the agency should permit electronic submission of rulemaking comments in this proceeding, and, if so, with what features. What is your recommendation? *Cf. Fund for Animals v. Norton*, 294 F.Supp. 2d 92 (D.D.C. 2003).

§ 5.4.2 FORMAL RULEMAKING

Procedures for so-called "formal" rulemaking are set forth in §§ 556 and 557 of the federal APA. Those sections require trial-type hearings, including the right to present evidence, cross-examine witnesses, and submit rebuttal evidence. In formal rulemaking, the record made before the agency in that proceeding is the exclusive basis for agency action. Ex parte communications, as defined by § 557(d), are prohibited; however, the separation of functions provisions of § 554(d) are inapplicable. Since the rights of private parties are much more detailed and extensive in formal rulemaking than in informal or even hybrid rulemaking, it is important to identify the circumstances in which formal rulemaking applies. Those circumstances are specified in § 553(c), which states that "[w]hen rules are required by statute to be made on the record after opportunity for an agency hearing, sections 556 and 557 of this title" are applicable. The following case construes this language.

UNITED STATES V. FLORIDA EAST COAST RAILWAY CO.
410 U.S. 224 (1973)

[During the 1960s, railroads regularly borrowed boxcars from each other for the purpose of shipping freight. The borrowing railroad would pay the owner of the car a daily rental charge set by the Interstate Commerce Commission (ICC). Apparently the rental rates were so low that they encouraged railroads to hold onto cars owned by other companies, rather than invest in cars of their own. The result was a nationwide shortage of boxcars. Thus, Congress directed the ICC to increase the rental charges.

In adopting rules to implement this mandate, the ICC refused to grant protesting railroads a trial-type hearing. Two lower courts held that this refusal violated §§ 556 and 557 of the APA, which in their view applied to this case by virtue of § 553(c). The railroads also argued that the agency's refusal violated § 1(14)(a) of the Interstate Commerce Act, which provides that the ICC "after hearing" can establish rules with respect to car service.

The Supreme Court disagreed, in an opinion written by Justice Rehnquist. The Court noted that one of the lower courts that had addressed the APA issue had

> observed that it was "rather hard to believe that the last sentence of § 553(c) was directed only to the few legislative sports where the words 'on the record' or their equivalent had found their way into the statute book." This is, however, the language which Congress used, and since there are statutes on the books that do use these very words, adherence to that language cannot be said to render the provision nugatory or ineffectual. We recognized in [*United States v. Allegheny-Ludlum Steel Corp.*, 406 U.S. 742 (1972),] that the actual words "on the record" and "after . . . hearing" used in § 553 were not words of art, and that other statutory language having the same meaning could trigger the provisions of §§ 556 and 557 in rulemaking proceedings. But we adhere to our conclusion, expressed in that case, that the phrase "after hearing" in § 1(14)(a) of the Interstate Commerce Act does not have such an effect.

The Court also rejected the railroads' argument that the ICC's procedures had failed to satisfy the "hearing" requirement of § 1(14)(a), even if they did satisfy § 553 of the APA. Justice Rehnquist wrote:

> The term "hearing" in its legal context undoubtedly has a host of meanings. Its meaning undoubtedly will vary, depending on whether it is used in the context of a rulemaking-type proceeding or in the context of a proceeding devoted to the adjudication of particular disputed facts. It is by no means apparent what the drafters of . . . the first part of § 1(14)(a) of the Interstate Commerce Act, meant by the term. . . . What is apparent, though, is that the term was used in granting authority to the Commission to make rules and regulations of a prospective nature. . . . [C]onfronted with a grant of substantive authority made after the Administrative Procedure Act was enacted, we think that reference to that Act, in which Congress devoted itself exclusively to questions such as the nature and scope of hearings, is a satisfactory basis for determining what is meant by the term "hearing" used in another statute. Turning to that Act, we are convinced that the term "hearing" as used therein does not necessarily embrace either the right to present evidence

orally and to cross-examine opposing witnesses, or the right to present oral argument to the agency's decisionmaker.

The Court went on to conclude that, because the Commission had complied with all of the § 553 notice-and-comment requirements, the hearing requirement of § 1(14)(a) of the Act was also met.

Finally, the Court decided that the Constitution did not require any different result. (The Court's constitutional analysis is excerpted in § 2.5.) Justices Douglas and Stewart dissented.]

NOTES AND QUESTIONS

1. *The trigger for formal rulemaking.* According to the *Florida East Coast* case, when a statute authorizes rulemaking of general applicability, it does not require an agency to go beyond the informal procedures of § 553 unless the statute explicitly provides that the rule be made after a hearing on the record, or uses language very similar to that. In effect, the Court adopted a strong presumption against the invocation of APA formal rulemaking.

In this connection, recall *Dominion Energy Brayton Point v. Johnson*, excerpted in § 3.1.1, which addressed the question of whether a statute calling for a "hearing" triggers trial-type procedures under the federal APA in the context of *adjudication*. In that case, the court deferred to the agency's reading of the relevant statute, because that reading was reasonable and the statute was unclear. As a practical matter, is there a difference between the approaches taken in *Florida East Coast* and *Dominion Energy*?

2. *Statutory "hearing" requirements in rulemaking.* Notice that *Florida East Coast* held not only that the ICC proceeding was not governed by §§ 556 and 557 of the APA, but also that the "hearing" mandate of the Interstate Commerce Act gave the railroads no broader right to be heard than they would have possessed under the APA alone. Is this a convincing interpretation of that Act?

3. *The merits of mandatory trial-type rulemaking proceedings.* Studies of agencies' experiences with formal rulemaking have resulted in harsh criticisms of their utility. One reason for opposition to trial-type hearings in rulemaking is their perceived inefficiency. The classic example is a Food and Drug Administration formal rulemaking to decide whether peanut butter should be required to have 87 or 90 percent peanuts. The proceeding began in 1959 and ended in 1968, generating 7,736 pages of transcript. *Corn Products Co. v. FDA*, 427 F.2d 511 (3d Cir. 1970).

In upholding the Federal Power Commission's use of notice and comment procedures, rather than trial-type procedures, to issue a rule fixing a nationwide rate for natural gas sales, another court of appeals remarked:

> Were the Commission to have allowed all interested parties to submit oral testimony and conduct oral cross-examination on an undertaking so massive and novel as setting a national rate for new

gas, the proceeding would have taken years, and the Commission's power to effectively regulate the industry would have been destroyed.

Shell Oil Co. v. FPC, 520 F.2d 1061, 1076 (5th Cir. 1975).

A second concern is that the use of trial-type hearings in rulemaking has been found to obstruct agency action and frustrate agency regulatory goals. Professor Hamilton noted in a report to the Administrative Conference:

> [T]he primary impact of . . . [trial-type] procedural requirements [in rule making] is often not, as one might otherwise have expected, the testing of agency assumptions by cross-examination, or the testing of agency conclusions by courts on the basis of substantial evidence of record. Rather these procedures either cause the abandonment of the program, . . . the development of techniques to reach the same regulatory goal but without a hearing, . . . or the promulgation of noncontroversial regulations by a process of negotiation and compromise. . . . In practice, therefore, the principal effect of imposing [formal requirements on] rulemaking . . . has often been the dilution of the regulatory process rather than the protection of persons from arbitrary action.

Robert W. Hamilton, *Procedures for the Adoption of Rules of General Applicability: The Need for Procedural Innovation in Administrative Rulemaking,* 60 CAL. L. REV. 1276, 1312–13 (1972).

A third reason for the opposition to trial-type proceedings in rulemaking is a belief that they are unsuitable for determining most issues presented in rulemaking proceedings. Trial-type procedures, which include the right to present evidence, cross-examine witnesses, and present rebuttal evidence, are usually considered to be most helpful in settling disputed facts of a specific nature about particular persons and circumstances. Rulemaking procedures, on the other hand, are designed to formulate general policy. The formation of such policy may be based in part on general legislative facts, but only rarely on specific facts, and in the end is based upon value judgments. Thus, it is argued, the *desirability* of a certain policy cannot be proven through trial-type procedures—although, admittedly, the resolution of some subsidiary specific factual premises of such a policy may sometimes be aided by their use.

Against the background of these appraisals, the Administrative Conference recommended that "Congress should repeal formal ('on-the-record') or other adjudicative fact-finding procedures in rulemaking in any existing statutes mandating such procedures." ACUS Recommendation 93–4, *Improving the Environment for Agency Rulemaking,* 58 Fed. Reg. 4630 (1994).

4. *Fadeout.* Unsurprisingly, in view of the foregoing criticisms, trial-type hearings for the purpose of promulgating rules of general applicability have all but disappeared from federal practice. The statute that required

formal rulemaking in the peanut butter episode was repealed in 1990. Other formal rulemaking statutes do survive, such as provisions that authorize regulations to prohibit the "taking" of marine mammals, 16 U.S.C. § 1373(d), or to amend the schedule of controlled substances, 21 U.S.C. § 811(a). Even in these areas, however, administrators seem to do their best to avoid actually using this procedure. *See, e.g., Hemp Industries Ass'n v. DEA*, 357 F.3d 1012 (9th Cir. 2004) (rejecting DEA effort to classify hemp products as controlled substances without using formal rulemaking).

These days, indeed, one sometimes encounters the phrase "formal rulemaking" in opinions written by judges who actually mean to refer to notice-and-comment rulemaking, which traditionally has been called "*informal* rulemaking." *E.g., Wyeth v. Levine*, 555 U.S. 555, 580 (2009); *National Cable & Telecomms. Ass'n v. Brand X Internet Services*, 545 U.S. 967, 1004 (2005) (Breyer, J., concurring); *Washington State Dep't of Social & Health Services v. Guardianship Estate of Keffeler*, 537 U.S. 371, 385 (2003); *Flores v. USCIS*, 718 F.3d 548, 551 (6th Cir. 2013). This imprecision typically occurs when a judge means to draw a contrast between legislative rules, which generally must be promulgated through notice-and-comment procedures, and interpretive rules or policy statements, which may be promulgated *even more* informally, i.e., without notice and comment. (These and other exemptions from § 553 rulemaking requirements are discussed in detail in § 6.1.) To avoid confusion, this casebook uses the term "formal rulemaking" to refer exclusively to rules issued in conformity with the trial-type procedures of §§ 556–57. Still, the imprecision just described is a telling sign of how uncommon the formal rulemaking process of the APA has become.

5. *Legislative revival of formal rulemaking?* A bill now before Congress would empower private persons to force an agency to utilize trial-type procedures under APA §§ 556–57 to resolve certain core issues in important rulemaking proceedings. See Regulatory Accountability Act (RAA), H.R. 2122, 113th Cong. §§ 3(b), 5 (2013) (proposed §§ 553(e), 556(g)). The House of Representatives passed a prior version of the RAA in 2011. H.R. 3010, 112th Cong. (2011). This obligation would apply to proceedings involving "high-impact rules" (those expected to impose at least $1 billion in annual costs on the economy), and sometimes to proceedings to promulgate "major rules" (imposing at least $100 million in annual costs). The issues considered at the hearing would include, among others, whether the factual predicate of the rule is supported by evidence, whether any alternative to the proposed rule would achieve the statutory objectives at lower cost, and whether the proposed rule's benefits would justify a failure to adopt such a lower cost alternative. All issues in the proceeding that were not subject to formal rulemaking would be resolved through the usual notice and comment process.

The ABA Section of Administrative Law and Regulatory Practice submitted comments strongly opposing these provisions, largely for reasons suggested in N.3. *Comments on H.R. 3010, The Regulatory Accountability Act of 2011*, 64 ADMIN. L. REV. 619, 650–54 (2012). Professor Nielson, however, argues that the administrative law community should rethink its longstanding opposition to formal rulemaking. He notes that trial-type procedure, specifically including hearings with cross-examination, is recognized throughout the legal system as an effective tool for eliciting truth, perhaps even on issues of legislative fact. Thus, he says, administrative lawyers should question whether indiscriminate opposition to formal rulemaking is well grounded. Although he does not specifically endorse the Regulatory Accountability Act, he suggests that requiring formal rulemaking for expensive rules might be a good place to start, because "for more important rules, more procedure is appropriate." Aaron Nielson, *In Defense of Formal Rulemaking* (forthcoming in 75 OHIO ST. L.J. (2014)). Are these arguments well taken?

6. *State law.* The 2010 MSAPA does not require any trial-type procedures in rulemaking. The agency need not allow any hearing "[u]nless a hearing is required by law of this state other than this [act]," § 306(c), although an agency may provide one in its discretion. But even when a hearing is available, the specifications for such a hearing in § 306(c)–(e) are quite skeletal, like a town hall meeting. The Act's "contested case" provisions for a trial-type hearing apply solely to adjudication. § 401.

7. *Problem.* Mercy Hospital Corp. owns and has operated for almost 100 years a non-profit hospital that has provided free services to poor people in Jefferson County. The directors have decided to convert to a publicly-held for-profit corporation operating a profit-making hospital. After this conversion takes place, Mercy Hospital will offer no free services to the poor.

By statute, a conversion of a corporation from non-profit to profit status must be approved by the Department of Corporations (DOC). Such approval can be granted only on terms that are "fair, just and equitable" to the public. A statute provides that DOC must provide a "fair hearing" in such cases.

Jay, the director of Jefferson Fund for the Homeless (JFH), sent a letter to DOC stating that the conversion should be approved only on condition that Mercy be required to contribute $50,000,000 to charities serving the poor in Jefferson County. The letter argued that Mercy was presently worth well in excess of that sum and it would be unjust and inequitable to allow that value to pass into private hands. The letter further urged that DOC should establish a general policy of requiring similarly situated nonprofit hospitals to contribute to charity as a condition of converting to for-profit status.

Rhoda, the head of DOC, commenced two rulemaking proceedings: one to prescribe the general policy proposed by Jay, and another to approve Mercy's application with the condition envisioned by that policy. (She characterized the latter proceeding as rulemaking on the ground that it would authorize a "corporate reorganization" within the meaning of 5 U.S.C. § 551(4).) She treated both matters as notice-and-comment proceedings, with no oral testimony or cross-examination permitted. Evidence could be submitted only in writing.

Rhoda has denied Mercy's request that it be allowed to cross-examine Jay in each proceeding. Should the request be granted if DOC is subject to i) the federal APA, ii) the 2010 MSAPA, iii) no APA?

§ 5.4.3 HYBRID RULEMAKING AND THE LIMITS ON JUDICIAL SUPERVISION OF ADMINISTRATIVE PROCEDURE

As noted earlier, Congress has enacted a variety of "hybrid rulemaking" statutes. These statutes instruct specific agencies to make rules using procedures that are somewhat more elaborate than APA informal rulemaking:

> Although the [federal] APA does not contain an oral hearing requirement for informal rulemaking, some laws enacted in the 1970s do contain requirements that the agency hold a "public hearing" or provide interested persons "an opportunity for the oral presentation of data, views, or arguments" in rulemaking. . . . Statutes calling for a legislative-type hearing include the Occupational Safety and Health Act (1970); the Consumer Product Safety Act (1972); the Safe Drinking Water Act (1974); the Energy Policy and Conservation Act (1975); the Clean Water Act (1977); the Federal Mine Safety and Health Amendment Act (1977); and the Endangered Species Act Amendments (1978).

> A few of these hybrid rulemaking statutes require not only a legislative-type hearing but also an opportunity for interested persons to question or cross-examine opposing witnesses. These include the Magnuson-Moss Warranty—Federal Trade Commission Improvement Act (1975); the Securities Acts Amendments (1975); and the Toxic Substances Control Act (1976). . . .

> The enactment of statutes requiring an oral hearing likely reflected the growing complexity of the issues involved in informal rulemaking, the perceived need to probe the accuracy of public comments on these issues, and the strong belief among legislators in the value of oral communication between regulators and the regulated.

JEFFREY S. LUBBERS, A GUIDE TO FEDERAL AGENCY RULEMAKING 282 (5th ed. 2012).

At around the same time as these legislative developments, reviewing courts occasionally held that specific agency rulemaking proceedings had been conducted improperly because of an agency's failure to permit procedural devices that would supplement the usual notice and comment procedures. Because of their wide potential applicability, these court decisions were studied closely by the administrative law bar.

The advent of hybrid rulemaking led to a debate within the Court of Appeals for the District of Columbia Circuit over the issue of whether procedure rather than substance should be emphasized in judicial review of rulemaking. For example, in *International Harvester Co. v. Ruckelshaus,* 478 F.2d 615, 652 (D.C. Cir. 1973), Judge David Bazelon suggested that the courts should not "scrutinize the technical merits of each decision" but should "establish a decision-making process which assures a reasoned decision. . . ." The debate came to a head in *Ethyl Corp. v. EPA,* 541 F.2d 1 (D.C. Cir. 1976). In a concurring opinion Judge Bazelon again warned: "Because substantive review of mathematical and scientific evidence by technically illiterate judges is dangerously unreliable, . . . we will do more to improve administrative decision-making by concentrating our efforts on strengthening administrative procedures." Another concurrence, by Judge Leventhal, replied: "Our obligation [of substantive review] is not to be jettisoned because our initial technical understanding may be meagre when compared to our initial grasp of FCC or freedom of speech questions. . . . Better no judicial review at all than a charade that gives the imprimatur without the substance of judicial confirmation that the agency is not acting unreasonably." Ultimately, the Supreme Court resolved this argument in an unusually definitive opinion.

VERMONT YANKEE NUCLEAR POWER CORP. V. NRDC
435 U.S. 519 (1978)

[The Atomic Energy Commission (AEC, now the Nuclear Regulatory Commission) has regulatory authority over nuclear energy. Before a utility can start constructing a nuclear power plant, it must obtain a construction permit from the AEC. Applications for construction permits undergo extensive safety and environmental review by the AEC staff. A public adjudicatory hearing occurs before the permit can be granted.

At issue in Vermont Yankee's application was the environmental effect of the disposal and storage of highly toxic nuclear waste produced by operating the plant. Because this is a recurring issue, the AEC conducted a rulemaking proceeding to determine how the nuclear waste storage issue should be resolved in each licensing proceeding. The objective was to settle the issue so it would not have to be relitigated in every single license application (analogously to the grid regulations in *Campbell,* § 3.2).

The proposed and final AEC rule specified numerical values for the environmental impact of waste disposal; these values would be part of an overall cost-benefit analysis of whether the permit should be granted. The values assigned were so low that their practical effect would be that the AEC would essentially ignore the waste disposal problem. This approach was based on the AEC's determination that in the future methods of storage of nuclear waste would be developed that would render the wastes non-hazardous.

The only support in the record for this conclusion was a 20-page report by Dr. Pittman of the AEC staff. The Natural Resources Defense Council (NRDC) and others sought to cross-examine Dr. Pittman, but the AEC refused to allow cross-examination. On appeal, the D.C. Circuit reversed in an opinion by Judge Bazelon. According to the court of appeals, Pittman's report had offered "conclusory reassurances" but little detailed backup on precisely how the wastes could be safely handled in the future.]

REHNQUIST, J.:

In 1946, Congress enacted the Administrative Procedure Act, which as we have noted elsewhere was not only "a new, basic and comprehensive regulation of procedures in many agencies," *Wong Yang Sung v. McGrath*, 339 U.S. 33 (1950), but was also a legislative enactment which settled "long-continued and hard-fought contentions, and enacts a formula upon which opposing social and political forces have come to rest." *Id.* Section 553 dealing with rulemaking, requires in subsection (b) that "notice of proposed rule making shall be published in the Federal Register," . . . describes the contents of that notice, and goes on to require in subsection (c) that after the notice the agency "shall give interested persons an opportunity to participate in the rule making through submission of written data, views, or arguments with or without opportunity for oral presentation. After consideration of the relevant matter presented, the agency shall incorporate in the rules adopted a concise general statement of their basis and purpose." Interpreting this provision of the Act in *United States v. Allegheny-Ludlum Steel Corp.,* 406 U.S. 742 (1972), and *United States v. Florida East Coast R. Co.,* 410 U.S. 224 (1973), we held that generally speaking this section of the Act established the maximum procedural requirements which Congress was willing to have the courts impose upon agencies in conducting rulemaking procedures. Agencies are free to grant additional procedural rights in the exercise of their discretion, but reviewing courts are generally not free to impose them if the agencies have not chosen to grant them. This is not to say necessarily that there are no circumstances which would ever justify a court in overturning agency action because of a failure to employ procedures beyond those required by the statute. But such circumstances, if they exist, are extremely rare. . . .

[In this case,] [r]espondents appealed from both the Commission's adoption of the rule [dealing with the environmental effects of the uranium fuel cycle] and its decision to grant Vermont Yankee's license [to operate a nuclear power plant] to the Court of Appeals for the District of Columbia Circuit. . . .

With respect to the challenge of Vermont Yankee's license, the court [of appeals] first [held] that in the absence of effective rulemaking proceedings, the Commission must deal with the environmental impact of fuel reprocessing and disposal in individual licensing proceedings. . . . The court then examined the rulemaking proceedings and, despite the fact that it appeared that the agency employed all the procedures required by 5 U.S.C. § 553 and more, the court determined the proceedings to be inadequate and overturned the rule. Accordingly, the Commission's determination with respect to Vermont Yankee's license was also remanded for further proceedings. . . .

After a thorough examination of the opinion itself, we conclude that . . . the majority of the Court of Appeals struck down the rule because of the perceived inadequacies of the procedures employed in the rulemaking proceedings. . . . The court conceded that absent extraordinary circumstances it is improper for a reviewing court to prescribe the procedural format an agency must follow, but it likewise clearly thought it entirely appropriate to "scrutinize the record as a whole to insure that genuine opportunities to participate in a meaningful way were provided. . . ." The court also refrained from actually ordering the agency to follow any specific procedures, . . . but there is little doubt in our minds that the ineluctable mandate of the court's decision is that the procedures afforded during the hearings were inadequate. . . .

In prior opinions we have intimated that even in a rulemaking proceeding when an agency is making a " 'quasi-judicial' determination by which a very small number of persons are exceptionally affected, in each case upon individual grounds," in some circumstances additional procedures may be required in order to afford the aggrieved individuals due process. *Florida East Coast R. Co.,* quoting from *Bi-Metallic Investment Co.* [§ 2.5]. It might also be true, although we do not think the issue is presented in this case and accordingly do not decide it, that a totally unjustified departure from well-settled agency procedures of long standing might require judicial correction.

But this much is absolutely clear. Absent constitutional constraints or extremely compelling circumstances the "administrative agencies 'should be free to fashion their own rules of procedure and to pursue methods of inquiry capable of permitting them to discharge their multitudinous duties.' " . . . Respondent NRDC argues that . . . 5 U.S.C. § 553 . . . merely establishes lower procedural bounds and that a court may routinely require more than the minimum when an agency's proposed rule addresses complex or technical factual issues or "Issues of

Great Public Import. . . ." We have, however, previously shown that our decisions reject this view. We also think the legislative history . . . does not bear out its contention. . . . In short, all of this leaves little doubt that Congress intended that the discretion of the *agencies* and not that of the courts be exercised in determining when extra procedural devices should be employed.

There are compelling reasons for construing [§ 553] in this manner. In the first place, if courts continually review agency proceedings to determine whether the agency employed procedures which were, in the court's opinion, perfectly tailored to reach what the court perceives to be the "best" or "correct" result, judicial review would be totally unpredictable. And the agencies, operating under this vague injunction to employ the "best" procedures and facing the threat of reversal if they did not, would undoubtedly adopt full adjudicatory procedures in every instance. Not only would this totally disrupt the statutory scheme, through which Congress enacted "a formula upon which opposing social and political forces have come to rest," but all the inherent advantages of informal rulemaking would be totally lost.

Secondly, it is obvious that the court in these cases reviewed the agency's choice of procedures on the basis of the record actually produced at the hearing, and not on the basis of the information available to the agency when it made the decision to structure the proceedings in a certain way. This sort of Monday morning quarterbacking not only encourages but almost compels the agency to conduct all rulemaking proceedings with the full panoply of procedural devices normally associated only with adjudicatory hearings.

Finally, and perhaps most importantly, this sort of review fundamentally misconceives the nature of the standard for judicial review of an agency rule. The court below uncritically assumed that additional procedures will automatically result in a more adequate record because it will give interested parties more of an opportunity to participate in and contribute to the proceedings. But informal rulemaking need not be based solely on the transcript of a hearing held before an agency. Indeed, the agency need not even hold a formal hearing. Thus, the adequacy of the "record" in this type of proceeding is not correlated directly to the type of procedural devices employed, but rather turns on whether the agency has followed the statutory mandate of the Administrative Procedure Act or other relevant statutes. If the agency is compelled to support the rule which it ultimately adopts with the type of record produced only after a full adjudicatory hearing, it simply will have no choice but to conduct a full adjudicatory hearing prior to promulgating every rule. In sum, this sort of unwarranted judicial examination of perceived procedural shortcomings of a rulemaking proceeding can do nothing but seriously interfere with that process prescribed by Congress.

In short, nothing in the APA, . . . the circumstances of this case, the nature of the issues being considered, past agency practice, or the statutory mandate under which the Commission operates permitted the court to review and overturn the rulemaking proceeding on the basis of the procedural devices employed (or not employed) by the Commission so long as the Commission employed at least the statutory *minima,* a matter about which there is no doubt in this case.

There remains, of course, the question of whether the challenged rule finds sufficient justification in the administrative proceedings that it should be upheld by the reviewing court. Judge Tamm, concurring in the result reached by the majority of the Court of Appeals, thought that it did not. There are also intimations in the majority opinion which suggest that the judges who joined it likewise may have thought the administrative proceedings an insufficient basis upon which to predicate the rule in question. We accordingly remand so that the Court of Appeals may review the rule as the Administrative Procedure Act provides. We have made it abundantly clear before that when there is a contemporaneous explanation of the agency decision, the validity of that action must "stand or fall on the propriety of that finding, judged, of course, by the appropriate standard of review. If that finding is not sustainable on the administrative record made, then the Comptroller's decision must be vacated and the matter remanded to him for further consideration." *Camp v. Pitts,* 411 U.S. 138, 143 (1973). The court should engage in this kind of review and not stray beyond the judicial province to explore the procedural format [beyond that required by the APA] or to impose upon the agency its own notion of which procedures are "best" or most likely to further some vague, undefined public good. . . .

Reversed and remanded.

[BLACKMUN and POWELL, JJ., did not participate.]

NOTES AND QUESTIONS

1. *Responses to Vermont Yankee.* If the main objective of the Supreme Court's unanimous, strongly worded opinion was to send a message to the lower courts, it has been quite successful. In subsequent years, the federal courts have been careful to avoid imposing procedural requirements on agencies in rulemaking without at least purporting to find support in statutory or other provisions of law. *Vermont Yankee* principles have also found support in state courts, although most have not yet addressed the issue. *Brown v. D.C. Dep't of Empl. Servs.,* 83 A.3d 739 (D.C. 2014); *Tri-State Generation & Transmission Ass'n v. Envtl. Quality Council,* 590 P.2d 1324 (Wyo. 1979). Few, if any, cases have even professed to find one of the "extremely rare" circumstances that the Court said might justify an exception to the general ban on judicially created rulemaking procedures in addition to those of § 553. Whether the courts have adhered to the "spirit" of *Vermont*

Yankee in their performance of the functions that the Court did allow them to exercise is, however, less clear, as subsequent notes in this section will discuss.

Meanwhile, scholarly opinion about *Vermont Yankee* has been divided. *See* Cooley B. Howarth, Jr., *Informal Agency Rulemaking and the Courts: A Theory for Procedural Review*, 61 WASH. U.L.Q. 891, 913–25 (1984) (surveying commentators' views). Professor Davis contended that *Vermont Yankee* was wrong to forbid courts from creating common law rulemaking requirements to supplement those provided in APA § 553. He argued that the Supreme Court improperly ignored APA § 559, which provides that this Act does "not limit or repeal additional requirements imposed by statute or otherwise *recognized by law*." (Emphasis added). Section 559 makes clear, Davis said, that the APA imposes only minimum, not maximum, procedural requirements. In his view, court-created administrative common law is necessary to ensure an acceptable administrative law system. *See* Kenneth Culp Davis, *Administrative Common Law and the* Vermont Yankee *Opinion*, 1980 UTAH L. REV. 3. Professor Byse, on the other hand, commended the Court for recognizing that the judiciary must respect the procedural decisions mandated by Congress, and that agencies, not courts, are in the best position to evaluate the efficacy of their factfinding procedures. Clark Byse, Vermont Yankee *and the Evolution of Administrative Procedure: A Somewhat Different View*, 91 HARV. L. REV. 1823 (1978). Over time, the Byse view seems to have prevailed. *See* Jack M. Beermann & Gary Lawson, *Reprocessing* Vermont Yankee, 75 GEO. WASH. L. REV. 856 (2007). But which view is more persuasive?

2.   *Hybrid rulemaking statutes after Vermont Yankee.* The Supreme Court's opinion in *Vermont Yankee* also effectively marked the demise of congressional legislation imposing trial-type procedural formalities in rulemaking. The 1970s statutes described at the beginning of this section find no counterparts in recent federal legislation.

One possible explanation for this change in congressional behavior—in addition to the *Vermont Yankee* case itself—is that empirical studies of the actual operation of hybrid rulemaking have raised serious doubts about its effectiveness. After a detailed study by Professor Barry B. Boyer of the FTC's experience with a statutory rulemaking scheme that included an express right to conduct cross-examination and present rebuttal evidence on disputed issues of fact, the Administrative Conference concluded that there was "compelling evidence" that trial-type hearing procedure "is not an effective means of controlling an agency's discretion in its exercise of a broad delegation of legislative power which has not acquired, in law, specific meaning." ACUS Recommendation 80–1, *Trade Regulation Rulemaking Under the Magnuson-Moss Warranty–Federal Trade Commission Improvement Act*, 45 Fed. Reg. 46,772 (1980). *But see* William D. Dixon, *Rulemaking and the Myth of Cross-Examination*, 34 ADMIN. L. REV. 389 (1982) (a more positive assessment by the FTC's chief presiding officer).

Similarly, Professor (now Judge) Stephen Williams conducted a study of several cases in which appellate courts had invalidated a rule because of an agency's failure to allow more procedural opportunities than § 553 prescribed. Williams looked at what actually happened after each of these cases returned to the agency on remand. He found that most of the litigants that had won a right to cross-examination abandoned it or used it only as a bargaining chip. In the only case in which challengers actually engaged in cross-examination on remand, they derived little benefit from it. Stephen F. Williams, *"Hybrid Rulemaking" under the Administrative Procedure Act: A Legal and Empirical Analysis*, 42 U. CHI. L. REV. 401, 436–45 (1975).

3. *Vermont Yankee and judicial interpretations of § 553.* To what extent does *Vermont Yankee* undermine or call into question judicial interpretations of the notice and comment provisions of the federal APA, such as the logical outgrowth doctrine or the duty to disclose scientific information underlying a proposed rule? Reconsider the *Chocolate Manufacturers, Nova Scotia*, and *Portland Cement* cases discussed in § 5.3.

4. *Substantive review after Vermont Yankee.* What does the Supreme Court's opinion imply about judicial review of the substance of agency rules? On remand in the *Vermont Yankee* litigation itself, the D.C. Circuit revisited the NRC's waste disposal rule and struck it down again, this time on the theory that the rule was arbitrary and capricious. Again the Supreme Court reversed the court of appeals. *Baltimore Gas & Elec. Co. v. NRDC,* 462 U.S. 87 (1983). The Court found that the agency had carefully balanced environmental and economic factors, and added that a court must give great deference to an agency's predictions, within the area of its expertise, at the frontiers of science. *See* § 9.4 N.3. Yet the Court did not condemn intensive judicial review of rules on their merits in the same strong terms as it had used to dress down the D.C. Circuit in *Vermont Yankee*; and only a few weeks later, the Court strongly reaffirmed "hard look" review in the *State Farm* case, reprinted at § 9.3.2. It seems, therefore, that—in terms of the *Ethyl* debate mentioned at the beginning of this section—the Supreme Court has rejected the "Bazelon" position, and the "Leventhal" position has prevailed.

Yet, might a court's power to hold an agency rule arbitrary and capricious serve as an indirect means of controlling the agency's procedural choices, which *Vermont Yankee* supposedly forbids? The Court commented on this possibility in *Pension Benefit Guaranty Corp. (PBGC) v. LTV Corp.*, 496 U.S. 633 (1990). The Court recognized that in the leading case of *Citizens to Preserve Overton Park, Inc. v. Volpe*, 401 U.S. 402 (1971), it had authorized a district court to remand that case to the agency for a fuller explanation of the agency's reasoning at the time of the administrative action. The Court said in *PBGC*:

[A]lthough one initially might feel that there is some tension between *Vermont Yankee* and *Overton Park*, the cases are not necessarily inconsistent. *Vermont Yankee* stands for the general proposition that courts are not free to impose upon agencies specific procedural requirements that have no basis in the APA. At most, *Overton Park* suggests that § 706(2)(A) of the APA, which directs a court to ensure that an agency action is not arbitrary and capricious . . ., imposes a general "procedural" requirement of sorts by mandating that an agency take whatever steps it needs to provide an explanation that will enable the court to evaluate the agency's rationale at the time of decision.

At times, the "steps" that courts exhort agencies to take in order to facilitate judicial review do seem to carry rather strong implications for the agencies' procedural choices. In *National Lime Ass'n v. EPA*, 627 F.2d 416, 452–53 (D.C. Cir. 1980), the court described its standard of review for EPA rulemaking as evincing

> a concern that variables be accounted for, that the representativeness of test conditions [be] ascertained, that the validity of tests be assured and the statistical significance of results determined, . . . coupled with a requirement that assumptions be revealed, that the rejection of alternate theories or abandonment of alternate courses of action be explained and that the rationale for the ultimate decision be set forth in a manner which permits the public to exercise its statutory prerogative of comment and the courts to exercise their statutory responsibility upon review.

Doesn't this sort of statement amount to a serious subversion of the principle of agency autonomy that the Court was trying to preserve in *Vermont Yankee*? Isn't even *PBGC* something of a retreat from that principle?

5. *Vermont Yankee in adjudication.* The principal case dealt with informal rulemaking; should its teachings also apply to informal adjudication? In *PBGC v. LTV, supra,* the PBGC (an agency that regulates pension systems) ordered a company to resume responsibility for billions of dollars' worth of pension obligations to its employees, notwithstanding the company's resort to bankruptcy proceedings. The court of appeals held that the agency's highly informal procedures had been inadequate, because PBGC had "neither apprised LTV of the material on which it was to base its decision, [given] LTV an adequate opportunity to offer contrary evidence, proceeded in accordance with ascertainable standards, . . . nor provided [LTV] a statement showing its reasoning in applying those standards." In reversing the decision of the court of appeals and sustaining the agency procedures used in this case, the Supreme Court stated:

> [T]o support its ruling, the court focused on "fundamental fairness" to LTV. . . . But the court did not point to any provision in [the agency's enabling act] or the APA which gives LTV the procedural rights the court identified. Thus, the court's holding runs afoul of *Vermont Yankee.* . . .
>
>   . . . The determination in this case . . . was lawfully made by informal adjudication, the minimal requirements for which are set

forth in § 555 of the APA, and do not include such elements. A failure to provide them where the Due Process Clause itself does not require them (which has not been asserted here) is therefore not unlawful.

The Court did not explain why it believed that the principles of *Vermont Yankee*, developed in the context of informal rulemaking, should also apply to informal adjudication. Was this extension justified? Examine the text of § 555 of the APA, on which the Court relied. Does it appear to play the same role in structuring informal adjudication as § 553 does in structuring informal rulemaking?

6.   *Problem.* The Madison Department of Pollution Control undertook a rulemaking proceeding for the purpose of setting ambient water quality standards governing discharges of industrial pollutants into the state's waterways. The proposed standards would set numerical limits on discharges of cadmium, copper, and zinc.

John represents the Committee for Prosperity, an industrial group whose members sometimes discharge these metallic substances into waterways as an incident of their manufacturing operations. In response to the Department's notice of proposed rulemaking, John filed comments arguing that the proposed standards would be too expensive and would confer minimal environmental benefits in comparison with the less stringent standards that they would replace. After considering these and other comments, the Department adopted a final rule that was identical to its proposed rule.

On behalf of the Committee, John has filed for judicial review and makes two arguments on appeal. First, he contends that the Department's exploration of the benefits and costs of the proposed limits was superficial. He asks the court to remand the rules with instructions that the Department must hold a second comment period, so that the Committee and other members of the public would be able to engage the agency more fully on the issues.

Second, John points out that the Department, in the explanation accompanying its final rule, relied heavily on a report prepared by Martha, an outside consultant. Her report, which she prepared after the rulemaking proceeding had begun, evaluated the costs and environmental benefits of the proposed discharge standards. John contends that Martha's report was methodologically flawed. He complains that the Department never disclosed or mentioned the report to him and other members of the public until it adopted the final rule.

How should the court respond to these claims if Madison has adopted (a) an administrative procedure act similar to the federal APA, or (b) the 2010 MSAPA? In connection with John's second argument, you should review § 5.3.2. *Cf. Industrial Liaison Comm. v. Williams*, 527 N.E.2d 274 (N.Y. 1988).

§ 5.5 PROCEDURAL REGULARITY IN RULEMAKING

This section focuses on the process of decision in rulemaking proceedings and on objections that interested persons outside the agency might lodge against those proceedings. It considers ex parte contacts by outsiders with the agency, bias of the agency heads, and a requirement that the agency head be personally familiar with the record before deciding. Section 3.3 focused on similar problems as they arise in *adjudication*. Solutions to these problems require tradeoffs between judicial and institutional approaches to decisionmaking—that is, between the procedural norms of the courtroom and the distinctive needs of a bureaucratic organization. One of the dominant themes of this section will be whether and to what extent these tradeoffs should be revised when the context changes from adjudication to rulemaking.

§ 5.5.1 ROLE OF AGENCY HEADS

Recall the discussion of *Morgan I*, § 3.3.1. That case obligates the person who takes responsibility for an agency decision to have at least some personal familiarity with the record. In *Morgan I* the Court described the proceedings as "quasi-judicial," but they actually involved ratesetting for fifty market agencies on a classwide basis. Today we would describe those proceedings as formal rulemaking. But should the *Morgan I* principle apply with equal force to *informal* rulemaking?

The federal APA and the various MSAPAs specifically provide that agency decisionmakers must actually consider the written and oral submissions received in the course of the rulemaking proceeding. *See, e.g.,* federal APA § 553(c); 2010 MSAPA § 306(c); 1961 MSAPA § 3(a)(2). However, this requirement does not necessarily mean that the agency head must personally preside at an oral proceeding or personally read all written submissions. In practice, it is seldom feasible for an agency head to perform these functions personally, although in the end it is the agency head who must personally make the determination whether to adopt proposed rules and in what form.

Section 306(e) of the 2010 MSAPA explicitly provides that others may preside at oral rulemaking proceedings and prepare summaries for subsequent personal consideration by the agency head. Both the federal APA and state APAs have been construed in the same manner. An agency head need not read all (or even any) of the written submissions, transcripts and summaries, but must understand their contents so that he or she can make an informed decision. *See Massachusetts State Pharm. Ass'n v. Rate Setting Comm'n*, 438 N.E.2d 1072, 1078 (Mass. 1982). In *National Small Shipments Traffic Conf. v. ICC*, 725 F.2d 1442, 1450–51 (D.C. Cir. 1984), the court said that commissioners may rely on summaries of the record prepared by their staff. "At some point, however, staff-prepared synopses may so distort the record that an agency decisionmaking body can no longer rely on them in meeting its obligations under the law ... to accord 'consideration' to relevant comments submitted for the record by interested parties." Thus, if staff members systematically suppressed all comments on one side of a question, the agency decisionmakers would need to take independent steps to familiarize themselves with those comments.

However, persons who wish to challenge a rule are usually not free to examine an agency head in court to ascertain whether he or she understood the record assembled during the rulemaking proceeding. Recall *Morgan IV,* discussed in § 3.3.1 N.5, holding that such examination is normally improper. Because of this principle, violations of *Morgan I* are in most cases impossible to prove, even where they occur.

Problem. Thirteen days after a new Commissioner of the Food and Drug Administration took office, he signed and issued voluminous regulations setting standards for special dietary foods. During those thirteen days he had also signed fourteen other final regulations, thirteen proposed regulations, and six other notices. Manufacturers of dietary foods sought to take a deposition of the new Commissioner to determine whether he had in fact given sufficient consideration to their 1000 pages of formal exceptions. The record also contained 20,000 additional letters, not to mention 32,000 pages of testimony and thousands of pages of exhibits, reflecting hearings lasting almost two years. The petitioners argued that the objective circumstances raised enough doubt about whether he had actually given sufficient consideration to their views to warrant the unusual step of discovery directed to that issue. What result? *See National Nutritional Foods Ass'n v. FDA,* 491 F.2d 1141 (2d Cir. 1974).

§ 5.5.2 EX PARTE COMMUNICATIONS AND POLITICAL INFLUENCE IN RULEMAKING

During the course of every rulemaking proceeding, an agency acquires a voluminous amount of material concerning the proposed rule. The compilation of this material is known as the rulemaking record. The record serves three basic functions: it aids public participation, it provides materials helpful to the agency in making a decision, and it facilitates judicial review of the agency decision. Although the rulemaking record serves these important functions, the federal APA, the 1961 MSAPA, and the many state acts based on that Model Act are silent with respect to the creation and maintenance of any official agency record in rulemaking. Section 302 of the 2010 MSAPA, on the other hand, provides for a rulemaking record and specifies the materials it must include.

To what extent may persons outside an agency engage in off-the-record, ex parte communications with an agency about a proposed rule? In *formal* rulemaking the answer is clear. Since such rulemaking must be conducted according to the requirements of §§ 556–57 of the federal APA, ex parte communications are forbidden in that kind of rulemaking, and if they nevertheless occur the agency must disclose their substance on the public record. *See* APA § 557(d). On the other hand, in *informal* rulemaking, the assumption for many years was that the federal APA neither banned ex parte communications nor required the inclusion of such communications in the agency rulemaking record. It was early noted that the APA does not

> require the formulation of rules upon the exclusive basis of any "record" made in informal rulemaking proceedings. . . . Accordingly . . . an agency is free to formulate rules [in informal notice and comment rulemaking] upon the basis of materials in its files and the knowledge and experience of the agency, in addition to the materials adduced in public rulemaking proceedings.

U.S. DEP'T OF JUSTICE, ATTORNEY GENERAL'S MANUAL ON THE ADMINISTRATIVE PROCEDURE ACT 31–32 (1947).

HOME BOX OFFICE, INC. V. FCC
567 F.2d 9 (D.C. Cir. 1977)

Before WRIGHT and MACKINNON, CIRCUIT JUDGES, and WEIGEL, DISTRICT JUDGE.

PER CURIAM:

[This case involved a challenge to FCC rules that would have limited the types of programming and advertising that could appear on pay cable channels and subscription television. For example, sports events and feature films on those outlets would have been sharply restricted. The purpose of the rules was to prevent subscription television and cable operators from outbidding regular broadcasters for the right to present these popular shows. The Commission hoped the rules would protect the economic viability of regular broadcast stations, so that the owners of those stations would continue to be able to produce public service programs and serve viewers who could only afford to watch "free" television.]

It is apparently uncontested that a number of participants before the Commission sought out individual commissioners or Commission employees for the purpose of discussing *ex parte* and in confidence the merits of the rules under review here. In fact, the Commission itself solicited such communications in its notices of proposed rulemaking. . . .

. . . It is important to note that many contacts occurred in the crucial period between the close of oral argument . . . and the adoption of the *First Report and Order* . . . when the rulemaking record should have been closed while the Commission was deciding what rules to promulgate. The information submitted to this court by the Commission indicates that during this period broadcast interests met some 18 times with Commission personnel, cable interests some nine times, motion picture and sports interests five times each, and "public interest" intervenors not at all.

Although it is impossible to draw any firm conclusions about the effect of *ex parte* presentations upon the ultimate shape of the pay cable rules, the evidence is certainly consistent with often-voiced claims of undue industry influence over Commission proceedings, and we are particularly concerned that the final shaping of the rules we are reviewing here may have been by compromise among the contending industry forces, rather than by exercise of the independent discretion in the public interest the Communications Act vests in individual commissioners. . . .

Even the possibility that there is here one administrative record for the public and this court and another for the Commission and those "in the know" is intolerable. Whatever the law may have been in the past, there can now be no doubt that implicit in the decision to treat the promulgation of rules as a "final" event in an ongoing process of administration is an assumption that an act of reasoned judgment has occurred, an assumption which further contemplates the existence of a body of material—documents, comments, transcripts, and statements in various forms declaring agency expertise or policy—with reference to which such judgment was exercised. Against this material, "the full administrative record that was before [an agency official] at the time he made his decision," *Citizens to Preserve Overton Park, Inc. v. Volpe,* [401 U.S. 402, 420 (1971)], it is the obligation of this court to test the actions of the Commission for arbitrariness or inconsistency with delegated authority. Yet here agency secrecy stands between us and fulfillment of our obligation. As a practical matter, *Overton Park's* mandate means that the public record must reflect what representations were made to an agency so that relevant information supporting or refuting those representations may be brought to the attention of the reviewing courts by persons participating in agency proceedings. This course is obviously foreclosed if communications are made to the agency in secret and the agency itself does not disclose the information presented. Moreover, where, as here, an agency justifies its actions by reference only to information in the public file while failing to disclose the substance of other relevant information that has been presented to it, a reviewing court cannot presume that the agency has acted properly, *Citizens to*

Preserve Overton Park, Inc. v. Volpe, supra, but must treat the agency's justifications as a fictional account of the actual decisionmaking process and must perforce find its actions arbitrary.

The failure of the public record in this proceeding to disclose all the information made available to the Commission is not the only inadequacy we find here. Even if the Commission had disclosed to this court the substance of what was said to it *ex parte,* it would still be difficult to judge the truth of what the Commission asserted it knew about the television industry because we would not have the benefit of an adversarial discussion among the parties. The importance of such discussion to the proper functioning of the agency decisionmaking and judicial review processes is evident in our cases. We have insisted, for example, that information in agency files or consultants' reports which the agency has identified as relevant to the proceeding be disclosed to the parties for adversarial comment. Similarly, we have required agencies to set out their thinking in notices of proposed rulemaking. This requirement not only allows adversarial critique of the agency but is perhaps one of the few ways that the public may be apprised of what the agency thinks it knows in its capacity as a repository of expert opinion. From a functional standpoint, we see no difference between assertions of fact and expert opinion tendered by the public, as here, and that generated internally in an agency: each may be biased, inaccurate, or incomplete—failings which adversary comment may illuminate. Indeed, the potential for bias in private presentations in rulemakings which resolve "conflicting private claims to a valuable privilege," *Sangamon Valley Television Corp. v. United States,* 269 F.2d 221, 224 [(D.C. Cir. 1959)], seems to us greater than in cases where we have reversed agencies for failure to disclose internal studies. . . .

Equally important is the inconsistency of secrecy with fundamental notions of fairness implicit in due process and with the ideal of reasoned decisionmaking on the merits which undergirds all of our administrative law. Certainly any ambivalence about [this inconsistency] has been removed by recent congressional and presidential actions. In the Government in the Sunshine Act, for example, Congress has declared it to be "the policy of the United States that the public is entitled to the fullest practicable information regarding the decisionmaking processes of the Federal Government," and has taken steps to guard against ex parte contacts in formal agency proceedings. . . .

From what has been said above, it should be clear that information gathered *ex parte* from the public which becomes relevant to a rulemaking will have to be disclosed at some time. On the other hand, we recognize that informal contacts between agencies and the public are the "bread and butter" of the process of administration and are completely appropriate so long as they do not frustrate judicial review or raise serious questions of fairness. Reconciliation of these considerations in a manner which will reduce procedural uncertainty leads us to conclude that communications which are received prior to issuance of a formal notice of rulemaking do not, in general, have to be put in a public file. Of course, if the information contained in such a communication forms the basis for agency action, then, under well-established principles, that information must be disclosed to the public in some form. Once a notice of proposed rulemaking has been issued, however, any agency official or employee who is or may reasonably be expected to be involved in the decisional process of the rulemaking proceeding, should "refus[e] to discuss matters relating to the disposition of a [rulemaking proceeding] with any interested private party, or an attorney or agent for any such party, prior to the [agency's] decision. . . ." If *ex parte* contacts nonetheless occur, we think that any written document or a summary of any oral communication must be placed in the public file established for each rulemaking docket immediately after the communication is received so that interested parties may comment thereon. . . .

[Concurring opinions by MACKINNON, J., and WEIGEL, J., are omitted.]

SIERRA CLUB V. COSTLE
657 F.2d 298 (D.C. Cir. 1981)

[The Environmental Protection Agency (EPA) adopted a regulation governing the emissions of sulfur dioxide by new coal-fired electric generators. In part, the rulemaking involved a struggle between Western states that produce low sulfur coal and Eastern states that produce high sulfur coal. Extremely high stakes were involved. On this appeal, one issue raised by the Environmental Defense Fund (EDF) was whether the rule was invalid because of an "ex parte blitz" that began after the close of the comment period. The "blitz" included meetings between the agency and private persons, executive branch officials, and elected officials. According to EDF, the agency had been on the verge of adopting stricter limits on sulfur dioxide emissions, but it backed down because of these meetings, in which the White House tried to influence EPA to adopt a less costly solution, and representatives of Eastern coal interests, including the National Coal Association and Senator Robert Byrd of West Virginia, sought a standard that would be more acceptable to their interests.

After spending about sixty pages discussing and rejecting substantive attacks on the rule, the court turned to the post-comment period meetings held with individuals outside of the EPA. The court's opinion was written by WALD, J.:]

[The rule was issued under the authority of the 1977 Amendments to the Clean Air Act, which] required the agency to establish a "rulemaking docket" for each proposed rule which would form the basis of the record for judicial review. The docket must contain, *inter alia*, "[a]ll documents . . . which become available after the proposed rule has been published and which the Administrator [of EPA] determines are of central relevance to the rulemaking. . . ."

. . . Oral face-to-face discussions are not prohibited anywhere, anytime, in the [Clean Air] Act. The absence of such prohibition may have arisen from the nature of the informal rulemaking procedures Congress had in mind. Where agency action resembles judicial action, where it involves formal rulemaking, adjudication, or quasi-adjudication among "conflicting private claims to a valuable privilege," the insulation of the decisionmaker from ex parte contacts is justified by basic notions of due process to the parties involved. But where agency action involves informal rulemaking of a policymaking sort, the concept of ex parte contacts is of more questionable utility.

Under our system of government, the very legitimacy of general policymaking performed by unelected administrators depends in no small part upon the openness, accessibility, and amenability of these officials to the needs and ideas of the public from whom their ultimate authority derives, and upon whom their commands must fall. As judges we are insulated from these pressures because of the nature of the judicial process in which we participate; but we must refrain from the easy temptation to look askance at all face-to-face lobbying efforts, regardless of the forum in which they occur, merely because we see them as inappropriate in the judicial context. Furthermore, the importance to effective regulation of continuing contact with a regulated industry, other affected groups, and the public cannot be underestimated. Informal contacts may enable the agency to win needed support for its program, reduce future enforcement requirements by helping those regulated to anticipate and shape their plans for the future, and spur the provision of information which the agency needs. The possibility of course exists that in permitting ex parte communications with rulemakers we create the danger of "one administrative record for the public and this court and another for the Commission." *Home Box Office.* Under the Clean Air Act procedures, however, "[t]he promulgated rule may not be based (in part or whole) on any information or data which has not been placed in the docket. . . ." Thus EPA must justify its rulemaking solely on the basis of the record it compiles and makes public.

Regardless of this court's views on the need to restrict all post-comment contacts in the informal rulemaking context, however, it is clear to us that Congress has decided not to do so in the statute which controls this case. As we have previously noted:

Where Congress wanted to prohibit *ex parte* contacts it clearly did so. Thus [the] APA . . . forbids *ex parte* contacts when an "adjudication" is underway. . . . If Congress wanted to forbid or limit *ex parte* contact in every case of informal rulemaking, it certainly had a perfect opportunity of doing so when it enacted the Government in the Sunshine Act [in 1976, adding § 557(d) to the APA]. . . . *That it did not extend the ex parte contact provisions of the amended section 557 to section 553—even though such an extension was urged upon it during the hearing— is a sound indication that Congress still does not favor a per se prohibition or even a "logging" requirement in all such proceedings.*

Lacking a statutory basis for its position, EDF would have us extend our decision in *Home Box Office, Inc. v. FCC* to cover all meetings with individuals outside EPA during the post-comment period. Later decisions of this court, however, have declined to apply *Home Box Office* to informal rulemaking of the general policymaking sort involved here, and there is no precedent for applying it to the procedures found in the Clean Air Act Amendments of 1977.

It still can be argued, however, that if oral communications are to be freely permitted after the close of the comment period, then at least some adequate summary of them must be made in order to preserve the integrity of the rulemaking docket, which under the [Clean Air Act] must be the sole repository of material upon which EPA intends to rely. The statute does not require the docketing of all post-comment period conversations and meetings, but we believe that a fair inference can be drawn that in some instances such docketing may be needed in order to give practical effect to section 307(d)(4)(B)(i) [of that Act,] which provides that all *documents* "of central relevance to the rulemaking" shall be placed in the docket as soon as possible after their availability. This is so because unless *oral* communications of central relevance to the rulemaking are also docketed in some fashion or other, information central to the justification of the rule could be obtained without ever appearing on the docket, simply by communicating it by voice rather than by pen, thereby frustrating the command of section 307 that the final rule not be "based (in part or whole) on any information or data which has not been placed in the docket."

EDF is understandably wary of a rule which permits the agency to decide for itself when oral communications are of such central relevance that a docket entry for them is required. Yet the statute itself vests EPA with discretion to decide whether "documents" are of central relevance and therefore must be placed in the docket; surely EPA can be given no less discretion in docketing oral communications, concerning which the statute has no explicit requirements whatsoever. Furthermore, this court has already recognized that the relative significance of various communications to the outcome of the rule is a factor in determining whether their disclosure is required. A judicially imposed blanket requirement that all post-comment period oral communications be docketed would, on the other hand, contravene our limited powers of review, would stifle desirable experimentation in the area by Congress and the agencies, and is unnecessary for achieving the goal of an established, procedure-defined docket, *viz.,* to enable reviewing courts to fully evaluate the stated justification given by the agency for its final rule.

Turning to the particular oral communications in this case, we find that only two of the nine contested meetings were undocketed by EPA. [One was an informational briefing by EPA to Senate aides, which was not the sort of meeting that would require docketing. The other was a meeting with President Carter and other high-ranking White House officials. The court thus turned to the distinctive issues presented by intra-executive branch meetings:]

We have already held that a blanket prohibition against meetings during the post-comment period with individuals outside EPA is unwarranted, and this perforce applies to meetings with White House officials. . . .

[I]t is hard to believe Congress was unaware that intra-executive meetings and oral comments would occur throughout the rulemaking process. We assume, therefore, that unless expressly forbidden by Congress, such intra-executive contacts may take place, both during and after the public comment period; the only real issue is whether they must be noted and summarized in the docket. The court recognizes the basic need of the President and his White House staff to monitor the consistency of executive agency regulations with Administration policy. He and his White House advisers surely must be briefed fully and frequently about rules in the making, and their contributions to policymaking considered. The executive power under our Constitution, after all, is not shared—it rests exclusively with the President. . . . To ensure the President's control and supervision over the Executive Branch, the Constitution—and its judicial gloss—vests him with the powers of appointment and removal, the power to demand written opinions from executive officers, and the right to invoke executive privilege to protect consultative privacy. In the particular case of EPA, Presidential authority is clear since it has never been considered an "independent agency," but always part of the Executive Branch.

The authority of the President to control and supervise executive policymaking is derived from the Constitution; the desirability of such control is demonstrable from the practical realities of administrative rulemaking. Regulations such as those involved here demand a careful weighing of cost, environmental, and energy considerations. They also have broad implications for national economic policy. Our form of government simply could not function effectively or rationally if key executive policymakers were isolated from each other and from the Chief Executive. Single mission agencies do not always have the answers to complex regulatory problems. An over-worked administrator exposed on a 24-hour basis to a dedicated but zealous staff needs to know the arguments and ideas of policymakers in other agencies as well as in the White House.

We recognize, however, that there may be instances where the docketing of conversations between the President or his staff and other Executive Branch officers or rulemakers may be necessary to ensure due process. This may be true, for example, where such conversations directly concern the outcome of adjudications or quasi-adjudicatory proceedings; there is no inherent executive power to control the rights of individuals in such settings. Docketing may also be necessary in some circumstances where a statute like this one *specifically requires* that essential "information or data" upon which a rule is based be docketed. But in the absence of any further Congressional requirements, we hold that it was not unlawful in this case for EPA not to docket a face-to-face policy session involving the President and EPA officials during the post-comment period, since EPA makes no effort to base the rule on any "information or data" arising from that meeting. Where the President himself is directly involved in oral communications with Executive Branch officials, Article II considerations—combined with the strictures of *Vermont Yankee*—require that courts tread with extraordinary caution in mandating disclosure beyond that already required by statute.

The purposes of full-record review which underlie the need for disclosing ex parte conversations in some settings do not require that courts know the details of every White House contact, including a Presidential one, in this informal rulemaking setting. After all, any rule issued here with or without White House assistance must have the requisite *factual support* in the rulemaking record, and under this particular statute the Administrator may not base the rule in whole or in part on any "*information or data*" which is not in the record, no matter what the source. The courts will monitor all this, but they need not be omniscient to perform their role effectively. Of course, it is always possible that undisclosed Presidential prodding may direct an outcome that *is* factually based on the record, but different from the outcome that would have obtained in the absence of Presidential involvement. In such a case, it would be true that the political process did affect the outcome in a way the courts could not police. But we do not believe that Congress intended that the courts convert informal rulemaking into a rarified technocratic process, unaffected by political considerations or the presence of Presidential power. In sum, we find that the existence of intra-Executive Branch meetings during the post-comment period, and the failure to docket one such meeting involving the President, violated neither the procedures mandated by the Clean Air Act nor due process.

Finally, EDF challenges the rulemaking on the basis of alleged Congressional pressure, citing principally two meetings with Senator Byrd. EDF asserts that under the controlling case law the political interference demonstrated in this case represents a separate and independent ground for invalidating this rulemaking. . . .

D.C. Federation [*v. Volpe*, 459 F.2d 1231 (D.C. Cir. 1971), discussed in § 3.3.3 N.4,] requires that two conditions be met before an administrative rulemaking may be overturned simply on the grounds of Congressional pressure. First, the content of the pressure upon the Secretary is designed to force him to decide upon factors not made relevant by Congress in the applicable statute. . . . Second, the Secretary's determination must be affected by those extraneous considerations.

In the case before us, there is no persuasive evidence that either criterion is satisfied. Senator Byrd requested a meeting in order to express "strongly" his already well-known views that the SO_2 standards' impact on coal reserves was a matter of concern to him. . . . Americans rightly expect their elected representatives to voice their grievances and preferences concerning the administration of the laws. We believe it entirely proper for Congressional representatives vigorously to represent the interests of their constituents before administrative agencies engaged in informal, general policy rulemaking, so long as individual Congressmen do not frustrate the intent of Congress as a whole as expressed in statute, nor undermine applicable rules of procedure. Where Congressmen keep their comments focused on the substance of the proposed rule—and we have no substantial evidence to cause us to believe Senator Byrd did not do so here[539]—administrative agencies are expected to balance Congressional pressure with the pressures emanating from all other sources. To hold otherwise would deprive the agencies of legitimate sources of information and call into question the validity of nearly every controversial rulemaking.

---

[539] The only hint we are provided that extraneous "threats" were made comes from a newspaper article which states, in part:

> The ceiling decision came after two weeks of what one Senate source called "hard-ball arm-twisting" by Byrd and other coal state Senators. Byrd summoned [EPA Administrator] Costle and White House adviser Stuart Eizenstat *strongly hinting* that the Administration needs his support on strategic arms limitation treaty (SALT) and the windfall profits tax, according to Senate and Administration sources.

The Washington Post, May 5, 1979, at A–1 (emphasis supplied). We do not believe that a single newspaper account of strong "hint[s]" represents substantial evidence of extraneous pressure significant enough to warrant a finding of unlawful congressional interference.

NOTES AND QUESTIONS

1. *Contrasting views.* Obviously *Home Box Office* and *Sierra Club* present diametrically opposing views on the subject of ex parte communications in informal rulemaking. Which perspective is more persuasive?

Consider the reasoning of *Home Box Office*. There Judge Wright (generally considered to be the author of the court's per curiam opinion) emphasized the reviewing court's interest in conducting effective review of the merits of the FCC rule. Is a prohibition of ex parte communications in rulemaking necessary in order to enable courts to review the "full administrative record," as he suggests? Does *Sierra Club* effectively answer this point?

The court in *Home Box Office* seemed to be particularly concerned that the rulemaking record on judicial review will not reflect an agency's actual basis of decision unless it contains all ex parte communications to the agency. Was the court correct to say that, under the circumstances of this case, it "cannot presume that the agency has acted properly"? Is the court's concern limited to the problem of ex parte communications or is it a problem inherent in all administrative decisionmaking processes? Professor Nathanson responds:

> So far as judicial review is concerned, if the formulation given is an appropriate one under the governing statute, that should be sufficient to sustain the administrative action. It might be that administrative action was also motivated by some other policy considerations which could not be so easily articulated or which had no relation to the acknowledged purposes of the statute or the agency. Such ulterior purposes might or might not be suggested by disclosure of ex parte communications. Even so it is hard to see why the existence of such ulterior motives should be the proper concern of a reviewing court, any more than it would be if the court were reviewing the reasonableness of legislation.

Nathaniel L. Nathanson, *Report to the Select Committee on Ex Parte Communications in Informal Rulemaking Proceedings*, 30 ADMIN. L. REV. 377, 395 (1978). Do you agree with Nathanson?

Home Box Office relied on considerations of "fundamental fairness." Such fairness concerns are well recognized in the context of formal adjudication; why are they of "questionable utility" in informal rulemaking, as the court in *Sierra Club* asserts? Because ex parte contacts in informal rulemaking are not unfair at all? Or because any such unfairness is outweighed by beneficial aspects of ex parte contacts, or is beyond the authority of the courts to rectify?

2. *Political rulemaking.* Note that *Sierra Club* rests on an assumption that politics has a large role to play in rulemaking. For an even blunter endorsement of a political, rather than judicial or technocratic, model of the

rulemaking process, consider Professor (now Justice) Scalia's reaction to the court's reasoning in *Home Box Office*. He urged that oral ex parte communications be allowed in rulemaking and that they be excluded from the official agency rulemaking record:

> It is unquestionably true that the regulated industries have had—to use the censorious phrase adopted by the *Home Box Office* case—"undue" influence in the rulemaking decisions of their governing agencies. The court might have added that Ralph Nader, Common Cause, and the Sierra Club have also had "undue" influence—in the sense that their positions, like those of the proximately affected industries, have been given greater weight than positions espoused by, let us say, private citizens such as you and me. The rulemaking process has assuredly not been an open forum producing an ultimate decision which values each presentation on the basis of its intrinsic intellectual worth, with no regard to the *political power* of its proponent.... This process of accommodating public desires, including the ardent support or vehement opposition of interest groups most proximately affected, is an essential part of the democratic process, however untidy and unanalytic it may be.... An agency will be operating politically blind if it is not permitted to have frank and informal discussions with members of Congress and the vitally concerned interest groups; and it will often be unable to fashion a politically acceptable (and therefore enduring) resolution of regulatory problems without some process of negotiation off the record.

Antonin Scalia, *Two Wrongs Make a Right: The Judicialization of Standardless Rulemaking*, REGULATION, July–Aug. 1977, at 38, 40–41.

Scalia concluded that a prohibition of ex parte communications would increase the likelihood that agency rulemaking would be politically unacceptable to the legislature and the people. This, in turn, would lead to three undesirable consequences. First, since it will be more difficult for an agency to gauge the political acceptability of its rules, the legislature will be required to intervene into agency rulemaking to avoid an increased number of unacceptable rules. Second, this increased need for intervention will generate tension between the agencies and Congress, making it increasingly difficult for them to get along on a day-to-day basis. Third, substantial and unnecessary costs would be imposed on regulated persons and agencies when rules turn out in the end to be politically unacceptable and, therefore, are reversed by action of the legislature.

Does Scalia—or for that matter *Sierra Club*—press the political model of rulemaking too far? Consider the analysis of Professor Glen Robinson, who was a member of the FCC at the time of *Home Box Office*, and who came to view that case's position with ambivalence:

> In support of allowing ex parte contacts is the argument from participation: ex parte contacts promote such participation by

lessening the burdens thereof. . . . Burdening information flows with the formality of notice to other parties and incorporation of information into an official record . . . may be enough to discourage valuable communications with interested persons.

Moreover, informal communications can facilitate a real dialogue on policy issues. . . . Confronted with often prodigious quantities of information in the form of briefs and written comments, the decision makers find themselves searching for some way to get to the heart of the matter. . . . Ex parte communications between officials and outside parties is a way of checking staff-provided information and interpretation. It is a means of avoiding the problem of "staff capture," which is one of the most frustrating problems confronting higher echelon agency officials.

However, if the foregoing considerations argue against restrictions on ex parte contacts, they do so equivocally. . . . When interested persons are able to present their facts and arguments to individual agency members and staff off the record, there is no check on the reliability of information presented to the decisionmakers. This raises obvious questions of fairness, as well as substantive problems of effectiveness and efficiency. . . . Regulatory policymakers are often forced to place great reliance on oral briefing and discussion because of the massive quantities of paper confronting them. However, this produces a situation where even the most carefully produced commentary of one party can be negated by the offhand comments of another. Informal exchanges reinforce the natural disposition of busy agency officials to define data as the plural of anecdote. . . .

As to the point that ex parte communications help to promote a real dialogue among the parties, which, inter alia, facilitates compromise and negotiated settlement, it must be asked whether this is the proper aim of agency rule making. . . . Bargaining may or may not be the appropriate means for resolving disputes (it depends on the nature of the interests at stake), but in no circumstance is it appropriate without rules that prevent public policy decisions turning on who was able to contact whom, when, and so forth. This is the whole point of having a structured rule-making process. . . . [T]he notion that agencies are constrained by legal standards and formal processes, if it means anything, must mean that the administrative process is constrained by tighter standards of regularity and objectivity [than mere assessment of the intensity of the leading protagonists' preferences]. . . . If what we are looking for is some set of constraints on the process that will help to ensure reasonably principled judgments by administrative decision makers, then it is necessary to set some formal boundaries on the kind of influences that are appropriate. The rule of law demands no less.

GLEN O. ROBINSON, AMERICAN BUREAUCRACY: PUBLIC CHOICE AND PUBLIC
LAW 144–49 (1991). For a fuller discussion, see Ernest Gellhorn & Glen O.
Robinson, *Rulemaking "Due Process": An Inconclusive Dialogue*, 48 U. CHI. L.
REV. 201 (1981).

3. *Switching off HBO.* As *Sierra Club* notes, the *Home Box Office* case
met with strong criticism almost from the moment it was decided. Soon other
panels of the same court began questioning it and trying to narrow its reach.
See, e.g., Action for Children's Television v. FCC, 564 F.2d 458 (D.C. Cir.
1977). No doubt the decision in *Vermont Yankee* the following year also raised
doubts about the permissibility of the court's holding. In any event, ever since
the announcement of the *Sierra Club* opinion, judicial efforts to purge ex
parte communications from informal rulemaking have essentially vanished
from the case law. Nor have state courts shown any inclination to embrace
the broad principles of *Home Box Office* in ordinary notice and comment
rulemaking. *See, e.g., Boyles v. Miss. State Oil & Gas Board,* 794 So.2d 149
(Miss. 2001); *Mass. State Pharm. Ass'n v. Rate Setting Comm'n,* 438 N.E.2d
1072 (Mass. 1982); *Citizens Ass'n of Georgetown v. Zoning Comm'n,* 392 A.2d
1027 (D.C. 1978).

Notice, however, that *Sierra Club* did indicate that ex parte contacts
may be restricted where agency action involves "quasi-adjudication among
'conflicting private claims to a valuable privilege.'" That phrase was drawn
from *Sangamon Valley Television Corp. v. United States,* 269 F.2d 221 (D.C.
Cir. 1959), which was also cited in *Home Box Office. Sangamon* was an FCC
proceeding that involved the allocation of television channels between two
communities. A Channel 2 slot on the VHF spectrum would be assigned to
either the St. Louis market or the Springfield, Illinois, market. The other
market would get a less profitable UHF frequency. Strictly speaking, this
was a rulemaking proceeding, because the allocation of slots was to be
permanent and thus could affect an indefinite number of licensees in the two
cities over time. In the short run, however, two existing broadcasters in St.
Louis and Springfield knew that one of them would be the main immediate
beneficiary of the FCC's decision. The Commission decided to assign Channel
2 to St. Louis, but when the court learned that the St. Louis broadcaster had
engaged in extensive ex parte lobbying of FCC commissioners (including
visiting them in their offices, taking them to lunch, and sending them turkeys
at Christmas), it invalidated the FCC's decision, stating that "basic fairness
requires such a proceeding to be carried on in the open." In light of *Vermont
Yankee,* should the court in *Sierra Club* have declared that the *Sangamon*
holding was no longer viable?

4. *Written summary of ex parte communications.* Relying upon a
specific provision in the Clean Air Act, the *Sierra Club* case requires a
summary in the agency rulemaking record of oral and written ex parte
communications if EPA finds them to be "of central relevance to the
rulemaking." This obligation stops short of the *Home Box Office* requirement
that *all* ex parte contacts during a rulemaking proceeding must be
summarized for the record. Could a court impose the *Sierra Club* obligation

in ordinary § 553 rulemaking, in the absence of a similar statute? *See Board of Regents of Univ. of Wash. v. EPA*, 86 F.3d 1214 (D.C. Cir. 1996).

In any event, some agencies have imposed upon themselves a duty to reveal at least some oral contacts. *See* JEFFREY S. LUBBERS, A GUIDE TO FEDERAL AGENCY RULEMAKING 307–09 (5th ed. 2012). For example, EPA now requires that the public record of its rulemaking proceedings (not just those under the Clean Air Act) must include ex parte written comments, as well as summaries of "significant new factual data or information likely to affect the final decision received during a meeting." Regulations of the Federal Emergency Management Agency similarly require disclosure of summaries of outside communications with "significant information and argument respecting the merits of the proposed rule." *Id.*

Contrast the approach of the 2010 MSAPA. It requires all *written* materials relied on or consulted by an agency to be included in the record; but it does not prohibit *oral* ex parte communications, nor does it require any disclosure of them in the rulemaking record (except where the agency chose to prepare a transcript of them). §§ 302(b)(3), 306(b); *see* ARTHUR EARL BONFIELD, STATE ADMINISTRATIVE RULE MAKING 340–41 (1986) (defending a similar approach in the 1981 MSAPA). Are the EPA and FEMA policies too strict? Or is the MSAPA approach too lenient?

5. *Executive branch intervention in rulemaking.* Presidents (and governors) frequently have an intense interest in pending agency rulemaking proceedings, because such rules may either obstruct or promote their own political agendas. For example, the President may be concerned that a rule would be too costly to business, or that it may not do enough to protect the public. Did the court in *Sierra Club* hold the President to a more lenient standard than other interested persons? Is a double standard justified?

In *Sierra Club*, the court cited ACUS Recommendation 80–6, *Intragovernmental Communications in Informal Rulemaking Proceedings*, 45 Fed. Reg. 86,407 (1980), which recommended that rulemaking agencies "should be free to receive written or oral policy advice at any time from the President, advisers to the President, the Executive office of the President, or other administrative bodies," without any duty of disclosure except to the extent these communications "contain material factual information (as distinct from indications of governmental policy) pertaining to or affecting a proposed rule." However, eight members of ACUS filed a separate statement, stating in part:

> We oppose this recommendation because we believe that Executive Branch agencies should be encouraged to disclose, not withhold, all of the factors which may have influenced their decisions in informal rulemaking. The public's right to know the reasons for a decision far outweighs agency decisionmakers' rights to secrecy. . . .

This recommendation extends beyond the President and his closest advisors and allows all Executive Branch agencies to involve themselves secretly in informal rulemaking. In our view agencies should be encouraged to provide their views during the public comment period so that the public might respond, or at least be aware of the views expressed. The recommendation actually encourages Executive Branch agencies as well as the White House to wait until the public record is closed before making their views known. . . .

In all likelihood this recommendation will expose agency heads to increased political pressures [based on] considerations other than those made relevant by the statutes which the particular rulemaking implements. Moreover, the courts will be unable to serve as a check upon consideration of statutorily irrelevant factors since they cannot review that which is not disclosed.

Who had the better of this argument? *See generally* Paul R. Verkuil, *Jawboning Administrative Agencies: Ex Parte Contacts by the White House*, 80 COLUM. L. REV. 943 (1980).

Since 1981 Presidents have entrusted the Office of Information and Regulatory Affairs (OIRA), a subdivision of the Office of Management and Budget (OMB), with a supervisory role over agency rulemaking. Political and policy factors, as well as purely technical factors, may influence OIRA in its performance of this role. In a subsequent recommendation, ACUS proposed that "official written policy guidance" from OIRA to rulemaking agencies should be disclosed when a proposed or final rule is published, but oral communications need not be. ACUS Recommendation 88–9, *Presidential Review of Agency Rulemaking*, § 5(a), 54 Fed. Reg. 5207 (1989). This and other openness requirements have since been imposed by a presidential executive order. *See* § 7.6 NN.2, 7. ACUS's later recommendation did not, however, apply to ad hoc intervention in rulemaking by the President personally.

6. *Congressional intervention in rulemaking.* The language in *Sierra Club* endorsing congressional advocacy of constituents' interests before administrative agencies has been frequently quoted. Following out its logic, suppose an agency generally requires disclosure of ex parte contacts in rulemaking (either under a specific statute like the Clean Air Act or under agency regulations). Should members of Congress be required to submit their comments for the record during the comment period just like any other interested person? Or should they be exempted from disclosure under the same circumstances as those in which intra-executive contacts would be exempted pursuant to the ACUS recommendation discussed in the preceding note?

Notice footnote 539 of *Sierra Club*, discussing the allegation that Senator Byrd (who at the time was Senate Majority Leader) had offered to trade his support for the SALT treaty for concessions on the sulfur dioxide rule. Was the petitioners' problem that they did not have enough proof, or that the senator's conduct would not have warranted invalidation of the rule even if it had been proved?

7. *Problem.* The Madison Transportation Department (MTD) is responsible for planning the development of public transit systems in the state. Recently the department had to determine the route for an extension of the Monroe City subway system from one of its existing stations to a nearby airport. The most controversial question was whether the new line should run along the east side or the west side of Van Buren Park. Fillmore University lies along most of the eastern edge of the park, and it hoped for a subway stop on the east side for the convenience of its students and faculty. Tyler Corp., an office equipment company, has a headquarters building on the west side of the park. It favored the western route, with a stop benefiting its customers and employees. Either of the two stops would also be conveniently accessible for a few neighboring small businesses and residences.

MTD commenced a notice and comment rulemaking proceeding to decide the route question. The lengthiest comments were submitted by the university and the company, each promoting its preferred route on the basis of factors such as the number of passengers who would use the new line, cost of construction, prospects for commercial development near the new station, etc. After receiving these and other written submissions, MTD held a town-meeting style public hearing about the route question. Sixty days later the department announced that it had chosen the western route.

Soon afterwards, press accounts described how lobbyists from the Tyler company had visited the state capitol after the comment period and met with department officials to urge selection of the western route. Reportedly they assured MTD that Tyler was planning a huge expansion of its operations at its facility in Monroe City, although for competitive reasons these plans had not been spelled out in Tyler's public statement. Fillmore wants to know whether it has any grounds for legal challenge because of Tyler's ex parte contacts. Assume that the department will not contest the truth of the press stories, but that no statutes or regulations purport to prohibit, or require disclosure of, oral ex parte communications during the department's rulemaking proceedings.

§ 5.5.3 BIAS AND PREJUDGMENT

Recall the material in § 3.3.5 on the various forms of bias that disqualify an adjudicatory decisionmaker. Which, if any, of those forms should disqualify a rulemaker? What would be the statutory or constitutional basis for such disqualification?

ASSOCIATION OF NATIONAL ADVERTISERS, INC. V. FTC
627 F.2d 1151 (D.C. Cir. 1979)

[In 1978, the FTC issued a notice of proposed rulemaking that suggested restrictions regarding television advertising directed toward children. The rule would have banned televised advertising for any product that is directed to children too young to understand the selling purpose of the ad. It also would have banned ads for sugared food products directed to children. Several trade associations sued to prohibit Michael Pertschuk, Chairman of the FTC, from participating in the proceeding.

Before the issuance of the notice, Pertschuk had written and spoken extensively in a variety of settings about children's television. In one speech, he referred to the "moral myopia of children's television advertising" and declared that "advertisers seize on the child's trust and exploit it as a weakness for their gain." He went on to ask: "Shouldn't society apply the law's strictures against commercial exploitation of children, and the law's solicitude for the health of children to ads that threaten to cause imminent harm—harm which ranges from increasing tooth decay and malnutrition to injecting unconscionable stress into the parent-child relationship?" He said in a letter: "Setting legal theory aside, the truth is that we've been drawn into this issue because of the conviction . . . that one of the evils flowing from the unfairness of children's advertising is the resulting distortion of children's perceptions of nutritional values." In an interview with *Newsweek*, he said: "Commercialization of children has crept up on us without scrutiny or action. It is a major, serious problem. I am committed to taking action." The plaintiffs produced many other quotations from Pertschuk to similar effect.]

TAMM, J: . . .

The district court, citing this court's decision in *Cinderella Career & Finishing Schools, Inc. v. FTC*, 425 F.2d 583 (D.C. Cir. 1970) [excerpted in § 3.3.5], found that Chairman Pertschuk had prejudged issues involved in the rulemaking and ordered him disqualified. We hold that the *Cinderella* standard is not applicable to the Commission's rulemaking proceeding. An agency member may be disqualified from such a proceeding only when there is a clear and convincing showing that he has an unalterably closed mind on matters critical to the disposition of the rulemaking. Because we find that the appellees have failed to demonstrate the requisite prejudgment, the order of the district court is reversed. . . .

In *Cinderella*, we held that the standard for disqualifying an administrator in an adjudicatory proceeding because of prejudgment is whether "a disinterested observer may conclude that [the decisionmaker] has in some measure adjudged the facts as well as the law of a particular case in advance of hearing it." . . .

The district court in the case now before us held that "the standard of conduct delineated in *Cinderella*" governs agency decisionmakers participating in a section 18 proceeding. Section 18 [of the FTC Act, added by the Magnuson-Moss Warranty—Federal Trade Commission Improvement Act of 1974,] authorizes the Commission to promulgate rules designed to "define with specificity acts or practices which are unfair or deceptive." . . . The district court ruled that a section 18 proceeding, notwithstanding the appellation rulemaking, "is neither wholly legislative nor wholly adjudicative." According to the district court, the "adjudicative aspects" of the proceeding render *Cinderella* applicable.

The appellees . . . emphasize two allegedly "adjudicatory aspects" of a section 18 proceeding: (1) interested persons are entitled [by statute] to limited cross-examination of those who testify to disputed issues of material fact, and (2) [according to statute] a reviewing court must set aside any rule not supported by substantial evidence in the rulemaking record taken as a whole.

The district court's characterization of section 18 rulemaking as a . . . quasi-adjudicative proceeding ignores the clear scheme of the APA. Administrative action pursuant to the APA is either adjudication or rulemaking. The two processes differ fundamentally in purpose and focus. . . .

. . . Congress has, in [section 18] and elsewhere, enacted specific statutory rulemaking provisions that require more procedures than those of section 553 but less than the full procedures required under sections 556 and 557. The presence of procedures not mandated by section 553, however, does not, as the appellees urge, convert rulemaking into quasi-adjudication. The appellees err by focusing on the details of administrative process rather than the nature of administrative action.

[T]he Commission's children's advertising inquiry is designed to determine whether certain acts or practices will, in the future, be considered to contravene the FTC Act. The proceeding is not adjudication or quasi-adjudication. It is a clear exercise of the Commission's rulemaking authority.

The appellees also argue that we must apply *Cinderella* because it involves a factual prejudgment similar to the one now before us. In *Cinderella*, Chairman Dixon made statements that reflected prejudgment that Cinderella Career & Finishing Schools, Inc. had engaged in certain acts. In this case, the appellees accuse Chairman Pertschuk of prejudging issues of material fact in the children's television proceeding. We find that the appellees' argument belies a misunderstanding of the factual basis of rules.

The factual predicate of a rulemaking decision substantially differs in nature and in use from the factual predicate of an adjudicatory decision. The factual predicate of adjudication depends on ascertainment of [adjudicative facts, whereas rulemaking turns on ascertainment of legislative facts]. . . .

. . . As we already have noted, legislative facts adduced in rulemaking partake of agency expertise, prediction, and risk assessment. In *Cinderella*, the court was able to cleave fact from law in deciding whether Chairman Dixon had prejudged particular factual issues. In the rulemaking context, however, the factual component of the policy decision is not easily assessed in terms of an empirically verifiable condition. Rulemaking involves the kind of issues "where a month of experience will be worth a year of hearings."

The legitimate functions of a policymaker, unlike an adjudicator, demand interchange and discussion about important issues. We must not impose judicial roles upon administrators when they perform functions very different from those of judges. . . .[38]

The *Cinderella* view of a neutral and detached adjudicator is simply an inapposite role model for an administrator who must translate broad statutory commands into concrete social policies. If an agency official is to be effective he must engage in debate and discussion about the policy matters before him. As this court has recognized before, "informal contacts between agencies and the public are the 'bread and butter' of the process of administration." . . .

Section 18 outlines a process by which the Commission must form a preliminary view on a proposed rule, must hear comment from concerned parties, and in some cases, must hold trial-type proceedings before deciding whether to promulgate a rule. There is no doubt that the purpose of section 18 would be frustrated if a Commission member had reached an irrevocable decision on whether a rule should be issued prior to the Commission's final action. At the same time, the Commission could not exercise its broad policymaking power under section 18 if administrators were unable to discuss the wisdom of various regulatory positions. That discussion necessarily involves the broad, general characterizations of reality that we label legislative fact.

---

[38] . . . As one commentator has observed in a slightly different context:

Agencies are created to maintain or to restructure certain areas of private activity in light of expressed statutory policies. Thus, unlike courts, agencies should be positive actors, not passive adjudicators. . . . [A]n agency should not apologize for being predisposed to implementing the goals that Congress has set for it. To call such an attitude "bias" . . . misses this central point.

Pedersen, *The Decline of Separation of Functions in Regulatory Agencies*, 64 VA. L. REV. 991, 994 (1978).

Accordingly, a Commissioner should be disqualified only when there has been a clear and convincing showing that the agency member has an unalterably closed mind on matters critical to the disposition of the proceeding. The "clear and convincing" test is necessary to rebut the presumption of administrative regularity. The "unalterably closed mind" test is necessary to permit rulemakers to carry out their proper policy-based functions while disqualifying those unable to consider meaningfully a section 18 hearing.

Chairman Pertschuk's remarks, considered as a whole, represent discussion, and perhaps advocacy, of the legal theory that might support exercise of the Commission's jurisdiction over children's advertising. The mere discussion of policy or advocacy on a legal question, however, is not sufficient to disqualify an administrator. To present legal and policy arguments, Pertschuk not unnaturally employed the factual assumptions that underlie the rationale for Commission action. The simple fact that the Chairman explored issues based on legal and factual assumptions, however, did not necessarily bind him to them forever. Rather, he remained free, both in theory and in reality, to change his mind upon consideration of the presentations made by those who would be affected.

In outlining his legal theory of "unfairness," Pertschuk suggested that children might be harmed by overconsumption of sugared products and that they might not be able to comprehend the purpose of advertising. Insofar as these conclusions are ones of fact, they are certainly of legislative facts. . . .

The appellees have a right to a fair and open proceeding; that right includes access to an impartial decisionmaker. Impartial, however, does not mean uninformed, unthinking, or inarticulate. The requirements of due process clearly recognize the necessity for rulemakers to formulate policy in a manner similar to legislative action. The standard enunciated today will protect the purposes of a section 18 [rulemaking] proceeding, and, in so doing, will guarantee the appellees a fair hearing. . . .

Reversed.

LEVENTHAL, J., concurring:

I concur in Judge Tamm's opinion for the court. . . . The application of [the disqualification] test must take into account important differences in function and functioning between the agencies and court systems. . . . In the case of agency rulemaking, . . . the decision-making officials are appointed precisely to implement statutory programs, and with the expectation that they have a personal disposition to enforce them vigilantly and effectively. . . .

One can hypothesize beginning an adjudicatory proceeding with an open mind, indeed a blank mind, a tabula rasa devoid of any previous knowledge of the matter. In sharp contrast, one cannot even conceive of an agency conducting a rulemaking proceeding unless it had delved into the subject sufficiently to become concerned that there was an evil or abuse that required regulatory response. It would be the height of absurdity, even a kind of abuse of administrative process, for an agency to embroil interested parties in a rulemaking proceeding, without some initial concern that there was an abuse that needed remedying, a concern that would be set forth in the accompanying statement of the purpose of the proposed rule. . . .

MACKINNON, J., dissenting: . . .

In my opinion the "unalterably closed mind", where it exists, in many cases is practically impossible to prove, imposes too high a barrier to the public's obtaining fair decisionmakers and is a higher standard than the Supreme Court has applied in its recent decisions. I would require any Federal Trade Commissioner to recuse himself, or failing that to be disqualified, upon a showing by a preponderance of the evidence that he could not participate fairly in the formulation of the rule because of substantial bias or prejudgment with respect to any critical fact that must be resolved in such formulation.

Also, in my view the majority opinion places too much reliance on the strict rulemaking/adjudication dichotomy, applied in earlier cases under the Administrative Procedure Act. The Magnuson-Moss Act creates a rulemaking procedure that combines elements of *both* rulemaking and adjudication, as those functions are exercised under the Administrative Procedure Act, and this blending of the two procedures makes it impossible to look at Magnuson-Moss rulemaking as anything but a combination of the two. . . .

It is true that legislators are not required to make findings of fact to support their legislation and that they cannot be disqualified by any court for bias, but there are other safeguards in the legislative process that compensate for the absence of such safeguards as are expressly imposed or implicit in the administrative process. First of all, legislators are *elected* by the voters of their district, and those in the House are elected for a relatively short term—only two years. They can be turned out very quickly if any bias they disclose offends their constituents. Secondly, there is a protection in the sheer size of Congress—535 members of the House and Senate—that implicitly diffuses bias and guarantees that impermissible bias of individual members will not control. There is safety in numbers and a biased Congressman soon loses influence among the other members, if he ever acquired any. Also, the two house system and the Presidential veto are tremendous guarantees that legislation will not be the result of individual bias or even the impermissible bias of one house. . . .

I would not restrict members of a regulatory commission in their public discussion of policy issues, and there is nothing in the requirement that rules should be promulgated after fair hearings by unbiased Commissioners that would prohibit administrators from discussing "the wisdom of various regulatory positions." The office of the Commissioner contemplates some such activity but that does not justify their overstepping ordinary bounds of reasonableness to become loud advocates and spend three months haranguing the public with their prejudgment on basic factual issues that they must eventually decide. [W]hen a decisionmaker, who must rise above partisanship, descends to vigorous and consistent advocacy over a substantial period of time and commits himself in the public mind, he jeopardizes his ability to make fair determinations and in extreme cases, such as we have here, he should be disqualified from subsequently posing as a fair decisionmaker on the subject of his advocacy.

NOTES AND QUESTIONS

1. *The "unalterably closed mind" standard.* Is the disqualification test articulated in *ANA* desirable? The court argues that an agency head needs to "discuss" policy options with various constituencies. Even accepting that proposition, shouldn't the courts disqualify officials who become advocates for anticipated regulations, as Pertschuk obviously did? For comprehensive analyses of the *ANA* issue, see Ernest Gellhorn & Glen O. Robinson, *Rulemaking "Due Process": An Inconclusive Dialogue*, 48 U. CHI. L. REV. 201 (1981); Alfred S. Neely, IV, *The Duty to Act Fairly: An Alternative to the "Unalterably Closed Mind" Standard for Disqualification of Administrators in Rulemaking*, 16 NEW ENG. L. REV. 733 (1981); Peter L. Strauss, *Disqualification of Decisional Officials in Rulemaking*, 80 COLUM. L. REV. 990 (1980).

2. *Judicial authority.* As the basis for its authority to enforce any disqualification standard in *ANA*, the court relied on the Magnuson-Moss Act. Subsequently, federal courts have also invoked the "unalterably closed mind" standard in ordinary § 553 rulemaking. *See, e.g., Air Transp. Ass'n v. Nat'l Mediation Bd.*, 663 F.3d 476, 487 (D.C. Cir. 2011); *PLMRS Narrowband Corp. v. FCC*, 182 F.3d 995 (D.C. Cir. 1999); *Alaska Factory Trawler Ass'n v. Baldridge*, 831 F.2d 1456 (9th Cir. 1987). They have not addressed the question of whether this latter move is permissible under *Vermont Yankee*. Is it? *Cf.* Jack M. Beermann & Gary Lawson, *Reprocessing* Vermont Yankee, 75 GEO. WASH. L. REV. 856, 888–92 (2007) (no).

3. *Formalized rulemaking.* Did the court properly discount the significance of the hybrid rulemaking procedures that Congress had adopted in the Magnuson-Moss Act? Would the court also apply the *ANA* test in a situation in which Congress had mandated *formal* rulemaking under APA §§ 556–57?

4. *ANA and adjudication.* One of the plaintiffs in this case was the Kellogg Company. Suppose that, instead of launching a rulemaking proceeding, the FTC had filed an administrative complaint against Kellogg, seeking a cease and desist order that would prohibit the company from running the same sorts of advertisements that were under attack in *ANA*. Also suppose that Pertschuk had made exactly the same public pronouncements as in the real case, but that neither he nor the Commission contended that Kellogg's ads or products were materially different from those of any other cereal manufacturer. The Commission was simply using the Kellogg proceeding as a test case. Should Pertschuk have been disqualified from participating in the hypothetical case? If so, why? Should the *Cinderella* test be understood as applying only to prejudgments of adjudicative facts?

5. *State cases.* State courts seem to agree with federal courts that "bias in the sense of crystallized point of view about issues of law or policy is almost universally deemed no ground for disqualification." *N.H. Milk Dealers' Ass'n v. N.H. Milk Control Bd.*, 222 A.2d 194, 198 (N.H. 1966). In that relatively early decision, the court refused to disqualify the Board chairman for having voted for a rule that would eliminate milk price controls, notwithstanding his acknowledgement that his views had been consistent since the days when he had been a legislator who had sponsored a bill to terminate the board's authority to maintain those controls. The court in *Milk Dealers* did say that "prejudgment concerning issues of fact in a particular case" would be a basis for disqualification. Whether the court's reference to a "particular case" would include a controversy over legislative facts in a rulemaking proceeding was not clear from the opinion. That may not have been a salient issue in 1966. In more recent state cases, however, the *ANA* standard has found some acceptance *See, e.g., Fogle v. H & G Restaurant, Inc.*, 654 A.2d 449, 459–60 (Md. 1995) (refusing disqualification); *Citizens for a Better Environment v. Pollution Control Board*, 504 N.E.2d 166 (Ill. App. 1987) (same).

Consider, however, *Mahoney v. Shinpoch*, 732 P.2d 510 (Wash. 1987). The state of Washington, like other states, provides public assistance payments, known as SSP, to needy blind, elderly, and disabled persons who also receive such benefits from the federal Social Security Administration. The federal agency distributes both sets of benefits in a single check. In 1983 Congress passed an increase in federal benefits, but allowed states to reduce their SSP benefits to offset the increase. The Washington legislature adopted a budget contemplating the use of this option, and on October 18, 1985, the Department of Social and Health Services (DSHS) commenced rulemaking proceedings to implement that intention. A hearing on that proposed rule was scheduled to be held on November 26. On November 7, nineteen days before the scheduled hearing, DSHS wrote a letter to the Social Security Administration indicating that "the state is opting to revise the SSP per the Social Security Amendments of 1983," and the federal agency notified SSP recipients that their benefits would reflect DSHS's intended reduction.

The court concluded that the DSHS letter demonstrated that the agency had made its decision before it had considered public comment on the proposed rule and, therefore, that the rule violated the state APA (similar to 1961 MSAPA § 3(a)(2)). The court wrote:

> DSHS asks us to view its November 7 directive to the Social Security Administration as merely a preliminary signalling of an intention. . . . Looking at the letter in a light most favorable to DSHS, we nevertheless must conclude that the agency had already fixed on its decision. The letter contains no conditional or qualifying language, such as "the state is considering revising the SSP" or "the state *may* revise the SSP." . . .

> Full consideration of public comment prior to agency action is both a statutory and constitutional imperative. . . . The APA contains no harmless error provision permitting an agency not to consider public comment even when the public comment proves unpersuasive; rulemaking conducted without substantial compliance with APA requirements is per se invalid.

Is this case inconsistent with *ANA*? Or is the question in *Mahoney* actually somewhat different from that in *ANA*?

6.   *Problem.* Until recently, Madison engaged in extensive regulation of oil pipelines within the state. Pursuant to legislation, the Madison Public Utilities Commission is considering deregulation of the oil pipeline industry. Sludge Pipeline Co. sought to disqualify Henry, an elected member of the PUC, from participating in all present and future phases of rulemaking directed at oil pipeline deregulation.

In the two years before the attempted disqualification, Henry had become a zealous and active opponent of deregulation legislation, expressing his views in speeches, press releases, and testimony to legislative committees. His unfavorable opinion of Sludge, a proponent of the legislation, also was clear. He referred to Sludge personnel as "jackals in lambskins" and the deregulation bill as "the biggest premeditated robbery since Jesse James rode the plains, except he had more ethics. He only stole from the rich!" One press release said that Sludge was "lying to the public" and that deregulation was "nothing more than a hoax and a planned rip-off of the public."

The trial court disqualified Henry from consideration of the pending rulemaking proceeding and all future deregulation rulemaking proceedings. The case is now on appeal to the Madison Supreme Court. Should Henry have been disqualified at all? If so, should the court order his removal from (a) the pending deregulation rulemaking, (b) any future rulemaking proceedings in which Sludge participates; or (c) all future MPUC proceedings in which Sludge is a party? Or should the court hold that, in any given future case, Sludge will have to move to disqualify Henry, and the court will have to decide the disqualification issue anew at that time? *See Northwestern Bell Tel. Co. v. Stofferahn*, 461 N.W.2d 129 (S.D. 1990).

§ 5.6   FINDINGS AND REASONS

Most administrative procedure acts expressly require an agency to provide a statement of reasons to accompany its final adoption of a rule. For example, § 553(c) of the federal APA requires a "concise general statement of . . . basis and purpose," and 2010 MSAPA § 313 calls for "a concise explanatory statement that contains (1) the agency's reasons for adopting the rule." On a theoretical level, these legal obligations are quite similar to the corresponding mandates applicable to adjudication, which we examined in § 4.3. In practice, however, reason-giving requirements often pose distinctive challenges in the context of rulemaking.

NATIONAL ASS'N OF INDEPENDENT INSURERS v. TEXAS DEP'T OF INSURANCE

925 S.W.2d 667 (Tex. 1996)

CORNYN, J.

This appeal by several insurance companies and insurance trade associations (the Insurers) challenges the validity of two administrative rules adopted by the State Board of Insurance (the Board). . . . The first rule, Rule 1000, prohibits insurance companies from refusing to sell certain types of insurance to prospective purchasers because they have had an insurance policy canceled by another insurer. . . .[2] The second rule, Rule 1003, prohibits insurers from conditioning the sale of automobile insurance on the purchase of another policy or denying an application because the applicant owns only one car.[3] The violation of these rules constitutes an unfair trade practice and subjects an insurer to sanctions.

The Insurers . . . argue, among other things, that these rules were not adopted in substantial compliance with procedural requirements for agency rulemaking contained in the [Texas] Administrative Procedure

---

[2] Rule 1000 states:

     The fact that another insurer canceled, non-renewed, or refused to insure an applicant shall not be a reason, in whole or in part, for an insurer or agent writing or offering personal automobile, residential property, life, accident or health insurance to refuse to insure or submit an application or binder or conditional receipt for that applicant. An insurer may base its decision whether to insure an applicant on the same factor on which another insurer made its adverse decision if that insurer would have based its decision on that factor without knowledge of the previous insurer's actions. . . . This rule does not prohibit an insurer or agent from asking if another insurer canceled, non-renewed or refused to insure the applicant.

[3] Rule 1003 states:

     An insurer or agent shall not condition the issuance, renewal, price, continuation, or amount of coverage of personal automobile insurance on the number of vehicles to be insured on the policy or on the purchase from the insurer or any affiliated insurer of any other policy or policies. This rule does not preclude the application of a type of discount as provided in a rate manual approved by the Texas Department of Insurance or the conditioning of the sale of any umbrella or excess coverage policy on the purchase of an underlying policy.

Act (APA) and are therefore invalid. The trial court held that the rules were valid, and the court of appeals affirmed. We agree with the Insurers, and therefore reverse the judgment of the court of appeals.

The Legislature has directed that when an administrative agency adopts a rule, it must at the same time state a reasoned justification for the rule. *See* Tex. Gov't Code § 2001.033. That is, the agency must explain how and why it reached the conclusions it did. The agency's order must present its justification "in a relatively clear, precise, and logical fashion." In addition to a reasoned justification, the order adopting the rule must include (1) a summary of the comments the agency received from interested parties; (2) a restatement of the factual basis for the rule; and (3) the reasons why the agency disagrees with the comments. Thus, section 2001.033 places an affirmative duty on an agency to summarize the evidence it considered, state a justification for its decision based on the evidence before it, and demonstrate that its justification is reasoned.

If an order does not substantially comply with these requirements, the rule is invalid. Tex. Gov't Code § 2001.035(a). An agency's order substantially complies with the reasoned justification requirement if it (1) accomplishes the legislative objectives underlying the requirement and (2) comes fairly within the character and scope of each of the statute's requirements in specific and unambiguous terms.

Provisions like section 2001.033 are designed to compel an administrative agency to articulate its reasoning and, in the process, more thoroughly analyze its rules. Requiring an agency to demonstrate a rational connection between the facts before it and the agency's rules promotes public accountability and facilitates judicial review. It also fosters public participation in the rulemaking process and allows interested parties to better formulate "specific, concrete challenges" to a rule.

Judicial review of administrative rulemaking is especially important because, although the executive and legislative branches may serve as political checks on the consequences of administrative rulemaking, the judiciary is assigned the task of policing the *process* of rulemaking. Given the vast power allocated to governmental agencies in the modern administrative state, and the broad discretion ordinarily afforded those agencies, judicial oversight of the rulemaking process represents an important check on government power that might otherwise exist without meaningful limits.

We now turn to the Board's orders for the two rules at issue. In adopting Rule 1000, the Board offered the following as a justification:

> Insurers should, on an independent basis, determine whether to insure an applicant in accordance with their individual underwriting guidelines. The fact that another

insurer has declined to write, canceled or nonrenewed a policy for an applicant, should not in whole or in part be the basis for an insurer declining to write the applicant. Such action is anti-competitive and results in the blacklisting of some consumers from the insurance market. This section will ensure that the possibility of unfair competition and unfair practices do not occur in the marketplace, and when it does, that there are appropriate remedies for the consumer.

The Board also stated that the rule "will result in greater fairness . . ., increased competition, and better informed consumers."

As we have emphasized, the order must explain the agency's reasoning in adopting the rule. The Board fails to explain anywhere in the order, why consideration of a previous denial, along with other permissible factors, is unfair or anti-competitive. It merely concludes that consideration of a previous denial, "in whole or in part," will lead to "blacklisting." The Board states that an insurer should rely on its own underwriting criteria in determining whether to insure an applicant, but has not explained why an insurer's consideration of a previous denial of insurance, as one of perhaps several factors, is unacceptable.

Without an explanation by the Board of its reasoning, we cannot know, and just as importantly, the public cannot know, why the Board reached the conclusions that it did. For example, it is not apparent whether the Board believes or has evidence that a previous denial of insurance has so little correlation with the risk of insurability that consideration of this factor, even as part of the insurer's decisionmaking process, is patently unfair. Or, perhaps, the Board believes that insurers will place greater weight on a previous denial than other factors, and that consideration of the previous denial, even in part, unfairly prevents some applicants from obtaining insurance. In any event, the Legislature has mandated that the reasoning an agency actually relied on appear in the order. If courts allow agencies to adopt conclusory rules such as Rule 1000, the purposes of section 2001.033—to provide meaningful public participation in the rulemaking procedure, to allow opponents of the rule to formulate specific challenges, and to ensure that the agency carefully considers and analyzes a rule before adopting it—will be eviscerated. We conclude therefore that the rule is invalid.

The Board's order adopting Rule 1003 is similarly deficient. In that order, the Board offers as a justification that:

Section 21.1003 will result in eliminating any practice of determining the company, coverage or price of personal automobile insurance on the basis of the number of vehicles to be insured on the policy. In addition, this section will also eliminate the practice of tying the sale of a personal automobile insurance policy to another policy, except in specific instances that such tie-in is allowed by the rule. This will result in greater fairness in the personal automobile insurance marketplace and greater availability and affordability of personal automobile insurance.

We hold that the Board has failed to explain why the prohibited practices are unfairly discriminatory or what effect these rules will have on consumers and the insurance market. The order makes no effort to explain why the "tying-in" of automobile coverage to an umbrella or excess coverage policy is acceptable, while linking coverage to other types of policies is an unfair practice. The order also fails to explain why conditioning the price of insurance on the number of vehicles to be insured should be prohibited, while giving a discount "as provided in a rate manual approved by the Texas Department of Insurance" is permissible. Nothing in the order sheds any light on the agency's rationale. Rather, the Board merely concludes that eliminating such practices will lead to "greater availability and affordability." Such conclusory statements, without an explanation of the agency's rationale, do not satisfy the reasoned justification requirement of the APA.

We do not suggest that the Board cannot provide reasoned justifications for both Rules 1000 and 1003. We merely hold that it has not yet done so. Because the Board has failed to meet the procedural requirements of section 2001.033 for Rules 1000 and 1003, we reverse the judgment of the court of appeals and render judgment that the Rules are invalid.

SPECTOR, J., joined by PHILLIPS, C.J., and GONZALEZ, J., concurring in part and dissenting in part.

I concur in the Court's judgment that the Board of Insurance failed to state a reasoned justification for Rule 1003. I respectfully dissent, however, from the Court's judgment invalidating Rule 1000.

The insurers challenged the rules under section 2001.035 of the Administrative Procedure Act (APA). Under that statute, a rule is not valid unless the agency's order is in substantial compliance with section 2001.033 of the APA, which requires that an order adopting a rule set forth a reasoned justification. I believe that the majority opinion requires more than substantial compliance by invalidating Rule 1000 based on a single phrase—"in part."

The Board's order adopting Rule 1000 stated that the prohibited actions are "anti-competitive and result[ ]in blacklisting of some consumers from the insurance market." It further provided that the rule would "result in greater fairness . . ., increased competition, and better informed consumers," while allowing insurers to base decisions on the same factors underlying another insurer's adverse decision. The order also noted that "an underwriter's function is to underwrite risk based on an individual company's underwriting guidelines" and that the rule was intended to ensure the "fair and equitable application of existing guidelines."

From its use of the term "blacklisting" in conjunction with references to the "equitable application of existing guidelines," the Board's reasoning is readily apparent. An insurer should not be free to reject out of hand an applicant who meets the company's own risk-based underwriting guidelines simply because another insurer previously rejected the applicant or cancelled the applicant's coverage. The order repeatedly made clear that an insurer is *not* required to act without knowledge of another insurer's decision. In fact, the Board incorporated a provision that specifically allows insurers to ask about an applicant's adverse experiences with other companies, so long as the insurer makes a decision based upon its own underwriting criteria.

Even though the Board's order identifies a justification for the rule as a whole, the majority holds the rule invalid based upon the agency's failure to address a single phrase. I agree with the Austin Court of Appeals, however, that "the reasoned justification requirement was not intended to be applied clause by clause but rather to the rule as a whole." I believe that the result of the majority opinion will be to require administrative agencies to provide justification for virtually every word in adopted rules in order to sustain their validity. This would, in effect, "impose a requirement under § 2001.033 for detailed findings of fact and conclusions of law." Nothing in the language of section 2001.033 hints that the Legislature intended to impose such an unworkable requirement.

Because I believe that the Board substantially complied with the reasoned justification requirement, I dissent from that portion of the Court's judgment invalidating Rule 1000. I concur in the remainder of the Court's judgment.

NOTES AND QUESTIONS

1.   *Merits of a reasons requirement.* The *Independent Insurers* opinion summarizes the practical advantages that have been said to flow from an agency's duty to give reasons in rulemaking. Professor Mashaw adds that the duty also serves a fundamental legitimating function: "Reason giving . . . treats persons as rational moral agents who are entitled to evaluate and participate in a dialogue about official policies on the basis of reasoned discussion. It affirms the individual as subject rather than object of the law." Jerry L. Mashaw, *Reasoned Administration: The European Union, the United States, and the Project of Democratic Governance*, 76 GEO. WASH. L. REV. 99, 118 (2007).

Not everyone, however, finds the case for a reasons requirement persuasive. Some state APAs permit agencies to issue rules without any written explanation at all. *See, e.g., District of Columbia Hosp. Ass'n v. Barry,* 498 A.2d 216 (D.C. App. 1985) (stating that the absence of such a requirement in the District of Columbia reflects "a deliberate policy choice" by legislative authorities); Md. Code Ann., State Gov't § 10–114. Professor Frohnmayer cites Utah as another example and defends the position of states that have made this choice:

> The rational-technical model [of rulemaking, implicit in the "reasons" requirement,] ignores the usual environment of state administrative decisionmaking. The typical state agency is not rich in staff depth. The two commodities in shortest supply in the typical state agency are likely to be political courage and executive time. The stock of each can be rapidly depleted by the burdens of this requirement. . . .
>
> Furthermore, the exercise of expert judgment—and that is often the essence of a discretionary rulemaking policy choice—is often a mixture of experience, values and refined intuition. Considerations leading to the act of policy judgment may not be . . . easily reducible to a set of "reasons." . . . These problems are compounded in circumstances typically encountered in state government. The agency decision may genuinely be collegial. [M]ulti-member citizen boards [may act] after hearing or reviewing hundreds of considerations from the affected public favoring or opposing a course of action. To expect the members of a body to reduce their reasoning, or to psychoanalyze that of their colleagues, into a conclusively binding set of reasons, ignores group psychology, risks extension of the decisionmaking process indefinitely, and maximizes the possibility that decisions will be based on the lowest common policy denominator. . . .

Dave Frohnmayer, *National Trends in Court Review of Agency Action: Some Reflections on the Model State Administrative Procedure Act and New Utah Administrative Procedure Act,* 3 BYU J. PUB. L. 1, 11–12 (1989). How persuasive is this analysis?

2. *Independent Insurers.* The question of whether an explanatory statement should be required at all is closely related to the question of how firmly existing requirements should be enforced. *Independent Insurers* presents the latter issue. Did the court apply § 2001.033 too stringently? The majority says that the political branches review the "consequences" of rulemaking, but "the judiciary is assigned the task of policing the *process* of rulemaking." How clear is it that the majority's objections to Rule 1000 are procedural rather than substantive?

In 1999, in the wake of this and other judicial decisions invalidating agency rules, the Texas legislature revised the state's APA. Now, in order to meet the "reasoned justification" requirement of § 2001.033, the agency's burden is to show "a rational connection between the factual basis for the rule and the rule as adopted." The new APA also provides that an agency substantially complies with that requirement if it "demonstrates in a relatively clear and logical fashion that the rule is a reasonable means to a legitimate objective." § 2001.035. This legislation has been explained as an effort "to make the standard for reasoned justification less strict." *Lower Laguna Madre Found. v. Texas Natural Resource Conserv. Comm'n*, 4 S.W.3d 419, 425 (Tex. Ct. App. 1999). Under the revised APA, do you think *Independent Insurers* would have been decided differently?

3.   *Federal law.* Section 553(c) of the federal APA calls for a "concise general statement . . . of basis and purpose," and a respected contemporaneous source described it in similarly modest terms: "Except as required by statutes providing for 'formal' rule making procedure, findings of fact and conclusions of law are not necessary. Nor is there required an elaborate analysis of the rules or of the considerations upon which the rules were issued. Rather, the statement is intended to advise the public of the general basis and purpose of the rules.'" ATTORNEY GENERAL'S MANUAL ON THE ADMINISTRATIVE PROCEDURE ACT 32 (1947). Over time, however, the federal courts have charted a different course. As the court in *Automotive Parts & Accessories Ass'n v. Boyd,* 407 F.2d 330, 338 (D.C. Cir. 1968), stated:

> [I]t is appropriate for us to . . . caution against an overly literal reading of the statutory terms 'concise' and 'general.' These adjectives must be accommodated to the realities of judicial scrutiny, which do not contemplate that the court itself will, by a laborious examination of the record, formulate in the first instance the significant issues faced by the agency and articulate the rationale of their resolution. We do not expect the agency to discuss every item of fact or opinion included in the submissions made to it in informal rule making. We do expect that, if the judicial review which Congress has thought it important to provide is to be meaningful, the "concise general statement of . . . basis and purpose" mandated by Section [553] will enable us to see what major issues of policy were ventilated by the informal proceedings and why the agency reacted to them as it did.

This is frequently quoted language. *See, e.g., City of Portland v. EPA*, 507 F.3d 706, 714 (D.C. Cir. 2007); *Simms v. NHTSA*, 45 F.3d 999, 1005 (6th Cir. 1995).

One tangible measure of the evolution of statements of basis and purpose in federal regulation comes from *Sierra Club v. Costle*, 657 F.2d 298 (D.C. Cir. 1981), excerpted in § 5.5.2. The rule involved in that case and its accompanying statement filled forty-three pages of very fine print in the Federal Register. (The record in that case contained over 2520 submissions, including almost 1400 rulemaking comments.) *Id.* at 314 n.22.

The *Auto Parts* gloss on § 553(c) tends to blur the contrast between the wording of that provision and the more detailed requirements that Congress has imposed on agencies engaged in *formal* proceedings (either rulemaking or adjudication). *See* APA § 557(c)(A). Why *shouldn't* the APA be read literally and as originally intended? Does *Auto Parts* violate the letter, or at least the intent, of *Vermont Yankee*?

4. *"Major issues of policy."* The court in *Auto Parts* says that only "major issues of policy" need be addressed in a statement of basis and purpose. That phrase is not self-defining, of course. In practice, federal courts tend to equate the question of whether a statement of basis and purpose was adequate with the question of whether the agency's explanation is sufficient to prevent the rule from being held arbitrary and capricious on the merits. *See, e.g., Indep. U.S. Tanker Owners Comm. v. Dole*, 809 F.2d 847 (D.C. Cir. 1987); *Trans-Pacific Freight Conf. v. Fed. Maritime Comm'n*, 650 F.2d 1235, 1249–50 (D.C. Cir. 1980).

A practical difficulty that agencies face when they try to comply with the dictates of *Auto Parts* is that an agency cannot always anticipate what issues a court will consider important. The unpredictability of this criterion gives the agency an incentive to plan for the "worst case" scenario. Thus, although the *Auto Parts* opinion, as quoted above, says that only "major issues of policy" need be addressed, some scholars argue that, in reality, the federal courts' approach to judicial review forces agencies to discuss their rules in extravagant detail, with debilitating effects on the overall rulemaking process. We treat this controversy in greater depth in § 9.3.2.

5. *Responses to comments.* Modern federal cases have declared that an agency must explain how and why it reacted to important comments it received during the course of the rulemaking proceeding. As the court stated in *Rodway v. USDA*, 514 F.2d 809, 817 (D.C. Cir. 1975):

> The basis and purpose statement is not intended to be an abstract explanation addressed to imaginary complaints. Rather, its purpose is, at least in part, to respond in a reasoned manner to the comments received, to explain how the agency resolved any significant problems raised by the comments, and to show how that resolution led the agency to the ultimate rule. . . . The basis and purpose statement is inextricably intertwined with the receipt of comments.

As *Independent Insurers* notes, a duty to respond to comments is expressly codified in the Texas APA. The 2010 MSAPA contains similar language. § 313(1) (agency must state its "reasons for not accepting substantial arguments made in testimony and comments"). In federal law, the obligation is presumably based on § 553(e), or on the "arbitrary and capricious" judicial review test in APA § 706(2)(A), or both. Is this gloss on the APA justified? If the agency has made an otherwise cogent case for its position, why does it have to rebut commentators?

The *Rodway* principle does not mean that an agency must respond to every argument it receives—only to arguments that are significant and material. In other words, the agency must address any comment that, if true, would require a change in the proposed rule. *See Sherley v. Sibelius*, 689 F.3d

776, 784 (D.C. Cir. 2012); *Louisiana Federal Land Bank Ass'n v. Farm Credit Admin.,* 336 F.3d 1075, 1080 (D.C. Cir. 2003); *Safari Aviation Inc. v. Garvey,* 300 F.3d 1144, 1151 (9th Cir. 2002). Comments that are speculative, or that do not show why or how they are relevant to the proceeding, need not be considered or answered. *See Public Citizen v. FAA,* 988 F.2d 186 (D.C. Cir. 1993) (unsupported speculation); *Northside Sanitary Landfill, Inc. v. Thomas,* 849 F.2d 1516 (D.C. Cir. 1988) (relevance of 420 pages of submitted documents was facially unclear and petitioner did not specifically explain their relevance).

In an adjudicative context, both courts and agencies are generally expected to respond to all, or nearly all, issues properly raised by the parties. Why should any lesser degree of responsiveness be expected from agencies in a rulemaking context? *See* Stephen Breyer, *Judicial Review of Questions of Law and Policy,* 38 ADMIN. L. REV. 363, 393 (1986).

6. *Post hoc rationalizations.* Aside from the mandate of APA § 553(c), a federal agency has a further reason to make sure that its statement of basis and purpose contains a full account of its justifications for adopting a rule: If the rule is challenged in court as arbitrary and capricious, the court normally will use the agency's contemporaneously stated reasoning as the sole basis for resolving the challenge. This is the *Chenery* doctrine, which we saw in the adjudication context. *See* § 4.3 N.5. "Post hoc rationalizations" for agency action are disfavored. The purpose of this principle is to ensure that agency heads, not staff lawyers, exercise the authority delegated to the agency: "If an order is valid only as a determination of policy or judgment which the agency alone is authorized to make and has not made, a judicial judgment cannot be made to do service for an administrative judgment." *SEC v. Chenery Corp.,* 318 U.S. 80, 88 (1943). Given this justification, should the policy of not relying on post hoc rationalizations by counsel apply to a question concerning the meaning of the APA, or of the statute under which the agency is acting? *See Bank of America v. FDIC,* 244 F.3d 1309, 1319–21 (11th Cir. 2001); Kevin M. Stack, *The Constitutional Foundations of* Chenery, 116 YALE L.J. 952, 965–66, 1008–10 (2007).

7. *Problem.* Under the Madison Workers' Compensation Act, health care providers such as hospitals treat injured workers and are then reimbursed by a compensation carrier, under rules issued by the Madison Worker Compensation Board. The Act provides that the reimbursement rates set by these rules must be "fair and reasonable and designed to ensure the quality of medical care and to achieve effective medical cost control."

Until recently the Board reimbursed providers for treating worker compensation cases by permitting them to recover a percentage of their usual charges, subject to certain ceilings imposed for the sake of cost containment. Last year, however, the Board proposed to replace this system with an entirely new one. The proposed system would divide all hospital and medical services into three categories (medical, surgical, and intensive care). For each category, the rule would prescribe a flat per diem reimbursement rate for any treatment falling within that category.

During the comment period, the Madison Hospital Organization, a trade association, filed comments criticizing the proposed rates as too rigid. The association argued that it would be unfair to reimburse open-heart surgery in a metropolitan hospital at the same per diem rate as an operation in a small hospital to repair a broken leg, merely because both are "surgery."

Late last year, after reviewing these and many other comments, the Board adopted its final rules, which were identical to the proposed rules in all respects pertinent to this problem. In its explanatory statement accompanying the rules, the Board stated in relevant part:

> The reimbursement level for each of the three categories was determined on the basis of a broad survey of participating providers' cost structures and billing data. Agency staff computed the average of providers' daily charges in each category and then adjusted the average figure downwards by ten percent in order to achieve cost containment. The new system will more accurately relate reimbursement to providers' actual costs and will also give them strong incentives to control their costs.

On judicial review, MHO contends that the Board's written explanation was too superficial. Moreover, MHO says, the Board completely ignored the association's argument that the agency should have postponed revising its reimbursement rates until it had gathered more data and studied the industry's challenges in greater depth. In reply to this last point, counsel for the Board contend that the Act had directed the Board to finalize its guidelines by the end of the year.

Should the court remand the rules for a better explanation? Assume, alternatively, that Madison's explanation requirements are based on those of the federal APA, the 2010 MSAPA, or the Utah APA (discussed in N.1 of this section). *Cf. Texas Hospital Ass'n v. Texas Workers' Compensation Comm'n*, 911 S.W.2d 884 (Tex. App. 1995).

§ 5.7 ISSUANCE AND PUBLICATION

Publication of agency rules is important, because it facilitates easy public access to their contents. That access allows affected parties to ascertain the relevant law and to adjust their conduct accordingly. Limited availability of agency rules creates a risk that individuals may be adversely affected by rules that were not only unknown to them, but that could not have been easily discovered. Because most people obey rules they know about, publication of rules also facilitates compliance with the law, thereby reducing the enforcement workload of agencies. Furthermore, the publication of rules communicates to the general public the standards by which agencies must operate, and the standards by which agencies may be measured. Publication of rules therefore helps to ensure that agencies as well as regulated parties follow the law. For all of these reasons, rules are required to be published and normally are not effective until a specified period after their publication.

Publication requirements for federal agency rules are contained in APA § 552(a)(1). These requirements, in approximately their present form, were added to the APA in 1967 as part of the Freedom of Information Act (FOIA), and some writers treat them as part of FOIA. (The main provisions of FOIA are discussed in § 8.1.)

In addition to meeting the publication requirements of the APA, federal agencies must also abide by the Federal Register Act (FRA), 44 U.S.C. §§ 1501–1511. The FRA requires the *Federal Register* to be published each federal working day. That publication includes all rules of "general applicability and legal effect" and notices of proposed rulemaking. In addition, FRA requires the publication of a complete codification of all documents having "general applicability and legal effect" that were published in the *Federal Register*. This publication is entitled the *Code of Federal Regulations* (C.F.R.) and consists of 50 titles that are arranged by subject matter similar to the U.S. Code. It is kept up to date by a process of continuous revision. Both the *Federal Register* and the C.F.R. are available online, and frequently updated, at the website of the Government Printing Office, *www.gpo.gov/fdsys/*.

The story of the FRA's origins provides a dramatic illustration of why it is needed. The Act was a by-product of *Panama Refining Co. v. Ryan*, 293 U.S. 388 (1935) (also discussed in § 7.2.1a.) That case considered the validity of the Petroleum Code, one of the codes of "fair competition" established during the Depression under the National Recovery Act (NRA):

> [T]here had not been devised, prior to NRA, any required, authorized, or even standard method of publishing administrative rules or decisions. It is true that Executive Orders (and codes were to be issued as such) were filed with the Secretary of State and published each year with the statutes at large. But it was not uncommon for the White House to retain orders which it preferred to keep from public view. And the Executive Orders embodying the codes were not (in many instances) even at the White House but here and there in the desk drawers of NRA officials! Such was the case with the Petroleum Code, held invalid in *Panama Refining Co. v. Ryan*. The industry used an unofficial copy. . . . When the brief [in *Panama Refining*] came to be written it occurred to the brief writer to examine the originals (which were found with some difficulty). He discovered the sickening fact that by reason of a mistaken use of terms—the Code had been amended out of

existence. . . . The President immediately supplied the missing provisions, thus making true the state of facts which had been assumed by all persons and all courts to have existed. Nevertheless the Supreme Court refused to treat the Code as properly before it. Those who heard and participated in the argument were struck by the almost gleeful eagerness with which the Court probed into the unsavory story (though it had previously been completely advised). A valuable consequence was the Federal Register Act [a few months later].

LOUIS L. JAFFE, JUDICIAL CONTROL OF ADMINISTRATIVE ACTION 61–62 (1965).

On the state level, § 201 of the 2010 MSAPA requires (with certain exceptions) the periodic publication and indexing of proposed and recently adopted state agency rules in a frequently issued publication similar to the *Federal Register,* as well as the compilation and indexing of such rules in a publication similar to the C.F.R. Today, the overwhelming number of states have both types of publications. Under the 2010 MSAPA, the state may disseminate this publication in electronic form, written form, or both. Most state codes of administrative regulations are available online. For a compilation, see *www.administrativerules.org.*

A general principle at both the federal and state level is that, absent good cause, a final rule does not become effective immediately upon publication or filing. Section 553(d) of the federal APA states that, in general, a final agency rule becomes effective no sooner than 30 days following publication of that final rule in the *Federal Register*; and § 317(a) of the 2010 MSAPA states that a rule will become effective 30 days after it is officially published.

An important function of the delayed effectiveness provision is "to afford persons affected a reasonable time to prepare for the effective date of a rule or rules or to take any other action which the issuance of rules may prompt." U.S. DEP'T OF JUSTICE, ATTORNEY GENERAL'S MANUAL ON THE ADMINISTRATIVE PROCEDURE ACT 36 (1947) (quoting from congressional reports). The delay has also proved to be of value to agencies, because it gives them time to detect and correct purely technical errors or omissions in newly adopted rules or to revise the rules in light of public reaction and unanticipated enforcement problems that surface during the pre-effective period.

NOTES AND QUESTIONS

1. *Publication of guidance documents.* Paragraph (1)(D) of federal APA § 552(a) requires publication in the *Federal Register* of both "substantive rules of general applicability adopted as authorized by law" (also called legislative rules) and "statements of general policy or interpretations of

general applicability" (also collectively called guidance documents or nonlegislative rules). These terms are discussed more fully in § 6.1.4. There is no real controversy about agencies' duty to publish their substantive rules in the *Federal Register* and C.F.R., and they do so routinely. However, questions concerning their responsibility to publish guidance documents have caused a great deal of uncertainty.

Part of the problem is that the APA is confusingly drafted. As just stated, one paragraph of § 552 provides for publication in the *Federal Register* of "statements of general policy or interpretations of general applicability formulated and adopted by the agency." 5 U.S.C. § 552(a)(1)(D). But another paragraph directs agencies to make available for public inspection and copying (and also to make available electronically) "those statements of policy and interpretations which have been adopted by the agency and are not published in the Federal Register." *Id.* § 552(a)(2)(B). The APA goes on to provide that if the agency does not make a document in this latter category available as the statute provides, the document "may be relied on, used, or cited as precedent by an agency against a party other than an agency only if . . . the party has actual and timely notice of the terms thereof." But still, it is clear from the statutory language that a document in this latter category need not be published in the *Federal Register*. Courts have had difficulty determining what pronouncements fall within paragraph (1)(D) as opposed to paragraph (2)(B).

Compounding the uncertainty is the fact that, at least according to some commentators, the phrasing of paragraph (1)(D) is unrealistically broad. Consider the comments of Professor Davis, whose analysis has been influential in this area:

> Probably a requirement that *all* interpretative rules be published cannot be responsibly imposed by a court, unless the court considers such questions as whether the requirement of publication extends to (1) a written memorandum from the agency head to the staff about how to interpret something, (2) such a memorandum to one staff member, (3) an informal ruling in a particular case that is buried in the file, (4) such a ruling that is occasionally regarded as a precedent, (5) such a ruling that is the foundation for all later decisions on the subject, (6) an opinion in a formal adjudication that may or may not become a precedent, (7) an adjudicative opinion that is explicitly written for the purpose of formulating a "rule" to guide future decisions, or (8) an opinion rejecting the old "rule" and establishing a new "rule." The list could be eighty-eight instead of eight.

1 KENNETH CULP DAVIS, ADMINISTRATIVE LAW TREATISE § 5:11 at 342 (2d ed.1978). Perhaps for this reason, courts tend to read paragraph (1)(D) narrowly. For example, according to the Ninth Circuit, "an administrative interpretation is not of general applicability [within the meaning of paragraph (1)(D)] if: '(1) only a clarification or explanation of existing laws or

regulations is expressed; and (2) no significant impact upon any segment of the public results.'" *Powderly v. Schweiker*, 704 F.2d 1092, 1098 (9th Cir. 1983) (quoting *Anderson v. Butz*, 550 F.2d 459 (9th Cir. 1977)). Is the *Powderly* interpretation consistent with the APA language? *See also Cathedral Candle Co. v. United States International Trade Comm'n*, 400 F.3d 1352 (Fed. Cir. 2005); *Nguyen v. United States*, 824 F.2d 697 (9th Cir. 1987).

As a real world matter, it appears that agencies publish guidance documents only sporadically and haphazardly. *See* Randy S. Springer, Note, *Gatekeeping and the* Federal Register: *An Analysis of the Publication Requirement of Section 552(a)(1)(D) of the Administrative Procedure Act*, 41 ADMIN. L. REV. 533 (1989). Agencies' widespread use of the Internet has ameliorated this situation, but a 2007 study found that only about half of the agencies make policy statements accessible at their websites. National Security Archive, *File Not Found: 10 Years After E-FOIA, Most Federal Agencies Are Delinquent* (March 12, 2007) (available at *www2.gwu.edu/~nsarchiv/NSAEBB/NSAEBB216/e-foia_audit_brief.pdf*).

2. *2010 MSAPA*. The 2010 MSAPA takes a different approach to publication of guidance documents. It does not require an agency to publish them in the official state bulletin (similar to the *Federal Register*). That publication obligation applies only to what the federal APA calls substantive rules—pronouncements that have the force of law. § 316. Instead, the MSAPA provides that a guidance document must be published on the agency's website. The agency may not "rely on a guidance document, or cite it as precedent against any party to a proceeding," unless it has been so published. § 311(e). This sanction is based directly on 5 U.S.C. § 552(a)(2) of the federal APA. As already noted, this APA provision applies to interpretive rules and policy statements that are *not* required to be published in the *Federal Register*. Does the MSAPA solve the problem highlighted in the preceding note?

3. *Incorporation by reference*. Many regulations provide that companies or individuals must comply with the standards set forth in a code prepared by a private industry organization. The code itself, however, is typically not published in the *Federal Register*. Instead, the agency simply cites to the code, which is published elsewhere. The APA permits such "incorporation by reference" with permission of the Director of the Office of Federal Register (OFR), if the material is "reasonably available" to affected persons. 5 U.S.C. § 552(a)(1). Federal policies favor this practice as a means of drawing upon industry expertise and harmonizing standards between the public and private sectors. *See also* 2010 MSAPA § 314(3) (incorporated material must be readily available "at no charge or for a reasonable charge").

In practice, however, these codes are frequently copyrighted, so that regulated entities can consult them only by purchasing a copy from the organization that created it. A code may cost hundreds of dollars, a price tag that would not be affordable for a small business, let alone for a public interest group that may wish to raise questions about whether the code is too weak to serve as a basis for compliance with the regulatory legislation. Furthermore, a business may be expected to comply with many such codes, so the collective cost may be prohibitive.

To improve public access to codes that have been incorporated by reference into regulations, the Administrative Conference has recommended that agencies should work with organizations on voluntary measures that can make codes publicly accessible (e.g., in an online read-only format) while also respecting the owner's intellectual property interests. ACUS Recommendation 2011–5, *Incorporation by Reference*, 77 Fed. Reg. 2257 (2012); *see* Emily S. Bremer, *Incorporation by Reference in an Open-Government Age*, 36 HARV. J.L. & PUB. POL'Y 131 (2013) (supporting this approach).

Some commentators consider these solutions too modest. They argue that the original purpose of allowing incorporation by reference—to allow the government to control printing costs and library space usage—is obsolete in the digital age. The option of Internet posting entails no such costs. More fundamentally, these commentators argue that it is intolerable to require people to comply with or be affected by legal requirements that they cannot afford to consult. Thus, they contend, the term "reasonably available" in § 552(a)(1) should now be interpreted to mean that all incorporated material must be accessible to the public online at both the proposed rule and final rule stages. Nina Mendelson, *Private Control over Access to Public Law: The Puzzling Federal Regulatory Use of Private Standards*, 112 MICH. L. REV. 737 (2013); Peter L. Strauss, *Private Standards Organizations and Public Law*, 42 WM & MARY BILL RTS. J. 497 (2013). These authors and others have petitioned OFR to revise its regulations accordingly, but so far that office has merely proposed to require an agency that incorporates by reference to state what efforts it has made to promote public access. 78 Fed. Reg. 60,784 (2013).

4. *Delayed effectiveness.* How does one measure the thirty days' minimum notice period required by APA § 553(d)? That question divided the court in *Rowell v. Andrus,* 631 F.2d 699 (10th Cir.1980). The Interior Department adopted an increase in the amounts to be paid by oil and gas lease owners from fifty cents per acre to a dollar per acre. The rule appeared in the Federal Register on January 5, 1977, with a stated effective date of February 1. The plaintiffs, applicants for leases who wanted to be charged the lower rate, argued that the agency had violated § 553(d). The dissent said that plaintiffs were in no position to claim any unfair surprise, because the agency had proposed the increase nine months earlier, plaintiffs had undoubtedly heard about it then, and the final rule was identical to the proposed rule. The majority, however, said that the notice of proposed rulemaking could not serve as the required publication for purposes of § 553(d); the increase could not go into effect until thirty days after a separate publication of the final rule at the time of its adoption. Which view is preferable?

5.   *Remedy.* The court in *Rowell* went on to say that the Interior Department's breach of § 553(d) did not mean that the price increase on lease payments had to be vacated. Rather, the rule would simply go into effect thirty days after its publication. Does this holding leave agencies with an adequate incentive to comply with § 553(d)? Is it justifiable?

6.   *Exemptions from the deferred effectiveness requirements.* The federal APA allows an agency to make a rule effective immediately "for good cause found and published with the rule." 5 U.S.C. 553(d)(3). This provision is discussed in greater detail in § 6.1.1 N.7. Similarly, 2010 MSAPA allows an agency to set an earlier effective date for an emergency rule. 2010 MSAPA § 317(d). There is a comparable provision in 1961 MSAPA § 4(b)(2).

The federal APA also provides that an agency need not delay the effective date of newly adopted rules if they grant an exemption or relieve a restriction. § 553(d)(1). Since such rules confer benefits rather than impose burdens on regulated persons, those persons usually do not need and do not want a delayed effective date. They want the rules to be effective as soon as possible. Finally, the federal APA allows interpretive rules and general statements of policy to be immediately effective. § 553(d)(2). In effect, the 2010 MSAPA does the same, because § 317 applies only to rules, not to guidance documents.

7.   *Midnight regulations.* Typically, when control of the White House shifts from Republican to Democratic or vice versa, the outgoing administration adopts a large number of rules at the very end of its term, and the incoming administration looks for ways to nullify these "midnight regulations" (so-called by analogy to the "midnight judgeships" underlying *Marbury v. Madison*). When President Reagan took office, his administration asked agencies to postpone for sixty days the effective dates of all recently-promulgated regulations, so that the new administration would have time to decide which ones to retain and which ones to modify or rescind. The incoming administration of President Clinton requested each agency to immediately withdraw all rules that had been submitted to the Office of the Federal Register but not actually published. And when Presidents George W. Bush and Barack Obama took office, their chiefs of staff requested agencies to take *both* of these measures. Measures of this kind naturally bring supporters of the old and new administrations into direct conflict and elicit partisan controversy.

The tactic of withdrawing rules before the Office of the Federal Register has published them has been upheld in the courts as a permissible use of an option provided by that office's internal procedures. *Kennecott Utah Copper Corp. v. United States Dep't of Interior,* 88 F.3d 1191 (D.C.Cir.1996). However, the tactic of postponing the effective dates of rules that have already been promulgated stands on a less secure legal footing. According to some case law, the effective date specified in a rule is an essential element of the rule and thus may not be postponed without a new rulemaking proceeding. *Envtl. Defense Fund v. Gorsuch,* 713 F.2d 802, 813–16 (D.C. Cir.

1983); *NRDC v. EPA*, 683 F.2d 752 (3d Cir. 1982); *see also NRDC v. Abraham*, 355 F.3d 179, 202–04 (2d Cir. 2004) (doubting that agencies have an inherent right to reconsider already-issued regulations without instituting new notice and comment proceedings). For analysis of the legal issues, see Kathryn A. Watts, *Regulatory Moratoria*, 61 DUKE L.J. 1883, 1939–49 (2012) (also discussed in § 7.6 N.13). The Administrative Conference has invited Congress to consider enacting legislation that would expressly allow an incoming presidential administration a 60-day review period in which to evaluate midnight rules issued by the outgoing administration. ACUS Recommendation 2012–2, *Midnight Rules*, 77 Fed. Reg. 47,802 (2012).

The study underlying the ACUS recommendation found little substance to the frequently heard criticism that agency rules promulgated at the last minute have often been hastily made or promulgated for the purpose of making it harder for the incoming administration to abandon its predecessor's policies. *See* Jack M. Beermann, *Midnight Rules: A Reform Agenda*, 2 MICH. J. ENVTL. & ADMIN. L. 285 (2013). Even so, one can argue that the turnover in party control implies that the voters no longer support those policies. Moreover, the outgoing administration cannot be held politically accountable for post-election rules. In this light, does the ACUS recommendation go far enough? Should an outgoing administration be forbidden to issue significant rules after the election? *See* H.R. 4607, 112th Cong. (2012) (proposing such a ban). Should the APA be amended to allow an incoming administration to revoke a midnight regulation without having to conduct full rulemaking proceedings?

8.   *Problem.* The Madison Meat Inspection Act (MMIA) requires the Madison Department of Health to conduct safety inspections of "all meat food products prepared in any slaughtering, rendering, packing, or similar establishment." Because the term "packing" is generally understood to refer to the wholesale meat industry, the Act has long been construed as exempting "retail" outlets such as ordinary grocery stores and restaurants.

Last year the Department received a complaint from a consumer who alleged that she had become ill after eating a sausage pizza purchased at one of Alvin's grocery stores. Alvin operates a chain of thirteen groceries in Monroe City, Madison. The stores sell pizza by the slice at delicatessen counters. Alvin's staff prepares the pizzas at a central kitchen facility attached to one of the stores and distributes them to the other stores by refrigerator truck. One month later, the Secretary of the Department sent a memorandum, labeled Bulletin 260, to agency staff members, in which he said: "To dispel any confusion that may exist, I write to clarify that, in our view, the term 'packing or similar establishment' in the MMIA includes a grocery kitchen facility in which meat pizzas are prepared for offsite purchase. The slicing and handling of sausage and pepperoni during pizza-making is certainly 'preparation' of a meat food product. Moreover, the 'retail' exemption does not apply, because the centralized preparation and distribution of pizzas makes such operations akin to those of a wholesaler."

Soon afterwards, department inspectors arrived at Alvin's pizza kitchen to conduct an inspection pursuant to the new policy, although they did not mention the bulletin (which had never been posted on the agency's website). Alvin allowed the inspection only under protest. The inspectors determined that Alvin would have to remodel the kitchen in order to meet the design and temperature control requirements expected of packinghouses. They also issued a notice directing him to come into compliance immediately or face monetary penalties. Alvin requested the Secretary to grant him relief from these measures, but the Secretary declined to intervene.

Being without further recourse within the agency, Alvin filed suit in an appropriate court. He learned about Bulletin 260 for the first time during discovery in this court action. While the action was pending, the department initiated a notice-and-comment rulemaking proceeding to adopt the substance of Bulletin 260 as a legislative rule. Shortly after the comment period, the department adopted the final rule (without change). The rule, designated as Regulation 36, said it was "effective immediately." The accompanying statement did not explain why immediate effectiveness was imposed.

In his court action, Alvin contends that, because Bulletin 260 was never published in the Madison Register, his company cannot be penalized for any actions it took prior to the effective date of Regulation 36. He also contends that Regulation 36 is unlawful because it provided for immediate effectiveness instead of allowing a preparation period. Alvin asks the court to vacate Regulation 36, or at least to postpone its effective date until thirty days after the court has resolved all questions about the legality of the department's jurisdiction over Alvin's pizza-making operations. How should the court respond, if Madison follows (i) federal law, or (ii) the 2010 MSAPA? *Cf. D & W Food Centers, Inc. v. Block*, 786 F.2d 751 (6th Cir. 1986).

§ 5.8   REGULATORY ANALYSIS

A regulatory analysis is an intensive, formal examination by an agency of the merits of a proposed rule. It is intended to involve a more detailed and systematic assessment than is inherent in the ordinary process of notice-and-comment rulemaking. At their best, regulatory analyses can aid careful consideration of the desirability of particular rules by structuring agency consideration of their costs and benefits, their advantages and disadvantages, and the various alternatives available. In addition, regulatory analyses can help to focus public attention on, and public discussion of, proposed rules in a manner that can improve the ultimate agency decision. On the other hand, analysis requirements should not unduly hamper an agency's ability to fulfill its basic mission. An issue explored in this section is whether existing regulatory analysis schemes are well designed to reconcile these competing objectives. *See generally* Symposium, *The Contemporary Regulatory State*, 33 FORDHAM URB. L.J. 953 (2006).

The most common variety of regulatory analysis utilizes the methods of economics to evaluate whether the benefits of a proposed rule compare favorably with its costs. A regulatory analysis that has this focus is also frequently known as a cost-benefit analysis or CBA (some writers prefer "benefit-cost analysis"). Stakeholders and commentators have carried on a vigorous and often heated debate about the merits of this technique.

In general, judges play a relatively small role in monitoring agencies' cost-benefit analyses. Many statutes and executive orders that require agencies to engage in such analysis expressly prohibit, or sharply limit, judicial review of the agency's compliance with those requirements.

§ 5.8.1 REGULATORY ANALYSIS IN FEDERAL AGENCIES: ESSENTIALS

Two of the authors of the following readings went on to serve in the Obama administration. Professor Sunstein became Administrator of the Office of Information and Regulatory Affairs, and Professor Heinzerling became Associate Administrator for the Office of Policy at the Environmental Protection Agency.

CASS R. SUNSTEIN, THE COST-BENEFIT STATE: THE FUTURE OF REGULATORY PROTECTION
20–27 (2002)

What does a cost-benefit state do? And what does CBA involve? First and foremost, a government committed to CBA will attempt to analyze the consequences of regulations, on both the cost and benefit side. Such an analysis will include quantitative and qualitative accounts of expected effects, including, for example, a statement of the expected lives saved, curable cancers prevented, asthma attacks averted, and much more. Where science does not permit specific predictions, government should produce ranges, as, for example, in a statement that the regulation will save between 100 and 240 lives per year. Whenever possible, expected benefits should be translated into monetary equivalents, not because a life is really worth, say, $6 million, but to permit sensible comparisons and priorities.

These ideas should be limited to regulations of a certain magnitude, such as those that impose costs of at least $50 million per year. Many regulations do not impose substantial costs, and for routine or low-cost measures a formal analysis should not be required (and it has not been under the relevant executive orders). . . .

Quantification will be difficult or even impossible in some cases. For arsenic in drinking water, government cannot really come up with specific numbers to link exposure levels to deaths and illnesses. At this stage, science is able to produce only ranges of anticipated benefits, which are not precise but are nonetheless highly illuminating. For regulations protecting airport security in the face of terrorist threats, quantification of the benefits is at best a guess. We do not know the magnitude of the risks, and a full-scale cost-benefit analysis would be silly. But even here, an effort to be as specific as possible about costs and anticipated efficacy is likely to help us to promote airport security in the most reasonable manner.

Thus far I have been discussing CBA as a *procedural* requirement— as a requirement that information be compiled and disclosed. But the cost-benefit state imposes a substantive requirement as well. In order to proceed, an agency should be required to conclude, in ordinary circumstances, that the benefits justify the costs, and to explain why. If, for example, a regulation is expected to save 80 lives, each valued at $6 million, and it would cost $200 million, it is fully justified. But if a regulation is expected to save four lives and cost $400 million, an agency should ordinarily be barred from issuing it. If an agency seeks to proceed even though the benefits do not justify the costs, it should have to explain itself—by saying, for example, that those at risk are young children, and that because they cannot protect themselves, and because a number of years of life are involved, unusual steps should be taken.

At this point, it might be possible to question whether a large amount of money (say, $400 million) would really be too much to spend to save a small number of lives (say, two). Who is to say that $400 million is too much? The best answer is heavily pragmatic. Each of us has limited resources, and we do not spend all of our budget on statistically low risks. We spen[d] a certain amount, and not more, to protect against the risks associated with poor diet, motor vehicle accidents, fires, floods, and much more. In allocating our resources, we set priorities, partly to use resources to prevent the more serious safety problems and partly to use them on other things we care about, such as education, recreation, food, and entertainment. The same is true for governments, which cannot sensibly spend huge amounts on small hazards. If an agency requires a $400 million expenditure to save two lives, it will be expending resources that might well be spent on other matters, including the saving of more lives. . . . It is not as if people are, with respect to some risk, either "safe" or "unsafe." The real questions are whether and how to reduce the risks to which they are now subject. Cost-benefit analysis is a tool for ensuring good answers to those questions.

None of this suggests that the government should be rigidly bound by the "bottom line." Cost-benefit analysis ought not to place agencies in an arithmetic straightjacket. The benefits should ordinarily be required to exceed the costs, but regulators might reasonably decide that the numbers are not decisive if, for example, children are mostly at risk, or if the relevant hazard is faced mostly by poor people, or if the hazard at issue is involuntarily incurred or extremely difficult to control. . . .

Many of the most popular defenses of CBA come from neoclassical economics. For economists, goods should be measured in accordance with private "willingness to pay." The idea is not as strange as it might seem. Each of us must make choices about how much to spend for additional increments of safety—by, for example, buying smoke alarms or especially strong locks, or taking certain jobs. Everyone is, as a practical matter, willing to pay a certain amount—no more and no less—to increase the current level of safety; each of us will demand a certain amount to be subject to an additional level of risk. Studies suggest, for example, that the value of a statistical life, measured in terms of private willingness to pay, is between $3 million and $8 million. If a regulation will save 20 lives per year, it will produce between $60 million and $160 million in benefits. It follows that we can assess the value of proposed regulations by comparing their aggregated costs to their aggregated benefits, thus measured. Suppose that the regulation would also produce $40 million in other benefits, because of the morbidity and aesthetic gains that it would generate. If the same regulation would cost $200 million, it would fail CBA.

But there are some problems with using private willingness to pay as the basis for assessing regulatory benefits. . . . The strongest arguments for CBA seem to rest not with neoclassical economics but with common sense, informed by behavioral economics and cognitive psychology. The basic idea here is that it is exceedingly difficult to choose the appropriate level of regulation without looking at both the benefit and cost sides. . . . Sometimes people are alert to the dangers at issue but fail to see the problems, economic and otherwise, with eliminating or reducing those dangers. CBA has the advantage of putting both sides of the picture before the public and relevant officials. And if people's emotions are getting in the way—as they sometimes do in the domain of risk, especially when a bad outcome would be catastrophic but its probability is tiny— CBA can have a salutary "cooling effect."

. . . Well-organized private groups very often exploit the cognitive mechanisms just described by pushing regulation, or nonregulation, in their preferred directions. And all too often, citizens and their representatives do not attend to the serious questions at stake, or the actual consequences of competing approaches. CBA can improve the process and substance of decisions by allowing people to evaluate agency decisions in an informed way, not clouded by evasions of the central issues. There is [thus] a strong *democratic* case for CBA, one that does not depend on controversial claims from neoclassical economics.

LISA HEINZERLING & FRANK ACKERMAN, PRICING THE PRICELESS: COST-BENEFIT ANALYSIS OF ENVIRONMENTAL PROTECTION

1–2 (2002)

Proponents of cost-benefit analysis make two basic arguments in its favor. First, use of cost-benefit analysis ostensibly leads to more "efficient" allocation of society's resources by better identifying which potential regulatory actions are worth undertaking and in what fashion. Advocates of cost-benefit analysis also contend that this method produces more objective and more transparent government decision-making by making more explicit the assumptions and methods underlying regulatory actions.

In fact, cost-benefit analysis is incapable of delivering what it promises. First, cost-benefit analysis cannot produce more efficient decisions because the process of reducing life, health, and the natural world to monetary values is inherently flawed.

Efforts to value life illustrate the basic problems. Cost-benefit analysis implicitly equates the risk of death with death itself, when in fact they are quite different and should be accounted for separately in considering the benefits of regulatory actions. Cost-benefit analysis also ignores the fact that citizens are concerned about risks to their families and others as well as themselves, ignores the fact that market decisions are generally very different from political decisions, and ignores the incomparability of many different types of risks to human life. The kinds of problems which arise in attempting to define the value of human life in monetary terms also arise in evaluating the benefits of protecting human health and the environment in general.

Second, the use of discounting systematically and improperly downgrades the importance of environmental regulation. While discounting makes sense in comparing alternative *financial* investments, it cannot reasonably be used to make a choice between preventing noneconomic harms to present generations and preventing similar harms to future generations. Nor can discounting reasonably be used even to make a choice between harms to the current generation; the choice between preventing an automobile fatality and a cancer death should not turn on prevailing rates of return on financial investments. In addition, discounting tends to trivialize long-term environmental risks, minimizing the very real threat our society faces from potential catastrophes and irreversible environmental harms, such as those posed by global warming and nuclear waste.

Third, cost-benefit analysis ignores the question of *who* suffers as a result of environmental problems and, therefore, threatens to reinforce existing patterns of economic and social inequality. Cost-benefit analysis treats questions about equity as, at best, side issues, contradicting the widely shared view that equity should count in public policy. Poor countries, communities, and individuals are likely to express less "willingness to pay" to avoid environmental harms simply because they have fewer resources. Therefore, cost-benefit analysis would justify imposing greater environmental burdens on them than on their wealthier counterparts. With this kind of analysis, the poor get poorer.

Finally, cost-benefit analysis fails to produce the greater objectivity and transparency promised by its proponents. For the reasons described above, cost-benefit analysis rests on a series of assumptions and value judgments that cannot remotely be described as objective. Moreover, the highly complex, resource-intensive, and expert-driven nature of this method makes it extremely difficult for the public to understand and participate in the process. Thus, in practice, cost-benefit analysis is anything but transparent.

Beyond these inherent flaws, cost-benefit analysis suffers from serious defects in practical implementation. Many benefits of public health and environmental protection have not been quantified and cannot easily be quantified given the limits on time and resources; thus, in practice, cost-benefit analysis is often akin to shooting in the dark. Even when the data gaps are supposedly acknowledged, public discussion tends to focus on the misleading numeric values produced by cost-benefit analysis while relevant but non-monetized factors are simply ignored. Finally, the cost side of cost-benefit analysis is frequently exaggerated, because analysts routinely fail to account for the economies that can be achieved through innovative efforts to meet new environmental standards.

Real-world examples of cost-benefit analysis demonstrate the strange lengths to which this flawed method can be taken. For example, the consulting group Arthur D. Little, in a study for the Czech Republic, concluded that encouraging smoking among Czech citizens was beneficial to the government because it caused citizens to die earlier and thus reduced government expenditures on pensions, housing, and health care. In another study, analysts calculated the value of children's lives saved by car seats by estimating the amount of time required to fasten the seats correctly and then assigning a value to the time based on the mothers' actual or imputed hourly wage. These studies are not the work of some lunatic fringe; on the contrary, they apply methodologies that are perfectly conventional within the cost-benefit framework.

NOTES AND QUESTIONS

1.   *Cost-benefit analysis mandates.* A series of presidential executive orders have long mandated that federal executive-branch agencies engage in

cost-benefit analysis, at least in important cases. These presidential directives first reached full-blown form with Executive Order 12,291, 46 Fed.Reg. 13,193 (1981), which was issued by President Reagan and retained by President George H.W. Bush. That order was later supplanted by Executive Order 12,866, 58 Fed.Reg. 51,735 (1993), adopted by President Clinton and retained in its essential features by Presidents George W. Bush and Obama. The orders were and are implemented by the Office of Information and Regulatory Affairs (OIRA), a branch of the Office of Management and Budget (OMB). (The role of these and other executive orders in facilitating supervision of the agencies by OIRA, and ultimately by the President, is the subject of § 7.6. The present section deals primarily with the impact of regulatory analysis requirements within the agencies themselves.) Although E.O. 12,866 applies to most legislative rulemaking, the order prescribes a full-blown CBA only in limited circumstances—for rules that are likely to have an annual effect on the economy of $100 million or more, or to have a material adverse effect on the economy, productivity, jobs, etc. E.O. 12,866, §§ 3(f)(1), 6(a)(3)(C).

In addition, the Unfunded Mandates Reform Act of 1995 requires that any agency rule that imposes costs of $100 million on state or local governments, or on the private sector, must be accompanied by a cost-benefit statement. 2 U.S.C. § 1532(a). A court can require administrators to prepare the statement if they have failed to do so, but the court cannot overturn the rule on the basis of the agency's failure to prepare the statement or the inadequacy of a statement the agency did prepare. *Id.* § 1571; *see Allied Local & Regional Mfrs. Caucus v. EPA*, 215 F.3d 61, 80–81 (D.C. Cir. 2000). Probably because of this weak enforcement structure, this aspect of the act has had little impact in practice.

2. *Cost-benefit decisional criteria.* E.O. 12,866 not only requires agencies to study costs and benefits, but also provides, with several qualifications, that agency action must be guided by cost-benefit considerations. "Each agency shall assess both the costs and benefits of [an] intended regulation and, recognizing that some costs and benefits are difficult to quantify, propose or adopt a regulation only upon a reasoned determination that the benefits of the intended regulation justify its costs." § 1(b)(6). The Reagan order had been much firmer in its language. It provided, for example, that "[r]egulatory action shall not be undertaken unless the potential benefits to society for the regulation outweigh the potential costs to society;" and "[a]mong alternative approaches to any given regulatory objective, the alternative involving the least net cost to society shall be chosen." E.O. 12291, §§ 2(b), 2(d). Was the Reagan version too confining? Or is the Clinton version too open-ended?

3. *Is CBA cost-justified?* The scholarly literature debating the merits of CBA is enormous, including much additional writing by Sunstein, Heinzerling, and Ackerman. For further commentary supporting CBA, see, e.g. MURRAY L. WEIDENBAUM, BUSINESS AND GOVERNMENT IN THE GLOBAL MARKETPLACE 179–88 (7th ed. 2004); Stephen F. Williams, *Squaring the*

Vicious Circle, 53 ADMIN. L. REV. 257 (2001). For further criticisms of CBA, see, e.g., Thomas O. McGarity, *A Cost-Benefit State,"* 50 ADMIN. L. REV. 7 (1998); Sidney A. Shapiro & Christopher H. Schroeder, *Beyond Cost-Benefit Analysis: A Pragmatic Reorientation*, 32 HARV. ENVTL. L. REV. 433 (2008); *cf.* Richard W. Parker, *Grading the Government*, 70 U. CHI. L. REV. 1345 (2003) (critiquing "regulatory scorecards"). Another book assumes that CBA is here to stay but argues that it should be reformed to diminish the influence of anti-regulatory biases. RICHARD L. REVESZ & MICHAEL A. LIVERMORE, RETAKING RATIONALITY: HOW COST-BENEFIT ANALYSIS CAN BETTER PROTECT THE ENVIRONMENT AND OUR HEALTH (2008).

For an intermediate view, see Sally Katzen, *Cost-Benefit Analysis: Where Should We Go From Here?*, 33 FORDHAM URB. L.J. 1313 (2006). Katzen, who was President Clinton's OIRA Administrator, supports the use of CBA in principle. She suggests, however, that it has not lived up to its potential because, in many cases, it is underfunded or is performed so late in the decisionmaking process that it is merely used to rationalize results reached on other grounds. Indeed, empirical studies have cast doubt on the extent to which agencies actually carry out and rely on CBAs. *See, e.g.*, Cary Coglianese, *Empirical Analysis and Administrative Law*, 2002 U. ILL. L. REV. 1111, 1120–25 (2002).

4. *CBA mandates in substantive statutes.* At the federal level, a handful of substantive statutes in addition to TSCA require (or at least can be construed to require) the agencies that administer them to conduct and rely on CBA during rulemaking. *See* Hahn, *supra*, at 889–91. A statute that imposes this obligation expressly is the Safe Drinking Water Act, 42 U.S.C. § 300g–1(b). A highly publicized controversy in 2001 over EPA's proposed emission levels for arsenic in drinking water arose out of this requirement. *See* Symposium, 90 GEO. L.J. 2255 (2002). *See also* 49 U.S.C. §§ 60102(b)(3), (b)(6) (pipeline safety). Other statutes contain more general language, such as provisions authorizing agencies to regulate "unreasonable" adverse environmental effects. *See* 7 U.S.C. § 136a(a) (pesticides). Under these latter provisions, the extent to which an agency must conduct a formal cost-benefit analysis and reach conclusions consistent with it is a matter of interpretation. For example, a 1996 statute requires the SEC to consider the effect of any new rule on "efficiency, competition, and capital formation." 15 U.S.C. §§ 78c(f), 80a–2(c). Recent D.C. Circuit case law has interpreted this language to require rigorous analysis of costs and benefits. *See Business Roundtable v. SEC*, 647 F.3d 1144 (D.C. Cir. 2011). This interpretation has profoundly influenced rulemaking in the area of financial regulation. *See, e.g.*, Bruce Kraus & Connor Raso, *Rational Boundaries for SEC Cost-Benefit Analysis*, 30 YALE J. ON REG. 289 (2013).

5. *Legal constraints.* E.O. 12,866 states repeatedly that it applies only "to the extent permitted by law." §§ 1(b), 9. Similar disclaimers were included in the predecessor order, E.O. 12,291. Thus, if a statute directs an agency to issue a rule that even the agency itself would not deem cost-justified, the agency must follow the statute. An example is the Occupational Safety and

Health Act, under which OSHA had an obligation to adopt standards "to the extent feasible" to protect employees from risks of inhaling cotton dust. The Court said that the plain meaning of "feasible" is "capable of being done," and thus the standards must require as much protection as the technology and the economic viability of the employers permitted, regardless of what cost-benefit analysis might imply. *American Textile Mfrs. Inst. v. Donovan,* 452 U.S. 490, 506–09 (1981) (*Cotton Dust*); *see also Whitman v. American Trucking Ass'ns, Inc.,* 531 U.S. 457 (2001) (excerpted in § 7.2). In *Entergy Corp. v. Riverkeeper, Inc.,* 556 U.S. 208 (2009), however, the Court distinguished those two cases and made clear that the determination of whether a statute permits CBA has to be worked out on a case-by-case basis. The Court deferred to the EPA's determination that one section of the Clean Water Act does authorize CBA, but it acknowledged that other sections of the Act may not. The Court said that EPA's mandate to rely on the "best technology available" was ambiguous, because it did not specify the basis on which the technology had to be "best." Thus, under *Chevron,* EPA could construe it to refer to the most efficient solution, which a CBA could illuminate.

6. *Judicial review of analysis requirements.* On the federal level, judicial review of agencies' compliance with CBA obligations is usually quite limited. Section 10 of E.O. 12,866 provides that the order "is intended only to improve the internal management of the Federal Government and does not create any right or benefit . . . enforceable at law or equity." The predecessor order, E.O. 12,291, contained almost identical language. The courts have respected this intention: they have consistently declined to review agencies' compliance with these orders. *Michigan v. Thomas,* 805 F.2d 176, 187 (6th Cir. 1986); *Alliance for Natural Health US v. Sebelius,* 775 F. Supp. 2d 114, 135 n.10 (D.D.C. 2011). In this context, unreviewability means that the agency's failure to perform the analysis in the prescribed manner will not, standing alone, cause a court to set aside the rule. It does not mean, however, that a court must ignore the conclusions that an agency reached while conducting a regulatory analysis. Normally, the agency's analysis and data will be added to the rulemaking record, and on appeal the court will take account of this material as it decides whether the rule is reasonable on the merits. *Michigan v. Thomas, supra; see Nat'l Ass'n of Home Builders v. EPA,* 682 F.3d 1031, 1040 (D.C. Cir. 2012) (agency's reliance on a CBA must be reasonable, but judicial review thereof is deferential).

7. *Specialized regulatory analyses.* Even prior to the Reagan executive order prescribing broad use of CBA, Congress had provided for more specialized forms of regulatory analysis of agency rules. Since 1969 the National Environmental Policy Act (NEPA) has instructed all agencies to prepare a detailed environmental impact statement in connection with "major Federal actions significantly affecting the quality of the human environment." *See* 42 U.S.C. §§ 4321–61. The purpose is to force agencies to become more sensitive to the (frequently unintended) environmental consequences of their actions.

Similarly, the Regulatory Flexibility Act (RFA), 5 U.S.C. §§ 601 et seq., first adopted in 1980, requires agencies to consider and to embody in an analysis the impact of proposed rules on "small entities"—primarily small businesses, although "small (not-for-profit) organizations" and "small governmental jurisdictions" are also included. The requirement sweeps broadly and is not limited to "significant" rules. This Act attempts to correct for a perceived tendency among agencies to overlook the implications of their actions for the small business community. *See* Paul R. Verkuil, *A Critical Guide to the Regulatory Flexibility Act*, 1982 DUKE L.J. 213. At first, the RFA specifically forbade judicial review of the obligations it imposed. Thus, courts refused to hear claims arising under that Act, much as they have declined to hear claims arising under E.O. 12,866. *See Small Refiner Lead Phase-Down Task Force v. USEPA*, 705 F.2d 506, 537–39 (D.C. Cir. 1983) (court cannot review compliance with RFA, but can consider material in the analysis in reviewing a rule under the arbitrary and capricious test).

In 1996, responding to criticism that the RFA was not fulfilling its goals, Congress adopted legislation to strengthen it. *See* Small Business Regulatory Enforcement Fairness Act of 1996 (SBREFA), Pub.L.No. 104–121. One change wrought by SBREFA was to permit judicial review of alleged RFA violations. Courts can now redress such violations in about the same manner as they have previously redressed violations of the environmental impact statement requirements of NEPA. *See Associated Fisheries of Maine v. Daley*, 127 F.3d 104 (1st Cir. 1997) (reviewing agency's compliance with RFA for good faith and reasonableness). "These changes were long sought by the small business community, which came to believe, as the [new] Act's sponsors noted, that many agencies gave the RFA lip service at best. The question is whether judicial review will improve compliance, and thus serve the purposes of the Act, more than it will complicate and slow the regulatory process." Thomas O. Sargentich, *The Small Business Regulatory Enforcement Fairness Act*, 49 ADMIN. L. REV. 123, 128 (1997). Was this change in the law desirable?

8. *Problem.* The Middle East oil embargo of 1973 resulted in waiting lines at gas stations, shortages of home heating oil, and other painful disruptions in the United States. In the wake of this crisis, Congress passed the Energy Policy and Conservation Act of 1975 (EPCA). The accompanying Senate report noted that the goals of the Act were to "decrease dependence on foreign imports, enhance national security, achieve the efficient utilization of scarce resources, and guarantee the availability of domestic energy supplies at prices consumers can afford." Under the Act (as it existed at the time of this problem), the National Highway Traffic Safety Administration (NHTSA) sets corporate average fuel economy (CAFE) standards that motor vehicle manufacturers must achieve in designated model years. "Passenger cars" are regulated separately from "light trucks" (a term that the statute defines as including minivans and sport utility vehicles, although in practice those vehicles are frequently used primarily to transport passengers). The statute directs NHTSA, when regulating light trucks, to impose CAFE standards at "the maximum feasible average fuel economy level that the [agency] decides

the manufacturers can achieve in that model year." § 32902(a). Further, "[w]hen deciding maximum feasible average fuel economy under this section, [NHTSA] shall consider technological feasibility, economic practicability, the effect of other motor vehicle standards of the Government on fuel economy, and the need of the United States to conserve energy." *Id.* § 32902(f).

In a recent rulemaking proceeding, NHTSA announced new CAFE standards for light trucks for the upcoming model years. They included a modest increase in the average level of fuel economy (in miles per gallon) that manufacturers would have to meet, but not as much of an increase as environmentalists had sought. The agency explained that, in determining the new standard, it had relied on a CBA that it had prepared pursuant to Executive Order 12,866. In preparing this analysis, the agency had assigned monetary values to factors such as the benefits of fuel savings to the consumer, the costs to manufacturers of developing new technologies, and externalities such as the crash and noise costs associated with driving. NHTSA did not, however, assign a monetary value to the beneficial effects that reduced carbon dioxide emissions would have on the accumulation of greenhouse gases that lead to global warming. Consequently, it did not take account of that factor in its comparison of costs with benefits. Responding to the Smart Energy Coalition, an environmental group that had urged the agency to include climate change issues in its determination, NHTSA said that it did not believe those issues were within its statutory mandate. In any event, the agency said, those benefits were too diffuse and uncertain to be considered in a regulatory analysis.

The Coalition now appeals, arguing that NHTSA should not have prepared or relied on a CBA in this proceeding, because the statutory standard of setting "maximum feasible" levels foreclosed it from doing so. Moreover, the Coalition argues, if the agency was going to use cost-benefit analysis at all, it should have included climate change effects in its determination. In the Coalition's view, the agency's reliance on this flawed CBA rendered its decision to adopt the new CAFE standards arbitrary and capricious. How should the court rule? *Cf. Center for Biological Diversity v. NHTSA*, 538 F.3d 1172 (9th Cir. 2008); Jonathan S. Masur & Eric A. Posner, *Climate Regulation and the Limits of Cost-Benefit Analysis*, 99 CAL. L. REV. 1557 (2011).

§ 5.8.2 REGULATORY ANALYSIS IN FEDERAL AGENCIES: ELABORATIONS

CORROSION PROOF FITTINGS V. EPA
947 F.2d 1201 (5th Cir. 1991)

SMITH, J.:

The Environmental Protection Agency (EPA) issued a final rule under section 6 of the Toxic Substances Control Act (TSCA), [15 U.S.C.

§ 2605(a)], to prohibit the future manufacture, importation, processing, and distribution of asbestos in almost all products. . . . Asbestos is a naturally occurring fibrous material that resists fire and most solvents. Its major uses include heat-resistant insulators, cements, building materials, fireproof gloves and clothing, and motor vehicle brake linings. Asbestos is a toxic material, and occupational exposure to asbestos dust can result in mesothelioma, asbestosis, and lung cancer. . . . The EPA estimates that this rule will save either 202 or 148 lives, depending upon whether the benefits are discounted, at a cost of approximately $450–800 million, depending upon the price of substitutes. . . .

[Section 6(a) of] TSCA provides, in pertinent part, as follows:

(a) Scope of regulation.—If the Administrator finds that there is a *reasonable basis* to conclude that the manufacture, processing, distribution in commerce, use, or disposal of a chemical substance or mixture, or that any combination of such activities, presents or will present an *unreasonable risk of injury* to health or the environment, the Administrator shall by rule apply one or more of the following requirements to such substance or mixture to the extent necessary *to protect adequately* against such risk using the *least burdensome* requirements. (Emphasis added [by the court].)

As the highlighted language shows, Congress did not enact TSCA as a zero-risk statute. The EPA, rather, was required to consider both alternatives to a ban and the costs of any proposed actions and to "carry out this chapter in a reasonable and prudent manner [after considering] the environmental, economic, and social impact of any action." [TSCA § 2(c).] [The court also concluded that, because TSCA requires the EPA to select the "least burdensome requirements," the agency should have calculated the costs and benefits of adopting intermediate measures, instead of simply calculating the costs and benefits of adopting a total ban versus doing nothing. Mere "consideration" of those intermediate measures was not enough.]

Furthermore, we are concerned about some of the methodology employed by the EPA in making various of the calculations that it did perform. . . . Although various commentators dispute whether it ever is appropriate to discount benefits when they are measured in human lives, we note that it would skew the results to discount only costs without according similar treatment to the benefits side of the equation. . . . Because the EPA must discount costs to perform its evaluations properly, the EPA also should discount benefits to preserve an apples-to-apples comparison, even if this entails discounting benefits of a non-monetary nature.

When the EPA does discount costs or benefits, however, it cannot choose an unreasonable time upon which to base its discount calculation. Instead of using the time of injury as the appropriate time from which to discount, as one might expect, the EPA instead used the time of exposure. . . . Such an approach might be proper when the exposure and injury are one and the same, such as when a person is exposed to an immediately fatal poison, but is inappropriate for discounting toxins in which exposure often is followed by a substantial lag time before manifestation of injuries.

Of more concern to us is the failure of the EPA to compute the costs and benefits of its proposed rule past the year 2000, and its double-counting of the costs of asbestos use. In performing its calculus, the EPA only included the number of lives saved over the next thirteen years, and counted any additional lives saved as simply "unquantified benefits." The EPA and intervenors now seek to use these unquantified lives saved to justify calculations as to which the benefits seem far outweighed by the astronomical costs. For example, the EPA plans to save about three lives with its ban of asbestos pipe, at a cost of $128–227 million (*i.e.*, approximately $43–76 million per life saved). Although the EPA admits that the price tag is high, it claims that the lives saved past the year 2000 justify the price.

Such calculations not only lessen the value of the EPA's cost analysis, but also make any meaningful judicial review impossible. . . . Unquantified benefits can, at times, permissibly tip the balance in close cases. They cannot, however, be used to effect a wholesale shift on the balance beam. Such a use makes a mockery of the requirements of TSCA that the EPA weigh the costs of its actions before it chooses the least burdensome alternative. . . .

The final requirement the EPA must satisfy before engaging in any TSCA rulemaking is that it only take steps designed to prevent "unreasonable" risks. . . . Even taking all of the EPA's figures as true, and evaluating them in the light most favorable to the agency's decision . . ., the agency's analysis results in figures as high as $74 million per life saved. For example, the EPA states that its ban of asbestos pipe will save three lives over the next thirteen years, at a cost of $128–227 million ($43–76 million per life saved), depending upon the price of substitutes; that its ban of asbestos shingles will cost $23–34 million to save 0.32 statistical lives ($72–106 million per life saved); that its ban of asbestos coatings will cost $46–181 million to save 3.33 lives ($14–54 million per life saved); and that its ban of asbestos paper products will save 0.60 lives at a cost of $4–5 million ($7–8 million per life saved). . . .

The EPA's willingness to argue that spending $23.7 million to save less than one-third of a life reveals that its economic review of its regulations, as required by TSCA, was meaningless. As the petitioners' brief and our review of EPA caselaw reveals, such high costs are rarely, if ever, used to support a safety regulation. If we were to allow such cavalier treatment of the EPA's duty to consider the economic effects of its decisions, we would have to excise entire sections and phrases from the language of TSCA. Because we are judges, not surgeons, we decline to do so.[23] . . .

[In the end, the court upheld a minor part of the rule (relating to products that were no longer sold in the United States), but it remanded the principal portions to the agency for further consideration. On remand, the EPA decided not to proceed with the asbestos regulation and has never issued it.]

NOTES AND QUESTIONS

1. *TSCA aftermath.* Largely as a result of the Fifth Circuit's decision in *Corrosion Proof Fittings*, EPA has all but abandoned rulemaking under § 6(a) of TSCA. EPA does regularly monitor *new* toxic substances under other provisions of TSCA. But the agency makes almost no attempt to exercise its authority under § 6(a) to ban substances that are already in use, because of doubts that it can meet the burden of proof imposed by *Corrosion Proof Fittings*. Indeed, only five toxic substances have ever been successfully regulated pursuant to that section. *See* Government Accountability Office, *Chemical Regulation: Options Exist to Improve EPA's Ability to Assess Health Risks and Manage Its Chemical Review Program*, GAO–05–458, at 27–29 (2005). Not surprisingly, some commentators have scathingly criticized the court's decision. *See, e.g.,* Thomas O. McGarity, *The Courts and the Ossification of Rulemaking: A Response to Professor Seidenfeld*, 75 TEX. L. REV. 525, 541–49 (1997). Do you think that the court's demanding expectations were warranted by a fair reading of the language of § 6(a)? Should the court have interpreted the statute more leniently?

2. *Valuation problems.* As the principal readings in the preceding section suggested, one of the most controversial questions about cost-benefit analysis is how, or even whether, agencies can legitimately use dollar values corresponding to the lives that a particular rule would save (or put at risk). Regulations in the areas of health, safety, and the environment pose the problem most sharply. Who has the better of this argument—Sunstein or Heinzerling & Ackerman? In practice, federal agencies use a variety of figures to represent the "value of a statistical life," and the trend is upwards. Recently used figures have ranged from $6.1 million to $9.1 million.

---

[23] . . . As the petitioners point out, the EPA regularly rejects, as unjustified, regulations that would save more lives at less cost. For example, over the next 13 years, we can expect more than a dozen deaths from ingested *toothpicks*—a death toll more than twice what the EPA predicts will flow from the quarter-billion-dollar bans of asbestos pipe, shingles, and roof coatings.

Binyamin Appelbaum, *As U.S. Agencies Put More Value on a Life, Businesses Fret*, N.Y. TIMES, Feb. 16, 2011.

The court in *Corrosion Proof Fittings* was disturbed because, according to its interpretation of the data, some of the product bans encompassed by the asbestos rule would have resulted in much higher costs per life saved than the above values. Notice, however, that the court reached this conclusion by focusing on particular applications of the rule in which this ratio was especially unfavorable. Meanwhile, the court also mentioned that the overall rule would save 148 to 202 lives, at a cost of approximately $450–800 million. By dividing out those figures, one could conclude that, *in the aggregate*, the rule would have cost somewhere between $2.2 million and $5.4 million per life saved—a not uncommon valuation level at that time. Would that have been a fairer basis for assessing the impact of the rule?

3. *Discounting.* A standard practice in CBA is to assign lower monetary values to benefits and costs that will accrue in the long run than to similar benefits and costs that will accrue in the short run. One author explains: "If two individuals of the same age are exposed to a latent harm from an environmental carcinogen and to a risk of instantaneous death, respectively, the person exposed to the carcinogen stands to lose fewer life-years and to lose them later in life. Discounting is an appropriate technique for taking account of the latter factor." Richard L. Revesz, *Environmental Regulation, Cost-Benefit Analysis, and the Discounting of Human Lives*, 99 COLUM. L. REV. 941, 1016 (1999). Notice, however, the critique of discounting in the monograph by Heinzerling and Ackerman. Are the criticisms well taken? In *Corrosion Proof Fittings*, the court declares that EPA should have discounted the benefits of the asbestos rule based on the date of injury (i.e., when symptoms appeared), rather than from the date of exposure to asbestos. Is that claim persuasive? For a sampling of the extensive literature on discounting, see Revesz, *supra*; Symposium, *Intergenerational Equity and Discounting*, 74 U. CHI. L. REV. 1 (2007).

4. *Regulatory Accountability Act.* The proposed Regulatory Accountability Act (RAA), also discussed in § 5.4.2 N.5, would require an agency to discuss a large number of "rulemaking considerations" in its written explanations accompanying the proposed and final rule in ordinary notice-and-comment rulemaking. To cite only a few examples, the agency would need to consider "[t]he specific nature and significance of the problem the agency may address with a rule (including the degree and nature of risks the problem poses and the priority of addressing those risks compared to other matters or activities within the agency's jurisdiction), whether the problem warrants new agency action, and the countervailing risks that may be posed by alternatives for new agency action," as well as "[a]ny reasonable alternatives for a new rule or other response identified by the agency or interested persons. . . ." *See* H.R. 2122, 113th Cong. § 3(b) (2013) (proposed §§ 553(b), (d), (f)). In the preceding Congress, the House of Representatives passed an almost identical bill, H.R. 3010, with Republicans uniformly supporting it and almost all Democrats opposing it.

Many of the prescribed inquiries are already found in presidential executive orders, but proponents of the RAA have argued that agencies would take them more seriously if they were codified in the APA, so that they would be enforceable in court. However, critics of the bill have argued that such legislation would greatly impede the rulemaking process and encourage agencies to make policy through less publicly visible means, such as guidance documents (which are not subject to the APA rulemaking process, *see* § 6.1.4) or case-by-case adjudication. For a critique of the bill's "considerations" requirements, see ABA Section of Administrative Law and Regulatory Practice, *Comments on H.R. 3010, The Regulatory Accountability Act of 2011*, 64 ADMIN. L. REV. 619, 628–37 (2012).

5. *Supermandates.* The bill discussed in the preceding note would require a rulemaking agency to give consideration to certain factors "[n]otwithstanding any other provision of law." For example, the agency would be required to consider, in connection with a proposed rule, "the potential costs and benefits associated with potential alternative rules . . . including direct, indirect, and cumulative costs and benefits and estimated impacts on jobs (including an estimate of the net gain or loss in domestic jobs), economic growth, innovation, and economic competitiveness," even if these factors were irrelevant to the agency's decision under its enabling statute. H.R. 2122, 113th Cong. § 3(b) (2013) (proposed § 553(b)(6)). In addition to overriding existing limitations on the scope of an agency's *analysis* obligations, the bill would also change the grounds on which they may *act*. For example, an agency would be required to adopt the "least costly rule considered during the rule making . . . that meets relevant statutory objectives" unless the agency can justify a higher cost alternative "based on interests of public health, safety or welfare that are clearly within the scope of the statutory provision authorizing the rule." *Id.* (proposed § 553(f)(3)).

Override provisions of this kind are known as "supermandates." For support of such a requirement, see Christopher DeMuth, *The Regulatory State*, NAT'L AFFAIRS, Summer 2012, at 70, 78–84 (2012). For opposition, see the ABA Section's *Comments on H.R. 3010, supra*, at 639–43. Can supermandates be defended as devices by which Congress takes responsibility for choosing the values that should drive the nation's regulatory policies? Would they promote or retard political accountability? *Cf.* William W. Buzbee, *Regulatory Reform or Statutory Muddle: The "Legislative Mirage" of Single-Statute Regulatory Reform*, 5 NYU ENVTL. L.J. 298 (1996) (discussing supermandates in earlier APA reform bills).

6. *Specialized analyses by executive order.* Several executive orders direct federal agencies to write regulatory analyses in specialized areas. One order, issued by President Reagan, instructs agencies to assess the impact of any proposed rule on federalism values; other orders have required assessment of impacts on trade, property rights, the family, etc. The proliferation of such requirements led the ABA to adopt a resolution in 1992 that "urge[d] the President and Congress to exercise restraint in the overall

number of required rulemaking impact analyses. . . ." According to the supporting report:

> [A] study conducted . . . during a three-month period revealed that of the 717 rules issued, none contained a "Takings" impact statement . . ., or a "Trade" impact statement . . ., and only three had either a "Family" or "Federalism" impact statement. . . . Even supporters of rulemaking review concede that some of the current required reviews are not, and should not, be taken seriously. Retention of these requirements may demean the importance of other reviews [and] have the effect of stymieing appropriate and necessary rulemaking.

117 ABA ANN. REP. 469, 470–71 (1992).

Would it be better if all of these mandates were fully enforced? Professor Seidenfeld has assembled a list of *twenty* statutes and executive orders that may govern the federal rulemaking process under various circumstances. Mark Seidenfeld, *A Table of Requirements for Federal Administrative Rulemaking*, 27 FLA. ST. U.L. REV. 533 (2000).

7. *Administrative guidelines.* The Office of Information and Regulatory Affairs (OIRA) and its parent agency, OMB, have published a variety of statements to guide agencies in fulfilling their regulatory analysis responsibilities. Among them are memoranda on cost-benefit analysis principles; guidance on assessing and managing risks to health, safety, and the environment; and a bulletin that directs agencies to provide for independent peer review of influential scientific information that they intend to disseminate to the public. These policies are available at OMB's website, *www.whitehouse.gov/omb*. OMB's authority to prescribe such policies was bolstered by the so-called Information Quality Act or IQA (also known as the Data Quality Act). This statute, enacted in 2000, requires every agency, under OMB direction, to issue guidelines "ensuring and maximizing the quality, objectivity, utility, and integrity of information (including statistical information) disseminated by the agency." 44 U.S.C. § 3516 note. Congress adopted this mandate by attaching a 227-word amendment to an omnibus appropriations bill, without hearings, a committee report, or other explanation. What concerns, if any, does this enactment history raise about the IQA and the guidelines adopted under it? *See generally* Sidney A. Shapiro, *OMB and the Politicization of Risk Assessment*, 37 ENVTL. L. 1083 (2007).

The IQA also directs agencies to "establish administrative mechanisms allowing affected persons to seek and obtain correction of information maintained and disseminated by the agency." Agencies do sometimes revise their reports, websites, etc., in response to requests tendered under the Act, but the courts have so far been unwilling to allow private persons to bring suit to force a correction. *See, e.g., Salt Institute v. Leavitt*, 440 F.3d 156 (4th Cir. 2006).

§ 5.8.3 REGULATORY ANALYSIS IN THE STATES

1. *State regulatory analysis mandates.* Most states have amended their APAs (or in a few instances have used executive orders) to require cost-benefit or other regulatory analyses in rulemaking. A wealth of information on state systems, including a state-by-state survey, can be found in JASON A. SCHWARTZ, 52 EXPERIMENTS WITH REGULATORY REVIEW: THE POLITICAL AND ECONOMIC INPUTS INTO STATE RULEMAKINGS (2010), *policyintegrity.org/publications/detail/52–experiments-with-regulatory-review.* This report ranks the effectiveness of each state's program on a variety of metrics and reaches a harsh conclusion: "With exceedingly few (if any) trained economists, limited time, and strained budgets, most state agencies struggle to assess the basic costs of regulations and completely forgo any rigorous analysis of benefits or alternative policy choices. Based on a fifteen-point scale, no state scores an A; the average grade nationwide is a D+. . . ." *Id.* at iii. Compare the reaction of the counsel to the North Carolina Rules Review Commission: "While there is certainly always room for improvement, if not one of the 52 units of government surveyed merited an 'A,' that may say something about the grading. Perhaps what the report considers the ideal is not in fact what any state wants." Bobby Bryant, *A Review of "52 Experiments With Regulatory Review . . .,"* ADMIN. LAWYER [N.C. Bar Ass'n Admin. L. Sec.], March 2011, at 7, 8, *administrativelaw.ncbar.org/media/11610068/almar11.pdf.*

To the extent that Schwartz's critique is well founded, what factors may have contributed to the current difficulties? *See* Richard Whisnant & Diane DeWitt Cherry, *Economic Analysis of Rules: Devolution, Evolution, and Realism,* 31 WAKE FOREST L. REV. 693, 696–97 (1996): "The states' experience with economic analysis is problematic and unique for three main reasons: the lack of resources typically devoted to analysis of rules at the state level, the absence of staff expertise to conduct additional benefit-cost analysis, and the minimal state judicial expertise to review these analyses." *See also* Robert W. Hahn, *State and Federal Regulatory Reform: A Comparative Analysis,* 29 J. LEGAL STUD. 873. 875–78 (2000).

2. *California experience.* The ABA Administrative Law Section takes a pessimistic view of regulatory analysis requirements as they have played out in California:

> In 1947, California adopted APA provisions for rulemaking that were modeled on the federal APA. In 1979, however, the state adopted a much more detailed set of APA rulemaking provisions. The statute calls for specialized findings and explanations and for numerous impact statements. These provisions require constant fine-tuning and have been amended on numerous occasions.

The intense regulation of regulatory agencies contained in the California APA has had a variety of adverse consequences. Specialized and experienced lawyers (rather than staff non-lawyers) must supervise every step of every rulemaking process. The state's APA generates a large amount of boilerplate findings, because agencies lack resources to perform all of the required studies. The process has become slow and cumbersome and consumes large quantities of staff resources. As a result, agencies can complete work on fewer regulations, particularly in a time of declining budgets like the present. This has adverse effects on public health and safety. The detailed provisions of the state's APA also provide many opportunities for lawyers to challenge rules on judicial review because of minor procedural infirmities. The California experience suggests that a simpler statutory structure like the existing federal APA, regulated sensibly and flexibly by court decisions, is better than a minutely detailed statutory prescription of rulemaking procedure.

ABA Section of Admin. Law and Reg. Practice, *Comments on H.R. 3010, The Regulatory Accountability Act of 2011*, 64 ADMIN. L. REV. 619, 635–36 (2012). *See also* Michael Asimow, *A Lethal Injection of California Administrative Law*, ADMIN. & REG. L. NEWS, Fall 2013, at 4, 4.

3. *Triggering regulatory analysis.* Some states require regulatory analyses for all rules. *E.g.,* N.Y. State APA Law § 202–a; W.Va. Code § 29A–3–5. Usually, however, such analyses are required only under limited circumstances. One justification for these limitations is that the preparation of careful, technically proficient regulatory analyses can be burdensome and expensive. At the federal level, estimates of the dollar cost of a CBA typically range between $100,000 to several times that sum, depending on the particular rule. *See, e.g.,* Whisnant & Cherry, *supra,* at 720. Nor is money the only source of concern:

> If the regulatory analysis requirement were not limited, opponents of proposed rules could request the issuance of these time-consuming and expensive statements simply to harass agencies, or to delay their rule making without any compensating public benefit. Moreover, if agencies were required to issue such an analysis [upon request] in every instance of rule making, . . . agencies would be likely to compile those statements in a haphazard way, to divert resources to that task from more essential functions, or to de-emphasize policy making by rule in favor of increased law making by ad hoc adjudicatory orders that could subsequently be relied upon as precedent.

ARTHUR EARL BONFIELD, STATE ADMINISTRATIVE RULE MAKING 214 (1986).

Like the federal executive oversight order, *see* § 5.8.1 N.1, state APAs often use a dollar-cost criterion to identify those rules for which regulatory analysis should be required. Compare the approach taken by 2010 MSAPA § 305(a). That section provides that an agency "shall prepare a regulatory analysis for a proposed rule that has an estimated economic impact of more than $[ ]," but it leaves the dollar figure blank. Legislators are expected to fill in the blank for their particular state. The official Comment advises states to set the amount "carefully so that the number of regulatory analyses prepared by any agency are proportionate to the resources that are available," but states do not have to take that advice.

4.   *State-level judicial review.* Although § 305(f) of the 2010 MSAPA limits judicial review of regulatory analyses, it does so to a lesser extent than does E.O. 12,866. It instructs courts to uphold a rule if the agency made a "good faith effort to comply" with regulatory analysis requirements. Does § 305(f) limit judicial review sufficiently? Too much?

In a number of states with regulatory analysis requirements in their APAs, the statute does not explicitly limit the judicial role in reviewing the contents of those analyses. Nevertheless, some courts seem disinclined to police these requirements very aggressively. *See Northeast Ohio Regional Sewer Dist. v. Shank*, 567 N.E.2d 993 (Ohio 1991); *Methodist Hospitals of Dallas v. Texas Industrial Accident Board*, 798 S.W.2d 651 (Tex. App. 1990); *Citizens for Free Enterprise v. Dept. of Revenue*, 649 P.2d 1054 (Colo. 1982). In *Methodist Hospitals*, the Board issued a rule setting the amounts that hospitals would receive for treating workers' compensation patients. By statute, it was required to file a "public benefit-cost note showing [on a yearly basis] (A) the public benefits to be expected as a result of adoption of the proposed rule; and (B) the probable economic cost to persons who are required to comply with the rule." The Board's note stated that "[f]or each year . . . the public benefit anticipated . . . will be provision of a uniform standard for fair and reasonable fees . . . that should result in: (1) improved delivery and quality of health facility goods and services to claimants; and (2) reduced premiums for employers. . . ." The description of costs was that "public health facilities should experience impact on revenue resulting from [the rate ceiling, the facility's payment ratio, and administrative costs]." Rejecting the argument that the Board should have assigned monetary amounts to these propositions, the court held that the Board had substantially complied with the statute. Do you agree?

5.   *Regulatory flexibility in the states.* About half the states have adopted "regulatory flexibility" laws, according to the Small Business Administration, *www.sba.gov/advo/laws/law_modeleg.html*. One such law was at issue in *Unified Loans, Inc. v. Pettijohn*, 955 S.W.2d 649 (Tex. App. 1997). The statute provided that, before adopting a rule that "would

have an adverse economic effect on small businesses," an agency must prepare a statement analyzing the compliance costs of the rule for small businesses and comparing these costs with the compliance costs that large businesses would incur. In 1994, the state consumer credit commissioner promulgated rules that required pawnbrokers to meet minimum standards regarding matters such as insurance, record-keeping, and safes and alarm systems. The commissioner's impact statement was brief, asserting that the rule would have no effect on small businesses, because small pawnshops were already complying with these requirements or would not have to incur additional expenses in order to do so. The court reversed, observing that the record contained no evidence substantiating the commissioner's assertions. The court also said that the commissioner must publish the required analysis along with the notice of *proposed* rulemaking. This would enable interested persons to comment on the analysis and would induce the agency to take account of their concerns in adopting the final rule. Finally, the commissioner argued that he should not have to prepare the statement unless a proposed rule would have a *disproportionate* effect on small businesses as compared with larger ones. The court again disagreed, noting that the above-quoted statutory language did not contain that limitation. Do you agree?

6. *Problem.* The Madison Transportation Department (MTD) has statutory authority to adopt "such reasonable measures as are adequate to meet the need" for vehicle safety. Recently MTD officials noticed a rash of newspaper stories about fatal traffic collisions attributed to the inattention of drivers who were talking on cell telephones at the time of their accidents. Shortly afterwards, the agency proposed a rule that would prohibit any driver from using a handheld phone while operating a motor vehicle. The ban would be enforced by state police, like other traffic offenses. The MTD notice pointed out that a number of states have already imposed analogous restrictions. The agency also asserted that, according to studies it had reviewed, a driver's risk of an accident increases substantially while he or she is using a cell phone. Thus, according to the notice, the ban would save lives and reduce injuries and associated health care costs.

Keep in Touch (KIT), an industry group funded by wireless telephone companies, filed comments questioning the wisdom of the proposed rule. KIT submitted its own study, conducted by Grace. Her study suggested that the benefits of a ban on drivers' use of handheld cell phones would be low, because the risks that such drivers incur, though not nonexistent, are no higher than those incurred by drivers who use "hands-free" phones or engage in other behavior that society does not regulate, such as reading a map or tuning a radio. Grace also maintained that the ban would be widely ignored unless the state devoted substantial resources to enforcement. KIT urged the department to commission a cost-benefit analysis to study the proposed rule. Such an analysis would show, KIT predicted, that the asserted benefits of the rule (many of which would not be realized until years or decades in the future) would be outweighed by the costs of enforcement, not to mention the reduction in personal freedom and convenience that the ban would entail.

Larry is a state representative who sympathizes with KIT's views (and frequently makes cell phone calls from his car). He is drafting legislation to define the regulatory analysis responsibilities of the MTD in "significant rulemaking proceedings" (of which the pending cell phone proceeding would be one). At present, the Madison APA contains no provisions on regulatory analysis. Larry's bill would provide that in significant MTD rulemaking proceedings (a) the department must conduct a regulatory analysis, applying the standards in 2010 MSAPA § 305(c); (b) the department may not issue a rule unless it finds, pursuant to such a regulatory analysis, that the benefits of the rule will be commensurate with its costs; and (c) on judicial review, a court may set aside a rule if it finds that the department did not make a good faith effort to comply with the mandates of the new legislation. You are an aide to Larry. What advice will you give him about these proposed provisions? Must the agency conduct a CBA even without new legislation? Should the bill be amended? *Cf.* Robert W. Hahn & Patrick M. Dudley, *The Disconnect Between Law and Policy Analysis: A Case Study of Drivers and Cell Phones,*" 55 ADMIN. L. REV. 127 (2003).

§ 5.9   NEGOTIATED RULEMAKING

JEFFREY S. LUBBERS, A GUIDE TO FEDERAL AGENCY RULEMAKING
190–94 (5th ed. 2012)

In [the Negotiated Rulemaking Act of 1990 (NRA), now codified at 5 U.S.C. §§ 561–70,] Congress endorsed the use by agencies of an alternative procedure known as "negotiated rulemaking." This procedure, sometimes called "regulatory negotiation" or "reg-neg," has been used by a fair number of agencies to bring interested parties into the rule-drafting process at an early stage, under circumstances that foster cooperative efforts to achieve solutions to regulatory problems. Where successful, negotiated rulemaking can lead to better, more acceptable rules, based on a clearer understanding of the concerns of all affected interests. Negotiated rules may be easier to enforce and less likely to be challenged in litigation.

[In the ordinary rulemaking process, any] agency contacts with regulated parties or the general public while the agency is considering or drafting a proposed rule are usually informal and unstructured.

Typically, there is no opportunity for interchange of views among potentially affected parties, even where an agency chooses to conduct a hearing.

The dynamics of the rulemaking process tend to encourage interested parties to take extreme positions in their written and oral statements—in pre-proposal contacts as well as in comments on any published proposed rule. They may choose to withhold information that they view as damaging. A party may appear to put equal weight on every argument, giving the agency little clue as to the relative importance it places on the various issues. There is usually little willingness among commenters to recognize the legitimate viewpoints of others. The adversarial atmosphere often contributes to the expense and delay associated with regulatory proceedings, as parties try to position themselves for the expected litigation. What is lacking is an opportunity for the parties to exchange views and to focus on finding constructive, creative solutions to problems.

In negotiated rulemaking, the agency, with the assistance of one or more neutral advisers known as "convenors," assembles a committee of representatives of all affected interests to negotiate a proposed rule. The goal of the process is to reach consensus on a text that all parties can accept. The agency should be represented at the table by an official who is sufficiently senior to be able to speak authoritatively on behalf of the agency. Negotiating sessions, however, are chaired not by the agency representative, but by a neutral mediator or facilitator skilled in assisting in the resolution of multiparty disputes.

Negotiated rulemaking is clearly not suitable for all agency rulemaking. The Negotiated Rulemaking Act sets forth [in § 563(a)] several criteria to be considered when an agency determines whether to use reg-neg. These include (1) whether there are a limited number of identifiable interests—usually not more than 25, including any relevant government agencies—that will be significantly affected by the rule; (2) whether a balanced committee can be convened that can adequately represent the various interests and negotiate in good faith to reach a consensus on a proposed rule; (3) whether the negotiation process will not unreasonably delay issuance of the rule; (4) whether the agency has adequate resources to support the negotiating committee; and (5) whether the agency—to the maximum extent consistent with its legal obligations—will use a committee consensus as the basis for a proposed rule. . . .

In addition, there should be a number of diverse issues that participants can rank according to their own priorities, so that each of the participants may be able to find room for compromise on some of the issues as an agreement is sought. However, it is essential that the issues to be negotiated not require compromise of principles so fundamental to the parties that meaningful negotiations are impossible. Parties must indicate a willingness to negotiate in good faith, and no single interest should be able to dominate the negotiations.

The goal of the committee is to reach consensus on a draft rule. The word "consensus" is usually understood in this context to mean that each interest represented, including the agency, concurs in the result, unless all members of the committee agree at the outset to a different meaning. Negotiators try to reach a consensus through a process of evaluating their own priorities and making trade-offs to achieve an acceptable outcome on the issues of greatest importance to them. . . .

If consensus is achieved by the committee, the agency ordinarily would publish the draft rule based on that consensus in a notice of proposed rulemaking—and the agency would have committed itself in advance to doing so. Such a commitment is not an abdication of the agency's statutory responsibility, for there would not be consensus without the agency's concurrence in the committee's proposed rule. Even negotiations that result in less than full consensus on a draft rule can still be very useful to the agency by narrowing the issues in dispute, identifying information necessary to resolve issues, ranking priorities, and finding potentially acceptable solutions.

Negotiated rulemaking should be viewed as a supplement to the rulemaking provisions of the APA. This means that the negotiation sessions generally take place prior to issuance of the notice and the opportunity for the public to comment on a proposed rule. In some instances, negotiations may be appropriate at a later stage of the proceeding. But it should be emphasized that negotiated rulemaking does not in any way reduce the agency's obligations to follow the APA process, to produce a rule within its statutory authority, or to adequately explain the result.

WILLIAM FUNK, WHEN SMOKE GETS IN YOUR EYES: REGULATORY NEGOTIATION AND THE PUBLIC INTEREST— EPA's WOODSTOVE STANDARDS

18 ENVTL. L. 55 (1987)

Regulatory negotiation is a recent development in administrative law. Philip Harter provided its first real description and justification in [*Negotiating Regulations: A Cure for Malaise*, 71 GEO. L.J. 1 (1982)]. . . .

Since Harter's article, several agencies, including especially the Environmental Protection Agency (EPA), have experimented with negotiating proposed regulations according to Harter's formula, as reflected in the recommendations of the Administrative Conference of the United States. Assessments of those experiments have been uniformly positive, even where the regulatory negotiation failed to result in a proposed or final regulation. One of the most recent experiments resulted in an EPA proposed rule to establish emission limitations for residential woodstoves under the Clean Air Act.

It is the thesis of this Article that this proposed rule is not authorized by the Clean Air Act, and that the process of developing the rule by regulatory negotiation directly contributed to this unlawful proposal. Moreover, this Article concludes that the nature of regulatory negotiation has the tendency to obscure, if not pervert, the public interest to the benefit of private interests, and that the regulatory negotiation of the woodstove emission limitation is a case study of such a perversion.

. . . Under section 111 [of the Clean Air Act, the principal provision on which the woodstove standard purportedly rests], a "stationary source" is "any building, structure, facility, or installation which emits or may emit any air pollutant." . . . After the effective date of any standard of performance under this section, it is unlawful for "any owner or operator of any new source to operate such source in violation" of that standard. . . .

The prohibitions in the regulations run primarily to the manufacturers and retailers of woodstoves, not to the [residential] operators of the stoves. . . . There is some difficulty in fitting the proposed rule . . . to the statutory scheme. . . . [The] terms "building, structure, facility, or installation" [in section 111] are clearly not the terms one would choose to use to indicate a consumer product a person buys at a store, brings home, and uses there. . . . [Compounding the doubtful legality of the woodstove rule is] the fact that section 111 only applies to "owners or operators" of sources; there is no mention of manufacturers or importers of sources, unlike every other statutory scheme governing consumer products. . . .

[Also questionable] is the portion of the proposed rule which requires any woodstove sold meeting the applicable emission limits to have affixed to the stove a removable label that shows its estimated emissions, efficiency, and heat output data. This label . . . has nothing to do with pollution control but is an informative label that will enable consumers to make more informed choices concerning woodstove purchases. Nothing in section 111 would authorize such a label. . . .

In the absence of a regulatory negotiation, it is highly likely that a number of commenters would have objected to the particular method of regulating woodstoves under section 111, if not to the basic concept of their regulation under section 111. Unable to rely on their "inside" ability to achieve a regulation that would meet their substantive objections, commenters would have an interest in raising legal objections to the rule. The negotiation process, however, not only mutes legal objections, it does bring the parties in interest "inside" the substantive rulemaking process.

In the case of woodstoves, for example, it meant that manufacturers and environmentalists could negotiate which woodstoves would be regulated at what level according to what timetable.

. . . The Regulatory Impact Analysis . . . states unambiguously that "the stringency of the [standard] in terms of the maximum grams of emissions per hour was negotiated." In other words, the maximum emission rate is not something derived by scientific method, but rather derived through the relative power of the negotiating parties.

This is not to say that the scientific information or statistical methods described in the preamble to the proposed rule were irrelevant in the negotiations. To the contrary, data and statistical methods may provide negotiating power to one side or the other. But other matters, such as concessions or agreements on other features of the proposed rule, may also provide negotiating power to one side or the other. Knowing that the numerical limits were "negotiated," rather than determined solely on the basis of the data and methodology described in the preamble, we are left not knowing *what* role the data and methodology played, if any. . . .

The concept of regulatory negotiation stands [a rulemaking agency's traditional] role on its head, first, by reducing the agency to the level of a mere participant in the formulation of the rule, and second, by essentially denying that the agency has any responsibility beyond giving effect to the consensus achieved by the group. [While] the agency technically has the final decision, this power becomes theoretical at best where the agency has already agreed beforehand along with all the other participants to seek consensus in good faith, to support the consensus result, and in particular to publish as a proposed rule the rule developed by that consensus. . . .

This fundamental change in the role of the agency in the rulemaking process is mirrored by the fundamental change in the underlying theoretical justification for the eventual rule. As Harter admits: "[U]nder the traditional . . . process, the legitimacy of the rule rests on a resolution of complex factual materials and rational extrapolation from those facts, guided by the criteria of the statute. Under regulatory negotiation, however, the regulation's legitimacy would lie in the overall agreement of the parties." Stated another way, the parties to the rule are happy with it; therefore, it matters not whether the rule is rational or lawful. Discretion delegated to the agency by Congress is effectively exercised by the group of interested parties, constrained only by the need to obtain consensus. The law no longer directs or even necessarily constrains the outcome but has become merely a factor in the give-and-take necessary to achieve consensus. . . .

Reliance on the absence of disagreement as evidence of legitimacy for a regulation puts a premium on assuring that the negotiating group adequately represents all affected interests. There are, however, both practical and theoretical limitations on the number of interests that may be represented and the quality of representation each interest may obtain. Where the interest is strong enough to make itself known and felt, little difficulty arises—either that interest will be represented in the negotiation or the negotiation in the end will not likely be successful. More problematic is where the interest is not well defined, organized, or strong. . . . For example, in the woodstove negotiation, the Consumer Federation of America (CFA) was supposed to represent the interests of the consumer, but consumers, as the CFA would be the first to admit, are hardly a homogenous entity. The CFA may have represented the interests associated with the mentality of a *Consumers Reports* reader, but it did not appear to lobby on behalf of poor, rural folk for whom the rule will provide little benefit and perhaps significant burden. Moreover, the fact that these people do not comment on the proposed rule or challenge a final rule in court hardly establishes that the rule is fair and wise as to them.

. . . However, it is not the purpose of this Article to conclude that regulatory negotiation is necessarily bad and should be shot dead in its tracks. To the contrary, the practical benefits of regulatory negotiation cannot be gainsaid, and if they have not received much attention here, it is only because there are ample other sources. It is of no small moment when the professional defenders of the environment, the affected industry, and government entities can achieve consensus on how to deal with a particular source of pollution. Rather, it is the purpose of this Article to demonstrate that regulatory negotiation . . . fundamentally alters the dynamics of traditional administrative rulemaking from a search for the public interest, however imperfect that search may be, to a search for a consensus among private parties representing particular interests.

Only after one recognizes this fundamental change can one fully assess the advantages and disadvantages of regulatory negotiation as an alternative to traditional administrative rulemaking. Up to now, the debate over regulatory negotiation has revolved around its feasibility and methods to improve its "success" rate. Now, however, the debate should include the appropriateness of private interests determining the public values at stake in the rulemaking. In some cases the issues to be decided in the negotiation may be so bounded that any threat to public values disappears. In other cases the negotiation may claim as its subject matter issues which properly should be decided only by an agency.

NOTES AND QUESTIONS

1. *Legal context.* Obviously, the theory and practice of negotiated rulemaking draw directly upon the philosophy and techniques of the

alternative dispute resolution movement. (Recall the Administrative Dispute Resolution Act, discussed in § 4.1.3, which applies ADR techniques to agency *adjudication*.) As Funk mentions, the Administrative Conference provided much of the initial impetus for the development of negotiated rulemaking. Although regulatory negotiation was generally viewed as permissible even without specific authorizing legislation, Congress enacted the NRA in 1990 in order to encourage use of the technique and to standardize its procedures. At first the NRA was adopted on a temporary basis, but in 1996 Congress renewed it to continue indefinitely.

2. *Reg-neg in the states.* A number of states have enacted legislation similar to the NRA or have experimented more informally with regulatory negotiation. *See* Fla. Stat. § 120.54(d) (2010); Idaho Code Ann. § 67–5220 (1995); Mont. Code Ann. § 2–5–101 (2007); Neb. Rev. Stat. § 84–921 (2008); Okla. Stat. tit. 74, § 485(B) (2010); Tex. Gov't Code Ann. § 2008.001 (West 2008); Wash. Rev. Code § 34.05.310(2)(a) (2009); Ind. R. Ct. A.D.R. 1.1; N.Y. Exec. Order 20 § II ¶ 9 (Mar. 2008). The 2010 MSAPA also provides for negotiated rulemaking in § 303(b)–(c). The MSAPA provision recites that "[t]he agency shall consider whether to use [the consensus recommendation of a negotiated rulemaking committee] as the basis for a proposed rule under Section 304, but the agency is not required to propose or adopt the recommendation." § 303(c). No such language appears in the NRA or the state statutes just mentioned. Does the MSAPA language make a difference?

3. *Candidates for reg-neg.* Although success with negotiated rulemaking can serve to expedite the regulatory process by avoiding a court appeal, negotiations sometimes fail—in which case the net effect of the effort may be greater delay. Therefore, as the Lubbers reading emphasizes, an agency must exercise great care in its selection of issues that it will attempt to resolve through negotiation. Consider this example: In 1987 the Department of Transportation convened an advisory committee to negotiate issues of how airlines should accommodate passengers with disabilities. Among the matters on the agenda were: making aircraft restrooms more accessible to passengers who used wheelchairs; setting training requirements for airline employees on how to treat disabled passengers; and determining whether exit row seating, which normally is subject to special restrictions because of safety concerns, would be available to passengers who were blind. The negotiations were partly successful, but not entirely so. Why do you suppose that was? *See Despite Impasse, Parties Praise DOT's Non-discrimination Reg-neg*, 2 ADR REP. (BNA) 117 (1988).

4. *Criticisms.* Funk's article is accurate in its initial observation that participants in regulatory negotiation usually come away satisfied with the process. Nevertheless, he criticizes the process for subjecting rulemaking to inordinate influence by well-organized interest groups, to the detriment of the overall public interest and the rule of law. How valid is the contrast, in this regard, between negotiated rulemaking and the ordinary process of notice and comment rulemaking? Isn't the latter also somewhat political? To the extent that negotiated rulemaking is particularly vulnerable to the

tendencies Funk identifies, are these vices an acceptable price to pay for the virtues of reg-neg, as summarized by Lubbers? For a continuation of this debate, see Cary Coglianese, *Empirical Analysis and Administrative Law*, 2002 U. ILL. L. REV. 1111, 1131–36 (2002); Symposium, 46 DUKE L.J. 1255 (1997); Jody Freeman, *Collaborative Governance in the Administrative State*, 45 UCLA L. REV. 1 (1997).

5. *Judicial review.* One of the chief attractions of a successfully negotiated rule, from an agency's point of view, is that affected interests usually do not seek judicial review of it. Indeed, most negotiated rules (including the woodstove rule) have not been challenged in court. Occasionally, however, the process misfires and an appeal occurs. Should courts be unusually deferential when they review a negotiated rule? *See* Michael Herz, *Some Thoughts on Judicial Review and Collaborative Governance*, 2009 J. DISP. RESOL. 361. In federal practice, the NRA provides that "[a] rule which is the product of negotiated rulemaking and is subject to judicial review shall not be accorded any greater deference by a court than a rule which is the product of other rulemaking procedures." § 570. Does this mean that the agency must demonstrate to a court that it has made the same legal determinations, performed the same studies, and engaged in the same reasoning as if it had not used negotiated rulemaking? Or would that expectation make regulatory negotiation unworkable or meaningless? *See generally* Patricia M. Wald, *ADR and the Courts: An Update*, 46 DUKE L.J. 1445 (1997).

6. *"Reneging" in reg-neg.* Suppose an agency proposes a rule to the public that departs from the consensus reached earlier by a negotiated rulemaking committee. Has the agency negotiated in bad faith, and is there anything that the disappointed negotiator can do about it? According to Chief Judge Posner, the answers are "no" and "no." *USA Group Loan Services, Inc. v. Riley,* 82 F.3d 708, 714–15 (7th Cir. 1996):

> During the negotiations, an official of the Department of Education promised the servicers that the Department would abide by any consensus reached by them unless there were compelling reasons to depart. The propriety of such a promise may be questioned. It sounds like an abdication of regulatory authority to the regulated, the full burgeoning of the interest-group state, and the final confirmation of the "capture" theory of administrative regulation. . . .

> We have doubts about the propriety of the official's promise to abide by a consensus of the regulated industry, but we have no doubt that the Negotiated Rulemaking Act did not make the promise enforceable. . . . The practical effect of enforcing it would be to make the Act extinguish notice and comment rulemaking in all cases in which it was preceded by negotiated rulemaking; the comments would be irrelevant if the agency were already bound by promises that it had made to the industry. . . . The Act simply

creates a consultative process in advance of the more formal arms' length procedure of notice and comment rulemaking.

Do you agree with the court's "doubts about the propriety" of an agency's pledging that it will be strongly inclined to adopt whatever deal the negotiating committee endorses? Is that an "abdication of regulatory authority to the regulated"? On the other hand, even if an agency must remain open to changing the consensus agreement if it receives comments that demonstrate a need for revision, shouldn't the department at least have *proposed* the agreement in its notice of proposed rulemaking? If the courts are not going to forbid "bad faith" such as that of the department here, does an agency have any good reasons to adhere to an agreement it reaches during regulatory negotiation?

7. *Notice of variance.* If the agency does propose the consensus agreement as a proposed rule, but later finds itself inclined to adopt a different final rule, should it be expected to notify the participants to the agreement about this newfound intention? The D.C. Circuit has said no. *See City of Portland v. EPA*, 507 F.3d 706 (D.C. Cir. 2007): "[N]either the Negotiated Rulemaking Act nor any other statute we know of requires an agency to provide more detailed notice of possible changes in its draft rules just because they evolve from negotiated rulemaking. Indeed, adopting the cities' suggestion would make it easier for disappointed parties to overturn negotiated rules than non-negotiated rules, thus discouraging agencies from engaging in negotiated rulemaking—exactly the opposite of what Congress intended." Do you agree? If such notice is not required now, should the NRA be amended to require it?

8. *Waning.* The use of negotiated rulemaking remains relatively rare. Professor Funk believes the main reason is that "agencies are averse to losing control over the regulatory outcome for which they are responsible both legally and politically." William Funk, *Public Participation and Transparency in Administrative Law—Three Examples as an Object Lesson*, 61 ADMIN. L. REV. 171, 194 (spec. ed. 2009). Professor Lubbers has other explanations but agrees that the technique has not flourished as much as its early proponents foresaw. *See* Jeffrey S. Lubbers, *Achieving Policymaking Consensus: The (Unfortunate) Waning of Negotiated Rulemaking*, 49 S. TEX. L. REV. 987 (2008).

9. *Problem.* Under § 18 of the Federal Insecticide, Fungicide and Rodenticide Act (FIFRA), the EPA Administrator has authority to grant "emergency" exemptions from pesticide restrictions. An exemption allows farmers in a given area to make short-term use of a pesticide that is still undergoing testing for safety. Eligibility for an exemption turns in part on whether farmers will suffer "significant economic loss" if relief is denied. EPA and congressional committees became concerned that the agency's program for implementing this authority needed overhauling; grants of exemptions were increasing rapidly, threatening the integrity of the regulatory regime. The agency convened a negotiating committee to draft new rules. Four

environmental groups, four state organizations, four agricultural user groups, two manufacturers, the Department of Agriculture, and EPA were represented. After four months the participants arrived at a consensus agreement, and EPA published it as a proposed rule, inviting comments.

The American Farm Bureau Federation, one of the signatories to the consensus agreement, filed comments proposing a change in the proposal. The proposed rule stated that "significant economic loss" must be determined only in terms of decreased crop yield. Thus, for example, no exemption could be granted to resist an infestation that merely caused harmless spotting on apples. The Federation argued that significant economic loss should be determined in terms of overall profitability; this test would allow a different result in the apples example, because consumers might refuse to buy the fruit. The Federation contended that the agency's proposal would be ineffective, unfairly restrictive, and contrary to congressional intent.

EPA adopted its proposed rule without material change. In its statement of basis and purpose, the agency said in relevant part: "While the Federation's argument has some logical appeal in the abstract, the negotiating committee decided to use a crop-yield definition of economic loss. We believe it is in the public interest to adhere to that agreement, which enjoys broad support from affected interests. The committee concluded that the proposal will allow farmers to sustain reasonable profit margins, and we do not disagree." How should the court respond to this line of argument? (In real life, only the events described in the first paragraph above actually occurred; EPA adopted the committee's proposal as a final rule without controversy. 51 Fed. Reg. 1896 (1986).)

CHAPTER 6

POLICYMAKING ALTERNATIVES

■ ■ ■

Chapter 5 outlined the basic procedures used in rulemaking. It focused primarily on the notice and comment models prescribed in the federal and state APAs (supplemented in some instances by additional procedures, such as those prescribed in regulatory analysis statutes and executive orders). Important as it is, however, notice and comment rulemaking does not exist in a vacuum. Rather, it constitutes only one element in the overall enterprise of agency policymaking.

As they carry out their policymaking responsibilities, agencies have a number of procedural tools at their disposal, and many choices to make. Sometimes they can elect to adopt a rule without resorting to the procedural steps explained in the preceding chapter. Sometimes they can avoid rulemaking procedure by enunciating a new policy through case-by-case adjudication, in the manner of a common law court. They may decline to launch a new policymaking initiative if they prefer to devote their attention to other priorities. And sometimes they can decide to soften an existing policy by granting waivers from an otherwise applicable regulation. Although each of these choices involves significant elements of discretion, all are bounded by legal obligations, which are explored in this chapter.

§ 6.1   EXEMPTIONS FROM RULEMAKING PROCEDURE

§ 6.1.1 GOOD CAUSE EXEMPTIONS

Federal and state APAs contain exemptions providing that notice and comment proceedings may be omitted in particular circumstances for good cause. These exemptions provide some flexibility so that the need to observe usual rulemaking procedures can, in appropriate situations, be reconciled with the equally important need to conduct government administration in an expeditious, effective, and economical manner.

Read federal APA § 553(b)(B). It exempts rules from usual notice and comment procedures when it would be "unnecessary, impracticable, or contrary to the public interest" for the agency to follow them. The agency must make an explicit finding at the time of issuance that good cause exists and must give reasons to support that finding. Numerous court decisions have declared that the good cause exemptions from notice-and-comment procedure must be "narrowly construed and reluctantly countenanced." *See, e.g., Mack Trucks, Inc. v. EPA,* 682 F.3d 87, 93 (D.C. Cir. 2012); *United States v. Valverde,* 628 F.3d 1159, 1164 (9th Cir. 2010). Similarly, 1961 MSAPA § 3(b), adopted in many states, and 2010 MSAPA § 309 generally limit emergency rulemaking to cases involving "an imminent peril to the public health, safety, or welfare."

Despite this clear message in statutes and judicial case law, however, agencies do rely on the exemption with some frequency. A scholar who examined every issue of the *Federal Register* published during a six-month period found that agencies expressly invoked the exemption in twenty-five percent of the rules they issued. In other instances, he said, agencies appeared to rely on it by implication, so that the true figure might be closer to thirty-three percent. Juan J. Lavilla, *The Good Cause Exemption to Notice and Comment Rulemaking Requirements Under the Administrative Procedure Act,* 3 ADMIN. L.J. 317, 338–39 & n.86 (1989). "Although this figure would seem to be excessive," he added, "an examination of the actual cases where the clause is invoked does not reveal general misuse." *Id.* at 339–40. Over time the percentage of rules as to which agencies invoke good cause has remained about the same. *See* Gov't Accountability Office, *Federal Rulemaking: Agencies Could Take Additional Steps to Respond to Public Comments,* GAO–13–21, at 8, 15 (2012).

A separate provision in the APA, 5 U.S.C. § 553(d)(3), provides that for "good cause" an agency may dispense with the normal requirement that a rule may not become effective until thirty days after its issuance. The two exemptions are commonly invoked simultaneously, because an agency that is in a hurry to move forward with a rule often wishes to avoid both a comment period and a delay in effectiveness.

JIFRY v. FEDERAL AVIATION ADMINISTRATION
370 F.3d 1174 (D.C. Cir. 2004)

ROGERS, J.:

Petitions filed by two non-resident alien pilots challenge certain aviation regulations adopted in the wake of the September 11, 2001 terrorist attacks. From the establishment of the Transportation Security Administration ("TSA") in November 2001 to the promulgation of the challenged regulations in January 2003, aviation security has undergone a fundamental transformation. The pilots contend that the new procedures resulting in the revocation of their airman certificates issued by the Federal Aviation Administration ("FAA") violated the Administrative Procedure Act ("APA"). . . .

. . . The two pilots, Jifry and Zarie, are citizens of Saudi Arabia who have used their FAA certificates to pilot flights abroad, but have not operated Saudi Arabian Airlines flights to the United States in the past nine and four years, respectively. On August 14, 2002, the TSA sent letters to the FAA requesting that Captain Jifry and Captain Zarie have their airman certificates revoked, stating that "based upon information available to us," they presented "a security risk to civil aviation or national security." The FAA notified Jifry and Zarie by letters of August 20, 2002, that their airman certificates would be revoked because the Acting Under Secretary of Transportation for Security . . . had determined that they presented risks to aviation or national security. The FAA revoked the pilots' certificates, and the pilots appealed the revocations to the National Transportation Safety Board ("NTSB"). An administrative law judge ("ALJ") held a telephonic pre-hearing conference on January 17, 2003, and ordered that the FAA and the TSA provide a privilege log and that depositions of key witnesses take place by mid-February.

A week later, on January 24, 2003, the FAA dismissed the revocation actions against Jifry and Zarie, and in conjunction with the TSA, published, without notice and comment, new regulations governing the suspension and revocation of airman certificates for security reasons. The new FAA regulation provides for automatic suspension by the FAA of airman certificates upon written notification from the TSA that the pilot poses a security threat and, therefore, is not eligible to hold an airman certificate. . . . On January 24, 2003, the TSA also served an Initial Notice of Threat Assessment designating Jifry and Zarie as security threats, and the FAA suspended their certificates. . . .

. . . The pilots contend that the regulations of January 2003 are invalid because they were unlawfully promulgated without notice and comment. . . . They maintain that the "good cause" exception does not apply. . . .

Generally, the "good cause" exception to notice and comment rulemaking is to be "narrowly construed and only reluctantly countenanced." The exception excuses notice and comment in emergency situations, or where delay could result in serious harm. The latter circumstance is applicable here in examining the TSA's determination that "the use of notice and comment prior to issuance of the [January 2003 regulations] could delay the ability of TSA and the FAA to take effective action to keep persons found by TSA to pose a security threat from holding an airman certificate," and was "necessary to prevent a possible imminent hazard to aircraft, persons, and property within the United States."

The pilots contend that the "good cause" exception does not apply because the FAA already had unlimited power to revoke a certificate immediately if it believed an airman to be a security risk, and the TSA was already authorized to make security assessments under 49 U.S.C. § 114(f). While true, the pilots fail to acknowledge that at the time the challenged regulations were adopted, the FAA's power to suspend or revoke certificates was permissive only. . . . As the respondents explain, the January 2003 regulations mandated a "streamlined process" by which an individual's pilot certificate would be automatically suspended or revoked by the FAA upon notification by the TSA that a pilot posed a security threat. The TSA and FAA deemed such regulations necessary "in order to minimize security threats and potential security vulnerabilities to the fullest extent possible." Given the respondents' legitimate concern over the threat of further terrorist acts involving aircraft in the aftermath of September 11, 2001, agencies had "good cause" for not offering advance public participation.

NOTES AND QUESTIONS

1.   *Urgent rules.* Little if any distinction is drawn between the "impracticable" and "contrary to the public interest" criteria in the good cause exemption. Both terms are construed as coming into play when an agency has an overriding need to take immediate action. Rules that are designed to meet a serious health or safety problem, or some other risk of irreparable harm, often qualify for exemption on this basis. *See, e.g., Hawaii Helicopter Operators Ass'n v. FAA,* 51 F.3d 212, 214 (9th Cir. 1995) (safety rule designed to counteract growing number of helicopter accidents); *Northern Arapahoe Tribe v. Hodel,* 808 F.2d 741, 750–52 (10th Cir. 1987) (urgent need for hunting regulations where season had begun and herds could dwindle to extinction). Yet, pursuant to the policy of narrow construction of the exemption, courts sometimes refuse to accept an agency's assertion of urgency at face value. *See Action on Smoking and Health v. CAB,* 713 F.2d 795, 801–02 (D.C. Cir. 1983) (fact that existing rule is confusing and difficult to enforce does not furnish good cause to replace it without prior notice).

Another line of cases has found good cause on the basis of a statutory deadline for the issuance of rules. *See, e.g., Methodist Hospital of Sacramento v. Shalala,* 38 F.3d 1225 (D.C. Cir. 1994). This rationale is unlikely to succeed, however, if the court believes that the agency itself was dilatory and brought the deadline pressure on itself. *Council of Southern Mountains, Inc. v. Donovan,* 653 F.2d 573, 581 (D.C. Cir. 1981).

2.   *Terrorism cases.* Does the fact that the rule in *Jifry* was adopted sixteen months after 9/11 cast doubt on the court's holding that the FAA had good cause to dispense with notice and comment? Compare *Jewish Community Action v. Comm'r of Public Safety,* 657 N.W.2d 604 (Minn. 2003). Minnesota's good cause provision exempts rules that are intended to address a "serious and immediate threat to the public health, safety, or welfare," In

this case the state department of public safety adopted, without notice and comment, a rule that would tighten the requirements for proof of identity on applications for drivers' licenses. For example, applicants would need to submit proof of lawful presence in the United States and a full-face, unobscured photo (despite any religious objections to being photographed). The agency explained that the restrictions would impede terrorists from blending into society and planning sabotage schemes from the inside. The court held, however, that the department had not adequately demonstrated that public rulemaking proceedings would be contrary to the public interest. To make this showing, the court concluded, the department must "reasonably quantify the delay that will occur if formal rulemaking is undertaken; show with reasonable particularity how the public interest will likely be harmed by that delay; and demonstrate specifically how the exempt rulemaking procedure will better serve the public interest." Is this requiring too much?

3. *State law. Jewish Community Action* tacitly raises the question of whether the precise wording of a state's rulemaking exemption for urgent rules makes any difference in outcomes. Section 3(b) of the 1961 MSAPA, adopted in many states, provides:

> If an agency finds that an imminent peril to the public health, safety, or welfare requires adoption of a rule upon fewer than 20 days' notice and states in writing its reasons for that finding, it may proceed without prior notice or hearing or upon any abbreviated notice and hearing that it finds practicable, to adopt an emergency rule.

Section 3–108(a) of the 1981 MSAPA embraced the "impracticable, unnecessary, or contrary to the public interest" language of the federal APA, but the 2010 MSAPA reverts to the language of the 1961 Act. *See* 2010 MSAPA § 309. It has been argued that this return to the older language was intended to express a preference for a relatively narrow exemption for emergency rulemaking. *See* Babette E.L. Boliek, *Agencies in Crisis? An Examination of State and Federal Agency Emergency Powers*, 81 FORDHAM L. REV. 3338, 3375–78 (2013). The 2010 Act adds, however, that threatened loss of federal funding for an agency program qualifies as a justification for emergency rulemaking. Statutes in some eighteen states contain a similar provision on compliance with federal mandates. *Id.* at 3386 n.265.

4. *Interim-final rules.* Agencies that adopt a rule in reliance on the "impracticable" or "public interest" prongs of the good cause exemption usually request comments on the rule *after* it becomes effective. Such rules are often called "interim-final" rules, because they are both interim (they will be reconsidered and perhaps revised or replaced in light of the comments received) and final (they go into effect immediately). The Administrative Conference of the United States has recommended that the interim-final technique be used in connection with all rules expedited under the "impracticable" or "public interest" tests. ACUS Recommendation 95–4, 60 Fed. Reg. 43,110 (1995), and agencies now routinely do so. *See* Michael

Asimow, *Interim–Final Rules: Making Haste Slowly*, 51 ADMIN. L. REV. 703, 712–15 (1999).

In a survey of numerous interim-final rules, Asimow found that nearly half remained unrevised after three years' time. *Id.* at 736–37. In that regard, consider § 3(b) of the 1961 MSAPA, which provides that rules issued on the basis of its good cause exemption "may be effective for a period of not longer than 120 days [renewable once for a period not exceeding ___ days]," although the subsequent adoption of an identical rule through the usual notice-and-comment procedures is not precluded. A similar time limit appears in 2010 MSAPA § 309 and in the laws of most states. Boliek, *supra*, at 3345. Should a 120-day limit on the shelf life of an interim-final rule be adopted at the federal level? *See* Asimow, *supra*, at 738–40.

Finally, suppose an agency adopts an interim-final rule, and then, upon receiving and considering public comments, adopts a similar rule to last indefinitely. Later a court finds that the interim-final rule failed to qualify under the APA's good cause exemption because the agency failed to demonstrate exigent circumstances. In this situation, some cases have invalidated not only the interim-final rule, but also the final one. *See, e.g., New Jersey v. USEPA*, 626 F.2d 1038, 1049–50 (D.C. Cir. 1980). These cases have expressed mistrust of the post-promulgation comment process, because of doubts "that persons would bother to submit their views or that the [agency] would seriously consider their suggestions after the regulations are a *fait accompli.*" *Id. But see Federal Express Corp. v. Mineta*, 373 F.3d 112 (D.C. Cir. 2004). The *Federal Express* case upheld such a final rule, noting that the agency had invited and taken seriously the post-adoption comments it received on the interim-final rule. The ACUS recommendation encourages courts not to reject a final rule simply because it has supplanted an improperly adopted interim-final rule. Do you agree?

5. *"Unnecessary" rulemaking procedures.* When are usual rulemaking procedures "unnecessary" within the meaning of the federal APA good cause exemption? The legislative history of the federal act indicates that the exemption should apply when comment is "unnecessary so far as the public is concerned, as would be the case if a minor or merely technical amendment in which the public is not particularly interested were involved." *APA Legislative History*, S. Doc. No. 79–248, at 200 (1946) (Senate report); *id.* at 248 (House report). An example would be a rule that makes a "technical correction" by reinstating a rule that was earlier dropped by mistake in a recodification of an agency's regulations. *United States v. Sutton*, 795 F.2d 1040, 1053–54 (Temp. Emer. Ct. App. 1986). *Sutton* is one of the very few cases upholding the invocation of this exemption. Why do you suppose there are so few? Another example is a repeal of Coast Guard regulations that had become meaningless because of the destruction of the bridge to which they referred. 52 Fed. Reg. 670 (1987).

Public comment is also considered "unnecessary" when the agency has absolutely no discretion about the contents of its rule, as where its task is merely to make a mathematical calculation or ascertain an objective fact. Since nothing the public might say could affect the rule, the agency has good cause to forego a comment period.

A third situation in which the exemption has been invoked grew out of the EPA's approval, without notice and comment proceedings, of implementation plans tendered by state governments under the Clean Air Act. Two circuits held that APA public procedures were "unnecessary," because EPA was acting under a congressional deadline and the details of the plans had all been aired during proceedings at the state level. *Duquesne Light Co. v. EPA,* 481 F.2d 1 (3d Cir. 1973), *vacated on other grounds,* 427 U.S. 902 (1976); *Appalachian Power Co. v. EPA,* 477 F.2d 495 (4th Cir. 1973). Do you agree with this analysis? What if there had been no statutory deadline? Ellen R. Jordan, *The Administrative Procedure Act's "Good Cause" Exemption,* 36 ADMIN. L. REV. 113, 132–33 (1984) (questioning reasoning of these cases).

6. *Direct final rules.* ACUS has recommended that when an agency plans to rely on the "unnecessary" prong of the good cause exemption, it should issue its rule using "direct final rulemaking." *See* ACUS Recommendation 95–4, *supra*; Ronald M. Levin, *Direct Final Rulemaking,* 64 GEO. WASH. L. REV. 1 (1995). Direct final rulemaking is a streamlined variation on the normal § 553 procedure. Agencies use it for issuing rules that they consider totally noncontroversial. Under this procedure, the agency publishes the rule and announces that if no adverse comment is received within a specified time period, the rule will become effective as of a specified later date. But if even a single adverse comment is received, the agency withdraws the rule and republishes it as a proposed rule under the normal notice-and-comment procedure. For example, the Clean Air Act state implementation plans mentioned in the previous note are now routinely adopted through direct final rulemaking; most survive the process with no controversy. Moreover, the Agriculture Department used this technique to authorize importation of meat products from the Czech Republic (rather than from "Czechoslovakia," as under the prior rule) and to update its technical standards for scales used for weighing grain. *Id.* at 4, 7. The technique has also made headway at the state level. *See* Va. Code Ann. § 2.2–4012.1. The 2010 MSAPA provides for direct final rulemaking and makes it the exclusive means by which an agency can expedite a rule that it expects will be noncontroversial. § 310.

Would it be going too far to say that when an agency succeeds in issuing a rule through this technique, the rule should automatically be deemed to have satisfied the "good cause" exemption? Why might an agency choose to use the "direct final rulemaking" device instead of simply adopting the rule without any public involvement, as the "unnecessary" exemption permits?

7. *Immediate effectiveness.* As we saw in § 5.7, the federal APA provides that an agency usually must allow regulated parties thirty days' preparation time before a final rule goes into effect, but the agency may

shorten or eliminate that waiting period if it can establish "good cause" for doing so. 5 U.S.C. § 553(d)(3). Like the § 553(b)(B) good cause exemption, this provision is intended to accommodate situations in which the government has urgent reasons to act quickly. Again, however, courts sometimes respond skeptically to government pleas of urgency.

An example of this skepticism is *United States v. Gavrilovic,* 551 F.2d 1099 (8th Cir. 1977), in which the Drug Enforcement Agency issued a rule classifying mecloqualone as a Schedule I drug (the most strictly controlled category) and made the rule immediately effective, citing the dangers of the drug and the congressional desire for preventive controls. Defendants, who were manufacturing the drug in a warehouse disguised as a T-shirt company, were arrested 21 days later. Ultimately, the court overturned their conviction, because the DEA had not shown good cause for making the regulation effective in fewer than 30 days. The court said that the government's haste in promulgating the rule had been directly motivated by a desire to suppress the activities of these defendants. Yet, the court continued, the government did not need the Schedule I classification for that purpose: these defendants were not registered as drug manufacturers, so their operations could have been civilly enjoined immediately. The court said that the government's burden of justification under § 553(d)(3) is heavy when its rule creates criminal liability for previously lawful conduct. Was *Gavrilovic* correctly decided?

8.   *Problem.* A child who came to be known as "Baby Doe" was born with Down syndrome as well as a blockage in his digestive tract. His parents refused to consent to surgery to correct the blockage, and the child died a few days later. The incident gave rise to nationwide controversy about the ethics of withholding life-sustaining medical treatment from newborn infants with severe physical or mental defects.

About a year later, the Secretary of Health and Human Services (HHS) promulgated an interim-final rule to address the issues in the Baby Doe incident. Hospitals were directed to post conspicuous notices declaring that discriminatory denial of food or care to handicapped infants violated federal law (a reference to the Rehabilitation Act of 1973). The notices invited anyone with knowledge of such discrimination to call a toll-free "hotline" at HHS to report the violation. Hospitals were also directed to provide access to their records and facilities to officials investigating alleged discrimination of the "Baby Doe" variety. Access would have to be provided outside of normal business hours if HHS officials deemed such access necessary to protect the life or health of a handicapped infant.

Explaining her failure to allow prior notice and comment on the rule, the Secretary noted that investigators already had authority to obtain access to hospital records and facilities. The extension of this authority to compulsory access outside of normal business hours was a "minor technical change and necessary to meet emergency situations." More generally, she said, "[a]ll modifications made by the interim final rule are necessary to protect life from imminent harm. Any delay would leave lives at risk." The regulation was set to go into effect in fifteen days, which the Secretary estimated was the minimum time needed to set up the hotline apparatus.

After the comment period, the Secretary issued a final rule that was essentially the same as the previous rule. Was the interim-final rule procedurally valid? How about the final rule? *See American Academy of Pediatrics v. Heckler,* 561 F. Supp. 395 (D.D.C. 1983).

§ 6.1.2 EXEMPTED SUBJECT MATTER

Both federal and state APAs provide categorical exemptions from the usual notice-and-comment requirements for rules relating to certain governmental functions. Unlike the good cause exemptions, discussed in the preceding section, the categorical exemptions are not based upon an evaluation of the particular circumstances surrounding an individual rulemaking. Instead, they represent a generalized judgment that *all* rules falling into the defined categories should be exempt, regardless of individual circumstances.

The policy of narrow construction of rulemaking exemptions also applies to these provisions, at least at the federal level. Indeed, that policy is bolstered by indications in the legislative history of the APA that these exemptions apply only " 'to the extent' that the excepted subject matter is clearly and directly involved." *APA Legislative History,* S. Doc. No. 79–248, at 257 (1946) (House committee report). Moreover, these exemptions are inapplicable to the extent other law requires an agency to follow usual rulemaking procedures for any of the rules within the excepted categories. Even so, many observers believe that some of the exemptions are still too broad and should be repealed or substantially narrowed by legislative action.

NOTES AND QUESTIONS

1.   *Proprietary matters.* Federal APA § 553(a)(2) excludes rules relating to "public property, loans, grants, benefits, or contracts" from all of the provisions of § 553, including notice and comment procedure as well as the requirements for deferred effective date and the right to petition. Consider some of the activities that can potentially come within the broad sweep of this exemption: the sale or lease of public lands or of mineral, timber, or grazing rights in such lands; the use of national forests and national parks; loans to local government for urban mass transportation systems, small business loans, disaster loans, and student loans; grants-in-aid programs; pensions, social security old age and disability payments, and such welfare programs as food stamps; and government contracts for the procurement of land, goods, or services, and for construction of any kind. The exemption means that, in all of these areas, affected people have no right under the APA to influence the

contents of agency rules. It also means that agencies covered by the exemption may become out of touch with public needs and desires.

The exemption is apparently an outgrowth of the right-privilege distinction, which in recent decades has been rejected in due process law. *See* § 2.2.1 N.1. The Administrative Conference has recommended that the proprietary matters exemption should be repealed. *See* ACUS Recommendation 69–8, 38 Fed. Reg. 19,782 (1969). This recommendation was based on Arthur Earl Bonfield, *Public Participation in Federal Rulemaking Relating to Public Property, Loans, Grants, Benefits, or Contracts*, 118 U. PA. L. REV. 540 (1970).

2. *Waiver of exemptions.* In its recommendation opposing the proprietary matters exemption, ACUS called on agencies to utilize rulemaking procedures in these areas without awaiting a legislative command to do so. Numerous agencies have followed this advice by issuing regulations waiving any reliance on the exemption.

When an agency adopts a procedural rule that commits it to follow § 553 procedure, despite a statutory exemption, it is required to conform to its own rule. *See Alcaraz v. Block,* 746 F.2d 593, 611 (9th Cir. 1984); *Rodway v. USDA,* 514 F.2d 809, 813–14 (D.C. Cir. 1975). Should a similar requirement apply to an agency that has not formally adopted such a rule but does routinely provide notice and comment in exempt situations? *See Malek-Marzban v. INS,* 653 F.2d 113, 116 (4th Cir. 1981) (no).

In 2013 the Department of Agriculture (USDA) rescinded its rule that had waived reliance on the proprietary matters exemption. It explained that the rulemaking process now takes longer than it did when the waiver was first adopted. Often the delay results in little benefit, because many rules attract little public interest. USDA also emphasized that Congress had never rescinded the exemption, despite ACUS's longstanding recommendation. 78 Fed. Reg. 33,045 and 64,194 (2013). Are these reasons persuasive?

3. *Proprietary matters in state law.* The 1981 MSAPA contained no exemption with the broad scope of federal APA § 553(a)(2), but it did contain narrower exemptions for rules that, for example, "establishe[d] specific prices to be charged for particular goods or services sold by an agency" or that concerned "care of agency owned or operated facilities." § 3–116(3)–(5). The 2010 MSAPA, however, completely eliminates proprietary exemptions.

4. *Agency management and personnel.* Under federal APA § 553(a)(2), rules "relating to agency management or personnel" are excepted from all rulemaking requirements. Although this exemption is codified in the same sentence of the APA as the proprietary matters exemption, ACUS did *not* call for its repeal. Nevertheless, the scope of the exemption is uncertain. The legislative history of the APA contains indications that the exemption should not apply to rules that have a substantial effect on persons outside of the national government. Indeed, some case law reflects that assumption. Thus, for example, a rule that prohibited agencies from removing administrative

law judges from pending cases by reassigning them to other duties was not exempt, because it implicated "not only the rights of an individual ALJ being removed, but also the broader interest of the public in having private rights adjudicated by persons who have some independence from the agency opposing them." *Tunik v. MSPB*, 407 F.3d 1326 (Fed. Cir. 2005).

But another court reached a contrasting result in *Stewart v. Smith*, 673 F.2d 485, 496–500 (D.C. Cir. 1982). That case involved a rule by which the Bureau of Prisons announced that it would refuse to consider persons over thirty-four years of age for employment within correctional facilities. (According to the court, a statutory exception to the age discrimination laws permitted such a policy.) The court held, 2–1, that § 553 procedures were not required, because of the agency management and personnel exemption. Do you agree with the procedural holding?

In practice, the effect of the federal APA personnel exemption has been reduced somewhat by other statutes. The Federal Civil Service Reform Act of 1978, for example, requires the Office of Personnel Management to follow notice and comment procedures in formulating government-wide personnel rules unless they are "temporary in nature and . . . necessary to be implemented expeditiously as the result of an emergency." 5 U.S.C. §§ 1103(b)(3), 1105.

The 2010 MSAPA effectively adopts the *Tunik* analysis: it excludes from the definition of rule or guidance document a statement that "concerns only the internal management of an agency and which does not affect private rights or procedures available to the public. §§ 102(14), 102(30)(A). A similarly worded exemption is found in § 1(7)(A) of the 1961 MSAPA and in the acts of many states. *See Evans v. State*, 914 A.2d 25, 77–80 (Md. 2006) (manual prescribing lethal injection methods did not fit within that exemption).

5. *Military and foreign affairs functions.* Federal APA § 553(a)(1) exempts a rule from all rulemaking procedures "to the extent there is involved . . . a military or foreign affairs function of the United States." Like the proprietary matters exemption, this provision seems much broader than necessary. The Administrative Conference has proposed that Congress should narrow it. *See* ACUS Recommendation 73–5, 39 Fed. Reg. 4847 (1974); Arthur Earl Bonfield, *Military and Foreign Affairs Function Rulemaking Under the APA*," 71 MICH. L. REV. 221 (1972). Again, nonstatutory developments have made the exemption less influential than it might be. The Department of Defense has established a general policy favoring notice and comment procedures in the development of rules that have a direct or substantial effect on the public and do not involve classified information. DOD Administrative Instruction No. 102, § E3.2 (2006).

Meanwhile, agencies and courts have had to work out the boundaries of the existing exemption. Some applications are relatively straightforward, as with regulations implementing international trade agreements. *See Int'l Bhd. of Teamsters v. Pena,* 17 F.3d 1478 (D.C. Cir. 1994); *American Ass'n of*

Exporters & Importers v. United States, 751 F.2d 1239, 1249 (Fed. Cir. 1985). In *Independent Guard Ass'n v. O'Leary,* 57 F.3d 766 (9th Cir. 1995), amended, 69 F.3d 1038 (9th Cir. 1995), however, the court held that the exemption did *not* apply to a rule governing drug abuse by armed guards at a site at which the Department of Energy researched, produced, and tested nuclear explosive devices for the military. Wackenhut, a private contractor, hired and supervised the guards. The rule provided for random drug testing and permanent disqualification from duty for any employee who had ever used hallucinogens. The court said that DOE, although a "civilian" agency, does perform some "military functions" to which the rulemaking exemption could apply. Nevertheless:

> The legislative history and relevant case law direct that exceptions to the APA be narrowly construed, and that the exception can be invoked only where the activities being regulated directly involve a military function. If the Secretary's position were adopted, and contractor support activities held to be within the scope of the military function exception, maintenance staff, custodial help, food service workers and even window washers could find their undoubtedly necessary support tasks swept within the exception's ambit, and DOE regulations affecting their employment exempt from notice and comment. Neither the statute, nor common sense, requires such a result.

> We do not mean to imply that the military function exception can never apply to a contractor's services. Indeed, at argument IGAN conceded that contractor employees could perform a military function within the meaning of the APA. For example, if they were making military weapons, they might well be performing such a function. The record shows that the guards employed and supervised by Wackenhut were performing duties similar to those performed by civilian security guards everywhere. They were no more performing a "military function" than civilian contract guards employed to guard judges are performing a "judicial function." The exemption should not be stretched to encompass civilian support services.

6.   *Problem.* Suppose that the rule in *Independent Guard Ass'n* had barred civilian guards from using hallucinogens while serving on duty, or within twenty-four hours of such service. Would it be exempted from notice and comment obligations by the military function exemption? By the agency management and personnel exemption?

§ 6.1.3 PROCEDURAL RULES

"Rules of agency organization, procedure, or practice" are exempted from usual notice and comment procedures by federal APA § 553(b)(A). There is no similar exemption for such rules in the MSAPAs or in state APAs. A constant problem in the law is to distinguish "procedure" from "substance." Nevertheless, such a distinction must be drawn under this exemption.

PUBLIC CITIZEN V. DEPARTMENT OF STATE
276 F.3d 634 (D.C. Cir. 2002)

TATEL, J.:

[This case arose out of Public Citizen's request for various State Department records, including documents describing the department's current system for managing and archiving word processing files and e-mail messages.]

When the State Department responds to Freedom of Information Act requests, it generally declines to search for documents produced after the date of the requester's letter. Challenging this "date-of-request cutoff" policy, appellant claims that the Department promulgated it without notice and opportunity to comment as required by the Administrative Procedure Act. . . .

. . . The Department responds that its cut-off policy is procedural and thus covered by the APA's exemption from notice and comment for "rules of agency organization, procedure, or practice," 5 U.S.C. § 553(b)(3)(A). According to Public Citizen, the cut-off policy cannot be considered procedural because it "substantially . . . affects rights" by "needlessly multiplying the number of FOIA requests that must be submitted to obtain access to records." We have, however, characterized agency rules as procedural even where their effects were far harsher than the Department's date-of-request cut-off policy. For example, . . . we found an agency rule establishing a cut-off date for the filing of radio license applications to be procedural even though the failure to observe the rule cost appellants a radio broadcast license. *Ranger v. FCC*, 294 F.2d 240 (D.C. Cir. 1961).

As we recognized in *American Hospital Ass'n v. Bowen*, 834 F.2d 1037, 1047 (D.C. Cir. 1987), over time, our circuit in applying the 553 exemption for procedural rules has gradually shifted focus from asking whether a given procedure has a substantial impact on parties to inquiring more broadly whether the agency action encodes a substantive value judgment. This "gradual move," we noted, "reflects a candid recognition that even unambiguously procedural measures affect parties to some degree." *Id.* More recently, in *JEM Broadcasting Co. v. FCC*, we found that FCC "hard look rules," which required the dismissal of flawed license applications without leave to amend, were procedural despite their sometimes harsh effects. 22 F.3d 320 (D.C. Cir. 1994). In doing so, we rejected the argument that the rules encoded substantive value judgments because they valued applications without errors over those with minor errors. Clarifying the *American Hospital* standard, we held that in referring to "value judgments" in that case, we had not intended to include "judgments about what mechanics and processes are most efficient" because to do so would "threaten[ ] to swallow the procedural exception to notice and comment, for agency housekeeping rules often embody [such] judgments."

Because the Department's cut-off policy applies to all FOIA requests, making no distinction between requests on the basis of subject matter, it clearly encodes no "substantive value judgment." To be sure, the policy does represent a "judgment" that a date-of-request cut-off promotes the efficient processing of FOIA requests, but a "judgment about procedural efficiency . . . cannot convert a procedural rule into a substantive one." *James V. Hurson Assocs., Inc. v. Glickman*, 229 F.3d 277, 282 (D.C. Cir. 2000). Consequently, we agree with the district court that the Department's cutoff policy represents a prototypical procedural rule properly promulgated without notice and comment.

[The court went on to hold, however, that the cut-off policy was unreasonable on the merits, because it unnecessarily curtailed requesters' FOIA rights. The court said that the Department could at least have extended its searches for disclosable documents up through the date on which it actually conducted the search, as opposed to the date on which the request was submitted.]

NOTES AND QUESTIONS

1.   *Substance and procedure—rationale.* State APAs do not exempt procedural rules from notice and comment procedures. Why does the federal APA do so? Suppose, for example, that an agency publishes a new set of practice rules providing for discovery, adversary hearings, administrative appeals, etc., in civil penalty actions. *Cf. Air Transport Ass'n v. Dep't of Transp.*, 900 F.2d 369 (D.C. Cir. 1990), *remanded,* 498 U.S. 1077 (1991), *vacated as moot,* 933 F.2d 1043 (D.C. Cir. 1991). Assuming that these are "procedural rules," why should an agency be permitted to issue them without notice and comment? The exemption has been variously explained as reflecting "a congressional judgment that such rules, because they do not directly guide public conduct, do not merit the administrative burdens of public input proceedings," *United States Dep't of Labor v. Kast Metals Corp.*, 744 F.2d 1145 (5th Cir. 1984), or as based on an agency's need for "latitude in organizing [its] internal operations." *Batterton v. Marshall*, 648 F.2d 694 (D.C. Cir. 1980). Are these satisfactory answers?

2.   *Competing tests.* As the *Public Citizen* opinion notes, the case law delimiting the scope of the procedural rule exemption has not been uniform. Judicial opinions applying a "substantial impact" criterion have not entirely disappeared. *See, e.g., Phillips Petroleum Co. v. Johnson*, 22 F.3d 616 (5th Cir. 1994). As between that test and the "encodes a substantive value judgment" test, which is preferable? Did the court in *Public Citizen* apply the

latter test persuasively? Couldn't it be argued that the State Department rule did rest on a "substantive value judgment" about requesters' disclosure rights?

3. *ACUS recommendation.* The Administrative Conference recommended that the procedural rule exemption should be construed to apply to a rule "when it both (a) relates solely to agency methods of internal operations or of interacting with regulated parties or the public, and (b) does not (i) significantly affect conduct, activity, or a substantive interest that is the subject of agency jurisdiction, or (ii) affect the standards for eligibility for a government program." ACUS Recommendation 92–1, 57 Fed. Reg. 30,102 (1992); *see also* Jeffrey S. Lubbers & Nancy G. Miller, *The APA Procedural Rule Exemption: Looking for a Way to Clear the Air*, 6 ADMIN. L.J. AM. U. 481 (1992) (the article on which the recommendation was based). Would this formulation be an improvement on the case-law tests discussed in the principal case? How should *JEM Broadcasting* and *Public Citizen* be decided under the ACUS test?

4. *Enforcement.* A number of cases applying the procedural rule exemption have involved documents in which an agency maps out an enforcement plan. For example, in the *American Hospital* decision cited in the principal case, the Department of Health and Human Services published a seventy-page manual of instructions for peer review organizations (PROs) in the Medicare program. The PROs reviewed hospitals' decisions regarding admission of patients in order to curb excessive reimbursements. The manual told PROs to pay particular attention to admissions for certain types of medical care, including cardiac pacemaker implantations and other invasive procedures where a pattern of abuse had been identified. Rejecting a claim that HHS should have issued the manual using the rulemaking process, the court deemed the manual to be a procedural rule: "This is not a case in which HHS has urged its reviewing agents to utilize a different standard of review in specified medical areas; rather, it asks only that they examine a greater share of operations in given medical areas." Was the case correctly decided? Didn't the manual rest on the agency's "substantive value judgment" in favor of preventing excessive reimbursements?

5. *Problem.* The Occupational Safety and Health Administration adopted, without notice and comment, a directive setting forth a "Cooperative Compliance Program" (CCP). Under this initiative, workplaces with the worst safety records would be targeted for inspections, but OSHA would forego the inspection for any employer that enrolled in a "comprehensive safety and health program." Employers would agree to conduct their own inspections at regular intervals, to investigate "near-miss" incidents, and maintain grievance procedures for their employees. They also would agree to adhere to a list of safety recommendations approved by OSHA, including best-practices recommendations issued by industry organizations and suppliers. OSHA intended the CCP to be a creative experiment in "cooperative governance," whereby employers would have a choice between traditional command-and-

control enforcement and a cooperative partnership relationship with the agency.

The Chamber of Commerce sues for a declaration that the directive was unlawfully adopted without public rulemaking proceedings. It contends that the CCP improperly uses the threat of burdensome inspections to induce employers to observe higher safety standards than OSHA has the budgetary resources, or the evidence, to impose through the regular rulemaking process. OSHA, however, contends that the directive was validly adopted as a procedural rule and thus was exempt from the requirements of APA § 553. Who should prevail in this case? *Cf. Chamber of Commerce of the United States v. United States Dep't of Labor,* 174 F.3d 206 (D.C. Cir. 1999).

§ 6.1.4 GUIDANCE DOCUMENTS

§ 6.1.4a Legislative Rules and Guidance Documents

Legislative rules are rules issued by an agency pursuant to an express or implied grant of authority to issue rules with the force of law. Because they can directly alter the rights and obligations of citizens, they are often considered to be the most important type of agency rules, and most of the cases examined in the preceding chapter concerned the procedural requirements that must accompany their issuance.

Legislative rules are sometimes known as "substantive rules." That usage can be misleading, because it undesirably implies a contrast with "procedural rules." Actually, procedural rules are often legislative rules. They may have the force of law, and, therefore, be binding both on the members of the public that interact with the agency and on the issuing agency itself. *See Service v. Dulles,* 354 U.S. 363, 388 (1957), and *Vitarelli v. Seaton,* 359 U.S. 535 (1959) (holding agencies bound by procedural rules they had previously adopted). Nevertheless, the term "substantive rules," as a synonym for legislative rules, is in common use, as the next principal case illustrates.

Also vital to the administrative process, however, are guidance documents (also known as nonlegislative rules). These are agency rules that do not have the force of law, as they are not based upon delegated authority to issue such rules. (That is, either the agency did not possess such authority or chose not to use it.) Agencies issue large numbers of guidance documents, and many are of great practical importance:

> Members of the public who live and do business in the shadow of regulation need to learn what the agency thinks the law means and how discretion may be exercised. Increasing the level of people's understanding about what the law requires of them is a good thing for society; it reduces the number of unintentional law violations, and it reduces the transaction costs incurred in planning private transactions. Agency staff members also

require authoritative information about these subjects in order
to apply the law consistently, fairly, and efficiently.

Michael Asimow, *California Underground Regulations*, 44 ADMIN. L. REV.
43, 43 (1992). Indeed, many agencies generate dozens or hundreds of
pages of guidance documents for every page of legislative rules they
promulgate. Moreover, according to some scholars, the tendency for
agencies to rely on guidance documents as instruments of policy
development is now on the increase, because of the recent growth in
procedural hurdles that agencies must surmount when they attempt to
promulgate legislative rules. *See* § 5.1 N.1. Agencies' widespread use of
guidance documents is a reality that administrative law must
accommodate, but it also creates risks of abuses. Some of the legal
system's efforts to curb such abuses are explored in this section.

The preeminent characteristic of a legislative rule, inherent in its
having "the force of law," is that it is binding and enforceable in the same
way as other species of effective law. *See* Thomas W. Merrill, *The* Accardi
Principle, 74 GEO. WASH. L. REV. 569 (2006). So, for example, the United
States Supreme Court has noted that a "regulation . . . made by . . . [a]
commission in pursuance of constitutional statutory authority . . . has the
same force as though prescribed in terms by the statute." *Atchison, T. &
S.F. Ry. Co. v. Scarlett,* 300 U.S. 471, 474 (1937). Violation of a valid
legislative rule, therefore, is often a basis for imposing civil and criminal
sanctions.

More particularly, valid legislative rules are binding on *private
persons;* as we have seen in cases such as *Heckler v. Campbell,* excerpted
in § 3.2, they can extinguish citizens' right to be heard on the issues that
they address. At the same time, legislative rules are also binding on the
issuing agency, which must adhere to them until such time as they may
be revoked or invalidated by a court. *United States v. Nixon,* 418 U.S. 683,
694–96 (1974); *Tew v. City of Topeka Police & Fire Civil Service Comm'n,*
697 P.2d 1279, 1282–83 (Kan. 1985). Consequently, an agency may not
violate its own legislative rules, although it may be able to waive them if
it has authority to do so. *See* § 6.4. Finally, legislative rules are
sometimes said to be "binding on the courts." That notion, however, is
somewhat less helpful to understanding, because the circumstances
under which courts may invalidate administrative rules are governed by
a complex body of doctrines that cannot be captured very well in a short
phrase. *See* Chapter 9.

In contrast, guidance documents are not binding on agencies or
citizens. *See Vietnam Veterans of America v. Secretary of Navy,* 843 F.2d
528, 536–38 (D.C. Cir. 1988). They can sometimes have *some* constraining
effects on subsequent agency action, such as in a case in which the
agency's failure to explain why it did not adhere to the guidance

document renders the action arbitrary and capricious. But this constraining effect results from the agency's misuse of its discretion, not from a belief that the guidance document is "law."

Guidance documents are commonly subdivided into "interpretive rules" and "general statements of policy." Federal APA §§ 553(b)(A) and 553(d)(2) exempt both those two categories of rules from the usual notice and comment and delayed effectiveness procedures. (Actually, the APA uses the word "interpretative," but most writers prefer the briefer term "interpretive.") Most of the federal case law on guidance documents has grown out of efforts to determine whether a given rule should have been issued using notice and comment procedures. This has proved a difficult task in practice. Meanwhile, many state APAs do not exempt interpretive rules and policy statements from rulemaking procedural requirements; state law thus offers some revealing contrasts with the federal model.

§ 6.1.4b Policy Statements

PROFESSIONALS AND PATIENTS FOR CUSTOMIZED CARE V. SHALALA

56 F.3d 592 (5th Cir. 1995)

WIENER, J.:

In this challenge brought pursuant to the Administrative Procedure Act (APA), Plaintiff-Appellant Professionals and Patients for Customized Care (P2C2) contends that the district court erred in concluding that Food & Drug Administration (FDA) Compliance Policy Guide 7132.16 (CPG 7132.16) is not a substantive rule and thus is not subject to the APA's notice-and-comment requirement. Finding no reversible error, we affirm.

In 1992, the FDA promulgated CPG 7132.16 to address what the agency perceived to be a burgeoning problem in the pharmaceutical industry—the manufacture of drugs by establishments with retail pharmacy licenses. Pharmacies have long engaged in the practice of traditional compounding, the process whereby a pharmacist combines ingredients pursuant to a physician's prescription to create a medication for an individual patient. This type of compounding is commonly used to prepare medications that are not commercially available, such as diluted doses for children and altered forms of medications for easier consumption.

Pharmacies that practice traditional compounding are regulated primarily by state law, and the drugs that they blend are exempt from many federal misbranding provisions. Drug manufacturers and their products, however, are subject to rigorous federal oversight.

By the 1990s, the FDA had become aware that many establishments with retail pharmacy licenses were purchasing large quantities of bulk drug substances; combining those substances into specific drug products before ever receiving any valid prescriptions; and then marketing those drug products to practitioners and patients. The FDA suspected that establishments engaged in this large-scale speculative "compounding" were doing so to circumvent those new drug, adulteration, and misbranding provisions of the Food, Drug, and Cosmetic Act (Act) that regulate the manufacture of drugs.

To combat this perceived problem, the FDA issued CPG 7132.16, in an effort to establish the following "policy":

POLICY

FDA recognizes that a licensed pharmacist may compound drugs extemporaneously after receipt of a valid prescription for an individual patient. . . .

Pharmacies that do not otherwise engage in practices that extend beyond the limits set forth in this CPG may prepare drugs in very limited quantities before receiving a valid prescription, provided they can document a history of receiving valid prescriptions that have been generated solely within an established profession practitioner-patient-pharmacy relationship and provided further that they maintain the prescription on file for all such products dispensed at the pharmacy as required by state law.

If a pharmacy compounds finished drugs from bulk active ingredient materials considered to be unapproved new drug substances, . . . such activity must be covered by an FDA-sanctioned investigation new drug application. . . .

Pharmacies may not, without losing their status as retail entities, compound, provide, and dispense drugs to third parties for resale to individual patients. . . .

FDA may, in the exercise of its enforcement discretion, initiate federal enforcement actions against entities and responsible persons when the scope and nature of a pharmacy's activity raises the kind of concerns normally associated with a manufacturer and that results in significant violations of the new drug, adulteration, or misbranding provisions of the Act.

This CPG goes on to identify nine factors that the FDA "will consider" in determining whether to initiate an enforcement action, but explains that the "list of factors is not intended to be exhaustive and other factors may be appropriate for consideration in a particular case." [The nine factors included "[s]oliciting business . . . to compound specific drug products," "[u]sing commercial scale manufacturing or testing equipment for compounding drug products," and "[d]istributing inordinate amounts of compounded products out of state."]

The FDA issued CPG 7132.16 without complying with APA notice-and-comment procedures, as the agency considered CPG 7132.16 to be for internal guidance. The FDA explains that CPG 7132.16 was intended to be used within the agency, primarily by FDA district offices, as an aid in identifying those pharmacies that manufacture drugs under the guise of traditional compounding.

P2C2, an organization comprising individuals and entities engaged in the practice of pharmacy, . . . filed suit in federal district court, claiming that CPG 7312.16 is invalid because it is a substantive rule issued in violation of the APA's notice-and-comment requirement. [The district court disagreed.] . . .

If CPG 7312.16 were a substantive rule it would be unlawful, for it was promulgated without the requisite notice-and-comment. The pivotal issue in this case, therefore, is whether CPG 7312.16 is a substantive rule. Although the APA itself does not define "substantive rules," "interpretive rules," or "statements of policy," courts over the years have developed a body of jurisprudence that is helpful in drawing the necessary—but often illusory—distinctions among the three types of rules. . . . In analyzing these criteria, we are to give some deference, "albeit 'not overwhelming,'" to the agency's characterization of its own rule. . . .

. . . As we noted in *Panhandle Producers & Royalty Owners Ass'n v. Economic Regulatory Administration*, [847 F.2d 1168 (5th Cir. 1988) (quoting *Pacific Gas & Electric Co. v. FPC*, 506 F.2d 33, 38–39 (D.C. Cir. 1974))]:

"A properly adopted substantive rule establishes a standard of conduct which has the force of law. In subsequent administrative proceedings involving a substantive rule, the issues are whether the adjudicated facts conform to the rule and whether the rule should be waived or applied in that particular instance. The underlying policy embodied in the rule is not generally subject to challenge before the agency.

"A general statement of policy, on the other hand, does not establish a 'binding norm.' It is not finally determinative of the issues or rights to which it is addressed. The agency cannot apply or rely upon a general statement of policy as law because a general statement of policy only announces what the agency seeks to establish as policy. A policy statement announces the agency's tentative intentions for the future. When the agency applies the policy in a particular situation, it must be prepared to support the policy just as if the policy statement had never been issued. An agency cannot escape its responsibility to present evidence and reasoning supporting its substantive rules by announcing binding precedent in the form of a general statement of policy."

1.   *Agency Deference: FDA's Characterization*

In analyzing whether an agency pronouncement is a statement of policy or a substantive rule, the starting point is "the agency's characterization of the rule." It is undisputed that the FDA has consistently classified the instant rule as a statement of policy. The rule is self-described as "Policy," and it was promulgated as a "compliance policy guide." . . . But as we observed in *Brown Express, Inc. v. United States*, [607 F.2d 695 (5th Cir. 1979)], " '[t]he label that the particular agency puts upon its given exercise of administrative power is not, for our purposes, conclusive; rather, it is what the agency does in fact.' " We therefore turn now to those matters of substance.

2.   *Binding Effect of CPG 7132.16*

A touchstone of a substantive rule is that it establishes a binding norm. As the Eleventh Circuit has observed:

> The key inquiry . . . is the extent to which the challenged policy leaves the agency free to exercise its discretion to follow or not to follow that general policy in an individual case, or on the other hand, whether the policy so fills out the statutory scheme that upon application one need only determine whether a given case is within the rule's criteria. As long as the agency remains free to consider the individual facts in the various cases that arise, then the agency action in question has not established a binding norm.

[*Ryder Truck Lines, Inc. v. United States*, 716 F.2d 1369, 1377 (11th Cir. 1983).] P2C2 argues that CPG 7132.16 establishes a binding norm, as it imposes on compounding pharmacists significant new obligations. Most of these new obligations are manifested in the nine "factors," which, according to P2C2, are tantamount to binding norms. . . . To ascertain whether CPG 7132.16 creates binding norms, we first consider its plain language and then address the manner in which it had been implemented by the FDA.

a.   *Plain Language of CPG 7132.16 . . .*

We observe initially the statement of CPG 7132.16 that the FDA "will consider" the nine factors in determining whether to initiate an enforcement action against a pharmacy. We also note that, even though the mandatory tone of the factors is undoubtedly calculated to encourage compliance, CPG 7132.16 affords an opportunity for individual determinations. It expressly provides that "[t]he foregoing list of factors is not intended to be exhaustive," recognizes that "other factors may be appropriate for consideration in a particular case," and states that, even if the factors are present, the FDA retains discretion whether to bring an enforcement action. . . .

b.   *FDA's Enforcement of CPG 7132.16*

P2C2 urges that, even if the plain language of the rule does not create a binding norm, the agency has *treated* CPG 7132.16 as though it establishes binding norms, and thus we should hold that it does. P2C2 reminds us that the pertinent inquiry is not only what CPG 7132.16 states that the agency will do, but also, " 'what the agency does in fact.' "

P2C2 relies on numerous informal agency communications as evidence that the FDA has treated CPG 7132.16 as establishing a binding norm. P2C2 cites in particular to evidence that, since CPG 7132.16's promulgation: (1) the FDA has used the nine factors listed in CPG 7132.16 when inspecting pharmacies, and has relied on those factors to determine whether federal enforcement actions were warranted; (2) in numerous letters the FDA has warned pharmacies that they were engaged in drug manufacturing, rather than traditional compounding, because they were conducting some, or all, of the activities listed in CPG 7132.16, and (3) the FDA has furnished copies of CPG 7132.16 to pharmacists who inquired about the legal restrictions on drug compounding. P2C2's reliance is misplaced.

The fact that FDA inspectors refer to CPG 7132.16 to help determine whether a pharmacy is engaged in traditional compounding or drug manufacturing is not particularly probative whether the rule is substantive. . . . Indeed, what purpose would an agency's statement of policy serve if agency employees could not refer to it for guidance?

More probative of the nature of CPG 7132.16, however, is the language used by the FDA in warning letters to pharmacies. In one such letter, the FDA wrote that firms engaged in activities that "exceed the limits of CPG 7132.16 are considered manufacturers and are subject to all the provisions of the Act." We would not dispute that if this statement were viewed in a vacuum, one could be led to conclude that the FDA was in fact treating CPG 7132.16 as a binding norm. But statements are not to be considered out of context or in isolation, and in that very same letter the FDA clearly stated that CPG 7132.16 was only used by the agency as "internal guidance." Moreover, informal communications often exhibit a lack of "precision of draftsmanship" and such internal inconsistencies are not unexpected, which is why such documents are generally entitled to limited weight. We cannot conclude, in light of all of the other circumstances, that these warning letters are sufficient to transform CPG 7132.16 into a substantive rule.

As with that use of CPG 7132.16, we do not find particularly probative the fact that the FDA enclosed copies of CPG 7132.16 in letters responding to some pharmacists' questions regarding the legality of compounding activities. . . . [T]he letters made clear that CPG 7132.16 was used for guidance, but that the FDA retained discretion to conduct an individualized inquiry and to consider other factors outside the list. . . .

We cannot conclude that the FDA has treated the factors in CPG 7132.16 as binding norms. Rather, the agency has used CPG 7132.16 for guidance to help identify those pharmacies that might be engaged in drug manufacturing activities under the guise of compounding.

3.   *Degree of Enforcement Discretion Accorded FDA*

Even if CPG 7132.16 does not create binding norms, argues P2C2, the rule so narrowly constricts FDA enforcement discretion that the CPG should be deemed to be a substantive rule. P2C2 contends that CPG 7132.16 acts essentially to identify those pharmacies against which the FDA will bring enforcement actions, thereby denying the agency any semblance of discretion. We disagree.

True, the FDA had even greater discretion in bringing enforcement actions before CPG 7132.16 issued; prior to that time inspectors were apparently provided with no official guidance whatsoever. In that sense, therefore, CPG 7132.16 has "channeled" the FDA's enforcement discretion, providing direction—where once there was none—by helping determine whether a pharmacy is engaged in traditional compounding or drug manufacturing. But all statements of policy channel discretion to some degree—indeed, that is their purpose. . . .

In our view, CPG 7132.16 merely identifies some indicia of drug manufacturing; it neither compels the conclusion that a pharmacy is engaged in drug manufacturing nor provokes an automatic or nondiscretionary response from the agency. Rather, FDA inspectors are free to consider in toto those nine factors, as well as others, and then, based on that guidance and their own judgment, decide whether the pharmacy in question is engaged in drug manufacturing. Such is the nature of a discretionary rule, not of a substantive one.

[The court concluded by harmonizing its holding with the case law defining general statements of policy and interpretive rules.]

. . . As we agree, then, that CPG 7132.16 is not a substantive rule, and thus is not subject to APA notice-and-comment requirements, the district court's judgement is, in all respects,

AFFIRMED.

NOTES AND QUESTIONS

1. *Criticisms of guidance documents.* Agencies are frequently accused of circumventing normal rulemaking procedures by using guidance documents in an inflexible or coercive way. Too often, it is argued, agency staff turn a deaf ear to criticisms of a policy statement, and citizens feel obliged to comply with the statement because they lack the resources or nerve to resist. In this fashion, guidance documents are said to become, in practical effect, as binding on private parties as legislative rules are. Professor Anthony has summarized the objections that this recurrent situation provokes:

> In such cases, affected persons and the public generally will not have been accorded a regularized notice of the agencies' actions or an assured opportunity to participate in their development. Citizens or lawyers in Pocatello, or even in Washington, sometimes do not have ready access to the guidances or manuals that agencies are using to bind them. And when they do, they can be confused about the legal import of documents like these, and frustrated at their inability to escape the practical obligations or standards the documents impose. Often, in order to win a needed approval, they must accept the conditions demanded by the nonlegislative rule, and thereby as a practical matter surrender the opportunity to obtain court review of the offending conditions. The agencies, for their part, might not have issued these pronouncements so freely if legislative rulemaking procedures had had to be followed.

Robert A. Anthony, *Interpretive Rules, Policy Statements, Guidances, Manuals, and the Like—Should Federal Agencies Use Them to Bind the Public?*, 41 DUKE L.J. 1311, 1372 (1992). Guidance documents can also be problematic for persons who stand to benefit from a regulatory scheme, such as environmentalists or consumers. If the agency does not allow these persons to be heard when it adopts the document, they are unlikely to have any other forum, such as an enforcement proceeding, at which they can air any disagreements with the agency's policy. *See* Nina A. Mendelson, *Regulatory Beneficiaries and Informal Agency Policymaking*, 92 CORNELL L. REV. 397 (2007).

Concerns about the abuse of guidance documents have led some authorities to define "binding effect" in expansive terms. In a frequently quoted dictum, Judge Randolph cited to Anthony's article and declared: "If an agency acts as if a document issued at headquarters is controlling in the field, if it treats the document in the same manner as it treats a legislative rule, if it bases enforcement actions on the policies or interpretations formulated in the document, if it leads private parties or State permitting authorities to believe that it will declare permits invalid unless they comply with the terms of the document, then the agency's document is for all practical purposes 'binding.'" *Appalachian Power Co. v. EPA*, 208 F.3d 1015, 1021 (D.C. Cir. 2000). Does this passage carry the notion of a "binding norm" too far? Should an agency have to use notice and comment for every document that it will consult as a basis for taking enforcement actions, or that contains instructions that staff are expected to treat as "controlling in the field"?

2. *Support for guidance documents.* The literature also contains vigorous defenses of agencies' use of guidance documents. According to Professor Strauss, Anthony's argument does not adequately take into account the competing equities of people who *want* the advice that guidance documents provide:

> Professor Anthony sees in a potential *complainant* about the policy judgments entailed in [the Nuclear Regulatory Commission's] technical specifications for nuclear power plants, a party bound in practical effect by those guidelines.... But ... [f]rom the perspective of an applicant whose chief interest is to build a plant that will meet NRC standards, receiving such guidance from the agency where possible is strongly preferable to being left to speculate about the details of agency policies and to pay for case-by-case demonstration that it has met those policies' demands. The NRC *may* leave these issues to determination first in negotiations with uninstructed staff and then in the adjudicatory licensing proceedings in which the applicant bears the burden of showing that its design will satisfy safety requirements. Do we wish to encourage it to do so?

Peter L. Strauss, *The Rulemaking Continuum*, 41 DUKE L.J. 1463, 1481–82 (1992). In a later article he elaborated:

> Agency administration is aided when central officials can advise responsible bureaucrats how they should apply agency law. Citizens are better off if they can know about these instructions and rely on agency positions, with the assurance of equal treatment such central advice permits, than if they are remitted to the discretion of local agents and "secret law."

Peter L. Strauss, *Publication Rules in the Rulemaking Spectrum: Assuring Proper Respect for an Essential Element*, 53 ADMIN. L. REV. 803, 808 (2001).

The experience of California suggests what would happen if the exemption for guidance documents were eliminated. Although state APAs generally require pre-adoption procedure for guidance documents, with only very limited exemptions, agencies in many states are permitted to ignore the requirement with impunity. In California, however, the requirement is vigorously enforced. As a practical reality, then, "underground regulations," meaning guidance documents adopted without full compliance with the APA rulemaking formalities, are considered invalid. Michael Asimow, *California Underground Regulations*, 44 ADMIN. L. REV. 43, 44–45 (1992).

Asimow's study showed that the California system had numerous negative consequences for agencies in that state. Because of the costs and delays of rulemaking procedure, most agencies stopped issuing guidance documents entirely. In many cases, agencies found it quicker and cheaper to go to the legislature and change the statute than to adopt guidance documents through rulemaking. Other agencies relied on techniques of dubious validity to provide interpretive guidance (such as announcing "tentative" policy positions but never finalizing them, or sending out identical letters to numerous regulated parties but never generalizing them). Other agencies simply defied the law, adopting guidance documents without advance procedures, and gambling that they wouldn't be challenged. Indeed, the study pointed out that, by a conservative estimate, 100,000 to 200,000 underground regulations were being enforced by California state agencies at that time. *Id.* at 56–61.

You will recall that, according to some scholars, increases in the procedural burdens associated with rulemaking have caused agencies to issue fewer rules. *See* § 5.1 N.1. Asimow's study maintains that this chilling effect is particularly powerful in the case of guidance documents:

> The reason for this assumption is that nonlegislative rules are different from other bureaucratic outputs in one critical respect: normally the regulatory program can function without them. Legislative rules are usually necessary to set a regulatory program in motion, particularly if the agency's statute is not self-executing. Similarly, an agency must adjudicate the cases on its docket and respond to complaints. But nonlegislative rules can be dispensed with because an agency is not usually required to issue them. Their primary function is to diminish uncertainty, but the agency is not required to diminish uncertainty.
>
> The costs of uncertainty are largely borne by the members of the public, not by agency officials. For that reason, public uncertainty is an externality that agency utility-maximizers need not take into account. Thus an agency may well choose to muddle through without producing any guidance documents, or it may find some informal way to communicate the information. . . . [S]ince the production of nonlegislative rules can usually be deferred until additional resources become available, such rules must often be losers in the unending internal struggle for resources.

Asimow, *supra,* at 64–65.

3. *Policy statements v. legislative rules.* Although the *P2C2* opinion is phrased in terms of determining whether the CPG was a substantive rule (or legislative rule), its analysis is basically the same as courts typically use in deciding whether a document is *not* such a rule, but, instead, a general statement of policy. Either way, the essential question is whether the document establishes a "binding norm." The rationale for the distinction appears to be as follows: When an agency makes a discretionary decision that is guided by a past policy statement, an individual can argue that the agency should disregard the policy statement and treat his case differently. However, if a discretionary decision is prescribed by a legislative rule, the

agency has not left itself free to reconsider. In the latter situation, therefore, the individual should have a chance to influence the rule at the time it is adopted, because it will be binding at the time it is applied. Frequently, however, it is difficult for courts to determine whether an agency has, in fact, left itself free to reconsider. As can be seen from *P2C2*, and the two following notes, the data for their determinations may come from the language of the purported policy statement, or from the agency's implementation of it, or both.

4. *Mandatory language.* The court in *P2C2* did not think that the language of the FDA's compliance practice guide was binding, but in other circumstances courts have often found that a document should not be considered a policy statement because its wording indicated that the agency was not open to reexamining its position. *See, e.g., General Electric Co. v. EPA*, 290 F.3d 377 (D.C. Cir. 2002).

An interesting example of this logic at work is *CropLife America v. EPA*, 329 F.3d 876 (D.C. Cir. 2003). The Environmental Protection Agency sets tolerance levels for pesticide residues on food, in part by considering whether a pesticide would cause unreasonable risks to human health. In evaluating these risks, EPA used to rely regularly on research studies, conducted by third parties, that tested human exposure to pesticides. Beginning in 1998, however, the agency began to reexamine its use of third-party human data. It commissioned various studies of the ethical and scientific questions surrounding this practice. At length, in October 2001, the agency announced that it would continue using human data, making decisions about its propriety on a case-by-case basis.

This announcement, however, triggered renewed criticism from environmental groups. In December 2001, EPA responded by placing a moratorium on the use of third-party human test data. The agency said that it would request advice on this subject from the National Academy of Sciences. In a press release announcing this request, EPA stated: "During the Academy's consideration of the issues and until a policy is in place, the Agency will not consider or rely on any such human studies in its regulatory decision making [except where EPA is] legally required to consider or rely on any such human study during this interim period. . . ."

Pesticide manufacturers filed for review, arguing that the December press release constituted a binding regulation and thus was void because it had been issued without notice and comment. The court agreed, remarking that the unequivocal language of the announcement "created a 'binding norm' that is 'finally determinative of the issues or rights to which it is addressed.' . . . EPA's stated rule is binding on petitioners, who are now barred from relying on third-party human studies (even in cases where such studies formerly were approved), and is binding on the agency because EPA has made it clear that it simply 'will not consider' human studies." Does it make sense to say that, if the agency wants to institute a moratorium on using human test data while it is considering what its long-term policy should be, it must first resort to notice and comment procedure?

Against this background, was the result in *P2C2* correct? Suppose you are a pharmacist who has received one of the FDA's warning letters. You want to take the position that you should be permitted to compound drugs for resale to third parties, and also that you should not have to retain records of past compounded prescriptions. Judging from the language of CPG 7132.16, would you expect that the FDA will be open to serious consideration of your position?

5. *Binding effects in practice.* Members of the public sometimes complain that an agency policy statement has been *applied* against them in a binding fashion. Recall the *Flagstaff* case in § 4.4.2 N.2, in which the FCC was reversed for relying on "established policies" (embodied in a policy statement) instead of meeting the challengers' arguments head-on. A similar case is *McLouth Steel Products Corp. v. Thomas,* 838 F.2d 1317, 1320 (D.C. Cir. 1988). McLouth, which produced sludge as a byproduct at its steel factory, petitioned the EPA to exclude the sludge from regulation as a hazardous waste. EPA refused after using a mathematical model to predict the extent to which lead and cadmium in the sludge would contaminate the nearby groundwater. The model had been adopted without notice and comment. The court agreed with McLouth that EPA was invalidly treating the model as a legislative rule. The notice announcing the model sounded as though the agency had made up its mind; and, more significantly, when McLouth and another steel company raised objections to the model in their petitions for individual relief, EPA brushed the objections aside by saying that questions about the model were no longer open for consideration. The court thus instructed EPA either to subject the model to § 553 proceedings or "reconsider McLouth's delisting petition with full recognition that [the] issues are open."

Compare *Panhandle Producers & Royalty Owners Ass'n v. Economic Regulatory Admin. (ERA),* 847 F.2d 1168 (5th Cir. 1988), a case cited in *P2C2.* Domestic producers of natural gas challenged an ERA order authorizing imports of gas from Canada. The order had been based on a guideline in which the Secretary of Energy had prescribed a presumption favoring such imports. Plaintiffs alleged that the guideline was invalid because it had not been issued through rulemaking procedures. The court rejected this argument, stating: "Even though the ERA looked to the Guidelines for presumptions and burdens of proof, the ERA responded fully to each argument made by opponents of the order, without merely relying on the force of the policy statement. . . . The ERA did not give the Guidelines undue weight by refusing endlessly to reconsider the principles established in [past] cases." Is the court's result consistent with its statement (quoted in *P2C2*) that an agency must be "prepared to support the policy just as if the policy statement had never been issued"? If so, how? *See also Catawba County v. EPA,* 571 F.3d 20, 34 (D.C. Cir. 2009) (upholding EPA memo that prescribed rebuttable presumption regarding state compliance plans and encouraged, but did not require, states to address nine factors); *Steeltech, Ltd. v. USEPA*, 273 F.3d 652, 655–56 (6th Cir.2001) (upholding decision of ALJ who "expressly stated that the [guidance document] was not a rule and that she had the discretion to depart from [it], if appropriate," but who adhered to the document upon determining "that the present case does not present circumstances that raise policy issues not accounted for in the [document]").

The impact of guidance documents on subsequent agency adjudications is sometimes compared with that of case law precedents. *See* Strauss, *The Rulemaking Continuum, supra,* at 1472–73, 1486; John F. Manning, *Nonlegislative Rules,* 72 GEO. WASH. L. REV. 893, 934–37 (2004); Ronald M. Levin, *Nonlegislative Rules and the Administrative Open Mind,* 41 DUKE L.J. 1497, 1500–02 (1992).

6.   *State law.* A comprehensive survey of the states' treatment of guidance documents appears in Michael Asimow, *Guidance Documents in the States: Toward a Safe Harbor,* 54 ADMIN. L. REV. 631 (2002). Although ambiguities in states' laws militate against exact figures in this area, the study found that approximately thirty-one jurisdictions (including the District of Columbia) effectively exempt guidance documents from APA rulemaking procedures. Fourteen have accomplished this feat by creative construction of state APAs that probably were not intended to contain such an exemption. Seventeen others have explicit statutory exemptions. These thirty-one jurisdictions include all but two of the fifteen states with the largest populations (the exceptions being Ohio and California). On the other hand, twelve states adhere more or less faithfully to APA provisions in which no exemption is provided, and statutes in eight more states specifically prohibit agencies from promulgating guidance documents without APA procedures. *Id.* at 637–44, 651.

7.   *Guidance documents and the 2010 MSAPA.* The 2010 MSAPA takes an innovative approach to guidance documents. Like the federal APA, it allows agencies to issue them without engaging in notice and comment. Unlike federal law, however, it expressly provides that the term "rule" does not include guidance documents. § 102(27)(F). The Act then sets forth in § 311 a set of procedural obligations pertaining specifically to guidance documents, including the following:

(b)   An agency that proposes to rely on a guidance document to the detriment of a person in any administrative proceeding must afford the person an adequate opportunity to contest the legality or wisdom of a position taken in the document. The agency may not use a guidance document to foreclose consideration of issues raised in the document.

(c)   A guidance document may contain binding instructions to agency staff members if, at an appropriate stage in the administrative process, the agency's procedures provide an affected person an adequate opportunity to contest the legality or wisdom of a position taken in the document.

(d) If an agency proposes to act in an adjudication at variance with a position expressed in a guidance document, it shall provide a reasonable explanation for the variance. If an affected person in an adjudication may have relied reasonably on the agency's position, the explanation must include a reasonable justification for the agency's conclusion that the need for the variance outweighs the affected person's reliance interest.

Under MSAPA § 311, a private person who contends that an agency is using a guidance document in an improperly coercive manner would not have to argue that the document is really a (legislative) rule. Rather, the person would simply contend that the agency had violated subsection (b). Is this approach an improvement on the federal model? For analysis of § 311, see Ronald M. Levin, *Rulemaking Under the 2010 Model State Administrative Procedure Act*, 20 WIDENER L.J. 855, 875–84 (2011).

The provision in subsection (c) for mandatory instructions to staff is based on similar language in Office of Management and Budget, Final Bulletin for Agency Good Guidance Practices, 72 Fed. Reg. 3432, 3436–37 (2007). Is it consistent with *CropLife* and *McLouth*?

8. *Problem.* The Federal Communications Act permits the FCC to assess monetary penalties for violations of that Act, such as sending false distress communications or failing to maintain a current license. The FCC issued, without notice and comment, what it termed a "policy statement" setting forth a schedule of base penalties for computing such sanctions. For example, the base penalty for a false distress signal was $20,000 for broadcasters and $80,000 for common carriers (including telephone companies). The schedule also provided for upward adjustments from the base figure in cases of "substantial economic gain," downward adjustments for "voluntary disclosure of violations," etc. The explanation accompanying the penalty schedule added that the FCC reserved discretion to depart from the schedule in particular cases.

An association of telephone companies petitioned for reconsideration, questioning why the base penalties for them were higher than for broadcasters. The Commission declined to revise the schedule, observing that the association's concerns would be more appropriately addressed in the context of specific cases.

Later the association challenged the penalty schedule in court, arguing that the FCC should have complied with § 553 procedures before issuing the schedule. The evidence before the court indicated that the FCC had made use of the schedule in fifty cases since its promulgation and had followed the figures listed in the schedule in forty-two of those cases. In the other eight cases, the FCC had imposed more lenient fines than the schedule prescribed, but the agency's brief written opinions in those cases were unclear as to whether these departures had involved downward adjustments pursuant to the guidelines themselves, or instead had involved completely independent decisions.

Should the plaintiff's challenge under § 553 succeed? *Cf. United States Tel. Ass'n v. FCC*, 28 F.3d 1232 (D.C. Cir. 1994).

§ 6.1.4c Interpretive Rules

NOTES AND QUESTIONS

1.   *Intent to make law.* Although there is broad agreement that the exemption for general statements of policy should depend in some fashion on whether a rule is "binding," there is much less agreement as to the best way to apply the exemption for interpretive rules. Broadly speaking, courts tend to classify a rule as interpretive or legislative by asking whether the agency possessed, and intended to exercise, delegated authority to make law, as opposed to interpreting existing text. A common formulation asks whether the agency intends to clarify the law or instead to make substantive changes in the law. *See, e.g., Sprint Corp. v. FCC*, 315 F.3d 369 (D.C. Cir. 2003); *Splane v. West*, 216 F.3d 1058 (Fed. Cir. 2000); *Orengo Caraballo v. Reich*, 11 F.3d 186, 195 (D.C. Cir. 1993). *See generally* Michael Asimow, *Nonlegislative Rules and Regulatory Reform*, 1985 DUKE L.J. 381, 393–97.

In some situations, that judgment is relatively easy to make. Among the various situations in which a court can assume that an agency must have intended to use its legislative rulemaking authority, the "clearest case is where, in the absence of a legislative rule by the agency, the legislative basis for agency enforcement would be inadequate." *American Mining Congress v. MSHA*, 995 F.2d 1106, 1109 (D.C. Cir. 1993). That is, if the enabling legislation imposes no liability itself, but instead authorizes the implementing agency to enunciate rules that would create liability, Congress must have intended for the agency to utilize its legislative authority to flesh out the statute. Without implementing rules, the statute could not be "interpreted" as requiring anything. *Id.; see also Oceana, Inc. v. Locke*, 670 F.3d 1238 (D.C. Cir. 2011).

Conversely, a rule is plainly *not* legislative, but rather interpretive, if the agency has no legislative rulemaking authority at all with respect to the subject area of the rule. For example, the EEOC has no authority to promulgate legislative rules to define the scope of the antidiscrimination laws, so its guidelines on that subject are all interpretive. *General Electric Co. v. Gilbert*, 429 U.S. 125, 141 (1976). Case law addressing whether or not an agency should be held to possess legislative rulemaking authority was examined in § 5.1 N.2.

In other situations, however, the agency's intentions may be hard to discern. Part of the problem is that a rule that ascribes a meaning to a statutory term may be either interpretive or legislative. (A famous example of the latter is *Chevron U.S.A. Inc. v. NRDC*, 467 U.S. 837 (1984), excerpted in

§ 9.2.2, in which the EPA used a legislative rule to define "stationary source" in the Clean Air Act to mean an entire factory rather than an individual piece of equipment.) Courts sometimes give particular weight to the agency's own characterization of a rule as legislative or interpretive, *see, e.g., Chrysler Corp. v. Brown,* 441 U.S. 281, 312–16 (1979), excerpted in § 8.1, but, as in the case of policy statements, judicial second-guessing of such characterizations is quite common.

Two types of inquiries are prominent in the case law. One examines the *substance* of the so-called interpretive rule to determine whether it can be legitimately characterized as "interpretation." The other examines the *process* through which the agency implements the rule. The following notes discuss these two approaches.

2. *"Interpretation" v. "arbitrary choice."* The well-known case of *Hoctor v. USDA,* 82 F.3d 165 (7th Cir. 1996), exemplifies the former approach. That case arose under the Animal Welfare Act, which authorizes the Department of Agriculture (USDA) to adopt rules "to govern the humane handling, care, treatment, and transportation of animals by dealers." Using notice and comment procedure, USDA adopted a rule entitled "Structural Strength" requiring that a facility housing animals "must be constructed of such material and of such strength as appropriate for the animals involved." USDA later adopted an internal memorandum addressed to its inspectors, in which it said that all dangerous animals must be kept inside a perimeter fence at least eight feet high. Mr. Hoctor, a dealer in big cats, was penalized because the perimeter fence surrounding one of his pens was only six feet high. He argued that the memorandum should have been adopted through notice and comment, but USDA defended it as an interpretive rule. Judge Posner, writing for the court, rejected this defense:

> Even if . . . the eight-foot rule is consistent with, even in some sense authorized by, the structural-strength regulation, it would not necessarily follow that it is an interpretive rule. It is that only if it can be derived from the regulation by a process reasonably described as interpretation. . . .
>
> . . . [U]nless a statute or regulation is of crystalline transparency, the agency enforcing it cannot avoid interpreting it, and the agency would be stymied in its enforcement duties if every time it brought a case on a new theory it had to pause for a bout, possibly lasting several years, of notice and comment rulemaking. . . .
>
> At the other extreme from what might be called normal or routine interpretation is the making of reasonable but arbitrary (not in the "arbitrary or capricious" sense) rules that are consistent with the statute or regulation under which the rules are promulgated but not derived from it, because they represent an arbitrary choice among methods of implementation. A rule that turns on a number is likely to be arbitrary in this sense. There is no way to reason to an

eight-foot perimeter-fence rule as opposed to a seven-and-a-half foot fence or a nine-foot fence or a ten-foot fence. None of these candidates for a rule is uniquely appropriate to, and in that sense derivable from, the duty of secure containment.... The rule is arbitrary in the sense that it could well be different without significant impairment of any regulatory purpose.

But this does not make the rule a matter of indifference to the people subject to it. There are thousands of animal dealers, and some unknown fraction of these face the prospect of having to tear down their existing fences and build new, higher ones at great cost. The concerns of these dealers are legitimate and since, as we are stressing, the rule could well be otherwise, the agency was obliged to listen to them before settling on a final rule and to provide some justification for that rule, though not so tight or logical a justification as a court would be expected to offer for a new judge-made rule. Notice and comment is the procedure by which the persons affected by legislative rules are enabled to communicate their concerns in a comprehensive and systematic fashion to the legislating agency.

Id at 170–71 (paragraphing altered). Many other cases employ similar reasoning to distinguish interpretive from legislative rules. *See, e.g., Catholic Health Initiatives v. Sebelius*, 617 F.3d 490 (D.C. Cir. 2010); *Paralyzed Veterans of America v. D.C. Arena L.P.,* 117 F.3d 579, 588 (D.C. Cir. 1997) ("the distinction . . . likely turns on how tightly the agency's interpretation is drawn linguistically from the actual language of the statute"); *United Technologies Corp. v. EPA,* 821 F.2d 714, 719–20 (D.C. Cir. 1987) (interpretive rule must be "based on specific statutory provisions" rather than on "an agency's power to exercise its judgment as to how best to implement a general statutory mandate"). Is Judge Posner's reasoning persuasive? *Cf.* John F. Manning, *Nonlegislative Rules*, 72 GEO. WASH. L. REV. 893, 923–27 (2004) (arguing that the distinction between interpretation and policymaking is unmanageable, because it is solely a matter of degree).

3. *Contrasting case law.* If one requirement of an interpretive rule is that it can be "derived by interpretation," some cases do not seem to enforce the requirement very stringently. In *Shalala v. Guernsey Memorial Hospital,* 514 U.S. 87 (1995), an informal Medicare guideline provided that, for reimbursement purposes, losses that hospitals incurred when they refinanced their debts should be "amortized" (spread over a period of many years), instead of being recognized in full in the year the transaction occurred. The guideline purported to implement (i) a statute that simply said that the Medicare program should bear its fair share of costs, and (ii) a regulation authorizing reimbursement of costs that are "appropriate and helpful in . . . maintaining the operation of patient care facilities." The Court found that, although these provisions said nothing about the timing of loss recognition, the guideline was lawfully adopted as an interpretive rule. *Id.* at 97–99. Similarly, in *American Mining Congress, supra,* the Mine Safety and Health

Administration issued a "program policy letter" stating that if the chest x-ray of a miner measured 1/0 or higher (the fourth most severe of twelve possible ratings), it would be regarded as a "diagnosis" of black lung disease that would trigger reporting obligations. The court held that the letter was an interpretive rule that construed the term "diagnosis" in an existing legislative regulation. Can holdings such as *Guernsey* and *American Mining* be reconciled with the reasoning of the *Hoctor* opinion?

4.   *Lack of binding effect.* Near the end of the *Hoctor* opinion, Judge Posner described the USDA internal memorandum as setting forth a flat rule and suggested that the case would have been different if the memo had said that an eight foot fence criterion was only presumptive and could be overcome in particular instances. To this extent, *Hoctor* can be seen as ultimately resting on the same kind of "binding norm" reasoning that underlies the policy statement exemption. *See* Peter L. Strauss, *Publication Rules in the Rulemaking Spectrum: Assuring Proper Respect for an Essential Element,* 53 ADMIN. L. REV. 803, 815–16, 842–43 (2001) (endorsing this reading of *Hoctor*). Similarly, in *Catholic Health Initiatives, supra,* the D.C. Circuit found that the "interpretation" in an agency manual did not flow fairly from the substance of the underlying statute and regulations; but the court also emphasized that "it is enforced" in a "rigid" way. 617 F.3d at 494, 496 & n.6.

Indeed, some cases seem to blur the distinction between interpretive rules and policy statements, with little concern for possible differences between the two categories. *See, e.g., Erringer v. Thompson, supra; Appalachian Power Co. v. EPA,* 208 F.3d 1015 (D.C. Cir. 2000); *New York City Employees' Retirement System v. SEC,* 45 F.3d 7 (2d Cir. 1995); *Alaska v. United States Dep't of Transp.,* 868 F.2d 441 (D.C. Cir. 1989); *National Ass'n of Reg. Utility Comm'rs v. DOE,* 851 F.2d 1424, 1431 (D.C. Cir. 1988). Thus, concerns about binding effect can loom large even when a rule is characterized as interpretive.

A related trend is the increasing use of the term "guidance documents" to apply generically to both subcategories of nonlegislative rules. The trend may reflect an intuition that the uses, and abuses, of both kinds of guidance documents are roughly similar as a practical matter. For example, 2010 MSAPA § 311 applies the same provisions to all guidance documents, drawing no distinction between interpretive rules and policy statements.

However, there are also cases that declare, or at least assume, that the exemptions for interpretive rules and policy statements are sharply distinct. *Syncor Int'l Corp. v. Shalala,* 127 F.3d 90, 94 (D.C. Cir. 1997); *Paralyzed Veterans, supra.* Should the trend toward analyzing interpretive rules using "binding norm" reasoning be encouraged? Or are there good reasons to continue to treat the two kinds of guidance documents separately?

The federal Office of Management and Budget has published a bulletin on "good guidance practices" that might be thought to straddle these competing perspectives. For the most part, its advice for proper use of guidance documents does not distinguish between interpretive rules and policy statements. However, it does indicate that staff members who draft interpretive rules, as distinguished from policy statements, may freely use mandatory terms like "shall" and "must." Final Bulletin for Agency Good Guidance Practices, 72 Fed. Reg. 3432, 3436–37 (2007). Is there a valid justification for this distinction? Why should mandatory language be more readily tolerated in the context of an interpretive rule? *Cf. American Mining*, 995 F.2d at 1111.

5. *Inconsistency with the interpreted provision.* In *Guernsey, supra,* the Supreme Court did not try to limit interpretive rules to any particular mode of reasoning, but the Court did indicate that the Medicare guideline would have been invalid if it had been inconsistent with the regulation that it purported to interpret. A comparable analysis underlay the holding in *National Family Planning & Reproductive Health Ass'n v. Sullivan*, 979 F.2d 227 (D.C. Cir. 1992). After the Supreme Court had upheld the "gag rule" by which the Department of Health and Human Services had forbidden personnel in federally funded clinics to give abortion counseling to their patients, *Rust v. Sullivan,* 500 U.S. 173 (1991), the Department decided to modify that ban. On instructions from President Bush, the Department issued directives providing that the gag rule would no longer apply to doctors, but only to other clinic personnel. The directives had not been preceded by notice and comment, and the court held that they were not exempt as interpretive rules. According to the court, "It is a maxim of administrative law that: 'If a second rule repudiates or is irreconcilable with [a prior legislative rule], the second rule must be an amendment of the first; and, of course, an amendment to a legislative rule must itself be legislative.'" *See also Hemp Industries Ass'n v. DEA*, 333 F.3d 1082 (9th Cir. 2003) (adopting a similar rationale).

Why would a court in a case like *National Family Planning* hold the challenged rule procedurally invalid, instead of simply holding that it was invalid on the merits by virtue of being inconsistent with the legal text it was supposed to be interpreting? *Cf. Fertilizer Institute v. EPA*, 935 F.2d 1303, 1308 (D.C. Cir. 1991) (holding that an EPA pronouncement was within the interpretive rule exemption but untenable on the merits, and stating: "Simply because an agency may fail to interpret a statute correctly does not mean that the agency has not in fact interpreted it.").

6. *Interpretive reversals.* In an extension of the *National Family Planning* reasoning, a number of cases, especially in the D.C. Circuit, have held that a purported interpretive rule is invalid if it is inconsistent with *a prior interpretation of a legislative rule. Mortgage Bankers Ass'n v. Harris*, 720 F.3d 966 (D.C. Cir. 2013); *Alaska Professional Hunters Ass'n v. FAA*, 177 F.3d 1030 (D.C. Cir. 1999); *Shell Offshore, Inc. v. Babbitt*, 238 F.3d 622 (5th Cir. 2001). As the court said in *Paralyzed Veterans of America v. D.C. Arena L.P.*, 117 F.3d 579, 586 (D.C. Cir. 1997): "Once an agency gives its regulation an interpretation, it can only change that interpretation as it would formally modify the regulation itself, through the process of notice and comment rulemaking." Administrative law scholars have generally rejected this

reasoning, however, and the case law is not unanimous. At least six circuits have concluded "that changes in interpretations do not require notice and comment because both the original and current positions constitute interpretive rules." *Warshauer v. Solis*, 577 F.3d 1330, 1338 (11th Cir. 2009) (compiling cases). Has the D.C. Circuit's position a logical foundation? So far, courts have not prohibited agencies from using interpretive rules to revise their interpretations of regulatory *statutes*. Is this discrepancy justified? For a thorough review of all these issues, see Richard W. Murphy, Hunters *for Administrative Common Law*, 58 ADMIN. L. REV. 917 (2006).

7. *Problem.* The Madison Nonpublic Schools Act provides that "the courses of study at any nonpublic school shall be of the same standard as provided by the general school laws of the state." By its terms the Act applies to "any primary- or secondary-level school in the state other than a public school," and the Madison Supreme Court has construed the Act to apply to home schools. The Madison Board of Education has legislative rulemaking authority to implement the Act.

Without prior notice or a comment period, the Board recently adopted a set of "Home School Compliance Guidelines." The document had the stated aim of advising parents who engage in home-schooling about their legal obligations under the Nonpublic Schools Act. According to the guidelines, every home school must provide instruction in classes on social studies and science, during a school year lasting at least 180 days. The Board said that it inferred the 180-day requirement from the fact that, under Madison's school aid statute, a public school district that holds fewer than 180 days of classes forfeits some of its state aid. (Madison provides no financial aid to home schools.)

The Board then mailed a copy of the guidelines to all known home school families in Madison. The mailing instructed them to complete and return the attached information forms, in order to confirm that they were in compliance with the stated "legal requirements." It added that violations of the Nonpublic Schools Act may be redressed through administrative penalty proceedings. One recipient of this mailing was Irene. She has little confidence in the public schools of Madison, so she is educating her three school-age children at home, in cooperation with a private school at which the children take a few classes. She has now filed suit to challenge the guidelines as having been adopted unlawfully. The Board contends that they were validly adopted as interpretive rules.

Assume that Madison's law on rulemaking procedure is equivalent to federal law. How should the litigation be resolved? *Cf. Clonlara, Inc. v. State Board of Education*, 501 N.W.2d 88 (Mich. 1993).

§ 6.2   REQUIRED RULEMAKING

Reread § 5.1, which suggested some advantages and disadvantages of adjudication and rulemaking as agency lawmaking modalities. Although the decision to make law by rule rather than by order or vice versa has significant consequences, courts have generally been reluctant to interfere with an agency's choice of lawmaking procedures. That is particularly true in the federal courts. *See* Russell L. Weaver, *Chenery II: A Forty-year Retrospective*, 40 ADMIN. L. REV. 161 (1988). In the states, however, the picture is more mixed. Most states appear to follow the principle that agencies generally have discretion to make their law either by order or by rule. A significant minority, however, have moved in the direction of requiring agencies to make law by rule rather than by order, at least in some circumstances. Some have acted by statute, and others have reached this result through case law. Their experience offers an interesting study in contrasts with the federal model. *See generally* Arthur Earl Bonfield, *State Administrative Policy Formulation and the Choice of Lawmaking Methodology*, 42 ADMIN. L. REV. 121 (1990)

Much of the federal case law in this area has centered on the National Labor Relations Board, an agency that wields major policymaking power in structuring labor-management relations but virtually always relies on case-by-case adjudication, rather than rulemaking, to do so. As many other agencies began to use substantive rulemaking extensively in the 1960s and 1970s, the Board's preference attracted broad professional criticism. *See, e.g.,* Merton C. Bernstein, *The NLRB's Adjudication-Rule Making Dilemma Under the Administrative Procedure Act*, 79 YALE L.J. 571 (1970). The controversy came to a head in the following decision.

NLRB v. BELL AEROSPACE CO.
416 U.S. 267 (1974)

MR. JUSTICE POWELL delivered the opinion of the Court.

[Among the issues in this case is] whether the Board must proceed by rulemaking rather than by adjudication in determining whether certain buyers are "managerial employees." . . .

[The United Auto Workers petitioned the NLRB to hold] a representation election to determine whether the union would be certified as the bargaining representative of the buyers in the purchasing and procurement department at [Bell Aerospace's New York] plant. The company opposed the petition on the ground that the buyers were "managerial employees" and thus were not covered by the [National Labor Relations] Act. . . .

[The court of appeals, in an opinion written by Judge Henry Friendly, held that the Board had applied the wrong legal standard in deciding that these buyers were covered by the Act. Then the court remanded the case with instructions to commence a rulemaking proceeding to examine the question of the Act's coverage of managerial employees. The court argued: "The Board was prescribing a new policy, not just with respect to 25 buyers in Wheatfield, N.Y., but in substance . . . 'to fit all cases at all times.' . . . Yet the Board did not even attempt to inform industry and labor organizations . . . of its proposed new policy and to invite comment thereon, as it has sometimes done in the past. . . . [T]he argument for rule-making is especially strong when the Board is proposing to reverse a long-standing and oft-repeated policy on which industry and labor have relied. . . . [W]hen the Board has so long been committed to a position, it should be particularly sure that it has all available information before adopting another, in a setting where nothing stands in the way of a rule-making proceeding except the Board's congenital disinclination to follow [that] procedure. . . ."

[The Supreme Court upheld the lower court's position on the labor law question and then turned to the procedural issue:]

[T]he present question is whether on remand the Board must invoke its rulemaking procedures if it determines, in light of our opinion, that these buyers are not "managerial employees" under the Act. The Court of Appeals thought that rulemaking was required because *any* Board finding that the company's buyers are not "managerial" would be contrary to its prior decisions and would presumably be in the nature of a general rule designed "to fit all cases at all times."

A similar issue was presented to this Court in its second decision in *SEC v. Chenery Corp.,* 332 U.S. 194 (1947) *(Chenery II).* There, the respondent corporation argued that in an adjudicative proceeding the Commission could not apply a general standard that it had formulated for the first time in that proceeding. Rather, the Commission was required to resort instead to its rulemaking procedures if it desired to promulgate a new standard that would govern future conduct. In rejecting this contention, the Court first noted that the Commission had a statutory duty to decide the issue at hand in light of the proper standards and that this duty remained "regardless of whether those standards previously had been spelled out in a general rule or regulation." The Court continued:

> The function of filling in the interstices of the [Public Utility Holding Company] Act should be performed, as much as possible, through this quasi-legislative promulgation of rules to be applied in the future. But any rigid requirement to that effect would make the administrative process inflexible and incapable of dealing with many of the specialized problems which arise. . . . Not every principle essential to the effective administration of a statute can or should be cast immediately into the mold of a general rule. Some principles must await their own development, while others must be adjusted to meet particular, unforeseeable situations. *In performing its important functions in these respects, therefore, an administrative agency must be equipped to*

act either by general rule or by individual order. To insist upon one form of action to the exclusion of the other is to exalt form over necessity.

In other words, problems may arise in a case which the administrative agency could not reasonably foresee, problems which must be solved despite the absence of a relevant general rule. Or the agency may not have had sufficient experience with a particular problem to warrant rigidifying its tentative judgment into a hard and fast rule. *Or the problem may be so specialized and varying in nature as to be impossible of capture within the boundaries of a general rule.* In those situations, the agency must retain power to deal with the problems on a case-to-case basis if the administrative process is to be effective. There is thus a very definite place for the case-by-case evolution of statutory standards. (Emphasis added.)

The Court concluded that "the choice made between proceeding by general rule or by individual, *ad hoc* litigation is one that lies primarily in the informed discretion of the administrative agency.". . .

And in *NLRB v. Wyman-Gordon Co.*, 394 U.S. 759 (1969), the . . . plurality opinion of Mr. Justice Fortas . . . recognized that "adjudicated cases may and do . . . serve as vehicles for the formulation of agency policies, which are applied and announced therein," and that such cases "generally provide a guide to action that the agency may be expected to take in future cases." The concurring opinion of Mr. Justice Black . . . also noted that the Board had both adjudicative and rulemaking powers and that the choice between the two was "within its informed discretion."

The views expressed in *Chenery II* and *Wyman-Gordon* make plain that the Board is not precluded from announcing new principles in an adjudicative proceeding and that the choice between rulemaking and adjudication lies in the first instance within the Board's discretion. Although there may be situations where the Board's reliance on adjudication would amount to an abuse of discretion or a violation of the Act, nothing in the present case would justify such a conclusion. Indeed, there is ample indication that adjudication is especially appropriate in the instant context. As the Court of Appeals noted, "[t]here must be tens of thousands of manufacturing, wholesale and retail units which employ buyers, and hundreds of thousands of the latter." Moreover, duties of buyers vary widely depending on the company or industry. It is doubtful whether any generalized standard could be framed which would have more than marginal utility. The Board thus has reason to proceed with caution, developing its standards in a case-by-case manner with attention to the specific character of the buyers' authority and duties in each company. The Board's judgment that adjudication best serves this purpose is entitled to great weight.

The possible reliance of industry on the Board's past decisions with respect to buyers does not require a different result. It has not been shown that the adverse consequences ensuing from such reliance are so substantial that the Board should be precluded from reconsidering the issue in an adjudicative proceeding. Furthermore, this is not a case in which some new liability is sought to be imposed on individuals for past actions which were taken in good-faith reliance on Board pronouncements. Nor are fines or damages involved here. In any event, concern about such consequences is largely speculative, for the Board has not yet finally determined whether these buyers are "managerial."

It is true, of course, that rulemaking would provide the Board with a forum for soliciting the informed views of those affected in industry and labor before embarking on a new course. But surely the Board has discretion to decide that the adjudicative procedures in this case may also produce the relevant information necessary to mature and fair consideration of the issues. Those most immediately affected, the buyers and the company in the particular case, are accorded a full opportunity to be heard before the Board makes its determination. . . .

[Four Justices dissented on labor law grounds. All concurred in the portion of the opinion reprinted here.]

NOTES AND QUESTIONS

1. *Bell Aerospace.* In light of the analysis by the court of appeals, was the Supreme Court's ruling persuasive? As a practical matter, *Bell Aerospace* has been an overwhelming success in subsequent federal cases. Exceptions have been few and far between. *See* N. 5 below. Its reception among scholars, however, has been mixed. Professor Manning supports the Court's deference. He argues that any mandatory rulemaking doctrine would run into unmanageable questions of degree, because "all written laws leave some ambiguity (and thus discretion) at the margins," and any judicial effort to decide how much ambiguity is too much would have the "feel of arbitrary line-drawing." John F. Manning, *Nonlegislative Rules*, 72 GEO. WASH. L. REV. 893, 909–14 (2004). Professor Bressman, however, favors a judicially enforced "preference" for notice and comment rulemaking, so that agencies would at least have to justify their failure to rely on that procedure. Lisa Schultz Bressman, *Beyond Accountability: Arbitrariness and Legitimacy in the Administrative State*, 78 N.Y.U. L. REV. 461, 541–51 (2003). *See also* M. Elizabeth Magill, *Agency Choice of Policymaking Form*, 71 U. CHI. L. REV. 1383, 1412–25 (2004) (skeptically contrasting the courts' persistent failure to supervise agencies' policymaking forms with their intensive scrutiny of other discretionary choices). Should courts take on a larger role than *Bell Aerospace* seems to contemplate?

2. *Purely prospective adjudication.* Justice Powell's opinion in *Bell Aerospace* somewhat understated the ambivalence reflected in the Court's earlier decision in *NLRB v. Wyman-Gordon Co.*, 394 U.S. 759 (1969). That badly fractured case arose out of a Board-sponsored election to allow Wyman-Gordon's employees to decide whether to unionize and, if so, which union should be their exclusive bargaining representative. The Board ordered the company to furnish the competing unions a list of the names and addresses of its employees for electioneering purposes. The Board had instituted the practice of list disclosure in *Excelsior Underwear, Inc.,* 156 N.L.R.B. 1236 (1966), calling it "a requirement that will be applied in all election cases." However, the Board had declined to apply its new requirement to the companies involved in the *Excelsior* case itself.

Justice Fortas's plurality opinion for four Justices in *Wyman-Gordon* chastised the Board for its persistent failure to utilize APA rulemaking procedure. The avoidance of the APA was particularly glaring in *Excelsior*, he continued, because the Board did not even apply the list requirement to the case in which it was announced. While acknowledging that agencies can and do make law through case-by-case adjudication, he insisted that such precedents are not " 'rules' in the sense that they must, without more, be obeyed by the affected public." In separate opinions, Justices Douglas and Harlan also condemned the Board's circumvention of rulemaking procedure.

Ultimately, however, Justice Fortas concluded that the Board's failure to employ rulemaking in this instance was irrelevant, because Wyman-Gordon itself had been "specifically directed by the Board to submit a list." Thus, "[e]ven though the direction to furnish the list was followed by citation to *Excelsior,* it is an order in the present case that the respondent was required to obey." Justice Black wrote a concurring opinion that basically anticipated the broadly deferential stance of *Bell Aerospace* and was joined by two other Justices. Thus, through the combined effect of the Fortas and Black opinions, the Board's decision was upheld.

Today, having been eclipsed by *Bell Aerospace, Wyman-Gordon* is a largely forgotten decision. Is its low profile deserved? How significantly, if at all, did the decision limit the Board's ability to demand *Excelsior* lists from future employers without engaging in rulemaking?

Would it at least make sense for courts to hold that the Board may not do what it did in *Excelsior*—adopt a case law principle in an adjudicative case and then decline to apply it in that very proceeding? In the realm of civil litigation, the Court has taken steps in the direction of disapproving prospective-only judicial holdings. *Harper v. Virginia Dep't of Taxation*, 509 U.S. 86 (1993). In administrative law, however, no such absolute rule prevails. What objections could be advanced against a judicial doctrine that puts pressure on agencies to make their adjudicative lawmaking retroactive?

3. *Willingness to reconsider.* If the Board's lawmaking by adjudication in *Bell Aerospace* was valid, or at least not open to judicial correction, under what circumstances would that device be impermissible? In *Mercy Hospitals*

of Sacramento, Inc. v. Local 250, Hosp. & Institutional Workers Union, 217 N.L.R.B. 765 (1975), the Board announced a policy that registered nurses at nonprofit hospitals may always be represented by a separate bargaining unit. A hospital challenged that policy and sought a larger bargaining unit in *NLRB v. St. Francis Hosp.,* 601 F.2d 404, 414–17 (9th Cir. 1979), but the Board refused to receive evidence to support this position. The Ninth Circuit reversed:

> The key question raised herein is whether the *per se* policy established in the Board's *Mercy* decision . . . is consistent with the congressional directive. . . . Further, one may question the fairness of a policy that is applied without a chance for an effected [sic] party to demonstrate that its situation does not fall within the scope of the policy or otherwise to argue why the policy should not be applied in its case. This is especially so herein because the Board . . . has, on more than one occasion, placed registered nurses in the same bargaining unit as other health care professionals, as the Hospital argued it should do in this case. . . .
>
> . . . Because we find the Hospital's proffered evidence as to the appropriateness of an all-professional unit to be definitely relevant and because we do not believe that the Board's *Mercy* decision can or should control this case, we find the refusal to receive the Hospital's evidence herein to be arbitrary and capricious.

What was wrong with the Board's adjudicative lawmaking in this case? How was the case different from *Bell Aerospace*? Would the result have been different if the Board had used § 553 rulemaking? *Cf. American Hosp. Ass'n v. NLRB,* 499 U.S. 606 (1991), discussed in § 3.2 N.2.

4. *Reliance and retroactivity. Bell Aerospace* alludes to three situations in which reliance interests might require a "different result." They are situations in which: (1) the adverse consequences of retrospective adjudicative lawmaking would be substantial to parties who had relied on past decisions of the agency; (2) new liability is sought to be imposed retrospectively by adjudication on individuals for past actions which were taken in good-faith reliance on agency pronouncements; or (3) fines or damages are involved. In current federal practice, the "different result" that courts would prescribe under such circumstances would generally not be a directive to engage in rulemaking proceedings. Instead, the court would probably hold on the merits that the agency order was a violation of due process or was arbitrary and capricious in its application to that particular case, so that the complaining litigant would not have to comply with it. *See, e.g., FCC v. Fox Television Stations, Inc. (Fox II),* 132 S. Ct. 2307 (2012), § 4.5.1; *Microcomputer Technology Institute v. Riley,* 139 F.3d 1044 (5th Cir. 1998); *Pfaff v. HUD,* 88 F.3d 739, 747–50 (9th Cir. 1996); *Stoller v. CFTC,* 834 F.2d 262, 265 (2d Cir. 1987). If otherwise valid, however, the precedent itself would stand, and the agency would be free to enforce it in the future

against parties who did have timely notice of it. *McDonald v. Watt,* 653 F.2d 1035, 1041–46 (5th Cir. 1981).

Recall *Retail, Wholesale & Dep't Store Union v. NLRB,* 466 F.2d 380, 390 (D.C. Cir. 1972), discussed in § 4.5.1 N.4. According to that case, when an agency seeks to apply a new case law principle retroactively, a reviewing court should apply a balancing test in order to decide whether that application is arbitrary and capricious. Under that test, the court should consider, among other factors, the statutory interest in applying the new rule to the case at hand, as well as the possible burdens of applying the new rule retroactively to a party, especially if that party had relied on the agency's former policy.

Is the *Retail Union* remedy for unfairly retroactive agency lawmaking better or worse than the approach of the lower court in *Bell Aerospace,* i.e., holding that the agency must institute rulemaking proceedings if it wants to consider overruling its prior case law?

5. *Abuse of discretion.* According to *Bell Aerospace,* "there may be situations where the Board's reliance on adjudication would amount to an abuse of discretion. . . ." Among the few federal cases to find that an agency has abused its discretion in this sense is *Ford Motor Co. v. FTC,* 673 F.2d 1008 (9th Cir. 1981). In that case the Federal Trade Commission issued a cease and desist order against Francis Ford, a retail automobile dealer. The Commission found the repossession practices used by Francis Ford against its defaulting purchasers to be a violation of Section 5 of the FTC Act. The court of appeals vacated the order, stating: "Ultimately . . . we are persuaded to set aside this order because the rule of the case made below will have general application. It will not apply just to Francis Ford. Credit practices similar to those of Francis Ford are widespread in the car dealership industry; and the U.C.C. section the FTC wishes us to interpret [adversely to Francis Ford] exists in 49 states." *Id.* at 1009–10.

Is *Ford Motor Co.* distinguishable from *Bell Aerospace? See* Richard K. Berg, *Re-examining Policy Procedures: The Choice Between Rulemaking and Adjudication,* 38 ADMIN. L. REV. 149, 155–58 (1986); Ford Motor Co. v. FTC: *No Rule without a Rulemaking?,* REGULATION, Sept./Oct. 1981, at 13. For better or worse, federal court decisions purporting to discern exceptions to *Bell Aerospace* have essentially vanished from the federal case law after the early 1980s. *See* William D. Araiza, *Agency Adjudication, the Importance of Facts, and the Limitations of Labels,* 57 WASH. & LEE L. REV. 351 (2000).

6. *Benefit programs.* One additional Supreme Court case has suggested that an agency must execute specified lawmaking by rule rather than by order, despite the absence of a statute explicitly requiring that approach. In *Morton v. Ruiz,* 415 U.S. 199, 231–35 (1974), the issue was whether welfare benefits should be paid to those Indians who live near but not on reservations. According to *Ruiz,* if the Bureau of Indian Affairs did not have sufficient funds to pay all eligible beneficiaries, "it would be incumbent upon [the agency] to develop an eligibility standard to deal with this

problem. . . . But in such a case the agency must, at a minimum, let the standard be generally known so as to assure that it is being applied consistently and so as to avoid both the reality and the appearance of arbitrary denial of benefits to potential beneficiaries. . . . No matter how rational or consistent with congressional intent a particular decision might be, the determination of eligibility cannot be made on an ad hoc basis by the dispenser of the funds."

Ruiz was decided a few months before *Bell Aerospace,* which did not even cite it. Thus, most commentators have regarded *Ruiz* as an outlier that cannot be reconciled with the main body of federal law on required rulemaking. Do you agree?

7. *Judicial presumption.* State courts have experimented with bolder approaches to required rulemaking than have ever prevailed in the federal courts. Perhaps the most widely noted of these state-level experiments has been the opinion of Justice Hans Linde in *Megdal v. Oregon State Bd. of Dental Exam'rs*, 605 P.2d 273 (Ore. 1980). The Board revoked the petitioner's dental license because he had fraudulently obtained malpractice coverage for dentists in his California office by falsely representing that they were employed in Oregon. The applicable statute prohibited "unprofessional conduct." The court remanded the case because the Board had not adopted rules to elaborate on this vague statutory standard. Justice Linde pointed out that the Board did have rulemaking authority. He reasoned that the legislature "should not be assumed to be insensitive to the importance of fair notice of grounds that may lead to loss of one's profession or occupation." In fact, a number of other professional licensing schemes did specifically require an administrative board to make policy through rules. The court inferred from this statutory pattern that "the legislative purpose is to provide for the further specification of the standard by rules, unless a different understanding is shown. . . ."

Megdal had at least the potential to become the fount of a broad presumption favoring rulemaking in similar circumstances. *See* Bonfield, *supra*, at 161. In practice, however, Oregon courts have not adhered to this broad reading. Later cases have indicated that the legislature's intentions regarding mandatory rulemaking should be ascertained on the basis of multiple indicia of legislative intent, rather than through a widely applicable presumption. *See, e.g., Coffey v. Bd. of Geologist Exam'rs*, 235 P.3d 678, 681–82 (Ore. 2010); *Trebesch v. Employment Div.*, 710 P.2d 136, 139–40 (Ore. 1985).

8. *Rulemaking required by due process.* An alternative potential route to required rulemaking, which the court in *Megdal* considered but ultimately eschewed, would be through the federal due process clause. Indeed, a handful of federal and state cases have held that in some circumstances due process requires agencies to take adverse actions against an individual only in accordance with standards previously expressed in statutes or rules. *See White v. Roughton*, 530 F.2d 750 (7th Cir. 1976) (denial of welfare benefits

under a local program); *Soglin v. Kauffman,* 418 F.2d 163 (7th Cir. 1969) (expulsion of a university student for "misconduct"); *Elizondo v. State Dep't of Revenue,* 570 P.2d 518 (Colo. 1977) (denial of probationary drivers' licenses); *Pa. State Bd. of Pharmacy v. Cohen,* 292 A.2d 277 (Pa. 1972) (revocation of pharmacist's license for "grossly unprofessional conduct). Note, however, that these decisions all date from the 1970s or before. Would there be a good case for reviving this line of authority? *See* Bonfield, *supra,* at 165–72.

9. *Other state cases.* Cases in states other than Oregon have also required agencies to elaborate the major contours of their law by rule, despite the absence of an express statutory requirement. Some of these cases have held a particular agency action invalid because that action was deemed to be a rule *de facto* but had been issued without observance of ordinary rulemaking procedures. *See, e.g., CBS Inc. v. Comptroller of the Treasury,* 575 A.2d 324, 330 (Md. 1990); *Las Vegas Transit System, Inc. v. Las Vegas Strip Trolley,* 780 P.2d 1145 (Nev. 1989); *In re Hibbing Taconite Co.,* 431 N.W.2d 885, 894–95 (Minn. App. 1988); *Metromedia v. Director, Div. of Taxation,* 478 A.2d 742 (N.J. 1984); Bonfield, *supra,* at 152–53. In other state cases, particular agency adjudicatory actions have been held invalid because they made legal or policy decisions that, in the court's view, should have been made by rule instead. *See Rodriguez v. Service Lloyds Insurance Co.,* 997 S.W.2d 248 (Tex. 1999); *Tenn. Cable Television Ass'n v. Tennessee Public Serv. Comm'n,* 844 S.W.2d 151 (Tenn. App. 1992); *Aluli v. Lewin,* 828 P.2d 802 (Hawaii 1992); *Matter of Bessemer Mountain,* 856 P.2d 450 (Wyo. 1993). The latter cases have reached this result by relying primarily on policy considerations, as opposed to a *Megdal*-like presumption about the legislature's expectations.

10. *1981 MSAPA.* Section 2–104(3) of the 1981 MSAPA provides that "as soon as feasible, and to the extent practicable, [each agency must] adopt rules, in addition to those otherwise required . . . embodying appropriate standards, principles, and procedural safeguards, that the agency will apply to the law it administers." According to the reporter for that Act, "[t]his model statutory provision embodies a clear legislative determination that the values of *prompt* elaboration of agency law by rule and *detailed* elaboration of agency law by rule are to be preferred over the competing general values of agency convenience or agency preference for ad hoc law making in the course of adjudications. As a result, the MSAPA provision would fundamentally change existing law in most states. . . ." Bonfield, *supra,* at 145. Iowa adopted the same language in 1998. *See* Iowa Code § 17A.3(1)(c). *See also* Utah Code Ann. § 63G–3–201 (a differently phrased statutory provision on required rulemaking). The 2010 MSAPA, however, discontinues the 1981 experiment and contains no provision on required rulemaking.

11. *Presumptive rulemaking under Florida law.* In 1991, Florida adopted a version of the 1981 MSAPA required-rulemaking standard. By statute, "rulemaking is not a matter of agency discretion." Agencies are required to use rulemaking as a means for making statements of general applicability and future effect to the extent that it is "feasible and

practicable" to do so. Agencies bear the burden of showing that rulemaking is not feasible or practicable. Fla. Stat. Ann. § 120.54(1)(a). In practice, no other state has pursued a required-rulemaking policy as forcefully as Florida has.

Unsurprisingly, the effect of the "presumptive rulemaking" provision, as it has come to be known, was an immediate and substantial increase in the number of agency rules. That development sparked a sharp reaction. The governor claimed that presumptive rulemaking resulted in a "proliferation of overly-precise rules [and] overwhelming red tape and deprives agency decision-makers of the ability to exercise good judgment and common sense." In 1996, the legislature sharply revised the rulemaking structure, although it did not repeal the presumptive rulemaking provision. *See* Jim Rossi, *The 1996 Revised Florida Administrative Procedure Act: A Rulemaking Revolution or Counter-Revolution?*, 49 ADMIN. L. REV. 345 (1997).

Among the changes enacted in 1996 was one provision (discussed in § 6.4 N.6) that made waivers or variances from existing rules *mandatory* under certain broadly defined circumstances. Another provision (discussed in § 5.1 N.3) limited agency rulemaking power to situations in which an agency is implementing a specific provision of law; agencies may no longer adopt rules that merely are deemed reasonably related to the purposes of the underlying legislation. A third provision revised the APA's regulatory analysis requirements and enabled private parties to enforce them more easily. A fourth provision abolished the presumption of validity normally accorded to agency rules—it shifted the burden of proof to agencies when their proposed rules are challenged in hearings before the Florida central panel. In subsequent years the Florida rulemaking system has remained unstable. The APA has been amended several more times to impose further constraints on the rulemaking process.

To what extent, if at all, does the Florida rulemaking counter-revolution cast doubt on the desirability of required rulemaking provisions such as those of the 1981 MSAPA?

12. *Problem.* Madison University (MU) student disciplinary rules (adopted after appropriate notice and comment procedures) provide that a student can be suspended or expelled for "conduct inappropriate for a student." A Student Discipline Board (SDB), consisting of both faculty and students, administers the student disciplinary rules.

Mark, an MU student, received 185 tickets for illegal parking in MU parking lots. After providing notice and a trial-type hearing, the SDB suspended Mark from school for six months, holding that such flagrant disregard of the MU parking rules was "conduct inappropriate for a student." In its opinion the Board stated: "Suspension is clearly not an excessive sanction for a student who has committed over 150 parking infractions." The SDB had never before treated a parking or traffic violation as a violation of the student disciplinary rules.

(a)   Should the SDB's decision be reversed because of insufficient prior rulemaking? Assume, alternatively, that MU is (i) a federal government institution; (ii) a state university in a state that has adopted the 2010 MSAPA; or (iii) a state university in a state that has adopted the 1981 MSAPA.

(b)   Suppose that, a year after Mark's case, Belinda accumulated 175 parking tickets and was brought before the SDB. By this time a new group of faculty and students had rotated onto the Board. The SDB suspended Belinda, stating in its decision that "to distinguish between 175 and 185 tickets would be artificial, so we must follow the precedent set in Mark's case." It refused to even consider Belinda's argument that the precedent should be reconsidered or overruled. Should the SDB's decision in Belinda's case be reversed?

§ 6.3   RULEMAKING PETITIONS AND AGENCY AGENDA-SETTING

Section 553(e) of the federal APA, § 6 of the 1961 MSAPA, and § 318 of the 2010 MSAPA all authorize members of the public to petition an agency for the issuance, amendment, or repeal of a rule. The worthwhile objectives of these provisions have resulted in their widespread incorporation in state APAs.

Perhaps the most important purpose of the petition for rulemaking is to force an agency to re-examine the status quo. A petition might request that the agency undertake additional regulation, or that the agency repeal or modify existing rules that are not working properly or have become obsolete. Such petitions bring to the agency's attention situations requiring prompt action and thus help to insure more responsive government.

Another important purpose of petitions for rulemaking is to supply a means for focused public input when an agency has adopted a rule without advance notice and comment under one of the § 553 exemptions. *See Guardian Fed. Sav. & Loan Ass'n v. FSLIC,* 589 F.2d 658, 668 (D.C. Cir. 1978). Similarly, even when an agency has provided advance notice and comment, some members of the public who did not know about the proposed rule, or who did not participate in the process, may be dissatisfied with the final rule and wish to persuade the agency to modify it. The right to file a rulemaking petition may help them.

The 1961 and 2010 MSAPA provisions just cited require a statement of reasons upon denial of a rulemaking petition. Federal APA § 553(e) does not require any such statement, but § 555(e) of that Act requires a brief statement of the grounds for denial of any application or petition filed with an agency. *See Auer v. Robbins,* 519 U.S. 452, 459 (1997) (proper remedy for allegedly obsolete regulations is "a petition to the agency for rulemaking, § 553(e), denial of which must be justified by a statement of reasons, § 555(e), and can be appealed to the courts"). The requirement of an explanatory statement is important, because it forces agencies to consider carefully their precise reasons for any such denial, thereby discouraging automatic or impulsive dismissals of rulemaking petitions. The required written statement also facilitates judicial review.

From the government's point of view, rulemaking petitions give rise to concerns about the extent to which an agency will be able to determine its own priorities and workload, notwithstanding pressures from outsiders. This concern surfaces not only when the agency is asked to commence a proceeding, but also when outside parties seek to hasten the completion of a proceeding that the agency has already begun. This section examines a number of contexts in which the law seeks to reconcile these competing private and governmental interests.

MASSACHUSETTS V. ENVIRONMENTAL PROTECTION AGENCY
549 U.S. 497 (2007)

[Massachusetts and other parties petitioned the EPA to regulate greenhouse gases emitted by new motor vehicles. Such rules would, they argued, help to combat global warming. Section 202(a)(1) of the Clean Air Act (CAA), 42 U.S.C. § 7521(a)(1), provides: "The [EPA] Administrator shall by regulation prescribe . . . standards applicable to the emission of any air pollutant from any . . . new motor vehicle engines, which in his judgment cause, or contribute to, air pollution which may reasonably be anticipated to endanger public health or welfare. . . ." The key term "air pollutant" means "any air pollution agent . . . including any physical, chemical, biological, radioactive . . . substance or matter which is emitted into or otherwise enters the ambient air." *Id.* § 7602(g).

EPA declined to adopt regulations concerning new motor vehicle emissions, concluding that the term "air pollutant" does not include greenhouse gases such as carbon dioxide. In any event, the agency said, a causal link between greenhouse gases produced by human activities and global warming had not been "unequivocally established." In that light, the agency continued, "[w]e do not believe . . . that it would be either effective or appropriate for EPA to establish [greeenhouse gas] standards for motor vehicles at this time." EPA noted that such regulations would conflict with the President's comprehensive approach to the problem of climate change, such as the creation of non-regulatory programs to encourage voluntary private sector reductions in greenhouse gas emissions, and might hamper the President's ability to persuade developing nations to reduce emissions. The petitioners sought judicial review of EPA's refusal to act.

The Court initially held, by a 5–4 vote, that petitioners had standing to sue. This portion of the opinion is discussed in § 11.1.2 N.5. The same five-Justice majority then reached the merits and overturned EPA's decision not to engage in rulemaking:]

STEVENS, J. . . .

The scope of our review of the merits of the statutory issues is narrow. As we have repeated time and again, an agency has broad discretion to choose how best to marshal its limited resources and personnel to carry out its delegated responsibilities. That discretion is at its height when the agency decides not to bring an enforcement action. Therefore, in *Heckler v. Chaney*, 470 U.S. 821 (1985) [excerpted in § 10.5], we held that an agency's refusal to initiate enforcement proceedings is ordinarily not subject to judicial review. [The Court concluded, however, that the *Chaney* rule of unreviewability should not apply to agency denials of rulemaking petitions. This part of the Court's opinion is quoted in § 10.5 N.4.] Refusals to promulgate rules are thus susceptible to judicial review, though such review is "extremely limited" and "highly deferential."

[The Court determined that EPA had misinterpreted § 7602(g) and that the statutory definition of an "air pollutant" clearly included greenhouse gases such as carbon dioxide.]

The alternative basis for EPA's decision—that even if it does have statutory authority to regulate greenhouse gases, it would be unwise to do so at this time—rests on reasoning divorced from the statutory text. While the statute does condition the exercise of EPA's authority on its formation of a "judgment," that judgment must relate to whether an air pollutant "cause[s], or contribute[s] to, air pollution which may reasonably be anticipated to endanger public health or welfare." Put another way, the use of the word "judgment" is not a roving license to ignore the statutory text. It is but a direction to exercise discretion within defined statutory limits.

If EPA makes a finding of endangerment, the Clean Air Act requires the agency to regulate emissions of the deleterious pollutant from new motor vehicles. EPA no doubt has significant latitude as to the manner, timing, content, and coordination of its regulations with those of other agencies. But once EPA has responded to a petition for rulemaking, its reasons for action or inaction must conform to the authorizing statute. Under the clear terms of the Clean Air Act, EPA can avoid taking further action only if it determines that greenhouse gases do not contribute to climate change or if it provides some reasonable explanation as to why it cannot or will not exercise its discretion to determine whether they do. To the extent that this constrains agency discretion to pursue other priorities of the Administrator or the President, this is the congressional design.

EPA has refused to comply with this clear statutory command. Instead, it has offered a laundry list of reasons not to regulate. For example, EPA said that a number of voluntary executive branch programs already provide an effective response to the threat of global warming, that regulating greenhouse gases might impair the President's ability to negotiate with "key developing nations" to reduce emissions, and that curtailing motor-vehicle emissions would reflect "an inefficient, piecemeal approach to address the climate change issue."

Although we have neither the expertise nor the authority to evaluate these policy judgments, it is evident they have nothing to do with whether greenhouse gas emissions contribute to climate change. Still less do they amount to a reasoned justification for declining to form a scientific judgment. In particular, while the President has broad authority in foreign affairs, that authority does not extend to the refusal to execute domestic laws. . . .

Nor can EPA avoid its statutory obligation by noting the uncertainty surrounding various features of climate change and concluding that it would therefore be better not to regulate at this time. If the scientific uncertainty is so profound that it precludes EPA from making a reasoned judgment as to whether greenhouse gases contribute to global warming, EPA must say so. That EPA would prefer not to regulate greenhouse gases because of some residual uncertainty—which . . . is in fact all that it said—is irrelevant. The statutory question is whether sufficient information exists to make an endangerment finding.

In short, EPA has offered no reasoned explanation for its refusal to decide whether greenhouse gases cause or contribute to climate change. Its action was therefore "arbitrary, capricious, . . . or otherwise not in accordance with law." We need not and do not reach the question whether on remand EPA must make an endangerment finding, or whether policy concerns can inform EPA's actions in the event that it makes such a finding. Cf. *Chevron*. We hold only that EPA must ground its reasons for action or inaction in the statute. . . .

SCALIA, J., joined by ROBERTS, C.J., THOMAS, J., and ALITO, J., dissenting. . . .

[Justice Scalia emphasized that, according to CAA § 202(a)(1), the EPA Administrator must regulate motor vehicle emissions "which *in his judgment* cause, or contribute to, air pollution which may reasonably be anticipated to endanger public health or welfare" (emphasis added). He continued:]

The question thus arises: Does anything *require* the Administrator to make a "judgment" whenever a petition for rulemaking is filed? Without citation of the statute or any other authority, the Court says yes. Why is that so? . . . Where does the CAA say that the EPA Administrator is required to come to a decision on this question whenever a rulemaking petition is filed? The Court points to no such provision because none exists. . . .

I am willing to assume, for the sake of argument, that the Administrator's discretion in this regard is not entirely unbounded—that if he has no reasonable basis for deferring judgment he must grasp the nettle at once. The Court, however, with no basis in text or precedent, rejects all of EPA's stated "policy judgments" as not "amount[ing] to a reasoned justification," effectively narrowing the universe of potential reasonable bases to a single one: Judgment can be delayed *only* if the Administrator concludes that "the scientific uncertainty is [too] profound." The Administrator is precluded from concluding *for other reasons* "that it would . . . be better not to regulate at this time." Such other reasons—perfectly valid reasons—were set forth in the agency's statement. . . .

[T]he statute says *nothing at all* about the reasons for which the Administrator may *defer* making a judgment—the permissible reasons for deciding not to grapple with the issue at the present time. Thus, the various "policy" rationales that the Court criticizes are not "divorced from the statutory text," except in the sense that the statutory text is silent, as texts are often silent about permissible reasons for the exercise of agency discretion. The reasons the EPA gave are surely considerations executive agencies *regularly* take into account (and *ought* to take into account) when deciding whether to consider entering a new field: the impact such entry would have on other Executive Branch programs and on foreign policy. There is no basis in law for the Court's imposed limitation. . . . As the Administrator acted within the law in declining to make a "judgment" for the policy reasons above set forth, I would uphold the decision to deny the rulemaking petition on that ground alone. . . .

NOTES AND QUESTIONS

1. *"Extremely narrow" judicial review.* In *Massachusetts* the Court says that judicial review of an agency's refusal to commence a rulemaking proceeding is available but "extremely limited." Similar assertions pervade the case law. For example, in *Defenders of Wildlife v. Gutierrez*, 532 F.3d 913 (D.C. Cir. 2008), environmentalists petitioned the National Marine Fisheries Service to adopt an emergency rule to protect North Atlantic right whales (a severely endangered species) from collisions with ships. The suggested rule would have required ships to reduce their speeds during certain periods. NMFS denied the petition, explaining that an emergency rule would detract agency resources from the promulgation of a final, comprehensive rule. The court upheld this decision, remarking that " 'an agency's refusal to institute rulemaking proceedings is at the high end of the range' of levels of deference we give to agency action under our 'arbitrary and capricious' review." The

court said that it had overturned such refusals "only in the rarest and most compelling of circumstances," and that this was not such a case, although three years had elapsed since the petition denial, and NMFS had still not issued a final rule.

Why *should* courts review petition denials more deferentially than they would review other decisions? An influential opinion by Judge McGowan contains one answer:

> An agency's discretionary decision *not* to regulate a given activity is inevitably based, in large measure, on factors not inherently susceptible to judicial resolution—*e.g.,* internal management considerations as to budget and personnel; evaluations of its own competence; weighing of competing policies within a broad statutory framework. Further, even if an agency considers a particular problem worthy of regulation, it may determine for reasons lying within its special expertise that the time for action has not yet arrived. . . . The circumstances in the regulated industry may be evolving in a way that could vitiate the need for regulation, or the agency may still be developing the expertise necessary for effective regulation.

Natural Resources Defense Council, Inc. v. SEC, 606 F.2d 1031 (D.C. Cir.1979). *But see* William V. Luneburg, *Petitioning Federal Agencies for Rulemaking: An Overview of Administrative and Judicial Practice and Some Recommendations for Improvement,* 1988 WIS. L. REV. 1, 48–50 (questioning the validity of the distinction between petition denials and other decisions).

2. *Massachusetts v. EPA.* Does the Court's disposition of the merits in *Massachusetts* undercut its claim that its review is "highly deferential"? Notice that the opinion refers several times to the EPA's broad discretion in handling rulemaking petitions. In that light, can you articulate precisely what error the Court thinks the agency made, and should that error have been fatal? Did the opinion really leave the EPA free to decline on remand to regulate greenhouse gases? For assessments of the principal case, see, e.g., Jody Freeman & Adrian Vermeule, Massachusetts v. EPA: *From Politics to Expertise,* 2007 SUP. CT. REV. 51; Kathryn A. Watts & Amy J. Wildermuth, Massachusetts v. EPA: *Breaking New Ground on Issues Other Than Global Warming,* 102 NW. U. L. REV. 1029 (2008); Eric Biber, *The Importance of Resource Allocation in Administrative Law,* 60 ADMIN. L. REV. 1 (2008).

3. *Jurisdictional issues.* Even   before   *Massachusetts,*   some circumstances that could justify a judicial decision to overturn an agency's refusal to commence rulemaking proceedings were well recognized. For example, in *NAACP v. FPC,* 520 F.2d 432 (D.C. Cir. 1975), *aff'd,* 425 U.S. 662 (1976), the plaintiff asked the Federal Power Commission to adopt rules requiring its regulatees to observe equal employment opportunity practices. The Commission declined on the basis that it had no jurisdiction to do so. The D.C. Circuit disagreed and vacated the agency's decision. However, as the court later explained, the *NAACP* case "[did not] compel the agency to

actually institute rulemaking proceedings. Rather, [the] agency was required on remand to *reconsider* its denial of the petition, in light of the correct interpretation of the law as enunciated by the court. . . ." *WWHT, Inc. v. FCC,* 656 F.2d 807, 819 (D.C. Cir. 1981). How well does this precedent account for the *Massachusetts* decision?

4.   *State case.* In *Rios v. Dep't of Labor & Industries,* 39 P.3d 961 (Wash.2002), the Supreme Court of Washington reversed a workplace safety agency's refusal to require mandatory blood testing for agricultural pesticide handlers. That refusal was arbitrary and capricious, the court concluded, because a technical advisory group of experts convened by the agency had found that such a program would be feasible and protective of workers. The department had not disputed the advisory group's findings. Nevertheless, it had declined to proceed with rulemaking on the ground that its limited budget and staff resources should not necessarily be devoted to designing and defending a blood testing program as opposed to more manageable projects. The court found that argument unpersuasive, however, because the department had already invested time and resources into studying the merits of a testing program and appointing an advisory group to evaluate it. Did this holding intrude too far on the agency's prerogatives?

5.   *Deadline for response.* Even if courts cannot or will not supervise the petitioning process closely, an APA can impose constraints on the process at the agency level. Section 318 of the 2010 MSAPA requires that an agency act on a petition within sixty days, either to deny the petition or to initiate rulemaking proceedings. The 1961 MSAPA provision, adopted by many states, requires such an agency response within thirty days. Federal APA § 553(e), however, contains no time limit provision. As a result, petitions are often filed with a federal agency and never heard of again. Should the federal act be amended to provide that an agency must respond to a rulemaking petition within a specified number of days? *See* Luneburg, *supra,* at 16–17.

6.   *Reexamination of existing rules.* Even without a formal proposal from outsiders, an agency can conduct internal reviews of its rules to determine which ones should be changed or abandoned. *See generally* ACUS Recommendation 95–3, 60 Fed. Reg. 43,109 (1995); Neil R. Eisner & Judith S. Kaleta, *Federal Agency Review of Existing Regulations,* 48 ADMIN. L. REV. 139 (1996); Sidney A. Shapiro, *Agency Priority Setting and the Review of Existing Agency Rules,* 48 ADMIN. L. REV. 370, 372 (1996).

Sometimes such reviews are mandatory. The Regulatory Flexibility Act requires agencies to reexamine all of their existing rules that have a significant economic impact on a substantial number of small entities (mainly small businesses). The agency must review any given rule within ten years of adopting it, and public input must be invited. 5 U.S.C. § 610. President Obama has made retrospective review of regulations a priority of his administration. *See, e.g.,* Exec. Order 13,610, 77 Fed. Reg. 28,469 (2012); Exec. Order 13,563, § 6, 76 Fed. Reg. 3821 (2011); COUNCIL OF ECONOMIC ADVISERS, SMARTER REGULATIONS THROUGH RETROSPECTIVE REVIEW 1 (2012),

www.whitehouse.gov/sites/default/files/lookback_report_rev_final.pdf
(declaring that plans submitted by agencies under this program would result
in more than 500 rule changes and more than $10 billion in savings). At the
state level, see, e.g., Mo. Rev. Stat. § 536.175 (requiring state agencies to
review all of their rules every five years).

Congressional critics of agency regulation have introduced bills in recent
sessions to require broader and more frequent reviews and to bring the courts
into the process. *See* H.R. 309, 113th Cong. (2013); H.R. 3392, 112th Cong.
(2011). Should legislation of this kind be enacted? A study by the GAO
indicates that reviews of existing rules can be useful, but mandatory reviews
are far less likely to lead to a conclusion that a rule needs a change than are
reviews that an agency undertakes voluntarily. Government Accountability
Office, *Reexamining Regulations: Opportunities Exist to Improve Effectiveness
and Transparency of Retrospective Reviews*, GAO–07–791, at 30–34 (2007).

7. *Retrospective review in individual statutes.* Some individual
regulatory statutes also require agencies to review existing rules. The Dodd-
Frank Act requires the Consumer Financial Protection Bureau to assess the
effectiveness of each of its significant rules within five years of its effective
date. 12 U.S. C. § 5512(d). In addition, the Telecommunications Act of 1996
directs the FCC to review telecommunications rules every two years "to
determine whether any such regulation is no longer necessary in the public
interest as the result of meaningful economic competition," and to repeal or
modify any rule deemed not to be necessary. 47 U.S.C. § 161(a)(2). As the
FCC construed this provision, "necessary" did not mean "indispensable," but
simply referred to the same "necessary in the public interest" standard that
the Commission uses in deciding whether to adopt a rule in the first place.
Does that interpretation unduly frustrate the deregulatory, pro-competitive
purposes that generally underlay the 1996 Act? *See Cellco Partnership v.
FCC*, 357 F.3d 88 (D.C. Cir. 2004).

8. *Delay in completing rulemaking proceedings.* Even after an agency
has launched a rulemaking proceeding, it may stir controversy by not issuing
a final rule as quickly as proponents had expected or hoped. Congress has
frequently responded to apparent foot-dragging on agencies' part by enacting
deadlines for the completion of particular proceedings. *See generally* Jacob E.
Gersen & Anne Joseph O'Connell, *Deadlines in Administrative Law*, 156 U.
PA. L. REV. 923 (2008). Such deadlines have been widely criticized as
ineffective and counterproductive. *See* ACUS Recommendation 78–3, 43 Fed.
Reg. 27,509 (1978); Alden F. Abbott, *The Case Against Federal Statutory and
Judicial Deadlines: A Cost-Benefit Analysis*, 39 ADMIN. L. REV. 171 (1987).
Declaring that Congress has imposed far more deadlines on EPA than the
agency could possibly meet, one scholar says that this device provokes a
"deadline-litigation syndrome" that "transfers responsibility for setting
agency priority from top administrators to interest groups. . . . It is hard to
imagine a worse way to apportion agency resources." R. Shep Melnick,
Administrative Law and Bureaucratic Reality, 44 ADMIN. L. REV. 245, 249–50
(1992).

However, when Congress prescribes such a deadline, should a court enforce it in a suit brought by a would-be beneficiary of the proposed rule? Some courts do. *See, e.g., Forest Guardians v. Babbitt*, 174 F.3d 1178, 1187 (10th Cir. 1999) (" 'shall' means shall"). The D.C. Circuit, however, sometimes declines to do so, out of "respect for the autonomy and comparative institutional advantage of the executive branch." *See, e.g., In re Barr Labs, Inc.* 930 F.2d 72 (D.C. Cir. 1991). Professor Pierce, although highly critical of Congress for imposing deadlines without providing agencies the resources with which to meet them, disagrees with the D.C. Circuit's approach: "A court cannot deviate from [such] clear commands without doing violence to the principle of legislative supremacy. That principle is too valuable to sacrifice even when adherence to the principle is certain to produce a plethora of unintended adverse effects. . . . When the legislative branch is the sole source of a problem, the courts should leave its solution solely to the legislative branch." Richard J. Pierce, Jr., *Judicial Review of Agency Actions in a Period of Diminishing Agency Resources*, 49 ADMIN. L. REV. 61, 77–84, 93 (1997). Do you agree? For a reply, see Patricia M. Wald, *Judicial Review in the Time of Cholera*, 49 ADMIN. L. REV. 659, 663–64 (1997).

Even in the absence of a statutory deadline, private citizens sometimes seek the courts' aid in inducing agencies to conclude a protracted proceeding. *See* APA § 706(1) (reviewing court shall "compel agency action unlawfully withheld or unreasonably delayed"). Judicial relief in this sort of suit is highly discretionary. According to *In re International Chemical Workers Union*, 958 F.2d 1144, 1149–50 (D.C. Cir. 1992), a court must consider four factors in determining whether an agency's delay was unreasonable:

> First, the "court should ascertain the length of time that has elapsed since the agency came under a legal duty to act." . . . Second, "the reasonableness of the delay must be judged 'in the context of the statute' which authorizes the agency's action." . . . Third, the court must examine the consequences of the agency's delay. . . . Finally, the court should give due consideration in the balance to "any plea of administrative error, administrative convenience, practical difficulty in carrying out a legislative mandate, or need to prioritize in the face of limited resources."

In this case the Occupational Safety and Health Administration had spent six years postponing action on a proposed new standard for occupational exposure to cadmium. The court held the delay unreasonable and imposed a five-month deadline on the agency for the issuance of such a rule. In doing so, the court relied upon the availability of compelling evidence concerning the toxicity of cadmium and the agency's numerous failures to meet past deadlines it had announced for that action. "There is a point when the court must 'let the agency know, in no uncertain terms, that enough is enough,' . . . and we believe that point has been reached." *See generally* Neil R. Eisner, *Agency Delay in Informal Rulemaking*, 3 ADMIN. L.J. 7 (1989).

9. *Lapse of rulemaking proceedings.* In at least a dozen states, statutes place an outside limit on the rulemaking period. A typical provision is Cal. Gov't Code § 11346.4(b), which provides that the effective period of a notice of proposed rulemaking is one year. If the agency cannot finish in a year, it must start over. Elsewhere the allowed time period may be as short as 90 days after the end of the comment period, Ala. Code § 41–22–6(b), or as long as four years, Wis. Stat. § 227.14(6)(c). Section 307 of the 2010 MSAPA contains an optional two-year lapse proceeding (but allows the agency to extend that period for good cause. Is such a lapse provision a good idea? The federal APA does not contain one. Does the maxim "justice delayed is justice denied" have force in the rulemaking context? Or does a time limit invite overly rushed decisionmaking, especially in complex rulemaking proceedings? For criticism of the state time limits, see Ronald M. Levin, *Rulemaking Under the 2010 Model State Administrative Procedure Act*, 20 WIDENER L.J. 855, 866–71 (2011).

10. *Problem.* In the Horse Protection Act, Congress sought to curtail the practice of deliberately injuring show horses to improve their performance in the ring. This practice, called soring, may involve fastening chains or similar equipment on a horse's front limbs. As a result of wearing chains, the horse suffers intense pain as its forefeet touch the ground. This pain causes it to adopt a high-stepping gait that is highly prized in show horses.

The Act contains a statement of findings declaring that "(1) the soring of horses is cruel and inhumane; [and] (2) horses shown or exhibited which are sore, where such soreness improves the performance of such horse, compete unfairly with horses which are not sore. . . ." The Act accordingly prohibits the "showing or exhibiting, in any horse show or horse exhibition, of any horse which is sore;" imposes criminal penalties for violations of this ban; and empowers the Secretary of Agriculture to issue rules to carry out the provisions of the Act.

Initially, the Secretary promulgated regulations forbidding the training of horses through the use of chains that weighed more than ten ounces. In the statement of basis and purpose accompanying these regulations, the Secretary stated that he had commissioned a study by veterinary medicine researchers at a prominent university to evaluate the effectiveness of these measures.

The university study was completed three years later. It suggested that training chains weighing eight to ten ounces caused horses to suffer lesions, bleeding, and inflammation. The Horse Defense Alliance submitted a letter highlighting these findings and asking that the regulations be strengthened. The HDA was dismayed when, several months later, the Secretary wrote back to state: "I have reviewed your letter and the referenced studies. I have also consulted informally with industry representatives, who doubt that the allowable weight of action devices can be lowered while retaining the desired gait. As presently advised I believe that the most effective method of enforcing the Act is to continue the current regulations."

On review, should the court sustain the Secretary's decision? If it does not, what relief should it prescribe? *See American Horse Protection Ass'n v. Lyng,* 812 F.2d 1 (D.C. Cir. 1987).

§ 6.4   WAIVERS OF RULES

Rules apply across the board. They may work fairly and well in the generality of cases, but they sometimes produce harsh or unanticipated consequences when applied in particular situations. Agencies often entertain requests for waivers in cases in which the applicants can demonstrate that the rule does not work appropriately in their cases. But are waivers consistent with the rule of law? Isn't there a danger of favoritism or that too many waivers will completely undermine a rule?

WAIT Radio v. FCC
418 F.2d 1153 (D.C. Cir. 1969)

LEVENTHAL, J.:

WAIT Radio brings this appeal to protest a decision by the Federal Communications Commission rejecting as unacceptable its application for authority to operate its station on an unlimited time basis. We think the Commission erred by not giving adequate reasons for denying and refusing to hold a hearing on appellant's request for waiver of certain FCC rules and we remand for further consideration.

WAIT operates a Chicago AM radio station on a frequency of 820 kHz, one of the so-called clear channels. Under FCC "clear channel" rules certain AM frequencies are designated as clear channels that can be used at night only by specified stations that broadcast a signal to "white areas," sparsely populated regions that have no local radio service. . . . As a result, WAIT operates on a sunrise to sunset basis.

WAIT filed an application requesting a waiver of the clear channel rules. Its proposal included plans for constructing a directionalized antenna that would beam its signal away from "white" areas that were being served by [two clear channel stations in] Fort Worth/Dallas, Texas. WAIT's application asserted that by confining its signal, its . . . beam would not interfere with . . . the signal from the Texas stations except in regions that receive primary groundwave service from at least one other station, and its ostensible violation of Commission rules would not conflict with the policy underlying the "clear channel" rules.

In support of its waiver request WAIT further alleged that its programming of "good" music and forum discussions on matters of public interest is a unique AM service in the Chicago area. . . . The application further alleged that the present fluctuating broadcast schedule, dependent on the actual time of sunrise and sunset, and no evening service, is a disadvantage. WAIT makes particular reference to its distinctive adult audience, able during the evening hours to listen to, and understand, serious social, political and educational programs. . . .

The Commission rejected WAIT's request . . . and ordered that the application be returned as unacceptable. WAIT appeals. . . .

We hold that the Commission must state its basis for decision with greater care and clarity than was manifested in its disposition of WAIT's claims, and remand for a clearer statement of reasons.

1.   Two strands of doctrine apply to the judicial review of administrative determinations. First is the principle that an agency or commission must articulate with clarity and precision its findings and the reasons for its decisions. The importance of this requirement is inherent in the doctrine of judicial review. . . .

Of course busy agency staffs are not expected to dot "i's" and cross "t's." Our decisions recognize the presumption of regularity. We adhere to "salutary principles of judicial restraint." . . .

2.   The tension between these principles is heightened when a court undertakes to review administrative action on an application for waiver. Presumptions of regularity apply with special vigor when a Commission acts in reliance on an established and tested agency rule. An applicant for waiver faces a high hurdle even at the starting gate. "When an applicant seeks a waiver of a rule, it must plead with particularity the facts and circumstances which warrant such action." Yet an application for waiver has an appropriate place in the discharge by an administrative agency of its assigned responsibilities. The agency's discretion to proceed in difficult areas through general rules is intimately linked to the existence of a safety valve procedure for consideration of an application for exemption based on special circumstances.

The salutary presumptions do not obviate the need for serious consideration of meritorious applications for waiver, and a system where regulations are maintained inflexibly without any procedure for waiver poses legal difficulties. The Commission is charged with administration in the "public interest." That an agency may discharge its responsibilities by promulgating rules of general application which, in the overall perspective, establish the "public interest" for a broad range of situations, does not relieve it of an obligation to seek out the "public interest" in particular, individualized cases. A general rule implies that a commission need not re-study the entire problem de novo and reconsider policy every time it receives an application for waiver of the rule. On the other hand, a general rule, deemed valid because its overall objectives are in the public interest, may not be in the "public interest" if extended to an applicant who proposes a new service that will not undermine the policy, served by the rule, that has been adjudged in the public interest. An agency need not sift pleadings and documents to identify such applications, but allegations such as those made by petitioners, stated with clarity and accompanied by supporting data, are not subject to perfunctory treatment, but must be given a "hard look."[9]

3.   These principles are not easily reduced to a quantifiable formula for deciding when an agency disposing of a waiver application has crossed the line from the tolerably terse to the intolerably mute. There are strong indications that the boundary has been transgressed in the case before us. The Commission's order suggested, and perhaps even required, that WAIT's waiver application may not be entertained because it failed to proceed broadside against the clear channel policy. . . . This approach is without merit. The very essence of waiver is the assumed validity of the general rule, and also the applicant's violation unless waiver is granted. And as already noted, provision for waiver may have a pivotal importance in sustaining the system of administration by general rule.

The somewhat perfunctory treatment in the Commission's opinion is capped by the startling statement . . . that the application is subject to dismissal out of hand because it revealed that in the absence of waiver there would be a violation of the Commission's rules.[12]

4.   The court's insistence on the agency's observance of its obligation to give meaningful consideration to waiver applications emphatically does not contemplate that an agency must or should tolerate evisceration of a rule by waivers. On the contrary a rule is more likely to be undercut if it does not in some way take into account considerations of hardship, equity, or more effective implementation of overall policy, considerations that an agency cannot realistically ignore, at least on a continuing basis. The limited safety valve permits a more rigorous adherence to an effective regulation.

Sound administrative procedure contemplates waivers, or exceptions granted only pursuant to a relevant standard—expressed at least in decisions accompanied by published opinions, especially during a period when an approach is in formation, but best expressed in a rule that obviates discriminatory approaches. The agency may not act out of unbridled discretion or whim in granting waivers any more than in any other aspect of its regulatory function. The process viewed as a whole leads to a general rule, and limited waivers or exceptions granted pursuant to an appropriate general standard. This combination of a

---

[9]   The agency is not bound to process in depth what are only generalized pleas, a requirement that would condemn it to divert resources of time and personnel to hollow claims. The applicant for waiver must articulate a specific pleading, and adduce concrete support, preferably documentary. Even when an application complies with these rigorous requirements, the agency is not required to author an essay for the disposition of each application. It suffices, in the usual case, that we can discern the "why and wherefore."

[12]   . . . It is manifest error to deny a waiver on the ground that there would be a violation in the absence of the waiver sought.

general rule and limitations is the very stuff of the rule of law, and with diligent effort and attention to essentials administrative agencies may maintain the fundamentals of principled regulation without sacrifice of administrative flexibility and feasibility.

5.   We have identified deficiencies in the FCC's opinion rejecting the application for waiver. We have examined the significance of the waiver procedure and pointed out that it is not necessarily a step-child, but may be an important member of the family of administrative procedures, one that helps the family stay together. . . .

We think the pleading filed by WAIT, supported by data sufficient to overcome the initial hurdle, was entitled to reflective consideration. . . . We do not rule on substantive contentions, but remand for further consideration.

So ordered.

[A dissenting opinion by DANAHER, J., is omitted. On remand, the FCC again denied a waiver, writing a longer opinion, and the court affirmed. *WAIT Radio v. FCC*, 459 F.2d 1203 (D.C. Cir. 1972).]

NOTES AND QUESTIONS

1.   *Hospitality to administrative waivers.* There is a substantial scholarly literature on waivers. In general, academic opinion accords with Judge Leventhal's position, endorsing waivers as a necessary corrective to the rigidity of rules. Professors Glicksman and Shapiro, describing waivers as a means of fine-tuning regulation at the "back end" of the policy implementation process, cite some of the benefits:

A back-end adjustment process has a number of policy advantages. First, it permits agencies to preserve relatively stringent baseline risk-reduction standards while still accommodating concerns that the application of these stringent rules will cause irrational or unfair results in particular cases. . . .

Second, [u]nlike rulemaking, in which regulators must attempt to anticipate problems before they occur in the context of writing general rules, incremental adjustments permit regulators to consider concrete problems, one at a time, in the context of specific circumstances. The back-end process can also make adjustments to circumstances that cannot be anticipated at the time a rule was written. A back-end adjustment process can also reduce the number of challenges to regulations and the need to use enforcement proceedings to interpret rules and make policy.

Third, a back-end adjustment process can increase the legitimacy of the regulatory program that contains the back-end process by reducing the frustrations likely to result from the application of regulatory requirements in ways that produce harsh or anomalous results. . . .

Finally, but hardly least of all, a back-end process is one of the ways that regulators can take costs into account when Congress eschews the use of a cost-benefit test to establish the level of regulation.

Robert L. Glicksman & Sidney A. Shapiro, *Improving Regulation Through Incremental Adjustment*, 52 U. KAN. L. REV. 1179, 1185–86 (2004). For fuller discussion, see Jim Rossi, *Waivers, Flexibility, and Reviewability*, 72 CHI.–KENT L. REV. 1359 (1997); Peter H. Schuck, *When the Exception Becomes the Rule*, 1984 DUKE L.J. 163; Alfred C. Aman, Jr., *Administrative Equity: An Analysis of Exceptions to Administrative Rules*," 1982 DUKE L.J. 277.

2. *Must waivers be available?* A broad reading of *WAIT Radio* and the above scholarly literature might suggest that *every* significant rule must leave room for some sort of meaningful opportunity to apply for a waiver. We saw in § 3.2 that the Supreme Court seemed to throw cold water on that proposition in *FCC v. WNCN Listeners Guild*, 450 U.S. 582 (1981), and arguably in *Heckler v. Campbell*, 461 U.S. 458 (1983). There the Court upheld regulations in the face of objections that they lacked waiver provisions. In those situations, however, the issue arose only incidentally, because the cases did not involve actual requests for waivers.

Lower courts have faced the question more directly and have made clear that the policy of *WAIT Radio* has its limits: " '[S]trict adherence to a general rule may be justified by the gain in certainty and administrative ease, even if it appears to result in some hardship in individual cases.' " *BellSouth Corp. v. FCC*, 162 F.3d 1215, 1225 (D.C. Cir. 1999) (quoting *Turro v. FCC*, 859 F.2d 1498, 1500 (D.C. Cir. 1988)).

Indeed, some agencies have steadfastly refused to grant any waivers from certain of their rules, and the courts have acquiesced in this refusal. A well-known example (also discussed in § 3.2 N.3) is the Federal Aviation Administration's rule that prohibited any large commercial airliner from taking off under the command of a pilot aged 60 or more. The rule came into force in 1959, and over the ensuing half century the FAA never waived it, although pilots filed numerous petitions seeking individual exemptions. The FAA's long-held position was that after age 60, physical abilities decline and the risk of sudden incapacitation in flight increases; and that, although some pilots in their sixties remained fully qualified, no medical test was reliable enough to distinguish them from more dangerous ones. Repeated court challenges to this policy occasionally resulted in remands for fuller explanation, but in the end the FAA always prevailed. For example, despite doubts about the medical evidence, the majority in *Baker v. FAA*, 917 F.2d 318 (7th Cir. 1990), deferred to the expert agency, observing that "safety is the dominant and controlling consideration."

Eventually, in 2007, the FAA commenced a rulemaking proceeding to reexamine the age limit, and this proceeding was cut short when Congress itself raised the limit to age 65. Pub. L. No. 110–135 (2007). During its long reign, however, the age 60 rule caused a good deal of hardship. As a dissenter in *Baker* noted: "Pilots with tens of thousands of hours of flight time and flawless records, and who pass every physical test with flying colors, suddenly find themselves grounded on their sixtieth birthdays, even though [they] are still deemed qualified to pilot planes with thirty passengers or less." 917 F.2d at 323 (Will, J., dissenting). Should courts have demanded that the FAA devise a more flexible policy sooner, by at least seriously considering waivers?

3. *Abuse of discretion review.* Assuming that an agency is willing to consider granting waivers in some instances, how far can a court go in second-guessing the agency's refusal to grant one in a particular case? In *Alizoti v. Gonzales*, 477 F.3d 448 (6th Cir. 2007), the Board of Immigration Appeals ordered the petitioner deported to her native Albania, but she moved to reopen her case on the ground that she had recently married a U.S. citizen, which would entitle her to an adjustment of status. She had reason to assume that the Department of Homeland Security had issued the necessary form to confirm the fact of her marriage, but her statement that it had done so turned out to be mistaken, and the Board denied her motion. Later, after the department had belatedly completed the proper paperwork, she asked the BIA to reconsider, but the BIA denied this motion also, stating that its rules did not permit "new evidence" to be considered on such a motion. The BIA could have waived the procedural defect and treated the second motion as merely supplementing the first, but it refused to do so.

On appeal to the Sixth Circuit, a dissenting judge vigorously condemned the Board's "inertia or inattention" to the particulars of Alizoti's case. He argued that none of the administrative errors that had prevented the Board from taking account of her marital status were her fault. He declared: "The purpose of vesting jurisdiction in this Court to correct errors includes this kind of fundamental error on which a deportation order turns." But the panel majority did not agree: "[T]his case seemingly cries out for a common sense waiver of procedural defects. However, that discretion vests firmly with the BIA in these circumstances, and we should be careful not to disturb the exercise of it. To do otherwise would require this Court to conduct a *de novo* review, rather than reviewing for abuse of discretion. . . . In the short run, we may satisfy a sense of justice, while in the long run bringing chaos to the review process." Should the court have reversed?

4. *Structured waiver programs.* Agencies are not always reluctant to entertain requests for waivers. In fact, some rely heavily on waiver programs as a tool of regulatory policy. The exceptions process at the Department of Energy in the 1970's and 1980's is an example. *See* Aman, *supra;* Schuck, *supra.* A more recent example is the Environmental Protection Agency's Excellence and Leadership Program (Project XL), under which EPA gives regulated entities, within limits, the flexibility to devise their own strategies

to comply with pollution regulations, instead of doing it the agency's way. *See* Dennis D. Hirsch, *Project XL and the Special Case: The EPA's Untold Success Story*, 26 COLUM. J. ENVTL. L. 219 (2001); Marshall J. Breger, *Regulatory Flexibility and the Administrative State*, 32 TULSA L.J. 325, 331–33 (1996).

5.   *Potential dangers of waivers.* As a species of deregulation, waiver programs can give rise to charges that the agency is enforcing its mandate too leniently. Another potential problem is that an agency might grant waivers on the basis of favoritism or other impermissible considerations. Because the exceptions process is usually less visible than the rule-writing process, it triggers particular concerns about the need to ensure agency accountability. *See* Breger, *supra,* at 339–44, 347–49. Glicksman and Shapiro have suggested safeguards to apply at the federal level, including a notice and comment process for proposed waivers, legislative-type hearings, and required publicity on the agency's website. Glicksman & Shapiro, *supra*, at 1238–45. Some states *prohibit* waivers unless the agency has enunciated rules to channel its discretion in awarding them. *See* N.C. Gen. Stat. § 150B–19(6); N.H. Rev. Stat. Ann. § 541–A:22; Vt. Stat. Ann. tit. 3, § 845. Iowa has adopted that restriction and several others—for example, the applicant must show by "clear and convincing evidence" that the waiver "would not prejudice the substantial legal rights of any person." Iowa Code § 17A.9A.

6.   *Florida provision.* A Florida statute *requires* that agencies grant waivers or variances when (1) the person subject to a rule demonstrates that the purpose of the underlying statute will be or has been achieved by other means; and (2) application of a rule would create a substantial hardship or would violate principles of fairness. Fla. Stat. Ann. § 120.542.

Prior to this legislation, Florida law had been widely interpreted as prohibiting waivers or variances, except by agencies that had previously provided for such action in published rules. The proponents of the waiver statute favored it as "part of a political compromise to introduce flexibility into the regulatory process without sacrificing the apparent values of Florida's presumptive rulemaking mechanism." Jim Rossi, *The 1996 Revised Florida Administrative Procedure Act: A Rulemaking Revolution or Counter-Revolution?,"* 49 ADMIN. L. REV. 345, 356 (1997). Would you give the legislature high marks for promoting flexibility in the regulatory process? Should other states emulate the Florida example?

7.   *Big waiver.* Somewhat different from the authority to waive requirements for individual persons or companies in exceptional circumstances is the authority to waive requirements of a congressionally established program on a large scale. Professors Barron and Rakoff call the latter species of administrative discretion "big waiver." David J. Barron & Todd D. Rakoff, *In Defense of Big Waiver*, 113 Colum. L. Rev. 265 (2013). For example, the Education Department has permitted many states and localities to receive grants under the No Child Left Behind Act, although their plans to improve teaching and academic achievement are considerably different from those originally contemplated by that Act. Similarly, the Department of

Health and Human Services has authorized states to operate health care insurance exchanges in ways that differ substantially from the model that Congress established in the Affordable Care Act. All of these actions were taken pursuant to detailed statutory provisions that expressly allowed the administering agency to grant waivers based on specific findings that the central purposes of the statute (quality education and affordable health insurance, respectively) would be equally or better served by waiving some of its requirements.

Barron and Rakoff suggest several reasons why Congress finds such statutory provisions attractive. It has found that "the characteristic pathology of large federal spending programs [has been] a statutory rigidity that precluded innovation and cost-effectiveness over time. The cure for that disease [is] not greater congressional micromanagement—through ex post legislative revision to reduce agency discretion, such as setting timelines for action—but rather, the delegation of administrative discretion to inject a measure of flexibility and vitality into systems that risked having run their course." *Id.* at 296–97. This can be particularly true in fields like education and health care, in which federal regulation is already extensive and the requirements of multiple statutes need to be harmonized.

How persuasive are these explanations? Writing about the numerous waivers granted by HHS in the early stages of implementing the ACA, Professor Hamburger warned of the risks of favoritism and of the use of waivers as a means "to co-opt political support for insupportable laws . . . by offering relief to the most powerful of those who might demand repeal." Moreover, "[w]aivers . . . undermine the political process by permitting lawmakers to escape the political consequences of drafting onerous laws. Lawmakers ordinarily have reason to worry about imposing severe rules. Waivers, however, remove the incentives for responsibly moderate legislation. . . . Even more seriously, waivers are a threat to government by and under law." Philip Hamburger, *Can Health-Care Waivers Be Justified?*, NAT'L REV. ONLINE, Feb. 18, 2011. In this light, is "big waiver" a power that the executive branch should have?

8.   *Problem.* According to a 1937 regulation of the Federal Highway Administration (FHWA), drivers of commercial trucks operating in interstate commerce must possess at least 20/40 vision in each eye (measured with or without corrective lenses). For many years, however, drivers who have the required vision in only one eye have qualified for commercial licenses under state law. Such licenses allow them to drive in *intrastate* commerce. Recently, against the background of numerous legal and societal initiatives to curb discrimination against the disabled, the FHWA decided to conduct a study to determine whether to amend its safety regulation.

The agency said that preliminary, but inconclusive, studies indicated that the accident records of these "monocular" drivers are no worse than those of drivers with normal sight, presumably because the monocular drivers have learned to adapt their driving practices to take account of their disability. Thus, the agency announced that it would waive the regulation for certain monocular truck drivers, so that they could serve as subjects in a controlled experiment that would compare their safety experience with the experience of drivers who were already qualified under federal law. The program was open only to drivers who were licensed under state law and had maintained accident-free records for three years. This experiment, the FHWA said, would serve the public interest in furthering the employment of qualified drivers with impaired vision.

The Highway Safety League, a public interest group composed of insurance companies and law enforcement associations, challenged the waiver program in court, arguing that by statute any waiver must be "consistent with public safety" and the FHWA had not made a determination as to whether drivers participating in the experiment would pose risks to other cars on the road. In fact, the agency's own statement indicated uncertainty on that point. The court agreed and remanded the rule. After further deliberation, the agency reaffirmed its commitment to the waiver program, concluding that initial experience with it had been satisfactory and strengthened the belief that the participation of monocular drivers in the study was "consistent with public safety."

At this point, Bert, a monocular truck driver with a record of 22 accident-free years on the road, applied for a waiver of the safety regulation. He stated that he had not known about the experimental program until after the deadline for applying to join it had expired. The deputy administrator of FHWA refused his request in a brief letter, stating that "if we were to grant your request for a waiver, it could set a precedent and we might have to allow it for everyone, making it impossible for us to enforce the regulation during this transition period." Bert has filed for review in court, arguing that the denial of his waiver request was unlawful.

Questions: (a) Do you agree with the court's ruling in the suit brought by the Highway Safety League? (b) How should the court respond to Bert's suit? Would the result change if FHWA's enabling statute contained a provision like the Florida waiver statute? *Cf. Rauenhorst v. United States Dep't of Transp.,* 95 F.3d 715 (8th Cir. 1996); *Advocates for Highway and Auto Safety v. FHWA,* 28 F.3d 1288 (D.C. Cir. 1994)

CHAPTER 7

CONTROL OF AGENCIES BY THE
POLITICAL BRANCHES OF GOVERNMENT

■ ■ ■

§ 7.1 INTRODUCTION

An examination of the role of political bodies in controlling agency action requires consideration of two fundamental constitutional principles: *separation of powers* and *checks and balances*. The founders created three distinct branches of government, each authorized to exercise its own specialized powers. They also believed that each branch must be protected against encroachment by the others, and each must be in a position to curb arbitrary or unwise actions by the others.

Administrative agencies, which are barely mentioned in the federal Constitution, have often been regarded as posing threats to the constitutional structure. They typically possess delegated authority to make rules, to adjudicate individual cases, to engage in law enforcement, and to conduct other activities related to those functions. Yet these are the functions normally entrusted to the three branches of government that the Constitution establishes in express and detailed terms. Nevertheless, most people today concede that this combination of functions within a single administrative unit is legitimate and a practical necessity in modern government. *See* Peter L. Strauss, *The Place of Agencies in Government: Separation of Powers and the Fourth Branch*, 84 COLUM. L. REV. 573 (1984).

Some of the actions that the named branches of government take in order to supervise agency action may themselves offend separation of powers principles. A given branch might attempt to perform a task that more properly belongs elsewhere, or might attempt to restrain other branches from carrying out their constitutionally assigned functions. The legal system has to resolve these interbranch conflicts. Sometimes the controversy focuses on the language of the Constitution. At other times, it may involve an appeal to the general design of our tripartite governmental structure—for the "separation of powers doctrine" shapes the relationships among branches even where no specific constitutional provision is at issue.

Another relevant distinction is between what scholars call "formalist" and "functionalist" approaches to separation of powers issues. A formalist analysis assumes that various types of activities fall categorically inside or outside the scope of a given branch's purview. Thus, a judge influenced by formalism is likely to endorse bright-line restrictions on political entities, with little or no overt reliance on policy considerations. Constitutional requirements that are formalist in this sense can be based on either specific language in the Constitution or on more generalized separation of powers notions. A court that employs a functionalist approach, on the other hand, openly weighs competing interests that militate in favor of or against a given restriction on the powers of a branch of government. Balancing tests and questions of degree play a prominent role in functionalist arguments. One source of unpredictability in separation of powers law is that courts differ among themselves about whether to adopt formalist or functionalist premises, and a single court (including the U.S. Supreme Court) may follow both approaches in varying contexts. *See* Peter L. Strauss, *Formal and Functional Approaches to Separation of Powers Questions—A Foolish Inconsistency?*, 72 CORNELL L. REV. 488 (1987).

The problems of separation of powers and checks and balances in state agencies may differ from the situation under federal law. First, some state agencies are directly created by state constitutions, giving such agencies a status equivalent to the legislature and governor. Second, some state officials are directly elected by the voters, which provides a form of direct accountability. When an agency has constitutional status, or when agency heads are elected, the normal legislative and executive checks on agency action may not be applicable or may apply in a different way.

In this chapter, we first consider how far the legislature may go in vesting agencies with legislative and adjudicative powers. We then inquire into the means by which the legislature and chief executive may control the exercises of agency authority, and also into the circumstances in which such efforts at control exceed permissible bounds.

§ 7.2   DELEGATION OF LEGISLATIVE POWER TO AGENCIES

§ 7.2.1 THE NONDELEGATION DOCTRINE AND FEDERAL AGENCIES

Article I of the federal Constitution vests legislative power in Congress and authorizes Congress to enact laws that are necessary and proper means of implementing its powers. Despite the Necessary and Proper Clause, however, the *nondelegation doctrine* maintains that Congress' power to delegate its legislative authority is limited.

The nondelegation doctrine invokes both separation of powers and checks and balances arguments. The separation of powers argument is that the Constitution assigned all legislative power to the legislature; therefore Congress cannot transfer any part of that power to administrative agencies. The checks and balances argument recognizes that delegation to agencies may be inevitable, but insists that the legislature impose adequate limits on the discretion such agencies can exercise. It remains a source of continuing controversy whether courts can or should enforce the nondelegation doctrine by invalidating improper delegations.

§ 7.2.1a From *Field* to the New Deal

Marshall Field & Co. v. Clark, 143 U.S. 649 (1892), sounded themes of both separation of powers and checks and balances. A statute empowered the President to raise tariffs and suspend trade with foreign countries "for such time as he shall deem just." The President was to take this action if he deemed the tariffs imposed by such countries on American goods to be unequal and unreasonable. (Congress ordinarily makes decisions on the imposition of import tariffs. Why would it have delegated such an important power to the President?)

The Supreme Court stated the nondelegation doctrine broadly. "That Congress cannot delegate legislative power to the President is a principle universally recognized as vital to the integrity and maintenance of the system of government ordained by the Constitution." This assertion was dubious, given that Congress had frequently delegated broad powers to the President or other executive branch officials without any judicial challenge. Such delegations occurred during the First and Second Congresses, suggesting that the founders had little concern with delegation issues. For example, the First Congress granted military pensions "under such regulations as the President of the United States may direct."

Despite its assertion that the nondelegation principle was vital to the integrity of constitutional government, the Court upheld the delegation:

As the suspension was absolutely required when the President ascertained the existence of a particular fact, it cannot be said that in ascertaining that fact and in issuing his proclamation, in obedience to the legislative will, he exercised the function of making laws. Legislative power was exercised when Congress declared that the suspension should take effect upon a named contingency. What the President was required to do was simply in execution of the act of Congress. It was not the making of law. He was the mere agent of the law-making department to ascertain and declare the event upon which its expressed will was to take effect. It was a part of the law itself as it left the hands of Congress that [favorable tariff provisions] should be suspended, in a given contingency, and in [such cases] certain duties should be imposed.

143 U.S. at 693.

Of course, the power given to the President in the *Field* case was far more significant than a mere power to "ascertain the fact" of whether a "given contingency" had occurred. It was indeed "the making of law." A decision about whether foreign tariffs are unequal and unreasonable, and thus justify retaliation, calls for subtle judgment and entails deeply political as well as economic calculations.

From the time of the *Field* case until the early 1930's, the Supreme Court continued to assert that a nondelegation doctrine existed. Yet it upheld every delegation in a line of cases that involved steadily more sweeping transfers of power to federal agencies. In those cases, the Court applied the nondelegation doctrine by attempting to ascertain whether Congress had established an "intelligible principle" or a "primary standard" to guide the delegate in making the decision. The most frequently cited case is *J. W. Hampton Jr. & Co. v. United States,* 276 U.S. 394 (1928), which noted that "if Congress shall lay down by legislative act *an intelligible principle* to which the person or body authorized to [regulate] is directed to conform, such legislative action is not a forbidden delegation of legislative power." During this period the Court upheld delegations to the Federal Trade Commission to prohibit "unfair methods of competition" and to the predecessor of the Federal Communications Commission to regulate the airwaves as the "public convenience, interest or necessity requires." *FTC v. Gratz,* 253 U.S. 421 (1920); *Federal Radio Comm'n v. Nelson Bros. Bond & Mortgage Co.,* 289 U.S. 266 (1933). Of course, vague standards like "unfair methods of competition" and "public convenience, interest or necessity" really furnish no guidance to anyone.

In 1935, the Supreme Court twice held statutes unconstitutional under the nondelegation doctrine. Both provisions were contained in the National Industrial Recovery Act (NIRA) of 1933, an early New Deal measure passed in the depths of the Great Depression. These cases were the first and the last Supreme Court decisions to overturn statutes as invalid legislative delegations to administrative agencies. They must be viewed in light of the extreme judicial activism of the early 1930's, an attitude that resulted in the invalidation of numerous New Deal laws on other grounds, including a lack of congressional power to enact the particular statute.

NIRA contained various legislative findings about the economic emergency and declared congressional policy that there should be cooperation among trade groups, including labor and management, to revive the economy, relieve unemployment, increase production and consumption, and conserve natural resources. Thus the Act apparently contained a wealth of "standards" and "intelligible principles" to guide the delegate.

The first delegation case arose under § 9 of NIRA, a provision that allowed the President to ban from interstate commerce the shipment of oil produced in violation of a state agency's order (so-called "hot oil"). The background of this provision was that new oil discoveries in Texas led to massive overproduction. Each producer pumped as fast as possible lest other producers deplete the pool. The result was a drastic fall in the price of oil, waste of a non-renewable resource, and complete disorganization of the oil industry.

Texas set up a state agency to control the amount that each producer could pump, but the interstate nature of the oil business meant that state regulation couldn't work without help from the federal government. The language and legislative history of § 9 indicated that it was intended to provide that help by making interstate shipment of "hot oil" a federal crime when the President deemed such a ban desirable.

In *Panama Refining Co. v. Ryan*, 293 U.S. 388 (1935), the Supreme Court invalidated this delegation. It declared:

> In every case in which the question has been raised, the Court has recognized that there are limits of delegation which there is no constitutional authority to transcend. We think that section 9(c) goes beyond those limits. As to the transportation of oil production in excess of state permission, the Congress has declared no policy, has established no standard, has laid down no rule. There is no requirement, no definition of circumstances and conditions in which the transportation is to be allowed or prohibited.

293 U.S. at 430. Only Justice Cardozo dissented, pointing out that the statute defined the precise act which the President was to perform and, in context, made abundantly clear the circumstances in which it should be performed. Was *Panama* consistent with *Field v. Clark?*

The second decision invalidated a much more important and vastly more sweeping delegation. The background of § 3 of NIRA was the catastrophic depression engulfing the American economy. Unemployment exceeded 25%, wages and prices plummeted, banks and businesses of every sort failed. NIRA was an attempt to reverse the terrifying downward spiral of the Depression and start the economy moving upward again. Section 3 empowered the President to adopt "codes of fair competition" for any industry. The codes would prescribe maximum and minimum prices to be charged, wages, hours and working conditions of labor, levels of production, and many other competitive practices which previously had been determined by market forces. Violations of a code were a criminal offense.

In *A.L.A. Schechter Poultry Corp. v. United States,* 295 U.S. 495 (1935), the Supreme Court invalidated § 3 under the nondelegation doctrine. *Schechter* arose under the poultry code. In addition to setting poultry prices, the code required retailers to take all the chickens offered to them by wholesalers; they could no longer pick and choose. Schechter Poultry, a wholesaler in New York, was convicted of a crime because it permitted retailers to reject chickens.

The Supreme Court held unanimously that the delegation to the President to adopt "codes of fair competition" was invalid because NIRA lacked an adequate standard to govern the drafting of codes. The Court objected to the lack of any procedure for adopting the codes. It also questioned the involvement of dominant private producers in proposing and writing a code that would bind their competitors. It distinguished the earlier cases that upheld delegations to various agencies to prevent "unfair methods of competition" or to act in the "public interest." In these situations, unlike NIRA, Congress created agencies to enforce the law in accordance with defined and fair procedures.

Moreover, as Justice Cardozo pointed out in his concurring opinion, the statutes involved in the earlier precedents were different from NIRA in that they focused on practices that would generally be considered oppressive or unfair or upon economically unsound practices in specific industries. NIRA went much further. It extended to the entire economy and entailed a "roving commission" to achieve positive reform of industrial practice. "The extension becomes as wide as the field of industrial regulation. If that conception shall prevail, anything that Congress may do within the limits of the commerce clause for the betterment of business may be done by the President upon the recommendation of a trade association by calling it a code. This is delegation running riot. No such plenitude of power is susceptible of transfer. The statute, however, aims at nothing less, as one can learn both from its terms and from the administrative practice under it." *Id.* at 553. Even if there was a measure of truth in this description, was the Court justified in blocking Congress's effort to come to grips with the desperate conditions of the Depression?

§ 7.2.1b From the New Deal to the Modern Era

Following the *Schechter* and *Panama* decisions, the Supreme Court returned to its pre-1930's practice of giving lip service to the nondelegation doctrine, while upholding ever more sweeping and vague delegations. For example, in *Yakus v. United States,* 321 U.S. 414 (1944), the Court upheld (with a single dissent) a delegation in the Emergency Price Control Act of 1942 to the Price Administrator to fix maximum prices. Like NIRA, the 1942 Act was designed to deal comprehensively with an economic emergency—in this case, the inflationary spiral generated by World War II. The standard for fixing prices was that such prices had to be "generally fair and equitable." The Administrator had to ascertain and give due consideration to the prices prevailing in October, 1941, and was required to furnish a statement of the considerations involved in setting particular prices.

Yakus was convicted of selling beef for a price in excess of a ceiling set by the Administrator. In responding to the claim that the statute was an unlawful delegation, the Supreme Court stated:

> The Constitution as a continuously operative charter of government does not demand the impossible or the impracticable. . . . The essentials of the legislative function are the determination of the legislative policy and its formulation and promulgation as a defined and binding rule of conduct—here the rule, with penal sanctions, that prices shall not be greater than those fixed by maximum price regulations which conform to standards and will tend to further the policy which Congress has established. . . . It is no objection that the determination of facts and the inferences to be drawn from them in the light of the statutory standards and declaration of policy call for the exercise of judgment, and for the formulation of subsidiary administrative policy within the prescribed statutory framework. . . .
>
> Congress is not confined to that method of executing its policy which involves the least possible delegation of discretion to administrative officers. . . . It is free to avoid the rigidity of such a system, which might well result in serious hardship, and to choose instead the flexibility attainable by the use of less restrictive standards. . . . Only if we could say that there is an absence of standards for the guidance of the Administrator's action, so that it would be impossible in a proper proceeding to ascertain whether the will of Congress has been obeyed, would we be justified in overriding its choice of means for effecting its declared purpose of preventing inflation.

Id. at 424–26.

The Court quickly distinguished *Schechter* on the ground that NIRA failed to provide standards for the codes of fair competition and because the delegation to write the codes was to private companies in the industries to be regulated rather than to public officials. *Panama Refining* was not mentioned. Although cases like *Yakus* (and there have been many) suggest that the Supreme Court is unwilling to invalidate a statute on the basis of unlawful delegation, the *Schechter* and *Panama* cases have never been overruled.

§ 7.2.1c Revival of the Nondelegation Doctrine?

Despite the Supreme Court's post-1935 practice of never invalidating a delegation, interest in the nondelegation doctrine has never entirely faded away. In the following cases, individual Justices called for a reinvigoration of the doctrine; and the majority, although not heeding that call, can arguably be seen as having at least taken the doctrine seriously.

INDUSTRIAL UNION DEPARTMENT, AFL–CIO V. AMERICAN PETROLEUM INSTITUTE
448 U.S. 607 (1980)

[The Occupational Safety and Health Act delegates authority to the Secretary of Labor to adopt safety and health standards for the workplace. Under § 3(8), the standards must be "reasonably necessary or appropriate to provide safe or healthful . . . places of employment." Section 6(b)(5) of the Act also directs the Secretary, when setting standards for toxic materials, "to set the standard which most adequately assures, to the extent feasible . . . that no employee will suffer material impairment of health. . . ."

The Occupational Safety and Health Administration (OSHA), which discharges the Secretary's responsibilities under this statute, construed "feasible" in § (6)(b)(5) to mean that the agency must set standards at the safest possible level that is technologically feasible and that would not cause material economic impairment of the industry. The *Industrial Union* case involved the standard for benzene, an industrial chemical which in high concentration causes leukemia and other illnesses. OSHA set the standard for benzene at 1 part per million (ppm), although OSHA's research did not directly establish that there is danger to the health of workers at levels of concentration below 10 ppm. In the agency's view, workplace exposure to benzene entailed at least some cancer risk, and the statute did not require it to determine how large that risk was.

A four-Justice plurality, in an opinion written by STEVENS, J., overturned the benzene standard. Interpreting § 3(8), the plurality held that OSHA must find, before promulgating a standard, that it is necessary and appropriate to remedy a *significant risk* of material health impairment:]

In the absence of a clear mandate in the Act, it is unreasonable to assume that Congress intended to give the Secretary the unprecedented power over American industry that would result from the Government's view of §§ 3(8) and 6(b)(5), coupled with OSHA's cancer policy. Expert testimony that a substance is probably a human carcinogen—either because it has caused cancer in animals or because individuals have contracted cancer following extremely high exposures—would justify the conclusion that the substance poses some risk of serious harm no matter how minute the exposure and no matter how many experts testified that they regarded the risk as insignificant. That conclusion would in turn justify pervasive regulation limited only by the constraint of feasibility. In light of the fact that there are literally thousands of substances used in the workplace that have been identified as carcinogens or suspect carcinogens, the Government's theory would give OSHA power to impose enormous costs that might produce little, if any, discernible benefit.

If the Government were correct in arguing that neither § 3(8) nor § 6(b)(5) requires that the risk from a toxic substance be quantified sufficiently to enable the Secretary to characterize it as significant in an understandable way, the statute would make such a "sweeping delegation of legislative power" that it might be unconstitutional under the Court's reasoning in *Schechter Poultry* and *Panama Refining*. A construction of the statute that avoids this kind of open-ended grant should certainly be favored.

[REHNQUIST, J., concurred in the judgment, arguing that § 6(b)(5) was invalid under the nondelegation doctrine:]

[I]n my opinion decisions such as *Panama Refining* suffer from none of the excesses of judicial policymaking that plagued some of the other decisions of that era. The many later decisions that have upheld congressional delegations of authority to the Executive Branch have done so largely on the theory that Congress may wish to exercise its authority in a particular field, but because the field is sufficiently technical, the ground to be covered sufficiently large, and the Members of Congress themselves not necessarily expert in the area in which they choose to legislate, the most that may be asked under the separation-of-powers doctrine is that Congress lay down the general policy and standards that animate the law, leaving the agency to refine those standards, "fill in the blanks," or apply the standards to particular cases. These decisions, to my mind, simply illustrate the above-quoted principle stated more than 50 years ago by Mr. Chief Justice Taft [in the *J. W. Hampton* case] that delegations of legislative authority must be judged "according to common sense and the inherent necessities of the governmental co-ordination."

Viewing the legislation at issue here in light of these principles, I believe that it fails to pass muster. Read literally, the relevant portion of § 6(b)(5) is completely precatory, admonishing the Secretary to adopt the most protective standard if he can, but excusing him from that duty if he cannot. In the case of a hazardous substance for which a "safe" level is either unknown or impractical, the language of § 6(b)(5) gives the

Secretary absolutely no indication where on the continuum of relative safety he should draw his line. Especially in light of the importance of the interests at stake, I have no doubt that the provision at issue, standing alone, would violate the doctrine against uncanalized delegations of legislative power. For me the remaining question, then, is whether additional standards are ascertainable from the legislative history or statutory context of § 6(b)(5) or, if not, whether such a standardless delegation was justifiable in light of the "inherent necessities" of the situation. [The legislative history of the statute failed to clarify the meaning of "to the extent feasible"]. . . .

Finally, as indicated earlier, in some cases this Court has abided by a rule of necessity, upholding broad delegations of authority where it would be "unreasonable and impracticable to compel Congress to prescribe detailed rules" regarding a particular policy or situation. But no need for such an evasive standard as "feasibility" is apparent in the present cases. In drafting § 6(b)(5), Congress was faced with a clear, if difficult, choice between balancing statistical lives and industrial resources or authorizing the Secretary to elevate human life above all concerns save massive dislocation in an affected industry. . . . That Congress chose, intentionally or unintentionally, to pass this difficult choice on to the Secretary is evident from the spectral quality of the standard it selected. . . .

As formulated and enforced by this Court, the nondelegation doctrine serves three important functions. First, and most abstractly, it ensures to the extent consistent with orderly governmental administration that important choices of social policy are made by Congress, the branch of our Government most responsive to the popular will. . . . Second, the doctrine guarantees that, to the extent Congress finds it necessary to delegate authority, it provides the recipient of that authority with an "intelligible principle" to guide the exercise of the delegated discretion. . . . Third, and derivative of the second, the doctrine ensures that courts charged with reviewing the exercise of delegated legislative discretion will be able to test that exercise against ascertainable standards.

I believe the legislation at issue here fails on all three counts. The decision whether the law of diminishing returns should have any place in the regulation of toxic substances is quintessentially one of legislative policy. For Congress to pass that decision on to the Secretary in the manner it did violates, in my mind, John Locke's caveat—reflected in the cases cited earlier in this opinion—that legislatures are to make laws. Nor, as I think the prior discussion amply demonstrates, do the provisions at issue or their legislative history provide the Secretary with any guidance that might lead him to his somewhat tentative conclusion that he must eliminate exposure to benzene as far as technologically and economically possible. Finally, I would suggest that the standard of "feasibility" renders meaningful judicial review impossible. . . .

If we are ever to reshoulder the burden of ensuring that Congress itself make the critical policy decisions, these are surely the cases in which to do it. It is difficult to imagine a more obvious example of Congress simply avoiding a choice which was both fundamental for purposes of the statute and yet politically so divisive that the necessary decision or compromise was difficult, if not impossible, to hammer out in the legislative forge. Far from detracting from the substantive authority of Congress, a declaration that the first sentence of § 6(b)(5) of the Occupational Safety and Health Act constitutes an invalid delegation to the Secretary of Labor would preserve the authority of Congress. If Congress wishes to legislate in an area which it has not previously sought to enter, it will in today's political world undoubtedly run into opposition no matter how the legislation is formulated. But that is the very essence of legislative authority under our system. It is the hard choices, and not the filling in of the blanks, which must be made by the elected representatives of the people. When fundamental policy decisions underlying important legislation about to be enacted are to be made, the buck stops with Congress and the President insofar as he exercises his constitutional role in the legislative process.

[The concurring opinion of POWELL, J., argued that the statute required OSHA to set a standard on the basis of a cost-benefit analysis. MARSHALL, J., dissented (joined by BRENNAN, WHITE, and BLACKMUN, JJ.). Marshall argued that OSHA's interpretation of the Act was completely consistent with congressional intent. As to delegation, he wrote:]

. . . While my brother Rehnquist eloquently argues that there remains a place for [the nondelegation] doctrine in our jurisprudence, I am frankly puzzled as to why the issue is thought to be of any relevance here. The nondelegation doctrine is designed to assure that the most fundamental decisions will be made by Congress, the elected representatives of the people, rather than by administrators. Some minimal definiteness is therefore required in order for Congress to delegate its authority to administrative agencies. Congress has been sufficiently definite here. The word "feasible" has a reasonably plain meaning, and its interpretation can be informed by other contexts in which Congress has used it. . . . In short, Congress has made the "critical policy decisions" in these cases. . . .

The plurality's apparent suggestion that the nondelegation doctrine might be violated if the Secretary were permitted to regulate definite but nonquantifiable risks is plainly wrong. Such a statute would be quite definite and would thus raise no constitutional question under *Schechter*

Poultry. Moreover, Congress could rationally decide that it would be better to require industry to bear "feasible" costs than to subject American workers to an indeterminate risk of cancer and other fatal diseases.

[In a case decided the following year, the Court upheld OSHA's interpretation of the word "feasible" in § 6(b)(5). REHNQUIST, J., dissented again on nondelegation grounds, and BURGER, C.J., joined his dissent. *American Textile Mfrs. Inst. v. Donovan*, 452 U.S. 490 (1981).]

WHITMAN V. AMERICAN TRUCKING ASS'NS, INC.
531 U.S. 457 (2001)

SCALIA, J.:

[The Clean Air Act (CAA) requires the EPA Administrator to promulgate national ambient air quality standards (or NAAQS) for each air pollutant for which "air quality criteria" have been issued. CAA § 109(b)(1) instructs the EPA to set NAAQS "the attainment and maintenance of which . . . are requisite to protect the public health" with "an adequate margin of safety." In 1997, the Administrator revised the NAAQS for particulate matter (PM) and ozone. The D.C. Circuit held that § 109(b)(1) violated the nondelegation doctrine because it found that EPA had interpreted the statute to provide no "intelligible principle" to guide the agency's exercise of authority. The court thought that EPA might be able to avoid the unconstitutional delegation by adopting a restrictive construction of § 109(b)(1). Therefore, instead of declaring § 109(b)(1) unconstitutional, the court remanded the NAAQS to EPA.

The Supreme Court first held that the statute precludes EPA from considering costs in applying § 109(b)(1). Justice Scalia declared that the most natural reading of the statutory language supported this conclusion. He then continued:] We have [in the past] refused to find implicit in ambiguous sections of the CAA an authorization to consider costs that has elsewhere, and . . . often, been expressly granted.

Accordingly, to prevail in their present challenge, respondents must show a textual commitment of authority to the EPA to consider costs in setting NAAQS under § 109(b)(1). . . . Congress, we have held, does not alter the fundamental details of a regulatory scheme in vague terms or ancillary provisions—it does not, one might say, hide elephants in mouseholes. Respondents' textual arguments ultimately founder upon this principle.

Their first claim is that § 109(b)(1)'s terms "adequate margin" and "requisite" leave room to pad health effects with cost concerns. . . . [We] find it implausible that Congress would give to the EPA through these modest words the power to determine whether implementation costs should moderate national air quality standards. [The Court rejected as equally unpersuasive several other textual arguments tendered by respondents.]

It should be clear from what we have said that the canon requiring texts to be so construed as to avoid serious constitutional problems has no application here. No matter how severe the constitutional doubt, courts may choose only between reasonably available interpretations of a text. The text of § 109(b), interpreted in its statutory and historical context and with appreciation for its importance to the CAA as a whole, unambiguously bars cost considerations from the NAAQS-setting process, and thus ends the matter for us as well as the EPA. We therefore affirm the judgment of the Court of Appeals on this point.

III

. . . The Court of Appeals held that [§ 109(b)] as interpreted by the Administrator did not provide an "intelligible principle" to guide the EPA's exercise of authority in setting NAAQS. "[The] EPA," it said, "lacked any determinate criteria for drawing lines. It has failed to state intelligibly how much is too much." The court hence found that the EPA's interpretation (but not the statute itself) violated the nondelegation doctrine. We disagree.

In a delegation challenge, the constitutional question is whether the statute has delegated legislative power to the agency. Article I, § 1, of the Constitution vests "all legislative Powers herein granted . . . in a Congress of the United States." This text permits no delegation of those powers, and so we repeatedly have said that when Congress confers decisionmaking authority upon agencies *Congress* must "lay down by legislative act an intelligible principle to which the person or body authorized to [act] is directed to conform." *J. W. Hampton.* We have never suggested that an agency can cure an unlawful delegation of legislative power by adopting in its discretion a limiting construction of the statute. . . . The idea that an agency can cure an unconstitutionally standardless delegation of power by declining to exercise some of that power seems to us internally contradictory. The very choice of which portion of the power to exercise—that is to say, the prescription of the standard that Congress had omitted—would *itself* be an exercise of the forbidden legislative authority. Whether the statute delegates legislative power is a question for the courts, and an agency's voluntary self-denial has no bearing upon the answer.

[However, § 109(b)(1) satisfies the intelligible principle standard because the term "requisite"] "mean[s] sufficient, but not more than necessary." These limits on the EPA's discretion . . . resemble the Occupational Safety and Health Act provision requiring the agency to " 'set the standard which most adequately assures, to the extent feasible, on the basis of the best available evidence, that no employee will suffer any impairment of health' "—which the Court upheld in [*Industrial Union*] . . . .

The scope of discretion § 109(b)(1) allows is in fact well within the outer limits of our nondelegation precedents. In the history of the Court we have found the requisite "intelligible principle" lacking in only two statutes, one of which provided literally no guidance for the exercise of discretion, and the other of which conferred authority to regulate the entire economy on the basis of no more precise a standard than stimulating the economy by assuring "fair competition." See *Panama Refining*; *Schechter Poultry*. . . . In short, we have almost never felt qualified to second-guess Congress regarding the permissible degree of policy judgment that can be left to those executing or applying the law.

It is true enough that the degree of agency discretion that is acceptable varies according to the scope of the power congressionally conferred. While Congress need not provide any direction to the EPA regarding the manner in which it is to define "country elevators," which are to be exempt from new-stationary-source regulations governing grain elevators, it must provide substantial guidance on setting air standards that affect the entire national economy. But even in sweeping regulatory schemes we have never demanded, as the Court of Appeals did here, that statutes provide a "determinate criterion" for saying "how much [of the regulated harm] is too much." . . . "[A] certain degree of discretion, and thus of lawmaking, inheres in most executive or judicial action." *Mistretta v. United States,* 488 U.S. 361, 417 (Scalia, J., dissenting). Section 109(b)(1) of the CAA, which to repeat we interpret as requiring the EPA to set air quality standards at the level that is "requisite"—that is, not lower or higher than is necessary—to protect the public health with an adequate margin of safety, fits comfortably within the scope of discretion permitted by our precedent. . . .

THOMAS, J., concurring.

. . . Although this Court since 1928 has treated the "intelligible principle" requirement as the only constitutional limit on congressional grants of power to administrative agencies, the Constitution does not speak of "intelligible principles." Rather, it speaks in much simpler terms: "*All* legislative Powers herein granted shall be vested in a Congress." U.S. Const., Art. 1, § 1 (emphasis added). I am not convinced that the intelligible principle doctrine serves to prevent all cessions of legislative power. I believe that there are cases in which the principle is intelligible and yet the significance of the delegated decision is simply too great for the decision to be called anything other than "legislative."

As it is, none of the parties to this case has examined the text of the Constitution or asked us to reconsider our precedents on cessions of legislative power. On a future day, however, I would be willing to address the question whether our delegation jurisprudence has strayed too far from our Founders' understanding of separation of powers.

STEVENS, J., with whom SOUTER, J., joins, concurring in part and concurring in the judgment. . . . [It would be clearer if we recognized that the statute delegates legislative power to the EPA but is constitutional because it provides an intelligible principle. This approach is better than the approach taken by the majority, which pretends that the rulemaking authority delegated to the EPA is not "legislative power."]

BREYER, J., concurring in part and concurring in the judgment. [Breyer argued that regulators must often balance the costs and benefits of regulations. "Other things being equal, we should read silences or ambiguities in the language of regulatory statutes as permitting, not forbidding, this type of rational regulation." But in this case the language of § 109 and its legislative history make it clear that such balancing is not permissible.]

NOTES AND QUESTIONS

1. *Purposes of the standards requirement.* According to Justice Rehnquist's opinion in *Industrial Union,* what are the purposes of the requirement that a statute contain an "intelligible standard?" Are his arguments persuasive? Where, aside from the language of the statute, might such standards be found?

2. *Safeguards and nondelegation.* Professor Davis argued that courts should insist on "safeguards" to prevent agencies from abusing discretion rather than "standards." Kenneth Culp Davis, *A New Approach to Delegation,* 36 U. CHI. L. REV. 713 (1969). Recall the importance of "checks and balances" in our constitutional system. Davis contended that safeguards serve a checking function that is more effective than vague legislative standards. Such safeguards could include, for example, a system in which agencies regularly state findings and reasons for their decisions and use precedents as a guide. *Id.* at 726. Davis also argued that "when legislative bodies have failed to provide standards, the courts should not hold the delegation unlawful but should require that the administrators must as rapidly as feasible supply the standards." *Id.* at 725. The Supreme Court rejected the latter argument in *American Trucking.*

3. *Arguments for reviving nondelegation doctrine.* David Schoenbrod believes that courts should invalidate statutes that state only the *goals* that Congress wishes to achieve (like providing safe workplaces or cleaning up the air) but leave to agencies the hard decisions about *means.* He wrote:

> Statutes that purport to give lawmaking power to an agency
> actually entail a sharing of lawmaking power among several groups,
> including the agency, the most powerful members of the legislative
> committees with jurisdiction over the agency, their counterparts in

the White House, and concentrated interests [such as regulated industries]. Concurrently, political benefits accrue to legislators and the president. First, they can claim credit for the promised benefits of a regulatory program, yet shift blame for the disappointments and costs of the program to the agency. Second, with delegation they increase their opportunities to obtain campaign contributions and other favors from concentrated interests.

[The ways] in which legislators can use delegation to maximize their credit and minimize their blame help to explain why delegation systematically produces the delay, complexity, and confusion that the Clean Air Act illustrates. As former EPA Administrator Lee Thomas put it, "Everybody is accountable and nobody is accountable under the way [Congress] is setting it up, but [the legislators] have got a designated whipping boy."

POWER WITHOUT RESPONSIBILITY 82, 93 (1993). While still a law professor, Justice Scalia wrote the following analysis of Rehnquist's *Industrial Union* opinion:

There are several problems with revivification of the unconstitutional delegation doctrine. . . . [especially] the difficulty of enunciating how much delegation is too much. The relevant factors are simply too multifarious. . . . A doctrine so vague, it may be said, is no doctrine at all, but merely an invitation to judicial policy making in the guise of constitutional law. This fear is indeed the reason for the alleged demise of the doctrine—because its use in 1935 paralleled the Court's now discredited use of the due process clause to impose its own notions of acceptable social legislation. But surely vague constitutional doctrines are not automatically unacceptable. . . . And the risk of vagueness here is much less than elsewhere. Decisions under the due process clause . . . are an absolute impediment to governmental action. A decision based on the unconstitutional delegation doctrine is not; it merely requires the action to be taken in a different fashion. . . .

[I]n modern circumstances the unconstitutional delegation doctrine, far from permitting an increase in judicial power, actually reduces it. For now that judicial review of agency action is virtually routine, it is the courts, rather than the agencies, that can ultimately determine the content of standardless legislation. In other words, to a large extent judicial invocation of the unconstitutional delegation doctrine is a self-denying ordinance— forbidding the transfer of legislative power not to the agencies, but to the courts themselves. The benzene case is illustrative. In giving content to a law which in fact says no more than that OSHA should ensure "safe places of employment" (whatever that means) and should maximize protection against toxic materials "to the extent feasible" (whatever that means), it was the plurality of the Court, rather than OSHA, that ended up doing legislator's work.

So even with all its Frankenstein-like warts, knobs, and (concededly) dangers, the unconstitutional delegation doctrine is worth hewing from the ice. The alternative appears to be continuation of the widely felt trend toward government by bureaucracy or (what is no better) government by courts. . . .

Antonin Scalia, *A Note on the Benzene Case*, REGULATION, July/Aug. 1980, at 27–28. Note that Scalia had a chance to put his theory into action in *American Trucking* but passed up the opportunity.

4. *Arguments against reviving nondelegation doctrine.* Richard Stewart opposes any effort to revive the nondelegation doctrine:

[A]ny large-scale enforcement of the nondelegation doctrine would clearly be unwise . . . . . [T]here appear to be serious institutional constraints on Congress' ability to specify regulatory policy in meaningful detail. Legislative majorities typically represent coalitions of interests that must not only compromise among themselves but also with opponents. Individual politicians often find far more to be lost than gained in taking a readily identifiable stand on a controversial issue of social or economic policy. Detailed legislative specification of policy would require intensive and continuous investigation, decision, and revision of specialized and complex issues. Such a task would require resources that Congress has in most instances, been unable or unwilling to muster. . . .

Finally there are serious problems in relying upon the judiciary to enforce the nondelegation doctrine. A court may not properly insist on a greater legislative specification of policy than the subject matter admits of. But how is the judge to decide the degree of policy specification that is possible? . . . Given such subjective standards, and the controversial character of decisions on whether to invalidate legislative delegations, such decisions will almost inevitably appear partisan, and might often be so.

Richard B. Stewart, *The Reformation of American Administrative Law*, 88 HARV. L. REV. 1667, 1695–97 (1975).

In challenging the views of Schoenbrod and other theorists, Jerry Mashaw points out that private special interests seeking to redistribute wealth to themselves might prefer a narrow delegation that answers the hard questions in ways favorable to themselves. "No one has been able to demonstrate any systematic relationship between improving accountability, or enhancing the public welfare, or respecting the rule of law, and the specificity of legislation. . . . If that is the case, then surely the Supreme Court has been wise to leave the choice of statutory generality to the legislature itself." JERRY L. MASHAW, GREED, CHAOS, AND GOVERNANCE 147–48 (1997).

Mashaw argues that broad delegations of power actually *promote* democratic values, because the President is accountable for the decisions of executive agencies:

> The voter's vision of presidential electoral politics is arguably quite different [from the way the voters are assumed to choose representatives in Congress]. . . . Citizens vote for a president based almost wholly on a perception of the difference that one or another candidate might make to general governmental policies. If this description of voting in national elections is reasonably plausible, then the utilization of vague delegations to administrative agencies takes on significance as a device for facilitating responsiveness to voter preferences expressed in presidential elections. The high transactions costs of legislating specifically suggests that legislative activity directed to the modification of administration mandates will be infrequent. Agencies will thus persist with their statutory empowering provisions relatively intact over substantial periods of time.

> . . . Indeed one can reasonably expect that a president will be able to affect policy in a four-year term only because being elected president entails acquiring the power to exercise, direct, or influence policy discretion. The group of executive officers we commonly call "the administration" matters only because of the relative malleability of the directives that administrators have in their charge. If congressional statutes were truly specific with respect to the actions that administrators were to take, presidential politics would be a mere beauty contest. *Id.* at 152–53.

Eric Posner and Adrian Vermeule have challenged the nondelegation doctrine on a more fundamental level. They argue that prudential arguments against the doctrine are

> entirely too respectful of the alleged constitutional rule limiting the scope or terms of statutory grants of authority to the executive. In our view there just is no constitutional nondelegation rule, nor has there ever been. . . . Nondelegation is nothing more than a controversial theory that floated around the margins of nineteenth century constitutionalism—a theory that wasn't clearly adopted by the Supreme Court until 1892 [in *Field v. Clark*], and even then only in dictum. The Court's invocation of the rule to invalidate two statutes in 1935 was nothing more than a local aberration. . . .

> To be clear about our thesis, we agree that the Constitution bars the "delegation of legislative power." In our view, however, the content of that prohibition is the following: Neither Congress nor its members may delegate to anyone else the authority to vote on

federal statutes or to exercise other de jure powers of federal legislators. What we argue, in contradiction of the usual view, is that a statutory grant of authority to the executive branch or other agents can never amount to a delegation of legislative power. A statutory grant of authority to the executive isn't a transfer of legislative power, but an exercise of legislative power.

Eric A. Posner & Adrian Vermeule, *Interring the Nondelegation Doctrine*, 69 U. CHI. L. REV. 1721, 1722–23 (2002). Gary Lawson takes sharp exception to the Posner-Vermeule thesis on originalist grounds, positing that some statutes delegating unlimited authority violate the Necessary and Proper Clause of Article I. *Discretion as Delegation: The "Proper" Understanding of the Nondelegation Doctrine*, 73 GEO. WASH. L. REV. 235 (2005) (arguing that if a statute outlawed all interstate transactions that did not promote "goodness and niceness," and authorized the President to define the contents of the statute, it would violate the nondelegation doctrine).

5. *Judicial review.* In a frequently quoted remark, Judge Leventhal once wrote that "Congress has been willing to delegate its legislative powers broadly—and the courts have upheld such delegations—because there is court review to assure that the agency exercises the delegated power within statutory limits." *Ethyl Corp. v. EPA*, 541 F.2d 1, 68 (D.C. Cir. 1976) (en banc) (concurring opinion). Thus, the availability of judicial review can ameliorate concerns about delegation, and its absence can aggravate them. This proposition seems to be at work in *Touby v. United States*, 500 U.S. 160, 168–69 (1991). There the Court rejected a nondelegation challenge to a provision in the Controlled Substances Act that allowed the Drug Enforcement Administration to temporarily designate a drug as a controlled substance on an expedited basis when "necessary to avoid an imminent hazard to the public safety." Among the bases for this challenge was the fact that the statute said that such a DEA order "is not subject to judicial review." The Court parried this argument by finding that, despite its literal language, the prohibition on judicial review referred only to preenforcement challenges; it did not prevent accused drug dealers from contesting the validity of the order as a defense to a criminal prosecution.

6. *Narrow construction of statutes.* In *Mistretta v. United States*, 488 U.S. 361, 374 n.7 (1989), the Court remarked: "In recent years, our application of the nondelegation doctrine principally has been limited to the interpretation of statutory texts, and, more particularly, to giving narrow constructions to statutory delegations that might otherwise be thought to be unconstitutional." Justice Stevens' plurality opinion in *Industrial Union* seems to bear out this observation. It interpreted § 3(8) of the OSHA Act to avoid the problem that the statute might violate the nondelegation doctrine. Before promulgating a standard for toxic materials, he said, OSHA must find that it is "necessary and appropriate to remedy a *significant risk* of material health impairment." Yet the "significant risk" requirement does not appear in the language of the statute, and the four dissenters vigorously objected to it.

Touby, discussed in the preceding note, offers another example of judicial narrowing.

These holdings could be defended as reflecting the judicial policy of construing statutes to avoid constitutional problems if such an interpretation is (in the words of *American Trucking*) "reasonably available." Yet, is strained interpretation of a broad statute really a better response to delegation concerns than outright invalidation of the statute? Professor Manning suggests not: "If the point of the nondelegation doctrine is to ensure that Congress makes important statutory policy, a strategy that requires the judiciary, in effect, to rewrite the terms of a duly enacted statute cannot be said to serve the interests of that doctrine." John F. Manning, *The Nondelegation Doctrine as a Canon of Avoidance*, 2000 SUP. CT. REV. 223, 228.

7. *Nondelegation canons.* Professor Sunstein suggests that, in order to effectuate constitutional and other public policy values, courts should regularly read administrative statutes in light of interpretive principles that he calls "nondelegation canons." For example, such canons prevent agencies (absent a clear congressional statement) from applying a statute retroactively or from interpreting a statute to preempt state law. Sunstein writes: "The relevant canons operate as nondelegation principles, and they are designed to ensure that Congress decides certain contested questions on its own." He argues that the use of these clear-statement rules is superior to enforcement of the nondelegation doctrine. "Courts do not ask the hard-to-manage question whether the legislature has exceeded the permissible level of discretion, but pose instead the far more manageable question whether the agency has been given the discretion to decide something that (under the appropriate canon) only legislatures may decide." Cass R. Sunstein, *Nondelegation Canons*, 67 U. CHI. L. REV. 315 (2000). *But see* David M. Driesen, *Loose Canons: Statutory Construction and the New Nondelegation Doctrine*, 64 U. PITT. L. REV. 1 (2002), which criticizes the Sunstein thesis and argues that narrowly construing statutes to avoid the nondelegation doctrine poses the same dangers as does the nondelegation doctrine itself.

8. *Problem—bird flu.* In 2001, Congress enacted a statute that authorized the Director of the Public Health Service (PHS) to adopt regulations to deal with public health emergencies. The statute contained no standards or any definition of "public health emergency" but it stated that the regulations could impose federal criminal penalties on persons who violated them.

Last year, the PHS Director adopted rules (without notice and comment) concerning a potential human bird flu epidemic. Under the rules, in the event that cases of bird flu are detected, all persons in areas to be designated by the local public health director are quarantined, meaning they must remain in their residences until further notice. Violators are punishable by fine or imprisonment for up to one year. A quarantine must be announced in the local print media and on television and be published in the Federal Register. Nobody challenged these regulations in court.

Several months ago, several cases of bird flu were detected in Oak City. The local public health director announced a quarantine on all Oak City residents and the quarantine was announced repeatedly in all local newspapers and on all television stations. Next day, Mary, knowing about the quarantine, left her home by car to buy groceries for her family in a nearby city. She was caught by the police and prosecuted in federal court for violating the regulation. You represented Mary at her trial and argued that the regulations were procedurally and substantively invalid and that the statute violated the nondelegation doctrine. However, all defenses were rejected and she was sentenced to six months in prison. There were no additional cases of bird flu in Oak City or elsewhere in the U.S. and nobody died from the disease. On appeal of Mary's conviction, what are the prospects for reversal of the conviction?

9. *Problem—Indian lands.* Section 5 of the Indian Reorganization Act of 1934 provides: "The Secretary of the Interior is hereby authorized, in his discretion, to acquire, through purchase, relinquishment, gift, exchange, or assignment, any interest in lands, water rights, or surface rights to land . . . for the purpose of providing land for Indians." 25 U.S.C. § 465. The statute makes two million dollars per year available to the Secretary for this purpose. The Secretary decided to use her authority under § 425 to acquire 150 acres of land in the State of Madison. The tract would be held in trust for the benefit of a federally recognized tribe that intended to construct and operate a casino on that site. The state government opposed this project, because Indian lands are exempt from state property taxes and because it did not support an expansion of legalized gambling in Madison.

The state brought suit against the Secretary, alleging that § 5 violates the nondelegation doctrine. The district judge agreed. He wrote:

> The statute contains no limits or guidance as to where, when, or why the Secretary may acquire land for the benefit of Indians. She could potentially acquire land from private citizens to provide Indian tribes or individual Indians with a residential subdivision, a retirement home, a children's playground, or a golf course. This is too much unchecked power to entrust to any one official.

> The unfettered grant of power in § 5 is all the more disturbing in light of case law holding that the Secretary's authority under § 5 is so broad that its exercise is not susceptible of judicial review (*Florida v. U.S. Dep't of Interior*, 768 F.2d 1248 (11th Cir. 1985)). Congress must make the choice as to the grounds on which the Secretary may acquire land for Indians. It is hardly clear that, if it did so, acquisition of so large a parcel for a casino would be one of those grounds.

The Secretary contends that the purpose of the Act is to enable Indians to achieve economic security and tribal self-governance, and that § 5 is adequately limited if it is construed as designed for that purpose. However, the quotations from legislative history that underlie this argument cannot alter the plain language of § 5, which is entirely openended.

The Secretary files an appeal. What result? *Cf. Michigan Gambling Opposition v. Kempthorne*, 525 F.3d 23 (D.C. Cir. 2008); *South Dakota v. U.S. Dep't of Interior*, 69 F.3d 878 (8th Cir. 1995), *vacated*, 519 U.S. 919 (1996).

§ 7.2.2 THE NONDELEGATION DOCTRINE AND STATE AGENCIES

The nondelegation doctrine has much greater practical significance at the state level than at the federal level. Why the difference between state and federal law? One factor may be the strong separation of powers language found in about thirty-five state constitutions. For example, the Illinois constitution provides: "The legislative, executive and judicial branches are separate. No branch shall exercise powers properly belonging to another." Ill. Const., art. II, § 1. Consider whether the federal courts should emulate state courts in more strongly enforcing the nondelegation doctrine or whether state courts should follow the federal courts in giving only lip service to the doctrine.

THYGESEN V. CALLAHAN
385 N.E.2d 699 (Ill. 1979)

MORAN, J.:

[This case involved a challenge, on grounds of undue delegation, to § 19.3 of the Illinois currency exchange act, which provided:]

"The Director [of Financial Institutions] shall, by rules adopted in accordance with the Illinois Administrative Procedure Act, formulate and issue, within 120 days from the effective date of this amendatory Act, schedules of maximum rates which can be charged for check cashing and writing of money orders by community currency exchanges and ambulatory currency exchanges. Such rates may vary according to such circumstances and conditions as the Director determines to be appropriate. The schedule so established may be modified by the Director from time to time by the same procedure." . . .

. . . For this court's most recent and comprehensive pronouncement on the delegation of power to administrative agencies, we defer to *Stofer v. Motor Vehicle Casualty Co.*, 369 N.E.2d 875 (1977). In *Stofer,* the court reaffirmed its adherence to the guiding principle that intelligible standards or guidelines must accompany legislative delegations of power. This court, thus, implicitly recognized both the constitutional dimensions of the principle (Ill. Const.1970, art. IV, sec. 1) and the practical functions which standards continue to serve. Intelligible standards help guide the administrative agency in the application of the statutes involved and, thereby, safeguard against the unwarranted or unintended extension of legislative delegation. They tend to insure that the legislature does not abdicate to the agency the legislature's primary responsibility to determine, from among the policy alternatives, those objectives the legislation is meant to achieve. Moreover, intelligible standards are indispensable to a meaningful judicial review of any action ultimately taken by the administrative agency. . . .

In an attempt to endow the requisite of intelligible standards with a conceptual foundation, the *Stofer* court declared that a legislative delegation is valid if it sufficiently identifies:

> (1) The *persons* and *activities* potentially subject to regulations;

> (2) the *harm* sought to be prevented; and

> (3) the general *means* intended to be available to the administrator to prevent the identified harm.

In *Stofer,* the legislature had delegated to the Director of Insurance the power to promulgate a standard policy as a means of ensuring uniformity in the insurance of identical risks. The legislation clearly satisfied the first prong of the test by specifying that the regulation was to apply to fire and lightning insurance issued in Illinois. As to the second prong, the court noted that the legislature had articulated its intention to prevent a chaotic proliferation of disparate fire insurance policies. In discussing the general *means* intended to be available to the Director to prevent the identified harm (the third prong), the court cautioned:

> "[H]ad the legislature left the Director completely free to promulgate a 'reasonable' uniform fire insurance policy, we would have serious doubts as to the constitutionality of such uncabined discretion. We find, however, that the legislature has provided substantial additional standards defining the harm sought to be prevented and thereby limit[ed] the Director's discretion."

The court then referred to a related statutory provision which delegated to the Director the power to order the discontinuation of any policy which contained "inconsistent, ambiguous or misleading clauses, or [any] exceptions or conditions that will unreasonably or deceptively affect the risks that are purported to be assumed by the policy. . . ." The court, reasoning that the delegated authority to promulgate a reasonable uniform policy necessarily incorporated the above-quoted limitation, held that the Director's discretion was limited sufficiently to withstand constitutional scrutiny.

Here, as in *Stofer,* the legislature clearly satisfied the first prong of the test. Those subject to regulation under § 19.3 of the currency exchange act are community and ambulatory currency exchanges, and the regulation is limited to the activities of cashing checks and issuing money orders. In contrast to *Stofer,* the legislature made no attempt to identify the "harm sought to be prevented" in delegating to defendant the power to set maximum rates and did not sufficiently identify the "means . . . intended to be available . . . to prevent the identified harm." Section 19.3 is devoid of any reference to the harm to be remedied. The currency exchange act contains no other provision which indicates, explicitly or implicitly, general purposes which the legislature might have intended to foster with respect to setting rates for cashing checks and issuing money orders.

The legislature's failure to convey, within the Act, the harm which it sought to remedy by the setting of maximum rates, is compounded by its failure to set forth any meaningful standards to guide defendant in setting the maximum rates. The only provision cited by defendant which in any way guides defendant's discretion in setting maximum rates is an omnibus provision which states:

> "The Director may make and enforce such *reasonable,* relevant regulations, directions, orders, decisions and findings as may be necessary for the execution and enforcement of this Act *and the purposes sought to be attained herein.*"

As we have already discussed, the Act fails to identify any purposes which the legislature might have sought to attain by providing for the establishment of maximum check-cashing and money-order rates. Defendant refers to various provisions in the Act that, he contends, limit his discretion to the promulgation of maximum rates which promote economic benefit and stability to both the currency exchange and the public. The provisions cited by defendant, however, apply to regulatory matters, such as the issuance of licenses and the appointment of advisory board members, which are totally unrelated to the promulgation of maximum check-cashing and money-order rates. We find that the only statutory limitation on defendant's discretion in establishing maximum rates is that the rates be *reasonable.* This court, in *Stofer,* rightfully expressed serious doubt as to the constitutionality of such "uncabined discretion." Here, where the legislature has not only failed to provide any additional standards to guide defendant's discretion, but has failed to communicate to defendant the harm it intended to prevent, it is clear that the legislature has unlawfully delegated its power to set such maximum rates.

NOTES AND QUESTIONS

1. *Delegation in the states.* Many state supreme courts insist that a delegation of authority to an agency may not be upheld absent adequate statutory standards that constrain the agency's discretion. Assuming a state strongly enforces the nondelegation doctrine, is *Thygesen* a persuasive application of the doctrine?

The Illinois statute involved in *Thygesen* provided that the agency had to comply with the rulemaking procedures of the state APA when it established rates for check cashing services. However, the court seemed indifferent to the presence of these procedural safeguards. A number of states have substituted consideration of safeguards for standards. See § 7.2.1 N.2. In a case involving a delegation challenge to a building code, the Oregon Supreme Court said:

> It is now apparent that the requirement of expressed standards has, in most instances, been little more than a judicial fetish for legislative language, the recitation of which provides no additional safeguards to persons affected by the exercise of the delegated authority. Thus, we have learned that it is of little or no significance in the administration of a delegated power that the statute which generated it stated the permissible limits of its exercise in terms of such abstractions as "public convenience, interest or necessity" or "unjust or unreasonable," or "for the public health, safety, and morals" and similar phrases accepted as satisfying the standards requirement.

> As pointed out in Davis on Administrative Law, the important consideration is not whether the statute delegating the power expresses standards, but whether the procedure established for the exercise of the power furnishes adequate safeguards to those who are affected by the administrative action. . . . We believe that the appeals procedure provided a sufficient safeguard to persons wishing to contest administrative action in the enforcement of the code.

Warren v. Marion County, 353 P.2d 257 (Ore. 1960). Similarly, see *Barry & Barry, Inc. v. Dep't of Motor Vehicles*, 500 P.2d 540 (Wash. 1972).

However, the safeguards approach was squarely rejected by the Florida Supreme Court. That court overturned a delegation of authority to an agency to identify the areas in the state in which development should be regulated to protect "environmental, historical, natural, or archeological resources of regional or statewide importance." Because the statute transferred the fundamental policy decision to the agency of which areas were to be protected, it was invalid despite Florida's extensive system of procedural safeguards on the rulemaking process. *Askew v. Cross Key Waterways*, 372 So.2d 913 (Fla. 1978).

Professor Rossi lists twenty states as maintaining a "strong" nondelegation doctrine, which insists that the authority-delegating statute contain meaningful standards, including Illinois, Florida, and Texas. He lists seven states that follow the Washington-Oregon approach, which he calls the "weak version" of the nondelegation doctrine. Finally, he lists twenty-three states that follow a "moderate" version of the doctrine. These "moderate approach" states combine consideration of standards and safeguards and tend to accept legislative declarations of policy in place of more precise standards. *See* Jim Rossi, *Institutional Design and the Lingering Legacy of Antifederalist Separation of Powers Ideals in the States*, 52 VAND. L. REV. 1167, 1191–1201 (1999). In short, most states at least purport to take the nondelegation doctrine seriously and require the legislature to articulate meaningful standards (or at least meaningful declarations of policy) that guide the agencies in their exercise of discretion.

2. *Supersized delegation?* A recent target of nondelegation reasoning was a widely publicized measure promoted by Mayor Michael Bloomberg of New York City. On his recommendation, the city's Board of Health prohibited restaurants, movie theatres, and food carts from serving sugared sodas in cups larger than sixteen ounces in size. This "portion cap" was intended to ameliorate rising obesity rates in the city. An appellate court held the cap unconstitutional, declaring that, " '[as] an arm of the executive branch of government, an administrative agency may not, in the exercise of rule-making authority, engage in broad-based public policy determinations.' " Although the words of the city charter authorized the Board to regulate "all matters affecting the health of the City," the court insisted that " '[e]nactments conferring authority on administrative agencies in broad or general terms must be interpreted in light of the limitations that the Constitution imposes.' " An interpretation that would allow the Board to regulate all matters having some relation to the public health would amount to "unfettered delegation of legislative power." *N.Y. Statewide Coalition of Hispanic Chambers of Commerce v. N.Y. City Dep't of Health & Mental Hygiene*, 970 N.Y.S.2d 200 (App. Div. 2013).

The court was particularly troubled by the fact that the Board had openly balanced concerns of public health against economic costs, such as by allowing certain exemptions. Moreover, it argued, the city council and state assembly had earlier considered bills that targeted the same policy area, but these measures had failed to pass, indicating that "the legislature remains unsure about how best to approach the issue of excessive sugary beverage consumption." Were these good reasons to disapprove of the rule?

3. *Incorporation by reference of future federal law.* All states operate programs that are funded in part by the national government. These programs require that the states abide by federal rules, even though those rules are constantly changing. As a result, many state statutes incorporate

federal statutes and regulations by reference or authorize state agencies to adopt federal law by reference in their rules. The 2010 MSAPA lets individual states choose whether or not rules that incorporate federal law by reference may include *future* amendments. § 314(2). The same problem arises where a state tax statute mirrors a federal tax statute; the state statute provides that the state tax law automatically changes when the federal law changes. Should statutes that incorporate *future* changes in federal law be treated as an unlawful delegation of power to the federal government?

The Supreme Court of Michigan has endorsed a lenient test for evaluating state statutes that allegedly delegate legislative authority to a federal agency. The issue was the validity of a statute providing that a company could not be held liable for producing any drug that had been approved by the federal Food and Drug Administration as safe and effective. The court held that the statute did not unconstitutionally delegate power when it incorporated standards set by some other entity, so long as those standards have "independent significance." *Taylor v. SmithKline Beecham Corp.*, 658 N.W.2d 127 (Mich. 2003). "The FDA does not decide who may bring a products liability action in Michigan; rather, the FDA, for its own reasons that are independent of Michigan tort law, simply makes a factual finding regarding the safety and efficacy of drugs. It is the Michigan Legislature that has determined the legal consequences that flow from that finding." Similarly, *McFaddin v. Jackson*, 738 S.W.2d 176 (Tenn. 1987), upheld a state inheritance tax law that incorporated future changes in the federal estate tax.

For a contrasting view, see *Oklahoma City v. State ex rel. Okla. Dep't of Labor*, 918 P.2d 26 (Okla. 1995). The case involved the state's version of the federal Davis-Bacon Act. These Acts require governmental units to pay prevailing wages on construction projects. The Oklahoma statute delegated determination of local prevailing wages to the federal Labor Department. The court invalidated the Act because it left "an important determination to the unrestricted and standardless discretion of unelected bureaucrats. Worse, it delegates to an administrative arm of the federal government."

One commentator has written:

> The state adoption of federal law issue should be addressed in terms of the governmental policies being sought, and the substantive area being regulated. In matters where uniform regulation among the states and the federal government is desirable in order to implement a consistent national and local policy, to further identical state and federal goals, and to combat one "evil" which impacts on both the national and local level equally, and where the area being regulated involves matters which are highly technical, requires a level of expertise beyond that available to the states, requires a commitment of resources greater than what can be allocated by the states, and requires constant revision and quick response to new developments, state adoption of federal law should be encouraged.

This is especially true if the state adoption of federal law would not create additional significant burdens on regulated persons, and if the efficiency of the regulatory process would be improved by state adoption.

Arnold Rochvarg, *State Adoption of Federal Law—Legislative Abdication or Reasoned Policymaking*, 36 ADMIN. L. REV. 277, 298–99 (1984). Under Rochvarg's analysis, were *Taylor, McFaddin,* and *Oklahoma City* correctly decided? *See also* Jim Rossi, *Separation of Powers and State Implementation of Federally Inspired Regulatory Programs and Standards*, 46 WM. & MARY L. REV. 1343, 1363–70 (2005).

4.   *Problem.* The Madison state constitution requires that the annual state budget be balanced. Because the state encountered unexpected budget deficits in recent years, the legislature passed a statute requiring the Budget Commission, an executive agency, to make such cuts in the current year's appropriations as are necessary to bring the budget into balance. The cuts must reduce the deficit, not impair an essential government function, and not harm the public interest.

Because of a shortfall in tax revenues, the Commission had to cut state spending by $600,000,000. Therefore, it cut various spending items, including one for the construction of housing for homeless families. Children who would have received this housing sue to restore the appropriation. Assuming they have standing and that the case is otherwise justiciable, is the Commission's action valid? *See Chiles v. Children A, B, C, D, E, and F*, 589 So.2d 260 (Fla. 1991).

§ 7.2.3   DELEGATIONS TO PRIVATE ENTITIES

Legislatures sometimes delegate governmental authority, including the power to make rules or adjudicate disputes, to private persons or entities. Such delegations raise serious issues, because private delegatees may not be subject to direct political controls nor to due process, administrative procedure laws, freedom of information laws, or judicial review. Moreover, they may have a conflict of interest.

1.   *Legal framework.* In an early case, the U.S. Supreme Court invalidated a federal statute under which the maximum hours and minimum wages agreed upon by a majority of affected miners and mine-operators were made binding upon the rest of them. *Carter v. Carter Coal Co.,* 298 U.S. 238 (1936). The Court in *Carter* stressed the peculiar dangers inherent in a delegation of governmental authority to private parties: Such a delegation "is not even delegation to an official or an official body, presumptively disinterested, but to private persons whose interests may be and often are adverse to the interests of others in the same business." *Id.* at 311.

Since 1936, however, the federal courts have upheld a number of delegations of governmental authority to private enterprises. See Gillian

E. Metzger, *Privatization and Delegation*, 103 COLUM. L. REV. 1367, 1438–45 (2003). Programs in which a private entity merely implements policies set by a government body do not pose a serious problem. Also permissible are arrangements in which rules promulgated by the government will go into effect only if a majority or supermajority of regulated persons votes to endorse them. *Currin v. Wallace.* 306 U.S. 1 (1939). In addition, a private organization may even be empowered to write standards to implement a government program, if these standards are essentially advisory or are subject to being overridden by a politically accountable government entity. *Sunshine Anthracite Coal Co. v. Adkins,* 310 U.S. 381 (1940). For instance, one court of appeals upheld a federal statute authorizing a private securities dealer association to issue rules and discipline its members for violation of those rules. However, the statutory scheme contained an important check: both the rules and the disciplinary proceedings were subject to Securities and Exchange Commission (SEC) review. *Todd & Co., Inc. v. SEC,* 557 F.2d 1008, 1012 (3d Cir. 1977).

2. *Getting off track.* Modern judicial tolerance for public-private partnerships does have outer boundaries, if one may judge from *Ass'n of Am. R.Rs. v. U.S. Dep't of Transp.,* 721 F.3d 666 (D.C. Cir. 2013). This case involved the National Railroad Passenger Corporation, a federally chartered corporation better known as Amtrak. Amtrak operates passenger trains on tracks that belong to privately owned railroads. It is entitled to priority in the usage of these tracks, and a railroad that fails to give Amtrak such priority is subject to a penalty. The standards used to determine the railroads' liability are prescribed jointly by the Federal Railroad Administration and by Amtrak. If those two entities do not agree, either can refer the issue to binding arbitration.

The court held that this delegation of regulatory power to Amtrak went beyond the scope of prior case law and was unconstitutional. Here, Amtrak had standard-setting authority, and the FRA could not necessarily override it; if the matter went to arbitration, the FRA would not get the last word. The court pointed out that, as in *Carter,* Amtrak had a conflict of interest, because tough standards would be good for its own profit margins.

As the court recognized, its premise that Amtrak is indeed a private entity was debatable. After all, the federal government owns all of Amtrak's preferred stock, most members of its Board of Directors are appointed by the President, and the Supreme Court has held that Amtrak is a government actor for purposes of the First Amendment. *Lebron v. Nat'l R.R. Passenger Corp.,* 513 U.S. 374 (1995). On the other hand, Congress itself has characterized Amtrak as a for-profit corporation, not a government instrumentality; and its website is *amtrak.com*, not *amtrak.gov*. Amid these mixed signals, the court chose to regard Amtrak as private for purposes of this case, because its mission is to maximize profits, and its quasi-independent status enables the government to avoid accountability for its actions.

3. *Privatization in broader perspective.* In recent years, functions that were previously carried out by government employees have increasingly been contracted out to private parties. For example, the George W. Bush administration made heavy use of private military contractors in fighting the wars in Iraq and Afghanistan, including such debatable functions as the care and interrogation of prisoners. Outsourcing has continued apace during the Obama administration. Today private entities administer Medicare and Medicaid claims, operate welfare facilities, run charter schools, etc.

Even when the contracted function does not involve rulemaking or adjudication, such privatization raises a set of difficult issues. For example, is it more efficient for jobs to be done by private workers who are less likely to be unionized than government employees and are not subject to civil service protections, and by private entities that aren't encumbered by administrative procedure laws? Will the jobs be done as well by private contractors who see themselves as serving clients to make a profit rather than carrying out government functions in the public interest? When should government require private entities who want to take over public jobs to engage in competitive bidding? How should government hold private contractors accountable? Do the same methods of legislative, executive, and judicial oversight that we use to hold public agencies accountable work for private contractors? Can we depend on market forces to hold private contractors accountable? *See generally* Jody Freeman, *Extending Public Law Norms Through Privatization*, 116 HARV. L. REV. 1285 (2003) (urging that government attempt to impose public law norms on private contractors).

One limitation on contracting out is that it is improper to delegate "inherent government functions" to non-government entities. As Verkuil points out, "the Secretary of Defense cannot delegate the power to conduct the war in Iraq to the Rand Corporation any more than the Attorney General can leave it to private . . . counsel to decide when to prosecute." Paul R. Verkuil, *Public Law Limitations on Privatization of Government Functions*, 84 N.C.L. REV. 397, 425 (2006). However, the definition of "inherent government functions" is contested. *See* Office of Mgmt. & Budget Circular A–76 (attempting a definition); Verkuil, *supra,* at 436–40.

In light of the above, under what circumstances, if at all, should a state or the federal government be allowed to delegate to a private entity the authority to run a prison? *See* Ira P. Robbins, *The Impact of the Delegation Doctrine on Prison Privatization*, 35 UCLA L. REV. 911, 929–

52 (1988); Metzger, *supra*, at 1499–1501. For other commentaries on legal and policy issues arising from privatization, see, e.g., Harold J. Krent, *The Private Performing the Public: Delimiting Delegations to Private Parties*, 65 U. MIAMI L. REV. 507 (2011); Kathleen Clark. *Ethics, Employees and Contractors: Financial Conflicts of Interest In and Out of Government*, 62 ALA. L. REV. 961 (2011); Jon D. Michaels, *Privatization's Pretensions*, 77 U. CHI. L. REV. 717 (2010).

4. *State entities exercising federal power*. Delegation of federal regulatory authority to state governments does not pose nearly as troubling a situation as delegation to private entities. After all, federal-state relationships are inherent in our constitutional system, and "cooperative federalism" is often highly prized. *See* Harold J. Krent, *Federal Power, Non-Federal Actors: The Ramifications of* Free Enterprise Fund, 79 FORDHAM L. REV. 2425 (2011). Even in this context, however, Congress must affirmatively authorize any such delegation; a federal agency may not unilaterally decide to delegate some of its decisionmaking authority to a state government. *See U.S. Telecom. Ass'n v. FCC*, 359 F.3d 554, 565–68 (D.C. Cir. 2004). Why not?

5. *State law*. Questions about delegations to private persons or entities can also arise at the state level. For example, *Texas Boll Weevil Eradication Found. v. Lewellen*, 952 S.W.2d 454 (Tex. 1997), invalidated a legislative scheme whereby a private foundation was empowered to establish boll weevil eradication zones and conduct elections of cotton farmers within each zone. If a majority of cotton farmers in a zone voted favorably, the foundation assessed each farmer a fixed amount (whether or not they agreed and whether or not their crop was infested) and spent the money on projects to eradicate the dreaded weevil. Farmers who failed to pay the assessment were guilty of a misdemeanor, and their crop was destroyed whether or not infested with weevils.

The court noted: "We believe it axiomatic that courts should subject private delegations to a more searching scrutiny than their public counterparts." The court employed a multi-factor test in making its determination. Factors that suggested invalidity of the delegation included: the foundation was subject to only minimal control by a state agency; the foundation not only made rules, it also had power to apply them to particular farmers; the foundation board members (themselves cotton farmers) had a pecuniary interest in the foundation's activity; the foundation's rules were backed up by the criminal law; the delegation of authority was not limited by cost or duration; there was no guarantee that the board members would have any special training or experience; and the legislature provided few statutory standards to guide the Foundation.

Could the Texas legislature redraft the boll weevil eradication program to pass constitutional muster without turning it into just another agency-run regulatory scheme?

§ 7.3   DELEGATION OF ADJUDICATORY POWER TO AGENCIES

This section examines the legitimacy of delegations of adjudicatory power to agencies—the power to determine the rights or duties of particular persons based on their individual circumstances. The materials pertaining to delegations of rulemaking power are equally applicable here. The presence of standards and safeguards seems relevant to the propriety of delegating adjudicatory as well as rulemaking power. Indeed, some of the cases considered in the prior section involved delegations of adjudicatory authority.

The federal judicial power was vested in Article III judges—judges with life tenure and protection against salary reduction—to ensure unbiased consideration of cases and to ensure that the other branches could not deprive the judiciary of its essential functions. A delegation of adjudicatory power to agencies transfers to them authority that appears to belong exclusively to the judicial branch. This section considers whether such delegations run afoul of the requirements of Article III of the United States Constitution or comparable provisions in state constitutions.

The Court spoke to this issue in an important early case, *Crowell v. Benson,* 285 U.S. 22 (1932). *Crowell* concerned a federal workers' compensation statute that provided benefits based on strict liability if an "employee" was injured while working on "navigable waters." The statute empowered an administrative agency to conduct the necessary adjudications. Despite the fact that the statute at issue in *Crowell* displaced a common law cause of action and affected a pre-existing relationship based on a common law employment contract, the Supreme Court upheld the delegation to the agency to try such cases.

The Court distinguished between matters of "public rights" (arising between the government and private persons) and matters of "private rights" (involving the liability of one private person to another). Because Congress could relegate public rights matters entirely to executive authority, it could also take the lesser step of requiring that such rights be adjudicated in administrative rather than judicial tribunals. The Court gave examples of these tribunals: "Familiar illustrations of administrative agencies created for the determination of such matters are found in connection with the exercise of the congressional power as to interstate and foreign commerce, taxation, immigration, the public lands, public health, the facilities of the post office, pensions and payments to veterans." *Id.* at 51.

In *Crowell* itself, however, "private rights" were involved—i.e., the tort liability of an employer to an employee. This fact made the case closer, but the Court upheld the constitutionality of the system anyway. It did so by assuming that Article III courts were assured of a substantial role in the adjudication process. The Court held that Article III judges must have *independent power* to decide all issues of law and "questions of constitutional and jurisdictional fact" on review of the agency's decision. Jurisdictional facts were those on which the agency's jurisdiction depended—in *Crowell,* whether an employment relationship existed and whether the injury occurred on navigable waters. But factual disputes that were neither constitutional nor jurisdictional could be resolved administratively, subject to only deferential judicial review.

In subsequent years, the Court has essentially abandoned the "constitutional and jurisdictional facts" aspect of *Crowell* (*see* § 9.1.2). For decades, however, *Crowell* was taken to have established the more fundamental proposition that administrative adjudication is compatible with Article III of the Constitution.

The picture became more complicated after *Northern Pipeline Constr. Co. v. Marathon Pipe Line Co.,* 458 U.S. 50 (1982). In that case, the Supreme Court invalidated a statute that assigned the trial of all the issues in a bankruptcy case, including breach of contract issues, to bankruptcy judges. Because those judges were not appointed according to the requirements of Article III, they lacked life tenure and salary protection. Writing for a plurality of four, Justice Brennan asserted that, with only a few historically based exceptions, cases that involve "private rights" must be decided by Article III judges. Justices Rehnquist and O'Connor concurred in the result but on a narrower ground that was limited to contract disputes. Although it arose in a bankruptcy setting, *Northern Pipeline* implicitly raised questions as to whether the *Crowell* Court's generally permissive attitude toward administrative adjudication would long survive. The following case shed some light on that issue.

COMMODITY FUTURES TRADING COMMISSION V. SCHOR

478 U.S. 833 (1986)

[The Commodity Exchange Act (CEA) created the Commodity Futures Trading Commission (CFTC) as an independent agency to regulate trading in commodity futures. CEA empowered the CFTC to award reparations (damages) to customers from their brokers for violations of the Act or regulations. CFTC regulations provided that in such cases brokers could submit counterclaims against their customers. The brokers could also choose to assert their counterclaims in court.

Schor incurred heavy commodity trading losses in his account with Conti. His account reflected a large debit balance (*i.e.* an amount owed to Conti). Schor commenced a reparation proceeding against Conti before the CFTC, and Conti counterclaimed for the amount of the debit balance (essentially a claim for contract damages). The CFTC held for Conti on both claim and counterclaim. Schor contends that the delegation to the CFTC to try the counterclaim violates Article III.]

O'CONNOR, J.:

Article III, § 1 directs that the "judicial Power of the United States shall be vested in one supreme Court and in such inferior Courts as the Congress may from time to time ordain and establish," and provides that these federal courts shall be staffed by judges who hold office during good behavior, and whose compensation shall not be diminished during tenure in office. Schor claims that these provisions prohibit Congress from authorizing the initial adjudication of common law counterclaims by the CFTC, an administrative agency whose adjudicatory officers do not enjoy the tenure and salary protections embodied in Article III . . . . .

Although our precedents in this area do not admit of easy synthesis, they do establish that the resolution of claims such as Schor's cannot turn on conclusory reference to the language of Article III. Rather, the constitutionality of a given congressional delegation of adjudicative functions to a non-Article III body must be assessed by reference to the purposes underlying the requirements of Article III. This inquiry, in turn, is guided by the principle that "practical attention to substance rather than doctrinaire reliance on formal categories should inform application of Article III." *Thomas* [*v. Union Carbide Agric. Prods. Co.*, 473 U.S. 568 (1985).]

Article III, § 1 serves both to protect the role of the independent judiciary within the constitutional scheme of tripartite government, and to safeguard litigants' right to have claims decided before judges who are free from potential domination by other branches of government. . . . Article III, § 1 safeguards the role of the Judicial Branch in our tripartite system by barring congressional attempts to transfer jurisdiction [to non-Article III tribunals] for the purpose of emasculating constitutional courts, and thereby preventing the encroachment or aggrandizement of one branch at the expense of the other. . . .

In determining the extent to which a given congressional decision to authorize the adjudication of Article III business in a non-Article III tribunal impermissibly threatens the institutional integrity of the Judicial Branch, the Court has declined to adopt formalistic and unbending rules. *Thomas.* Although such rules might lend a greater degree of coherence to this area of the law, they might also unduly constrict Congress' ability to take needed and innovative action pursuant to its Article I powers. Thus, in reviewing Article III challenges, we have weighed a number of factors, none of which has been deemed determinative, with an eye to the practical effect that the congressional action will have on the constitutionally assigned role of the federal judiciary.

Among the factors upon which we have focused are the extent to which the "essential attributes of judicial power" are reserved to Article III courts, and, conversely, the extent to which the non-Article III forum exercises the range of jurisdiction and powers normally vested only in Article III courts, the origins and importance of the right to be adjudicated, and the concerns that drove Congress to depart from the requirements of Article III.

An examination of the relative allocation of powers between the CFTC and Article III courts in light of the considerations given prominence in our precedents demonstrates that the congressional scheme does not impermissibly intrude on the province of the judiciary. The CFTC's adjudicatory powers depart from the traditional agency model in just one respect: the CFTC's jurisdiction over common law counterclaims. While wholesale importation of concepts of pendent or ancillary jurisdiction into the agency context may create greater constitutional difficulties, we decline to endorse an absolute prohibition on such jurisdiction out of fear of where some hypothetical "slippery slope" may deposit us. . . .

[T]here is little practical reason to find that this single deviation from the agency model is fatal to the congressional scheme. Aside from its authorization of counterclaim jurisdiction, the CEA leaves far more of the "essential attributes of judicial power" to Article III courts than did that portion of the Bankruptcy Act found unconstitutional in *Northern Pipeline*.

The CEA scheme in fact hews closely to the agency model approved by the Court in *Crowell v. Benson*. The CFTC, like the agency in *Crowell*, deals only with a "particularized area of law," whereas the jurisdiction of the bankruptcy courts found unconstitutional in *Northern Pipeline* extended to broadly "all civil proceedings arising under title 11 or arising in or *related to* cases under title 11."

CFTC orders, like those of the agency in *Crowell*, but unlike those of the bankruptcy courts under the 1978 Act, are enforceable only by order of the District Court. CFTC orders are also reviewed under the same "weight of the evidence" standard sustained in *Crowell*, rather than the more deferential standard found lacking in *Northern Pipeline*. The legal rulings of the CFTC, like the legal determinations of the agency in *Crowell*, are subject to *de novo* review. Finally, the CFTC, unlike the bankruptcy courts under the 1978 Act, does not exercise "all ordinary powers of district courts," and thus may not, for instance, preside over jury trials or issue writs of habeas corpus.

Of course, the nature of the claim has significance in our Article III analysis quite apart from the method prescribed for its adjudication. The counterclaim asserted in this case is a "private" right for which state law provides the rule of decision. It is therefore a claim of the kind assumed to be at the "core" of matters normally reserved to Article III courts. Yet this conclusion does not end our inquiry; just as this Court has rejected any attempt to make determinative for Article III purposes the distinction between public rights and private rights, there is no reason inherent in separation of powers principles to accord the state law character of a claim talismanic power in Article III inquiries.

We have explained that "the public rights doctrine reflects simply a pragmatic understanding that when Congress selects a quasi-judicial method of resolving matters that 'could be conclusively determined by the Executive and Legislative Branches,' the danger of encroaching on the judicial powers" is less than when private rights, which are normally within the purview of the judiciary, are relegated as an initial matter to administrative adjudication. . . . Accordingly, where private, common law rights are at stake, our examination of the congressional attempt to control the manner in which those rights are adjudicated has been searching. See, *e.g., Northern Pipeline*. In this litigation, however, "[l]ooking beyond form to the substance of what" Congress has done, we are persuaded that the congressional authorization of limited CFTC jurisdiction over a narrow class of common law claims as an incident to the CFTC's primary, and unchallenged, adjudicative function does not create a substantial threat to the separation of powers. . . .

When Congress authorized the CFTC to adjudicate counterclaims, its primary focus was on making effective a specific and limited federal regulatory scheme, not on allocating jurisdiction among federal tribunals. Congress intended to create an inexpensive and expeditious alternative forum through which customers could enforce the provisions of the CEA against professional brokers. Its decision to endow the CFTC with jurisdiction over such reparations claims is readily understandable given the perception that the CFTC was relatively immune from political pressures, and the obvious expertise that the Commission possesses in applying the CEA and its own regulations. This reparations scheme itself is of unquestioned constitutional validity. *Crowell v. Benson.*

It was only to ensure the effectiveness of this scheme that Congress authorized the CFTC to assert jurisdiction over common law counterclaims. . . . [T]he CFTC's assertion of counterclaim jurisdiction is limited to that which is necessary to make the reparations procedure workable. The CFTC adjudication of common law counterclaims is incidental to, and completely dependent upon, adjudication of reparations claims created by federal law, and in actual fact is limited to claims arising out of the same transaction or occurrence as the reparations claim.

In such circumstances, the magnitude of any intrusion on the Judicial Branch can only be termed *de minimis.* Conversely, were we to hold that the Legislative Branch may not permit such limited cognizance of common law counterclaims at the election of the parties, it is clear that we would "defeat the obvious purpose of the legislation to furnish a prompt, continuous, expert and inexpensive method for dealing with a class of questions of fact which are peculiarly suited to examination and determination by an administrative agency specially assigned to that task." *Crowell v. Benson.*

[BRENNAN and MARSHALL, JJ. dissented, arguing that the delegation to CFTC to adjudicate state-law counterclaims offended both the system of checks and balances and the right of litigants to impartial adjudication by life-tenured judges. They found the case indistinguishable from *Northern Pipeline.*]

NOTES AND QUESTIONS

1. *Public and private rights.* According to the plurality opinion in *Northern Pipeline,* Congress could almost never delegate authority to a non-Article III tribunal to decide questions of private rights. The concurring opinion in that case argued more narrowly that Congress at least could not delegate authority to decide typical state law contract issues. But in *Schor,* as well as the *Thomas* case it cited, the Court deemphasized the distinction between public and private rights. It used a pragmatic, functionalist analysis to decide that some private rights cases may be adjudicated by non-Article III tribunals. Thus the public rights/private rights distinction has become quite muddy.

Notice, however, what was *not* in dispute: The plurality in *Northern Pipeline* did not question the validity of administrative adjudication in the context of disputes between the individual and the government, because these were by definition "public rights." Of course, such disputes constitute the bulk of administrative adjudication.

2. *Further developments in the bankruptcy context.* After *Northern Pipeline,* Congress rewrote the laws governing the bankruptcy courts. Under the revised law, bankruptcy judges (who are not Article III judges) can adjudicate creditors' claims against the bankruptcy estate as well as counterclaims filed by the bankrupt person against such creditors. This did not mean, however, that the system was now safe from constitutional challenge, as the Court demonstrated in *Stern v. Marshall,* 131 S.Ct. 2594 (2011).

Stern arose from the bankruptcy proceeding of Vickie Marshall (also known as Anna Nicole Smith), who was the widow of billionaire J. Howard Marshall. Pierce Marshall, who was J. Howard's son, submitted a creditor's claim for defamation against Vickie. Vickie then filed a counterclaim against Pierce for the tort of interfering with J. Howard's plan to leave money to her. The bankruptcy court found in favor of Vickie on both claims. It rejected Pierce's defamation claim but entered judgment for over $400 million for Vickie on her counterclaim against Pierce.

In a 5–4 decision, the Supreme Court held that a non-Article III judge could not decide Vickie's counterclaim, because it concerned a matter of private rights—a traditional tort action that was not dependent on any statute and bore none of the earmarks of public rights. The Court distinguished *CFTC v. Schor*, noting that the counterclaim in *Schor* was decided by a federal agency that possessed considerable subject-matter expertise and was responsible for administering a regulatory scheme; the agency's ability to decide counterclaims was important to the functioning of that scheme. (The dissent in *Stern* argued that the ability of bankruptcy judges to decide counterclaims was also critical to the efficient functioning of the bankruptcy law.)

Stern acknowledged that the public rights doctrine remains muddy. The public rights category covers not only cases in which the government is a party but also some private v. private disputes that arise out of federal regulatory statutes "or in which resolution of the claim by an expert government agency is deemed essential to a limited regulatory objective within the agency's authority." The Court made clear that it was not addressing cases that involve the government as litigant. For the present, therefore, the capacity of regulatory agencies to administer their programs through adjudication is not in jeopardy; what seems uncertain is the extent to which agencies can also assert pendent or ancillary jurisdiction over claims that are factually related to their substantive responsibilities but arise under some other source of law, such as common-law tort or contract.

3.   *Public and private rights in broader perspective.* The distinction between public and private rights is sometimes criticized as lacking a sound policy foundation. Critics say that the benefit that Article III affords to the public—the protection of a life-tenured judiciary—is just as valuable, if not more valuable, in cases involving public rights, where government is one of the litigants, as opposed to cases involving private rights, where the government is not involved.

Theorists have explored the question of where the line between permissible and impermissible forms of agency adjudication *should* be drawn. Fallon argues that if a statute provides for judicial review of agency determinations of both fact and law by an Article III court, a delegation of adjudicatory power to an agency should be allowable regardless of whether the case involves public rights or private rights (with the exception of the imposition of criminal sanctions, which can be done only by courts). *See*

Richard H. Fallon, Jr., *Of Legislative Courts, Administrative Agencies, and Article III*, 101 HARV. L. REV. 915 (1988). *But see* Caleb Nelson, *Adjudication in the Political Branches*, 107 COLUM. L. REV. 559 (2007). Nelson argues in favor of the traditional public/private right distinction and distinguishes private rights to person or property from private privileges. Non-Article III courts, in Nelson's view, can adjudicate questions of public rights and private privileges but not "core" private rights. *See also* Richard H. Fallon, Jr., *Jurisdiction-Stripping Reconsidered*, 96 VA. L. REV. 1043, 1122–26 & n.377 (2010) (responding to Nelson and refining his own theory).

4. *Incursions on the tort system.* A number of state decisions have insisted that adjudication of private rights of the sort traditionally handled by courts cannot be vested in administrative agencies. In *Wright v. Central Du Page Hosp. Ass'n*, 347 N.E.2d 736 (Ill. 1976), the court invalidated a scheme for adjudication of medical malpractice disputes by a panel of a judge, a doctor, and an attorney. The court stated that the scheme violated the Illinois Constitution because it vested essentially judicial functions in nonjudicial personnel, and because it impaired plaintiff's constitutionally protected interests in trial by jury.

Similarly, *In re Opinion of the Justices*, 179 A. 344 (N.H. 1935), advised that the adjudication of negligence cases arising out of auto accidents could not be transferred to an agency. The court concluded that "the function of trying and deciding litigation is strictly and exclusively for the judiciary when it is between private parties, neither of whom seeks to come under the protection of a public interest and to have it upheld and maintained for his benefit. The function cannot be executive unless executive activity may embrace litigation in general. If the proposed jurisdiction might be bestowed, the limits of executive authority would be almost without bounds and indefinite encroachment on judicial power would be possible."

Transfer of medical malpractice cases to administrative "health courts" has also been proposed at the federal level. For analysis of whether such a scheme could comply with Article III, see E. Donald Elliott et al., *Administrative "Health Courts" for Medical Injury Claims: The Federal Constitutional Issues*, 33 J. HEALTH POL., POL'Y & L. 761, 777–87 (2008); Amy Widman & Francine A. Hochberg, *Federal Administrative Health Courts are Unconstitutional: A Reply to Elliott, Narayan, and Nasmith*, 33 J. HEALTH POL., POL'Y & L. 799, 820–24 (2008).

5. *Jury trials.* The Seventh Amendment to the U.S. Constitution provides: "In Suits at common law, where the value in controversy shall exceed twenty dollars, the right of trial by jury shall be preserved. . . ."

Congress can avoid jury trials by removing certain types of civil disputes from courts to agencies. In *Atlas Roofing Co. v. Occupational Safety and Health Rev. Comm'n*, 430 U.S. 442 (1977), an employer challenged the validity of a statute authorizing OSHRC (an adjudicating agency separate from OSHA) to impose civil money penalties ranging up to $10,000 per violation of rules requiring employers to maintain safe workplaces. The

Supreme Court held that the employer had no right to a jury under the Seventh Amendment because the civil penalties were a means of enforcing a "public right" rather than a "private right." "Congress is not required by the Seventh Amendment to choke the already crowded federal courts with new types of litigation or prevented from committing some new types of litigation to administrative agencies with special competence in the relevant field. This is the case even if the Seventh Amendment would have required a jury where the adjudication of those rights is assigned to a federal court of law instead of an administrative agency."

The Court observed that OSHRC decisions were judicially reviewable both as to law and fact. "Thus these cases do not present the question whether Congress may commit the adjudication of fines for [the] violation [of these public rights] to an administrative agency without any sort of intervention by a court at any stage of the proceedings." *Atlas* was followed under a state constitution in *National Velour Corp. v. Durfee*, 637 A.2d 375 (R.I. 1994) (no right to jury trial when environmental agency imposes $205,000 civil penalty). In *Tull v. United States,* 481 U.S. 412 (1987), a *court* imposed a civil penalty under the Clean Water Act. The Supreme Court held that the defendant had a right to a jury trial on the question of whether civil penalties should be imposed (but not on the issue of the amount of the penalties). Thus the right to a jury trial turned on whether a court (*Tull*) or an agency (*Atlas Roofing*) imposes a civil penalty. The Seventh Amendment can also trigger a right to jury trial in bankruptcy court; the Court applies the same type of distinctions between public and private rights that underlay *Northern Pipeline* and *Stern. Granfinanciera, S.A. v. Nordberg*, 492 U.S. 33 (1989).

6.   *Remedies and penalties.* Only the judiciary may impose a sentence of imprisonment. *Wong Wing v. United States,* 163 U.S. 228 (1896), indicated that a person may be temporarily detained by an agency pending proceedings to decide whether exclusion or expulsion as an illegal alien is appropriate, and that an alien may be administratively excluded or expelled from the country. However, an illegal alien may not be sentenced to prison without the protection of a judicial trial. Similarly, an agency cannot impose a criminal fine, because of constitutional restrictions applicable to the criminal process.

Nevertheless, a legislature can delegate to an agency the power to adopt rules, the violation of which will be crimes to be punished by a court. In these situations, the legislature has decided that violations of the rules will be criminal offenses. *See, e.g., United States v. Grimaud,* 220 U.S. 506 (1911) (criminal conviction for violation of agency's grazing rules). And, as *Atlas Roofing* makes clear, agencies can impose civil penalties.

Courts may be reluctant, however, to permit agencies to award the same types of remedies that courts traditionally have imposed. In *McHugh v. Santa Monica Rent Control Bd.*, 777 P.2d 91 (Cal. 1989), the California Supreme Court upheld the power of a local rent control board to award restitution to tenants of excess rentals. This holding depended on two determinations: i) the decision to empower the agency to dispense this remedy was reasonably necessary to effectuate the agency's legitimate regulatory purpose of making a scheme of rent control work (as opposed to an attempt to transfer traditional common law claims from the courts to an agency); and ii) the courts retained their essential checking power through adequate judicial review.

In *McHugh*, the Court invalidated several additional remedies. First, the statute authorized tenants to collect the amount of excess rents by withholding them from future rent payments. This violated the principle of check because it was a self-executing remedy that enabled the tenant to collect their restitution before the courts would have an opportunity to judicially review the Board's award of restitution. Second, the Board was authorized to assess punitive damages (a multiple of the excess rents). The Court found that the award of punitive damages was not reasonably necessary to effectuate rent control and presented a risk of arbitrary administrative action. Do you agree that the remedies of rent withholding and punitive damages are not reasonably necessary to effectuate a scheme of rent control?

    7.   *Problem.* A recent state statute transferred adjudication of all moving traffic violations and parking tickets to a newly formed Traffic Agency. The purpose of the statute was to lessen congestion in the criminal courts and to assure expedited treatment of such offenses. If the Traffic Agency finds that a violation has been proved by a preponderance of the evidence, it may impose penalties of up to $1,000 per violation. Your client Ralph is charged with speeding. Can he object to trial of his case before the Traffic Agency? *See Van Harken v. City of Chicago*, 103 F.3d 1346 (7th Cir. 1997); *Rosenthal v. Hartnett*, 326 N.E.2d 811 (N.Y. 1975). What if the Traffic Agency were a federal agency created to adjudicate cases involving alleged moving traffic violations and parking tickets on federal lands?

§ 7.4   LEGISLATIVE CONTROLS

    The legislature can control agency action by inserting specific language in the agency's enabling act. However, for reasons explored in § 7.2, legislatures have frequently been unable or unwilling to be very specific in enabling legislation. Instead, they have typically vested agencies with broad discretion under open-ended statutory delegations of authority. When a legislature finds an exercise of that authority unacceptable, it can respond by narrowing the agency's enabling act or by overturning the specific agency action deemed objectionable.

    However, enactment of a statute to overcome agency action is difficult, in part because it requires the concurrence of both houses of the legislature and the chief executive (or, if the latter vetoes the legislature's action, an override of that veto by a supermajority of both houses). That is why many legislatures have turned to the "legislative veto." This section examines the rise and decline of that device, as well as other methods by which legislatures exercise continuing influence over agency actions.

§ 7.4.1 THE LEGISLATIVE VETO AND CONTROL OF FEDERAL AGENCIES

The term "legislative veto" describes a mechanism that allows legislators to invalidate or suspend agency action by less cumbersome means than the enactment of a statute. For example, it might provide for disapproval of an agency rule solely by a resolution passed by one or two houses of the legislature, or by a legislative committee, without any participation by the chief executive.

The legislative veto device made its first appearance in a smattering of laws passed at both the federal and state levels in the 1930's. It became particularly popular in the 1970's, as legislatures stepped up their search for responses to the burgeoning administrative state and what they regarded as "overregulation." More recently, however, the use of the legislative veto has withered in the face of constitutional challenges, exemplified most notably by the decision that follows.

IMMIGRATION AND NATURALIZATION SERVICE V. CHADHA
462 U.S. 919 (1983)

[Section 244(a)(1) of the Immigration and Nationality Act provides that the Attorney General shall have discretion to "suspend" the deportation of an otherwise deportable alien who meets certain statutory standards, one of which is that deportation would cause "extreme hardship." The Attorney General delegated this power to the INS.

Chadha was an East Indian who had been born in Kenya and held a British passport; he had been admitted on a student visa but had overstayed the expiration date. Following an on-the-record hearing, an immigration judge held that Chadha was deportable but ordered that deportation be suspended because Chadha met the "extreme hardship" requirements of the statute.

Section 244(c)(1) provides that the Attorney General must report all suspensions of deportation to Congress; and § 244(c)(2) provides that if, during the legislative session in which the suspension is reported or the next session, either the House or the Senate passes a resolution "stating in substance that it does not favor the suspension of such deportation," the effect will be to "veto" the suspension.

Chadha's suspension was reported to Congress and remained outstanding for a year and a half. At almost the last possible moment, a resolution was introduced in the House to veto deportation suspensions of six aliens, including that of Chadha. The sponsor of the resolution stated that, in the Judiciary Committee's view, those aliens had not met the statutory requirement of undue hardship, but he did not elaborate. There was no debate and no recorded vote. Because the resolution passed, Chadha was ordered to be deported. He questions the constitutionality of the legislative veto provision in § 244(c)(2).

The Court first held that the provision for legislative veto was "severable" from the provision for suspension of deportation. Consequently, if the veto were invalidated, the INS decision suspending Chadha's deportation would remain in effect.]

BURGER, C.J.: . . .

We turn now to the question whether action of one House of Congress under § 244(c)(2) violates strictures of the Constitution. We begin, of course, with the presumption that the challenged statute is valid. . . .

By the same token, the fact that a given law or procedure is efficient, convenient, and useful in facilitating functions of government, standing alone, will not save it if it is contrary to the Constitution. Convenience and efficiency are not the primary objectives—or the hallmarks—of democratic government and our inquiry is sharpened rather than blunted by the fact that Congressional veto provisions are appearing with increasing frequency in statutes which delegate authority to executive and independent agencies. . . .

JUSTICE WHITE undertakes [in his dissent] to make a case for the proposition that the one-House veto is a useful "political invention," and we need not challenge that assertion. We can even concede this utilitarian argument although the long range political wisdom of this "invention" is arguable. . . . But policy arguments supporting even useful "political inventions" are subject to the demands of the Constitution which defines powers and, with respect to this subject, sets out just how those powers are to be exercised.

Explicit and unambiguous provisions of the Constitution prescribe and define the respective functions of the Congress and of the Executive in the legislative process. Since the precise terms of those familiar provisions are critical to the resolution of this case, we set them out verbatim. Art. I provides:

"All legislative Powers herein granted shall be vested in a Congress of the United States, which shall consist of a Senate *and* a House of Representatives." Art. I, § 1.

"Every Bill which shall have passed the House of Representatives and the Senate, *shall,* before it becomes a Law, be presented to the President of the United States; . . ." Art. I, § 7, cl. 2.

"Every Order, Resolution, or Vote to which the Concurrence of the Senate and House of Representatives may be necessary (except on a question of Adjournment) *shall be* presented to the President of the United States; and before the Same shall take Effect, *shall be* approved by him, or being disapproved by him, shall be repassed by two thirds of the Senate and House of Representatives, according to the Rules and Limitations prescribed in the Case of a Bill." Art. I, § 7, cl. 3.

These provisions of Art. I are integral parts of the constitutional design for the separation of powers. . . . [T]he purposes underlying the Presentment Clauses, Art. I, § 7, cls. 2, 3, and the bicameral requirement of Art. I, § 1 and § 7, cl. 2, guide our resolution of the important question presented in this case. . . .

The records of the Constitutional Convention reveal that the requirement that all legislation be presented to the President before becoming law was uniformly accepted by the Framers. Presentment to the President and the Presidential veto were considered so imperative that the draftsmen took special pains to assure that these requirements could not be circumvented. During the final debate on Art. I, § 7, cl. 2, James Madison expressed concern that it might easily be evaded by the simple expedient of calling a proposed law a "resolution" or "vote" rather than a "bill." As a consequence, Art. I, § 7, cl. 3, was added.

The decision to provide the President with a limited and qualified power to nullify proposed legislation by veto was based on the profound conviction of the Framers that the powers conferred on Congress were the powers to be most carefully circumscribed. It is beyond doubt that lawmaking was a power to be shared by both Houses and the President. . . . The President's role in the lawmaking process also reflects the Framers' careful efforts to check whatever propensity a particular Congress might have to enact oppressive, improvident, or ill-considered measures. . . .

The bicameral requirement of Art. I, §§ 1, 7 was of scarcely less concern to the Framers than was the Presidential veto and indeed the two concepts are interdependent. By providing that no law could take effect without the concurrence of the prescribed majority of the Members of both Houses, the Framers reemphasized their belief, already remarked upon in connection with the Presentment Clauses, that legislation should not be enacted unless it has been carefully and fully considered by the Nation's elected officials. . . .

We see therefore that the Framers were acutely conscious that the bicameral requirement and the Presentment Clauses would serve essential constitutional functions. The President's participation in the legislative process was to protect the Executive Branch from Congress and to protect the whole people from improvident laws. The division of the Congress into two distinctive bodies assures that the legislative power would be exercised only after opportunity for full study and debate in separate settings. The President's unilateral veto power, in turn, was limited by the power of two thirds of both Houses of Congress to overrule a veto thereby precluding final arbitrary action of one person. It emerges clearly that the prescription for legislative action in Art. I, §§ 1, 7 represents the Framers' decision that the legislative power of the Federal government be exercised in accord with a single, finely wrought and exhaustively considered, procedure. . . .

When any Branch acts, it is presumptively exercising the power the Constitution has delegated to it. When the Executive acts, it presumptively acts in an executive or administrative capacity as defined in Art. II. And when, as here, one House of Congress purports to act, it is presumptively acting within its assigned sphere.

Beginning with this presumption, we must nevertheless establish that the challenged action under § 244(c)(2) is of the kind to which the procedural requirements of Art. I, § 7 apply. Not every action taken by either House is subject to the bicameralism and presentment requirements of Art. I. Whether actions taken by either House are, in law and fact, an exercise of legislative power depends not on their form but upon "whether they contain matter which is properly to be regarded as legislative in its character and effect."

Examination of the action taken here by one House pursuant to § 244(c)(2) reveals that it was essentially legislative in purpose and effect. In purporting to exercise power defined in Art. I, § 8, cl. 4 to "establish an uniform Rule of Naturalization," the House took action that had the purpose and effect of altering the legal rights, duties and relations of persons, including the Attorney General, Executive Branch officials and Chadha, all outside the legislative branch. . . .

The legislative character of the one-House veto in this case is confirmed by the character of the Congressional action it supplants. Neither the House of Representatives nor the Senate contends that, absent the veto provision in § 244(c)(2), either of them, or both of them acting together, could effectively require the Attorney General to deport an alien once the Attorney General, in the exercise of legislatively delegated authority,[16] had determined the alien should remain in the

---

[16] Congress protests that affirming the Court of Appeals in these cases will sanction "lawmaking by the Attorney General. . . . Why is the Attorney General exempt from submitting his proposed changes in the law to the full bicameral process?" To be sure, some administrative agency action—rulemaking, for example—may resemble "lawmaking." See 5 U.S.C. § 551(4), which defines an agency's "rule" as "the whole or part of an agency statement of general or particular applicability and future effect designed to implement, interpret, or prescribe *law* or policy. . . ." This Court has referred to agency activity as being "quasi-legislative" in character.

United States. Without the challenged provision in § 244(c)(2), this could have been achieved, if at all, only by legislation requiring deportation. . . .

The nature of the decision implemented by the one-House veto in this case further manifests its legislative character. After long experience with the clumsy, time consuming private bill procedure, Congress made a deliberate choice to delegate to the Executive Branch, and specifically to the Attorney General, the authority to allow deportable aliens to remain in this country in certain specified circumstances. It is not disputed that this choice to delegate authority is precisely the kind of decision that can be implemented only in accordance with the procedures set out in Art. I. Disagreement with the Attorney General's decision on Chadha's deportation—that is, Congress' decision to deport Chadha—no less than Congress' original choice to delegate to the Attorney General the authority to make that decision, involves determinations of policy that Congress can implement in only one way; bicameral passage followed by presentment to the President. Congress must abide by its delegation of authority until that delegation is legislatively altered or revoked. . . .

. . . There are but four provisions in the Constitution, explicit and unambiguous, by which one House may act alone with the unreviewable force of law, not subject to the President's veto: [initiation of impeachments by the House; and impeachment trials, approval of presidential appointments, and ratification of treaties by the Senate]. . . . Since it is clear that the action by the House under § 244(c)(2) was not within any of the express constitutional exceptions authorizing one House to act alone, and equally clear that it was an exercise of legislative power, that action was subject to the standards prescribed in Article I. . . .

Clearly, however, "[i]n the framework of our Constitution, the President's power to see that the laws are faithfully executed refutes the idea that he is to be a lawmaker."

When the Attorney General performs his duties pursuant to § 244, he does not exercise "legislative" power. The bicameral process is not necessary as a check on the Executive's administration of the laws because his administrative activity cannot reach beyond the limits of the statute that created it—a statute duly enacted pursuant to Art. I, §§ 1, 7. The constitutionality of the Attorney General's execution of the authority delegated to him by § 244 involves only a question of delegation doctrine. The courts, when a case or controversy arises, can always "ascertain whether the will of Congress has been obeyed," and can enforce adherence to statutory standards.

It is clear, therefore, that the Attorney General acts in his presumptively Art. II capacity when he administers the Immigration and Nationality Act. Executive action under legislatively delegated authority that might resemble "legislative" action in some respects is not subject to the approval of both Houses of Congress and the President for the reason that the Constitution does not so require. That kind of Executive action is always subject to check by the terms of the legislation that authorized it; and if that authority is exceeded it is open to judicial review as well as the power of Congress to modify or revoke the authority entirely. A one-House veto is clearly legislative in both character and effect and is not so checked; the need for the check provided by Art. I, §§ 1, 7, is therefore clear. Congress' authority to delegate portions of its power to administrative agencies provides no support for the argument that Congress can constitutionally control administration of the laws by way of a congressional veto.

The veto authorized by § 244(c)(2) doubtless has been in many respects a convenient shortcut; the "sharing" with the Executive by Congress of its authority over aliens in this manner is, on its face, an appealing compromise. In purely practical terms, it is obviously easier for action to be taken by one House without submission to the President; but it is crystal clear from the records of the Convention, contemporaneous writings and debates, that the Framers ranked other values higher than efficiency. . . . There is no support in the Constitution or decisions of this Court for the proposition that the cumbersomeness and delays often encountered in complying with explicit Constitutional standards may be avoided, either by the Congress or by the President. . . .

We hold that the Congressional veto provision in § 244(c)(2) is severable from the Act and that it is unconstitutional.

POWELL, J., concurring in the judgment.

The Court's decision, based on the Presentment Clauses, Art. I, § 7, cls. 2 and 3, apparently will invalidate every use of the legislative veto. The breadth of this holding gives one pause. Congress has included the veto in literally hundreds of statutes, dating back to the 1930s. Congress clearly views this procedure as essential to controlling the delegation of power to administrative agencies. One reasonably may disagree with Congress' assessment of the veto's utility, but the respect due its judgment as a coordinate branch of Government cautions that our holding should be no more extensive than necessary to decide this case. In my view, the case may be decided on a narrower ground. When Congress finds that a particular person does not satisfy the statutory criteria for permanent residence in this country it has assumed a judicial function in violation of the principle of separation of powers. Accordingly, I concur only in the judgment. . . .

Functionally, the [separation of powers] doctrine may be violated in two ways. One branch may interfere impermissibly with the other's performance of its constitutionally assigned function. Alternatively, the doctrine may be violated when one branch assumes a function that more properly is entrusted to another. This case presents the latter situation. . . .

On its face, the House's action appears clearly adjudicatory. The House did not enact a general rule; rather it made its own determination that six specific persons did not comply with certain statutory criteria. It thus undertook the type of decision that traditionally has been left to other branches. Even if the House did not make a *de novo* determination, but simply reviewed the Immigration and Naturalization Service's findings, it still assumed a function ordinarily entrusted to the federal courts. Where, as here, Congress has exercised a power "that cannot possibly be regarded as merely in aid of the legislative function of

Congress," the decisions of this Court have held that Congress impermissibly assumed a function that the Constitution entrusted to another branch.

The impropriety of the House's assumption of this function is confirmed by the fact that its action raises the very danger the Framers sought to avoid—the exercise of unchecked power. In deciding whether Chadha deserves to be deported, Congress is not subject to any internal constraints that prevent it from arbitrarily depriving him of the right to remain in this country. Unlike the judiciary or an administrative agency, Congress is not bound by established substantive rules. Nor is it subject to the procedural safeguards, such as the right to counsel and a hearing before an impartial tribunal, that are present when a court or an agency adjudicates individual rights. The only effective constraint on Congress' power is political, but Congress is most accountable politically when it prescribes rules of general applicability. When it decides rights of specific persons, those rights are subject to "the tyranny of a shifting majority."

WHITE, J., dissenting.

Today the Court not only invalidates § 244(c)(2) of the Immigration and Nationality Act, but also sounds the death knell for nearly 200 other statutory provisions in which Congress has reserved a "legislative veto." For this reason, the Court's decision is of surpassing importance. And it is for this reason that the Court would have been well-advised to decide the case, if possible, on the narrower grounds of separation of powers, leaving for full consideration the constitutionality of other congressional review statutes operating on such varied matters as war powers and agency rulemaking, some of which concern the independent regulatory agencies.

The prominence of the legislative veto mechanism in our contemporary political system and its importance to Congress can hardly be overstated. It has become a central means by which Congress secures the accountability of executive and independent agencies. Without the legislative veto, Congress is faced with a Hobson's choice: either to refrain from delegating the necessary authority, leaving itself with a hopeless task of writing laws with the requisite specificity to cover endless special circumstances across the entire policy landscape, or in the alternative, to abdicate its lawmaking function to the executive branch and independent agencies. To choose the former leaves major national problems unresolved; to opt for the latter risks unaccountable policymaking by those not elected to fill that role. Accordingly, over the past five decades, the legislative veto has been placed in nearly 200 statutes. The device is known in every field of governmental concern: reorganization, budgets, foreign affairs, war powers, and regulation of trade, safety, energy, the environment and the economy. . . .

Even this brief review suffices to demonstrate that the legislative veto is more than "efficient, convenient, and useful." It is an important if not indispensable political invention that allows the President and Congress to resolve major constitutional and policy differences, assures the accountability of independent regulatory agencies, and preserves Congress' control over lawmaking. Perhaps there are other means of accommodation and accountability, but the increasing reliance of Congress upon the legislative veto suggests that the alternatives to which Congress must now turn are not entirely satisfactory.

The history of the legislative veto also makes clear that it has not been a sword with which Congress has struck out to aggrandize itself at the expense of the other branches—the concerns of Madison and Hamilton. Rather, the veto has been a means of defense, a reservation of ultimate authority necessary if Congress is to fulfill its designated role under Article I as the nation's lawmaker. While the President has often objected to particular legislative vetoes, generally those left in the hands of congressional committees, the Executive has more often agreed to legislative review as the price for a broad delegation of authority. To be sure, the President may have preferred unrestricted power, but that could be precisely why Congress thought it essential to retain a check on the exercise of delegated authority. . . .

. . . There is no question that a bill does not become a law until it is approved by both the House and the Senate, and presented to the President. Similarly, I would not hesitate to strike an action of Congress in the form of a concurrent resolution which constituted an exercise of original lawmaking authority. I agree with the Court that the President's qualified veto power is a critical element in the distribution of powers under the Constitution, widely endorsed among the Framers, and intended to serve the President as a defense against legislative encroachment and to check the "passing of bad laws through haste, inadvertence, or design." The Federalist No. 73, at 458 (A. Hamilton). The records of the Convention reveal that it is the first purpose which figured most prominently but I acknowledge the vitality of the second. *Id.,* at 443. I also agree that the bicameral approval required by Art. I, §§ 1, 7 "was of scarcely less concern to the Framers than was the Presidential veto," and that the need to divide and disperse legislative power figures significantly in our scheme of Government. All of this . . . is entirely unexceptionable.

It does not, however, answer the constitutional question before us. The . . . Court properly recognizes that it "must establish that the challenged action under § 244(c)(2) is of the kind to which the procedural requirements of Art. I, § 7 apply" and admits that "not every action taken by either House is subject to the bicameralism and presentation requirements of Art. I." . . .

. . . The Court's holding today that all legislative-type action must be enacted through the lawmaking process ignores that legislative authority is routinely delegated to the Executive branch, to the independent regulatory agencies, and to private individuals and groups. . . . If Congress may delegate lawmaking power to independent and executive agencies, it is most difficult to understand Article I as forbidding Congress from also reserving a check on legislative power for itself. Absent the veto, the agencies receiving delegations of legislative or quasi-legislative power may issue regulations having the force of law without bicameral approval and without the President's signature. It is thus not apparent why the reservation of a veto over the exercise of that legislative power must be subject to a more exacting test. In both cases, it is enough that the initial statutory authorizations comply with the Article I requirements. . . .

The central concern of the presentation and bicameralism requirements of Article I is that when a departure from the legal status quo is undertaken, it is done with the approval of the President and both Houses of Congress—or, in the event of a presidential veto, a two-thirds majority in both Houses. This interest is fully satisfied by the operation of § 244(c)(2). The President's approval is found in the Attorney General's action in recommending to Congress that the deportation order for a given alien be suspended. The House and the Senate indicate their approval of the Executive's action by not passing a resolution of disapproval within the statutory period. Thus, a change in the legal status quo—the deportability of the alien—is consummated only with the approval of each of the three relevant actors. The disagreement of any one of the three maintains the alien's pre-existing status. . . .

It is true that the purpose of separating the authority of government is to prevent unnecessary and dangerous concentration of power in one branch. For that reason, the Framers saw fit to divide and balance the powers of government so that each branch would be checked by the others. Virtually every part of our constitutional system bears the mark of this judgment.

But the history of the separation of powers doctrine is also a history of accommodation and practicality. . . . This is the teaching of *Nixon v. Administrator of General Services,* 433 U.S. 425 (1977), which, in rejecting a separation of powers objection to a law requiring that the Administrator take custody of certain presidential papers, set forth a framework for evaluating such claims:

> [I]n determining whether the Act disrupts the proper balance between the coordinate branches, the proper inquiry focuses on the extent to which it prevents the Executive Branch from accomplishing its constitutionally assigned functions. Only

where the potential for disruption is present must we then determine whether that impact is justified by an overriding need to promote objectives within the constitutional authority of Congress.

Section 244(c)(2) survives this test. The legislative veto provision does not "prevent the Executive Branch from accomplishing its constitutionally assigned functions." . . .

A legislative check on an inherently executive function, for example that of initiating prosecutions, poses an entirely different question. But the legislative veto device here—and in many other settings—is far from an instance of legislative tyranny over the Executive. It is a necessary check on the unavoidably expanding power of the agencies, both executive and independent, as they engage in exercising authority delegated by Congress.

I regret that I am in disagreement with my colleagues on the fundamental questions that this case presents. But even more I regret the destructive scope of the Court's holding. It reflects a profoundly different conception of the Constitution than that held by the Courts which sanctioned the modern administrative state. Today's decision strikes down in one fell swoop provisions in more laws enacted by Congress than the Court has cumulatively invalidated in its history. I fear it will now be more difficult "to insure that the fundamental policy decisions in our society will be made not by an appointed official but by the body immediately responsible to the people."

[JUSTICE REHNQUIST dissented, arguing that the suspension and veto provisions were not severable. JUSTICE WHITE agreed.]

NOTES AND QUESTIONS

1. *"Legislative" acts.* The majority holds that the House's veto of the Attorney General's decision to suspend deportation was "legislative"—and invalid because of a failure to satisfy the bicameralism and presentment provisions of the United States Constitution. Do you agree that the House's action was "legislative"? Why is a decision as to whether Chadha may stay in the United States "legislative" if a House of Congress makes it, but not if the Attorney General does?

2. *Legislative veto versus delegation.* Assuming the House's action in Chadha's case was "legislative," should the House's failure to comply with the bicameralism and presentment safeguards have been fatal to the constitutionality of that action? Notice the dissent's argument that, if Congress may delegate the decision on Chadha's fate to an administrative agency, it should also be able to delegate that decision to a subunit of itself. Does the majority have a persuasive reply? Why isn't the fact that the

Immigration and Nationality Act was enacted through the Article I, § 7 process a sufficient answer to the constitutional challenge in this case?

3. *Legislative vetoes of agency adjudications.* The statute at issue in *Chadha* was somewhat exceptional. At the time of the Supreme Court's decision, legislative veto schemes were usually regarded as a tool by which legislatures could supervise administrative *rulemaking,* as opposed to agency decisions about individuals such as Mr. Chadha. Indeed, Justice Powell's concurrence focuses on the adjudicative nature of the matter at hand, arguing that the House had no business overturning an agency order of that kind. Was he right? If the procedure was, indeed, unconstitutional for the reasons Powell identifies, would the addition of bicameralism and presentment guarantees have cured the problem?

4. *Extension of Chadha to rulemaking.* The Court evidently intended its *Chadha* opinion to apply to both adjudication and rulemaking situations. Only a few weeks after *Chadha,* without even pausing to write an opinion, the Court affirmed two lower court decisions that had struck down legislative veto provisions in a rulemaking context. In one of these cases, Congress had empowered the Federal Trade Commission to adopt consumer protection rules, subject to a two-house veto provision. In other words, any such rule was to be ineffective if both houses of Congress disapproved it through a concurrent resolution (a resolution that is not submitted to the President for his approval or veto). In 1981 the FTC adopted a rule covering used car warranties, but Congress vetoed it. The court of appeals held that the legislative veto provision was invalid and, as noted, the Supreme Court summarily affirmed. *Consumers Union v. FTC,* 691 F.2d 575 (D.C. Cir. 1982), *aff'd sub nom. United States Senate v. FTC,* 463 U.S. 1216 (1983). In a companion case, the Court struck down a one-house legislative veto provision pertaining to FERC gas pricing rules. *Process Gas Consumers Group v. Consumer Energy Council,* 463 U.S. 1216 (1983).

5. *Policy issues.* Justice White's dissent argues that the legislative veto is a desirable political invention that "allows the President and Congress to resolve major constitutional and policy differences, assures accountability of independent regulatory agencies, and preserves Congress' control over lawmaking." Others have portrayed the practical consequences of this "invention" in much less flattering terms. A prominent study of several federal regulatory programs in which agency rules were subject to legislative veto found that the device led to a number of problems:

> [T]he practices observed here violate the ideal of equal access to the rulemaking process. . . . Those groups having greater resources or prior influence with congressional committees have an additional chance to affect agency action not available to those without such resources or influence. . . .

> [T]he review process was necessarily an attempt by Congress to second-guess the agency without the benefit of all the facts the agency had developed. . . . As a result of Congress' heavy workload,

even the committee members were not normally as familiar with a rule under review as agency personnel, or as a reviewing court would be. . . .

. . . Most of the effective review occurred at the committee or subcommittee level, often focusing on the concerns of a single chairman or member. . . . [T]he power of review was really exercised by congressional committees and their staffs, [which] inevitably are bodies of relatively narrow composition compared to Congress as a whole.

. . . Since the veto provides an easier method for altering agency policy, it reduces the incentive of the oversight committees to sponsor legislation. Because the veto is negative, and because it reduces pressure on committees to report legislation affirmatively resolving policy disputes with agencies, it increases substantially the chance that no policy will be formed by Congress or by the agency.

Harold H. Bruff & Ernest Gellhorn, *Congressional Control of Administrative Regulation: A Study of Legislative Vetoes*, 90 HARV. L. REV. 1369, 1414–18, 1423 (1977). How many of these difficulties were attributable to the veto device itself, and how many would be inherent in any vigorous legislative oversight scheme?

6. *Reality check.* The *Chadha* decision has essentially eliminated the legislative veto as a tool for disapproving administrative rules, but the device has not disappeared entirely. Most notably, Congress has continued to enact provisions requiring agencies to obtain the approval of appropriations committees for various expenditures. Because these measures have made Congress more willing to grant particular kinds of authority, Presidents have sometimes acquiesced in them, despite their seeming unconstitutionality. LOUIS FISHER, CONSTITUTIONAL CONFLICTS BETWEEN CONGRESS AND THE PRESIDENT 151–54 (5th ed. 2007) (noting that more than 500 post-*Chadha* legislative vetoes have been enacted). Even where it does not use the legislative veto itself, Congress has found other means of challenging agency actions that it finds undesirable and has remained a vigilant counterforce to the executive. *See id.*; JESSICA KORN, THE POWER OF SEPARATION: AMERICAN CONSTITUTIONALISM AND THE MYTH OF THE LEGISLATIVE VETO 116–21 (1996).

7. *Congressional Review Act.* A variation on the legislative veto was enacted as part of the Contract with America Advancement Act of 1996, P.L. 104–121, codified at 5 U.S.C. §§ 801–08. Familiarly known as the Congressional Review Act (CRA), this statute applies throughout the federal government. It requires that virtually all rules of general applicability, adopted by virtually all agencies (including independent agencies), be submitted to Congress and to the Government Accountability Office (GAO) before they take effect. The rule must be accompanied by a report containing various items of information about the rule.

The CRA distinguishes between major and non-major rules. A major rule is one determined to be economically significant by OIRA under Executive Order 12,866. *See* § 7.6 N.2. There are about 50–100 major rules each year. A non-major rule may take effect whenever the agency determines, but a major rule cannot take effect for at least 60 calendar days after it is submitted to Congress (or, in some situations, a longer period).

In case of either major or non-major rules, Congress can nullify the rule by enacting a joint resolution of disapproval. A joint resolution is like a statute; it must be approved by both houses and signed by the President (or repassed by two-thirds of each house if the President vetoes it). The statute provides for a fast-track system of congressional consideration of disapproval resolutions, although Congress is not bound by the fast tracking system and can proceed more slowly if it wishes. On the other hand, where Congress does not enact a disapproval resolution, courts are instructed not to draw any inferences about Congress' attitude toward the rule.

Does the CRA procedure meet the constitutional requirements set forth in *Chadha*? More generally, is the CRA a wise enhancement of legislative oversight of the agencies? Or is it just another costly hurdle that agencies must jump over to adopt rules, and a tempting backdoor route by which special interests may thwart unwelcome rules? *See generally* Morton Rosenberg, *The Critical Need for Effective Congressional Review of Agency Rules: Background and Considerations for Incremental Reform* (ACUS, July 18, 2012), available at *www.acus.gov/report/congressional-review-act-report*; Daniel Cohen & Peter L. Strauss, *Congressional Review of Agency Regulations*, 49 ADMIN. L. REV. 95 (1997).

In 2001, a broad regulation issued by the Occupational Safety and Health Administration to prevent ergonomic injuries in the workplace became the first (and, to date, the only) rule to be disapproved by Congress under the CRA. Pub. L. 107–5 (2001). The override was very popular with business interests, which had argued that the rule was unworkable and could cost up to $100 billion to implement. Supporters of the OSHA regulation, however, expressed dismay that Congress spent less than a week considering disapproval of a rule on which OSHA had worked for ten years. An exceptional historical circumstance made the CRA an attractive weapon for opponents of the ergonomics rule. The rule had been issued in November 2000, in the waning weeks of the Clinton Administration. By the time the CRA resolution came before Congress the following March, a newly installed President George W. Bush was available, and more than willing, to sign it. *See* Rosenberg, *supra*, at 12–14.

8.   *Scope of the CRA.* The statute's definition of rule is not limited to those rules that can be adopted only after notice and comment rulemaking. The definition includes interpretive rules, policy statements, and a vast array of other documents issued by an agency. As a result of this broad coverage, the GAO received more than 42,000 CRA-eligible rules during the first decade of the CRA's existence, although only twenty-eight resolutions to

disapprove rules were actually introduced in Congress. GAO, *Federal Rulemaking: Perspectives on 10 Years of Congressional Review Act Implementation*, GAO–06–601T, at 3–4 (2006). Supporters of the law have argued that its wide scope is necessary, because many non-major rules embody questionable decisions; moreover, agencies must not be allowed to shield new policies from congressional scrutiny by burying them in supposedly nonbinding documents such as policy statements. However, a resolution of the American Bar Association has recommended that the process should apply only to major rules and other limited classes of high-impact rules (although other rules could be included on an individual basis at the request of a congressional committee). 122–2 ABA REP. 465 (August 1997). Should Congress follow this recommendation?

9. *Effect of CRA disapproval.* The CRA provides that, if a rule is disapproved, the agency may not re-issue the rule in substantially the same form unless Congress enacts legislation allowing it to do so. 5 U.S.C. § 801(b)(2). This provision could create significant difficulties, because it could place an entire rule off limits, even though Congress might object to only a small part of it. Moreover, a resolution of disapproval is a simple "no"; it does not explain to the agency how the rule might be successfully redrafted. Courts would have to decide whether a later rule is sufficiently different from the disapproved earlier rule to pass muster. The ABA resolution mentioned in N.8 proposes that § 801(b)(2) be replaced by a requirement that, when an agency proposes a substitute rule, it must explain how the new rule meets the objections raised against the old rule. Does this alternative go to the opposite extreme, by giving agencies too much latitude to readopt a similar (or even identical) rule to the one that Congress has already repudiated?

10. *REINS Act.* The House of Representatives has twice voted to enact a bill known as the Regulations From the Executive in Need of Scrutiny Act, or REINS Act. H.R. 367, 113th Cong. (2013); H.R. 10, 112th Cong. (2011). Under the bill, no "major rule" could go into effect unless endorsed in a joint resolution of Congress. A joint resolution, like a statute, requires concurrence of the House and Senate, plus a presidential signature or a two-thirds override of his veto in each chamber. The Act follows common usage in defining a "major rule" as, roughly speaking, a rule that would have a $100 million effect on the nation's economy. Rules that are not "major" would remain subject to the Congressional Review Act, as at present. In each of the two House votes on the Act, all Republicans voted in favor of it, and all but a handful of Democrats opposed it.

Under the REINS Act, a joint resolution to approve a given rule would be considered under special legislative procedures to ensure a timely vote; for example, it could not be filibustered in the Senate. Congressional passage of a joint resolution would cause the major rule to go into effect, but normal judicial review of the rule would remain available: its enactment "shall not extinguish or affect any claim, whether substantive or procedural, against any alleged defect in a rule." H.R. 367, § 3 (proposed § 805(c)).

The bill contains the following explanation of its purpose:

> The purpose of this Act is to increase accountability for and transparency in the federal regulatory process. Section 1 of article I of the United States Constitution grants all legislative powers to Congress. Over time, Congress has excessively delegated its constitutional charge while failing to conduct appropriate oversight and retain accountability for the content of the laws it passes. By requiring a vote in Congress, the REINS Act will result in more carefully drafted and detailed legislation, an improved regulatory process, and a legislative branch that is truly accountable to the American people for the laws imposed upon them.

Id. § 2. *Should* the legislature be accountable for every major rule—or is it sufficient that that the *executive* branch is accountable for its exercises of delegated authority? Would the REINS Act be constitutional, or is it too much like the legislative veto condemned in *Chadha*? How well would the Act work in a Congress in which, as at present, the House and Senate have widely divergent philosophical views regarding regulation and have often been unable to agree on compromise positions?

For commentary on the Act, see Jonathan Adler, *Placing "REINS" on Regulations: Assessing the Proposed REINS Act,* 16 N.Y.U. J. LEGIS. & PUB. POL'Y 1 (2013) (supporting the Act); Jonathan Siegel, *The REINS Act and the Struggle to Control Agency Rulemaking,* 16 N.Y.U. J. LEGIS. & PUB. POL'Y 131 (2013) (calling the Act constitutional but unwise); Sally Katzen with Julian Ginos, *A Response to Professors Adler and Siegel Addressing the Constitutionality of the REINS Act,* 2013 N.Y.U. J. LEGIS. & PUB. POL'Y QUORUM 13 (challenging its constitutionality).

11. *Separation of powers.* Post-*Chadha* cases from the Supreme Court have reinforced the constitutional constraints on Congress's ability to control administrative actions, but the Court's doctrinal analysis has not been consistent. Instead of relying squarely on textual provisions, such as the bicameralism and presentment clauses involved in *Chadha,* the Court has sometimes used the separation of powers doctrine in its nontextual aspect. *See* § 7.1. Remember how Justices Powell and White drew attention to that doctrine in their separate opinions in *Chadha*.

One such case was *Bowsher v. Synar,* 478 U.S. 714 (1986), more fully discussed in § 7.5.2b N.3. There the Court found implicit in the Constitution a "command . . . that Congress play no direct role in the execution of the laws." *Id.* at 736. Therefore, Congress may not remove an officer who is engaged in executive functions, *even if it complies with the bicameralism and presentment clauses of the Constitution.* Even the possibility of such removal disqualifies an officer from wielding executive power. In *Bowsher* itself, this meant that the Comptroller General (who headed a congressional support agency and by statute could have been removed by Congress) could not perform the "executive" task of determining how much spending would have to be cut from the federal budget in order to meet the deficit reduction targets of the Gramm-Rudman balanced budget legislation.

In *Metropolitan Washington Airports Authority v. Citizens for the Abatement of Aircraft Noise, Inc.*, 501 U.S. 252 (1991), a federal statute provided for a regional airport authority (MWAA) that was controlled by a Review Board composed of nine members of Congress. The Board was authorized to veto any decisions made by MWAA. The Court held that the structure of this Board was unconstitutional. In effect, the Board was an agent of Congress. Thus, if the Board's actions were deemed to be legislative, *Chadha* required that they be exercised in conformity with the bicameralism and presentment requirements. On the other hand, if the Board's actions were considered to be executive, the separation of powers doctrine as interpreted in *Bowsher* would not permit a congressional agent to exercise them at all.

The implication of *MWAA* seems to be that characterizations of a congressional action as "legislative" or "executive" have become less important. Either way, Congress is apparently unable to take legally binding action through a means other than the full enactment process, except in the limited areas identified in *Chadha*. If that interpretation proves correct, does it tie Congress's hands too tightly?

12. *Presidential revision.* The Court revisited the reasoning of *Chadha* when it struck down the Line Item Veto Act in *Clinton v. City of New York*, 524 U.S. 417 (1998). The newly elected Republican Congress had adopted the Act in 1996, as part of the "Contract With America." It was intended as a substitute for the "line item veto" authority wielded by many governors. Under the federal Act, the President would sign an appropriations bill in the usual way but could then send a message to Congress stating that he intended to "cancel" particular expenditures authorized in the bill. The cancellations would become effective unless overridden by a "disapproval bill" (a new piece of legislation enacted through the Article I, § 7 procedures).

President Clinton used this authority to cancel funds that would have underwritten New York City's system of providing medical care to the indigent. The City brought suit. The Court held the Act unconstitutional, asserting that the cancellation procedure would have allowed the President, in legal and practical effect, to amend the appropriations act by repealing a portion of it. The Presentment Clause of the Constitution did not allow him to do that unilaterally. To permit the President to "create a different law—one whose text was not voted on by either House of Congress or presented to the President for his signature"—would alter the carefully drawn lawmaking procedures of Article I, § 7, according to the Court.

Justices Scalia, Breyer, and O'Connor dissented. They protested that the Act, although somewhat misleadingly named, was simply a delegation of authority to the President. It was no different in substance from numerous well-accepted laws that have authorized Presidents, in their discretion, to decline to spend money appropriated by Congress for particular purposes.

But the Court disagreed: "The critical difference between this statute and all its predecessors . . . is that unlike any of them, this Act gives the President the unilateral power to change the text of duly enacted statutes."

Is that distinction meaningful? Moreover, why should the Court have struck down a law that augmented the powers of the President relative to Congress, when it was the legislative branch itself that had conferred, and could repeal or override, those new powers? One answer may come from Justice Kennedy's concurrence, which saw the Line Item Veto Act as a threat to the liberties of individual citizens: it "establishes a new mechanism which gives the President the sole ability to hurt a group that is a visible target, in order to disfavor the group or to extract further concessions from Congress."

Recall the "big waiver" statutory provisions discussed in § 6.3 N.7. These provisions give a presidential administration broad authority to waive compliance with major components of a regulatory program, such as the No Child Left Behind Act or the Affordable Care Act. Does *Clinton v. City of New York* cast doubt on their validity? *See* David J. Barron & Todd D. Rakoff, *In Defense of Big Waiver*, 113 COLUM. L. REV. 265, 312–18 (2013).

13. *Problem.* Congress adopted the (fictional) Drug Labeling Improvements Act at a time when the Food and Drug Administration (FDA) was pursuing a number of proposed regulations to require that labels on pharmaceutical products must contain fuller disclosure of potential health risks. Among the principal supporters of the FDA's efforts was People for Safer Meds (PSM), an organization of patients who could be affected by inadequate warnings. Congress, however, entertained many doubts about the wisdom of those measures. Accordingly, it wrote a special mechanism for legislative oversight into the Act.

The Act provides that the FDA shall no longer have authority to adopt rules regulating drug labeling. The agency may, however, *propose* rules for consideration by Congress. In developing these proposals, the agency must comply with § 553 of the APA and all other procedures normally required in a rulemaking proceeding, The internal procedures of the House of Representatives and Senate were amended to provide that, whenever the FDA tenders such a rule proposal, a bill to approve the proposal is immediately introduced in each chamber. If neither House takes any action within sixty days, the bill is automatically deemed to have been passed by each of the respective chambers and is sent to the President for his signature (or veto, which may be overridden as in the case of other presidential vetoes). The approval process is terminated, however, if either chamber votes during that period not to approve the proposed rule. In that event, the proposed rule does not take effect.

The Act goes on to provide that if a rule is approved as provided in the Act (either through the automatic deeming process or through affirmative votes), the effect is merely to cure the deficiency in the FDA's rulemaking authority. Affected persons may nevertheless challenge the validity of the rule in court under the APA or otherwise, invoking the same grounds as would be available in cases involving other rules. No court may construe the circumstances of congressional consideration as expressing either endorsement or disapproval of the contents of the rule.

A few months ago the FDA completed action on a new rule to require stricter warnings on packages of cold pills, but the bill to approve it was voted down by the Senate, thanks to energetic lobbying by the drug industry and the timely intervention of an influential committee chair. PSM has now brought suit for a declaratory judgment that the approval procedure in the Act is unconstitutional and that the rule has, therefore, gone into effect after all. PSM argues that the Act's procedure is too much like the one-House veto system struck down in *Chadha*. Counsel for the House and Senate, supported by the drug industry, contend that the approval system in the Act is a valid exercise of the constitutional prerogatives of the House and Senate under Article I, § 5, cl. 2, which states that "[e]ach House may determine the Rules of its Proceedings." Should the court grant the relief sought by PSM? Is the approval procedure in the Act constitutionally permissible, and is it a good idea? *Cf.* Morton Rosenberg, *Whatever Happened to Congressional Review of Agency Rulemaking?: A Brief Overview, Assessment, and Proposal for Reform*, 51 ADMIN. L. REV. 1051, 1083–90 (1999).

§ 7.4.2 LEGISLATIVE CONTROLS IN THE STATES

1. *State legislative vetoes.* Many state legislatures have adopted legislative veto provisions, often authorizing a single legislative committee to exercise disapproval authority over agency regulations. For a detailed, state-by-state survey of these systems, see JASON A. SCHWARTZ, 52 EXPERIMENTS WITH REGULATORY REVIEW: THE POLITICAL AND ECONOMIC INPUTS INTO STATE RULEMAKINGS (2010), *http://policyintegrity.org.* For narrative overviews, see Jerry L. Anderson & Christopher Poynor, *A Constitutional and Empirical Analysis of Iowa's Administrative Rules Review Committee Procedure*, 61 DRAKE L. REV. 1, 16–26 (2012); Jim Rossi, *Institutional Design and the Lingering Legacy of Antifederalist Separation of Powers Ideals in the States*, 52 VAND. L. REV. 1167, 1201–16 (1999). Courts in at least a dozen states have held such provisions unconstitutional, in line with *Chadha. See, e.g., Mo. Coalition for the Envir. v. Joint Comm. on Admin. Rules,* 948 S.W.2d 125 (Mo. 1997); *State v. A.L.I.V.E. Voluntary,* 606 P.2d 769 (Alaska 1980). However, some states, including Connecticut, Iowa, and Nevada, have explicit provisions for legislative veto in their constitutions. And one state supreme court, relying heavily on Justice White's analysis, has squarely upheld a two-house legislative veto scheme for administrative rules. *Mead v. Arnell,* 791 P.2d 410 (Idaho 1990); *see* Phillip M. Barber, Mead v. Arnell: *The Legislative Veto and Too Much Separation of Powers,* 27 IDAHO L. REV. 157 (1991).

Professor Devlin has argued that creative methods of facilitating legislative control over administration may be more defensible at the state level than at the federal level:

Congress is in session for the bulk of each year and is endowed with a large and professional staff. It thus enjoys a substantial institutional capacity to gather information on a continuous basis and to deal with emergencies as they arise. In marked contrast, many state legislatures meet for only short and intermittent sessions, and the legislators themselves are often only part-time politicians with other livelihoods that require attention. State legislative staffs are smaller and less regimented than their federal counterparts. [These factors] tend to make state legislators far less able than members of Congress to exercise influence through informal oversight mechanisms, such as hearings or direct contact with administrators.

[Moreover,] states today do not operate in a legal vacuum, but rather are subject to the restraining influence of paramount federal law. This pervasive background of federal law is especially salient in the area of individual rights, providing a "floor" beneath which protection of individual liberties may not fall. In particular, the Federal Bill of Rights and, to a lesser extent, the Federal Civil Rights and Voting Rights statutes, provide a potentially significant degree of protection against anti-democratic or oppressive acts by state authorities. . . . [And] all of these rights can be vindicated in the federal courts, a system that is by design independent of any control by state authorities.

. . . [T]he unique position of states as actors within a federal system may, rightly understood, free state courts construing state constitutions to concentrate somewhat less on remote and hypothetical concerns about the prevention of oppression, in order to concentrate more on the other concerns that underlie distribution of powers analysis—concerns such as maintaining efficiency, preserving accountability, and preventing any branch from abdicating its responsibilities.

John Devlin, *Toward a State Constitutional Analysis of Allocation of Powers: Legislators and Legislative Appointees Performing Administrative Functions*, 66 TEMP. L. REV. 1205, 1228–35 (1993). Does it follow that states should uphold the legislative veto?

2. *Suspensive veto.* May a state adopt a statute that authorizes a legislative committee to suspend an agency rule for a limited period of time? Some state constitutions specifically authorize this procedure, including those of Michigan, Nevada, and South Dakota, but legislatures

have also instituted the device in states that lack such direct constitutional support. *See, e.g.,* Alaska Stat. § 24.20; Ga. Code Ann. § 50–13–4(f). The 2010 MSAPA contains a provision of this type. §§ 703(a), (d).

Statutory versions of this device have led to constitutional challenges. For example, in *Martinez v. Dep't of Industry, Labor, & Human Relations [DILHR],* 478 N.W.2d 582, 585–87 (Wis. 1992), a statute allowed the legislature's Joint Committee for Review of Administrative Rules (JCRAR) to suspend a rule for any of the following reasons: (1) absence of statutory authority; (2) an emergency relating to public health, safety or welfare; (3) failure to comply with legislative intent; (4) conflict with state law; (5) changed circumstances; or (6) arbitrariness and capriciousness, or imposition of an undue hardship. The committee was required, immediately after imposing any suspensive action, to introduce a bill in each house to repeal the suspended rule. If neither of those bills was enacted as a law, the rule would go into effect, and the committee could not suspend it again.

In *Martinez,* DILHR adopted a regulation allowing employers to pay a "sub-minimum wage" to short-term workers. The JCRAR suspended it for failing to comply with statutory intent and imposing an undue hardship on workers. However, DILHR regarded the suspension as unconstitutional and instructed employers that they could pay the sub-minimum wage anyway. Eventually DILHR raised the wage level, but twelve migrant workers, who had been paid at the lower rate, filed suit against the agency. They claimed that the JCRAR suspension had been lawful and that DILHR should therefore require employers to pay back wages to any employee who had been subjected to the sub-minimum wage that the agency had illegally prescribed.

The Wisconsin Supreme Court agreed with the workers and upheld the suspensive veto device. The court noted that it interpreted the separation of powers principles of the Wisconsin state constitution liberally, because those principles are only implied—unlike the constitutions of many other states, which contain express separation of powers provisions. Consequently, in Wisconsin, a sharing of powers between the legislative and executive branches is not inappropriate unless it demonstrably disturbs "the balance between the three branches of government," interferes with "their respective independence and integrity," or causes a "concentration of unchecked power in the hands of any one branch." The court concluded that the JCRAR authority to suspend an agency rule did not cause any of these evils. The legislative and executive branches "share inherent interests in the legislative creation and oversight of administrative agencies," so that this was not a situation where "one branch interferes with a constitutionally guaranteed 'exclusive zone' of authority vested in another branch." Furthermore, the court said, "legislative power may be delegated . . . so long as adequate standards for conducting the allocated power are in place," and the statute vesting the JCRAR with authority to suspend agency rules contained "sufficient procedural safeguards . . . to prevent unauthorized decisions by the committee."

The court also said that the JCRAR temporary suspensive power did not violate the bicameralism or presentment provisions of the state constitution, because "only the formal bicameral enactment process coupled with executive action can make permanent a rule suspension." The court was convinced that the "full involvement of both houses of the legislature and the governor are critical elements [of the statutory scheme] and these elements distinguish Wisconsin from the [otherwise similar] statutory schemes" found to be unconstitutional in other states. It stressed that this statute was "carefully designed so that the people of this state, through their elected representatives, will continue to exercise a significant check on the activities of nonelected bureaucrats . . . [and that it] provides a legislative check . . . which prevents potential agency overreaching."

In New Hampshire the state supreme court has also endorsed a suspensive veto in dictum, *Opinion of the Justices,* 431 A.2d 783, 789 (N.H. 1981). But in Kentucky such a statute was held unconstitutional. *Legislative Research Comm'n v. Brown,* 664 S.W.2d 907, 917–19 (Ky. 1984). *See also* Philip P. Frickey, *The Constitutionality of Legislative Committee Suspension of Administrative Rules: The Case of Minnesota,* 70 MINN. L. REV. 1237 (1986) (arguing against the validity of Minnesota's suspensive veto, which has since been repealed). Was *Martinez* correctly decided?

3.   *Grounds for objection.* Notice that the suspensive veto statute in *Martinez* provided a limited list of grounds on which the legislative committee was authorized to object to an agency rule. This is a fairly common feature among legislative review statutes of various kinds. Some provide that a veto or suspension is permitted only if the review committee believes that a rule is unauthorized by statute. *See* Idaho Code § 67–5218. Section 3–204(d) of the 1981 MSAPA, discussed more fully in the next note, instructs the legislature's review committee to object to a rule only if it is beyond the agency's procedural or substantive authority. In other states, however, the grounds for objection are essentially unrestricted. *See* N.H. Rev. Stat. Ann. § 541–A:13(IV)(c) (committee may object to rule as being not "in the public interest").

Supporting the 1981 MSAPA approach, Bonfield argues that the ARRC should not be authorized to object to a rule on pure policy grounds, because "such a committee power would divest the agencies of the very discretion that they were authorized to exercise by statute. It would also deny the public the benefit of the agencies' expertise on policy matters within their lawful authority. Finally, a power of this kind would permit the administrative rules review committee to impugn otherwise legal action taken by agencies pursuant to authorizations by the legislature as a whole, and would thereby allow that committee to undercut actions of its principal." *See* ARTHUR EARL BONFIELD, STATE ADMINISTRATIVE RULE MAKING 521 (1986). Another scholar agrees, adding that pure policy review would give too much influence to well-connected interest groups. Carl A. Auerbach, *Bonfield on State Administrative Rulemaking: A Critique*, 71 MINN. L. REV. 543, 568 (1987).

The effectiveness of such limits has been questioned. " 'It would doubtless be unrealistic to assume that a group of state legislators would be content to make judgments about the *legal* power of administrative agencies, and ignore the *political* implications of administrative policies as these are revealed in actual application in specific instances. Legislative review of administrative rule-making is almost certain, in the United States, to be *political* review.' " *State ex rel. Barker v. Manchin*, 279 S.E.2d 622, 632 n.5 (W. Va. 1981) (quoting political scientist Glendon Schubert). Indeed, an empirical study of legislative review in Iowa found that the legislature's review committee "often acts based on policy disagreement," despite the nominal limits on its authority. Anderson & Poynor, *supra*, at 53–54. Yet, even assuming that legislators' compliance with statutory grounds for objections will be imperfect, are such limitations desirable in principle, and, therefore, perhaps worth a try? Which issue is a legislator better qualified to address: the consistency of a rule with statutory intent, or the political acceptability of the rule? *See* Harold H. Bruff & Ernest Gellhorn, *Congressional Control of Administrative Regulation: A Study of Legislative Vetoes*, 90 HARV. L. REV. 1369, 1429–30 (1977).

Finally, if a statute does prescribe specific grounds on which the review committee may intervene, should the courts entertain allegations that the committee has overstepped those limits? In *Mead v. Arnell*, 791 P.2d 410 (Idaho 1990), after upholding the constitutionality of the legislative veto, the court held that a *particular* use of the device had been unlawful. The veto was supposed to be employed only if the challenged rule exceeded the agency's statutory authority; but the legislature had not expressly found this to be the case, and, indeed, had apparently objected to the rule because of perceived procedural and factual errors in the agency's decision. Such judicial review of the merits of a legislative veto has, however, been extremely rare.

4. *Burden-shifting.* Section 3–204(d) of the 1981 MSAPA assigns a reviewing role to an "administrative rules review committee" (ARRC), consisting of three members from each of the two houses of the legislature (§ 3–203). The committee may object to all or a portion of a rule that it considers to be "beyond the procedural or substantive authority delegated

to the adopting agency." The committee must file a concise statement of its reasons for objecting, and the agency may then respond in writing. But if the committee does not withdraw its objection, the burden will be on the agency to establish the validity of the rule in any subsequent judicial review proceedings. (Normally, the challenger bears the burden of showing that the rule is *not* valid.) Among states that have provisions similar to § 3–204(d) are Iowa, Minnesota, Montana, New Hampshire, North Dakota, and Vermont.

The official Comment to § 3–204(d) suggests that this device is not a legislative veto because it only authorizes the ARRC to "alter one aspect of the procedure by which *the legality of the rule will be finally determined by the courts.*" In light of the fact that legislatures regularly allocate the burden of persuasion in civil litigation, the Comment argues that the shift in the burden of persuasion authorized by that provision is legitimate. Furthermore, it is "logical to shift to the agency the burden of demonstrating the validity of a rule in subsequent litigation when a more politically accountable and independent body [like the ARRC] objects thereto." For a fuller explication of the case for § 3–204(d), see BONFIELD, *supra,* at § 8.3.3. *But see* Anderson & Poynor, *supra*, at 68–79 (arguing that Iowa's statute allowing burden-shift by committee violates separation of powers principles).

Are the above arguments for § 3–204(d) persuasive? Is it constitutional? Desirable?

5. *Affirmative approval statutes.* A few states have adopted legislation under which rules must be affirmatively approved by the legislature. These measures are comparable to the REINS Act proposals at the federal level (*see* § 7.4.1 N.10). In West Virginia, a 1982 statute provides that, "[u]nless lawfully promulgated as an emergency rule, a legislative rule is only a proposal by the agency and has no legal force or effect until promulgated by specific authorization of the Legislature." W. Va. Code § 29A–1–2(d); *see also id.* § 29A–3–9. In practice, the legislature ratifies agency rules by passing omnibus bills grouped into subject matter categories. *See Swiger v. UGI/Amerigas, Inc.*, 613 S.E.2d 904 (W. Va. 2005). However, the state's highest court does not treat this procedure as preventing it from evaluating legislative rules under the same judicial review standards that courts use in other jurisdictions. *See id.* at 910–11.

In Florida, the legislature passed a statute in 2010 (overriding the governor's veto) under which, "[i]f the adverse impact or regulatory costs of [a] rule exceed [$1 million dollars in the aggregate within five years, as estimated by the agency], the rule may not take effect until it is ratified by the Legislature." Fla. Stat. Ann. § 120.541(3). The legislature's first act ratifying a "million dollar rule" came two years later, approving a regulation that updated standards for the storage and handling of liquefied petroleum gases. The approval legislation contained language declaring that its enactment would not preempt any challenge based on lack of authority or violation of rulemaking requirements. Fla. Stat. ch. 2012–101.

When the West Virginia and Florida legislatures assume responsibility for an agency's rule by adopting a statute to ratify it, why shouldn't the courts treat the rule as a *statute* and defer to it accordingly?

6. *Problem.* You are counsel to a senator in the Madison legislature, which is considering adopting a suspensive veto statute modeled on the Wisconsin provision described in N.3. What would you advise as to the proposal's constitutionality and desirability? Assume that Madison's constitution has no explicit separation of powers provision.

§ 7.4.3 OTHER LEGISLATIVE CONTROLS

Aside from amendment or repeal of substantive legislation and the various forms of legislative veto, what other mechanisms are available to Congress or a state legislature to control administrative agencies? This section provides a brief survey. For a comprehensive discussion, see Jack M. Beermann, *Congressional Administration*, 43 SAN DIEGO L. REV. 61 (2006).

a. *Oversight committees.* Most states have adopted formal continuing legislative oversight mechanisms to review the legality and desirability of agency rules. *See generally* ARTHUR EARL BONFIELD, STATE ADMINISTRATIVE RULE MAKING § 8.3.1 (1986); L. Harold Levinson, *Legislative and Executive Veto of Rules of Administrative Agencies: Models and Alternatives*, 24 WM. & MARY L. REV. 79 (1982). These oversight functions are normally performed by special standing joint legislative committees. Committees of this kind are typically authorized to hold public hearings on proposed or adopted agency rules, to give advice to agencies concerning such rules, and to submit bills to the legislature to overcome by statute rules that the agency declines to withdraw on its own.

In Congress, responsibility for oversight of federal agencies is much more diffused. The authorization committees of Congress are responsible for considering legislation in a particular area—such as commerce or energy or labor. These committees also supervise the agencies that implement previously enacted legislation in those particular areas. In addition, the House Committee on Oversight and Government Reform and the Senate Committee on Homeland Security and Governmental Affairs maintain oversight over a variety of types of government business, including many issues that involve administrative agencies.

Moreover, an agency's budget request is annually scrutinized by the appropriations committees of each house. Specialized subcommittees of the appropriations committees are expert in the work of each agency. Their investigations of the manner in which the agency is spending money can touch upon virtually everything the agency does. Finally, senatorial hearings to consider the confirmation of politically appointed personnel (such as agency heads) often focus on policy issues and involve scrutiny of an agency's performance. This would be especially likely to occur if the individual is seeking reappointment to the job or is being promoted from the staff level to the agency head level.

b. *Investigations and hearings.* The many standing committees of Congress and state legislatures constantly investigate the manner in which agencies spend money as well as discharge their responsibilities. Thus they hold hearings, request agencies to furnish written reports or studies, and write committee reports. Inadequate legislative staffing and less professionalism in some state legislatures appears to make this form of oversight less effective in some states than at the federal level.

Some legislative committee hearings draw the attention of print or broadcast media and generate a great deal of publicity. At times, the proceedings become quite adversarial, and committee members seem more interested in scoring political points than in obtaining information. Preparing for legislative committee hearings, and actually testifying, often consumes a large fraction of the time of an agency head. *See* Richard J. Lazarus, *The Neglected Question of Congressional Oversight of EPA: Quis Custodiet Ipsos Custodes (Who Shall Watch the Watchers Themselves)?*, 54 L. & CONTEMP. PROB. 205 (1991).

In connection with a legislative investigation, an agency may be requested to furnish information or documents; if these are not forthcoming, the legislative committee sometimes exercises its subpoena power to obtain documents that the agency prefers not to disclose. The extent to which an agency can withhold documents from the legislature, upon a claim of executive privilege, remains unsettled, in part because most of these conflicts are resolved through negotiation. *See generally* LOUIS FISHER, THE POLITICS OF EXECUTIVE PRIVILEGE (2004); Josh Chafetz, *Executive Branch Contempt of Congress*, 76 U. CHI. L. REV. 1083 (2009). However, in a recent decision involving a congressional inquiry into "Operation Fast and Furious," a drug enforcement operation that went awry, the court reaffirmed its past position that such disputes are potentially justiciable. *Comm. on Oversight & Gov't Reform v. Holder*, 2013 WL 5428834 (D.D.C. 2013) (citing *Comm. on the Judiciary v. Miers*, 558 F. Supp. 2d 53 (D.D.C. 2008)).

In addition to committee investigations, legislative investigative agencies may be employed for oversight purposes. The federal Government Accountability Office (GAO), headed by the Comptroller General, is an example of such a legislative agency. The GAO is concerned primarily with the efficiency of federal government operation and with the manner in which government funds are used. Much of its time is spent in studying executive branch activities and evaluating particular programs. The GAO can launch an investigation on its own initiative or at the request of a member of Congress or a committee. Its subpoena powers are limited, *see Walker v. Cheney*, 230 F. Supp. 2d 51 (D.D.C. 2002), but normally agencies cooperate with GAO inquiries.

A few states have also created an office of ombudsman, usually located in the legislative branch. Such an office is typically authorized to receive and investigate citizen complaints about any state agency or aspect of the state administrative process, and to make a report and recommendation to the legislature and/or governor on such complaints. The office may have various names, such as Ombuds, Citizens' Aide, or Public Counsel. *See, e.g.,* Hawaii Rev.Stat. § 96–2; Iowa Code ch. 601G; Neb.Rev.Stat. §§ 81–8, 240–254. The most potent oversight weapon of this body is usually publicity for its investigations and recommendations. Proposals for a *congressional* office of constituent assistance have been offered over the years, but most members of Congress believe that contacts made by their own offices (discussed below) are an adequate or even superior alternative. Thus, ombudsman offices at the federal level tend to be situated within the agencies themselves. *See* David R. Anderson & Diane M. Stockton, *Federal Ombudsmen: An Underused Resource*, 5 ADMIN. L. J. 275 (1991).

c.　*Funding measures.* Congress and state legislatures appropriate funds for every unit of government—usually every year, although in some states it occurs every other year. Consequently, the appropriations mechanism provides a convenient way to achieve legislative objectives without altering the statutes which furnish authority to agencies. For example, measures appropriating money to an agency sometimes contain provisions cutting the amount spent on one agency function while increasing another—thus altering an agency's priorities. Similarly, an activity can be deliberately underfunded, thus preventing effective enforcement. Indeed, appropriation measures sometimes bar an agency from spending any money in carrying out a particular program or enforcing a particular regulation. *See* Beermann, *supra*, at 84–90; Neal Devins, *Regulation of Government Agencies Through Limitation Riders*, 1987 DUKE L.J. 456. In recent years, appropriations have become entangled with budget politics. As a result, many funding decisions are made by chamber leaders, bypassing the normal committee process.

Often, legislative action in the appropriation process falls short of the enactment of binding legislation. Instead, a committee report (or even a statement in committee or on the floor) will contain an admonition to the agency about how it should conduct its business. While not binding, such statements are likely to influence the persons responsible for spending the appropriated funds. *See* JESSICA KORN, THE POWER OF SEPARATION: AMERICAN CONSTITUTIONALISM AND THE MYTH OF THE LEGISLATIVE VETO 40 (1996).

d. *Direct contacts.* Individual members of Congress and state legislatures consider that their responsibilities include making direct contacts with units of government that are causing problems for their constituents. *See generally* JOHN R. JOHANNES, TO SERVE THE PEOPLE: CONGRESS AND CONSTITUENCY SERVICE (1984); Ronald M. Levin, *Congressional Ethics and Constituent Advocacy in an Age of Mistrust*, 95 MICH. L. REV. 1, 16–31 (1996). For example, at the federal level, legislative staff members frequently contact the Department of Veterans Affairs or the Social Security Administration on behalf of constituents. For the most part, these contacts are relatively harmless requests by staff for "status reports" about pending matters, or attempts to cut through red tape for a constituent who is inexperienced in dealing with bureaucracy. Responding to such requests, however, can consume a considerable portion of agency resources. When these contacts turn into efforts to influence the outcome of a pending matter, such as an adjudication or a grantmaking decision, serious questions of propriety can arise, especially if the participation is off-the-record. *See* § 3.3.3.

§ 7.5   EXECUTIVE CONTROL: PERSONNEL DECISIONS

Presidents and governors indirectly control agency action by exercising their authority to appoint and discharge officials who execute the laws. This section considers the scope of this authority, as well as the extent to which Congress or a state legislature may limit, or even share in, the exercise of appointment and removal powers.

§ 7.5.1 APPOINTMENT OF OFFICERS

§ 7.5.1a Federal Appointments

BUCKLEY V. VALEO
424 U.S. 1 (1976)

[Under legislation adopted in 1974, the Federal Election Commission] consists of eight members. The Secretary of the Senate and the Clerk of the House of Representatives are *ex officio* members of the Commission without the right to vote. Two members are appointed by the President pro tempore of the Senate "upon the recommendations of the majority leader of the Senate and the minority leader of the Senate." Two more are to be appointed by the Speaker of the House of Representatives, likewise upon the recommendations of its respective majority and minority leaders. The remaining two members are appointed by the President. . . .

Appellants urge that since Congress has given the Commission wide-ranging rulemaking and enforcement powers with respect to the substantive provisions of the Act, Congress is precluded under the principle of separation of powers from vesting in itself the authority to appoint those who will exercise such authority. Their argument is based on the language of Art. II, § 2, cl. 2, of the Constitution, which provides in pertinent part as follows:

> [The President] shall nominate, and by and with the Advice and Consent of the Senate, shall appoint . . . all other Officers of the United States, whose Appointments are not herein otherwise provided for, and which shall be established by Law: but the Congress may by Law vest the Appointment of such inferior Officers, as they think proper, in the President alone, in the Courts of Law, or in the Heads of Departments."

. . . We think . . . that any appointee exercising significant authority pursuant to the laws of the United States is an "Officer of the United States," and must, therefore, be appointed in the manner prescribed by § 2, cl. 2, of that Article. . . . [S]urely the Commissioners before us are at the very least such "inferior Officers" within the meaning of that Clause.[162] . . . While the second part of the Clause authorizes Congress to vest the appointment of the officers described in that part in "the Courts of Law, or in the Heads of Departments," neither the Speaker of the House nor the President *pro tempore* of the Senate comes within this language.

The phrase "Heads of Departments," used as it is in conjunction with the phrase "Courts of Law," suggests that the Departments referred to are themselves in the Executive Branch or at least have some connection with that branch. While the Clause expressly authorizes Congress to vest the appointment of certain officers in the "Courts of Law," the absence of similar language to include Congress must mean that neither Congress nor its officers were included within the language "Heads of Departments" in this part of cl. 2.

Thus with respect to four of the six voting members of the Commission, neither the President, the head of any department, nor the Judiciary has any voice in their selection. . . .

We are . . . told by appellees and amici that Congress had good reason for not vesting in a Commission composed wholly of Presidential appointees the authority to administer the Act, since the administration

---

[162] "Officers of the United States" does not include all employees of the United States, but there is no claim made that the Commissioners are employees of the United States rather than officers. Employees are lesser functionaries subordinate to officers of the United States. . . .

of the Act would undoubtedly have a bearing on any incumbent President's campaign for re-election. While one cannot dispute the basis for this sentiment as a practical matter, it would seem that those who sought to challenge incumbent Congressmen might have equally good reason to fear a Commission which was unduly responsive to Members of Congress whom they were seeking to unseat. But such fears, however rational, do not by themselves warrant a distortion of the Framers' work.

Appellee Commission and amici finally contend . . . that whatever shortcomings the provisions for the appointment of members of the Commission might have under Art. II, Congress had ample authority under the Necessary and Proper Clause of Art. I to effectuate this result. We do not agree. . . . Congress could not, merely because it concluded that such a measure was "necessary and proper" to the discharge of its substantive legislative authority, pass a bill of attainder or ex post facto law contrary to the prohibitions contained in § 9 of Art. I. No more may it vest in itself, or in its officers, the authority to appoint officers of the United States when the Appointments Clause by clear implication prohibits it from doing so.

. . . [T]he Commission's powers fall generally into three categories: functions relating to the flow of necessary information—receipt, dissemination, and investigation; functions with respect to the Commission's task of fleshing out the statute—rulemaking and advisory opinions; and functions necessary to ensure compliance with the statute and rules—informal procedures, administrative determinations and hearings, and civil suits.

Insofar as the powers confided in the Commission are essentially of an investigative and informative nature, falling in the same general category as those powers which Congress might delegate to one of its own committees, there can be no question that the Commission as presently constituted may exercise them. . . .

But when we go beyond this type of authority to the more substantial powers exercised by the Commission, we reach a different result. The Commission's enforcement power, exemplified by its discretionary power to seek judicial relief, is authority that cannot possibly be regarded as merely in aid of the legislative function of Congress. A lawsuit is the ultimate remedy for a breach of the law, and it is to the President, and not to the Congress, that the Constitution entrusts the responsibility to "take Care that the Laws be faithfully executed." Art. II, § 3.

We hold that these provisions of the Act, vesting in the Commission primary responsibility for conducting civil litigation in the courts of the United States for vindicating public rights, violate Art. II, § 2, cl. 2, of the Constitution. Such functions may be discharged only by persons who are "Officers of the United States" within the language of that section.

All aspects of the Act are brought within the Commission's broad administrative powers: rulemaking, advisory opinions, and determinations of eligibility for funds and even for federal elective office itself. These functions, exercised free from day-to-day supervision of either Congress or the Executive Branch, are more legislative and judicial in nature than are the Commission's enforcement powers, and are of kinds usually performed by independent regulatory agencies or by some department in the Executive Branch under the direction of an Act of Congress. Congress viewed these broad powers as essential to effective and impartial administration of the entire substantive framework of the Act. Yet each of these functions also represents the performance of a significant governmental duty exercised pursuant to a public law. While the President may not insist that such functions be delegated to an appointee of his removable at will, *Humphrey's Executor v. United States,* 295 U.S. 602 (1935), none of them operates merely in aid of congressional authority to legislate or is sufficiently removed from the administration and enforcement of public law to allow it to be performed by the present Commission. These administrative functions may therefore be exercised only by persons who are "Officers of the United States."

NOTES AND QUESTIONS

1. *Buckley.* The Federal Election Commission makes numerous decisions that can profoundly affect the competition between the two major political parties in the United States. Isn't it extreme to read the Constitution as requiring that *all* members of the Commission must be chosen by the President—who of course will always be a Republican or a Democrat? Should the Court have read the Necessary and Proper Clause more generously, to avoid this anomaly?

2. *Principal versus inferior officers.* Notice the Court's distinction in *Buckley* between principal officers, who must be selected by the President with the advice and consent of the Senate, and inferior officers, whom Congress may allow to be appointed by "the President alone, [by] the Courts of Law, or [by] the Heads of Departments." The Court has had difficulty distinguishing between the two categories.

In *Morrison v. Olson,* 487 U.S. 654 (1988), the Court upheld a statute that allowed a special court to appoint an independent counsel to investigate and prosecute possible violations of federal law by high ranking executive officials. Chief Justice Rehnquist, writing for seven Justices, admitted that the line between principal and inferior officers was far from clear. Nevertheless, the Court said, the independent counsel was clearly an inferior officer. She was subject to removal by a higher executive branch officer (the Attorney General), even though she possessed a degree of independent discretion in the exercise of the powers of her office. Further, her duties were limited to the investigation of certain federal crimes; she could only act within the scope of the jurisdiction conferred by the special court; and her position was temporary, in that she was "appointed essentially to accomplish a specific task, and when that task is over the office is terminated." *Id.* at 671–72.

Justice Scalia, in dissent, contended that the independent counsel was not an inferior officer and, therefore, had to be appointed by the President. *Id.* at 715–23. He denied that the job was as limited in power or duration as the majority maintained. More fundamentally, he argued that the status of being an inferior officer should depend primarily on whether one is subordinate to some other official. Because the independent counsel could be removed under only very limited circumstances, she was "*independent* of, not *subordinate* to, the President and the Attorney General," according to Scalia. Who had the better of this argument?

The majority opinion also addressed the appellees' contention that the Appointments Clause should not be construed to allow *judicial* officials to appoint a prosecutor, whose functions were basically *executive*. *Id.* at 673–77. Quoting from an earlier case, the Court acknowledged that " 'incongruous' interbranch appointments" were prohibited by the Constitution. But there was nothing incongruous about the appointment of the independent counsel by a special court, because judicial appointments of prosecutors had a long history. "Indeed, in light of judicial experience with prosecutors in criminal cases, it could be said that courts are especially well qualified to appoint prosecutors. This is not a case in which judges are given power to appoint an officer in an area in which they have no special knowledge or expertise, as in, for example, a statute authorizing the courts to appoint officials in the Department of Agriculture or the Federal Energy Regulatory Commission." *Id.* at 676 n.13. Besides, the Court added, "Congress of course was concerned when it created the office of independent counsel with the conflicts of interest that could arise in situations when the Executive Branch is called upon to investigate its own high-ranking officers. If it were to remove the appointing authority from the Executive Branch, the most logical place to put it was in the Judicial Branch." *Id.* at 677. (Other aspects of *Morrison* are addressed in § 7.5.2b.)

3.   *More inferiority complexities.* In *Edmond v. United States,* 520 U.S. 651 (1997), the Court held that members of the Coast Guard Court of Criminal Appeals, a tribunal that hears appeals in court-martial cases, were inferior rather than principal officers. Thus, they could be appointed by the Secretary of Transportation. Justice Scalia, writing for the Court, observed that some of the factors relied on in *Morrison* were absent here, because these military judges did not have the kind of case-specific jurisdiction or limited tenure that an independent counsel had. Nevertheless:

> Generally speaking, the term "inferior officer" connotes a relationship with some higher ranking officer or officers below the President: whether one is an "inferior" officer depends on whether he has a superior. . . . [I]n the context of a clause designed to preserve political accountability relative to important government

assignments, we think it evident that 'inferior officers' are officers whose work is directed and supervised at some level by others who were appointed by presidential nomination with the advice and consent of the Senate."

That test was satisfied in this instance, because the Judge Advocate General (a subordinate of the Secretary of Transportation) exercised administrative oversight over the Coast Guard court and had authority to remove its judges without cause; moreover, decisions of the Coast Guard court were reviewable on the merits by the Court of Appeals for the Armed Forces. Justice Souter concurred separately, arguing that, although the supervision under which the Coast Guard judges worked did not conclusively show that they were "inferior officers," the issue was close enough to justify the Court's deferring to the judgment of the political branches.

After *Edmond*, is the *Morrison* analysis no longer authoritative? Commentators suggested as much during the investigation of President Clinton by Independent Counsel Kenneth Starr. *E.g.*, Akhil Reed Amar, *Intratextualism*, 112 HARV. L. REV. 747, 810–11 & n.243 (1999). That theory was not tested in litigation, however, until almost a decade later. Following the leak in 2003 of a CIA agent's identity to columnist Robert Novak, Acting Attorney General James Comey appointed Patrick Fitzgerald, the U.S. Attorney for the Northern District of Illinois, as a special counsel to investigate the leak. In his letter to Fitzgerald, Comey "delegate[d] all the authority of the Attorney General with respect to the Department's investigation . . ., [to be exercised] independent of the supervision or control of any officer of the Department." The investigation culminated in the conviction of I. Lewis Libby, an aide to Vice President Cheney, on perjury and obstruction of justice charges. The defense argued that Fitzgerald was a principal officer, because no other officer directed or supervised his work, as *Edmond* requires for inferior officers. Therefore, the defense theory ran, Fitzgerald's appointment as special counsel had been unconstitutional, because it had not been made by the President. The district court rejected this reasoning. *United States v. Libby*, 429 F. Supp. 2d 27 (D.D.C. 2006). The President later commuted Libby's prison sentence, but the underlying conviction remained in effect after Libby withdrew his appeal. Had he pursued the appeal, should he have succeeded?

4. *Courts of law and department heads.* The ground rules for determining who can appoint "inferior officers" remain somewhat indeterminate. In *Freytag v. Commissioner*, 501 U.S. 868 (1991), a statute created the Tax Court as an independent Article I legislative court with both regular judges and special trial judges. The statute provided that the special trial judges (comparable to magistrate judges in the Article III district courts) would be appointed by the chief judge of the court. The taxpayers in *Freytag* contended that this appointment scheme was inconsistent with the requirements of the Constitution. The Supreme Court unanimously disagreed, but the Justices were sharply divided as to their reasons for this conclusion.

In an opinion for five members of the Court, Justice Blackmun asserted that the Tax Court exercised judicial power and thus was one of the "Courts of Law" mentioned in the Appointments Clause. At the same time, he rejected the argument that the Tax Court could be considered a "department" within the meaning of the clause, because that term referred only to "executive divisions like the Cabinet-level departments." Blackmun refused to read the term "department" broadly, because the Appointments Clause "reflects our Framers' conclusion that widely distributed appointment power subverts democratic government. Given the inexorable presence of the administrative state, a holding that every organ in the Executive Branch is a department would multiply indefinitely the number of actors eligible to appoint." *Id.* at 885.

The Court added, however, that the term "Department" might not be "strictly limit[ed]" to Cabinet departments: "We do not address here any question involving an appointment of an inferior officer by the head of one of the principal agencies, such as the Federal Trade Commission, the Securities Exchange Commission, the Federal Energy Regulatory Commission, the Central Intelligence Agency, or the Federal Reserve Bank of St. Louis." *Id.* at 887 n.4.

Four concurring Justices, in an opinion by Justice Scalia, rejected the basis for the majority's holding, noting that the Appointments Clause "refers to '*the* Courts of Law.' . . . The definite article 'the' obviously narrows the class of eligible 'Courts of Law' to those Courts of Law envisioned by the Constitution. Those are Article III courts, and the Tax Court is not one of them." *Id.* at 902 (concurrence). However, Scalia maintained that the appointment of special trial judges was valid "because the Tax Court is a 'Department' and the Chief Judge is its head." *Id.* at 901. He saw no reason to limit the phrase 'the Heads of Departments' in the Appointments Clause to Cabinet officials. *Id.* at 915–22. According to Scalia, the Clause was not intended to prevent diffusion of appointment authority within the executive branch, as the majority supposed; instead, its purpose was to keep appointments out of the hands of Congress, so that legislators could not appoint their friends to various government jobs. *Id.* at 904. Which analysis is more persuasive, the majority's or the concurrence's?

5.   *Inferiority and removability.* In *Free Enterprise Fund v. Public Company Accounting Oversight Board*, 130 S.Ct. 3138 (2010), also discussed in § 7.5.2 NN.4–6, the Court held that the structure of the PCAOB, an entity established by the Sarbanes-Oxley Act of 2002, was unconstitutional. The Securities and Exchange Commission, which had appointed the Board, could remove its members only for good cause, and the President, in turn, presumably could remove Commission members themselves only for good cause. According to the Court, this dual level of tenure protection unduly weakened presidential authority over the Board. Therefore, the Act's restriction of the grounds on which the SEC could remove Board members should be treated as a nullity.

The Court then turned to the plaintiffs' contention that, under the Appointments Clause, the SEC should not have been empowered to appoint the members of the Board in the first place. The Court noted that *Freytag* had left open the question of whether the SEC was a "Department" for Appointments Clause purposes. Adopting the position of Justice Scalia in that case, the Court answered this question affirmatively, explaining that the SEC is "a freestanding component of the Executive Branch, not subordinate to or contained within any other such component." In addition, the SEC commissioners are collectively the "Heads" of that Department. As to the question of whether the Board members were "principal officers" who could only be appointed by the President with senatorial confirmation, the Court said this:

> We held in *Edmond v. United States*, 520 U.S. 651 (1997), that "[w]hether one is an 'inferior' officer depends on whether he has a superior," and that " 'inferior officers' are officers whose work is directed and supervised at some level" by other officers appointed by the President with the Senate's consent. In particular, we noted that "[t]he power to remove officers" at will and without cause "is a powerful tool for control" of an inferior. As explained above, the statutory restrictions on the Commission's power to remove Board members are unconstitutional and void. Given that the Commission is properly viewed, under the Constitution, as possessing the power to remove Board members at will, and given the Commission's other oversight authority, we have no hesitation in concluding that under *Edmond* the Board members are inferior officers whose appointment Congress may permissibly vest in a "Hea[d] of Departmen[t]."

Does a simple test of "being a subordinate and being removable at will" prove too much? Even Deputy Secretaries of Cabinet departments have superiors (their respective Secretaries), yet they have traditionally been appointed with the advice and consent of the Senate. Does *Free Enterprise Fund* indicate that Congress could allow all of them to be appointed by the President alone?

The D.C. Circuit relied on the remedial holding of *Free Enterprise Fund* in a case involving the validity of the appointment of copyright royalty judges (CRJs). *Intercollegiate Broad. System, Inc. v. Copyright Royalty Bd.*, 684 F.3d 1332 (D.C. Cir. 2012). These judges had authority to set default rates for royalties that webcasters would owe to holders of copyrights for sound recordings. They were appointed by the Librarian of Congress and could be removed by him, but only for "misconduct or neglect of duty." The court held that the CRJs were "principal officers" because (1) their decisions had enormous economic consequences for industry members; (2) the Librarian's ability to remove them from office was very limited; and (3) their rate determinations were not reviewable or correctible by any other executive officer. Citing *Free Enterprise Fund*, however, the court decided to cure the defect in the CRJs' appointments by invalidating the removal restriction. If the CRJs were readily removable, the court said, they would be subject to enough supervision to make them "inferior officers." Their appointments by the Librarian (whom the court considered a "head of department") could thus be upheld.

6. *Employees.* Notice footnote 162 of *Buckley,* which explains that mere "employees" of an agency (who do not exercise "significant authority pursuant to the laws of the United States") need not be hired pursuant to the Appointments Clause at all. Obviously, neither the President, the courts, nor the department heads should have to be involved in hiring every desk clerk or field inspector who works for the federal government. However, it is sometimes difficult to say who is an "employee," as opposed to being an "Officer of the United States." For example, in *Landry v. FDIC,* 204 F.3d 1125 (D.C. Cir. 2000), an administrative law judge at the Federal Deposit Insurance Corporation (a bank regulatory agency) recommended that Landry be removed as vice president of a Louisiana bank. The FDIC agreed. Upholding their actions, the court held that the FDIC's ALJs were "employees" and thus did not have to be appointed in conformity with the Appointments Clause. The court acknowledged that these ALJs performed many of the typical duties of administrative law judges, such as conducting trials and enforcing compliance with discovery orders. Nevertheless, they (unlike the special trial judges of the Tax Court in *Freytag*) could never render final decisions on their own. Under FDIC rules, they could only make "recommended" decisions, which the agency could reconsider de novo. (Responding to Landry's assertion that the FDIC had not actually reviewed his case de novo, the court said that this accusation merely called into question the agency's carefulness, not its authority.)

Can Congress itself appoint "employees" as civil servants? Perhaps not—the Appointments Clause would not be an obstacle, but the separation of powers doctrine might be. *See Springer v. Government of Philippine Islands,* 277 U.S. 189, 202 (1928) (construing the Philippine Organic Act, assumed to be based on the U.S. Constitution): "Legislative power, as distinguished from executive power, is the authority to make laws, but not to enforce them or appoint the agents charged with the duty of such enforcement. The latter are executive functions." Do you think this case would be followed today?

7. *Qualifications.* Legislatures regularly prescribe the qualifications that executive appointees to various agencies must meet. Years ago Justice Brandeis listed some of the many congressional specifications for various offices: for example, in some cases Congress has required that certain offices may be held only by residents of a particular state, by persons who speak a certain language, by persons who have passed an examination, or (at one time) by persons who show "habitual temperance in the use of intoxicating liquors." *Myers v. United States,* 272 U.S. 52, 265–74 (1926) (dissent). More common today are requirements that the membership of multimember commissions must be balanced as between political parties. Are the bipartisan membership requirements constitutionally valid, or do they impinge too far on the chief executive's appointment discretion? *See* Note,

Congressional Restrictions on the President's Appointment Power and the Role of Longstanding Practice in Constitutional Interpretation, 120 HARV. L. REV. 1914, 1925–26 (2007) (suggesting that they may not be valid).

In practice, Presidents usually accept and comply with statutory qualifications requirements without protest. However, a provision in the Department of Homeland Security Appropriations Act enacted in 2006 did give rise to a real-world controversy. Congress there provided that an Administrator of the Federal Emergency Management Agency "shall be appointed from among individuals who have (A) a demonstrated ability in and knowledge of emergency management and homeland security; and (B) not less than 5 years of executive leadership and management experience in the public or private sector." Pub. L. No. 109–295, § 611(11) (2006) (codified at 6 U.S.C. § 313(c)(2)). When signing this legislation, President Bush stated that this provision "purports to limit the qualifications of the pool of persons from whom the President may select the appointee in a manner that rules out a large portion of those persons best qualified by experience and knowledge to fill the office," but nevertheless the executive branch would "construe [it] in a manner consistent with the Appointments Clause of the Constitution." 42 WEEK. COMP. PRES. DOC. 1742 (2006). Was his objection well taken?

8. *Recess appointments.* The Recess Appointments Clause of the Constitution provides: "The President shall have Power to fill up all Vacancies that may happen during the Recess of the Senate, by granting Commissions which shall expire at the End of their next Session." Art. II, § 2, cl. 3. Opinions differ as to several aspects of this provision, including whether the President may exercise this power during a recess that occurs *within* a session of the Senate, and also whether the Senate may block recess appointments by holding brief "pro forma" sessions while most senators are away. These and other questions are currently before the Supreme Court in *NLRB v. Noel Canning*, No. 12–1281, a suit challenging the validity of President Obama's use of recess appointments to install three members of the National Labor Relations Board. A decision is expected by the end of the 2013 Term.

9. *Problem.* Each judicial district in the federal court system has a United States Attorney who is the chief federal law enforcement officer for that district. He or she heads an office that prosecutes criminal cases and represents the United States in civil litigation. Normally, U.S. Attorneys are appointed to a four-year term by the President, subject to confirmation by the Senate. However, in the event of a vacancy, the Attorney General may appoint an interim U.S. Attorney to serve for up to 120 days (or less if a replacement is appointed and confirmed within that period). If no successor has qualified for the position when the 120-day period expires, "the district court for such district will appoint a United States Attorney to serve until the vacancy is filled." 28 U.S.C. § 546(d). A U.S. Attorney, whether or not appointed on an interim basis, may be removed only by the President.

Six years ago, Brenda, the chief judge of the U.S. District Court for the District of Madison, appointed Gail as an interim U.S. Attorney. Since then, due to political disagreements between the President and the Senate, no one has been appointed to a regular term as U.S. Attorney for this district, and so Gail has continued to serve in that capacity.

Steve is under federal indictment on drug charges in Madison. He moves to exclude Gail from participating in his prosecution, because her continued service as U.S. Attorney violates the Appointments Clause and the principle of separation of powers. Should his motion be granted? *Cf. United States v. Hilario*, 218 F.3d 19 (1st Cir. 2000); Ross E. Wiener, *Inter-Branch Appointments After the Independent Counsel: Court Appointment of United States Attorneys*, 86 MINN. L. REV. 363 (2001).

§ 7.5.1b State Appointments

1. *Constitutional provisions.* State governors appoint most executive branch officers, some with and some without legislative confirmation. Other state executive branch officials are elected by the voters rather than appointed. In some instances, the governor must share the appointment power with the legislature or other governmental officials. *See* 45 COUNCIL OF STATE GOVERNMENTS, THE BOOK OF THE STATES 171–76 (2013).

These differences among states are partly a result of the wide variety of state constitutional provisions on this subject. "Some [state constitutions] vest a general power to make administrative appointments in the governor . . ., while others leave it to the legislature to decide the method by which officials will be appointed—including, in some cases, reserving that power to itself. . . . [I]n other states the text is, on its face, remarkably unclear. . . ." John Devlin, *Toward a State Constitutional Analysis of Allocation of Powers: Legislators and Legislative Appointees Performing Administrative Functions*, 66 TEMP. L. REV. 1205, 1237–38 (1993).

2. *Separation of powers.* In states in which the constitution does not expressly limit the appointment power to the governor, the courts have resorted to general separation of powers principles in order to sort out the respective prerogatives of the governmental branches. *See id.* at 1242–50. Some state courts have ruled that appointments are inherently executive and, therefore, may only be made by the governor. *See, e.g., Opinion of the Justices*, 309 N.E.2d 476 (Mass. 1974) (holding that neither the legislature nor the judiciary could constitutionally appoint members of a commission with responsibility for setting government-wide policies for electronic data transmissions and telecommunications). Prominent in these cases is the suggestion that, if powers are to remain *separated,* officials who enact the laws should play no role in selecting the personnel who will implement them.

Contrast *Marine Forests Soc'y v. Cal. Coastal Comm'n,* 113 P.3d 1062 (Cal. 2005). That case upheld a statute that provided for appointments to the California Coastal Commission, a powerful state agency that controls all land development within 1000 yards of California's long coastline. The governor appoints four of its twelve members, the Senate Rules Committee appoints four, and the Speaker of the Assembly appoints four. The supreme court declined to follow federal law as expressed in *Buckley v. Valeo*. It explained that the state constitution contains no language like the Appointments Clause of the federal Constitution, and the state has had a long history of legislative appointments. Moreover, the California legislature has plenary power (unlike Congress, which has only limited powers), and the executive function is divided among a number of elected officials (unlike the President, who is a unitary executive).

The court's analysis was ultimately pragmatic. It emphasized that the division of appointive authority between the executive and legislative branches would tend to prevent any one state actor (possibly unsympathetic to coastal regulation) from appointing the entire membership. The court added that the state constitution does impose *some* limits on the legislature's power to give itself appointing authority, although those limits were not transgressed here. The appropriate inquiry, it said, was whether a statute improperly intrudes upon a core zone of executive authority (such as by empowering the legislature to appoint a confidential advisor to the governor) or retains undue legislative control over an appointee's executive actions. The court strongly hinted that the latter circumstance would have been implicated if the legislature had retained the power to *remove* a commissioner who had been legislatively appointed. (In fact, the former version of the statute had indeed asserted such power, but the legislature had deleted that provision after losing an earlier round of this case in the court of appeal.)

3. *Regulating politics.* In cases that, like *Buckley*, involve regulation of the political process, state courts have displayed a variety of approaches. In *Parcell v. State,* 620 P.2d 834 (Kan. 1980), six members of the state Governmental Ethics Commission were appointed by legislative party leaders and five by the governor, although the governor was entitled to appoint its chairperson. The commission's membership had to be balanced with regard to political party affiliation. The commission had rulemaking and report-collecting responsibilities, but could not initiate enforcement actions on its own. Parcell, a political candidate who was under investigation for failing to file campaign reports with the commission, challenged the constitutionality of the agency's composition.

The court endorsed a balancing test consisting of four criteria: (1) the nature of the powers being exercised by the agency; (2) the degree of control being exercised by the legislature; (3) whether the legislature's objective was to cooperate with the executive branch, as opposed to establishing its superiority in an executive domain; and (4) the practical results of this blending of legislative and executive powers. Applying this standard, the court upheld the commission's structure, calling it "a cooperative venture rather than the usurpation of power by the legislative branch from the executive branch." The goal of the underlying legislation was to increase public trust in elected officials, and the appointment scheme " 'gives the Commission needed independence should it be called upon to investigate those officials who appointed some of its members.' "

The court in *State Bd. of Ethics for Elected Officials v. Green,* 566 So.2d 623 (La. 1990), reached a similar result, although the board in that case did have the responsibility for filing suit against suspected violators of the campaign finance disclosure laws. Two members of this board were appointed by the Senate, two by the House, and the fifth had to be a retired or former judge appointed by the governor. The court upheld the scheme because "the appointees are not subject to such significant legislative control that the Legislature can be deemed to be performing executive functions." (Would this structure satisfy the *Parcell* test?)

But a third state supreme court refused to follow *Parcell* and *Green,* noting that its case law has "rejected the notion of a 'blending' of powers in favor of a more strict separation of powers." *Spradlin v. Arkansas Ethics Comm'n,* 858 S.W.2d 684 (Ark. 1993). One member of the election commission had to be appointed by the chief justice of the state. The court held this scheme unconstitutional, because the commission "is not related to the administration of justice and is not part of the judicial department of government." The commission did not act in a judicial capacity, because it could not enter binding orders, as a court does; it could only issue warnings or report findings to law enforcement authorities. Was the case correctly decided?

4. *Legislators as appointees.* Constitutional limits on the ability of the legislature to place its own members in administrative positions tend to be particularly strict. The Incompatibility Clause of the federal Constitution provides: "[N]o Person holding any Office under the United States, shall be a Member of either House during his Continuance in Office." Art. I, § 6, cl.2. Most state constitutions contain similar clauses, although they vary in their stringency. *See* Devlin, *supra,* at 1239–40.

Even when an incompatibility clause does not apply, many state court decisions rely on the separation of powers doctrine to bar legislators from holding executive branch jobs. *See, e.g., State ex rel. Wallace v. Bone,* 286 S.E.2d 79 (N.C. 1982); *Book v. State Office Building Comm'n,* 149 N.E.2d 273 (Ind. 1958); *Greer v. State,* 212 S.E.2d 836 (Ga. 1975). Recall that in the *MWAA* case, § 7.4.1 N.11, the U.S. Supreme Court reached a similar holding on separation of powers grounds, even though it might well have relied on the federal Incompatibility Clause instead. State decisions do not fall easily into any single pattern. *See State ex rel. Schneider v. Bennett,* 547 P.2d 786 (Kan. 1976) (using the same four-factor test as in *Parcell* to uphold "a cooperative effort between the executive department and the legislative department . . . to insure prompt state action in the event of a major disaster"); *J.F. Ahern Co. v. Wis. State Bldg. Comm'n,* 336 N.W.2d 679 (Wis. Ct. App. 1983); *State ex rel. McLeod v. Edwards,* 236 S.E.2d 406 (S.C. 1977). *See generally* Devlin, *supra,* at 1250–64.

A notable episode in Rhode Island raised these issues in a dramatic fashion. For many years the General Assembly exercised control over numerous administrative agencies, by setting up boards of directors to oversee them. The legislature appointed many of these directors (243 members of 73 boards), and legislators themselves were often among the appointees. Thus the Assembly came to dominate some of the most powerful state agencies, including the Coastal Commission, the commission that nominated candidates for judicial appointment, and even the Ethics Commission. In 2000, the state supreme court upheld the composition of the Lottery Commission, a majority of whose members were legislators who had been appointed by the Senate and House leadership. *Almond v. Rhode Island Lottery Comm'n,* 756 A.2d 186 (2000). However, critics of the status quo responded with a grassroots referendum campaign for a constitutional amendment. Proponents of the amendment argued that the concentration of both legislative and executive power in the same officials' hands, with a resulting lack of checks and balances, had given rise to a host of problems, including patronage abuses, petty retaliation against administrators, ineffective regulation of financial institutions, and, as the final straw, the attempted cover-up of a sexual harassment scandal. Ultimately, in November 2004, a referendum to adopt the amendment passed with a vote of 78 percent of the electorate. It instituted an appointments system modeled on the Appointments Clause of the federal Constitution. It also prohibited legislators from serving on a board that wields executive power. *See generally In re Request for Advisory Opinion from the House of Reps. (Coastal Resources Mgmt. Council),* 961 A.2d 930 (R.I. 2008); Carl T. Bogus, *The Battle for Separation of Powers in Rhode Island,* 56 ADMIN. L. REV. 77 (2004).

Consider *Alexander v. State ex rel. Allain,* 441 So.2d 1329 (Miss. 1983). The court invalidated several functions of the Commission on Budget and Accounting, an entity composed of the governor and several legislators. Among these functions was to prepare an executive budget for enactment by the legislature. The court said that, although the governor does submit a budget proposal, and the legislature ultimately adopts a budget, the "constitutional imperative that the powers of government be divided into separate and distinct departments ... renders unconstitutional the organization of any commission or agency on which both legislators and members of the executive branch serve as voting members." Was this holding sound?

5.   *Problem.* A recently enacted Madison statute, S.B. 234, provides that the Chief Justice of the Madison Supreme Court shall appoint the Director of the state's Office of Administrative Hearings (OAH). The Director serves as the chief administrative law judge of the state. Like other ALJs, he hears testimony, applies rules of evidence, and writes findings of fact and conclusions of law in contested cases. These cases might come from any of Madison's administrative agencies. The Director also is responsible for administrative tasks within OAH, such as designating particular ALJs to preside over specific types of cases, hiring hearing officers for certain assignments, and resolving disciplinary complaints against ALJs (including, potentially, removing an ALJ for just cause).

Implementing the new statute, Madison's Chief Justice, Anna, has appointed Gunther to be the Director of OAH. Stuart, a respondent in a license revocation proceeding pending before Gunther, has filed a court action, claiming that Gunther was appointed illegally. He relies on § 1 of the Madison constitution, which provides that "[t]he legislative, executive, and judicial powers of the State government shall be forever separate and distinct from each other." How should Stuart's claim be resolved? *Cf. State ex rel. Martin v. Melott*, 359 S.E.2d 783 (N.C. 1987).

§ 7.5.2 REMOVAL OF OFFICERS

§ 7.5.2a The Rise of the Independent Agency

Except in its provisions on impeachment, the federal Constitution does not expressly speak to the question of removing administrative officials from office. The subject was debated in the first Congress, in the context of legislation that created the position of Secretary of State. Apparently, the sense of Congress in 1789 was that the President could remove the Secretary of State whether Congress gave him removal power or not.

The 1867 Tenure of Office Act challenged the view that the principal officers of government had to serve at the President's pleasure. This statute forbade presidential removal of designated cabinet members without the consent of the Senate. President Andrew Johnson dismissed the Secretary of War, in violation of the Tenure of Office Act. That action led to the President's impeachment by the House; but a Senate vote to convict him failed by a single vote.

The constitutional issues surrounding the Tenure of Office Act did not reach the Supreme Court until *Myers v. United States,* 272 U.S. 52 (1926). The issue arose in connection with a suit for back pay by a postmaster in Oregon whom President Wilson had discharged without cause. The discharge violated a statute (passed a few years after the Tenure of Office Act) that required the consent of the Senate for the appointment and also for the suspension or removal of a postmaster.

Chief Justice Taft (who had earlier been President) wrote for the Court that Congress could not limit the President's removal power over any officer of the United States whom the President had appointed. Consequently, both the Tenure of Office Act (which had long since been repealed) and the statute relating to postmasters were invalid. In part, this holding was grounded on the notion that the power to remove is an incident of the power to appoint. *Id.* at 119. More significantly, the Court emphasized the President's constitutional duty to take care that the laws "be faithfully executed":

> The ordinary duties of officers prescribed by statute come under the general administrative control of the President by virtue of the general grant to him of the executive power, and he may properly supervise and guide their construction of the statutes under which they act in order to secure that unitary and uniform execution of the laws which Article II of the Constitution evidently contemplated in vesting general executive power in the President alone. Laws are often passed with specific provision for the adoption of regulations by a department or bureau head to make the law workable and effective. The ability and judgment manifested by the official thus empowered, as well as his energy and stimulation of his subordinates, are subjects which the President must consider and supervise in his administrative control. Finding such officers to be negligent and inefficient, the President should have the power to remove them. Of course there may be duties so peculiarly and specifically committed to the discretion of a particular officer as to raise a question whether the President may overrule or revise the officer's interpretation of his statutory duty in a particular instance. Then there may be duties of a quasi-judicial character imposed on executive officers and members of executive tribunals whose decisions after hearing affect interests of individuals, the discharge of which the President can not in a particular case properly influence or control. But even in such a case he may consider the decision after its rendition as a reason for removing the officer, on the ground that the discretion regularly entrusted to that officer by statute has not been on the whole intelligently

or wisely exercised. Otherwise he does not discharge his own constitutional duty of seeing that the laws be faithfully executed.

Id. at 135. Less than a decade later, however, the Court was suggesting that some of the language in *Myers* had been too broad.

HUMPHREY'S EXECUTOR V. UNITED STATES
295 U.S. 602 (1935)

[The Federal Trade Commission Act provided that a commissioner could be removed only for "inefficiency, neglect of duty, or malfeasance in office." Despite this limitation, President Roosevelt wrote to request the resignation of the chairman of the FTC, William Humphrey, who had been appointed by President Hoover. Instead of invoking one of the statutory grounds, Roosevelt's letter said: "I do not feel that your mind and my mind go along together on either the policies or the administering of the Federal Trade Commission, and, frankly, I think it is best for the people of the country that I should have a full confidence." The chairman refused to resign, but Roosevelt discharged him. After Humphrey's death, his estate sued to recover his salary. SUTHERLAND, J., wrote for the Court:]

The commission is to be non-partisan; and it must, from the very nature of its duties, act with entire impartiality. It is charged with the enforcement of no policy except the policy of the law.... Like the Interstate Commerce Commission, its members are called upon to exercise the trained judgment of a body of experts "appointed by law and informed by experience." ...

The office of a postmaster is so essentially unlike the office now involved that the decision in the *Myers* case cannot be accepted as controlling our decision here. A postmaster is an executive officer restricted to the performance of executive functions. He is charged with no duty at all related to either the legislative or judicial power....

The Federal Trade Commission is an administrative body created by Congress to carry into effect legislative policies embodied in the statute in accordance with the legislative standard therein prescribed, and to perform other specified duties as a legislative or as a judicial aid. Such a body cannot in any proper sense be characterized as an arm or an eye of the executive. Its duties are performed without executive leave and, in the contemplation of the statute, must be free from executive control. In administering the provisions of the statute in respect of "unfair methods of competition"—that is to say in filling in and administering the details embodied by that general standard—the commission acts in part quasi-legislatively and in part quasi-judicially. ...

We think it plain under the Constitution that illimitable power of removal is not possessed by the President in respect of officers of the character of those just named. The authority of Congress, in creating quasi-legislative or quasi-judicial agencies, to require them to act in discharge of their duties independently of executive control cannot well be doubted; and that authority includes, as an appropriate incident, power to fix the period during which they shall continue in office, and to forbid their removal except for cause in the meantime. For it is quite evident that one who holds his office only during the pleasure of another, cannot be depended upon to maintain an attitude of independence against the latter's will.

NOTES AND QUESTIONS

1.   *Independent agencies.* The *Humphrey's Executor* decision fostered the development of the so-called "independent agencies." The Federal Reserve Board, the Nuclear Regulatory Commission, the Securities and Exchange Commission, and the Federal Communications Commission are familiar examples of agencies that are considered independent and thus not subject to direct presidential control. Theoretically, at least, Congress creates an independent agency in the hope of lessening political influence over its decisions; the idea is that, free of direct executive control, the agency can perform its administrative functions impartially and regulate purely in the public interest. For comprehensive surveys of the independent agencies and the principles under which they operate, see DAVID E. LEWIS & JENNIFER L. SELIN, SOURCEBOOK OF UNITED STATES EXECUTIVE AGENCIES 46–59 (ACUS 2012); Marshall J. Breger & Gary J. Edles, *Established by Practice: The Theory and Operation of Independent Federal Agencies*, 52 ADMIN. L. REV. 1111 (2000). Congress has codified a list of agencies that are generally regarded as independent. 44 U.S.C. § 3502(5).

The most fundamental characteristic of an independent agency is that its head or heads may not be removed by the President, except for "good cause." In that respect such agencies differ from "executive" agencies, whose top officers serve at the pleasure of the President. Independent agencies are usually constituted as multi-member boards or commissions. (But not all of them: for example, the Social Security Administration was reorganized in 1994 as an "independent agency within the executive branch," headed by a single Commissioner.) Statutory requirements of staggered terms and party balance among the members of these agencies are intended to bolster their independence. The executive branch agencies, on the other hand, are typically Cabinet departments, headed by a Secretary. (But not all of them: for example, the EPA is an executive branch agency, but not a Cabinet department.)

Some jurists and commentators argue that the concept of agency "independence" should be defined by a cluster of attributes, no one of which is crucial. *See Free Enter. Fund v. PCAOB*, 130 S. Ct. 3138, 3183 (2010) (Breyer,

J., dissenting); Kirti Datla & Richard L. Revesz, *Deconstructing Independent Agencies (and Executive Agencies)*, 98 CORNELL L. REV. 769 (2013); Lisa Schultz Bressman & Robert B. Thompson, *The Future of Agency Independence*, 63 VAND. L. REV. 599 (2010) (exploring the emergence of "hybrid agencies," especially in financial regulation). However, the association of independent agencies with tenure protections is at least roughly correct, and it is the premise on which much constitutional doctrine has been built. *See* Adrian Vermeule, *Conventions of Agency Independence*, 113 COLUM. L. REV. 1163, 1168–81 (2013).

2. *Supreme Court analysis.* Do you agree with *Myers* that the separation of powers doctrine should guarantee the President the right to discharge some administrative officers, even if Congress has legislated to the contrary? If so, how persuasively did *Humphrey's Executor* delimit the circumstances in which Congress may prescribe "independence"? Can one effectively distinguish between the "purely executive" administrative functions performed by Myers and the "quasi-legislative" and "quasi-adjudicative" functions performed by Humphrey? Cf. *City of Arlington v. FCC*, 133 S. Ct. 1863, 1873 n.4 (2013) (Scalia, J.) ("Agencies make rules . . . and conduct adjudications . . . and have done so since the beginning of the Republic. These activities take 'legislative' and 'judicial' forms, but they are exercises of—indeed, under our constitutional structure they *must be* exercises of—the 'executive Power.' Art. II, § 1, cl. 1."). Indeed, why should Congress be allowed to set up *any* "independent agencies" that are outside the direct control of the President? *See generally* Peter M. Shane, *Independent Policymaking and Presidential Power: A Constitutional Analysis*, 57 GEO. WASH. L. REV. 596 (1989); Peter L. Strauss, *The Place of Agencies in Government: Separation of Powers and the Fourth Branch*, 84 COLUM. L. REV. 573, 611–16 (1984).

3. *Removal of adjudicators.* In *Wiener v. United States,* 357 U.S. 349 (1958), the Court invalidated President Eisenhower's removal of a member of the War Claims Commission. Congress had established the commission, with a three year life span, to resolve claims concerning injuries to person or property during World War II. The statute said nothing about the circumstances under which a commissioner could be removed. The Court held, however, that because the Commission had been created to "adjudicate according to law," the philosophy of *Humphrey's Executor* precluded the President from removing its members simply because he wanted his own appointees to serve instead.

Does it make sense for the Court to have implied a right of tenure where Congress did not see fit to specify one? Can the logic of *Wiener* be extended to justify tenure for members of agencies that perform a wider range of functions than the War Claims Commission did, such as the FCC and SEC?

4. *The significance of independence.* In practice, independent agencies and executive agencies have important similarities as well as important differences. *See, e.g.,* Susan Bartlett Foote, *Independent Agencies Under*

Attack: A Skeptical View of the Importance of the Debate," 1988 DUKE L.J. 223, 232–37; Glen O. Robinson, *Independent Agencies: Form and Substance in Executive Prerogative,* 1988 DUKE L.J. 238, 241–50; Strauss, *supra,* at 583–96. The similarities are particularly evident in routine operations. Both kinds of agencies function in about the same way (carrying out rulemaking, adjudication, and law enforcement) and are subject identically to the APA and to judicial review. Indeed, most of the principles of law discussed in this book apply identically to independent and executive agencies. In addition, all agencies are staffed (below the top levels) by civil service employees, who are protected against discharge except for cause (and thus often resist new initiatives).

At the policymaking level, agency structure often makes more of a difference, especially in independent agencies with bipartisan membership requirements. According to one study, recent trends toward polarization in national politics are augmenting the disparities: "[I]t is taking Presidents longer and longer to appoint a majority of commissioners from their political party. Furthermore, opposition-party commissioners are not turncoats loyal to the President who appoints them; instead, today's opposition-party commissioners are ideological partisans committed to the agenda of the opposition party. Thus, statutory limits on the President's appointment and removal powers are effective: opposition-party members do not share the President's priorities and Presidents are unable to quickly appoint a majority of commissioners. . . . At the same time, party polarization also explains why today's independent agencies are more likely to agree with presidential preferences once the President appoints a majority of his party to the agency." Neal Devins & David E. Lewis, *Not-So Independent Agencies: Party Polarization and the Limits of Institutional Design,* 88 B.U.L. REV. 459, 461 (2008).

In other respects, also, independent agencies do appear to have somewhat more autonomy from presidential control than executive branch agencies have. In addition to their protection from removal without cause, the heads of independent agencies typically appoint the agency staff on their own authority; in executive agencies, the White House often plays a larger role in staffing decisions. Moreover, independent agencies tend to have somewhat greater authority to conduct their own litigation than executive branch agencies. The White House has to date exempted the independent agencies from formal participation in executive oversight of rulemaking proceedings (*see* § 7.6 N.6). They also can face less scrutiny of their communications with Congress, such as through advance submission of draft statutes or testimony. *See* Strauss, *supra,* at 589–90.

But even this distinction can be exaggerated. All agencies submit budgetary requests each year to the Office of Management and Budget, and all are treated alike in the President's budget as submitted to Congress. In addition, the President usually has power to choose which of the several agency heads of multi-member independent agencies will be the chair. The chair, who makes a great many important practical decisions for the agency, is likely to be a person with whom the President has a good working relationship. In short, the de facto independence of an agency from presidential control can depend more on political factors than on whether the agency is formally independent. *Id.* at 583–596. According to Foote, *supra,* at 237:

> Does the structure of administrative agencies matter? My answer is a resounding "it depends." Independence is one factor among many in the complex political environment in which regulatory policy is made. When Congress is strong, it can impose its imprint on the structure of the administrative state through the creation of independent agencies. When the balance of power shifts, however, formal structures cannot prevent pressure, even domination, by the executive branch. There are many other critical factors that influence regulatory outcomes, including powerful business interests and the public at large. . . . Separation of powers may be of greater importance to constitutional theorists than to regulators.

§ 7.5.2b Removal Issues in the Modern Era

Humphrey's Executor has always been a controversial decision. During the 1980s, criticism of the case became particularly prominent. Proponents of the so-called "unitary executive" theory maintained that all agencies that perform functions of an executive nature should be under the effective control of the President. *See FTC v. American National Cellular, Inc.,* 810 F.2d 1511 (9th Cir. 1987) (rejecting an attempt to litigate anew the constitutionality of the FTC's independent status); Geoffrey P. Miller, *Independent Agencies,* 1986 SUP. CT. REV. 41. Acting in an atypical context, the Supreme Court responded to this debate in the following case.

MORRISON v. OLSON

487 U.S. 654 (1988)

[The 1978 Ethics in Government Act created a special court (the Special Division) that was authorized, in response to a request by the Attorney General, to appoint an independent counsel to investigate and prosecute possible violations of federal law by certain high ranking government officials. The Act provided that the Attorney General could remove the independent counsel, but only for "good cause." Pursuant to the procedures outlined in the Act, the Special Division appointed Morrison an independent counsel to investigate Assistant Attorney General Olson's alleged obstruction of a congressional inquiry. Olson moved to quash certain subpoenas issued by a grand jury at Morrison's request. He argued that the Act creating the office of independent counsel was unconstitutional and, therefore, that Morrison had no authority to proceed. The district court held that the Act was valid. The court of appeals reversed, holding that the Act violated the Appointments Clause and the principle of separation of powers. In an opinion joined by seven members of the Supreme Court, REHNQUIST, C.J., first rejected the Appointments Clause challenge, *see* § 7.5.1 N.2, and then continued:]

We now turn to consider whether the Act is invalid under the constitutional principle of separation of powers. Two related issues must be addressed. The first is whether the provision of the Act restricting the Attorney General's power to remove the independent counsel to only those instances in which he can show "good cause," taken by itself, impermissibly interferes with the President's exercise of his constitutionally appointed functions. The second is whether, taken as a whole, the Act violates the separation of powers by reducing the President's ability to control the prosecutorial powers wielded by the independent counsel. . . .

Unlike both *Bowsher [v. Synar,* 478 U.S. 714 (1986),] and *Myers,* this case does not involve an attempt by Congress itself to gain a role in the removal of executive officials other than its established powers of impeachment and conviction. The Act instead puts the removal power squarely in the hands of the Executive Branch; an independent counsel may be removed from office "only by the personal action of the Attorney General, and only for good cause." There is no requirement of congressional approval of the Attorney General's removal decision, though the decision is subject to judicial review. In our view, the removal provisions of the Act make this case more analogous to *Humphrey's Executor v. United States,* 295 U.S. 602 (1935), and *Wiener v. United States,* 357 U.S. 349 (1958), than to *Myers* or *Bowsher.* . . .

Appellees contend that *Humphrey's Executor* and *Wiener* are distinguishable from this case because they did not involve officials who performed a "core executive function." They argue that our decision in *Humphrey's Executor* rests on a distinction between "purely executive" officials and officials who exercise "quasi-legislative" and "quasi-judicial" powers. In their view, when a "purely executive" official is involved, the governing precedent is *Myers,* not *Humphrey's Executor.* And, under *Myers,* the President must have absolute discretion to discharge "purely" executive officials at will.

We undoubtedly did rely on the terms "quasi-legislative" and "quasi-judicial" to distinguish the officials involved in *Humphrey's Executor* and *Wiener* from those in *Myers,* but our present considered view is that the determination of whether the Constitution allows Congress to impose a "good cause"-type restriction on the President's power to remove an official cannot be made to turn on whether or not that official is classified as "purely executive." The analysis contained in our removal cases is designed not to define rigid categories of those officials who may or may not be removed at will by the President,[28] but to ensure that Congress does not interfere with the President's exercise of the "executive power" and his constitutionally appointed duty to "take care that the laws be faithfully executed" under Article II. *Myers* was undoubtedly correct in its holding, and in its broader suggestion that there are some "purely executive" officials who must be removable by the President at will if he is to be able to accomplish his constitutional role. But as the Court noted in *Wiener,*

> The assumption was short-lived that the *Myers* case recognized the President's inherent constitutional power to remove officials no matter what the relation of the executive to the discharge of their duties and no matter what restrictions Congress may have imposed regarding the nature of their tenure.

At the other end of the spectrum from *Myers,* the characterization of the agencies in *Humphrey's Executor* and *Wiener* as "quasi-legislative" or "quasi-judicial" in large part reflected our judgment that it was not essential to the President's proper execution of his Article II powers that these agencies be headed up by individuals who were removable at will.[30] We do not mean to suggest that an analysis of the functions served by the officials at issue is irrelevant. But the real question is whether the removal restrictions are of such a nature that they impede the President's ability to perform his constitutional duty, and the functions of the officials in question must be analyzed in that light.

Considering for the moment the "good cause" removal provision in isolation from the other parts of the Act at issue in this case, we cannot say that the imposition of a "good cause" standard for removal by itself unduly trammels on executive authority. There is no real dispute that the functions performed by the independent counsel are "executive" in the sense that they are law enforcement functions that typically have been undertaken by officials within the Executive Branch. As we noted above, however, the independent counsel is an inferior officer under the Appointments Clause, with limited jurisdiction and tenure and lacking policymaking or significant administrative authority. Although the counsel exercises no small amount of discretion and judgment in deciding how to carry out her duties under the Act, we simply do not see how the President's need to control the exercise of that discretion is so central to the functioning of the Executive Branch as to require as a matter of

---

[28] . . . [I]t is hard to dispute that the powers of the FTC at the time of *Humphrey's Executor* would at the present time be considered "executive," at least in some degree.

[30] The terms also may be used to describe the circumstances in which Congress might be more inclined to find that a degree of independence from the Executive, such as that afforded by a "good cause" removal standard, is necessary to the proper functioning of the agency or official. It is not difficult to imagine situations in which Congress might desire that an official performing "quasi-judicial" functions, for example, would be free of executive or political control.

constitutional law that the counsel be terminable at will by the President.[31]

Nor do we think that the "good cause" removal provision at issue here impermissibly burdens the President's power to control or supervise the independent counsel, as an executive official, in the execution of her duties under the Act. This is not a case in which the power to remove an executive official has been completely stripped from the President, thus providing no means for the President to ensure the "faithful execution" of the laws. Rather, because the independent counsel may be terminated for "good cause," the Executive, through the Attorney General, retains ample authority to assure that the counsel is competently performing her statutory responsibilities in a manner that comports with the provisions of the Act.[32] Although we need not decide in this case exactly what is encompassed within the term "good cause" under the Act, the legislative history of the removal provision also makes clear that the Attorney General may remove an independent counsel for "misconduct." Here, as with the provision of the Act conferring the appointment authority of the independent counsel on the special court, the congressional determination to limit the removal power of the Attorney General was essential, in the view of Congress, to establish the necessary independence of the office. We do not think that this limitation as it presently stands sufficiently deprives the President of control over the independent counsel to interfere impermissibly with his constitutional obligation to ensure the faithful execution of the laws.

The final question to be addressed is whether the Act, taken as a whole, violates the principle of separation of powers by unduly interfering with the role of the Executive Branch. Time and again we have reaffirmed the importance in our constitutional scheme of the separation of governmental powers into the three coordinate branches. . . . On the other hand, we have never held that the Constitution requires that the three Branches of Government "operate with absolute independence." . . . In the often-quoted words of Justice Jackson,

> "While the Constitution diffuses power the better to secure liberty, it also contemplates that practice will integrate the dispersed powers into a workable government. It enjoins upon its

---

[31] We note by way of comparison that various federal agencies whose officers are covered by "good cause" removal restrictions exercise civil enforcement powers that are analogous to the prosecutorial powers wielded by an independent counsel. See, *e.g.*, 15 U.S.C. § 45(m) (giving the FTC the authority to bring civil actions to recover civil penalties for the violations of rules respecting unfair competition); 15 U.S.C. §§ 2061, 2071, 2076(b)(7)(A) (giving the Consumer Product Safety Commission the authority to obtain injunctions and apply for seizure of hazardous products).

[32] Indeed, during the hearings on the 1982 amendments to the Act, a Justice Department official testified that the "good cause" standard contained in the amendments "would make the special prosecutor no more independent than officers of the many so-called independent agencies in the executive branch."

branches separateness but interdependence, autonomy but reciprocity." *Youngstown Sheet & Tube Co. v. Sawyer,* 343 U.S. 579, 635 (1952) (concurring opinion).

We observe first that this case does not involve an attempt by Congress to increase its own powers at the expense of the Executive Branch. Unlike some of our previous cases, most recently *Bowsher v. Synar,* this case simply does not pose a "dange[r] of congressional usurpation of Executive Branch functions." Indeed, with the exception of the power of impeachment—which applies to all officers of the United States—Congress retained for itself no powers of control or supervision over an independent counsel. . . .

Similarly, we do not think that the Act works any *judicial* usurpation of properly executive functions. . . .

Finally, we do not think that the Act "impermissibly undermine[s]" the powers of the Executive Branch, or "disrupts the proper balance between the coordinate branches [by] prevent[ing] the Executive Branch from accomplishing its constitutionally assigned functions." It is undeniable that the Act reduces the amount of control or supervision that the Attorney General and, through him, the President exercises over the investigation and prosecution of a certain class of alleged criminal activity. The Attorney General is not allowed to appoint the individual of his choice; he does not determine the counsel's jurisdiction; and his power to remove a counsel is limited. Nonetheless, the Act does give the Attorney General several means of supervising or controlling the prosecutorial powers that may be wielded by an independent counsel. Most importantly, the Attorney General retains the power to remove the counsel for "good cause," a power that we have already concluded provides the Executive with substantial ability to ensure that the laws are "faithfully executed" by an independent counsel. No independent counsel may be appointed without a specific request by the Attorney General, and the Attorney General's decision not to request appointment if he finds "no reasonable grounds to believe that further investigation is warranted" is committed to his unreviewable discretion. The Act thus gives the Executive a degree of control over the power to initiate an investigation by the independent counsel. In addition, the jurisdiction of the independent counsel is defined with reference to the facts submitted by the Attorney General, and once a counsel is appointed, the Act requires that the counsel abide by Justice Department policy unless it is not "possible" to do so. Notwithstanding the fact that the counsel is to some degree "independent" and free from Executive supervision to a greater extent than other federal prosecutors, in our view these features of the Act give the Executive Branch sufficient control over the independent counsel to ensure that the President is able to perform his constitutionally assigned duties.

In sum, we conclude today that ... the Act does not violate the separation of powers principle by impermissibly interfering with the functions of the Executive Branch. The decision of the Court of Appeals is therefore

Reversed.

SCALIA, J., dissenting.

[Justice Scalia emphasized that in separation of powers disputes between Congress and the President, neither can be presumed to be correct. Then he stressed that Article II, § 1, cl. 1 of the Constitution vests the executive power in *the President.* His dissent continued:]

As I described at the outset of this opinion, this does not mean *some of* the executive power, but *all of* the executive power. It seems to me, therefore, that the decision of the Court of Appeals invalidating the present statute must be upheld on fundamental separation-of-powers principles if the following two questions are answered affirmatively: (1) Is the conduct of a criminal prosecution (and of an investigation to decide whether to prosecute) the exercise of purely executive power? (2) Does the statute deprive the President of the United States of exclusive control over the exercise of that power? Surprising to say, the Court appears to concede an affirmative answer to both questions, but seeks to avoid the inevitable conclusion that since the statute vests some purely executive power in a person who is not the President of the United States it is void.

The Court concedes that "[t]here is no real dispute that the functions performed by the independent counsel are 'executive'." ... Governmental investigation and prosecution of crimes is a quintessentially executive function.

As for the second question, whether the statute before us deprives the President of exclusive control over that quintessentially executive activity: The Court does not, and could not possibly, assert that it does not. That is indeed the whole object of the statute. Instead, the Court points out that the President, through his Attorney General, has at least *some* control. That concession is alone enough to invalidate the statute, but I cannot refrain from pointing out that the Court greatly exaggerates the extent of that "some" presidential control. "Most importan[t]" among these controls, the Court asserts, is the Attorney General's "power to remove the counsel for 'good cause.'" This is somewhat like referring to shackles as an effective means of locomotion. As we recognized in *Humphrey's Executor v. United States,* 295 U.S. 602 (1935)—indeed, what *Humphrey's Executor* was all about—limiting removal power to "good cause" is an impediment to, not an effective grant of, presidential control.... Congress, of course, operated under no such illusion when it enacted this statute, describing the "good cause" limitation as "protecting the independent counsel's ability to act independently of the President's direct control" since it permits removal only for "misconduct."

Moving on to the presumably "less important" controls that the President retains, the Court notes that no independent counsel may be appointed without a specific request from the Attorney General. As I have discussed above, the condition that renders such a request mandatory (inability to find "no reasonable grounds to believe" that further investigation is warranted) is so insubstantial that the Attorney General's discretion is severely confined. And once the referral is made, it is for the Special Division to determine the scope and duration of the investigation. And in any event, the limited power over referral is irrelevant to the question whether, *once appointed,* the independent counsel exercises executive power free from the President's control. Finally, the Court points out that the Act directs the independent counsel to abide by general Justice Department policy, except when not "possible." The exception alone shows this to be an empty promise. . . . Almost all investigative and prosecutorial decisions—including the ultimate decision whether, after a technical violation of the law has been found, prosecution is warranted—involve the balancing of innumerable legal and practical considerations. [This balancing] is the very essence of prosecutorial discretion. To take this away is to remove the core of the prosecutorial function, and not merely "some" presidential control.

As I have said, however, it is ultimately irrelevant *how much* the statute reduces presidential control. . . . We should say here that the President's constitutionally assigned duties include *complete* control over investigation and prosecution of violations of the law, and that the inexorable command of Article II is clear and definite: the executive power must be vested in the President of the United States. . . .

The Court has, nonetheless, replaced the clear constitutional prescription that the executive power belongs to the President with a "balancing test." What are the standards to determine how the balance is to be struck, that is, how much removal of presidential power is too much? Once we depart from the text of the Constitution, just where short of that do we stop? The most amazing feature of the Court's opinion is that it does not even purport to give an answer. . . .

In my view, moreover, even as an ad hoc, standardless judgment the Court's conclusion must be wrong. . . . Perhaps the boldness of the President himself will not be affected—though I am not even sure of that. (How much easier it is for Congress, instead of accepting the political damage attendant to the commencement of impeachment proceedings against the President on trivial grounds—or, for that matter, how easy it is for one of the President's political foes outside of Congress—simply to trigger a debilitating criminal investigation of the Chief Executive under this law.) But as for the President's high-level assistants, who typically have no political base of support, it is as utterly unrealistic to think that they will not be intimidated by this prospect, and that their advice to him and their advocacy of his interests before a hostile Congress will not be affected, as it would be to think that the Members of Congress and their staffs would be unaffected by replacing the Speech or Debate Clause with a similar provision. It deeply wounds the President, by substantially reducing the President's ability to protect himself and his staff. That is the whole object of the law, of course, and I cannot imagine why the Court believes it does not succeed.

Besides weakening the Presidency by reducing the zeal of his staff, it must also be obvious that the institution of the independent counsel enfeebles him more directly in his constant confrontations with Congress, by eroding his public support. Nothing is so politically effective as the ability to charge that one's opponent and his associates are not merely wrongheaded, naive, ineffective, but, in all probability, "crooks." And nothing so effectively gives an appearance of validity to such charges as a Justice Department investigation and, even better, prosecution. The present statute provides ample means for that sort of attack, assuring that massive and lengthy investigations will occur, not merely when the Justice Department in the application of its usual standards believes they are called for, but whenever it cannot be said that there are "no reasonable grounds to believe" they are called for. The statute's highly visible procedures assure, moreover, that unlike most investigations these will be widely known and prominently displayed. . . .

Since our 1935 decision in *Humphrey's Executor v. United States*, . . . it has been established that the line of permissible restriction upon removal of principal officers lies at the point at which the powers exercised by those officers are no longer purely executive. Thus, removal restrictions have been generally regarded as lawful for so-called "independent regulatory agencies," such as the Federal Trade Commission, the Interstate Commerce Commission, and the Consumer Products Safety Commission, which engage substantially in what has been called the "quasi-legislative activity" of rulemaking, and for members of Article I courts, such as the Court of Military Appeals, who engage in the "quasi-judicial" function of adjudication. It has often been observed, correctly in my view, that the line between "purely executive" functions and "quasi-legislative" or "quasi-judicial" functions is not a clear one or even a rational one. But at least it permitted the identification of certain officers, and certain agencies, whose functions were entirely within the control of the President. Congress had to be aware of that restriction in its legislation. Today, however, *Humphrey's Executor* is swept into the dustbin of repudiated constitutional principles. "[O]ur present considered view," the Court says, "is that the determination of whether the Constitution allows Congress to impose a 'good cause'-type restriction on the President's power to remove an official cannot be made to turn on whether or not that official is classified as 'purely executive.' " What *Humphrey's Executor* (and presumably *Myers*) really means, we are now told, is not that there are any "rigid categories of those officials who may or may not be removed at will by the President," but simply that Congress cannot "interfere with the President's exercise of the 'executive power' and his constitutionally appointed duty to 'take care that the laws be faithfully executed.' "

. . . There are now no lines. If the removal of a prosecutor, the virtual embodiment of the power to "take care that the laws be faithfully executed," can be restricted, what officer's removal cannot? This is an open invitation for Congress to experiment. What about a special Assistant Secretary of State, with responsibility for one very narrow area of foreign policy, who would not only have to be confirmed by the Senate but could also be removed only pursuant to certain carefully designed restrictions? Could this possibly render the President "[un]able to accomplish his constitutional role"? Or a special Assistant Secretary of Defense for Procurement? The possibilities are endless, and the Court does not understand what the separation of powers, what "[a]mbition . . . counteract[ing] ambition," Federalist No. 51 (Madison), is all about, if it does not expect Congress to try them. . . .

Only someone who has worked in the field of law enforcement can fully appreciate the vast power and the immense discretion that are placed in the hands of a prosecutor with respect to the objects of his investigation. . . . Under our system of government, the primary check against prosecutorial abuse is a political one. The prosecutors who exercise this awesome discretion are selected and can be removed by a President, whom the people have trusted enough to elect. Moreover, when crimes are not investigated and prosecuted fairly, nonselectively, with a reasonable sense of proportion, the President pays the cost in political damage to his administration. . . . The President is directly dependent on the people, and since there is only *one* President, *he* is responsible. The people know whom to blame, whereas "one of the weightiest objections to a plurality in the executive . . . is that it tends to conceal faults and destroy responsibility." [Federalist No. 70 (Hamilton).] . . .

That is the system of justice the rest of us are entitled to, but what of that select class consisting of present or former high-level Executive Branch officials? . . . An independent counsel is selected, and the scope of his or her authority prescribed, by a panel of judges. What if they are politically partisan, as judges have been known to be, and select a prosecutor antagonistic to the administration, or even to the particular individual who has been selected for this special treatment? There is no remedy for that, not even a political one. . . .

[A]n additional advantage of the unitary Executive [is] that it can achieve a more uniform application of the law. Perhaps that is not always achieved, but the mechanism to achieve it is there. The mini-Executive that is the independent counsel, however, operating in an area where so little is law and so much is discretion, is intentionally cut off from the unifying influence of the Justice Department, and from the perspective that multiple responsibilities provide. What would normally be regarded as a technical violation (there are no rules defining such things), may in his or her small world assume the proportions of an indictable offense. What would normally be regarded as an investigation that has reached the level of pursuing such picayune matters that it should be concluded, may to him or her be an investigation that ought to go on for another year. How frightening it must be to have your own independent counsel and staff appointed, with nothing else to do but to investigate you until investigation is no longer worthwhile—with whether it is worthwhile not depending upon what such judgments usually hinge on, competing responsibilities. And to have that counsel and staff decide, with no basis for comparison, whether what you have done is bad enough, willful enough, and provable enough, to warrant an indictment. How admirable the constitutional system that provides the means to avoid such a distortion. And how unfortunate the judicial decision that has permitted it.

. . . Today's decision on the basic issue of fragmentation of executive power is ungoverned by rule, and hence ungoverned by law. It extends into the very heart of our most significant constitutional function the "totality of the circumstances" mode of analysis that this Court has in recent years become fond of. Taking all things into account, we conclude that the power taken away from the President here is not really *too* much. The next time executive power is assigned to someone other than the President we may conclude, taking all things into account, that it *is* too much. . . . This is not analysis; it is ad hoc judgment. . . . I prefer to rely upon the judgment of the wise men who constructed our system, and of the people who approved it, and of two centuries of history that have shown it to be sound. Like it or not, that judgment says, quite plainly, that "[t]he executive Power shall be vested in a President of the United States."

NOTES AND QUESTIONS

1. *Morrison.* Does the Court's analysis in *Morrison* satisfactorily explain its holding on the removal issue? How can one tell whether a removal restriction "impede[s] the President's ability to perform his constitutional duty"? And does *Morrison* constitute, as Justice Scalia charges, an invitation to Congress to experiment with giving tenure to numerous other officers, such as assistant secretaries in the State or Defense Department? If you find

the Court's reasoning unconvincing, could the result be justified on a stronger basis? (Consider, as one possibility, the somewhat different separation of powers test articulated in *Nixon v. Administrator of General Services,* 433 U.S. 425, 433 (1977), quoted in Justice White's dissent in *Chadha.*)

In the years following *Morrison,* the "unitary executive" theory has continued to attract spirited support from some scholars and spirited opposition from others. *See generally* Symposium, *Presidential Power in Historical Perspective: Reflections on Calabresi and Yoo's the Unitary Executive,* 12 U. PA. J. CONST. L. 241 (2010). The theory has also been invoked from time to time by presidential administrations, most notably that of President George W. Bush. *See* § 7.6 N.8. Is *Morrison* compatible with that theory?

2. *Demise of the independent counsel statute.* On June 30, 1999, the independent counsel provisions of the Ethics in Government Act automatically expired when Congress failed to renew them. The decision to allow the statute to expire was supported by legislative leaders of both parties, as well as by the Justice Department and even Independent Counsel Kenneth Starr (although his investigation of President Clinton did not end immediately, because the expiration of the law did not affect independent counsel who had already been appointed). Some twenty independent counsel had been appointed under the expired Act and had collectively spent an estimated $150 million on investigations and prosecutions. *See generally* Panel, *The Independent Counsel Statute,* 51 ADMIN. L. REV. 627 (1999).

Does hindsight indicate that the independent counsel statute did "impede the President's ability to perform his constitutional duty," and thus should have been declared unconstitutional after all, on the basis of the *Morrison* Court's own standard?

3. *Legislative removal.* While *Humphrey's Executor, Wiener,* and *Morrison* declare that Congress may limit the President's power to remove some agency officials, it does not follow that Congress may retain for itself the power to remove officials engaged in administrative functions. Indeed, Congress lacks that power, according to *Bowsher v. Synar,* 478 U.S. 714 (1986), which is discussed in *Morrison.* There the Court struck down part of the Gramm-Rudman Act, a budget-balancing measure enacted in 1985. The Act provided for an automatic reduction in appropriations for nearly all federal spending programs if the projected budget deficit for a particular year exceeded a certain level. (This same mechanism was later incorporated into the Budget Control Act of 2011 and became the basis for deep budget cuts known as "sequestration" beginning in 2013.)

But who would be responsible for making the complex and difficult estimate of the size of the projected deficit? The Act assigned this determination to the Comptroller General, who heads the Government Accountability Office. Under the 1921 law which created that post, the Comptroller General may be removed by a joint congressional resolution (which the President could veto) for inefficiency, neglect of duty, or malfeasance. However, Congress had never exercised this power or even threatened to do so.

The Court held that the Comptroller General's duties under the Act were clearly "executive" in nature: "Interpreting a law enacted by Congress to implement the legislative mandate is the very essence of 'execution' of the law." Thus, since Congress had reserved the right to remove the Comptroller General (by a route other than impeachment), it had in effect retained control over the execution of the law. Such control was unacceptable, because of "the command of the Constitution that the Congress play no direct role in the execution of the laws."

In a concurring opinion, Justice Stevens, joined by Justice Marshall, argued that the real flaw in the Gramm-Rudman Act was that the Comptroller General was an agent of Congress. That officer was part of the legislative branch not only because the authority to remove him was vested in Congress, but also, and much more importantly, because most of his other duties were intended to aid Congress in the process of passing laws and appropriating money. But, the concurrence continued, when Congress seeks to make policy that will bind the nation, it must do so by following Article I legislative procedures, as *Chadha* had held. The same must be true when Congress delegates power to one of its own agents rather than to the Executive or an independent agency.

Justice White's dissent argued that the carefully limited and never used congressional power to remove the Comptroller was of no practical significance. There was no genuine likelihood that the Comptroller General would be subservient to Congress. Justice Blackmun's dissent argued that the Court should strike down the removal power by stating that it would refuse to uphold a removal and save the Gramm-Rudman Act.

Of course, *Bowsher* only denies Congress a *formal* role in discharging agency officials. On an informal level, members of Congress can exert enormous influence on an administration's decisions about whether particular agency officials will stay or go. It has even been suggested that "congressional pressure is responsible for more firings and reassignments of executive branch personnel than is presidential action." *See* LOUIS FISHER, CONSTITUTIONAL CONFLICTS BETWEEN CONGRESS AND THE PRESIDENT 80 (5th ed. 2007).

4.   *Dual-level removal protection.* In *Free Enterprise Fund v. PCAOB*, 130 S.Ct. 3138 (2010), the Court announced new limits on Congress's ability to confer tenure protection on executive officials. The case was an outgrowth of the Sarbanes-Oxley Act of 2002, which Congress had adopted in the wake of a string of company failures that had been facilitated by questionable accounting practices. Among other measures, the Act created a new entity, the Public Company Accounting Oversight Board, to write rules for the accounting profession, audit individual firms, and investigate and adjudicate discipline cases. The Securities and Exchange Commission had authority to disapprove or revise any of the Board's rules and sanctions.

The Court focused on the fact that the Board members were appointed by the SEC, which could remove them only for cause. The majority also assumed that the SEC members themselves could be removed by the President only for cause. In an opinion by Chief Justice Roberts, the Court held "that the dual for-cause limitations on the removal of Board members contravene the Constitution's separation of powers." He elaborated:

> The added layer of tenure protection makes a difference. Without a layer of insulation between the Commission and the Board, the Commission could remove a Board member at any time, and therefore would be fully responsible for what the Board does. The President could then hold the Commission to account for its supervision of the Board, to the same extent that he may hold the Commission to account for everything else it does. . . .
>
> A second level of tenure protection changes the nature of the President's review. . . . The Commissioners are not responsible for the Board's actions. They are only responsible for their own determination of whether the Act's rigorous good-cause standard is met. And even if the President disagrees with their determination, he is powerless to intervene—unless that determination is so unreasonable as to constitute "inefficiency, neglect of duty, or malfeasance in office." *Humphrey's Executor*. . . .
>
> By granting the Board executive power without the Executive's oversight, this Act subverts the President's ability to ensure that the laws are faithfully executed—as well as the public's ability to pass judgment on his efforts.

To cure the constitutional violation, the Court struck down the Act's provision under which the SEC could remove Board members only for "cause." Thus, the members would be subject to one level of tenure protection rather than two. See § 7.5.2a N.5.

Justice Breyer, joined by Justices Stevens, Ginsburg, and Sotomayor, dissented, arguing in part:

> [T]he "for cause" restriction before us will not restrict presidential power significantly. For one thing, the restriction directly limits, not the President's power, but the power of an already independent agency. . . . [S]o long as the President is *legitimately* foreclosed from removing the *Commissioners* except for cause (as the majority assumes), nullifying the Commission's power to remove Board members only for cause will not resolve the problem the Court has identified: The President will *still* be "powerless to intervene" by removing the Board members if the Commission reasonably decides not to do so.
>
> In other words, the Court fails to show why *two* layers of "for cause" protection . . . impose any more serious limitation upon the *President's* powers than *one* layer. . . .

At the same time, Congress and the President had good reason for enacting the challenged "for cause" provision. First and foremost, the Board adjudicates cases. This Court has long recognized the appropriateness of using "for cause" provisions to protect the personal independence of those who even only sometimes engage in adjudicatory functions. *Humphrey's Executor*; see also *Wiener*. . . .

Moreover, in addition to their adjudicative functions, the Accounting Board members supervise, and are themselves, technical professional experts. . . . [H]istorically, this regulatory subject matter—financial regulation—has been thought to exhibit a particular need for independence. . . .

. . . [G]iven *Morrison,* where the Court upheld a restriction that significantly interfered with the President's important historic power to control criminal prosecutions, a "'purely executive'" function, the constitutionality of the present restriction would seem to follow *a fortiori*. . . . [T]he Accounting Board's adjudicatory responsibilities, the technical nature of its job, the need to attract experts to that job, and the importance of demonstrating the nonpolitical nature of the job to the public strongly justify a statute that assures that Board members need not fear for their jobs when competently carrying out their tasks, while still maintaining the Commission as the ultimate authority over Board policies and actions.

The majority responded:

According to the dissent, Congress may impose multiple levels of for-cause tenure between the President and his subordinates when it "rests agency independence upon the need for technical expertise." . . . No one doubts Congress's power to create a vast and varied federal bureaucracy. But where, in all this, is the role for oversight by an elected President? . . .

One can have a government that functions without being ruled by functionaries, and a government that benefits from expertise without being ruled by experts. Our Constitution was adopted to enable the people to govern themselves, through their elected leaders. The growth of the Executive Branch, which now wields vast power and touches almost every aspect of daily life, heightens the concern that it may slip from the Executive's control, and thus from that of the people. This concern is largely absent from the dissent's paean to the administrative state. . . .

In fact, the multilevel protection that the dissent endorses "provides a blueprint for extensive expansion of the legislative power." In a system of checks and balances, "[p]ower abhors a vacuum," and one branch's handicap is another's strength. . . .

Congress has plenary control over the salary, duties, and even existence of executive offices. Only Presidential oversight can counter its influence. . . .

. . . The point is not to take issue with for-cause limitations in general; we do not do that. The question here is far more modest. We deal with the unusual situation, never before addressed by the Court, of two layers of for-cause tenure. And though it may be criticized as "elementary arithmetical logic," two layers are not the same as one.

Does the majority make a persuasive case that dual levels of removal protection should be impermissible? For commentaries on the decision, see, e.g., Richard H. Pildes, Free Enterprise Fund, *Boundary-Enforcing Decisions, and the Unitary Executive Branch Theory of Government Administration*, 6 DUKE J. CONST. L. & PUB. POL'Y 1 (spec. issue 2010); Peter L. Strauss, *On the Difficulties of Generalization—PCAOB in the Footsteps of* Myers, Humphrey's Executor, Morrison, *and* Freytag, 32 CARDOZO L. REV. 2255 (2011).

5. *Ramifications of Free Enterprise Fund.* In his dissent, Justice Breyer warned that the majority's holding could potentially affect "hundreds, perhaps thousands of high-level government officials" who could be described as entitled to two levels of statutory protection. Among them may be "most of the leadership of the Nuclear Regulatory Commission (including that agency's executive director as well as the directors of its Office of Nuclear Reactor Regulation and Office of Enforcement), virtually all of the leadership of the Social Security Administration, the executive directors of the Federal Energy Regulatory Commission and the Federal Trade Commission, as well as the general counsels of the Chemical Safety Board, the Federal Mine Safety and Health Review Commission, and the National Mediation Board." Also potentially affected would be administrative law judges, who generally may be removed from office only for cause by the Merit Systems Protection Board. MSPB members themselves are protected from removal by the President, except for cause. The majority refused to address any of these possibilities, in part because some of the details in the PCAOB's statutory protections had no direct parallels in other statutes.

Professor Strauss has suggested that the statutory structure of the PCAOB may indeed have been unique in the sense that it created an independent *agency* within another independent agency. If the opinion is read as applying only to that situation, he suggests, it is less problematic than if it is read (as Justice Breyer does) as condemning dual levels of for-cause protection enjoyed by *individual officers*. Strauss, *supra*, at 2278–82. How readily does the Court's reasoning lend itself to this limiting interpretation?

6. *Functionalism and formalism.* Notice that *Morrison* displayed a flexible mode of analysis, looking to a variety of factors in order to decide whether, in the particular circumstances, a statute intruded unduly on the President's ability to carry out his duties. The case can thus be regarded as

"functionalist" in its analytical style. *See* § 7.1. Similarly, *CFTC v. Schor* openly relied on interest-balancing when it decided whether common law counterclaims could be adjudicated in an administrative tribunal. *See also Mistretta v. United States,* 488 U.S. 361 (1989) (upholding the constitutionality of the United States Sentencing Commission, an "independent commission in the judicial branch," on the basis that its structure did not *unduly* strengthen or weaken the judicial branch). In his dissent in *Free Enterprise Fund,* Justice Breyer defended this method:

> [A] functional approach permits Congress and the President the flexibility needed to adapt statutory law to changing circumstances. That is why the "powers conferred upon the Federal Government by the Constitution were phrased in language broad enough to allow for the expansion of the Federal Government's role" over time. . . .

> Federal statutes . . . create a host of different organizational structures. . . . The functional approach required by our precedents recognizes this administrative complexity and, more importantly, recognizes the various ways presidential power operates within this context—and the various ways in which a removal provision might affect that power. . . .

But that opinion was, of course, a dissent. The majority opinion in *Free Enterprise Fund* could be better described as exemplifying a "formalist" method that does not directly incorporate policy considerations into its separation of powers analysis. *Chadha, Bowsher,* and *MWAA,* and *Clinton v. New York* are also commonly regarded as examples of formalist reasoning. Is there a logical reason for this variation in methodological approaches?

7.   *State constitutions.* "State constitutional provisions relating to the power of the governor to remove public officials vary dramatically from state to state." THOMAS C. MARKS, JR. & JOHN F. COOPER, STATE CONSTITUTIONAL LAW 65 (2d ed. 2003). Most state constitutions, unlike the federal one, explicitly vest removal authority in the chief executive. In many states, however, this authority is less than absolute. The provision may limit removal to "for cause" situations, or may authorize the legislature to impose similar constraints.

Even where a constitution provides that the governor may "remove any officer appointed by him for incompetency, neglect of duty or malfeasance in office," some courts have in effect treated the removal power as plenary. They have said that the governor need not give reasons for his decision, nor allow any kind of hearing before he acts; nor will the courts review the decision. *State ex rel. Duran v. Anaya,* 698 P.2d 882 (N.M. 1985); *Wilcox v. People ex rel. Lipe,* 90 Ill. 186 (1878) (removal of park commissioners). In Illinois, *Wilcox* was regarded as authoritative for almost a century. *See Adams v. Walker,* 492 F.2d 1003 (7th Cir. 1974). In *Lunding v. Walker,* 359 N.E.2d 96 (Ill. 1976), however, the court limited *Wilcox,* concluding that the constitutional provision should be read to harmonize with *Myers* and

Humphrey's Executor. Thus, the governor's removal of a member of the State Board of Elections for failing to file a financial disclosure statement, as required by the governor's executive order, was judicially reviewable. The court based this conclusion on the independent nature of the election board and noted that it might still follow *Wilcox* in a case involving a "purely executive officer directly responsible to the Governor." Can you justify *Wilcox? Lunding?*

In line with *Bowsher*, state courts have also held or suggested that *legislative* removal of agency officials offends separation of powers principles. *Schisler v. State*, 907 A.2d 175 (Md. 2006); *see also Marine Forests Soc'y v. Cal. Coastal Comm'n*, 113 P.3d 1062 (Cal. 2005), discussed in § 7.5.1b N.2.

8.   *Good cause.* The statutory language involved in Humphrey's case, allowing removal for "inefficiency, neglect of duty, or misconduct," is typical of statutes that allow an officer to be dismissed only for "cause" (or "good cause"), but the meaning of this criterion has rarely been litigated in federal courts. *See* Marshall J. Breger & Gary J. Edles, *Established by Practice: The Theory and Operation of Independent Federal Agencies*," 52 ADMIN. L. REV. 1111, 1144–46 (2000). The traditional assumption is that "good cause" narrowly limits the President's power to remove an official. See *Mistretta v. United States*, 488 U.S. 361, 410–11 (1989) (this limitation on the removal power "is specifically crafted to prevent the President from exercising 'coercive influence' over independent agencies" and thus to "safeguard the independence of the Commission"). However, the majority in *Morrison* treated the possibility of removal for good cause as affirmatively demonstrating the sufficiency of the President's control over an independent counsel. Moreover, when the Court held in *Bowsher* that Congress could not reserve the right to remove the Comptroller General for good cause, it stated that the statutory restrictions were "very broad" and "could sustain removal . . . for any number of actual or perceived transgressions of the legislative will." *Bowsher*, 478 U.S. at 729. Should one conclude that the conventional understanding of "good cause" is obsolete? *See* Lawrence Lessig & Cass R. Sunstein, *The President and the Administration*, 94 COLUM. L. REV. 1, 110–11 (1994).

9.   *Case law on good cause.* At the state level, an occasional case does turn on the meaning of a "cause" criterion. In *Ariz. Indep. Redistricting Comm'n v. Brewer*, 275 P.3d 1267 (Ariz. 2012), the governor of Arizona, a Republican, removed the chair of a redistricting commission that had reportedly been considering adoption of an electoral map that would benefit Democrats. The statutory test for removal was "substantial neglect of duty, gross misconduct in office, or inability to discharge the duties of office." The governor's stated explanations were that certain meetings of the commission had violated the open meetings requirement of the state constitution (although it was not clear that the meetings in question were governed by that requirement) and that the redistricting plan did not meet constitutional criteria (although the plan was still in draft form). Two weeks later, the state

supreme court unanimously ordered the chair reinstated, declaring that neither of the governor's reasons constituted legal cause for removal.

A more closely contested case was *Levy v. Acting Governor*, 767 N.E.2d 66 (Mass. 2002). Applying a statute that permitted her to remove any gubernatorial appointee "for cause," the governor dismissed two members of the Massachusetts Turnpike Authority. The firing grew out of disagreements about the MTA's administration of the "Big Dig," a massive and hugely expensive highway construction project in central Boston. The crux of the dispute was the members' decision to postpone for six months a scheduled increase in highway tolls. The state's political leaders had earlier agreed to endorse the immediate increase, and MTA's vote to change that plan resulted in an immediate drop in the Authority's bond ratings. The governor concluded that the members' actions had been "fiscally irresponsible, . . . damaging the Authority's credit outlook, and creating financial instability."

By a 4–3 vote, the Supreme Judicial Court held that the firing had been improper. The majority said that the earlier political consensus had not been a binding agreement. Moreover, the members had consulted counsel, staff, and the public before voting for the delay. Thus, the court concluded, the instant case "involves a difference of opinion over policy that, in the circumstances, does not constitute substantial evidence of cause to remove." The court distinguished past cases in which it had accorded virtually blanket deference to "removal[s] of public officials over whom an executive had broad supervisory or managerial responsibility and control, or oversight, or whose position existed to aid the executive in carrying out policies." The MTA's enabling statute contemplated a greater degree of autonomy because "the Legislature has determined that the public would be better served by an independent Authority that operates more like a business than a government agency, . . . free from the changing winds of politics." In short, "the Governor's powers over the Authority do not include the power to remove its members for any reason advanced in 'good faith and honest judgment,' or an honest dispute over policy." The dissenters argued that the "cause" standard was at least broad enough to encompass removal for "maladministration or fiscal irresponsibility," which in their view was involved here.

Finally, in *Bouton v. Farrelly*, 122 Fed. Appx. 562, 565 (3d Cir. 2004), the governor of the Virgin Islands discharged an administrative hearing officer for repeatedly failing to wear a coat and tie to work, as required by an agency dress code. Applying Virgin Islands law, the Third Circuit held that this decision satisfied a statutory "removal for cause" standard. Do you agree? *See generally* Eric R. Daleo, Note, *The Scope and Limits of the New Jersey Governor's Authority to Remove the Attorney General and Others "For Cause,"* 39 RUTGERS L.J. 393, 433–39 (2008).

10. *Inferring tenure.* Even where a legislature has the power to confer removal protection on a government official, the relevant statute may leave room for debate as to whether the legislature intended to do so. Both federal and state courts have often had to resolve such debates. Many cases recite

the maxim that "[i]n the absence of specific provision to the contrary, the power of removal from office is incident to the power of appointment." *Keim v. United States,* 177 U.S. 290, 293 (1900). But that is only a starting point.

Where the term of office is unspecified, courts are strongly inclined to find that the officer serves at the pleasure of the appointing authority. Otherwise, the individual would be able, by avoiding misconduct, to remain in office for life—a conclusion that the courts have understandably been reluctant to reach. *Shurtleff v. United States,* 189 U.S. 311 (1903) (upholding removal without cause, even though the statute expressly specified grounds for removal!); *Kalaris v. Donovan,* 697 F.2d 376 (D.C. Cir. 1983). In *Kalaris* the court held that members of the Benefits Review Board, a workers' compensation tribunal within the Department of Labor, could be removed by the Secretary of Labor without a showing of cause. Despite the purely judicial nature of the Board's functions, the court held that the *Wiener* case, discussed in § 7.5.2a N.3, was not controlling, in part because of the indefinite duration of the Board members' terms.

Where an officer has been appointed for a specific number of years, results vary more widely. Sometimes, if the agency has a structure and functions resembling those of a typical independent agency, a court will infer a legislative intention that its members should be removable only for cause. *See, e.g., FEC v. NRA Political Victory Fund,* 6 F.3d 821, 826 (D.C. Cir. 1993), *cert. dismissed,* 513 U.S. 88 (1994) (Federal Election Commission). On the other hand, in *Parsons v. United States,* 167 U.S. 324, 338–39 (1897), the Court held that the President may freely remove U.S. Attorneys before their four year terms expire. And the Pennsylvania Supreme Court has adopted a compromise position: A statute fixing the term of an officer implies tenure in situations in which members of an agency serve *staggered terms.* If they have fixed terms that by law can expire concurrently, they serve at the pleasure of the appointing authority. *Schluraff v. Rzymek,* 208 A.2d 239 (Pa.1965).

The status of the members of the SEC has generated significant controversy recently. As one court of appeals noted a generation ago, "it is commonly understood" that the Commission's members may be removed only for cause. *SEC v. Blinder, Robinson & Co.,* 855 F.2d 677, 681 (10th Cir. 1988). In *Free Enterprise Fund,* the majority *assumed* that this was so (and relied on that assumption in reaching its "double-for-cause" holding), because the parties had agreed with that premise. In his dissenting opinion, however, Justice Breyer questioned this assumption. He pointed out that the Securities Exchange Act is silent on the issue of tenure for SEC commissioners, and that this omission could be explained by the fact that the Commission had been created after *Myers* and before *Humphrey's Executor,* i.e., at a time when "for cause" removal requirements were considered unconstitutional. Although Breyer did not take a position on the issue himself, his dissent has fueled doubts about whether SEC commissioners are indeed protected from at-will removal, as has been generally assumed for many years. *See* Note, *The SEC Is Not an Independent Agency,* 126 HARV. L. REV. 781 (2013). Is the traditional supposition justified, in the absence of statutory language supporting it? *Cf.* Adrian Vermeule, *Conventions of Agency Independence*, 113 COLUM. L. REV. 1163, 1218–22 (2013).

11. *Problem.* The Publius River Port Authority (PRPA) was established to construct and operate bridges spanning the Publius River; to construct and maintain facilities for transporting passengers across the river; and to improve and develop the ports on each bank. The river runs between the states of Madison and Hamilton. The governor of each state appoints four commissioners to the PRPA, which was created by an interstate compact between the two states. Such compacts must be approved by Congress, and their terms are interpreted and applied according to federal law.

The compact provides that Madison's representatives on the PRPA "are appointed by the Governor of Madison for terms of five years," subject to confirmation by the Madison Senate. Three years ago, Marjorie, the governor of Madison, appointed Jane to serve on the PRPA. Last week, the recently elected governor, Alex, told Jane that he was disappointed about her vote for a new chairperson of the PRPA. He asked for Jane's resignation. She refused and was notified the next day that Alex intended to remove her from office.

(a) Jane has filed suit to enjoin Alex from removing her. How should the case be resolved?

(b) Now assume that the Publius River runs entirely within the boundaries of Madison, and the PRPA is exclusively a creature of Madison state law. Should the result in Jane's suit change? *Cf. Pievsky v. Ridge,* 98 F.3d 730 (3d Cir. 1996); *Alcorn v. Wolfe,* 827 F. Supp. 47 (D.D.C. 1993).

§ 7.6   EXECUTIVE OVERSIGHT

Exercise of the power to appoint and remove officials is by no means the only tool by which Presidents and governors exert influence over administrative action. Agencies normally maintain a significant working relationship with the chief executive. The President or governor typically coordinates agencies' activities, defends them against political opposition, and prevails upon them to pursue the policies of "the administration."

Presidents and governors often use *executive orders* to prescribe policies for the executive branch. An executive order is not legally binding by its very existence, although it can have the force of law if based on statutory or constitutional authority. *See National Ass'n of Gov't Employees v. FLRA,* 179 F.3d 946 (D.C. Cir. 1999); Kevin M. Stack, *The Statutory President,* 90 IOWA L. REV. 539, 550–52 (2005). Persons outside the government can argue in court that an executive order exceeds the chief executive's authority, such as in the *Youngstown* case discussed below in N.1. *See Chamber of Commerce v. Reich,* 74 F.3d 1322 (D.C. Cir. 1996). Legal obligations aside, however, members of the executive branch will normally comply with these orders, for presidents and governors tend to have many tools of persuasion at their command.

White House intervention in regulatory affairs occurs in part through a structured system for presidential review of agency rulemaking. As discussed earlier in § 5.8.1, the Office of Information and Regulatory Affairs (OIRA), a division of the Office of Management and Budget (OMB), regularly conducts oversight of significant rulemaking proceedings on behalf of the White House. This function received a broad charter when President Reagan issued Executive Order 12,291, 46 Fed. Reg. 13,193 (1981). A related directive, Executive Order 12,498, 50 Fed. Reg. 1036 (1985), created a "regulatory planning" process, under which agencies would submit their anticipated rulemaking initiatives to OIRA each year for approval. President Clinton, upon taking office, promulgated a revised version of both directives in Executive Order 12,866, 58 Fed. Reg. 51,735 (1993). This order has survived with minor amendments and supplementation through the second Bush administration and the Obama administration.

The OIRA review process is not, however, the only medium by which the White House controls or influences ongoing agency actions. Less formal instances of ad hoc intervention by White House staff have also been important, particularly during the administrations of President Clinton and his successors.

Meanwhile, a few states have also developed executive oversight programs, some following the federal model and others displaying a quite different emphasis.

EXECUTIVE ORDER 12,866
REGULATORY PLANNING AND REVIEW
58 Fed. Reg. 51,735 (1993)

[B]y the authority vested in me as President by the Constitution and laws of the United States of America, it is hereby ordered as follows:

Sec. 1.   *Statement of Regulatory Philosophy and Principles.* . . .

(b)   *The Principles of Regulation*: [A]gencies should adhere to the following principles, to the extent permitted by law and where applicable:
. . .

(6)   Each agency shall assess both the costs and the benefits of the intended regulation and, recognizing that some costs and benefits are difficult to quantify, propose or adopt a regulation only upon a reasoned determination that the benefits of the intended regulation justify its costs.

Sec. 2.   *Organization.*

(a)   *The Agencies.* Because Federal agencies are the repositories of significant substantive expertise and experience, they are responsible for developing regulations and assuring that the regulations are consistent with applicable law, the President's priorities, and the principles set forth in this Executive order.

(b) *The Office of Management and Budget.* Coordinated review of agency rulemaking is necessary to ensure that regulations are consistent with applicable law, the President's priorities, and the principles set forth in this Executive order, and that decisions made by one agency do not conflict with the policies or actions taken or planned by another agency. The Office of Management and Budget (OMB) shall carry out that review function. . . .

Sec. 3. *Definitions.*

(b) "Agency," unless otherwise indicated, means any authority of the United States that is an "agency" . . . other than those considered to be independent regulatory agencies. . . .

(f) "Significant regulatory action" means any regulatory action that is likely to result in a rule that may

(1) Have an annual effect on the economy of $100 million or more or adversely affect in a material way the economy, a sector of the economy, productivity, competition, jobs, the environment, public health or safety, or State, local, or tribal governments or communities;

(2) Create a serious inconsistency or otherwise interfere with an action taken or planned by another agency;

(3) Materially alter the budgetary impact of entitlements, grants, user fees, or loan programs or the rights and obligations of recipients thereof; or

(4) Raise novel legal or policy issues arising out of legal mandates, the President's priorities, or the principles set forth in this Executive order.

Sec. 4. *Planning Mechanism.* . . . [T]o the extent permitted by law:

(a) *Agencies' Policy Meeting.* Early in each year's planning cycle, the Vice President shall convene a meeting of the [President's policy advisors] and the heads of agencies to seek a common understanding of priorities and to coordinate regulatory efforts to be accomplished in the upcoming year.

(c) *The Regulatory Plan.* For purposes of this subsection, the term "agency" or "agencies" shall also include those considered to be independent regulatory agencies. . . .

(1) . . . [E]ach agency shall prepare a Regulatory Plan (Plan) of the most important significant regulatory actions that the agency reasonably expects to issue in proposed or final form

in that fiscal year or thereafter. The Plan shall be approved personally by the agency head. . . .

(5) If the Administrator of OIRA believes that a planned regulatory action of an agency may be inconsistent with the President's priorities or the principles set forth in this Executive order or may be in conflict with any policy or action taken or planned by another agency, the Administrator of OIRA shall promptly notify, in writing, the affected agencies, the [President's policy advisors], and the Vice President. . . .

Sec. 6.   *Centralized Review of Regulations.*

(a) *Agency Responsibilities.* . . .

(3) . . . (C) For those matters identified as, or determined by the Administrator of OIRA to be, a significant regulatory action within the scope of section 3(f)(1), the agency shall . . . provide to OIRA [a cost-benefit analysis] developed as part of the agency's decisionmaking process (unless prohibited by law). . . .

(b) *OIRA Responsibilities.* The Administrator of OIRA shall provide meaningful guidance and oversight so that each agency's regulatory actions are consistent with applicable law, the President's priorities, and the principles set forth in this Executive order and do not conflict with the policies or actions of another agency. . . .

(1) OIRA may review only actions identified by the agency or by OIRA as significant regulatory actions. . . .

(2) [In most cases OIRA must complete its review within 90 calendar days after it receives the agency's regulatory analysis.] . . .

(C) The review process may be extended (1) once by no more than 30 calendar days upon the written approval of the Director and (2) at the request of the agency head.

(3) For each regulatory action that the Administrator of OIRA returns to an agency for further consideration of some or all of its provisions, the Administrator of OIRA shall provide the issuing agency a written explanation for such return . . .

(4) [This paragraph commits OIRA to several openness requirements, including disclosures regarding communications between OIRA and persons not employed by the federal government.]

Sec. 7.   *Resolution of Conflicts.*

To the extent permitted by law, disagreements or conflicts between or among agency heads or between OMB and any agency that cannot be resolved by the Administrator of OIRA shall be resolved by the President, or by the Vice President acting at the request of the President, with the relevant agency head (and, as appropriate, other interested government officials). . . .

At the end of this review process, the President, or the Vice President acting at the request of the President, shall notify the affected agency and the Administrator of OIRA of the President's decision with respect to the matter. . . .

Sec. 9. *Agency Authority.* Nothing in this order shall be construed as displacing the agencies' authority or responsibilities, as authorized by law.

Sec. 10. *Judicial Review.* Nothing in this Executive order shall affect any otherwise available judicial review of agency action. This Executive order is intended only to improve the internal management of the Federal Government and does not create any right or benefit, substantive or procedural, enforceable at law or equity by a party against the United States, its agencies or instrumentalities, its officers or employees, or any other person. . . .

NOTES AND QUESTIONS

1. *Case law background.* Supreme Court guidance regarding the proper relationship between the President and the federal agencies has been sparse. An early case that defined some of the outer boundaries of that relationship was *Kendall v. United States ex rel. Stokes,* 37 U.S. (12 Pet.) 524, 610–12 (1838). Congress had passed a special law to resolve a dispute between the postmaster general and a contract carrier for the Post Office. The law directed the postmaster to pay the amount owed to the carrier, as calculated by the solicitor of the treasury. The postmaster refused to pay, claiming that the President had instructed him not to comply. The Court upheld a writ of mandamus against the postmaster:

> There are certain political duties imposed upon many officers in the executive department, the discharge of which is under the direction of the President. But it would be an alarming doctrine, that congress cannot impose upon any executive officer any duty they may think proper, which is not repugnant to any rights secured and protected by the constitution; and in such cases, the duty and responsibility grow out of and are subject to the control of the law, and not to the direction of the President. And this is emphatically the case, where the duty enjoined is of a mere ministerial character. . . .

> It was urged at the bar, that the postmaster general was alone subject to the direction and control of the President, with respect to the execution of the duty imposed upon him by this law, and this right of the President is claimed, as growing out of the obligation

imposed upon him by the constitution, to take care that the laws be faithfully executed. This is a doctrine that cannot receive the sanction of this court. . . . To contend that the obligation imposed on the President to see the laws faithfully executed, implies a power to forbid their execution, is a novel construction of the constitution, and entirely inadmissible. . . .

Another important historical milestone was *Youngstown Sheet & Tube Co. v. Sawyer,* 343 U.S. 579 (1952). President Truman used an executive order to direct the Secretary of Commerce to take control of the nation's steel mills for the purpose of preventing a strike during the Korean War. The Supreme Court held this seizure invalid.

Justice Black's opinion for the Court took a straightforward approach to the separation of powers issue. It argued that the President's seizure was not authorized by statute and could not be justified by his independent constitutional powers as commander-in-chief. "Nor," Black continued, "can the seizure order be sustained because of the several constitutional provisions that grant executive power to the President. In the framework of our Constitution, the President's power to see that the laws are faithfully executed refutes the idea that he is to be a lawmaker. The Constitution . . . is neither silent nor equivocal about who shall make laws which the President is to execute. The first section of the first article says that 'All legislative Powers herein granted shall be vested in a Congress of the United States. . . .' " *Id.* at 585–88.

The well-known concurring opinion of Justice Jackson in the *Youngstown* case took a more flexible view of the President's power. Justice Jackson sketched three situations. In the first, where "the President acts pursuant to an express or implied authorization of Congress, his authority is at its maximum." In the second, the President acts in the absence of statutes supporting or prohibiting his action. Here the President "can only rely on his own independent constitutional powers," and, therefore, he has less authority than in the first situation; "but there is a zone of twilight in which he and Congress may have concurrent authority, or in which its distribution is uncertain. Therefore, congressional inertia, indifference or quiescence may sometimes, at least as a practical matter, enable, if not invite, measures on independent presidential responsibility. In this area, any actual test of power is likely to depend on the imperatives of events and contemporary imponderables rather than on abstract theories of law." In the third situation, the President takes action that is "incompatible with the expressed or implied will of Congress." In this situation "his power is at its lowest ebb, for then he can rely only upon his own constitutional powers minus any constitutional powers of Congress over the matter." *Id.* at 634–38.

Jackson concluded that the *Youngstown* situation fit into the third category and was impermissible. Congress had specified conditions under which the President could seize private property; those conditions had not been met. By implication, Congress had forbidden seizures under other circumstances. In essence, a majority of the Court apparently believed that, in the event of a conflict between Congress and the President concerning matters over which they each have constitutional competence to act, the conflict should be resolved in favor of Congress.

2. *Evolution of OIRA oversight.* The initial years of the formal oversight program, during the Reagan administration, were stormy ones. Relations between OIRA and the agencies were often marked by mutual suspicion. Moreover, countless academic and journalistic critiques accused OIRA of interfering with legitimate rulemaking initiatives. *See, e.g.,* Alan B. Morrison, *OMB Interference with Agency Rulemaking: The Wrong Way to Write a Regulation,* 99 HARV. L. REV. 1059 (1986). Rivalry between agencies and presidential reviewers continued during the George H.W. Bush years. A particular target of complaint was the Council on Competitiveness, which was established within Vice President Quayle's office to supervise OIRA's functions. It operated with a strong deregulatory emphasis and few regularized procedures. *See, e.g.,* Peter M. Shane, *Political Accountability in a System of Checks and Balances: The Case of Presidential Review of Rulemaking,* 48 ARK. L. REV. 161, 165–73 (1995).

When President Clinton took office, the drafters of E.O. 12,866 kept the basic mission of OIRA intact but revised the order in several ways. First, they limited the number of rules that OIRA would be expected to review. Now, OIRA reviews only rules that it deems "significant" (as defined in § 3(f)). Intensive review, including a formal cost-benefit study, is reserved for rules that fall within § 3(f)(1). The latter, which are informally called "economically significant," are typically rules with a $100 million economic impact. The drafters also revised the order's regulatory analysis criteria to take fuller account of qualitative, judgmental considerations (as was discussed in § 5.8.1 N.2); and they adopted procedural reforms aimed at avoiding delays and exposing more OIRA operations to public scrutiny. The new executive order also put an increased emphasis on planning, so that OIRA and the agencies could more often resolve their differences at an early stage in the rulemaking process. For these reasons—and perhaps others, such as differences between the ideological positions of the Clinton administration and those of its two predecessors—the public witnessed fewer public struggles between OIRA and rulemaking agencies during the Clinton years. (For helpful comparisons between the two executive orders, see Shane, *supra,* at 174–92; Richard H. Pildes & Cass R. Sunstein, *Reinventing the Regulatory State,* 62 U. CHI. L. REV. 1, 16–33 (1995).)

Upon taking office, President George W. Bush made few changes in E.O. 12,866. The one significant revision that he did make was to eliminate what had been a significant role for the Vice President in supervising the review process. Executive Order 13,258, 67 Fed.Reg. 9385 (2002). Bush adopted additional amendments in 2007. Among other adjustments, they extended OIRA review to apply not only to "regulatory actions" (rules that have the force of law), but also to "guidance documents" (interpretive rules and policy statements), although the review procedures for the latter were relatively modest. *See* Executive Order 13,422, 72 Fed.Reg. 2763, § 9 (2007). President Obama rescinded the Bush changes at the outset of his administration (Executive Order 13,497, 74 Fed.Reg. 6113 (2009)), but he informally retained the guidance document review policy anyway. Two years later Obama issued an oversight order that "supplement[ed]" the Clinton order. It added some new presidential priorities and revised phrasing, but it made no fundamental changes in the earlier order's structure or approach. Executive Order 13,563, 76 Fed. Reg. 3821 (2011).

3.   *Merits of executive oversight.* Recall the strong endorsement of presidential oversight of rulemaking in *Sierra Club v. Costle,* § 5.5.2, and the reasons given for that endorsement. Of course, the court's vote of confidence preceded any experience under E.O. 12,291. Moreover, it pertained to the actions of the President personally, as opposed to a review office acting on his behalf. Do the court's arguments also support the OIRA oversight program? According to some observers, they do:

> [T]here are strong reasons for creating and maintaining an executive office entrusted with the job of coordinating modern regulation, promoting sensible priority setting, and ensuring conformity with the President's basic mission. In view of the wide array of regulatory programs administered by modern government, the absence of such an office would probably guarantee duplication, parochial perspectives, and inefficiency. A number of separate agencies and programs deal with environmental and other risks, and it is therefore important to share information, to reduce inconsistency, and to devote scarce resources to places where they will do the most good.

Pildes & Sunstein, *supra,* at 16. More particularly, Professor Pierce argues that OIRA's oversight at least compares favorably with judicial review of whether a major rule displays "reasoned decisionmaking":

> OIRA has significant advantages over courts in performing this review function.... OIRA is staffed by an interdisciplinary team of social and natural scientists. Its reviewers know how to read and interpret conflicting studies and analyses. By contrast, generalist judges and their bright young law clerks typically know virtually nothing about the disciplines relevant to the policy disputes resolved in a major rulemaking.... OIRA also can devote more resources to the review process than can a federal court.... [I]t seems unlikely that any judge ever gets very far into the 10,000 to 250,000 page record of a major rulemaking. Judges necessarily rely on the briefs of the parties and the selected excerpts from the record submitted by the parties as their near exclusive basis for obtaining a picture of the rulemaking. The lawyers that represent petitioners in rulemaking review proceedings are experts at distorting that picture....

OIRA's flexibility advantage inheres in its ability to engage in expeditious, two-way communications with a rulemaking agency. . . . OIRA typically communicates its questions and concerns within a week or two of receiving an agency's proposed final rule, and the agency often responds to OIRA's satisfaction within a week or two thereafter. . . . The OIRA review process always is completed in a small fraction of the time required for completion of the process of judicial application of the duty to engage in reasoned decisionmaking.

Finally, OIRA is more politically accountable than a reviewing court. [R]ulemaking is, and should be, a political process. . . . Moreover, the president will be held politically accountable for the results of the OIRA review process. . . . By contrast, no one can be held politically accountable for analogous judicial decisions [although judges often] exercise significant power to veto policy decisions based on each judge's political and ideological perspective.

Richard J. Pierce, Jr., *Seven Ways to Deossify Agency Rulemaking*, 47 ADMIN. L. REV. 59, 70–71 (1995).

Some commentators maintain, however, that OIRA's actual track record does not measure up to the aspirations claimed for it:

> . . . Proponents of centralized executive review of agency decisionmaking [initially] justified it with reference to two goals: the promotion of political accountability, interagency coordination, rational priority setting, and cost-effective rulemaking (the harmonizing function); and the curbing of the regulatory excesses of overzealous bureaucrats bent on promoting their agencies' narrow agendas (the checking function).
>
> In practice, however, Reagan-era centralized review did a lot of checking and not much harmonizing. . . . Given the Reagan administration's "professed aim . . . to cut back significantly, if not actually to destroy, the regulatory system established by Congress," its commitment to deregulation at the expense of harmonization is hardly surprising. . . . What is surprising, however, is that the basic contours of the Reagan-era executive review mechanism remain in place today. . . . [M]any of the features of OMB review create a profound institutional bias against regulation—a bias which is inexplicable except with reference to the implicit Reagan-era belief that agencies will systematically overregulate.
>
> [A]dvocates justify this bias with reference to a simple and remarkably stable story, namely, that health and safety agencies are frequently captured by prohealth and prosafety constituencies, leading systematically to overzealous and inefficient regulation. . . . But the claim that agencies are systematically biased in a proregulatory direction finds little support in public choice theory,

the political science literature, or elsewhere. Standard public choice accounts would suggest that agencies could easily (and more plausibly) reflect antiregulatory interests. Moreover, even if we believed that some agencies (say, the Environmental Protection Agency (EPA)) had proregulatory biases, other federal agencies (say, the Department of Energy (DOE)) would be likely to have corresponding antiregulatory proclivities. A one-size-fits-all executive review process that automatically disfavors regulation is therefore inappropriate. . . . Even if the regulatory state were in fact characterized by zealous agencies captured by powerful interest groups, . . . OMB review is a poorly designed solution to that problem for the simple reason that OMB's location within the Executive Office of the President does not immunize it from any pathologies that affect other agencies.

Nicholas Bagley & Richard L. Revesz, *Centralized Oversight of the Regulatory State*, 106 COLUM. L. REV. 1260, 1261–63 (2006). *But see* John D. Graham, *The Evolving Role of the U.S. Office of Management and Budget in Regulatory Policy*, 1 REV. ENVTL. ECON. & POL'Y 171, 173 (2007) (discussing several examples of pro-regulatory interventions by OIRA).

In subsequent years, empirical studies of OIRA oversight have shed more light on the review process but have by no means dispelled controversy about it. A study of oversight during the Clinton years reached largely favorable conclusions about it. Steven Croley, *White House Review of Agency Rulemaking: An Empirical Investigation*, 70 U. CHI. L. REV. 821 (2003). Not surprisingly, a survey of political appointees at the EPA found that those officials, whose rules OIRA often challenged during the give-and-take of the review process, had a less laudatory perspective. Lisa Schultz Bressman & Michael P. Vandenbergh, *Inside the Administrative State: A Critical Look at the Practice of Presidential Control*, 105 MICH. L. REV. 47 (2006). In still other articles, however, political scientists caution that the overall impact of OIRA oversight may not be as extensive as is often hoped (or feared). Cary Coglianese, *The Rhetoric and Reality of Regulatory Reform*, 25 YALE J. ON REG. 85, 91–95 (2008); Stuart Shapiro, *Presidents and Process: A Comparison of the Regulatory Process Under the Clinton and Bush (43) Administrations*, 23 J.L. & POL. 393, 409–10, 415–18 (2007).

4. *Legality of executive oversight.* Like its predecessor orders, E.O. 12,866 repeatedly declares that its prescriptions apply only "to the extent permitted by law." But to what "extent" is a presidential review program "permitted"? Congress has not explicitly authorized presidential review, but this program has been widely assumed to fall, at the very least, within the second, "zone of twilight" category that Justice Jackson identified in *Youngstown* as the proper mode of analysis for actions that Congress has neither authorized nor prohibited. According to commentators who support the program, its legality is rooted in the President's constitutional duty to "take Care that the Laws be faithfully executed," and also in a less well known clause of the Constitution under which the President may "require the

Opinion, in writing, of the principal Officer in each of the executive Departments, upon any Subject relating to the Duties of their respective Offices." Art. II, § 2, cl. 1. *See* Peter L. Strauss, *The Place of Agencies in Government: Separation of Powers and the Fourth Branch*, 84 COLUM. L. REV. 573, 653–62 (1984).

On the other hand, could it be argued that Congress has implicitly directed the President *not* to get involved in the agencies' rulemaking? If so, OIRA's operations would presumably fall into the third, and most disfavored, of Justice Jackson's three categories. This thesis would be supportable if regulatory legislation were interpreted as implying that an agency head should make his or her decision without White House participation. Such a suggestion was made in the early years of the Reagan oversight program. *See* Morton Rosenberg, *Beyond the Limits of Executive Power: Presidential Control of Agency Rulemaking Under Executive Order 12,291*, 80 MICH. L. REV. 193 (1981). In subsequent years, however, wholesale attacks on the validity of OIRA review have ebbed. Nevertheless, *particular* exercises of OIRA's authority can still pose legal problems. For example, agencies are not allowed to use the pendency of OIRA review as a justification for their failure to comply with applicable statutory deadlines. *See NRDC v. EPA*, 797 F. Supp. 194, 198 (E.D.N.Y. 1992); *Envtl. Defense Fund v. Thomas*, 627 F. Supp. 566 (D.D.C. 1986) (ordering immediate promulgation of rule despite OMB's "interference").

More generally, *Kendall* has commonly been read to mean that if a matter is entrusted to an agency official, the President cannot lawfully require the official to act at variance with the statutory mandate. Notice, however, that in *Kendall* the postmaster's duty was considered ministerial. What if an agency head has been given discretion—can the President (or, perhaps, the President's designee) order the agency head to exercise it in a particular way? Could the President fire the agency head for failing to comply with that directive? Consider the reasoning of *Sierra Club v. Costle*, 657 F.2d 298 (D.C. Cir. 1981), excerpted in § 5.5.2, and *Myers v. United States*, 272 U.S. 52 (1926), quoted in § 7.5.2a. *See generally* Peter L. Strauss, *Overseer, or "The Decider"?: The President in Administrative Law*, 75 GEO. WASH. L. REV. 696, 705–15 (2007).

5.   *Where the buck stops.* What happens if White House officials and the rulemaking agency reach an impasse? Professor McGarity cites an incident involving Vice President George H.W. Bush, to whom President Reagan had delegated a degree of supervisory authority under E.O. 12,291. OSHA proposed a rule to require labeling for hazardous substances in the workplace. OMB's assessment of the rule's likely benefits differed from OSHA's. The issue reached the Vice President, who ultimately sided with OSHA. THOMAS O. MCGARITY, REINVENTING RATIONALITY: THE ROLE OF REGULATORY ANALYSIS IN THE FEDERAL BUREAUCRACY 100 (1991). As two commentators have remarked, "the fact that [Vice President Bush] endorsed OSHA's regulatory approach is perhaps less revealing than the fact that he

believed it to be his decision whether OSHA would prevail." Pildes & Sunstein, *supra,* at 24 n.95.

Against this background, consider the conflict resolution role of the President and Vice President in E.O. 12,866. As between the President and the rulemaking agency, does the order purport to say who has the last word? *See* §§ 7, 9. Who *should* have the last word?

6. *Independent agencies.* Both E.O. 12,291 and E.O. 12,866 exempted independent agencies' rulemaking proceedings from OIRA review (although the latter order includes the independent agencies in its provisions for government-wide planning of rulemaking initiatives). The Justice Department has maintained that the President does have authority to prescribe OIRA review of rulemaking by independent agencies, but the White House has chosen to avoid the controversy that such an extension of the oversight program would be likely to engender. The proposed Independent Agency Regulatory Analysis Act, a bill now pending in the Senate, would expressly affirm the President's authority to extend OIRA oversight to independent agencies' rulemaking (although the bill would not authorize OIRA to block a rule that it did not favor). S. 1173, 113th Cong. (2013).

ACUS has recommended that, "[a]s a matter of principle, presidential review of rulemaking should apply to independent regulatory agencies to the same extent as it applies to the rulemaking of Executive Branch departments and other agencies." ACUS Recommendation 88–9, *Presidential Review of Agency Rulemaking,* 54 Fed. Reg. 5207 (1989). The American Bar Association has taken the same position. Defending this view, two scholars write:

> From the standpoint of sound regulatory policy, fashioned in a process of informal rulemaking, we believe that there is no meaningful difference between the "independent" agencies and those agencies to which the two executive orders are currently applicable. The two categories of agencies engage in regulatory activities that are, from a functional standpoint, indistinguishable. Indeed, often those activities concern the same or similar subject areas; consider the overlapping work of the Department of Justice and the Federal Trade Commission. The same considerations that justify a coordinating presidential role with respect to "executive" agencies apply with full force to those characterized as "independent."

Peter L. Strauss & Cass R. Sunstein, *The Role of the President and OMB in Informal Rulemaking,* 38 ADMIN. L. REV. 181, 205 (1986). Wouldn't such an extension defeat the congressional goal of keeping the independent agencies' actions apolitical and free of presidential influence? *See* Harold H. Bruff, *Presidential Management of Agency Rulemaking,* 57 GEO. WASH. L. REV. 533, 590–93 (1989).

7. *Implementation of OIRA oversight.* Controversies about the manner in which OIRA implements its oversight responsibilities in practice have

continued down to the present day. The objections stem in part from opposition to or doubts about the intrinsic value of cost-benefit analysis and other forms of regulatory analysis. *See* § 5.8.1. Aside from that critique, observers sometimes fault the *process* by which OIRA carries out that assignment.

Describing the process from the vantage point of his recent service as Administrator of OIRA, Professor Sunstein explains that fewer than twenty percent of the rules that OIRA reviews are "economically significant" (meaning that the agency must prepare a formal cost-benefit analysis). Cass R. Sunstein, *The Office of Information and Regulatory Affairs: Myths and Realities*, 126 HARV. L. REV. 1838, 1851 (2013). For other rules, an important aspect of OIRA's role is to coordinate a dialogue in which other regulatory agencies, as well as the White House staff, react to the initiating agency's proposal. OIRA then works to reconcile these often conflicting perspectives. *Id.* at 1854–59. Is this a beneficial function? For some doubts, see Sidney A. Shapiro, *Does OIRA Improve the Rulemaking Process? Cass Sunstein's Incomplete Defense*, ADMIN. & REG. L. NEWS, Fall 2013, at 6.

As discussed in N.2, the Clinton order was designed in part to induce OIRA to act promptly and more openly. The agency's track record has not fully lived up to this aspiration. A persistent criticism is that OIRA's review process should be more transparent. *See* Lisa Heinzerling, *Inside EPA: A Former Insider's Reflections on the Relationship Between the Obama EPA and the Obama White House*, 31 PACE ENVTL. L. REV. 337 (2014); Nina A. Mendelson, *Disclosing "Political" Oversight of Agency Decision Making*, 108 MICH. L. REV. 1127 (2010).

Moreover, delays in OIRA's completion of its review responsibilities became especially severe during 2012; many proposed rules that agencies had submitted for review were held up for months. (What might account for this behavior?) By 2013 OIRA had begun to make considerable progress in clearing its backlog, but the recent pattern of delays led the Administrative Conference—which on the whole is a strong supporter of OIRA review—to express concern about the situation and make suggestions for improving turnaround times. ACUS Statement No. 18, *Improving the Timeliness of OIRA Review*, 78 Fed. Reg. 76,275 (2013). According to Heinzerling, *supra*, at 371, delays often occur when OIRA asks the agency to request a postponement. Is this consistent with § 6(b)(2) of the executive order?

8. *Presidential administration.* Long before she joined the Supreme Court, now-Justice Elena Kagan served on the domestic policy staff in the Clinton White House. She evaluates that experience in a widely discussed law review article. Elena Kagan, *Presidential Administration*, 114 HARV. L. REV. 2245 (2001). She explains that, during the Clinton years, the White House did not limit its participation in administrative decisionmaking to the OIRA review process. The President himself issued numerous directives to various agencies, instructing them to pursue regulatory initiatives as a central feature of his governing strategy. *Id.* at 2290–99. He also made a

habit of announcing these initiatives at public events, thus effectively committing his administration to going forward with them. *Id.* at 2299–302. Does this kind of presidential "ownership" of rulemaking proceedings raise any concerns other than those that may be associated with OIRA review? *See* Peter L. Strauss, *Presidential Rulemaking*, 72 CHI.–KENT L. REV. 965 (1997).

Defending the emergence of "presidential administration," Kagan argues that regulatory statutes that appear on their face to entrust discretionary judgments to an agency head should be construed as allowing the President to direct that official to take particular regulatory actions, unless there is affirmative evidence that Congress intends to disallow such presidential authority. Very few statutes do contain such affirmative evidence, so the Kagan presumption of statutory construction, if followed, would sweep broadly. She bases this argument on the President's political accountability: he has incentives to stay in touch with public sentiments. She also emphasizes a President's distinctive capacity to bring energy and leadership to the task of governing. 114 HARV. L. REV. at 2331–46. However, Kagan parts company with the "unitary executive" theorists (*see* § 7.5.2b N.1), in that she assumes that Congress does have the power to preclude the President from substituting judgment for the named official, so long as the legislative will is clear. She also acknowledges that her proposal cannot be applied to independent agencies, because a statute that prevents the President from removing an official except for cause must logically be understood as forbidding the President to override that official's policy choices more directly. *Id.* at 2320, 2323, 2326–27.

Even with those qualifications, however, the Kagan thesis has elicited strong rebuttals from other scholars. Professor Sargentich argues that Presidents often respond to narrow political pressures, just as other political actors do; and, as far as dynamism goes, "one person's energy can be another person's mistake." He sees presidential administration as antithetical to a well-functioning system of checks and balances. Thomas O. Sargentich, *The Emphasis on the Presidency in U.S. Public Law: An Essay Critiquing Presidential Administration*, 59 ADMIN. L. REV. 1 (2007). *See also* Kevin M. Stack, *The President's Statutory Powers to Administer the Laws*, 106 COLUM. L. REV. 263 (2006); Lisa Schultz Bressman, *Beyond Accountability: Arbitrariness and Legitimacy in the Administrative State*, 78 N.Y.U. L. REV. 461 (2003).

Whatever its merits, "presidential administration" has outlived the Clinton Administration. The second President Bush was well known for his expansive and controversial ideas about the powers of the presidency, particularly in the context of national security. His approach to regulatory issues reflected similar aspirations and elicited similar criticisms. According to Dean Krent, all modern Presidents have staked out positions reflecting a "unitary executive" model of government, but President Bush's version surpassed those of his predecessors and might be described as resting on a theory of "unilateral" presidential powers. Harold J. Krent, *From a Unitary to a Unilateral Presidency*, 88 B.U.L. REV. 523 (2008). President Obama's pronouncements about presidential prerogatives have been more restrained, but from the outset of his administration he and his advisors have played an active role in management of regulation. *See* John F. Cooney, *Chief Executive Obama*, ADMIN. & REG. L. NEWS, Spring 2009, at 21. A well-publicized aspect of this management was his designation of "czars" on the White House staff to coordinate administration policy in various subject areas. *See* Adam J. Saiger, *Obama's "Czars" for Domestic Policy and the Law of the White House Staff*, 79 FORDHAM L. REV. 2577 (2011).

9. *State executive review.* Several states have executive review programs modeled on OIRA's functions. *See* Ariz. Rev. Stat. Ann. § 41–1051 et. seq.; Colo. Rev. Stat. § 24–4–103(2.5); Ohio Rev. Code Ann. § 107.51 et seq.; 4 Pa. Code § 1.374. In other states, gubernatorial review is integrated with the functions of the legislature's rules review committee. *See* Md. Code Ann., State Gov't § 10–111.1; Wash.Rev. Code Ann. § 34.05.640(3). *See also* Va. Code Ann. § 2.2–4013 (rules are submitted for review to governor, who may suggest changes or order brief suspension, but may not cancel the rule). For a state-by-state survey, see JASON A. SCHWARTZ, 52 EXPERIMENTS WITH REGULATORY REVIEW: THE POLITICAL AND ECONOMIC INPUTS INTO STATE RULEMAKINGS (2010), *http://policyintegrity.org*.

New York's executive oversight program, established by Governor George Pataki, led to a rarity: a judicial opinion (albeit a dissenting one) that actually addressed the validity of the program. In *Rudder v. Pataki*, 675 N.Y.S.2d 653 (App. Div. 1998), *aff'd*, 711 N.E.2d 978 (N.Y. 1999), the state health department proposed a rule that would have required that all directors of social work departments in the state's urban hospitals must hold a master's degree in social work. The Governor's Office of Regulatory Reform (GORR) opposed the rule. On its recommendation, the "review committee" (consisting of the governor's secretary, counsel, budget director, and director of state operations) prohibited the rule from taking effect. A coalition of social work agencies and others went to court to challenge the legality of GORR, which had been established by executive order, but the suit failed for want of standing. However, two dissenters in the Appellate Division found that the plaintiffs had standing. Reaching the merits, they asserted that the governor's program violated the doctrine of separation of powers insofar as it empowered a review entity to block rules from taking effect. It "actually nullifies specific grants of rulemaking authority given to the agencies and divests these statutory rulemaking bodies of the discretion given them by the Legislature. . . . [T]he lay members of the Governor's committee are given absolute veto power over rules prescribed by the Commissioner, regardless of the professional expertise required to properly assess and evaluate them." 675 N.Y.S.2d at 193 (Mercure, J., dissenting). Does that critique apply equally to the federal program? Governor Andrew Cuomo eliminated the GORR when he took office in 2011.

10. *Executive review in California.* In California, the Office of Administrative Law (OAL), an executive-branch agency, must approve virtually all administrative rules. *See* Cal. Govt. Code §§ 11349 et seq.

Created in 1979, OAL functions as a surrogate for judicial review. It decides whether a rule is "necessary" based on substantial evidence in the rulemaking record. It also decides whether a rule meets tests of legality ("consistency") and whether the agency complied with APA procedural requirements. It serves as the state's English teacher—deciding whether the meaning of the rule will be easily understood by those persons directly affected by it. And it asks whether the rule is duplicative of other statutes or rules and whether the agency has cited to the relevant authorities under which the rule is issued.

If OAL disapproves a rule, the agency can resubmit it within 120 days. However, if a resubmitted rule comes after 120 days, or its substantive provisions have been significantly changed, the agency must begin the rulemaking process anew. There is an opportunity for an appeal to the governor, but this is seldom attempted and seldom successful.

Like their federal counterparts, OAL and the agencies had an antagonistic and hostile relationship until the early 1990's. Now, however, OAL is viewed as constructive and useful, by both agency staff and members of the public. It seems to function fairly smoothly. Leadership changes at OAL and agencies' growing familiarity with OAL's ways are among the reasons for this changed atmosphere.

Notice, however, the differences between OAL and OIRA. The latter's function is openly political. It is designed to improve inter-agency coordination, to analyze whether the benefits of a regulation justify its costs, and to make certain that regulations are consistent with the President's priorities. In contrast, OAL's function is not explicitly political and is not intended to further any particular method of analysis. It does not receive political input from the governor. Instead, it is designed to serve a judicial-review type of function and to improve the drafting of rules. Given the availability of judicial review, is this layer of executive review needed or appropriate? If it is, should OIRA's role be changed to make it more like OAL's?

11. *Gubernatorial vetoes.* In some states, rules may not take effect without the governor's approval. *See* Hawaii Rev. Stat. § 91–3(c); Neb. Rev. Stat. § 84–908; 75 Okla. Stat. § 308.1. In these states the governor may decline to approve a rule for any reason. In Wyoming, each rule requires the governor's approval, which must be denied unless the rule is authorized, consistent with the legislative purpose, and procedurally valid. The law is unclear as to whether the governor may withhold approval for other reasons as well. *See* Wyo. Stat. § 16–3–103(d); Barton R. Voigt, Comment, *Wyoming's Administrative Regulation Review Act*, 14 LAND & WATER L. REV. 189 (1979). In a few other states, a rule may go into effect without gubernatorial involvement, but the governor may rescind the rule by disapproving it within a short period following its promulgation. *See* Ind. Code § 4–22–2–34; Iowa Code § 17.4(6); La. Rev. Stat. Ann. § 49:970.

12. *The plural executive.* In most states the executive branch is not even arguably "unitary," because important executive officials are elected separately from the governor. *See* § 7.5.1b N.1. Frequently they are members of a different political party from the governor's. The potential for conflicts within the executive branch is obvious. The conflicts can become especially visible when the attorney general, who is constitutionally charged with representing agencies headed by gubernatorial appointees, disagrees with them about the legality or desirability of their policies. *See generally* William P. Marshall, *Break Up the Presidency?: Governors, State Attorneys General, and Lessons from the Divided Executive*, 115 Yale L.J. 2446 (2006).

13. *Regulatory moratoria.* Presidents, as well as governors in at least ten states, have occasionally imposed moratoria on rulemaking by all agencies. Sometimes they suspend ongoing rulemaking proceedings at the beginning of their terms in order to take stock of the prior administration's initiatives. In other situations they have instituted freezes on rulemaking to dramatize their intention to reduce overregulation or to set a more "business-friendly" tone for their administrations. Legislative bills have been introduced for similar reasons.

In Florida, an action of this kind led to a judicial rebuff. Governor Rick Scott issued an executive order that created a new executive oversight entity within his office and directed all agencies to "immediately suspend all rulemaking." After a court challenge was commenced, the governor revised the order to state that all new rulemaking must be cleared in advance with the new review entity. The Florida Supreme Court viewed the revision as mere "sleight of hand" that did not alter the essential nature of the order. It then found that the governor's suspension of rulemaking violated separation of powers principles. *Whiley v. Scott*, 79 So.3d 702 (Fla. 2011). According to the court, "rulemaking is a legislative function," and the governor's order "encroach[es] upon the Legislature's delegation of its rulemaking power as set forth in the Florida Statutes." *Id.* at 710, 713. More specifically, the legislature had prescribed a rulemaking process in the state APA, and the governor was not entitled to supersede it. The court did not pass on the validity of the remainder of Governor Scott's order. Two justices dissented, arguing that the governor, as chief executive, had authority to manage the administrative process, and that nothing in the state APA was inconsistent with this program. How persuasive was the majority's reasoning? Would it have been more persuasive if the original order had not been revised? (Soon afterwards, the legislature overturned the court's holding by ratifying the contested parts of the governor's order. Fla. Stat. ch. 2012–116.)

In a comprehensive study of regulatory moratoria at the federal and state levels, Professor Watts argues that protracted or indefinite freezes ("hard moratoria") are ill-advised and improper, because they foster uncertainty, invite legal challenges (as in *Whiley*), and do not demonstrably reduce compliance costs anyway. She takes a more benign view of temporary ("soft") moratoria on rulemaking. If limited in duration, she says, they can be a legally defensible and legitimate response to "midnight rulemaking" by a prior administration. Kathryn A. Watts, *Regulatory Moratoria*, 61 DUKE L.J. 1883 (2012). For more on midnight rulemaking, see § 5.7 N.9.

14. *Problem.* Recently the Department of Pollution Control (DPC), an executive branch agency in the state of Madison, announced rules designed to regulate municipal incinerators, which are a significant source of air pollution. Soon afterwards, a local newspaper published an article purporting to give the inside story as to why some of the restrictions that DPC had tentatively endorsed in its notice of proposed rulemaking were eliminated from the final version of the rules. Among the details in the story were the following:

One of these abandoned proposals was a ban on burning lead-acid automobile batteries in city incinerators. According to the newspaper, Bonita, a policy analyst with the Madison Office of Information and Regulatory Affairs (MOIRA), questioned the proposed ban in a face-to-face meeting with Chad, the chair of DPC. Bonita pointed out that the burning of vehicle batteries is already regulated under other environmental laws. She argued that, although DPC had claimed that the incinerator rule would produce even greater environmental benefits, the studies on which it was relying had methodological problems. Chad didn't want to conduct further studies, because he was eager to get the overall package of rules onto the books soon. Moreover, he thought that her proposed solution was reasonable, although not the one he would have chosen on his own. Accordingly, Chad, who wanted to be seen as a team player, agreed to support Bonita's recommendation.

That discussion proceeded in a cooperative fashion, but another aspect of the negotiations went less smoothly. Bonita challenged the agency's proposed requirement that cities must develop programs to recycle old newspapers, in order to minimize the quantity of newsprint that would be burned in municipal incinerators. When Chad resisted dropping the recycling requirement, Bonita insisted: "I have it straight from the governor that this change is imperative. We're really hearing from the mayors on this. They say the kind of recycling you would require is just too expensive and wouldn't have much effect on pollution anyway. So, we aren't just asking you to drop this—we're telling you." Chad reluctantly replied, "All right—but only because the governor says we have to do this."

The Alliance for a Clean Environment intends to petition the agency to reconsider its omission of the vehicle battery and recycling requirements. As counsel to the Alliance, you are asked whether the group can fairly argue that, if the newspaper's story is true, MOIRA or DPC acted unlawfully or inappropriately. How would you respond? *Should* any of their activities be prohibited? (a) Assume that MOIRA conducts its oversight activities pursuant to a state executive order that is substantially identical to federal E.O. 12,866, and that Madison's judicial case law is the same as federal law. (b) Alternatively, assume that the governor of Madison must sign off on all regulations issued by state agencies. *Cf. New York v. Reilly,* 969 F.2d 1147 (D.C. Cir. 1992).

CHAPTER 8

FREEDOM OF INFORMATION AND OTHER OPEN GOVERNMENT LAWS

■ ■ ■

This chapter addresses statutes that relate to the issue of governmental openness and transparency. It asks whether government documents and functions should be open to public scrutiny. It also considers whether such openness might be viewed as a political check on agency action, like the legislative and executive controls discussed in chapter 7. The chapter concentrates on freedom of information legislation and also considers open meeting laws and the Federal Advisory Committee Act.

§ 8.1 FREEDOM OF INFORMATION

The federal Freedom of Information Act (often referred to as FOIA) was originally enacted in 1966. It was amended and strengthened in 1974, at a time when mistrust of government was rampant. In 1996 it was amended to take account of electronic records. FOIA was again amended in 2007 by the OPEN Government Act in ways that made agencies more accountable for responding to FOIA requests.

The Act consists of three parts, all found in § 552 of the APA:

(i)   Under APA § 552(a)(1) (parts of which were in the original 1946 APA), an agency must *publish* certain important information, including a statement of its organization and procedure, as well as its substantive rules of general applicability. *See* § 5.7. Statements of general policy and interpretations of general applicability must also be published. If any of this material is not published, a person without actual and timely knowledge of its terms cannot be adversely affected by it.

(ii)   Under APA § 552(a)(2), an agency must *make available* (but not necessarily publish) specified additional material. This includes final opinions, staff manuals, instructions to staff that affect the public, and policy statements and interpretations of particular (rather than general) applicability. This requirement is discussed in § 5.7 N.1 and in the *Sears, Roebuck* case which follows. (At the state level, obligations similar to those of §§ 552(a)(1) and (a)(2) are imposed by 2010 MSAPA § 203; *see also* the discussion in § 5.7 N.2.)

Material covered by § 552(a)(2) must be indexed, and, for records created after November 1, 1996, must be placed in a computer database. Material covered by this provision may not be used adversely to a person unless these requirements are met or the person had actual and timely knowledge of its contents. *See Smith v. NTSB*, 981 F.2d 1326 (D.C. Cir. 1993) (decision suspending pilot's license set aside because agency failed to make publicly available a staff instruction setting the penalties for such violations).

(iii) Most important, under APA § 552(a)(3), an agency *must furnish any reasonably described record* requested by any person for any reason. This provision was revolutionary at the time of its enactment. It's what people usually mean when they discuss FOIA.

If an agency refuses to furnish the record (or fails to act within the very short time frame described in § 552(a)(6)), the requester is entitled to go to federal district court to compel disclosure. A requester who substantially prevails in court can recover attorney's fees. The agency has the burden to justify non-disclosure on the basis of one of the nine exemptions to the Act's disclosure requirements contained in § 552(b). To satisfy its burden, the agency must claim and justify an exemption for each document (or part of a document) through a detailed index (usually called a *Vaughn* index). The court decides the matter de novo (i.e. without deferring to the agency's judgment).

The 1996 E-FOIA amendments require the government to place on the Internet previously released records that are likely to be the subject of additional requests (as well as § 552(a)(2) materials created after November 1, 1996). It requires the government to supply documents in the format requested (such as CD-ROM). It permits agencies to establish multiple tracks, delaying complex requests and satisfying simple ones first. It also permits requesters to request expedited processing if they can demonstrate a compelling need for the information (such as a reporter working on deadline). The 2007 OPEN Government Act created a new agency, the Office of Government Information Services (OGIS). OGIS serves as a FOIA ombudsman, assisting members of the public with FOIA problems and mediating FOIA disputes between requesters and agencies.

Comparable provisions have been adopted in every state and in many foreign countries. See Burt A. Braverman & Wesley R. Heppler, *A Practical Review of State Open Records Laws*, 49 GEO. WASH. L. REV. 720 (1981); John M. Ackerman & Irma E. Sandoval-Ballesteros, *The Global Explosion of Freedom of Information Laws*, 58 ADMIN. L. REV. 85 (2006). See Wikipedia's impressive list of FOIA laws by country. http://en.wikipedia.org/wiki/Freedom_of_information_laws_by_country

There is a sharp difference of opinion about whether the benefits of laws like FOIA or similar state acts outweigh the costs. During hearings on the e-rulemaking amendments in 1992, Senator Patrick Leahy stated: "FOIA proves that the best way to combat the coverups, the mistakes, and the secrecy that undermine faith in our democratic system is to expose them to public view."

Against these benefits must be weighed the substantial costs of FOIA's commitment to disclose whatever document is requested. At the federal level, FOIA's costs are far in excess of what its drafters ever imagined. In 2012, the federal government received more than 650,000 requests for information under FOIA, of which about 95% were granted in whole or in part. (See foia.gov for up-to-date statistics about FOIA.) Many requests appear to involve efforts by one business to obtain information about another business for private gain. Many agencies are hopelessly backlogged with FOIA requests and cannot possibly comply with its time requirements. The delays can run to many years. A single request can be enormously time consuming; one company's request to the Navy was estimated to include several million documents that spanned 10,000 linear feet. Thomas M. Susman, *Introduction to the Issues, Problems, and Relevant Law*, 34 ADMIN. L. REV. 117, 118 (1982).

It is difficult to estimate the cost to government, but estimates range between about $50 million and $250 million per year or more. A large number of agency employees, who would otherwise be engaged in carrying out agency programs, are instead employed to respond to FOIA requests—searching for documents, redacting (deleting) material from records that are partly exempt from disclosure (sometimes word-by-word review is needed), making copies, or reviewing disclosure decisions by other employees. This work is laborious and unpopular with the government employees assigned to do it.

Thousands of FOIA cases have been filed in the already swamped federal courts; the cases often receive priority (28 U.S.C. § 1657) and require the judge to conduct a painstaking in-camera review of a mass of documents. The U.S. Supreme Court has decided dozens of FOIA cases, and the Arkansas Supreme Court has decided over three dozen. John Watkins, *The Arkansas Freedom of Information Act: Time for a Change*, 44 ARK. L. REV. 535 (1991). While still a law professor, Justice Scalia wrote:

> FOIA . . . is the Taj Mahal of the Doctrine of Unanticipated Consequences, the Sistine Chapel of Cost Benefit Analysis Ignored . . . The foregoing defects [of excessive costs and burdens on government and the courts] . . . might not be defects in the best of all possible worlds. They are foolish extravagances only because we do not have an unlimited amount of federal money to spend, an unlimited number of agency employees to assign, an unlimited number of judges to hear and decide cases. We must,

alas, set some priorities—and unless the world is mad the usual
FOIA request should not be high on the list.

Antonin Scalia, *The Freedom of Information Act Has No Clothes*,
REGULATION, March/April 1982, at 15, 17–18.

To alleviate the burden on courts of resolving FOIA cases, Illinois,
Connecticut, Minnesota and Utah route FOIA disputes to an independent
agency for decision. *See* Sarah Klaper, *The Sun Peeking Around the
Corner: Illinois' New Freedom of Information Act as a National Model,* 10
CONN. PUB. INT. L. J. 63 (2010). The FOIA agency's decision is judicially
reviewable, but at least a reviewing court need not consider the case de
novo, as it must do under federal law and the law of most states. In New
York, an independent agency provides advisory opinions about FOIA
issues, to which courts often grant deference. *Miracle Mile Assocs. v.
Yudelson,* 417 N.Y. Supp. 2d 142 (App. Div. 1979).

In evaluating FOIA, it is necessary to take account of its nine
exemptions. If FOIA is too costly, one policy alternative is to broaden the
existing exemptions or create new ones. Or are these exceptions already
too broad? The following discussion considers two of the exemptions in the
federal act: § 552(b)(5), discussed in *Sears, Roebuck,* and § 552(b)(4),
discussed in *Chrysler.*

§ 8.1.1 PROTECTING DELIBERATION: § 552(b)(5)

NLRB v. SEARS, ROEBUCK & CO.
421 U.S. 132 (1975)

WHITE, J.:

The National Labor Relations Board (the Board) and its General
Counsel seek to set aside an order of the United States District Court
directing disclosure to respondent, Sears, Roebuck & Co. (Sears),
pursuant to the Freedom of Information Act, 5 U.S.C. § 552 (Act), of
certain memoranda, known as "Advice Memoranda" and "Appeals
Memoranda," and related documents generated by the Office of the
General Counsel in the course of deciding whether or not to permit the
filing with the Board of unfair labor practice complaints. . . .

[When an employer or union believes that an unfair labor practice
has occurred, it files a "charge" with an NLRB regional director. The
regional director decides whether or not to issue a "complaint" and thus
set the Board's adjudicatory process into motion. If the director refuses to
issue a complaint and the charging party disagrees with that decision, the
charging party can appeal the director's decision to the General Counsel
who makes the ultimate decision whether a complaint should issue. This
decision is embodied in an "appeal memorandum." In some situations, a

regional director seeks advice from the General Counsel before deciding whether to issue a complaint. The advice is furnished in a document called an "advice memorandum." Sears requested that the General Counsel disclose under FOIA all advice memos and appeal memos issued within the previous five years concerning a specific legal issue, but the General Counsel refused.]

As the Act is structured, virtually every document generated by an agency is available to the public in one form or another, unless it falls within one of the Act's nine exemptions. Certain documents described in 5 U.S.C. § 552(a)(1) such as "rules of procedure" must be published in the Federal Register; others, including "final opinions . . . made in the adjudication of cases," "statements of policy and interpretations which have been adopted by the agency," and "instructions to staff that affect a member of the public," described in 5 U.S.C. § 552(a)(2), must be indexed and made available to a member of the public on demand. Finally, and more comprehensively, all "identifiable records" must be made available to a member of the public on demand. 5 U.S.C. § 552(a)(3). The Act expressly states, however, that the disclosure obligation "does not apply" to those documents described in the nine enumerated exempt categories listed in § 552(b).

Sears claims, and the courts below ruled, that the memoranda sought are expressions of legal and policy decisions already adopted by the agency and constitute "final opinions" and "instructions to staff that affect a member of the public," both categories being expressly disclosable under § 552(a)(2) of the Act, pursuant to its purposes to prevent the creation of "secret law." In any event, Sears claims, the memoranda are nonexempt "identifiable records" which must be disclosed under § 552(a)(3). The General Counsel, on the other hand, claims that the memoranda sought here are not final opinions under § 552(a)(2) and that even if they are "identifiable records" otherwise disclosable under § 552(a)(3), they are exempt under § 552(b), principally as "intra-agency" communications under § 552(b)(5) (Exemption 5), made in the course of formulating agency decisions on legal and policy matters. . . .

It is clear, and the General Counsel concedes, that Appeals and Advice Memoranda are at the least "identifiable records" which must be disclosed on demand, unless they fall within one of the Act's exempt categories. It is also clear that, if the memoranda do fall within one of the Act's exempt categories, our inquiry is at an end, for the Act "does not apply" to such documents. Thus our inquiry, strictly speaking, must be into the scope of the exemptions which the General Counsel claims to be applicable—principally Exemption 5 relating to "intra-agency memorandums." The General Counsel also concedes, however, and we hold for the reasons set forth below, that Exemption 5 does not apply to any document which falls within the meaning of the phrase "final opinion

... made in the adjudication of cases." 5 U.S.C. § 552(a)(2)(A). The General Counsel argues, therefore, as he must, that no Advice or Appeals Memorandum is a final opinion made in the adjudication of a case and that all are "intra-agency" memoranda within the coverage of Exemption 5. . . .

A

The parties are in apparent agreement that Exemption 5 withholds from a member of the public documents which a private party could not discover in litigation with the agency. Since virtually any document not privileged may be discovered by the appropriate litigant, if it is relevant to his litigation, and since the Act clearly intended to give any member of the public as much right to disclosure as one with a special interest therein, it is reasonable to construe Exemption 5 to exempt those documents, and only those documents, normally privileged in the civil discovery context. The privileges claimed by petitioners to be relevant to this case are (i) the "generally . . . recognized" privilege for "confidential intra-agency advisory opinions. . . ." disclosure of which "would be injurious to the consultative functions of government . . ." (sometimes referred to as "executive privilege"), and (ii) the attorney-client and attorney work-product privileges generally available to all litigants.

(i)

That Congress had the Government's executive privilege specifically in mind in adopting Exemption 5 is clear. . . . The cases uniformly rest the privilege on the policy of protecting the "decision making processes of government agencies," and focus on documents "reflecting advisory opinions, recommendations and deliberations comprising part of a process by which governmental decisions and policies are formulated." . . . [T]he "frank discussion of legal or policy matters" in writing might be inhibited if the discussion were made public; and the "decisions" and "policies formulated" would be the poorer as a result. As a lower court has pointed out, "there are enough incentives as it is for playing it safe and listing with the wind," and as we have said in an analogous context, "[h]uman experience teaches that those who expect public dissemination of their remarks may well temper candor with a concern for appearances . . . to the detriment of the decisionmaking process." *United States v. Nixon*, 418 U.S. 683, 705 (1974).

Manifestly, the ultimate purpose of this long-recognized privilege is to prevent injury to the quality of agency decisions. The quality of a particular agency decision will clearly be affected by the communications received by the decisionmaker on the subject of the decision prior to the time the decision is made. However, it is difficult to see how the quality of a decision will be affected by communications with respect to the decision occurring after the decision is finally reached; and therefore equally difficult to see how the quality of the decision will be affected by forced disclosure of such communications, as long as prior communications and the ingredients of the decisionmaking process are not disclosed. Accordingly, the lower courts have uniformly drawn a distinction between pre-decisional communications, which are privileged, and communications made after the decision and designed to explain it, which are not.[19]

This distinction is supported not only by the lesser injury to the decisionmaking process flowing from disclosure of postdecisional communications, but also, in the case of those communications which explain the decision, by the increased public interest in knowing the basis for agency policy already adopted. The public is only marginally concerned with reasons supporting a policy which an agency has rejected, or with reasons which might have supplied, but did not supply, the basis for a policy which was actually adopted on a different ground. In contrast, the public is vitally concerned with the reasons which did supply the basis for an agency policy actually adopted. These reasons, if expressed within the agency, constitute the "working law" of the agency and have been held by the lower courts to be outside the protection of Exemption 5. Exemption 5, properly construed, calls for "disclosure of all 'opinions and interpretations' which embody the agency's effective law and policy, and the withholding of all papers which reflect the agency's group thinking in the process of working out its policy and determining what its law shall be."

This conclusion is powerfully supported by the other provisions of the Act. The affirmative portion of the Act, expressly requiring indexing of "final opinions," "statements of policy and interpretations which have been adopted by the agency," and "instructions to staff that affect a member of the public," 5 U.S.C. § 552(a)(2), represents a strong congressional aversion to "secret [agency] law," and represents an affirmative congressional purpose to require disclosure of documents which have "the force and effect of law." We should be reluctant, therefore, to construe Exemption 5 to apply to the documents described in 5 U.S.C. § 552(a)(2); and with respect at least to "final opinions," which not only invariably explain agency action already taken or an agency decision already made, but also constitute "final dispositions" of matters by an agency, Exemption 5 can never apply.

---

[19] We are aware that the line between predecisional documents and postdecisional documents may not always be a bright one. Indeed, even the prototype of the postdecisional document—the "final opinion"—serves the dual function of explaining the decision just made and providing guides for decisions of similar or analogous cases arising in the future. In its latter function, the opinion is predecisional; and the manner in which it is written may, therefore, affect decisions in later cases. For present purposes it is sufficient to note that final opinions are primarily postdecisional—looking back on and explaining, as they do, a decision already reached or a policy already adopted—and that their disclosure poses a negligible risk of denying to agency decisionmakers the uninhibited advice which is so important to agency decisions.

(ii)

It is equally clear that Congress had the attorney's work-product privilege specifically in mind when it adopted Exemption 5 and that such a privilege had been recognized in the civil discovery context by the prior case law. The case law clearly makes the attorney's work-product rule of *Hickman v. Taylor*, 329 U.S. 495 (1947), applicable to Government attorneys in litigation. Whatever the outer boundaries of the attorney's work-product rule are, the rule clearly applies to memoranda prepared by an attorney in contemplation of litigation which set forth the attorney's theory of the case and his litigation strategy.

B

Applying these principles to the memoranda sought by Sears, it becomes clear that Exemption 5 does not apply to those Appeals and Advice Memoranda which conclude that no complaint should be filed and which have the effect of finally denying relief to the charging party; but that Exemption 5 does protect from disclosure those Appeals and Advice Memoranda which direct the filing of a complaint and the commencement of litigation before the Board.

(i)

Under the procedures employed by the General Counsel, Advice and Appeals Memoranda are communicated to the Regional Director after the General Counsel, through his Advice and Appeals Branches, has decided whether or not to issue a complaint; and represent an explanation to the Regional Director of a legal or policy decision already adopted by the General Counsel. In the case of decisions not to file a complaint, the memoranda effect as "final" a "disposition" as an administrative decision can—representing, as it does, an unreviewable rejection of the charge filed by the private party. Disclosure of these memoranda would not intrude on predecisional processes, and protecting them would not improve the quality of agency decisions, since when the memoranda are communicated to the Regional Director, the General Counsel has already reached his decision and the Regional Director who receives them has no decision to make—he is bound to dismiss the charge. Moreover, the General Counsel's decisions not to file complaints together with the Advice and Appeals Memoranda explaining them, are precisely the kind of agency law in which the public is so vitally interested and which Congress sought to prevent the agency from keeping secret.

For essentially the same reasons, these memoranda are "final opinions" made in the "adjudication of cases" which must be indexed pursuant to § 552(a)(2)(A). The decision to dismiss a charge is a decision in a "case" and constitutes an "adjudication": an "adjudication" is defined under the Administrative Procedure Act, of which § 552 is a part, as "agency process for the formulation of an order," § 551(7); an "order" is defined as "the whole or a part of a final disposition, whether affirmative [or] negative . . . of an agency in a matter . . ." § 551(6); and the dismissal of a charge, as noted above, is a "final disposition." Since an Advice or Appeals Memorandum explains the reasons for the "final disposition" it plainly qualifies as an "opinion"; and falls within § 552(a)(2)(A). . . .

(ii)

Advice and Appeals Memoranda which direct the filing of a complaint, on the other hand, fall within the coverage of Exemption 5. The filing of a complaint does not finally dispose even of the General Counsel's responsibility with respect to the case. The case will be litigated before and decided by the Board; and the General Counsel will have the responsibility of advocating the position of the charging party before the Board. The Memoranda will inexorably contain the General Counsel's theory of the case and may communicate to the Regional Director some litigation strategy or settlement advice. Since the Memoranda will also have been prepared in contemplation of the upcoming litigation, they fall squarely within Exemption 5's protection of an attorney's work product. At the same time, the public's interest in disclosure is substantially reduced by the fact that the basis for the General Counsel's legal decision will come out in the course of litigation before the Board; and that the "law" with respect to these cases will ultimately be made not by the General Counsel but by the Board or the courts.

We recognize that an Advice or Appeals Memorandum directing the filing of a complaint—although representing only a decision that a legal issue is sufficiently in doubt to warrant determination by another body— has many of the characteristics of the documents described in § 552(a)(2). Although not a "final opinion" in the "adjudication" of a "case" because it does not effect a "final disposition," the memorandum does explain a decision already reached by the General Counsel which has real operative effect—it permits litigation before the Board; and we have indicated a reluctance to construe Exemption 5 to protect such documents. We do so in this case only because the decisionmaker—the General Counsel—must become a litigating party to the case with respect to which he has made his decision. The attorney's work-product policies which Congress clearly incorporated into Exemption 5 thus come into play and lead us to hold that the Advice and Appeals Memoranda directing the filing of a complaint are exempt whether or not they are, as the District Court held, "instructions to staff that affect a member of the public. . . ."

C

Petitioners assert that the District Court erred in holding that documents incorporated by reference in nonexempt Advice and Appeals Memoranda lose any exemption they might previously have held as "intra-agency" memoranda. We disagree.

The probability that an agency employee will be inhibited from freely advising a decisionmaker for fear that his advice, if adopted, will become public is slight. First, when adopted, the reasoning becomes that of the agency and becomes its responsibility to defend. Second, agency employees will generally be encouraged rather than discouraged by public knowledge that their policy suggestions have been adopted by the agency. Moreover, the public interest in knowing the reasons for a policy actually adopted by an agency supports the District Court's decision below. Thus, we hold that, if an agency chooses *expressly* to adopt or incorporate by reference an intra-agency memorandum previously covered by Exemption 5 in what would otherwise be a final opinion, that memorandum may be withheld only on the ground that it falls within the coverage of some exemption other than Exemption 5.

NOTES AND QUESTIONS

1.   *Governmental assertion of FOIA exemptions.* Early in his first term, President Clinton issued a memorandum calling upon agencies to "renew their commitment" to FOIA. Under the Clinton approach, the Department applied a presumption of disclosure, meaning that it should assert that an exemption applies only where disclosure would be harmful to an interest protected by an exemption. The George W. Bush administration reversed the Clinton policy. It announced that there is no presumption of disclosure and that it would defend any non-disclosure decision that had a substantial legal basis.

On his first day in office, President Obama issued a memorandum that reversed the Bush FOIA policy and called for all agencies and departments to adopt a presumption in favor of Freedom of Information Act requests. 74 Fed. Reg. 4683 (2009). The Obama memorandum called for online publication of as much information as possible without waiting for a FOIA request. The memorandum called for each agency to create and institutionalize a culture of open government. Obama's open government initiative led to creation of FOIA.gov, an all-purpose website that is a goldmine of information. For example, it has a handy list of FOIA contact information within every government agency and includes frequently requested documents.

Should the government resist disclosure of documents that might be covered by a FOIA exemption if disclosure would not harm the interest of the government or of private parties?

2.   *FOIA exemption (5)—deliberative documents.* A document that would normally be privileged from discovery in civil litigation is exempt from FOIA disclosure under exemption (5). The most important such privilege is the government's right to withhold records that would expose its deliberative processes. As *Sears* explains, this privilege applies to governmental documents that are both "pre-decisional" and "deliberative." What is the rationale for the deliberative process privilege? Does the deliberative process privilege diminish the value of FOIA as a political check on agencies?

In applying the deliberative process privilege, courts often distinguish between factual and non-factual material. The notion is that disclosure of factual material even in pre-decisional memoranda would not have a detrimental effect on the decision-making process. However, even factual material is exempt "when disclosure would so expose the deliberative process within an agency that it must be deemed exempted." *Trentadue v. Integrity Committee*, 501 F.3d 1215, 1226–29 (10th Cir. 2007). The New York statute explicitly provides that its deliberative process exemption applies neither to "statistical or factual tabulations or data" nor to "instructions to staff that affect the public." Public Officers Law § 87(g).

A provision comparable to the deliberative process exemption exists in about one-third of state open records laws. In numerous others it has been recognized by judicial decisions. *See, e.g., City of Colorado Springs v. White*, 967 P.2d 1042 (Colo. 1998). However, in many states these exemptions are significantly narrower than federal exemption (5). For example, many states exempt only preliminary drafts of government reports, not other pre-decisional communications. Michigan exempts intra-agency communications only if the agency "shows that in the particular instance the public interest in encouraging frank communication between officials and employees of public bodies clearly outweighs the public interest in disclosure." *See Bukowski v. City of Detroit*, 732 N.W.2d 75 (Mich. 2007); Braverman & Heppler, *supra*, at 743–45.

California applies a similar balancing test to all requested information under its Public Records Act. Thus the California statute gives courts considerably more discretion to create FOIA exceptions than does the federal act. Under authority of that statute, the California Supreme Court adopted the deliberative process privilege (which had not existed in the California statute prior to that decision). *See Times Mirror Co. v. Superior Court*, 813 P.2d 240 (Cal. 1991) (denying disclosure of governor's appointment schedules for five years in order to preserve his ability to hold candid discussions).

Sears also applied the work-product privilege under the FOIA (5) exemption. In *Kent Corp. v. NLRB*, 530 F.2d 612, 622–24 (5th Cir. 1976), Kent sought disclosure of "final investigative reports" prepared by NLRB regional board attorneys (for cases in which the regional director refused to issue a complaint). These reports contained both legal theories and analyses of factual materials. The court held that both the legal and the factual portions of these reports fell under the work-product privilege and thus were exempt from FOIA disclosure. The work-product privilege "is based on the public policy of preserving the independence of lawyers through the avoidance of unwarranted intrusion into their private files and mental processes . . . and since the litigants before the Labor Board are legion, the evil of harassment . . . is correspondingly multiplied. The function of deciding controversies might soon be overwhelmed by the duty of answering questions about them."

FOIA exemption (5) also includes a privilege for presidential communications. The term "executive privilege" (referred to in the *Sears* opinion) covers both the presidential privilege and the deliberative process privilege (discussed in *Sears*). The presidential privilege covers communications with the President. In addition, it covers documents authored by, or solicited and received by, members of the White House staff with significant responsibility for formulating advice to be given to the President. *See Judicial Watch, Inc. v. United States Dep't of Justice*, 365 F.3d 1108 (D.C. Cir. 2004) (presidential privilege does not extend to documents concerning pardon applications that are not solicited by or received by the President or his senior advisers). The presidential privilege is broader than the deliberative process privilege involved in *Sears*, because the presidential privilege covers factual materials and post-decisional documents. *See In re Sealed Case*, 121 F.3d 729 (D.C. Cir. 1997). *See generally* Michael N. Kennedy, *Escaping the Fishbowl: A Proposal to Fortify the Deliberative Process Privilege,* 99 Nw. U. L. Rev. 1769 (2005), which advocates a merger of the deliberative process and presidential privileges.

3.   *Final opinions and exemption (5).* *Sears* held that post-decisional appeals or advice memos are "final opinions." Under § 552(a)(2)(A), final opinions must be routinely made available (as distinguished from being furnished on specific request) and must be indexed. Exemption (5) does not apply to final opinions because such opinions are considered to state the agency's effective law and policy. If undisclosed, these opinions would be "secret law." What's wrong with secret law?

The final paragraph of the opinion requires disclosure of an exempt document if "an agency chooses *expressly* to adopt or incorporate by reference" [emphasis is in the original] an exempt intra-agency memorandum . . . in what otherwise would be a final opinion." This language has caused difficulty in subsequent cases. In *National Council of La Raza v. Dep't of Justice,* 411 F.3d 350 (2d Cir. 2005), the Attorney General repeatedly referred in letters and press conferences to an exempt pre-decisional memorandum from the Office of Legal Council (OLC) as to whether state and local government could legally enforce immigration laws. This was "express" adoption of the memo as a justification for a newly announced federal government policy. As a result the memo had to be disclosed.

Another passage in *Sears* has also been difficult to apply. What is the "working law" of the agency? The *Sears* opinion said: "In contrast, the public is vitally concerned with the reasons which did supply the basis for an agency policy actually adopted. These reasons, if expressed within the agency, constitute the 'working law' of the agency and have been held by the lower courts to be outside the protection of Exemption 5." *See* APA § 552(a)(2)(B), calling for the agency to make public (without request) "statements of policy and interpretations which have been adopted by the agency and are not published in the Federal Register."

Thus memoranda that state an agency's policy decision as to how it will discharge its functions, and that are in fact followed by agency staff, are treated as "working law" that must be disclosed even if the documents were pre-decisional and deliberative in nature. *See Public Citizen, Inc. v. Office of Mgmt. & Budget,* 598 F.3d 865, 874–77 (D.C. Cir. 2010). The *Public Citizen* case involved a request for documents from OMB that indicate which agencies may submit materials to Congress and bypass prior OMB clearance. The documents in question list the agencies currently allowed to bypass OMB and the reasons for allowing the bypass. Thus the documents aren't deliberative; instead, they state the working law of the agency and must be disclosed.

4.   *FOIA as discovery.* Why did Sears want the documents? Why did the NLRB want to keep them confidential? Sears had filed a charge with a regional director who refused to issue a complaint after receiving an advice memorandum from the General Counsel. Sears was in the process of preparing an appeal to the General Counsel of that refusal. The Court observed:

> Sears' rights under the Act are neither increased nor decreased by reason of the fact that it claims an interest in the Advice and Appeals Memoranda greater than that shared by the average member of the public. The Act is fundamentally designed to inform the public about agency action and not to benefit private litigants.

421 U.S. at 143 n.10. The *Sears* case is a good example of one of the most important functions of FOIA—and one of its most controversial. It is used as a technique for discovery in pending administrative or judicial litigation. *See generally* Edward A. Tomlinson, *Use of the Freedom of Information Act for Discovery Purposes,* 43 MD. L. REV. 119 (1984).

A litigator might prefer to conduct discovery through a FOIA request, because agency rules may provide only for very limited discovery or none at all. *See* § 4.1.2 N.7. When discovery is available, it is provided only at defined times (i.e. after a complaint is filed) and is controlled by an adjudicator (an administrative presiding officer or a judge if the case is in court). Under conventional discovery rules, a party can resist production of irrelevant or excessively burdensome materials. But when documents are demanded under FOIA, there are no such limits. Unless an exemption applies, all of the requested documents must be promptly disclosed.

On the other hand, the regular discovery process offers litigants some advantages over FOIA. For example, a person making a FOIA request must ordinarily pay the costs of search and duplication. *See* § 552(a)(4)(A). No such costs are imposed in discovery. Discovery sometimes offers processes such as depositions and interrogatories that are unavailable under FOIA. Finally, discovery privileges might be less protective to the government than the FOIA exemptions. For example, although the deliberative process privilege involved in *Sears* is also applicable to a request for documents in discovery, a court may require disclosure of the documents upon a showing of special need. *See, e.g., United States v. Nixon,* 418 U.S. 683 (1974) (documents and tapes protected by executive privilege must be disclosed, because they were needed in the prosecution of a criminal case).

Should FOIA be amended to preclude requests by persons engaged in litigation with the agency, thus remitting such persons to conventional discovery? Or do such litigants have the strongest claim for FOIA disclosure? ACUS recommended that a party in litigation against the government be required to notify government counsel of any FOIA requests relevant to the proceeding. But it did not recommend closing FOIA to parties in litigation. *See* ACUS Recommendation 83–4, *The Use of the Freedom of Information Act for Discovery Purposes,* 48 Fed. Reg. 57,463 (1983).

5. *Related exemptions.* The Government's interest in secrecy is protected by a number of exceptions in addition to FOIA exemption (5). Thus information that is classified as secret is protected from disclosure under exemption (1). Government employees make millions of decisions to classify information each year, and the amount of information classified has greatly increased since 9/11. While many such decisions are appropriate, others may be intended more to cover up embarrassing material than to protect national security. Exemption (1) permits the court to conduct an in-camera review of whether the document should be classified. *See* 5 U.S.C. § 552(a)(4)(B). Nevertheless, judges tend to be quite deferential in second-guessing classification decisions and usually accept affidavits from intelligence or military officials at face value. *See Bassiouni v. CIA,* 392 F.3d 244 (7th Cir.2004) (upholding CIA's refusal to itemize which documents or files included requester's name); Meredith Fuchs, *Judging Secrets: The Role Courts Should Play in Preventing Unnecessary Secrecy,* 58 ADMIN. L. REV. 131 (2006). As mentioned earlier, on his first day in office, President Obama called for a new culture of government transparency. Less than a year later, he issued an executive order that sharply limited the government's ability to classify materials as secret. Exec. Order 13,526, 75 Fed. Reg. 707 (2009).

FOIA exemption (3) protects information specifically exempted by another statute if the other statute leaves no discretion on the issue or establishes particular criteria for withholding. There are many such statutes. One, for example, protects virtually all CIA documents from disclosure. *See Berman v. CIA,* 501 F.3d 1136 (9th Cir. 2007).

Exemption (2) covers material "relating solely to the internal personnel rules and practices of an agency." The Supreme Court has construed this exemption quite narrowly, so that it covers only material relating to government personnel practices, such as documents relating to employee parking. See *Dep't of the Air Force v. Rose,* 425 U.S. 352 (1976) (exemption (2) does not cover case summaries of ethics decisions by the Air Force Academy, because they do not involve routine personnel practices but instead are important to the public—but they must be redacted to remove names of individual cadets); *Milner v. Dep't of the Navy,* 131 S. Ct. 1259 (2011) (exemption (2) does not cover data and maps relating to the storage of explosives by the Navy, because the documents do not relate to personnel practices—even though disclosure might threaten the security of the base). In *Milner,* the Court pointed out that the government could classify the documents as secret under exemption (1) if disclosure would really be dangerous and could even do so after receiving a FOIA request. Alternatively, it could persuade Congress to pass a statute that exempts the materials from disclosure and then rely on exemption (3) to keep them secret.

Exemption (7) protects the government's interest in the confidentiality of many law enforcement files and manuals. For example, a document that might disclose the identity of a confidential source is protected. Similarly, material that would disclose law enforcement techniques or guidelines is exempt if disclosure might facilitate circumvention of the law.

§ 8.1.2 CONFIDENTIAL PRIVATE INFORMATION: § 552(b)(4)

CHRYSLER CORP. v. BROWN
441 U.S. 281 (1979)

[Executive Orders 11246 and 11275 prohibit government contractors (such as Chrysler) from engaging in employment discrimination on the basis of race or sex. Regulations adopted by the Office of Federal Contract Compliance Programs (OFCCP) require contractors to file with the Defense Logistics Agency (DLA) detailed reports on their affirmative action plans and the composition of their workforce.

OFCCP regulations provide that such reports shall be made available for public inspection and copying "if it is determined that the requested inspection or copying furthers the public interest and does not impede any of the functions of OFCCP or the Compliance Agencies except in the case of records, disclosure of which is prohibited by law." OFCCP proposed to furnish Chrysler's affirmative action plan to a requester. Chrysler sought to enjoin this release, asserting that FOIA exemption (4) prevented disclosure of the material (a so-called "reverse FOIA" suit).]

REHNQUIST, J.:

The expanding range of federal regulatory activity and growth in the Government sector of the economy have increased federal agencies' demands for information about the activities of private individuals and corporations. These developments have paralleled a related concern about secrecy in Government and abuse of power. [FOIA] was a response to this concern, but it has also had a largely unforeseen tendency to exacerbate the uneasiness of those who comply with governmental demands for information. For under the FOIA third parties have been able to obtain Government files containing information submitted by corporations and individuals who thought that the information would be held in confidence. . . .

II

Chrysler contends that the nine exemptions in general, and Exemption 4 in particular, reflect a sensitivity to the privacy interests of private individuals and nongovernmental entities. That contention may be conceded without inexorably requiring the conclusion that the exemptions impose affirmative duties on an agency to withhold information sought. . . .

That the FOIA is exclusively a disclosure statute is, perhaps, demonstrated most convincingly by examining its provision for judicial relief. Subsection (a)(4)(B) gives federal district courts "jurisdiction to enjoin the agency from withholding agency records and to order the production of any agency records improperly withheld from the complainant." That provision does not give the authority to bar disclosure, and thus fortifies our belief that Chrysler, and courts which have shared its view, have incorrectly interpreted the exemption provisions of the FOIA. The Act is an attempt to meet the demand for open government while preserving workable confidentiality in governmental decisionmaking. . . .

III

Chrysler contends, however, that even if its suit for injunctive relief cannot be based on the FOIA, such an action can be premised on the Trade Secrets Act, 18 U.S.C. § 1905. The Act provides:

> Whoever, being an officer or employee of the United States . . . makes known in any manner or to any extent not authorized by law any information coming to him in the course of his employment . . . which information concerns or relates to the trade secrets, processes, operations, style of work, or apparatus . . . of any person [or] firm . . . shall be fined not more than $1,000, or imprisoned not more than one year, or both; and shall be removed from office or employment. . . .

A

The Court of Appeals held that § 1905 was not applicable to the agency disclosure at issue here because such disclosure was "authorized by law" within the meaning of the Act [referring to the OFCCP regulations]. . . . Chrysler contends here that these agency regulations are not "law" within the meaning of § 1905. It has been established in a variety of contexts that properly promulgated, substantive agency regulations have the "force and effect of law. . . ."

In order for a regulation to have the "force and effect of law," it must have certain substantive characteristics and be the product of certain procedural requisites. The central distinction among agency regulations found in the APA is that between "substantive rules" on the one hand and "interpretative rules, general statements of policy, or rules of agency organization, procedure, or practice" on the other. . . . We described a substantive rule—or a "legislative-type rule"—as one "affecting individual rights and obligations. . . ."

But in order for such regulations to have the "force and effect of law," it is necessary to establish a nexus between the regulations and some delegation of the requisite legislative authority by Congress. . . . We think that it is clear that when it enacted these statutes, Congress was not concerned with public disclosure of trade secrets or confidential business information. [Rather, they are housekeeping statutes, civil rights laws, etc.]

There is also a procedural defect in the OFCCP disclosure regulations which precludes courts from affording them the force and effect of law. That defect is a lack of strict compliance with the APA. . . . Certainly regulations subject to the APA cannot be afforded the "force and effect of law" if not promulgated pursuant to the statutory procedural minimum found in that Act. . . . [When he adopted the rules in question, the Secretary declared that they were interpretive rules, general statements of policy, or rules of procedure, so that notice and comment was not required.] We need not decide whether these regulations are properly characterized as "interpretative rules." It is enough that such regulations are not properly promulgated as substantive rules, and therefore not the product of procedures which Congress prescribed as necessary prerequisites to giving a regulation the binding force of law. An interpretative regulation or general statement of policy cannot be the "authorization by law" required by § 1905. . . .

IV

While Chrysler may not avail itself of any violations of the provisions of § 1905 in a separate cause of action, any such violations may have a dispositive effect on the outcome of judicial review of agency action pursuant to the APA. . . . [W]e conclude that DLA's decision to disclose the Chrysler reports is reviewable agency action and Chrysler is a person "adversely affected or aggrieved". . . . We believe any disclosure that violates § 1905 is "not in accordance with law" within the meaning of 5 U.S.C. § 706(2)(A). . . .

NOTES AND QUESTIONS

1. *The (4) exemption.* Under FOIA exemption (4), an agency may refuse to disclose information previously submitted to it in confidence.

Exemption (4) covers "trade secrets and commercial or financial information obtained from a person and privileged or confidential."

The key variable in applying exemption (4) is whether the material in question was provided to the government voluntarily or under compulsion. If a private submitter provided confidential information voluntarily and an agency disclosed it, the submitter would probably refuse to provide such information in the future. If, however, the information was submitted under compulsion, disclosure would not dry up the future flow of the information, but it might still affect the reliability and accuracy of the information and it would break the government's promise to keep the information confidential.

If the confidential information is submitted to the government voluntarily, it falls under exemption (4) if "it is of a kind that would customarily not be released to the public by the person from whom it was obtained." If the information is submitted to the government under compulsion (like the information involved in *Chrysler*), it falls under exemption (4) if disclosure is likely to cause substantial harm to the competitive position of the person from whom the information was obtained. *Critical Mass Energy Project v. NRC,* 975 F.2d 871 (D.C. Cir. 1992).

2.   *Disclosure of confidential material.* Government obtains a vast amount of confidential material from private parties through its regulatory, procurement, licensing, and law enforcement activity. Sometimes agencies wish to disclose such information instead of keeping it confidential. In theory, the *Chrysler* decision provides adequate protection, since the information that agencies are forbidden to disclose under § 1905 is the same as information the agency may refuse to disclose under exemption (4). *CNA Financial Corp. v. Donovan*, 830 F.2d 1132 (D.C. Cir. 1987).

One practical problem is that agencies may disclose confidential information by accident. Low-level staff members who are responsible for responding to FOIA requests may overlook material that should be kept confidential. Many submitters stamp their material "confidential" to alert agency personnel to such claims. Another practical problem is that agencies sometimes fail to inform the submitter of confidential information that they intend to disclose. This problem was remedied by Executive Order 12,600, 52 Fed. Reg. 23,781 (1987), which requires agencies to notify the submitters of confidential information that they propose to release the information, thus providing the submitters an opportunity to present objections to disclosure. *See also* N. Y. Public Officers Law § 89(5), which requires that an agency maintain material submitted in confidence separately from other material and notify the submitter if it proposes to disclose such material. Submitters are entitled to immediate judicial review if the agency proposes to release the material.

3.   *Reverse FOIA and the Trade Secrets Act. Chrysler* refused to accept the "reverse-FOIA" theory. Instead, it seized on the Trade Secrets Act as a judicially enforceable tool to prohibit agency disclosures of confidential material. The Trade Secrets Act is traceable to legislation originally enacted

in 1864, largely to prevent leaks of information by corrupt internal revenue agents. The section reads more like a rather clumsy attempt to deter and punish crooked government employees than a provision designed to limit agency discretion to disclose confidential business documents.

From the point of view of information submitters who wish to prevent disclosure, § 1905 has some flaws. In addition to the practical problems mentioned in N.2, the agency can adopt a rule permitting it to disclose the information and thus get around § 1905. Why did the Court decide that OFCCP's rule did not permit it to disclose the reports at issue in Chrysler?

4. *Privacy exemptions—judicial weighing.* A few other FOIA exemptions are intended to protect privacy interests. FOIA exemption (6) prevents disclosure of material (such as personnel or medical files) that would constitute a clearly unwarranted invasion of personal privacy. This exemption requires a court to balance the public's interest in disclosure against the private interest in preserving privacy. *See Dep't of Defense v. FLRA*, 510 U.S. 487 (1994), which concerned a request by a union to obtain the home addresses of non-member federal employees.

The Court upheld the government's refusal to supply the information under exemption (6), despite the Union's claim that the information was needed for collective bargaining purposes. The Court emphasized that the particular needs of the requestor to obtain the information would not be considered. The public's interest in disclosure of this particular information was slight, since it would tell the public nothing about what the Government is up to. In contrast, the invasion of the privacy interest of the federal employees is quite substantial.

Another exemption that protects privacy is (7)(C), for "records or information compiled for law enforcement purposes . . . to the extent that the production of such law enforcement records or information . . . (C) could reasonably be expected to constitute an unwarranted invasion of personal privacy." *FCC v. AT&T, Inc.*, 131 S.Ct. 1177 (2011), involved a request for documents that AT&T had submitted during an FCC investigation of that company. The Court unanimously held that "personal privacy" in this exemption refers to individuals, not to corporations. Corporations may be "persons" for many constitutional purposes, but Congress couldn't have intended to refer to corporations in using the term "personal privacy." Chief Justice Roberts concluded his opinion for the Court by remarking: "We trust that AT&T will not take it personally."

When it does apply, however, exemption (7)(C) does involve a weighing of interests, as exemption (6) does. Should this sort of weighing be employed when the government seeks to take advantage of other FOIA exemptions, such as exemptions (4) and (5)?

5. *Problem.* Gloria is a psychology professor at Madison University (MU). She is researching the effect on parents of having been subjected to physical abuse in childhood. The work has no commercial application but

requires substantial outside funding. Gloria applied to the National Institute of Mental Health (NIMH), a federal grantmaking agency, and received a $400,000 grant.

Gloria's application set forth the methodology for her research and the results she hoped to achieve. As part of its peer review process, NIMH submits each application to a committee of professors who write candid appraisals. The committee recommends which applications should be granted or denied and creates a priority list for granted applications in case funds are not sufficient for all of them. John, NIMH's director, makes the ultimate decision on each application. He writes a detailed report on his reasons for each decision. NIMH promised its applicants that all of the above material would remain confidential.

Bob, a psychology professor at Adams State University, filed a FOIA request to receive Gloria's application, the appraisals written by peer reviewers, the minutes of the committee's deliberation, and John's report.

(a) Assume that NIMH refuses to disclose any of the information and Bob brings a FOIA action to compel its disclosure. What part of the material, if any, is exempt from disclosure?

(b) Assume that NIMH proposes to disclose the information. Gloria seeks judicial review of this decision. Can she prevent the disclosure? *See Washington Research Project v. HEW*, 504 F.2d 238 (D.C. Cir. 1974).

§ 8.2 THE SUNSHINE AND ADVISORY COMMITTEE ACTS

§ 8.2.1 SUNSHINE ACTS

In 1976, the federal government enacted the Government in the Sunshine Act, 5 U.S.C. § 552b, which requires public meetings at multi-member agencies (agencies headed by a single individual are not covered). These open meeting laws are often referred to as "sunshine laws." All fifty states have sunshine laws applicable to local government and about half of them apply to state government agencies as well. *See* Teresa Pupillo, Note, *The Changing Weather Forecast: Government in the Sunshine in the 1990s—An Analysis of State Sunshine Laws,* 71 WASH. U.L.Q. 1165 (1993). In general, sunshine laws require that members of the agency head hold their meetings in public unless the meeting falls under a statutory exemption. An agency must publish advance public notice of such meetings including the agenda.

In many states, violation of open meeting laws by public officials can subject the officials to civil money penalties or even criminal prosecution. *See Rangra v. Brown,* 566 F.3d 515 (5th Cir. 2009), involving the criminal prosecution of several local government officials for violating the Texas Open Meeting Act (TOMA) by exchanging private emails about whether to call a council meeting. The court held that the First Amendment fully protects the speech of elected officials and that TOMA punishes speech based on its content. As a result, the restrictions on that speech are subject to strict scrutiny. The Fifth Circuit later granted en banc consideration of the *Rangra* decision (which had the effect of vacating it); ultimately, the case was dismissed as moot because the council members had left office. A subsequent Fifth Circuit decision seems contrary to *Rangra*, because it holds that TOMA is content-neutral, thus triggering only intermediate First Amendment scrutiny. *Asgeirsson v. Abbott*, 696 F.3d 454 (5th Cir. 2012). In any event, whether open meeting law provisions that impose civil or criminal penalties on elected officials who speak to each other in private might violate the First Amendment remains a live issue. *See* Steven J. Mulroy, *Sunlight's Glare: How Overbroad Open Government Laws Chill Free Speech and Hamper Effective Democracy*, 78 TENN. L. REV. 309 (2011).

a.   *Costs and benefits of sunshine laws.* The primary benefit of open meeting laws is to provide a political check on agency action. One court summarized the purposes of the federal act:

> Congress enacted the Sunshine Act to open the deliberations of multi-member federal agencies to public view. It believed that increased openness would enhance citizen confidence in government, encourage higher quality work by government officials, stimulate well-informed public debate about government programs and policies, and promote cooperation between citizens and government. In short, it sought to make government more fully accountable to the people.

Common Cause v. NRC, 674 F.2d 921, 928 (D.C. Cir. 1982).

However, numerous scholars and agency officials have pointed out that sunset laws create some serious problems. Because such laws contain no exemption parallel to FOIA exemption (5), pre-decisional communications among a quorum of agency members must be open to the public. Professor Richard Pierce writes:

> GSA [that is, the Government in the Sunshine Act] renders collegiality impossible in a collegial body that heads an agency . . . Because of GSA, meetings among members of multi-member agencies are infrequent; such agencies often make important decisions through notational voting with no prior deliberation; and communications at open meetings are grossly distorted by the presence of the public. Commissioners are reluctant to express their true views for fear that they will expose their ignorance or uncertainty with respect to issues of fact, policy, and laws. They attempt to disguise their uncertainties with stilted and contrived discussions that greatly impede the kind of

frank exchange of views that is essential to high-quality decisionmaking by a collegial body. . . . It is highly unlikely, for instance, that the Supreme Court would have issued its unanimous, bold decision in *Brown v. Board of Education* . . . if the Justices had been required to conduct the decade-long debate that preceded *Brown* only in public meetings.

1 RICHARD J. PIERCE, JR., ADMINISTRATIVE LAW TREATISE § 5.18 (5th ed. 2010).

In addition to notational voting, mentioned by Pierce, agencies sometimes engage in seriatim one-on-one meetings between the agency head and the various members (such meetings are exempt from sunshine laws if two members are not enough to be a quorum). The Act can also be circumvented by having staff members representing their bosses engage in deliberative meetings; the agency heads then rubber-stamp the staff decision in an open meeting without further discussion. Yet multi-member agencies exist so that members with diverse viewpoints can discuss and decide policy issues in a collegial manner; this goal is thwarted by the various techniques used to get around the requirements of open meeting laws.

In applying sunshine acts, courts have wrestled with the definition of "meeting," the requirement that agencies publish agendas of their meetings in advance, the application of the exemptions, and the sanctions for violation of the acts.

b. *Definition of meeting.* If the term "meeting" is defined too broadly, a sunshine act would prevent informal discussions between agency members; but if it is defined too narrowly, the members can easily circumvent it by making collegial decisions in secret, then rubber stamping them in brief public sessions.

In *Moberg v. Indep. School Dist. No. 281*, 336 N.W.2d 510, 518 (Minn. 1983) (emphasis added), the Court considered a series of informal discussions between members of a school board who were seeking to break a deadlock over an important policy issue. It said:

> We therefore hold that "meetings" subject to the requirements of the Open Meeting Law are those gatherings of a quorum or more members of the governing body . . . at which members *discuss, decide, or receive information as a group* on issues relating to the official business of that governing body. Although "chance or social gatherings" are exempt from the requirements of the statute . . . a quorum may not, as a group, discuss or receive information on official business in any setting under the guise of a private social gathering. The statute does not apply to letters or telephone conversations between fewer than a quorum.

Appellants correctly point out that this rule may be circumvented by serial face-to-face or telephone conversations between board members to marshall their votes on an issue before it is initially raised at a public hearing. It does not follow that two-or three-person conversations should be prohibited, however, because officials who are determined to act furtively will hold such discussions anyway, or might simply use an outsider as an intermediary. There is a way to illegally circumvent any rule the court might fashion, and therefore it is important that the rule not be so restrictive as to lose the public benefit of personal discussion between public officials while gaining little assurance of openness. Of course, serial meetings in groups of less than a quorum for the purposes of avoiding public hearings or fashioning agreement on an issue may also be found to be a violation of the statute depending upon the facts of the individual case.

In contrast to *Moberg,* the U.S. Supreme Court excluded information-gathering meetings from the federal Sunshine Act. *FCC v. ITT World Communc'ns, Inc.,* 466 U.S. 463 (1984). The *ITT* case involved a committee of FCC members who engaged in consultation with their foreign counterparts. The FCC committee was itself treated as an "agency," because it had power to approve certain applications. But its consultations were not "meetings," because they did not concern such approvals. According to the Court, a "meeting" occurs only when the agency *deliberates on matters within its formal delegated authority,* whereas the meetings in question were background discussions and exchanges of views with non-agency members. "Informal background discussions that clarify issues and expose varying views" are not "meetings," because Congress thought that keeping such discussions private was necessary for the effective conduct of agency business.

Should agencies be permitted to close their meetings to the public when the meeting will consist only of "discussions" as opposed to "deliberations?" Is it possible to make that distinction? *See* RICHARD K. BERG ET. AL., AN INTERPRETIVE GUIDE TO THE GOVERNMENT IN THE SUNSHINE ACT 226–28 (2d ed. 2005).

c.   *Advance publication of agendas.* In order for open meeting statutes to be a meaningful political check on government, members of the public must be able to attend the meetings. This requires reasonable advance publication of the time and place of the meeting and the agenda. Yet an overly rigid application of this rule would prevent agencies from dealing with important new business that demands immediate attention. Thus the Texas Supreme Court held that a school board violated the act when it notified the public that it would consider "personnel" and "litigation" matters. The public was entitled to a more specific agenda, in this case that the Board was going to consider the appointment of a new school superintendent and a major desegregation lawsuit—even though it was legally entitled to go into closed session on these matters. *Cox Enterprises v. Board of Trustees of Austin Indep. School Dist.*, 706 S.W.2d 956 (Tex. 1986).

d.   *Exemptions.* The exemptions to the federal act closely parallel the FOIA exemptions, except, as already mentioned, for the absence of a deliberative communication exemption. Generally speaking, if an agency could resist a FOIA demand, it could close a meeting which considers the same sort of information. Where a meeting or part of a meeting falls within an exemption, it can be closed, but the rest of the meeting, dealing with non-exempt matters, must be kept open.

There are several exemptions in the federal Sunshine Act not found in FOIA. One is for information that, if prematurely disclosed, would frustrate agency action. § 552b(c)(9)(B). This exemption is quite narrow. For example, premature disclosure of an embargo would cause the goods to be exported before the agency had time to act. *Common Cause v. NRC, supra.*

Another Sunshine exception not found in FOIA concerns discussions of pending civil litigation or of the initiation, conduct, or disposition of formal agency adjudication. Thus the agency can close a meeting where it discusses how to decide an appeal from an ALJ decision. But it must hold open meetings at which it makes decisions about rulemaking.

e.   *Sanctions for Sunshine violations.* Like FOIA, open meeting laws allow any person to seek judicial enforcement and allow the award of attorney's fees to a substantially prevailing party. Many state laws provide for civil money penalties, contempt citations, or even criminal penalties for violations of open meeting laws.

Under the federal act, a court cannot invalidate agency action simply because a closed meeting should have been open. However, many state laws give courts discretion to invalidate the action taken at an improperly closed meeting. A court must exercise such discretion sparingly, however. The possibility of invalidation of action taken at a closed meeting leaves the finality of government action in limbo, perhaps for many years, while litigation winds its way through the courts. Moreover, invalidation might be extremely detrimental to the public interest if the result is to abrogate agency rules protective of health or safety.

§ 8.2.2   FEDERAL ADVISORY COMMITTEE ACT (FACA)

The Federal Advisory Committee Act (FACA) was enacted in 1972. *See* 5 U.S.C. App. 2. An article provides background on FACA:

[FACA's enactment should not] suggest that agencies began to receive advice from nongovernmental entities only in 1972. Much to the contrary, the FACA was designed to formalize and routinize what was already an age-old institution. . . . [T]here is a common understanding that the great growth of advisory committees occurred after World War II, generally in response to the increased government regulation occasioned by the New Deal and perhaps by increased government and industry cooperation during the war. . . .

And yet, while the institution to which FACA's passage gave discipline and organization has a long heritage, advisory committees before and since the Act have until recently been largely "Beltway" phenomena—established by and for agency officials inside Washington and with Washington-oriented memberships. Lately, however, advisory committees have been and are being established throughout the country. As a result, field-level agency personnel, as well as potential committee members in various regions, have of necessity become familiar with FACA, thereby raising the important if uncelebrated Act's general visibility and, with that visibility, urgent questions about how it is (and should be) interpreted, applied, and administered.

Steven P. Croley & William F. Funk, *The Federal Advisory Committee Act and Good Government*, 14 YALE J. ON REG. 451, 453, 458–59 (1997).

FACA requires that the membership of an advisory committee "be fairly balanced in terms of the points of view represented and the functions to be performed . . ." The document setting up the committee must "contain appropriate provisions to assure that the advice and recommendations of the advisory committee will not be inappropriately influenced by the appointing authority or by any special interest . . ."

FACA requires that a detailed charter of each advisory committee be filed with the agency. Notice of committee meetings must be published in advance in the Federal Register, and the meetings must be open to the public (except under the same exemptions that apply to the Sunshine Act). All of the Committee's records and documents must be open to the public (except under the same exceptions that apply to FOIA). Detailed minutes must be kept. A designated agency employee must be present at every such meeting and must approve the agenda. There are detailed record-keeping requirements.

An "advisory committee" covered by FACA includes every "committee . . . or other similar group . . . established or utilized" by the President or an agency to obtain advice. This definition is broad enough to cover any meeting of two or more persons with agency staff. It could, in theory, apply "any time the President seeks the views of the NAACP before nominating commissioners to the Equal Employment Opportunity Commission, or asks the leaders of an American Legion Post he is visiting for the organization's opinion on some aspect of military policy" or asks the Republican National Committee for advice about picking the cabinet. *Public Citizen v. Department of Justice*, 491 U.S. 440, 453 (1989).

Giving the word "utilized" a narrow meaning to avoid these extreme outcomes, *Public Citizen* held that the ABA's Standing Committee on the Federal Judiciary was not covered by FACA, even though it advises the President and the Attorney General about the qualifications of potential nominees for federal judgeships. Drawing on the legislative history of FACA, the Court (by a 6–3 majority) held that the only committees that are covered by FACA are those established directly or indirectly by the President, an agency, or a quasi-public entity. Clearly, this definition left out the Committee in question, which was created by the ABA. The Court also pointed out that a contrary construction of FACA would raise grave constitutional issues. It might infringe on the President's power to nominate federal judges and violate the separation of powers.

Early in his administration, President George W. Bush established the National Energy Policy Development Group (NEPDG) to advise him about a national energy plan. NEPDG was established within the Executive Office of the President, and Vice President Cheney was assigned to direct the group and preside at meetings. Ultimately, NEPDG issued a controversial report that urged more aggressive exploitation of domestic fossil fuel resources.

Various groups took the position that NEPDG was an advisory committee that functioned in violation of FACA. For example, NEPDG's meetings were closed to the public and it never made available its minutes or records. These groups asserted that NEPDG consisted not only of government officials such as cabinet secretaries, but also of numerous private individuals (including Kenneth Lay, CEO of the failed Enron Corp.), functioning as "de facto members." The Government denied that any private individuals could properly be regarded as members of NEPDG; as a result, argued the Government, NEPDG was exempt from FACA since its membership consisted entirely of government officials.

The groups filed suit to enforce FACA and sought discovery to determine whether private individuals had taken part in NEPDG deliberations. The trial court allowed discovery to proceed. The D.C. Circuit refused to intervene by issuing a writ of mandamus to the lower court, holding that the Vice President must assert executive privilege if he wishes to withhold information. The Supreme Court reversed. *Cheney v. United States District Court*, 542 U.S. 367 (2004). It held that discovery orders addressed to high officials of the executive branch, such as the Vice

President, raise serious issues of separation of powers and threaten intrusion on the President's ability to consult with other executive officials. Therefore, such discovery demands must be as narrow as possible. Here, however, the plaintiff's discovery demands were extremely broad and burdensome.

On remand, the D.C. Circuit unanimously ordered the case dismissed. *In re Cheney,* 406 F.3d 723 (D.C. Cir. 2005) (en banc). The court held that FACA does not apply where "the President has given no one other than a federal official a vote in or, if the committee acts by consensus, a veto over the committee's decisions." Since there was no indication that, under this test, NEPDG had any members other than federal officials, the court dismissed the case without reaching the discovery issues. The court was heavily influenced by the separation-of-powers problems of applying FACA to an advisory committee that was so deeply involved in providing confidential policy advice to the President.

CHAPTER 9

SCOPE OF JUDICIAL REVIEW

■ ■ ■

The doctrines that fix the scope of judicial review define the court's checking power over the actions of administrative agencies. If the line is placed in a way that favors agencies too much, the vital principle of judicial check will be sacrificed. But if it is placed in a way that disfavors agencies too much, they will be unable to carry out their regulatory roles, and judges will expend excessive resources on the reviewing function.

The scope of review varies depending on what kind of issue a court is examining at a particular time. Courts will often say that, in reviewing an agency's *fact findings* or *policy choices*, they cannot substitute their judgment for that of the agency. In other words, they will *defer* to the agency's view. With respect to the *legality* of agency action, courts are much likelier to claim the power to substitute their judgment for that of the agency. Accordingly, this chapter is organized around the various types of issues that can arise during judicial review and the types of judicial inquiries that respectively apply to them.

However, a number of factors can complicate this picture. In the first place, a typical administrative decision rests on multiple determinations, any or all of which may be drawn into question on appeal. Thus, the reviewing court will often have to vary the nature of its analysis in the course of deciding a single case.

Second, even the generalizations just mentioned are only a starting point. They are far from clear-cut, especially as they are applied by federal courts. On legal issues, federal courts have imposed limitations on their own powers through the so-called *Chevron* doctrine. And on policy issues, the courts often overturn an agency's decision by claiming that the agency did not analyze its position carefully enough, even though the policy may not be inherently unreasonable.

As you consider the material that follows, keep in mind the relationship between the scope of judicial review and the common legislative practice of delegating power to agencies. After all, a delegation of authority to an agency suggests that the agency has primary responsibility for resolution of matters falling within the bounds of that grant, meaning that the court should deference to the agency's determination. On the other hand, this justification for deference does not apply insofar as the legislature settles a matter by a statutory command, thereby circumscribing its delegation to the agency. Of course, all this leaves an initial question to be determined: how far did the legislature delegate discretion to the agency to decide a particular matter?

§ 9.1   REVIEW OF AGENCY FINDINGS OF BASIC FACT IN FORMAL PROCEEDINGS

An agency's findings of basic fact determine what happened and why, or who did what to whom, with what state of mind. When legislatures and courts undertake to specify the scope of a reviewing court's power to overturn an agency's findings of basic fact, they can choose from a variety of well-known formulas. These formulas can be arrayed as follows, starting with those that provide for the largest judicial powers and finishing with the smallest:

i.   *Trial de novo.* The court receives evidence on its own and redecides the case. *See* APA § 706(2)(F); 2010 MSAPA § 508(a)(3)(E). In a sense, a court with power to rehear the case does not engage in judicial review at all, because it can decide the case without referring to the evidence considered by the agency. There are a number of examples in state and federal administrative law of de novo judicial trials on specific issues of fact determined initially by an agency. They will be discussed in § 9.1.2.

ii.   *Independent judgment on the evidence.* The court decides the case on the record made by the agency but need not give any deference to agency fact findings. This formula is infrequently employed in federal administrative law (except with reference to a few constitutionally sensitive issues) but is sometimes employed in the states, especially in California. Independent judgment will be discussed in § 9.1.2.

iii.   *Clearly erroneous.* The court reverses if it "is left with the definite and firm conviction that a mistake has been committed." *United States v. United States Gypsum Co.,* 333 U.S. 364, 395 (1948). Sometimes this test is referred to as the "manifest weight of the evidence" test. It is the standard used by a federal court of appeals to review the decision of a trial judge when there is no jury. Fed. R. Civ. P. 52(a). It was used in the 1961 Model State APA, § 15(g)(5), and in a substantial number of states.

iv.   *Substantial evidence.* The court cannot reverse if a *reasonable person* could have reached the same conclusion as the agency. This is the standard normally used in reviewing agency fact findings in formal adjudication, APA § 706(2)(E), as discussed in *Universal Camera* below. It is used in many states and is the standard set forth under 2010 MSAPA § 508(a)(3)(D). It is also equivalent to the standard used by a trial court in deciding whether to take a matter from the jury, Fed. R. Civ. P. 50(a), and by a federal court of appeals in reviewing the findings of a jury. The Supreme Court has often equated the substantial evidence test in administrative law with the court's power to review a jury verdict. *See, e.g., Allentown Mack Sales & Serv., Inc. v. NLRB*, 522 U.S. 359 (1998).

v. *Arbitrary and capricious.* In federal law, the substantial evidence test of APA § 706(2)(E) applies by its terms only "in a case subject to sections 556 and 557 of [the APA] or otherwise reviewed on the record of an agency hearing provided by statute." Thus, it basically is used only in formal adjudication or formal rulemaking (and a few other situations specified by statute). Agency factfinding in informal proceedings, whether adjudication or rulemaking, is reviewed under § 706(2)(A). That clause authorizes a reviewing court to reverse the agency only if its findings are arbitrary, capricious, or an abuse of discretion. Similarly, the substantial evidence test in the 2010 MSAPA applies only "in a contested case." For other cases, the arbitrariness test of § 508(a)(3)(C) is available. Because the arbitrariness test also boils down to an assessment of the reasonableness of agency action, the scrutiny it entails probably does not differ significantly from the substantial evidence test. That similarity will be discussed in § 9.4 N.2.

vi. *Some evidence.* The court cannot reverse if there is some evidence in support of the agency's conclusion. Sometimes this is called the "scintilla" test. It is uncommon in administrative law, but it was employed in judicial review of the determinations of selective service boards. *Estep v. United States,* 327 U.S. 114 (1946). It is also occasionally found at the state level. For example, "some evidence" is the test used by the Ohio Supreme Court in reviewing workers' compensation decisions. *State ex rel. AutoZone, Inc. v. Industrial Comm'n*, 883 N.E.2d 372 (Ohio 2008). When courts use the "some evidence" test, they obviously intend to greatly restrict judicial power to second-guess an agency's fact findings.

vii. *Facts not reviewable at all.* A statute may preclude any judicial review of an agency's factual determinations. Some statutes take this approach even though they do allow review of an agency's procedures and its determinations of law. The issue of preclusion of review is treated in § 10.4.

It is important to master the verbal formulas of scope of review doctrine, because they provide the language with which litigants and courts communicate with each other. However, you should not assume that the above gradations among verbal formulas necessarily reveal very much about the likelihood that a reviewing court will reject an agency's fact findings. Indeed, the divergences can be significant. An illuminating empirical study found that claimants in Social Security disability benefits cases succeed on judicial review about half the time, although the statutory standard of review, "substantial evidence," is theoretically quite deferential. Conversely, Congress has prescribed a "de novo" standard of review for Freedom of Information Act appeals, but courts actually uphold the government about ninety percent of the time in FOIA cases. Even "reverse FOIA" plaintiffs (persons who sue to prevent the government from voluntarily releasing information that they have submitted) succeed about twice as often as FOIA plaintiffs do, although they have to overcome the nominally very deferential "arbitrary or capricious" test. Paul R. Verkuil, *An Outcomes Analysis of Scope of Review Standards*, 44 WM. & MARY L. REV. 679 (2002).

It is fair to ask why judicial practice sometimes seems inconsistent with the relative intensity of review apparently prescribed by these statutes. The answer may be, at least in part, that judicial perceptions about the underlying dynamics of various programs and the reliability of the agencies that respectively implement them inevitably exert a strong influence on results.

§ 9.1.1 THE SUBSTANTIAL EVIDENCE AND CLEARLY ERRONEOUS TESTS

UNIVERSAL CAMERA CORP. v. NLRB
340 U.S. 474 (1951)

[The NLRB charged that Universal had fired an employee named Imre Chairman in retaliation for his testimony at a previous NLRB hearing. That allegation, if proved, would mean that Universal had committed an unfair labor practice. Universal responded that Chairman had been discharged for being insubordinate during a quarrel that occurred about a month after he gave the testimony.

The hearing in an unfair labor practice case is conducted by a hearing examiner (now called an ALJ), who renders an initial decision. The losing party can then appeal to the Board. In this case the hearing examiner believed the company's witnesses, but a panel of Board members reversed his decision and awarded Chairman reinstatement and back pay.

In an opinion by Judge Learned Hand, the Second Circuit affirmed the Board, finding that there was substantial evidence in support of the Board's findings. The court decided that it should attach no importance to the agency's rejection of the hearing examiner's findings.]

FRANKFURTER, J.:

The essential issue raised by this case . . . is the effect of the Administrative Procedure Act and . . . the Taft-Hartley Act on the duty of Courts of Appeals when called upon to review orders of the National Labor Relations Board.

I

. . . . The Wagner Act provided: "The findings of the Board as to the facts, if supported by evidence, shall be conclusive." This Court read "evidence" to mean "substantial evidence," and we said that "[s]ubstantial evidence is more than a mere scintilla. It means such relevant evidence as a reasonable mind might accept as adequate to support a conclusion." *Consolidated Edison Co. v. NLRB*, 305 U.S. 197, 229 (1938). Accordingly, it "must do more than create a suspicion of the existence of the fact to be established. . . . [I]t must be enough to justify, if the trial were to a jury, a refusal to direct a verdict when the conclusion sought to be drawn from it is one of fact for the jury." *NLRB v. Columbian Enameling & Stamping Co.*, 306 U.S. 292, 300 (1939).

The very smoothness of the "substantial evidence" formula as the standard for reviewing the evidentiary validity of the Board's findings established its currency. But the inevitably variant applications of the standard to conflicting evidence soon brought contrariety of views and in due course bred criticism. Even though the whole record may have been canvassed in order to determine whether the evidentiary foundation of a determination by the Board was "substantial," the phrasing of this Court's process of review readily lent itself to the notion that it was enough that the evidence supporting the Board's result was "substantial" when considered by itself. . . .

Criticism of so contracted a reviewing power reinforced dissatisfaction felt in various quarters with the Board's administration of the Wagner Act in the years preceding the war. . . .

[T]he legislative history of [the APA] hardly speaks with that clarity of purpose which Congress supposedly furnishes courts in order to enable them to enforce its true will. On the one hand, the sponsors of the legislation indicated that they were reaffirming the prevailing "substantial evidence" test. But with equal clarity they expressed disapproval of the manner in which the courts were applying their own standard. The committee reports of both houses refer to the practice of agencies to rely upon "suspicion, surmise, implications, or plainly incredible evidence," and indicate that courts are to exact higher standards "in the exercise of their independent judgment" and on consideration of "the whole record."

Similar dissatisfaction with too restricted application of the "substantial evidence" test is reflected in the legislative history of the Taft-Hartley Act. The bill as reported to the House provided that the "findings of the Board as to the facts shall be conclusive unless it is made to appear to the satisfaction of the court either (1) that the findings of fact are against the manifest weight of the evidence, or (2) the findings of fact are not supported by substantial evidence." The bill left the House with this provision. Early committee prints in the Senate provided for review by "weight of the evidence" or "clearly erroneous" standards. But, as the Senate Committee Report relates, "it was finally decided to conform the statute to the corresponding section of the Administrative Procedure Act where the substantial evidence test prevails. In order to clarify any ambiguity in that statute, however, the committee inserted the words" questions of fact, if supported by substantial evidence *on the record considered as a whole. . . .*'"...

It is fair to say that in all this Congress expressed a mood. And it expressed its mood not merely by oratory but by legislation. As legislation that mood must be respected, even though it can only serve as a standard for judgment and not as a body of rigid rules assuring sameness of application. . . . [One conclusion that emerges from this history is that] the scope of review under the Taft-Hartley Act is [no] different from that under the Administrative Procedure Act.

Whether or not it was ever permissible for courts to determine the substantiality of evidence supporting a Labor Board decision merely on the basis of evidence which in and of itself justified it, without taking into account contradictory evidence or evidence from which conflicting inferences could be drawn, the new legislation definitely precludes such a theory of review and bars its practice. The substantiality of evidence must take into account whatever in the record fairly detracts from its weight. This is clearly the significance of the requirement in both statutes that courts consider the whole record. Committee reports and the adoption in the Administrative Procedure Act of the minority views of the Attorney General's Committee demonstrate that to enjoin such a duty on the reviewing court was one of the important purposes of the movement which eventuated in that enactment.

To be sure, the requirement for canvassing "the whole record" in order to ascertain substantiality does not furnish a calculus of value by which a reviewing court can assess the evidence. Nor was it intended to negative the function of the Labor Board as one of those agencies presumably equipped or informed by experience to deal with a specialized field of knowledge, whose findings within that field carry the authority of an expertness which courts do not possess and therefore must respect. Nor does it mean that even as to matters not requiring expertise a court may displace the Board's choice between two fairly conflicting views, even though the court would justifiably have made a different choice had the matter been before it de novo. Congress has merely made it clear that a reviewing court is not barred from setting aside a Board decision when it cannot conscientiously find that the evidence supporting that decision is substantial, when viewed in the light that the record in its entirety furnishes, including the body of evidence opposed to the Board's view.

There remains, then, the question whether enactment of these two statutes has altered the scope of review other than to require that substantiality be determined in the light of all that the record relevantly presents. A formula for judicial review of administrative action may afford grounds for certitude but cannot assure certainty of application. Some scope for judicial discretion in applying the formula can be avoided only by falsifying the actual process of judging or by using the formula as an instrument of futile casuistry. It cannot be too often repeated that judges are not automata. . . . To find the change so elusive that it cannot be precisely defined does not mean it may be ignored. We should fail in our duty to effectuate the will of Congress if we denied recognition to expressed Congressional disapproval of the finality accorded to Labor Board findings by some decisions of this and lower courts, or even of the atmosphere which may have favored those decisions.

We conclude, therefore, that the Administrative Procedure Act and the Taft-Hartley Act direct that courts must now assume more responsibility for the reasonableness and fairness of Labor Board decisions than some courts have shown in the past. Reviewing courts must be influenced by a feeling that they are not to abdicate the conventional judicial function. Congress has imposed on them responsibility for assuring that the Board keeps within reasonable grounds. That responsibility is not less real because it is limited to enforcing the requirement that evidence appear substantial when viewed, on the record as a whole, by courts invested with the authority and enjoying the prestige of the Courts of Appeals. The Board's findings are entitled to respect; but they must nonetheless be set aside when the record before a Court of Appeals clearly precludes the Board's decision from being justified by a fair estimate of the worth of the testimony of witnesses or its informed judgment on matters within its special competence or both. . . .

Our power to review the correctness of application of the present standard ought seldom to be called into action. Whether on the record as a whole there is substantial evidence to support agency findings is a question which Congress has placed in the keeping of the Courts of Appeals. This Court will intervene only in what ought to be the rare instance when the standard appears to have been misapprehended or grossly misapplied.

II.

. . . The decision of the Court of Appeals is assailed on two grounds. It is said (1) that the court erred in holding that it was barred from taking into account the report of the examiner on questions of fact insofar as that report was rejected by the Board, and (2) that the Board's order was not supported by substantial evidence on the record considered as a whole, even apart from the validity of the court's refusal to consider the rejected portions of the examiner's report.

The latter contention is easily met. . . . [I]t is clear from the court's opinion in this case that it in fact did consider the "record as a whole," and did not deem itself merely the judicial echo of the Board's conclusion. The testimony of the company's witnesses was inconsistent, and there was clear evidence that the complaining employee had been discharged by an officer who was at one time influenced against him because of his appearance at the Board hearing. On such a record we could not say that it would be error to grant enforcement.

The first contention, however, raises serious questions to which we now turn.

III.

The Court of Appeals deemed itself bound by the Board's rejection of the examiner's findings because the court considered these findings not "as unassailable as a master's." They are not. Section 10(c) of the Labor Management Relations Act provides that "If upon the preponderance of the testimony taken the Board shall be of the opinion that any person named in the complaint has engaged in or is engaging in any such unfair labor practice, then the Board shall state its findings of fact. . . ." The responsibility for decision thus placed on the Board is wholly inconsistent with the notion that it has power to reverse an examiner's findings only when they are "clearly erroneous." Such a limitation would make so drastic a departure from prior administrative practice that explicitness would be required. . . .

We are aware that to give the examiner's findings less finality than a master's and yet entitle them to consideration in striking the account, is to introduce another and an unruly factor into the judgmatical process of review. But we ought not to fashion an exclusionary rule merely to reduce the number of imponderables to be considered by reviewing courts.

The Taft-Hartley Act provides that "The findings of the Board with respect to questions of fact if supported by substantial evidence on the record considered as a whole shall be conclusive." Surely an examiner's report is as much a part of the record as the complaint or the testimony. According to the Administrative Procedure Act, "All decisions (including initial, recommended, or tentative decisions) shall become a part of the record. . . ." [§ 557(c)]. . . .

It is therefore difficult to escape the conclusion that the plain language of the statutes directs a reviewing court to determine the substantiality of evidence on the record including the examiner's report. . . . Nothing in the statutes suggests that the Labor Board should not be influenced by the examiner's opportunity to observe the witnesses he hears and sees and the Board does not. Nothing suggests that reviewing courts should not give to the examiner's report such probative force as it intrinsically commands. To the contrary, § 11 of the Administrative Procedure Act contains detailed provisions designed to maintain high standards of independence and competence in examiners. Section 10(c) of the Labor Management Relations Act requires that examiners "shall issue ... a proposed report, together with a recommended order." Both statutes thus evince a purpose to increase the importance of the role of examiners in the administrative process. High standards of public administration counsel that we attribute to the Labor Board's examiners both due regard for the responsibility which Congress imposes on them and the competence to discharge it. . . .

We do not require that the examiner's findings be given more weight than in reason and in the light of judicial experience they deserve. The "substantial evidence" standard is not modified in any way when the Board and its examiner disagree. We intend only to recognize that evidence supporting a conclusion may be less substantial when an impartial, experienced examiner who has observed the witnesses and lived with the case has drawn conclusions different from the Board's than when he has reached the same conclusion. The findings of the examiner are to be considered along with the consistency and inherent probability of testimony. The significance of his report, of course, depends largely on the importance of credibility in the particular case. To give it this significance does not seem to us materially more difficult than to heed the other factors which in sum determine whether evidence is "substantial." . . .

We therefore remand the cause to the Court of Appeals. On reconsideration of the record it should accord the findings of the trial examiner the relevance that they reasonably command in answering the comprehensive question whether the evidence supporting the Board's order is substantial. But the court need not limit its reexamination of the case to the effect of that report on its decision. We leave it free to grant or deny enforcement as it thinks the principles expressed in this opinion dictate.

Judgment vacated and cause remanded.

BLACK and DOUGLAS, JJ., concur with parts I and II of this opinion but as to part III agree with the opinion of the court below.

NOTES AND QUESTIONS

1. *Rationales for substantial evidence test.* The substantial evidence test is designed to limit an appellate court's power to reverse agency fact findings. Why should courts be expected to apply that test as opposed to a less deferential test? Some possible explanations might be:

i.   Agencies specialize and develop expertise in the areas they regulate. Their fact-finding process reflects that expertise, and thus their findings should receive only limited judicial scrutiny.

ii.   When it creates a regulatory program, the legislature usually delegates to an agency all of the powers necessary to execute the legislative scheme, including the power to adjudicate and to find facts. Because fact-finding is an essential element of the delegated power, the legislature intends a court to respect those findings, absent a serious error by the agency.

iii.   The narrowness of the reviewing power discourages disappointed litigants from appealing, thus conserving the resources of both courts and agencies.

iv.   Courts are likely to have a different political orientation than agencies. An agency is expected to carry out the objective set by the legislature and to reflect the views of the executive who appointed its members. A reasonableness scope of review limits the ability of a court to impose its values in place of the agency's values.

Suppose a court believes, in a particular case, that some or all of these rationales are not implicated—for example, because the issue involved is simple and does not require specialized knowledge, or because the agency heads are not really experts. May the court take a less deferential approach to its review? *See Elliott v. Commodity Futures Trading Comm'n*, 202 F.3d 926, 940 (7th Cir. 2000) (Easterbrook, J., dissenting), stating that, before joining the CFTC, the commissioners in the majority below had been a lawyer, a banker, and a manager of an agricultural conservation program; the dissenting commissioner was the only member who had actually been a trader. If true, should these facts matter? *See id.* at 935 (Cudahy, J., for the panel majority).

2.   *The whole record.* The *Universal Camera* opinion holds that, when reviewing for substantiality of evidence, the court must consider the "whole record," as opposed to simply considering whether the record contains evidence that reasonably *supports* the agency's finding. Does this principle give the reviewing court too much leeway to second-guess the agency? Some state courts have appeared to think so. *See, e.g., Campbell v. Board for Volunteer Firefighters*, 45 P.3d 216 (Wash. App. 2002).

In *Yao v. Board of Regents*, 649 N.W.3d 356 (Wis. App. 2002), the University of Wisconsin discharged an assistant professor of physiology for tampering with a colleague's laboratory experiments. Surveillance videotapes and the testimony of his accusers supported the charges, but Dr. Yao testified on his own behalf and also pointed out that portions of the videotapes had been erased through carelessness. In upholding the university's action, the court did discuss the evidence on both sides, but it insisted that it had no obligation to follow the "whole record" principle of *Universal Camera*. The court pointed out that the Wisconsin scope of review statute had recently been amended. The new provision said that the court "shall not substitute its judgment for that of the agency as to the weight of the evidence," and may review whether fact findings are "supported by substantial evidence in the record." As the court noted, the latter phrase had been amended to *omit* the words "in view of the entire record as submitted." Should the court have adhered to the federal standard anyway?

3. *Disagreement between agency and ALJ.* In *Universal Camera,* the NLRB overturned fact findings made by its hearing examiner (hearing examiners are now called ALJs). The dispute concerned the credibility of witnesses whom the examiner had heard and the Board had not.

Both the Second Circuit and the Supreme Court rejected the analogy between a hearing officer and a master appointed by a trial court to take testimony. A trial court cannot reverse a master's findings unless it finds them clearly erroneous. Fed. R. Civ. P. 53(e)(2). Agency heads have more power to reverse an examiner's findings than that. Why is the relationship between a court and a master different from that between an agency and its ALJ? Consider the statement in APA § 557(b) that, in reviewing a hearing examiner's decision, the agency head "has all the powers which it would have in making the initial decision," and the similar language of 2010 MSAPA §§ 414(e), 415(b).

Judge Hand's first opinion in *Universal Camera* stated that a reviewing court has no middle ground between disregarding an agency's reversal of its examiner and making the examiner's findings as unassailable as those of a master. 179 F.2d 749, 753 (2d Cir.1950). Did the Supreme Court identify a middle ground? Where is that ground located?

On remand, Judge Hand went to the opposite extreme: he ruled that "an examiner's findings on veracity must not be overruled without a very substantial preponderance in the testimony as recorded." 190 F.2d 429, 430 (2d Cir. 1951). The Supreme Court later disapproved this approach, since it appeared to equate the relationship between ALJs and agency heads with that of masters and trial courts. *FCC v. Allentown Broadcasting Corp.,* 349 U.S. 358 (1955).

Under *Universal Camera,* if agency heads reverse an ALJ's credibility findings, this disagreement is treated by courts reviewing the agency heads' decision under the substantial evidence test as a *minus factor.* According to one formula, the reviewing court requires the agency heads "to fully articulate [their] reasons" for disagreeing with an ALJ on credibility questions; the court then decides "with heightened scrutiny" whether the heads' decision is supportable. *Aylett v. Secretary of Housing & Urban Devel.,* 54 F.3d 1560 (10th Cir. 1995) (reversing HUD's decision that housing discrimination took place, where ALJ believed the landlord). *But see Hall v. U.S. Dep't of Labor,* 476 F.3d 847, 860 (10th Cir. 2007) (upholding, despite "heightened scrutiny," administrative review board's rejection of ALJ's credibility determination, where board found that "the ALJ evaluated only

Dr. Hall's credibility, despite the fact that 50 witnesses testified, 40 of whom testified against Dr. Hall").

The heightened scrutiny reasoning applies most clearly to disagreements between ALJs and agency heads about the credibility of witnesses—and especially to that subset of credibility determinations that depend on assessment of the demeanor of a witness. As to other factual issues, should the agency heads be free to substitute their judgment without the disagreement being treated as a minus factor? For example, imagine an antitrust case before the FTC in which the ALJ makes detailed fact findings about the relevant market. Could the agency heads make different fact findings on this subject without running into a *Universal Camera* problem?

4. *Agency-ALJ disagreements in the states.* Not all states follow *Universal Camera* on this issue. Under the Florida and Montana APAs, an agency cannot reject or modify an ALJ's findings of fact if the findings are based on "competent substantial evidence." Interpreting this statute, a Florida court reviewing a medical board decision stated that the board could override the ALJ's findings only where the issue requires "special knowledge and expertise in the practice of medicine." The issue was whether a doctor had prescribed inappropriate amounts of an opiate to patients in pain. The ALJ thought not; the medical board reversed. The court reversed the board decision, stating that "the circumstances of this case do not present a unique question that is not susceptible to ordinary methods of proof, resolution of which falls within the special expertise of the board to the point that the board may overturn the findings of the hearing officer when those findings are based upon competent substantial evidence in the record." *Johnston v. Dep't of Prof. Reg.*, 456 So.2d 939 (Fla. App. 1984). Is this a sounder approach to the problem than the *Universal Camera* approach? Does it appropriately enhance the status of the ALJ in the adjudicatory process? Does it enhance the status of the ALJ too much?

Traditionally, in California, reviewing courts ignored the fact findings of ALJs. Agency heads were free to substitute their own findings about witness credibility, even though they never heard or saw the witness. However, a 1995 amendment to the APA changed this rule:

> If the factual basis for the decision includes a determination based substantially on the credibility of a witness, the statement shall identify any specific evidence of the observed demeanor, manner, or attitude of the witness that supports the determination, and on judicial review the court shall give great weight to the determination to the extent the determination identifies the observed demeanor, manner, or attitude of the witness that supports it.

Cal. Gov't Code § 11425.50(b). Does this provision codify *Universal Camera*? The statutory comment indicates that this was the intent. Or does the provision go even further than *Universal Camera* in enhancing the status of ALJs vis-à-vis agency heads?

5. *Supreme Court review of court of appeals.* In *Universal Camera*, the Court noted that it would seldom overturn a court of appeals decision applying the substantial evidence test. However, in *Allentown Mack Sales & Serv., Inc. v. NLRB*, 522 U.S. 359 (1998), the Court did exactly that.

The issue in *Allentown Mack* was whether an employer had a "reasonable doubt, based on objective considerations, that the Union continued to enjoy the support of a majority of the bargaining unit employees." Only an employer that entertains such a doubt is permitted to conduct a poll of its employees to find out whether they in fact continue to support the union. The NLRB held that various statements made by employees to the employer were insufficient to raise a reasonable doubt. But the Court concluded: "Giving fair weight to Allentown's circumstantial evidence, we think it quite impossible for a rational factfinder to avoid the conclusion that Allentown had reasonable good-faith grounds to doubt—to be *uncertain about*—the union's retention of majority support." Four Justices dissented.

One possible reason for the Court's departure from its normal practice of leaving substantial evidence cases to the courts of appeals is that it wanted to make a more general point. Apparently the NLRB had applied a different (and much more demanding) standard for deciding "reasonable doubt" than the words of that test suggested. This undisclosed standard violated the norm of reasoned decisionmaking. This aspect of the case is discussed further in § 9.3.1 N.7.

Should *Universal Camera* be interpreted to mean that the Supreme Court will display *deference* toward a lower court's application of the substantial evidence test? Or only that the Court will seldom *review* such applications but will apply the same test as the lower court in cases that it does review? *Allentown Mack* is an example of the latter approach, but other cases follow the former one. *See FTC v. Standard Oil Co.*, 355 U.S. 396, 400–01 (1958).

In some states, the supreme court reviews agency factfindings as if the lower court decision had not occurred. *See, e.g., Jackson County Pub. Hosp. v. Pub. Employment Rel. Bd.*, 280 N.W.2d 426, 429 (Iowa 1979). Another alternative is to give less scrutiny to lower court decisions that agree with agency decisions, but more scrutiny to lower court decisions that disagree with agency decisions. *Clowes v. Terminix Int'l*, 538 A.2d 794, 801 (N.J. 1988). Should state supreme courts follow the *Standard Oil* model and defer to lower court decisions applying the substantial evidence test?

6. *"Clearly erroneous" review.* As noted above, many states apply the "clearly erroneous" rule to agency fact findings, rather than the substantial evidence rule. This was the approach used in § 15(g)(5) of the 1961 MSAPA. Congress has also prescribed this standard of review in a few federal administrative contexts, such as for judicial review of decisions of the Tax Court.

In the abstract, review for clear error can be distinguished from substantial evidence review. "Common experience suggests . . . that when two persons are arguing in good faith, whether in court or otherwise, one may think the other clearly wrong without going so far as to claim that no reasonable person could reach the other's conclusion." Robert L. Stern, *Review of Findings of Administrators, Judges and Juries: A Comparative Analysis*, 58 HARV. L. REV. 70, 81 (1944). Judge Posner argues, however, that, realistically speaking, the distinction between the two standards is immaterial:

> Defenders of the [asserted] difference will point out that administrative proceedings often involve technical issues on which the agency is expert and the reviewing court is not. But court cases often involve issues on which the trial judge has an equally great advantage over the reviewing court—the factual issues may be esoteric ones that the judge was able to immerse himself in and the reviewing court, which has limited exposure to a case, was not. So it is not obvious that a blanket distinction between the standard for review of agency findings and the standard for review of judicial findings is warranted, and in any event the cognitive limitations that judges share with other mortals may constitute an insuperable obstacle to making distinctions any finer than that of plenary versus deferential review. . . .

> But here we must note a difference between the questionable judicial attempt to multiply standards of review and the unavoidable heterogeneity in the application of a given standard across the full range of cases governed by it. . . . The more technical the issue resolved by the agency, the less likely the reviewing court is to feel comfortable second-guessing the agency's resolution. As a practical matter, having nothing to do with the precise articulation of the standard of review, the agency's finding will receive greater judicial respect in such a case.

School Dist. of Wis. Dells v. Z.S., 295 F.3d 671, 674–75 (7th Cir. 2002).

The Supreme Court made similar points in *Dickinson v. Zurko*, 527 U.S. 150 (1999). For many years, the Court of Appeals for the Federal Circuit (a specialized court charged with handling patent and other matters) used the "clearly erroneous" test in its review of decisions by the Patent and Trademark Office to deny patent applications. It reaffirmed that practice in the course of reversing an administrative decision to reject Zurko's application for a patent on a computer security system. The PTO appealed to the Supreme Court. In an opinion by Justice Breyer, the Court examined the Federal Circuit's practice and held that an APA standard—presumably, "substantial evidence"—should apply instead.

In resolving this dispute, however, the Court acknowledged that the difference between the clearly erroneous and substantial evidence tests is subtle—"so fine that (apart from the present case) we have failed to uncover a single instance in which a reviewing court conceded that use of one standard rather than the other would in fact have produced a different outcome." As the Court explained, the choice of standard of review may have less influence on outcomes than such case-specific factors as "a finding's dependence upon agency expertise or the presence of internal agency review." Thus, the expertise of the Federal Circuit in patent matters may "play a more important role in assuring proper review than would a theoretically somewhat stricter standard."

As matters turned out, the choice between the substantial evidence standard and the clearly erroneous standard made no difference in this case, either. On remand from the Supreme Court, the Federal Circuit again reversed the Patent Office, finding that the agency's refusal to grant a patent to Zurko was unsupported by substantial evidence. *In re Zurko*, 258 F.3d 1379 (Fed. Cir. 2001).

If there is no practical difference between substantial evidence review and clearly erroneous review, why have litigants like Zurko, not to mention legislative drafters like the authors of the 1961 MSAPA, devoted so much effort to trying to replace the former with the latter?

7.   *Problem.* Madison law prohibits discrimination by any business establishment on the basis of race, religion, gender, or sexual orientation. Ted, a gay man, was a member of City Health Club. On April 2, Joe (a staff member of the Club) overheard Ted making a date with another male Club member. As Ted was leaving the Club, Mark (the manager) asked Ted to come into the office and discuss his conduct. Ted told him to drop dead and left the Club. That day, Mark terminated Ted's membership. Mark's letter stated that termination occurred because Ted's conduct had offended a member of the staff and because he had refused to discuss the matter with management.

Ted complained to the Civil Rights Commission (CRC), which enforces the anti-discrimination law. Gloria, the CRC's ALJ, found that Ted had been terminated because his conduct had offended a staff member and because of his refusal to discuss it, not because of his sexual orientation. Consequently, she denied relief.

Ted appealed the decision to the full CRC, which reversed. Its opinion stated that Ted had been terminated because of his sexual orientation, not because of his conduct. It found that the Club was trying to rid itself of gay members. It also found that Joe had not been offended, and that Ted's conduct could not be the basis for terminating him, whether Joe was offended or not. Thus it awarded Ted compensatory and punitive damages, as well as attorney's fees, as permitted by the statute.

Should a court reverse this decision, assuming the state subscribes to (i) the substantial evidence on the whole record test? (ii) the clearly erroneous test?

Suppose the CRC had agreed with Gloria, and Ted sought judicial review. What result? *See Blanding v. Sports & Health Club, Inc.,* 373 N.W.2d 784 (Minn. App. 1985).

§ 9.1.2 INDEPENDENT JUDGMENT AND DE NOVO REVIEW

As just discussed, the prevailing test for judicial review of basic facts in both federal and state courts is a reasonableness test (substantial evidence on the whole record), although many states use the clearly erroneous test. This subsection explores instances in which a much broader scope of basic fact review is employed. In limited circumstances both federal and state courts will substitute their own judgment for agency judgment on the basis of the record made before the agency, or even conduct a trial de novo.

1. *Constitutional and jurisdictional fact.* An odd collection of Supreme Court decisions in the 1920s and 1930s generated uncertainty and controversy over the proper role of de novo judicial review in administrative law. The Court held that certain issues of "constitutional fact" required independent judicial judgment. The clearest example was agency decisionmaking about whether public utility rates were "confiscatory" (i.e., constituted takings). *St. Joseph Stock Yards Co. v. United States,* 298 U.S. 38 (1936) (prescribing de novo judicial judgment as applied to the agency hearing record); *Ohio Valley Water Co. v. Ben Avon Borough,* 253 U.S. 287 (1920) (prescribing de novo trial).

A related line of cases called for independent judicial judgment in the resolution of fact issues that were "fundamental or 'jurisdictional' in the sense that their existence is a condition precedent to the operation of the statutory scheme." *Crowell v. Benson,* 285 U.S. 22, 54 (1932) (also discussed in § 7.3). The Court held that one such "jurisdictional fact" was the issue of whether a person whom the government proposed to deport was actually a citizen rather than an alien. *Ng Fung Ho v. White,* 259 U.S. 276 (1922). *Crowell* extended this notion to apply to two narrow issues arising under the Longshoremen's and Harbor Workers' Act (a federal statute providing benefits for persons injured in the course of employment on navigable waters). Those issues were whether an employment relationship existed and whether the injury occurred on navigable waters.

In modern times, these cases have become obsolete. *Crowell's* jurisdictional fact teachings under the Longshoremen's Act were never extended beyond the facts of that case, and the Court has said that this holding has not survived. *Northern Pipeline Construction Co. v. Marathon Pipe Line Co.,* 458 U.S. 50, 82 n.34 (1982). The ratemaking cases have become essentially irrelevant, because of the evolution of the constitutional law of public utility regulation. Under modern ratemaking principles, any method of valuation is permitted, provided that the final result of the ratemaking process is reasonable in the sense that the rates cover the utility's costs. *FPC v. Hope Natural Gas Co.,* 320 U.S. 591 (1944). From today's perspective the *Ng Fung Ho* requirement that the court must independently determine citizenship in a deportation case probably makes the most sense. A fundamental liberty interest was involved, and that issue (unlike the complex questions raised in utility ratemaking) is well within judicial competence. Yet even that case is no longer important, because Congress has codified the de novo trial right, and the Court now treats the subject as raising questions of statutory construction rather than constitutional interpretation. *Agosto v. INS,* 436 U.S. 748 (1978).

De novo review of fact issues on which constitutional rights depend does retain vitality outside the realm of administrative law. *See Gonzales v. Carhart,* 550 U.S. 124 (2007) (abortion legislation); *Bose Corp. v. Consumers Union,* 466 U.S. 485 (1984) (First Amendment limitations on defamation liability); Henry P. Monaghan, *Constitutional Fact Review,* 85 COLUM. L. REV. 229 (1985).

2. *De novo review in federal courts today.* In certain unusual situations, like the citizenship question in immigration cases, Congress requires that an administrative decision be reviewed by a de novo trial. One such example is an administrative disqualification of a food retailer from the food stamp program. It is reviewed by a trial de novo in either state or federal court. *See Warren v. United States,* 932 F.2d 582 (6th Cir. 1991) (court makes its own findings based on preponderance of the evidence and is not limited to matters in the administrative record). Similarly, under the Patent Act of 1952, certain appeals from the decisions of the Patent and Trademark Office can be determined by de novo factfinding in district court. *Kappos v. Hyatt,* 132 S. Ct. 1690, 1696 (2011).

Another instance of de novo review involves judicial review of a school board decision under the Individuals with Disabilities Education Act (IDEA). IDEA calls for appropriate educational placements for disabled children. In IDEA cases, the court receives the record of the administrative proceeding, takes additional evidence at the request of a party, and basing its decision on the preponderance of the evidence, grants appropriate relief. *See Ojai Unified School Dist. v. Jackson,* 4 F.3d 1467 (9th Cir. 1993). Why would Congress call for this sort of judicial review in food stamp, patent, and IDEA cases?

Perhaps the most prominent statute providing for de novo review of federal agencies' decisions is the Freedom of Information Act (FOIA). As discussed in § 8.1, FOIA requires agencies, upon request, to disclose any information in their possession to "any person" unless the information falls within any of nine statutory exemptions. If the agency denies the request, Congress has provided a right of review in district court. FOIA directs the court to "determine the matter de novo," and "the burden is on the agency to sustain its action." 5 U.S.C. § 552(a)(3)(B). Yet, as mentioned in the introductory note to § 9.1, the government almost always wins these cases. Does this mean that the right of de novo review should be repealed as unrealistic, or that the courts should change their behavior? For an argument supporting the latter view, see Nathan Slegers, Comment, *De Novo Review Under the Freedom of Information Act: The Case Against Judicial Deference to Agency Decisions to Withhold Information*, 43 SAN DIEGO L. REV. 209 (2006).

3. *State law.* State statutes requiring de novo trials for review of particular administrative decisions are not uncommon. *See, e.g., Weeks v. Personnel Bd. of Review,* 373 A.2d 176 (R.I. 1977) (review of decision to discharge police officer), which cites cases from other states.

In the mid-twentieth century Texas developed a unique hybrid that is sometimes known as "substantial evidence de novo." In this system, a "jury would decide whether substantial evidence admitted in court supported the decision the agency had made on some other basis. Specifically, the jury would decide whether a reasonable person, presented with the evidence presented to the jury, could rationally have reached the decision that the agency had in fact made." Pete Schenkkan, *Texas Administrative Law: Trials, Triumphs, and New Challenges*, 7 TEX. TECH. ADMIN. L.J. 288, 300–02 (2006). With faint praise, Schenkkan argues that "[s]ubstantial evidence de novo was less crazy than it seems." He notes that most agencies did not hold formal hearings or compile administrative records, and the agencies themselves carried little credibility. Yet the Texas Supreme Court would not allow "true" de novo review, in which the trial court would actually replace the agency decision with one of its own. Thus, the hybrid, in which a loss for the agency would lead to a remand, was viewed as the next best option.

Eventually Texas adopted a version of the 1961 MSAPA, including orderly hearing processes at the agency level. As legislators grew more comfortable with this system, substantial evidence review in the courts became standard. Nevertheless, the Texas APA contemplates that the legislature may prescribe de novo review (or at least substantial evidence de novo) for specific agencies or types of cases. It has done so in various contexts, such as in workers' compensation cases. *Id.* at 305–07. Do you agree that substantial evidence de novo is "less crazy than it seems"?

4. *California independent judgment rule.* Some state systems provide for judicial review of agency fact-findings without trial de novo but under an independent judgment standard. *See Frick v. City of Salina,*

208 P.3d 739 (Kan. 2009) (applying a statute that so provided in the specific context of housing relocation benefits). California provides the leading example. The applicable statute, Cal. Code Civ. Proc. § 1094.5, provides that agency fact findings should in general be overturned only if they are not supported by "substantial evidence in the light of the whole record." However, "in cases in which the court is authorized by law to exercise its independent judgment on the evidence, abuse of discretion is established if the court determines that the findings are not supported by the weight of the evidence."

The independent judgment test of § 1094.5 was originally (but is no longer) grounded in state constitutional law; it has been maintained and steadily expanded through judicial discretion. It applies only if the agency decision "substantially affects a vested, fundamental right." The courts determine the applicability of that key phrase on a case-by-case basis, and the case law is often criticized as vague and unpredictable. For example, the California Supreme Court has held that the loss of a professional license substantially affects a vested, fundamental right. *Bixby v. Pierno,* 481 P.2d 242, 254 (Cal. 1971). "Too often," the court explained, "the independent thinker or crusader is subjected to the retaliation of the professional or trade group; the centripetal pressure toward conformity will often destroy the advocate of reform. . . . Before his license is revoked, such an individual, who walks in the shadow of the governmental monoliths, deserves the protection of a full and independent judicial hearing." And in *Frink v. Prod,* 643 P.2d 476, 482, 484 (Cal. 1982), the court concluded that "the right of the needy disabled to public assistance is of such significance as to require independent judgment review," because "[w]hile the degree to which the right is vested may not be overwhelming, the degree of fundamentalness is."

In *Fukuda v. City of Angels,* 977 P.2d 693 (Cal. 1999), the California Supreme Court was urged to abandon the independent judgment rule, in a case challenging a city's dismissal of a policeman. Instead, the court reaffirmed it. Does the California approach strike you as a good idea, and do these cases seem to be appropriate candidates for its use?

5. *Problem.* Recall the problem about Ted's membership termination by City Health Club in § 9.1.1 N.7. Suppose it arose in California. Would the court have power to exercise independent judgment if the CRC had found in Ted's favor? The Club's favor? Suppose the case was before a health club licensing board which revoked City's license because of repeated incidents of sexual orientation discrimination?

§ 9.2 REVIEW OF ISSUES OF LEGAL INTERPRETATION

In the course of its work, an agency constantly interprets and reinterprets the meaning of the words in legal texts such as statutes or its own prior rules or decisions. For example, an agency might engage in the process of legal interpretation in rendering an adjudicative decision, in engaging in legislative or interpretive rulemaking, or in giving advice to the public.

A court might take any of three approaches when reviewing such interpretations. Under one approach, the court would decide the interpretive issue on its own and give no deference to the agency. The agency's view would receive no more weight than the court gives to the view of the private litigants opposing the agency.

At the opposite extreme, sometimes referred to as the "reasonableness" or "strong deference" approach, the courts would treat interpretive issues largely as they treat agency findings of basic fact under the substantial evidence test. The court would accept the agency's interpretation of a statute or other text if the interpretation was "reasonable"; it would not substitute its own preferred interpretation for that of the agency. In many respects the *Chevron* case illustrates this approach, although only within limits (for example, such deference comes into play only if the court decides that the statute is ambiguous).

In between these poles is a third approach that involves what is sometimes called "weak deference." It resembles the first approach in that it allows the court to substitute its judgment for the agency. On the other hand, it also resembles the second approach, because the court is expected, at least under some circumstances, to give "weight" to the agency's position. The *Connecticut Medical Society* case, which follows, illustrates this approach.

As you might suppose, all of these approaches shade into one another. For instance, a court that purports to employ a substitution of judgment approach, but that grants some degree of deference to the agency's interpretation, may for all practical purposes really be using a "reasonableness" approach. Conversely, if a court employing the "reasonableness" approach conducts an intensive examination of the statute's history and policy to assess whether the statute is "ambiguous" or whether the agency's interpretation of an ambiguous statute is "reasonable," its analysis may in effect merge with the substitution of judgment approach.

§ 9.2.1 STATE LAW APPROACHES

CONNECTICUT STATE MEDICAL SOCIETY v. CONNECTICUT BOARD OF EXAMINERS IN PODIATRY

546 A.2d 830 (Conn. 1988)

HULL, J.:

[The Podiatry Board issued a declaratory ruling that the ankle is part of the foot, so that podiatrists could treat ankle ailments. It noted that "podiatrists in Connecticut have conservatively treated minor sprains, strains and fractures of the foot or ankle for many years without any regulatory or reimbursement questions being raised." The Medical Society sought judicial review, claiming that the ruling was contrary to § 20–50, Ct. Gen'l Statutes, which provides: "Podiatry is defined to be the diagnosis, prevention, and treatment of foot ailments . . ." Relying on the dictionary definition of "foot," the trial court overturned the Podiatry Board's ruling.]

STANDARD OF REVIEW . . .

[The Board claims] that the court substituted its judgment for that of the agency as to the weight of the evidence on questions of fact . . . [and] that the court erred in failing to afford "special deference" to the board's factual findings, and to time-tested agency interpretations.

The standard of judicial review of administrative agency rulings is well established. [The Connecticut APA] permits modification or reversal of an agency's decision "if substantial rights of the appellant have been prejudiced because the administrative findings, inferences, conclusions, or decisions are: (1) In violation of constitutional or statutory provisions; (2) in excess of the statutory authority of the agency; (3) made upon unlawful procedure; (4) affected by other error of law; (5) clearly erroneous in view of the reliable, probative, and substantial evidence on the whole record; or (6) arbitrary or capricious or characterized by abuse of discretion or clearly unwarranted exercise of discretion." The trial court may not retry the case or substitute its judgment for that of the agency on the weight of the evidence or questions of fact. Rather, an agency's factual and discretionary determinations are to be accorded considerable weight by the courts.

On the other hand, it is the function of the courts to expound and apply governing principles of law. This case presents a question of law turning upon the interpretation of a statute. Both the board and the trial court had to construe § 20–50 to determine the permissible scope of podiatry practice in Connecticut. In our view, this is purely a question of law, requiring that the intent of the legislature be discerned. Such a question invokes a broader standard of review than is ordinarily involved in deciding whether, in light of the evidence, the agency has acted unreasonably, arbitrarily, illegally or in abuse of its discretion.

Ordinarily, we give great deference to the construction given a statute by the agency charged with its enforcement. We agree with the trial court, however, that, in this case, the board's interpretation of § 20–50 is not entitled to any special deference. Ordinarily, the construction and interpretation of a statute is a question of law for the courts where the administrative decision is not entitled to special deference, particularly where, as here, the statute has not previously been subjected to judicial scrutiny or time-tested agency interpretations. . . .

The podiatrists . . . claim that "a practical construction placed on legislation over many years" will be accorded special deference by a reviewing court. We have accorded deference to such a time-tested agency interpretation of a statute, but only when the agency has consistently followed its construction over a long period of time, the statutory language is ambiguous, and the agency's interpretation is reasonable. The defendants rely on the fact that podiatrists have long performed the procedures in question in this case. We disagree that such practices constitute time-tested agency interpretation of the statute. Further, we do not consider the board's knowledge of and acquiescence in certain podiatric practices to rise to the level of statutory construction entitled to judicial deference. . . .

The board's contention that the issue presented was a mixed question of law and fact is also without merit. Interpretation of the statute should effect the intent of the legislature and not expand the law's meaning to accommodate unauthorized practices simply because they have been performed in the past . . .

INTERPRETATION OF THE TERM "FOOT"

. . . "In construing a statute, this court will consider its plain language, its legislative history, its purpose and the circumstances surrounding its enactment." . . . When a statute does not define a term, it is appropriate to look to the common understanding expressed in the law and in dictionaries. Webster's Third New International Dictionary defines "foot" as "[t]he terminal part of the vertebrate leg upon which an individual stands consisting in most bipeds (as man) and in many quadrupeds (as the cat) of all the structures (as heel, arches, and digits) below the ankle joint." . . .

. . . The podiatrists, relying on the testimony of the state health commissioner (commissioner) at a hearing before [a legislative committee in 1935, when the Act was revised], claim that [a statutory] change was made to authorize the board to define the scope of podiatric practice in Connecticut. . . . We are unconvinced that the assertions of the commissioner are entitled to the weight the podiatrists urge us to accord them. "While relevant to our inquiry, [excerpts from legislative proceedings] are by no means conclusive in determining legislative intent. . . . As to occurrences at legislative public hearings, these are not admissible as a means of interpreting a legislative act and may not be considered." . . . Further, our examination of the statutory scheme as it now exists belies such a conclusion.

[T]he podiatry statutes both authorize the practice of podiatry and define its limits . . . The provisions limiting the scope of podiatry and, thus, tempering the expansion, however, are the predominant theme of the statutes. This is in marked contrast to chapter 370 of the General Statutes, entitled "Medicine and Surgery," wherein the scope of practice of medicine and surgery is not defined. . . . We conclude, therefore, that it was not the intention of the legislature to empower the board to define the scope of podiatry practice in Connecticut.

The podiatrists rely heavily on *Finoia v. Winchester Repeating Arms Co.*, 34 A.2d 636 (1943), in which we interpreted "hands" as used in a workers' compensation statute in its common anatomical sense as including the wrist and not the forearm . . . We can see no basis, however, for translating that statement into a declaration that the legislature intended the foot to include the ankle within the meaning of the podiatry statutes . . .

There is no error.

NOTES AND QUESTIONS

1. *Independent judgment.* The *Connecticut Medical* opinion acknowledges that, with respect to factual determinations, it would not substitute its judgment for that of the agency. That proposition is, of course, consistent with the teachings of *Universal Camera*. But, the opinion continues, the issue of the meaning of "foot" invokes the independent judgment of the court because it involves a "legal issue." What justifies this distinction? Do the arguments used to justify deference under *Universal Camera* not apply in this situation? Who has more expertise in making professional judgments of the kind involved here—an experienced agency or a generalist court? If at least some of the rationales for deference do apply to legal issues as well as factual ones, does the court's relatively intrusive scope of review for legal issues rest on persuasive countervailing considerations?

2. *Interpretive weight.* Even though *Connecticut Medical* declares that the exposition of governing law is a question for the judiciary, the court also says that it will "[o]rdinarily . . . give great deference" to a statutory interpretation rendered by an agency charged with its enforcement. This is a mode of analysis sometimes called "weak deference." For a fuller exposition of how such a review standard can operate, and how it differs from review for reasonableness, see *Yamaha Corp. v. State Bd. of Equalization*, 960 P.2d 1031 (Cal. 1998). Yamaha bought certain musical instruments out of state,

stored them in California, and later gave them away as promotional gifts. The Board determined that these purchases were subject to California's use tax, even when the instruments were given to out-of-state recipients. In a refund suit brought by Yamaha, the court of appeal upheld the Board's determination, relying on a brief published staff opinion or "annotation" contained in the Board's Business Taxes Law Guide. The court of appeal indicated that it would defer to the Board's view if it was not arbitrary and capricious. The California Supreme Court, in an opinion by Justice Janice Rogers Brown (now a judge on the federal D.C. Circuit), held that this was erroneous:

> In effect, the Court of Appeal held the annotations were entitled to the same "weight" or "deference" as "quasi-legislative" rules.
>
> We reach a different conclusion. An agency interpretation of the meaning and legal effect of a statute is entitled to consideration and respect by the courts; however, unlike quasi-legislative regulations adopted by an agency to which the Legislature has confided the power to "make law," and which, if authorized by the enabling legislation, bind this and other courts as firmly as statutes themselves, the binding power of an agency's *interpretation* of a statute or regulation is contextual: Its power to persuade is both circumstantial and dependent on the presence or absence of factors that support the merit of the interpretation. . . .
>
> . . . To quote the statement of the Law Revision Commission in a recent report, "The standard for judicial review of agency interpretation of law is the *independent judgment* of the court, giving *deference* to the determination of the agency *appropriate* to the circumstances of the agency action."
>
> Whether judicial deference to an agency's interpretation is appropriate and, if so, its extent—the "weight" it should be given— is thus fundamentally *situational*. A court assessing the value of an interpretation must consider a complex of factors material to the substantive legal issue before it, the particular agency offering the interpretation, and the comparative weight the factors ought in reason to command.

Developing this theme, Justice Brown went on to identify

> two broad categories of factors relevant to a court's assessment of the weight due an agency's interpretation: Those "indicating that the agency has a comparative interpretive advantage over the courts," and those "indicating that the interpretation in question is probably correct."
>
> In the first category are factors that "assume the agency has expertise and technical knowledge, especially where the legal text to be interpreted is technical, obscure, complex, open-ended, or entwined with issues of fact, policy, and discretion. . . . The second

group of factors . . .—those suggesting the agency's interpretation is likely to be correct—includes indications of careful consideration by senior agency officials ("an interpretation of a statute contained in a regulation adopted after public notice and comment is more deserving of deference than [one] contained in an advice letter prepared by a single staff member"), evidence that the agency "has consistently maintained the interpretation in question, especially if [it] is long-standing" ("[a] vacillating position . . . is entitled to no deference"), and indications that the agency's interpretation was contemporaneous with legislative enactment of the statute being interpreted. . . .

The court went on to equate its approach with that of Justice Robert Jackson's opinion in *Skidmore v. Swift & Co.* 323 U.S. 134 (1944). "*Skidmore* deference" is discussed in detail in § 9.2.4.

3. *Application of law to fact.* In *Connecticut Mutual* and *Yamaha*, the courts faced what they assumed were pure questions of law. After a court has determined the applicable law as an abstract matter, however, it must proceed to apply that law to the facts. That task requires it to reach some conclusion about whether to treat the question of law application as legal (which would mean the court should use independent judgment) or factual (which would usually bring into play a more deferential standard such as substantial evidence). This problem arises in many legal contexts, and, unfortunately, there is no universally accepted method for making that classification. Sometimes courts make the classification by overtly relying on policy considerations, such as "a determination that, as a matter of the sound administration of justice, one [institutional] actor is better positioned than another to decide the issue in question." *Miller v. Fenton*, 474 U.S. 104, 113–14 (1985). The court might also make that choice depending on how it wants to review the issue. If it decides to substitute judgment, it identifies the issue as one of law, while if it decides that the agency's application is acceptable, it identifies the issue as one of fact or discretion. Of course, application issues involve law, fact, and discretion—which is the reason they are often referred to as "mixed questions of law and fact."

4. *Delegation of authority.* One solution to the conundrum just mentioned, which is distinctive to the field of administrative law, rests on the concept of delegation. It proceeds from the premise that when a statute empowers an administrative agency to make legally binding decisions in a subject area, the statute should generally be read as granting the agency discretion to interpret such language, except insofar as the court finds particular meanings to reside in the statute "as a matter of law." This reasoning would allow the court to separate out the "legal" and "factual" elements of the decision under review by inquiring into the scope of the delegation. *See* Ronald M. Levin, *Interpreting Questions of Law in Administrative Law*, 74 GEO. L.J. 1, 23–29 (1985) (developing this analysis in a federal law context). Note that in *Connecticut Medical* the court rejected the commissioner's assertion that the legislature had delegated to the Podiatry

Board the task of defining the scope of podiatric practice in the state. If, however, the court had concluded that the Board did possess such delegated lawmaking authority, its disposition could have taken a very different path.

Helpful insights on this line of reasoning emerge from *McPherson v. Employment Division*, 591 P.2d 1381 (Or. 1979). The petitioner in that case appealed from a decision of the Employment Division denying her unemployment compensation on the ground that she had left her employment voluntarily and without good cause. The court noted that it was "undisputed that claimant left work voluntarily and that she did so because of the 'sexist' behavior of male employees with whom she was assigned to work and who objected to her doing 'men's work.'" The question before the court was whether this reason constituted "good cause." In an opinion by Justice Hans Linde, the court wrote:

> Agency decisions interpreting a legal term in applying it to particular facts are sometimes said to pose a "mixed question of law and fact." . . . When such a determination is reviewed, [the Oregon APA] calls for separating the elements of the mixture that are "facts" from those that interpret the law. . . .
>
> "Facts," it has been said, are those elements entering into the decision that describe phenomena and events without reference to their significance under the law in question, or to put it another way, as they might be described by a lay person unaware of the disputed legal issue. In that sense, the claimant's reasons for quitting her employment and the events that led up to them are questions of fact. The meaning of the words "good cause" . . . on the other hand, is plainly a question of law. But that is not the end of the inquiry into the scope of judicial review, for this question of law in turn leads to the question how far [the Unemployment Compensation Law] entrusts to the agency the determination of what kind of reasons are "good cause" to leave employment and what kind of reasons are not. . . .
>
> . . . Like standards such as "fair" or "unfair," "undue" or "unreasonable," or "public convenience and necessity," "good cause" in its own terms calls for completing a value judgment that the legislature itself has only indicated: evaluating what are "good" reasons for giving up one's employment and what are not. Judicial review of such evaluations, though a "question of law," requires a court to determine how much the legislature has itself decided and how much it has left to be resolved by the agency. For an agency decision is not [invalid] if the agency's elaboration of a standard like "good cause" is within the range of its responsibility for effectuating a broadly stated statutory policy. . . .
>
> . . . The history of Oregon's unemployment compensation law shows that some range of agency responsibility for defining "good cause" was intended. [The administrator] is directed to "determine

all questions of general policy and promulgate rules and regulations and be responsible for the administration of this chapter." . . .

[In this case the Division apparently construed a prior opinion of the court as establishing, as a matter of law, that "offensive character habits of fellow workers, however distasteful, will not constitute good cause."] [T]his assumption takes an improperly narrow view of the Division's own responsibility to define "good cause" within the overall policy and provisions of the Unemployment Compensation Law. . . .

The law does not extend its benefits to a worker who has a job and voluntarily gives it up without "good cause." But it also does not impose upon the employee the one-dimensional motivation of Adam Smith's "economic man." The workplace is the setting of much of the worker's daily life. The statute does not demand as a matter of law that he or she sacrifice all other than economic objectives and, for instance, endure racial, ethnic, or sexual slurs or personal abuse, for fear that abandoning an oppressive situation will disqualify the worker from unemployment benefits. . . .

. . . We cannot discern what criteria of "good cause" the agency might have applied on its own in the absence of [its erroneous] assumption. This does not mean that on the present record the Court of Appeals or this court might not have reached the same result. That, however, is not our assignment but the Division's, subject only to review whether its assessment of the kind of reasons that are "good cause" to leave employment is "unlawful in substance." For these reasons, the case must be remanded to the Division for reconsideration. . . .

In this connection, notice that Justice Linde frames the question as one of determining "how far" the statute delegates authority. This formulation suggests that if a challenger demonstrates that the agency's view is outside the range of possibilities that the statute leaves open, the court can find an error of law and reverse. In *McPherson*, if the Board were to decide upon the remand that, in its considered judgment, the "good cause" language of the Unemployment Compensation Law should not be read to encompass claims of a hostile work environment, should the court affirm?

5.   *State overview.* Among state courts generally, the most prevalent attitude toward deference on issues of law is some version of the weak deference model articulated in *Connecticut State Medical Society* and *Yamaha.* For helpful surveys of the cases, see WILLIAM N. ESKRIDGE, JR., ET AL., CASES AND MATERIALS ON LEGISLATION: STATUTES AND THE CREATION OF PUBLIC POLICY 1258–61 (4th ed. 2007); Michael Pappas, *No Two-Stepping in the Laboratories: State Deference Standards and Their Implications for Improving the* Chevron *Doctrine,* 39 MCGEORGE L. REV. 977 (2008); Anuradha Vaitheswaran & Thomas A. Mayes, *The Role of Deference in Judicial Review of Agency Action: A Comparison of Federal Law, Uniform*

State Acts, and the Iowa APA, 27 J. NAT'L ASS'N ADMIN. L. JUDICIARY 402, 420–25 (2007). A minority of jurisdictions follow *Chevron. See* § 9.2.2 N.8. On the other hand, some state cases read as though they will accord no deference whatsoever to administrative views, although it is not clear that any jurisdiction adheres to this position consistently. *See, e.g., Kansas Dep't of Revenue v. Powell*, 232 P.3d 856 (Kan. 2010). As discussed in the article just cited, Iowa has a unique statutory provision that addresses matters "vested by a provision of law in the discretion of the agency." A court *shall* defer to the agency's view on matters that have been so vested; *should not* defer on matters that have *not* been so vested; and *shall not* defer on the question of *whether* they have been so vested. Iowa Code § 17A.19(11).

6.   *Problem.* Dr. Sherman specialized in the treatment of obesity. He believed that the best treatment for obesity was the use of a combination of amphetamine and barbiturate drugs in conjunction with diet. He routinely prescribed the same drugs for every patient. Patients were told to call if they had any adverse reaction to the drugs and to return in two weeks.

Dr. Sherman testified that he had studied the problem of obesity extensively, had served 48,000 patients, and had never been sued for malpractice. He testified that none of the drugs he prescribed could adversely affect any medical condition.

Several other doctors testified that the method of treatment used by Dr. Sherman was a fraud, that it could not help patients, was likely to produce addiction, and could adversely affect other medical conditions.

The State Medical Board revoked Dr. Sherman's license to practice medicine on the ground that this method of treatment was a "fraud and deceit in the practice of medicine" (one of the statutory grounds for discipline of physicians). What should be the scope of judicial review of the Board's finding that Dr. Sherman's method of treatment was a "fraud and deceit in the practice of medicine"? *See Sherman v. Board of Regents*, 266 N.Y.S.2d 39 (App. Div. 1966), *aff'd*, 225 N.E.2d 559 (N.Y. 1967).

§ 9.2.2 THE *CHEVRON* DOCTRINE

CHEVRON U.S.A. INC. V. NATURAL RESOURCES DEFENSE COUNCIL
467 U.S. 837 (1984)

[The Clean Air Act requires that, in "nonattainment areas" (i.e., localities that have not met EPA's air quality standards), a company may not construct a "new or modified major stationary source" of air pollution unless it obtains a permit. Such a permit may not be issued unless the applicant complies with strict emissions limitations.

An EPA legislative regulation allowed states to treat an entire plant as a single "stationary source." Under this approach, if a plant contained several pollution-emitting devices, it could install or modify one piece of equipment without meeting the permit requirements if the alteration would not increase the total emissions from the plant. For example, a plant might install a new device that increased pollution if, at the same time, it altered or abandoned other equipment that produced an equal or greater amount of pollution. This approach was sometimes referred to as the "bubble" concept, because it treated a single plant as if it were encased in an imaginary "bubble" with a small hole in it. So long as the total amount of pollution escaping through the imagined hole did not increase, the permit obligation would not be triggered. The bubble approach was attractive to industry because it gave companies broad flexibility to make economical choices about which devices to install or alter.

The issue before the Court was whether the statutory term "stationary source" could refer to an entire plant (as EPA maintained in the "bubble" regulation) rather than a single pollution-emitting piece of equipment within a plant. The court of appeals found that the statute and legislative history were inconclusive, but it decided that EPA's interpretation was contrary to the congressional purpose of improving air quality in nonattainment areas. Thus it invalidated the "bubble" regulation.]

STEVENS, J:

... When a court reviews an agency's construction of the statute which it administers, it is confronted with two questions. First, always, is the question whether Congress has directly spoken to the precise question at issue. If the intent of Congress is clear, that is the end of the matter; for the court, as well as the agency, must give effect to the unambiguously expressed intent of Congress.[9] If, however, the court determines Congress has not directly addressed the precise question at issue, the court does not simply impose its own construction on the statute, as would be necessary in the absence of an administrative interpretation. Rather, if the statute is silent or ambiguous with respect to the specific issue, the question for the court is whether the agency's answer is based on a permissible construction of the statute.[11]

"The power of an administrative agency to administer a congressionally created ... program necessarily requires the formulation of policy and the making of rules to fill any gap left, implicitly or

---

[9] The judiciary is the final authority on issues of statutory construction and must reject administrative constructions which are contrary to clear congressional intent. If a court, employing traditional tools of statutory construction, ascertains that Congress had an intention on the precise question at issue, that intention is the law and must be given effect.

[11] The court need not conclude that the agency construction was the only one it permissibly could have adopted to uphold the construction, or even the reading the court would have reached if the question initially had arisen in a judicial proceeding.

explicitly, by Congress." If Congress has explicitly left a gap for the agency to fill, there is an express delegation of authority to the agency to elucidate a specific provision of the statute by regulation. Such legislative regulations are given controlling weight unless they are arbitrary, capricious, or manifestly contrary to the statute. Sometimes the legislative delegation to an agency on a particular question is implicit rather than explicit. In such a case, a court may not substitute its own construction of a statutory provision for a reasonable interpretation made by the administrator of an agency.

We have long recognized that considerable weight should be accorded to an executive department's construction of a statutory scheme it is entrusted to administer, and the principle of deference to administrative interpretations

> has been consistently followed by this Court whenever decision as to the meaning or reach of a statute has involved reconciling conflicting policies, and a full understanding of the force of the statutory policy in the given situation has depended upon more than ordinary knowledge respecting the matters subjected to agency regulations ... If this choice represents a reasonable accommodation of conflicting policies that were committed to the agency's care by the statute, we should not disturb it unless it appears from the statute or its legislative history that the accommodation is not one that Congress would have sanctioned.

In light of these well-settled principles it is clear that the Court of Appeals misconceived the nature of its role in reviewing the regulations at issue. Once it determined, after its own examination of the legislation, that Congress did not actually have an intent regarding the applicability of the bubble concept to the permit program, the question before it was not whether in its view the concept is "inappropriate" in the general context of a program designed to improve air quality, but whether the Administrator's view that it is appropriate in the context of this particular program is a reasonable one. Based on the examination of the legislation and its history which follows, we agree with the Court of Appeals that Congress did not have a specific intention on the applicability of the bubble concept in these cases, and conclude that the EPA's use of that concept here is a reasonable policy choice for the agency to make. . . .

The legislative history . . . does not contain any specific comment on the "bubble concept" or the question whether a plantwide definition of a stationary source is permissible under the permit program. It does, however, plainly disclose that in the permit program Congress sought to accommodate the conflict between the economic interest in permitting capital improvements to continue and the environmental interest in improving air quality. . . .

[T]he plantwide definition [of stationary source] is fully consistent with one of those concerns—the allowance of reasonable economic growth—and, whether or not we believe it most effectively implements the other, we must recognize that the EPA has advanced a reasonable explanation for its conclusion that the regulations serve the environmental objectives as well. Indeed, its reasoning is supported by the public record developed in the rulemaking process, as well as by certain private studies. . . .

. . . The fact that the agency has from time to time changed its interpretation of the term "source" does not, as respondents argue, lead us to conclude that no deference should be accorded the agency's interpretation of the statute. An initial agency interpretation is not instantly carved in stone. On the contrary, the agency, to engage in informed rulemaking, must consider varying interpretations and the wisdom of its policy on a continuing basis. . . .

In [this case,] the Administrator's interpretation represents a reasonable accommodation of manifestly competing interests and is entitled to deference: the regulatory scheme is technical and complex, the agency considered the matter in a detailed and reasoned fashion, and the decision involves reconciling conflicting policies. Congress intended to accommodate both interests, but did not do so itself on the level of specificity presented by this case. Perhaps that body consciously desired the Administrator to strike the balance at this level, thinking that those with great expertise and charged with responsibility for administering the provision would be in a better position to do so; perhaps it simply did not consider the question at this level; and perhaps Congress was unable to forge a coalition on either side of the question, and those on each side decided to take their chances with the scheme devised by the agency. For judicial purposes, it matters not which of these things occurred.

Judges are not experts in the field, and are not part of either political branch of the Government. Courts must, in some cases, reconcile competing political interests, but not on the basis of the judges' personal policy preferences. In contrast, an agency to which Congress has delegated policy-making responsibilities may, within the limits of that delegation, properly rely upon the incumbent administration's views of wise policy to inform its judgments. While agencies are not directly accountable to the people, the Chief Executive is, and it is entirely appropriate for this political branch of the Government to make such policy choices—resolving the competing interests which Congress itself either inadvertently did not resolve, or intentionally left to be resolved by the agency charged with the administration of the statute in light of everyday realities.

When a challenge to an agency construction of a statutory provision, fairly conceptualized, really centers on the wisdom of the agency's policy, rather than whether it is a reasonable choice within a gap left open by Congress, the challenge must fail. In such a case, federal judges—who have no constituency—have a duty to respect legitimate policy choices made by those who do. The responsibilities for assessing the wisdom of such policy choices and resolving the struggle between competing views of the public interest are not judicial ones: "Our Constitution vests such responsibilities in the political branches."

We hold that the EPA's definition of the term "source" is a permissible construction of the statute which seeks to accommodate progress in reducing air pollution with economic growth. "The Regulations which the Administrator has adopted provide what the agency could allowably view as . . . [an] effective reconciliation of these twofold ends. . . ."

The judgment of the Court of Appeals is reversed.

REHNQUIST, O'CONNOR, and MARSHALL, JJ. did not participate.

NOTES AND QUESTIONS

1. *Chevron's impact. Chevron* is by far the most prominent federal case on judicial review of agencies' statutory interpretations. It has been cited thousands of times by the courts and has generated extensive controversy. Many, probably most, lower courts regularly treat it as the starting point for their analysis of the merits of an administrative rule or order. By any measure it is a landmark decision with which every administrative lawyer must be familiar.

At the same time, some cautionary notes are in order. According to one empirical study, the Supreme Court has since 1984 relied on *Chevron* in fewer than half of the cases in which one might logically have expected it to be cited. *See* William N. Eskridge, Jr. & Lauren E. Baer, *The Continuum of Deference: Supreme Court Treatment of Agency Statutory Interpretations from* Chevron *to* Hamdan," 96 GEO. L.J. 1083, 1120–23 (2008). Indeed, if one can judge from archival records of the Court's internal deliberations, the Justices probably did not initially anticipate that this opinion—issued in a case in which only six Justices participated—would come to be regarded as a watershed pronouncement on scope of review. They apparently considered it a routine environmental case. The canonical status of the *Chevron* test came about because of the importance that lawyers, scholars, and lower courts soon ascribed to it. *See* Thomas W. Merrill, *The Story of* Chevron: *The Making of an Accidental Landmark*, in ADMINISTRATIVE LAW STORIES ch. 10 (Peter L. Strauss ed. 2006). In subsequent years, however, the Court has followed the lead of these authorities and now frequently relies on the two-step *Chevron* standard of review in its opinions.

You should also bear in mind that case law has identified a number of circumstances in which the *Chevron* test does not (or may not) apply. These exceptions are discussed in §§ 9.2.3 NN. 5–7 and § 9.2.4.

2. *Strong deference.* The two-step inquiry described at the beginning of the excerpted opinion can be described as prescribing "strong" deference to an agency's interpretation of a statute that it administers. The logic behind that label is that if the court determines that the statute is ambiguous on the issue presented, and that the agency's position on that issue is reasonable, deference is mandatory.

To some degree, this policy of deference rests on the widely accepted idea that when a court finds that the legislature has entrusted responsibility for a given set of matters to an administrative agency, the court should accept reasonable determinations that fall within the scope of that delegation. *Connecticut Medical* and *McPherson*, § 9.2.1, reflect support for this proposition. For an argument that deferential review under these circumstances is compatible with the court's duty to "say what the law is," as prescribed in *Marbury v. Madison*, 5 U.S. (1 Cranch) 137 (1803), see Henry P. Monaghan, Marbury *and the Administrative State*, 83 COLUM. L. REV. 1 (1983). However, the *Chevron* test goes significantly further, because the Court indicates that it will *presume,* at step one, that Congress intended to delegate discretion to the agency to resolve any given issue, unless the statute "clearly" indicates otherwise. Statutory ambiguity may reflect a deliberate delegation, or may have resulted from inadvertence or political calculation, the Court says, but "[f]or judicial purposes, it matters not which of these things occurred."

What, if anything, justifies the "strong" deference prescribed in *Chevron?* The opinion refers to EPA's expertise and political accountability. Another suggestion has been that *Chevron* serves the salutary purpose of centralization: it tends to ensure that critical policy decisions will be made by a single administering agency rather than diffused among scattered courts in multiple circuits across the country. Peter L. Strauss, *One Hundred Fifty Cases Per Year: Some Implications of the Supreme Court's Limited Resources for Judicial Review of Agency Action*, 87 COLUM. L. REV. 1093 (1987). Collectively, are these rationales persuasive?

3. *Academic perspectives.* Law review commentary on *Chevron* has been voluminous and cannot be adequately summarized here. Important treatments include: Stephen Breyer, *Judicial Review of Questions of Law and Policy*, 38 ADMIN. L. REV. 236 (1986); Antonin Scalia, *Judicial Deference to Administrative Interpretations of Law*, 1989 DUKE L.J. 511; Thomas W. Merrill, *Judicial Deference to Executive Precedent*, 101 YALE L.J. 969 (1992); Michael Herz, *Deference Running Riot: Separating Interpretation and Lawmaking Under* Chevron, 6 ADMIN. L.J. AM. U. 187 (1992).

Illustrative of academic support for *Chevron* is this assessment in 1 RICHARD J. PIERCE, JR., ADMINISTRATIVE LAW TREATISE 160–63 (5th ed. 2010):

> The *Chevron* Court's reconceptualization of the process of statutory construction is an enormous improvement over the inconsistent and wooden characterizations of the process that dominated judicial decisionmaking in the pre-*Chevron* era. . . . Understanding *Chevron* requires acceptance of a reality courts have often denied. Many questions concerning the meaning to be given statutes cannot be characterized as issues of law. If Congress has resolved a policy dispute in the process of enacting a statute, an agency or court can, and must, adopt Congress' resolution. . . . This is the situation governed by *Chevron* step one. . . .
>
> Congress cannot, and does not, resolve all policy disputes when it enacts a statute, however. For a variety of reasons . . . Congress leaves many policy issues open. When Congress drafts a statute that does not resolve a policy dispute that later arises under the statute, some institution must resolve that dispute. The institution called upon to perform this task is not engaged in statutory interpretation. . . . It is not resolving an issue of "law." Rather, it is resolving an issue of policy. That is the situation governed by *Chevron* step two. . . . In other words, policy disputes within the scope of authority Congress has delegated an agency are to be resolved by agencies rather than courts.
>
> . . . The *Chevron* Court's reasoning in support of this institutional allocation of responsibility is based on political accountability—a value central to the concept of democratic government. . . .

On the other hand, *Chevron* has elicited numerous negative, or at least skeptical, assessments from the scholarly world. A well-known statement of this critique was that of Professor Farina, who wrote in part:

> A crucial aspect of the capacity for external control upon which the permissibility of delegating regulatory power hinged was judicial policing of the terms of the statute. . . . The constitutional accommodation ultimately reached in the nondelegation cases implied that principal power to say what the statute means must rest *outside* the agency, in the courts. Hence, a key assumption of *Chevron's* "judicial usurpation" argument—that Congress may give agencies primary responsibility not only for making policy within the limits of their organic statutes, but also for defining those limits whenever the text and surrounding legislative materials are ambiguous—is fundamentally incongruous with the constitutional course by which the Court came to reconcile agencies and separation of powers.

Cynthia R. Farina, *Statutory Interpretation and the Balance of Power in the Administrative State*, 89 COLUM. L. REV. 452, 487–88 (1989).

4.   *The two step test.* The ABA Section of Administrative Law and Regulatory Practice has endorsed a helpful overview of the two-step *Chevron* test as it has evolved through subsequent case law:

> Under step one of the *Chevron* test, the reviewing court determines whether the statutory meaning with respect to the precise issue before it is "clear" (and thus, not "ambiguous"). Step one of *Chevron* does not dictate that courts use any particular method of statutory interpretation. However, the court should use "the traditional tools of statutory construction" to determine whether the meaning of the statute is clear with respect to the precise issue before it. For most judges, these tools include examination of the text of the statute, dictionary definitions, canons of construction, statutory structure, legislative purpose, and legislative history.

> If the statutory meaning on the precise issue before the court is not clear, or if the statute is silent on that issue, the court is required to defer to the agency's interpretation of the statute if that interpretation is "reasonable" or "permissible" (step two of *Chevron*).

> While there is no single, established method of conducting the step two analysis, two interrelated approaches are most prominent. First, courts regularly examine the same statutory materials relied on in step one, seeking to determine whether the statute, even if subject to more than one interpretation, can support the particular interpretation adopted by the agency. For example, the court might find that the statutory context, viewed as a whole, clearly rules out the option the agency selected, or a premise on which it relied. (Some courts, however, make essentially the same inquiry within step one when they determine whether the agency interpretation violates the clear meaning of the statute. As a practical matter, the court's review of these legal issues is not affected by which step is deemed to be involved. In either case, the court is measuring the interpretation against congressionally established limitations.)

> Second, in addition to engaging in conventional statutory construction, or in some cases instead of engaging in it, courts at step two of *Chevron* evaluate whether the agency, in reaching its interpretation, reasoned from statutory premises in a well-considered fashion. Courts may look, for example, to whether the interpretation is supported by a reasonable explanation and is logically coherent, or they may ask whether the agency interpretation is arbitrary and capricious in substance. In this regard, the step two inquiry tends to merge with review under the arbitrary and capricious standard.

ABA Section of Administrative Law and Regulatory Practice, A Blackletter Statement of Federal Administrative Law 34-35 (2d ed. 2013).

In some cases, judicial invocations of the *Chevron* test can sound perfunctory. Consider, as one example, the First Circuit's *one-paragraph* analysis applying *Chevron* to the "public hearing" provision of the Clean Water Act in *Dominion Energy*, § 3.1.1. Indeed, some critics believe that *Chevron* creates an unhealthy temptation for judges not to try very hard to understand or consider a challenger's objections. Yet the brevity of a court's discussion may simply reflect the absence of any particularly viable legal theory that the challenger could have deployed. In *Dominion Energy* itself, after all, even the petitioners agreed that the hearing provision of the Clean Water Act was ambiguous. Regardless, the following notes explain how the *Chevron* test can operate when the court does apply it conscientiously.

5. *Applying step one.* The question posed by the first *Chevron* step is whether "Congress has directly addressed the precise question at issue"—in other words, whether the court can find that the agency's interpretation violates the clear meaning of the statute. This inquiry leaves a good deal to the judgment of the reviewing court in a particular case. In practice, it can be quite searching. The full range of what *Chevron* calls "traditional tools of statutory construction" may come into play, as is discussed more fully in § 9.2.3. For the moment, however, consider *MCI Telecomms. Corp. v. AT&T*, 512 U.S. 218 (1994), which is an example of a clash between the Justices about the applicability of *Chevron* step one. The Federal Communications Commission sought to exempt all long-distance telephone companies except the most dominant one (AT&T) from the obligation to file tariffs (rate schedules) with the Commission. The FCC relied on its statutory authority to "modify any requirement" imposed by the Communications Act. The Court rejected this action in an opinion by Justice Scalia, arguing that the new policy was too radical a departure from the premises of the Act to be described as a "modification." This was true, he continued, because, according to virtually every dictionary, " 'to modify' means to change moderately or in minor fashion." Scalia declined to defer to the FCC, because "an agency's interpretation of a statute is not entitled to deference when it goes beyond the meaning that the statute can bear." Three Justices dissented, contending that the Communications Act should be read flexibly to allow the FCC to respond to changing conditions in the long-distance telephone market.

As *MCI* illustrates, and cases discussed in § 9.2.3 elaborate, judges often prove to be quite willing to find a statute to be "clear" with respect to an interpretive issue in controversy. Moreover, the Court did not say in *MCI* that the statute under consideration was entirely unambiguous—only that it could not mean what the agency said it meant.

6. *Applying step two.* At step two of *Chevron*, the question for the court is whether the agency's interpretation of a statutory provision is "unreasonable." An agency is less likely to lose at this stage, but reversals

under step two do occur. *See* Christopher H. Schroeder & Robert L. Glicksman, Chevron, State Farm, *and EPA in the Courts of Appeals During the 1990s*, 31 ENVTL. L. REP. 10,371, 10,375–77 (2001) (survey of environmental cases in which "[a]t Step One EPA loses 59% of the time," but "once EPA got beyond Step One, it was upheld 92% of the time").

There is more than a little uncertainty about how the second step is supposed to work. While some cases engage in a more or less rubber-stamp analysis of the reasonableness of the agency interpretation, other decisions have more bite. Among the latter, some are simply statutory interpretation under a different name and could just as well have been decided under step one, as the ABA statement indicates. For present purposes we focus on a different application: A court may say that the agency's interpretation is "unreasonable" because it fails to implement a statutory mandate in a sufficiently *reasoned* manner. The following cases illustrate this approach:

• In *NRDC v. Daley*, 209 F.3d 747 (D.C. Cir. 2000), the Commerce Department set a yearly quota on the fishing industry's harvesting of summer flounder, which is a species threatened with depletion. The court found the quota unreasonable, because it admittedly had only an 18% chance of meeting the conservation goals that Congress had directed the agency to achieve.

• In *Republican Nat'l Comm. v. FEC*, 76 F.3d 400 (D.C. Cir. 1996), the Federal Election Campaign Act provided that a political committee must use its "best efforts" to induce contributors to identify their employers and occupations when sending in a donation. The Federal Election Commission's regulations instructed the committees to include in their solicitation letters a mandatory statement advising donors that federal law required them to submit this information (which was not so). The court said that "best efforts" was an ambiguous term, but the agency had read it in an unreasonable way: "Although the mandatory statement's language may well produce higher reporting rates, we doubt that Congress authorized the Commission to achieve this purpose by misleading donors."

It is widely acknowledged that this approach to the step two issue overlaps the arbitrary and capricious test of the APA to a considerable degree. In *Judulang v. Holder*, 132 S.Ct. 476 (2011), also discussed in § 9.3.1 N.1, the Court, in a unanimous opinion written by Justice Kagan, found that a deportation policy of the Board of Immigration Appeals was arbitrary and capricious, because it lacked support in either the language or the policies of the governing statute. In a footnote, Justice Kagan mentioned that the government had urged the Court to decide the case by applying the second step of *Chevron*. "Were we to do so," she replied, "our analysis would be the same, because under *Chevron* step two, we ask whether an agency interpretation is 'arbitrary or capricious in substance.' " *Id.* at 484 n.7. *See also Verizon Commc'ns., Inc. v. FCC*, 535 U.S. 467, 527 n.27 (2002). Lower courts have been making similar suggestions for years. *See, e.g., Shays v. FEC*, 414 F.3d 76, 96–97 (D.C. Cir. 2005); *General Am. Transp. Corp. v. ICC*,

872 F.2d 1048, 1053 (D.C. Cir. 1989) (stating that both of those tests "require us to determine whether the [agency,] in effecting a reconciliation of competing statutory aims, has rationally considered the factors deemed relevant by the Act"); Ronald M. Levin, *The Anatomy of* Chevron: *Step Two Reconsidered*, 72 CHI.–KENT L. REV. 1253, 1263–77 (1997).

The arbitrary and capricious test is discussed in §§ 9.3 and § 9.4. That test does encompass some inquiries that *Chevron* step two does not, such as whether the agency action has adequate factual support and is consistent with precedent. But courts do not appear to use step two to accomplish anything that could not be accomplished equally well under either *Chevron* step one or the arbitrary and capricious test.

7. *Chevron and stare decisis.* When an agency adopts one interpretation of an ambiguous regulatory statute and the interpretation is judicially upheld, should the agency be free to adopt a different interpretation later, if the interpretation would otherwise be entitled to *Chevron* deference? In general, yes, according to *Nat'l Cable & Telecomms. Ass'n v. Brand X Internet Servs.*, 545 U.S. 967 (2005). The question in *Brand X* was whether providers of high-speed cable modem Internet service are common carriers for purposes of the Communications Act (meaning that they would be subject to FCC rate regulation, would not be able to discriminate among customers, etc.). The FCC found that they were not common carriers, and the Supreme Court upheld that answer under *Chevron* in an opinion by Justice Thomas. Before reaching that issue, however, Thomas criticized the court of appeals for having been too quick to reject the FCC's view in favor of one of its own prior precedents, in which it had held that the common carrier provisions did apply. According to Thomas, "[a] court's prior judicial construction of a statute trumps an agency construction otherwise entitled to *Chevron* deference only if the prior court decision holds that its construction follows from the unambiguous terms of the statute and thus leaves no room for agency discretion." This holding was in line with the position of commentators who had argued that a stricter approach to stare decisis would impede an agency's ability to engage in policymaking over time. *See*, e.g., Kenneth A. Bamberger, *Provisional Precedent: Protecting Flexibility in Administrative Policymaking*, 77 N.Y.U. L. REV. 1272 (2002).

The Court's statement of its holding was not limited to lower court opinions. In a two-sentence concurrence, however, Justice Stevens said that he joined the majority opinion but believed that the Court's account of the stare decisis effect of a court of appeals decision "would not necessarily be applicable to a decision by this Court that would presumably remove any pre-existing ambiguity." Justice Scalia dissented. He objected to the majority's implication that an agency could be permitted to disagree with what the Supreme Court has previously declared to be the best interpretation of a regulatory statute. This result, he contended, was "not only bizarre [but] probably unconstitutional," because "Article III courts do not sit to render decisions that can be reversed or ignored by executive officers." Whose view is preferable?

8.   *Chevron in the states.* A few state courts have adopted the *Chevron* test for use in evaluating the actions of state agencies. *See, e.g., Nunnally v. D.C. Metro. Police Dep't*, 80 A.3d 1004 (D.C. 2013); *Olmstead v. Dep't of Telecomms. & Cable*, 999 N.E.2d 125 (Mass. 2013); *Forest Ecol. Network v. Land Use Reg. Comm'n*, 39 A.3d 74, 91 (Me. 2012); *Appalachian Power Co. v. State Tax Dep't*, 466 S.E.2d 424 (W. Va. 1995). Most state courts, however, have not. They adhere to a variety of tests that are, or at least profess to be, less deferential. *See* § 9.2.1 N.5. A striking illustration is *State ex rel. Celebrezze v. National Lime & Stone Co.*, 627 N.E.2d 538 (Ohio 1994), concluding, on facts almost identical to those of *Chevron*, that "any uncertainty with regard to the interpretation of [the Ohio air pollution statute] and rules promulgated thereunder should be construed in favor of the person or entity (manufacturer or otherwise) affected by the law."

Is *Chevron* less appropriate at the state level than at the federal level? Consider these views:

> While the states have not adopted a uniform approach to agency deference, most states share common attributes that, this Comment argues, justify denying state agencies *Chevron*-like deference on *Chevron*'s own terms. State judges are in most cases more directly politically accountable than state agency officials and federal judges due to their necessary involvement in electoral politics. State courts also have a long, rich history of engaging in common law making that state agencies and federal courts do not, making them well-suited to fill statutory gaps independently. Finally, deference based on technical expertise is less warranted at the state level due to the typical subject matter of state agency action.

D. Zachary Hudson, Comment, *A Case for Varying Interpretive Deference at the State Level*, 119 YALE L.J. 373, 375 (2009). *See also* Pete Schenkkan, *Texas Administrative Law: Trials, Triumphs, and New Challenges*, 7 TEX. TECH. ADMIN. L.J. 288, 317–18 (2006); William R. Andersen, Chevron *in the States: An Assessment and a Proposal*, 58 ADMIN. L. REV. 1017 (2006); Michael Asimow, *The Scope of Judicial Review of Decisions of California Administrative Agencies*, 42 UCLA L. REV. 1157, 1206–08 (1995) (recommending that California should not follow *Chevron*).

9.   *Problem.* Six years ago, Madison enacted a statute relating to cleanup of oil spills. Section 201 of the Act requires any person responsible for an oil spill to pay "damages for injury to natural resources" to the Madison Environmental Quality Agency (MEQA). Section 203 provides: "Damages recovered under § 201 can be spent only on restoration of the resource or acquisition of a substitute. The measure of damages under § 201 shall not be limited by the amount needed to restore the resource."

MEQA has power to adopt regulations to implement the statute and also has power to adjudicate the amount of any damages to be paid under § 201. The Report of the Senate Environmental Affairs Committee stated: "Section

201 is intended to provide funds to MEQA to restore any resources destroyed by a spill and also to encourage oil companies to take appropriate precautions to prevent spills."

Last year, Petrol Oil Co.'s tanker went aground and sank off a remote part of the Madison coast. The resulting oil spill killed 300 fur seals and destroyed their breeding area. MEQA, which had adopted no regulations under § 201, conducted an adjudicatory proceeding to determine Petrol's liability for damages. The Sierra Club intervened in the proceeding. The Petrol case was the first to apply § 201.

MEQA's decision construed § 201 so that the amount of damages would be the market value of the natural resource destroyed, or the cost of restoring the resource, whichever is less. The seals were worth $15 each (the value of their fur) for a total of $4500. The oil soaked beach area is worth $3000. As a result, MEQA assessed damages of $7500. The cost of restoring the breeding area and bringing back the colony of seals is $30,000,000.

Sierra Club seeks judicial review of this decision. The Madison courts generally apply *Chevron*. How should the court rule? *See Ohio v. Dep't of Interior*, 880 F.2d 432 (D.C. Cir. 1989).

§ 9.2.3 STATUTORY INTERPRETATION AND THE *CHEVRON* DOCTRINE

The interplay between *Chevron* and statutory interpretation is difficult to assess in the abstract. One way of exploring it is to examine the kinds of arguments that courts commonly deploy as they determine whether a statute has a "clear meaning" that the agency failed to heed. This section surveys several such arguments, and also commences an examination (continued in § 9.2.4) of various types of cases in which *Chevron* does not come into play in the first place.

FDA v. BROWN & WILLIAMSON TOBACCO CORP.
529 U.S. 120 (2000)

O'CONNOR, J.:

This case involves one of the most troubling public health problems facing our Nation today: the thousands of premature deaths that occur each year because of tobacco use. In 1996, the Food and Drug Administration (FDA), after having expressly disavowed any such authority since its inception, asserted jurisdiction to regulate tobacco products. . . . Pursuant to this authority, it promulgated regulations intended to reduce tobacco consumption among children and adolescents. The agency believed that, because most tobacco consumers begin their use before reaching the age of 18, curbing tobacco use by minors could substantially reduce the prevalence of addiction in future generations and thus the incidence of tobacco-related death and disease.

[W]e believe that Congress has clearly precluded the FDA from asserting jurisdiction to regulate tobacco products. Such authority is inconsistent with the intent that Congress has expressed in the FDCA's overall regulatory scheme and in the tobacco-specific legislation that it has enacted subsequent to the FDCA. In light of this clear intent, the FDA's assertion of jurisdiction is impermissible.

I

The FDCA grants the FDA, as the designee of the Secretary of Health and Human Services, the authority to regulate, among other items, "drugs" and "devices." The Act defines "drug" to include "articles (other than food) intended to affect the structure or any function of the body." 21 U.S.C. § 321(g)(1)(C). It defines "device," in part, as "an [article] which is . . . intended to affect the structure or any function of the body." § 321(h). . . .

On August 28, 1996, the FDA issued a final rule [in which it] determined that nicotine is a "drug" and that cigarettes and smokeless tobacco are "drug delivery devices," and therefore it had jurisdiction under the FDCA to regulate tobacco products as customarily marketed— that is, without manufacturer claims of therapeutic benefit. . . . The access regulations prohibit the sale of cigarettes or smokeless tobacco to persons younger than 18; require retailers to verify through photo identification the age of all purchasers younger than 27; prohibit the sale of cigarettes in quantities smaller than 20; prohibit the distribution of free samples; and prohibit sales through self-service displays and vending machines except in adult-only locations. [The rules also limited advertising practices and required additional labeling on tobacco product packages.]

Respondents, a group of tobacco manufacturers, retailers, and advertisers, filed suit in United States District Court for the Middle District of North Carolina challenging the regulations. . . . The District Court [upheld the regulations, except for the advertising restrictions.] . . . The Court of Appeals for the Fourth Circuit reversed, holding that Congress has not granted the FDA jurisdiction to regulate tobacco products.

II.

The FDA's assertion of jurisdiction to regulate tobacco products is founded on its conclusions that nicotine is a "drug" and that cigarettes and smokeless tobacco are "drug delivery devices." [T]he FDA found that tobacco products are "intended" to deliver the pharmacological effects of satisfying addiction, stimulation and tranquilization, and weight control. . . . As an initial matter, respondents take issue with the FDA's reading of "intended." . . . We need not resolve this question, however, because assuming, *arguendo*, that a product can be "intended to affect the structure or any function of the body" absent claims of therapeutic or medical benefit, the FDA's claim to jurisdiction contravenes the clear intent of Congress.

... Because this case involves an administrative agency's construction of a statute that it administers, our analysis is governed by *Chevron*. . . . In determining whether Congress has specifically addressed the question at issue, a reviewing court should not confine itself to examining a particular statutory provision in isolation. The meaning—or ambiguity—of certain words or phrases may only become evident when placed in context. It is a "fundamental canon of statutory construction that the words of a statute must be read in their context and with a view to their place in the overall statutory scheme." . . . Similarly, the meaning of one statute may be affected by other Acts, particularly where Congress has spoken subsequently and more specifically to the topic at hand. In addition, we must be guided to a degree by common sense as to the manner in which Congress is likely to delegate a policy decision of such economic and political magnitude to an administrative agency.

A

... Viewing the FDCA as a whole, it is evident that one of the Act's core objectives is to ensure that any product regulated by the FDA is "safe" and "effective" for its intended use. This essential purpose pervades the FDCA. . . .

In its rulemaking proceeding, the FDA quite exhaustively documented that "tobacco products are unsafe," "dangerous," and "cause great pain and suffering from illness." . . . These findings logically imply that, if tobacco products were "devices" under the FDCA, the FDA would be required to remove them from the market. . . .

The FDA apparently recognized this dilemma and concluded, somewhat ironically, that tobacco products are actually "safe" within the meaning of the FDCA. In promulgating its regulations, the agency conceded that "tobacco products are unsafe, as that term is conventionally understood." Nonetheless, the FDA reasoned that, in determining whether a device is safe under the Act, it must consider "not only the risks presented by a product but also any of the countervailing effects of use of that product, including the consequences of not permitting the product to be marketed." Applying this standard, the FDA found that, because of the high level of addiction among tobacco users, a ban would likely be "dangerous." In particular, current tobacco users could suffer from extreme withdrawal, the health care system and available pharmaceuticals might not be able to meet the treatment demands of those suffering from withdrawal, and a black market offering cigarettes even more dangerous than those currently sold legally would likely develop. . . .

... [T]he FDA's judgment that leaving tobacco products on the market "is more effective in achieving public health goals than a ban" is no substitute for the specific safety determinations required by the FDCA's various operative provisions. . . . The inescapable conclusion is that there is no room for tobacco products within the FDCA's regulatory scheme. If they cannot be used safely for any therapeutic purpose, and yet they cannot be banned, they simply do not fit.

B

In determining whether Congress has spoken directly to the FDA's authority to regulate tobacco, we must also consider in greater detail the tobacco-specific legislation that Congress has enacted over the past 35 years. At the time a statute is enacted, it may have a range of plausible meanings. Over time, however, subsequent acts can shape or focus those meanings. The "classic judicial task of reconciling many laws enacted over time, and getting them to 'make sense' in combination, necessarily assumes that the implications of a statute may be altered by the implications of a later statute." This is particularly so where the scope of the earlier statute is broad but the subsequent statutes more specifically address the topic at hand. . . .

Congress has enacted six separate pieces of legislation since 1965 addressing the problem of tobacco use and human health. Those statutes, among other things, require that health warnings appear on all packaging and in all print and outdoor advertisements; prohibit the advertisement of tobacco products [on television; and make certain block grants to states contingent on their forbidding sales of tobacco products to minors.]

In adopting each statute, Congress has acted against the backdrop of the FDA's consistent and repeated statements that it lacked authority under the FDCA to regulate tobacco absent claims of therapeutic benefit by the manufacturer. In fact, on several occasions over this period, and after the health consequences of tobacco use and nicotine's pharmacological effects had become well known, Congress considered and rejected bills that would have granted the FDA such jurisdiction. Under these circumstances, it is evident that Congress' tobacco-specific statutes have effectively ratified the FDA's long-held position that it lacks jurisdiction under the FDCA to regulate tobacco products. Congress has created a distinct regulatory scheme to address the problem of tobacco and health, and that scheme, as presently constructed, precludes any role for the FDA. . . .

C

Finally, our inquiry into whether Congress has directly spoken to the precise question at issue is shaped, at least in some measure, by the nature of the question presented. Deference under *Chevron* to an agency's construction of a statute that it administers is premised on the theory that a statute's ambiguity constitutes an implicit delegation from Congress to the agency to fill in the statutory gaps. In extraordinary cases, however, there may be reason to hesitate before concluding that Congress has intended such an implicit delegation. Cf. Breyer, Judicial Review of Questions of Law and Policy, 38 Admin. L. Rev. 363, 370 (1986) ("A court may also ask whether the legal question is an important one. Congress is more likely to have focused upon, and answered, major questions, while leaving interstitial matters to answer themselves in the course of the statute's daily administration").

This is hardly an ordinary case. Contrary to its representations to Congress since 1914, the FDA has now asserted jurisdiction to regulate an industry constituting a significant portion of the American economy. In fact, the FDA contends that, were it to determine that tobacco products provide no "reasonable assurance of safety," it would have the authority to ban cigarettes and smokeless tobacco entirely. Owing to its unique place in American history and society, tobacco has its own unique political history. . . .

. . . [W]e are confident that Congress could not have intended to delegate a decision of such economic and political significance to an agency in so cryptic a fashion. To find that the FDA has the authority to regulate tobacco products, one must not only adopt an extremely strained understanding of "safety" as it is used throughout the Act—a concept central to the FDCA's regulatory scheme—but also ignore the plain implication of Congress' subsequent tobacco-specific legislation. It is therefore clear, based on the FDCA's overall regulatory scheme and the subsequent tobacco legislation, that Congress has directly spoken to the question at issue and precluded the FDA from regulating tobacco products.

. . . For these reasons, the judgment of the Court of Appeals for the Fourth Circuit is affirmed.

BREYER, J., with whom STEVENS, SOUTER, and GINSBURG, JJ., join, dissenting.

The Food and Drug Administration (FDA) has the authority to regulate "articles (other than food) intended to affect the structure or any function of the body. . . ." Unlike the majority, I believe that tobacco products fit within this statutory language.

In its own interpretation, the majority nowhere denies the following two salient points. First, tobacco products (including cigarettes) fall within the scope of this statutory definition, read literally. . . . Second, the statute's basic purpose—the protection of public health—supports the inclusion of cigarettes within its scope. Unregulated tobacco use causes "more than 400,000 people [to] die each year from tobacco-related illnesses, such as cancer, respiratory illnesses, and heart disease." Indeed, tobacco products kill more people in this country every year "than . . . AIDS, car accidents, alcohol, homicides, illegal drugs, suicides, and fires, *combined.*" . . .

I

. . . After studying the FDCA's history, experts have written that the statute "is a purposefully broad delegation of discretionary powers by Congress," J. O'Reilly, 1 Food and Drug Administration § 6.01, p. 6–1 (2d ed.1995), and that, in a sense, the FDCA "must be regarded as a *constitution*" that "establishes general principles" and "permits implementation within broad parameters" so that the FDA can "implement these objectives through the most effective and efficient controls that can be devised." Hutt, Philosophy of Regulation Under the Federal Food, Drug and Cosmetic Act, 28 Food Drug Cosm.L.J. 177, 178–179 (1973) (emphasis added). This Court, too, has said that the "historical expansion of the definition of drug, and the creation of a parallel concept of devices, clearly show . . . that Congress fully intended that the Act's coverage be as broad as its literal language indicates—and equally clearly, broader than any strict medical definition might otherwise allow."
. . .

II

[In Parts II.A. and II.B. of his dissent, Justice Breyer rejected the tobacco companies' contentions that tobacco is not a "device" that is "intended to affect . . . any function of the body," as required by the FDCA.]

C

The majority nonetheless reaches the "inescapable conclusion" that the language and structure of the FDCA as a whole "simply do not fit" the kind of public health problem that tobacco creates. That is because, in the majority's view, the FDCA requires the FDA to ban outright "dangerous" drugs or devices (such as cigarettes); yet, the FDA concedes that an immediate and total cigarette-sale ban is inappropriate.

This argument . . . fails to take into account the fact that a statute interpreted as requiring the FDA to pick a more dangerous over a less dangerous remedy would be a perverse statute, *causing*, rather than preventing, unnecessary harm whenever a total ban is likely the more dangerous response. . . .

[T]he statute's language does not restrict the FDA's remedial powers in this way. . . . [S]urely the agency can determine that a substance is comparatively "safe" (*not* "dangerous") whenever it would be *less* dangerous to make the product available (subject to regulatory requirements) than suddenly to withdraw it from the market. . . . Indeed, the FDA already seems to have taken this position when permitting distribution of toxic drugs, such as poisons used for chemotherapy, that are dangerous for the user but are not deemed "dangerous to health" in the relevant sense. . . .

[T]o read the statute to forbid the agency from taking account of the realities of consumer behavior either in assessing safety or in choosing a remedy could increase the risks of harm. . . . Why would Congress insist that the FDA ignore such realities, even if the consequent harm would occur only unusually, say, where the FDA evaluates a product . . . that is already on the market, potentially habit forming, or popular? . . .

In my view, where linguistically permissible, we should interpret the FDCA in light of Congress' overall desire to protect health. That purpose requires a flexible interpretation that both permits the FDA to take into account the realities of human behavior and allows it, in appropriate cases, to choose from its arsenal of statutory remedies. A statute so interpreted easily "fits" this, and other, drug- and device-related health problems.

III

In the majority's view, laws enacted since 1965 require us to deny jurisdiction, whatever the FDCA might mean in their absence. But why? Do those laws contain language barring FDA jurisdiction? The majority must concede that they do not. . . . [W]hatever individual Members of Congress after 1964 may have assumed about the FDA's jurisdiction, the laws they enacted did not embody any such "no jurisdiction" assumption. And one cannot automatically *infer* an antijurisdiction intent, as the majority does, for the later statutes are both (and similarly) consistent with quite a different congressional desire, namely, the intent to proceed without interfering with whatever authority the FDA otherwise may have possessed. [T]he subsequent legislative history is critically ambivalent, for it can be read *either* as (a) "ratifying" a no-jurisdiction assumption, *or* as (b) leaving the jurisdictional question just where Congress found it. And the fact that both inferences are "equally tenable" prevents the majority from drawing from the later statutes the firm, antijurisdiction implication that it needs.

IV

I now turn to the final historical fact that the majority views as a factor in its interpretation of the subsequent legislative history: the FDA's former denials of its tobacco-related authority. . . . In my view, the FDA's change of policy, like the subsequent statutes themselves, does nothing to advance the majority's position. . . .

What changed? For one thing, the FDA obtained evidence sufficient to prove the necessary "intent" despite the absence of specific "claims." . . .

Moreover, scientific evidence of adverse health effects mounted, until, in the late 1980's, a consensus on the seriousness of the matter became firm.... Finally, administration policy changed. Earlier administrations may have hesitated to assert jurisdiction for the reasons prior Commissioners expressed. Commissioners of the current administration simply took a different regulatory attitude.

Nothing in the law prevents the FDA from changing its policy for such reasons. By the mid-1990's, the evidence needed to prove objective intent—even without an express claim—had been found. The emerging scientific consensus about tobacco's adverse, chemically induced, health effects may have convinced the agency that it should spend its resources on this important regulatory effort....

V

One might nonetheless claim that ... courts, when interpreting statutes, should assume in close cases that a decision with "enormous social consequences" should be made by democratically elected Members of Congress rather than by unelected agency administrators. Cf. *Kent v. Dulles*, 357 U.S. 116, 129 (1958) (assuming Congress did not want to delegate the power to make rules interfering with exercise of basic human liberties). If there is such a background canon of interpretation, however, I do not believe it controls the outcome here.

Insofar as the decision to regulate tobacco reflects the policy of an administration, it is a decision for which that administration, and those politically elected officials who support it, must (and will) take responsibility. And the very importance of the decision taken here, as well as its attendant publicity, means that the public is likely to be aware of it and to hold those officials politically accountable. Presidents, just like Members of Congress, are elected by the public. Indeed, the President and Vice President are the *only* public officials whom the entire Nation elects. I do not believe that an administrative agency decision of this magnitude—one that is important, conspicuous, and controversial—can escape the kind of public scrutiny that is essential in any democracy. And such a review will take place whether it is the Congress or the Executive Branch that makes the relevant decision....

The upshot is that the Court today holds that a regulatory statute aimed at unsafe drugs and devices does not authorize regulation of a drug (nicotine) and a device (a cigarette) that the Court itself finds unsafe. Far more than most, this particular drug and device risks the life-threatening harms that administrative regulation seeks to rectify. The majority's conclusion is counter-intuitive. And, for the reasons set forth, I believe that the law does not require it.

Consequently, I dissent.

NOTES AND QUESTIONS

1.   *Brown & Williamson.* This case dramatically demonstrates the breadth of inquiries that can come into play in the first *Chevron* step. The Court assumes for the sake of argument that the tobacco regulations would fit within the literal language of the specific authorizing provisions of the FDCA, 21 U.S.C. § 321. Nevertheless, it finds a contrary "clear intent of Congress" by relying on the structure of the FDCA; related statutes and the context in which Congress enacted them; and a "common sense" judgment about what kinds of issues Congress would entrust to an administrative agency. Is its reasoning persuasive?

In 2009, Congress enacted the Family Smoking Prevention and Tobacco Control Act, Pub. L. No. 111–31, 123 Stat. 1776. This Act explicitly gives the FDA jurisdiction over tobacco products, with many detailed provisions. The Act directed the FDA to reissue its 1996 rule (with certain exceptions). The FDA reissued the rule in 2010, although some of its advertising and marketing requirements have been stalled, perhaps permanently, due to First Amendment challenges. What, if anything, does the passage of this legislation suggest as to whether the Court reached the correct result when it invalidated the FDA's regulation in *Brown & Williamson*?

2.   *Legislative purpose.* An important premise of Justice Breyer's dissent is that the FDCA should be read in a manner that facilitates the general objectives of the Act and avoids "perverse" consequences. Indeed, he appears to endorse the notion that the Act should be read like a "constitution." Should that principle extend as far as Breyer would take it? *Cf. Rodriguez v. United States*, 480 U.S. 522, 525–26 (1987) ("[N]o legislation pursues its purposes at all costs. Deciding what competing values will or will not be sacrificed to the achievement of a particular objective is the very essence of legislative choice—and it frustrates rather than effectuates legislative intent simplistically to assume that whatever furthers the statute's primary objective must be the law.").

3.   *Canons.* Canons of construction are among the "traditional tools" to which courts look in determining whether an agency interpretation violates the clear intent of Congress. Justice O'Connor's premises that a statutory provision should be construed to harmonize with the Act of which it is a part, as well as with related legislation, are only two such canons. *See generally* Kenneth A. Bamberger, *Normative Canons in the Review of Administrative Policymaking*, 118 YALE L.J. 64 (2008). Consider a few examples of how other canons can interact with *Chevron*:

a.   *Constitutional avoidance.* The canon that statutes should be construed to avoid constitutional problems has been frequently deployed to overturn an agency statutory interpretation under *Chevron* step one. In *Solid Waste Agency of Northern Cook County v. Army Corps of Eng'rs,* 531 U.S. 159 (2001), a group of cities wanted to construct a solid waste disposal facility at the site of an abandoned gravel pit. The Army Corps directed them to obtain a landfill permit under the Clean Water Act, because the facility would disrupt ponds at the site. The Court concluded that the Act, which applies to "navigable waters," did not allow the Corps to regulate the ponds, which were not adjacent to any open waters. Even if the Act were otherwise unclear, the opinion by Chief Justice Rehnquist added, the Court would not defer to the agency's interpretation, because that construction would raise significant constitutional difficulties. The Court was plainly dubious about the government's theory that the Act was constitutional because protection of the habitat of migratory birds at the site would have a significant effect on interstate commerce. *See also Rapanos v. United States*, 547 U.S. 715, 738 (2006) (plurality opinion) (using similar reasoning in the same statutory context); *Clark v. Martinez*, 543 U.S. 371 (2005) (endorsing constitutional avoidance in the immigration context).

Yet the Court has not always given controlling weight to the constitutional avoidance canon. An earlier Rehnquist opinion found a statute ambiguous and upheld the agency's interpretation under *Chevron*. The effect was to uphold the validity of a regulation that banned doctors in federally funded family planning centers from discussing abortion with patients, although four dissenters thought the regulation raised significant First Amendment problems and thus should have been invalidated under Chevron step one. *Rust v. Sullivan*, 500 U.S. 173 (1991). Should an agency's interpretation that would otherwise be upheld under *Chevron* be rejected if it would *raise a serious constitutional question*—or only if that interpretation *would actually be unconstitutional*? *See* Thomas W. Merrill & Kristin E. Hickman, Chevron's *Domain*, 89 GEO L.J. 833, 914–15 (2001) (preferring the latter alternative).

b. *Retroactivity*. Recall the maxim disfavoring retroactive laws, as discussed in *Bowen v. Georgetown Hospital*, § 5.2 N.3. The Court applied this principle to find a statute unambiguous under *Chevron* step 1 in *INS v. St. Cyr*, 533 U.S. 289 (2001). In 1996 immigration reform legislation, Congress provided that aliens who plead guilty to certain felonies are automatically deportable and are ineligible for discretionary relief from the Attorney General. The Court held that the law was inapplicable to aliens like St. Cyr who had entered into plea agreements prior to the effective date of the statute (a point on which the statute was not explicit). Justice Stevens rejected the INS's reliance on *Chevron* by writing (somewhat paradoxically?):

> We only defer . . . to agency interpretations of statutes that, applying the normal "tools of statutory construction," are ambiguous. Because a statute that is ambiguous with respect to retroactive application is construed under our precedent to be unambiguously prospective, there is, for *Chevron* purposes, no ambiguity in such a statute for an agency to resolve.

c. *Lenity*. What should a court do if an administrative decision construes a regulatory statute that might also be enforced in a criminal prosecution? Should the court adhere to the "rule of lenity," the traditional maxim under which ambiguous criminal laws are construed to favor the defendant? Or should it apply *Chevron*, which dictates that ambiguous administrative statutes should generally be construed to favor the government? The problem has no obvious or universally endorsed answer. In *United States v. Thompson/Center Arms Co.*, 504 U.S. 505, 517–18 & n.10 (1992), the Court narrowly construed a tax statute in a refund suit brought by a firearms manufacturer. The Court relied on lenity, noting that "this tax statute has criminal applications, and we know of no other basis for determining when the essential nature of a statute is 'criminal.'" Although the present suit was civil, the Court assumed that any subsequent prosecution would have to adhere to the holding in this case. *See also FCC v. American Broadcasting Co.*, 347 U.S. 284, 296 (1954) (holding, in a facial challenge to FCC regulations, that a TV quiz show is not a prohibited "lottery"; the anti-lottery statute could have been enforced criminally, and "[t]here cannot be one construction for the Federal Communications Commission and another for the Department of Justice.").

However, in *NLRB v. Oklahoma Fixture Co.*, 332 F.3d 1284, 1286–87 (10th Cir. 2003) (en banc), the Board held that an employer was required to collect union membership dues from employee paychecks and transmit them to the union. Although the holding turned on interpretation of an exemption from a criminal provision, the Tenth Circuit upheld the Board's position as a reasonable construction of an ambiguous statute. Citing the Board's expertise and the need for a uniform national interpretation of the statute, the court said that the Board was entitled to "some deference." *See generally* Elliot Greenfield, *A Lenity Exception to* Chevron *Deference*, 58 BAYLOR L. REV. 1 (2006) (lenity should trump *Chevron*); Sanford N. Greenberg, *Who Says It's a Crime?:* Chevron *Deference to Agency Interpretations of Regulatory Statutes that Create Criminal Liability*, 58 U. PITT. L. REV. 1 (1996) (*Chevron* should trump lenity).

4. *Legislative history.* Both commentators and judges have debated the appropriateness of consulting legislative history documents, such as committee reports and excerpts from floor debates, in construing statutes. In *Chevron* itself, the Court treated legislative history as relevant to determining whether a statute was ambiguous. However, the argument has heated up since then. Justice Scalia, who joined the Court shortly after *Chevron* was decided, has been the Court's most tenacious opponent of reliance on legislative history. *See, e.g., INS v. Cardoza-Fonseca*, 480 U.S. 421, 452–53 (1987) (Scalia, J., concurring) ("Judges interpret laws rather than reconstruct legislators' intentions. Where the language of those laws is clear, we are not free to replace it with an unenacted legislative intent."). *See also* ANTONIN SCALIA & BRYAN A. GARNER, READING LAW: THE INTERPRETATION OF LEGAL TEXTS 369–90 (2012). (Is his concurrence in the majority opinion in *Brown & Williamson* consistent with this stance?)

Justice Breyer, on the other hand, has been a prominent defender of judicial reliance on legislative history: "Legislative history helps a court understand the context and purpose of a statute. . . . Should one not look to the background of a statute, the terms of the debate over its enactment, the factual assumptions the legislators made, the conventions they thought applicable, and their expressed objectives in an effort to understand the statute's relevant context, conventions, and purposes?" Stephen G. Breyer, *On the Uses of Legislative History in Interpreting Statutes*, 65 S. CAL. L. REV. 845, 848 (1992).

On the whole, the assault on legislative history has not yet prevailed. *See Zuni Public School District No. 89 v. Dep't of Educ.*, 550 U.S. 81 (2007); *Gonzales v. Oregon*, 546 U.S. 243 (2006); William N. Eskridge, Jr. & Lauren E. Baer, *The Continuum of Deference: Supreme Court Treatment of Agency Statutory Interpretations from* Chevron *to* Hamdan," 96 GEO. L.J. 1083, 1135–36 (2008). However, the Court's practice is not entirely consistent. In some cases the Court has rephrased the *Chevron* step one inquiry by saying that it will defer to a reasonable agency interpretation unless the *text* of the controlling statute forecloses the agency's position. *See generally* Linda Jellum, Chevron*'s Demise: A Survey of* Chevron *from Infancy to Senescence*, 59 ADMIN. L. REV. 725, 761–71 (2007). Would this be a desirable modification of *Chevron* step one? What difficulties might it engender? *See* Thomas W. Merrill, *Textualism and the Future of the* Chevron *Doctrine*, 72 WASH. U.L.Q. 351 (1994).

5. *Major questions.* In *Brown & Williamson* the Court suggested that the FDA's interpretation did not merit *Chevron* deference because the "economic and political significance" of this case made it "extraordinary." Is that suggestion persuasive? Notice that the Court relied in this connection on an article by Justice Breyer. Indeed, Breyer has continued to suggest that a court should be less willing to infer that Congress desires *Chevron* deference where "an unusually basic legal question is at issue." *Nat'l Cable & Telecomms. Ass'n v. Brand X Internet Servs.*, 545 U.S. 967, 1004 (2005) (concurring opinion). Does his dissent in *Brown & Williamson* offer a persuasive reason for not following that reasoning here? More generally, to what extent do you agree that the importance of an issue makes it unlikely that Congress gave an agency authority to resolve it? For evaluations of the major questions principle, see Abigail R. Moncrieff, *Reincarnating the "Major Questions" Exception to* Chevron *Deference as a Doctrine of Noninterference (or Why* Massachusetts v. EPA *Got It Wrong)*, 60 ADMIN. L. REV. 593 (2008); Cass R. Sunstein, Chevron *Step* Zero, 92 VA. L. REV. 187, 236–47 (2006).

6. *Related limitations.* Somewhat akin to the "major questions" limitation is—or rather, was—the claim made by some judges and scholars that a reviewing court need not afford *Chevron* deference to an agency's construction of the scope of its own jurisdiction. Recently the Supreme Court decisively rejected the proposed limitation in an opinion by Justice Scalia. The Court argued that jurisdictional questions are analytically no different from other questions of statutory authority that are routinely resolved using the *Chevron* framework. *City of Arlington v. FCC*, 133 S.Ct. 1833 (2013).

Another, perhaps more enduring variation on the major questions theme stems from the Court's opinion in *Whitman v. American Trucking Ass'ns*,

Inc., § 7.2.1. In rejecting the claim that the Clean Air Act allows the EPA to consider cost factors in setting national ambient air quality standards, Justice Scalia wrote: "Congress, we have held, does not alter the fundamental details of a regulatory scheme in vague terms or ancillary provisions—it does not, one might say, hide elephants in mouseholes." A case that Scalia cited in support of this statement was *Brown & Williamson*. Is this a fair characterization of Justice O'Connor's reasoning? Regardless, Scalia's colorful "mouseholes" metaphor has been invoked in a number of subsequent majority and dissenting opinions. *See, e.g., Coeur Alaska, Inc. v. Southeast Alaska Conservation Council*, 557 U.S. 261, 303 (2009) (Ginsburg, J., dissenting); *Entergy Corp. v. Riverkeeper, Inc.*, 556 U.S. 208, 239 (2009) (Stevens, J., dissenting); *Gonzales v. Oregon*, 546 U.S. 243, 267 (2006). Is it a helpful interpretive principle? Two commentators find it somewhat appealing in the abstract, as a "nondelegation canon" (*see* § 7.2.1 N.7), but they nevertheless "reluctantly" conclude that it is unworkable as a judicial doctrine, because it

> cannot be applied in a consistent fashion. How do we know whether an agency interpretation *alters* the *fundamental* details of a regulatory scheme rather than simply defining or clarifying those details? And how do we know that the relied-upon statutory provision is "ancillary" to the aim of the statute rather than constituent of it? In other words, we cannot easily know that what we find in the mousehole is truly an elephant—and not just a rather plump mouse. Nor can we easily determine that a statutory provision is sufficiently unimportant to be a mousehole—and not just a rather cramped circus tent. . . . It should be no surprise, then, that the Court applies the elephants-in-mouseholes doctrine seemingly haphazardly; those in the majority one day are in the dissent the next, and vice versa.

Jacob Loshin & Aaron Nielson, *Hiding Nondelegation in Mouseholes*, 62 ADMIN. L. REV. 19, 45 (2010).

7. *Other questions that Congress is unlikely to have delegated.* Although the limitations on *Chevron* deference discussed in the preceding two notes have been controversial, there is little if any disagreement about a related notion: Courts must decide on their own, without deference, issues arising under generic statutes such as the APA and the Freedom of Information Act. *Collins v. NTSB*, 351 F.3d 1246, 1252 (D.C. Cir. 2003); *American Airlines, Inc. v. DOT*, 202 F.3d 788, 796 (5th Cir. 2000). Those statutes exist for the very purpose of curbing agency power. Moreover, no single agency administers these acts; thus, no single agency's interpretation of them can be controlling. Although the basic principle is well established, there can still be debate about what circumstances bring it into play. Recall the question raised in *Dominion Energy Brayton Point v. Johnson*, § 3.1.1, as to whether the right to formal adjudication should be analyzed as involving an interpretation of the agency's enabling statute (thus inviting *Chevron* deference) or of the APA (thus inviting independent judicial determination). Similarly, courts have not afforded *Chevron* deference to agencies'

interpretations of statutes that determine the availability or timeliness of judicial review proceedings. *See Shweika v. Dep't of Homeland Sec.*, 723 F.3d 710, 717–18 (6th Cir. 2013) (compiling cases).

The Court has also said that *Chevron* does not apply to an agency's interpretation of a statutory private right of action, because Congress cannot be assumed to have delegated to an agency the power to determine the circumstances under which one private person may bring suit in court against another private person. *Adams Fruit Co. v. Barrett*, 494 U.S. 638 (1990). But is that so clear? *See* Richard J. Pierce, Jr., *Agency Authority to Define the Scope of Private Rights of Action*, 48 ADMIN. L. REV. 1 (1996) (criticizing *Adams Fruit*).

8.   *Problem.* Section 9 of the Endangered Species Act of 1973 (ESA) forbids any person to "take" an endangered or threatened species. Section 3(1) also provides that "[t]he term 'take' means to harass, harm, pursue, hunt, shoot, wound, kill, trap, capture, or collect, or to attempt to engage in any such conduct." According to a legislative regulation adopted by the Secretary of the Interior after notice and comment in 1975, the term "harm" in this statutory definition "may include significant habitat modification or degradation where it actually kills or injures wildlife by significantly impairing essential behavioral patterns, including breeding, feeding, or sheltering." 50 C.F.R. § 17.3. The Secretary considers habitat protection crucial to the survival of numerous endangered species. Many landowners, however, have discovered that ESA restrictions greatly impair their ability to use their private property for productive uses.

In 1982 Congress amended § 10(a) of the ESA to authorize the Secretary to issue "incidental take permits" to enable private parties to engage in an otherwise prohibited taking that "is incidental to, and not the purpose of, the carrying out of an otherwise lawful activity." Congress took no action at that time in response to the Secretary's habitat modification regulation.

Bill, a representative of the Interior Department, contacted Sam, who operated a lumber company. Bill told Sam that his logging activities were impairing forests that provided critical habitat for an endangered species of woodpecker. Relying on 50 C.F.R. § 17.3, Bill directed Sam to cease timber harvesting in those forests and reminded him that knowing violations of the ESA are subject to criminal penalties.

Sam feared that enforcement of these restrictions would lead to layoffs and financial ruin for his company. After exhausting all available administrative channels for relief, Sam filed suit to challenge the validity of § 17.3. He argued that the regulation was an end-run around § 5 of the ESA, which authorizes the Secretary to acquire land by purchase as an aid to protecting endangered species. In this connection he cited to a remark by Representative Sullivan, the floor manager of the bill that became the ESA:

> For the most part, the principal threat to animals stems from the destruction of their habitat. . . . [The bill] will meet this problem by

providing funds for acquisition of critical habitat through the use of the land and water conservation fund. It will also enable the Department of Agriculture to cooperate with willing landowners who desire to assist in the protection of endangered species, but who are understandably unwilling to do so at excessive cost to themselves.

The district court held that the regulation was invalid, relying on dictionary definitions of "take" such as one in the Oxford English Dictionary: "[t]o catch, capture (a wild beast, bird, fish, etc.)." The court also cited the statutory construction maxim *noscitur a sociis* ("a word is known by its associates"), reasoning that the surrounding words of § 3(1), such as "shoot," "wound," and "kill," indicate that "take" refers to the direct use of force, or at least some conduct directed at individual animals, not indirect actions such as modifying the habitat of an animal population.

The department appeals. What result? *Cf. Babbitt v. Sweet Home Chapter of Communities for a Great Oregon*, 515 U.S. 687 (1995).

§ 9.2.4 INFORMAL INTERPRETATIONS AND THE *SKIDMORE* ALTERNATIVE

Despite the status of *Chevron* as a leading case, federal courts do not use it to review every statutory interpretation adopted by an administrative agency. Debates over the circumstances in which *Chevron* should or should not apply have generated an ample case law. *See generally* Thomas W. Merrill & Kristin E. Hickman, Chevron's Domain, 89 GEO. L.J. 833 (2001). The threshold question of whether a court should apply the two-step *Chevron* test to a given agency interpretation has acquired the informal nickname "Step Zero." The preceding section discussed some of the factors that can militate against *Chevron* deference, and this section continues that exploration.

One of the most controversial of these threshold questions concerns the extent to which *Chevron* deference should depend on the *format* in which an agency interpretation appears. For example, the EPA's bubble interpretation in *Chevron* was part of a legislative rule. Necessarily, then, despite its broad language, that case did not squarely decide what standard of review should apply to a less formally developed pronouncement, such as an interpretive rule or policy statement. In the decades leading up to *Chevron*, however, a highly respected pronouncement on judicial deference to interpretive rules was the opinion of Justice Robert Jackson in *Skidmore v. Swift & Co.*, 323 U.S. 134, 137–40 (1944). In this private suit for overtime pay under the Fair Labor Standards Act, Jackson explained how the courts should take account of interpretive bulletins issued by the Wage-Hour Administrator in the Department of Labor:

Congress did not utilize the services of an administrative agency to find facts and to determine in the first instance whether particular cases fall within or without the Act. Instead, it put this responsibility on the courts. But it did create the office of Administrator, impose upon him a variety of duties, endow him with powers to inform himself of conditions in industries and employments subject to the Act, and put on him the duties of bringing injunction actions to restrain violations. . . . He has set forth his views of the application of the Act under different circumstances in an interpretative bulletin and in informal rulings. They provide a practical guide to employers and employees as to how the office representing the public interest in its enforcement will seek to apply it. . . .

. . . The rulings of this Administrator are not reached as a result of hearing adversary proceedings in which he finds facts from evidence and reaches conclusions of law from findings of fact. They are not, of course, conclusive, even in the cases with which they directly deal, much less in those to which they apply only by analogy. They do not constitute an interpretation of the Act or a standard for judging factual situations which binds a district court's processes, as an authoritative pronouncement of a higher court might do. But the Administrator's policies are made in pursuance of official duty, based upon more specialized experience and broader investigations and information than is likely to come to a judge in a particular case. They do determine the policy which will guide applications for enforcement by injunction on behalf of the Government. Good administration of the Act and good judicial administration alike require that the standards of public enforcement and those for determining private rights shall be at variance only where justified by very good reasons. The fact that the Administrator's policies and standards are not reached by trial in adversary form does not mean that they are not entitled to respect. This Court has long given considerable and in some cases decisive weight to Treasury Decisions and to interpretative regulations of the Treasury and of other bodies that were not of adversary origin.

We consider that the rulings, interpretations and opinions of the Administrator under this Act, while not controlling upon the courts by reason of their authority, do constitute a body of experience and informed judgment to which courts and litigants may properly resort for guidance. The weight of such a judgment in a particular case will depend upon the thoroughness evident in its consideration, the validity of its reasoning, its consistency with earlier and later pronouncements, and all those factors which give it power to persuade, if lacking power to control.

The emergence of *Chevron* as a leading case gave rise to the question of whether and under what circumstances *Skidmore* deference would continue to survive. Beginning in 2000, the Supreme Court has offered some answers to that question.

CHRISTENSEN V. HARRIS COUNTY
529 U.S. 576 (2000)

THOMAS, J.:

Under the Fair Labor Standards Act of 1938 (FLSA), States and their political subdivisions may compensate their employees for overtime by granting them compensatory time or "comp time," which entitles them to take time off work with full pay. § 207(*o*). If the employees do not use their accumulated compensatory time, the employer is obligated to pay cash compensation under certain circumstances.

Petitioners are 127 deputy sheriffs employed by . . . Harris County, Texas, and its sheriff. . . . As petitioners accumulated compensatory time, Harris County became concerned that it lacked the resources to pay monetary compensation to employees who worked overtime after reaching the statutory cap on compensatory time accrual and to employees who left their jobs with sizable reserves of accrued time. As a result, the county began looking for a way to reduce accumulated compensatory time. It wrote to the United States Department of Labor's Wage and Hour Division, asking "whether the Sheriff may schedule non-exempt employees to use or take compensatory time." The Acting Administrator of the Division replied [in a letter that this would be impermissible except pursuant to a prior agreement. Nevertheless, despite the absence of such an agreement], Harris County implemented a policy under which the employees' supervisor sets a maximum number of compensatory hours that may be accumulated. . . .

Petitioners sued, claiming that the county's policy violates the FLSA. . . . [The Court disagreed. In Part II of its opinion, the Court asserted that § 207(*o*) only means that an employee must be *allowed* to use comp time. It says nothing about whether an employee can be *compelled* to use comp time. The Court continued:]

III

In an attempt to avoid the conclusion that the FLSA does not prohibit compelled use of compensatory time, petitioners and the United States contend that we should defer to the Department of Labor's opinion letter, which takes the position that an employer may compel the use of compensatory time only if the employee has agreed in advance to such a practice. Specifically, they argue that the agency opinion letter is entitled to deference under our decision in *Chevron.* . . .

Here, however, we confront an interpretation contained in an opinion letter, not one arrived at after, for example, a formal adjudication or notice-and-comment rulemaking. Interpretations such as those in opinion letters—like interpretations contained in policy statements, agency manuals, and enforcement guidelines, all of which lack the force of law— do not warrant *Chevron*-style deference. See, *e.g., Reno v. Koray*, 515 U.S. 50, 61 (1995) (internal agency guideline, which is not "subject to the rigors of the Administrative Procedure Act, including public notice and comment," entitled only to "some deference"). Instead, interpretations contained in formats such as opinion letters are "entitled to respect" under our decision in *Skidmore*, but only to the extent that those interpretations have the "power to persuade." As explained above, we find unpersuasive the agency's interpretation of the statute at issue in this case.

Of course, the framework of deference set forth in *Chevron* does apply to an agency interpretation contained in a regulation. But in this case the Department of Labor's regulation does not address the issue. The regulation provides only that "the agreement or understanding [between the employer and employee] *may* include other provisions governing the preservation, use, or cashing out of compensatory time so long as these provisions are consistent with [§ 207(o)]" (emphasis added). Nothing in the regulation even arguably requires that an employer's compelled use policy *must* be included in an agreement. . . .

Seeking to overcome the regulation's obvious meaning, the United States asserts that the agency's opinion letter interpreting the regulation should be given deference under our decision in *Auer v. Robbins*, 519 U.S. 452 (1997). In *Auer*, we held that an agency's interpretation of its own regulation is entitled to deference. See also *Bowles v. Seminole Rock & Sand Co.*, 325 U.S. 410 (1945). But *Auer* deference is warranted only when the language of the regulation is ambiguous. The regulation in this case, however, is not ambiguous—it is plainly permissive. To defer to the agency's position would be to permit the agency, under the guise of interpreting a regulation, to create *de facto* a new regulation. Because the regulation is not ambiguous on the issue of compelled compensatory time, *Auer* deference is unwarranted.

SOUTER, J., concurring.

I join the opinion of the Court on the assumption that it does not foreclose a reading of the Fair Labor Standards Act of 1938 that allows the Secretary of Labor to issue regulations limiting forced use.

SCALIA, J., concurring in part and concurring in the judgment.

I join the judgment of the Court and all of its opinion except Part III, which declines to give effect to the position of the Department of Labor in this case because its opinion letter is entitled only to so-called "*Skidmore* deference." *Skidmore* deference to authoritative agency views is an anachronism, dating from an era [prior to] our watershed decision in *Chevron*, which established the principle that "a court may not substitute its own construction of a statutory provision for a reasonable interpretation made by the administrator of an agency." While *Chevron* in fact involved an interpretive regulation, the rationale of the case was not limited to that context.... Quite appropriately, therefore, we have accorded *Chevron* deference not only to agency regulations, but to authoritative agency positions set forth in a variety of other formats....

[STEVENS, J., jointed by GINSBURG and BREYER, JJ., dissented on the merits. BREYER, J., joined by GINSBURG, J., also wrote a concurrence responding to Justice Scalia. He said: "[T]o the extent there may be circumstances in which *Chevron*-type deference is inapplicable—*e.g.*, where one has doubt that Congress actually intended to delegate interpretive authority to the agency (an 'ambiguity' that *Chevron* does not presumptively leave to agency resolution)—I believe that *Skidmore* nonetheless retains legal vitality."]

[Later the same month the Court granted certiorari in the following case, which enabled it to speak more comprehensively on the *Skidmore* issue.]

UNITED STATES v. MEAD CORP.

533 U.S. 218 (2001)

SOUTER, J.

The question is whether a tariff classification ruling by the United States Customs Service deserves judicial deference. The Federal Circuit rejected Customs's invocation of *Chevron* in support of such a ruling, to which it gave no deference. We agree that a tariff classification has no claim to judicial deference under *Chevron*, there being no indication that Congress intended such a ruling to carry the force of law, but we hold that under *Skidmore* the ruling is eligible to claim respect according to its persuasiveness....

[Customs makes] tariff rulings before the entry of goods by [issuing] "ruling letters" setting tariff classifications for particular imports.... Most ruling letters contain little or no reasoning, but simply describe goods and state the appropriate category and tariff. A few letters, like the Headquarters ruling at issue here, set out a rationale in some detail.

Respondent, the Mead Corporation, imports "day planners," three-ring binders with pages having room for notes of daily schedules and phone numbers and addresses, together with a calendar and suchlike. . . . In January 1993, . . . Customs . . . issued a Headquarters ruling letter classifying Mead's day planners as "Diaries . . ., bound" subject to tariff. . . . Mead [subsequently] went to the United States Court of Appeals for the Federal Circuit, [which] held that Customs classification rulings should not get *Chevron* deference. . . . The Court of Appeals accordingly gave no deference at all to the ruling classifying the Mead day planners and rejected the agency's reasoning as to both "diary" and "bound." . . .

. . . We hold that administrative implementation of a particular statutory provision qualifies for *Chevron* deference when it appears that Congress delegated authority to the agency generally to make rules carrying the force of law, and that the agency interpretation claiming deference was promulgated in the exercise of that authority. Delegation of such authority may be shown in a variety of ways, as by an agency's power to engage in adjudication or notice-and-comment rulemaking, or by some other indication of a comparable congressional intent. . . .

[A]gencies charged with applying a statute necessarily make all sorts of interpretive choices, and while not all of those choices bind judges to follow them, they certainly may influence courts facing questions the agencies have already answered. . . . Justice Jackson summed things up in *Skidmore*. . . .

Since 1984, we have identified a category of interpretive choices distinguished by an additional reason for judicial deference. This Court in *Chevron* recognized that Congress not only engages in express delegation of specific interpretive authority, but that "[s]ometimes the legislative delegation to an agency on a particular question is implicit." Congress, that is, may not have expressly delegated authority or responsibility to implement a particular provision or fill a particular gap. Yet it can still be apparent from the agency's generally conferred authority and other statutory circumstances that Congress would expect the agency to be able to speak with the force of law when it addresses ambiguity in the statute or fills a space in the enacted law, even one about which "Congress did not actually have an intent" as to a particular result. When circumstances implying such an expectation exist, a reviewing court . . . is obliged to accept the agency's position if Congress has not previously spoken to the point at issue and the agency's interpretation is reasonable.

. . . It is fair to assume generally that Congress contemplates administrative action with the effect of law when it provides for a relatively formal administrative procedure tending to foster the fairness and deliberation that should underlie a pronouncement of such force. Thus, the overwhelming number of our cases applying *Chevron* deference have reviewed the fruits of notice-and-comment rulemaking or formal adjudication. That said, and as significant as notice-and-comment is in pointing to *Chevron* authority, the want of that procedure here does not decide the case, for we have sometimes found reasons for *Chevron* deference even when no such administrative formality was required and none was afforded.[13] . . . There are, nonetheless, ample reasons to deny *Chevron* deference here. . . .

. . . Customs does not generally engage in notice-and-comment practice when issuing [ruling letters], and their treatment by the agency makes it clear that a letter's binding character as a ruling stops short of third parties; Customs has regarded a classification as conclusive only as between itself and the importer to whom it was issued, and even then only until Customs has given advance notice of intended change. . . .

Indeed, to claim that classifications have legal force is to ignore the reality that 46 different Customs offices issue 10,000 to 15,000 of them each year. Any suggestion that rulings intended to have the force of law are being churned out at a rate of 10,000 a year at an agency's 46 scattered offices is simply self-refuting. Although the circumstances are less startling here, with a Headquarters letter in issue, none of the relevant statutes recognizes this category of rulings as separate or different from others. . . .

To agree with the Court of Appeals that Customs ruling letters do not fall within *Chevron* is not, however, to place them outside the pale of any deference whatever. *Chevron* did nothing to eliminate *Skidmore*'s holding that an agency's interpretation may merit some deference whatever its form, given the "specialized experience and broader investigations and information" available to the agency, and given the value of uniformity in its administrative and judicial understandings of what a national law requires.

There is room at least to raise a *Skidmore* claim here, where the regulatory scheme is highly detailed, and Customs can bring the benefit of specialized experience to bear on the subtle questions in this case. . . .

Since the *Skidmore* assessment called for here ought to be made in the first instance by the Court of Appeals for the Federal Circuit or the Court of International Trade, we go no further than to vacate the judgment and remand the case for further proceedings consistent with this opinion.

SCALIA, J., dissenting: . . .

---

[13] In *NationsBank of N. C., N. A. v. Variable Annuity Life Ins. Co.*, 513 U.S. 251, 256–257 (1995), we quoted longstanding precedent concluding that "the Comptroller of the Currency is charged with the enforcement of banking laws to an extent that warrants the invocation of [the rule of deference] with respect to his deliberative conclusions as to the meaning of these laws."

The Court's new doctrine is neither sound in principle nor sustainable in practice.

As to principle: The doctrine of *Chevron*—that all *authoritative* agency interpretations of statutes they are charged with administering deserve deference—was rooted in a legal presumption of congressional intent, important to the division of powers between the Second and Third Branches. When, *Chevron* said, Congress leaves an ambiguity in a statute that is to be administered by an executive agency, it is presumed that Congress meant to give the agency discretion, within the limits of reasonable interpretation, as to how the ambiguity is to be resolved. . . .

The basis in principle for today's new doctrine can be described as follows: The background rule is that ambiguity in legislative instructions to agencies is to be resolved not by the agencies but by the judges. Specific congressional intent to depart from this rule must be found—and while there is no single touchstone for such intent it can generally be found when Congress has authorized the agency to act through (what the Court says is) relatively formal procedures such as informal rulemaking and formal (and informal?) adjudication, and when the agency in fact employs such procedures. The . . . Court's principal criterion of congressional intent to supplant its background rule seems to me quite implausible. There is no necessary connection between the formality of procedure and the power of the entity administering the procedure to resolve authoritatively questions of law. . . . [C]ertain significant categories of rules—those involving grant and benefit programs, for example, are exempt from the requirements of informal rulemaking. *See* 5 U.S.C. § 553(a)(2). Under the Court's novel theory, when an agency takes advantage of that exemption its rules will be deprived of *Chevron* deference, i.e., authoritative effect. Was this either the plausible intent of the APA rulemaking exemption, or the plausible intent of the Congress that established the grant or benefit program? . . .

As for the practical effects of the new rule:

The principal effect will be protracted confusion. [T]he one test for *Chevron* deference that the Court enunciates is wonderfully imprecise: whether "Congress delegated authority to the agency generally to make rules carrying the force of law, . . . as by . . . adjudication[,] notice-and-comment rulemaking, or . . . some other [procedure] indicati[ng] comparable congressional intent." But even this description does not do justice to the utter flabbiness of the Court's criterion, [which also looks to] a grab-bag of other factors . . .

And finally, the majority's approach compounds the confusion it creates by breathing new life into the anachronism of *Skidmore*, which sets forth a sliding scale of deference. . . . [In] an era when federal statutory law administered by federal agencies is pervasive, and when the ambiguities (intended or unintended) that those statutes contain are innumerable, totality-of-the-circumstances *Skidmore* deference is a recipe for uncertainty, unpredictability, and endless litigation. . . .

To decide the present case, I would adhere to the original formulation of *Chevron*. . . . I would uphold the Customs Service's construction. . . .

[On remand, the Federal Circuit applied *Skidmore*, concluded that the Customs ruling did not have "power to persuade," and set it aside again. *Mead Corp. v. United States*, 283 F.3d 1342 (Fed. Cir. 2002).]

NOTES AND QUESTIONS

1.   *Christensen.* The Court declares in *Christensen* that opinion letters and guidance documents do not warrant deference under *Chevron*. A leading academic defense of this view is Robert A. Anthony, *Which Agency Interpretations Should Bind Citizens and Courts?*, 7 YALE J. ON REG. 1 (1990). Do the principal rationales for *Chevron* deference (expertise, political accountability, etc.) apply less forcefully to interpretations in informal formats?

2.   *Skidmore.* Just what is *Skidmore* deference? In the most comprehensive study to date of decisions applying that doctrine in the federal courts of appeals, Hickman and Krueger observe that various panels understand the doctrine in different ways. Some apply *Skidmore* according to an "independent judgment" model, in which the court can treat the agency interpretation as relevant but need not uphold it unless the court itself is ultimately persuaded that it is correct. *Christensen* reads as though the Court were following this model. Kristin E. Hickman & Matthew D. Krueger, *In Search of the Modern* Skidmore *Standard*," 107 COLUM. L. REV. 1235, 1251–55 (2007). Others follow a "sliding scale" approach, in which the court does generally owe *deference* to an agency interpretation, but the extent of that deference depends on contextual factors such as those identified in *Skidmore* itself (consistency, thoroughness of consideration, etc.). *Mead* seems to endorse this model. *Id.* at 1255–59. One court of appeals has explained the latter concept this way:

> At times, the Court has characterized the degree of deference to particular agency interpretations of statutes as depending on "the extent that the interpretations have the 'power to'" persuade. *Christensen.* We are confident that the Court did not mean for that standard to reduce to the proposition that "we defer if we agree." If that were the guiding principle, *Skidmore* deference would entail no deference at all. Instead, we believe the Supreme Court intends for us to defer to an agency interpretation of the statute that it administers if the agency has conducted a careful analysis of the statutory issue, if the agency's position has been consistent and reflects agency-wide policy, and if the agency's position constitutes a reasonable conclusion as to the proper construction of the statute,

even if we might not have adopted that construction without the benefit of the agency's analysis.

Cathedral Candle Co. v. Int'l Trade Comm'n, 400 F.3d 1352, 1366 (Fed. Cir. 2005).

Hickman and Krueger report that about three quarters of their sample of circuit court opinions seem to follow the "sliding scale" approach. *Id.* at 1271. At one end of the "scale," some cases find the contextual deference factors weighty and accord "distinctly *Chevron*-like" deference to the agency. At the other end of this spectrum, some cases conclude that the deference factors weaken the agency's position; these cases display little or no deference. Other cases fall between these two poles. *Id.* at 1295–99. Overall, Hickman and Krueger report that circuit cases applying *Skidmore* are fairly deferential, upholding agencies about sixty percent of the time. *Id.* at 1275. They say this is still not as deferential as *Chevron*, citing another study that found an affirmance rate in circuits applying *Chevron* of 89 percent at step two (or 73 percent overall if step one affirmances are added in). *Id.* at 1276 & n.214 (citing an earlier study by Orin S. Kerr).

On the other hand, other research suggests that the disparity disappears almost entirely in the Supreme Court. The Court has been found to rule in agencies' favor in 73.5 percent of the cases applying *Skidmore* and 76.2 percent of the cases applying *Chevron*. William N. Eskridge, Jr. & Lauren E. Baer, *The Continuum of Deference: Supreme Court Treatment of Agency Statutory Interpretations from* Chevron *to* Hamdan," 96 GEO. L.J. 1083, 1143 (2008). Indeed, the Court often remarks that it need not decide which of the two standards applies in a particular case, because it would reach the same result under either one. *See, e.g., General Dynamics Land Systems, Inc. v. Cline,* 540 U.S. 581, 600 (2004).

To what extent, if at all, do the research findings just summarized undermine the utility of the distinction between "strong" *Chevron* deference and "weak" *Skidmore* deference? Or should the distinction be justified on some other basis? Perhaps the most important difference between the two standards is not how demanding they are, but instead the manner in which they are to be applied. Under *Chevron* the reviewing court is expected to analyze the merits using the structured two-step test that revolves around a threshold finding of ambiguity; but the *Skidmore* approach contemplates a more free-form weighing of various prudential and contextual factors in a single interpretive "step."

3. *Mead.* Like *Chevron*, *Mead* has triggered voluminous commentary. *See* Administrative Law Discussion Forum, 54 ADMIN. L. REV. 565 (2002), containing a half dozen articles about the case (and other articles touching on it indirectly). One focus of controversy is its apparent premise that courts should make ad hoc judgments about the propriety of *Chevron* deference in a particular situation, instead of relying on clear-cut rules.

This is a long-held view of Justice Breyer's, and in a post-*Mead* decision he found an opportunity to press it even more forcefully. *Barnhart v. Walton*, 535 U.S. 212, 221–22 (2002). Writing for eight Justices (all except Justice Scalia), Breyer stated that a legislative rule that the Social Security Administration had adopted after *Walton's* case reached the courts was not too tardy to receive *Chevron* deference. He then added that, *regardless*, the agency had long espoused the same interpretation in informal pronouncements and did not necessarily have to resort to notice-and-comment rulemaking to qualify for *Chevron* deference. He concluded: "In this case, the interstitial nature of the legal question, the related expertise of the Agency, the importance of the question to administration of the statute, the complexity of that administration, and the careful consideration the Agency has given the question over a long period of time all indicate that *Chevron* provides the appropriate legal lens through which to view the legality of the Agency interpretation here at issue." Breyer took a similar totality-of-circumstances approach in *Long Island Care at Home, Ltd. v. Coke*, 551 U.S. 158, 173–74 (2007). (Indeed, Justice Breyer appears to favor that contextual approach even outside the context of informal agency pronouncements. *See City of Arlington v. FCC*, 133 S. Ct. 1863, 1875–77 (2013) (Breyer, J., concurring).)

Amid the emphasis in *Mead* and *Barnhart* on flexibility, has the Court given adequate guidance about when *Chevron* should apply? Some think not. *See* Cass R. Sunstein, Chevron *Step Zero*, 92 VA. L. REV. 187, 228 (2006) (*Christensen, Mead*, and *Barnhart* "force[ ] courts to undertake complex inquiries when it is far from clear that anything at all is gained by the ultimate conclusion that *Skidmore*, rather than *Chevron*, provides the governing standard"); Adrian Vermeule, Mead *in the Trenches*," 71 GEO. WASH. L. REV. 347, 355–58 (2003) (*Mead* may be "a failed experiment"); Lisa Schultz Bressman, *How* Mead *Has Muddled Judicial Review of Agency Action*, 58 VAND. L. REV. 1443 (2005).

4. *Congressional intent.* Is *Mead's* benchmark of asking whether "Congress would expect the agency to be able to speak with the force of law" helpful? Congress surely does not often deliberate on such esoteric questions as whether to apply *Chevron* or *Skidmore* to a particular decision, or what the standard of review of a guidance document should be.

Justice Breyer has argued, however, that attention to what a reasonable member of Congress *would* want can be a useful fiction:

> [P]articular circumstances can generate clear (if narrow and specific) legal answers; and those answers may make more sense than answers that would flow from a more absolute, overarching interpretive rule. As important, those answers make *democratic* sense. In all likelihood a hypothetical reasonable member of Congress *would* have decided the delegation/deference question so as to help the statute work better to achieve its ends. And those ends usually reflect the general desires of the public. Use of the

fiction thereby helps the statute work better, in both the functional and the democratic sense of the term.

STEPHEN BREYER, ACTIVE LIBERTY: INTERPRETING OUR DEMOCRATIC CONSTITUTION 106–08 (2005). Is this persuasive?

5. *Rules of thumb.* If, indeed, the *Mead* reasoning is too indeterminate, what should be the alternative? Some favor a force of law test for deciding whether *Chevron* will apply. Thomas W. Merrill, *The* Mead *Doctrine: Rules and Standards, Meta-Rules and Meta-Standards*, 54 ADMIN. L. REV. 807 (2002); Robert A. Anthony, *Keeping* Chevron *Pure*, 5 GREEN BAG 2D 371 (2002). This is basically what the Court said in *Christensen*, and some language in *Mead* also supports this position. In this context, "force of law" presumably means something like the binding effect that distinguishes legislative rules from guidance documents. *See* § 6.1.4. But why should the presence or absence of force of law, or binding effect, determine the standard of review? It has been argued that the one has very little to do with the other. *See, e.g.,* David J. Barron & Elena Kagan, Chevron*'s Nondelegation Doctrine*, 2001 SUP. CT. REV. 201, 216–19.

Another possibility is that the choice between *Skidmore* and *Chevron* should turn directly on the extent and adequacy of the procedures the agency used in arriving at its interpretation. *See* Bressman, *supra.* Much of the reasoning of *Mead* would support such a test. Under this approach, however, what should be the standard for judicial review of those legislative rules (such as foreign affairs rules) that can lawfully be issued without any public participation because of an APA exemption? Should judges feel free, for example, to set aside a rule on a foreign affairs matter unless they conclude that the reasoning on which it rests has "power to persuade"? *See City of New York v. Permanent Mission of India*, 618 F.3d 172 (2d Cir. 2010) (upholding, under *Chevron*, State Department rule protecting foreign missions to the United Nations from local property taxes, although the rule was validly issued without notice and comment).

Finally, Barron and Kagan propose a revised view of *Mead*, in which the key inquiry should not be what *kind* of decision the agency made or *how* the agency made it,, but rather *who* within the agency made it. If the decision was made by the officer whom Congress expressly named in the statute that delegates authority (normally the agency head), *Chevron* would apply. If it was made by an underling to whom the statutory delegatee had subdelegated the decision, *Skidmore* would apply instead. Barron & Kagan, *supra*, at 235–36. The authors call this an "administrative nondelegation" standard. According to the authors, their distinction is attractive because a policy of giving greater deference to interpretations that have the imprimatur of the statutory delegatee would have beneficial effects on administration. For example, agency heads should be given an incentive to review interpretations emanating from their agencies, because these officers are the most visible figures in their agencies and thus can be held accountable for their interpretations through the political process. Moreover, the augmented expectation that the agency head might review subordinates' work would induce the latter to act more rigorously and thoughtfully than they otherwise might. *Id* at 242–44. The authors also argue that their proposed test is manageable, because it is relatively easy to determine whether a statutory delegatee has or has not endorsed his or her agency's position. *Id*. at 250–51. Whatever its merits, however, the authors' proposed reinterpretation of *Mead* does not yet seem to attracted support from any judges (including any named Kagan).

6. *Informal adjudication.* Under *Mead*, *Chevron* certainly governs interpretations that agencies adopt in formal adjudication, but its applicability to informal adjudications is less clear and may depend on individual circumstances. In adjudicative situations that are not exactly APA formal proceedings but nevertheless entail highly structured evidentiary presentations, the Court has had no trouble concluding that *Chevron* does apply. *INS v. Aguirre-Aguirre*, 526 U.S. 415, 425 (1999). But the *Nationsbank* case, cited in note 13 of the *Mead* opinion, involved an informal letter ruling, yet *Mead* reaffirmed that case's reliance on *Chevron*, too. The factual holding of *Mead* sheds an uncertain light on this issue. Recall from the opinion that the customs ruling in that case was binding on the Mead Corporation but not on other stationery importers. Thus, it had the force of law in some sense, but not in every sense.

The court in *Managed Pharmacy Care v. Sebelius*, 716 F.3d 1235, 1246–49 (9th Cir. 2013), spoke more directly to this issue. There, the California legislature approved reductions in Medicaid reimbursement rates, and the Centers for Medicare and Medicaid Services (CMS) approved these rates. A group of pharmacies, hospitals, and patients challenged CMS's decision as unlawful under the Medicaid Act. The court held that "despite the lack of formal procedures available for interested parties, the Secretary's exercise of discretion in the 'form and context' of a [state plan amendment] approval deserves *Chevron* deference." It was clear that the Secretary had acted with the force of law, because "Congress explicitly granted the Secretary authority to determine whether a State's Medicaid plan complies with federal law."

An earlier case from the same court takes a contrasting view. *Wilderness Soc'y v. United States Fish & Wildlife Serv.*, 353 F.3d 1051, 1067 (9th Cir. 2003) (en banc). The FWS granted a permit for a salmon enhancement project in Alaska. Environmentalists brought suit, contending the permit violated the Wilderness Act by introducing a "commercial enterprise" into a wilderness area. The court of appeals agreed that the Act unambiguously supported the plaintiffs, but went on to say that, even if this were not so, it would set aside the permit. In reaching the latter conclusion, the court applied *Skidmore*, because "this case involves only an agency's application of law in a particular permitting context and not an interpretation of a statute that will have the force of law generally for others in similar circumstances." Thus, issuance of the permit was not "the exercise of a congressionally delegated lawmaking function." *See also High Sierra Hikers Ass'n v.*

Blackwell, 390 F.3d 630 (9th Cir. 2004) (following *Wilderness Society*). Is the Ninth Circuit's position in *Wilderness Society* attractive?

The D.C. Circuit's position on whether to apply *Chevron* deference to informal adjudication seems to be "it depends." In *Fox v. Clinton*, 684 F.3d 67 (D.C. Cir. 2012), the plaintiff, a Jewish American by birth, obtained Israeli citizenship by invoking that country's "law of return." He then applied to the State Department for a "certificate of loss of nationality" (CLN). Betancourt, the Director of the Office of Policy Review and Interagency Liaison in the State Department, sent him a letter rejecting his application. When Fox sued, the court found *Chevron* inapplicable to its review of that letter. It distinguished past cases in which

> the reviewing courts deferred to agency interpretations of statutes within their domains of delegated authority, because the challenged interpretations satisfied the factors laid out in *Barnhart*; and the agency interpretations were clearly intended to have general applicability and the force of law. The resulting actions were thus easily subject to meaningful judicial scrutiny, because the agency decisions were thoroughly explained.
>
> We cannot say the same of the Betancourt Letter, particularly because there is nothing in it to give deference to. Indeed, in some ways, it is even less deserving of *Chevron* deference than was the opinion letter at issue in *Christensen*. In *Christensen*, at least, the challenged letter offered the issuing agency's general policy position with respect to a provision of the Fair Labor Standards Act, with supporting references to corresponding regulations. Here, by contrast, the Department offered little more than uncited, conclusory assertions of law in a short, informal document that does not purport to set policy for future CLN determinations. And the Betancourt Letter is premised on highly questionable assumptions about foreign law, i.e., Israel's Nationality Law and Law of Return, with respect to which the agency is owed no deference.

Id. at 78.

7. *Litigating positions.* The Court has declined to apply *Chevron* to "agency litigating positions that are wholly unsupported by regulations, rulings, or administrative practice." *Bowen v. Georgetown University Hospital*, 488 U.S. 204, 212 (1988). It has been said that the "reluctance to defer to agency counsel stems from two concerns. First, appellate counsel's interpretation may not reflect the views of the agency itself. Second, it is likely that 'a position established only in litigation may have been developed hastily, or under special pressure,' and is not the result of the agency's deliberative processes." *National Wildlife Fed'n v. Browner*, 127 F.3d 1126, 1129 (D.C. Cir. 1997). The former of these two concerns about "post hoc rationalizations" is an outgrowth of the *Chenery* doctrine, as we saw in § 4.3 N.5 and § 5.6 N.6. The latter concern can come into play even when the agency head personally endorses the legal position in question. On the other

hand, when an agency adopts an interpretation using the full notice-and-comment rulemaking process, it can qualify for *Chevron* deference even if the advent of litigation provided the impetus for the regulation. *Barnhart v. Walton, supra.*

8.   *Problem. Chevron* principles played a small but notable role in the famous case of Elian Gonzalez, the six-year-old Cuban boy whose contested immigration status sparked political turmoil in Florida and a lively international debate during 1999 and 2000. A small boat carrying Elian and his mother from Cuba to the United States capsized off the coast of Florida. The mother did not survive, but Elian was rescued and taken to Florida alone. His father, Juan Miguel, who had remained in Cuba, sought to have him brought home, but Cuban-American groups in Miami passionately opposed returning the boy to live under the authoritarian regime in his native land. Working in cooperation with those groups, Elian's great-uncle Lazaro filed an application for political asylum on the boy's behalf, as his "next friend," with the Immigration and Naturalization Service. An application signed by Elian himself was also filed.

Although a federal statute provides that "any alien" may petition for asylum, the INS took the position that neither a young child nor his non-parental relative has legal capacity to file an application over the opposition of his parent. This policy may have been devised specifically in response to the Elian controversy. In any event, it was apparently first expressed in writing in a memorandum that the INS General Counsel submitted to the INS Commissioner after the agency had received the petitions in this case. Two days after the submission of this memorandum, an INS district director sent a letter to Lazaro and the lawyers for Elian, summarily rejecting the applications as legally void. A week later, the Attorney General sent the applicants another letter, declining to overrule this decision.

Lazaro then filed for review in Florida district court, which dismissed his suit. On appeal, the Eleventh Circuit affirmed the dismissal, relying squarely on *Chevron.* The court said that it was "not untroubled by the degree of obedience that the INS policy appears to give to the wishes of parents, especially parents who are outside this country's jurisdiction." However, the court continued, "[b]ecause we cannot say that this element of the INS policy . . . is unreasonable, we defer to the INS policy." The court also acknowledged that it had "worries" about the agency's adherence to this policy even where, as in this case, the parent lived in a communist-totalitarian country that violates human rights. "Nonetheless," the court said, "we cannot properly conclude that the INS policy is totally unreasonable in this respect." *Gonzalez v. Reno,* 212 F.3d 1338 (11th Cir. 2000), *rehearing denied,* 215 F.3d 1243 (11th Cir. 2000).

Had this case arisen after *Mead,* should the court have deferred under *Chevron?*

§ 9.2.5 INTERPRETATION OF REGULATIONS

For decades, federal cases have declared that an agency's interpretation of *its own legislative regulation* should be given "controlling weight unless it is "plainly erroneous or inconsistent with the regulation." *Bowles v. Seminole Rock & Sand Co.*, 325 U.S. 410, 414 (1945). That language is commonly regarded as prescribing "strong deference" on a level with *Chevron* itself. In *Auer v. Robbins*, 519 U.S. 452, 462 (1997) (Scalia, J.), the Court unanimously adhered to this test. Accordingly, as *Christensen* illustrates, this doctrine, which has traditionally been known as *Seminole Rock* deference, is now often called "*Auer* deference." Recently, however, the Court seems to have taken steps in the direction of a more flexible approach to this venerable doctrine.

CHRISTOPHER V. SMITHKLINE BEECHAM CORP.
132 S. Ct. 2156 (2012)

[The Fair Labor Standards Act requires employers to compensate employees for working overtime, but it excludes from this protection any "outside salesman" as defined by regulations of the Secretary of Labor. A Department of Labor regulation defined that term as "any employee . . . [w]hose primary duty is . . . making sales within the meaning of section 3(k) of the Act." According to § 3(k), "sale" "includes any sale, exchange, contract to sell, consignment for sale, shipment for sale, or other disposition."

Because consumers can buy a prescription drug only if a doctor prescribes it, pharmaceutical companies employ "detailers" whose job is to visit medical offices, provide doctors with information about the company's products, and try to persuade the doctors to prescribe these products for their patients. Plaintiffs Christopher and Buchanan were detailers for one such drug company, SmithKline. They brought suit against the company, seeking overtime pay. SmithKline defended on the ground that the "outside salesman" exemption applied.

When the dispute reached the Supreme Court, the DOL filed an amicus brief supporting the plaintiffs and contending that its regulation is not satisfied unless the employee actually transfers title to the property at issue to the consumer. Plaintiffs argued that the Court should give controlling deference to that interpretation of the regulation, but the Court disagreed:]

ALITO, J. . . . .

Although *Auer* ordinarily calls for deference to an agency's interpretation of its own ambiguous regulation, even when that interpretation is advanced in a legal brief, this general rule does not apply in all cases. Deference is undoubtedly inappropriate, for example, when the agency's interpretation is " 'plainly erroneous or inconsistent with the regulation.' " And deference is likewise unwarranted when there is reason to suspect that the agency's interpretation "does not reflect the agency's fair and considered judgment on the matter in question." This might occur when the agency's interpretation conflicts with a prior interpretation, or when it appears that the interpretation is nothing more than a "convenient litigating position," or a " '*post hoc* rationalizatio[n]' advanced by an agency seeking to defend past agency action against attack."

In this case, there are strong reasons for withholding the deference that *Auer* generally requires. Petitioners invoke the DOL's interpretation of ambiguous regulations to impose potentially massive liability on respondent for conduct that occurred well before that interpretation was announced. To defer to the agency's interpretation in this circumstance would seriously undermine the principle that agencies should provide regulated parties "fair warning of the conduct [a regulation] prohibits or requires." Indeed, it would result in precisely the kind of "unfair surprise" against which our cases have long warned.

This case well illustrates the point. Until 2009, the pharmaceutical industry had little reason to suspect that its longstanding practice of treating detailers as exempt outside salesmen transgressed the FLSA. The statute and regulations certainly do not provide clear notice of this. . . .

Even more important, despite the industry's decades-long practice of classifying pharmaceutical detailers as exempt employees, the DOL never initiated any enforcement actions with respect to detailers or otherwise suggested that it thought the industry was acting unlawfully. . . .

Our practice of deferring to an agency's interpretation of its own ambiguous regulations undoubtedly has important advantages, but this practice also creates a risk that agencies will promulgate vague and open-ended regulations that they can later interpret as they see fit, thereby "frustrat[ing] the notice and predictability purposes of rulemaking." *Talk America, Inc. v. Michigan Bell Telephone Co.*, 131 S.Ct. 2254, 2266 (2011) (Scalia, J., concurring). . . .

Accordingly, whatever the general merits of *Auer* deference, it is unwarranted here. We instead accord the Department's interpretation a measure of deference proportional to the " 'thoroughness evident in its consideration, the validity of its reasoning, its consistency with earlier and later pronouncements, and all those factors which give it power to persuade.' " *United States v. Mead Corp.*, 533 U. S. 218, 228 (2001) (quoting *Skidmore v. Swift & Co.*, 323 U. S. 134, 140 (1944)).

[Applying *Skidmore*, the Court concluded that DOL's "transfer of title" interpretation was unpersuasive. The department had developed its view without allowing an opportunity for public comment; it had vacillated on the issue; and its current interpretation was at odds with the statutory text, which defines sales to include consignments. In short, the Court felt free to interpret the regulation without any deference to the agency. Given that premise, the majority found that the plaintiffs were, indeed, "outside salesmen" for FLSA purposes, because their promotional work fit within the phrase "other disposition" in § 3(k). The Court observed that "[o]btaining a nonbinding commitment from a physician to prescribe one of respondent's drugs [was] the most that petitioners were able to do to ensure the eventual disposition of the products that respondent sells." Moreover, plaintiffs had "all of the external indicia of salesmen," such as working away from the office with minimal supervision.

BREYER, J., joined by GINSBURG, SOTOMAYOR, and KAGAN, JJ., dissented. He agreed with the majority that, in view of the government's shifting views as to the meaning of DOL's regulations, "we should not give the Solicitor General's current interpretative view any especially favorable weight." Thus, he was willing to assume that the Court should make "an independent examination of the statute's language and the related Labor Department regulations." On the merits of the dispute, however, he argued that the detailers provided information to doctors and *encouraged* sales, but they did not *make* sales. Thus, they were not "outside salesmen" as defined in the DOL's regulations.]

NOTES AND QUESTIONS

1. *Christopher.* The upshot of *Christopher* seems to be that the Court will sometimes support strong deference to agencies' interpretations of their regulations, but its decision about whether to do so will depend on the circumstances of a particular case. *Cf. Barnhart v. Walton,* § 9.2.4 N.3. This development raises several questions. First, on a general level, do the arguments in favor of *Chevron* deference to agencies' statutory interpretation apply to an agency's interpretation of its own regulation, as *Seminole Rock* and *Auer* apparently presupposed? If so, does *Christopher* articulate convincing reasons for not applying that standard of review in this case? Perhaps the most prominent factor invoked by Justice Alito is the unfair surprise that would result from applying the DOL position to Christopher's and Buchanan's lawsuit. This argument recalls the *Fox II* due process right to fair notice, discussed in § 4.5. Is that consideration pertinent to the interpretation of the regulation, or only to the question of whether it should be applied retroactively? If a detailer sued SmithKline for overtime pay solely with regard to a period of time in which the company was on notice of the DOL interpretation, should *Auer* apply?

2. *Format issues.* Recall Justice Thomas's invocation of the *Auer*-*Seminole Rock* deference test in *Christensen,* § 9.2.4. Was his adherence to that test at odds with his conclusion elsewhere in that opinion that informal

pronouncements construing *statutes* deserve only *Skidmore* deference? For criticism of the Court's seeming double standard, see Robert A. Anthony & Michael Asimow, *The Court's Deferences—A Foolish Inconsistency*, ADMIN. & REG. L. NEWS, Fall 2000, at 10. Inconsistent or not, the courts continue to apply *Auer* to interpretations of regulations in opinion letters. *D.L. v. Baltimore*, 706 F.3d 257, 259 (4th Cir. 2013); *Bassiri v. Xerox Corp.*, 463 F.3d 927, 930 (9th Cir. 2006); *Drake v. FAA*, 291 F.3d 59, 67–69 (D.C. Cir. 2002). Indeed, the Court's continued willingness to defer (or at least consider deferring) to regulatory interpretations in government litigation briefs, as in *Auer* and *Christopher*, can also be seen as in tension with the reasoning of *Christensen* and *Mead*.

3. *Parroting.* The Court has held that if a regulation merely "parrots" statutory language, the agency's interpretation of it does not qualify for *Auer* deference. *Federal Express Corp. v. Holowecki*, 552 U.S. 389, 398–99 (2008); *Gonzales v. Oregon*, 546 U.S. 243, 257 (2006). As the Court wrote in *Gonzales*: "An agency does not acquire special authority to interpret its own words when, instead of using its expertise and experience to formulate a regulation, it has elected merely to paraphrase the statutory language." In *Christopher*, however, the DOL regulation specifically relied on § 3(k) of the FLSA, and the majority and dissenters joined issue over the meaning of *that* provision. Why, then, did Justice Alito think *Auer* deference was implicated in the case at all?

4. *Montesquieu and Manning.* In *Christopher*, Justice Alito cited in passing to Justice Scalia's concurring opinion in *Talk America v. Michigan Bell Tel. Co.* In that opinion, Scalia said that he had become "increasingly doubtful" about the validity of the deference principle of the *Auer* case (which he himself had written). He argued that *Auer* deference is very different from *Chevron* deference:

> When Congress enacts an imprecise statute that it commits to the implementation of an executive agency, it has no control over that implementation (except, of course, through further, more precise, legislation). The legislative and executive functions are not combined. But when an agency promulgates an imprecise rule, it leaves *to itself* the implementation of that rule, and thus the initial determination of the rule's meaning.... It seems contrary to fundamental principles of separation of powers to permit the person who promulgates a law to interpret it as well. "When the legislative and executive powers are united in the same person, or in the same body of magistrates, there can be no liberty...." [quoting Montesquieu, *Spirit of the Laws*].

Furthermore, he argued, "deferring to an agency's interpretation of its own rule encourages the agency to enact vague rules which give it the power, in future adjudications, to do what it pleases." This critique was largely based on an article by Professor John Manning, who argues that agencies' interpretations of their own rules should be governed by *Skidmore*. John F. Manning, *Constitutional Structure and Judicial Deference to Agency*

Interpretations of Agency Rules, 96 COLUM. L. REV. 612, 655–668 (1996). In a post-*Christopher* case, Scalia repeated and elaborated on this critique and dissented outright from the majority's use of *Auer* deference. *Decker v. Nw. Envtl. Def. Ctr.*, 133 S.Ct. 632 (2012). In a concurring opinion in *Decker*, Chief Justice Roberts and Justice Alito said that the propriety of such deference had not been adequately briefed in that case but was an important question that the Court may want to consider in a future case.

Do you agree with this critique of *Auer*? As to the separation of powers concern, Judge Posner has noted that the Supreme Court itself sometimes announces new principles of law (as in *Chevron*) and later elaborates on what they mean; if courts can do that, he asks, why can't agencies? Richard A. Posner, *Can't Justice Scalia learn a little science?*, SLATE, June 24, 2013. As to the matter of perverse incentives, recall from § 6.2 that federal courts give agencies wide latitude to decide how far they will develop their policies through rulemaking, as opposed to other modes of decisionmaking. Do those precedents cast doubt on the idea that courts should alter their deference principles in order to induce agencies to engage in rulemaking more often than they now do? *See* Scott H. Angstreich, *Shoring Up* Chevron: *A Defense of* Seminole Rock *Deference to Agency Regulatory Interpretations*, 34 U.C. DAVIS L. REV. 49 (2000).

Finally, does the Scalia-Manning critique give unduly short shrift to the affirmative benefits of *Auer* deference? By hypothesis, the affected interpretations will all fall within what the court considers to be the agency's sphere of delegated authority (if they didn't, they would be set aside under *Chevron*). In the above-cited column, Judge Posner comments that the incentives point

> is a valid concern, but it doesn't justify a blanket refusal to grant some deference, some leeway, to agency interpretations of their own regulations. The regulation may deal with a highly technical matter that the agency understands better than a court would; its interpretation may be in the nature of explanation and clarification rather than alteration. Scalia proposes that in all cases in which an agency's interpretation of its own regulation is challenged, the reviewing court should resolve the challenge 'by using the familiar tools of textual interpretation.' Those tools are notably unreliable, especially when dealing with a technical regulation. In *Decker*, the regulation concerned storm water runoff from logging roads.

5. *A purposivist approach.* Aside from the issue of deference, the methods by which courts construe regulations are roughly similar to the techniques they use when construing administrative statutes. *See* § 9.2.3. Professor Stack has, however, recently advocated a methodological approach that is intended to respond to the distinctive context of judicial interpretation of regulations. Kevin M. Stack, *Interpreting Regulations*, 111 MICH. L. REV. 355 (2012). Under his "purposive" approach, a court should resolve ambiguities in the text of a regulation by looking primarily to the purposes

expressed in the preamble or "statement of basis and purpose" that an agency files with a rule pursuant to APA § 553(c). Stack notes that, in statutory interpretation, courts often hesitate to rely on congressional committee reports and floor statements, because they may be poorly thought out or may reflect the views of a faction that are not shared by other members of the legislative coalition. But a preamble, he contends, will usually be a credible source of insight into the rulemaking agency's intentions, because (1) it is an official statement by the administrative decisionmaker, not by a subset thereof, and (2) it is usually a fairly coherent and internally consistent document (because courts require high standards of rationality through the hard look doctrine). Is this analysis persuasive? How well can it serve as the basis for a general framework for judicial interpretation of regulations?

6.   *Problem.* Long term care facilities that participate in Medicare and Medicaid are subject to inspections conducted by state agencies on behalf of the federal Centers for Medicare and Medicaid Services (CMS). During an inspection of the Marsh Nursing Home, surveyors from the Madison Department of Aging observed that several of the breakfast plates had eggs with runny yolks. The cook explained that he had accommodated requests by some of the elderly residents for "soft-cooked eggs." Nevertheless, the surveyors reported that the home had served unpasteurized eggs in an undercooked, and therefore unsafe, manner.

A regulation adopted by CMS after notice and comment proceedings provides that a facility must "[s]tore, prepare, distribute, and serve food under sanitary conditions." 42 C.F.R. § 483.35(i). CMS has published an operations manual that provides in relevant part:

> Cooking is a critical control point in preventing foodborne illness. Cooking to heat all parts of food to the temperature and for the time specified below will either kill dangerous organisms or inactivate them. . . . Foods should reach the following internal temperatures:
> . . .
>> Unpasteurized eggs when cooked to order in response to resident request and to be eaten promptly after cooking—145 degrees F for 15 seconds (the white should be completely set and the yolk congealed).

On the basis of the surveyors' report, CMS determined that Marsh had violated the regulation as explicated in the manual. It suspended Marsh's provider-of-care agreement and imposed a $5000 fine.

Marsh demanded a formal adjudicative hearing on these sanctions. At the hearing, Marsh's cook explained the manner in which he had cooked the eggs on the occasion in question. Marsh's dietician testified that she had tested the temperature of eggs cooked according to this method and found that they had temperatures ranging from 153 to 156 degrees for the specified period, even though the yolks were soft or slightly runny. CMS staff conceded all of these points but said that the regulation and manual required a congealed yolk as well as the stated temperature range. The ALJ vacated the suspension but upheld the $5000 fine. The department's appeals board affirmed.

On judicial review, Marsh submits that the undisputed evidence shows that it complied with the temperature provision. It argues that the language in the manual about a firm yolk is best read as merely advisory, and it had no way of anticipating that CMS would interpret the regulation as requiring it to meet both the temperature criterion and the firm-yolk criterion. What standard of review should the court apply in this appeal, and how should it rule? *Cf. Elgin Nursing & Rehab. Ctr. v. HHS*, 718 F.3d 488 (5th Cir. 2013).

§ 9.3 JUDICIAL REVIEW OF DISCRETIONARY DETERMINATIONS

§ 9.3.1 BASIC CONCEPTS

A great variety of administrative action is judicially reviewed under § 706(2)(A) of the APA and corresponding provisions in state law, such as 2010 MSAPA § 508(a)(3)(C): "arbitrary, capricious, an abuse of discretion, or otherwise not in accordance with law." This review standard is referred to as the "arbitrary and capricious" or "abuse of discretion" test (the terms are interchangeable).

Courts use the arbitrary and capricious test in reviewing the *discretionary* element of all kinds of formal and informal agency actions, including both adjudicative and rulemaking proceedings. The present section, § 9.3, examines this use of the test. Moreover, as noted at the beginning of § 9.1, the arbitrary-capricious standard is often applied to review of *factfinding* in informal proceedings. This topic is examined in § 9.4. Finally, the arbitrary-capricious standard overlaps to some extent the "reasonableness" standard applied to agency *legal* interpretations under *Chevron* step two. *See* § 9.2.2 N.6.

CITIZENS TO PRESERVE OVERTON PARK, INC. v. VOLPE
401 U.S. 402 (1971)

[This well-known case involved review of a decision by the Secretary of Transportation to grant funds to build an interstate highway through a park. A statute prohibited the use of parks for highways unless "there is no feasible and prudent alternative" route. The Secretary did not explain why there was no feasible and prudent alternative route.

In an opinion by MARSHALL, J., the Court interpreted the statute to mean that the Secretary could not approve a parkland route unless each alternative route was unsound from an engineering point of view (i.e., not "feasible") or would present "unique problems" (i.e., not "prudent"). A threshold problem for the Court was that the Secretary had not rendered findings that would reveal whether he had actually applied this test. As discussed in § 4.3 N.3, the Court decided that, on remand, the district court should conduct a factual inquiry into what the Secretary's reasons had been—a judicial review procedure that almost certainly would not be allowable today.

Of greater interest for present purposes is the Court's discussion as to how the district court should *review* the Secretary's application of the "no feasible and prudent alternative" test, assuming that the forthcoming inquiry showed that he had indeed applied it.

The Court noted that the "substantial evidence" standard was not applicable. It applies only to formal rulemaking or formal adjudication, and the decision in *Overton Park* was neither. Although a hearing was required, it was merely a public hearing for the purpose of informing the community about the project and eliciting its views. Such a hearing "is not designed to produce a record that is to be the basis of agency action— the basic requirement for substantial evidence review." Therefore, the district court would have to apply the arbitrary and capricious test instead. Justice Marshall elaborated:

> . . . [T]he reviewing court [must] engage in a substantial inquiry. Certainly, the Secretary's decision is entitled to a presumption of regularity. But that presumption is not to shield his action from a thorough, probing, in-depth review.
>
> The court is first required to decide whether the Secretary acted within the scope of his authority. This determination naturally begins with a delineation of the scope of the Secretary's authority and discretion. As has been shown, Congress has specified only a small range of choices that the Secretary can make. . . .
>
> Section 706(2)(A) [further] requires a finding that the actual choice made was not "arbitrary, capricious, an abuse of discretion. . . ." To make this finding the court must consider whether the decision was based on a consideration of the relevant factors and whether there has been a clear error of judgment. Although this inquiry into the facts is to be searching and careful, the ultimate standard of review is a narrow one. The court is not empowered to substitute its judgment for that of the agency.

The Court's willingness in *Overton Park* to endorse "searching" judicial review of even a highly informal administrative action proved to be a harbinger of future developments. Also influential have been the "relevant factors" and "clear error of judgment" criteria by which the Court amplified on the arbitrary and capricious test. Since then, however, at least some courts have supplemented those criteria with intensive scrutiny of an agency's reasoning process, as the following discussion demonstrates.]

NOTES AND QUESTIONS

1. *Relevant factors.* As explained in *Overton Park*, a court's review under the arbitrary-capricious test begins with consideration of whether the action was "based on a consideration of the relevant factors." This inquiry largely turns on issues of legal *interpretation:* what are the boundaries of the agency's discretionary power?

In cases involving discretionary action, the questions of legal interpretation include determination of which factors a statute requires the agency to consider and which ones it should not consider. The Supreme Court provided a contemporary example of "relevant factors" analysis in *Judulang v. Holder*, 132 S.Ct. 476 (2011). In that case the Bureau of Immigration Appeals ruled that an alien could not qualify for discretionary relief from *deportation* unless the offense that underlay the proposed deportation was directly comparable to an offense that could justify *exclusion* of aliens who had never been admitted to the country. Yet the Board could identify no good reason for insisting on this symmetry. In a unanimous opinion by Justice Kagan, the Supreme Court held that "[t]he BIA has flunked [the relevant factors] test here. By hinging a deportable alien's eligibility for discretionary relief on the chance correspondence between statutory categories—a matter irrelevant to the alien's fitness to reside in this country—the BIA has failed to exercise its discretion in a reasoned manner." Thus, "the BIA's approach must be tied, even if loosely, to the purposes of the immigration laws or the appropriate operation of the immigration system."

In *Pension Benefit Guaranty Corp. v. LTV Corp.*, 496 U.S. 633 (1990), the Supreme Court put some limits on the courts' ability to prescribe "relevant factors" that an agency must consider in rendering a decision. In that case the PBGC (a governmental entity created to implement the Employee Retirement Income Security Act) ordered a company to resume its pension obligations upon emerging from bankruptcy. A court of appeals reversed this decision because of the PBGC's failure to discuss the policies expressed in various federal labor and bankruptcy statutes. The Supreme Court upheld the PBGC decision, saying:

> [T]here are numerous federal statutes that could be said to embody countless policies. If agency action may be disturbed whenever a reviewing court is able to point to an arguably relevant statutory policy that was not explicitly considered, then a very large number of agency decisions might be open to judicial invalidation. . . . [In addition], because the PBGC can claim no expertise in the labor and bankruptcy areas, it may be ill-equipped to undertake the difficult task of discerning and applying the "policies and goals" of these fields.

2.   *Clear error of judgment. Overton Park* says that, after resolving issues of legal interpretation, a court reviewing an agency's exercise of discretion under § 706(2)(A) must consider whether "there has been a clear error of judgment" in "the actual choice made." Facts, policy judgments, and discretion may all be called into question (unless the action is "committed to agency discretion," as discussed in § 10.5). Yet, according to the Court, the standard of review is "a narrow one."

Right after referring to the "clear error of judgment" criterion, the Court cited to LOUIS L. JAFFE, JUDICIAL CONTROL OF ADMINISTRATIVE ACTION 182 (1965). There Jaffe wrote that "a minute speck of dust on a window pane would hardly support a refusal [to license a dairy] based on uncleanliness." That would be an extreme case; how much less extreme an action could be and still fail the Court's test has never been precisely defined. (Note that, despite an unfortunate verbal similarity, this inquiry is *not* the same as the "clearly erroneous" test by which an appellate court reviews the findings of district courts under Rule 52(a) of the Federal Rules of Civil Procedure. *See NAACP v. FCC*, 682 F.2d 993, 998 n.4 (D.C. Cir. 1982).) In modern case law, courts are more likely to hold that an agency's explanation is inadequate than to hold that the bottom-line result is categorically unacceptable.

3.   *Other abuses of discretion.* Modern arbitrary and capricious review extends well beyond the tests articulated in *Overton Park*. Many cases can be better described as enforcing a norm of reasoned decisionmaking. The ABA Section of Administrative Law and Regulatory Practice has offered a checklist of kinds of agency errors that are sometimes held to constitute arbitrary and capricious action:

A.   The agency relied on factors that may not be taken into account under, or ignored factors that must be taken into account under, any authoritative source of law. (The caselaw often describes this ground as an element of the arbitrary and capricious test, although it seems more properly understood as a component of the court's legal analysis.)

B.   The action does not bear a reasonable relationship to statutory purposes or requirements.

C.   The asserted or necessary factual premises of the action do not withstand scrutiny under the relevant standard of review.

D.   The action is unsupported by any explanation or rests upon reasoning that is seriously flawed.

E.   The agency failed, without adequate justification, to give reasonable consideration to an important aspect of the problems presented by the action, such as the effects or costs of the policy choice involved, or the factual circumstances bearing on that choice.

F.   The action, where inconsistent with prior agency policies or precedents, fails to display an awareness of the change in position, fails to explain a changed view of the facts, or fails to consider serious reliance interests that its prior policy engendered.

G.   The agency failed, without an adequate justification, to consider or adopt an important alternative solution to the problem addressed in the action.

H.   The agency failed to consider substantial arguments, or respond to relevant and significant comments, made by the participants in the proceeding that gave rise to the agency action.

I.   The agency has imposed a sanction that is greatly out of proportion to the magnitude of the violation.

J.   The action fails in other respects to rest upon reasoned decisionmaking.

ABA SECTION OF ADMINISTRATIVE LAW AND REGULATORY PRACTICE, A BLACKLETTER STATEMENT OF FEDERAL ADMINISTRATIVE LAW 40–41 (2d ed. 2013). This list was designed as a *descriptive* account of the case law, not as an endorsement of all current doctrine. Moreover, the Section prefaced the list with an apt caveat: "In practice, application of these grounds varies according to the nature and magnitude of the agency action. Thus, a court will typically apply the criteria rigorously during judicial review of high-stakes rulemaking proceedings (a practice commonly termed 'hard look' review), but much more leniently when reviewing a routine, uncomplicated action."

Of course, a court does not have to address every item on this list in order to sustain an agency decision. Rather, the challenger will normally rely on whatever theory or theories may fit the facts of its case, and the court will only need to respond to those allegations. In the end, however, as *Overton Park* makes clear, arbitrary and capricious review is supposed to be for reasonableness, not rightness. In 1998, Iowa adopted a lengthy statutory list of review standards, based roughly on a predecessor version of the ABA statement. *See* Iowa Code § 17A.19(8).

Does this array of potential challenges under the arbitrary and capricious test give a court too much power to interfere with legitimate agency discretion?

4.   *Reasoned decisionmaking review in application.* A representative example of a court enforcing the norm of reasoned decisionmaking is *Salameda v. INS*, 70 F.3d 447 (7th Cir. 1995). Mr. Salameda was a Filipino who stayed in the United States beyond the term of his student visa. He and his wife thus became deportable, but they applied for discretionary suspension of deportation. To qualify for this relief, they first had to show that deportation would result in "extreme hardship." The Board of Immigration Appeals rejected their application, but the Seventh Circuit reversed that decision. In an opinion by Judge Posner, the court said that the question presented was "whether the INS's judicial officers addressed in a rational manner the questions that the aliens tendered for consideration.

They did not." Specifically, the court faulted the Board for failing to consider whether Mr. Salameda's record of local community service would intensify the hardship that would ensue from his being removed from that community. Moreover, the court thought the INS's failure to name the Salamedas' young son as an additional party to the proceeding was an "ignoble ploy," because it enabled the Board to avoid considering the hardship to the son that deportation would bring about. The Board needed to consider this "novel interpretive question" as well. A dissent by Judge Easterbrook strongly disputed the majority's contention that the Board needed to take account of either of these issues. In addition, the dissent argued that deportation to the Philippines might be "hardship," but could not fairly be considered "extreme hardship."

As the *Salameda* decision illustrates, modern arbitrary and capricious review can serve as a means by which courts can insist that agencies spell out their reasoning carefully—but such review can also appear to be, or actually be, inappropriate judicial second-guessing of a legitimate administrative decision. The ramifications of this development are examined more fully in § 9.3.2.

5.   *Resource constraints.* A background issue in the *Salameda* case was whether courts should make allowances when agencies simply lack the resources necessary to do their assigned job. At that time, four BIA members had to deal with a caseload of over 14,000 new appeals per year! The result was an ever-lengthening queue of cases, sloppy and rushed decisionmaking, and a twelve-year delay in *Salameda.* In his dissent, Judge Easterbrook wrote: "A short-handed INS is hard pressed to keep up with the flow of new cases, let alone address the evolving circumstances in ongoing ones. It is inevitable that in the process some arguments will be dealt with in passing, or not at all, and that judges disposed to question any of the Board's decisions won't want for opportunity. But should we seek to use that opportunity?" For the majority, Judge Posner responded that "understaffing is not a defense to a violation of principles of administrative law." Since the time of that case, the BIA has acquired more adjudicators and support staff, but judges have continued to insist that resource limitations are no excuse for arbitrary decisionmaking. *See Recinos de Leon v. Gonzales*, 400 F.3d 1185, 1193–94 (9th Cir. 2005); *Zhen Li Iao v. Gonzales*, 400 F.3d 530 (7th Cir. 2005) (Posner, J.). In agencies generally, the problem of underfunding has persisted and in some ways gotten worse. Is it realistic for reviewing courts to ignore budgetary constraints? *See* Richard J. Pierce, *Judicial Review of Agency Actions in a Period of Diminishing Agency Resources*, 49 ADMIN. L. REV. 61 (1997).

6.   *Sanctions.* In *Butz v. Glover Livestock Comm'n Co.*, 411 U.S. 182 (1973), the agency found that a licensee had negligently weighed livestock. It imposed a twenty-day suspension, even though in the past it had never suspended a license except in cases of intentional and flagrant violations. The court of appeals reversed the suspension because of this disparate treatment, but the Supreme Court reversed.

The Court held that the decision below "was an impermissible intrusion into the administrative domain." The agency's choice of sanction is not to be overturned unless found to be "unwarranted in law or without justification in fact." The Court held that there is no legal requirement that licensees be treated uniformly or that license suspension can occur only in cases of intentional or flagrant violation. Since the licensee had been warned about short-weighting in the past, there was sufficient factual justification for the sanction. "The fashioning of an appropriate and reasonable remedy is for the Secretary, not the court." Courts have, by and large, heeded the Court's admonition to exercise restraint in this area. *See, e.g., Coosemans Specialties, Inc. v. Dep't of Agric.*, 482 F.3d 560, 566–67 (D.C. Cir. 2007); *Andershock's Fruitland v. USDA*, 151 F.3d 735 (7th Cir. 1998). Yet one can find occasional judicial decisions in which sanctions have been rejected as disproportionate. *See, e.g., Morgan v. Secretary of Housing & Urban Devel.*, 985 F.2d 1451 (10th Cir. 1993) (reducing civil penalty from $10,000 to $500 for mobile home park owner who had discriminated against families with children but whose first-time offense was not egregious).

In Maryland, judicial oversight of sanctions may be even more lenient than in the federal system. In *Md. Aviation Admin. v. Noland*, 873 A.2d 1145 (Md. 2005), a paramedic who worked for the state aviation agency struck a combative psychiatric patient who had become violent. At his discipline hearing, Noland pleaded that he had acted without malice and in self-defense, but the agency terminated him and barred him from future employment with the government. On appeal, a lower court remanded the decision for explicit consideration of various mitigating factors that suggested the sanction might have been too harsh. But the state's highest court ruled that this remand was unwarranted: "[W]hen the discretionary sanction imposed upon an employee by an adjudicatory administrative agency is lawful and authorized, the agency need not justify its exercise of discretion by findings of fact or reasons articulating why the agency decided upon the particular discipline." The sanction is presumed to be correct, and the employee has the burden of "persuad[ing] the reviewing court that . . . the decision was 'so extreme and egregious' that it constituted 'arbitrary or capricious' agency action." The court's refusal to require the agency to make findings to justify its choice of sanction is criticized in Arnold Rochvarg, *Judicial Review of Administrative Sanctions: Why* Noland *Should Be Abandoned*, 44 MD. BAR J. 24 (2011).

7.   *Reasoned decisionmaking and the Chenery rule.* According to the *Chenery* rule, a court cannot affirm an agency decision on a ground within the agency's discretion other than the one relied on by the agency in the decision under review. *See SEC v. Chenery Corp.*, 318 U.S. 80, 88 (1943). In short, the court cannot exercise the agency's discretion. *See generally* Kevin M. Stack, *The Constitutional Foundations of* Chenery," 116 YALE L.J. 952 (2007).

One corollary of this principle, as we have seen earlier (§§ 4.3 N.5, § 5.6 N.6, § 9.2.4 N.7), is that post hoc rationalizations by appellate counsel normally cannot substitute for a determination by the actual agency decisionmaker. *Chenery* also has a number of other implications for judicial review.

First, when an agency takes an action in the mistaken belief that it is legally required to do so, the court cannot uphold the decision, even if the action was one that the agency could lawfully have taken in its discretion. *See Prill v. NLRB*, 755 F.2d 941, 947–50 (D.C. Cir. 1985), remanding a Board order that dismissed a claim that an employee had engaged in protected concerted activities. The court said that, "contrary to the Board's view, the statutory language does not compel it to adopt its present definition of 'concerted activities,' but rather gives the Board substantial responsibility to determine the scope of that provision in light of its own policy judgment and expertise." (Recall the similar reasoning in *McPherson v. Employment Div.*, § 9.2.1 N.4.)

Second, when an agency rests its action on a premise that the reviewing court considers impermissible, the court cannot uphold the action by deciding that the agency was actually applying a different, unacknowledged premise, even if the latter premise would have been permissible. *Allentown Mack Sales & Service, Inc. v. NLRB*, 522 U.S. 359 (1998); *Gifford Pinchot Task Force v. Fish & Wildlife Serv.*, 378 F.3d 1059, 1072 n.9 (9th Cir. 2004).

Third, if the court finds that an agency's exercise of discretion is arbitrary and capricious, it normally must remand the case to the agency for reconsideration, instead of resolving the remaining issues on its own or prescribing a specific outcome. *See, e.g., National Ass'n of Home Builders v. Defenders of Wildlife*, 551 U.S. 644 (2007); *INS v. Orlando Ventura*, 537 U.S. 12 (2002); *Federal Power Comm'n v. Idaho Power Co.*, 344 U.S. 17 (1952); *FCC v. Pottsville Broad. Co.*, 309 U.S. 134 (1940). In *Idaho Power*, the court of appeals found that the Commission had included an improper condition in a license. The court modified the license by striking the condition, but the Supreme Court held that this relief had been impermissible. Rather, the court of appeals had to give the agency a choice of whether to eliminate the condition or issue no license at all. The principle of these cases has its limits: a reviewing court can take more definitive action if a particular outcome is legally required or self-evident. *Fleshman v. West*, 138 F.3d 1429, 1433 (Fed. Cir. 1998). But the courts apply this exception narrowly, in order to preserve the agency's primacy within the sphere of its discretion.

8. *Problem—teacher dismissal.* A local school board discharged two tenured high school teachers for misconduct. Both had taught in the district for thirty years.

At Alice's hearing, testimony by her ex-husband revealed that Alice had, over a period of years, taken home for her own use $35 of school supplies (paper, pens, tape, etc.). She admitted that it was true.

Bob was discharged for insubordination. The evidence showed that parents had complained to the principal and the school board about Bob's use of the book *Catcher in the Rye* in English class two years ago. They objected to the "explicit street language" used in the book. After a discussion with the principal, Bob agreed not to use the book again. Last month, however, Bob again assigned *Catcher in the Rye*. When summoned to a conference with the principal to discuss this, Bob walked out and refused to discuss it any further.

Alice and Bob seek judicial review. They question only the Board's choice to discharge them instead of imposing some lesser sanction such as a reprimand in their file. How should the court rule? *See Pell v. Board of Educ.*, 313 N.E.2d 321 (N.Y. 1974); *Harris v. Mechanicville Cent. Sch. Dist.*, 380 N.E.2d 213 (N.Y. 1978).

9. *Problem—free drinks.* The NLRB conducted a representation election for electricians employed by Ampere, Inc., to determine whether the United Electrical Workers should become their exclusive union representative. The election was held at a local hotel. While it was in progress, the local union's business manager camped out in a nearby cocktail lounge and treated about a dozen of the electricians to unlimited free drinks, reminding them not to "forget how to vote." The union won the election by a vote of 13 to 5. Ampere refused to bargain with the union, causing the Board to hold that the company had committed an unfair labor practice.

In its opinion, the Board ruled that the election had been valid, there being no direct evidence of coercion or excessive inebriation among the workers. The Board also said that this result followed easily from *Galvanics, Inc.*, an earlier Board case in which a union had provided free lunches (tuna sandwiches and soda) to workers while a representation election was in progress.

Ampere appeals, contending that the business manager's hospitality in this case had interfered with the workers' exercise of free choice, and that the Board should have considered the risk that condoning the union's conduct in this case could cause employers and unions to vie for workers' support in future elections through rival drinking parties. Ampere also contends that the Board's reliance on the *Galvanics* case overlooked significant differences between the two situations. Should the appeal succeed? *Cf. NLRB v. Labor Services, Inc.*, 721 F.2d 13 (1st Cir. 1983).

§ 9.3.2 POLICY, POLITICS, AND THE HARD LOOK

In exercising their delegated rulemaking power, agencies necessarily make policy. As the preceding section explained, courts use the "arbitrary and capricious" test to review these policy choices. Federal courts sometimes engage in penetrating "hard look" review of these choices, and at other times engage in more deferential "soft look" review. Whether the former goes too far, or the latter not far enough, has been a subject of continuing debate over the years. Some of the state courts, meanwhile, employ a very deferential mode of review that the federal courts abandoned long ago.

MOTOR VEHICLE MANUFACTURERS ASS'N V. STATE FARM MUTUAL AUTOMOBILE INS. CO.

463 U.S. 29 (1983)

[The National Traffic and Motor Vehicle Safety Act of 1966 directs the Secretary of Transportation or his delegate to issue motor vehicle safety standards that "shall be practicable, shall meet the need for motor vehicle safety, and shall be stated in objective terms." 15 U. S. C. § 1392(a). The Secretary has delegated this authority to the National Highway Traffic Safety Administration (NHTSA). This case concerned the issue of whether NHTSA should require "passive restraints," meaning either airbags or automatic seatbelts. The need for regulation arose out of the fact that relatively few people buckle up on their own. A passive restraint requirement would be very costly for auto manufacturers but would have enormous safety benefits: if everyone actually wore seatbelts or were protected by passive restraints, there would be 12,000 fewer traffic deaths and 100,000 fewer serious injuries each year.

This issue was the subject of 60 rulemaking notices; a passive restraint requirement was imposed, amended, rescinded, and reimposed. At one point, NHTSA required an "ignition interlock," which prevented cars from starting until seatbelts were attached; this was unpopular and was banned by statute. Eventually, NHTSA adopted Motor Vehicle Safety Standard 208 in 1977. The Standard required cars produced after 1982 to be equipped with passive restraints.

In 1981, pursuant to a deregulatory initiative of the Reagan administration, NHTSA delayed the effective date of the 1977 standard. After a notice and comment proceeding, NHTSA rescinded the standard.

NHTSA explained that it could not find that the standard would produce significant safety benefits. The industry had decided that virtually all cars would be produced with *automatic detachable belts* (rather than airbags). Once this type of belt is unbuckled, it loses its automatic feature until it is rebuckled. Thus, Standard 208 might not significantly increase usage of restraints at all.

Since the standard would cost $1 billion to implement, NHTSA did not believe it reasonable to impose such costs on manufacturers and consumers without more adequate assurance of sufficient safety benefits. In addition, NHTSA concluded that automatic restraints might have an adverse effect on the public's attitude toward safety, "poisoning popular sentiment toward efforts to improve occupant restraint systems in the future." Insurance companies challenged the rescission, which the D.C. Circuit held arbitrary and capricious.]

WHITE, J.: . . . .

III

Unlike the Court of Appeals, we do not find the appropriate scope of judicial review to be the "most troublesome question" in the case. [The statute indicates] that motor vehicle safety standards are to be promulgated under the informal rulemaking procedures of § 553 of the [APA]. The agency's action in promulgating such standards therefore may be set aside if found to be "arbitrary, capricious, an abuse of discretion, or otherwise not in accordance with law." § 706(2)(A). *Citizens to Preserve Overton Park v. Volpe,* 401 U.S. 402 (1971). We believe that the rescission or modification of an occupant protection standard is subject to the same test. . . .

Petitioner [MVMA] disagrees, contending that the rescission of an agency rule should be judged by the same standard a court would use to judge an agency's refusal to promulgate a rule in the first place—a standard Petitioner believes considerably narrower than the traditional arbitrary and capricious test. [*See* § 6.3 NN.1–2.] We reject this view. The Motor Vehicle Safety Act expressly equates orders "revoking" and "establishing" safety standards; neither that Act nor the APA suggests that revocations are to be treated as refusals to promulgate standards. Petitioner's view would render meaningless Congress' authorization for judicial review of orders revoking safety rules. Moreover, the revocation of an extant regulation is substantially different than a failure to act. Revocation constitutes a reversal of the agency's former views as to the proper course. "A settled course of behavior embodies the agency's informed judgment that, by pursuing that course, it will carry out the policies committed to it by Congress. There is, then, at least a presumption that those policies will be carried out best if the settled rule is adhered to." Accordingly, an agency changing its course by rescinding a rule is obligated to supply a reasoned analysis for the change beyond that which may be required when an agency does not act in the first instance.

In so holding, we fully recognize that "regulatory agencies do not establish rules of conduct to last forever," and that an agency must be given ample latitude to "adapt their rules and policies to the demands of changing circumstances." But the forces of change do not always or necessarily point in the direction of deregulation. In the abstract, there is no more reason to presume that changing circumstances require the rescission of prior action, instead of a revision in or even the extension of current regulation. If Congress established a presumption from which judicial review should start, that presumption—contrary to petitioners' views—is not *against* safety regulation, but *against* changes in current policy that are not justified by the rulemaking record. While the removal of a regulation may not entail the monetary expenditures and other costs of enacting a new standard, and accordingly, it may be easier for an agency to justify a deregulatory action, the direction in which an agency chooses to move does not alter the standard of judicial review established by law. . . .

[U]nder [the arbitrary and capricious] standard, a reviewing court may not set aside an agency rule that is rational, based on consideration of the relevant factors and within the scope of the authority delegated to the agency by the statute. We do not disagree with this formulation.[9] The scope of review under the "arbitrary and capricious" standard is narrow and a court is not to substitute its judgment for that of the agency. Nevertheless, the agency must examine the relevant data and articulate a satisfactory explanation for its action including a "rational connection between the facts found and the choice made." *Burlington Truck Lines v. United States,* 371 U.S. 156 (1962). In reviewing that explanation, we must "consider whether the decision was based on a consideration of the relevant factors and whether there has been a clear error of judgment." *Citizens to Preserve Overton Park v. Volpe, supra.*

Normally, an agency rule would be arbitrary and capricious if the agency has relied on factors which Congress has not intended it to consider, entirely failed to consider an important aspect of the problem, offered an explanation for its decision that runs counter to the evidence before the agency, or is so implausible that it could not be ascribed to a difference in view or the product of agency expertise. The reviewing court should not attempt itself to make up for such deficiencies: "We may not supply a reasoned basis for the agency's action that the agency itself has not given." *SEC v. Chenery Corp.,* 332 U.S. 194 (1947). We will, however, "uphold a decision of less than ideal clarity if the agency's path may reasonably be discerned." For purposes of this case, it is also relevant that Congress required a record of the rulemaking proceedings to be compiled and submitted to a reviewing court, 15 U.S.C. § 1394, and intended that agency findings under the Motor Vehicle Safety Act would be supported by "substantial evidence on the record considered as a whole" [citing committee reports]. . . .

V

The ultimate question before us is whether NHTSA's rescission of the passive restraint requirement of Standard 208 was arbitrary and capricious. We conclude, as did the Court of Appeals, that it was. We also conclude, but for somewhat different reasons, that further consideration of the issue by the agency is therefore required. We deal separately with the rescission as it applies to airbags and as it applies to seatbelts.

---

[9] The Department of Transportation suggests that the arbitrary and capricious standard requires no more than the minimum rationality a statute must bear in order to withstand analysis under the Due Process Clause. We do not view as equivalent the presumption of constitutionality afforded legislation drafted by Congress and the presumption of regularity afforded an agency in fulfilling its statutory mandate.

A

The first and most obvious reason for finding the rescission arbitrary and capricious is that NHTSA apparently gave no consideration whatever to modifying the Standard to require that airbag technology be utilized. Standard 208 sought to achieve automatic crash protection by requiring automobile manufacturers to install either of two passive restraint devices: airbags or automatic seatbelts. . . . The agency has now determined that the detachable automatic belts will not attain anticipated safety benefits because so many individuals will detach the mechanism. . . . Given the effectiveness ascribed to airbag technology by the agency, the mandate of the Safety Act to achieve traffic safety would suggest that the logical response to the faults of detachable seatbelts would be to require the installation of airbags. At the very least this alternative way of achieving the objectives of the Act should have been addressed and adequate reasons given for its abandonment. But the agency not only did not require compliance through airbags, it did not even consider the possibility in its 1981 rulemaking. Not one sentence of its rulemaking statement discusses the airbags-only option. Because, as the Court of Appeals stated, "NHTSA's . . . analysis of airbags was nonexistent," what we said in *Burlington Truck Lines v. United States, supra,* is apropos here:

> There are no findings and no analysis here to justify the choice made, no indication of the basis on which the [agency] exercised its expert discretion. We are not prepared to and the [APA] will not permit us to accept such . . . practice. . . . Expert discretion is the lifeblood of the administrative process, but "unless we make the requirements for administrative action strict and demanding, *expertise,* the strength of modern government, can become a monster which rules with no practical limits on its discretion."

We have frequently reiterated that an agency must cogently explain why it has exercised its discretion in a given manner, and we reaffirm this principle again today.

The automobile industry has opted for the passive belt over the airbag, but surely it is not enough that the regulated industry has eschewed a given safety device. For nearly a decade, the automobile industry waged the regulatory equivalent of war against the airbag and lost—the inflatable restraint was proven sufficiently effective. Now the automobile industry has decided to employ a seatbelt system which will not meet the safety objectives of Standard 208. This hardly constitutes cause to revoke the standard itself. Indeed, the Motor Vehicle Safety Act was necessary because the industry was not sufficiently responsive to safety concerns. The Act intended that safety standards not depend on current technology and could be "technology-forcing" in the sense of inducing the development of superior safety design. . . .

. . . [P]etitioners recite a number of difficulties that they believe would be posed by a mandatory airbag standard. These range from questions concerning the installation of airbags in small cars to that of adverse public reaction. But these are not the agency's reasons for rejecting a mandatory airbag standard. Not having discussed the possibility, the agency submitted no reasons at all. The short—and sufficient—answer to petitioners' submission is that the courts may not accept appellate counsel's *post hoc* rationalizations for agency action. It is well-established that an agency's action must be upheld, if at all, on the basis articulated by the agency itself.

Petitioners also invoke our decision in *Vermont Yankee* as though it were a talisman under which any agency decision is by definition unimpeachable. Specifically, it is submitted that to require an agency to consider an airbags-only alternative is, in essence, to dictate to the agency the procedures it is to follow. Petitioners both misread *Vermont Yankee* and misconstrue the nature of the remand that is in order. In *Vermont Yankee,* we held that a court may not impose additional procedural requirements upon an agency. We do not require today any specific procedures which NHTSA must follow. Nor do we broadly require an agency to consider all policy alternatives in reaching decision. It is true that a rulemaking "cannot be found wanting simply because the agency failed to include every alternative device and thought conceivable by the mind of man . . . regardless of how uncommon or unknown that alternative may have been. . . ." But the airbag is more than a policy alternative to the passive restraint standard; it is a technological alternative within the ambit of the existing standard. We hold only that given the judgment made in 1977 that airbags are an effective and cost-beneficial life-saving technology, the mandatory passive-restraint rule may not be abandoned without any consideration whatsoever of an airbags-only requirement.

B

Although the issue is closer, we also find that the agency was too quick to dismiss the safety benefits of automatic seatbelts. NHTSA's critical finding was that, in light of the industry's plans to install readily detachable passive belts, it could not reliably predict "even a 5 percentage point increase as the minimum level of expected usage increase." The Court of Appeals rejected this finding because there is "not one iota" of evidence that Modified Standard 208 will fail to increase nationwide seatbelt use by at least 13 percentage points, the level of increased usage necessary for the standard to justify its cost. Given the lack of probative evidence, the court held that "only a well-justified refusal to seek more evidence could render rescission non-arbitrary."

Petitioners object to this conclusion. In their view, "substantial uncertainty" that a regulation will accomplish its intended purpose is sufficient reason, without more, to rescind a regulation. We agree with petitioners that just as an agency reasonably may decline to issue a safety standard if it is uncertain about its efficacy, an agency may also revoke a standard on the basis of serious uncertainties if supported by the record and reasonably explained. Rescission of the passive restraint requirement would not be arbitrary and capricious simply because there was no evidence in direct support of the agency's conclusion. It is not infrequent that the available data does not settle a regulatory issue and the agency must then exercise its judgment in moving from the facts and probabilities on the record to a policy conclusion. Recognizing that policymaking in a complex society must account for uncertainty, however, does not imply that it is sufficient for an agency to merely recite the terms "substantial uncertainty" as a justification for its actions. The agency must explain the evidence which is available, and must offer a "rational connection between the facts found and the choice made." Generally, one aspect of that explanation would be a justification for rescinding the regulation before engaging in a search for further evidence.

In this case, the agency's explanation for rescission of the passive restraint requirement is *not* sufficient to enable us to conclude that the rescission was the product of reasoned decisionmaking. To reach this conclusion, we do not upset the agency's view of the facts, but we do appreciate the limitations of this record in supporting the agency's decision. We start with the accepted ground that if used, seatbelts unquestionably would save many thousands of lives and would prevent tens of thousands of crippling injuries. Unlike recent regulatory decisions we have reviewed, *Industrial Union Department v. American Petroleum Institute,* 448 U.S. 607 (1980), the safety benefits of wearing seatbelts are not in doubt and it is not challenged that were those benefits to accrue, the monetary costs of implementing the standard would be easily justified. We move next to the fact that there is no direct evidence in support of the agency's finding that detachable automatic belts cannot be predicted to yield a substantial increase in usage. The empirical evidence on the record, consisting of surveys of drivers of automobiles equipped with passive belts, reveals more than a doubling of the usage rate experienced with manual belts. Much of the agency's rulemaking statement—and much of the controversy in this case—centers on the conclusions that should be drawn from these studies. The agency maintained that the doubling of seatbelt usage in these studies could not be extrapolated to an across-the-board mandatory standard because the passive seatbelts were guarded by ignition interlocks and purchasers of the tested cars are somewhat atypical. Respondents insist these studies demonstrate that Modified Standard 208 will substantially increase seatbelt usage. We believe that it is within the agency's discretion to pass upon the generalizability of these field studies. This is precisely the type of issue which rests within the expertise of NHTSA, and upon which a reviewing court must be most hesitant to intrude.

But accepting the agency's view of the field tests on passive restraints indicates only that there is no reliable real-world experience that usage rates will substantially increase. To be sure, NHTSA opines that "it cannot reliably predict even a 5 percentage point increase as the minimum level of increased usage." But this and other statements that passive belts will not yield substantial increases in seatbelt usage apparently take no account of the critical difference between detachable automatic belts and current manual belts. A detached passive belt does require an affirmative act to reconnect it, but—unlike a manual seat belt—the passive belt, once reattached, will continue to function automatically unless again disconnected. Thus, inertia—a factor which the agency's own studies have found significant in explaining the current low usage rates for seatbelts—works in *favor* of, not *against,* use of the protective device. Since 20 to 50% of motorists currently wear seatbelts on some occasions, there would seem to be grounds to believe that seatbelt use by occasional users will be substantially increased by the detachable passive belts. Whether this is in fact the case is a matter for the agency to decide, but it must bring its expertise to bear on the question.

The agency is correct to look at the costs as well as the benefits of Standard 208. The agency's conclusion that the incremental costs of the requirements were no longer reasonable was predicated on its prediction that the safety benefits of the regulation might be minimal. Specifically, the agency's fears that the public may resent paying more for the automatic belt systems is expressly dependent on the assumption that detachable automatic belts will not produce more than "negligible safety benefits." When the agency reexamines its findings as to the likely increase in seatbelt usage, it must also reconsider its judgment of the reasonableness of the monetary and other costs associated with the Standard. In reaching its judgment, NHTSA should bear in mind that Congress intended safety to be the preeminent factor under the Motor Vehicle Safety Act. . . .

The agency also failed to articulate a basis for not requiring nondetachable belts under Standard 208. It is argued that the concern of the agency with the easy detachability of the currently favored design would be readily solved by a continuous passive belt, which allows the occupant to "spool out" the belt and create the necessary slack for easy extrication from the vehicle. The agency did not separately consider the continuous belt option, but treated it together with the ignition interlock device. . . . The agency was concerned that use-compelling devices would "complicate the extrication of [an] occupant from his or her car" [and] might trigger adverse public reaction.

By failing to analyze the continuous seatbelts option in its own right, the agency has failed to offer the rational connection between facts and judgment required to pass muster under the arbitrary-and-capricious standard. [When General Motors proposed a continuous passive belt system in 1978,] NHTSA was satisfied that this belt design assured easy extricability. . . . While the agency is entitled to change its view on the acceptability of continuous passive belts, it is obligated to explain its reasons for doing so.

The agency also failed to offer any explanation why a continuous passive belt would engender the same adverse public reaction as the ignition interlock. . . . We see no basis for equating the two devices: the continuous belt, unlike the ignition interlock, does not interfere with the operation of the vehicle. More importantly, it is the agency's responsibility, not this Court's, to explain its decision.

VI

"An agency's view of what is in the public interest may change, either with or without a change in circumstances. But an agency changing its course must supply a reasoned analysis. . . ." *Greater Boston Television Corp. v. FCC*, 444 F.2d 841, 852 [(D.C. Cir. 1970)]. . . . [T]he agency has failed to supply the requisite "reasoned analysis" in this case. Accordingly, we vacate the judgment of the Court of Appeals and remand the case to that court with directions to remand the matter to the NHTSA for further consideration consistent with this opinion.

[REHNQUIST, J., joined by BURGER, C.J. and POWELL and O'CONNOR, JJ., joined most of the Court's opinion but dissented from Part V.B. They argued that NHTSA had adequately explained its decision to reject the automatic seatbelt alternative. It was reasonable for NHTSA to accept studies indicating that such belts would not save enough lives to be worth the cost.]

The agency's changed view of the standard seems to be related to the election of a new President of a different political party. It is readily apparent that the responsible members of one administration may consider public resistance and uncertainties to be more important than do their counterparts in a previous administration. A change in administration brought about by the people casting their votes is a perfectly reasonable basis for an executive agency's reappraisal of the costs and benefits of its programs and regulations. As long as the agency remains within the bounds established by Congress,* it is entitled to assess administrative records and evaluate priorities in light of the philosophy of the administration.

NOTES AND QUESTIONS

1. *Hard look review.* Traditionally, judicial review of an agency's policy decisions under the arbitrary-capricious standard was extremely deferential, perhaps close to the "minimum rationality" test for the validity of *statutes* under substantive due process. "[W]here the regulation is within the scope of authority legally delegated, the presumption of the existence of facts justifying its specific exercise attaches alike to statutes, to municipal ordinances, and to orders of administrative bodies." *Pacific States Box & Basket Co. v. White,* 296 U.S. 176, 186 (1935). As note 9 of *State Farm* points out, federal courts now reject this approach.

Today, the phrase "hard look" often is used to describe the modern review function of federal courts. *State Farm* is the leading example. What is meant by hard look review? *See* Mark Seidenfeld, *Demystifying Deossification: Rethinking Recent Proposals to Modify Judicial Review of Notice and Comment Rulemaking,* 75 TEX. L. REV. 483, 491–92 (1997):

> Essentially, under the hard look test, the reviewing court scrutinizes the agency's reasoning to make certain that the agency carefully deliberated about the issues raised by its decision. . . . Courts require that agencies offer detailed explanations for their actions. The agency's explanation must address all factors relevant to the agency's decision. A court may reverse a decision if the agency fails to consider plausible alternative measures and explain why it rejected these for the regulatory path it chose. If an agency route veers from the road laid down by its precedents, it must justify the detour in light of changed external circumstances or a changed view of its regulatory role that the agency can support under its authorizing statute. The agency must allow broad participation in its regulatory process and not disregard the views of any participants. In addition to these procedural requirements, courts have, on occasion, invoked a rigorous substantive standard by remanding decisions that the judges believed the agency failed to justify adequately in light of information in the administrative record.

Do you see an inconsistency between hard look review and the principle of *Vermont Yankee? See* § 5.4.3 N.4.

2. *Scholarly evaluations of hard look review.* Is hard look review appropriate? Some argue that it allows unelected and inexpert judges to

---

*   Of course, a new administration may not refuse to enforce laws of which it does not approve, or to ignore statutory standards in carrying out its regulatory functions. But in this case, as the Court correctly concludes, Congress has not required the agency to require passive restraints.

substitute their own judgments and values for those of an expert agency, even though the agency was legislatively designated to make the choice. But others argue that it is a necessary corrective to bureaucratic tendencies to build empires, be captured by the regulated industry, or act unreasonably, maliciously, politically, carelessly, or inconsistently. Compare these views:

a.   One criticism of hard look review is that it makes rulemaking very costly and time-consuming. This is the "ossification" critique that was described in § 5.1 N.1. According to Thomas O. McGarity, *Some Thoughts on "Deossifying" the Rulemaking Process*, 41 DUKE L.J. 1385, 1412 (1992):

> Many observers have concluded that substantive judicial review has had a profound impact on the way agencies make rules. Fully aware of the consequences of a judicial remand, the agencies are constantly "looking over their shoulders" at the reviewing courts in preparing supporting documents, in writing preambles, in responding to public comments, and in assembling the rulemaking "record." Because they can never know what issues dissatisfied litigants will raise on appeal, they must attempt to prepare responses to all contentions that may prove credible to an appellate court, no matter how ridiculous they may appear to agency staff. Having gone to the considerable effort of a successful rulemaking, the agencies are understandably reluctant to change their rules to adapt to experience with the rules or changed circumstances. . . .

See also Richard J. Pierce, Jr., *"Waiting for Vermont Yankee III, IV, and V?: A Response to Beermann and Lawson*, 75 GEO. WASH. L. REV. 902, 909–10 (2007) ("hard-look review adds years to each major rulemaking, adds many millions of dollars in procedural costs to each rulemaking, and produces rulemaking 'records' that usually exceed 10,000 pages. As a result, agencies are extremely reluctant to use informal rulemaking."). *But see* William S. Jordan, III, *Ossification Revisited: Does Arbitrary and Capricious Review Significantly Interfere with Agency Ability to Achieve Regulatory Goals Through Informal Rulemaking?*, 94 NW. U. L. REV. 393, 394 (2000) (concluding, in a study of D.C. Circuit remands of rules between 1985 and 1995, that hard look review "did not significantly impede agencies in the pursuit of their policy goals during the decade under review").

b.   Even if one accepts the ossification diagnosis as descriptively correct, there remains the question of whether hard look review is worth its costs. *See, e.g.,* Thomas O. Sargentich, *The Critique of Active Judicial Review of Administrative Agencies: A Reevaluation*, 49 ADMIN. L. REV. 599, 632–34 (1997):

> It is true, as many have pointed out, that reasonableness review can be extremely burdensome. Courts should be reasonable in imposing reasonableness requirements. Also, courts should not use the reasonableness inquiry simply to substitute their views for those of an agency, as the Supreme Court noted in *Overton Park*. . . . These concerns are real but not definitive. To establish that modern

reasonableness review should be jettisoned and that a minimal rationality test should be substituted in its place, one needs to show that there is little value in reasonableness review, not just that its abuse can occur. . . .

[O]ne ought to pay attention to certain negative tendencies of bureaucracies in general. Don't bureaucracies have tendencies not only toward secrecy but also toward aggressively protecting their own power? Don't bureaucracies sometimes act too quickly, without adequate thought or deliberation, in the formulation of policy? (They certainly can act too slowly, but the opposite possibility also occurs). Can't bureaucracies be effectively captured by narrow interest groups? Don't bureaucracies sometimes act significantly on the basis of inertia and habit, without adapting to changing circumstances or responding to individual situations?

Each of these rhetorical questions presupposes a need for checks on agency decisionmaking. Courts are well attuned to provide those checks. Active judicial review can help to deter the worst abuses of power and to give staff inside an agency levers with which to bargain in the development of policy that serves statutory aims.

c.   According to a study of published appellate rulings from 1996 to 2006 involving review of decisions of the EPA and the NLRB, judges' votes in hard look review cases are significantly influenced by ideology. Judges appointed by Democratic Presidents are significantly more likely to vote for liberal outcomes than are judges appointed by Republican Presidents, and the reverse is true for conservative outcomes. Thomas J. Miles & Cass R. Sunstein, *The Real World of Arbitrariness Review*, 75 U. CHI. L. REV. 761, 766–67 (2008). On the other hand, an earlier study by the same authors reached a very similar conclusion about cases involving review of agency interpretations of law under *Chevron*. *Id* at 768. Thus, the study leaves room for debate as to how much these tendencies are attributable to hard look review as such.

In any event, another body of literature discounts (but does not totally dismiss) the influence of ideology and emphasizes that judges applying hard look review frequently reach decisions that would not be predicted from the party of their appointing President. Douglas H. Ginsburg, *The Behavior of Federal Judges: A View from the D.C. Circuit*, 97 JUDICATURE 109 (2013); William S. Jordan, III, *Judges, Ideology, and Policy in the Administrative State: Lessons from a Decade of Hard Look Remands of EPA Rules*, 53 ADMIN. L. REV. 45 (2001); Harry T. Edwards, *Collegiality and Decision Making on the D.C. Circuit*, 84 VA. L. REV. 1335 (1998).

3.   *A place for politics?* Justice Rehnquist's dissent in *State Farm* has been widely discussed because of its candid argument that an agency may legitimately "assess administrative records and evaluate priorities in light of the philosophy of the administration." Elaborating on this theme, Professor

Watts has argued that, at least in a rulemaking context, courts should allow agencies to justify their discretionary decisions by explicitly acknowledging that they have been influenced by the President, Congress, or other officials. Kathryn A. Watts, *Proposing a Place for Politics in Arbitrary and Capricious Review*, 119 YALE L.J. 2 (2009). She notes that the majority opinion in *State Farm* has been widely interpreted to require a basically technocratic approach to hard look review, and agencies have responded by writing their rulemaking preambles to reflect that approach. Yet, she argues, this technocratic focus stands in sharp contrast to *Chevron*'s acceptance of political accountability as a justification for deference when courts review agencies' *statutory interpretations*. In her view, an agency's proximity to the political process should be a source of legitimacy in both spheres.

Accordingly, Watts proposes that courts should read enabling statutes to allow agencies to consider political influences in the rulemaking context, unless the statute demonstrably requires otherwise. She adds, however, that courts should make this accommodation only where the government officials exerting the political influence appeal to policy considerations or public values—not to "raw politics or pure partisanship."

For a skeptical reaction to Watts' analysis, see Mark Seidenfeld, *The Irrelevance of Politics for Arbitrary and Capricious Review*, 90 WASH. U. L. REV. 141 (2012). Seidenfeld acknowledges that agencies may often legitimately act with political *motives*, but he argues that courts should evaluate a rule without regard to such impulses. Otherwise, he suggests, hard look cannot serve its proper function of ensuring that agencies engage in rigorous analysis of scientific or technical subjects in accordance with congressional mandates.

4. *Consistency.* In *State Farm*, the Court was unanimous in holding that NHTSA's unexplained turnaround in its position on airbags was arbitrary and capricious. Also, recall the holding in *UAW v. NLRB*, § 4.4.2, that "an administrative agency is not allowed to change direction without some explanation of what it is doing and why." But what kind of explanation does an agency need to give when it departs from a prior policy or precedent?

The Court addressed that issue in *FCC v. Fox Television Stations, Inc.*, 556 U.S. 502 (2009). This case (*Fox I*) was an earlier round in the litigation that culminated in *Fox* II, the due process case excerpted in § 4.5. As explained more fully there, the case arose out of the FCC's decision that Fox had violated the Communication Act's ban on "indecent" language when it broadcast "fleeting expletives" in the remarks of celebrities at awards ceremonies. Prior to this case, the Commission had been tolerant of incidental, casually uttered expletives on television broadcasts, but its order in the Fox proceeding changed that policy. The Second Circuit found the FCC order arbitrary and capricious, because the Commission did not make clear " 'why the original reasons for adopting the [displaced] rule or policy are no longer dispositive' " as well as " 'why the new rule effectuates the statute as well as or better than the old rule.'" The Supreme Court rejected this reasoning in a 5–4 opinion by Justice Scalia:

> [O]ur opinion in *State Farm* neither held nor implied that every agency action representing a policy change must be justified by reasons more substantial than those required to adopt a policy in the first instance. . . .
>
> To be sure, the requirement that an agency provide reasoned explanation for its action would ordinarily demand that it display awareness that it is changing position. An agency may not, for example, depart from a prior policy sub silentio or simply disregard rules that are still on the books. And of course the agency must show that there are good reasons for the new policy. But it need not demonstrate to a court's satisfaction that the reasons for the new policy are better than the reasons for the old one; it suffices that the new policy is permissible under the statute, that there are good reasons for it, and that the agency believes it to be better, which the conscious change of course adequately indicates. This means that the agency need not always provide a more detailed justification than what would suffice for a new policy created on a blank slate. Sometimes it must—when, for example, its new policy rests upon factual findings that contradict those which underlay its prior policy; or when its prior policy has engendered serious reliance interests that must be taken into account. It would be arbitrary or capricious to ignore such matters. In such cases it is not that further justification is demanded by the mere fact of policy change; but that a reasoned explanation is needed for disregarding facts and circumstances that underlay or were engendered by the prior policy. . . .

Justice Breyer, in a dissent joined by Justices Stevens, Souter, and Ginsburg, thought this analysis too lenient:

> To explain a change requires more than setting forth reasons why the new policy is a good one. It also requires the agency to answer the question, "Why did you change?" And a rational answer to this question typically requires a more complete explanation than would prove satisfactory were change itself not at issue. . . . Thus, the agency must explain *why* it has come to the conclusion that it should now change direction. Why does it now reject the considerations that led it to adopt that initial policy? What has changed in the world that offers justification for the change? What other good reasons are there for departing from the earlier policy?

Who had the better of this argument? For academic commentary on *Fox I*, see Ronald M. Levin, *Hard Look Review, Policy Change, and* Fox Television, 65 U. MIAMI L. REV. 555 (2011); Richard W. Murphy, *Politics and Policy Change in American Administrative Law*, 28 WINDSOR Y.B. ACCESS JUST. 325 (2010).

5.   *Variations on the consistency theme. Fox I* makes it relatively easy for agencies to change policy direction after a change in political leadership. In *National Ass'n of Home Builders v. EPA*, 682 F.3d 1032 (D.C. Cir. 2012), the court confirmed that this freedom to alter policy applies to rulemaking as well as adjudication. A 1992 statute required the EPA to adopt regulations concerning remodeling of older rental property that contained lead-based paint. In 2008 (during the George W. Bush administration), the EPA adopted implementing rules that contained an opt-out provision for housing units in which no pregnant women or children under the age of six resided. In 2010 (during the Obama administration), the EPA removed the opt-out provision. Industry plaintiffs objected that the agency had revised its policy without identifying any evidence or experience that was not available to it when it included the opt-out provision in the original rule. However, the court upheld the revised rule on the authority of *Fox I*. It noted that the EPA had acknowledged it was changing direction. The agency had also presented a reasonable explanation for the new rule, i.e., that it would provide more complete protection to various affected populations. That the original rule was consistent with congressional intent did not matter, so long as the revised rule was also permissible under the statute.

According to some case law, the duty of explaining a departure from precedent applies only when *the agency* changes course. That ALJs or other subordinate officials reach inconsistent decisions in unappealed cases is not objectionable. If a party is aggrieved by such a discrepancy, the remedy is to appeal to the agency head. *Ho v. Donovan*, 569 F.3d 677, 682 (7th Cir. 2009); *see also Comcast Corp. v. FCC*, 526 F.3d 763, 769 (D.C. Cir. 2008) (FCC need not justify an inconsistency between its present action and prior decisions by its Media Bureau, because "an agency is not bound by unchallenged staff decisions"). Do these cases let agencies off the hook too easily?

6.   *Judicial remedies.* Traditionally, when a court found a rule to be arbitrary and capricious, it would routinely vacate and remand the rule to the agency for further consideration. The consequence would be that no rule would be on the books until such time as the agency fixed the problem with the vacated rule. In recent decades, however, a number of courts have experimented with "remand without vacation." That is, they have, as a matter of judicial discretion, allowed a remanded rule to remain in effect while the agency is curing the error that caused the rule to be sent back. This device can allow the court to avoid short-run disruption of an ongoing regulatory program or protect private persons who have made resource commitments in reliance on the rule.

Despite its practical advantages, however, remand without vacation (or, as it is sometimes called, "remand without vacatur") has given rise to a number of objections. Can it be reconciled with the language of the APA, which provides that a reviewing court *"shall . . . hold unlawful and set aside"* an agency action that violates one of the Act's review standards? 5 U.S.C. § 706 (emphasis added). *See Checkosky v. SEC*, 23 F.3d 452, 490–93 (D.C. Cir. 1994) (Randolph, J., dissenting) (claiming that the APA prohibits remand without vacation). As yet, no appellate court has held the device to be unlawful. Yet policy issues persist. Is the device fair to the challenger, who has convinced the court that the agency acted unlawfully but gets no immediate benefit from the court's disposition? Does the remand without vacation device encourage courts to reverse agency actions too readily, since the disruptive effect of their holdings will be avoided? What can the court do to ensure that the agency will have an adequate incentive to cure its error expeditiously? For an analysis supporting the use of remand without vacation, see Ronald M. Levin, *"Vacation" at Sea: Judicial Remedies and Equitable Discretion in Administrative Law*, 53 D<small>UKE</small> L.J. 291 (2003).

The Administrative Conference has endorsed the device and has suggested criteria to guide its use: "In determining whether the remedy of remand without vacatur is appropriate, courts should consider equitable factors, including whether: (a) correction is reasonably achievable in light of the nature of the deficiencies in the agency's rule or order; (b) the consequences of vacatur would be disruptive; and (c) the interests of the parties who prevailed against the agency in the litigation would be served by allowing the agency action to remain in place." ACUS Recommendation 2013–6, *Remand Without Vacatur*, 78 Fed. Reg. 76,272 (2013); *see* Stephanie J. Tatham, *The Unusual Remedy of Remand Without Vacatur* (2013) (consultant's report available at *acus.gov*). Would the rule underlying *Chocolate Manufacturers Ass'n v. Block*, § 5.3.1, have been a good candidate for remand without vacation? How about the rule underlying *FDA v. Brown & Williamson*, § 9.2.3?

In Texas, remand without vacation is the default practice. A remanded rule "shall remain effective unless the court finds good cause to invalidate [it]." Tex. Gov't Code § 2001.040. Should the federal courts emulate the Texas model?

7. *State court review of discretionary action.* Many states take an extremely deferential approach to review of agency rules. This approach requires that a rule be upheld if there was a conceivable basis for the agency's decision, with the burden on the challenger to demonstrate the lack of any such basis. Under this model, the agency is not required to explain the rule at the time it was adopted. In meeting the challenge, the agency is not limited to the evidence that it considered at the time it adopted the rule.

Massachusetts is one such state. For example, in *Salisbury Nursing & Rehab. Ctr., Inc. v. Div. of Admin. Law Appeals*, 861 N.E.2d 429 (Mass. 2007), the state devised a temporary plan for reimbursement of nursing homes that participated in Medicaid. This plan included a "total payment adjustment" (TPA) provision under which a home's 1998 reimbursement rate was capped at 109% of its 1997 rate. Salisbury challenged the validity of the rule, arguing that the TPA perversely penalized the most efficient nursing homes, but the court rejected its claim in broad language:

> "The plaintiff has the burden of showing that the regulation is invalid or illegal." To do so, the plaintiff must establish the "absence

of any conceivable ground" upon which the regulation may be upheld. This is because "[w]e accord to a regulation, including a rate regulation, the same deference we extend to a statute." In conducting our review, "we must apply all rational presumptions in favor of the validity of the administrative action and not declare it void unless its provisions cannot by any reasonable construction be interpreted in harmony with the legislative mandate." . . .

Salisbury has not met its burden of showing that there is no ground on which to uphold the TPA regulation. . . . Even if Salisbury were correct in its claim that the TPA regulations are poorly designed with respect to "efficiently operated" facilities, that is not sufficient to defeat the regulation. The question here is not whether the TPA is the best or most sensible way to control costs, but whether it bears a rational relationship to the agency's statutory authority and directive. Clearly it does. In reviewing a regulation, this court does not substitute its judgment concerning the wisdom of the regulation for that of the agency. . . .

. . . Once a court has determined that a regulation satisfies the statutory requirements, the task of judicial review is done. We will not otherwise inquire into the details of how a regulation operates in practice, or the degree of precision with which its application takes into account the many variations it may encounter. . . . Salisbury cannot meet its burden by arguing that the TPA caused it financial harm, or that the regulation could have been drafted in a way that would have caused less harm. Neither of these, even if true, would make the regulation arbitrary or capricious.

Id. at 436–38. *See also, e.g., Borden v. Comm'r of Pub. Health*, 448 N.E.2d 367 (Mass. 1983).

However, many states have moved closer to the federal model, although few have embraced true hard look review. *See, e.g., Mechanical Contractors of Alaska, Inc. v. State*, 91 P.3d 240, 247 (Alaska 2004) ("To determine if a regulation is reasonable, we examine whether the agency has taken a hard look at the salient problems and has genuinely engaged in reasoned decision making.") (internal quotation marks omitted); *Washington Indep. Tel. Ass'n v. Wash. Utils. & Transp. Comm'n*, 64 P.3d 606 (Wash. 2003) ("agency action is arbitrary and capricious if it is willful and unreasoning and taken without regard to the attending facts or circumstances") William Funk, *Rationality Review of State Administrative Rulemaking*, 43 ADMIN. L. REV. 147, 153–56 (1991). For example, *Liberty Homes, Inc. v. Department of Industry*, 401 N.W.2d 805 (Wis. 1987), involved a rule that prohibited concentrations of formaldehyde over .4 ppm in mobile homes. The court noted that it would not presume the presence of facts supporting the rule. Instead, it would apply the arbitrary and capricious test by asking whether, based on facts in the record, the agency could reasonably have concluded that the rule would effectuate the legitimate governmental objective it is directed to implement. The record consisted both of materials considered by the agency and additional materials introduced by either side in the trial court. Thus the court exercised review for rationality, but not precisely federal-style hard look review. Ultimately, it upheld the rule.

The 1961 MSAPA, § 15(g)(6), allowed a court to reverse if administrative decisions were "arbitrary or capricious or characterized by abuse of discretion or clearly unwarranted exercise of discretion." This section, especially the last clause, could be read as calling for a fairly hard look. However, it applied only to review of "contested cases"—essentially adjudication. The 2010 MSAPA follows the exact language of federal APA § 706(2)(A) and applies it to all reviewable agency actions. 2010 MSAPA § 508(a)(3)(C). This is not to say, however, that the acceptance of this sort of APA language at the state level has been uncontroversial. *See* Donald W. Brodie & Hans A. Linde, *State Court Review of Administrative Action: Prescribing the Scope of Review*, 1977 ARIZ. ST. L.J. 537, 553–60 (commending the Florida APA for omitting the "accordion-like" epithets "arbitrary," "capricious," and "abuse").

8.   *Problem*. The Surface Transportation Board, a subdivision of the U.S. Department of Transportation, regulates rail service in interstate commerce. Federal law provides that a rail carrier may abandon any part of its railroad lines "only if the Board finds that the present or future public convenience and necessity require or permit the abandonment." 49 U.S.C. § 10903(d). In a leading case, *Midlands Rail Co.*, the Board stated in 1996 that this provision requires it to "balance the competing benefits and burdens of the abandonment on all interested parties in an inherently fact-specific process." The same statutory provision also governs applications for "adverse abandonment." This occurs when an interested person petitions the Board to force an abandonment of a rail line over the objections of the carrier. Typically, the Board uses adverse abandonment to dispossess owners of track lines that have been out of use for a decade or more, so that the land may be devoted to more productive uses.

Diamond Railroad operates a terminal facility that it leases from the city of Monroe. At this waterfront site, it transports rail cars by barge across the Publius River to connecting rail lines. Monroe applied to the Board for adverse abandonment of the terminal and adjacent trackage. The city stated that it aspired to redevelop the waterfront area sometime in the future. Several members of the local congressional delegation, who were also members of the House and Senate transportation committees, filed supportive comments.

Diamond and eight freight shippers opposed the application for adverse abandonment. The shippers stated that they made use of Diamond's barge operations and would be injured if it were ousted from service.

The Board granted the city's application. Its opinion said in relevant part: "We recognize that we have never before granted an application for adverse abandonment of a rail line that was currently in use. However, the time has come for a new approach. As we have held in *Midlands* and other cases, we exercise our broad authority in this area through an inherently fact-specific process. Here, the terminal is owned by the city, which as a government entity represents all of its citizens, not just the businesses that use Diamond's services. The city has concluded that its property should be put to other public uses, as have members of Congress from the region. We will not block the city from using its property as it wishes absent an overriding need for the rail service. There is no such need, because the shippers do have other options, including barge connections across the Publius River 150 miles upriver from Monroe."

On judicial review, Diamond and the disappointed shippers contend that the Board's decision was arbitrary and capricious. Should the court agree? *Cf. N.Y. Cross Harbor R.R. v. Surface Transp. Bd.*, 374 F.3d 1177 (D.C. Cir. 2004).

§ 9.4 REVIEW OF FACT ISSUES IN INFORMAL PROCEEDINGS

1. *Factual errors as arbitrariness.* As earlier sections of this chapter have chronicled, courts have traditionally used the substantial evidence test to engage in serious scrutiny of agency actions in formal proceedings, and the APA codifies this standard in § 706(2)(E). *See* § 9.1.1 above. However, no APA standard expressly provides for review of the facts in informal proceedings (aside from the almost never used provision for de novo review, § 706(2)(F)). Moreover, the arbitrary and capricious test in APA § 706(2)(A) was originally considered extremely lenient, on a par with the test courts use in evaluating the constitutionality of legislation. *See* § 9.3.2 N.1.

This state of affairs could not persist indefinitely. Beginning in the 1960s, agencies began using informal rulemaking, rather than formal adjudication, to make extremely important regulatory decisions. *See* § 5.1. In the federal system and many of the states, administrative lawyers and members of the public could not accept the idea that there should be no serious judicial scrutiny of the facts underlying these rules. Courts turned to § 706(2)(A) for this purpose, because it was the only plausible statutory standard available. In the modern era, therefore, the arbitrary and capricious test, which is most naturally read as focusing on misuses of *discretion*, serves an important second function as a standard for review of *fact* findings in proceedings to which the substantial evidence test does not apply.

2. *Substantial evidence v. arbitrary and capricious.* The above developments have given rise to the question of how the substantial evidence test compares with the arbitrary and capricious test. In a leading case, Judge Scalia discerned an "emerging consensus of the Courts of Appeals" that the distinction between the two standards is "largely semantic." *Ass'n of Data Processing Service Orgs. v. Board of*

Govs., Fed. Reserve System, 745 F.2d 677, 680–86 (D.C. Cir. 1984). This does not mean, he explained, that the distinction is pointless. In a case governed by APA § 706(2)(E), the substantial evidence provision, the agency must support its factual assertions in an evidentiary record compiled with all the procedural opportunities and safeguards that accompany formal proceedings. However, he continued, this does not mean that the amount of factual support needed to satisfy the substantial evidence test is different from that needed to satisfy the arbitrary and capricious test.

The D.C. Circuit's decision in *Data Processing* has been widely cited as authoritative in other circuits. In addition, the Supreme Court has taken note of the *Data Processing* reasoning (without squarely endorsing it). *Dickinson v. Zurko,* 527 U.S. 150, 158 (1999).

The *Data Processing* analysis recognizes that the two tests are functionally similar. Both call for reasonableness review, and both require the agency to muster a sufficient factual basis in the record (however that record is assembled) for the result it has reached. Recall that the legislative history of the Motor Vehicle Safety Act (discussed in *State Farm*) said that the findings of the agency must be supported by "substantial evidence on the record considered as a whole." However, the statute itself called only for arbitrary and capricious review and the Court made nothing of the difference.

Special issues arise, however, in connection with several regulatory statutes in which Congress has explicitly provided that judicial review of legislative rules must be governed by the substantial evidence test. For example, occupational safety and health standards adopted by OSHA must be supported by substantial evidence. 29 U.S.C. § 655(f). Some cases have maintained that when Congress deliberately calls for substantial evidence review, it intends more rigorous judicial scrutiny than would occur under the assertedly "more deferential" arbitrary and capricious test. *See, e.g., Color Pigments Mfrs. Ass'n v. OSHA,* 16 F.3d 1157, 1160 (11th Cir. 1994); *see also Corrosion Proof Fittings v. EPA,* 947 F.2d 1201 (5th Cir. 1991) (excerpted on other issues in § 5.8). In *Data Processing,* however, Scalia argued that "[o]ne should not be too quick . . . to impute such a congressional intent." He suggested that "substantial evidence" in such a provision should be interpreted to mean what it usually means, not some "ineffable" standard that would be more stringent. 745 F.2d at 685–86. Which view is more persuasive? *See generally* Matthew J. McGrath, Note, *Convergence of the Substantial Evidence and Arbitrary and Capricious Standards of Review During Informal Rulemaking,* 54 GEO. WASH. L. REV. 541 (1986). The issue has considerable relevance today, because a bill currently pending in Congress would impose the substantial evidence test for judicial review of any rule that is likely to cost the economy a billion dollars or more. S. 1029, 113th Cong. (2013)

(proposed §§ 551(16), 553(e)(2)). Considering the magnitude of the stakes in such proceedings, should this provision be enacted?

3.   *Soft look and judgmental or predictive facts.* When it rescinded Standard 208, NHTSA concluded that seat belt usage would not increase much even if automatic seat belts were mandatory. This was a prediction—nobody could know for sure. NHTSA argued that courts must accept an agency's prediction, particularly when it relied on agency expertise. This is an important issue, because most health, safety, and environmental regulations rely on predictions, computer modeling, extrapolations, and other techniques by which government tries to minimize risks in the face of economic or scientific uncertainty.

In *Baltimore Gas & Elec. Co. v. NRDC*, 462 U.S. 87, 103 (1983), the Supreme Court upheld a Nuclear Regulatory Commission rule that was premised on a conclusion that permanent storage of nuclear waste would have no significant environmental impact. This was a newer version of the rule considered in the *Vermont Yankee* case. As in *Vermont Yankee,* the court of appeals had invalidated the rule. The Supreme Court said:

> [A] reviewing court must remember that the Commission is making predictions, within its area of special expertise, at the frontiers of science. When examining this kind of scientific determination, as opposed to simple findings of fact, a reviewing court must generally be at its most deferential.

Id. at 103. The Court has made similar observations in less science-laden contexts. In upholding a Federal Communications Commission rule that prohibited common ownership between newspapers and broadcasters in certain circumstances, the Court said that "complete factual support in the record for the Commission's judgment or prediction is not possible or required; 'a forecast of the direction in which the future public interest lies necessarily involves deductions based on the expert knowledge of the agency.'" *FCC v. National Citizens Comm. for Broadcasting*, 436 U.S. 775, 814 (1978). The Court reached a similar conclusion in the "fleeting expletives" case, *Fox I*, discussed in § 9.3.2 N.4. Justice Scalia wrote:

> There are some propositions for which scant empirical evidence can be marshaled, and the harmful effect of broadcast profanity on children is one of them. One cannot demand a multiyear controlled study, in which some children are intentionally exposed to indecent broadcasts (and insulated from all other indecency), and others are shielded from all indecency. It is one thing to set aside agency action under the Administrative Procedure Act because of failure to adduce empirical data that can readily be obtained. *See, e.g., State Farm* (addressing the costs and benefits of mandatory passive

restraints for automobiles). It is something else to insist upon obtaining the unobtainable.

Fox Television Stations, Inc. v. FCC, 556 U.S. 502, 519 (2009).

Recall, however, the admonition in *State Farm* that, when data are inconclusive, an agency may not "merely recite the terms 'substantial uncertainty' as a justification for its actions." It must nevertheless "offer a 'rational connection between the facts found and the choice made.' " *See also NRDC v. Herrington*, 768 F.2d 1355, 1391 (D.C. Cir. 1985) ("DOE may resolve even substantial factual uncertainties in the exercise of its informed expert judgment; but it may not tolerate needless uncertainties in its central assumptions when the evidence fairly allows investigation and solution of those uncertainties."). For a review and critique of the judgmental or predictive facts doctrine, see Emily Hammond Meazell, *Super Deference, the Science Obsession, and Judicial Review as Translation of Agency Science*, 109 MICH. L. REV. 733 (2011).

4. *State-level judgmental facts.* Consider *Citizens for Free Enterprise v. Dep't of Revenue*, 649 P.2d 1054 (Colo. 1982). The revenue department issued a regulation requiring that establishments with liquor licenses must observe standards of "orderly and inoffensive conduct." The regulation included "specific standards governing minimum clothing to be worn by hostesses," "proscription of specified sexually-oriented physical contact," etc.

In a judicial review proceeding brought by bar owners, dancers, and others, the Supreme Court of Colorado upheld the rule. The court initially observed that the legislature had amended the state's APA to require that agency rules must be based on a rulemaking record and must be accompanied by a statement of basis and purpose. The court appeared to regard the Colorado system as at least somewhat similar to the federal system. Nevertheless, the opinion argued, "courts should display sensitivity to the range and nature of determinations that must be made by an administrative agency. [Some] regulations may be based primarily upon policy considerations, with factual determinations playing a tangential or unimportant role. In that context, specific factual support for the regulation should not be required, although the reasoning process that leads to its adoption must be defensible." The court referred specifically to the language from *National Citizens Committee for Broadcasting* just quoted.

In this case, "the record before the department contained testimony by various police officers concerning the law enforcement problems associated with establishments permitting the activities proscribed by the . . . regulation, and several letters from law enforcement officers stating that establishments of this nature foster increased criminal activity. . . . [T]he depth of experience that the police officers possessed in law enforcement as related to liquor-licensed premises entitles the department to give weight to their statements." In the court's view, the causal connection between the regulated activities and increased crime was not susceptible of definitive resolution, but "in light of the materials presented to the department, the breadth and judgmental or predictive nature of the determinations made by the department, and the substantial element of policy choice inherent in the department's action, we conclude that the department has acted reasonably in promulgating the . . . regulation." *Id.* at 1064–65. Was this a proper use of the "judgmental facts" doctrine?

5. *Open or closed record—federal law.* A recurring judicial review issue concerns the contents of the record that a court considers in reviewing agency action. Under one approach, a court is limited to the materials considered by the agency (the "closed record" approach). Under a second approach, that record can be supplemented by additional evidence in the form of testimony or affidavits (the "open record" approach). Formal proceedings, of course, have always been reviewed "on the record," *see* 5 U.S.C. § 706(2)(E), but historically this was not true of informal proceedings.

Overton Park brought about a major shift in the federal courts' practice in this regard. In addressing the factual basis by which the district court should determine whether the Secretary's highway routing decision had been arbitrary and capricious, the Court said: "[T]here is an administrative record that allows the full, prompt review of the Secretary's action that is sought without additional delay which would result from having a remand to the Secretary. . . . Thus it is necessary to remand this case to the District Court for plenary review of the Secretary's decision. That review is to be based on the full administrative record that was before the Secretary at the time he made his decision."

Ironically, the Court was mistaken on this point. It turned out that no administrative record had actually been compiled, and the process of reconstructing it during the remand proceedings proved laborious. Peter L. Strauss, Citizens to Preserve Overton Park v. Volpe—*Of Politics and Law, Young Lawyers and the Highway Goliath*, in ADMINISTRATIVE LAW STORIES 259, 320–21, 326 (Peter L. Strauss ed. 2006). Nevertheless, federal agencies came to understand that, to survive judicial review, they would need to maintain records to support their decisions in informal proceedings.

Today, judicial review of informal actions on a closed "administrative record" has become firmly established in federal law. In *IMS, P.C. v. Alvarez*, 129 F.3d 618, 623–24 (D.C. Cir. 1997), the court summarized federal practice as follows:

It is a widely accepted principle of administrative law that the courts base their review of an agency's actions on the materials that were before the agency at the time its decision was made. . . . [citing *Overton Park* and *Camp v. Pitts*, 411 U.S. 138 (1973), which stated]: "In applying the [arbitrary and capricious] standard, the focal point for judicial review should be the administrative record already in existence, not some new record made initially in the reviewing court." It is not necessary that the agency hold a formal hearing in compiling its record, for "the APA specifically contemplates judicial review on the basis of the agency record compiled in the course of informal agency action in which a hearing has not occurred."

See generally ACUS Recommendation 2013–4, *The Administrative Record in Informal Rulemaking*, 78 Fed. Reg. 41,358 (2013) (containing guidelines regarding the compilation and use of rulemaking records).

There are a few exceptions to the federal closed record rule. *See Lands Council v. Regional Forester of Region One*, 395 F.3d 1019, 1030 (9th Cir. 2005): "In limited circumstances, district courts are permitted to admit extra-record evidence: (1) if admission is necessary to determine 'whether the agency has considered all relevant factors and has explained its decision,' (2) if 'the agency has relied on documents not in the record,' (3) 'when supplementing the record is necessary to explain technical terms or complex subject matter,' or (4) 'when plaintiffs make a showing of agency bad faith.'" However, the court added: "Though widely accepted, these exceptions are narrowly construed and applied." *See generally* Leland E. Beck, *Agency Practices and Judicial Review of Administrative Records in Informal Rulemaking* 66–74 (2013) (consultant's report underlying the above ACUS recommendation, available at *acus.gov*); James N. Saul, Comment, *Overly Restrictive Administrative Records and the Frustration of Judicial Review*, 38 ENVTL. L. 1301 (2008).

6. *Open or closed record—state adjudication.* Some states follow an open record approach. *See Lake Sunapee Protective Ass'n v. N.H. Wetlands Bd.*, 574 A.2d 1368, 1373 (N.H. 1990). California courts, which review *rules* on a closed record (as discussed in the next note), have adhered to an open record approach for "informal or ministerial actions." *Western States Petroleum Ass'n v. Superior Court*, 888 P.2d 1268, 1277 (Cal. 1995). The 2010 MSAPA borrows from the California model. *See* § 507(b) (providing for an open record on judicial review if "the agency action was ministerial or was taken on the basis of a minimal or no administrative record").

There are credible arguments for using an open record methodology, particularly at the state level, where many agencies make decisions with a minimum of procedural formality. The written file for such decisions may be fragmentary at best, or highly disorganized. This fact of life probably helps to explain why many state courts have refrained from following the lead of *Overton Park* by demanding support for informal agency decisions in a contemporaneously compiled record.

7. *Open or closed record—state rulemaking.* In the case of rulemaking, however, practice at the state level is mixed, with substantial support for the closed-record approach.

In the rulemaking context, the open record approach has some positive features. Parties who have an interest in a particular matter may not have known about the agency proceeding and thus may have failed to furnish timely input. Even if they knew about it, they may not have participated or retained counsel to help them participate effectively. Thus it may seem unfair to prevent them from introducing relevant evidence at the time of judicial review.

Moreover, the closed record approach impels both the agency and private parties to place into the record every conceivable piece of relevant information in their possession, lest they be prevented from relying on it at the judicial review stage. This could increase costs and cause serious delays at the agency level. Yet building a massive record may be unnecessary, because the agency action may never be judicially reviewed or particular arguments may never be raised in court. Thus an open record may simplify and speed up the agency decisionmaking process.

However, many states have adopted the closed record approach to judicial review of rulemaking, just as the federal courts have. So does the 2010 MSAPA. *See* §§ 302, 507(a). One factor that militates in favor of that approach is judicial economy. An open record approach insures lengthy trials in which either side is free to bring in new expert witnesses or economic analyses to buttress its position. In addition, an open record encourages private parties to engage in strategic behavior called "sandbagging"—that is, holding back evidence until the judicial review stage so that the agency never gets to pass on that evidence. A more fundamental argument for the closed record approach was offered by a leading California decision:

> Were we to hold that courts could freely consider extra-record evidence in these circumstances, we would in effect transform the highly deferential substantial evidence standard of review . . . into a de novo standard, and under that standard the issue would be not whether the administrative decision was rational in light of the evidence before the agency but whether it was the wisest decision given all the available scientific data. The propriety or impropriety of a particular legislative decision is a matter for the Legislature and the administrative agencies to

which it has lawfully delegated quasi-legislative authority; such matters are not appropriate for the judiciary. . . .

[If parties could introduce scientific testimony in court that was not produced before the agency, this] would seriously undermine the finality of quasi-legislative administrative decisions. Any individual dissatisfied with a regulation could hire an expert who is likewise dissatisfied to prepare a report or give testimony explaining the grounds for his disagreement, introduce this evidence in a traditional mandamus proceeding, and, if he can persuade the court that the report raises a question regarding the wisdom of the regulation, obtain an order reopening the rulemaking proceedings. . . .

Western States Petroleum Ass'n v. Superior Court, supra, at 1274, 1278; see *Carrancho v. Cal. Air Resources Bd.*, 4 Cal. Rptr. 3d 536, 549–50 (Ct. App. 2003).

8.   *Problem.* By statute, OSHA must set standards for exposure of workers to toxic chemicals at a level that "most adequately assures, to the extent feasible, that no employee will suffer material impairment of health." As you may recall from earlier chapters, "feasible" in this context means technologically and economically feasible, regardless of what the agency might deem justified on the basis of a cost-benefit analysis. *American Textile Mfrs. Inst. v. Donovan*, 452 U.S. 490 (1981) (*Cotton Dust*), § 5.8 N.7. However, OSHA may not regulate a substance unless it poses a "significant risk." *Industrial Union Dept. v. American Petroleum Inst.*, 448 U.S. 607 (1980) (*Benzene*), § 7.2.1c. The statute also provides that OSHA standards must be sustained if supported by substantial evidence in the record considered as a whole.

Ethylene oxide (EtO) is a hazardous chemical used to sterilize hospital instruments. In 1971, OSHA adopted a standard that workers must not be exposed to more than 50 parts per million (ppm) of EtO averaged over a workday. Since 1971, there has been increasing (though inconclusive) evidence that EtO causes cancer and spontaneous abortion. Last year, after a lengthy notice and comment proceeding, OSHA found that any exposure to EtO presented a significant health risk; it set an exposure limit of 1 ppm averaged over a workday. Compliance with this standard will cost hospitals many millions of dollars over the next few years. A standard of 5 ppm would save the industry 85% of those costs.

OSHA relied on several studies in support of the standard. According to the Hogstedt study, there were 3 deaths from leukemia at a Swedish hospital out of 230 workers (all exposed to significant EtO) when only 0.2 deaths would normally be expected in a similar group. The Bushy Run study indicated that rats exposed to 100 ppm of EtO every day for a year developed various cancers; rats exposed to 60 ppm developed fewer cancers. However, the rats also developed a severe viral ailment during the study. The Hemminki study indicated that nurses exposed to EtO while pregnant reported on questionnaires that they had a higher rate of spontaneous abortion than a control group. However, the nurses studied knew the purpose of the questionnaire was to test the effects of EtO on pregnant women.

The level of 1 ppm was set by extrapolating the results of the Bushy Run study to humans by making a series of mathematical assumptions. OSHA found that there would be between 12 and 23 additional cancer deaths even at a level of 1 ppm, but it found that it was not technically or economically feasible to set a zero tolerance.

At the same time as it originally proposed the 1 ppm limit for exposure to EtO averaged over an eight-hour workday, OSHA also proposed a short-term exposure limit (STEL)—that no single exposure to EtO could exceed 10 ppm, no matter how brief. The Office of Management and Budget objected to the STEL (on the grounds of excessive cost and lack of benefit), and OSHA decided not to adopt any STEL. Its stated reason was that the 1 ppm limit offered sufficient protection, especially because it would induce hospitals to lower short-term exposures so as to meet the eight-hour average.

Industry groups seek review of the 1 ppm standard. Public interest groups seek review of the decision not to adopt a STEL. What should the court decide? *See Public Citizen Health Research Group v. Tyson,* 796 F.2d 1479 (D.C. Cir. 1986).

CHAPTER 10

REVIEWABILITY OF AGENCY DECISIONS

■ ■ ■

The previous chapter made clear the indispensable role of judicial review in controlling illegal or unreasonable agency action, but it also demonstrated that courts frequently defer to agency judgments. The next two chapters concern additional limitations on judicial review. Chapter 10 begins with a treatment of the availability of and limitations on judicial remedies. It considers two additional remedies: damage actions against an official or against an agency and recovery of attorney fees from an agency. It then considers doctrines that make agency action unreviewable: preclusion of review and commitment to agency discretion. It concludes with the problems of reviewing agency inaction and undue delay. Chapter 11 considers problems of standing (whether a particular plaintiff can challenge agency action) and timing (whether judicial review is premature).

Of course, quite apart from these legalistic limitations, judicial review may be useless for practical reasons. A great deal of money (or some other quite serious issue) must be at stake to justify a client's decision to take the agency to court and incur heavy attorneys' fees in what may well prove to be a losing cause. In addition, obtaining judicial relief is likely to take several years or more. Sometimes, the harm from the agency's action may already be done and it may be irremediable. Once a person is out of business or a product has been banned, it may be impossible to start up again, regardless of what a court might say. Even if review is successful, the remedy may be a remand to the agency which may take the same action for different reasons, thus starting the process anew. Also, the client may conclude that going to court would be imprudent because it could antagonize the agency that will continue to regulate it. In short, it is often better to accept an unfavorable result and move on without seeking judicial review.

As you consider judicial review from the point of view of a private client, the many limitations on review may seem frustratingly technical. However, there is another side to this coin. Judicial interference with agencies has significant systemic costs as well as benefits. Judicial review, particularly of complex agency action or of legislative rules, can consume enormous resources, particularly the time and energy of agency lawyers and of judges. Judicial review can congest appellate dockets, thus exacerbating an already serious problem. And the public interest is not always served by the substitution of a less-informed judicial view for a better-informed agency view.

Consider also the balance of resources: we often think of an ordinary person (say a taxpayer, welfare recipient, or professional licensee) up against a huge, unfeeling bureaucracy. But sometimes the balance is quite different. The private party may be a Fortune 500 corporation with virtually unlimited resources that can be deployed to prevent or at least delay unfavorable agency action such as a new environmental rule. The agency is often seriously underfunded and understaffed. Budget constraints may prevent it from hiring sufficient staff to enable it to discharge its statutory responsibilities. It probably cannot match the resources of many of its private-sector opponents and may be compelled to settle a case or give up rather than defend its actions in court. During the long years that judicial review is pending in court, a regulated business enterprise often can continue polluting or selling a product that harms the public. In other situations, judicial review may be launched by well-funded public interest groups. They can use the review process to fight public or private plans to build a highway, a dam, a shopping mall or a nuclear power plant. These plans can be sidetracked indefinitely or even killed by delays and rising construction costs. Perhaps the projects should not be built, but the decision should not be a function of whether tenacious opponents can litigate them to death. In short, beware of accepting claims that more judicial review is always a good thing.

§ 10.1 PROCEDURAL ELEMENTS: JURISDICTION AND CAUSE OF ACTION

In order to seek the assistance of a court in reviewing agency action: (i) the court must have jurisdiction and (ii) the plaintiff must plead a recognized cause of action that provides the needed relief.

§ 10.1.1 JURISDICTION OF THE REVIEWING COURT

a. *Statutory review.* The statute that creates an agency often explicitly lays out the road to judicial review of its actions—what court has jurisdiction, who can seek review, time limits for seeking review, and so on. Ordinarily, that procedure is exclusive and no other route can be pursued.

At the federal level, the trend is to lodge responsibility for statutory review of rules and final orders in appellate rather than trial courts. In most states, judicial review begins at the trial court level. Unfortunately, statutes are not always clear about where a particular agency action should be reviewed. In construing ambiguous review statutes, courts often prefer appellate court, not trial court, review unless there is a need for additional evidence to be taken, in which case a trial court is preferred. *See, e.g., Citizens Awareness Network, Inc. v. United States*, 391 F.3d 338, 345–47 (1st Cir. 2004), holding that the court of appeals was the proper court to review a procedural rule adopted by the Nuclear Regulatory Commission, even though the statute provided for appellate court review only of "orders."

There are persuasive reasons to prefer appellate court review. Judicial review is an appellate function, so appellate judges may be better at it than trial judges. In general, appellate judges are likely to be more experienced and, on the whole, better qualified than trial judges to decide issues with public policy dimensions. Important matters may get more careful consideration from a three-judge appellate panel than from a single-judge trial court. The waiting line may be shorter at the appellate than at the trial court level. Finally, the matter may well be appealed anyway, so why bother with a costly and unnecessary trial court proceeding?

On the other hand, if the class of matters produces a large volume of cases that involve relatively small stakes and seldom raise significant legal or policy issues, trial court jurisdiction may be preferable. Trial court review is less costly for the judicial system, since only one judge works on the case rather than three. In addition, it may be more convenient for litigants to go to court in their home town than in the state capital or some other distant city.

Thus, consider Social Security cases, which are reviewed by federal district courts. Since there are a large and increasing number of such cases, the decision to lodge them in trial courts seems sensible. Some writers suggest that a specialized Social Security court would be an even better choice. A Social Security court would relieve a heavy burden on the district courts and might produce more informed, quicker, and more consistent results. Specialized Article I courts already exist to decide tax cases and veterans' claims, so a Social Security court would not be unprecedented. Opponents of a Social Security court argue that it might be captured by the Social Security Administration and be less sympathetic to claimants than are the federal district judges. The opponents also believe that cases should be decided by generalist judges with a broader perspective rather than by specialized judges. For a good treatment of the contrasting views, see Paul R. Verkuil & Jeffrey S. Lubbers, *Alternative Approaches to Judicial Review of Social Security Disability Cases*, 55 ADMIN. L. REV. 731, 752–58 (2003).

In contrast, immigration cases go straight to the federal court of appeals. There is a heavy volume of such cases and they represent a serious drain on the time of appellate courts. It might make sense to send them to district court first.

b.   *Review under a general statute:* If no statute provides for review of the actions of a particular agency, state law usually provides that specific courts (usually trial courts) have jurisdiction to review agency action. Review is usually available under the authority of an administrative procedure statute. For example, under New York Civil Practice Law and Rules Art. 78, review of an administrative decision is commenced in a trial court and is transferred to an appellate court if it entails review of formal adjudication.

c.   *Non-statutory review.* If neither a specific nor a general review statute confers jurisdiction to review a particular type of case, the person seeking review must file a civil action against the agency or the official under normal jurisdictional and venue provisions. Thus under 28 U.S.C. § 1331, which covers actions "arising under the Constitution, laws, or treaties of the United States," federal district courts have jurisdiction to conduct judicial review of the actions of any federal agency or official.

In prior years, the doctrine of sovereign immunity sometimes barred the courthouse door. This doctrine immunized the United States from being sued without its consent. Consequently, a litigant seeking non-statutory judicial review had to sue a federal official instead of the agency itself. Such actions were permitted only if the official acted under an unconstitutional statute or outside the powers conferred by statute. *See, e.g., Larson v. Domestic & Foreign Commerce Corp.*, 337 U.S. 682 (1949). The serious injustices resulting from the doctrine of sovereign immunity led Congress to abolish it in 1976 in cases seeking non-monetary relief against federal agencies. *See* APA §§ 702 (all material after the first sentence) and 703 (middle sentence). We consider the narrower federal waiver of immunity in suits for money damages in § 10.2.

In an action seeking judicial review of federal agency action under § 1331, the plaintiff may file suit in any judicial district where a defendant resides, or the cause of action arose, or any real property involved in the action is situated, or (if no real property is involved) the plaintiff resides. 28 U.S.C. § 1391(e). The defendant is the United States, the agency by its official title, or the appropriate officer. APA § 703; Fed. R. Civ. P. 25(d)(2).

Once federal jurisdiction under § 1331 is established, the federal APA comes into play. The APA does not itself provide for federal jurisdiction, but it provides the ground rules for judicial review once jurisdiction is otherwise established. *Califano v. Sanders,* 430 U.S. 99 (1977). Sections 701 to 706 establish what action is reviewable, who can seek review, when it can be sought, the nature of the reviewing court's power, and the scope of review.

§ 10.1.2   NON-STATUTORY REVIEW: FORMS OF ACTION

If no statute establishes the rules for reviewing agency action, the plaintiff must state a claim for relief in a trial court under other state or federal law. This subchapter concerns non-monetary relief, meaning that the plaintiff seeks a court order that an agency must do or not do something. Monetary relief is addressed in § 10.2.

§ 10.1.2a   Injunction and Declaratory Judgment

Generally injunction and declaratory judgment are the most useful and non-technical forms of action. See APA § 703, specifically providing for "any applicable form of legal action, including actions for declaratory judgments or writs of prohibitory or mandatory injunction . . ." For all practical purposes, these are the same—it does not matter whether plaintiff seeks a *declaration* that agency action is illegal or an *injunction* ordering the agency to take action or refrain from taking action. One caution, however: if the plaintiff seeks a mandatory injunction (*i.e.* ordering the agency to do something as opposed to stop doing something), the court may treat the action as one for *mandamus*, which brings in its wake a series of complexities that are treated below. Both injunction and declaratory judgment are equitable remedies and thus *discretionary*. If a court believes that an injunction or declaration against the government would cause harm to the public that outweighs the benefit to the plaintiff, or the remedies are for some other reason inappropriate, it can refuse to grant relief.

The federal courts have long recognized injunction as an administrative remedy. In *American School of Magnetic Healing v. McAnnulty*, 187 U.S. 94 (1902), the plaintiff sought relief from an order by the post office cutting off its mail because of fraud. Previous Supreme Court decisions had ruled that common law writs like mandamus and certiorari were not available in federal court (see below). No problem: the Supreme Court held that plaintiff could obtain an injunction requiring the post office to deliver its mail if it established that the fraud order was erroneous.

§ 10.1.2b   Mandamus

American courts inherited the prerogative writs from England. Each writ developed separately to enable the judges to correct a particular injustice and each had its own limitations, which American courts often preserved. Sometimes they did so even though a statute purports to dispense with the writs in favor of an administrative review petition. Each state has its own body of statutes and case law relating to the prerogative writs.

Mandamus is used to compel ("mandate") action that an agency official refuses to take—for example, to issue a license or hold a hearing. A mandamus plaintiff must show that the defendant owes a "clear legal duty" to act, the desired action is "ministerial" rather than "discretionary," and the plaintiff has exhausted all other avenues of relief. In some states, the writ will correct abuse of discretion.

Mandamus in the federal courts began auspiciously with *Marbury v. Madison,* 5 U.S. (1 Cranch) 137 (1803). In *Marbury,* the Supreme Court held that mandamus would lie to require Madison to issue Marbury his judicial commission (but only in a lower court, not by an original action in the Supreme Court). However, a few years later the Court held that federal courts outside the District of Columbia could not issue mandamus. *McIntire v. Wood,* 11 U.S. (7 Cranch) 504 (1813); *Kendall v. United States ex rel. Stokes,* 37 U.S. (12 Pet.) 524 (1838).

Federal courts outside the District evaded this limitation by issuing injunctions that were prohibitory in form but mandatory in effect, as in *American School of Magnetic Healing* discussed above. The equity tradition made it possible to provide flexible and adequate relief, even if it was affirmative in character. However, other courts held that the mandamus tradition prevailed even though plaintiff sought an injunction instead of mandamus.

The inability of federal courts outside the District to issue mandamus changed in 1962 with the enactment of 28 U.S.C. § 1361, which provides: "The district courts shall have original jurisdiction of any action in the nature of mandamus to compel an officer or employee of the United States or any agency thereof to perform a duty owed to the plaintiff." To obtain the writ, a plaintiff must establish that the defendant owes it a clear, non-discretionary duty and plaintiff has exhausted all other available remedies. *Heckler v. Ringer*, 466 U.S. 602, 616 (1984). *See, e.g., Wolcott v. Sibelius*, 635 F.3d 757 (5th Cir. 2011). Wolcott was a doctor who supplied services to Medicare recipients. Social Security disputed whether it was liable to pay claims arising from those services. Wolcott won an ALJ decision that the claims were payable. Still, a contractor for Social Security refused to pay. The court determined that Wolcott had a clear legal right to payment and had no other remedy. Therefore, he was entitled to a writ of mandamus ordering Social Security to pay the claims.

Most federal courts construe the applicable statute to determine the scope of the official's discretionary power and will grant the writ of mandamus if the official exceeded his authority or abused discretion and the plaintiff has no other remedy. On the other hand, a D.C. Circuit en banc opinion seemingly restricted mandamus under § 1361 to its common law traditions. *See In re Cheney*, 406 F.3d 723 (D.C. Cir. 2005) (also discussed in § 8.2.2): "[M]andamus is drastic; it is available only in extraordinary situations; it is hardly ever granted; those invoking the court's mandamus jurisdiction must have a clear and indisputable right to relief; and even if the plaintiff overcomes all these hurdles, whether mandamus relief should issue is discretionary." And if that wasn't emphatic enough, the court continued: "[A] plaintiff's legal grounds supporting the government's duty to him must be clear and compelling. This does not mean that mandamus actions are ruled out whenever the statute allegedly creating the duty is ambiguous. The district court still must interpret the underlying statute, as must we. But if there is no clear and compelling duty under the statute as interpreted, the district court must dismiss the action." [Internal quotation marks and citations omitted.]

Generally, counsel should avoid § 1361 and seek an injunction or declaratory judgment under § 1331 instead. It should not matter whether the desired relief is affirmative or negative. After all, as already mentioned, APA § 703 permits "writs of prohibitory or mandatory injunction" and APA § 706(1) provides that a court can "compel agency action unlawfully withheld." (*See* § 10.6 for further discussion of the review of agency inaction.)

§ 10.1.2c   Certiorari

Certiorari is a writ directed to an inferior tribunal (which could be a court or an administrative body) that requires the latter to certify a copy of the record and convey it to the reviewing court. Traditionally, review lay only for absence of jurisdiction or for an error of law that appeared on the face of the record. Certiorari is designed to provide judicial review of *judicial* action based upon a record hearing, rather than action having a "legislative" or "administrative" character. Certiorari remains important in many states, particularly in reviewing adjudicatory decisions of local agencies or school boards.

In an early decision, the Supreme Court held that *federal* courts could not grant certiorari to review a fraud order by the post office. *Degge v. Hitchcock*, 229 U.S. 162 (1913). As a result, injunction and declaratory judgment emerged to fill the gap—remedies happily free of the ancient restrictions on certiorari.

§ 10.1.2d   Other Writs

Prohibition lies to prevent an inferior judicial body (including an agency) from initiating a case over which it lacks jurisdiction. Quo warranto is used to test the right to an office. Section 703 of the APA includes habeas corpus as an administrative remedy. Habeas has been used to review orders relating to the confinement of aliens or mentally ill persons and to review decisions that interfere with the liberty of a member of the military (such as a refusal to discharge the member).

Persons detained as enemy aliens at Guantanamo Bay, Cuba, successfully used habeas to litigate the legality of their confinement despite Congressional attempts to preclude habeas review. *Boumediene v. Bush*, 553 U.S. 723 (2008).

§ 10.2 DAMAGE ACTIONS AS A FORM OF JUDICIAL REVIEW

This subchapter considers damage actions against officials or against government. If a private individual has already been harmed by government action, damages may be the only useful remedy. In addition, negligent infliction of economic or physical harm by government personnel could not be prevented by any form of prospective relief. In other situations, damage actions may be a plausible alternative to hearings required by due process. See § 2.4 N.2. Finally, the existence of a tort remedy may serve as a potent deterrent against illegal government action. The subject of common law and constitutional torts committed by government officials has grown enormously in recent years. Complex statutes govern many aspects of the problem. Courses in torts and civil rights cover much of the ground. Therefore, this subchapter is a superficial survey of the area and focuses largely on damage remedies as a form of review of agency action.

§ 10.2.1   TORT LIABILITY OF GOVERNMENT

Historically, the doctrine of sovereign immunity protected government from monetary liability unless it consented to be sued. But government has often given its consent to be sued for money damages.

§ 10.2.1a   The Federal Tort Claims Act

In 1946 Congress abolished the federal government's immunity from tort liability. The Federal Tort Claims Act, 28 U.S.C. §§ 1346(b) and 2671–80 ("FTCA") makes the federal government liable for the wrongful acts of its employees committed within the scope of their employment. Broadly speaking, the federal government is vicariously liable in tort if a private employer would be liable under state law. However, there are a number of differences between suing the government and suing private employers.

i. *Intentional torts.* The general rule is that the government is not liable for intentional torts. However, there are important exceptions. The government is liable for injuries arising out of assault, battery, false imprisonment, false arrest, abuse of process, or malicious prosecution, if these torts were committed by federal investigative or law enforcement officers. § 2680(h). The government is also liable for other intentional torts such as trespass or conversion, but not for defamation, misrepresentation, or interference with contract rights.

ii. *Discretionary functions.* The most important FTCA exemption immunizes the government from damages for any claim "based upon the exercise or performance or the failure to exercise or perform a discretionary function or duty on the part of a federal agency or an employee of the Government, whether or not the discretion involved be abused." § 2680(a). Although the Supreme Court has addressed the discretionary function exception on several occasions, it remains difficult to apply to concrete situations. For a critique of the exception and the way the Supreme Court has interpreted it, see Mark C. Niles, "*Nothing But Mischief": The Federal Tort Claims Act and the Scope of Discretionary Immunity,* 54 ADMIN. L. REV. 1275, 1315–35 (2002).

High-level policy judgments about how to implement a regulatory program fall within the discretionary function exception. The more difficult problem is whether actions taken at the operational level are discretionary functions. If a government employee took action that was not permissible under a statute or regulation, the government cannot claim that a discretionary function was involved. The key issue is whether a discretionary action involved policy judgment. *United States v. Gaubert,* 499 U.S. 315 (1991), held that the discretionary function exception applied to the actions of managers appointed by a federal agency to run an insolvent bank. These managers were permitted by agency policy to exercise judgment, and these judgments are grounded in regulatory policy.

Gaubert stated: "When established governmental policy, as expressed or implied by statute, regulation, or agency guidelines, allows a Government agent to exercise discretion, it must be presumed that the agent's acts are grounded in policy when exercising that discretion. For a complaint to survive a motion to dismiss, it must allege facts which would support a finding that the challenged actions are not the kind of conduct that can be said to be grounded in the policy of the regulatory regime. The focus of the inquiry is not on the agent's subjective intent in exercising the discretion conferred by statute or regulation, but on the nature of the actions taken and on whether they are susceptible to policy analysis." *Id.* at 324–25.

Gaubert noted that there are some obviously discretionary acts performed by government agents that are not within the discretionary function exception because these acts cannot be said to be based on the purposes that the regulatory regime seeks to accomplish. For example, if one of the banking officials negligently drove a car on a mission connected with his official duties and caused an accident, the exception would not apply. "Although driving requires the constant exercise of discretion, the official's decisions in exercising that discretion can hardly be said to be grounded in regulatory policy." *Id.* at 325 n.7.

§ 10.2.1b   State and Local Government Liability

State court actions. Traditionally, state government was completely immune from tort liability. Local government was immune from liability arising out of "governmental" functions but liable for claims arising out of "proprietary" functions. Sometimes the governmental/proprietary distinction was changed into a discretionary/ministerial distinction (similar to that in the FTCA). Although it is easy to classify many functions as either "governmental" or "proprietary" (it is "governmental" to fight fires, "proprietary" to operate a bus company), the distinction gave rise to a vast and confusing body of case law. The governmental/proprietary distinction was rejected by the United States Supreme Court in construing the discretionary function exception of the FTCA. *Indian Towing Co. v. United States,* 350 U.S. 61 (1955).

In the great majority of states (around 40), statutes have rendered state and local government vicariously liable for most torts committed by government employees. Most of the states have exceptions parallel to those in the FTCA. Many have additional exceptions such as action caused by reliance on statutes, denial or revocation of a license, or the plan or design of public improvements. *See* Lawrence Rosenthal, *A Theory of Governmental Damages Liability: Torts, Constitutional Torts, and Takings,* 9 U. PA. J. CONST. L. 797, 806 (2007). Some states impose a cap on liability (apparently to limit exposure to judgments in excess of insurance policy limits). As under the FTCA, courts and legislatures struggle to define the circumstances in which government is different from the private sector and thus to carve out some remaining sphere of immunity. *See, e.g., Kentucky Dep't of Banking & Securities v. Brown,* 605 S.W.2d 497 (Ky. 1980) (state is not liable for negligence of bank examiners in failing to detect bank fraud, since bank auditing has no private sector counterpart).

Federal court actions. The Eleventh Amendment deprives federal courts of jurisdiction over suits against a state. It applies both to actions seeking damages and those seeking non-monetary relief. The Eleventh Amendment does not provide immunity to *local* government entities— only to states. *Mt. Healthy City School Dist. v. Doyle,* 429 U.S. 274 (1977).

The Eleventh Amendment does not preclude a federal court from granting *injunctive* relief against a state *official* (as opposed to the state itself), if the official's authority is based upon an unconstitutional statute or if the official's action is otherwise contrary to federal law. *Ex parte Young,* 209 U.S. 123 (1908). For example, a phone company was permitted to sue the members of the Maryland Public Service Commission for injunctive relief because the Commission compelled the company to provide services to its competitor, allegedly in violation of federal law. *Verizon Maryland Inc. v. Public Service Comm'n of Maryland*, 535 U.S. 635 (2002). Nor does the Eleventh Amendment preclude, in most cases, actions against officials in their *individual* capacity (discussed below).

Congress can override the Eleventh Amendment by enacting a statute enacted under the authority of section five of the Fourteenth Amendment, but only if its intention to do so is unmistakably clear. The power to override the Eleventh Amendment extends only to measures that remedy or deter violations of rights *already* guaranteed by the Fourteenth Amendment. In addition, "there must be a congruence and proportionality between the injury to be prevented or remedied and the means adopted to that end." *Kimel v. Florida Bd. of Regents*, 528 U.S. 62 (2000).

Congress cannot override state sovereign immunity by enacting private rights of action under the Commerce Clause. *Seminole Tribe of Florida v. Florida*, 517 U.S. 44 (1996). Indeed, the Court has ruled that state sovereign immunity is a fundamental (though not expressly stated) constitutional principle that is broader than the Eleventh Amendment. For that reason, Congress lacks power to authorize actions against states *even in state courts,* a doctrine that obviously does not rely on the Eleventh Amendment. *Alden v. Maine,* 527 U.S. 706 (1999). However, these cases recognize an important exception: state sovereign immunity does not extend to an action by *the federal government* against a state, only to actions brought by non-governmental entities.

The *Seminole* rule also applies to cases brought against states in federal administrative agencies. *FMC v. South Carolina State Ports Auth.,* 535 U.S. 743 (2002). A federal statute allows shipping companies to bring an action in the Federal Maritime Commission (FMC) against ports that engage in illegal discrimination. Such cases are heard by ALJs, and the agency heads make the final agency decision. In the *South Carolina* case, a private cruise line pursued a discrimination action against the state before the FMC. The Court held that Congress lacks power to create a right of action by a private party against a state in an administrative agency.

In dissent, Justice Breyer argued that FMC proceedings should be considered federal government enforcement actions rather than private enforcement. (As noted above, state sovereign immunity does not apply to actions brought by the federal government against a state.) The FMC's decision is not self-enforcing; normally the Attorney General goes to federal court to enforce the FMC's decision. If the state seeks judicial review, it sues the federal government in court. Beyond this, Breyer argued that the decision departs from consistent constitutional interpretations that empower the government to deal with changing social, economic and technological conditions.

§ 10.2.2   TORT LIABILITY OF OFFICIALS

Officials may commit common law torts or constitutional torts (meaning actions that violate the Constitution but are not otherwise tortious). If a federal official acting within the scope of employment is charged with a common law tort, the Westfall Act requires that the action against the individual be dismissed. Such actions must be brought against the United States under the FTCA. See 28 U.S.C. § 2679(b)(1), (d)(1). However, if the official is charged with a constitutional tort, or if the official acted outside the scope of employment, the Westfall Act does not apply and the tort action against the official can proceed. *Id.* § 2679(b)(2). State law on this issue varies greatly but in many states any tort action brought against a state official is dismissed and the state is substituted as the defendant.

§ 10.2.2a   Bases of Liability for Constitutional Torts

Section 1983 (which was enacted in 1871) makes state and local government officials liable for actions that violate rights protected under the federal constitution *or* federal statutes. 42 U.S.C. § 1983. Section 1983 suits can be brought in state or federal courts. Such suits can be brought against local government entities (but not state government entities). A prevailing party under § 1983 is entitled to compensatory damages, to injunctive relief, to punitive damages from individual (but not governmental) defendants, and to reasonable attorney's fees. 42 U.S.C. § 1988.

There is no statute parallel to § 1983 that makes *federal officials* personally liable for constitutional or statutory violations. However, the Supreme Court has filled that gap. In *Bivens v. Six Unknown Named Agents of Federal Bureau of Narcotics,* 403 U.S. 388 (1971), the Court held that a right of action arises from the Fourth Amendment. That right permits the victims of an unlawful search and seizure to sue the responsible federal law enforcement officials for damages.

At the same time, the Court has vacillated in applying *Bivens,* holding that it does not apply in cases where there are "special factors counseling hesitation." For example, social security disability recipients were denied a *Bivens* remedy, despite allegations of due process violations, because they already have extensive statutory rights. *Schweiker v. Chilicky,* 487 U.S. 412 (1988). Prisoners denied medical care in a private prison were denied a *Bivens* remedy because state tort law provided adequate remedies. *Minneci v. Pollard,* 132 S.Ct. 617 (2012). In addition, even in the absence of alternative remedies, "a *Bivens* remedy is a subject of judgment: the federal courts must make the kind of remedial determination that is appropriate for a common-law tribunal, paying particular heed, however, to any special factors counseling hesitation before authorizing a new kind of federal litigation." *Wilkie v. Robbins*, 551 U.S. 537 (2007). *Wilkie* refused to recognize a *Bivens* claim against federal officials for retaliating against a landowner who refused to grant an easement to the government. Although sympathetic, the majority felt that it could not frame a judicial standard that would avoid an onslaught of new *Bivens* claims in the federal courts.

§ 10.2.2b   Immunity from Liability

Courts have worked out elaborate doctrines of both qualified and absolute immunity from constitutional tort liability in light of two rationales: (1) the injustice of subjecting to liability officers required by their jobs to exercise discretion, and (2) the danger that the threat of such liability would deter them from doing their jobs decisively. *Scheuer v. Rhodes*, 416 U.S. 232 (1974).

The leading federal authority on immunity of officials from constitutional tort liability is *Butz v. Economou*, 438 U.S. 478 (1978). That case involved an action for constitutional tort (under *Bivens*) against officials of the Department of Agriculture (USDA). Economou, a regulated commodity broker, complained that USDA had revoked his license without due process and in retaliation for his exercise of First Amendment rights. The case has three holdings:

(i) Agency prosecutors and adjudicators, including ALJs, are entitled to *absolute* immunity from damage suits (like judges and criminal prosecutors).

(ii) Other law enforcement officials (including the heads of agencies) have only *qualified* immunity from damage suits (defined below).

(iii) The rules of qualified immunity are the same in actions against state officials under § 1983 and against federal officials under *Bivens*.

The *Butz* decision also recognized that officials charged with *common law torts*, and acting within the scope of their authority, enjoy absolute immunity. This reflected prior law. *Barr v. Matteo*, 360 U.S. 564 (1959) (agency head who issued defamatory press release within the scope of his employment had absolute immunity). Today, this holding is less important because of the Westfall Act mentioned above—common law tort actions against officials are dismissed and the United States is substituted as a defendant. At that point, the various defenses under the FTCA come into play.

The President enjoys *absolute* immunity from damage actions. Presidential aides have absolute immunity in connection with highly sensitive activity. *Nixon v. Fitzgerald,* 457 U.S. 731 (1982); *Harlow v.*

Fitzgerald, 457 U.S. 800 (1982). Members of Congress enjoy immunity for actions in a legislative capacity under the Speech and Debate Clause (Art. I, § 6) and state legislators have comparable immunity. *Tenney v. Brandhove,* 341 U.S. 367 (1951). Legislative immunity probably extends to agency officials engaged in rulemaking. *Redwood Village Partnership, Inc. v. Graham,* 26 F.3d 839 (8th Cir. 1994).

Other officials whose actions violated constitutional norms are entitled only to *qualified immunity.* Officials with qualified immunity are personally liable only if the right that was violated was "clearly established," meaning that "it would be clear to a reasonable officer that his conduct was unlawful in the situation he confronted." *Saucier v. Katz,* 533 U.S. 194 (2001). This test is objective, meaning that it does not matter whether officials are even aware of the limitation or whether they acted "maliciously." *Harlow v. Fitzgerald,* 457 U.S. 800 (1982); *Davis v. Scherer,* 468 U.S. 183 (1984). An objective test makes it easier to resolve cases quickly on summary judgment, since the defendant's "malice" or actual knowledge of constitutional law is not in issue.

Moreover, government officials are not vicariously liable for constitutional violations committed by their subordinates. The plaintiff must plead and prove that the defendants personally engaged in constitutionally prohibited actions. *Ashcroft v. Iqbal,* 556 U.S. 662 (2009). This case held that the plaintiff failed to allege specific facts showing that the Attorney General and FBI director personally ordered a roundup of Arab-Americans after 9/11 for the purpose of discriminating against them because of their religion or national origin. Consequently, the case had to be dismissed before the plaintiffs could conduct discovery to find out whether the defendants actually acted with the forbidden purpose.

Problem. The Commission on Pornography was appointed to study the impact of pornography on society and to recommend legal means by which its spread might be contained. The Commission concluded that erotic photographs in nationally circulated magazines provoke assaults against women. Such photographs are not "obscene" and thus cannot legally be suppressed under the First Amendment. The Commission singled out *Penthouse* for special criticism. Its report recommended that local citizens institute boycotts against "pornographers" who sell *Penthouse.* It named several retail chains as "pornographers" and thus possible boycott targets.

Mercury Stores was on the list of possible targets. It ignored the report and continued to sell *Penthouse.* As a result it was subjected to picketing and boycotts in several states that caused it considerable damage. Mercury has asked for advice about suing the government or the Commission members for damages. Analyze the prospects for litigation if

(a) The Commission was appointed by the President of the United States;

(b) The Commission was appointed by a state governor.

Cf. Penthouse International, Ltd. v. Meese, 939 F.2d 1011 (D.C. Cir. 1991); *Playboy Enterprises, Inc. v. Meese*, 639 F. Supp. 581 (D.D.C. 1986).

§ 10.3 RECOVERY OF FEES

Like all litigation, administrative adjudication is time consuming and costly. A client must take account of those costs in deciding whether to challenge an adverse agency decision; many times the cost of litigation simply makes it impracticable to proceed. The cost of litigation is a particularly severe problem for public interest plaintiffs. Typically, public interest groups (such as environmental, civil rights, or consumer protection organizations) are underfunded. Even if many people agree with them, the free rider effect makes it difficult and costly to obtain voluntary contributions (free riders refuse to contribute since they can receive the benefits of the litigation whether they contribute or not). Yet to challenge agency action, such a group must be prepared for years of costly litigation against skilled, determined and well-funded adversaries.

For these reasons, a vitally important remedial issue is whether a prevailing party can obtain an award of attorney's fees (as well as other costs such as expert witness fees). Many statutory provisions authorize a court to require the losing party to pay the winner's fees. Such statutes may make it feasible to pursue litigation against the government that otherwise would be too costly. However, fee-shifting statutes could make agencies too cautious in taking regulatory action since they might have to absorb a substantial fee award from their existing budget if they lose. This subchapter explores a range of issues arising under fee-shifting statutes.

NOTES AND QUESTIONS

1. *The American rule.* In *Wilderness Society v. Morton*, 495 F.2d 1026 (D.C. Cir.1974), the court held that public interest environmental groups were entitled to an award of attorney's fees for their efforts (4500 hours of lawyers' time) in halting the trans-Alaska pipeline. The rationale was that they had served as a "private attorney general" by vindicating important environmental interests. See § 11.1.1 for discussion of the "private attorney general" theory in the law of standing to seek judicial review.

The Supreme Court reversed. *Alyeska Pipeline Service Co. v. Wilderness Society*, 421 U.S. 240 (1975). *Alyeska* held that under the "American rule," each party in litigation must bear its own attorneys' fees, absent a fee-shifting statute or some other exception (such as bad faith or creation of a common fund in a class action). There is no exception for suits brought by a private attorney general vindicating an important public interest.

However, not all states follow *Alyeska. See Serrano v. Priest,* 569 P.2d 1303 (Cal. 1977), which upheld an $800,000 fee award to public interest law firms that won a major case relating to the constitutionality of public school financing. *Serrano* was later codified by Cal. Code of Civ. Proc. § 1021.5, which provides that a court may award attorneys' fees to a successful party in any action that resulted in the enforcement of an important right affecting the public interest if (a) a significant benefit has been conferred on the general public or a large class of persons and (b) the necessity and financial burden of private enforcement make the award appropriate.

2. *Statutes providing for fees.* Numerous federal statutes provide that the losing party must pay the prevailing party's fees. For example, a prevailing plaintiff in a § 1983 action is entitled to recover attorneys' fees unless special circumstances render an award unjust. 42 U.S.C. § 1988. (*See* § 10.2.2a for discussion of § 1983 actions.)

Like a number of other environmental statutes, § 304 of the Clean Air Act provides for attorneys' fees if the trial court determines that an award is "appropriate." In *Western States Petroleum Ass'n v. EPA,* 87 F.3d 280, 286 (9th Cir. 1996), a group of plaintiffs consisting of air pollution dischargers successfully challenged an EPA regulation. The court decided that an award of attorney's fees was not "appropriate" because the plaintiffs did not contribute substantially to the goals of the Clean Air Act and were financially able to litigate without a fee award.

3. *Reasonable attorneys' fees.* To shift attorney fees, the court must determine what a reasonable fee would be. Generally, fees are calculated by the "lodestar method," which requires a court to multiply the hours reasonably spent on a case by a reasonable hourly rate. The lodestar includes not only the cost of litigating the case but also the cost of litigating about a reasonable fee (so-called "fees on fees").

In all but rare and extraordinary cases, the attorney is limited to the lodestar amount, even if the attorney's services were superior and the client won an extraordinary victory. *Perdue v. Kenny A.,* 559 U.S. 542 (2010). The *Perdue* case was a class action brought on behalf of 3000 children in the Georgia foster care system. Plaintiffs claimed that deficiencies in that system abridged the constitutional and statutory rights of the children. After working roughly 30,000 hours on the case, the attorneys won an enormous victory on the children's behalf. The trial judge stated that the attorneys exhibited a "higher degree of skill, commitment, dedication and professionalism than the Court has seen displayed by the attorneys in any other case during its 27 years on the bench." The trial court awarded fees based on the lodestar of $6 million and enhanced them by 75%.

The Supreme Court overturned the enhancement in *Perdue,* holding that the lodestar calculation "cabins the discretion of trial judges, permits meaningful judicial review, and produces reasonably predictable results." This approach rules out an enhancement for the quality of the attorney's performance or the results obtained. The *Perdue* decision recognized only one kind of exception to its rule that fees cannot exceed the lodestar. The exception might arise in very lengthy cases in which counsel experienced a long delay in recovering its fee or in recovering expenses advanced in litigating the case. These enhancements would be measured strictly by the length of that delay times a reasonable interest rate. Four Justices dissented in *Perdue,* arguing that the trial court should have discretion to enhance the lodestar in extraordinary cases and that discretion to do so had not been abused in the *Perdue* case.

4. *Equal Access to Justice Act.* Under the Equal Access to Justice Act (EAJA), enacted in 1980 and expanded several times, Congress departed substantially from the American rule. EAJA provides that a prevailing party (other than the United States) is entitled to attorneys' fees and other expenses unless the government's position was "substantially justified" or special circumstances make an award unjust. More than 30 states have adopted similar provisions. Susan M. Olson, *How Much Access to Justice From State "Equal Access to Justice Acts"?,* 71 CHI.–KENT L. REV. 547 (1995).

EAJA consists of two related statutes: Under 5 U.S.C. § 504, an agency shall award fees and expenses to a prevailing party unless an ALJ finds that the agency's position was substantially justified. Section 504 covers the costs of a formal agency adjudication (other than ratemaking or granting a license) in which the government is represented by counsel. Section 504 is inapplicable to cases to which the APA adjudication provisions do not apply. *Ardestani v. INS,* 502 U.S. 129 (1991) (EAJA is inapplicable to deportation case because deportation hearings are not under the APA). (*See* § 3.1.1 for discussion of when the APA applies to adjudicated cases.)

Under 28 U.S.C. § 2412(d), a court shall award to a prevailing party fees and expenses incurred in any civil action (except a tort action) brought by or against the United States unless the court finds that the government's position was substantially justified. Section 2412(d) permits an award of fees incurred in the course of judicial review of agency action, regardless of whether the APA adjudication provisions applied at the agency level.

Both §§ 504 and 2412(d) permit awards only to parties who need assistance in litigating against the government. Broadly speaking, awards can be made only to an individual whose net worth did not exceed $2 million or to a business whose net worth did not exceed $7 million and which had not more than 500 employees. However, tax exempt charitable organizations (such as most public interest law firms) qualify regardless of their net worth. Small local government units also qualify. Should an award also be available to a trade association that has a $3.3 million budget and 36 employees, if its members include multi-billion dollar corporations? *See Texas Food Industry Ass'n v. Dep't of Agric.,* 81 F.3d 578 (5th Cir. 1996) (answering yes by 2–1 vote).

The amount that can be paid under EAJA includes reasonable attorney fees plus the cost of expert witnesses and paralegals and the costs of necessary studies. However, attorney fees cannot exceed $125 per hour (adjusted for inflation since 1996 when the $125 figure was established by statute). Even when increased for inflation, the $125 per hour figure is far below the amount currently charged by most lawyers. A recent case described the figure as "rather chintzy" but explained that Congress was reluctant about "forking over government money to people litigating against the government." *Matthew-Sheets v. Astrue,* 653 F.3d 560, 562 (7th Cir. 2011). This case suggests that the inflation adjustment is not automatic but that the attorney seeking fees must justify the reasonableness of the inflation-adjusted hourly rate.

The hourly figure can be adjusted upward if a special factor (such as limited availability of qualified attorneys for the proceedings involved) justifies a higher fee. The exception for "limited availability" applies only to attorneys with some distinctive knowledge or specialized skill, such as a specialty like patent law or knowledge of foreign law or language. *Pierce v. Underwood,* 487 U.S. 552 (1988).

Under both sections 504 and 2412, the government has the burden to show that its "position" (both its litigation position and its original action) was "substantially justified." "Substantially justified" means that the government's position had a "reasonable basis in both law and fact." *Pierce v. Underwood, supra.*

The government can sustain its burden to show that its position was substantially justified even if it lost the underlying case. For example, in *Bricks, Inc. v. EPA,* 426 F.3d 918 (7th Cir. 2005), the issue was whether a company's wetland was hydrologically connected to navigable waters (in which case the company violated the Clean Water Act by filling in the wetland without first securing a permit to do so). EPA's ALJ held that a violation had occurred, but the Environmental Appeals Board (EAB) reversed, finding that the EPA failed to prove the hydrological connection by a preponderance of the evidence. Nevertheless, the court held that EPA's position was substantially justified. EPA lost because EAB had doubts about the credibility and consistency of its evidence, but the case was not a "slam dunk" for the company, and the EPA prosecutors could not have predicted they would lose.

5.   *Fee awards when the agency settles.*   Most federal fee-shifting statutes provide for an award of fees only to a "prevailing party." Generally, a prevailing party is one who secured administrative or judicial relief by winning on the merits of at least one of its claims as the result of a judgment or a consent decree. *Buckhannon Board & Care Home, Inc. v. West Va. Dep't of Health and Human Resources,* 532 U.S. 598 (2001).

A party is not entitled to a fee award simply because its lawsuit brought about the desired effect through a *voluntary change* in defendant's conduct. In *Buckhannon,* the plaintiff filed suit under the Americans with Disabilities

Act, hoping to invalidate a state statute because it was preempted by federal law. The state legislature changed the statute, and the defendant moved to dismiss the lawsuit as moot. Although plaintiff's lawsuit was the "catalyst" for the legislative action, plaintiff was not a "prevailing party," because the change did not come about as the result of a judicial judgment or consent decree. Later decisions have applied *Buckhannon* to other federal fee-shifting statutes including the Equal Access to Justice Act, discussed in N.4.

Some authority indicates that *Buckhannon* is not applicable to statutes (discussed in N.2) allowing the award of fees "when appropriate" or which do not contain "prevailing party" language. For example, the Endangered Species Act (ESA) allows the court to award fees to "any party, whenever the court determines such award is appropriate." In *Ass'n of Cal. Water Agencies v. Evans*, 386 F.3d 879 (9th Cir. 2004), landowners sued in federal court in California, complaining about designation of certain streams as critical habitats for endangered species. Similar litigation in another circuit settled, which made the California litigation moot, so it was dismissed. The settlement secured the relief that the plaintiffs were seeking, so they sued to recover attorneys' fees under the catalyst theory. The court held that a fee award was "appropriate." It distinguished *Buckhannon* because ESA does not contain the "prevailing party" language that was construed in *Buckhannon*.

The *Buckhannon* rule may have perverse effects. It discourages the plaintiff from agreeing to a settlement offer that it might otherwise have accepted, because by settling rather than trying the case, the plaintiff loses the ability to seek attorney's fees. By the same token, it encourages the government defendant to engage in "strategic capitulation," meaning that after fighting the case, the government concedes defeat at the last moment to avoid liability for fees. When the government folds at the last minute (even after a trial but before the case is decided) the plaintiff is not treated as a "prevailing party." *See Goldstein v. Moatz*, 445 F.3d 747 (4th Cir. 2006), holding that there is no "tactical mooting" exception to *Buckhannon*.

6.   *Problem.* Assume the state of Monroe adopts provisions identical to EAJA and to Cal. Code of Civ. Proc. § 1021.5 (quoted in N.1).

The Monroe Civil Rights Act prohibits discrimination by landlords on the basis of race and sex. Your clients Mary and Bernice are lesbians who sought to rent an apartment from Ruth. Ruth refused to rent to them, stating that she did not feel they were financially responsible. However, Mary and Bernice believe that Ruth decided not to rent to them because she disapproves of their sexual orientation. They both have good jobs and believe there was no basis to question their financial responsibility. However, Mary went through bankruptcy three years ago.

After an adjudicatory hearing, the Monroe Civil Rights Commission (MCRC) ruled i) Ruth refused to rent to Ruth and Mary because she believed that Mary was not financially responsible; ii) the Civil Rights Act does not apply to discrimination on the basis of sexual orientation. On judicial review, a superior court judge ruled i) substantial evidence supported MCRC's ruling that Ruth's decision was based on concerns about Mary's financial responsibility; ii) the Civil Rights Act does apply to discrimination on the basis of sexual orientation.

Your fees in representing Mary and Bernice before the Commission total $15,000 (60 hours at $250 per hour). Your fees in representing them on judicial review total $10,000 (40 hours at $250 per hour). These fees were paid by the Monroe Gay Rights Action League. How much, if any, of these fees can MCRC be compelled to pay?

§ 10.4 PRECLUSION OF JUDICIAL REVIEW

Administrative action is presumed to be judicially reviewable, but this presumption can be rebutted. APA § 701(a)(1) provides: "This chapter applies . . . except to the extent that—(1) statutes preclude judicial review . . ." What happens if judicial review seems inconsistent with a statutory scheme, but the legislature did not explicitly preclude judicial review?

BOWEN V. MICHIGAN ACADEMY OF FAMILY PHYSICIANS
476 U.S. 667 (1986)

[Medicare Part A provides Social Security recipients with hospitalization insurance. Part B provides coverage for non-hospital medical procedures. The Department of Health and Human Services (HHS) adopted a regulation under Part B providing lower payments to allopathic family physicians than to other physicians. The issue was whether the Medicare Act precludes judicial review of this regulation. Section 1395ff of that Act provides for judicial review of adverse *eligibility* determinations under both Parts A and B, but it authorizes judicial review of *amount* determinations only under Part A. HHS argues that this omission means that courts cannot review regulations relating to the determination of amounts payable to Part B providers.]

STEVENS, J.:

. . . We begin with the strong presumption that Congress intends judicial review of administrative action. From the beginning "our cases [have established] that judicial review of a final agency action by an aggrieved person will not be cut off unless there is persuasive reason to believe that such was the purpose of Congress." *Abbott Laboratories v. Gardner,* 387 U.S. 136 (1967). In *Marbury v. Madison,* 5 U.S. 137 (1803), a case itself involving review of executive action, Chief Justice Marshall insisted that "[t]he very essence of civil liberty certainly consists in the right of every individual to claim the protection of the laws." . . .

Committees of both Houses of Congress have endorsed this view in undertaking the comprehensive rethinking of the place of administrative agencies in a regime of separate and divided powers that culminated in the passage of the Administrative Procedure Act (APA). . . . [The APA legislative history states that] Congress ordinarily intends that there be judicial review, and emphasized the clarity with which a contrary intent must be expressed:

> . . . To preclude judicial review under this bill a statute, if not specific in withholding such review, must upon its face give clear and convincing evidence of an intent to withhold it. The mere failure to provide specially by statute for judicial review is certainly no evidence of intent to withhold review.

This standard has been invoked time and again when considering whether the Secretary has discharged "the heavy burden of overcoming the strong presumption that Congress did not mean to prohibit all judicial review of his decision." *Dunlop v. Bachowski,* 421 U.S. 560 (1975).

Subject to constitutional constraints, Congress can, of course, make exceptions to the historic practice whereby courts review agency action. The presumption of judicial review is, after all, a presumption, and "like all presumptions used in interpreting statutes, may be overcome by," *inter alia,* "specific language or specific legislative history that is a reliable indicator of congressional intent," or a specific congressional intent to preclude judicial review that is "fairly discernible in the detail of the legislative scheme." *Block v. Community Nutrition Inst.,* 467 U.S. 340 (1984). . . .

Section 1395ff on its face is an explicit authorization of judicial review, not a bar. As a general matter, "[t]he mere fact that some acts are made reviewable should not suffice to support an implication of exclusion as to others. The right to review is too important to be excluded on such slender and indeterminate evidence of legislative intent." *Abbott Laboratories v. Gardner.*

In the Medicare program, however, the situation is somewhat more complex. . . . [I]ndividuals aggrieved by delayed or insufficient payment with respect to benefits payable under Part B are afforded an "opportunity for a fair hearing by the *carrier.*" In comparison . . . a similarly aggrieved individual under Part A is entitled "to a hearing thereon by the *Secretary* . . . and to judicial review."

"In the context of the statute's precisely drawn provisions," we held in *United States v. Erika, Inc.,* 456 U.S. 201 (1982), that the failure "to authorize further review for determinations of the amount of Part B awards . . . provides persuasive evidence that Congress deliberately intended to foreclose further review of such claims." Not limiting our consideration to the statutory text, we investigated the legislative history which "confirm[ed] this view," and disclosed a purpose to "avoid overloading the courts with trivial matters," "a consequence which would unduly ta[x]" the federal court system with "little real value" to be derived by participants in the program.

Respondents' federal-court challenge to the validity of the Secretary's regulation is not foreclosed by § 1395ff as we construed that provision in *Erika*. The reticulated statutory scheme . . . simply does not speak to challenges mounted against the *method* by which such amounts are to be determined rather than the *determinations* themselves. As the Secretary has made clear, "the legality, constitutional or otherwise, of any provision of the Act or regulations relevant to the Medicare Program" is not considered in a "fair hearing" held by a carrier to resolve a grievance related to a determination of the amount of a Part B award. As a result, an attack on the validity of a regulation is not the kind of administrative action that we described in *Erika* as an "amount determination" which decides "the amount of the Medicare payment to be made on a particular claim" and with respect to which the Act impliedly denies judicial review. . . .

[The Court also discussed § 1395ii, which states that § 405(h) of the Social Security Act applies to Medicare cases. The latter section precludes any federal court action against Social Security other than as provided in the Act.]

In light of Congress' express provision for carrier review of millions of what it characterized as "trivial" claims, it is implausible to think it intended that there be *no* forum to adjudicate statutory and constitutional challenges to regulations promulgated by the Secretary. The Government nevertheless maintains that this is precisely what Congress intended to accomplish. . . . [W]e will not indulge the Government's assumption that Congress contemplated review by carriers of "trivial" monetary claims, but intended no review at all of substantial statutory and constitutional challenges to the Secretary's administration of Part B of the Medicare program. This is an extreme position, and one we would be most reluctant to adopt without a showing of "clear and convincing evidence" to overcome the "strong presumption that Congress did not mean to prohibit all judicial review" of executive action. We ordinarily presume that Congress intends the executive to obey its statutory commands and, accordingly, that it expects the courts to grant relief when an executive agency violates such a command. That presumption has not been surmounted here.

NOTES AND QUESTIONS

1. *Implied preclusion.* In *United States v. Erika, Inc.,* 456 U.S. 201 (1982), the Court interpreted the same provisions that were at issue in *Michigan Academy,* holding that Congress *impliedly* precluded judicial review of Medicare's determination that it would pay only a certain amount

for kidney dialysis supplies used in Medicare Part B. How did the Court distinguish *Michigan Academy* from *Erika?*

2. *Interpreting preclusive statutes.* Courts frequently construe apparently preclusive statutory language to permit some form of review. Thus a statute providing that certain agency action is "final" is often read to permit review of the action on some grounds or by some means. *See, e.g., Shaughnessy v. Pedreiro,* 349 U.S. 48 (1955) ("shall be final" means final in administrative branch and is not intended to preclude judicial review). One commentator discerned some general patterns in these holdings:

> [T]he Court has been developing what might be considered a "common law of preclusion." A critical reading of recent case law . . . indicates that the Court tends to allow some issues to be precluded more readily than other issues. At the top of the scale . . . the presumption against preclusion of constitutional grievances against an agency is practically irrebuttable. The Court also has proved less willing to find preclusion in cases involving administrative rules than in cases involving agency adjudication, and less willing to foreclose legal challenges than factual ones, especially where the legal issues are not within the administering agency's expertise. At the bottom of the hierarchy are issues of fact and application of law to fact, which the Court allows to be precluded more readily than any others.
>
> In most of these cases, the Court also found technical grounds for reading the statutes to support these results; thus the Court's lawmaking was peripheral and somewhat covert. Yet these holdings clearly have been informed by practical judgments about the relative importance of judicial review of various kinds of issues. . . .

Ronald M. Levin, *Understanding Unreviewability in Administrative Law,* 74 MINN. L. REV. 689, 739–40 (1990).

Congress has attempted to preclude judicial review (either through direct appeals or habeas corpus) in a wide variety of situations involving application of the immigration laws, especially in cases of denial of discretionary relief to persons subject to deportation. For example, the REAL ID Act of 2005, 8 U.S.C. § 1159(b), allows direct review only of "constitutional claims or questions of law" arising out of deportation orders and cuts off habeas corpus review of such orders.

Another statute (the Immigration Reform and Immigrant Responsibility Act or IIRIRA) precludes review of discretionary deportation decisions by the Attorney General when a *statute* authorized the Attorney General to exercise discretion. In *Kucana v. Holder,* 558 U.S. 233 (2010), the Court held that IIRIRA did not preclude review of a discretionary decision authorized by a *regulation* rather than by a statute. It remarked that any lingering doubt on this score would be dispelled by a familiar principle of statutory construction: the presumption favoring judicial review of administrative action. When a statute is reasonably susceptible to divergent interpretation, we adopt the reading that accords with traditional understandings and basic principles: that executive determinations generally are subject to judicial review. We have consistently applied that interpretive guide to legislation regarding immigration, and particularly to questions concerning the preservation of federal-court jurisdiction. Because the presumption favoring interpretations of statutes to allow judicial review of administrative action is well settled, the Court assumes that Congress legislatives with knowledge of the presumption. It therefore takes clear and convincing evidence to dislodge the presumption. [Quotation marks and citations omitted.]

3. *Preclusion of constitutional claims.* Perhaps the most important language in *Michigan Academy* is its final footnote, which reads:

Our disposition avoids the "serious constitutional question" that would arise if we construed § 1395ii to deny a judicial forum for constitutional claims arising under Part B of the Medicare program. *Johnson v. Robison,* 415 U.S. 361 (1974). *See Yakus v. United States,* 321 U.S. 414 (1944); *St. Joseph Stock Yards Co. v. United States,* 298 U.S. 38, 84 (1936) (Brandeis, J., concurring); Gunther, *Congressional Power to Curtail Federal Court Jurisdiction: An Opinionated Guide to the Ongoing Debate,* 36 STAN. L .REV. 895, 921, n. 113 (1984) ("[A]ll agree that Congress cannot bar all remedies for enforcing federal constitutional rights"). Cf. Hart, *The Power of Congress to Limit the Jurisdiction of the Federal Courts: An Exercise in Dialectic,* 66 HARV. L. REV. 1362, 1378–79 (1953).

This footnote highlights an unresolved constitutional question: to what extent can Congress preclude judicial review of constitutional issues, either in the Supreme Court or in the lower federal courts? For example, could Congress preclude the federal courts from considering the constitutionality of state abortion statutes? Could it deny courts power to issue the writ of habeas corpus as a means to challenge deportation orders? As the *Michigan Academy* footnote suggests, the Court often avoids such issues by construing apparently unambiguous preclusion statutes to permit review of constitutional issues. In *Webster v. Doe,* 486 U.S. 592 (1988), for example, the Court held that a statute precluded judicial review of the merits of the CIA's decision to discharge an employee who was admittedly homosexual, but did not prevent review of his constitutional claims: "Where Congress intends to preclude judicial review of constitutional claims its intent to do so must be clear."

Justice Scalia's dissent in *Webster* argued strongly that Congress had foreclosed review of all of the plaintiff's claims, including those based on the Constitution, and Congress could properly do so. His argument was based on the fact that the Constitution leaves to Congress the creation of lower federal courts and thus, by inference, the jurisdiction of those courts. Art. III, § 1. Even as to the Supreme Court, Article III confers "appellate Jurisdiction, both as to Law and Fact, with such Exceptions, and under such Regulations as the Congress shall make." Art. III, § 2, cl. 2. Other scholars take issue with Scalia's view and argue that the Constitution prohibits Congress from precluding judicial review of constitutional issues, both in the lower federal courts, and in the Supreme Court's review of state court constitutional decisions. We cannot do justice to this debate here. *See, e.g.,* Richard H. Fallon, *Jurisdiction-Stripping Reconsidered,* 96 VA. L. REV. 1043 (2010); James E. Pfander, *Jurisdiction-Stripping and the Supreme Court's Power to Supervise Inferior Tribunals,* 78 TEX. L. REV. 1433 (2000).

4.   *Time limits on challenge to rules.* A number of statutes provide for review of rules only during a short period such as sixty days. As a result, persons against whom a rule is enforced may be unable to challenge the rule—even though they didn't even find out about it during the sixty-day period.

Courts typically interpret such statutes to permit the persons who are the subject of an enforcement action to raise substantive objections to the rule during the enforcement proceedings (such as that the agency lacked authority to adopt it). In addition, arguments that the rule doesn't apply to the challenger are always allowed, because they are not, strictly speaking, challenges to the *validity* of the rule. However, the courts generally do not allow such persons to raise procedural objections (such as the agency's failure to comply with APA notice-and-comment procedures). *Indep. Cmty. Bankers of Am. v. Board of Govs. of Federal Reserve System,* 195 F.3d 28 (D.C. Cir. 1999) (substantive attacks on rule considered); *JEM Broadcasting Co. v. FCC,* 22 F.3d 320 (D.C. Cir. 1994) (procedural attack rejected). See ACUS Recommendation 82–7, *Judicial Review of Rules in Enforcement Proceedings,* 47 Fed. Reg. 58,208 (1982); Ronald M. Levin, *Statutory Time Limits on Judicial Review of Rules: Verkuil Revisited,* 32 CARDOZO L. REV. 2203 (2011).

Sometimes, however, Congress not only imposes a time limit but explicitly prohibits the subject of an enforcement action from challenging the validity of a rule outside the statutory period, even in a criminal prosecution. The prototype for such statutes is *Yakus v. United States,* 321 U.S. 414 (1944), which involved regulations setting maximum prices for goods during wartime. The regulations could be challenged by an action brought in the Emergency Court of Appeals within sixty days after the regulation was promulgated, but the statute provided that persons who were criminally prosecuted for violating a price regulation could not question its validity.

Yakus was criminally charged with violating a regulation that set a ceiling price for meat. He had failed to challenge the regulation within sixty days of its adoption. Over a strong dissent by Justice Rutledge, the Court held that he could not challenge the regulation in his criminal trial. However, the majority reserved the question of whether Congress could preclude a *constitutional* challenge to the regulation. Should *Yakus* be treated as a precedent applicable only in a wartime emergency?

In *Adamo Wrecking Co. v. United States,* 434 U.S. 275 (1978), the Court considered a criminal statute that explicitly prohibited judicial review of EPA emission standards after a thirty-day period, even in later civil or criminal enforcement actions. The Court distinguished *Yakus* and allowed a criminal defendant to raise a limited challenge to the rule under which it was prosecuted. The defendant was charged with emitting an air pollutant in violation of an EPA emission standard. It was permitted to raise the defense that the rule in question was not an "emission standard" (but the Court stated that the defendant would not have been allowed to raise procedural objections to the rule or to claim it was arbitrary and capricious). In his concurring opinion, Justice Powell argued that Adamo would also have been allowed to raise constitutional challenges despite the preclusion statute. Powell also thought that *Yakus* should be limited to situations involving wartime emergencies.

One potential way to get around a statute that sets a deadline for filing for review of a rule is to petition the agency to repeal or amend the rule on the ground that the original rule violated the underlying statute. *See* APA § 553(e), which permits anyone to petition an agency to issue, amend, or repeal a rule. If the agency rejects the petition, the party could then seek judicial review of that action. Courts have not permitted this type of end run around preclusion statutes that *expressly* bar any judicial review after the statutory time limit runs out. *See American Road & Transp. Bldrs. Ass'n v. EPA,* 588 F.3d 1109, 1113 (D.C. Cir. 2009). They do allow it when the statutory language does not explicitly forbid review after the deadline. *Id.* at 1112. In the latter situation, the conflict with congressional expectations is less clear, and the presumption favoring reviewability controls.

Under § 503(a) of the 2010 MSAPA, procedural challenges of rules are barred two years after the effective date of the rule. However, the MSAPA imposes no time limit on non-procedural challenges.

5. *State law.* The states vary considerably in their approach to preclusion of judicial review. Some states allow the legislature to preclude review, apparently without any exceptions. *Delagorges v. Board of Educ.,* 410 A.2d 461 (Conn. 1979); *Appeal of K-Mart Corp.,* 654 P.2d 470 (Kan. 1982).

Some states allow only limited preclusion. *See, e.g., New York City Dep't of Envtl. Protection. v. New York City Civil Serv. Comm'n,* 579 N.E.2d 1385 (N.Y. 1991). In that case, a hearing officer ruled that a local government employee should be discharged for assault, but the Civil Service Commission reversed that decision. The employer appealed. A statute precluded review of Civil Service Commission decisions. The court held that the legislature could preclude review of the merits of an administrative decision (which were the only issues before the court). However, it also stated that the legislature could not preclude review of claims that the agency had acted illegally, unconstitutionally, or in excess of jurisdiction.

At the other extreme, constitutional provisions in some states require the courts to provide judicial review despite apparently preclusive statutes enacted by the legislature. Thus the Pennsylvania constitution and statutes guarantee the right of appeal to the courts from state and local adjudicatory decisions. Pa. Const. Art.5, § 9; 2 Pa. Stats. 701(a), 751. However, the right of appeal extends only to review of adjudicatory decisions, not rulemaking. *Concerned Citizens of Chestnut Hill Township v. Dep't of Envtl. Resources,* 632 A.2d 1 (Pa. Cmwlth. Ct. 1993). In Indiana and New Jersey, apparently no limits can be placed on the right of judicial review. *See Board of School Trustees v. Barnell,* 678 N.E.2d 799 (Ind. App. 1997); *Hirth v. City of Hoboken,* 766 A.2d 803 (N.J. App. Div. 2001).

6.   *Problem.* Monroe state employees are entitled to a pension if they are compelled to retire because of a permanent work-related disability. The Monroe Personnel Agency (MPA) adjudicates questions arising under the disability retirement program. The applicable statute provides that MPA decisions "are final and conclusive and are not subject to judicial review."

Joan claims that she is unable to continue working in her state job as a data analyst because of injuries to her wrists arising out of the repetitive motions of typing on a computer keyboard. Dr. Bruce, a physician in general practice appointed by MPA to examine Joan, filed a written report concluding that Joan's wrist injury was mild and would not prevent her from working as a data analyst (with some slight changes in the placement of her keyboard). He also stated that the injury would clear up by itself. Consequently, he concluded that Joan did not qualify for a pension.

Joan's lawyer requested Dr. Bruce to appear at the hearing but he declined to do so, saying he was too busy. MPA has subpoena power, but the ALJ refused to issue a subpoena because it was agency practice to rely on written physician reports. At the hearing, Joan presented testimony of two doctors who specialized in repetitive motion injuries. Both concluded that Joan's injury was disabling and permanent. Joan's counsel moved to exclude Dr. Bruce's report, but the ALJ denied the motion. The ALJ's decision rejected Joan's claim because he decided that Dr. Bruce's report was more persuasive than the testimony of Joan's physicians. MPA adopted the ALJ's decision.

Is MPA's decision judicially reviewable? *See Lindahl v. OPM,* 470 U.S. 768 (1985); *Czerkies v. United States Dep't of Labor,* 73 F.3d 1435 (7th Cir. 1996); *New York City Dep't of Envtl. Protec. v. New York City CSC,* 579 N.E.2d 1385 (N.Y. 1991).

§ 10.5   COMMITMENT TO AGENCY DISCRETION

Section 9.3 considered the scope of judicial review of an agency's exercise of discretion. You should review that material now. This section considers agency action that is unreviewable because it is "committed to agency discretion by law." APA § 701(a)(2). Thus the APA contemplates two kinds of agency discretion—that which is reviewable under APA § 706(2)(A) ("arbitrary, capricious, an abuse of discretion, or otherwise not in accordance with law") and that which is not reviewable at all.

HECKLER V. CHANEY
470 U.S. 821 (1985)

[Chaney was a prisoner sentenced to death by lethal injection under Texas law. He wrote to the Food and Drug Administration (FDA), alleging that the use of drugs for capital punishment violated the Food, Drug, and Cosmetic Act (FDCA), because such use had not been approved as "safe and effective." He petitioned the FDA to take enforcement action to prevent the violation. The FDA Commissioner refused to do so. He disagreed with Chaney's construction of the law and also relied on his discretion not to enforce the Act in cases where there is no serious danger to the public health or a blatant scheme to defraud. The lower court held that the FDA's refusal to take enforcement action was reviewable and an abuse of discretion.]

REHNQUIST, J.:

. . . [T]his case turns on the important question of the extent to which determinations by the FDA *not to exercise* its enforcement authority over the use of drugs in interstate commerce may be judicially reviewed. That decision in turn involves the construction of two separate but necessarily interrelated statutes, the APA and the FDCA.

The APA's comprehensive provisions for judicial review of "agency actions" are contained in 5 U.S.C. §§ 701–706. Any person "adversely affected or aggrieved" by agency action, see § 702, including a "failure to act," is entitled to "judicial review thereof," as long as the action is a "final agency action for which there is no other adequate remedy in a court," see § 704. The standards to be applied on review are governed by the provisions of § 706. But before any review at all may be had, a party must first clear the hurdle of § 701(a). That section provides that the chapter on judicial review "applies, according to the provisions thereof, except to the extent that—(1) statutes preclude judicial review; or (2) agency action is committed to agency discretion by law." Petitioner urges that the decision of the FDA to refuse enforcement is an action "committed to agency discretion by law" under § 701(a)(2).[2]

This Court has not had occasion to interpret this second exception in § 701(a) in any great detail. On its face, the section does not obviously lend itself to any particular construction; indeed, one might wonder what

---

[2] . . . Respondents have not challenged the statement that all they sought were certain enforcement actions, and this case therefore does not involve the question of agency discretion not to invoke rulemaking proceedings.

difference exists between § 701(a)(1) and § 701(a)(2). The former section seems easy in application; it requires construction of the substantive statute involved to determine whether Congress intended to preclude judicial review of certain decisions. . . . But one could read the language "committed to agency discretion *by law*" in § (a)(2) to require a similar inquiry. In addition, commentators have pointed out that construction of § (a)(2) is further complicated by the tension between a literal reading of § (a)(2), which exempts from judicial review those decisions committed to agency "discretion," and the primary scope of review prescribed by § 706(2)(A)—whether the agency's action was "arbitrary, capricious, or an *abuse of discretion.*" How is it, they ask, that an action committed to agency discretion can be unreviewable and yet courts still can review agency actions for abuse of that discretion? . . . [W]e think there is a proper construction of § (a)(2) which satisfies each of these concerns.

This Court first discussed § (a)(2) in *Citizens to Preserve Overton Park v. Volpe*, 401 U.S. 402 (1971). That case dealt with the Secretary of Transportation's approval of the building of an interstate highway through a park in Memphis, Tennessee. The relevant federal statute provided that the Secretary "shall not approve" any program or project using public parkland unless the Secretary first determined that no feasible alternatives were available. . . . After setting out the language of § 701(a), the Court stated:

> Similarly, the Secretary's decision here does not fall within the exception for action "committed to agency discretion." This is a very narrow exception. . . . The legislative history of the Administrative Procedure Act indicates that it is applicable in those rare instances where "statutes are drawn in such broad terms that in a given case there is no law to apply."

The above quote answers several of the questions raised by the language of § 701(a), although it raises others. First, it clearly separates the exception provided by § (a)(1) from the § (a)(2) exception. The former applies when Congress has expressed an intent to preclude judicial review. The latter applies in different circumstances; even where Congress has not affirmatively precluded review, review is not to be had if the statute is drawn so that a court would have no meaningful standard against which to judge the agency's exercise of discretion. In such a case, the statute ("law") can be taken to have "committed" the decisionmaking to the agency's judgment absolutely. This construction avoids conflict with the "abuse of discretion" standard of review in § 706—if no judicially manageable standards are available for judging how and when an agency should exercise its discretion then it is impossible to evaluate agency action for "abuse of discretion." In addition, this construction satisfies the principle of statutory construction [that every statutory clause should be given some effect], by identifying a separate class of cases to which § 701(a)(2) applies.

To this point our analysis does not differ significantly from that of the Court of Appeals. That court purported to apply the "no law to apply" standard of *Overton Park*. We disagree, however, with that court's insistence that the "narrow construction" of § (a)(2) required application of a presumption of reviewability even to an agency's decision not to undertake certain enforcement actions. Here we think the Court of Appeals broke with tradition, case law, and sound reasoning.

Overton Park did not involve an agency's refusal to take requested enforcement action. It involved an affirmative act of approval under a statute that set clear guidelines for determining when such approval should be given. Refusals to take enforcement steps generally involve precisely the opposite situation, and in that situation we think the presumption is that judicial review is not available. This Court has recognized on several occasions over many years that an agency's decision not to prosecute or enforce, whether through civil or criminal process, is a decision generally committed to an agency's absolute discretion. This recognition of the existence of discretion is attributable in no small part to the general unsuitability for judicial review of agency decisions to refuse enforcement.

The reasons for this general unsuitability are many. First, an agency decision not to enforce often involves a complicated balancing of a number of factors which are peculiarly within its expertise. Thus, the agency must not only assess whether a violation has occurred, but whether agency resources are best spent on this violation or another, whether the agency is likely to succeed if it acts, whether the particular enforcement action requested best fits the agency's overall policies, and indeed, whether the agency has enough resources to undertake the action at all. An agency generally cannot act against each technical violation of the statute it is charged with enforcing. The agency is far better equipped than the courts to deal with the many variables involved in the proper ordering of its priorities. Similar concerns animate the principles of administrative law that courts generally will defer to an agency's construction of the statute it is charged with implementing, and to the procedures it adopts for implementing that statute.

In addition to these administrative concerns, we note that when an agency refuses to act it generally does not exercise its *coercive* power over an individual's liberty or property rights, and thus does not infringe upon areas that courts often are called upon to protect. Similarly, when an agency *does* act to enforce, that action itself provides a focus for judicial review, inasmuch as the agency must have exercised its power in some manner. The action at least can be reviewed to determine whether the agency exceeded its statutory powers. Finally, we recognize that an agency's refusal to institute proceedings shares to some extent the characteristics of the decision of a prosecutor in the Executive Branch not to indict—a decision which has long been regarded as the special province of the Executive Branch, inasmuch as it is the executive who is charged by the Constitution to "take care that the Laws be faithfully executed." U.S. Const., Art. II, § 3.

We of course only list the above concerns to facilitate understanding of our conclusion that an agency's decision not to take enforcement action should be presumed immune from judicial review under § 701(a)(2). For good reasons, such a decision has traditionally been "committed to agency discretion," and we believe that the Congress enacting the APA did not intend to alter that tradition. In so stating, we emphasize that the decision is only presumptively unreviewable; the presumption may be rebutted where the substantive statute has provided guidelines for the agency to follow in exercising its enforcement powers.[4] Thus, in establishing this presumption in the APA, Congress did not set agencies free to disregard legislative direction in the statutory scheme that the agency administers. Congress may limit an agency's exercise of enforcement power if it wishes, either by setting substantive priorities, or by otherwise circumscribing an agency's power to discriminate among issues or cases it will pursue. . . .

[The Court referred to *Dunlop v. Bachowski*, 421 U.S. 560 (1975).] The statute in that case provided that the Secretary of Labor "shall" sue to set aside a union election "if he finds probable cause to believe that a violation . . . has occurred." Thus, the statute being administered quite clearly withdrew discretion from the agency and provided guidelines for exercise of its enforcement power. [In contrast, the FDCA's] general provision for enforcement, § 372, provides only that "the [Commissioner] is *authorized* to conduct examinations and investigations. . . ."

[The Court of Appeals placed considerable weight on an FDA policy statement that seemed to constrain enforcement discretion. However,] the statement was attached to a rule that was never adopted. Whatever force such a statement might have, and leaving to one side the problem of whether an agency's rules might under certain circumstances provide courts with adequate guidelines for informed judicial review of decisions not to enforce, we do not think the language of the agency's "policy

---

4   We do not have in this case a refusal by the agency to institute proceedings based solely on the belief that it lacks jurisdiction. Nor do we have a situation where it could justifiably be found that the agency has "consciously and expressly adopted a general policy" that is so extreme as to amount to an abdication of its statutory responsibilities. See, *e.g., Adams v. Richardson,* 480 F.2d 1159 ([D.C. Cir.] 1973) (en banc). Although we express no opinion on whether such decisions would be unreviewable under § 701(a)(2), we note that in those situations the statute conferring authority on the agency might indicate that such decisions were not "committed to agency discretion."

statement" can plausibly be read to override the agency's express assertion of unreviewable discretion contained in [a separate] rule.

. . . The FDA's decision not to take the enforcement actions requested by respondents is therefore not subject to judicial review under the APA. The general exception to reviewability provided by § 701(a)(2) for action "committed to agency discretion" remains a narrow one, see *Overton Park,* but within that exception are included agency refusals to institute investigative or enforcement proceedings, unless Congress has indicated otherwise. In so holding, we essentially leave to Congress, and not to the courts, the decision as to whether an agency's refusal to institute proceedings should be judicially reviewable. No colorable claim is made in this case that the agency's refusal to institute proceedings violated any constitutional rights of respondents, and we do not address the issue that would be raised in such a case. Cf. *Johnson v. Robison,* 415 U.S. 361 (1974); *Yick Wo v. Hopkins,* 118 U.S. 356 (1886).

The fact that the drugs involved in this case are ultimately to be used in imposing the death penalty must not lead this Court or other courts to import profound differences of opinion over the meaning of the Eighth Amendment to the United States Constitution into the domain of administrative law. *Reversed.*

MARSHALL, J., concurring in the judgment.

. . . [R]efusals to enforce, like other agency actions, are reviewable in the absence of a "clear and convincing" congressional intent to the contrary, but . . . such refusals warrant deference when, as in this case, there is nothing to suggest that an agency with enforcement discretion has abused that discretion. . . . [Justice Brennan concurred in the majority opinion but wrote briefly to point out the numerous issues left open in that opinion.]

NOTES AND QUESTIONS

1.   *Heckler v. Cheney—the sequel.* In *Cheney,* the relevant statute left it up to the FDA to decide whether to take enforcement action against a misbranded or unapproved drug. The Court held that the FDA's decision not to take enforcement action against drugs used for lethal injection was committed to agency discretion and thus unreviewable.

The conventional protocol for lethal injection requires three drugs. The first is an anesthetic called sodium thiopental. In 2009, U.S. companies stopped making sodium thiopental. The drug is made in Britain by Dream Pharma Ltd. States that need the drug for administering lethal injection have to import it. The drug has never been approved by the FDA and Dream Pharma is unlicensed. The statute (21 U.S.C. § 381(a)) provides that misbranded or unapproved drugs, or drugs made by an unlicensed manufacturer, *shall* be refused admission into the U.S.

Several death row prisoners sought an injunction to prevent the FDA from allowing importation of sodium thiopental. The district court granted the injunction and the D.C. Circuit affirmed. *Cook v. FDA,* 733 F.3d 1 (D.C. Cir. 2013). The court distinguished *Cheney* because the statute in question gives the FDA no discretion to allow importation of the drugs. As a result of the *Cook* case, states wishing to conduct execution by lethal injection have turned to other drugs that have less of a track record and, in some cases, questionable legal status.

2.   *The expanding circle.* Although the *Overton Park* decision (quoted in *Heckler v. Chaney*) stated that the § 701(a)(2) exception is "very narrow," the Supreme Court has periodically broadened it. In addition to the *Chaney* decision, the Court held the following decisions are committed to agency discretion:

•   An agency's decision not to continue to fund a health program out of its lump sum appropriation. *Lincoln v. Vigil,* 508 U.S. 182 (1993).

•   An agency's refusal to reconsider its own decision. *ICC v. Brotherhood of Locomotive Engineers,* 482 U.S. 270 (1987).

•   The CIA director's decision to terminate an employee who was an admitted homosexual. The director, who gave no reasons, acted under a statute providing that "The [CIA] Director may, in his discretion, terminate the employment of any officer or employee of the Agency whenever he shall deem such termination necessary or advisable in the interests of the United States . . ." *Webster v. Doe,* 486 U.S. 592 (1988), also discussed in § 10.4.

•   The President's decision to accept or reject a list of military base closings proposed to him by the Defense Base Closure and Realignment Commission. *Dalton v. Specter,* 512 U.S. 1247 (1994).

3.   *No law to apply.* In *Overton Park,* the Court stated that action is committed to agency discretion only when "statutes are drawn in such broad terms that in a given case there is no law to apply." Similarly, *Chaney* states that action is unreviewable if a "statute is drawn so that a court would have no meaningful standard against which to judge the agency's exercise of discretion." In *Webster v. Doe, supra,* the Court emphasized the word "deem" in the statute relating to discharge of CIA employees:

> This standard fairly exudes deference to the Director, and appears to us to foreclose the application of any meaningful judicial standard of review. Short of permitting cross-examination of the Director concerning his views of the Nation's security and whether the discharged employee was inimical to those interests, we see no basis on which a reviewing court could properly assess an Agency termination decision.

However, the issue of whether agency action is "committed to agency discretion" is partly a policy question, not simply a matter of whether there is "law to apply" or whether the statute uses verbs like "deem." As it did in *Chaney,* the Court typically offers pragmatic and policy reasons for its conclusion. In *Webster v. Doe*, for example, the Court relied on the entire structure of the Act and the peculiar need for protecting intelligence sources and assuring the reliability and trustworthiness of CIA employees. Recall, however, as discussed in § 10.4 N.3, that the Court also held that the CIA's decision *was* reviewable on *constitutional* grounds.

Justice Scalia's concurring opinion in *Webster* criticizes the "law to apply" test:

> The key to understanding the "committed to agency discretion *by law*" provision of § 701(a)(2) lies in contrasting it with the "*statutes* preclude judicial review" provision of § 701(a)(1). Why "statutes" for preclusion, but the much more general term "law" for commission to agency discretion? The answer is, as we implied in *Chaney,* that the latter was intended to refer to "the 'common law' of judicial review of agency action"—a body of jurisprudence that had marked out, with more or less precision, certain issues and certain areas that were beyond the range of judicial review. That jurisprudence included principles ranging from the "political question" doctrine, to sovereign immunity . . . to official immunity, to prudential limitations upon the courts' equitable powers, to what can be described no more precisely than a traditional respect for the functions of the other branches. . . .

> All this law, shaped over the course of centuries and still developing in its application to new contexts, cannot possibly be contained within the phrase "no law to apply." It is not surprising, then, that although the Court recites the test it does not really apply it. . . . It is not really true "that a court would have no meaningful standard against which to judge the agency's exercise of discretion . . ." The standard set forth in § 102(c) . . . "necessary or advisable in the interests of the United States," at least excludes dismissal out of personal vindictiveness, or because the Director wants to give the job to his cousin. Why, on the Court's theory, is respondent not entitled to assert the presence of such excesses, under the "abuse of discretion" standard of § 706?

For further criticism of *Overton Park*'s "no law to apply" test, see Ronald M. Levin, *Understanding Unreviewability in Administrative Law,* 74 MINN. L. REV. 689, 734–40 (1990).

4. *Review of enforcement decisions.* While the *Chaney* decision agreed with *Overton Park* that the exception in § 701(a)(2) is "very narrow" in cases of affirmative agency action, it held that an agency decision *not* to enforce the law is presumed unreviewable. What reasons does it give for this presumption? The opinion mentions several possible exceptions to the presumption. How many can you list? Why did Justice Rehnquist take such care to mention the issues he was *not* deciding?

In *Chaney,* the Court holds that Congress imposed no limits on the FDA's enforcement discretion. Is this delegation of power invalid? How would Chief Justice Rehnquist reconcile his concurring opinion in the *Benzene* case, § 7.2.1c, with his conclusion in *Chaney* that there was no law to apply so that the agency's inaction could not be reviewed?

Chaney articulated a presumption that an agency's refusal to take enforcement action is unreviewable, but the presumption can be rebutted "where the substantive statute has provided guidelines for the agency to follow in exercising its enforcement powers." *Dunlop v. Bachowski,* cited in the *Cheney* opinion, was an example of such a case. The statute provided that the Secretary of Labor "shall" sue to set aside a union election "if he finds probable cause to believe that a violation . . . has occurred."

However, subsequent case law suggests that even the use of the mandatory word "shall" does not necessarily rebut the presumption of unreviewability. In *Sierra Club v. Jackson,* 648 F.3d 848 (D.C. Cir. 2011), several utilities sought to construct power plants in an area of Kentucky that met federal air pollution standards (a so-called "attainment area"). The statute required the utilities to get a permit to do so. Kentucky issued the permits but because Kentucky's permitting statute did not meet federal requirements, these permits were not valid. The federal EPA declined to seek an injunction to block construction, and Sierra Club sought judicial review of the EPA's non-enforcement decision. The Clean Air Act provided: "The [EPA] Administrator *shall,* and a state may, take such measures, including issuance of an order, or seeking injunctive relief, as *necessary* to prevent the construction or modification of a major emitting facility proposed to be constructed" in an attainment area. The court decided that the word "necessary" in this statute created a situation in which there was "no law to apply" and refused to overturn the EPA's decision. Couldn't the court have read this section to require the EPA to take *some* action to prevent construction of the power plants?

5. *Refusal to make a rule.* Footnote 2 of the *Chaney* opinion reserved the question of whether an agency's decision not to engage in rulemaking is reviewable. The Court considered that issue in *Massachusetts v. EPA,* 549 U.S. 497 (2007) (also discussed in § 6.3). The relevant statute stated that the Administrator of EPA "shall by regulation prescribe" standards relating to air pollution caused by motor vehicles which "in his judgment" endangers public health. EPA rejected a petition to adopt regulations that would limit motor vehicle emission of greenhouse gasses. The Court determined that EPA's rejection of the rulemaking petition was reviewable:

> As we have repeated time and again, an agency has broad discretion to choose how best to marshal its limited resources and personnel to carry out its delegated responsibilities. That discretion is at its height when the agency decides not to bring an enforcement action. *Heckler v. Chaney.* Some debate remains, however, as to the

rigor with which we review an agency's denial of a petition for rulemaking.

There are key differences between a denial of a petition for rulemaking and an agency's decision not to initiate an enforcement action. In contrast to non-enforcement decisions, agency refusals to initiate rulemaking "are less frequent, more apt to involve legal as opposed to factual analysis, and subject to special formalities, including a public explanation." They moreover arise out of denials of petitions for rulemaking which (at least in the circumstances here) the affected party had an undoubted procedural right to file in the first instance. Refusals to promulgate rules are thus susceptible to judicial review, though such review is "extremely limited" and "highly deferential."

Despite the *Massachusetts* case, if the statute that delegates authority to the agency includes no standard that constrains the agency's decision whether or not to adopt a regulation, the courts cannot review the agency's rejection of a rulemaking petition. *See Conservancy of Southwest Fla. v. U.S. Fish & Wildlife Serv.*, 677 F.3d 1073 (11th Cir. 2012). In that case, the Fish and Wildlife Service rejected a petition that it adopt a rule that would designate a critical habitat for the endangered Florida panther. The statute provided: "Critical habitat may be established for those species listed [before 1978] as threatened or endangered species for which no critical habitat has heretofore been established. . . ." The combination of the permissive "may" and the lack of any standard that constrained the Service's discretion led the court to rule that the rejection of the petition was unreviewable. It was concerned that the decision to initiate rulemaking "typically involves a complex balancing of factors, such as the agency's priorities and the availability of resources, that the agency is better equipped than courts to undertake."

6. *Agency inaction and rights of initiation.* Plaintiffs who complain of an agency's refusal to enforce the law are likely to be within the class of beneficiaries of the statutory scheme, and agency inaction may occur because of political pressures from powerful groups not to take action. We pursue the issues relating to judicial review of agency inaction in § 10.6. Suppose your clients petition EPA to take enforcement action against a particular environmental hazard, but the agency refuses. *Chaney* usually shuts the door on judicial review of that decision. What other remedies should your clients consider? Here are some possibilities.

• Consider the various loopholes left by the *Chaney* decision. For example, does a statute or an agency rule impose standards on the agency's enforcement decision? Has the agency "consciously and expressly adopted a general policy that is so extreme as to amount to an abdication of its statutory responsibilities?"

• Did the agency's non-enforcement decision contain an erroneous legal interpretation? It is unclear to what extent courts will decide legal issues that arise in connection with attempted review of an agency's non-enforcement decision. *See Crowley Caribbean Transport, Inc. v. Peña*, 37 F.3d 671 (D.C. Cir. 1994), in which the court refused to carve out for review a legal issue buried in an individualized enforcement decision. *Crowley* relied on a Supreme Court decision holding that an agency's refusal to reconsider its prior decision was committed to agency discretion—and declining to review the legality of the agency's reasons for refusing to reconsider. *ICC v. Bhd. of Locomotive Eng'rs*, discussed above at N.1. *Crowley* suggested that it would have reached a different result if the agency had articulated its legal interpretation in a document that showed that the agency intended to apply it in a broad class of situations. Outside the D.C. Circuit, however, courts seem readier to review claims of legal error affecting a non-enforcement error, even if the *Crowley* test is not met. *See Montana Air Chapter No. 29 v. FLRA*, 898 F.2d 753, 756–57 (9th Cir. 1990).

• Try to cut EPA out of the picture by construing the statute to provide for a private right of action against the person creating the health hazard. Whether courts can or should imply private rights of action is discussed in § 11.2.5 N.4.

• Petition the agency to adopt a rule on the subject or a policy statement that would structure its discretion. See N.5, *supra.*

• Engage in political action—either through grass roots activism or lobbying the legislature to take corrective action.

7. *State law.* State law on the reviewability of discretionary action reflects many of the same tensions that appear in federal cases. Thus the Illinois Supreme Court states that it follows federal precedents on this issue (even though its judicial review statute contains no language about commitment to agency discretion). In *Hanrahan v. Williams*, 673 N.E.2d 251 (Ill. 1996), the court held that decisions by the parole board refusing to grant parole are not reviewable because the decision is committed to agency discretion. It stated that there were no criteria by which it could evaluate the agency decision—even though the statute in fact contained specific standards telling the board when to deny parole. The court noted that a parole decision is subjective and predictive and thus seems unsuitable for judicial review. But perhaps it also wanted to protect the courts from a wave of litigation brought by disappointed prisoners who have little to do but sit in their cells and draft legal documents.

In contrast, *Greer v. Illinois Housing Devel. Auth.*, 524 N.E.2d 561 (Ill. 1988), granted review of a decision by the Authority to provide financing to a low-income housing development. The plaintiffs complained that the development would contain only very low-income tenants, in violation of a statute that required the Authority to make sure that the development avoided "*undue* income homogeneity among the tenants." At another point, the statute said that the number of units and rental levels shall be determined in such a way that "in the *sole judgment* of the Authority" the benefits of its low-cost financing would reduce rents below market levels.

Despite the italicized language, the court decided that the financing decision was not committed to agency discretion and could be reviewed under the arbitrary and capricious standard. The court evidently thought that the case presented important issues of public policy that deserved review.

The judicial review provisions of the 2010 MSAPA contain an exception for statutory preclusion of review (see § 10.4) but no exception for review of discretionary decisions. Section 501(b) provides: "Except to the extent that a statute of this state other than this [act] limits or precludes judicial review, a person that meets the requirements of this [article] is entitled to judicial review of final agency action." The term "agency action" is broadly defined to include (A) the whole or part of an order or rule; (B) the failure to issue an order or rule; or (C) an agency's performing or failing to perform a duty, function, or activity or to make a determination required by law. § 102(4). Like the federal APA, the 2010 Model Act provides that the scope of judicial review includes whether "the agency action is arbitrary, capricious, an abuse of discretion, or otherwise not in accordance with law." § 508(a)(3)(C). Thus the Model Act suggests that a court must review agency action for abuse of discretion even when no source of law provides legal standards for the court to apply. For example, the Model Act might require review in the case of an agency that refuses to exercise enforcement discretion, as in *Heckler v. Chaney,* or a refusal to grant parole as in *Hanrahan v. Wilson.*

8.   *Problem.* The Farmers Home Administration (FmHA) is a federal agency that makes loans to farmers. Section 19 of FmHA's statute provides: "At the request of the borrower, the Secretary of Agriculture may permit the deferral of principal and interest payments on any outstanding loan, and may forego foreclosure of any such loan, for such period as the Secretary deems necessary, upon a showing that the borrower is temporarily unable to make payments on the loan due to circumstances beyond the borrower's control without impairing the borrower's standard of living." Legislative history of § 19 said: "The section is intended to broaden FmHA's authority to cope with today's problems and be of greater service to farmers and the rural community."

Mary failed to make payments of principal or interest on her $250,000 FmHA loan because a disastrous drought wiped out her crop. FmHA foreclosed the loan and sold her farm. Mary appeals from the judgment of foreclosure. She had never requested FmHA to defer payments or to forego foreclosure because she did not know about § 19 until after foreclosure was completed. FmHA has never used its authority under § 19 to defer payments or forego foreclosure because it believes that the program is permissive, not mandatory. It has never notified any borrowers about its authority under § 19.

Should the court affirm the judgment of foreclosure and, if not, what relief should it grant? Suppose FmHA did occasionally exercise its § 19 authority—but declined to do so in Mary's case, despite a timely request on her part. Would that decision be reviewable? See *United States v. Markgraf,* 736 F.2d 1179 (7th Cir. 1984).

§ 10.6 AGENCY INACTION AND DELAY

NORTON V. SOUTHERN UTAH WILDERNESS ALLIANCE
542 U.S. 55 (2004)

SCALIA, J.

In this case, we must decide whether the authority of a federal court under the Administrative Procedure Act (APA) to "compel agency action unlawfully withheld or unreasonably delayed," § 706(1), extends to the review of the United States Bureau of Land Management's stewardship of public lands under certain statutory provisions and its own planning documents.

I.

Almost half the State of Utah, about 23 million acres, is federal land administered by the Bureau of Land Management (BLM), an agency within the Department of Interior. For nearly 30 years, BLM's management of public lands has been governed by the Federal Land Policy and Management Act of 1976 (FLPMA), 43 U.S.C. § 1701 et seq., which established a policy in favor of retaining public lands for multiple use management. "Multiple use management" is a deceptively simple term that describes the enormously complicated task of striking a balance among the many competing uses to which land can be put, "including, but not limited to, recreation, range, timber, minerals, watershed, wildlife and fish, and [uses serving] natural scenic, scientific and historical values." A second management goal, "sustained yield," requires BLM to control depleting uses over time, so as to ensure a high level of valuable uses in the future. To these ends, FLPMA establishes a dual regime of inventory and planning. Sections 1711 and 1712, respectively, provide for a comprehensive, ongoing inventory of federal lands, and for a land use planning process that "project[s] present and future use," given the lands' inventoried characteristics.

Of course not all uses are compatible. Congress made the judgment that some lands should be set aside as wilderness at the expense of commercial and recreational uses. A pre-FLPMA enactment, the Wilderness Act of 1964, provides that designated wilderness areas, subject to certain exceptions, "shall [have] no commercial enterprise and no permanent road," no motorized vehicles, and no manmade structures. 16 U.S.C. § 1133(c). The designation of a wilderness area can be made only by Act of Congress. [The Secretary must also identify "wilderness study areas" (WSAs), roadless lands of 5,000 acres or more that possess "wilderness characteristics."] Until Congress acts one way or the other, FLPMA provides that "the Secretary shall continue to manage [WSAs] . . . in a manner so as not to impair the suitability of such areas for preservation as wilderness." . . .

Aside from identification of WSAs, the main tool that BLM employs to balance wilderness protection against other uses is a land use plan— what BLM regulations call a "resource management plan." Land use plans, adopted after notice and comment, are "designed to guide and control future management actions." Generally, a land use plan describes, for a particular area, allowable uses, goals for future condition of the land, and specific next steps. Under FLPMA, "[t]he Secretary shall manage the public lands under principles of multiple use and sustained yield, in accordance with the land use plans . . . when they are available."

Protection of wilderness has come into increasing conflict with another element of multiple use, recreational use of so-called off-road vehicles (ORVs), which include vehicles primarily designed for off-road use, such as lightweight, four-wheel "all-terrain vehicles," and vehicles capable of such use, such as sport utility vehicles. According to the United States Forest Service's most recent estimates, some 42 million Americans participate in off-road travel each year, more than double the number two decades ago. United States sales of all-terrain vehicles alone have roughly doubled in the past five years, reaching almost 900,000 in 2003. The use of ORVs on federal land has negative environmental consequences, including soil disruption and compaction, harassment of animals, and annoyance of wilderness lovers. Thus, BLM faces a classic land use dilemma of sharply inconsistent uses, in a context of scarce resources and congressional silence with respect to wilderness designation. . . .

[SUWA] filed this action in the United States District Court for Utah against petitioners BLM, its Director, and the Secretary. [It] sought declaratory and injunctive relief for BLM's failure to act to protect public lands in Utah from damage caused by ORV use. SUWA made [two] claims that are relevant here: (1) that BLM had violated its non-impairment obligation under § 1782(a) by allowing degradation in certain WSAs; (2) that BLM had failed to implement provisions in its land use plans relating to ORV use . . . SUWA contended that it could sue to remedy these [two] failures to act pursuant to the APA's provision of a cause of action to "compel agency action unlawfully withheld or unreasonably delayed." 5 U.S.C. § 706(1). [The District Court dismissed the claims but the 10th Circuit reversed]

II

[Both] claims at issue here involve assertions that BLM failed to take action with respect to ORV use that it was required to take. Failures to act are sometimes remediable under the APA, but not always. We begin by considering what limits the APA places upon judicial review of agency inaction.

The APA authorizes suit by "[a] person suffering legal wrong because of agency action, or adversely affected or aggrieved by agency action within the meaning of a relevant statute." § 702. Where no other statute provides a private right of action, the "agency action" complained of must be "final agency action." § 704. "Agency action" is defined in § 551(13) to include "the whole or a part of an agency rule, order, license, sanction, relief, or the equivalent or denial thereof, *or failure to act*." The APA provides relief for a failure to act in § 706(1): "The reviewing court shall . . . compel agency action unlawfully withheld or unreasonably delayed."

Sections 702, 704, and 706(1) all insist upon an "agency action," either as the action complained of (in §§ 702 and 704) or as the action to be compelled (in § 706(1)). The definition of that term begins with a list of five categories of decisions made or outcomes implemented by an agency—"agency rule, order, license, sanction [or] relief." § 551(13). All of those categories involve circumscribed, discrete agency actions, as their definitions make clear: "an agency statement of . . . future effect designed to implement, interpret, or prescribe law or policy" (rule); "a final disposition . . . in a matter other than rule making" (order); a "permit . . . or other form of permission" (license); a "prohibition . . . or taking [of] other compulsory or restrictive action" (sanction); or a "grant of money, assistance, license, authority," etc., or "recognition of a claim, right, immunity," etc., or "taking of other action on the application or petition of, and beneficial to, a person" (relief). §§ 551(4), (6), (8), (10), (11).

The terms following those five categories of agency action are not defined in the APA: "or the equivalent or denial thereof, or failure to act." § 551(13). But an "equivalent . . . thereof" must also be discrete (or it would not be equivalent), and a "denial thereof" must be the denial of a discrete listed action (and perhaps denial of a discrete equivalent).

The final term in the definition, "failure to act," is in our view properly understood as a failure to take an *agency action*—that is, a failure to take one of the agency actions (including their equivalents) earlier defined in § 551(13). Moreover, even without this equation of "act" with "agency action" the interpretive canon of *ejusdem generis* would attribute to the last item ("failure to act") the same characteristic of discreteness shared by all the preceding items. . . . A "failure to act" is not the same thing as a "denial." The latter is the agency's act of saying no to a request; the former is simply the omission of an action without formally rejecting a request—for example, the failure to promulgate a rule or take some decision by a statutory deadline. The important point is that a "failure to act" is properly understood to be limited, as are the other items in § 551(13), to a *discrete* action.

A second point central to the analysis of the present case is that the only agency action that can be compelled under the APA is action *legally required*. This limitation appears in § 706(1)'s authorization for courts to "compel agency action *unlawfully* withheld."[1] In this regard the APA carried forward the traditional practice prior to its passage, when judicial review was achieved through use of the so-called prerogative writs— principally writs of mandamus under the All Writs Act, 28 U.S.C. § 1651(a). The mandamus remedy was normally limited to enforcement of "a specific, unequivocal command . . ." [or] the ordering of a " 'precise, definite act . . . about which [an official] had no discretion whatever." As described in the Attorney General's Manual on the APA, a document whose reasoning we have often found persuasive, § 706(1) empowers a court only to compel an agency "to perform a ministerial or non-discretionary act," or "to take action upon a matter, without directing *how* it shall act."

Thus, a claim under § 706(1) can proceed only where a plaintiff asserts that an agency failed to take a *discrete* agency action that it is *required* to take. These limitations rule out several kinds of challenges. The limitation to discrete agency action precludes the kind of broad programmatic attack we rejected in *Lujan v. Nat'l Wildlife Fed'n,* 497 U.S. 871 (1990) [which held that BLM's "land withdrawal review program," involving the status of thousands of parcels of public lands, was not "agency action" that plaintiffs could challenge under § 706(2)].

The limitation to *required* agency action rules out judicial direction of even discrete agency action that is not demanded by law (which includes, of course, agency regulations that have the force of law). Thus, when an agency is compelled by law to act within a certain time period, but the manner of its action is left to the agency's discretion, a court can compel the agency to act, but has no power to specify what the action must be. . . .

III

A.   With these principles in mind, we turn to SUWA's first claim, that by permitting ORV use in certain WSAs, BLM violated its mandate to "continue to manage [WSAs] . . . in a manner so as not to impair the suitability of such areas for preservation as wilderness. . . ." Section 1782(c) is mandatory as to the object to be achieved, but it leaves BLM a great deal of discretion in deciding how to achieve it. It assuredly does not mandate, with the clarity necessary to support judicial action under § 706(1), the total exclusion of ORV use.

SUWA argues that § 1782 *does* contain a categorical imperative, namely the command to comply with the non-impairment mandate. It contends that a federal court could simply enter a general order

---

[1]   Of course, § 706(1) also authorizes courts to "compel agency action . . . unreasonably delayed"—but a delay cannot be unreasonable with respect to action that is not required.

compelling compliance with that mandate, without suggesting any particular manner of compliance. [However,] general deficiencies in compliance . . . lack the specificity requisite for agency action.

The principal purpose of the APA limitations we have discussed—and of the traditional limitations upon mandamus from which they were derived—is to protect agencies from undue judicial interference with their lawful discretion, and to avoid judicial entanglement in abstract policy disagreements which courts lack both expertise and information to resolve. If courts were empowered to enter general orders compelling compliance with broad statutory mandates, they would necessarily be empowered, as well, to determine whether compliance was achieved— which would mean that it would ultimately become the task of the supervising court, rather than the agency, to work out compliance with the broad statutory mandate, injecting the judge into day-to-day agency management. . . . The prospect of pervasive oversight by federal courts over the manner and pace of agency compliance with such congressional directives is not contemplated by the APA.

B.   SUWA's second claim is that BLM failed to comply with certain provisions in its land use plans, thus contravening the requirement that "[t]he Secretary shall manage the public lands . . . in accordance with the land use plans . . . when they are available." [SUWA] alleged that BLM had violated a variety of commitments in its land use plans, but over the course of the litigation these have been reduced to . . . one relating to . . . the 1990 ORV implementation plan for the Henry Mountains area, [namely] that "in light of damage from ORVs in the Factory Butte area," . . . "the [plan] obligated BLM to conduct an intensive ORV monitoring program." This claim is based upon the plan's statement that the Factory Butte area "will be monitored and closed if warranted." SUWA does not contest BLM's assertion in the court below that informal monitoring has taken place for some years, but it demands continuing implementation of a monitoring program. [The Court ruled that the statements in the plan merely indicated the agency's general intentions and were not legally enforceable commitments.]

. . . Quite unlike a specific statutory command requiring an agency to promulgate regulations by a certain date, a land use plan is generally a statement of priorities; it guides and constrains actions, but does not (at least in the usual case) prescribe them. It would be unreasonable to think that either Congress or the agency intended otherwise, since land use plans nationwide would commit the agency to actions far in the future, for which funds have not yet been appropriated . . .

Of course, an action called for in a plan may be compelled when the plan merely reiterates duties the agency is already obligated to perform, or perhaps when language in the plan itself creates a commitment binding on the agency. But allowing general enforcement of plan terms would lead to pervasive interference with BLM's own ordering of priorities. For example, a judicial decree compelling immediate preparation of all of the detailed plans called for in the San Rafael plan would divert BLM's energies from other projects throughout the country that are in fact more pressing. And while such a decree might please the environmental plaintiffs in the present case, it would ultimately operate to the detriment of sound environmental management. Its predictable consequence would be much vaguer plans from BLM in the future— making coordination with other agencies more difficult, and depriving the public of important information concerning the agency's long-range intentions.

We therefore hold that the Henry Mountains plan's statements to the effect that BLM will conduct "use supervision and monitoring" in designated areas—like other "will do" projections of agency action set forth in land use plans—are not a legally binding commitment enforceable under § 706(1). That being so, we find it unnecessary to consider whether the action envisioned by the statements is sufficiently discrete to be amenable to compulsion under the APA. . . .

The judgment of the Court of Appeals is reversed, and the case is remanded for further proceedings consistent with this opinion.

NOTES AND QUESTIONS

1. *Reviewability of an agency's failure to act.* The APA includes "failure to act" in its definition of "agency action." APA §§ 551(13). It allows a reviewing court to "compel agency action unlawfully withheld or unreasonably delayed." § 706(1). Clearly, therefore, an agency's failure to take action could be the subject of judicial review, as in *Massachusetts v. EPA*, discussed in §§ 6.3 and § 10.5 N.5, *supra*, which involved refusal to initiate a rulemaking process following a petition for rulemaking.

Under *SUWA*, an agency's failure to act is reviewable agency action only if it involves failure to take a "discrete" action that is legally "required." What does the court mean by "discrete" action? Are you convinced by the Court's construction of § 551(13) that "failure to act" refers only to "failure to take discrete action?" Why did BLM's failure to prevent ORV use within the WSA not meet the "agency action" test? Would the "agency action" test have been satisfied if SUWA requested BLM to ban ORV use in the WSA, and BLM refused to do it?

2. *Administrative delay.* What if BLM never got around to acting on SUWA's request to ban ORV use in the WSA? Under the APA, "within a reasonable time, each agency shall proceed to conclude a matter presented to it" and it requires a reviewing court to "compel agency action unlawfully withheld or unreasonably delayed." *See* APA §§ 555(b), 706(1).

A court asked to remedy agency foot-dragging faces a dilemma: an order to expedite one matter may delay other matters or force the agency to decide a matter before it is prepared to do so. After all, an agency has broad discretion with respect to the deployment of its limited resources. Thus a court should hesitate before imposing its own timing priorities.

In *Heckler v. Day*, 467 U.S. 104 (1984), a group of Vermont applicants for Social Security disability benefits brought a class action to force a speed-up in claims processing. In fact, administration of the disability program is characterized by agonizing delays. Recall *Mathews v. Eldridge*, § 2.3. The trial court ordered that the state agency complete its reconsideration of negative initial decisions within 90 days and that Social Security schedule hearings before ALJs within 90 days. In a 5–4 decision, the Supreme Court set the decision aside. While Congress was concerned about sluggish administration of the disability program, it had repeatedly rejected mandatory deadline schemes because deadlines might jeopardize the quality and uniformity of decisions. The Supreme Court deferred to that congressional judgment. Moreover, the Court observed, it made no sense to impose rigid deadlines in Vermont but not in other states, since Social Security might simply shift resources from other states to Vermont.

The leading case on judicial power to remedy agency delay is *Telecomm. Research and Action Center (TRAC) v. FCC*, 750 F.2d 70 (D.C. Cir. 1984). The *TRAC* decision cautioned that a rule of reason must be employed. If a statute contains a timetable for agency action, that provision might supply content for a judicial decision mandating that the agency follow the timetable. In addition, *TRAC* noted that delays are less tolerable if human health and welfare are at stake instead of money; the court must consider the effect of expediting review on agency activities of higher or competing priority; and the court must evaluate the interests prejudiced by delay. *TRAC* was an action to compel the FCC to decide the issue of the disposition of AT&T overcharges. Since the FCC assured the court that it was working diligently on the matter and had established deadlines, the court did not compel the agency to act, but it retained jurisdiction until final disposition, because the delay to date had been unjustifiable.

3. *Judicial review of resource allocation disputes.* In many cases of agency inaction or delay, the real issue is judicial reluctance to dictate an agency's priorities or resource allocations. In addition to *SUWA*, consider *Heckler v. Chaney* and *Lincoln v. Vigil* in § 10.5; *Heckler v. Day*, in N.2 above; *Lujan v. Defenders of Wildlife* in § 11.1; and *Lujan v. Nat'l Wildlife Fed'n*, which is discussed in the *SUWA* opinion. While courts are rightly cautious about reordering agency priorities, they must balance this reluctance against their obligation to enforce statutory commands (such as the non-impairment of WSAs, which was at issue in *SUWA*).

Are you convinced by the Court's contention that review of SUWA's claims would threaten "judicial entanglement in abstract policy disagreements which courts lack both expertise and information to resolve"?

Or that "allowing general enforcement of [land use] plan terms would lead to pervasive interference with BLM's own ordering of priorities" and "divert BLM's energies from other project throughout the country that are in fact more pressing"?

Was there a remedy that might have avoided entangling the court in the problem of ongoing forest management? Considering the political power of forty-two million ORV users and the ORV equipment manufacturers, was there a need for judicial involvement to safeguard the environmental interest in these potential wilderness lands? Note that continued ORV use can create a dirt road that renders the area unsuitable for designation as wilderness (since a wilderness area can have no roads).

For discussion of *SUWA,* see Eric Biber, *The Importance of Resource Allocation in Administrative Law: A Case Study of Judicial Review of Agency Inaction under the Administrative Procedure Act,* 60 ADMIN. L. REV. 1 (2008); Lisa Schultz Bressman, *Judicial Review of Agency Inaction: An Arbitrariness Approach,* 79 N.Y.U. L. REV. 1657, 1705–09 (2004); William Araiza, *In Praise of a Skeletal APA: Norton v. Southern Utah Wilderness Alliance, Judicial Remedies for Agency Inaction, and the Questionable Value of Amending the APA,* 56 ADMIN. L. REV. 979 (2004).

4.   *Problem.* City is undergoing substantial gentrification. Especially in the Kenwood neighborhood, younger, affluent home buyers are purchasing and improving older houses now occupied by ethnically diverse working class families. This has caused a sharp increase in rents. Last year the City Council adopted an ordinance that called on the Planning Department to conduct a study of the economic impact of gentrification and the steps that City should take to mitigate the hardships experienced by Kenwood renters. Joe, the mayor of City, has quietly instructed the Department to defer the study indefinitely, since Joe is in favor of the gentrification movement (which is producing an increase in tax revenues and a decline in crime). Joe's order was leaked to the press.

Gloria, an African-American resident of Kenwood, fears that her family will be driven out of the neighborhood by rising rents. They would probably have to move to an area that is much further from her job and that lacks many of the amenities of Kenwood. She has consulted you about the possibilities of getting some kind of court order that would require the Department to conduct the study. She lacks the resources to pay a fee. What is your advice? (Assume that state law follows federal law but that Gloria will have standing to sue under state law.)

CHAPTER 11

STANDING TO SEEK JUDICIAL REVIEW AND THE TIMING OF JUDICIAL REVIEW

■ ■ ■

This chapter considers several important obstacles to seeking judicial review. First, it addresses the issue of standing—can a particular plaintiff seek review? Second, it considers timing issues—has the plaintiff sought review prematurely?

§ 11.1 STANDING TO SEEK REVIEW

§ 11.1.1 BACKGROUND AND HISTORY OF STANDING LAW

A person seeking judicial review is usually the *object* of agency action, meaning that the agency has required the person to do or not do something or refused the person's application for a government benefit or license. For example, persons might seek judicial review of agency rules or orders that require them to pay money or cease and desist from a business practice or that deny an application for a license. Normally, a person who is the object of administrative action has no problem establishing standing to challenge that action.

However, standing becomes an issue when a person is harmed indirectly by agency action that regulates or fails to regulate someone else. Potential plaintiffs often claim that the action is unlawful because they were the intended *beneficiary* of a law that the government action allegedly violated. For example, suppose Agency A issues a license to B to open a bank. C, an existing bank in the same town, believes that B's license was granted unlawfully. However, C's standing to seek judicial review of Agency A's action is questionable. C suffers harm from unwanted competition, but the agency has not required C to do or not do anything.

Historically, most standing disputes arose out of cases of this sort. Under the traditional "legal interest" test, parties like C often lacked standing to sue. The "legal interest" test required a court to analyze whether a party would have a common law right to prevent the unwanted competition or other injury. Under our free market system, there is no right in tort, property, or contract law to be protected from competition;

consequently, plaintiffs like C lacked standing. Thus, in *Tennessee Electric Power Co. v. TVA*, 306 U.S. 118 (1939), private power companies wished to prevent the Tennessee Valley Authority (a federal agency) from competing with them. They contended that the Constitution does not allow the federal government to enter the power business. However, they lacked standing to raise this issue, because they had no common law right to be free from competition. Politically, this narrow approach to standing served the interests of Supreme Court Justices who wanted to protect New Deal legislation from challenges by activist judges.

"Statutory standing" was an exception to the "legal interest" test. In *FCC v. Sanders Brothers Radio Station*, 309 U.S. 470 (1940), the FCC granted a license to a radio station that would compete with one operated by Sanders. The Communications Act provided that anyone "aggrieved or whose interests were adversely affected" by an FCC licensing decision could seek review. Since Sanders was "aggrieved" or "adversely affected," it had standing to challenge the FCC's order. The case makes it clear that Congress has the power to confer standing on a competitor in order to promote the public interest in a correct application of federal law, even though the FCC was not required to take account of the interest of competitors. In effect, the statute deputized Sanders to serve as a "private attorney general."

Some cases also recognized statutory standing where Congress evidenced a specific intention to benefit the plaintiff's class. Thus *Hardin v. Kentucky Utilities Co.*, 390 U.S. 1 (1968), held that a competitor of TVA had standing to challenge its actions because Congress enacted a statute protecting such competitors.

The next two subchapters address modern standing law, first considering constitutional limitations on standing, then limitations that arise from statutes. As you read the numerous standing cases that follow, consider whether a particular standing decision is really a surrogate for a decision on the merits—are judges voting to grant or deny standing because they wish to decide, or to avoid, the underlying legal questions in the case?

§ 11.1.2   CONSTITUTIONAL STANDING DOCTRINES

In part, standing to sue in federal court is a constitutional doctrine, one of several access restrictions encompassed under the nebulous term "justiciability." Under Article III, a federal court can only entertain "cases" or "controversies." The case or controversy requirement means that a person seeking judicial assistance must have a sufficient stake in the dispute. Federal courts must resolve questions of Article III standing before reaching other issues, even if they could readily dismiss the case on the merits and thus avoid a difficult standing analysis. *Steel Co. v.*

Citizens for a Better Environment, 523 U.S. 83 (1998). As a result, federal cases that wrestle with the murky principles of standing law have proliferated.

LUJAN V. DEFENDERS OF WILDLIFE
504 U.S. 555 (1992)

SCALIA, J.:

[The Endangered Species Act (ESA) requires federal agencies to consult with the Secretary of the Interior to ensure that actions funded by the agency are unlikely to jeopardize the habitat of an endangered species. Plaintiff is an environmental organization. It challenges a rule promulgated by the Secretary of the Interior. The rule provides that funding agencies need not consult the Secretary as to actions outside the United States. As a result, the Agency for International Development (AID) is not required to consult with the Secretary about projects that might threaten the habitat of the Asian elephant and leopard in Sri Lanka and the Nile crocodile in Egypt.]

II

. . . Over the years, our cases have established that the irreducible constitutional minimum of standing contains three elements: First, the plaintiff must have suffered an "injury in fact"—an invasion of a legally-protected interest which is (a) concrete and particularized,[1] and (b) actual or imminent, not conjectural or hypothetical. Second, there must be a causal connection between the injury and the conduct complained of—the injury has to be fairly . . . traceable to the challenged action of the defendant, and not . . . the result of the independent action of some third party not before the court. Third, it must be likely, as opposed to merely speculative, that the injury will be redressed by a favorable decision. . . .

When the suit is one challenging the legality of government action or inaction, the nature and extent of facts that must be averred (at the summary judgment stage) or proved (at the trial stage) in order to establish standing depends considerably upon whether the plaintiff is himself an object of the action (or foregone action) at issue. If he is, there is ordinarily little question that the action or inaction has caused him injury, and that a judgment preventing or requiring the action will redress it. When, however, as in this case, a plaintiff's asserted injury arises from the government's allegedly unlawful regulation (or lack of regulation) of someone else, much more is needed. In that circumstance, causation and redressability ordinarily hinge on the response of the regulated (or regulable) third party to the government action or

---

[1] By particularized, we mean that the injury must affect the plaintiff in a personal and individual way.

inaction—and perhaps on the response of others as well. The existence of one or more of the essential elements of standing depends on the unfettered choices made by independent actors not before the courts and whose exercise of broad and legitimate discretion the courts cannot presume either to control or to predict, and it becomes the burden of the plaintiff to adduce facts showing that those choices have been or will be made in such manner as to produce causation and permit redressability of injury. . . .

III

We think the Court of Appeals failed to apply the foregoing principles in denying the Secretary's motion for summary judgment. Respondents had not made the requisite demonstration of (at least) injury and redressability.

A

Respondents' claim to injury is that the lack of consultation with respect to certain funded activities abroad "increas[es] the rate of extinction of endangered and threatened species." Of course, the desire to use or observe an animal species, even for purely aesthetic purposes, is undeniably a cognizable interest for purpose of standing. . . . But the "injury in fact" test requires more than an injury to a cognizable interest. It requires that the party seeking review be himself among the injured . . . To survive the Secretary's summary judgment motion, respondents had to submit affidavits or other evidence showing, through specific facts, not only that listed species were in fact being threatened by funded activities abroad, but also that one or more of respondents' members would thereby be "directly" affected apart from their "special interest in the subject."

With respect to this aspect of the case, the Court of Appeals focused on the affidavits of two Defenders' members—Joyce Kelly and Amy Skilbred. . . . Ms. Skilbred averred that she traveled to Sri Lanka in 1981 and "observed th[e] habitat" of "endangered species such as the Asian elephant and the leopard" at what is now the site of the Mahaweli Project funded by the Agency for International Development (AID), although she "was unable to see any of the endangered species;" "this development project," she continued, "will seriously reduce endangered, threatened, and endemic species habitat including areas that I visited [which] may severely shorten the future of these species;" that threat, she concluded, harmed her because she "intend[s] to return to Sri Lanka in the future and hope[s] to be more fortunate in spotting at least the endangered elephant and leopard." When Ms. Skilbred was asked at a subsequent deposition if and when she had any plans to return to Sri Lanka, she reiterated that "I intend to go back to Sri Lanka," but confessed that she had no current plans: "I don't know [when]. There is a civil war going on right now. I don't know. Not next year, I will say. In the future." [Ms. Kelly furnished similar allegations concerning her plans to observe the Nile crocodile.]

We shall assume for the sake of argument that these affidavits contain facts showing that certain agency-funded projects threaten listed species—though that is questionable. They plainly contain no facts, however, showing how damage to the species will produce "imminent" injury to Mss. Kelly and Skilbred. That the women "had visited" the areas of the projects before the projects commenced proves nothing. . . . And the affiants' profession of an "inten[t]" to return to the places they had visited before—where they will presumably, this time, be deprived of the opportunity to observe animals of the endangered species—is simply not enough. Such "some day" intentions—without any description of concrete plans, or indeed even any specification of when the some day will be—do not support a finding of the "actual or imminent" injury that our cases require.

Besides relying upon the Kelly and Skilbred affidavits, respondents propose a series of novel standing theories. The first, inelegantly styled "ecosystem nexus," proposes that any person who uses any part of a "contiguous ecosystem" adversely affected by a funded activity has standing even if the activity is located a great distance away. This approach, as the Court of Appeals correctly observed, is inconsistent with our opinion in *Lujan v. National Wildlife Federation*, which held that a plaintiff claiming injury from environmental damage must use the area affected by the challenged activity and not an area roughly "in the vicinity" of it. 497 U.S. 871, 887–889 (1990). . . .

Respondents' other theories are called, alas, the "animal nexus" approach, whereby anyone who has an interest in studying or seeing the endangered animals anywhere on the globe has standing; and the "vocational nexus" approach, under which anyone with a professional interest in such animals can sue. Under these theories, anyone who goes to see Asian elephants in the Bronx Zoo, and anyone who is a keeper of Asian elephants in the Bronx Zoo, has standing to sue because the Director of AID did not consult with the Secretary regarding the AID-funded project in Sri Lanka. This is beyond all reason . . .

B

Besides failing to show injury, respondents failed to demonstrate redressability. [Even if plaintiffs prevailed on the merits, the funding agencies might not be bound by a court decision in the plaintiff's favor, because they were not parties to the suit. Therefore, they might refuse to consult with the Secretary. Moreover, the funding agencies typically supply only a small fraction of the total cost for a foreign project; if that fraction were eliminated, it is unclear whether the projects would be stopped and the danger to the animals thus eliminated. Only three Justices concurred with Justice Scalia's opinion in part III B, so it does not represent an opinion of the Court.]

IV

The Court of Appeals found that respondents had standing for an additional reason: because they had suffered a "procedural injury." The so-called "citizen-suit" provision of the ESA provides, in pertinent part, that "any person may commence a civil suit on his own behalf to enjoin any person, including the United States and any other governmental instrumentality or agency . . . who is alleged to be in violation of any provision of this chapter." The court held that, because [the ESA] requires interagency consultation, the citizen-suit provision creates a "procedural right" to consultation in all "persons"—so that anyone can file suit in federal court to challenge the Secretary's . . . failure to follow the assertedly correct consultative procedure, notwithstanding their inability to allege any discrete injury flowing from that failure.

To understand the remarkable nature of this holding one must be clear about what it does not rest upon: This is not a case where plaintiffs are seeking to enforce a procedural requirement the disregard of which could impair a separate concrete interest of theirs (e.g., the procedural requirement for a hearing prior to denial of their license application, or the procedural requirement for an environmental impact statement before a federal facility is constructed next door to them).[7] Nor is it simply a case where concrete injury has been suffered by many persons, as in mass fraud or mass tort situations. Nor, finally, is it the unusual case in which Congress has created a concrete private interest in the outcome of a suit against a private party for the government's benefit, by providing a cash bounty for the victorious plaintiff. Rather, the court held that the injury-in-fact requirement had been satisfied by congressional conferral upon all persons of an abstract, self-contained, noninstrumental "right" to have the Executive observe the procedures required by law. We reject this view.

We have consistently held that a plaintiff raising only a generally available grievance about government—claiming only harm to his and every citizen's interest in proper application of the Constitution and laws, and seeking relief that no more directly and tangibly benefits him than it

---

[7]   There is this much truth to the assertion that "procedural rights" are special: The person who has been accorded a procedural right to protect his concrete interests can assert that right without meeting all the normal standards for redressability and immediacy. Thus, under our case-law, one living adjacent to the site for proposed construction of a federally licensed dam has standing to challenge the licensing agency's failure to prepare an Environmental Impact Statement, even though he cannot establish with any certainty that the Statement will cause the license to be withheld or altered, and even though the dam will not be completed for many years. . . .

does the public at large—does not state an Article III case or controversy. . . .

To be sure, our generalized-grievance cases have typically involved Government violation of procedures assertedly ordained by the Constitution rather than the Congress. But there is absolutely no basis for making the Article III inquiry turn on the source of the asserted right. Whether the courts were to act on their own, or at the invitation of Congress, in ignoring the concrete injury requirement described in our cases, they would be discarding a principle fundamental to the separate and distinct constitutional role of the Third Branch—one of the essential elements that identifies those "Cases" and "Controversies" that are the business of the courts rather than of the political branches. . . .

If the concrete injury requirement has the separation-of-powers significance we have always said, the answer must be obvious: To permit Congress to convert the undifferentiated public interest in executive officers' compliance with the law into an "individual right" vindicable in the courts is to permit Congress to transfer from the President to the courts the Chief Executive's most important constitutional duty, to "take Care that the Laws be faithfully executed," Art. II, § 3. It would enable the courts, with the permission of Congress, "to assume a position of authority over the governmental acts of another and co-equal department," and to become "virtually continuing monitors of the wisdom and soundness of Executive action." We have always rejected that vision of our role. . . .

Nothing in this contradicts the principle that "[t]he . . . injury required by Art. III may exist solely by virtue of "statutes creating legal rights, the invasion of which creates standing." *Linda R.S. v. Richard D.*, 410 U.S. 614 (1973). Both of the cases used by *Linda R. S.* as an illustration of that principle involved Congress's elevating to the status of legally cognizable injuries concrete, de facto injuries that were previously inadequate in law (namely, injury to an individual's personal interest in living in a racially integrated community and injury to a company's interest in marketing its product free from competition). . . . We hold that respondents lack standing to bring this action and that the Court of Appeals erred in denying the summary judgment motion filed by the United States . . .

KENNEDY, J. with whom SOUTER, J. joins, concurring in part and concurring in the judgment.

. . . I also join Part IV of the Court's opinion with the following observations. As government programs and policies become more complex and far-reaching, we must be sensitive to the articulation of new rights of action that do not have clear analogs in our common-law tradition. . . . In my view, Congress has the power to define injuries and articulate chains of causation that will give rise to a case or controversy where none existed before, and I do not read the Court's opinion to suggest a contrary view. In exercising this power, however, Congress must at the very least identify the injury it seeks to vindicate and relate the injury to the class of persons entitled to bring suit. The citizen-suit provision of ESA does not meet these minimal requirements, because while the statute purports to confer a right on "any person . . . to enjoin . . . the United States and any other governmental instrumentality or agency . . . who is alleged to be in violation of any provision of this chapter," it does not of its own force establish that there is an injury in "any person" by virtue of any "violation." . . .

STEVENS, J., concurring in the judgment. [Stevens disagreed with the majority's views on standing, but he concurred in reversal on the basis that the consultation requirement in ESA does not apply to activities in foreign countries.]

BLACKMUN, J., with whom O'CONNOR, J., joins, dissenting. [Respondents raised genuine issues of fact, sufficient to survive summary judgment, as to injury in fact and redressability.] I question the Court's breadth of language in rejecting standing for "procedural" injuries. I fear the Court seeks to impose fresh limitations on the constitutional authority of Congress to allow citizen-suits in the federal courts for injuries deemed "procedural" in nature . . . In conclusion, I cannot join the Court on what amounts to a slash-and-burn expedition through the law of environmental standing. In my view, "[t]he very essence of civil liberty certainly consists in the right of every individual to claim the protection of the laws, whenever he receives an injury." *Marbury v. Madison*. . . .

NOTES AND QUESTIONS

1. *Injury in fact.* The *Defenders of Wildlife* opinion concedes that the type of aesthetic or environmental injury claimed by Kelly and Skilbred *could have* satisfied the injury in fact requirement. Why did they fail to pass the test? Must they have an airline ticket to Sri Lanka or Egypt in hand when they file suit?

Can a plaintiff satisfy the requirement that an alleged injury be "imminent" by arguing that the injury will *probably* occur? According to the 5–4 decision in *Clapper v. Amnesty Int'l*, 133 S.Ct. 1138 (2013), the answer is no. The injury must be "certainly impending." "An objectively reasonable likelihood" that it will occur is insufficient. *Clapper* involved a constitutional attack on 50 U.S.C. § 1881a, a provision enacted in 2008 that greatly broadened the government's ability to monitor communications between U.S. and foreign persons. Under the revised law, the foreign monitoring targets need not be agents of a foreign power but could be anyone who might produce "foreign intelligence information." No showing of probable cause was required. Surveillance programs under § 1881a must be approved by the secret FISA court, but the court was no longer required to approve each particular target, just the generalized surveillance program.

Some of the plaintiffs were attorneys who represent foreign persons accused of terrorism-related offenses (or held in detention at Guantanamo). Other plaintiffs were human rights advocates who work with persons considered to be terrorists by the U.S. government. The plaintiffs argued that there was an objectively reasonable likelihood that their email and phone communications with their foreign contacts would be intercepted. But the Court said that this probabilistic showing of injury was insufficient because it relied on a chain of speculation. Plaintiffs speculated that the FISA court would approve the surveillance in question and that the plaintiffs' particular conversations would be among those targeted for surveillance. According to the majority, the plaintiff need not show that the harms are "literally certain" to occur but they must establish more than a "reasonable likelihood" that they will occur.

In addition, the plaintiffs argued that they were required to take immediate precautions against possible surveillance, such as avoiding conversations, speaking in generalities, or traveling abroad to have the conversations in person. But the Court said that this also was inadequate; a plaintiff could not convert a speculative concern about future harm into a present harm just by taking precautions or buying a plane ticket. *See* F. Andrew Hessick, *Probabilistic Standing,* 106 Nw. U.L. Rev. 55 (2012), criticizing decisions like *Clapper* and arguing that Article III does not create a threshold of risk of potential harms. Instead, Hessick suggests, courts should develop a doctrine under which they can abstain from deciding claims alleging small risks of harm.

The "certainly impending" language is among the stricter formulas the Court has used to describe the imminence requirement. Whether the Court will adhere to this stringent test remains to be seen. Three years earlier, the Court found that organic farmers had standing to challenge an Agriculture Department order that permitted the sale of genetically modified alfalfa seeds. *Monsanto Co. v. Geertson Seed Farms*, 561 U.S. 139 (2010). The farmers had demonstrated a "substantial risk" that if these seeds were planted, their own crops would also be contaminated through cross-pollination. That risk would force them to spend money to test their crops in order to be able to sell alfalfa in the organic market, which would demand assurances of purity. In *Clapper*, the Court acknowledged that *Monsanto* and other cases had used a "substantial risk" test, but did not disapprove those cases. Rather, it asserted that "to the extent that the 'substantial risk' standard is relevant and is distinct from the 'clearly impending' requirement, [the *Clapper* plaintiffs] fall short of even that standard."

2. *Associations as plaintiffs.* The plaintiff in *Defenders* was the environmental organization Defenders of Wildlife, which paid the attorneys and made the strategic decisions. As an association, Defenders has standing

only if one or more members could have sued on their own. Since neither Kelly nor Skilbred had standing, Defenders also lacked standing.

The ability of associations to seek review on behalf of their members is quite important. Only established organizations can overcome the "free rider" problem, meaning that people are unwilling to pay for something they can get for free. Similarly, only established organizations can overcome the problem of "transaction costs," because it is difficult and costly to assemble a new group to fund a lawsuit.

Under *Hunt v. Washington State Apple Advertising Comm'n*, 432 U.S. 333 (1977), an association has standing to sue on behalf of its members when a) one or more of its members would otherwise have standing to sue in their own right, b) the interests the association seeks to protect are germane to the organization's purpose, and c) neither the claim nor the relief requested requires the participation of individual members in the lawsuit. In practice, the latter two requirements are easily met, so the organization can sue if it can identify at least one member who can claim the requisite injury in fact.

However, an organization with a large membership cannot simply set forth a general description of its members and rely on a statistical probability that some fraction of them will suffer an injury in fact. In *Summers v. Earth Island Institute*, 555 U.S. 488 (2009), the Sierra Club and other environmental organizations filed suit to challenge Forest Service regulations governing the sale of timber on lands damaged by forest fires. These regulations provided that the Service did not have to comply with statutory procedures for notice, comment, and appeal when the affected forest areas were small in size. The Court, speaking through Justice Scalia, refused to accept assurances that at least some of the Sierra Club's 700,000 members were likely in the near future to visit forests to which the regulations applied. Rather, the plaintiffs would have to furnish affidavits pertaining to the plans of particular individuals.

3.   *Public actions.* Most of the cases discussed in this sub-chapter are "public actions," meaning that ideologically motivated plaintiffs seek to compel government to regulate others. The plaintiffs care mostly about vindicating a non-selfish interest (usually environmental or consumer in nature), but the law of standing requires them to claim that they have suffered some sort of individualized harm. The injury in question must be imminent rather than speculative, particularized to the plaintiff rather than generalized to many citizens, and concrete rather than ideological or abstract. These standing rules are relatively recent judicial innovations with little historical grounding and are often difficult to apply.

The leading federal authority for denying standing in a public action is *Sierra Club v. Morton,* 405 U.S. 727 (1972). The Sierra Club sought to enjoin a ski development in Mineral King, a pristine area of the Sierras. It claimed standing based on its historic interest in the conservation of the Sierras and other wilderness areas. The Court held that Sierra Club lacked standing because it had failed to allege that it or its members had suffered injury in fact. A historic commitment to conservation is not enough.

In dissent, Justice Douglas argued that standing should be granted to an "inanimate object about to be despoiled, defaced, or invaded by roads and bulldozers and where injury is the subject of public outrage." However, no other Justice ever was willing to go that far. Sierra Club amended its complaint to allege that several of its members camped in Mineral King. The amended complaint survived a motion to dismiss. Ultimately the developer abandoned the project.

Some states permit "public actions." For example, *Common Cause v. Board of Supervisors*, 777 P.2d 610 (Cal. 1989), allowed a public interest group to sue a county for failing to implement a voter registration law. The Court stated: "Where the question is one of public right and the object of the mandamus is to procure the enforcement of a public duty, the relator need not show that he has any legal or special interest in the result, since it is sufficient that he is interested as a citizen in having the laws executed and the duty in question enforced. . . . The question in this case involves a public right to voter outreach programs, and plaintiffs have standing as citizens to seek its vindication." Florida, however, rejects the public action concept; even groups who had intervened in administrative hearings to raise environmental concerns lack standing to seek review unless their members will personally suffer an adverse effect from the decision under review. *LEAF v. Clark*, 668 So.2d 982 (Fla. 1996).

Which makes better sense—the California rule granting standing to well-funded associations in cases involving public issues, or the federal and Florida rule denying such groups standing unless an identified member demonstrably meets the injury in fact test? What's wrong with granting standing to "ideological" plaintiffs? Is the problem that such plaintiffs may do a poor job of presenting their case, thus depriving the courts of the adversarial clash necessary to decide difficult issues? Or would the courts be flooded with cases if outraged citizens were allowed to sue? Or is the concern that such cases inevitably present difficult remedial problems and a strict standing doctrine is necessary to avoid plunging the court into solving such problems? Or is the real explanation based on separation of powers doctrine, as urged in cases like *Defenders*? If so, what is the separation of powers problem?

4. *Causation and redressability.* To establish standing under Article III, a plaintiff that has been "injured in fact" must establish that the injury is "fairly traceable" to the conduct complained of (the causation requirement) and also that it is "likely" that the injury will be redressed by a favorable decision (the redressability requirement). Needless to say, the quoted words infuse significant indeterminacy into standing doctrine. Note that the causation and redressability requirements often overlap. For example, in Part III.B of *Defenders,* the plurality could have said either that the Secretary's failure to require consultation by the funding agencies was not

the cause of plaintiff's injury (causation) or that requiring the Secretary to engage in consultation would not remedy the plaintiff's injury (redressability).

Lower courts encounter difficulty applying these tests and some cases seem much stricter than others. As an example of a strict approach, *see National Wrestling Coaches Ass'n v. Dep't of Education*, 366 F.3d 930 (D.C. Cir. 2004). The coaches complained that colleges were eliminating men's wrestling programs because of a DOE "policy interpretation." The policy set forth enforcement guidelines for Title IX of the Education Amendments of 1972 which bans sex discrimination in federally funded educational programs. The policy stated that one of the tests of an institution's compliance would be whether intercollegiate athletic opportunities for male and female students are provided in numbers proportionate to their enrollments.

The coaches claimed that colleges were dropping unprofitable men's sports programs (such as wrestling) in order to devote the resources to women's sports. The court held that plaintiffs lacked standing on redressability grounds. It explained that the colleges (which were not parties to the case) might not restore the wrestling programs even if the court invalidated the challenged interpretation. After all, Title IX and other implementing regulations would remain on the books and would continue to encourage colleges to cancel men's sports. Colleges would continue to confront difficult budgetary problems of financing sports like wrestling. And Bucknell explained that its "gender equity plan," which included cancellation of the wrestling program, was "not only a matter of federal law but also morally the right thing to do."

The coaches argued that if they prevailed, they would have "better odds" of retaining their wrestling programs, but "a quest for ill-defined 'better odds' is not close to what is required to satisfy the redressability prong of Article III." The treatments of this issue in the majority opinion and the dissent each consume about ten pages in the Federal Reporter, indicating the complexity of the issues and the number of irreconcilable precedents on both sides.

5. *The global warming case—Massachusetts v. EPA.* In *Massachusetts v. EPA,* 549 U.S. 497 (2007), the Court (by a sharply divided 5–4 majority) took a different tack from *Defenders* on the issues of injury in fact, causation, and redressability. (We discuss other aspects of this important case in §§ 6.3 and 10.5.) The underlying issue in *Massachusetts* was whether the EPA violated the Clean Air Act by failing to adopt rules limiting greenhouse gas emissions from motor vehicles. However, since global warming harms everyone in the world (but not necessarily in imminent fashion), would anyone have standing to challenge EPA's decision?

The Court held that Massachusetts had standing because it alleged that its own coastal property was being consumed by rising sea levels caused by global warming. Needless to say, it is difficult to prove that changes in the coastline are caused by rising sea levels that are caused by climate change that is caused by human emissions of greenhouse gases from cars driven in America—and that all this harm is "imminent."

Massachusetts' ability to sue was somehow enhanced because it is a "quasi-sovereign," litigating on behalf of all of its citizens, although it is not clear precisely how this factor changes the analysis. Quoting from *Georgia v. Tennessee Copper Co.*, 206 U.S. 230 (1907), a case in which Georgia sought to protect its citizens from air pollution originating outside its borders, the Court said: "This is a suit by a State for an injury to it in its capacity of *quasi-*sovereign. In that capacity the State has an interest independent of and behind the titles of its citizens, in all the earth and air within its domain. It has the last word as to whether its mountains shall be stripped of their forests and its inhabitants shall breathe pure air."

As to causation and redressability, the Court said:

> *Causation.* EPA does not dispute the existence of a causal connection between man-made greenhouse gas emissions and global warming. At a minimum, therefore, EPA's refusal to regulate such emissions "contributes" to Massachusetts' injuries. EPA nevertheless maintains that its decision not to regulate greenhouse gas emissions from new motor vehicles contributes so insignificantly to petitioners' injuries that the agency cannot be haled into federal court to answer for them. For the same reason, EPA does not believe that any realistic possibility exists that the relief petitioners seek would mitigate global climate change and remedy their injuries. That is especially so because predicted increases in greenhouse gas emissions from developing nations, particularly China and India, are likely to offset any marginal domestic decrease.

> But EPA overstates its case. Its argument rests on the erroneous assumption that a small incremental step, because it is incremental, can never be attacked in a federal judicial forum. Yet accepting that premise would doom most challenges to regulatory action. Agencies, like legislatures, do not generally resolve massive problems in one fell regulatory swoop. They instead whittle away at them over time, refining their preferred approach as circumstances change and as they develop a more nuanced understanding of how best to proceed. That a first step might be tentative does not by itself support the notion that federal courts lack jurisdiction to determine whether that step conforms to law.

> And reducing domestic automobile emissions is hardly a tentative step. Even leaving aside the other greenhouse gases, the United States transportation sector emits an enormous quantity of carbon dioxide into the atmosphere . . . that accounts for more than 6% of worldwide carbon dioxide emissions. . . .

> *The Remedy.* While it may be true that regulating motor-vehicle emissions will not by itself reverse global warming, it by no

means follows that we lack jurisdiction to decide whether EPA has a duty to take steps to slow or reduce it. Because of the enormity of the potential consequences associated with man-made climate change, the fact that the effectiveness of a remedy might be delayed during the (relatively short) time it takes for a new motor-vehicle fleet to replace an older one is essentially irrelevant. Nor is it dispositive that developing countries such as China and India are poised to increase greenhouse gas emissions substantially over the next century. A reduction in domestic emissions would slow the pace of global emissions increases, no matter what happens elsewhere . . .

In sum—at least according to petitioners' uncontested affidavits—the rise in sea levels associated with global warming has already harmed and will continue to harm Massachusetts. The risk of catastrophic harm, though remote, is nevertheless real. That risk would be reduced to some extent if petitioners received the relief they seek. We therefore hold that petitioners have standing to challenge the EPA's denial of their rulemaking petition.

6.   *Procedural errors.* In footnote 7 of the *Defenders* opinion, the Court discussed "procedural rights." For example, suppose an agency fails to prepare a required environmental impact statement (EIS) before building a dam. An EIS is an elaborate document that studies the costs and benefits of a proposed agency action that might adversely affect the environment. An EIS compels the agency to consider the environmental aspects of proposed action, but it does not require the agency to desist from the project regardless of environmental damage.

A person who can establish injury in fact from construction of the dam (for example that it will wipe out his favorite fishing stream) has standing to challenge the agency's failure to prepare an EIS. As footnote 7 in *Defenders* explains, this outcome entails relaxation of the usual causation, redressability, and imminence requirements. In many (perhaps most) cases, even if the agency prepares a proper EIS, it will go ahead and construct the project anyway. Still, the person injured by the negative environmental effect of the project has standing to challenge the agency's failure to prepare an EIS, since the preparation of the EIS might plausibly have made a difference in the outcome. *See* Richard J. Pierce, Jr., *Making Sense of Procedural Injury,* 62 ADMIN. L. REV. 1 (2010); *Florida Audubon Soc. v. Bentsen*, 94 F.3d 658 (D.C. Cir. 1996).

Why couldn't the plaintiffs in *Defenders* successfully assert that they had a "procedural right" to have AID consult the Secretary of the Interior and that the failure to follow that procedure should allow them to meet the injury in fact test?

7.   *Citizen suit provisions.* The *Defenders* case casts doubt on the validity of a number of environmental and other statutes that contain provisions allowing any citizen to seek judicial review of agency non-

enforcement decisions. Note the majority's separation of powers rationale: by attempting to confer standing on persons who cannot meet the injury in fact test, Congress interferes with the President's duty to "take care" that the laws be faithfully executed. Does this approach strengthen the separation of powers? Or weaken it?

Several states have adopted statutes allowing any citizen to sue to prevent unreasonable damage to natural resources. *See* Andrew J. Piela, Comment, *A Tale of Two Statutes*, 21 B.C. ENVTL. AFF. L. REV. 401 (1994), discussing experience under the Connecticut and Minnesota statutes. The Comment concludes that the Minnesota statute has worked well in opening the door to judicial review of all sorts of generalized environmental claims. On the other hand, the Michigan Supreme Court invalidated a statute allowing any person to maintain a lawsuit for the protection of air, water, and other natural resources. *Michigan Citizens for Water Conservation v. Nestlé Waters North America, Inc.*, 737 N.W.2d 447 (Mich. 2007). The *Nestlé* decision followed *Defenders* and held that the statute violated separation of powers under the Michigan constitution, even though the Michigan constitution has no express case or controversy requirement.

8. *Legislatively created interests.* The majority opinion in *Defenders* recognized that Congress can indirectly broaden standing when it creates new legal rights. The Kennedy-Souter concurrence (which provided two critical votes for the result) is even more forthright on this point, declaring that "Congress has the power to define injuries . . . that will give rise to a case or controversy where none existed before." In light of the concurrence, suppose Congress redrafted the ESA to declare that every citizen of the United States has an interest in the survival of any endangered species on the theories of "ecosystem nexus" or "animal nexus" rejected by the majority. With the addition of that provision, would a citizen suit provision be constitutional? If so, why did Justices Kennedy and Souter regard the actual case as different? See Heather Elliott, *Congress's Ability to Solve Standing Problems*, 91 B.U. L. REV. 159 (2011) (arguing that it is unlikely for both constitutional and practical reasons that Congress could solve the problems identified in the *Defenders* decision).

In the later case of *Federal Election Commission v. Akins*, 524 U.S. 11 (1998), the plaintiff complained that the FEC had failed to enforce the campaign finance law against the American Israel Public Affairs Committee (AIPAC, an organization that spent substantial sums on political activity). The law required a "political committee" to disclose information about its members and its campaign-related contributions and expenditures, but the FEC had ruled that AIPAC was not a political committee. Akins wished to obtain information about AIPAC in order to make voting decisions. Even though his injury (the lack of access to information) was shared by all voters, the Court held that he had standing. The statute that created a specific right to information overcame objections that Akins's injury was generalized.

Similarly, courts have held that an individual may sue an agency for information under the Freedom of Information Act, or for disclosure of meetings of advisory committees as required by the Federal Advisory Committee Act, without showing an injury to some other concrete interest. *Public Citizen v. United States Dep't of Justice*, 491 U.S. 440 (1989). On the other hand, in *Summers v. Earth Island Inst.*, *supra* N.2, the Court ruled that environmentalists lacked standing to sue the Forest Service for depriving them of what they alleged was their statutorily conferred right to file comments on the agency's plans for timber sales. The Court said that "deprivation of a procedural right without some concrete interest that is affected by the deprivation—a procedural right *in vacuo*—is insufficient to create Article III standing." Does *Summers* cast doubt on cases such as *Akins* and *Public Citizen*?

9.   *Taxpayer actions.* In many states, taxpayers have standing to challenge the legality of legislative or executive action, at either the state or local level, that allegedly involves an unlawful expenditure of public funds. *See, e.g., District of Columbia Common Cause v. District of Columbia*, 858 F.2d 1 (D.C. Cir. 1988), holding that a D.C. taxpayer has standing to challenge unlawful expenditure by the D.C. municipal government. The opinion made clear that the federal standing rules are not applicable to the District's courts. Typically the remedy sought is injunctive, and in some states a prevailing plaintiff is entitled to attorney's fees. Apparently the result has not been an unmanageable flood of litigation. *See generally* Susan L. Parsons, Comment, *Taxpayers' Suits: Standing Barriers and Pecuniary Restraints,* 59 TEMP. L.Q. 951 (1986). Despite the existence of a statute permitting taxpayer actions, however, New York courts have limited them to challenges to government appropriations, not to administrative decisions that are "essentially nonfiscal activities." *Rudder v. Pataki,* 711 N.E.2d 978 (N.Y. 1999).

In contrast to experience in the states, federal recognition of taxpayer actions has been extremely grudging. A federal taxpayer lacks standing to challenge the expenditure of federal funds unless it can demonstrate that a victory on the merits will reduce its taxes (which is seldom possible). The federal courts cannot entertain state taxpayer actions, either. *DaimlerChrysler Corp. v. Cuno*, 547 U.S. 332 (2006).

The ban on federal taxpayer suits has one exception. In *Flast v. Cohen*, 392 U.S. 83 (1968), the Court allowed a taxpayer standing to challenge as facially unconstitutional a government expenditure program benefitting religious schools. But the decision designed the test so narrowly that only establishment clause challenges could qualify. Several subsequent cases narrow *Flast* still further. *Hein v. Freedom from Religion Found., Inc.,* 551 U.S. 587 (2007), rejected taxpayer standing to challenge expenditures for conferences at which President Bush promoted his "faith-based" approach to social service programs. *Arizona Christian School Tuition Org. v. Winn,* 131 S. Ct. 1436 (2011), held that taxpayers had no standing to challenge a state law that gave other taxpayers a credit for their contribution to religious schools. Such "tax expenditure" provisions do not impose a tax on the plaintiff, so *Flast* is distinguishable. In both cases, Justices Scalia and Thomas argued that *Flast* is an anomaly that should be overruled.

10. *Problem.* The Madison Arts Fund (MAF) makes grants to an array of local arts organizations. According to MAF's regulations, between 15% and 25% of the annual grants should go to theatrical organizations, and the grants should be distributed equitably throughout the state. The regulations also provide that MAF grants should be used primarily, though not exclusively, to help new organizations get started as opposed to providing an annual subsidy.

For each of the last four years, MAF granted $200,000 to Dinner Theater Company in the city of Elm to offset Dinner's annual deficit. Dinner stages musicals and light comedy in a dinner theater format. Mort, the director of MAF, used to be the director of Dinner.

For several years, Ellen has been trying to start another theater company in the same city (Elm Theater or ET) to produce new plays. ET has not raised enough funds to produce any plays. Her troupe of actors is willing to work for free or for very low salaries. Ellen has applied three times for an MAF grant which would be used to match contributions from the community. Each time, MAF rejected her application, stating that Elm cannot support two theater companies.

Ellen believes that the grants to Dinner are an abuse of MAF's discretion. She points to Mort's pre-existing relationship to Dinner and to the fact that Dinner has been treated with undue favoritism. Its three grants were to offset operating expenses rather than to aid in development, and its cultural contribution is minimal.

Nate, a local attorney who loves avant garde theater, has volunteered to represent ET pro bono. What are the prospects for this lawsuit? Assume Madison follows federal standing law.

§ 11.1.3   STANDING UNDER THE APA AND THE ZONE OF INTERESTS TEST

Did the APA change the law as it existed in 1946? (*See* § 11.1.1 for discussion of the history of standing law.) Section 10(a) of the federal APA (now the first sentence of § 702) provides: "A person suffering legal wrong because of agency action, or adversely affected or aggrieved by agency action within the meaning of a relevant statute, is entitled to judicial review thereof." The Attorney General argued that § 10(a) merely codified but did not change standing law. ATTORNEY GENERAL'S MANUAL ON THE ADMINISTRATIVE PROCEDURE ACT 96 (1947). Between 1946 and 1970, the issue of whether the APA changed prior law remained unresolved. Nevertheless, the lower courts pushed the available precedents to the limit. They granted standing to many beneficiaries of statutory schemes, including consumers, users of polluted rivers, and television viewers injured by racist programming. The *ADPSO* case, which follows, finally answered the question of whether the APA changed prior standing law, by holding that indeed it did. However, the case also created a problematic new test for judicial review under the APA.

ASSOCIATION OF DATA PROCESSING SERVICE ORGS. (ADPSO) V. CAMP
397 U.S. 150 (1970)

[Petitioners sold data processing services. They challenged a ruling by the Comptroller of the Currency that national banks could provide data processing services. Petitioners alleged that the ruling violated the National Bank Act. The lower courts dismissed for lack of standing. The Court surveyed prior law and disapproved cases such as *Tennessee Electric Power,* which was discussed in § 11.1.1.]

DOUGLAS, J.:

. . . Generalizations about standing to sue are largely worthless as such. One generalization is, however, necessary and that is that the question of standing in the federal courts is to be considered in the framework of Article III which restricts judicial power to "cases" and "controversies." As we recently stated in *Flast v. Cohen*, 392 U.S. 83: "[I]n terms of Article III limitations on federal court jurisdiction, the question of standing is related only to whether the dispute sought to be adjudicated will be presented in an adversary context and in a form historically viewed as capable of judicial resolution." *Flast* was a taxpayer's suit. The present is a competitor's suit. And while the two have the same Article III starting point, they do not necessarily track one another.

The first question is whether the plaintiff alleges that the challenged action has caused him injury in fact, economic or otherwise. There can be no doubt but that petitioners have satisfied this test. The petitioners not only allege that competition by national banks in the business of providing data processing services might entail some future loss of profits for the petitioners, they also allege that respondent American National Bank & Trust Company was performing or preparing to perform such services for two customers for whom petitioner Data Systems, Inc., had previously agreed or negotiated to perform such services. . . .

[The second] question [is] whether the interest sought to be protected by the complainant is arguably within the zone of interests to be protected or regulated by the statute or constitutional guarantee in question. Thus the Administrative Procedure Act grants standing to a person "aggrieved by agency action within the meaning of a relevant statute." § 702. That interest, at times, may reflect "aesthetic, conservational, and recreational" as well as economic values. . . . We mention these noneconomic values to emphasize that standing may stem from them as well as from the economic injury on which petitioners rely here. Certainly he who is "likely to be financially" injured, *FCC v. Sanders Bros. Radio Station*, may be a reliable private attorney general to litigate the issues of the public interest in the present case. . . .

[Section] 4 of the Bank Service Corporation Act of 1962 . . . provides: "No bank service corporation may engage in any activity other than the performance of bank services for banks. . . ." We think . . . that § 4 arguably brings a competitor within the zone of interests protected by it.

That leaves the remaining question, whether judicial review of the Comptroller's action has been precluded. We do not think it has been. . . . We find no evidence that Congress in either the Bank Service Corporation Act or the National Bank Act sought to preclude judicial review of administrative rulings by the Comptroller as to the legitimate scope of activities available to national banks under those statutes. Both Acts are clearly "relevant" statutes within the meaning of § 702. The Acts do not in terms protect a specified group. But their general policy is apparent; and those whose interests are directly affected by a broad or narrow interpretation of the Acts are easily identifiable. It is clear that petitioners, as competitors of national banks which are engaging in data processing services, are within that class of "aggrieved" persons who, under § 702, are entitled to judicial review of "agency action."

Whether anything in the Bank Service Corporation Act or the National Bank Act gives petitioners a "legal interest" that protects them against violations of those Acts, and whether the actions of respondents did in fact violate either of those Acts, are questions which go to the merits and remain to be decided below. We hold that petitioners have standing to sue and that the case should be remanded for a hearing on the merits.

[In a case decided the same day as *Data Processing*, the Court held that tenant cotton farmers had standing to challenge a regulation that would allow them to pledge federal subsidy payments to their landlords as security for their rent obligation. The farmers met the "injury in fact" test by alleging that the regulation would allow landlords to demand such assignments, thus increasing their dependency on the landlords. The "zone of interests" test was also met, because the statute provides that "the Secretary shall provide adequate safeguards to protect the interests of tenants . . ." *Barlow v. Collins*, 397 U.S. 159 (1970).

JUSTICE BRENNAN, joined by JUSTICE WHITE, concurred in the results of both cases, but disagreed with their reasoning:]

. . . My view is that the inquiry in the Court's first step [injury in fact] is the only one that need be made to determine standing. I had thought we discarded the notion of any additional requirement when we discussed standing solely in terms of its constitutional content in *Flast v. Cohen.* By requiring a second, non-constitutional step [zone of interests] the Court comes very close to perpetuating the discredited requirement that conditioned standing on a showing by the plaintiff that the challenged governmental action invaded one of his legally protected interests . . .

Before the plaintiff is allowed to argue the merits, it is true that a canvass of relevant statutory materials must be made in cases challenging agency action. But the canvass is made, not to determine standing, but to determine an aspect of reviewability; that is, whether Congress meant to deny or to allow judicial review of the agency action at the instance of the plaintiff. The Court in the present cases examines the statutory materials for just this purpose but only after making the same examination during the second step of its standing inquiry. . . .

I submit that in making such examination of statutory materials an element in the determination of standing, the Court not only performs a useless and unnecessary exercise but also encourages badly reasoned decisions, which may well deny justice in this complex field. When agency action is challenged, standing, reviewability, and the merits pose discrete, and often complicated, issues which can best be resolved by recognizing and treating them as such. . . . Where, as in the instant cases, there is no express grant of review, reviewability has ordinarily been inferred from evidence that Congress intended the plaintiff's class to be a beneficiary of the statute under which the plaintiff raises his claim. . . . [S]light indicia that the plaintiff's class is a beneficiary will suffice to support the inference. . . .

[A]n approach that treats separately the distinct issues of standing, reviewability, and the merits, and decides each on the basis of its own criteria, assures that these often complex questions will be squarely faced, thus contributing to better reasoned decisions and to greater confidence that justice has in fact been done. The Court's approach does too little to guard against the possibility that judges will use standing to slam the courthouse door against plaintiffs who are entitled to full consideration of their claims on the merits. The Court's approach must trouble all concerned with the function of the judicial process in today's world.

NOTES AND QUESTIONS

1. *The zone of interests test.* In *ADPSO,* the Court held that a plaintiff must not only meet the injury in fact test but must also show that "the interest sought to be protected by the complainant is arguably within the *zone of interests* to be protected or regulated by the statute or constitutional guarantee in question." The zone of interests test seems to be derived from

the language "... within the meaning of a relevant statute" in the first sentence of APA § 702.

In *Lujan v. National Wildlife Fed'n*, 497 U.S. 871 (1990), Justice Scalia illustrated the test in a hypothetical that distinguishes "injury in fact" from "zone of interests:"

> The failure of an agency to comply with a statutory provision requiring "on the record" hearings would assuredly have an adverse effect upon the company that has the contract to record and transcribe the agency's proceedings; but since the provision was obviously enacted to protect the interests of the parties to the proceedings and not those of the reporters, that company would not be "adversely affected within the meaning" of the statute.

The Court tried to articulate the thrust of the zone of interests test in *Clarke v. Securities Industry Ass'n,* 479 U.S. 388 (1987):

> In cases where the plaintiff is not itself the subject of the contested regulatory action, the test denies a right of review if the plaintiff's interests are so marginally related to or inconsistent with the purposes implicit in the statute that it cannot reasonably be assumed that Congress intended to permit the suit. The test is not meant to be especially demanding; in particular, there need be no indication of congressional purpose to benefit the would-be plaintiff.

The zone test seems to make intuitive sense. Parties whose interests are only "marginally related to or inconsistent with the purposes implicit in the statute" (like the court reporter in Justice Scalia's hypo) should not be able to engage the federal courts in complex litigation testing the legality of agency action that favors someone else.

Nevertheless, as N.2 describes, the test is difficult for lower courts to apply in practice. It requires courts to analyze difficult statutory materials at the threshold of litigation to answer a question that Congress had never considered: did Congress intend to protect the interests of a particular class of plaintiffs when it enacted the statute in question? Are the interests of that particular class at least congruent with the interests Congress did intend to protect? Or are that plaintiff's interests only "marginally related to or inconsistent with the purposes implicit in the statute?"

Unlike the injury in fact test, which is rooted in Article III, the zone of interests test is an interpretation of language in § 702 of the APA, meaning that Congress could abolish it. Should it do so? In his concurring opinion in *ADPSO,* Justice Brennan argued that the Court should dispense with the zone test. Instead, he argued, a plaintiff that has been injured in fact would have standing unless statutory materials indicate that Congress intended to preclude review by that class of plaintiffs. *See* § 10.4 for discussion of statutory preclusion; and compare *Block v. Community Nutrition Institute,* 467 U.S. 340 (1984), which held that Congress intended to preclude review of milk marketing orders by milk consumers, but not by milk producers.

2.   *Applying the zone of interests test.* The Supreme Court has been inconsistent in defining and applying the zone test. For example, it is unclear whether the "relevant statute" that must benefit or protect the plaintiff means the very provision of the statute that the plaintiff claims the agency violated, or whether the test can be satisfied by any other provision of that statute, or even by a related statute (as in *ADPSO* itself). It is also unclear whether plaintiff must establish that Congress actually intended to benefit or protect the plaintiff (or its interests) or whether no such showing is needed so long as the plaintiffs' interest is at least congruent with, or not inconsistent with, the interests Congress intended to benefit. For general treatment of the indeterminacy of the zone test, see Jonathan R. Siegel, *Zone of Interests,* 92 GEO. L.J. 317 (2004).

The zone test received only cursory consideration in *ADPSO* and *Barlow v. Collins.* It was applied in undemanding fashion in *Clarke* (cited in N.1) and in *Match-E-Be-Nash-She-Wish Band of Pottawatomi Indians v. Patchak,* 132 S. Ct. 2199 (2012). That case involved § 465 of the Indian Reorganization Act (IRA). That section of the IRA authorized the Secretary of the Interior to acquire property "for the purpose of providing land for Indians." The Secretary acquired land on which a tribe sought to open a casino. Patchak was a neighbor of the seized property. He was opposed to the casino project on economic, aesthetic, and environmental grounds. His legal objection, however, was that the Secretary could not seize land for the tribe because the tribe had not been federally recognized when the IRA was enacted in 1934.

The Court held that Patchak satisfied the zone of interest test. It followed *Clarke,* noting that the test is not meant to be especially demanding and "we have always conspicuously included the word 'arguably' in the test to indicate that the benefit of any doubt goes to the plaintiff." The Court held that the IRA is concerned not only with title to land but also with the use of that land. The Secretary must consider land use issues, both those that would promote Indian economic development and those that might be detrimental to non-Indians. "And so neighbors to the use (like Patchak) are reasonable—indeed, predictable—challengers of the Secretary's decisions. Their interests, whether economic, environmental, or aesthetic, come within § 465's regulatory ambit." See also *Lexmark International, Inc. v. Static Control Components, Inc.,* 134 S. Ct. 1377 (2014) (Scalia, J.), which reaffirmed the quoted language in *Match-E-Be-Nash-She-Wish Band* and declared: "That lenient approach is an appropriate means of preserving the flexibility of the APA's omnibus judicial-review provision, which permits suit for violations of numerous statutes of varying character that do not themselves include causes of action for judicial review."

However, an earlier case seems inconsistent with the authorities summarized in the previous paragraph, and it shows that the zone test can have real bite. In *Air Courier Conference of America v. American Postal Workers Union,* 498 U.S. 517 (1991), postal workers sought to prevent the U.S. Postal Service (USPS) from allowing private courier services to deliver mail from the U.S. to foreign countries. The plaintiffs argued that this action would violate the Private Express Statute (PES), which gives USPS a monopoly over carrying the mail. The postal workers met the "injury in fact" test, since the decision could result in the loss of postal jobs, but they flunked the "zone of interests" test. Perhaps contrary to the dictum from *Clarke* quoted in N.1, the Court required that plaintiff demonstrate that Congress intended to protect their jobs when it enacted PES.

The Court pointed out that the PES was first enacted in 1792, when there were no postal employees. It was reconsidered in 1845. Both in 1792 and 1845, the purpose of the PES was to protect the postal service from competition, *not* to protect the jobs of postal workers. The right of postal workers to unionize was recognized in a 1970 statute (the Postal Reorganization Act or PRA), but that had nothing to do with the PES:

> To adopt petitioners' contention would require us to hold that the "relevant statute" in this case is the PRA, with all of its various provisions united only by the fact that they deal with USPS. But to accept this level of generality in defining the "relevant statute" could deprive the zone-of-interests test of virtually all meaning. . . . None of the documents constituting the PRA legislative history suggests that those concerned with postal reforms saw any connection between the PES and the provisions of the PRA dealing with labor-management relations . . .

Thus *Air Courier* seems inconsistent with both *Clarke* and *NCUA*. These mixed signals have confused lower courts and produced a maze of confusing precedents.

3. *Zone of interests in the states.* Many states have rejected the zone of interests test. *See Greer v. Illinois Housing Dev. Auth.*, 524 N.E.2d 561 (Ill. 1988) (zone test would "unnecessarily confuse and complicate the law"); *Iowa Bankers Ass'n v. Iowa Credit Union Dep't*, 335 N.W.2d 439 (Iowa 1983) ("We believe the legislature intended to make a judicial remedy available to any person or party who can demonstrate the requisite injury").

However, other states have accepted the zone test, even though their judicial review statutes do not contain the language ("within the meaning of a relevant statute") found in § 702 of the federal APA. *See Sun-Brite Car Wash, Inc. v. Board of Zoning and Appeals of North Hempstead*, 508 N.E.2d 130 (N.Y. 1987), in which a car wash challenged the grant of a zoning variance that permitted construction of another car wash across the street. The Court held that this sort of competitive injury was not among the interests served by the zoning law. Similarly, Florida and Pennsylvania have applied the zone test without considering the differences between state statutes and the federal APA. *Florida Med. Ass'n v. Dep't of Prof. Reg.*, 426 So.2d 1112 (Fla. App. 1983); *Nernberg v. City of Pittsburgh*, 620 A.2d 692 (Pa. Commw. 1993).

Section 505 of the 2010 MSAPA provides: "The following persons have standing to obtain judicial review of a final agency action: (1) a person aggrieved or adversely affected by the agency action; and (2) a person that has standing under law of this state other than this [act]." Does this leave room for the zone test?

4. *Third party standing.* Another non-constitutional limitation on standing is the rule that a plaintiff cannot assert the rights of third parties— only its own rights. This is often referred to as the *jus tertii* rule. The courts have frequently allowed exceptions to *jus tertii.* For example, a plaintiff can assert the rights of third parties when the latter are legally or practically disabled from suing or when there is a protected relationship (such as doctor-patient or vendor-purchaser) between the plaintiff and the third party.

5. *Standing of agencies.* Can a government official or an agency that is displeased with the decision of another agency seek judicial review of that decision? In general, if the plaintiff agency is viewed as a subordinate to the decisionmaker, it cannot seek review. In *National Ass'n of Securities Dealers (NASD), Inc.* v. *SEC,* 431 F.3d 803 (D.C. Cir. 2005), NASD (a private self-regulatory organization) disciplined a securities dealer. The dealer was entitled to seek review of the NASD order by another agency—the SEC. The SEC reversed the NASD decision, and NASD sought judicial review. The court held that NASD lacked standing to appeal the SEC decision. The court thought that allowing standing to NASD would be as unprecedented as allowing an ALJ to seek judicial review of a decision by the agency heads reversing the ALJ's initial decision. Similarly, see *Mortensen v. Pyramid Sav. & Loan Ass'n,* 191 N.W.2d 730 (Wis. 1971) (savings and loan commissioner cannot appeal decision of savings and loan review board).

However, if the plaintiff is a separate agency or governmental unit whose legal mission is jeopardized by the decision, it can seek judicial review. *See, e.g., Bradford Central School Dist. v. Ambach,* 436 N.E.2d 1256 (N.Y. 1982) (school board can seek review of decision by state education commissioner certifying a teacher). *See generally* Frederick Davis, *Standing of a Public Official to Challenge Agency Decisions: A Unique Problem of State Administrative Law,* 16 ADMIN. L. REV. 163 (1964).

Should government officials who disagree with agency decisions be allowed to appeal them? Could this be a valuable check on the tendency of agencies to be captured by the interests they regulate? Or would it entangle a court excessively in executive branch conflicts?

6. *Problem*: The shortnose sucker is a small fish and is an endangered species. It is found only in Lost Lake, a body of water formed by High Dam and controlled by the Bureau of Reclamation. To protect the sucker's habitat, the Secretary of the Interior adopted a rule under the Endangered Species Act prohibiting withdrawal of water stored in Lost Lake if it would diminish the lake's depth below 12 feet.

Ted's farm is downstream from High Dam. In dry years, Ted relies on irrigation water released by the Bureau from Lost Lake. Ted challenges the rule in District Court, alleging that the rule would prevent releases of water and thus his individual allocation of water would be decreased. Ted claims that the rulemaking record shows that the rule was not based on the "best scientific and commercial data available" as required by the statute. Ted believes that evidence in the record shows that the sucker can survive in water much shallower than 12 feet. Ted seeks judicial review.

　　i)　　If Ted seeks judicial review under the APA, does he have standing?

　　ii)　　If Ted seeks judicial review under the citizen suit provision of the Endangered Species Act (discussed in Part IV of *Defenders of Wildlife* in § 11.1.2), does he have standing? *See Bennett v. Spear*, 520 U.S. 154 (1997).

§ 11.2　TIMING OF JUDICIAL REVIEW

§ 11.2.1　　INTRODUCTION

This subchapter addresses issues of timing: when can a litigant get into court? Often, the question of whether judicial review of agency action can be obtained immediately—or only after protracted administrative proceedings—is critically important.

The four parts of this subchapter concern four different timing doctrines. Each is a separate hurdle. The four doctrines are closely related and sometimes overlap. They are often confused with one another. In principle, however, each of the four doctrines serves different functions, draws upon different bodies of precedent, and should be carefully distinguished. Thus a preliminary sketch of the doctrines, and how they differ from each other, may be helpful.

　　a.　　*Final agency action.* Litigants are sometimes dissatisfied with decisions taken by the agency *during* the administrative process. For example, an agency might exclude certain evidence at a hearing or refuse to take immediate action to remove a dangerous pesticide from the market. However, as a general rule, courts review only "final" agency action. This means that ordinarily—but not always—a litigant must complete the entire administrative process before a court will review decisions that the agency took along the way.

　　b.　　*Exhaustion of remedies.* A private party may have an administrative remedy available that it would like to skip before going to court. By the general rule—but not always—a court will not hear the case until the party has first exhausted all administrative remedies.

　　c.　　*Ripeness.* A private party may be threatened by agency action that can be anticipated but has not yet occurred. For example, an agency might adopt a new rule or policy, but not yet have enforced it against the plaintiff. A court may find such disputes are not yet "ripe" for review, meaning that it will await concrete application of the agency action to the party before reviewing its legality.

d. *Primary jurisdiction.* Both a trial court and an agency may have jurisdiction to deal with a particular problem. If the doctrine of "primary jurisdiction" applies, the trial court refrains from acting, so that the matter can be resolved by the agency first. Thus the courts become involved only by judicially reviewing the agency decision, as opposed to conducting the original trial. Primary jurisdiction differs significantly from the three timing doctrines mentioned above, each of which concerns the timing of judicial review of agency action. Primary jurisdiction usually comes into play in controversies between private litigants in which the agency is not a party, but the court may decide to dump the case into the agency's lap to make the initial decision in the case, even though it was properly in court.

This introduction has sketched the four timing doctrines as if they were simple, absolute rules. Nothing could be further from the truth. Each of the four doctrines is riddled with exceptions and qualifications. Many cases are judicially reviewed in the absence of final agency action, or despite a plaintiff's failure to exhaust administrative remedies, or before an administrative policy has been applied to the plaintiff. Similarly, the courts frequently retain jurisdiction because they have determined that the doctrine of primary jurisdiction is inapplicable.

§ 11.2.2   FINAL AGENCY ACTION

FTC v. STANDARD OIL CO. OF CALIFORNIA (SOCAL)
449 U.S. 232 (1980)

[In 1973, the FTC issued a complaint against major oil companies (including Socal), alleging that it had "reason to believe" they were engaging in unfair methods of competition. By statute, the FTC had to make this determination before issuing a complaint charging a party with an unfair method of competition. Socal moved to dismiss the complaint on the ground that the FTC did not have "reason to believe" that it had violated the Act, but the FTC denied the motion. In 1975 (while adjudication before an ALJ was pending), Socal filed a complaint in the district court seeking review of whether the FTC had "reason to believe" it was violating the Act. Socal argued that political pressure, arising from gasoline shortages in 1973, had induced the FTC to issue a complaint against the major oil companies despite insufficient investigation.

The issue was whether issuance of the complaint before administrative adjudication concludes is "final agency action" subject to judicial review. The district court dismissed the complaint, but the Ninth Circuit reversed. It held that the district court could inquire whether the Commission in fact had determined that it had "reason to believe" Socal was violating the Act.

The Supreme Court held that issuance of the complaint was reviewable only if it was "final agency action" or otherwise was "directly reviewable" under § 704 of the APA. It concluded that it was neither.]

POWELL, J.:

A

The Commission's issuance of its complaint was not "final agency action." The Court observed in *Abbott Laboratories v. Gardner*, 387 U.S. 136, 149 (1967) [discussed in § 11.2.4] that "[t]he cases dealing with judicial review of administrative actions have interpreted the 'finality' element in a pragmatic way." In *Abbott Laboratories*, for example, the publication of certain regulations by the Commissioner of Food and Drugs was held to be final agency action subject to judicial review in an action for declaratory judgment brought prior to any Government action for enforcement. The regulations were "definitive" statements of the Commission's position, and had a "direct and immediate . . . effect on the day-to-day business" of the complaining parties. . . .

By its terms, the Commission's averment of "reason to believe" that Socal was violating the Act is not a definitive statement of position. It represents a threshold determination that further inquiry is warranted and that a complaint should initiate proceedings. To be sure, the issuance of the complaint is definitive on the question whether the Commission avers reason to believe that the respondent to the complaint is violating the Act. But the extent to which the respondent may challenge the complaint and its charges proves that the averment of reason to believe is not "definitive" in a comparable manner to the regulations in *Abbott Laboratories* and the cases it discussed. . . .

Serving only to initiate the proceedings, the issuance of the complaint averring reason to believe has no legal force comparable to that of the regulation at issue in *Abbott Laboratories*, nor any comparable effect upon Socal's daily business. The regulations in *Abbott Laboratories* forced manufacturers to "risk serious criminal and civil penalties" for noncompliance, or "change all their labels, advertisements, and promotional materials; destroy stocks of printed matter; and invest heavily in new printing type and new supplies." Socal does not contend that the issuance of the complaint had any such legal or practical effect, except to impose upon Socal the burden of responding to the charges made against it. Although this burden certainly is substantial, it is different in kind and legal effect from the burdens attending what heretofore has been considered to be final agency action.

In contrast to the complaint's lack of legal or practical effect upon Socal, the effect of the judicial review sought by Socal is likely to be interference with the proper functioning of the agency and a burden for the courts. Judicial intervention into the agency process denies the agency an opportunity to correct its own mistakes and to apply its expertise. Intervention also leads to piecemeal review which at the least is inefficient and upon completion of the agency process might prove to have been unnecessary. Furthermore, unlike the review in *Abbott Laboratories*, judicial review to determine whether the Commission decided that it had the requisite reason to believe would delay resolution of the ultimate question whether the Act was violated. Finally, every respondent to a Commission complaint could make the claim that Socal had made. Judicial review of the averments in the Commission's complaints should not be a means of turning prosecutor into defendant before adjudication concludes.

In sum, the Commission's issuance of a complaint averring reason to believe that Socal was violating the Act is not a definitive ruling or regulation. It had no legal force or practical effect upon Socal's daily business other than the disruptions that accompany any major litigation. And immediate judicial review would serve neither efficiency nor enforcement of the Act. These pragmatic considerations counsel against the conclusion that the issuance of the complaint was "final agency action."

B

Socal relies, however, upon different considerations than these in contending that the issuance of the complaint is "final agency action."

Socal first contends that it exhausted its administrative remedies by moving in the adjudicatory proceedings for dismissal of the complaint. By thus affording the Commission an opportunity to decide upon the matter, Socal contends that it has satisfied the interests underlying the doctrine of administrative exhaustion. The Court of Appeals agreed. We think, however, that Socal and the Court of Appeals have mistaken exhaustion for finality. By requesting the Commission to withdraw its complaint and by awaiting the Commission's refusal to do so, Socal may well have exhausted its administrative remedy as to the averment of reason to believe. But the Commission's refusal to reconsider its issuance of the complaint does not render the complaint a "definitive" action. The Commission's refusal does not augment the complaint's legal force or practical effect upon Socal. Nor does the refusal diminish the concerns for efficiency and enforcement of the Act.

Socal also contends that it will be irreparably harmed unless the issuance of the complaint is judicially reviewed immediately. Socal argues that the expense and disruption of defending itself in protracted adjudicatory proceedings constitutes irreparable harm. As indicated above, we do not doubt that the burden of defending this proceeding will be substantial. But the expense and annoyance of litigation is part of the social burden of living under government. . . .

Socal further contends that its challenge to the Commission's averment of reason to believe can never be reviewed unless it is reviewed before the Commission's adjudication concludes. As stated by the Court of Appeals, the alleged unlawfulness in the issuance of the complaint "is likely to become insulated from any review" if deferred until appellate review of a cease-and-desist order. Socal also suggests that the unlawfulness will be "insulated" because the reviewing court will lack an adequate record and it will address only the question whether substantial evidence supported the cease-and-desist order.[11]

We are not persuaded by this speculation. The Act expressly authorizes a court of appeals to order that the Commission take additional evidence. Thus, a record which would be inadequate for review of alleged unlawfulness in the issuance of a complaint can be made adequate. We also note that the APA specifically provides that a "preliminary, procedural, or intermediate agency action or ruling not directly reviewable is subject to review on the review of the final agency action," § 704, and that the APA also empowers a court of appeals to "hold unlawful and set aside agency action ... found to be ... without observance of procedure required by law." § 706. Thus, assuming that the issuance of the complaint is not "committed to agency discretion by law," a court of appeals reviewing a cease-and-desist order has the power to review alleged unlawfulness in the issuance of a complaint. We need not decide what action a court of appeals should take if it finds a cease-and-desist order to be supported by substantial evidence but the complaint to have been issued without the requisite reason to believe. It suffices to hold that the possibility does not affect the application of the finality rule ...

Because the Commission's issuance of a complaint averring reason to believe that Socal has violated the Act is not "final agency action" under [§ 704] of the APA, it is not judicially reviewable before administrative adjudication concludes.[14] ...

JUSTICE STEVENS concurred in the judgment.

---

[11] The Court of Appeals additionally suggested that the complaint would be "insulated" from review because the alleged unlawfulness would be moot if Socal prevailed in the adjudication. These concerns do not support a conclusion that the issuance of a complaint averring reason to believe is "final agency action." To the contrary, one of the principal reasons to await the termination of agency proceedings is "to obviate all occasion for judicial review." Thus, the possibility that Socal's challenge may be mooted in adjudication warrants the requirement that Socal pursue adjudication, not shortcut it.

[14] By this holding, we do not encourage the issuance of complaints by the Commission without conscientious compliance with the "reason to believe" obligation in 15 U.S.C. § 45(b). The adjudicatory proceedings which follow the issuance of a complaint may last for months or years. They result in substantial expense to the respondent and may divert management personnel from their administrative and productive duties to the corporation. Without a well-grounded reason to believe that unlawful conduct has occurred, the Commission does not serve the public interest by subjecting business enterprises to these burdens.

NOTES AND QUESTIONS

1. *Final agency action.* Judicial review statutes frequently authorize the courts to review only "final orders," and § 704 of the APA also contains a finality requirement. Even when the adjective "final" does not appear, courts often construe the statute as if it did. *See, e.g., City of Dania Beach v. FAA,* 485 F.3d 1181 (D.C. Cir. 2007) (a reviewable order "must possess the quintessential feature of agency decisionmaking suitable for judicial review: finality").

In *Bennett v. Spear,* 520 U.S. 154, 177–78 (1997), the Court summarized earlier cases defining final orders under § 704:

> As a general matter, two conditions must be satisfied for agency action to be "final": First, the action must mark the "consummation" of the agency's decisionmaking process—it must not be of a merely tentative or interlocutory character. And second, the action must be one by which "rights or obligations have been determined," or from which "legal consequences will flow."

How does the two-part *Bennett* test apply to the "reason to believe" determination in *Socal?*

In *Sackett v. EPA,* 132 S.Ct. 1367 (2012), the Court applied the *Bennett v. Spear* analysis. It ruled that an "administrative compliance order" (or ACO) issued by the EPA is "final agency action" under the APA. The underlying issue was whether wetlands filled by Sackett on his property were "navigable waters" (the issue of whether wetlands are "navigable waters" is difficult and unclear). If the wetlands were navigable waters, Sackett needed a permit to fill them.

The Clean Water Act allows the EPA two options. It can issue an ACO, as it did in this case. If Sackett fails to comply with the ACO by removing the fill, severe civil monetary penalties accrue from the date of the ACO. There is no right to an administrative hearing before issuance of an ACO. The statute provides for a judicial hearing only if the EPA seeks to enforce the ACO in court. EPA's other option is to seek an injunction against the landowner requiring the landowner to remove the fill.

Under *Bennett v. Spear,* the Court held that the ACO was the "consummation" of the EPA's decisionmaking process. The compliance order determined legal rights and obligations and legal consequences flow from issuance of the order (including liability for monetary penalties if Sackett fails to remove the fill). Consequently it was a final order. The Supreme Court also held that immediate judicial review of the ACO was not impliedly precluded by the statute.

Can a reviewing court furnish meaningful judicial review of an ACO, given that the EPA did not furnish Sackett with a hearing? Does the ACO procedure satisfy the requirements of due process? See *General Electric Co. v. Jackson,* 610 F.3d 110 (D.C. Cir. 2010), upholding under due process a similar scheme relating to removal of toxic waste because the recipient of the order can get a full judicial hearing if it refuses to remove the waste; the court has discretion not to impose the civil penalties.

2.   *Can a non-final order be reviewed along with the final decision?* In *Socal*, the Court indicated that the FTC's "reason to believe" determination would be reviewable at the time that a court reviews the final FTC cease and desist order against the company, citing the second sentence of § 704. It even suggested that, if necessary, the court of appeals could order the FTC to take additional evidence to determine whether its determination was in bad faith. What arguments would the FTC make against review of the "reason to believe" determination at the time of review of the final order in the case?

3.   *When is a non-final order immediately reviewable? Socal* indicates that the courts may review a non-final agency action if significant legal *or practical* consequences flow from that action. Could Socal have argued that the "reason to believe" determination had sufficient practical consequences to justify immediate review?

An example of review of a non-final order because of its practical effect arose in several cases involving the pesticide DDT. By statute, EPA must cancel the registration of a pesticide (and thus prevent its sale) if it is unsafe. After EPA issues a "notice of cancellation," a lengthy administrative investigatory and adjudicatory process ensues. Thus it might take years before an unsafe pesticide can be banned. In the case of an "imminent hazard to health and safety," however, EPA can suspend a pesticide's registration and thereby remove it from the market immediately.

Public interest groups petitioned EPA to suspend the registration of DDT, but the agency took no action on the petition. Instead, it issued a notice of cancellation for some uses of DDT while continuing to study other uses. The court of appeals held that EPA's failure to take action on the petition to suspend registration was immediately reviewable. If DDT posed an "imminent" health hazard, the public would suffer irreparable injury during the lengthy cancellation process, because DDT would remain on the market. On two different occasions, the court remanded the matter to EPA, pressing it to suspend DDT's registration or explain why it had not done so. *Environmental Defense Fund, Inc. v. Hardin*, 428 F.2d 1093 (D.C. Cir. 1970) (*EDF I*); *Environmental Defense Fund, Inc. v. Ruckelshaus*, 439 F.2d 584 (D.C. Cir. 1971) (*EDF II*). Can these decisions be reconciled with the *Bennett v. Spear* standard?

If EPA had granted the suspension, would the manufacturer be eligible for immediate review of that action, as opposed to having to wait until EPA's final decision on permanent cancellation of DDT's registration? *Compare Nor-Am Agricultural Products, Inc. v. Hardin*, 435 F.2d 1151 (7th Cir. 1970) (en banc) (no), *with EDF II, supra*, at 589–92 (yes).

4.   *Catch-22.* The state of Massachusetts wanted to challenge the methodology used in the 1990 census, which cost it a House seat, but it was

defeated by a combination of administrative law doctrines. *Franklin v. Massachusetts*, 505 U.S. 788 (1992). By statute, the Secretary of Commerce conducts the census and reports the results to the President, who transmits a statement to Congress allocating the number of seats for each state.

The Court held that the Secretary of Commerce's action was not "final," and thus not reviewable under the APA, because it was subject to review and revision by the President before it would have any direct and immediate effect on anyone. Moreover, the President's decision was not reviewable under the APA, because the President is not an "agency." The APA is vague on whether the President falls within the definition of "agency" in § 551(1). The Court held that if Congress wants the President to be covered by broad procedural statutes like the APA, it must say so explicitly.

5. *Exhaustion, finality, and ripeness.* In *Socal,* the Court observed that Socal had exhausted its remedy on the "reason to believe" issue, but the agency action remained non-final. This illustrates that the exhaustion and finality requirements are distinct. Conversely, as we shall see in § 11.2.3, agency action can be final but the case can still be dismissed because of a failure to exhaust remedies. These two subsections concentrate on the finality requirement in connection with judicial review of agency adjudicatory decisions, while § 11.2.4 discusses the interplay between finality and ripeness in connection with judicial review of various forms of rules.

6. *Witch hunts and judicial review.* Socal claimed that the FTC's decision to prosecute was politically motivated (it occurred during a period of extreme public resentment of big oil companies) and was not based upon an adequate investigation. This claim was not implausible. What can a victim do if an agency prosecutes it for reasons relating to politics or public relations? Is immediate judicial review of the agency's decision to issue a complaint a good remedy? Do you think that footnote 14 of the *Socal* opinion will help?

7. *Problem.* By statute, the Madison Insurance Commission (MIC) has power to seek an injunction in court against unfair insurance practices. It also has power to conduct administrative adjudication against insurance companies leading to a cease and desist order. MIC believes that Security Insurance Co. has a practice of systematically denying undisputed health insurance benefit claims.

Recently, MIC sought an injunction against Security. After a six-day trial, a judge refused to issue the injunction on the grounds that MIC had failed to prove that Security had any such practice. MIC did not appeal this decision.

MIC has since issued an administrative complaint against Security. MIC's ALJ has rejected Security's argument that the administrative case is barred by issue preclusion (often referred to as collateral estoppel). The MIC agency heads refused to review this ruling. Security predicts that the administrative hearing will take at least two months and will cost it one million dollars in attorney's fees.

Security seeks immediate judicial review under the APA of the ALJ's ruling on issue preclusion. Should the court hear the case? *See Top Choice Distributors, Inc. v. United States Postal Service*, 138 F.3d 463 (2d Cir. 1998); *Town of Huntington v. New York State Div. of Human Rights*, 624 N.E.2d 678 (N.Y. 1993).

§ 11.2.3　　EXHAUSTION OF ADMINISTRATIVE REMEDIES

PORTELA-GONZALEZ V. SECRETARY OF THE NAVY
109 F.3d 74 (1st Cir. 1997)

SELYA, J.

In this appeal, plaintiff-appellant Astrid L. Portela-Gonzalez (Portela) challenges a summary judgment entered in favor of the Navy. . . . Portela worked for nearly three decades as a civilian employee at the Roosevelt Roads Naval Station. From 1985 forward, she occupied the position of sales manager at the Navy Exchange. She had an unblemished employment record and achieved consistently high performance ratings.

On December 14, 1989, Portela placed 28 articles of clothing on layaway at the Exchange, 25 of which were clearance sale items (known colloquially as "red tag" items). The anticipated purchase price of the merchandise was $484.10. When the Exchange slashed the prices of all red tag items even more drastically during the post-Christmas lull, Portela spied an opportunity for increased savings, canceled her layaway arrangement (paying a $5.00 penalty), and simultaneously repurchased the articles she had removed from layaway status for a price of $330.79. Portela contends that these machinations did not transgress any policy, rule, or regulation of the Exchange; the Navy contends otherwise.

On April 9, 1990, L.H. Arcement, Jr., the Officer in Charge (OIC) of the Navy Exchange, suspended Portela without pay pending anticipated disciplinary action. On May 29, Arcement notified Portela that she would be terminated for "applying an unauthorized 40% price reduction to red tagged clothing items you had placed on layaway in violation of the Exchange's layaway policy, resulting in a loss to the Exchange of $197.32." Pursuant to the controlling administrative procedure, contained in a Secretary of the Navy Instruction (SECNAVINST), the letter informed Portela of the charges against her and outlined her procedural rights.

Portela contested the proposed disciplinary action. On June 22, 1990, the OIC overrode Portela's grievance and terminated her employment as of July 3, 1990. The Navy advised Portela of her right to appeal this decision and she proceeded to do so. Her first appeal was heard pro forma by the OIC who, not surprisingly, affirmed his original determination. Her second appeal culminated in a full evidentiary hearing, following which Michael F. O'Brien, the Commanding Officer of the Roosevelt Roads Naval Station, upheld her termination.

Portela pursued the appellate process to the next level. On March 25, 1991, Rear Admiral H.D. Weatherson, Commander of the Naval Resale & Services Support Office, headquartered at Staten Island, New York, affirmed her termination. This decision informed Portela of her right to take a final administrative appeal to the Deputy Assistant Secretary of the Navy, Civilian Personnel Policy, Equal Employment Opportunity Office, in Washington, D.C. Rather than pursue this fourth level of administrative redress, Portela filed suit. . . . [The trial court] ruled that Portela had failed to exhaust available administrative remedies but nonetheless reached the merits of her suit in the exercise of its perceived discretion. Portela's victory proved ephemeral, however, as the court concluded that the Navy's actions were neither arbitrary nor capricious. This appeal ensued.

We agree with the district court that Portela impermissibly failed to exhaust her administrative remedies. We disagree, however, that the court had discretion, in the circumstances of this case, to relieve her of the onus of her omission.

A.   *The Exhaustion Doctrine.*

Starkly contoured, the exhaustion doctrine holds that "no one is entitled to judicial relief for a supposed or threatened injury until the prescribed administrative remedy has been exhausted." *Myers v. Bethlehem Shipbuilding Corp.*, 303 U.S. 41 (1938). In practice, the doctrine has softer edges than this language implies. Although exhaustion of administrative remedies is absolutely required if explicitly mandated by Congress, see *McCarthy v. Madigan*, 503 U.S. 140 (1992), courts have more latitude in dealing with exhaustion questions when Congress has remained silent. See *Darby v. Cisneros,* 509 U.S. 137 (1993); *McCarthy.* In such purlieus, the court of first instance possesses a modicum of discretion to relax the exhaustion requirement.

The Court's opinion in *McCarthy* is integral to an understanding of the parameters of this discretion. Although recognizing that the exhaustion doctrine ordinarily "serves the twin purposes of protecting administrative agency authority and promoting judicial efficiency," and, thus, should customarily be enforced, the Court identified "three broad sets of circumstances in which the interests of the individual weigh heavily against requiring administrative exhaustion."

First, a court may consider relaxing the rule when unreasonable or indefinite delay threatens unduly to prejudice the subsequent bringing of a judicial action. And, relatedly, if the situation is such that "a particular plaintiff may suffer irreparable harm if unable to secure immediate judicial consideration of his claim," exhaustion may be excused even though "the administrative decisionmaking schedule is otherwise reasonable and definite."

Second, *McCarthy* acknowledges that it sometimes may be inappropriate for a court to require exhaustion if a substantial doubt exists about whether the agency is empowered to grant meaningful redress. An agency, for example, may lack authority to grant the type of relief requested.

Finally, *McCarthy* teaches that the exhaustion rule may be relaxed where there are clear, objectively verifiable indicia of administrative taint. Thus, if the potential decisionmaker is biased or can be shown to have predetermined the issue, failure to exploit an available administrative remedy may be forgiven.

B.   *Application of the Doctrine.*

Congress has excluded Navy Exchange personnel from the strictures of the Administrative Procedure Act, and has not otherwise mandated that such employees always must exhaust administrative remedies as a condition precedent to suit. Accordingly, Portela's admitted failure to exercise the final level of available administrative review is not necessarily fatal to her claim; the effect of her omission depends instead upon whether the circumstances of her case can justify that omission. . . .

2.   *The Futility Exception.* The only question that remains is whether Portela's failure to mount the final rung of the administrative ladder is fatal to the court case. She argued below that the court should excuse her omission, asseverating that a final appeal to the Deputy Assistant Secretary of the Navy would have been a futile gesture because it would have resulted in an automatic affirmance of her dismissal. In theory, this is a good argument. Consistent with the exceptions limned by the *McCarthy* Court, we have recognized the inappropriateness of requiring exhaustion when further agency proceedings would be futile.

But the futility exception is not available for the asking. Reliance on the exception in a given case must be anchored in demonstrable reality. A pessimistic prediction or a hunch that further administrative proceedings will prove unproductive is not enough to sidetrack the exhaustion rule. Accordingly, "an essential element of the claim of futility . . . is that all reasonable possibilities of adequate administrative relief have been effectively foreclosed. . . ."

Portela cannot surmount this hurdle. The claim of futility is merely a self-serving pronouncement in the circumstances of this case. The evidence is uncontradicted that the Deputy Assistant Secretary is an impartial official who has reversed termination decisions affecting Navy

Exchange personnel in the past. Though the prognosis for Portela's unused administrative appeal may have been poor and her expectations modest, neither courts nor litigants are allowed to equate pessimism with futility. Because there is nothing in the record to suggest that Portela's lack of success at the previous levels of review necessarily signified that the final level of review would be an empty gesture, her failure to exhaust an available administrative remedy cannot be overlooked on the ground of futility.

3. *The District Court's Rationale.* To this point, we are in agreement with the court below. After finding the plaintiff's futility argument futile, however, the district judge nonetheless elected to relax the exhaustion requirement "in the interests of minimizing cost and delay in the judicial system and avoiding the waste of resources." The judge reasoned that a perceived waste of resources, in and of itself, can justify excusing nonexhaustion of administrative remedies. We think not.

Were we to adopt the lower court's reasoning, the resulting exception would swallow the exhaustion rule in a single gulp. Once an aggrieved party has brought suit, forcing her to retreat to any unused administrative appeal potentially wastes resources. The Supreme Court has disavowed such a resupinate approach. In *McKart v. United States*, 395 U.S. 185 (1969), the Court explained that a "primary purpose" of the exhaustion doctrine is "the avoidance of premature interruption of the administrative process." Consequently, it is generally inefficient to permit a party to seek judicial recourse without first exhausting her administrative remedies. Following this train of thought, the Court has concluded that, by and large, concerns regarding efficiency militate in favor of, rather than against, strict application of the exhaustion doctrine.

This view is steeped in real-world wisdom. Insisting on exhaustion forces parties to take administrative proceedings seriously, allows administrative agencies an opportunity to correct their own errors, and potentially avoids the need for judicial involvement altogether. Furthermore, disregarding available administrative processes thrusts parties prematurely into overcrowded courts and weakens an agency's effectiveness by encouraging end-runs around it.

4. *The Bottom Line.* To sum up, the futility exception is unavailable to Portela and the district court's professed reason for excusing her failure to exhaust administrative remedies neither passes muster on its own terms nor falls within any of the hallmark *McCarthy* exceptions.[6] Those conclusions dictate the result we must reach. The plaintiff left an

---

[6] We do not suggest that the three exceptions to the exhaustion rule delineated by the *McCarthy* Court comprise an exclusive compendium. But to the extent that other exceptions appropriately may lie, they must be on a par with the exceptions described by the Court. As explained in the text, the record here contains nothing which suggests a plausible basis for a further exception.

available administrative remedy untapped and the record in this case, howsoever construed, reveals no sufficiently excusatory circumstances to warrant spurning that remedy

First, there is no indication that full exhaustion would have caused undue prejudice, irreparable harm, or unusual hardship of any sort. Although Portela had already pursued a fairly lengthy administrative process, it had moved celeritously—the pavane began when the OIC terminated Portela's employment as of July 3, 1990, and ended when the NRSSO, in the person of Rear Admiral Weatherson, denied her penultimate administrative appeal on March 25, 1991—and the Deputy Assistant Secretary would have been required to respond to her final appeal "within 60 calendar days of receipt of the official record." Second, the agency (here, the Navy) was fully capable of granting all the relief that Portela originally sought, namely, reinstatement, reassignment, and quashing the charges against her. Third, there is no meaningful indication of any institutional bias. Fourth, the plaintiff has not identified any other special circumstance warranting relaxation of the exhaustion rule, and our careful perlustration of the record reveals none. It follows that the district court should have dismissed the complaint for failure of the plaintiff to exhaust available administrative remedies.

IV. CONCLUSION

It may seem hypertechnical to some that a person who believes herself aggrieved by agency action must jump through a series of hoops before she can seek out a judicial forum. But long-recognized concerns regarding agency autonomy and judicial efficiency weigh heavily in favor of requiring complete exhaustion of administrative remedies. When all is said and done, our system of justice depends on litigants' adherence to well-defined rules. Where, as here, a party decides unilaterally to forsake those rules, she does so at her peril.

We need go no further. The short of it is that Portela lacked a legally sufficient reason for leaping prematurely to a judicial venue. Thus, the district court should have dismissed her complaint for failure to exhaust available administrative remedies. In the end, however, the district court's error is of no moment; though the court entered judgment in favor of the Navy on an inappropriate ground, the Navy is nonetheless entitled to judgment. AFFIRMED.

NOTES AND QUESTIONS

1. *Exhaustion of remedies or exhaustion of litigants?* Portela-Gonzalez is a good example of a decision that requires a litigant to exhaust every link in a chain of intra-agency appeals. Requiring a litigant to resort to each such remedy is likely to cause delay and extra expense, but the remedies are unlikely to provide any meaningful relief. By the time Ms. Portela-Gonzalez

received Admiral Weatherson's decision, almost a year had elapsed since her suspension without pay from her job; the final step would require another sixty days from the time the Deputy Assistant Secretary received the official record (assuming the Secretary met the deadline). This does not seem like "celeritous" action, in the court's word; it seems sluggish, given the fact that the issues are simple and someone's livelihood is at stake.

Note that the Navy's decision in the *Portela-Gonzalez* case met the finality requirement discussed in § 11.2.2—once the petitioner failed to appeal Admiral Weatherson's decision, the Navy's action was final. Nevertheless, she lost the case because of a failure to exhaust remedies.

A party who is unable to secure judicial review because of a failure to exhaust remedies often can return to the agency and avail itself of the unexhausted remedy. However, this is not possible if the time for exhausting the remedy has expired (which was probably the case with the appeal to the Deputy Assistant Secretary in *Portela-Gonzalez*). When a court dismisses the case on exhaustion grounds and it is no longer possible to exhaust the remedy, the effect is to preclude judicial review entirely rather than to delay it.

2. *Exceptions to the exhaustion requirement.* The *Portela-Gonzalez* decision points out that there are two distinct exhaustion of remedies requirements. If a statute explicitly requires exhaustion of remedies as a prerequisite to subject matter jurisdiction, the reviewing court has no power to recognize any exhaustion exceptions. It must dismiss the case for lack of jurisdiction if the private party failed to exhaust remedies. However, if a statute provides for administrative remedies or even requires parties to exhaust them, but does not make exhaustion a jurisdictional prerequisite, a reviewing court has discretion to recognize exceptions and excuse a failure to exhaust. *See, e.g., Avocados Plus Inc. v. Veneman*, 370 F.3d 1243 (D.C. Cir. 2004) (stating that Congress must be quite explicit if it wishes to make exhaustion of remedies a jurisdictional requirement).

In discretionary exhaustion cases, courts engage in a balancing test to determine whether to excuse a failure to exhaust. *McCarthy v. Madigan,* cited in the opinion, observed:

> Administrative remedies need not be pursued if the litigant's interest in immediate judicial review outweighs the government's interests in the efficiency or administrative autonomy that the exhaustion doctrine is designed to further. Application of this balancing principle is intensely practical, because attention is directed to both the nature of the claim presented and the characteristics of the particular administrative procedure provided.

Nevertheless, exhaustion of remedies is the rule, and excuse of the exhaustion requirement is the exception. Courts usually refuse to excuse a failure to exhaust remedies.

In cases of discretionary exhaustion, courts generally begin by asking whether the case fits a number of established exhaustion exceptions. For example, the courts may excuse a failure to exhaust if an agency cannot provide the remedy that the plaintiff seeks. In *McCarthy,* a prisoner filed a damage action against prison officials for deliberate indifference to his medical condition, a potential Eighth Amendment violation. The prison's complaint procedures did not provide any right to money damages. Consequently, the Court held that exhaustion was not required. It was also influenced by the fact that the prison's procedures included extremely short deadlines; this created a risk that prisoners would miss the deadlines.

Congress promptly overruled the *McCarthy* decision. Under 42 U.S.C. § 1997e(a), a prisoner must exhaust "such administrative remedies as are available" before suing over prison conditions, even if those remedies do not include a provision for damages. *Booth v. Churner,* 532 U.S. 731 (2001). This outcome illustrates that courts cannot recognize exceptions in the case of jurisdictional exhaustion.

McCarthy also recognized exhaustion exceptions when the agency engaged in unreasonable delaying tactics, the plaintiff suffered irreparable harm from a delay in securing review, or there is clear evidence of some kind of bias or other "taint." *Portela-Gonzalez* also recognized an exception for futility—petitioner is not required to exhaust a remedy if it is clear that the remedy is useless. Why couldn't Portela-Gonzalez establish that the remedy of appealing to the Deputy Assistant Secretary of the Navy was futile?

The *McCarthy* opinion illustrates that courts often combine elements of several exceptions in deciding whether to excuse exhaustion. They also often consider such factors as the degree of injury from delaying review, the strength of petitioner's claim on the merits, whether agency consideration would facilitate judicial review by creating a record, and whether the petitioner appears to be attempting to manipulate the system.

What did the court mean in *Portela-Gonzalez* by saying that the exhaustion rule ordinarily "serves the twin purposes of protecting administrative agency authority and promoting judicial efficiency? Should the trial court in *Portela-Gonzalez* have exercised its discretion to reach the merits to prevent a waste of resources, even though none of the established exceptions seemed to quite fit the case?

3. *Exhaustion of remedies and issues of law or jurisdiction.* Under federal law, a party must exhaust remedies even though the dispute concerns a question of law or of the agency's jurisdiction (unless one of the established exceptions is applicable). The leading case is *Myers v. Bethlehem Shipbuilding Corp.* (cited in *Portela-Gonzalez*). In *Myers,* the employer in an NLRB proceeding argued that it was not operating in interstate commerce and, therefore, that the agency had no jurisdiction over it as a matter of law. Accordingly, it sought judicial intervention to stop the Board from holding a hearing. The Court said:

The contention is at war with the long-settled rule of judicial administration that no one is entitled to judicial relief for a supposed or threatened injury until the prescribed administrative remedy has been exhausted. That rule has been repeatedly acted on in cases where, as here, the contention is made that the administrative body lacked power over the subject matter.

A number of states disagree with the federal approach. They allow courts to rule on questions of law or jurisdiction before a petitioner has exhausted administrative remedies. *See Ward v. Keenan*, 70 A.2d 77 (N.J. 1949) (excusing failure to exhaust when the only issues are questions of law and agency expertise is not relevant in deciding the issue); *Sedlock v. Bd. of Trustees*, 854 N.E.2d 748 (Ill. App. 2006) (reviewing claim without exhaustion that agency lacks jurisdiction); *Kelleher v. Personnel Adm'r*, 657 N.E.2d 229 (Mass. 1995) (excusing failure to exhaust remedies where case presents a purely legal question of wide public significance). In *Watergate II Apartments v. Buffalo Sewer Auth.*, 385 N.E.2d 560 (N.Y. 1978), the court ruled that no exhaustion is required when a party makes a claim that agency action is wholly beyond its authority and resolution of the claim required no factual determinations. But in *Bankers Trust Corp. v. New York City Dep't of Finance*, 805 N.E.2d 92 (N.Y. 2003), the court distinguished *Watergate,* making clear that exhaustion is required in the case of a dispute over the application of a statute to undisputed facts. What is the rationale for excusing exhaustion in cases of legal or jurisdictional disputes?

4.   *Exhaustion of remedies under the APA.* In *Portela-Gonzalez*, the court mentions in passing that "Congress has excluded Navy Exchange personnel from the strictures of the Administrative Procedure Act." Had this not been so, the court's analysis might have been significantly different. The last sentence of APA § 704 provides:

> Except as otherwise expressly required by statute, agency action otherwise final is final for the purposes of this section whether or not there has been presented or determined an application for a declaratory order, for any form of reconsideration, or, unless the agency otherwise requires by rule and provides that the action meanwhile is inoperative, for an appeal to superior agency authority.

In *Darby v. Cisneros*, 509 U.S. 137 (1993), the Court held that this sentence in the APA relaxes not only the finality requirement (as its plain language indicates) but also the exhaustion of remedies requirement. In *Darby*, rules of the Department of Housing and Urban Development (HUD) provided that a party could appeal an ALJ decision in a debarment case to the Secretary and that the decision would be stayed during the pendency of such an appeal. But the rules did not *require* parties to take the appeal. As a result, the Court held that Darby could seek judicial review of an adverse ALJ decision without bothering to appeal to the Secretary first.

Three years later, HUD amended its procedural rules to require an appeal to the Secretary in debarment cases. 24 C.F.R. § 26.51. Since that time, therefore, litigants like Darby have had to exhaust that internal remedy before seeking judicial review.

Note that § 704 states that a party need not submit an application for an agency to *reconsider* its decision before going to court. In Illinois, a reconsideration petition is a remedy that a party must exhaust. *Castaneda v. Illinois Human Rights Comm'n*, 547 N.E.2d 437 (Ill. 1989). California disagrees. *Sierra Club v. San Joaquin Local Agency Formation Comm'n*, 981 P.2d 543 (Cal. 1999). In the latter case, the court said:

> . . . [T]he administrative record has been created, the claims have been sifted, the evidence has been unearthed, and the agency has already applied its expertise and made its decision as to whether relief is appropriate. The likelihood that an administrative body will reverse itself when presented only with the same facts and repetitive legal arguments is small . . . The only likely consequence [of requiring a reconsideration petition] is delay and expense for both the parties and the administrative agency prior to the commencement of judicial proceedings. . . .

If a party *does* submit a reconsideration petition, however, or if the agency decides on its own to reconsider its prior decision, the decision is no longer a final order and cannot be appealed until the reconsideration is completed. *ICC v. Bhd. of Locomotive Eng'rs*, 482 U.S. 270 (1987).

5. *Exhaustion and constitutional issues.* Should exhaustion of remedies be required if the plaintiff's only argument is that the statute being applied by the agency is unconstitutional? The general rule is that an agency lacks authority to determine the constitutionality of statutes. *See Singh v. Reno,* 182 F.3d 504, 510 (7th Cir. 1999); Glenn Justin Hovemann, Comment, *When Constitutional Issues Arise in Agency Adjudications: A Suggested Approach*, 65 ORE. L. REV. 413 (1986). Indeed, the California Constitution prohibits an agency from invalidating its own statute on constitutional grounds. Art. III, § 3.5. However, some states do permit agencies to resolve constitutional issues. *Cooper v. Eugene School Dist. No. 4J,* 723 P.2d 298 (Ore. 1986).

Where agencies are prohibited from deciding constitutional questions, a party who launches an on-the-face challenge to the constitutionality of a statute or regulation normally should not be required to exhaust remedies, since there is no effective administrative remedy. This principle applies both to substantive attacks (such as that the statute or regulation violates the First Amendment) and procedural attacks (such as that the statute or regulation violates procedural due process). *See, e.g., Lehman v. Pennsylvania State Police,* 839 A.2d 265 (Pa. 2003) (no exhaustion required for on-the-face attack on constitutionality of statute); *Riggs v. Long Beach,* 503 A.2d 284 (N.J. 1986) (same). (In an unusual case, however, the Court has held that a civil service statute did require exhaustion in such circumstances. A federal employee was required to present his constitutional claim to the Merit Systems Protection Board; although the MSPB would not consider it, the plaintiff could then appeal to the Federal Circuit and get it adjudicated there. *Elgin v. Dep't of Treasury*, 132 S.Ct. 2126 (2012).)

Exhaustion is often required in several situations that involve constitutional claims. First, if exhaustion is jurisdictional rather than discretionary, a court is likely to insist that even on-the-face constitutional claims be first presented to the agency. *See, e.g., Avocados Inc. v. Veneman, supra.* Even in this situation, exhaustion might not be required if the constitutional issue is wholly collateral to the issue on the merits and could not be effectively reviewed at the time the merits are reviewed. *See Mathews v. Eldridge*, § 2.3 (excusing exhaustion as to the issue of whether due process requires a pre-termination hearing in disability cases).

Second, exhaustion may be required if the case presents both constitutional and non-constitutional issues, since the party may win on the non-constitutional issue and thus render a decision of the constitutional issue unnecessary. *See Ticor Title Ins. Co. v. FTC*, 814 F.2d 731 (D.C. Cir. 1987), requiring a party to pursue its non-constitutional claims before the agency and declining to consider the argument that independent prosecuting and adjudicating agencies are unconstitutional. The court noted that the law on whether exhaustion is required in this situation is unclear and indicated that it might have considered the constitutional claim if that claim had seemed persuasive on the merits (it didn't—*see* § 7.5.2) or if irreparable injury had been shown. (Two other opinions in the *Ticor* case reached the same conclusion on the basis of finality and ripeness.)

Third, exhaustion is usually required if the plaintiff's constitutional attack is on the statute as applied to the plaintiff as opposed to an on-the-face attack. In these situations, the facts of the particular case are usually needed to decide the constitutional question and the agency decision will assist the court by assembling a factual record. *See Insurance Comm'r v. Equitable Life Assurance Soc.*, 664 A.2d 862 (Md. Ct. App. 1995); *Lehman v. Penn. State Police, supra.*

Fourth, if an agency is empowered under state law to rule on constitutional issues (including the validity of its own statute), a court may require exhaustion of remedies even in the case of an on-the-face constitutional attack. *Prince George's County v. Ray's Used Cars*, 922 A.2d 495 (Md. 2007).

6. *Issue exhaustion.* There is a third variation of the exhaustion requirement (besides the distinction between jurisdictional and discretionary exhaustion discussed in N.2). A party must have raised the very issue before every level of the agency that it intends to raise on judicial review. This rule is sometimes framed as "issue exhaustion," sometimes as "waiver." Thus, in *United States v. L.A. Tucker Truck Lines*, 344 U.S. 33, 37 (1952), the Court said: "Simple fairness to those who are engaged in the tasks of administration, and to litigants, requires as a general rule that courts should

not topple over administrative decisions unless the administrative body not only has erred but has erred against objection made at the time appropriate under its practice." As a general matter, the issue exhaustion requirement makes sense; if it didn't exist, parties might "sandbag" the government by not making their strongest legal arguments at the agency level, thus denying the agency an opportunity to respond to the objection.

In *Sims v. Apfel,* 530 U.S. 103 (2000), the Court allowed an applicant for Social Security disability to raise in court an issue that he had not raised before the agency's Appeals Council. The Court was influenced by the fact that private parties seeking disability are often unrepresented by counsel and may be quite unsophisticated. In addition, the hearings before the ALJ are non-adversarial; the government is not represented by counsel and the ALJ is supposed to develop the record and raise all appropriate issues. Moreover, although the statute requires exhaustion of remedies, neither the statute nor a regulation requires issue exhaustion in Social Security cases. The Court was closely divided and the critical fifth vote was Justice O'Connor, who relied on the fact that the agency had not warned claimants that they had to exhaust all issues before the Appeals Council.

7.   *Actions under 42 U.S.C. § 1983.* Section § 1983 provides remedies in cases where the plaintiff claims that state or local government officials have denied the plaintiff civil rights protected by the U. S. Constitution or by federal statutes. (*See* § 10.2.1b.) In *Patsy v. Florida Board of Regents*, 457 U.S. 496 (1982), the Court decided that exhaustion of state remedies is not required before bringing a civil rights suit in federal court under § 1983.

Ms. Patsy was employed by a public university in Florida and alleged that she had been discriminated against because of her age and sex. Patsy did not take advantage of the grievance procedure provided by the university for alleged race or sex discrimination. The Supreme Court held that a § 1983 plaintiff is not required to exhaust state remedies, no matter how adequate or easily exhausted those remedies might be. Does this mean that Ms. Patsy was not even required to complain to her boss about the alleged discrimination before filing suit? Is this wise policy? Why might Patsy prefer to avoid the state remedies and go directly to court?

8.   *Exhaustion in rulemaking.* In general, the requirement of exhaustion of remedies does not apply to rulemaking, as opposed to adjudication. It is obviously relevant that nobody is required to participate in a rulemaking proceeding. An unlimited number of parties might submit comments in a rulemaking proceeding, but only a small fraction of them actually do. Many who might be adversely affected by a rule don't even know about it in time to comment, or hadn't been born yet, or they may justifiably assume that other parties will raise the appropriate objections. The 2010 MSAPA spells this out: "A petitioner for judicial review of a rule need not have participated in the rulemaking proceeding on which the rule is based or have filed a petition to adopt a rule." 2010 MSAPA § 506(c).

With *issue* exhaustion, however, the governing principles in rulemaking are less well defined. Often an agency will have a good argument that a challenger should not be allowed to raise a particular issue on judicial review, because the failure by any commentator to raise that issue during the rulemaking process prevented the agency from responding in its statement of basis and purpose. This would be a form of "sandbagging" described in N.6. Should an agency have to respond to arguments (at least not to non-obvious arguments) that *nobody* ever made during the rulemaking process? This problem may have no across-the-board solution. On the one hand, an agency is expected to apply the criteria in its governing statute. If it does not, it is in a poor position to explain this failure by saying that nobody asked it to do so. On the other hand, an agency has a recognized duty to respond to significant issues raised during the comment period. *See* § 5.6 N.5. That principle necessarily implies that there are some issues that an agency doesn't need to address unless someone brings them up. *See Advocates for Highway and Auto Safety v. Federal Motor Carrier Safety Admin*, 429 F.3d 1136, 1148–50 (D.C. Cir. 2005) (party forfeited opportunity to seek review of claims that no commentator made during the rulemaking process, and these were not the kind of clear points that an agency should have considered on its own initiative).

Regardless, the issue exhaustion requirement should not apply to an issue that the petitioner could not have known about until the final rule was issued. *See CSX Transp. Co. v. Surface Transp. Bd.*, 584 F.3d 1076 (D.C. Cir. 2009). In *CSX*, the final rule varied sharply from the proposed rule, thus violating the requirement that the final rule be a "logical outgrowth" of the proposed rule (*see* § 5.3.1 NN.3–5). Obviously, the petitioner couldn't have raised this issue during the comment period, since the error was not apparent until the final rule was issued. The court held that the petitioner was not required to raise the issue through a motion for reconsideration before challenging the rule in court.

9.   *Problem.* Ann applied to receive payments of $400 per month under Madison's Aid for the Totally Disabled Program (ATD), which is administered by the Welfare Board. Ann is unable to work because of disabling psychiatric problems. She desperately needs the money and is facing eviction from her apartment. Until recently, Ann received money from her mother, but that source of funds has ended, because her mother lost her job. Recipients of ATD must be totally disabled (meaning unable to work) and also must meet strict tests based on financial need. The Board's rules provide that an applicant who has worked for any compensation whatever during the last six months is disqualified from receiving ATD.

Two years ago, Ann had a baby who was born with severe handicaps including Down's Syndrome. Under Madison's In-Home Supportive Services (IHSS) program, Ann received $200 per month to care for her baby. On March 2, Ann received a notice from the Welfare Board rejecting her application for ATD benefits on the ground that the IHSS payments are compensation for work. The notice stated that she could request a fair hearing with regard to her application on April 20. A decision in that hearing could be expected about six weeks later. If she is dissatisfied with the result of the fair hearing, she can file an appeal with the Welfare Board. Generally the Board takes about six months to decide an appeal.

You wish to seek immediate judicial review. You intend to question the Board's application of its no-compensation rule to IHSS payments. If the rule is found to be applicable to IHSS payments, you wish to challenge its consistency with statute and with the Constitution. If that fails, you want to urge the agency to waive its usual rules in the case of IHSS payments.

Will the court dismiss some or all of Ann's claims under the doctrine of exhaustion of remedies? Assume the state follows i) New Jersey law or ii) federal law. Should you request a Welfare Board fair hearing on April 6 even if you plan to go to court immediately? Assuming the court case is pending on April 6, should you attend that hearing and put on your case? If you do go through the agency hearing and lose at that level, should you appeal to the Welfare Board?

§ 11.2.4   RIPENESS

ABBOTT LABORATORIES v. GARDNER
387 U.S. 136 (1967)

[This case involved the labeling of prescription drugs that were sold both under a trade (or "proprietary" name) and at a lower price under a generic (or "established") name. In 1962, Congress amended the Food, Drug and Cosmetic Act to require makers of drugs with trade names to print the generic names on labels and other printed material. The statute said that the generic name had to appear "prominently and in type at least half as large as that used thereon for [the] proprietary name." The purpose of the law was to bring to the attention of doctors and patients the fact that many drugs sold under trade names are identical to drugs sold under generic names at lower prices.

The Food and Drug Administration (FDA) adopted a rule (which the Supreme Court assumed to be a legislative rule) requiring that the generic name appear on labels and other promotional material *every time* the trade name is used. The manufacturers of ninety percent of the nation's prescription drugs jointly brought the present case, seeking declaratory and injunctive relief against the rule. They argued that the FDA's rule was inconsistent with the statute. The court of appeals held that i) pre-enforcement review of FDA rules was precluded by statute, and ii) the regulation was not ripe for review. In effect, this meant that the manufacturers could not challenge the rules until the government brought suit to force them to comply (at which time they could assert the invalidity of the rule as a defense against enforcement). The Supreme

Court first held that Congress had not precluded pre-enforcement review of FDA regulations.]

HARLAN, J.:

... A further inquiry must, however, be made. The injunctive and declaratory judgment remedies are discretionary, and courts traditionally have been reluctant to apply them to administrative determinations unless these arise in the context of a controversy "ripe" for judicial resolution. Without undertaking to survey the intricacies of the ripeness doctrine it is fair to say that its basic rationale is to prevent the courts, through avoidance of premature adjudication, from entangling themselves in abstract disagreements over administrative policies, and also to protect the agencies from judicial interference until an administrative decision has been formalized and its effects felt in a concrete way by the challenging parties. The problem is best seen in a twofold aspect, requiring us to evaluate both the fitness of the issues for judicial decision and the hardship to the parties of withholding court consideration.

As to the former factor, we believe the issues presented are appropriate for judicial resolution at this time. First, all parties agree that the issue tendered is a purely legal one: whether the statute was properly construed by the Commissioner to require the established name of the drug to be used every time the proprietary name is employed. Both sides moved for summary judgment in the District Court, and no claim is made here that further administrative proceedings are contemplated. It is suggested that the justification for this rule might vary with different circumstances, and that the expertise of the Commissioner is relevant to passing upon the validity of the regulation. This of course is true, but the suggestion overlooks the fact that both sides have approached this case as one purely of congressional intent, and that the Government made no effort to justify the regulation in factual terms.

Second, the regulations in issue we find to be "final agency action" within the meaning of § [704 of the APA], as construed in judicial decisions. . . . The regulation challenged here, promulgated in a formal manner after announcement in the Federal Register and consideration of comments by interested parties is quite clearly definitive. There is no hint that this regulation is informal or only the ruling of a subordinate official, or tentative. It was made effective upon publication, and the Assistant General Counsel for Food and Drugs stated in the District Court that compliance was expected. . . . [The regulations] have the status of law and violations of them carry heavy criminal and civil sanctions. . . . Moreover, the agency does have direct authority to enforce this regulation in the context of passing upon applications for clearance of new drugs, or certification of certain antibiotics.

This is also a case in which the impact of the regulations upon the petitioners is sufficiently direct and immediate as to render the issue appropriate for judicial review at this stage. These regulations purport to give an authoritative interpretation of a statutory provision that has a direct effect on the day-to-day business of all prescription drug companies; its promulgation puts petitioners in a dilemma that it was the very purpose of the Declaratory Judgment Act to ameliorate. As the District Court found on the basis of uncontested allegations, "Either they must comply with the every time requirement and incur the costs of changing over their promotional material and labeling or they must follow their present course and risk prosecution." The regulations are clear-cut, and were made effective immediately upon publication; as noted earlier the agency's counsel represented to the District Court that immediate compliance with their terms was expected. If petitioners wish to comply they must change all their labels, advertisements, and promotional materials; they must destroy stocks of printed matter; and they must invest heavily in new printing type and new supplies. The alternative to compliance—continued use of material which they believe in good faith meets the statutory requirements, but which clearly does not meet the regulation of the Commissioner—may be even more costly. That course would risk serious criminal and civil penalties for the unlawful distribution of "misbranded" drugs.

It is relevant at this juncture to recognize that petitioners deal in a sensitive industry, in which public confidence in their drug products is especially important. To require them to challenge these regulations only as a defense to an action brought by the Government might harm them severely and unnecessarily. Where the legal issue presented is fit for judicial resolution, and where a regulation requires an immediate and significant change in the plaintiffs' conduct of their affairs with serious penalties attached to noncompliance, access to the courts under the Administrative Procedure Act and the Declaratory Judgment Act must be permitted, absent a statutory bar or some other unusual circumstance, neither of which appears here. . . .

The Government further contends that the threat of criminal sanctions for noncompliance with a judicially untested regulation is unrealistic; the Solicitor General has represented that if court enforcement becomes necessary, "the Department of Justice will proceed only civilly for an injunction . . . or by condemnation." We cannot accept this argument as a sufficient answer to petitioners' petition. This action at its inception was properly brought and this subsequent representation of the Department of Justice should not suffice to defeat it.

Finally, the Government urges that to permit resort to the courts in this type of case may delay or impede effective enforcement of the Act. We fully recognize the important public interest served by assuring prompt and unimpeded administration of the Pure Food, Drug, and Cosmetic Act, but we do not find the Government's argument convincing. First, in this particular case, a pre-enforcement challenge by nearly all prescription drug manufacturers is calculated to speed enforcement. If the Government prevails, a large part of the industry is bound by the decree; if the Government loses, it can more quickly revise its regulation.

The Government contends, however, that if the Court allows this consolidated suit, then nothing will prevent a multiplicity of suits in various jurisdictions challenging other regulations. The short answer to this contention is that the courts are well equipped to deal with such eventualities. The venue transfer provision, 28 U.S.C. § 1404(a), may be invoked by the Government to consolidate separate actions. Or, actions in all but one jurisdiction might be stayed pending the conclusion of one proceeding. A court may even in its discretion dismiss a declaratory judgment or injunctive suit if the same issue is pending in litigation elsewhere. . . .

Further, the declaratory judgment and injunctive remedies are equitable in nature, and other equitable defenses may be interposed. If a multiplicity of suits are undertaken in order to harass the Government or to delay enforcement, relief can be denied on this ground alone. The defense of laches could be asserted if the Government is prejudiced by a delay. . . .

In addition to all these safeguards against what the Government fears, it is important to note that the institution of this type of action does not by itself stay the effectiveness of the challenged regulation. There is nothing in the record to indicate that petitioners have sought to stay enforcement of the "every time" regulation pending judicial review. See 5 U.S.C. § 705. If the agency believes that a suit of this type will significantly impede enforcement or will harm the public interest, it need not postpone enforcement of the regulation and may oppose any motion for a judicial stay on the part of those challenging the regulation. It is scarcely to be doubted that a court would refuse to postpone the effective date of an agency action if the Government could show, as it made no effort to do here, that delay would be detrimental to the public health or safety. . . .

Reversed and remanded.

[On the same day as the *Abbott Laboratories* decision, the Court decided *Toilet Goods Ass'n v. Gardner*, 387 U.S. 158 (1967), holding that a different FDA rule was not ripe for pre-enforcement review. The rule in *Toilet Goods* provided that if a maker of color additives refused to permit FDA inspectors free access to its facility and formulae, FDA could immediately suspend certification service to the maker. Without FDA certification the additives could not be sold.

Although the regulation was "final" and its validity presented a legal issue, the Court held that the case was not ripe for immediate review. The rule provided that the FDA "may" order an inspection and, if it is refused, "may" suspend certification. How, if at all, the FDA would use this authority was not yet known. Thus, postponing review would help the Court to know about FDA's enforcement problems and the adequacy of safeguards to protect trade secrets. "We believe that judicial appraisal of these factors is likely to stand on a much surer footing in the context of a specific application of this regulation than could be the case in the framework of the generalized challenge made here."

Moreover, the Court was not impressed by the degree of hardship encountered by the additive makers. It was not comparable to that in the *Abbott* case,

> where the impact of the administrative action could be said to be felt immediately by those subject to it in conducting their day to day affairs. . . . This is not a situation in which primary conduct is affected—when contracts must be negotiated, ingredients tested or substituted, or special records compiled. . . . Moreover, no irremediable adverse consequences flow from requiring a later challenge to this regulation by a manufacturer who refuses to allow this type of inspection. . . . [R]efusal to allow an inspector here would at most lead only to suspension of certification services to the particular party, a determination that can then be promptly challenged through an administrative procedure, which in turn is reviewable by a court. Such review will provide an adequate forum for testing the regulation in a concrete situation.

JUSTICE FORTAS dissented in *Abbott Laboratories* and concurred in *Toilet Goods*. He contended that neither case was ripe for review "at this stage, under these facts and in this gross, shotgun fashion." He continued:]

The Court, by today's decisions, has opened Pandora's box. Federal injunctions will now threaten programs of vast importance to the public welfare. The Court's holding here strikes at programs for the public health. The dangerous precedent goes even further. [Fortas contended that some federal judge would be moved to grant a disruptive stay of the regulation.] I believe that this approach improperly and unwisely gives individual federal district judges a roving commission to halt the regulatory process, and to do so on the basis of abstractions and generalities instead of concrete fact situations, and that it impermissibly broadens the license of the courts to intervene in administrative action by means of a threshold suit for injunction rather than by the method provided by statute. . . .

[As to the "every time" rule,] the Court says that this confronts the manufacturer with a "real dilemma." But the fact of the matter is that the dilemma is no more than citizens face in connection with countless statutes and with the rules of the SEC, FTC, FCC, ICC, and other regulatory agencies. This has not heretofore been regarded as a basis for injunctive relief unless Congress has so provided. The overriding fact here is—or should be—that the public interest in avoiding the delay in implementing Congress' program far outweighs the private interest; and that the private interest which has so impressed the Court is no more than that which exists in respect of most regulatory statutes or agency rules. Somehow, the Court has concluded that the damage to petitioners if they have to engage in the required redesign and reprint of their labels and printed materials without threshold review outweighs the damage to the public of deferring during the tedious months and years of litigation a cure for the possible danger and asserted deceit of peddling plain medicine under fancy trademarks and for fancy prices which, rightly or wrongly, impelled the Congress to enact this legislation.

I submit that a much stronger showing is necessary than the expense and trouble of compliance and the risk of defiance. Actually, if the Court refused to permit this shotgun assault, experience and reasonably sophisticated common sense show that there would be orderly compliance without the disaster so dramatically predicted by the industry, reasonable adjustments by the agency in real hardship cases, and where extreme intransigence involving substantial violations occurred, enforcement actions in which legality of the regulation would be tested in specific, concrete situations. I respectfully submit that this would be the correct and appropriate result. Our refusal to respond to the vastly overdrawn cries of distress would reflect not only healthy skepticism, but our regard for a proper relationship between the courts on the one hand and Congress and the administrative agencies on the other. It would represent a reasonable solicitude for the purposes and programs of the Congress. And it would reflect appropriate modesty as to the competence of the courts. The courts cannot properly—and should not—attempt to judge in the abstract and generally whether this regulation is within the statutory scheme. Judgment as to the "every time" regulation should be made only in light of specific situations, and it may differ depending upon whether the FDA seeks to enforce it as to doctors' circulars, pamphlets for patients, labels, etc. . . .

NOTES AND QUESTIONS

1.   *The Abbott Labs equation.* Justice Harlan's opinion in *Abbott Labs* dominates the law of ripeness. Its statement of the rationale for the ripeness doctrine and its balancing test have been repeated and applied in countless federal and state decisions. Consider these questions: What is balanced

against what under the *Abbott Labs* test? How does the ripeness doctrine relate to the final order rule? Why were the *Abbott Labs* and *Toilet Goods* cases decided differently?

In practice, the *Abbott Labs* balance is normally struck in favor of immediate reviewability of legislative rules and similar pronouncements that have legal force. Indeed, "where the first prong of the ripeness test is met [because the challenge raises purely legal issues, including claims that the action is arbitrary and capricious or that the agency has violated the APA rulemaking provisions] and Congress has emphatically declared a preference for immediate review [for example, by providing a short statute of limitations for challenging a rule], no purpose is served by proceeding to the [hardship] prong." *Cement Kiln Recycling Coalition v. EPA*, 493 F.3d 207, 215 (D.C. Cir. 2007).

Nevertheless, there are occasional examples of documents having legal force that are considered unripe for immediate review. *See, e.g., American Petroleum Inst. v. EPA*, 683 F.3d 382 (D.C. Cir. 2012) (holding attack on regulations was unripe because agency had proposed new regulations that would change the regulatory scheme—but warning that agencies could not generally dodge review of regulations by proposing new ones); *North Am. Aviation Project v. National Transp. Safety Bd.*, 94 F.3d 1029 (6th Cir. 1996) (dismissing challenge to new NTSB rules of practice because they might never be applied to petitioner, and, if they were applied, court would then be better able to see how they would play out in practice).

The forest management plan adopted by the National Forest Service in *Ohio Forestry Ass'n v. Sierra Club*, 523 U.S. 726 (1998), is another example of a document that has legal force but is unripe for immediate review. The Sierra Club sought judicial review of provisions in the plan that authorized clear-cutting in a national forest in Ohio. The Court unanimously held the case was not ripe. Before any trees could be cut, a series of additional steps had to occur, including designation of specific areas within the forest for cutting and preparation of an environmental impact statement. First, the plan created no legal or practical harm to the Sierra Club, which could challenge the plan and subsequent action after the additional steps were taken. Challenging the plan all at once would obviously be cheaper and more convenient than pursuing many site-specific decisions, but saving litigation costs is an insufficient showing of hardship. Second, immediate judicial review could hinder agency efforts to refine its policies through application of the plan in practice. Third, the issues did not seem fit for immediate review because they raised technical questions that could be illuminated through a focus on specific parcels and specific proposals.

2. *Justice Fortas and predictions of doom.* Before Justice Fortas was appointed to the Supreme Court, he was a partner in a leading Washington D.C. law firm. He had ample experience in challenging administrative regulations and in using the courts to obstruct enforcement of unwelcome

rules. Thus his dissenting remarks about the risks of broadening pre-enforcement review of rules deserve careful consideration.

For several decades, the professional consensus was that *Abbott Labs* was rightly decided. Pre-enforcement review seemed to function well in clearing away legal doubts about the validity of regulations, thus allowing administration to proceed, or in immediately exposing legal problems that could be promptly corrected by the agency or by Congress. Recently, however, some scholars have questioned *Abbott Labs* and the strong presumption of pre-enforcement reviewability articulated in that case. They have identified pre-enforcement review as one of the causes of ossification of the rulemaking process.

Mashaw claims that pre-enforcement review often encourages regulated parties to litigate instead of comply with rules, since there is virtually no penalty (other than paying attorney fees) for launching a challenge. Pre-enforcement review requires courts to review a whole laundry-list of objections to the rules rather than the precise problems that emerge when regulated entities actually attempt to comply. Early review requires the agencies to anticipate every possible legal issue that anyone might raise, which produces massive rulemaking records and lengthy statements of basis and purpose. Mashaw continues:

> A period of attempted compliance, experimentation, and negotiation between the agency and affected parties, induced by the unavailability of immediate review, might well produce better rules, swifter compliance, and less litigation. Moving back toward the older regime of rulemaking review primarily at the time of enforcement thus has much to recommend it, for unnecessary judicial review simultaneously stultifies the policy process while imperiling judicial and administrative legitimacy.

Jerry L. Mashaw, *Improving the Environment of Agency Rulemaking: An Essay on Management, Games, and Accountability*, 57 L. & CONTEMP. PROB. 185, 236 (1994).

Seidenfeld takes issue with Mashaw's analysis. He contends that pre-enforcement review compels agencies to do a better job in writing their rules. He also argues that dispensing with pre-enforcement review would cut beneficiaries of a regulatory program (as opposed to regulated parties) out of the judicial review loop, since beneficiaries could not get into court to argue that a regulation was too weak. He also believes that in a regime of high penalties for non-compliance and uncertainty about the validity of a rule, regulated parties would have to comply even with rules they reasonably believe are invalid and that might well turn out to be invalid. Mark Seidenfeld, *Playing Games with the Timing of Judicial Review: An Evaluation of Proposals to Restrict Pre-Enforcement Review of Agency Rules*, 58 OHIO ST. L. J. 85 (1997). Both Mashaw and Seidenfeld rely heavily on game theory to make their points.

3. *Ripeness and guidance documents.* Under *Abbott Labs* and *Toilet Goods*, legislative rules are usually deemed ripe for pre-enforcement review. But how about interpretive rules and policy statements or other informal agency pronouncements, which are referred to in this and the following notes as "guidance documents"? Guidance documents are often held unripe for immediate review. Sometimes courts find that the documents do not cause immediate hardship, since by definition they are not legally binding. *See* § 6.1.4. Other decisions find that the issues raised by the challenge are not fit for immediate review because the validity of the agency's position will be clarified by information about how it is applied in practice.

In *National Park Hospitality Ass'n v. Dep't of the Interior*, 538 U.S. 803 (2003), a divided Court held that a guidance document known as § 51.3 was not ripe for review. It was embedded within a legislative rule adopted by the National Park Service and thus met the finality requirement. Section 51.3 provided that the Contract Disputes Act (CDA) is inapplicable to settlement of disputes under contracts between concessionaires and national parks. CDA allows persons that contract with the government to choose between an administrative and judicial forum to adjudicate contract disputes. Because the Park Service does not administer the CDA and had no delegated power to interpret it, § 51.3 had no legal force.

A trade group representing concessionaires sought immediate review, but the Court held that the group's members had suffered no hardship because the guidance document had neither legal nor practical effect on them. Granted, the controversy over the validity of § 51.3 gave rise to legal uncertainty, which may have affected concessionaires' decision on whether to bid on a park contract, but "if we were to follow petitioner's logic, courts would soon be overwhelmed with requests for what essentially would be advisory opinions because most business transactions could be priced more accurately if even a small portion of existing legal uncertainties were resolved." Although the question presented was purely legal, the Court thought that further developments might improve the courts' ability to make a decision about the scope of the CDA. Some concessionaires' contracts might fall within the CDA and others might not (although the Court did not identify what the basis for that distinction might be).

Justice Breyer's dissent took sharp issue with this analysis. He thought § 51.3 was ripe for review. The issue involved was purely legal and would not be illuminated by future developments. The legal uncertainty created by § 51.3 satisfied the hardship requirement. Potential concessionaires would make lower bids if they had to litigate contract disputes in court rather than in an agency.

Despite the implications of *National Park Hospitality,* pre-enforcement review of guidance documents is not uncommon. For example, in *Aviators for Safe and Fairer Regulation, Inc. v. FAA*, 221 F.3d 222 (1st Cir. 2000), a longstanding legislative regulation relating to air taxi services required that pilots must be allowed ten hours of rest in the 24-hour period preceding a new assignment. Without notice and comment, the agency issued a "notice of enforcement policy" stating that the term "rest" does not include a period during which the pilot is on call for a new assignment—even if the pilot isn't actually called. During such a period the pilot must leave a phone number, take calls, and accept the new assignment (after the ten-hour rest period is over). A trade association for air taxi companies attacked the notice, arguing that it was invalid on both procedural and substantive grounds.

The court found that the issue was ripe for immediate review. Under the *Abbott Labs* two-prong analysis, the "hardship" requirement was met, because the notice threatened enforcement against violators, which could involve a variety of penalties including license revocation. But if air taxi companies complied with the notice in order to avoid enforcement proceedings, they would have to make major changes in their operations, because they couldn't call pilots about their next assignment during the rest period. As for the "fitness for immediate review" criterion, the court thought that the notice was unambiguous and raised only legal issues. These issues would not be clarified by specific facts arising out of enforcement.

4. *Guidance documents and finality.* Controversies over whether a guidance document is ready for immediate judicial review can implicate issues of finality as well as ripeness. Recall that *Bennett v. Spear*, 520 U.S. 154 (1997), discussed in § 11.2.2 N.1, indicated that, "[a]s a general matter," agency action is final only if the action determines "rights or obligations," or "legal consequences will flow" from it. According to one line of cases, guidance documents are not final, because they are not legally binding, and no "legal consequences" flow from them. Consequently, the court can deny judicial review of a guidance document on the basis that it is not a final agency action, without needing to discuss whether the document is ripe for review.

For example, in *Center for Auto Safety v. National Highway Traffic Safety Administration*, 452 F.3d 798 (D.C. Cir. 2006), the agency (NHTSA) issued policy guidelines concerning "regional recalls" of cars. Cars are often recalled (and repaired for free by the manufacturer) because of safety-related defects. If the defect is likely to cause problems only in areas of harsh climate (for example, where salt is used to combat ice on the roads), the guidelines allow manufacturers to recall cars only in such areas. A public interest safety group challenged these guidelines, contending that all recall orders must be national in scope. However, the court held that the guidelines were not "final agency action." The court resolved the finality issue by deciding that the policy guidelines were not a legislative rule and thus had no legal consequences. It was irrelevant that the guidelines had important practical consequences (car owners outside the affected regions wouldn't get the defects fixed for free). The court did consider whether the guidelines were applied in a binding fashion. If they were treated as binding, they would not qualify for the APA rulemaking exemption (see § 6.1.4b). To that extent, the plaintiffs were in effect able to litigate the *procedural* validity of the guidelines. But the court's finality holding prevented it from reaching the plaintiffs' *substantive* argument—that the regional recall policy violated NHTSA's statutory obligations.

However, another line of cases seems inconsistent with *Center for Auto Safety*. In *Aviators, supra,* the court concluded that the notice of enforcement policy was final agency action. The court pointed out that it was not a mere proposal, and there was no indication that the agency planned to conduct further proceedings. Then the court turned directly to the *Abbott Labs* ripeness analysis, in which the practical impact of an action is an important criterion. Thus, the court apparently assumed that the finality of the notice of enforcement policy could be satisfied on the basis of its practical effect, even though it had no legal effect. Is this approach to finality allowable under *Bennett*? Is it more attractive than the *Center for Auto Safety* approach? *See generally* Gwendolyn McKee, *Judicial Review of Agency Guidance Documents: Rethinking the Finality Doctrine,* 60 ADMIN. L. REV. 371 (2008).

5. *Judicial stays.* The APA provides that an agency has discretion to stay the effective date of action taken by it, and a reviewing court has discretion to stay the agency action if the agency has refused to do so. APA § 705. Whether a stay will be granted may be the most critical timing issue of all. If the court refuses a stay, the damage to the petitioner may be irreparable; even if the petitioner ultimately wins on the merits, it may be too late to rectify the harm. However, if the court does stay the agency action, a law enforcement program may be sidetracked for years, with considerable damage to the public interest.

As the Supreme Court has stated:

> It takes time to decide a case on appeal. Sometimes a little; sometimes a lot. No court can make time stand still while it considers an appeal, and if a court takes the time it needs, the court's decision may in some cases come too late for the party seeking review. That is why it has always been held that as part of its traditional equipment for the administration of justice, a federal court can stay the enforcement of a judgment pending the outcome of an appeal. A stay does not make time stand still, but does hold a ruling in abeyance to allow an appellate court the time necessary to review it. . .

> The authority to hold an order in abeyance pending review allows an appellate court to act responsibly. A reviewing court must bring considered judgment to bear on the matter before it, but that cannot always be done quickly enough to afford relief to the party aggrieved by the order under review. The choice for a reviewing court should not be between justice on the fly or participation in what may be an "idle ceremony." The ability to grant interim relief is accordingly not simply "[a]n historic procedure for preserving rights during the pendency of an appeal," but also a means of ensuring that appellate courts can responsibly fulfill their role in the judicial process. At the same time, a reviewing court may not

resolve a conflict between considered review and effective relief by reflexively holding a final order in abeyance pending review. A stay is an intrusion into the ordinary processes of administration and judicial review, and accordingly is not a matter of right, even if irreparable injury might otherwise result to the appellant. The parties and the public, while entitled to both careful review and a meaningful decision, are also generally entitled to the prompt execution of orders that the legislature has made final. *Nken v. Holder,* 556 U.S. 418 (2009) (citations and quotation marks omitted).

Nken noted that the standards for granting a stay "have been distilled into consideration of four factors: (1) whether the stay applicant has made a strong showing that he is likely to succeed on the merits; (2) whether the applicant will be irreparably injured absent a stay; (3) whether issuance of the stay will substantially injure the other parties interested in the proceeding; and (4) where the public interest lies." These factors are usually called the *Virginia Petroleum* factors, after the case that first enunciated them. *Virginia Petroleum Jobbers Ass'n v. FPC,* 259 F.2d 921 (D.C. Cir. 1958).

Normally, these standards for deciding whether to grant a judicial stay are the same as the standards used in preliminary injunction cases. *See, e.g., Winter v. NRDC,* 555 U.S. 7, 20 (2008). However, in *Nken* itself Congress had passed a statute that imposed an unusually strict test for preliminary injunctions in cases involving the deportation of an alien. The Court construed the statute narrowly so that it could continue to adhere to its traditional criteria for ruling on stay applications in those immigration cases.

Under the first of the *Virginia Petroleum* factors, the decision about whether to grant a stay requires a court to "peek" at the merits, in order to make an intelligent assessment of the likelihood the applicant will prevail on the merits. *Cronin v. USDA,* 919 F.2d 439 (7th Cir. 1990), suggests that whenever possible the court should resolve both the stay request and the merits all at once rather than doing so in two separate proceedings. However, this is often not possible, since the decision on a stay must be made soon after the notice of appeal is filed, whereas the decision on the merits may be months or years away.

Note the discussion of judicial stays in both the Harlan and Fortas opinions in *Abbott Labs.* Harlan argues that pre-enforcement review of regulations won't harm the public interest, because courts can refuse to grant a stay. Fortas counters that some court, somewhere, undoubtedly would grant a stay despite harm to the public interest.

6. *Problem.* The "Superfund" Act provides for cleaning up toxic waste dumps. Without notice and comment, EPA adopted a policy statement called the Hazardous Ranking System (HRS). EPA intended HRS to serve as a guideline (to itself and to the public) in setting toxic waste cleanup priorities. HRS is a methodology for setting priorities as to which sites are most

dangerous and should be cleaned up first. HRS took account of many factors, such as the toxicity of the particular hazardous substance that might be released, the likelihood of release into the environment, and the threatened population or other sensitive environment. While HRS enabled the calculation of a danger "score" for a particular site, it did not set any cleanup priorities or single out any sites. Zolt Chemicals anticipates that the HRS methodology would place its toxic waste dump high on a cleanup priority list. Can Zolt Chemicals get immediate judicial review of HRS? *See Eagle-Picher Industries v. EPA*, 759 F.2d 905 (D.C. Cir. 1985). If so, should the court grant a stay?

§ 11.2.5   PRIMARY JURISDICTION

FARMERS INSURANCE EXCHANGE V. SUPERIOR COURT
826 P.2d 730 (Cal. 1992)

LUCAS, C.J.:

[The California Attorney General (sometimes referred to as The People) sued Farmers to require it to offer good driver discounts to its auto insurance customers. Count 1 was based on Insurance Code § 1861.02 which was enacted by the voters as an initiative and requires insurers to offer good driver discounts. However, the Court held that the Insurance Code vests enforcement of § 1861.02 exclusively in the Insurance Commissioner. Consequently, it upheld the lower court's decision which dismissed count 1.

The second count was based on the Unfair Practices Act, Business & Professions Code § 17000, which provides remedies in cases of illegal business practices. The Attorney General has power to enforce § 17000 through actions for injunction or civil penalties. Farmers argued that the second count should be dismissed under the doctrine of primary jurisdiction.]

III. THE PRIMARY JURISDICTION DOCTRINE

A.   Development of the Doctrine

The judicially created doctrine of "primary jurisdiction" (also referred to as the doctrine of "prior resort" or "preliminary jurisdiction") originated in *Texas & Pac. Ry. v. Abilene Cotton Oil Co.*, 204 U.S. 426 (1907) (hereafter *Abilene*), and as explained below, most of the development of the doctrine has occurred in the federal courts.

In *Abilene*, a shipper sued a railroad in state court under the common law to recover alleged unreasonable amounts charged for transporting interstate freight. . . . Under the Commerce Act, Congress granted the ICC power to hear such complaints by shippers, and to order reparations to those injured. Despite provisions of the Commerce Act allowing a litigant to elect between administrative enforcement of statutory rights and judicial enforcement of common law rights, the high court declined to allow the common law suit in the first instance. Instead, it ruled that in order to promote uniformity and consistency of rate regulations, the shipper "must . . . primarily invoke redress through the Interstate Commerce Commission." . . . The Court explained that "if, without previous action by the Commission, power might be exerted by courts and juries generally to determine the reasonableness of an established rate, it would follow that unless all courts reached an identical conclusion a uniform standard of rates in the future would be impossible, as the standard would fluctuate and vary, depending on the divergent conclusions reached as to reasonableness by the various courts called upon to consider the subject as an original question." . . .

The doctrine of *Abilene* was refined and clarified in *Great Northern Ry. v. Merchants Elevator Co.*, 259 U.S. 285 (1922). In *Merchants*, another case in which a shipper attempted to press suit against a railway to recover asserted overcharges, Justice Brandeis, speaking for the court, allowed the state court suit to proceed because the issue presented in that case—i.e., the proper interpretation of a tariff—was one of law and neither involved disputed facts, nor required the exercise of expertise possessed by the ICC. The court explained, "Preliminary resort to the Commission [is necessary when] . . . the enquiry is essentially one of fact and of discretion in technical matters; and uniformity can be secured only if its determination is left to the Commission. Moreover, that determination is reached ordinarily upon voluminous and conflicting evidence, for the adequate appreciation of which acquaintance with many intricate facts of transportation is indispensable; and such acquaintance is commonly to be found only in a body of experts. But what construction shall be given to a railroad tariff presents ordinarily a question of law which does not differ in character from those presented when the construction of any other document is in dispute."

In a third railroad shipping case, *United States v. Western Pac. R. Co.*, 352 U.S. 59 (1956), the shipper (the United States government) filed suit in the Court of Claims to recover alleged overcharges. The issue presented was similar to that in *Merchants*, *i.e.*, the construction of a railroad tariff. Specifically, the question posed was whether shipments of steel bomb cases filled with napalm gel should be classified as "incendiary bombs" (subject to a high first-class tariff rate) or merely "gasoline in steel drums" (subject to a lower, fifth-class rate).

The high court considered the factors articulated in *Abilene* and *Merchants*. . . . The court asserted that the term "incendiary bomb," as used in the tariff regulations, posed a question of construction that involves factors the adequate appreciation of which presupposes an acquaintance with many intricate facts of transportation possessed by the

ICC. Accordingly, the court concluded, "in the circumstances here presented the question of tariff construction, as well as that of the reasonableness of the tariff as applied, was within the exclusive primary jurisdiction of the Interstate Commerce Commission."

A more recent high court case illustrates both procedural and substantive aspects of the primary jurisdiction doctrine. In *Nader v. Allegheny Airlines*, 426 U.S. 290 (1976), the plaintiff filed a common law tort action for fraudulent misrepresentation against an airline that sold him a confirmed ticket on an overbooked flight, causing the plaintiff to miss his flight. . . . The high court [allowed the fraud case to proceed and declined to apply the primary jurisdiction doctrine]. It noted that under the administrative scheme at issue, individual consumers were "not even entitled" to initiate proceedings before the Civil Aeronautics Board. The fact that the plaintiff in the case before it had no authority to bring an administrative action, however, did not resolve the court's primary jurisdiction inquiry. . . . It concluded the proposed misrepresentation action posed no challenge to uniformity of regulation and that "the standards to be applied in an action for fraudulent misrepresentation are within the conventional competence of the courts, and the judgment of a technically expert body is not likely to be helpful in the application of these standards to the facts of this case." . . .

B.　The Primary Jurisdiction and Exhaustion Doctrines Compared

Petitioners assert throughout their briefs that the People should be required to "exhaust" their administrative remedies before pursuing their civil action in this case, [but] the applicable principle in this case is the primary jurisdiction doctrine, not the exhaustion doctrine.

Petitioners' mischaracterization is understandable because courts have often confused the two closely related concepts. "Both are essentially doctrines of comity between courts and agencies. They are two sides of the timing coin: Each determines whether an action may be brought in a court or whether an agency proceeding, or further agency proceeding, is necessary."

In *Western Pacific*, the high court explained: "Exhaustion applies where a claim is cognizable in the first instance by an administrative agency alone; judicial interference is withheld until the administrative process has run its course. Primary jurisdiction, on the other hand, applies where a claim is originally cognizable in the courts, and comes into play whenever enforcement of the claim requires the resolution of issues which, under a regulatory scheme, have been placed within the special competence of an administrative body; in such a case the judicial process is suspended pending referral of such issues to the administrative body for its views." [Unlike the People's first count, its claim under

§ 17000] is originally cognizable in the courts, and thus it triggers application of the primary jurisdiction doctrine.

C.   Policy Considerations Underlying the Primary Jurisdiction and Exhaustion Doctrines

The policy reasons behind the two doctrines are similar and overlapping. The exhaustion doctrine is principally grounded on concerns favoring administrative autonomy (i.e., courts should not interfere with an agency determination until the agency has reached a final decision) and judicial efficiency (i.e., overworked courts should decline to intervene in an administrative dispute unless absolutely necessary). As explained above, the primary jurisdiction doctrine advances two related policies: it enhances court decisionmaking and efficiency by allowing courts to take advantage of administrative expertise, and it helps assure uniform application of regulatory laws.

No rigid formula exists for applying the primary jurisdiction doctrine. Instead, resolution generally hinges on a court's determination of the extent to which the policies noted above are implicated in a given case.[9] This discretionary approach leaves courts with considerable flexibility to avoid application of the doctrine in appropriate situations, as required by the interests of justice. . . .

VI. Application of the Primary Jurisdiction Doctrine in This Case

First . . . the Insurance Commissioner has at his disposal a "pervasive and self-contained system of administrative procedure" to deal with the precise questions involved herein.

Second, and more important, based on the allegations in the People's complaint, there is good reason to require that these administrative procedures be invoked here. As we explain below, we conclude that considerations of judicial economy, and concerns for uniformity in application of the complex insurance regulations here involved, strongly militate in favor of a stay to await action by the Insurance Commissioner in the present case . . . [C]ourts have observed that questions involving insurance rate making pose issues for which specialized agency fact-finding and expertise is needed in order to both resolve complex factual questions and provide a record for subsequent judicial review. . . .

The People assert the claims at issue here "involve relatively simple factual determinations which do not require the detailed examination of experts within the Department of Insurance. . . . [On the contrary] the

---

[9]   Although this approach focuses on the benefits to be gained by courts (e.g. efficiency and uniform application of regulatory laws) and agencies (e.g. autonomy) under the primary jurisdiction doctrine, courts have also appropriately considered the alleged "inadequacy" of administrative remedies, and other factors affecting litigants, in determining whether the interests of justice militate against application of the doctrine in a particular case.

resolution of these questions mandates exercise of expertise presumably possessed by the Insurance Commissioner, and poses a risk of inconsistent application of the regulatory statutes if courts are forced to rule on such matters without benefit of the views of the agency charged with regulating the insurance industry. . . .

The determination of whether a given Good Driver Discount policy comports with the "20 percent discount" provision of the statute also calls for exercise of administrative expertise preliminary to judicial review. Inevitably, analysis of the People's claim will require "a searching inquiry into the factual complexities of [automobile] insurance ratemaking and the conditions of that market during the turbulent time here involved. To address the People's claim, one must inquire into the insurer's ratemaking process in order to determine what the rate would be for a given driver without the discount. Thereafter one must discern whether the rate offered on a given Good Driver Discount policy is 20 percent below what the insured would otherwise have been charged. . . .

VII. Conclusion

We conclude, based on the complaint as it stands, that a paramount need for specialized agency review militates in favor of imposing a requirement of prior resort to the administrative process, and . . . we reject any suggestion that the interests of justice militate against application of a prior resort requirement in this case.

Accordingly, the judgment of the Court of Appeal is reversed with directions to issue a writ of mandate directing the superior court to stay judicial proceedings in this case and retain the matter on the court's docket pending proceedings before the Insurance Commissioner, and to closely monitor the progress of the administrative proceedings to ensure against unreasonable delay of the People's civil action.

NOTES AND QUESTIONS

1.   *Primary jurisdiction and exclusive jurisdiction.* The issue presented in final order, exhaustion of remedies, or ripeness cases (§§ 11.2.2 to 11.2.4) is the timing of judicial review. In primary jurisdiction cases, the issue is not the timing of judicial review. Instead, primary jurisdiction cases present the problem of *concurrent* trial jurisdiction to try a case (as in the second count in *Farmers*). Then the question is: who goes first? If the court decides that the agency should go first, it has applied the doctrine of primary jurisdiction.

Primary jurisdiction cases usually involve disputes between parties *other than the regulatory agency* that controls the particular industry. Most such cases are between two private parties (like the shipper and the railroad, as in the various U.S. Supreme Court cases discussed in *Farmers*); others, like *Farmers*, are law enforcement cases brought by a state or federal attorney general. In contrast, when the case is brought by or against the regulatory agency, the issue is the timing of judicial review of the agency action and generally involves the doctrines of finality, exhaustion of remedies, or ripeness, rather than primary jurisdiction.

Primary jurisdiction cases are of two different kinds. If a court finds that the agency should go first, and the agency proceeding will dispose of all the issues in the case, the court dismisses the action. The matter returns to court only upon judicial review of the agency action. This is primary jurisdiction of the whole case. If the court finds that the agency cannot dispose of the entire case, the court stays the action, sends the parties to the agency, and retains jurisdiction to try the remaining issues after the agency is finished. This is primary jurisdiction of an issue or issues. Note the concluding paragraph of the court's opinion in *Farmers*. In a case of primary jurisdiction over issues, a court might simply ask the agency to express its views by filing an amicus brief instead of sending the case to the agency.

As already mentioned, primary jurisdiction issues arise only if the court and the agency have concurrent jurisdiction to make the initial decision in the case. If the legislature precludes judicial jurisdiction, thus making the agency's jurisdiction *exclusive,* there is no concurrent jurisdiction. The *Farmers* court so held as to the People's first count.

Alternatively, the statute might preclude agency jurisdiction, in which case the court cannot send it to the agency and must try the case itself. Thus, consider *Southern Utah Wilderness Alliance v. Bureau of Land Mgmt.*, 425 F.3d 735 (10th Cir. 2005) (this *SUWA* case is not the same one that is excerpted in § 10.6). The court ruled that the agency had no jurisdiction, so that the district court should have tried the case. The dispute concerned whether Utah counties could build or improve roads through public lands. Until 1976, counties could do so without permission under Rev. Stat. 2477, which was passed in 1866. In 1976, however, R.S. 2477 was repealed. Counties with pre-1976 rights of way could continue to use and maintain them.

In 1996, several Utah counties graded roads through public lands, claiming that they were maintaining pre-1976 rights of way. *SUWA* sought to enjoin this road-building. The District Court applied primary jurisdiction, sending the case to the BLM, which administers the public lands. BLM conducted an informal adjudication and ruled that all of the road building was illegal. The case returned to the District Court which held the counties liable for trespass.

The court ruled that BLM had no adjudicatory authority over R.S. 2477 disputes. The statute was silent on the issue, and BLM had never claimed such authority during 100 years of R. S. 2477 litigation. Indeed, it had previously maintained that it had no such authority. Thus it was improper to refer that case to BLM for the purpose of conducting an adjudication that would bind the parties.

2. *Rationale for primary jurisdiction.* Why should a court that has jurisdiction over a matter send the case (or some of the issues in that case) for trial before an agency? There needs to be some persuasive reason for the court not to exercise its statutory jurisdiction. The cases discussed in *Farmers* indicate that there may be three reasons for doing so: a need for uniform results, a need for the agency's expertise, or the possibility that an agency decision could immunize the practice from legal attack. On which of these rationales did the court rely in *Farmers*? *See generally* Kathryn A. Watts, *Adapting to Administrative Law's* Erie *Doctrine*, 101 Nw. U. L. Rev. 997, 1026–33 (2007) (discussing potential benefits of primary jurisdiction).

Note that the People in *Farmers* sought civil penalties under § 17000. The Insurance Commissioner did not have power to award that remedy. Courts sometimes identify the lack of remedy as a factor suggesting that primary jurisdiction should not apply. How did the court get around the problem in *Farmers*?

3. *Primary jurisdiction and the administration of justice.* Why did the Attorney General resist having the case sent to the Insurance Commissioner? Why did Farmers want the case to be sent there?

National Communications Ass'n v. AT&T Co., 46 F.3d 220, 225 (2d Cir. 1995), involved a dispute between AT&T and a relatively small wholesaler of long distance time. The dispute concerned the interpretation of AT&T's tariff. The court refused to send the case to the FCC under the primary jurisdiction doctrine. It said:

> Agency decisionmaking often takes a long time and the delay imposes enormous costs on individuals, society and the legal system. Delay in agency decisionmaking is often due to 1) large workload, 2) difficult issues, 3) inadequate funding and staffing, 4) poor organizational structure and management, 5) time-consuming decisionmaking procedures, 6) judicial review, 7) OMB review, and 8) intentional delay.

The parties estimated that the delay resulting from sending the case back to the FCC would be from two to five years. "Since the district court can conclude this matter far more expeditiously, a potential delay of even two years more than outweighs any benefit that might be achieved by having the FCC resolve this relatively simple factual dispute." One possible solution for the problem of agency delay is to send the case or a disputed issue to the agency, but on a short fuse. If the agency does not deal with the issue that is sent to it within 180 days, the court action resumes. *American Auto. Mfrs. Ass'n v. Dep't of Envtl. Protection*, 163 F.3d 74 (1st Cir. 1998).

4. *Private rights of action.* The primary jurisdiction doctrine comes into play when both a court and an agency have jurisdiction to hear the case. Many statutes provide for administrative or criminal remedies, but are unclear about whether private parties have a civil remedy to enforce the statute. The issue then becomes whether the court should imply a "private

right of action" into the statute. Only after it rules that a private right of action exists under the statute in question does the court reach the issue of whether the agency has primary jurisdiction.

The problem of whether a statute gives rise to an implied private right of action by a victim against the party that caused the harm is difficult and recurrent. At one time, the rule was that "it is the duty of the courts to be alert to provide such remedies as are necessary to make effective the congressional purpose" expressed in a regulatory statute. *J. I. Case Co. v. Borak*, 377 U.S. 426 (1964). Under that approach, courts tended to assume that a civil remedy to enforce a regulatory statute existed unless language in the statute indicated that Congress did not want private enforcement.

An intermediate approach appeared in *Cort v. Ash*, 422 U.S. 66 (1975), in which the Court set forth a four-factor test to determine whether Congress intended a private right of action. The factors were: i) is the plaintiff in a class for whose especial benefit the statute was enacted? ii) Is there evidence of legislative intent to create such a remedy or deny it? iii) Is it consistent with the underlying purposes of the legislative scheme to imply such a remedy? iv) Is the cause of action one traditionally relegated to state law so it would be inappropriate to create a right based solely on federal law? *Cort v. Ash* is often followed by the states. *See, e.g., Upperman v. Grange Indemnity Ins. Co.*, 842 N.E.2d 132 (Ohio C.P. 2005), implying a private right of action from a statute requiring insurance companies to file rate changes with the Ohio Insurance Department.

However, recent Supreme Court cases reject *Cort v. Ash* balancing. The Supreme Court will not imply a private right of action from a regulatory statute without affirmative evidence that Congress intended one. "Having sworn off the habit of venturing beyond Congress's intent, we will not accept respondents' invitation to have one last drink." *Alexander v. Sandoval*, 532 U.S. 275 (2001).

Alexander v. Sandoval is a striking example of the Supreme Court's new approach. An earlier case, *Cannon v. University of Chicago*, 441 U.S. 677 (1979), ruled that there is a private right of action under § 901 of Education Amendments of 1972. That section prohibits education programs receiving federal funds from engaging in sex discrimination. Section 902 specified a procedure whereby federal aid to an educational institution could be terminated for violating § 901. Applying the *Cort v. Ash* balancing test, the Court decided that there was a private right of action by victims of sex discrimination against educational institutions.

Alexander v. Sandoval involved a very similar situation, this time arising under Title VI of the Civil Rights Act of 1964. Section 601 prohibits discrimination on the basis of race, color, or national origin by recipients of federal funds. Section 602 authorizes federal agencies to effectuate the provisions of § 601 by issuing rules. The Justice Department adopted a rule under § 602 that broadened the reach of § 601 to cover cases of disparate impact discrimination (such as the use of an English-only driver's license test). The question was whether there is a private right of action to enforce that rule. In a 5–4 decision, the court held there was not. Essentially, the majority was determined not to broaden the *Cannon* precedent, absent a clear message from Congress that a private right of action was intended. It also made clear that no private right of action could arise from a regulation unless Congress had indicated that one should exist.

In dissent, Justice Stevens wrote: "According to [the majority's] analysis, the recognition of an implied right of action when the text and structure of the statute do not absolutely compel such a conclusion is an act of judicial self-indulgence. As much as we would like to help those disadvantaged by discrimination, we must resist the temptation to pour ourselves 'one last drink.' Overwrought imagery aside, it is the majority's approach that blinds itself to Congressional intent. While it remains true that, if Congress intends a private right of action to support statutory rights, the far better course is for it to specify as much when it creates these rights, its failure to do so does not absolve us of the responsibility to endeavor to discern its intent."

5.   *Problem.* Madison has legal casino gambling and heavily regulates the casino industry. A statute provides that the Casino Control Commission (CCC) shall have exclusive jurisdiction over all matters delegated to it. It provides that the CCC shall regulate the industry so as to create and preserve public confidence and trust in the integrity of casino operations.

Casinos must receive a license from CCC. The agency is empowered to suspend or revoke casino licenses, or assess civil penalties against casinos, for violation of CCC regulations. The statute also provides that the CCC can order restitution of any money unlawfully obtained by a casino. All adjudicatory matters (licensing, penalties, and restitution) are initiated by the CCC director. CCC's regulations prohibit casinos from allowing persons to gamble while intoxicated.

Leonard lost over $1,000,000 in one night playing blackjack at Dusty's Casino. He was served 12 free drinks during this period and was visibly very intoxicated. Leonard files suit in Madison superior court seeking to recover $1,000,000 from Dusty's and to recover an additional $3,000,000 in punitive damages. Dusty's moves to dismiss the action, arguing that the CCC has either exclusive jurisdiction or primary jurisdiction over the claim. *See Campione v. Adamar of N.J., Inc.,* 714 A.2d 299 (N.J. 1998); *Greate Bay Hotel & Casino v. Tose,* 34 F.3d 1227 (3d Cir. 1994). How should the court rule on this motion?

APPENDIX A

UNITED STATES CONSTITUTION
(SELECTED PROVISIONS)

■ ■ ■

Article I

Section 1. All legislative Powers herein granted shall be vested in a Congress of the United States, which shall consist of a Senate and House of Representatives.

Section 7. [1] All Bills for raising Revenue shall originate in the House of Representatives; but the Senate may propose or concur with Amendments as on other Bills.

[2] Every Bill which shall have passed the House of Representatives and the Senate, shall, before it become a Law, be presented to the President of the United States; If he approve he shall sign it, but if not he shall return it, with his Objections to that House in which it shall have originated, who shall enter the Objections at large on their Journal, and proceed to reconsider it. If after such Reconsideration two thirds of that House shall agree to pass the Bill, it shall be sent, together with the Objections, to the other House, by which it shall likewise be reconsidered, and if approved by two thirds of that House, it shall become a Law. But in all such Cases the Votes of both Houses shall be determined by yeas and Nays, and the Names of the Persons voting for and against the Bill shall be entered on the Journal of each House respectively. If any Bill shall not be returned by the President within ten Days (Sundays excepted) after it shall have been presented to him, the Same shall be a Law, in like Manner as if he had signed it, unless the Congress by their Adjournment prevent its Return, in which Case it shall not be a Law.

[3] Every Order, Resolution, or Vote to Which the Concurrence of the Senate and House of Representatives may be necessary (except on a question of Adjournment) shall be presented to the President of the United States; and before the Same shall take Effect, shall be approved by him, or being disapproved by him, shall be repassed by two thirds of the Senate and House of Representatives, according to the Rules and Limitations prescribed in the Case of a Bill.

Section 8. The Congress shall have Power . . .

[18] To make all Laws which shall be necessary and proper for carrying into Execution the foregoing Powers, and all other Powers vested by this Constitution in the Government of the United States, or in any Department or Officer thereof.

Section 9. [3] No Bill of Attainder or ex post facto law shall be passed.

[7] No Money shall be drawn from the Treasury, but in Consequence of Appropriations made by Law; and a regular Statement and Account of the Receipts and Expenditures of all public Money shall be published from time to time.

Article II

Section 1. [1] The executive Power shall be vested in a President of the United States of America. . . .

Section 2. [1] The President shall be Commander in Chief of the Army and Navy of the United States; . . . he may require the Opinion, in writing, of the principal Officer in each of the executive Departments, upon any Subject relating to the Duties of their respective Offices. . . .

[2] He shall have Power, by and with the Advice and Consent of the Senate, to make Treaties, provided two thirds of the Senators present concur; and he shall nominate, and by and with the Advice and Consent of the Senate, shall appoint Ambassadors, other public Ministers and Consuls, Judges of the supreme Court, and all other Officers of the United States, whose Appointments are not herein otherwise provided for, and which shall be established by Law; but the Congress may by Law vest the Appointment of such inferior Officers, as they think proper, in the President alone, in the Courts of Law, or in the Heads of Departments.

The President shall have Power to fill up all Vacancies that may happen during the Recess of the Senate, by granting Commissions which shall expire at the End of their next Session.

Section 3. He shall from time to time give to the Congress Information of the State of the Union, and recommend to their Consideration such Measures as he shall judge necessary and expedient; . . . he shall take Care that the Laws be faithfully executed, and shall Commission all the Officers of the United States.

Section 4. The President, Vice President and all civil Officers of the United States, shall be removed from Office on Impeachment for, and Conviction of, Treason, Bribery, or other high Crimes and Misdemeanors.

Article III

Section 1. The judicial Power of the United States, shall be vested in one supreme Court, and in such inferior Courts as the Congress may from time to time ordain and establish. . . .

Section 2. [1] The judicial Power shall extend to all Cases, in Law and Equity, arising under this Constitution, the Laws of the United States, and Treaties made, or which shall be made, under their Authority;—to all Cases affecting Ambassadors, other public Ministers and Consuls;—to all Cases of admiralty and maritime Jurisdiction;—to Controversies to which the United States shall be a Party;—to Controversies between two or more States;—between a State and Citizens of another State;—between Citizens of different States;—between Citizens of the same State claiming Lands under the Grants of different States, and between a State, or the Citizens thereof, and foreign States, Citizens or Subjects.

Amendment I [1791]

Congress shall make no law respecting an establishment of religion, or prohibiting the free exercise thereof; or abridging the freedom of speech, or of the press; or the right of the people peaceably to assemble, and to petition the Government for a redress of grievances.

Amendment IV [1791]

The right of the people to be secure in their persons, houses, papers, and effects, against unreasonable searches and seizures, shall not be violated, and no Warrants shall issue, but upon probable cause, supported by Oath or affirmation, and particularly describing the place to be searched, and the persons or things to be seized.

Amendment V [1791]

No person shall be held to answer for a capital, or otherwise infamous crime, unless on a presentment or indictment of a Grand Jury, except in cases arising in the land or naval forces, or in the Militia, when in actual service in time of War or public danger; nor shall any person be subject for the same offence to be twice put in jeopardy of life or limb; nor shall be compelled in any criminal case to be a witness against himself, nor be deprived of life, liberty, or property, without due process of law; nor shall private property be taken for public use, without just compensation.

Amendment VII [1791]

In Suits at common law, where the value in controversy shall exceed twenty dollars, the right of trial by jury shall be preserved, and no fact tried by a jury, shall be otherwise re-examined in any Court of the United States, than according to the rules of the common law.

Amendment XIV [1868]

Section 1. All persons born or naturalized in the United States, and subject to the jurisdiction thereof, are citizens of the United States and of the State wherein they reside. No State shall make or enforce any law which shall abridge the privileges or immunities of citizens of the United States; nor shall any State deprive any person of life, liberty, or property, without due process of law; nor deny to any person within its jurisdiction the equal protection of the laws.

APPENDIX B

FEDERAL ADMINISTRATIVE PROCEDURE ACT

UNITED STATES CODE, TITLE 5

■ ■ ■

Table of Sections

Sec.

CHAPTER 5—ADMINISTRATIVE PROCEDURE

§ 551.   Definitions.

For the purpose of this subchapter—

(1) "agency" means each authority of the Government of the United States, whether or not it is within or subject to review by another agency, but does not include—

(A) the Congress;

(B) the courts of the United States;

(C) the governments of the territories or possessions of the United States;

(D) the government of the District of Columbia;

or except as to the requirements of section 552 of this title—

(E) agencies composed of representatives of the parties or of representatives of organizations of the parties to the disputes determined by them;

(F) courts martial and military commissions;

(G) military authority exercised in the field in time of war or in occupied territory; or

(H) functions conferred by sections 1738, 1739, 1743, and 1744 of title 12; chapter 2 of title 41; subchapter II of chapter 471 of title 49; or sections 1884, 1891–1902, and former section 1641(b)(2), of title 50, appendix;

(2) "person" includes an individual, partnership, corporation, association, or public or private organization other than an agency;

(3) "party" includes a person or agency named or admitted as a party, or properly seeking and entitled as of right to be admitted as a party, in an agency proceeding, and a person or agency admitted by an agency as a party for limited purposes;

(4) "rule" means the whole or a part of an agency statement of general or particular applicability and future effect designed to implement, interpret, or prescribe law or policy or describing the organization, procedure, or practice requirements of an agency and includes the approval or prescription for the future of rates, wages, corporate or financial structures or reorganizations thereof, prices, facilities, appliances, services or allowances therefor or of valuations, costs, or accounting, or practices bearing on any of the foregoing;

(5) "rule making" means agency process for formulating, amending, or repealing a rule;

(6) "order" means the whole or a part of a final disposition, whether affirmative, negative, injunctive, or declaratory in form, of an agency in a matter other than rule making but including licensing;

(7) "adjudication" means agency process for the formulation of an order;

(8) "license" includes the whole or a part of an agency permit, certificate, approval, registration, charter, membership, statutory exemption or other form of permission;

(9) "licensing" includes agency process respecting the grant, renewal, denial, revocation, suspension, annulment, withdrawal, limitation, amendment, modification, or conditioning of a license;

(10) "sanction" includes the whole or a part of an agency—

(A) prohibition, requirement, limitation, or other condition affecting the freedom of a person;

(B) withholding of relief;

(C) imposition of penalty or fine;

(D) destruction, taking, seizure, or withholding of property;

(E) assessment of damages, reimbursement, restitution, compensation, costs, charges, or fees;

(F) requirement, revocation, or suspension of a license; or

(G) taking other compulsory or restrictive action;

(11) "relief" includes the whole or a part of an agency—

(A) grant of money, assistance, license, authority, exemption, exception, privilege, or remedy;

(B) recognition of a claim, right, immunity, privilege, exemption, or exception; or

(C) taking of other action on the application or petition of, and beneficial to, a person;

(12) "agency proceeding" means an agency process as defined by paragraphs (5), (7), and (9) of this section;

(13) "agency action" includes the whole or a part of an agency rule, order, license, sanction, relief, or the equivalent or denial thereof, or failure to act; and

(14) "ex parte communication" means an oral or written communication not on the public record with respect to which reasonable prior notice to all parties is not given, but it shall not include requests for status reports on any matter or proceeding covered by this subchapter.

§ 552. Public information; agency rules, opinions, orders, records, and proceedings [Freedom of Information Act— excerpts only.]

(a) Each agency shall make available to the public information as follows:

(1) Each agency shall separately state and currently publish in the Federal Register for the guidance of the public—

(A) descriptions of its central and field organization and the established places at which, the employees (and in the case of a uniformed service, the members) from whom, and the methods whereby, the public may obtain information, make submittals or requests, or obtain decisions;

(B) statements of the general course and method by which its functions are channeled and determined, including the nature and requirements of all formal and informal procedures available;

(C) rules of procedure, descriptions of forms available or the places at which forms may be obtained, and instructions as to the scope and contents of all papers, reports, or examinations;

(D) substantive rules of general applicability adopted as authorized by law, and statements of general policy or interpretations of general applicability formulated and adopted by the agency; and

(E) each amendment, revision, or repeal of the foregoing.

Except to the extent that a person has actual and timely notice of the terms thereof, a person may not in any manner be required to resort to, or be adversely affected by, a matter required to be published in the Federal Register and not so published. For the purpose of this paragraph, matter reasonably available to the class of persons affected thereby is deemed published in the Federal Register when incorporated by reference therein with the approval of the Director of the Federal Register.

(2) Each agency, in accordance with published rules, shall make available for public inspection and copying—

(A) final opinions, including concurring and dissenting opinions, as well as orders, made in the adjudication of cases;

(B) those statements of policy and interpretations which have been adopted by the agency and are not published in the Federal Register;

(C) administrative staff manuals and instructions to staff that affect a member of the public;

(D) copies of all records, regardless of form or format, which have been released to any person under paragraph (3) and which, because of the nature of their subject matter, the agency determines have become or are likely to become the subject of subsequent requests for substantially the same records; and

(E) a general index of the records referred to under subparagraph (D);

unless the materials are promptly published and copies offered for sale. For records created on or after November 1, 1996, within one year after such date, each agency shall make such records available, including by computer telecommunications or, if computer telecommunications means have not been established by the agency, by other electronic means. . . . A final order, opinion, statement of policy, interpretation, or staff manual or instruction that affects a member of the public may be relied on, used, or cited as precedent by an agency against a party other than an agency only if—

(i) it has been indexed and either made available or published as provided by this paragraph; or

(ii) the party has actual and timely notice of the terms thereof.

(3)(A) Except with respect to the records made available under paragraphs (1) and (2) of this subsection, each agency, upon any request for records which (i) reasonably describes such records and (ii) is made in accordance with published rules stating the time, place, fees (if any), and procedures to be followed, shall make the records promptly available to any person.

(B) In making any record available to a person under this paragraph, an agency shall provide the record in any form or format requested by the person if the record is readily reproducible by the agency in that form or format. Each agency shall make reasonable efforts to maintain its records in forms or formats that are reproducible for purposes of this section. . . .

(4)(A)(i) In order to carry out the provisions of this section, each agency shall promulgate regulations, pursuant to notice and receipt of public comment, specifying the schedule of fees applicable to the processing of requests under this section . . .

(B) On complaint, the district court of the United States in the district in which the complainant resides, or has his principal place of business, or in which the agency records are situated, or in the District of Columbia, has jurisdiction to enjoin the agency from withholding agency records and to order the production of any agency records improperly withheld from the complainant. In such a case the court shall determine the matter de novo, and may examine the contents of such agency records in camera to determine whether such records or any part thereof shall be withheld under any of the exemptions set forth in subsection (b) of this section, and the burden is on the agency to sustain its action. . . .

(E)(i)   The court may assess against the United States reasonable attorney fees and other litigation costs reasonably incurred in any case under this section in which the complainant has substantially prevailed. . . .

(b)   This section does not apply to matters that are—

(1)(A)   specifically authorized under criteria established by an Executive order to be kept secret in the interest of national defense or foreign policy and (B) are in fact properly classified pursuant to such Executive order;

(2) related solely to the internal personnel rules and practices of an agency;

(3) specifically exempted from disclosure by statute (other than section 552b of this title), if that statute — (A) (i) requires that the matters be withheld from the public in such a manner as to leave no discretion on the issue; or (ii) establishes particular criteria for withholding or refers to particular types of matters to be withheld; and (B) if enacted after the date of enactment of the OPEN FOIA Act of 2009, specifically cites to this paragraph.

(4) trade secrets and commercial or financial information obtained from a person and privileged or confidential;

(5) inter-agency or intra-agency memorandums or letters which would not be available by law to a party other than an agency in litigation with the agency;

(6) personnel and medical files and similar files the disclosure of which would constitute a clearly unwarranted invasion of personal privacy;

(7) records or information compiled for law enforcement purposes, but only to the extent that the production of such law enforcement records or information (A) could reasonably be expected to interfere with enforcement proceedings, (B) would deprive a person of a right to a fair trial or an impartial adjudication, (C) could reasonably be expected to constitute an unwarranted invasion of personal privacy, (D) could reasonably be expected to disclose the identity of a confidential source, including a State, local, or foreign agency or authority or any private institution which furnished information on a confidential basis, and, in the case of a record or information compiled by criminal law enforcement authority in the course of a criminal investigation or by an agency conducting a lawful national security intelligence investigation, information furnished by a confidential source, (E) would disclose techniques and procedures for law enforcement investigations or prosecutions, or would disclose guidelines for law enforcement investigations or prosecutions if such disclosure could reasonably be expected to risk circumvention of the law, or (F) could reasonably be expected to endanger the life or physical safety of any individual;

(8) contained in or related to examination, operating, or condition reports prepared by, on behalf of, or for the use of an agency responsible for the regulation or supervision of financial institutions; or

(9) geological and geophysical information and data, including maps, concerning wells.

Any reasonably segregable portion of a record shall be provided to any person requesting such record after deletion of the portions which are exempt under this subsection. The amount of information deleted, and the exemption under which the deletion is made, shall be indicated on the released portion of the record, unless including that indication would harm an interest protected by the exemption in this subsection under which the deletion is made. If technically feasible, the amount of the information deleted, and the exemption under which the deletion is made, shall be indicated at the place in the record where such deletion is made. . . .

(d) This section does not authorize withholding of information or limit the availability of records to the public, except as specifically stated in this section. This section is not authority to withhold information from Congress. . . .

§ 552a. Records maintained on individuals

[This section, known as the Privacy Act, is omitted.]

§ 552b. Open meetings

[This section, known as the Government in the Sunshine Act, is omitted.]

§ 553. Rule making

(a) This section applies, according to the provisions thereof, except to the extent that there is involved—

> (1) a military or foreign affairs function of the United States; or

> (2) a matter relating to agency management or personnel or to public property, loans, grants, benefits, or contracts.

(b) General notice of proposed rule making shall be published in the Federal Register, unless persons subject thereto are named and either personally served or otherwise have actual notice thereof in accordance with law. The notice shall include—

> (1) a statement of the time, place, and nature of public rule making proceedings;

> (2) reference to the legal authority under which the rule is proposed; and

> (3) either the terms or substance of the proposed rule or a description of the subjects and issues involved.

Except when notice or hearing is required by statute, this subsection does not apply—

> (A) to interpretative rules, general statements of policy, or rules of agency organization, procedure, or practice; or

> (B) when the agency for good cause finds (and incorporates the finding and a brief statement of reasons therefor in the rules issued) that notice and public procedure thereon are impracticable, unnecessary, or contrary to the public interest.

(c) After notice required by this section, the agency shall give interested persons an opportunity to participate in the rule making through submission of written data, views, or arguments with or without opportunity for oral presentation. After consideration of the relevant matter presented, the agency shall incorporate in the rules adopted a concise general statement of their basis and purpose. When rules are required by statute to be made on the record after opportunity for an agency hearing, sections 556 and 557 of this title apply instead of this subsection.

(d) The required publication or service of a substantive rule shall be made not less than 30 days before its effective date, except—

(1) a substantive rule which grants or recognizes an exemption or relieves a restriction;

(2) interpretative rules and statements of policy; or

(3) as otherwise provided by the agency for good cause found and published with the rule.

(e) Each agency shall give an interested person the right to petition for the issuance, amendment, or repeal of a rule.

§ 554. Adjudications

(a) This section applies, according to the provisions thereof, in every case of adjudication required by statute to be determined on the record after opportunity for an agency hearing, except to the extent that there is involved—

(1) a matter subject to a subsequent trial of the law and the facts de novo in a court;

(2) the selection or tenure of an employee, except a[n] administrative law judge appointed under section 3105 of this title;

(3) proceedings in which decisions rest solely on inspections, tests, or elections;

(4) the conduct of military or foreign affairs functions;

(5) cases in which an agency is acting as an agent for a court; or

(6) the certification of worker representatives.

(b) Persons entitled to notice of an agency hearing shall be timely informed of—

(1) the time, place, and nature of the hearing;

(2) the legal authority and jurisdiction under which the hearing is to be held; and

(3) the matters of fact and law asserted.

When private persons are the moving parties, other parties to the proceeding shall give prompt notice of issues controverted in fact or law; and in other instances agencies may by rule require responsive pleading. In fixing the time and place for hearings, due regard shall be had for the convenience and necessity of the parties or their representatives.

(c)   The agency shall give all interested parties opportunity for—

(1)   the submission and consideration of facts, arguments, offers of settlement, or proposals of adjustment when time, the nature of the proceeding, and the public interest permit; and

(2)   to the extent that the parties are unable so to determine a controversy by consent, hearing and decision on notice and in accordance with sections 556 and 557 of this title.

(d)   The employee who presides at the reception of evidence pursuant to section 556 of this title shall make the recommended decision or initial decision required by section 557 of this title, unless he becomes unavailable to the agency. Except to the extent required for the disposition of ex parte matters as authorized by law, such an employee may not—

(1)   consult a person or party on a fact in issue, unless on notice and opportunity for all parties to participate; or

(2)   be responsible to or subject to the supervision or direction of an employee or agent engaged in the performance of investigative or prosecuting functions for an agency.

An employee or agent engaged in the performance of investigative or prosecuting functions for an agency in a case may not, in that or a factually related case, participate or advise in the decision, recommended decision, or agency review pursuant to section 557 of this title, except as witness or counsel in public proceedings. This subsection does not apply—

(A)   in determining applications for initial licenses;

(B)   to proceedings involving the validity or application of rates, facilities, or practices of public utilities or carriers; or

(C)   to the agency or a member or members of the body comprising the agency.

(e)   The agency, with like effect as in the case of other orders, and in its sound discretion, may issue a declaratory order to terminate a controversy or remove uncertainty.

§ 555.   Ancillary matters

(a)   This section applies, according to the provisions thereof, except as otherwise provided by this subchapter.

(b) A person compelled to appear in person before an agency or representative thereof is entitled to be accompanied, represented, and advised by counsel or, if permitted by the agency, by other qualified representative. A party is entitled to appear in person or by or with counsel or other duly qualified representative in an agency proceeding. So far as the orderly conduct of public business permits, an interested person may appear before an agency or its responsible employees for the presentation, adjustment, or determination of an issue, request, or controversy in a proceeding, whether interlocutory, summary, or otherwise, or in connection with an agency function. With due regard for the convenience and necessity of the parties or their representatives and within a reasonable time, each agency shall proceed to conclude a matter presented to it. This subsection does not grant or deny a person who is not a lawyer the right to appear for or represent others before an agency or in an agency proceeding.

(c) Process, requirement of a report, inspection, or other investigative act or demand may not be issued, made, or enforced except as authorized by law. A person compelled to submit data or evidence is entitled to retain or, on payment of lawfully prescribed costs, procure a copy or transcript thereof, except that in a non-public investigatory proceeding the witness may for good cause be limited to inspection of the official transcript of his testimony.

(d) Agency subpenas authorized by law shall be issued to a party on request and, when required by rules of procedure, on a statement or showing of general relevance and reasonable scope of the evidence sought. On contest, the court shall sustain the subpena or similar process or demand to the extent that it is found to be in accordance with law. In a proceeding for enforcement, the court shall issue an order requiring the appearance of the witness or the production of the evidence or data within a reasonable time under penalty of punishment for contempt in case of contumacious failure to comply.

(e) Prompt notice shall be given of the denial in whole or in part of a written application, petition, or other request of an interested person made in connection with any agency proceeding. Except in affirming a prior denial or when the denial is self-explanatory, the notice shall be accompanied by a brief statement of the grounds for denial.

§ 556. Hearings; presiding employees; powers and duties; burden of proof; evidence; record as basis of decision

(a) This section applies, according to the provisions thereof, to hearings required by section 553 or 554 of this title to be conducted in accordance with this section.

(b) There shall preside at the taking of evidence—

(1) the agency;

(2) one or more members of the body which comprises the agency; or

(3) one or more administrative law judges appointed under section 3105 of this title.

This subchapter does not supersede the conduct of specified classes of proceedings, in whole or in part, by or before boards or other employees specially provided for by or designated under statute. The functions of presiding employees and of employees participating in decisions in accordance with section 557 of this title shall be conducted in an impartial manner. A presiding or participating employee may at any time disqualify himself. On the filing in good faith of a timely and sufficient affidavit of personal bias or other disqualification of a presiding or participating employee, the agency shall determine the matter as a part of the record and decision in the case.

(c) Subject to published rules of the agency and within its powers, employees presiding at hearings may—

(1) administer oaths and affirmations;

(2) issue subpenas authorized by law;

(3) rule on offers of proof and receive relevant evidence;

(4) take depositions or have depositions taken when the ends of justice would be served;

(5) regulate the course of the hearing;

(6) hold conferences for the settlement or simplification of the issues by consent of the parties or by the use of alternative means of dispute resolution as provided in subchapter IV of this chapter;

(7) inform the parties as to the availability of one or more alternative means of dispute resolution, and encourage use of such methods;

(8) require the attendance at any conference held pursuant to paragraph (6) of at least one representative of each party who has authority to negotiate concerning resolution of issues in controversy;

(9) dispose of procedural requests or similar matters;

(10) make or recommend decisions in accordance with section 557 of this title; and

(11) take other action authorized by agency rule consistent with this subchapter.

(d)   Except as otherwise provided by statute, the proponent of a rule or order has the burden of proof. Any oral or documentary evidence may be received, but the agency as a matter of policy shall provide for the exclusion of irrelevant, immaterial, or unduly repetitious evidence. A sanction may not be imposed or rule or order issued except on consideration of the whole record or those parts thereof cited by a party and supported by and in accordance with the reliable, probative, and substantial evidence. The agency may, to the extent consistent with the interests of justice and the policy of the underlying statutes administered by the agency, consider a violation of section 557(d) of this title sufficient grounds for a decision adverse to a party who has knowingly committed such violation or knowingly caused such violation to occur. A party is entitled to present his case or defense by oral or documentary evidence, to submit rebuttal evidence, and to conduct such cross-examination as may be required for a full and true disclosure of the facts. In rule making or determining claims for money or benefits or applications for initial licenses an agency may, when a party will not be prejudiced thereby, adopt procedures for the submission of all or part of the evidence in written form.

(e)   The transcript of testimony and exhibits, together with all papers and requests filed in the proceeding, constitutes the exclusive record for decision in accordance with section 557 of this title and, on payment of lawfully prescribed costs, shall be made available to the parties. When an agency decision rests on official notice of a material fact not appearing in the evidence in the record, a party is entitled, on timely request, to an opportunity to show the contrary.

§ 557.   Initial   decisions;   conclusiveness;   review   by   agency; submissions by parties; contents of decisions; record

(a)   This section applies, according to the provisions thereof, when a hearing is required to be conducted in accordance with section 556 of this title.

(b)   When the agency did not preside at the reception of the evidence, the presiding employee or, in cases not subject to section 554(d) of this title, an employee qualified to preside at hearings pursuant to section 556 of this title, shall initially decide the case unless the agency requires, either in specific cases or by general rule, the entire record to be certified to it for decision. When the presiding employee makes an initial decision, that decision then becomes the decision of the agency without further proceedings unless there is an appeal to, or review on motion of, the agency within time provided by rule. On appeal from or review of the initial decision, the agency has all the powers which it would have in making the initial decision except as it may limit the issues on notice or by rule. When the agency makes the decision without having presided at the reception of the evidence, the presiding employee or an employee qualified to preside at hearings pursuant to section 556 of this title shall first recommend a decision, except that in rule making or determining applications for initial licenses—

(1) instead thereof the agency may issue a tentative decision or one of its responsible employees may recommend a decision; or

(2) this procedure may be omitted in a case in which the agency finds on the record that due and timely execution of its functions imperatively and unavoidably so requires.

(c) Before a recommended, initial, or tentative decision, or a decision on agency review of the decision of subordinate employees, the parties are entitled to a reasonable opportunity to submit for the consideration of the employees participating in the decisions—

(1) proposed findings and conclusions; or

(2) exceptions to the decisions or recommended decisions of subordinate employees or to tentative agency decisions; and

(3) supporting reasons for the exceptions or proposed findings or conclusions.

The record shall show the ruling on each finding, conclusion, or exception presented. All decisions, including initial, recommended, and tentative decisions, are a part of the record and shall include a statement of—

(A) findings and conclusions, and the reasons or basis therefor, on all the material issues of fact, law, or discretion presented on the record; and

(B) the appropriate rule, order, sanction, relief, or denial thereof.

(d)(1) In any agency proceeding which is subject to subsection (a) of this section, except to the extent required for the disposition of ex parte matters as authorized by law—

(A) no interested person outside the agency shall make or knowingly cause to be made to any member of the body comprising the agency, administrative law judge, or other employee who is or may reasonably be expected to be involved in the decisional process of the proceeding, an ex parte communication relevant to the merits of the proceeding;

(B) no member of the body comprising the agency, administrative law judge, or other employee who is or may reasonably be expected to be involved in the decisional process of the proceeding, shall make or knowingly cause to be made to any interested person outside the agency an ex parte communication relevant to the merits of the proceeding;

(C) a member of the body comprising the agency, administrative law judge, or other employee who is or may reasonably be expected to be involved in the decisional process of such proceeding who receives, or who makes or knowingly causes to be made, a communication prohibited by this subsection shall place on the public record of the proceeding:

    (i)   all such written communications;

    (ii) memoranda stating the substance of all such oral communications; and

    (iii) all written responses, and memoranda stating the substance of all oral responses, to the materials described in clauses (i) and (ii) of this subparagraph;

(D) upon receipt of a communication knowingly made or knowingly caused to be made by a party in violation of this subsection, the agency, administrative law judge, or other employee presiding at the hearing may, to the extent consistent with the interests of justice and the policy of the underlying statutes, require the party to show cause why his claim or interest in the proceeding should not be dismissed, denied, disregarded, or otherwise adversely affected on account of such violation; and

(E) the prohibitions of this subsection shall apply beginning at such time as the agency may designate, but in no case shall they begin to apply later than the time at which a proceeding is noticed for hearing unless the person responsible for the communication has knowledge that it will be noticed, in which case the prohibitions shall apply beginning at the time of his acquisition of such knowledge.

(2) This subsection does not constitute authority to withhold information from Congress.

§ 558.   Imposition of sanctions; determination of applications for licenses; suspension, revocation, and expiration of licenses

(a) This section applies, according to the provisions thereof, to the exercise of a power or authority.

(b) A sanction may not be imposed or a substantive rule or order issued except within jurisdiction delegated to the agency and as authorized by law.

(c) When application is made for a license required by law, the agency, with due regard for the rights and privileges of all the interested parties or adversely affected persons and within a reasonable time, shall set and complete proceedings required to be conducted in accordance with sections 556 and 557 of this title or other proceedings required by law and shall make its decision. Except in cases of willfulness or those in which public health, interest, or safety requires otherwise, the withdrawal, suspension, revocation, or annulment of a license is lawful only if, before the institution of agency proceedings therefor, the licensee has been given—

(1) notice by the agency in writing of the facts or conduct which may warrant the action; and

(2) opportunity to demonstrate or achieve compliance with all lawful requirements.

When the licensee has made timely and sufficient application for a renewal or a new license in accordance with agency rules, a license with reference to an activity of a continuing nature does not expire until the application has been finally determined by the agency.

§ 559. Effect on other laws; effect of subsequent statute

This [Act does] not limit or repeal additional requirements imposed by statute or otherwise recognized by law. Except as otherwise required by law, requirements or privileges relating to evidence or procedure apply equally to agencies and persons. Each agency is granted the authority necessary to comply with the requirements of this subchapter through the issuance of rules or otherwise. Subsequent statute may not be held to supersede or modify this [Act], except to the extent that it does so expressly.

Subchapter III—Negotiated Rulemaking Procedure

[This subchapter, known as the Negotiated Rulemaking Act, is omitted.]

Subchapter IV—Alternative Means of Dispute Resolution in the Administrative Process

[This subchapter, known as the Administrative Dispute Resolution Act, is omitted.]

CHAPTER 6—THE ANALYSIS OF REGULATORY FUNCTIONS

[This chapter, known as the Regulatory Flexibility Act, is omitted.]

CHAPTER 7—JUDICIAL REVIEW

§ 701. Application; definitions

(a) This chapter applies, according to the provisions thereof, except to the extent that—

(1) statutes preclude judicial review; or

(2) agency action is committed to agency discretion by law.

(b) For the purpose of this chapter—

(1) "agency" means each authority of the Government of the United States, whether or not it is within or subject to review by another agency, but does not include—

(A) the Congress;

(B) the courts of the United States;

(C) the governments of the territories or possessions of the United States;

(D) the government of the District of Columbia;

(E) agencies composed of representatives of the parties or of representatives of organizations of the parties to the disputes determined by them;

(F) courts martial and military commissions;

(G) military authority exercised in the field in time of war or in occupied territory; or

(H) functions conferred by sections 1738, 1739, 1743, and 1744 of title 12; chapter 2 of title 41; subchapter II of chapter 471 of title 49; or sections 1884, 1891–1902, and former section 1641(b)(2), of title 50, appendix; and

(2) "person", "rule", "order", "license", "sanction", "relief", and "agency action" have the meanings given them by section 551 of this title.

§ 702. Right of review

A person suffering legal wrong because of agency action, or adversely affected or aggrieved by agency action within the meaning of a relevant statute, is entitled to judicial review thereof. An action in a court of the United States seeking relief other than money damages and stating a claim that an agency or an officer or employee thereof acted or failed to act in an official capacity or under color of legal authority shall not be dismissed nor relief therein be denied on the ground that it is against the United States or that the United States is an indispensable party. The United States may be named as a defendant in any such action, and a judgment or decree may be entered against the United States: *Provided,* That any mandatory or injunctive decree shall specify the Federal officer or officers (by name or by title), and their successors in office, personally responsible for compliance. Nothing herein (1) affects other limitations on judicial review or the power or duty of the court to dismiss any action or deny relief on any other appropriate legal or equitable ground; or (2) confers authority to grant relief if any other statute that grants consent to suit expressly or impliedly forbids the relief which is sought.

§ 703. Form and venue of proceeding

The form of proceeding for judicial review is the special statutory review proceeding relevant to the subject matter in a court specified by statute or, in the absence or inadequacy thereof, any applicable form of legal action, including actions for declaratory judgments or writs of prohibitory or mandatory injunction or habeas corpus, in a court of competent jurisdiction. If no special statutory review proceeding is applicable, the action for judicial review may be brought against the United States, the agency by its official title, or the appropriate officer. Except to the extent that prior, adequate, and exclusive opportunity for judicial review is provided by law, agency action is subject to judicial review in civil or criminal proceedings for judicial enforcement.

§ 704. Actions reviewable

Agency action made reviewable by statute and final agency action for which there is no adequate remedy in a court are subject to judicial review. A preliminary, procedural, or intermediate agency action or ruling not directly reviewable is subject to review on the review of the final agency action. Except as otherwise expressly required by statute, agency action otherwise final is final for the purposes of this section whether or not there has been presented or determined an application for a declaratory order, for any form of reconsideration, or, unless the agency otherwise requires by rule and provides that the action meanwhile is inoperative, for an appeal to superior agency authority.

§ 705. Relief pending review

When an agency finds that justice so requires, it may postpone the effective date of action taken by it, pending judicial review. On such conditions as may be required and to the extent necessary to prevent irreparable injury, the reviewing court, including the court to which a case may be taken on appeal from or on application for certiorari or other writ to a reviewing court, may issue all necessary and appropriate process to postpone the effective date of an agency action or to preserve status or rights pending conclusion of the review proceedings.

§ 706. Scope of review

To the extent necessary to decision and when presented, the reviewing court shall decide all relevant questions of law, interpret constitutional and statutory provisions, and determine the meaning or applicability of the terms of an agency action. The reviewing court shall—

(1) compel agency action unlawfully withheld or unreasonably delayed; and

(2) hold unlawful and set aside agency action, findings, and conclusions found to be—

(A) arbitrary, capricious, an abuse of discretion, or otherwise not in accordance with law;

(B) contrary to constitutional right, power, privilege, or immunity;

(C) in excess of statutory jurisdiction, authority, or limitations, or short of statutory right;

(D) without observance of procedure required by law;

(E) unsupported by substantial evidence in a case subject to sections 556 and 557 of this title or otherwise reviewed on the record of an agency hearing provided by statute; or

(F) unwarranted by the facts to the extent that the facts are subject to trial de novo by the reviewing court.

In making the foregoing determinations, the court shall review the whole record or those parts of it cited by a party, and due account shall be taken of the rule of prejudicial error.

CHAPTER 8—CONGRESSIONAL REVIEW OF AGENCY RULEMAKING

[This chapter, known as the Congressional Review Act, is omitted.]

[ADMINISTRATIVE LAW JUDGES]

§ 3105. Appointment of administrative law judges

Each agency shall appoint as many administrative law judges as are necessary for proceedings required to be conducted in accordance with sections 556 and 557 of this title. Administrative law judges shall be assigned to cases in rotation so far as practicable, and may not perform duties inconsistent with their duties and responsibilities as administrative law judges.

§ 7521. Actions against administrative law judges

(a) An action may be taken against an administrative law judge appointed under section 3105 of this title by the agency in which the administrative law judge is employed only for good cause established and determined by the Merit Systems Protection Board on the record after opportunity for hearing before the Board. . . . [Actions covered include removal, suspension, and reduction in grade or pay.]

§ 5372. Administrative law judges

. . . There shall be 3 levels of basic pay for administrative law judges [as specified in detail in this section].

§ 3344. Details; administrative law judges

An agency as defined by section 551 of this title which occasionally or temporarily is insufficiently staffed with administrative law judges appointed under section 3105 of this title may use administrative law judges selected by the Office of Personnel Management from and with the consent of other agencies.

§ 1305. Administrative law judges

For the purpose of sections 3105, 3344, 4301(2)(D), and 5372 of this title and the provisions of section 5335(a)(B) of this title that relate to administrative law judges, the Office of Personnel Management may, and for the purpose of section 7521 of this title, the Merit Systems Protection Board may investigate, require reports by agencies, issue reports, including an annual report to Congress, prescribe regulations, appoint advisory committees as necessary, recommend legislation, subpena witnesses and records, and pay witness fees as established for the courts of the United States.

APPENDIX C

MODEL STATE ADMINISTRATIVE PROCEDURE ACTS (SELECTED PROVISIONS)

UNIFORM LAW COMMISSIONERS

■ ■ ■

2010 Model State Administrative Procedure Act
[ARTICLE] 1
GENERAL PROVISIONS

§ 102. DEFINITIONS. In this [act]: ...

    (4) "Agency action" means:

        (A) the whole or part of an order or rule;

        (B) the failure to issue an order or rule; or

        (C) an agency's performing or failing to perform a duty, function, or activity or to make a determination required by law.

    (7) "Contested case" means an adjudication in which an opportunity for an evidentiary hearing is required by the federal constitution, a federal statute, or the constitution or a statute of this state. ...

    (14) "Guidance document" means a record of general applicability developed by an agency which lacks the force of law but states the agency's current approach to, or interpretation of, law, or describes how and when the agency will exercise discretionary functions. The term does not include records described in paragraph (30)(A), (B), (C), or (D). ...

    (23) "Order" means an agency decision that determines or declares the rights, duties, privileges, immunities, or other interests of a specific person. ...

    (29) "Record" means information that is inscribed on a tangible medium or that is stored in an electronic or other medium and is retrievable in perceivable form.

    (30) "Rule" means the whole or a part of an agency statement of general applicability that implements, interprets, or prescribes law or policy or the organization, procedure, or practice requirements of an

agency and has the force of law. The term includes the amendment or repeal of an existing rule. The term does not include:

(A) a statement that concerns only the internal management of an agency and which does not affect private rights or procedures available to the public;

(B) an intergovernmental or interagency memorandum, directive, or communication that does not affect private rights or procedures available to the public;

(C) an opinion of the Attorney General;

(D) a statement that establishes criteria or guidelines to be used by the staff of an agency in performing audits, investigations, or inspections, settling commercial disputes, negotiating commercial arrangements, or defending, prosecuting, or settling cases, if disclosure of the criteria or guidelines would enable persons violating the law to avoid detection, facilitate disregard of requirements imposed by law, or give an improper advantage to persons that are in an adverse position to the state;

(E) a form developed by an agency to implement or interpret agency law or policy; or

(F) a guidance document. ...

[ARTICLE] 2

PUBLIC ACCESS TO AGENCY LAW AND POLICY

§ 201. PUBLICATION, COMPILATION, INDEXING, AND PUBLIC INSPECTION OF RULEMAKING DOCUMENTS.

(a) The [publisher] shall administer this section and other sections of this [act] that require publication. The [publisher] shall publish the [administrative bulletin] and the [administrative code].

(b) The [publisher] shall publish in [electronic and written] [electronic or written] [electronic] [written] format all rulemaking-related documents listed in Section 202(c). The [publisher] shall prescribe a uniform numbering system, form, and style for proposed rules.

(c) The [publisher] shall maintain the official record of a rulemaking, including the text of the rule and any supporting documents, filed with the [publisher] by an agency. An agency engaged in rulemaking shall maintain the rulemaking record required by Section 302(b) for that rule.

(d) The [publisher] shall create and maintain an Internet website. The [publisher] shall make available on the Internet website the [administrative bulletin], the [administrative code], and any guidance document filed with the [publisher] by an agency.

(e) The [publisher] shall publish the [administrative bulletin] at least once [each month].

(f) The [administrative bulletin] must be provided in written form on request, for which the [publisher] may charge a reasonable fee.

(g) The [administrative bulletin] must contain:

(1) notices of proposed rulemaking prepared so that the text of the proposed rule shows the text of any existing rule proposed to be changed and the change proposed;

(2) newly filed final rules prepared so that the text of a newly filed amended rule shows the text of the existing rule and the change that is made;

(3) any other notice and material required to be published in the [administrative bulletin]; and

(4) an index.

(h) The [administrative code] must be compiled, indexed by subject, and published in a format and medium prescribed by the [publisher]. The rules of an agency must be published and indexed in the [administrative code].

(i) The [publisher] shall make the [administrative bulletin] and the [administrative code] available for public inspection and, for a reasonable charge, copying.

(j) The [publisher], with notification to the agency, may make minor nonsubstantive corrections in spelling, grammar, and format in a proposed or final rule. The [publisher] shall make a record of the corrections.

(k) The [publisher] shall make available on the [publisher's] Internet website, at no charge, all the documents provided by an agency under Section 202(c).

§ 202. PUBLICATION; AGENCY DUTIES.

(a) Unless the record is exempt from disclosure under law of this state other than this [act], an agency shall publish on its Internet website and, on request and for a reasonable charge, make available through the regular mail:

(1) each notice of a proposed rule under Section 304;

(2) each rule filed under Section 316;

(3) each summary of regulatory analysis required by Section 305;

(4) each declaratory order issued under Section 204;

(5) the index of declaratory orders prepared under Section 204(g);

(6) each guidance document issued under Section 311;

(7) the index of currently effective guidance documents prepared under Section 311(e);

(8) each final order in a contested case issued under Section 413, 414, or 415; and

(9) the index of final orders in contested cases prepared under Section 418(a).

(b) An agency may provide for electronic distribution to a person that requests electronic distribution of notices related to rulemaking or guidance documents. If a notice is distributed electronically, the agency need not transmit the actual notice but must send all the information contained in the notice.

(c) An agency shall file with the [publisher] in an electronic format acceptable to the [publisher]:

(1) notice of the adoption of a final rule;

(2) a summary of the regulatory analysis required by Section 305 for each proposed rule;

(3) each final rule;

(4) an index of currently effective guidance documents under Section 311(f); and

(5) any other notice or matter that an agency is required to publish under this [act].

§ 203. REQUIRED AGENCY PUBLICATION AND RECORDKEEPING.

An agency shall:

(1) publish a description of its organization, stating the general course and method of its operations and the methods by which the public may obtain information or make submissions or requests;

(2) publish a description of all formal and informal procedures available, including a description of all forms and instructions used by the agency;

(3) publish a description of the process for application for a license, available benefits, or other matters for which an application is appropriate, unless the process is prescribed by law other than this [act];

(4) adopt rules for the conduct of public hearings [if the standard procedural rules adopted under Section 205 do not include provisions for the conduct of public hearings];

(5) maintain the agency's current rulemaking docket required by Section 301(b); and

(6) maintain a separate, official, current, and dated index and compilation of all final rules filed with the [publisher], make the index and compilation available for public inspection and, for a reasonable charge, copying at the principal office of the agency [and online on the [publisher]'s Internet website], update the index and compilation at least [monthly], and file the index and the compilation and all changes to both with the [publisher].

§ 204. DECLARATORY ORDER.

(a) A person may petition an agency for a declaratory order that interprets or applies a statute administered by the agency or states whether or in what manner a rule, guidance document, or order issued by the agency applies to the petitioner.

(b) An agency shall adopt rules prescribing the form of a petition under subsection (a) and the procedure for its submission, consideration, and prompt disposition. The provisions of this [act] concerning formal, informal, or other applicable hearing procedure do not apply to an agency proceeding for a declaratory order, except to the extent provided in this [article] or to the extent the agency provides by rule or order.

(c) Not later than 60 days [or at the next regularly scheduled meeting of the agency, whichever is later,] after receipt of a petition under subsection (a), an agency shall issue a declaratory order in response to the petition, decline to issue the order, or schedule the matter for further consideration.

(d) If an agency declines to issue a declaratory order requested under subsection (a), it shall notify promptly the petitioner of its decision. The decision must be in a record and must include a brief statement of the reasons for declining. An agency decision to decline to issue a declaratory order is subject to judicial review for abuse of discretion. An agency failure to act within the applicable time under subsection (c) is subject to judicial action under Section 501(d).

(e) If an agency issues a declaratory order, the order must contain the names of all parties to the proceeding, the facts on which it is based, and the reasons for the agency's conclusion. If an agency is authorized not to disclose certain information in its records to protect confidentiality, the agency may redact confidential information in the order. The order has the same status and binding effect as an order issued in an adjudication and is subject to judicial review under Section 501.

(f)   An agency shall publish each currently effective declaratory order.

(g)   An agency shall maintain an index of all of its currently effective declaratory orders, file the index [annually] with the [publisher], make the index readily available for public inspection, and make available for public inspection and, for a reasonable charge, copying the full text of all declaratory orders to the extent inspection is permitted by law of this state other than this [act].

[ARTICLE] 3

RULEMAKING; PROCEDURAL REQUIREMENTS AND EFFECTIVENESS OF RULES

§ 302. RULEMAKING RECORD.

(a)   An agency shall maintain a rulemaking record for each proposed rule. Unless the record and any materials incorporated by reference are privileged or exempt from disclosure under law of this state other than this [act], the record and materials must be readily available for public inspection in the principal office of the agency and available for public display on the Internet website maintained by the [publisher]. If an agency determines that any part of the rulemaking record cannot be displayed practicably or is inappropriate for public display on the Internet website, the agency shall describe the part and note that the part is not displayed.

(b)   A rulemaking record must contain:

(1)   a copy of all publications in the [administrative bulletin] relating to the rule and the proceeding on which the rule is based;

(2)   a copy of any part of the rulemaking docket containing entries relating to the rule and the proceeding on which the rule is based;

(3)   a copy and, if prepared, an index, of all factual material, studies, and reports agency personnel relied on or consulted in formulating the proposed or final rule;

(4)   any official transcript of oral presentations made in the proceeding on which the rule is based or, if not transcribed, any audio recording or verbatim transcript of the presentations, and any memorandum summarizing the contents of the presentations prepared by the agency official who presided over the hearing;

(5)   a copy of all comments received by the agency under Section 306(a) in response to the notice of proposed rulemaking;

(6)   a copy of the rule and explanatory statement filed with the [publisher]; and

(7) any petition for agency action on the rule, except a petition governed by Section 204.

§ 303. ADVANCE NOTICE OF PROPOSED RULEMAKING; NEGOTIATED RULEMAKING.

(a) An agency may gather information relevant to the subject matter of a potential rulemaking proceeding and may solicit comments and recommendations from the public by publishing an advance notice of proposed rulemaking in the [administrative bulletin] and indicating where, when, and how persons may comment.

(b) An agency may engage in negotiated rulemaking by appointing a committee to comment or make recommendations on the subject matter of a proposed rulemaking under active consideration within the agency. In making appointments to the committee, the agency shall make reasonable efforts to establish a balance in representation among members of the public known to have an interest in the subject matter of the proposed rulemaking. At least annually, the agency shall publish in the [administrative bulletin] a list of all committees with their membership. Notice of a meeting of the committee must be published in the [administrative bulletin] at least [15 days] before the meeting. A meeting of the committee is open to the public.

(c) A committee appointed under subsection (b), in consultation with one or more agency representatives, shall attempt to reach a consensus on the terms or substance of a proposed rule. The committee shall present the consensus recommendation, if any, to the agency. The agency shall consider whether to use it as the basis for a proposed rule under Section 304, but the agency is not required to propose or adopt the recommendation.

(d) This section does not prohibit an agency from obtaining information and opinions from members of the public on the subject of a proposed rule by any other method or procedure.

§ 304. NOTICE OF PROPOSED RULE.

(a) At least [30] days before the adoption of a rule, an agency shall file notice of the proposed rulemaking with the [publisher] for publication in the [administrative bulletin]. The notice must include:

(1) a short explanation of the purpose of the proposed rule;

(2) a citation or reference to the specific legal authority authorizing the proposed rule;

(3) the text of the proposed rule;

(4) how a copy of the full text of any regulatory analysis of the proposed rule may be obtained;

(5) where, when, and how a person may comment on the proposed rule and request a hearing;

(6) a citation to and summary of each scientific or statistical study, report, or analysis that served as a basis for the proposed rule, together with an indication of how the full text of the study, report, or analysis may be obtained; and

(7) any summary of a regulatory analysis prepared under Section 305(d). ...

§ 305. REGULATORY ANALYSIS.

(a) An agency shall prepare a regulatory analysis for a proposed rule that has an estimated economic impact of more than $[   ]. The analysis must be completed before notice of the proposed rulemaking is published. The summary of the analysis prepared under subsection (d) must be published with the notice of proposed rulemaking.

(b) If a proposed rule has an economic impact of less than $[   ], the agency shall prepare a statement of minimal estimated economic impact.

(c) A regulatory analysis must contain:

(1) an analysis of the benefits and costs of a reasonable range of regulatory alternatives reflecting the scope of discretion provided by the statute authorizing the proposed rule; and

(2) a determination whether:

(A) the benefits of the proposed rule justify the costs of the proposed rule; and

(B) the proposed rule will achieve the objectives of the authorizing statute in a more cost-effective manner, or with greater net benefits, than other regulatory alternatives.

(d) An agency preparing a regulatory analysis under this section shall prepare a concise summary of the analysis.

(e) An agency preparing a regulatory analysis under this section shall submit the analysis to the [appropriate state agency].

(f) If an agency has made a good faith effort to comply with this section, a rule is not invalid solely because the regulatory analysis for the proposed rule is insufficient or inaccurate.

§ 306. PUBLIC PARTICIPATION.

(a) An agency proposing a rule shall specify a public comment period of at least [30] days after publication of notice of the proposed rulemaking during which a person may submit information and comment on the proposed rule. The information or comment may be submitted in an electronic or written format. The agency shall consider all information and comment on a proposed rule which is submitted pursuant to this subsection within the comment period.

(b) An agency may consider any other information it receives concerning a proposed rule during the rulemaking. Any information considered by the agency must be incorporated into the record under Section 302(b)(3). The information need not be submitted in an electronic or written format. Nothing in this section prohibits an agency from discussing with any person at any time the subject of a proposed rule.

(c) Unless a hearing is required by law of this state other than this [act], an agency is not required to hold a hearing on a proposed rule but may do so. A hearing must be open to the public, recorded, and held at least [10] days before the end of the public comment period.

(d) A hearing on a proposed rule may not be held earlier than [20] days after notice of its location, date, and time is published in the [administrative bulletin].

(e) An agency representative shall preside over a hearing on a proposed rule. If the representative is not the agency head, the representative shall prepare a memorandum summarizing the contents of the presentations made at the hearing for consideration by the agency head.

§ 307. TIME LIMIT ON ADOPTION OF RULE.

(a) An agency may not adopt a rule until the public comment period has ended.

(b) Not later than [two years] after a notice of proposed rulemaking is published, the agency shall adopt the rule or terminate the rulemaking by publication of a notice of termination in the [administrative bulletin]. [The agency may extend the time for adopting the rule once for an additional [two years] by publishing a statement of good cause for the extension but must provide for additional public participation as provided in Section 306 before adopting the rule.]

(c) An agency shall file an adopted rule with the [publisher] not later than [   ] days after the adoption of the rule.

(d) A rule is void unless it is adopted and filed within the time limits in this section.

§ 308. VARIANCE BETWEEN PROPOSED AND FINAL RULE. An agency may not adopt a rule that differs from the rule proposed in the notice of proposed rulemaking unless the final rule is a logical outgrowth of the rule proposed in the notice.

§ 309. EMERGENCY RULE. If an agency finds that an imminent peril to the public health, safety, or welfare or the loss of federal funding for an

agency program requires the immediate adoption of an emergency rule and publishes in a record its reasons for that finding, the agency, without prior notice or hearing or on any abbreviated notice and hearing that it finds practicable, may adopt an emergency rule without complying with Sections 304 through 307. The emergency rule may be effective for not longer than [180] days [renewable once for no more than [180] days]. The adoption of an emergency rule does not preclude the adoption of a rule under Sections 304 through 307. The agency shall file with the [publisher] a rule adopted under this section as soon as practicable given the nature of the emergency, publish the rule on its Internet website, and notify persons that have requested notice of rules related to that subject matter. This section does not prohibit the adoption of a new emergency rule if, at the end of the effective period of the original emergency rule, the agency finds that the imminent peril to the public health, safety, or welfare or the loss of federal funding for an agency program still exists.

§ 310. DIRECT FINAL RULE. If an agency proposes to adopt a rule which is expected to be noncontroversial, it may use direct final rulemaking authorized by this section and must comply with Section 304(a)(1), (2), (3), and (5), Section 304(b), and Section 313(1). The proposed rule must be published in the [administrative bulletin] with a statement by the agency that it does not expect the adoption of the rule to be controversial and that the proposed rule takes effect 30 days after publication if no objection is received. If no objection is received, the rule becomes final under Section 317(e). If an objection to the rule is received from any person not later than [ ] days after publication of the notice of the proposed rule, the proposed rule does not become final. The agency shall file notice of the objection with the [publisher] for publication in the [administrative bulletin], and may proceed with rulemaking under Sections 304 through 307.

§ 311. GUIDANCE DOCUMENT.

(a) An agency may issue a guidance document without following the procedures set forth in Sections 304 through 307.

(b) An agency that proposes to rely on a guidance document to the detriment of a person in any administrative proceeding shall afford the person an adequate opportunity to contest the legality or wisdom of a position taken in the document. The agency may not use a guidance document to foreclose consideration of issues raised in the document.

(c) A guidance document may contain binding instructions to agency staff members if, at an appropriate stage in the administrative process, the agency's procedures provide an affected person an adequate opportunity to contest the legality or wisdom of a position taken in the document.

(d) If an agency proposes to act in an adjudication at variance with a position expressed in a guidance document, it shall provide a reasonable explanation for the variance. If an affected person in an adjudication may have relied reasonably on the agency's position, the explanation must include a reasonable justification for the agency's conclusion that the need for the variance outweighs the affected person's reliance interest.

(e) An agency shall maintain an index of all of its effective guidance documents, publish the index on its Internet website, make all guidance documents available to the public, and file the index [annually] with the [publisher]. The agency may not rely on a guidance document, or cite it as precedent against any party to a proceeding, unless the guidance document is published on its Internet website.

(f) A guidance document may be considered by a presiding officer or final decision maker in an agency adjudication, but it does not bind the presiding officer or the final decision maker in the exercise of discretion.

(g) A person may petition an agency under Section 318 to adopt a rule in place of a guidance document.

(h) A person may petition an agency to revise or repeal a guidance document. Not later than [60] days after submission of the petition, the agency shall:

(1) revise or repeal the guidance document;

(2) initiate a proceeding to consider a revision or repeal; or

(3) deny the petition in a record and state its reasons for the denial.

§ 312. **REQUIRED INFORMATION FOR RULE.** A final rule filed by an agency with the [publisher] under Section 316 must contain the text of the rule and be accompanied by a record that contains:

(1) the date the final rule was adopted by the agency;

(2) a reference to the specific statutory or other authority authorizing the rule;

(3) any finding required by law as a prerequisite to adoption or effectiveness of the rule;

(4) the effective date of the rule; and

(5) the concise explanatory statement required by Section 313.

§ 313. **CONCISE EXPLANATORY STATEMENT.** When an agency adopts a final rule, the agency shall issue a concise explanatory statement that contains:

(1)   the agency's reasons for adopting the rule, including the agency's reasons for not accepting substantial arguments made in testimony and comments;

(2)   subject to Section 308, the reasons for any change between the text of the proposed rule contained in the notice of proposed rulemaking and the text of the final rule; and

(3)   the summary of any regulatory analysis prepared under Section 305(d).

§ 314. INCORPORATION BY REFERENCE. A rule may incorporate by reference all or any part of a code, standard, or rule that has been adopted by an agency of the United States, this state, or another state, or by a nationally recognized organization or association, if:

(1)   repeating verbatim the text of the code, standard, or rule in the rule would be unduly cumbersome, expensive, or otherwise inexpedient;

(2)   the reference in the rule fully identifies the incorporated code, standard, or rule by citation, place of inspection, and date[, and states whether the rule includes any later amendments or editions of the incorporated code, standard, or rule];

(3)   the code, standard, or rule is readily available to the public in written or electronic form at no charge or for a reasonable charge;

(4)   the rule states where copies of the code, standard, or rule are available from the agency adopting the rule for a reasonable charge, if any, or where copies are available from the agency of the United States, this state, another state, or the organization or association originally issuing the code, standard, or rule; and

(5)   the agency maintains a copy of the code, standard, or rule readily available for public inspection at the principal office of the agency.

§ 316. FILING OF RULE. An agency shall file in written and electronic form with the [publisher] each final rule. In filing a final rule, an agency shall use a standard form prescribed by the [publisher]. The agency shall file the rule not later than [ ] days after adoption. The [publisher] shall maintain a permanent register of all filed rules and concise explanatory statements for the rules. The [publisher] shall affix to each final rule a certification of the time and date of filing. The [publisher] shall publish the notice of each final rule in the [administrative bulletin].

§ 317. EFFECTIVE DATE OF RULE.

(a)   Except as otherwise provided in this section, [unless disapproved by the [rules review committee][,] [or] [withdrawn by the agency under Section 703,] a rule becomes effective [30] days after publication of the rule [in the administrative bulletin] [on the [publisher=s] Internet website].

(b) A rule may become effective on a date later than that established by subsection (a) if that date is specified in the rule or required by law other than this [act].

(c) A rule becomes effective immediately on its filing with the [publisher] or on any subsequent date earlier than that established by subsection (a) if it is required to be implemented by a certain date by law other than this [act].

(d) An emergency rule under Section 309 becomes effective on adoption by the agency.

(e) A direct final rule under Section 310 to which no objection is made becomes effective [30] days after publication, unless the agency specifies a later effective date.

§ 318. PETITION FOR ADOPTION OF RULE. Any person may petition an agency to adopt a rule. An agency shall prescribe by rule the form of the petition and the procedure for its submission, consideration, and disposition. Not later than [60] days after submission of a petition, the agency shall:

(1) deny the petition in a record and state its reasons for the denial; or

(2) initiate rulemaking.

[ARTICLE] 4

ADJUDICATION IN CONTESTED CASE

§ 401. CONTESTED CASE. This [article] applies to an adjudication made by an agency in a contested case.

§ 402. PRESIDING OFFICER.

(a) A presiding officer must be an administrative law judge assigned in accordance with Section 604(2), the individual who is the agency head, a member of a multi-member body of individuals that is the agency head, or, unless prohibited by law of this state other than this [act], an individual designated by the agency head.

(b) An individual who has served as investigator, prosecutor, or advocate at any stage in a contested case or who is subject to the authority, direction, or discretion of an individual who has served as investigator, prosecutor, or advocate at any stage in a contested case may not serve as the presiding officer in the same case. An agency head that has participated in a determination of probable cause or other preliminary determination in an adjudication may serve as the presiding officer or final decision maker in the adjudication unless a party demonstrates grounds for disqualification under subsection (c).

(c) A presiding officer or agency head acting as a final decision maker is subject to disqualification for bias, prejudice, financial interest, ex parte communications as provided in Section 408, or any other factor that would cause a reasonable person to question the impartiality of the presiding officer or agency head. A presiding officer or agency head, after making a reasonable inquiry, shall disclose to the parties any known facts related to grounds for disqualification which are material to the impartiality of the presiding officer or agency head in the proceeding.

(d) A party may petition for the disqualification of a presiding officer or agency head promptly after notice that the person will preside or, if later, promptly on discovering facts establishing a ground for disqualification. The petition must state with particularity the ground on which it is claimed that a fair and impartial hearing cannot be accorded or the applicable rule or canon of practice or ethics that requires disqualification. The petition may be denied if the party fails to exercise due diligence in requesting disqualification after discovering a ground for disqualification.

(e) A presiding officer or agency head whose disqualification is requested shall decide whether to grant the petition and state in a record facts and reasons for the decision. The decision to deny disqualification is not subject to interlocutory judicial review.

(f) If a substitute presiding officer is required, the substitute must be appointed [as required by law, or if no law governs,] by:

(1) the Governor, if the original presiding officer is an elected official; or

(2) the appointing authority, if the original presiding officer is an appointed official.

(g) If participation of the agency head is necessary to enable the agency to take action, the agency head may continue to participate notwithstanding a ground for disqualification or exclusion.

§ 403. CONTESTED CASE PROCEDURE.

(a) This section does not apply to an emergency adjudication under Section 407.

(b) An agency shall give notice of the agency decision to a person when the agency takes an action as to which the person has a right to a contested case hearing. The notice must be in writing, set forth the agency action, inform the person of the right, procedure, and time limit to file a contested-case petition, and provide a copy of the agency procedures governing the contested case.

(c) In a contested case, the presiding officer shall give all parties a timely opportunity to file pleadings, motions, and objections. The presiding officer may give all parties the opportunity to file briefs, proposed findings of fact and conclusions of law, and proposed recommended, initial, or final orders. The presiding officer, with the consent of all parties, may refer the parties in a contested case to mediation or other dispute resolution procedure.

(d) In a contested case, to the extent necessary for full disclosure of all relevant facts and issues, the presiding officer shall give all parties the opportunity to respond, present evidence and argument, conduct cross-examination, and submit rebuttal evidence.

(e) Except as otherwise provided by law other than this [act], the presiding officer may conduct all or part of an evidentiary hearing or a prehearing conference by telephone, television, video conference, or other electronic means. The hearing may be conducted by telephone or other method by which the witnesses may not be seen only if all parties consent [or the presiding officer finds that this method will not impair reliable determination of the credibility of testimony]. Each party must be given an opportunity to attend, hear, and be heard at the proceeding as it occurs. This subsection does not prevent an agency from providing by rule for electronic hearings.

(f) Except as otherwise provided in subsection (g), a hearing in a contested case must be open to the public. A hearing conducted by telephone, television, video conference, or other electronic means is open to the public if members of the public have an opportunity to attend the hearing at the place where the presiding officer is located or to hear or see the proceeding as it occurs.

(g) A presiding officer may close a hearing to the public on a ground on which a court of this state may close a judicial proceeding to the public or pursuant to law of this state other than this [act].

(h) Unless prohibited by law of this state other than this [act], a party, at the party's expense, may be represented by counsel or may be advised, accompanied, or represented by another individual.

(i) A presiding officer shall ensure that a hearing record is created that complies with Section 406.

(j) The decision in a contested case must be based on the hearing record and contain a statement of the factual and legal bases of the decision. If a finding of fact is set forth in language of a statute of this state other than this [act], it must be accompanied by a concise and explicit statement of the underlying facts supporting the finding of fact. The decision must be prepared electronically and, on request, made available in writing.

(k) Subject to Section 205, the rules by which an agency conducts a contested case may include provisions more protective than the requirements of this section of the rights of parties other than the agency.

(l) Unless prohibited by law of this state other than this [act], an agency may dispose of a contested case without a hearing by stipulation, agreed settlement, consent order, or default.

§ 404. EVIDENCE IN CONTESTED CASE. The following rules apply in a contested case:

(1) Except as otherwise provided in paragraph (2), all relevant evidence is admissible, including hearsay evidence, if it is of a type commonly relied on by a reasonably prudent individual in the conduct of the affairs of the individual.

(2) The presiding officer may exclude evidence in the absence of an objection if the evidence is irrelevant, immaterial, unduly repetitious, or excludable on constitutional or statutory grounds or on the basis of an evidentiary privilege recognized in the courts of this state. The presiding officer shall exclude the evidence if objection is made at the time the evidence is offered.

(3) If the presiding officer excludes evidence with or without objection, the offering party may make an offer of proof before further evidence is presented or at a later time determined by the presiding officer.

(4) Evidence may be received in a record if doing so will expedite the hearing without substantial prejudice to a party. Documentary evidence may be received in the form of a copy if the original is not readily available or by incorporation by reference. On request, parties must be given an opportunity to compare the copy with the original.

(5) Testimony must be made under oath or affirmation.

(6) Evidence must be made part of the hearing record of the case. Information or evidence may not be considered in determining the case unless it is part of the hearing record. If the hearing record contains information that is confidential, the presiding officer may conduct a closed hearing to discuss the information, issue necessary protective orders, and seal all or part of the hearing record.

(7) The presiding officer may take official notice of all facts of which judicial notice may be taken and of scientific, technical, or other facts within the specialized knowledge of the agency. A party must be notified at the earliest practicable time of the facts proposed to be noticed and their source, including any staff memoranda or data. The party must be afforded an opportunity to contest any officially noticed fact before the decision becomes final.

(8) The experience, technical competence, and specialized knowledge of the presiding officer or members of an agency head that is a multi-member body that is hearing the case may be used in evaluating the evidence in the hearing record.

§ 405. NOTICE IN CONTESTED CASE. ...

(c) In a contested case initiated by an agency, the agency shall give notice to the party against which the action is brought. The notice must contain:

(1) a statement that a case that may result in an order has been commenced against the party;

(2) a short and plain statement of the matters asserted, including the issues involved;

(3) a statement of the legal authority under which the hearing will be held citing the statutes and any rules involved; ...

§ 406. HEARING RECORD IN CONTESTED CASE.

(a) An agency shall maintain the hearing record created under Section 403(i) in each contested case. ...

(c) The hearing record constitutes the exclusive basis for agency action in a contested case.

§ 407. EMERGENCY ADJUDICATION PROCEDURE.

(a) Unless prohibited by law of this state other than this [act], an agency may conduct an emergency adjudication in a contested case under this section.

(b) An agency may take action and issue an order under this section only to deal with an imminent peril to the public health, safety, or welfare.

(c) Before issuing an order under this section, an agency, if practicable, shall give notice and an opportunity to be heard to the person to which the agency action is directed. The notice of the hearing and the hearing may be oral or written and may be by telephone, facsimile, or other electronic means.

(d) An order issued under this section must briefly explain the factual and legal reasons for using emergency adjudication procedures.

(e) To the extent practicable, an agency shall give notice to the person to which the agency action is directed that an order has been issued. The order is effective when signed by the agency head or the designee of the agency head.

(f) After issuing an order pursuant to this section, an agency shall proceed as soon as practicable to provide notice and an opportunity for a hearing following the procedure under Section 403 to determine the issues underlying the order.

(g) An order issued under this section may be effective for not longer than [180] days or until the effective date of any order issued under subsection (f), whichever is shorter.

§ 408. EX PARTE COMMUNICATIONS.

(a) In this section, "final decision maker" means the person with the power to issue a final order in a contested case.

(b) Except as otherwise provided in subsection (c), (d), (e), or (h), while a contested case is pending, the presiding officer and the final decision maker may not make to or receive from any person any communication concerning the case without notice and opportunity for all parties to participate in the communication. For the purpose of this section, a contested case is pending from the issuance of the agency's pleading or from an application for an agency decision, whichever is earlier.

(c) A presiding officer or final decision maker may communicate about a pending contested case with any person if the communication is required for the disposition of ex parte matters authorized by statute or concerns an uncontested procedural issue.

(d) A presiding officer or final decision maker may communicate about a pending contested case with an individual authorized by law to provide legal advice to the presiding officer or final decision maker and may communicate on ministerial matters with an individual who serves on the [administrative] [personal] staff of the presiding officer or final decision maker if the individual providing legal advice or ministerial information has not served as investigator, prosecutor, or advocate at any stage of the case, and if the communication does not augment, diminish, or modify the evidence in the record.

(e) An agency head that is the presiding officer or final decision maker in a pending contested case may communicate about that case with an employee or representative of the agency if:

(1) the employee or representative:

(A) has not served as investigator, prosecutor, or advocate at any stage of the case;

(B) has not otherwise had a communication with any person about the case other than a communication a presiding officer or final decision maker is permitted to make or receive under subsection (c) or (d) or a communication permitted by paragraph (2); and

(2) the communication does not augment, diminish, or modify the evidence in the agency hearing record and is:

(A) an explanation of the technical or scientific basis of, or technical or scientific terms in, the evidence in the agency hearing record;

(B) an explanation of the precedent, policies, or procedures of the agency; or

(C) any other communication that does not address the quality or sufficiency of, or the weight that should be given to, evidence in the agency hearing record or the credibility of witnesses.

(f) If a presiding officer or final decision maker makes or receives a communication in violation of this section, the presiding officer or final decision maker:

(1) if the communication is in a record, shall make the record of the communication a part of the hearing record and prepare and make part of the hearing record a memorandum that contains the response of the presiding officer or final decision maker to the communication and the identity of the person that communicated; or

(2) if the communication is oral, shall prepare a memorandum that contains the substance of the verbal communication, the response of the presiding officer or final decision maker to the communication, and the identity of the person that communicated.

(g) If a communication prohibited by this section is made, the presiding officer or final decision maker shall notify all parties of the prohibited communication and permit parties to respond in a record not later than 15 days after the notice is given. For good cause, the presiding officer or final decision maker may permit additional testimony in response to the prohibited communication.

(h) If a presiding officer is a member of a multi-member body of individuals that is the agency head, the presiding officer may communicate with the other members of the body when sitting as the presiding officer and final decision maker. Otherwise, while a contested case is pending, no communication, direct or indirect, regarding any issue in the case may be made between the presiding officer and the final decision maker. Notwithstanding any provision of [state open meetings law], a communication permitted by this subsection is not a meeting.

(i) If necessary to eliminate the effect of a communication received in violation of this section, a presiding officer or final decision maker may be disqualified under Section 402(d) and (e), the parts of the record pertaining to the communication may be sealed by protective order, or other appropriate relief may be granted, including an adverse ruling on the merits of the case or dismissal of the application.

§ 413. ORDERS: RECOMMENDED, INITIAL, OR FINAL.

(a) If the presiding officer is the agency head, the presiding officer shall issue a final order.

(b) Except as otherwise provided by law of this state other than this [act], if the presiding officer is not the agency head and has not been delegated final decisional authority, the presiding officer shall issue a recommended order. If the presiding officer is not the agency head and has been delegated final decisional authority, the presiding officer shall issue an initial order that becomes a final order [30] days after issuance, unless reviewed by the agency head on its own initiative or on petition of a party.

(c) A recommended, initial, or final order must be served in a record on each party and the agency head not later than [90] days after the hearing ends, the record closes, or memoranda, briefs, or proposed findings are submitted, whichever is latest. The presiding officer may extend the time by stipulation, waiver, or for good cause.

(d) A recommended, initial, or final order must separately state findings of fact and conclusions of law on all material issues of fact, law, or discretion, the remedy prescribed, and, if applicable, the action taken on a petition for a stay. The presiding officer may permit a party to submit proposed findings of fact and conclusions of law. The order must state the available procedures and time limits for seeking reconsideration or other administrative relief and must state the time limits for seeking judicial review of the agency order. A recommended or initial order must state any circumstances under which the order, without further notice, may become a final order.

(e) Findings of fact must be based exclusively on the evidence and matters officially noticed in the hearing record in the contested case.

Alternative A

(f) Hearsay evidence may be used to supplement or explain other evidence, but on timely objection, is not sufficient by itself to support a finding of fact unless it would be admissible over objection in a civil action.

Alternative B

(f) Hearsay evidence is sufficient to support a finding of fact if it constitutes reliable, probative, and substantial evidence. ...

§ 414. AGENCY REVIEW OF INITIAL ORDER. ...

(e) When reviewing an initial order, the agency head shall exercise the decision-making power that the agency head would have had if the agency head had conducted the hearing that produced the order, except to the extent that the issues subject to review are limited by law of this state other than this [act] or by order of the agency head on notice to the parties. In reviewing findings of fact in an initial order, the agency head shall consider the presiding officer's opportunity to observe the witnesses and to determine the credibility of witnesses. The agency head shall consider the hearing record or parts of the record designated by the parties. ...

§ 415. AGENCY REVIEW OF RECOMMENDED ORDER. ...

(b) When reviewing a recommended order, the agency head shall exercise the decision-making power that the agency head would have had if the agency head had conducted the hearing that produced the order, except to the extent that the issues subject to review are limited by law of this state other than this [act] or by order of the agency head on notice to the parties. In reviewing findings of fact in a recommended order, the agency head shall consider the presiding officer's opportunity to observe the witnesses and to determine the credibility of witnesses. The agency head shall consider the hearing record or parts that are designated by the parties. ...

[ARTICLE] 5

JUDICIAL REVIEW

§ 501. RIGHT TO JUDICIAL REVIEW; FINAL AGENCY ACTION REVIEWABLE.

(a) In this [article], "final agency action" means an act of an agency which imposes an obligation, grants or denies a right, confers a benefit, or determines a legal relationship as a result of an administrative proceeding. The term does not include agency action that is a failure to act.

(b) Except to the extent that a statute of this state other than this [act] limits or precludes judicial review, a person that meets the requirements of this [article] is entitled to judicial review of a final agency action.

(c) A person entitled to judicial review under subsection (b) of a final agency action is entitled to judicial review of an agency action that is not final if postponement of judicial review would result in an inadequate remedy or irreparable harm that outweighs the public benefit derived from postponing judicial review.

(d) A court may compel an agency to take action that is unlawfully withheld or unreasonably delayed.

§ 502. RELATION TO OTHER JUDICIAL REVIEW LAW AND RULES. ...

(b) This [article] does not limit use of or the scope of judicial review available under other means of review, redress, relief, or trial de novo provided by law of this state other than this [act]. Except to the extent that prior, adequate, and exclusive opportunity for judicial review is available under this [article] or under law of this state other than this [act], final agency action is subject to judicial review in civil or criminal proceedings for judicial enforcement.

§ 503. TIME TO SEEK JUDICIAL REVIEW OF AGENCY ACTION; LIMITATIONS.

(a) Judicial review of a rule on the ground of noncompliance with the procedural requirements of this [act] must be commenced not later than [two] years after the effective date of the rule. Judicial review of a rule or guidance document on other grounds may be sought at any time. ...

§ 504. STAYS PENDING APPEAL. A petition for judicial review does not automatically stay an agency decision. A challenging party may request the reviewing court for a stay on the same basis as stays are granted under the rules of [appellate] [civil] procedure [of this state], and the reviewing court may grant a stay regardless of whether the challenging party first sought a stay from the agency.

§ 505. STANDING. The following persons have standing to obtain judicial review of a final agency action:

(1) a person aggrieved or adversely affected by the agency action; and

(2) a person that has standing under law of this state other than this [act].

§ 506. EXHAUSTION OF ADMINISTRATIVE REMEDIES.

(a) Subject to subsection (d) or law of this state other than this [act] which provides that a person need not exhaust administrative remedies, a person may file a petition for judicial review under this [act] only after exhausting all administrative remedies available within the agency the action of which is being challenged and within any other agency authorized to exercise administrative review.

(b) Filing a petition for reconsideration or a stay of proceedings is not a prerequisite for seeking judicial review.

(c) A petitioner for judicial review of a rule need not have participated in the rulemaking proceeding on which the rule is based or have filed a petition to adopt a rule under Section 318.

(d) The court may relieve a petitioner of the requirement to exhaust any or all administrative remedies to the extent the administrative remedies are inadequate or the requirement would result in irreparable harm.

§ 507. AGENCY RECORD ON JUDICIAL REVIEW; EXCEPTIONS.

(a) If an agency was required by [Article] 3 or 4, or by law of this state other than this [act], to maintain an agency record during the proceeding that gave rise to the action under review, the court review is confined to that record and to matters arising from that record.

(b) In any case to which subsection (a) does not apply, the record for review consists of the unprivileged materials that agency decision makers directly or indirectly considered, or which were submitted for consideration by any person, in connection with the action under review, including information that is adverse to the agency's position. If the agency action was ministerial or was taken on the basis of a minimal or no administrative record, the court may receive evidence relating to the agency's basis for taking the action.

(c) The court may supervise an agency's compilation of the agency record. If a challenging party makes a substantial showing of need, the court may allow discovery or other evidentiary proceedings and consider evidence outside the agency record to:

(1) ensure that the agency record is complete as required by this [act] and other applicable law;

(2) adjudicate allegations of procedural error not disclosed by the record; or

(3) prevent manifest injustice.

§ 508. SCOPE OF REVIEW.

(a) Except as provided by law of this state other than this [act], in judicial review of an agency action, the following rules apply:

(1) The burden of demonstrating the invalidity of agency action is on the party asserting invalidity.

(2) The court shall make a ruling on each material issue on which the court's decision is based.

(3) The court may grant relief only if it determines that a person seeking judicial review has been prejudiced by one or more of the following:

(A) the agency erroneously interpreted the law;

(B) the agency committed an error of procedure;

(C) the agency action is arbitrary, capricious, an abuse of discretion, or otherwise not in accordance with law;

(D) an agency determination of fact in a contested case is not supported by substantial evidence in the record as a whole; or

(E) to the extent that the facts are subject to a trial de novo by the reviewing court, the action was unwarranted by the facts.

(b) In making a determination under this section, the court shall review the agency record or the parts designated by the parties and shall apply the rule of harmless error.

[ARTICLE] 6

OFFICE OF ADMININISTRATIVE HEARINGS

§ 601.   CREATION OF OFFICE OF ADMINISTRATIVE HEARINGS.

(a) In this [article], "office" means the [Office of Administrative Hearings].

(b) The [Office of Administrative Hearings] is created in the executive branch of state government [within the [   ] agency].

§ 606.   ADMINISTRATIVE LAW JUDGES; POWERS; DUTIES; DECISION MAKING AUTHORITY.

(a) In a contested case, unless the hearing is conducted by a presiding officer assigned under Section 402(a) other than an administrative law judge, an administrative law judge must be assigned to be the presiding officer. If the administrative law judge is delegated final decisional authority, the administrative law judge shall issue a final order. If the administrative law judge is not delegated final decisional authority, the administrative law judge shall issue to the agency head a recommended order in the contested case.

(b) Except as otherwise provided by law of this state other than this [act], if a contested case is referred to the office by an agency, the agency may not take further action with respect to the proceeding, except as a party, until a recommended, initial, or final order is issued. [This subsection does not prevent an appropriate interlocutory review by the agency or an appropriate termination or modification of the proceeding by the agency when authorized by law of this state other than this [act].]

(c) In addition to acting as the presiding officer in contested cases under this [act], subject to the direction of the chief administrative law judge, an administrative law judge may perform duties authorized by law of this state other than this [act].

[[ARTICLE] 7

RULES REVIEW

§ 701. [LEGISLATIVE RULES REVIEW COMMITTEE]. There is created a standing committee of the [Legislature] designated the [rules review committee].

§ 702. REVIEW BY [RULES REVIEW COMMITTEE].

(a) An agency shall file a copy of an adopted rule with the [rules review committee] at the same time it is filed with the [publisher]. An agency is not required to file an emergency rule adopted under Section 309 with the [rules review committee].

(b) The [rules review committee] may examine each rule in effect and each newly adopted rule to determine whether the:

(1) rule is a valid exercise of delegated legislative authority;

(2) statutory authority for the rule has expired or been repealed;

(3) rule is necessary to accomplish the apparent or expressed intent of the specific statute that the rule implements;

(4) rule is a reasonable implementation of the law as it applies to any affected class of persons; and

(5) agency complied with the regulatory analysis requirements of Section 305 and the analysis properly reflects the effect of the rule.

(c) The [rules review committee] may request from an agency information necessary to exercise its powers under subsection (b). The [rules review committee] shall consult with standing committees of the [Legislature] with subject matter jurisdiction over the subjects of the rule under examination.

(d) The [rules review committee] shall:

(1) maintain oversight over agency rulemaking; and

(2) exercise other duties assigned to it under this [article].

§ 703. [RULES REVIEW COMMITTEE] PROCEDURE AND POWERS.

(a) Not later than [30] days after receiving a copy of an adopted rule from an agency under Section 702, the [rules review committee] may:

(1) approve the adopted rule;

(2) disapprove the rule and propose an amendment to the adopted rule; or

(3) disapprove the adopted rule.

(b) If the [rules review committee] approves an adopted rule or does not disapprove and propose an amendment under subsection (a)(2) or disapprove under subsection (a)(3), the adopted rule becomes effective on the date specified in Section 317.

(c) If the [rules review committee] proposes an amendment to an adopted rule under subsection (a)(2), the agency may make the amendment and resubmit the rule, as amended, to the [rules review committee]. The amended rule must be one that the agency could have adopted on the basis of the record in the rulemaking proceeding and the legal authority granted to the agency. The agency shall provide an explanation for the amended rule as provided in Section 313. An agency is not required to hold a hearing on an amendment made under this subsection. If the agency makes the amendment, it shall give notice to the [publisher] for publication of the rule, as amended, in the [administrative bulletin]. The notice must include the text of the rule as amended. If the [rules review committee] does not disapprove the rule, as amended, or propose a further amendment, the rule becomes effective on the date specified under Section 317.

(d) If the [rules review committee] disapproves the adoption of a rule under subsection (a)(3), the adopted rule becomes effective on adjournment of the next regular session of the [Legislature] unless before adjournment the [Legislature] [adopts a [joint] [concurrent] resolution] [enacts a bill] sustaining the action of the committee.

(e) Before the effective date specified in Section 317, the agency may withdraw the adoption of a rule by giving notice of the withdrawal to the [rules review committee] and to the [publisher] for publication in the [administrative bulletin]. A withdrawal under this subsection terminates the rulemaking with respect to the adoption but does not prevent the agency from initiating new rulemaking for the same or substantially similar adoption.]

■ ■ ■

1981 Model State Administrative Procedure Act

§ 2–104. [Required Rule Making]

In addition to other rule-making requirements imposed by law, each agency shall:

(1) adopt as a rule a description of the organization of the agency which states the general course and method of its

operations and where and how the public may obtain information or make submissions or requests;

(2) adopt rules of practice setting forth the nature and requirements of all formal and informal procedures available to the public, including a description of all forms and instructions that are to be used by the public in dealing with the agency; [and]

(3) as soon as feasible and to the extent practicable, adopt rules, in addition to those otherwise required by this Act, embodying appropriate standards, principles, and procedural safeguards that the agency will apply to the law it administers [; and] [.]

[(4) as soon as feasible and to the extent practicable, adopt rules to supersede principles of law or policy lawfully declared by the agency as the basis for its decisions in particular cases.]

§ 3–107. [Variance between Adopted Rule and Published Notice of Proposed Rule Adoption]

(a) An agency may not adopt a rule that is substantially different from the proposed rule contained in the published notice of proposed rule adoption. However, an agency may terminate a rule-making proceeding and commence a new rule-making proceeding for the purpose of adopting a substantially different rule.

(b) In determining whether an adopted rule is substantially different from the published proposed rule upon which it is required to be based, the following must be considered:

(1) the extent to which all persons affected by the adopted rule should have understood that the published proposed rule would affect their interests;

(2) the extent to which the subject matter of the adopted rule or the issues determined by that rule are different from the subject matter or issues involved in the published proposed rule; and

(3) the extent to which the effects of the adopted rule differ from the effects of the published proposed rule had it been adopted instead.

§ 3–108. [General Exemption from Public Rule-making Procedures]

(a) To the extent an agency for good cause finds that any requirements of Sections 3–103 through 3–107 are unnecessary, impracticable, or contrary to the public interest in the process of adopting a particular rule, those requirements do not apply. The agency shall incorporate the required finding and a brief statement of its supporting reasons in each rule adopted in reliance upon this subsection.

(b) In an action contesting a rule adopted under subsection (a), the burden is upon the agency to demonstrate that any omitted requirements of Sections 3–103 through 3–107 were impracticable, unnecessary, or contrary to the public interest in the particular circumstances involved. ...

(c) Within [2] years after the effective date of a rule adopted under subsection (a), the [administrative rules review committee or the governor] may request the agency to hold a rule-making proceeding thereon according to the requirements of Sections 3–103 through 3–107. The request must be in writing and filed in the office of the [secretary of state]. The [secretary of state] shall immediately forward to the agency and to the [administrative rules editor] a certified copy of the request. Notice of the filing of the request must be published in the next issue of the [administrative bulletin]. The rule in question ceases to be effective [180] days after the request is filed. However, an agency, after the filing of the request, may subsequently adopt an identical rule in a rule-making proceeding conducted pursuant to the requirements of Sections 3–103 through 3–107.

§ 3–116. [Special Provision for Certain Classes of Rules]

Except to the extent otherwise provided by any provision of law, Sections 3–102 through 3–115 are inapplicable to:

(1) a rule concerning only the internal management of an agency which does not directly and substantially affect the procedural or substantive rights or duties of any segment of the public;

(2) a rule that establishes criteria or guidelines to be used by the staff of an agency in performing audits, investigations, or inspections, settling commercial disputes, negotiating commercial arrangements, or in the defense, prosecution, or settlement of cases, if disclosure of the criteria or guidelines would:

(i)   enable law violators to avoid detection;

(ii) facilitate disregard of requirements imposed by law; or

(iii) give a clearly improper advantage to persons who are in an adverse position to the state;

(3) a rule that only establishes specific prices to be charged for particular goods or services sold by an agency;

(4) a rule concerning only the physical servicing, maintenance, or care of agency owned or operated facilities or property;

(5) a rule relating only to the use of a particular facility or property owned, operated, or maintained by the state or any of its subdivisions, if the substance of the rule is adequately indicated by means of signs or signals to persons who use the facility or property;

(6) a rule concerning only inmates of a correctional or detention facility, students enrolled in an educational institution, or patients admitted to a hospital, if adopted by that facility, institution, or hospital;

(7) a form whose contents or substantive requirements are prescribed by rule or statute, and instructions for the execution or use of the form;

(8) an agency budget; [or]

(9) an opinion of the attorney general[; or] [.]

(10) [the terms of a collective bargaining agreement.]

§ 3–204. [Review by Administrative Rules Review Committee]

(a) The [administrative rules review committee] shall selectively review possible, proposed, or adopted rules and prescribe appropriate committee procedures for that purpose. The committee may receive and investigate complaints from members of the public with respect to possible, proposed, or adopted rules and hold public proceedings on those complaints.

(b) Committee meetings must be open to the public. Subject to procedures established by the committee, persons may present oral argument, data, or views at those meetings. The committee may require a representative of an agency whose possible, proposed, or adopted rule is under examination to attend a committee meeting and answer relevant questions. The committee may also communicate to the agency its comments on any possible, proposed, or adopted rule and require the agency to respond to them in writing. Unless impracticable, in advance of each committee meeting, notice of the time and place of the meeting and the specific subject matter to be considered must be published in the [administrative bulletin].

(c) The committee may recommend enactment of a statute to improve the operation of an agency. The committee may also recommend that a particular rule be superseded in whole or in part by statute. The [speaker of the house and the president of the senate] shall refer those recommendations to the appropriate standing committees. This subsection does not preclude any committee of the legislature from reviewing a rule on its own motion or recommending that it be superseded in whole or in part by statute.

[(d)(1)   If the committee objects to all or some portion of a rule because the committee considers it to be beyond the procedural or substantive authority delegated to the adopting agency, the committee may file that objection in the office of the [secretary of state]. The filed objection must contain a concise statement of the committee's reasons for its action.

(2)   The [secretary of state] shall affix to each objection a certification of the date and time of its filing and as soon thereafter as practicable shall transmit a certified copy thereof to the agency issuing the rule in question, the [administrative rules editor, and the administrative rules counsel]. The [secretary of state] shall also maintain a permanent register open to public inspection of all objections by the committee.

(3)   The [administrative rules editor] shall publish and index an objection filed pursuant to this subsection in the next issue of the [administrative bulletin] and indicate its existence adjacent to the rule in question when that rule is published in the [administrative code]. In case of a filed objection by the committee to a rule that is subject to the requirements of Section 2–101(g), the agency shall indicate the existence of that objection adjacent to the rule in the official compilation referred to in that subsection.

(4)   Within [14] days after the filing of an objection by the committee to a rule, the issuing agency shall respond in writing to the committee. After receipt of the response, the committee may withdraw or modify its objection.

[(5) After the filing of an objection by the committee that is not subsequently withdrawn, the burden is upon the agency in any proceeding for judicial review or for enforcement of the rule to establish that the whole or portion of the rule objected to is within the procedural and substantive authority delegated to the agency.]

(6) The   failure   of   the   [administrative   rules   review committee] to object to a rule is not an implied legislative authorization of its procedural or substantive validity.]

(e)   The committee may recommend to an agency that it adopt a rule. [The committee may also require an agency to publish notice of the committee's recommendation as a proposed rule of the agency and to allow public participation thereon, according to the provisions of Sections

3–103 through 3–104. An agency is not required to adopt the proposed rule.]

(f)   The committee shall file an annual report with the [presiding officer] of each house and the governor.

§ 4–201. [Applicability]

An adjudicative proceeding is governed by this chapter, except as otherwise provided by:

(1)   a statute other than this Act;

(2)   a rule that adopts the procedures for the conference adjudicative hearing or summary adjudicative proceeding in accordance with the standards provided in this Act for those proceedings;

(3)   Section 4–501 pertaining to emergency adjudicative proceedings; or

(4)   Section 2–103 pertaining to declaratory proceedings.

§ 4–213. [Ex parte Communications]

(a)   Except as provided in subsection (b) or unless required for the disposition of ex parte matters specifically authorized by statute, a presiding officer serving in an adjudicative proceeding may not communicate, directly or indirectly, regarding any issue in the proceeding, while the proceeding is pending, with any party, with any person who has a direct or indirect interest in the outcome of the proceeding, or with any person who presided at a previous stage of the proceeding, without notice and opportunity for all parties to participate in the communication.

(b)   A member of a multi-member panel of presiding officers may communicate with other members of the panel regarding a matter pending before the panel, and any presiding officer may receive aid from staff assistants if the assistants do not (i) receive ex parte communications of a type that the presiding officer would be prohibited from receiving or (ii) furnish, augment, diminish, or modify the evidence in the record.

(c)   Unless required for the disposition of ex parte matters specifically authorized by statute, no party to an adjudicative proceeding, and no person who has a direct or indirect interest in the outcome of the proceeding or who presided at a previous stage of the proceeding, may communicate, directly or indirectly, in connection with any issue in that proceeding, while the proceeding is pending, with any person serving as presiding officer, without notice and opportunity for all parties to participate in the communication.

(d) If, before serving as presiding officer in an adjudicative proceeding, a person receives an ex parte communication of a type that could not properly be received while serving, the person, promptly after starting to serve, shall disclose the communication in the manner prescribed in subsection (e).

(e) A presiding officer who receives an ex parte communication in violation of this section shall place on the record of the pending matter all written communications received, all written responses to the communications, and a memorandum stating the substance of all oral communications received, all responses made, and the identity of each person from whom the presiding officer received an ex parte communication, and shall advise all parties that these matters have been placed on the record. Any party desiring to rebut the ex parte communication must be allowed to do so, upon requesting the opportunity for rebuttal within [10] days after notice of the communication.

(f) If necessary to eliminate the effect of an ex parte communication received in violation of this section, a presiding officer who receives the communication may be disqualified and the portions of the record pertaining to the communication may be sealed by protective order.

(g) The agency shall, and any party may, report any willful violation of this section to appropriate authorities for any disciplinary proceedings provided by law. In addition, each agency by rule may provide for appropriate sanctions, including default, for any violations of this section.

§ 4–214. [Separation of Functions]

(a) A person who has served as investigator, prosecutor or advocate in an adjudicative proceeding or in its pre-adjudicative stage may not serve as presiding officer or assist or advise a presiding officer in the same proceeding.

(b) A person who is subject to the authority, direction, or discretion of one who has served as investigator, prosecutor, or advocate in an adjudicative proceeding or in its pre-adjudicative stage may not serve as presiding officer or assist or advise a presiding officer in the same proceeding.

(c) A person who has participated in a determination of probable cause or other equivalent preliminary determination in an adjudicative proceeding may serve as presiding officer or assist or advise a presiding officer in the same proceeding, unless a party demonstrates grounds for disqualification in accordance with Section 4–202.

(d) A person may serve as presiding officer at successive stages of the same adjudicative proceeding, unless a party demonstrates grounds for disqualification in accordance with Section 4–202.

■ ■ ■

1961 Model State Administrative Procedure Act

§ 1. [Definitions].

As used in this Act: ...

(2) "contested case" means a proceeding, including but not restricted to ratemaking, [price fixing], and licensing, in which the legal rights, duties, or privileges of a party are required by law to be determined by an agency after an opportunity for hearing; ...

(7) "rule" means each agency statement of general applicability that implements, interprets, or prescribes law or policy, or describes the organization, procedure, or practice requirements of any agency. The term includes the amendment or repeal of a prior rule, but does not include (A) statements concerning only the internal management of an agency and not affecting private rights or procedures available to the public, or (B) declaratory rulings issued pursuant to Section 8, or (C) intra-agency memoranda.

§ 3. [Procedure for Adoption of Rules].

(a) Prior to the adoption, amendment, or repeal of any rule, the agency shall:

(1) give at least 20 days' notice of its intended action. The notice shall include a statement of either the terms or substance of the intended action or a description of the subjects and issues involved, and the time when, the place where, and the manner in which interested persons may present their views thereon. The notice shall be mailed to all persons who have made timely request of the agency for advance notice of its rule-making proceedings and shall be published in [here insert the medium of publication appropriate for the adopting state];

(2) afford all interested persons reasonable opportunity to submit data, views, or arguments, orally or in writing. In case of substantive rules, opportunity for oral hearing must be granted if requested by 25 persons, by a governmental subdivision or agency, or by an association having not less than 25 members. The agency shall consider fully all written and oral submissions respecting the proposed rule. Upon adoption of a rule, the agency, if requested to do so by an interested person either prior to adoption or within 30 days thereafter, shall issue a concise statement of the principal reasons for and against its adoption, incorporating therein its reasons for overruling the considerations urged against its adoption.

(b) If an agency finds that an imminent peril to the public health, safety, or welfare requires adoption of a rule upon fewer than 20 days' notice and states in writing its reasons for that finding, it may proceed without prior notice or hearing or upon any abbreviated notice and hearing that it finds practicable, to adopt an emergency rule. The rule may be effective for a period of not longer than 120 days [renewable once for a period not exceeding (4) days], but the adoption of an identical rule under subsections (a)(1) and (a)(2) of this Section is not precluded.

(c) No rule hereafter adopted is valid unless adopted in substantial compliance with this Section. A proceeding to contest any rule on the ground of non-compliance with the procedural requirements of this Section must be commenced within 2 years from the effective date of the rule.

§ 6. [Petition for Adoption of Rules].

An interested person may petition an agency requesting the promulgation, amendment, or repeal of a rule. Each agency shall prescribe by rule the form for petitions and the procedure for their submission, consideration, and disposition. Within 30 days after submission of a petition, the agency either shall deny the petition in writing (stating its reasons for the denials) or shall initiate rule-making proceedings in accordance with Section 3.

§ 14. [Licenses]. ...

(c) No revocation, suspension, annulment, or withdrawal of any license is lawful unless, prior to the institution of agency proceedings, the agency gave notice by mail to the licensee of facts or conduct which warrant the intended action, and the licensee was given an opportunity to show compliance with all lawful requirements for the retention of the license. If the agency finds that public health, safety, or welfare imperatively requires emergency action, and incorporates a finding to that effect in its order, summary suspension of a license may be ordered pending proceedings for revocation or other action. These proceedings shall be promptly instituted and determined.

§ 15. [Judicial Review of Contested Cases]. ...

(g) The court shall not substitute its judgment for that of the agency as to the weight of the evidence on questions of fact. The court may affirm the decision of the agency or remand the case for further proceedings. The court may reverse or modify the decision if substantial rights of the appellant have been prejudiced because the administrative findings, inferences, conclusions, or decisions are:

(1) in violation of constitutional or statutory provisions;

(2) in excess of the statutory authority of the agency;

(3)   made upon unlawful procedure;

(4)   affected by other error of law;

(5)   clearly erroneous in view of the reliable, probative, and substantial evidence on the whole record; or

(6)   arbitrary or capricious or characterized by abuse of discretion or clearly unwarranted exercise of discretion.

INDEX

References are to Pages